NEWMAN AND HIS CRITICS

By the Same Author
What the Bells Sang: Essays and Reviews
The Saint Mary's Book of Christian Verse (ed.)
John Henry Newman, Difficulties of Anglicans, Volume I (ed.)
Newman and History
Adventures in the Book Pages: Essays and Reviews
Culture and Abortion
Newman and his Family
Newman and his Contemporaries

NEWMAN
AND
HIS CRITICS

Edward Short

GRACEWING

First published in England in 2024
by
Gracewing
2 Southern Avenue
Leominster
Herefordshire HR6 0QF
United Kingdom
www.gracewing.co.uk

All rights reserved.
No part of this publication may be reproduced, stored in a retrieval system, or transmitted in any form or by any means, electronic, mechanical, photocopying, recording or otherwise, without the written permission of the publisher.

© 2024 Edward Short

The right of Edward Short
to be identified as the author of this work
have been asserted in accordance with the
Copyright, Designs and Patents Act 1988.

ISBN 978 085244 772 2 (paperback edition)
ISBN 978 178182 973 8 (cased edition)
ISBN 978 178182 099 5 (e-pub)

Cover image:
John Henry Newman by George Richmond
chalk drawing, National Portrait Gallery

Cover design by Bernardita Peña Hurtado

Typeset by Word and Page, Chester, UK

CONTENTS

Acknowledgements	vii
Abbreviations	x
Preface	xii
1. Richard William Church	1
2. Richard Holt Hutton	99
3. Mark Pattison	149
4. Edwin Abbott Abbott	201
5. James Fitzjames Stephen	237
6. James Anthony Froude	291
7. Frederick Meyrick	355
8. Charles Kingsley	385
9. Wilfrid Ward	441
10. Ian Ker	519
Epilogue	561
Index	563

ACKNOWLEDGEMENTS

Many friends and acquaintances gave me good counsel and vital encouragement while I was researching and writing *Newman and his Critics*, and I am pleased to acknowledge their kind help. Father Ian Ker, the finest of Newman scholars, looked over most of the chapters in typescript and gave me the benefit of his exacting criticisms. I could have wished that he had seen my chapter on his own work but unexpected death put him beyond the world of typescripts. Father Dermot Fenlon, before he went to his equally sudden death, shared with me his insights into my subject. No one saw what Newman called the "inside of things" with anything like Father Fenlon's discernment: speaking with him about Newman was always revelatory. Father Guy Nicholls of the Oratory, whose *Unearthly Beauty: The Aesthetic of St John Henry Newman* (2019) is such an unusually astute contribution to Newman scholarship, shared his insights into the Cardinal with me, as did Bishop James Conley of Nebraska.

Father Carleton Jones, O.P, to whom I dedicate the book, was a source of continual good counsel, sympathy and abounding encouragement. He looked over all the chapters with unflagging generosity and drove me to persevere when other projects threatened the book's completion. Having Fr Carleton as a reader was not only a blessing but a joy, especially since he shares my delight in Newman's wonderful sense of humor. My readers will know what I mean when I say that one of his favorite passages from the *Letters & Diaries* is the one in which Newman writes to apologize to a young seminarian visiting the Oratory whom he was fearful he might have offended. "It is strange to write a note about nothing," Newman wrote the young man, "but such is my fate just now and for some time, that since I have nothing to say to you, I must either be silent or unseasonable. Many is the time I have stood over the fire at breakfast or looked at you at Recreation, hunting for something to say." [*LD*, xiii, 32] The author who only wrote in response to occasions could be at a compunctious loss when it came to small talk.

Others who gave me invaluable help include Brother Brian Grenier of Brisbane and Dr. James McGuire of Dublin. Dr. Andrew Nash and the late Dr. Don Briel were also full of encouragement, as was my stalwart good friend and devoted Newmanian in New York, Mr. Allen Roth. The extraordinarily well-read Mrs. Stephanie Mann read most of the chapters in typescript with a critical care for which I am deeply grateful. Fr. Richard Smith, pastor of St. Joachim—St. John the Evangelist in Beacon, New York, was another marvelously generous reader, whose delight in Newman echoes my own. Kenneth Jones, Esq., an admirable Johnsonian as well as Newmanian, gave me invaluable encouragement, as did Bishop John Oliver Barres of New York. Father Gerald Murray, whose witness to the vitality of the dogmatic principle has been such a source of strength to so many Catholics in our stormy age, gave me true Newmanian encouragement. The exuberant church historian Dr. Sheridan Gilley, who knows more about

Ward *père et fils* than anyone living or dead, looked over my chapter on Wilfrid Ward and cheered me on. Dr. Reinhard Hütter of the Catholic University of America gave his blessings to the hagiographical approach that I take to my subject, though I fear the systematic theologian in him might be inclined to find the rather unsystematic cast of my musings exasperating.

From Gracewing, I am profoundly grateful to Mr. Tom Longford, the most civilized of gentleman publishers, who stood by me foursquare while I wrested the book from the bean counters of Bedford Square. Since taking on the book, he has shown me not only good counsel but the most vital sympathy. The book I have written being a kind of study in sympathy, I could not have chosen a better publisher. The learned and stylish Clive Tolley of Word & Page gave the book its beautiful typesetting. Beauty in our drab, utilitarian age is not something one often associates with book production but in Dr. Tolley they are as inseparable as Liddell and Scott. For all of the care he lavished on the book I am more grateful to him than I can say.

Since I have written the book for the common reader "uncorrupted by literary prejudices," I am particularly grateful for those in my personal swim who enter into what I am doing in my work on Newman and these include Jeremy Paff, Caroline Nogier, Wendy Long, Andrew Roberts, Conrad Black, Jo Anne and Eugene Sylva, Jack Scarisbrick, Luanne Zurlo, Margaret Fernandez, James and Virginia McGlone, Carl Olson, Paul Beston, Neil Merkl, Robert Emmet Crotty, Timothy Landers, and James Grant, the author of brilliant books on John Adams, Walter Bagehot, Edmund Burke and Charles James Fox, as well as editor of that unfailingly witty paper, *Grant's Interest Rate Observer*.

The reader, above all others, whom I wish could have read what I have done is my father, John Francis Short, now long dead, who first introduced me to Newman when I was a boy in a little seaside town on the northern tip of the Jersey shore called Monmouth Beach. He gave me the old Dent Everyman editions of the *Discourses on the Scope and Nature of University Education* and the *Apologia*, both of which I still have in my library. I first began reading Newman for the same reason I first began reading C.S Forester and the Hornblower books (of which my father was immensely fond): to be close to him. If he were still around to read *Newman and his Critics*, he would doubtless be full of altogether warrantable criticism of its undeniable flaws, but he would also be moved, I dare say, to see that his introducing me to this splendid saint when my young heart yearned for the Truth had not been in vain. *Gratias tibi ago pater*.

Here, too, I should like to give thanks beyond all saying sweet to my mother, who would often recall the day we went to Willoughby's together in West 32nd Street to buy my first computer, after the old Royal manual typewriter that she had given me as a boy became inoperable. She believed in the scribbler in me when it was neither popular nor profitable, and I look forward to the day we meet again so that I can introduce her to the grandson she never met in life.

Lastly, and more than ever, I am indebted to my wife Karina and my children, Sophia and Sebastian, my love for whom always helps me to understand the love at the heart of Newman's work. Indeed, I can never look upon my children without recalling that charming letter that Newman sent J. R. Bloxam in March of 1840: "The children are vastly improved in singing," he wrote his Littlemore

Acknowledgements

curate, "and now that the organ is mute, their voices are so thrilling as to make one sick with love." Exulting in the voices of my own children, I know exactly what St John Henry Newman meant.

ABBREVIATIONS

References to Newman's works in the text are to the uniform edition of 1868–81 (36 vols.), published by Longmans, Green, and Co. until the stock was destroyed by the bombs of the Luftwaffe in the Battle of Britain. Abbreviations of works by Newman's critics are set out in the text.

Apo.	*Apologia pro Vita Sua*, ed. Martin J. Svaglic (Oxford, 1967)
Ath.	*Select Treatises of St Athanasius*
AW	John Henry Newman, *Autobiographical Writings*, ed. Henry Tristram (S&W, 1956)
Call.	*Callista: A Tale of the Third Century*
Campaign	*My Campaign in Ireland, Part I* edited by William Neville (privately printed, 1896)
CS	*Catholic Sermons of Cardinal Newman*, ed. at the Birmingham Oratory (London, 1957)
Cons.	*On Consulting the Faithful in Matters of Doctrine*, ed. John Coulson (London, 1961)
DA	*Discussions and Arguments on Various Subjects*
Dev.	*An Essay on the Development of Christian Doctrine*
Diff.	*Certain Difficulties Felt by Anglicans in Catholic Teaching*, 2 vols.
DNB	*Dictionary of National Biography*
Ess.	*Essays Critical and Historical*, 2 vols.
GA	*An Essay in Aid of a Grammar of Assent*, ed. I. T. Ker (Oxford, 1985)
HS	*Historical Sketches*, 3 vols.
Idea	*The Idea of a University*, ed. I. T. Ker (Oxford, 1976)
Jfc.	*Lectures on the Doctrine of Justification*
LD	*The Letters and Diaries of John Henry Newman*, ed. Charles Stephen Dessain *et al.*, vols. i–x (Oxford, 1978–2006), xi–xxii (London, 1961–72), xxiii–xxxii (Oxford, 1973–2006)
LG	*Loss and Gain: The Story of a Convert*
MD	*Meditations and Devotions of the late Cardinal Newman* (London, 1893)
Mir.	*Two Essays on Biblical and on Ecclesiastical Miracles*
Mix.	*Discourses addressed to Mixed Congregations*
Moz.	*Letters and Correspondence of John Henry Newman during his Life in the English Church*, ed. Anne Mozley, 2 vols. (London, 1891)
NO	*Newman the Oratorian: His Unpublished Oratorian Papers*, ed. Placid Murray, OSB, (Dublin, 1969)

Abbreviations

ODNB	*Oxford Dictionary of National Biography* (Oxford: Oxford University Press, 2004)
OS	*Sermons Preached on Various Occasions*
PS	*Parochial and Plain Sermons*, 8 vols.
Prepos.	*Present Position of Catholics in England*
SD	*Sermons bearing on Subjects of the Day*
SE	*Stray Essays on Controversial Points* (privately printed, 1890)
Short Studies	James Anthony Froude, *Short Studies on Great Subjects* (London: Longmans, Green and Co., 1905)
TP i	*The Theological Papers of John Henry Newman on Faith and Certainty*, ed. Hugo M. de Achaval, S. J., and J. Derek Holmes (Oxford, 1976)
TP ii	*The Theological Papers of John Henry Newman on Biblical Inspiration and on Infallibility*, ed. J. Derek Holmes (Oxford, 1979)
TT	*Tracts Theological and Ecclesiastical*
US	*Fifteen Sermons Preached before the University of Oxford* ed Earnest and Tracey (Oxford University Press, 2006)
VM	*The Via Media*, 2 vols.
VV	*Verses on Various Occasions*

PREFACE

At the end of the Preface to his English Dictionary (1755), in what James Boswell called a "clear, strong, and glowing style," Samuel Johnson wrote:

> In this work, when it shall be found that much is omitted, let it not be forgotten that much likewise is performed; and though no book was ever spared out of tenderness to the authour, and the world is little solicitous to know whence proceeded the faults of that which it condemns; yet it may gratify curiosity to inform it, that the English Dictionary was written with little assistance of the learned, and without any patronage of the great; not in the soft obscurities of retirement, or under the shelter of academick bowers, but amidst inconvenience and distraction, in sickness and in sorrow: and it may repress the triumph of malignant criticism to observe, that if our language is not here fully displayed, I have only failed in an attempt which no human powers have hitherto completed. If the lexicons of ancient tongues, now immutably fixed, and comprised in a few volumes, be yet, after the toil of successive ages, inadequate and delusive; if the aggregated knowledge, and co-operating diligence of the Italian academicians, did not secure them from the censure of Beni; if the embodied criticks of France, when fifty years had been spent upon their work, were obliged to change its oeconomy, and give their second edition another form, I may surely be contented without the praise of perfection, which, if I could obtain, in this gloom of solitude, what would it avail me? I have protracted my work till most of those whom I wished to please, have sunk into the grave, and success and miscarriage are empty sounds: I therefore dismiss it with frigid tranquillity, having little to fear or hope from censure or from praise.

Since I was keen on having *Newman and his Critics* please a few friends and family now "sunk into the grave," I can sympathize with Johnson, even though he was only forty-six when he completed the Dictionary and had nearly thirty more years to live. Why its completion should have caused him such gloom is, therefore, a nice question. Yes, he was given to melancholy, and, indeed, often wrote to escape or at least to beguile melancholy. Yes, his beloved wife, Tetty, had recently died. And, yes, the Dictionary hardly made his fortune, as he had hoped it might. But there was perhaps a deeper reason for Johnson's gloom, and the last of his *Idler* essays—No. 103—may explain why.

> Though the Idler and his readers have contracted no close friendship they are perhaps both unwilling to part. There are few things not purely evil, of which we can say, without some emotion of uneasiness, this is the last. Those who never could agree together, shed tears when mutual discontent has determined them to final separation; of a place which has been frequently visited, though without pleasure, the last look is taken with heaviness of heart; and the Idler, with all his chillness of tranquility, is not wholly unaffected by the thought that his last essay

is now before him. This secret horror of the last is inseparable from a thinking being whose life is limited, and to whom death is dreadful. We always make a secret comparison between a part and the whole; the termination of any period of life reminds us that life itself has likewise its termination; when we have done any thing for the last time, we involuntarily reflect that a part of the days allotted us is past, and that as more is past there is less remaining.

Such musings, now that I have come to the end of my stitchings and unstitchings, have more than a literary appeal. After all, with all my weaving done, I am nearer my own earthly end, and that is naturally an arresting thought. The rich proud cost of outworn buried age is coming due. What was it Newman once said? "There is something awful in the silent resistless sweep of time—and as years go on, and friends are taken away, one draws the thought of those who remain about one, as in cold weather one buttons up great coats and capes, for protection."

Yet, *mirabile dictu*, I feel no gloom on the completion of this book: only colossal relief. I have cast off an awful albatross—not as vexatious, certainly, as the one that plagued poor Coleridge's friend but vexatious enough—and now I look forward to delighting anew in the society of my wife and children. In the meantime, I hope my book does not meet with the reception S. T. C.'s poem met with from Johnson's friend, Charles Burney, who thought it "the strangest story of a cock and bull that we ever saw on paper"—"a rhapsody of unintelligible wildness and incoherence." In fact, none of the critics had anything good to say of the poem when it first came out and, as a result, *Lyrical Ballads* (1798) sold miserably—proof that the judgments of critics must always be read with due wariness, not excepting those who set themselves up, as I have set myself up, as critics of critics.

Since *Newman and his Critics* is the last book of the trilogy of books about Newman, which I began with *Newman and his Contemporaries* (2011) and continued with *Newman and his Family* (2013), I have made it a companion to those earlier books, my object always being to put Newman in his immediate historical context to show how he transcends that context.

In keeping with Newman's own approach to critics, especially its element of sympathy, which Gilbert Chesterton emulates so splendidly, I go to considerable lengths to treat each of the main figures in the book not as mere touts for this or that critical view but as men whose views were shaped by their lives. Why they espoused the views they espoused, what influence their different experiences had in shaping their views, not simply the views themselves command my attention. In other words, I show my critics sympathy, though this does not mean that I show their bad judgments sympathy.

Since all the best critics of Newman were either actual friends of his or entered into spiritual friendship with him, I pay a good deal of attention to friendship in the book. After all, Newman, as we all know, had a genius for friendship and it stands to reason that those who had the privilege of befriending him would have a better understanding of what he was about than those who did not. The other day I was speaking on the telephone with Fr Guy Nicholls of the Oratory and he made an amusing point when he said that we might never have had the *Apologia* if Kingsley had somehow managed to meet and befriend Newman. My warrant for giving the theme of friendship a certain prominence is also bolstered by Newman's own befriending of the saints, in whose letters he delighted. Then, again, I knew I had landed on a good *leitmotif* for the book when I came across something R. W. Southern said in that wonderful late masterpiece of his, *Scholastic Humanism and the Unification of Europe* (1995–2000), in which he speaks of the theme of friendship as pivotal for the life of the Church:

> The association of nature and humanity with reason and religion is central in all twelfth-century intellectual development, and it had a peculiar development in arguments on the subject of friendship. To mention only one: there were none more eagerly sought than the friendship between God and man. This may seem a commonplace theme, and one which has been debased by countless sentimentalities and trivialities. But it once was fresh, and it lifted a great weight from human lives. In the early Middle Ages God had appeared as Creator, Judge, Saviour, but not as a friend. By great labour and exertion, by crippling penances and gifts to the Church, by turning from the world to the monastic life, God's anger might be averted; but God was very difficult to approach, except through the mediation of the saints; more difficult still to appease, except through an endless burden of penances. Then quite suddenly the humanity of the Redeemer began to appear not simply as a divine stratagem to outwit the Devil, but as an expression of God's fellowship with mankind. In the light of this discovery, the terror faded, the sun shone, and prayers, poems, devotions of all kinds, mingling scholastic with monastic themes, began to pour forth to express the humanity of God.

Reading this, I soon realized that what unites all of Newman's best critics is precisely their shared interest in the saint's work as a means of entering into fellowship with God. Readers can see this perhaps most pronouncedly in both the chapter that begins the book on Dean Church and the one that ends it on Ian Ker.

The scope of the book is straightforward: I only chose a few of Newman's contemporary critics, favorable and unfavorable, and I only chose figures whom I found instructively insightful or wrongheaded. Having written of Gladstone, one of Newman's more exuberant critics in the trilogy's first book, I have not included him here, though I treat of him incidentally throughout the book. Lord Acton is another figure whom I might have included more fully, though readers will see that I do advert to him here and there. Whatever my omissions, I did take pains to include the criticisms of many figures who had particularly sensible or insensible things to say of Newman in passing, even though some of these are not "critics" in any formal sense. Admittedly, I deviate from the book's scope by including a final chapter on the work of Ian Ker, but I trust I do so justifiably, if only to share with my readers what I believe the insights of Newman's finest critic.

Edward Short
Astoria New York
19 March 2024
Feast of St Joseph

For
Carleton Parker Jones, O.P.
Faithful Friend, Sage Newmanian

I expect to have many criticisms ... but I have done my best—No work on which one has bestowed great pains can meet with an early verdict. What has cost time and trouble to assert, must cost time and trouble to refute—and then how few critics care to take that time and trouble.

John Henry Newman to W. J. Copeland (5 April 1874)

A mere conviction that Catholic thought is the clearest as well as the best disciplined, will not make a man a writer like Newman. But without that conviction Newman would not be a writer like Newman; and probably not a writer at all. It is useless for the æsthete (or any other anarchist) to urge the isolated individuality of the artist, apart from his attitude to his age. His attitude to his age is his individuality: men are never individual when alone.

G. K. Chesterton, *The Victorian Age in Literature* (1913)

An author places himself uncalled before the tribunal of Criticism, and solicits fame at the hazard of disgrace. Dullness or deformity are not culpable in themselves, but may be very justly reproached when they pretend to the honour of wit or the influence of beauty. If bad writers were to pass without reprehension, what should restrain them?

Samuel Johnson, *Lives of the English Poets* (1779–81)

I wonder you can for a moment lay stress on the dicta of reviewers. You must have had surely enough experience how utterly worthless, for the most part, the formal criticisms of the day are. In saying this I intend no disrespect to serious and earnest critics, from whom one can always gain good.

John Henry Newman to Francis William Newman (22 May 1860)

I am far from exempting the actions of Saints from criticism; but it seems to me that a Catholic should treat them in a devout and loving manner.

John Henry Newman to Sir John Acton (11 June 1861)

I am often led to call my life a history of failures. It is a great consolation to me to receive evidence, as I do from time to time, that all was not lost.

John Henry Newman to John Duke Coleridge (12 October 1864)

RICHARD WILLIAM CHURCH

⇐ 1 ⇒

Richard William Church and the Criticism of Friendship

The remembrance, the tradition of "Church of Oriel" was still fresh with us. His name was knit into the old Tractarian story; it mingled with the records of J. H. Newman, whose personality still exercised over us that intimate fascination which was so peculiarly his own. ... And now and again we trooped to St. Mary's, eager to see the hero of the Proctorial Veto in 1845; and we listened with deepened interest to the preacher, as we noted, with the naïve surprise of young men, the many faces among the congregation of dons. whom it was very rare to see at a University sermon. We began to recognise that strange consent, in later days so unique, which made men of every type and party, whatever their quarrels or differences, somehow, always, accept "Church of Oriel." Round every other name there was hot debate, attack and defence, challenge and counter-challenge. But no one ever discussed the worth or the authority of this name; it was an established matter, about which there was no division of opinion.

Canon Henry Scott Holland

I

Nothing was more characteristic of John Henry Newman than his delight in friendship. It exhibited not only his charm and *caritas* but the great store he placed on personal influence in the cure of souls. It also demonstrated his readiness to play his faithful part in the communion of saints, which was so vital to so many of Newman's English contemporaries, living as they did at a time when sanctity had become a neglected grace.[1] In addition to the depth, there was a catholicity to his friendships. The man who could name among his friends individuals as sharply different as John Keble, Edward Pusey, Hurrell Froude, Blanco White,

---

[1] In 1841, over ten years before he poped, Manning wrote Gladstone a letter in which he confessed that "I have been thinking of much of what we have said about developing the Catholic Element of the English Church. If we had but the visible undeniable note of Sanctity upon us—nothing should resist us." Manning to Gladstone (23 April 1841), *The Correspondence of Henry Edward Manning and William Ewart Gladstone Vol. 1: 1833–1844*, 4 vols, ed. Peter C. Erb (Oxford: Oxford University Press, 2013), i, 219.

Ambrose St. John, Maria Giberne, Edward Caswall, James Hope-Scott, Aubrey de Vere, Frederick Rogers (later Lord Blachford), Mary Holmes, Georgiana Fullerton, Ignatius Ryder, Thomas Arnold, Emily Bowles, the Duke of Norfolk, Henry Wilberforce, and Bishop William Ullathorne was not someone of limited sympathies. If Newman's talents were of a far-reaching versatility, he might almost have chosen his friends to accommodate the range of that versatility. Lawyers, poets, statesmen, priests, dons, historians, converts, artists, writers, administrators—all figured in what became the apostolate of his friendships. Yet, for our purposes, of all his friends, the most revelatory was Richard William Church, whom the Anglican historian John Henry Overton nicely called "the very flower of Oxford culture."[2] After all, Church, after being elected a Fellow of Oriel in 1838, became one of Newman's most trusted confidants during what the author of the *Oxford University Sermons* referred to as "those trying five years from 1841 to 1845," when, as he said, Church, among a few others, "did so much to comfort and uphold me by their patient, tender kindness and their zealous service in my behalf."[3] Later, Church would tell his friend W. J. Copeland: "I often wish ... that I had Boswellized. But unhappily, or happily, I didn't." Naturally, he would "mourn over the utterly faded details."[4] As Church's daughter Mary confirmed, from her father's residence in Oriel and his attendance at Newman's famous sermons at St. Mary's "a daily companionship" developed between the two men, "which grew into a friendship of the closest and most familiar kind."[5] Indeed, Church was present throughout Newman's protracted Anglican death-bed, a distinction which one should bear in mind whenever considering the authority of Church's classic history of the Oxford Movement. Then, again, nearly twenty years after the debâcle of Tract 90, Church also helped Newman to verify portions of his *Apologia pro Vita Sua* (1864), the composition of which proved so lacerating to the convert. At the time, Newman regarded the revisiting of his religious development "to defend," as he said, "my honesty while in the Church of England" as "one of the most painful trials in which I have ever been in my life."[6] Being a man and, indeed, a critic of the most discerning fellow feeling, Church instinctively understood this pain, appreciating, as he said, that the man who has converted is all too liable to being "thrown inward on himself, to watch and study with unhealthy eagerness the vicissitudes of what is to him the most interesting of histories, the history of his religious experience ... It is not everyone who can dare to repeat the experiment of St Augustine's confessions."[7] Yet when Newman and Church met unexpectedly in 1864 at the London home of their mutual friend Frederic Rogers, Church spoke warmly of his old friend's undiminished charm. For Church, Newman "was very little changed in look or

---

[2] John Henry Overton, *The Anglican Revival* (London: Blackie & Son, 1897), 133.
[3] Dedicatory Letter from Newman to Church (Advent, 1871), in *US*.
[4] Church quoted in B. A. Smith, *Dean Church: The Anglican Response to Newman* (Oxford: Oxford University Press, 1958), 54.
[5] *Life and Letters of Dean Church*, ed. Mary C. Church (London: Macmillan & Co., 1897), 22.
[6] Newman to R. W. Church (23 April 1864), *LD*, xxi, 100.
[7] Church quoted in B. A. Smith, *Dean Church: The Anglican Response to Newman* (Oxford: Oxford University Press, 1958), 282. Smith is one of the few really first-rate critical biographers of the Tractarians. His treatment of Chruch's wide-ranging work is superb. The passage from Church can also be found in his *Cathedral and University Sermons* (London: Macmillan, 1899, 284–5.

general manner or way of talking, except that he seemed almost stronger in body. He was in good spirits, very hearty, and talked very freely about all sorts of things; reminding us every now and then that he was across the border, but without embarrassment, and without any attempt to flaunt anything in our faces. It was a much more easy meeting than I could have supposed possible. We seemed to fall into the old ways of talking." After this happy reunion, Rogers and Church made Newman a present of a new violin, which prompted one of the Oratorian's most brilliant impromptu musings. "I really think it will add to my power of working," he said to Church. "I never wrote more than when I played the fiddle. … There must be some electric current passing from the strings through the fingers into the brain and down the spinal marrow. Perhaps thought is music."[8] With this long-standing, close attachment to a figure who even now is the subject of continual misrepresentation, Church became one of Newman's finest contemporary critics, writing rich, vivid, judicious accounts of his old mentor in *The Oxford Movement: 1833–1845* (1891), sermons from several collections of sermons, and various articles collected in his *Occasional Papers* (1897). In this chapter, I shall delve into Church's life and work to show how aspects of both enabled him to enter into and appraise Newman's unique achievement.

II

Richard William Church (1815–90) was born in Lisbon, the son of a wine merchant, John Dearman Church (1782–1828) and his wife, Bromley Caroline Metzener (d. 1845) of German ancestry. His paternal grandfather, Matthew Church hailed from Cork and was a member of the Society of Friends, which explains why John was not baptized into the Anglican Church until he was thirty-two. John's brother, Sir Richard Church (1784–1873) was the famous liberator of Greece, a dashing soldier who left a deep impression on the future writer of history in his nephew. When five years of age, Church traveled with his parents to the south of Italy to visit his uncle, who, after serving in the Napoleonic wars in Egypt, France, and Italy, entered the service of the King of Naples as Viceroy in Apulia, Terra di Bari and Terra d'Otranto, a role in which he restored order to the territories under his charge, rooted out brigandage, and broke the power of the secret societies that had long vexed the country. According to Church's daughter Mary, the editor of his letters, "Some dim memories of this journey, with its strange experiences and changing scenes and picturesque figures, remained in the boy's mind; the one clear impression which survived being the sight of brigands' heads stuck upon poles, in places along the roadside—left there as significant tokens of his uncle's authority."[9] Like Newman, he was fascinated by the exploits of soldiers and sailors: Southey's *Life of Nelson* (1813) was one of his favorite books.

From Lisbon, the family moved to the Casa Annalena in Florence across from the Boboli Gardens, where they stayed for ten years. When it came time to be enrolled in school, Church attended the English school at Leghorn, where his parents had friends among the place's expatriates. As these foreign connections

---

[8] Newman to R. W. Church (11 July 1865), *LD*, xxii, 9.
[9] Church, *Life and Letters*, 4.

attest, Church hailed from a strikingly cosmopolitan background, which gave him something of the same critical detachment that Newman had when it came to such inalienably English things as the National Church and Oxford. After all, Newman's father was a private banker in Lombard Street in the highly cosmopolitan City of London and his mother came from a distinguished Huguenot family from Normandy. Moreover, Church's background gave him an openness to the world beyond England, an openness which one can see in his letters from abroad. "For the last weeks I have been living among people who form the most grotesque contrasts to all that I have been accustomed to," he wrote his friend Frederick Rogers in 1847 while staying with his uncle in Athens.

> The difference of scene and dress is very soon got over, and the views of the Acropolis, and the rickety cabs driven below them by fierce moustached coachmen in red caps and white petticoats, do not move me more than St. Mary's and a Vice-Chancellor and pokers would do. But the company that I keep—quite, I assure you, the elite of Athens—is very different from all your people at Oxford.

Apropos this visit, G. Martin Murphy claims in the *Oxford Dictionary of National Biography* that Church's "travels and his contacts with European liberals … modified his innate toryism." If one reads Church himself on these matters, it is clear that Europe's Liberals did not so much modify as reinforce his "innate toryism." In his letter to Rogers about his stay in Athens, for example, he writes: "all my friends are strong Liberals, and I hear nothing but Liberalism all day long. No one here has any notion that an Englishman can be other than a Liberal; if he was not, he would be a sort of unintelligible contradictory monster, who by some accident had come to be bred in the great country of enlightened constitutionalism." Europe's Liberals may have reinforced certain Whiggish caricatures of English Liberalism but they hardly induced Church to second guess his Tory distaste for insurrection.

> Of course all our governments have acted more or less so as to foster the idea, and the English who come to live here, besides the strong temptations of a foreign residence to become real Liberals, can hardly help appearing to be so, unless they take the line of talking against England and English policy and proceedings. *Prime face*, it is taken for granted that an Englishman abhors Jesuits and despotism as the two greatest of evils, and would die—or at least give a good deal of money—to provide constitutions for all nations wanting them; and it is difficult to make the natives understand that one is quite content with one's freedom at home from thumb-screws and black-holes without violently sympathising with all the insurrectionists in Europe.[10]

The fact that Church would later repudiate Gladstonian liberalism once he saw its hapless architect truckling to Ireland's insurrectionists gives this passage additional point.

At the same time, Church's letters show that he was not unappreciative of what he saw as the positive aspects of religious liberalism, though he did not gloss

---

[10] Ibid., 93–4.

over its heterodoxy. "I have just been reading a book which I advise you to look into if it falls in your way," he wrote to Rogers in 1856, "the memoirs and letters of a certain Frederic Perthes, a German bookseller, which I have been much struck with. He was a man who made his trade a great work, and followed it in the highest spirit; a thoroughly fine fellow, overflowing with energy, and cleverness, and kindliness, and affectionateness of all kinds, an enthusiastic German … The curious thing is, how he is an instance showing how those Germans contrive to show deep religious earnestness—and what certainly has all the look of New Testament religion—without Church or any fixed creed, and with a most unrestrained intercourse with men of the most clashing opinions, Roman Catholics, rationalists, sceptics, and everything. His business and his very high character brought him into acquaintance and intimacy with a vast number of great German names—Niebuhr, Stolberg, Neander, Schleiermacher, Jacobi, and a hundred others, and their and his letters are given. And the book let's one into the real feelings and workings of all those wild German thinkers whose proceedings startle and astonish us so much. It shows us their domestic and undress side, and certainly, to my mind, abates the strong dislike and condemnation which we have been taught is the right thing to feel towards them. I don't mean that it reconciles me to their way of going on; but it does make one feel how very much without real knowledge has been a great deal of the broad abuse of Germanism that goes on; and how much real goodness, and often strong religious feeling there has been in quarters among them, where it has been *a priori* assumed to be incompatible with their speculative opinions."[11] Such fair-minded sympathy has its appeal, though it also shows that Church could be patient of error in ways that Newman might have found too uncritical.

Later, however, in an incisive review of Mrs. Humphry Ward's *Robert Elsmere* (1888), her novel about an Oxford clergyman who, losing his Anglican faith after reading Schelling and Strauss, turns, instead, to liberalism and social work, Church showed how his indulgent view of German Protestantism underwent a marked change. "German learning is decidedly imposing," he would write.

> But after all there are Germans and Germans; and with all that there has been of great in German work there has been also a large proportion of what is bad—conceited, arrogant, shallow, childish. German criticism has been the hunting-ground of an insatiable love of sport—may we not say, without irreverence, the scene of the discovery of a good many mares' nests? When the question is asked, why all this mass of criticism has made so little impression on English thought, the answer is, because of its extravagant love of theorizing.[12]

But there was a more fundamental objection still to the Germans and their "Germanism." "A so-called Christianity, ignoring or playing with Christ's resurrection, and using the Bible as a sort of Homer," Church wrote, "may satisfy a class of clever and cultivated persons. It may be to them the parent of high and

---

[11] Ibid., 176.
[12] Church, "The Author of 'Robert Elsmere' on a New Reformation," in *Occasional Papers Selected from the Guardian, the Times, and the Saturday Review 1846–1890*, 2 vols (London: Macmillan & Co., 1897), i, 185–6.

noble thoughts, and readily lend itself to the service of mankind. But it is well in so serious a matter not to confuse things. This new religion may borrow from Christianity as it may borrow from Plato, or from Buddhism, or Confucianism, or even Islam. But it is not Christianity. Robert Elsmere may be true to life, as representing one of those tragedies which happen in critical moments of history. But a Christianity which tells us to think of Christ doing good, but to forget and put out of sight Christ risen from the dead, is not true to life. It is as delusive to the conscience and the soul as it is illogical to reason."[13] Ian Ker, as my readers will see in my chapter on his work, lays great stress on the lengths to which Newman would go in his sermons to present his auditors with the Christ of Scripture, not Tübingen. To quote Reinhard Hütter, "Keenly identifying counterfeits and replacing them with the true currency of Christianity is one of Newman's enduring theological contributions."[14] The Newmanian critic in Church was certainly faithful to this defining aspect of his subject, since he knew, as Newman knew, that in Holy Scripture "we find the history of this world interpreted for us by a heavenly rule. When, then, a man, thus formed and fortified within, with these living principles in his heart, with this firm hold and sight of things invisible, with likings, opinions, views, aims moulded upon God's revealed law, looks abroad into the world, he does not come to the world for a revelation—he has one already."[15]

Like all of his contemporaries, Church experienced the rise of liberalism in the shadow of the French Revolution, the spectre of which haunted Paris, as he could attest in a letter of May, 1862.

> This evening ... I strolled up to the place where Louis XVI and Marie Antoinette were buried after their execution. It was then an out-of-the-way cemetery attached to the parish of the Madeleine, and there they were thrown in anyhow, and, I believe, quicklime thrown over the bodies. The place was afterwards, it is said, bought by a royalist, who turned it into an orchard, by way of turning away any suspicions; but he kept note of where the bodies were laid. Then at the Restoration, what was to be found was removed to St. Denis, and the ground purchased, and a Chapelle Expiatoire built on it. It is somehow one of the gloomiest places I remember seeing; surrounded by dead walls or high houses, with just a border of ivy running round the ground; and then a ponderously heavy building, a sort of cloister and chapel, enclosing the old burying-place, with great iron posts and iron chains fencing it round, and the arches of the cloisters as deep and heavy as they could be made. No doubt it was not meant to have all this gloomy look; but if any one had planned to convey all the melancholy and hopeless ideas connected with the fall of the old monarchy in the Place de la Concorde by embodying them in a dismal and dreary monument, he could not have succeeded better than Louis XVIII has done in this case. One street that continually is the street down which the carts passed to the place of execution; and the street leading to the Chapelle Expiatoire is the one up which the carts with the bodies must

---

[13] Ibid., 188–9.
[14] Reinhard Hütter, *John Henry Newman on Truth and its Counterfeits: A Guide for Our Times* (Washington: Catholic University Press, 2020), 4.
[15] Newman, "Waiting for Christ" (1840), *PPS*, vi, 251.

have come. And now all is so different, and yet all is marked with the tokens and suggestive memorials of what was done then.[16]

In reading Church's letters from abroad, one can also see that he was a typical Victorian in regarding travel as a species of education, something to which one was bound to submit with a certain conscientious dutifulness. "The heat interrupted sight-seeing in the middle of the day," he told one correspondent regarding his visit to Delphi in 1847; "and, as usual, I have some two or three points on my traveler's conscience, as having been carelessly seen."[17] Oddly enough, he did not get around to seeing the sights of Rome until 1882, though when he did, he found them puzzlingly unsatisfactory. Many of his Anglican contemporaries were content to find the place simply contemptible. Lady Margaret Brewster, for example, the author of *Work: or Plenty to Do and How to Do It* (1855) held that only those could take the place seriously who had lost "all sense of the ludicrous and all purity of taste."[18] Church responded to it with marked ambivalence. "It is hopeless to talk about Rome," he wrote his friend, Lord Blachford, who had been one of Newman's students at Oriel.

> My inclination was not strong to come here, and when I got here, and it was before my eyes in all its rugged picturesqueness, all my feeling was one almost of hatred to the place. It seemed such a mixture of all incompatible things—ruins and magnificence, waste and civilisation, tumbledown squalidness and untidiness, and stateliness and grandeur, such as one has never seen elsewhere; an anti-religious world and an ostentatiously religious world, really as worldly, and also an undeniably magnificent organisation of high religion quite unique. It was a real worry and vexation to have it all forced on one's thoughts and sight at every step, in every view one had, and every inscription or name that came across one. I can only say that my feeling the first day was of hatred such as I never felt to London or Paris. I had the feeling that it is the one city in the world, besides Jerusalem, on which we know that God's eye is fixed, and that He has some purpose or other about it—one can hardly tell whether of good or evil. A good deal of His purpose is visible—and what of the rest? I cannot tell you how this kind of uncertainty about what the real meaning of the whole thing was tormented and vexed me.[19]

Something of Church's misgivings about Rome might have stemmed from his very Englishness, even though what set him apart from so many of his English

---

[16] Church, *Life and Letters*, 163. Forgetting the carnage to which it gave rise, James Fitzjames Stephen saw the Revolution as a theatrical performance. "The swearing, the swaggering, the protesting was genuine in its way, though the actors in this strange melodrama seem to have had continually before their minds' eye the reflection that they were wonderfully fine fellows for figuring in such a performance. ... [T]hey liked the sentiment which their position created so much, that they could not resist the temptation of increasing their enjoyment by exaggerated language." *Selected Writings of James Fitzjames Stephen: On the Novel and Journalism*, ed. Christopher Ricks (Oxford: Oxford University Press, 2023), 224.

[17] Church quoted in John Pemble, *The Mediterranean Passion: Victorians and Edwardians in the South* (Oxford: Oxford University Press, 1987), 68.

[18] Lady Margaret Brewster, quoted *ibid.*, 226.

[19] Church to Lord Blachford (27 April 1882), Church, *Life and Letters*, 355.

contemporaries was the fact that he had ties to Italy that enabled him to transcend the usual English insularity. In *Spenser* (1879), however, which he contributed to the "English Men of Letters" series, he actually gave it as his opinion that the idea of the gentleman was not only an English idea, but one that had taken root in Elizabethan England. "In the Faerie Queene, Spenser has brought out, not the image of the great Gloriana, but in its various aspects a form of character which was then just coming on the stage of the world," Church writes, "and which has played a great part in it since."

> As he has told us, he aimed at presenting before us, in the largest sense of the word, the English gentleman. It was, as a whole, a new character in the world. It had not really existed in the days of feudalism and chivalry, though features of it had appeared, and its descent was traced from those times: but they were too wild and coarse, too turbulent and disorderly, for a character which, however ready for adventure and battle, looked to peace, refinement, order, and law as the true conditions of its perfection. In the days of Elizabeth, it was beginning to fill a large place in English life. It was formed amid the increasing cultivation of the nation, the increasing varieties of public service, the awakening responsibilities to duty and calls to self-command. Still making much of the prerogative of noble blood and family honours, it was something independent of nobility and beyond it. A nobleman might have in him the making of a gentleman: but it was the man himself of whom the gentleman was made. Great birth, even great capacity, were not enough; there must be added a new delicacy of conscience, a new appreciation of what is beautiful and worthy of honour, a new measure of the strength and nobleness of self-control, of devotion to unselfish interests. This idea of manhood, based not only on force and courage, but on truth, on refinement, on public spirit, on soberness and modesty, on consideration for others, was taking possession of the younger generation of Elizabeth's middle years. Of course, the idea was very imperfectly apprehended, still more imperfectly realized. But it was something which on the same scale had not been yet, and which was to be the seed of something greater. It was to grow into those strong, simple, noble characters, pure in aim and devoted to duty, the Falklands, the Hampdens, who amid so much evil form such a remarkable feature in the Civil Wars, both on the Royalist and the Parliamentary sides. It was to grow into that high type of cultivated English nature, in the present and the last century, common both to its monarchical and its democratic embodiments, than which, with all its faults and defects, our western civilization has produced few things more admirable.[20]

If Newman contrived to see in his gentleman a creature tailor-made to epitomize the limitations of natural virtue, "a creation not of Christianity, but of civilisation," Church saw in his a paean to the putative "new delicacy of conscience" of "the younger generation of Elizabeth's middle years," a fanciful reading of cultural history which might very well have disabled him from appreciating the wild, coarse, disorderly, turbulent societies that gave the world Rome.[21] This

[20] Richard William Church, *Spenser* (London: Macmillan & Co., 1879), 156–7.
[21] For Newman's idea of the gentleman, see *Idea*, 174. See also this instructive letter, written roughly a year after the publication of the *Idea*. "I have contrasted virtue without the grace of God with

reading can also be seen as lively proof that Church, for all of his openness to the cosmopolitan, and his wide cosmopolitan reading, was, at times, susceptible to views as narrowly English as those of Pusey or Keble.

After the death of Church's father in 1828, his mother returned to England and settled in Bath. Thereafter, Church was enrolled in Redlands, an Evangelical school in Bristol, which, if not a particularly brilliant place, did give him the training necessary to pursue the scholarly interests that would always animate his work. Indeed, browsing the city's bookstalls turned him into a confirmed bibliophile. It also gave him a certain independence of mind. As his daughter Mary, who brought out an edition of his letters, points out, "whilst on good terms, both with schoolfellows and masters, he went very much his own way, a reserved, serious, studious boy, loving books and already beginning to collect them."[22] Once he went up to Oxford, his wide reading doubtless enabled him to appreciate Newman's considerable learning. Apropos the training he received at Redlands, he would later write: "I suppose I sapped, was made to learn rules carefully ... The grind was the thing, and not a bad thing. It saved time afterwards."[23] Another preoccupation of Church's dates from his days in Bristol, which also nicely prepared him for his friendship with Newman.

> I remember questions arising in my thoughts as to whether we really could be so cocksure about the absolute truth of the Evangelical formulae, as was commonly taken for granted. One of the great watchwords was the right of private judgment: and we used on Sundays to have to find texts to prove it. And it used to occur to me, how then can we condemn the Socinians, who go wrongly by using it—they with the Roman Catholics being the special type of heretics whom we thought of, and looked at when we saw them, with a kind of awful curiosity and dismay.[24]

From Bristol, in 1832, Church went up to Wadham College because of its Evangelical character, though, like Newman, he would quickly outgrow his Evangelical susceptibilities. At the same time, his mother married Thomas Crokat of Leghorn, whose daughter married George Moberly, fellow and tutor of Balliol and lifelong friend of John Keble. Although Moberly was a vital mentor to Church, it was Charles Marriott who introduced the shy, diffident, bookish undergraduate to Newman in 1835. There are many good pen portraits in Church's history of Tractarian Oxford but the one he wrote of Marriott is special because it exhibits something of the portraitist's deep respect for the man who did him so signal a service. "He called on me the first term," Church recalled of Marriott.

---

virtue with it—and said that no merely natural virtue will be rewarded with heaven any more than beauty of person or high intellectual powers," Newman wrote his friend Emily Bowles. "Can ... a clergyman of the Church of England dispute this? ... I suppose he would say that the moral code of the world is not at variance with the Christian code, though St John says 'the world lieth in evil.' He must say that the world's 'pattern man' is held in favour in God's sight, though 'just, upright, conscientious' warriors and statesmen have in our own day been adulterers, and Scripture says, 'Ye adulterers, know ye not that the friendship of the world is enmity with God?'" Newman to Emily Bowles (15 October 1874), LD, xxvii, 137–8.

[22] Church, *Life and Letters*, 9.
[23] Ibid., 8.
[24] Ibid., 8–9.

> He had got his Oriel Fellowship, and I thought it an immense honour to be noticed by such a swell. I don't suppose I saw very much of him, but he never lost sight of me. His kindness and affection grew and never faltered to the day of his death. He was the earliest friend to whose undeniable superiority I could look up: others had been more or less my equals ... But no man, that I ever heard of, had such strange influence, the influence arising from sheer respect, in turbulent Oxford scenes among the undergraduates, as in the rows at the Union ... No one was so listened to, as if men believed in his sincerity and truth of purpose, and entire absence of indirect motives.[25]

Another striking thing about this portrait is that it manages to capture something of the portraitist's own purity of purpose, which was not overlooked by his examiners when he presented himself for the Oriel fellowship. As another candidate for the fellowship at the time, Mark Pattison memorably remarked:

> I presume that Church was Newman's candidate, though so accomplished a scholar ... need not have required any party push. I have always looked upon Church as the type of the Oriel fellow; Richard Michell [tutor of Lincoln] said, at the time of the election: "There was such a moral beauty about Church, that they could not help taking him."[26]

Pattison makes for a good contrast to Church with regard to Newman because, unlike Church, he did not simply befriend Newman: he adulated him, which resulted in his not only losing his Christian faith—the Oxford historian Vivian Green described it as evaporating into "a mere Platonic wraith"—but setting up the humanist scholar Joseph Scaliger (1484–1558) in Newman's place as the object of his hero worship.[27] Rationalist intellectualism would be the guiding light of his life, not faith, of which he always felt himself incapable, even though he was apparently tempted, however fleetingly, to follow Newman into the Church of Rome in October of 1845. "The popular theory," Meta Bradley, a confidant of Pattison, wrote to him in his old age, "is that you made up your mind to become RC but that you lost a particular train and next day you changed your mind! My own idea is that religion would never have suited your character." Whether it would have suited him or not, converting to Catholicism would have required him to abandon his fellowship, and the scholarly Pattison would have found that profoundly difficult.[28] Church, by contrast, would never be tempted to follow Newman into the Roman Church, convinced as he was that Anglicanism was a legitimate branch of the Universal Church, though he did follow Newman in seeing the dead end of learning divorced from faith, an end which would embitter most of Pattison's long despondent flight from faith.

It was while preparing for the Oriel examination that Church attended Newman's late-afternoon sermons at St. Mary's, later relating that hearing Newman deliver his sermon, "The Ventures of Faith" (1836) constituted something of an

---

[25] Ibid., 13–14.
[26] Mark Pattison, *Memoirs of an Oxford Don* (London: Macmillan, 1885), 163.
[27] V. H. H. Green, *Religion at Oxford and Cambridge* (London: SCM Press, 1964), 294.
[28] Ibid., 288–9.

epoch in his life. Later, he would supply his readers with some of the best criticism that the sermons have ever received, noting in particular how "form and matter are closely connected in the sermons, and depend on one another, as they probably do in all work of a high order." This, of course, is true enough, but Church went much deeper as to their contemporary and, indeed, perennial appeal.

> The matter makes and shapes the form with which it clothes itself. The obvious thing which presents itself in reading them is that, from first to last, they are a great systematic attempt to raise the whole level of religious thought and religious life. They carry in them the evidence of a great reaction and a scornful indignant rising up against what were going about and were currently received as adequate ideas of religion. The dryness and primness and meagerness of the common Church preaching, correct as it was in its outlines of doctrine, and sober and temperate in tone, struck cold on a mind which had caught sight, in the New Testament, of the spirit and life of its words. The recoil was even stronger from the shallowness and pretentiousness and self-display of what was popularly accepted as earnest religion; morally the preacher was revolted at its unctuous boasts and pitiful performance, and intellectually by its narrowness and meanness of thought and its thinness of colour in all its pictures of the spiritual life. From first to last, in all manner of ways, the sermons are a protest, first against coldness, but even still more against meanness, in religion. With coldness they have no sympathy, yet coldness may be broad and large and lofty in its aspects; but they have no tolerance for what makes religion little and poor and superficial, for what contracts its horizon and dwarfs its infinite greatness and vulgarizes its mystery. Open the sermons where we will, different readers will rise from them with very different results; there will be among many the strongest and most decisive disagreement; there may be impatience at dogmatic harshness, indignation at what seems overstatement and injustice, rejection of arguments and conclusions; but there will always be the sense of an unfailing nobleness in the way in which the writer thinks and speaks. It is not only that he is in earnest; it is that he has something which really is worth being in earnest for. He placed the heights of religion very high. If you have a religion like Christianity—this is the pervading note—think of it, and have it, worthily. People will differ from the preacher endlessly as to how this is to be secured. But that they will learn this lesson from the sermons, with a force with which few other writers have taught it, and that this lesson has produced its effect in our time, there can be no doubt.[29]

If there was a great bond between Newman and Church, despite their considerable religious differences, their shared impatience with "what makes religion little and poor and superficial" had a lot to do with it. Early and late, Church profoundly respected Newman for taking a torch to the Latitudinarianism that characterized so much English faith before he began preaching at St Mary's in the 1830s.[30]

---

[29] Church, "Newman's Parochial Sermons," in *Occasional Papers*, ii, 449–51.
[30] While Church admired the new rigor that Newman brought to Anglican preaching, he could also confess: "I do not like to hear the modest religion, the unobtrusive piety and benevolence of the last century depreciated. It undoubtedly did exist. I believe that there was a great deal of

Utterly dissatisfied with what he found current as religion, Dr. Newman sought, without leaving the old paths, to put before people a strong and energetic religion based, not on feeling or custom, but on reason and conscience, and answering, in the vastness of its range, to the mysteries of human nature, and in its power to man's capacities and aims. The Liberal religion of that day, with its ideas of natural theology or of a cold critical Unitarianism, was a very shallow one; the Evangelical, trusting to excitement, had worn out its excitement and had reached the stage when its formulas, poor ones at the best, had become words without meaning. Such views might do in quiet, easy-going times, if religion were an exercise at will of imagination or thought, an indulgence, an ornament, an understanding, a fashion; not if it corresponded to such a state of things as is implied in the Bible, or to man's many-sided nature as it is shown in Shakespeare. The sermons reflect with merciless force the popular, superficial, comfortable thing called religion which the writer saw before him wherever he looked, and from which his mind recoiled. Such sermons as those on the "Self-wise Enquirer" and the "Religion of the Day," with its famous passage about the age not being sufficiently "gloomy and fierce in its religion," have the one-sided and unmeasured exaggeration which seems inseparable from all strong expressions of conviction, and from all deep and vehement protests against general faults; but, qualify and limit them as we may, their pictures were not imaginary ones, and there was, and is, but too much to justify them. From all this trifling with religion the sermons ... appealed to conscience; and they appealed equally to reason and thought ... They viewed religion as if projected on a background of natural and moral mystery ... He claimed to read their hearts; and people felt that he did read them, their follies and their aspirations, the blended and tangled web of earnestness and dishonesty, of wishes for the best and truest, and acquiescence in makeshifts; understating what ordinary preachers make much of, bringing into prominence what they pass by without being able to see or to speak of it; keeping before his hearers the risk of mismanaging their hearts, of "all kinds of unlawful treatments of the soul."[31]

At the same time, Church recognized that it was from "the popular, superficial, comfortable" travesty of Christianity that the pernicious influence of Renan's *Vie de Jésus* (1863) arose, about which he writes:

> M. Renan repeatedly declares that his great aim is to save religion by relieving it of the supernatural. He does not argue; but instead of the old familiar view of the Great History, he presents an opposite theory of his own, framed to suit that combination of the revolutionary and the sentimental which just now happens to be in favour in the unbelieving schools. And this is the result: a representation

unheeded, unremembered religion in it which may put us to deep shame." R. W. Church, *Pascal and Other Sermons* (London: Macmillan, 1996), 269.

[31] Church, "Newman's Parochial Sermons," ii, 453–5. The quotation comes from "Obedience the Remedy for Religious Perplexity" (1830), *PS*,i, 18, 234–5. Apropos the sermons, W. J. Copeland wrote in his Preface to their republication in 1868, that "the spirit that dictated them pierced here and there through the cloud which hung over the future," warning of "impending trials and conflicts ... perplexities and dangers ... then only dimly seen or unheeded" and that the author of them providing, "as best he might, words of guidance and support, and consolation and encouragement" proved "an anchor of the soul in the coming storm." *PPS*, i, vii–viii.

which boldly invests its ideal with the highest perfections of moral goodness, strength, and beauty, and yet does not shrink from associating with it also and that, too, as the necessary and inevitable condition of success—a deliberate and systematic willingness to delude and insensibility to untruth. This is the religion and this is the reason which appeals to Christ in order to condemn Christianity.[32]

No one saw the differences between Newman and Renan more clearly than Wilfrid Ward, who nicely elaborated on Church's insight into Renan's hollow moralism. "Newman finds in each age of the Church a wonderful similarity in the ethical character of the Catholic amid all the differences in the ecclesiastical polity," Ward writes,

> and in the various stages of doctrinal development. The one identical Divine truth, the one Christian revelation is in each age acting on the faithful soul, and with the same ethical result. The two are correlative. The character arises from the apprehension (albeit partial) of revealed truth which presupposes the truths of natural religion. In Renan they are both absent. To Newman the *semper eadem* of Catholicism is a *depositum fidei*, a revelation of truth beyond complete human expression, deepening and supplementing the intimations of conscience, gradually secured at many points by fixed dogmatic propositions, but far exceeding those propositions, as the Divine necessarily exceeds the human. The Frenchman's brilliancy and quick perception of all that lies at the surface are equalled by his inability to apprehend those deeper facts in the soul, those phenomena of the human "conscience," which Newman had so carefully analysed, and of which he has spoken as the "shadow" of God, testifying to His existence as the shadow is a proof of the substance phenomena which are essential to the latter's view of revelation itself. With a keen, emotional sensitiveness to the beauties of Catholic worship, Renan appears to be almost without any sense of the abiding realities between which that worship and the dogmatic system form an imperfect link—the sinful human soul, and the everlasting God, Creator, ever-present Sustainer, and Redeemer. Consequently, to him the *semper eadem* to be looked for in Catholicism is simply the visible, tangible object with which he has been in contact from his youth. It is hardly an exaggeration to say that he looks for it in the candles, the vestments, the altars, the flowers, as well as in the symmetrical details of the Scholastic propositions learnt by him at St. Sulpice, and in the French Catholic surroundings of his youth, in Paris and Brittany. This Catholicism satisfies his feelings (to which he gives the name of his "moral nature") but the theological details which it involves cannot be reconciled with the conclusions of his reason.[33]

Like Newman, Church stood out from his contemporaries in acknowledging the awful appeal of the supernatural, which always gave his work a certain humility. "I never should be a metaphysician," he once confessed, "but the way in which assumptions excite no question, and people go on spinning arguments,

---

[32] Church, "Renan's 'Vie de Jésus,'" in *Occasional Papers*, ii, 203–4.
[33] Wilfrid Ward, "Newman and Renan," in *Problems and Persons* (London: Longmans, Green & Co., 1903), 290–2.

as if the whole of the invisible world was as easy to be understood as the theory of the steam-engine, has long been one of my standing wonders."[34] Beginning in 1838, Church became a close friend and confidante of Newman's and joined the Tractarians, about whom he wrote so incisively in his history of the Oxford Movement. (When Gladstone read the book, he wrote to Cardinal Manning: "I have been travelling over the scenes & thoughts of days long gone by in the very remarkable work of Dean Church. I will not say it is more remarkable than the *Apologia* but it is (to my mind) much more of a history."[35]) It was also at this time that Church became the friend of Frederic Rogers, later Lord Blachford (1811–89) and James Bowling Mozley (1813–78), with both of whom he would frequently correspond. In 1840, he wrote Rogers an interesting description of the latest news preoccupying Oxford, a description which nicely demonstrates that the future historian of Tractarianism, even as an undergraduate, was finely attuned to its intermural nuances. Another noteworthy aspect of the letter is that it makes reference to Newman's series of letters to the *Times* under the pseudonym, "Catholicus," which he would later publish as *The Tamworth Reading Room* (1841), at a time when most readers were unaware that it had been written by him.

> curious things have happened since I wrote last. I think I told you that the *Times* had been letting in letters signed Catholicus, against Sir R. Peel, criticising an address delivered by him to the Tamworth Reading Room, in which he took Lord Brougham's scientific natural-theology line; and not only had let them in, but puffed them in its leading article, without, however, giving up Peel. These said letters, signed Catholicus … were thought to smack strongly of Puseyism, and brought out furious attacks on the said Puseyites in the *Globe*; expostulations and remonstrances, on political and theological grounds, from the poor old *Standard*; and a triumphant Macaulayism in the *Morning Chronicle*, in which the writer, with great cleverness, drew a picture of the alliance between effete, plausible, hollow Toryism, with Puseyism, which he described as a principle which for earnestness and strength had had no parallel since the Reformers and Puritans, and rejoiced greatly over the prospect that Puseyism must soon blow Toryism to shivers. And the *Globe* admitted that people were most egregiously out in supposing that this same Puseyism was an affair of vestments and ceremonies; that it was, on the contrary, something far deeper and more dangerous. Such was the state of things out of doors last month.[36]

This also shows the lively interest Newman inspired beyond Oxford. Mocking Robert Peel and Henry Brougham, keen advocates of the "march of mind," the founders of the non-denominational Tamworth Reading Room, from which all theological books would be banned, called forth some of Newman's best satirical sallies. Church doubtless remembered these long-ago, heady days in 1885 when Newman wrote him a brief letter thanking him for delivering an "impressive" Easter Sermon and ending by saying, "It is 63 years today since I was elected at

---

[34] Church, *Life and Letters*, 174.
[35] William Gladstone to Henry Edward Cardinal Manning (7 April 1890), *The Correspondence of Henry Edward Manning and William Ewart Gladstone*, iv, 93–4.
[36] Church, *Life and Letters*, 27–8.

Oriel: the turning day of my life."[37]

In 1841, after the Provost of Oriel, Edward Hawkins refused to allow Newman to treat his tutorial as pastoral duties, Church showed his support for his friend by resigning his own tutorship.[38] In 1845, he again proved his loyalty by taking advantage of his role as junior proctor to help veto Convocation's proposed censure of Newman over Tract 90. When the resolution was rejected by cries of *non placet*, James Mozley recalled, it was "like a trumpet and cheered enormously."[39] The unseemly vindictiveness of Convocation's attack on Newman did not go unnoticed by Church. "Mistakes men may commit, and defeats they may undergo, and yet lose nothing that concerns their character for acting as men of a high standard ought to act," he wrote nearly 50 years after the dramatic events had taken place in the Sheldonian on that cold, snowy St. Valentine's Day.

> But in this case, mistakes and defeat were the least of what the Board brought on themselves. This was the last act of a long and deliberately pursued course of conduct; and if it was the last, it was because it was the upshot and climax, and neither the University nor any one else would endure that it should go on any longer. The proposed attack on Mr. Newman betrayed how helpless they were, and to what paltry acts of worrying it was, in their judgment, right and judicious to condescend. It gave a measure of their statesmanship, wisdom, and good feeling in defending the interests of the Church; and it made a very deep and lasting impression on all who were interested in the honour and welfare of Oxford.[40]

This unsparing reading of the matter is made doubly compelling by a letter that Church wrote to Newman in June of 1841 apropos a conversation that he had had with Hawkins. "He is puzzled about our own Divines," Church wrote. "He asked whether Andrewes, Bull, etc., would agree with No. 90. I said I did not know whether every one would agree with every word of the Tract, but that I thought they would strongly condemn and repudiate the censure of the Heads of Houses."[41] Church's biographer, B. A. Smith writes that the veto "could not hold up a great university for long," which is true enough, though Church's stand was an honourable stand against a dishonourable censure—a censure which made a mockery of what ought to have been the university's commitment to the

---

[37] Newman to R. W. Church (12 April 1885), *LD*, xxxi, 53.

[38] When Hawkins died, his widow wrote Newman and he replied: "I have followed his life year after year as I have not been able to follow that of others, because I knew just how many years he was older than I am, and how many days his birthday was from mine. These standing reminders of him personally sprang out of the kindness and benefits done to me by him close upon sixty years ago, when he was Vicar of St Mary's and I held my first curacy at St Clement's. Then, during two Long Vacations, we were day after day in the Common Room all by ourselves, and in Ch Ch [Christ Church] meadow. He used then to say that he should not live past forty; and he has reached, in the event, his great age. I never shall forget to pray for him, till I too go, and have mentioned his name in my Obituary book, which dear Mrs Pusey made for me in her last illness. May God be with you, and make up to you by His grace this supreme desolation." Newman to Mrs. Hawkins (21 November 1882), *LD*, xxx, 153.

[39] Mozley quoted in Wilfrid Ward, *William George Ward and the Oxford Movement* (London: Macmillan & Co., 1889), 342.

[40] R. W. Church, *The Oxford Movement: Twelve Years 1833–1845* (London: Macmillan & Co., 1891), 331.

[41] Church, *Life and Letters*, 41.

teaching of universal knowledge, let alone its gross discourtesy to Newman.[42] Pusey's indignation was fierce. "To me, the condemnation of Newman when he has retired successively from every means of influence, Tracts, *British Critic*, St. Mary's, intercourse with young men, residence, sermons, Lives of the Saints, and has won more souls to Christ than any besides, is beyond measure dreadful. I should expect some dreadful chastisement to follow. 'They entreated him shamefully and beat him, and sent him away empty.' [Luke 20:11] He has been, to an amazing extent, God's messenger to us for the good of souls, and now men would cast him out."[43]

As for Newman himself, when news reached him of what had transpired at the Sheldonian, he could not have shown more splendid indifference. Since that momentous time, some have sought to suggest that Newman might have converted as a result of the displeasure he incurred with the Heads of Houses; but his correspondence shows otherwise. "The matter now going on has not given me a moment's pain, nay or interest," he wrote. "I did not even open the letter at once in which came the information of what the Hebdomadal Board had done." For the serene convert, "Nothing that has yet *happened* all along, has *caused* me to take any step which I have taken—though much has happened heretofore to augment the pain under which I acted. But now I have no pain about these ecclesiastical movements—I am too far gone for that." There was nothing reactive about Newman's leaving the National Church. "The real cause of my successive acts lies much deeper, and is more terrible. It is an intense perception that the English Church is … heir to the heretical and schismatical Churches of third, four[th] and fifth centuries, the Novatians, Arians, the Donatists, the Lucerferians, the Nestorians, the Monophysites, those churches from which all the fathers tell me to come out.[44]

Church's own sense of the part he had played in staving off the censure of Newman was characteristically modest: "The only thing to relieve the day," he wrote his mother, "has been the extreme satisfaction I had in helping to veto the third iniquitous measure against Newman. It was worth while being proctor to have had the unmixed pleasure of doing this."[45] Later that year, in August, Church wrote again to his mother. (Like Newman, he never let the skirmishing of dons get in the way of his corresponding with his mother—who became a key confidant to her son throughout this period, as Newman's mother had been of his during his earlier years at Oriel.) "I wish I could persuade you that Oxford is a very enjoyable place in the Long Vacation," Church wrote. "One is very quiet with one other Fellow, one cat, one dog, and one jackdaw with clipped wings, for one's companions in College; and when I am in the sulks, I can go to a friend who lives just out of the town, and all but in the country, at the Observatory, and smoke a cigar with him, and look at Jupiter and Saturn through his telescopes."[46]

---

[42] Smith, *Dean Church: The Anglican Response to Newman*, 49.
[43] Pusey quoted in Henry Parry Liddon, *Life of Edward Bouverie Pusey*, 4 vols (London: Macmillan, 1893), ii, 432.
[44] Newman to Charles Miller (11 February 1845), LD, x, 545–6.
[45] Church, *Life and Letters*, 65.
[46] Ibid., 67.

This serenity (imparted, in part, by his friendship with the astronomer Manuel Johnson, at whose Observatory Newman spent his last night in Oxford) would steady Church when word of Newman's desolating secession came. "You will be distressed to hear what I have just this moment heard from himself, that Newman has left us, and joined the Church of Rome," he wrote.

> It is a matter on which I can say little at present. I will ask you to pardon me once for all for my reserve on these points. It is so intensely painful to me to talk of them with those who do not know the whole case, and who, naturally, from distance, cannot have it put before them, that it has seemed better to abstain from it altogether. I will only say that about myself personally you need not make yourself unhappy.—Ever your affectionate son, R. W. C.[47]

What is striking about this letter is that, on the very day he learned of the conversion, long before any of the legion misrepresentations of it had been made, Church recognized that "those who do not know the whole case" would not appreciate its import. One of the reasons why studying Newman's critics is so vital to understanding the man and his work is that so many of them were heedless or even dismissive of the "whole case" to which Church refers. That he was not gives his criticism of his friend its rare distinction.[48] Apropos Newman's hostile critics, we should always keep in mind that their distortions of the great man arise fundamentally from the limitations of their judgement and taste. The English Opium-Eater, Thomas de Quincey recognized this vis-à-vis the critics of Edmund Burke. "To say ... that a man is a great thinker ... is but another expression for saying that he has a *schematizing* (or, to use a plainer but less accurate expression, a figurative) understanding. In that sense ... Burke is figurative: but understood, as he has been understood by the long-eared race of his critics, not as thinking in and by his figures, but as deliberately laying them on by way of *enamel* or after ornament,—not as *incarnating*, but simply as *dressing* his thoughts in imagery—so understood, he is not the Burke of reality, but a poor fictitious Burke, modelled after the poverty of conception which belongs to his critics."[49] The same can be said of Newman's long-eared critics.

In the long wake of Newman's conversion, Church would retire to Whatley near Frome in Somerset, where he became pastor, tending to 200 parishioners and looking after the parochial school with his wife Helen, with whom he had four children—three girls, Edith, Helen and Mary, and a boy, Frederick, a brilliant classical scholar who would die in 1888 at the age of thirty-three. "Nothing that has happened to me in life has been like that moment when we saw that no breath came through his lips," Fred's bereaved father would write afterwards.[50] Before the young man's sudden death, Lord Justice Bowen, with whom Fred was

---

[47] Ibid.
[48] Cf. "every conversion is unique and nothing to have theories about." Flannery O'Connor to "A" (19 May 56), *Letters of Flannery O'Connor: The Habit of Being*, ed Sally Fitzgerald (New York: Farrar, Giroux and Strauss, 1979), 157.
[49] Thomas de Quincey, "Elements of Rhetoric (1828)", *Thomas de Quincey: Selected Writings*, ed. Robert Morrison (Oxford: Oxford University Press, 2019), 125–6. The quotation is from a review of Richard Whately's book, in which Quincey writes at length of his own interest in prose style.
[50] Church quoted in Smith, *Dean Church: The Anglican Response to Newman*, 304.

studying law, wrote Church a note that must have made the loss of his only son all the more lacerating: "I never saw any one in whom the 'star' of home shone so continuously and so brightly."[51]

As was the case with so many of his friends, Newman tended to befriend whole families, not just this or that member of the family, and the Church family was no exception. When Newman wrote Church in 1871 to tell him that he should like to dedicate the "acephalous" revision of his Oxford University Sermons to him, Church replied, "it will indeed be most delightful to me, and to my children, to have my name associated with yours."[52] In 1876, Newman wrote Church's daughter Helen a letter to thank her for the gift she and her sisters had given him of a copy of Lewis Carroll's nonsense verse, "The Hunting of the Snark," which sent him back to his own childhood.

> I recollect well my own thoughts and feelings … as I lay in my crib in the early spring, with outdoor scents, sounds and sights wakening me up, and especially the cheerful ring of the mower's scythe on the lawn, which Milton long before me had noted;—and how in coming down stairs slowly, for I brought down both feet on each step, I said to myself "This is June!" though what my particular experience of June was, and how it was broad enough to be a matter of reflection, I really cannot tell.

Then, again, when Church's twin daughters turned twenty, Newman wrote them a moving birthday letter.

> The Oratory
> February 21. 1878
>
> My dear Helen and Mary,
>   How shall I best show kindness to you on your birthday?
>   It is by wishing and praying that year by year you may grow more and more in God's favour and in inward peace,—in an equanimity and cheerfulness under all circumstances which is the fruit of faith, and a devotion which finds no duties difficult, for it is inspired by love.
>   This I do with all my heart, & am, My dear Children very affectionately yours,
>   John H. Newman[53]

Another thing that Church and Newman had in common was that they were both good and faithful pastors, though Newman was constrained to confess to one begging priest, who had written to ask for financial help with his parish: "to speak honestly, I have a great dislike of Bazaars; and cannot get myself to take part in them; so I cannot help you in any way."[54] Mary Church is vivid about her father's

---

[51] Lord Justice Bowen quoted *ibid.*, 301.
[52] *LD*, xxv, 413.
[53] Newman to Helen and Mary Church (21 February 1878), *LD*, xxviii, 315–16. Later, in his old age, when he found that he could not "count or keep time" musically, Newman would re-gift the fiddle Church had given him to his daughter Mary on her wedding day, intent that he "should not … go without getting it a good master or mistress." Mary was a proficient fiddler. Newman to R. W. Church (28 March 1883), *LD*, xxx, 198.
[54] Newman to John Sherlock (17 August 1879), *LD*, xxxi, 95*–96*. Sherlock was the priest of St. Michael's, Moor Street, Birmingham. As it was, Newman sent him a check for twenty quid. Newman's distaste for church bazaars cannot have been entirely separate from his distaste for the

tenure at Whatley, where he quickly endeared himself to his country parishioners.

> Paper chases for the boys (an amusement unheard of before at Whatley) became an institution of the place, and one in which he might be counted on to take a foremost part; and with the elder children there were long country walks in summer, when they were encouraged to search for wild flowers to be looked at afterwards with Mr. Church's microscope. It was not long before throughout the place the hesitating welcome which had awaited him as a stranger passed into a loyal and affectionate confidence. Although his work at Whatley was not untouched by those disappointments which every parish priest must know, the relationship which thus grew up between him and his people was never disturbed or weakened. They turned to him unquestioningly as their friend, as on one whose counsel they could rely, who could understand their perplexities, and who could be trusted to keep their secrets. They could not mistake the presence of a sympathy which honestly and naturally entered into the familiar and homely details of their everyday life, and into all that concerned them—their work, their children, their gardens—and which could be interested, as they said themselves, even in their pigs. ... By the old, and by the sick, and dying, his visits were eagerly looked for. It was no uncommon request that he would come and sit by the bedside of the sick, watching with them until the dreaded "turn of the night" had passed; and in any case of sudden or urgent illness, or to a dying person, he would be summoned in haste—roused, it might be, at night by the sound of pebbles thrown up against his window—for they longed not to pass away without the help of his presence and his prayers. And among the men of the village his influence was not less remarkable. The roughest and most turbulent of them did not question his authority, or refuse a respect which was never forgotten even in the free and frank intercourse which had grown up in the night schools or the cricket-field. No one took liberties with him, and men were quick to recognise a power which on occasion could flash out in prompt and stern rebuke of faults of conduct, in a way that was all the more impressive by its contrast with the gentleness of his usual manner. ... And the qualities by which he won his peculiar power over his people were those which made themselves felt in church and in his sermons. ... His sermons, short and clear and practical, carefully written so as to avoid the use of long or difficult words, or of any lengthened thread of argument, had the same simple reality and directness of purpose about them. None could mistake his meaning; but simple as his words were, they had a force and sincerity which made their way to the hearts and consciences of all those who gathered weekly to listen to him in the little village church.[55]

When Church preached his farewell sermon at Whatley, he spoke for all of those who have ever known the passing of an epoch in the life of a parish with the passing of a particularly beloved pastor. "Many thoughts, and I am sure yours also, go back to many solemn and many joyful days; to festivals and weddings

---

idea of the university exhibited by modern Oxbridge, according to which its teaching was a kind of "bazaar ... in which wares of all kinds are heaped together for sale in stalls independent of each other." *Idea*, 421.

[55] Church, *Life and Letters*, 166–8.

and christenings" Church told his parishioners; "to many a happy Christmas, and Christmas Eve, with the lighted church, and the holly leaves, in the dark winter night; to many a glad and peaceful Easter; to many a summer school-feast; to many a blessed Communion together … I see again the faces which used to be so familiar to me, which have now passed away. I cannot go along a road, through the woods or across a field, I cannot look out on a prospect, I cannot enter a house, but it brings back something—some bright day, some happy meeting, some fear, some deliverance, some heavy tidings, some summons to me to hasten, in the dark chill morning, or the late night, or the warm summer day—to deathbed, to take last leave before it was too late. How it all comes back, through all these years, as if it was only yesterday … And now it is all over. It is finished and done. Never more in this world will it be as it has been. Other things are before all of us now. For what is past, as far as we are concerned in it, there only remains the judgment."[56]

In comparison with Church's amiable leaves-taking, Newman's "Parting of Friends" is shot through with a kind of prophetical scorn, which cannot have endeared him to most English Protestants, even those enamoured of the Romanism of the Anglo-Catholics. Here, Newman likened his departure to the departures of Scripture, which he saw as so many "memorials and tokens of the Son of Man, when His work and His labour were coming to an end." No one could have heard this sermon and been tempted to indulge in any nostalgia for the good old days.

> Like Jacob, like Ishmael, like Elisha, like the Evangelist whose day is just passed, He kept feast before His departure; and, like David, He was persecuted by the rulers in Israel; and, like Naomi, He was deserted by His friends; and, like Ishmael, He cried out, "I thirst" in a barren and dry land; and at length, like Jacob, He went to sleep with a stone for His pillow, in the evening. And, like St. Paul, He had "finished the work which God gave Him to do," and had "witnessed a good confession"; and, beyond St. Paul, "the Prince of this world had come, and had nothing in Him." [1 Tim. 6.13. John 14.30.] "He was in the world, and the world was made by Him, and the world knew Him not. He came unto His own, and His own received Him not." [John 1.10, 11.] Heavily did He leave, tenderly did He mourn over the country and city which rejected Him. "When He was come near, He beheld the city, and wept over it, saying, If thou hadst known, even thou, at least in this thy day, the things which belong unto thy peace! but now they are hid from thine eyes." And again: "O Jerusalem, Jerusalem, which killest the prophets, and stonest them that are sent unto thee, how often would I have gathered thy children together, as a hen doth gather her brood under her wings, and ye would not! Behold, your house is left unto you desolate." [Luke 19.41, 42; 13.34, 35.]

The moral Newman drew from these memorials was the reverse of consoling.

> A lesson surely, and a warning to us all, in every place where He puts His Name, to the end of time; lest we be cold towards His gifts, or unbelieving towards His word, or jealous of His workings, or heartless towards His mercies. O mother

[56] Ibid., 309–10.

of saints! O school of the wise! O nurse of the heroic! of whom went forth, in whom have dwelt, memorable names of old, to spread the truth abroad, or to cherish and illustrate it at home! O thou, from whom surrounding nations lit their lamps! O virgin of Israel! wherefore dost thou now sit on the ground and keep silence, like one of the foolish women who were without oil on the coming of the Bridegroom? Where is now the ruler in Sion, and the doctor in the Temple, and the ascetic on Carmel, and the herald in the wilderness, and the preacher in the market-place? where are thy "effectual fervent prayers," offered in secret, and thy alms and good works coming up as a memorial before God? How is it, O once holy place, that "the land mourneth, for the corn is wasted, the new wine is dried up, the oil languisheth, … because joy is withered away from the sons of men?" "Alas for the day! … how do the beasts groan! the herds of cattle are perplexed, because they have no pasture, yea, the flocks of sheep are made desolate." "Lebanon is ashamed and hewn down; Sharon is like a wilderness, and Bashan and Carmel shake off their fruits." [Joel 1.10–18, Isa. 33.9.] O my mother, whence is this unto thee, that thou hast good things poured upon thee and canst not keep them, and bearest children, yet darest not own them? why hast thou not the skill to use their services, nor the heart to rejoice in their love? how is it that whatever is generous in purpose, and tender or deep in devotion, thy flower and thy promise, falls from thy bosom and finds no home within thine arms? Who hath put this note upon thee, to have "a miscarrying womb, and dry breasts," to be strange to thine own flesh, and thine eye cruel towards thy little ones? Thine own offspring, the fruit of thy womb, who love thee and would toil for thee, thou dost gaze upon with fear, as though a portent, or thou dost loathe as an offence;—at best thou dost but endure, as if they had no claim but on thy patience, self-possession, and vigilance, to be rid of them as easily as thou mayest. Thou makest them "stand all the day idle," as the very condition of thy bearing with them; or thou biddest them be gone, where they will be more welcome; or thou sellest them for nought to the stranger that passes by. And what wilt thou do in the end thereof?[57]

Despite such differences in their style of preaching, the deep personal affinity between Church and Newman can be seen in a characteristically charming letter that Church wrote to Rogers in 1870 after Newman had stayed with him for an evening at Whatley on his way to see his niece Louisa Deane in Bath. "I have not had time to tell you about Newman's visit, which was duly chronicled in the local papers," he wrote.

> It was very pleasant. He was very well and happy, walking and even running, though it was that very hot weather. I took him to Longleat, and you know how he lets himself go when he enjoys being out in the air on a fine day, and looking at what he thinks beautiful; and Marston and Longleat looked their best for him. He made himself quite at home with Helen and the children; with the children he compared notes about children's books, which has ended in their sending him, and his very heartily accepting, one of their books of nonsense, *Alice's Adventures in Wonderland*, which he did not know, and they thought he ought

[57] SD, 405–8.

to. He talked very freely and a great deal; neither seeking nor avoiding subjects, but taking everything as it turned up, and becoming very animated at times. It was curious to learn, what of course is very natural, only it does not occur to outsiders, that there are degrees, and considerable ones, in the "Infallibilist" party; and that the passing of the Definition, in the shape in which it is likely to be passed, is looked on by some of them as almost a failure, to be deplored and to be wretched about, as not going far enough. He is anxious about the future of his school at Birmingham. I should gather from what he said that the Jesuits pick up the most promising of the converts from us.[58]

In 1871, Gladstone succeeded in persuading Church to become Dean of St. Paul's, after several demurrals, one of which showed that it was not only Newman and his Roman Catholic friends with whom the former Tractarian felt obliged to differ. "I have felt all along and the more lately," Church wrote to Gladstone, "that my relations with my old friends at Oxford, and the line which they have taken so strongly—and I cannot say altogether inconsistently—makes my position difficult as to preferment. They think that what seems to me just and reasonable in present Church policy a compromise and trimming, and something worse: as perhaps I should have thought it 25 years ago. I do not think that clergymen ought to mind being called trimmers even by a great man like Dr. Pusey: but it is of consequence that they should be able to say that they are not time-servers."[59] Neither Church nor Newman, it is safe to say, were time-servers.

No sooner did Church take up the post than he was required to weigh in on the ritualist controversy, about which Leslie Stephen was memorably acid.

> What a queer place ... [England] is! My excellent brother, now Sir James Stephen, has been speechifying in defence of the ritualists for four or five days. He says that he could hardly keep his countenance. One main question is whether the sacramental bread is to be cut thick and square, or round and thin—like a die or a penny. And David Hume has been dead for a century! I blush for my race. If I laugh, people shriek "levity" and "cynicism." But the utter silliness of the whole business protects it even from laughter. I could as soon ridicule a baby six months old.[60]

For Church, the controversy was simply an opportunity to exercise charity and good sense at a time when neither quality was in much abundance. Blanco White's biographer, G. Martin Murphy is astute on this score. Although no ritualist himself, Church "took the view that the principle of toleration was at stake and he regarded the Public Worship Regulation Act of 1874 as a dangerous attempt to enforce liturgical uniformity through the courts: matters of belief and worship were not to be determined by case law."[61] As a result of his adroit conduct of the opposition to the Act, its coercive force was baffled.

---

[58] Church, *Life and Letters*, 189–90.
[59] Church quoted in Smith, *Dean Church: The Anglican Response to Newman*, 148.
[60] Leslie Stephen to Charles Eliot Norton (4 February 1877), *Life and Letters of Leslie Stephen*, ed. Frederic William Maitland (London: Duckworth & Co., 1906), 297.
[61] ODNB.

When Newman got word of Church's own unexpected elevation, he wrote his old friend: "Our Birmingham Paper and the Guardian say you are to be Dean of St. Paul's. What a different life for you from Whatley! You must doff your wide awake, and don the Shovel ... I always think of St. Gregory Nazianzen, when I hear of metropolitan dignities."[62] Henry James, who had occasion to see the ceremonial world of the City up close, described it in one of his stories with a certain fascinated recoil. "It was the world of cheerful commonplace and conscious gentility and prosperous density," he observed, "a full fed material insular world, a world of hideous florid plate and ponderous order and thin conversation."[63] The idea of Newman's old friend taking so prominent a position in such a society amused Newman—he was always appreciative of the comedy of pomp—and he wrote several letters on Church's change of fortune, in one of which he mused aloud as to why he should find the elevation of friends so disconcerting. "I wonder whether it is because I am a little man myself, that I feel melancholy to have associations broken by the elevation of my friends," he wrote Church shortly after their mutual friend Frederick Roger's elevation to the peerage as Lord Blachford.

> If you are writing to [Rogers] please to send him my warm congratulations—but I do not write myself to him, not only because I don't know his full direction, or whether or not he is a bird of passage on the lake, but especially because I cannot yet say "Dear Blackworthy."
>
> Can you? you are a Spartan if you can. You see I have not yet got to call you "My dear Dean," though from College recollections of other Deans, it is comparatively natural—but I must undergo some preparation of mind and many private rehearsals before I can change the "Dear Rogers" which I have used for forty years.
>
> Oh! how strange it would have been, if, when he presented himself to my room at Oriel for examination for entrance, I could have read in some magic mirror on my table the paragraph in the Times which announced his peerage! What a vanity every thing is! I do hope you may not have any city dinners to go to. Any how, *they* are most unpleasant vanities.[64]

While Dean, Church brought new vitality to the Cathedral, restoring its physical structures and sorting out its Byzantine finances. Although scholarly, he was never impractical—a trait he shared with Newman. For all of his learned attainments, he proved a capable and effective administrator. Nevertheless, as the old *DNB* noted, his motto throughout his tenure might have been that of John Colet: *Si vis divinus esse, late ut deus*—"He who aims at doing God's work must be content to have the true influence of such work lie deep and hidden from the world." Newman certainly sympathized with how uncongenial the retiring scholar in Church would find the demands of such high ecclesiastical office, however dutifully he managed to fulfil them. "I trust you will be able, in one way or another, to do a great deal of good in your new position," he wrote his

---

[62] Newman to R. W. Church (17 August 1851), *LD*, xxv, 384.
[63] Henry James, "Brooksmith" (1892) in *Henry James: Selected Stories*, ed. Gerard Hopkins (Oxford: Oxford University Press, 1957), 412.
[64] Newman to R. W. Church (13 October 1871), *LD*, xxv, 413.

friend. "Milman found time for much literary work at St Paul's—This surprises me—and I shall be truly glad to find that you find the like—but somehow I have an idea that Westminster might be a post of leisure, as other Deaneries, but not St Paul's. Is it not a mass of incorporated sheep, Sion College, City Companies, religious societies, Trinity etc Houses, over whom you are a quasi pastor, to the extent at least of preaching Sermons, eating dinners, making speeches, and entertaining at home, and to the serious interruption of reading and writing? I shall rejoice to know that you can be as literary as Milman."[65] At the same time he was typically solicitous about Church's poor wife. "I pity (if I ought to use the word) your wife, even more than you," he wrote. "She seems so made for the sweet country, and I, though born in London, and in the city, feel no attraction to the *fumum strepitumque Romae*,[66] and no pleasure to find others doomed to it."[67] Newman's distaste for the smoky noise of the city cannot have been dispelled by an encounter he had at St Paul's Cathedral, as he related to Church: "I stood just inside the door listening to the chanting of the Psalms, of which I am so fond," he wrote.

> First came Verger one, a respectful person, inquiring if I wanted a seat in the choir, half a mile off me. No, I said—I was content where I was. Then came a second, not respectful, with a voice of menace—I still said No. Then came a third, I don't recollect much about him, except that he said he could provide me with a seat. Then came Number 2 again, in a compulsory mood, on which I vanished.
>
> I am sure if I was a dissenter, or again one of Mr Bradlaugh's people, nothing would attract me more to the Church of England than to be allowed to stand at the door of a Cathedral—did not St Augustine while yet a Manichee, stand and watch St Ambrose? No verger turned him out.[68]

---

[65] Henry Hart Milman (1791–1868), the rationalist historian, insisted, like Gibbon, on treating Christianity merely in its externals. Church criticized this Socinian view of history in one of his essays. "[A] history of religion which inadequately understands and estimates religious belief and doctrine ... cannot be a perfect one." R. W. Church, "Dean Milman's Essays," in *Occasional Papers*, i, 158. Newman criticized it as well, seeing it, in essence, as an expression of historicism. "It is obvious that the whole system of Revelation may be viewed in various, nay antagonist aspects," he wrote. "[T]hey who with Mr. Milman love to regard the whole Christian history as much as possible as a thing of earth ... may eventually be led on to commit themselves to positive errors about it, and may accordingly be wantonly trifling with serious matters ... Christianity has an external aspect and an internal; it is human without, divine within. To attempt to touch the human element without handling also the divine, we may fairly deem unreal, extravagant, and sophistical ... [S]uch a person does not *mean* any harm; nor does the writer who determines, as far as he can, to view the Christian as a secular fact, to the exclusion of all theological truth. He gives a representation of it, such as it would appear to a man of the world. This, at least, is our *primâ facie* view of Mr. Milman's book." *Ess.*, ii, 187–8. Newman refers to Milman's *A History of Latin Christianity* (1840).
[66] Horace, *Odes*, 3.29.12—*fumum ... strepitumque Romae* ("the smoke ... and noise of Rome"). Thackeray helps himself to this tag as well. See William Makepeace Thackeray, *Vanity Fair: A Novel Without a Hero* (1847), ed. John Sutherland (Oxford: Oxford University Press, 1998), 842.
[67] Newman to R. W. Church (27 August 1871), *LD*, xxv, 391.
[68] Newman to Richard Wiliam Church (26 December 1872), *LD*, xxvi, 221. To another correspondent in 1865, Newman confessed: "I speak from my own nido, and know nothing of the parties and their currents in the great metropolis." Newman to T. F. Wetherell (5 September 1865), *LD*, xxii, 26.

No one would have appreciated the wry charm of this better than Church. After the death of his son in 1888, other deaths of close friends followed in battering succession—especially those of Lord Blachford, Newman, and Dr. Liddon; indeed, the last time he appeared in St. Paul's it was to attend Liddon's funeral. (He had not been able to attend Newman's funeral because of bronchitis and, instead, wrote two articles about his old friend for *The Guardian*.) Towards the end he appeared less and less in public; he spent most of his time putting final touches to his history of the Oxford Movement; he died on 9 December 1890 at Dover.

III

"No one," the historian Algernon Cecil wrote, "has ever made an attack on Church."[69] Nevertheless, his very likeability could obscure attributes of the man that were at once deeper and more characteristic than his winning affability. In the preface to Mary Church's *Life and Letters of Dean Church*, Francis Paget (1851–1911), the Dean of Christ Church and later Bishop of Oxford, whose "tall, willowy figure and impressive bearing made him a notable figure in any assembly," took perceptive note of qualities in his father-in-law that lay beneath the endearing affability: "The notes of patience and of justice are on all his work," Paget wrote, "even as one felt them in the way he spoke of men, in the weight he gave to the considerations which might fairly weigh with others, in the large allowance he would always make for the vast diversity of men's gifts and opportunities, for the inscrutable depth of every human life, for the unknown hindrances and difficulties and discouragements through which those who seem to advance slowly may be winning a heroic way." Here is that critical sympathy so redolent of Church's observations regarding the work of others, which, in the case of Newman, would prove so incisive. "But patient as he was, he could be angry when need came," Paget continued; "angry with a quiet and self-possessed intensity which made his anger very memorable. The sight of injustice, of strength or wealth presuming on its advantages, of insolence—(a word that came from his lips with a peculiar ring and emphasis),—called out in him something like the passion that has made men patriots when their people were oppressed, something of that temper which will always make tyranny insecure and persecution hazardous." This certainly is a side of the man that we do not usually associate with Church. And yet Paget identified a still deeper and more abiding, though largely hidden trait in his father-in-law: "a habitual feeling of which only those who knew him well, perhaps, became distinctly conscious, but which, when once it had been discovered, might be traced in much that he said and did." This was a trait that would certainly have recommended Church to Newman—indeed, Paget's very description of it echoes many of the convert's own preoccupations and convictions.

> It was as though he lived in constant recollection of something that was awful and even dreadful to him; something that bore with searching force on all men's ways and purposes and hopes and fears; something before which he knew himself to

[69] Algernon Cecil, *Six Oxford Thinkers* (London: John Murray, 1909), 155.

be, as it were, continually arraigned; something which it was strange and pathetic to find so little recognised in current views of life. He seemed to bear about with him a certain hidden, isolating, constraining, and ennobling fear, which quenched the dazzling light of many things that attract most men; a fear which would have to be clean got rid of before time-serving or unreality could have a chance with him. Whatever that fear was it told upon his work in many ways; it helped him, probably, in great things to be unworldly; it sustained with an imperious and ever-present sanction his sense and care for perfect justice, in act and word, in his own life and in his verdicts on the past: and it may well have borne a part in making his style what it was; for probably few men have ever written so well and stayed so simply anxious to write truly.[70]

In November of 1838, when Newman was first befriending Church, he delivered a sermon at St. Mary's entitled "Reverence, A Belief in God's Presence," in which he spoke of the same holy fear that consumed Church. "Though Moses was not permitted to enter the land of promise, he was vouchsafed a sight of it from a distance," Newman told his auditors. "We too, though as yet we are not admitted to heavenly glory, yet are given to see much, in preparation for seeing more. Christ dwells among us in His Church really though invisibly, and through its Ordinances fulfils towards us, in a true and sufficient sense, the promise of the text. We are even now permitted to 'see the King in His beauty,' to 'behold the land that is very far off.'" If Newman, like Church, was profoundly appreciative of God's Presence, he was no less appreciative of how unaware, indeed, heedless their contemporaries were of this fundamental reality.

> Such a view is strange to most men; they do not realize the presence of Christ, nor admit the duty of realizing it. Even those who are not without habits of seriousness, have almost or quite forgotten the duty. This is plain at once: for, unless they had, they would not be so very deficient in reverence as they are. It is scarcely too much to say that awe and fear are at the present day all but discarded from religion. Whole societies called Christian make it almost a first principle to disown the duty of reverence; and we ourselves, to whom as children of the Church reverence is as a special inheritance, have very little of it, and do not feel the want of it. Those who, in spite of themselves, are influenced by God's holy fear, too often are ashamed of it, consider it even as a mark of weakness of mind, hide their feeling as much as they can, and, when ridiculed or censured for it, cannot defend it to themselves on intelligible grounds.[71]

As we will see in a later chapter, Edwin Abbott Abbott saw in Newman's holy fear a yearning for a kind of false nostalgic peace. "Wherever fear of sin may lead him—fear, that is to say, of his notions of sin, and of his notions of punishment—there it must be his unalterable destiny to follow," the schoolmaster contended. "Finally, his paper schemes being reduced to a blank by contact with realities, he will go continuously onward—however tortuous may be his path, while he dallies with the inevitable, determines to be guided by reason, plays at

---

[70] Church, *Life and Letters*, xxi–xxii. The description of Paget comes from the *ODNB*.
[71] *PS*, v, 2.

justifying himself on grounds of logic, and strives to convince himself that he is a free agent to that ultimate shock which shall procure him peace by pulverizing his intellect; so that at last, after long toil and tension, his mind may fall back once more at rest in the relaxation and easy calm of that sweet peace which he had lost as a youth almost as soon as he had begun to enjoy it."[72] Abbott may have been one of the first critics to misread Newman's youthful Evangelical phase but he was not the last.[73]

IV

In studying the critical reception that Newman received from his contemporaries or near contemporaries, we must always be struck by the peculiarly English incomprehension that characterized some of it. Abbott was one of the more impudent examples of this incomprehension but there were others. When the poet Wilfrid Scawen Blunt reread *Loss and Gain* (1847), he was convinced that "Newman's mind ... seems never to have faced the real issue of belief and unbelief, those which have to be fought out with materialism."[74] Another example can be found in Sir Montstuart Grant Duff's diary. There, the diarist might have understood Newman's playful sense of the ironic, recalling as he did the convert taking him over his library at the Oratory in Edgbaston and mentioning "amongst other things that he had thought of buying a copy at Stewart's of the Bollandists for 130 guineas, but took a day to consider it, and in the meantime it was bought for the Free Kirk College in Edinburgh."[75] Yet when it came to Newman's religious life, Grant Duff was one with many of his English contemporaries in simply finding it baffling. "Long walk and talk with Lady Salisbury, now Mary, Lady Derby," one entry reads. "She remembered the day when it was rumoured in London that Newman had gone over. Manning said it was probably too true, and that Newman would end like Blanco White."[76] White's end was nicely captured by the chronicler of the Noetics, the Reverend William Tuckwell, who wrote in *Pre-Tractarian Oxford* (1909) of how White, upon renouncing the "cool sequestered vale of eclectic Anglicanism in which he had walked contentedly with Whately, Hawkins, and Hampden,"[77] settled in Liverpool, where he attended a Unitarian

---

[72] Edwin Abbott, *The Anglican Career of Cardinal Newman*, 2 vols (London: Macmillan, 1892), i, 64–5.
[73] For the latest reading of this phase, see Geertjan Zuijdwegt, *An Evangelical Adrift: The Making of John Henry Newman's Theology* (Washington: Catholic University of America Press, 2023). Another reading of Newman's relationship to Evangelicalism can be found in Ian Ker, *Newman and the Fullness of Christianity* (Edinburgh: T&T Clark, 1993), 19–30.
[74] Blunt's diary entry (1 March 1909) quoted in Philip Waller, *Writers, Readers and Reputations: Literary Life in Britain 1870–1918* (Oxford: Oxford University Press, 2006), 1033.
[75] Montstuart Elphinstone Grant Duff, *Notes from a Diary 1851–1872* (London: John Murray, 1911), 92.
[76] Ibid., 110. One can get a good sense of Newman's profound solicitude for the spiritual well-being of his friends by reading something he said to Gladstone after White's death. Despite the fact that Newman had not seen White for thirteen years and had received no letter from him since that time, Newman confessed that "his image haunts me more than the dearest friends whom I have lost, and I can fancy him before me, and have a vivid impression of his voice, countenance and manner." Newman to W. E. Gladstone (12 June 1845), *LD*, x, 700.
[77] William Tuckwell, *Pre-Tractarian Oxford: A Reminiscence of the Oriel "Noetics"* (London: Smith,

Chapel "at which Martineau was a frequent preacher; exchanging ... acquiescence for conviction, and finding in the worship and the teaching of his new associates peace such as he had never known before." Moreover, "a grant of £300 from the Royal Bounty Fund, obtained through Lord Holland's influence, placed him beyond the reach of pecuniary inconvenience." Despite this eleemosynary largesse, White's end was grim.

> Removed to Greenbank, the country house of Mr. Rathbone, he there spent the last five months of his life, in acute suffering, and latterly in absolute crippled helplessness. "God to me is Jesus, and Jesus is God—of course not in the sense of divines"—were his last recorded words: his twofold ruling passion, of devotion and of protest, strong in death.[78]

Whether Manning actually said what Lady Salisbury said he said may be questionable but what is not questionable is that many Englishmen did believe that by renouncing the Anglo-Catholic faith Newman was succumbing to something very much like the skepticism that overcame White. Manning himself said as much in an extraordinary letter that he wrote his friend William Gladstone after he had finished reading Newman's *Essay on the Development of Christian Doctrine* (1845):

> Newmans Book is a subject I could not begin upon yesterday: and now all I can say must be παχυλῶς καὶ τύπῳ [roughly and in outline].
>
> I have read it once with an extraordinary interest, I remember no book that so held my attention fast from beginning to end. It seemed as if the doubts, difficulties, and problems of the last ten years were suddenly brought to a focus external to my own mind, with the strength & light of another mind to whose powers I felt as nothing. It seemed to swallow me up with all the thoughts of years.
>
> But in the end I feel where I was. There are some things which go before all reasoning, & survive all objections: of the former kind as I feel, is the invocation of God alone, & of the latter, the reality of the English Church.
>
> The Book seems to me to be an admission that the Roman Pontificate, & the Invocation of the Blessed Virgin cannot be proved by the *quod semper*. The idea of development shews that a case must be made for after ages.
>
> On the whole, then, the great debate is where it was: with this gain. Even Newman has hardly moved its limits in advance against us. The evident & vast difficulty with which he had to wrestle comes out in a multitude of ways.
>
> Having said this I cannot but add that "the blast of the terrible ones is as a storm against the wall" [Isaiah, 25:4]. The Book is to me wonderful. In some things very unlike him. The English is latinized—& the style abrupt in parts, & even odd & freakish, implying, I fancy, the perils of a solitary, & intense intellect. Some things made me uncomfortable, & reminded me of people who have been affected by strange causes. Other parts, for breadth, depth, splendour, fullness, & beauty are almost beyond compare. The awful passage on St. Mary pp. 405,6. "Thus there was, &c." has no parallel that I know except the Paradiso C.XXXIII

Elder & Co., 1909), 254.
[78] *Ibid.*, 257.

"Vergine Madre figlia del tuo Figlio &c." The whole book exhibits an intellectual compass, & *movement* belonging to an order of minds wh[ich] live in a region above the reach of all except a few. And I anticipate great but very various effects from it. I think it will provoke some to scepticism, & more to doubts about the Blessed Trinity: not a few will it send, year by year, to Rome. I am afraid it will open a running sore in our poor body.[79]

Manning might have delighted in intrigue—as his fraught relationship with Newman shows—but he did recognize genuine beauty when he saw it.[80] The passage to which he refers from the *Essay on Development* does indeed exhibit all Newman's accustomed rhetorical zest.

> Thus there was "a wonder in heaven": a throne was seen, far above all created powers, mediatorial, intercessory; a title archetypal; a crown bright as the morning star; a glory issuing from the Eternal Throne; robes pure as the heavens; and a scepter over all; and who was the predestined heir of that Majesty? Who was that Wisdom, and what was her name, "the Mother of fair love, and fear, and holy hope," "exalted like a palm-tree in Engaddi, and a rose-plant in Jericho," "created from the beginning before the world" in God's counsels, and "in Jerusalem was her power"? The vision is found in the Apocalypse, a Woman clothed with the sun, and the moon under her feet, and upon her head a crown of twelve stars. The votaries of Mary do not exceed the true faith, unless the blasphemers of her Son came up to it. The Church of Rome is not idolatrous, unless Arianism is orthodoxy.[81]

Manning's reference to Dante's *Divine Comedy* in his commendation of this passage reminds us that Church was one of England's keenest admirers of Dante. He also happened to be the one contemporary critic of Newman who understood his hunger for religious reality best. For reasons I shall endeavor to show, Church understood this defining aspect of my subject intimately; indeed, for all his stubborn Anglicanism, he had something of that hunger himself; and it is reflected in his work on Dante. D. C. Lathbury, the editor of Gladstone's religious writings,

---

[79] Henry Edward Manning to William Ewart Gladstone (26 December 1845), *The Correspondence of Henry Edward Manning and William Ewart Gladstone*, ii, 175–6. Here, it should be noted, Manning was never as hostile to Newman as some suggest. The beautiful letter he wrote Newman in 1861—and quoted in his eulogy for the Oratorian nearly thirty years later—amply demonstrates as much. "'You have been a master-builder in this work,' Manning wrote Newman, 'and I a witness of its growth. You remained long at Oxford, still, with all its disfigurements, so dear to both of us; but I was removed to a distance, and had to work alone. Nevertheless to you I owe a debt of gratitude, for intellectual help and light, greater than to any one man of our time; and it gives me a sincere gratification now publicly to acknowledge, though I can in no way repay it.' I little thought in 1861 that I should have the consolation of repeating these words, as it were, over his grave." Manning quoted in Edmund Sheridan Purcell, *Life of Cardinal Manning*, 2 vols (London: Macmillan & Co., 1896), ii, 751.

[80] Cf. "He has taught us that beauty and truth are inseparable; that beauty resides essentially in the thought, so that nothing can make that to be beautiful which is not so in the plainest words that will convey the meaning. The English people have read the thoughts through his transparent words, and have seen the beauty of Eternal Truth as it shone forth in his mind." Manning in his eulogy of Newman, quoted in Purcell, *Life of Cardinal Manning*, ii, 751.

[81] John Henry Newman, *An Essay on the Development of Doctrine* (London: J Toovey, 1845), 405–6.

gives a good example of this in his book on Church, in which he says of Church's essay on Dante that it remains "the truest and the most eloquent tribute Dante's English disciples have paid to the *Divina Commedia*."[82] For Church, such disciples "know how often its seriousness has put to shame their trifling, its magnanimity their faintheartedness, its living energy their indolence, its stern and sad grandeur rebuked low thoughts, its thrilling tenderness overcome sullenness and assuaged distress, its strong faith quelled despair and soothed perplexity, its vast grasp imparted the sense of harmony to the view of clashing truths. They know how often they have found in times of trouble, if not light, at least that deep sense of reality, permanent though unseen, which is more than light can always give in the view which it has suggested to them of the judgments and the love of GOD."[83]

V

From this, one can see that Church is an admirable critic of Newman precisely because he entered into and shared so many of the great convert's preoccupations. Faith and reason, faith and the challenges of natural science, practice in relation to the profession of faith, and that inveterately misunderstood article, literary style—all receive admirable attention in Church's sermons and critical writings.

In the case of faith and reason, he entirely recognizes its centrality for Newman, even though he does not quite realize its force for any proper understanding of the unique force of Roman Catholicism.

> In the position claimed for the Church of England, confessedly unique and anomalous in the history of Christendom, between Roman authority and infallibility on one side, and Protestant freedom of private judgment on the other, the question would at once arise as to the grounds of belief. What, if any, are the foundations of conviction and certitude, apart from personal inquiry, and examination of opposing arguments on different sides of the case, and satisfactory logical conclusions? The old antithesis between Faith and Reason, and the various problems connected with it, could not but come to the front, and require to be dealt with. It is a question which faces us from a hundred sides, and, subtly and insensibly transforming itself, looks different from them all. It was among the earliest attempted to be solved by the chief intellectual leader of the movement, and it has occupied his mind to the last.[84]

As for science, a topic on which Newman is brilliant in his *Oxford University Sermons*, arguing as he does that it was a discipline profoundly fostered and refined by the Church throughout history, long before it became fallaciously regarded as her antithesis, the Dean reminds his readers that the fact that the Oxford Movement emerged at the same time that science was making so many of its headlong strides was not adventitious.[85] "[T]here was a great movement of

---

[82] D. C. Lathbury, *Dean Church* (Oxford and London: Mowbray, 1905), 204.
[83] R. W. Church, *Dante* (London: Hodder & Stoughton, 1850), 151–2. See also *Dante in English*, ed. Eric Griffiths and Matthew Reynolds (London: Penguin Books, 2005).
[84] Church, *Oxford Movement*, 255.
[85] Cf. "For instance, it is obvious that to be in earnest in seeking the truth is an indispensable

thought going on in the country," the Dean writes, a movement of both religious and scientific import.

> It was the time when Bentham's utilitarianism had at length made its way into prominence and importance. It had gained a hold on a number of powerful minds in society and political life. It was threatening to become the dominant and popular philosophy. It began, in some ways beneficially, to affect and even control legislation. It made desperate attempts to take possession of the whole province of morals. It forced those who saw through its mischief, who hated and feared it, to seek a reason, and a solid and strong one, for the faith which was in them as to the reality of conscience and the mysterious distinction between right and wrong. And it entered into a close alliance with science, which was beginning to assert its claims, since then risen so high, to a new and undefined supremacy, not only in the general concerns of the world, but specially in education.[86]

We can see this exaltation of science in Josephine Ward's *One Poor Scruple* (1899), in which the novelist says of one of her characters, with an irony all the more caustic for being understated: "Dr. Rule had taken full advantage of the position of a successful doctor in an age in which health is a mania. He felt himself to be on a platform that commanded an attentive audience. So he discoursed to it, chiefly in the reviews, on many things, on moral, on philosophical questions. But of course science was his strong point, and the heredity of disease was the strong point in his science. He enjoyed the position of a sage and of a confessor to many."[87] When a young classics scholar sent Newman a paper critical of the claims of this presumptuous science, Newman responded: "I can truly say that I warmly sympathise and concur with you in the substance of your argument, and am rejoiced to have evidence in it that there are those in the rising generation who will in their day make a successful stand against the tyranny under which we at present lie of a 'science falsely so called', which is so shallow, so audacious,

---

> requisite for finding it. Indeed, it would not be necessary to notice so evident a proposition, had it not been for the strange conduct of the ancient philosophers in their theories concerning nature and man. It seems as though only one or two of them were serious and sincere in their inquiries and teaching. Most of them considered speculations on philosophical subjects rather in the light of an amusement than of a grave employment,—as an exercise for ingenuity, or an indulgence of fancy,—to display their powers, to collect followers, or for the sake of gain. Indeed, it seems incredible that any men, who were really in earnest in their search after truth, should have begun with theorizing, or have imagined that a system which they were conscious they had invented almost without data, should happen, when applied to the actual state of things, to harmonize with the numberless and diversified phenomena of the world. Yet, though it seems to be so obvious a position when stated, that in forming any serious theory concerning nature, we must begin with investigation, to the exclusion of fanciful speculation or deference to human authority, it was not generally recognized or received as such, till a Christian philosopher [Bacon] forced it upon the attention of the world. And surely he was supported by the uniform language of the whole Bible, which tells us that truth is too sacred and religious a thing to be sacrificed to the mere gratification of the fancy, or amusement of the mind, or party spirit, or the prejudices of education, or attachment (however amiable) to the opinions of human teachers, or any of those other feelings which the ancient philosophers suffered to influence them in their professedly grave and serious discussions."
> John Henry Newman, "The Philosophical Temper First Enjoined by the Gospel" (1826), *US*, 19.

[86] Church, *Oxford Movement*, 18.
[87] Josephine Ward, *One Poor Scruple*, ed. Bonnie Lander Johnson and Julia Meszaros (Washington: Catholic University of America, 2023), 280.

so arrogant, and so widely accepted."[88] Here Newman saw eye to eye with Christopher Dawson, who recognized that "Physical science, in fact, is nothing more nor less than measurement. It does not reveal the intrinsic nature of things, but deals simply with their qualitative relations and variations. Instead of giving an exhaustive causal explanation of reality, it offers a translation of reality into mathematical symbols or imagery. Thus scientific laws have the same relation to nature that the printed score of Beethoven's sonatas has to the music."[89]

If Church, like Newman, recognized that the Christian apologist had to make the case for Christianity in circumstances in which science was attaining "an undefined supremacy," he also recognized that no apologetical hurdle should ever stay the Christian from putting his professed faith into practice. In a lovely sermon entitled "The Call of God" (1876), preached in Salisbury Cathedral to young Anglican ministers, Church gave voice to this most fundamental of Christian imperatives with stirring eloquence.

> In Him you see what you have to do. In Him you see the spirit in which to do it—what manner of men, in feeling, in character, in behaviour, in aim, they ought to be, who continue His ministry. In Him you learn what we are so ready to forget, that it is not merely the work done, but the way, the meaning, the temper in which the work is done, that shows whether we understand the Gospel story and what it teaches. In Him, in His way of working, all is complete, balanced, harmonious; there is nothing missing; there is nothing over grown or disproportionate. There is tenderness and sympathy which none can gauge; there is sternness and severity, rebuking and alarming; there is terrible judgment, which appalls and crushes. There is, in its place, the fearless rough word of righteous wrath; in its place, too, there is the gentle, sparing, pitying word of forgiveness and comfort. Does He despise men for their foolishness, and meanness of spirit? No, for these poor weak men He is ever helping and encouraging, condescending to their condition, bearing with their weakness, providing for their need. Does He care about what men care about, and what they can give Him? No, for He avoids their homage, and passes by without a look all that they admire and covet.[90]

Church's understanding of what, in vulgar terms, is understood as the debate between faith and science is always informed by his understanding of the debate's stakes, however confused its terms. "I do not think that the majority of those who follow this tremendous debate reflect, or in any degree realise what is involved in victory or defeat," he says in an excellent sermon entitled "Responsibility for Our Belief" (1877):

> It is not victory or defeat for a mere philosophical theory or criticism. It is not a question of something future and at a distance, something to be developed in time, something which raises the possibility of a future policy, which retards

---

[88] Newman to Edmond G. A. Holmes (13 August 1875), *LD*, xxvii, 344.
[89] Christopher Dawson, *Progress and Religion: An Historical Inquiry* (London: Sheed & Ward, 1929), 174.
[90] Richard William Church, *Human Life and its Conditions: Sermons Preached before the University of Oxford in 1876–1878* (London: Macmillan & Co., 1894), 188–91.

or brings near a future change in institutions. It is a present, instant result. If the opponents of Christianity are right, if the victory lies with them, it is much more than that Christians are mistaken, as men have been mistaken, and have corrected in time their mistakes, about science, about principles of government, about the policy or the economy of a state. It means that now as regards religion, as widely as men are living and acting, all that is now, is false, rotten, wrong. Our present hopes are utterly extinguished. We are living in a dream. We are wasting on an idol the best love, the highest affections, the purest tenderness which can dwell in human hearts.[91]

Appalled by the rationalists' blithe obliviousness to such stakes, Church echoes Newman, who told a correspondent in 1882 that while "it is of the first importance ... to show that there is no contradiction between scientific and religious truth ... it was not there ... that the shoe pinched." Why? For Newman, "it is not reason that is against us, it is imagination. ... The mind, after having to the utter neglect of the Gospels, lived in science, experiences, on coming back to the Scriptures, an utter strangeness in what it reads." Hence, for Newman, the defining axiom of the unshriven, uncatechized mind: "'Christianity is behind the age.'"[92]

None of Church's writings reveals the influence that Newman's profoundly practical faith had on the man more movingly than his cry for an understanding of the consequentiality of Christian faith, a cry we can also hear in a perceptive piece on Bishop Butler, about whom he says:

> As men are haunted by a permanent sense of the vice of the world, or its disease, or its pain, he was haunted by a sense of the flippant irreligion of his age. The absurdity of a shallowness which affected to see nothing in the claims of Christianity, or to give it up as exploded, was a torment to his love of reasonableness. The insolence which dared to mock at so solid and grave a thing irritated and perplexed him. It weighed on him as if it was a kind of public insanity such as is spoken of in Dean Tucker's anecdote of a conversation with him, when he speculated on the question whether whole communities might not like individuals go mad.[93]

On the matter of what Wilfrid Ward called Newman's "regal style" Church is always incisive. In all his commentary on Newman's writings, Church is careful to emulate Newman, first and foremost, in the precision with which he uses words.[94] A good, rather comical example of the care Newman took with words can be seen in a letter he wrote to Keble. "Pattison wishes me to tell you that friends of his, a lady and daughter, are going into your Parish," he told Keble. "So

---

[91] Ibid., 76–7.
[92] Newman to W. S. Lilly (13 December 1882), *LD*, xxx, 162, and Newman to W. S. Lilly (7 December 1882), *LD*, xxx, 159–60.
[93] Richard William Church, *Pascal and Other Sermons* (London: Macmillan & Co., 1896), 33. Cf. "There really should be lunatic asylums for nations as well as for individuals." Sydney Smith, *Lectures on American Debts* (1844). In post-prandial conversation, the Tudor historian J. J. Scarisbrick would often characterize the practical unbelief of his countrymen as a kind of societal madness from which only a relative few were immune.
[94] "Remember that you have always a listener,/ One who abhors all ostentation and pretence, all insolent carelessness—/One who takes men at their word in ways they think not of." R. W. Church, "Strong Words" (1874), *Pascal and Other Sermons*, 262.

far you must know … but what you do not know, and he wishes you to know, is, that they have come to Hursley to be 'under your superintendence.' I do not know what the phrase means, but when he and I had repeated it several times, and no light seemed thrown upon it, I dropped the subject. Perhaps he does not know either."[95]

Few who write of Newman do justice to his style, the peculiar beauty of which arises naturally from his entering into the true richness of his Christian themes. Church, however, perhaps because of his childhood in Italy, had an aesthete in him, and he revels in the style's beauty, without ever falling into the error of imagining—as James Joyce imagined—that the beauty of its manner is somehow detachable from its matter.[96] Speaking of the sermons, Church writes:

> We have learned to look upon Dr. Newman as one of the half-dozen or so of the innumerable good writers of the time who have fairly left their mark as masters on the language. Little, assuredly, as the writer originally thought of such a result, the sermons have proved a permanent gift to our literature, of the purest English, full of spring, clearness, and force. A hasty reader would perhaps at first only notice a very light, strong, easy touch, and might think, too, that it was a negligent one. But it was not negligence; real negligence means at bottom bad work, and bad work will not stand the trial of time. There are two great styles—the self-conscious, like that of Gibbon or Macaulay, where great success in expression is accompanied by an unceasing and manifest vigilance that expression shall succeed, and where you see at each step that there is or has been much care and work in the mind, if not on the paper; and the unconscious, like that of Pascal or Swift or Hume, where nothing suggests at the moment that the writer is thinking of anything but his subject, and where the power of being able to say just what he wants to say seems to come at the writer's command, without effort, and without his troubling himself more about it than about the way in which he holds his pen . But both are equally the fruit of hard labour and honest persevering self-correction; and it is soon found out whether the apparent negligence comes of loose and slovenly habits of mind, or whether it marks the confidence of one who has mastered his instrument, and can forget himself and let himself go in using it. The free unconstrained movement of Dr. Newman's style tells any one who knows what writing is of a very keen and exact knowledge of the subtle and refined secrets of language. With all that uncared-for play and simplicity, there was a fulness, a richness, a curious delicate music, quite instinctive and unsought for; above all, a precision and sureness of expression which people soon began to find were not within the power of most of those who tried to use language. Such English, graceful with the grace of nerve, flexibility, and power, must always have attracted attention; but it had also an ethical element which was almost inseparable from its literary characteristics.[97]

---

[95] Newman to John Keble (8 June 1844), *LD*, x, 259.
[96] James Joyce wrote that "nobody has ever written English prose that can be compared with that of a tiresome footling little Anglican parson who afterwards became a prince of the only true church." James Joyce to Harriet Shaw Weaver (1 May 1933), *Selected Letters of James Joyce* ed Richard Ellmann (London: Faber and Faber, 1975), 375.
[97] Church, "Newman's Parochial Sermons," in *Occasional Papers*, ii, 447–8.

For Church, "Two things powerfully determined the style of these sermons. One was the intense hold which the vast realities of religion had gained on the writer's mind, and the perfect truth with which his personality sank and faded away before their overwhelming presence; the other was the strong instinctive shrinking, which was one of the most remarkable and certain marks of the beginners of the Oxford movement, from anything like personal display, any conscious aiming at the ornamental and brilliant, any show of gifts or courting of popular applause. Morbid and excessive or not, there can be no doubt of the stern self-containing severity which made them turn away, not only with fear, but with distaste and repugnance, from all that implied distinction or seemed to lead to honour; and the control of this austere spirit is visible, in language as well as matter, in every page of Dr. Newman's sermons."[98] These are perceptive observations about the self-effacement and, indeed, austerity at the heart of Newman's sermons, and their lifelong impact on Church shows their perdurable appeal. Indeed, Ian Ker, in the writing of his magisterial biography of Newman, would exhibit something of the same self-effacement and austerity.

It is also worth including here what Church once wrote to a young divine eager to know how style is attained. "I would gladly help one who writes so kindly as you do, if I could do so," Church wrote. "But I have nothing to say. I have never studied style as such; and I hardly imagine to myself how it is to be studied. It has always seemed to me that thoughts brought their own words, which, of course, had to be considered and sifted; but the root of the expression must be in the thought itself, which, if it was real and worth anything, would suggest the expression." In these eminently Newmanian observations, we can readily see whence Church derived his appreciation of Newman's style. It is, therefore, not surprising that he should cite Newman as one of his models. "As you see," Church ended his letter to his young aspirant, "I am a bad expounder of the secrets of writing. When I was a boy, and at college, I did a great deal of translating from English into Latin, which is a great discipline in itself. Where one's stock of words came from, I cannot tell. But I suppose they come if one reads with care good English. Shakespeare, Wordsworth, Burke, Walter Scott, Defoe (Robinson Crusoe), Goldsmith, were, as far as I can remember, the books I used to value, as giving, besides their thoughts, the most delightful and striking ways of saying them. Besides these, I heard and read a good deal of Mr. Newman's preaching; and it is, I am sure, to him that I owe it, if I can write at all simply and with the wish to be real. Of course being accustomed to good models produces insensibly a habit of mind which dislikes and shrinks from what is merely conventional, unmeaning, and 'flash.'"[99]

One can see the extent of Church's literary indebtedness to Newman in the convert's advice to a student at Maynooth about style: "[E]veryone," he wrote, "must form his style for himself, and under a few general rules." For Newman, "First, a man should be in earnest, by which I mean, he should write, not for

---

[98] Ibid., 448–9.
[99] Church to the Rev. George Bainton (21 September 1887), *Life and Letters*, 392–3. For Church, Newman stood as "almost the unique cross between a true Briton of the proud school of Chatham and Burke, and the enthusiastic, devout, fervent Roman Catholic." Church quoted in Henry Tristram, *Newman and his Friends* (London: John Lane, The Bodley Head Ltd., 1933), 192.

the sake of writing, but to bring out his *thoughts*. He should never aim at being eloquent. He should keep his idea in view, and write sentences over and over again till he has expressed his meaning accurately, forcibly and in few words. He should aim at being understood by his hearers or readers. He should use words which are most likely to be understood—ornament and amplification will come to him spontaneously in due time, but he should never seek them. He must creep before he can fly, by which I mean that humility, which is a great Christian virtue, has a place in literary composition—He who is ambitious will never write well. But he who tries to say simply and exactly what he feels or thinks, what religion demands, what Faith teaches, what the Gospel promises, will be eloquent without intending it, and ... write better English than if he made a study of English literature."[100]

Although Church cites Newman as his contemporary model, he could also have cited Bishop Butler, about whose style he says: "He never wastes a word in fine writing, but he never spares one when it would make him more intelligible. His writing bears the impress of that severe economy and thriftiness of material which comes from a man having taken great trouble to arrange and prepare his work. With him, with all his abounding wealth of ideas, of penetrating and widely-travelled thought, the question about any particular idea or phrase is, not, as it is with so many of us, whether it is clever, or telling, or brilliant ... but, first and foremost ... whether it is true, and then, whether it is in place." Judging by these criteria, we can readily see that Butler was certainly a model for Newman, as well—especially the Newman of the Anglican sermons, which share the same "singular seriousness" that Church sees as characteristic of Butler's work. For Church, Butler "is as serious as a physician, with life and death hanging on the clearness of his thoughts and the courage of his resolve; as serious as a general with a terrible and evenly balanced battle on his hands. Such people are impatient of talk, and ornament, and literary cleverness; and so is he. With him the questions which were bandied about among ingenious and witty reasoners, about the truth and evidences of religion, were no questions of words or speculation, no mere interesting philosophical or historical problems, but of far more immediate and more tremendous earnest than any thing else in the world could be."[101] Reading this, thanks to Church, we begin to suspect that Newman took very much more from Butler than merely his notion of antecedent probability.

Then, again, like Newman, Church is an incisive student of history. One can see this in his commentary on Gibbon, whom the English naturally admired for reconfirming so many of their most cherished prejudices. "It is not too much to say that the common opinion of educated Englishmen about the history and character of everything derived from Byzantium or connected with it is based [on Gibbon's history]," Church wrote. Gibbon "brought out with incomparable force all that was vicious, all that was weak, in Eastern Christendom. He has read us the evil lesson of caring in their history to see nothing else; of feeling too much pleasure in the picture of a religion discredited, of a great ideal utterly and meanly baffled, to desire to disturb it by the inconvenient severity of accuracy and

---

[100] Newman to a Young Student at Maynooth (2 March 1868), *LD*, xxix, 44–5.
[101] Church, *Pascal and Other Sermons*, 30.

justice."[102] Yet, for Church, "the authority of Gibbon is not final. There is, after all, another side to the story." In his history, Gibbon's "immense and exact knowledge gave him every advantage in supporting what I must call the prejudiced conclusions of a singularly cold heart."[103] Doubtless, in making this altogether fair judgment of the work of so influential an historian, Church might very well have had Newman's equally just assessment in mind, where, in the *Idea of a University*, the convert deplored what he saw as Gibbon's "godless intellectualism."[104] Both, as it happens, were vindicated not only by the nineteenth-century historians Finlay and Freeman but by Peter Brown, whose *World of Late Antiquity* (1989) departed sharply from Gibbon. The history of Byzantium was not a tale of any "retreat from reality"; on the contrary, the "ever-closer links between humans and the divine" was a "source of energy and inspiration."[105] As Brown noted in his revisionist history, Byzantium exemplified, *par excellence*, that "sudden release of creativity such as often follows the shaking of an *ancien régime*."[106]

Church is also a frequent observer of the intellectual currents of his age, in which so many of Newman's critics were so highly invested, though his *obiter dicta* on these often confused matters are not always as discriminating as they might have been. Apropos socialism, for example, he says, sensibly enough, "One speaks of questions of wages and production in mere terms of the market, which make us forget that they relate to creatures with will and conscience, and to whom they bring suffering or pleasure; the other invades with the idea of duty the limits within which self-interest thought itself privileged and secure, and gravely queries whether property is lawful, and how far the gains of mere capital are compatible with morality." But, then, a good deal less sensibly, he says: "In a word, Socialism adopts the great commandment of charity as the scientific and practical basis of civilized legislation. This is its boast. It does not reject religion, like the old infidels; it professes to complete Christianity."[107] This might have been true of the aspirations of certain English socialists—one thinks of such well-meaning men as Maurice and Kingsley—but there was no thought of the "great commandment of charity" in the confiscatory socialism of the Continent, the deeply anti-Christian advocates of which only meant to complete in the nineteenth century what the Jacobins of France had left unfinished in the eighteenth. Of course, it goes without saying that no sustainable order can have any Christian warrant that is built upon the coveting of one's neighbor's goods.

Church had something of Newman's playful sense of humor. Church's son-in-law gave vivid expression to this: "The sense of humour seldom gets due credit for the good work it does or helps to do," Francis Paget wrote.

---

[102] R. W. Church, *Christianity and Civilization* (London: Macmillan & Co., 1914), 57.
[103] R. W. Church, *The Gifts of Civilization and other Sermons and Lectures* (London: Macmillan & Co., 1891), 190–1.
[104] *Idea*, 196.
[105] Peter Brown, *Journeys of the Mind: A Life in History* (Princeton: Princeton University Press, 2023), 378.
[106] Peter Brown, *The World of Late Antiquity: AD 150–750* (New York: Norton, 1989), 35.
[107] R. W. Church, "The French Revolution of 1848" (1848), *Essays and Reviews* (London: J. and C. Mozley, 1854), 394–5.

Men often mark the blunders that are made through lack of it; but they do not generally think of the real excellences of mind and character into which it enters, and which more or less depend on it for their preservation and advancement. It was in the late Dean of St. Paul's a very keen and delicate sense; it was delightful to tell him a good story, or to watch him as he saw some ludicrous position, or recalled some bit of misplaced pompousness: he had a quick eye for fun, and enjoyed it splendidly. And this sense of humour ministered to much that was both strong and charming in him; it bore a real part in making him what he was, and enabling him for the especial work he did. Without it he might hardly have been able to sustain the perfect simplicity and lightness of manner which saved him wholly from that suspicion of somehow liking homage, and that annoyance and unreality in receiving it, to which big people are sometimes liable.[108]

Examples abound of Church's delight in the ludicrous. Upon becoming a Proctor at Oriel in 1844, he wrote his mother about the police duties the position entailed. "I have every other week to post the police in various parts of the town, and to receive their report of the previous day," he wrote. "One goes at nine at night to a vaulted room underground, as dreary looking and grim as a melodrama would require;—table with pen and ink, feeble lamp, and sundry cutlasses disposed round the walls. One sits down in great dignity at a table, and then the police are marched in by batches of six. They enter like robbers or conspirators in a play, all belted and great-coated, looking fierce. 'All quiet last night?' passes your lips. All their heads begin to bob, as if they were hung on springs, and without stopping for three or four minutes, all their voices commence repeating, 'all quiet, sir,' as fast as they can; and when they have lost their breath, *exeunt* all bobbing. The first time I was present I fairly lost my gravity, as I should think most of my predecessors must have done before me."[109] Writing to William Copeland of the mourners at Keble's funeral in April of 1866, Church remarked: "At the service and funeral itself the church was crowded, and Rogers, Dean Hook, and I were glad to get a school children's bench in the corner. Yet it was a strange gathering. There was a meeting of old currents and new. Besides the people I used to think of with Keble, there was a crowd of younger men, who no doubt have as much right in them as we have, in their way—Mackonochie, Lowder, and that sort. Excellent good fellows, but who, one could not help being conscious, looked upon us as rather dark people, who don't grow beards, and do other proper things."[110] Then, again, there were the wry observations with which Church took up his duties as Dean of St. Paul's: "[Y]esterday I had my first city dinner with the Worshipful Company of Clockworkers," he tells his brother in one of his letters, "ate my first turtle and made my first speech. It is an odd mixture of intense bore and flashes of amusement."[111] While Dean, Church also had to contend with the Ritualists, though their controversies only refined his sense of the ridiculous.

---

[108] Church, *Life and Letters*, xviii.
[109] Ibid., 46–7.
[110] Ibid., 207.
[111] Ibid., 235.

My own feeling is much like yours about such things as vestments. I understand the frame of mind which, partly out of special reverence for our highest service, partly out of regard to what I suppose was early, if not the earliest usage, makes men wish for them. But for myself, I should feel very uncomfortable if I had to wear them; and, indeed, I have never seen a specimen except the cope which our Bishop wears once a year at the ordination on Trinity Sunday. I wish the congregation could have some constitutional voice in the matter. The difficulty is how to give it them. No doubt there is clerical despotism; but, I am assured, it is an evil not confined to Ritualists. It would be a curious study to investigate the various forms of despotism under which, especially, country parishes groan. A large place must be kept for female despotism.[112]

Church's criticism of Newman, like that of Wilfrid Ward, is rooted in sympathy, though he did not agree with Newman on any number of matters. Most notably, he regarded his friend's conversion as a "catastrophe." In his classic history of the Oxford Movement, he quotes from the retrospective musings of Isaac Williams, the Tractarian poet to suggest a cause for the "catastrophe."

> Possibly, after the catastrophe, [Williams] may, in looking back, have exaggerated his early alarms. But from the first he says he saw in Newman what he had learned to look upon as the gravest of dangers—the preponderance of intellect among the elements of character and as the guide of life. "I was greatly delighted and charmed with Newman, who was extremely kind to me, but did not altogether trust his opinions; and though Froude was in the habit of stating things in an extreme and paradoxical manner, yet one always felt conscious of a ground of entire confidence and agreement; but it was not so with Newman, even though one appeared more in unison with his more moderate views."[113]

For Williams, as for Church, Newman poped, in large measure, because he could not resist giving way to this streak of extremity in his nature, not to mention "the preponderance of intellect," even though, as I shall show, it was from Newman that Church learned his own wariness of this preponderance. We can see this clearly in Church's wonderful essay on Pascal's *Pensées*, in which he declares that

> no professed master of the spiritual life, no book of practical piety, ever laid down more distinctly the true method of seeking religious light. It is implied in every line of Pascal that truth in religion is absolutely, and from the very nature of the case, dependent on moral purity and faithfulness. "Revelation," as has been

---

[112] *Ibid.*, 242. Cf. E. B. Pusey, Letter, 2 January 1875, in H. P. Liddon *et al.*, *Life of E. B. Pusey*, 4 vols (London: 1897) iv, 279. "The whole extreme Ritualist party is practically infallibilist." The Public Worship Regulation Act of 1874 was designed to suppress the growth of ritualism in the Church of England, which was thought too Romanizing for the Protestant National Church. Although the imprisonment of four priests for contumacy between 1877 and 1882 brought the Act into disrepute, it was only in 1963 that it was repealed. Liddon claimed that the Act had arisen as the result of "an unreasoning panic, and with much apparent disregard of the historical structure and spiritual independence of the Church of England." While Church found the Ritualists extravagant, if devout and earnest, he was utterly opposed to imprisoning them. See Church, *Life and Letters*, 243–4.

[113] Church, *Oxford Movement*, 63.

said, "was not given to satisfy doubts, but to make us better men, and it is as we become better men that it becomes light and peace to our souls, even though to the end of life we shall find difficulties in it and in the world around us." It is the great warning of Pascal, that if men would find and know God, they must begin by trying to do His will; they must act according to the greatness of the occasion, and to the laws not of one part only, but of their whole human nature; they must prepare their souls, habits and tempers and will, as well as intellect.[114]

That Church should have quoted from the *Parochial and Plain Sermons* here confirms how it was Newman who impressed upon him the paramountcy of putting holiness before intellect. Indeed, it is often striking to see the extent to which Newman's influence *created* the critic in Church, even though that critic can be, as in this case, mistaken about Newman himself. Nevertheless, the lens through which Church saw Newman's conversion tended to be an Anglican lens, one through which many continue to see the conversion. For the historian of nineteenth-century Oxford, M. G. Brock, for example, Newman "had none of the cautious conformism of his seniors. Where his convictions pointed he followed; it was not in him to modify his message from prudence or alarm. He stands in the Oxford tradition of Wyclif and Wesley—inspired, disruptive and a stranger to moderation."[115] Then, again, the student of Englishry in Church saw in Newman's conversion a kind of impatience with Englishry. In one passage in his history of the Oxford Movement, he says:

> Dr. Pusey, Mr. Keble, Mr. Isaac Williams, Mr. Marriott, were quite unaffected by the disquieting apprehensions which were beginning to beset Mr. Newman. With a humbling consciousness of the practical shortcomings of the English-Church, with a ready disposition to be honest and just towards Rome, and even to minimise our differences with it, they had not admitted for a moment any doubt of the reality of the English Church. The class of arguments which specially laid hold of Mr. Newman's mind did not tell upon them—the peculiar aspect of early precedents, about which, moreover, a good deal of criticism was possible; or the large and sweeping conception of a vast, ever-growing, imperial Church, great enough to make flaws and imperfections of no account, which appealed so strongly to his statesmanlike imagination.[116]

In commending Keble and Williams's loyalty to the National Church, the historian of Tractarianism expressed the basis of his own, a basis which is always implicit in his criticism of Newman's rejection of this basis. "Their content with the Church in which they had been brought up, in which they had been taught religion, and in which they had taken service, their deep and affectionate loyalty and piety to it, in spite of all its faults, remained unimpaired," Church wrote, "and unimpaired, also, was their sense of vast masses of practical evil in the Roman

---

[114] Church, *Pascal and Other Sermons*, 22. The passage he quotes is from "Obedience the Remedy for Religious Perplexity" (1830), *PS*, i, 18.
[115] M. G. Brock, "The Oxford of Peel and Gladstone," in *The History of the University of Oxford*, ed. M. G. Brock and M. C. Curthoys (Oxford: Oxford University Press, 1997), vi, pt. 1, 69.
[116] Church, *Oxford Movement*, 267.

Church, evils from which they shrank both as Englishmen and as Christians, and which seemed as incurable as they were undeniable." If Church and Newman saw the "practical evil" of the Roman Church differently—Church seeing it as a formidable barrier to submission and Newman as an unavoidable corollary of human frailty and therefore an eminently scalable hurdle—they were agreed as to the unlikelihood of most Anglicans seeing the appeal of the ancient Church. Certainly, Pusey and Keble were not inclined to see it. "Beyond the hope which they vaguely cherished that some day or other, by some great act of Divine mercy, these evils might disappear, and the whole Church become once more united," Church pointed out, "there was nothing to draw them towards Rome; submission was out of the question, and they could only see in its attitude in England, the hostility of a jealous and unscrupulous disturber of their Master's work."[117] Still, Church's critical sympathy redounds to his credit here, because if he could not agree with Newman, indeed, if he actually chose to see his friend's conversion as catastrophic, he could nevertheless enter into and respect the complexity and depth of the conversion, about which he knew others would be less than sympathetic. "The change of religion, when it comes on a man gradually,—when it is not welcomed from the first, but, on the contrary, long resisted, must always be a mysterious and perplexing process," he was careful to acknowledge. Moreover, for Church, it was "hard to realise and follow by the person most deeply interested, veiled and clouded to lookers-on, because naturally belonging to the deepest depths of the human conscience, and inevitably, and without much fault on either side, liable to be misinterpreted and misunderstood."[118]

That Gladstone would remonstrate with Newman and the Catholic Church so vehemently over the Vatican decrees, and the definition of papal infallibility that were their issue, bears out Church's premonition, though no one now would deny, as Newman prophesied, that the Liberal Prime Minister "committed himself to a representation of ecclesiastical documents which will not hold ... None but the *Schola Theologorum* is competent to determine the force of Papal and Synodal utterances," especially since "the exact interpretation of them is a work of time."[119] Newman's response to his unscrupulous accuser was one that he could have equally directed to those who saw disloyalty in his repudiation of the National Church: "I see no inconsistency in my being at once a good Catholic and a good Englishman."[120] Over a hundred years later, Ian Ker would echo Newman's conviction when, recalling his undergraduate days at Oxford when he was deciding whether to become a Catholic or an Anglo-Catholic, he was "struck," as he said, by how "Roman Catholics seemed more English, at least in their straight-forwardness and lack of elaborate theories, than the rather exotic and esoteric Anglo-Catholics that I encountered."[121]

---

[117] *Ibid.*, 267–8.
[118] *Ibid.*, 268.
[119] *Diff.*, ii, 176.
[120] *Ibid.*, 176–7. Here Newman echoes Descartes, who, in *Discourse de la Méthode*, III, said he was "happy to give my obedience to the my country, keeping without fail to that religion in which, God be praised, I was brought up from childhood."
[121] Ian Ker, "The Hall and the Side Rooms: C. S. Lewis, Newman and Conversion," in *The Path to Rome: Modern Journeys to the Catholic Church*, ed. Dwight Longenecker (Leominster: Gracewing, 1999), 57.

VI

If moderation and compromise were the hallmarks of Anglicanism, Church was their most forbearing critic. In an essay on the seventeenth-century divine, Lancelot Andrewes, composed in 1870, Church wrote of the English Reformation and the anomalous National Church to which it gave rise in a way that might almost have been a belated response to Newman's *Lectures on Certain Difficulties felt by Anglicans* (1850), in which the recent convert had urged his erstwhile Tractarian friends to abjure the Via Media and join the Church of Rome. In response, Church wrote in gingerly defense of the National Church. "With a kind of gallant contempt for the protection of a theory, we in England shaped our measures as well as we could, to suit the emergencies which at the moment most compelled the attention of the steersman at the helm," he wrote. "The English Reformation ventured on its tremendous undertaking—the attempt to make the Church theologically, politically, socially different, while keeping it historically and essentially the same—with what seems the most slender outfit of appliances. Principles it had; but they were very partially explored, applied, followed out to consequences, harmonised, limited. It sprung from an idea, a great and solid one, even though dimly comprehended, but not from a theory or a system, such as that unfolded in Calvin's Institutes. Its public and avowed purpose—I do not say that of all its promoters—but its public purpose was, taking the actual historical Church of Augustine and Ethelbert, of Becket and Wolsey, of Warham and Pole, the existing historical representative and descendant of that supernatural Society which is traceable through all the ages to Apostolic days, to assert its rights, to release it from usurpation, to purge away the evils which this usurpation had created and fostered; and accepting the Bible as the Primitive Church had accepted it, and trying to test everything by Scripture and history, to meet the immediate necessities of a crisis which called not only for abolition, but for reconstruction and replacement."[122]

Yet, Church had to admit that if what had been done "bore the marks of a clear and definite purpose ... it also bore the unmistakable marks of haste and pressure, as well as violence. Laws—all but the most indispensable ones—canons, synods, tribunals, the adjustment of the differing elements of its constitution, were adjourned to a more convenient season, which, in fact, has never arrived. It began with arrangements avowedly provisional. On the great dogmatic controversies of the moment it defined cautiously, its critics said, imperfectly: it hardly had made up its own mind. For the systematic confessions of the Continent, it provided a makeshift in the Thirty-nine Articles, put to a use for which they were not originally designed."[123] For Newman such grave deficiencies in the National church would ultimately prove intolerable; for Church—and indeed for Pusey and Keble—they could always be negotiated.

Nevertheless, for Church, the Anglican Confession ensured four things: "1. It maintained the Episcopate and the Ordinal; 2. It put the English Bible into the hands of the people; 3. It gave them the English Book of Common Prayer; and 4. To bind all together with the necessary bond of authority, it substituted boldly and

---

[122] Church, *Pascal and Other Sermons*, 66–7.
[123] Ibid., 67.

confidently, in place of the rejected authority of the Pope, the authority, equally undefined, of the Crown, presumed to be loyally Christian and profoundly religious, and always acting in concert with the Church and its representatives." For Church, this was the Reformers' Via Media, "an attempt, genuine though rude and rough and not always successful" to reconcile such things as "antiquity and novelty, control and freedom, ecclesiastical and civil authority, the staid order of a Church as old as the nation and the vigour of a modern revolution of the age of the Renaissance, a very strong public government with an equally strong private fervour and enthusiasm; to stimulate conscience and the sense of individual responsibility, and yet to keep them from bursting all bounds; to overthrow a vast ancient power, strong in its very abuses and entrenched behind the prejudices as well as the great deeds of centuries, and yet to save the sensitive, delicate instincts of loyalty, reverence, and obedience; to make room in the same system of teaching for the venerable language of ancient Fathers, and also for the new learning of famous modern authorities."[124]

To which "famous modern authorities" Church was referring he never specifies, but if he had John Jewell, Stephen Gardiner, Richard Hooker, Bishop William Warburton, and William Palmer of Worcester in mind—all ardent advocates of the validity of the National Church—his special pleading could have no cogency.[125] His praise of Hooker's "theory" of the new Anglican faith, which he set out in an introduction to his edition of the *Ecclesiastical Polity* is a piece of literary, not theological criticism, though it is worth recalling that all Newman's best critics—whether Church, Hutton, Wilfrid Ward or Ian Ker were literary critics. It is also worth noting that all of these critics were sympathetic to Newman, a fact that recalls something T. S. Eliot once wrote: "[W]hat I want to say now is true of all literary criticism. I am sure that it is true of mine, that it is at its best when I have been writing of authors whom I greatly admire."[126] Eliot's pieces on

---

[124] Ibid., 67–8.
[125] In fairness, one should quote something Church wrote in an excellent piece on Lancelot Andrewes, delivered at King's College in 1877: "The stress of the Reformation had forced [the Church of Rome] to look narrowly into its own case ... Against the learning of Erasmus and the genius and thought of Calvin, it felt the necessity of something more than the stock arguments and quotations of its earlier defenders, Eck and Cajetan. And the result was remarkable. The order of the Jesuits arose to place, not merely enthusiasm and political unscrupulousness at the service of the Pope, but learning, the spirit of research, intellectual activity and literary skill. Vast scientific systems of theology, like the great work of Suarez, unfolded and established with philosophic calmness and strength the Roman doctrine. To match such works as these there was nothing—I do not say in England, but even in Germany and Switzerland. There was nothing to match the subtlety and comprehensiveness of the Controversies of Bellarmine. There was nothing to match the imposing historical picture presented in the annals of Baronius. Rome had much more to say for itself than had appeared to Cranmer or even to Jewell." These were lively concessions from a dean of St. Paul's. Church, *Pascal and Other Sermons*, 72–3.
[126] T. S. Eliot, *To Criticize the Critic: Eight Essays on Literature and Education* (Farrar, Straus & Giroux, 1963), 23. Eliot's appraisal of Andrewes would have delighted the dogmatist in Newman. "Bishop Andrewes ... tried to confine himself in his sermons to the elucidation of what he considered essential in dogma," Eliot wrote. "To persons whose minds are habituated to feed on the vague jargon of our time, when we have a vocabulary for everything and exact ideas about nothing ... when all dogma is in doubt except the dogma of sciences of which we have read in the newspapers, when the language of theology itself, under the influence of an undisciplined mysticism of popular philosophy, tends to be a language of tergiversation—Andrewes may seem pedantic and verbal. It is only when we have saturated ourselves in his prose, followed the movement of his thought,

Virgil, Dante, Donne, Ben Jonson, Shakespeare, Lancelot Andrewes and Samuel Johnson certainly bear this out. For Church, "Hooker, like Shakespeare and Bacon, may be said to have opened a new vein in the use of the English language. He shewed that it was possible to write of theology in English in a way which should at once raise the level of thought in the learned, and be of interest to the public."[127] This is doubtless true; but when it comes to the ecclesiastical theory that Richard Hooker recommended, we should also recall something Henry Chadwick said, when, considering how Newman and his Tractarian friends, Pusey and Keble viewed these vexatious matters, he observed how "They did not all share the same estimate of the Reformation, though it is safe to say that none of them sacrilised the sixteenth century as the breaking out of light after fifteen centuries of Stygian darkness, surely the most improbable of all interpretations of church history."[128]

As to the church cobbled together by Henry VIII and his daughter Elizabeth having anything to do with the teachings of the Fathers, Newman was memorably barbed in his King William Street lectures. Having shared with his readers the character of his own peculiar reliance on the authority of the Anglican divines when he was still trying to identify apostolic *bona fides* for the Via Media, Newman then asked on what Anglo-Catholics based their trust in this authority, and, of course, he answers that they based this authority on the Fathers, though, naturally, as Newman dryly remarks, they were "not very solicitous (if I dare speak for others) *how far* the Fathers *seemed* to tell for the Church of Rome."[129] Such delicate irony did not sit well with Aubrey de Vere. "The only part of [Newman's] mind which I do not like," the poet confessed, "is that which comes out of his vein of irony."[130] If one were to remove Newman's "vein of irony" from the lectures, or, indeed, from his work as a whole, one should have to remove a good deal of its rhetorical fireworks, not to mention its wisdom. Newman's use of irony is always exquisite, but it is especially masterly in *Anglican Difficulties*. At times, laugh-aloud funny and, at others, excoriating, it is always inseparable from the *caritas* that animates his appeals to his Anglo-Catholic friends. The point of Newman's irony is always to try to charm his friends out of their false positions, to make them see the absurdity of such falsity.[131] His little disquisition on the Anglo-Catholic view of the Fathers is a case in point. "On the whole," Newman

---

that we find his examination of words terminating in the ecstasy of assent." T. S. Eliot, "Lancelot Andrewes" (1926), *Selected Essays of T. S. Eliot* (New York: Harcourt Brace and Company, 1950), 304–5.

[127] Richard William Church, "Introduction," Richard Hooker, *The Laws of Ecclesiastical Polity*, ed. R. W. Church (Oxford: The Clarendon Press, 1905), xiv–xv.

[128] Henry Chadwick, "Newman's Significance for the Anglican Church," in *Newman: A Man for our Time* (London: SPCK, 1990), 61.

[129] *Diff.*, i, 145.

[130] Wilfrid Ward, *Memoir of Aubrey de Vere* (London: Longmans, Green, & Co., 1904), 182.

[131] Cf. " I was not unwilling to draw an opponent on step by step, by virtue of his own opinions, to the brink of some intellectual absurdity, and to leave him to get back as he could. I was not unwilling to play with a man, who asked me impertinent questions. I think I had in my mouth the words of the wise man, "Answer a fool according to his folly," especially if he was prying or spiteful. I was reckless of the gossip which was circulated about me; and, when I might easily have set it right, did not deign to do so. Also I used irony in conversation, when matter-of-fact men would not see what I meant.". *Apo.*, 45.

says, the Anglo-Catholics took it into their heads to believe that the Fathers "did not tell materially" for the Church of Rome.

> But it was no matter ... [that the Fathers] partially seemed to do so; for their great and deadly foe, their scorn, and their laughingstock, was that imbecile, inconsistent thing called Protestantism; and there could not be a more thorough refutation of its foundation and superstructure than was to be found in the volumes of the Fathers. There was no mistaking that the principles professed, and doctrines taught by those holy men, were utterly anti-Protestant; and, being satisfied of this, which was their principal consideration, it did not occur to them accurately to determine the range and bounds of the teaching of the early Church, or to reflect that, perhaps, they had as yet a clearer view of what it did not sanction, than, of what it did.[132]

And this, of course, had interesting consequences for the exercise of private judgment, precisely the thing of which the Anglo-Catholics most disapproved.

> They saw, then, that there simply was no opportunity at all for private judgment, if one wished to exercise it ever so much, as regards the question of the anti-Protestantism of the Fathers; it was a patent fact, open to all, written on the face of their works, that they were anti-Protestant; you might defer to them, you might reject them, but you could as little deny that they were essentially anti-Protestant, as you could deny that "the Romanists" were anti-Protestants. It was a matter of fact, a matter of sense, which Protestants themselves admitted or rather maintained; and here, in this public and undeniable fact, we have arrived at what the movement considered the ultimate resolution of its faith.[133]

Consequently, for Newman, "the Oxford Movement claimed to represent the theological and ecclesiastical teaching of the Fathers; and the Fathers, when interrogated, did but pronounce them to be the offspring of eclecticism, and the exponent of a State Church."[134]

Newman's use of the word "eclecticism" here reminds one of a telltale passage from *Lectures on the Prophetical Office* (1837), in which, even as an Anglo-Catholic, he could not conceal his uneasiness with an Anglo-Catholicism that abounded in altogether unavoidable eclecticism. "When men choose or reject from religious systems what they please, they furnish melancholy evidence of their want of earnestness; and when they put themselves above existing systems, as if these were suited only to the multitude or to bigoted partisans, they are supercilious and proud; and when they think they may create what they are to worship, their devotion cannot possess any high degree of reverence and godly fear. Surely, then, it may be said, such theorizing on religious subjects is nothing else than an indulgence in that undue use of reason." However, Newman, when still sworn to the Anglo-Catholic colors, could entertain the possibility that "the evil specified would cease in proportion as we were able to bring into

---

[132] *Diff.*, i, 145.
[133] *Ibid.*, 145–6.
[134] *Ibid.*, 426.

practical shape that system which is wanting." In other words, for the Anglo-Catholic Newman, "the true answer to the objection is simply this, that though Anglo-Catholicism is not practically reduced to system in its fulness, it does exist, in all its parts, in the writings of our divines, and in good measure is in actual operation, though with varying degrees of consistency and completeness in different places. There is no room for eclecticism in any elementary matter. No member of the English Church allows himself to build on any doctrine different from that found in our book of Common Prayer. That formulary contains the elements of our theology; and herein lies the practical exercise of our faith, which all true religion exacts. We surrender ourselves in obedience to it: we act upon it: we obey it even in points of detail where there is room for diversity of opinion. The Thirty-Nine Articles furnish a second trial of our humility and self-restraint. Again, we never forget that, reserving our fidelity to the Creed, we are bound to defer to Episcopal authority."[135] Here the strenuous champion of Anglo-Catholicism in Newman willy-nilly exposed its incoherence, especially when the bishops could not be bothered, as in the case of the Gorham ruling, to uphold the Creed.[136]

In the fifth lecture of *Anglican Difficulties*, having established the self-evident unsoundness of the Tractarian citadel, Newman proceeded to address his friends with the blunt, unsparing directness that was one of the hallmarks of his English style.

> My brethren, when it was at length plain that primitive Christianity ignored the National Church, and that the National Church cared little for primitive Christianity, or for those who appealed to it as her foundation; when Bishops spoke against them, and Bishops' courts sentenced them, and Universities degraded them, and the people rose against them, from that day their "occupation was gone." Their initial principle, their basis, external authority, was cut from under them; they had "set their fortunes on a cast"; they had lost; henceforward they had nothing left for them but to shut up their school, and retire into the country. Nothing else was left for them, unless, indeed, they took up some other theory, unless they changed their ground, unless they ceased to be what they were, and became what they were not; unless they belied their own principles, and strangely

[135] *VM*, i, 22–3.
[136] After the Bishop of Exeter refused in 1847 to install the Rev. George Cornelius Gorham (1787–1857) in a Devonshire parish due to his Calvinist reading of baptismal regeneration, an appeal was made to the Archbishop of Canterbury and the Privy Council, which then overturned the Bishop's decision. As a result of the Erastian ruling, many Anglicans went over to Rome, including Henry Edward Manning and James Hope-Scott. Writing an appeal for support for a ragged school on Saffron Hill (where Fagin ruled the roost with his young pickpockets) Dickens made mention of the Gorham ruling. "My Lords and Gentleman, can you, at the present time, consider this at least, and agree to do some thing a little easy! Dearly beloved brethren elsewhere, do you know that between Gorham controversies, and Pusey controversies and Newman controversies, and twenty other edifying controversies, a certain large class of minds in the community is gradually being driven out of all religion! Would it be well, do you think, to come out of the controversies for a little while, and be simply Apostolic thus low down!" Charles Dickens, "A Sleep to Startle Us," in *Household Words* (13 March 1852). See *The Dent Uniform Edition of Dickens' Journalism Vol. 3 "Gone Astray" and Other Pieces from Household Words*, ed. Michael Slater (London: J. M. Dent, 1998), 57.

forgot their own luminous and most keen convictions; unless they vindicated the right of private judgment, took up some fancy-religion, retailed the Fathers, and jobbed theology. They had but a choice between doing nothing at all, and looking out for truth and peace elsewhere.[137]

Doubtless with Newman's strictures in mind, Church had no choice but to write of the National Church's efforts "To bind all together with the necessary bond of authority" with a certain allowance for their impracticability. "The task was a difficult one," he wrote,

> as it was unique among the various projects opposed to it, or likened to it, going on at the same time in Western Christendom. Abroad, the idea of the English Reformation appeared, as it still appears abroad, an illogical and incomprehensible attempt to unite incompatible principles and elements. That government should interfere with religion, should change it, should impose it, was perfectly understood both by Protestants and Catholics. But that reformers in England, having broken with the Pope, should not make a clear sweep of the whole of the inherited system and begin afresh; that they should embarrass themselves by maintaining the continuity and identity of the existing Church with the historical Church of the past; that they should be so bold, yet so guarded and reticent—this was unintelligible, both at Rome, Paris and Madrid, and at Wittenberg, Jena, Basle and Geneva. It must have seemed to many—not merely to the worshippers of absolute hypotheses, but to cool and practical judges of the probabilities of human affairs—a very unpromising, if not forlorn and desperate venture. So daring a disregard of obvious inconsequence and anomaly; so delicate a balancing of conflicting tendencies; so apparently artificial and arbitrary restraints on their natural development; all, too, depending on the chances of a single life, and the personal influence of a character, did not wear the look of permanence.[138]

Nevertheless, Church never wavered in his dedication to this precarious National Church. As Canon Scott Holland once observed, "There was a sense in him of holding a fort against grim odds."[139]

---

[137] *Diff.*, i, 152–3.
[138] Church, *Pascal and Other Sermons*, 66–9.
[139] Canon Henry Scott Holland (1847–1918), Regius Professor of Divinity and Canon of Christ Church, who founded the Christian Social Union, quoted in George William Erskine Russell, *A Pocketful of Sixpences*. (London: E. G. Richards, 1907), 146. Apropos Gerard Manley Hopkins and Newman, the philosopher T. H. Green once wrote to Holland: "I am glad that you and Nettleship saw Hopkins. A step such as he has taken, tho' I can't quite admit it to be heroic, must needs be painful, and its pain should not be aggravated—as it is pretty sure to be—by separation from old friends. I never had his intimacy, but always liked him very much. I imagine him—perhaps uncharitably—to be one of those, like his ideal J. H. Newman, who instead of simply opening themselves to the revelation of God in the reasonable world, are fain to put themselves into an attitude—saintly, it is true, but still an attitude. True citizenship 'as unto the Lord' (which includes all morality) I reckon higher than 'saintliness' in the technical sense. The 'superior young man' of these days, however, does not seem to understand it, but hugs his own 'refined pleasures' or (which is but a higher form of the same) his personal sanctity. Whence, and not from heterodoxy, ruin threatens Christian society." Holland responded: "I will try to digest your remarks." *Henry Scott Holland: Memoir and Letters*, ed. Stephen Paget (London: John Murray, 1921), 29–30.

VII

There are many accounts of Newman's Anglican deathbed but few that capture its exquisite difficulties as empathetically as Church's. Certainly, he understood that the process of conversion "is all the more tangled when it goes on, not in an individual mind, travelling in its own way on its own path, little affected by others, and little affecting them, but in a representative person, with the responsibilities of a great cause upon him, bound by closest ties of every kind to friends, colleagues, and disciples, thinking, feeling, leading, pointing out the way for hundreds who love and depend on him." Of course, this was Newman's plight with a vengeance, and it is doubly commendable of Church to take it into account in his criticism of his old friend in light of the tendency of many of Newman's critics only to take it into account in order to find fault with the convert.[140] Church, in sharp contrast, evokes these circumstances to remind his readers that they demand not only our circumspection but our charity, especially since they continually required the most excruciating deliberations on Newman's part.

> How shall he speak, and how shall he be silent? How shall he let doubts and difficulties appear, yet how shall he suppress them?—Doubts which may grow and become hopeless, but which, on the other hand, may be solved and disappear. How shall he go on as if nothing had happened, when all the foundations of the world seem to have sunk from under him? Yet how shall he disclose the dreadful secret, when he is not yet quite sure whether his mind will not still rally from its terror and despair? He must in honesty, in kindness, give some warning, yet how much? and how to prevent it being taken for more than it means? There are counter-considerations, to which he cannot shut his eyes. There are friends who will not believe his warnings. There are watchful enemies who are on the look-out for proofs of disingenuousness and bad faith. He could cut through his difficulties at once by making the plunge in obedience to this or that plausible sign or train of reasoning, but his conscience and good faith will not let him take things so easily; and yet he knows that if he hangs on, he will be accused by and by, perhaps speciously, of having been dishonest and deceiving. So subtle, so shifting, so impalpable are the steps by which a faith is disintegrated; so evanescent, and impossible to follow, the shades by which one set of convictions pass into others wholly opposite; for it is not knowledge and intellect alone which come into play, but all the moral tastes and habits of the character, its likings and dislikings, its weakness and its strength, its triumphs and its vexations, its keenness and its insensibilities, which are in full action, while the intellect alone seems to be busy with its problems.[141]

Here, Church shows what a good critic he was of Newman precisely by bringing to bear Newman's own understanding of conversion—how it necessarily exhibits the assent of the whole man, not merely what might be regarded as the demands of logic.

Wilfrid Ward certainly recognized this as well, when he wrote in his life of

---

[140] For a good example of this peculiar fault-finding, see chapter below on James Anthony Froude.
[141] Church, *Oxford Movement*, 234–5.

Newman: "He does not care to project himself along a single line or many single lines of logical thought along which at best the mere logical *simulacrum* of his reader, not the whole concrete man, will follow him; but he would fain make a wide pathway wherein a traveller may move rejoicing, carrying with him all that is his." Indeed, for Ward, "He sometimes seems to shrink from abstractions as from attenuated truths and endeavours to frame his argument from concrete to concrete. His exercise of formal logic in practice is often wonderfully dexterous and subtle, but it is rather used as a sword for defence or attack than as his implement for building the walls of Jerusalem."[142] In the *Grammar of Assent*, Newman insisted on the limitations of logic, about which his Noetic friends at Oriel, particularly Richard Whately, were so blithely heedless.

> It is plain that formal logical sequence is not in fact the method by which we are enabled to become certain of what is concrete; and it is equally plain ... what the real and necessary method is. It is the cumulation of probabilities, independent of each other, arising out of the nature and circumstances of the particular case ... probabilities too fine to avail separately, too subtle and circuitous to be convertible into syllogisms, too numerous and various for such conversion, even were they convertible. As a man's portrait differs from a sketch of him, in having, not merely a continuous outline, but all its details filled in, and shades and colours laid on and harmonized together, such is the multiform and intricate process of ratiocination, necessary for our reaching him as a concrete fact, compared with the rude operation of syllogistic treatment.[143]

Interestingly enough, even the lapsed Tractarian Mark Pattison saw the inadequacy of this "rude operation" in the work of William Warburton (1698–1779), the Bishop of Gloucester, whose defense of the Erastianism at the heart of the National Church Newman had such fun mocking in *Anglican Difficulties*. "Warburton offers nothing to his readers that is short of moral certainty," Pattison writes. "His pages are full of the language of proof. It is evident; it necessarily follows. *The Divine Legation* is laid out on a syllogism, with a major and a minor premiss, separately established, and then the conclusion drawn. That all this logical array should fail to carry conviction on the instant, seemed to him a thing incredible. Those who withstood it must be men of perverse minds."[144]

---

[142] Wilfrid Ward, *The Life of John Henry Cardinal Newman*, 2 vols (London: Longman, Green & Co., 1912), ii, 357–8.

[143] GA, 288.

[144] Mark Pattison, "Life of Bishop Warburton," *National Review* (1863); *Essays by Mark Pattison*, ed. Henry Nettleship, 2 vols (Oxford: Clarendon Press, 1889), ii, 164–5. Cf. "In reviewing the *Divine Legation*, we cannot help being forcibly reminded of the *Homeric Studies* of Mr. Gladstone. The differences between the two men are many and radical; the intellectual character of the two works is the same. A comprehensive general reading; an heroic industry in marshalling the particulars of the proof; a dialectical force of arm which would twist a bar of iron to its purposes; and all brought to bear to prove a perverse and preposterous proposition. The mischief done by such powerful efforts of human reason is not in the diffusion of erroneous opinion on the subjects of which they treat, but in setting brilliant examples of a false method." *Ibid.*, 166. For a highly abstruse, amusing discussion of how Warburton improbably influenced Jacques Derrida, see John Milbank, "William Warburton: An Eighteenth Century Bishop Fallen among Post-Structuralists," *New Blackfriars*, 64, no. 757 (July/August 1983), 315–24.

To the High Church civil servant, Albert Smith, who had wondered whether *odium theologicum* somehow told against the Roman Church being the one, true, apostolic Church, Newman replied by making reference to a point he had made in *Anglican Difficulties* (1850): "Religion is so deeply interesting and sovereign a matter, and so possesses the whole man, when it once gains its due entrance into the mind, that it is not wonderful, that, as worldly men quarrel fiercely about worldly things, so, through the weakness of human nature, particular theologians have had unchristian disputes about Christian truths."[145] In yet another piece of Newman's correspondence—a letter he wrote to A. J. Hanmer (1817–1907), who joined the Anglican ministry in 1840 after coming down from St John's, Cambridge—we can also see him adverting to the difficulties implicit in conversion.

> My dear Sir,
> It is sad to me, to think that you still remain uncertain and unsettled; and, while others have seized and are enjoying the high calling offered to them, you are, if you will allow me to say so, wasting precious years in vanity. Having myself been called to the Church late in life, when my best days were gone, I feel for those who persevere in losing what cannot be recalled.
> You say that, "though you feel this" (the ground on which you rest your position,) "in a dry argumentative way, you constantly feel your position to be most painful." Others have had and have the same feeling. Is not this a reductio ad absurdum of that ground? Is it not the witness of heart and conscience, of the whole man, that that argument will not *work*, and therefore cannot be true, difficult as it may be to find what is the intellectual flaw in what seems so specious? It will serve as an excuse for the insincere, not as a stay for the earnest.
> Next, I cast my eyes over your ten difficulties, and I see that not one of them is (as I think) to your purpose. The question is, "Is the communion of Rome the Catholic Church?" and you answer in these ten difficulties that the Pope is not infallible. How does the argument run, "The Pope is not infallible, therefore the Church in communion with him is not the Catholic Church"? Bossuet would not have felt the force of this argument.
> If the Pope is infallible, the Church in communion with him *is* the Catholic Church; but it does not therefore follow that, if the Pope is not infallible, the Church in communion with him is not the Catholic Church.
> That is, there are other arguments to prove it; and to my mind the overbearingly convincing proof is this:—that were St Athanasius and St Ambrose in London now, they would go to worship, not to St Paul's Cathedral, but to Warwick Street or Moor Fields. This my own reading of history has made to me an axiom, and it converted me, though I cannot of course communicate the force of it to another. As an illustration of what I mean, I would direct you to an article in the Dublin, part of which Mr Ward reprinted in his Ideal, in which the prima facie appearance of the Church in the 4th and 5th centuries is drawn out: its altars, tombs, pilgrimages, processions, rites, relics, medals etc; whereas I hardly see a trace of the Church of the Fathers, as a *living, acting* being, in the Anglican com-

---

[145] Newman to Albert Smith (8 January 1868), LD, xxiv, 6. See also *Diff.*, i, 329.

munion. E.g. the Eucharistic Service of the Ancients and our High Mass would strike a stranger as the same, a priestly action with the congregation assisting and uniting with voice and posture; and so of other peculiarities. Again, an active intercommunion is a special characteristic of the Ancient Church; again, a combination of many nations in one etc etc Again, a one government.

Now, it is the old fallacy of division, and nothing else, to say, "*This* is not necessary to the Church, nor *that*, nor the *other*; therefore not *all together*." All these things *make up* together a great note of the Church. The Church was to be one and the same from Christ's first coming to His second. The modern Roman communion is unmistakeably like the Church of the Fathers; and this great argument is confirmed by finding that the Church of England is unmistakeably unlike it.[146]

A month after Newman wrote this letter, he had occasion to send another. "My dear Hamner," he wrote, "I have been very anxious to hear from you, and I congratulate you on your having joined the Church with all my heart. We shall be truly glad to see you on Christmas Eve, as you propose."[147] Here was but one of the many Anglicans Newman converted in his lifetime, a welcome exception to those whose religion Newman described as "based upon self and the world, a mere *civilization* ... which they ingraft upon the selfish and worldly habits of an unrenewed heart."[148]

At the same time, the Oratorian was always leery of anyone's converting precipitately. Indeed, one of the reasons why he always felt odd man out with the Brompton Oratory and, indeed, with Manning, is that he thought their being based in London naturally tempted them to involve themselves with scalps of an unreliable prominence.[149] In a letter to Church, Newman wondered how

---

[146] Newman to A. J. Hamner (18 November 1849), *LD*, xiii, 295–6. Hanmer had first seen Newman in 1839 preaching at St Mary the Virgin in Oxford—it was his father who had introduced him to Newman, as it was my father who introduced him to me—and later Hamner even tried his vocation at the Oxford Oratory, before settling in Manchester, from which he would stay in touch with Newman. After visiting Littlemore in 1845, Hamner received a most moving letter from Newman in which the convert wrote: "I am now so convinced of the truth and divinity of the Catholic Church, that I am pained about persons who are external to it in a way in which I was not before." Indeed, Newman went further and shared with the unsettled young Hamner that "if a person *be* external to the aids and graces of the Church, he cannot have the true gift of faith, and can at best but rule his course by reason, which is an uncertain guide—and almost involves doubt as its attendant. Persons then, in waiting to be certain, may be waiting for that which from the nature of the case cannot be theirs." Newman to A. J. Hamner (11 December 1845), *LD*, xi, 60. In 1864, Newman commiserated with Hanmer when the American Civil War adversely affected his Lancashire cotton mill. See *LD*, xxi, 328.

[147] Newman to A. J. Hanmer (19 December 1849), *LD*, xiii, 343.

[148] Newman, "Knowledge of God's Will without Obedience" (1832), *PPS*, i, 30.

[149] The diplomatist James Bryce (1838–1922) recognized the qualities in Manning that made him such a good Archbishop of Westminster. "No one in our time, hardly even Cardinal Newman, has done so much to sap and remove the old Protestant fears and jealousies of Rome, fears and jealousies which had descended from days when they were less unreasonable than the liberality or indifference of our times will allow. Truly the Roman Church is a wonderful institution, fertile beyond any other, since in each succeeding age she has given birth to new types of force suited to the conditions she has to deal with. In Manning she developed a figure full of a kind of charm and strength which could hardly have found due scope within a Protestant body: a man who never obtruded a claim, yet never yielded one; who was the loyal servant of a spiritual despotism,

Dr. Wiseman felt when one of his showier scalps defected. "It is too true poor Sibthorp has come back—calling the Church of Rome the πόρνη μεγάλη [great whore] of the Revelations; and comparing the Church of England to a stiff, cross, uninteresting old maid by the side of a most fascinating adulteress. … What must Dr. Wiseman's feelings be, for so hastily ordaining him?"[150] Richard Waldo Sibthorp (1792–1879), an evangelical incumbent of St James's Church, Ryde, Isle of Wight, converted to Rome in 1842, reverted to the Anglican ministry in 1843, and reconverted in 1864, though he never outgrew his evangelical views and expressly asked that the Anglican service be read over his grave.[151]

The value of Church's testimony to Newman's developing religious opinions while on his Anglican deathbed is that he gives an honest—indeed, heart-felt—personal interpretation of that development, which is also impeccably Anglo-Catholic. It also contrasts markedly with the lack of any testimony to the same development from Pusey, whose reticence on the matter was of a piece with his inability to answer Newman's criticisms of the Via Media, and this despite the fact that he would strive to rehabilitate the mediatorial theory after Newman converted. Church's counter-claims may be unpersuasive—facts were demonstrably *not* against the Roman Church being the whole Church, as he says—but at least he responded to what was, in effect, Newman's challenge to all Anglo-Catholics who insisted on clinging to the Anglican "wreck," as he called the National Church.[152] "No theory would take in and suit all the facts, which the certainties of history and experience presented," Church wrote, implicitly rejecting Catholicism's claims of infallibility.

> Neither in England, nor in Rome, and much less anywhere else, did the old, to which all appealed, agree with the new; it might agree variously in this point or

yet apparently in sympathy with democratic ideas and movements; equally welcome among the poorest Irish of his diocese and at the gatherings of the great; ready to join in every good work with those most opposed to his own doctrines, yet standing detached as the austere and unbending representative of a world-embracing power." James Bryce, *Studies in Contemporary Biography* (London: Macmillan & Co., 1903), 259–60.

[150] Newman to R. W. Church (7 October 1843), *LD*, ix, 554.

[151] See *ODNB*. Cf. "When [Sibthorp] returned to Oxford after his reception, he called on me with a view to my conversion, but he only threw me back by the 'methodistical' character, as I felt them to be, of the reasons which he gave for the step which he had taken." Newman to John Fowler (12 April 1881), *LD*, xxix, 363.

[152] Asking himself why he bothered to write the King William Street lectures that he would gather together in *Anglican Difficulties* (1850) Newman answered: "It is this keen feeling that my life is wearing away, which overcomes the lassitude which possesses me, and scatters the excuses which I might plausibly urge to myself for not meddling with what I have left for ever, which subdues the recollection of past times, and which makes me do my best, with whatever success, to bring you to land from off your wreck, who have thrown yourselves from it upon the waves, or are clinging to its rigging, or are sitting in heaviness and despair upon its side. For this is the truth: the Establishment, whatever it be in the eyes of men, whatever its temporal greatness and its secular prospects, in the eyes of faith is a mere wreck. We must not indulge our imagination, we must not dream: we must look at things as they are; we must not confound the past with the present, or what is substantive with what is the accident of a period. Ridding our minds of these illusions, we shall see that the Established Church has no claims whatever on us, whether in memory or in hope; that they only have claims upon our commiseration and our charity whom she holds in bondage, separated from that faith and that Church in which alone is salvation. If I can do aught towards breaking their chains, and bringing them into the Truth, it will be an act of love towards their souls, and of piety towards God." *Diff.*, i, 4–5.

in that, in others there were contrarieties which it was vain to reconcile. Facts were against the English claim to be a Catholic Church—how could Catholicity be shut up in one island? How could England assert its continuity of doctrine? Facts were against the Roman claim to be an infallible, and a perfect, and the whole Church—how could that be perfect which was marked in the face of day with enormous and undeniable corruptions? How could that be infallible which was irreconcilable with ancient teaching? How could that be the whole Church, which, to say nothing of the break up in the West, ignored, as if it had no existence, the ancient and uninterrupted Eastern Church? Theory after theory came up, and was tried, and was found wanting. Each had much to say for itself, its strong points, its superiority over its rivals in dealing with the difficulties of the case, its plausibilities and its imaginative attractions. But all had their tender spot, and flinched when they were touched in earnest. In the confusions and sins and divisions of the last fifteen centuries, profound dis organisation had fastened on the Western Church. Christendom was not, could not be pretended to be, what it had been in the fourth century; and whichever way men looked the reasons were not hard to see. The first and characteristic feeling of the movement, one which Mr. Newman had done so much to deepen, was that of shame and humiliation at the disorder at home, as well as in every part of the Church. It was not in Rome only, or in England only; it was everywhere. What had been peculiar to Anglicanism among all its rivals, was that it had emphatically and without reserve confessed it. With this view of the dislocation and the sins of the Church, he could at once with perfect consistency recognise the shortcomings of the English branch of the Church, and yet believe and maintain that it was a true and living branch. The English fragment was not what it should be, was indeed much that it should not be; the same could be said of the Roman, though in different respects. This, as he himself reminds us, was no new thing to his mind when the unsettlement of 1839 began. "At the end of 1835, or the beginning of 1836, I had the whole state of the question before me, on which, to my mind, the decision between the Churches depended." It did not, he says, depend on the claims of the Pope, as centre of unity; "it turned on the Faith of the Church"; "there was a contrariety of claims between the Roman and Anglican religions"; and up to 1839, with the full weight of Roman arguments recognised, with the full consciousness of Anglican disadvantages, he yet spoke clearly for Anglicanism. Even when misgivings became serious, the balance still inclined without question the old way. He hardly spoke stronger in 1834 than he did in 1841, after No. 90.[153]

VIII

The degree to which Newman "spoke clearly for Anglicanism" immediately before or after Tract 90 is, of course, arguable, though Church's belief that he did is important to bear in mind, especially when we consider why he and so many others refused to budge from the National Church in the wake of his friend's secession. Clearly, when one reads Church, one has the sense that one reason he

---

[153] Church, *Oxford Movement*, 274-6. Church quotes *Apo.*, 111-13.

remained where he was is that he found Newman's defense of the Via Media so compelling that he could not repudiate it, even after Newman repudiated it. After all, for Church, Newman had been not only "the living soul and the inspiring genius" of the Oxford Movement but "the founder, we may almost say, of the Church of England as we know it."[154] The man to whom Newman had confided so many of his hopes for a truly apostolical Anglicanism could never accept that those hopes were lost.[155] Francis Paget confirms this steely independence in Newman's friend. Indeed, for Paget, this "independence had a peculiar quality, due in part at least to one great experience in the Dean's life. He had been a disciple; and he had gone straight on, holding his own unshaken course, when his master had swerved off and left him. The enthusiasm and inspiration which Mr. Newman could infuse had filled his heart: then came the great loss of 1845; and after that he could be no man's disciple; he must think for himself, with no dependence on another's thoughts. Independent he would anyhow have come to be, by the necessary bent of his own nature, and as a matter of duty to himself. But Mr. Newman's secession hastened his development in this regard; and it gave to the independence of his mind a distinctive beauty. For independence, admirable as it is, is apt to be somewhat unconciliatory and uninviting, apt to discourage the approach of kindness by showing too plainly the strength if not the pride of self-sufficiency. In him it was refined and chastened by an undertone of pathos. He was detached from many things that entangle men; he seemed ready to detach himself from more; and with him peculiarly one felt how the strong-hold of a true man's life is not near the frontier, but somewhere far away, remote and lonely and aloft." If one looks at photographs of Church, one can see what Paget is saying here. The Dean does have a kind of sweet detachedness about him. Doubtless, the fondness Paget had for Dante, which Church so ardently shared, enabled him to appreciate the inner serenity of the man. "But that great experience of disappointment," Paget goes on to say, "which had pressed forward the work of his detachment, the realisation of his independence, was felt in the result: felt through a certain quiet and simple gravity, verging towards sadness, and guarding independence from all touch of hardness or ungentleness or indifference or pride. It was in his courage of decision that the robust, unhampered energy of an independent mind declared itself most plainly. All his reverence for the rights of others and for the full scope that they should have and use, all his dislike of ill-grounded positiveness, all his insistence on the limitation of our knowledge, all his resolute recollection of our vast uncertainty and ignorance, did not stay him from saying clearly what, so far as he could judge, he clearly saw. So he dealt with the great problems of speculation, with the questions of political and social life, with the difficulties that men come to in their own separate experience. He never forgot the humility that becomes men in this dimly-lighted world, and the determined

---

[154] Church quoted in Charles Stephen Dessain's "Introduction," in *LD*, xi, xxvii, which is taken from the obituary he wrote for his friend, *The Guardian* (13 August 1890).

[155] Cf. "In Oxford, University life [after Newman's defection] was resumed under its ordinary conditions," Mary Church writes, "and men went back to their various occupations; the Tractarians who had not followed Newman in his final step having to meet as best they might the tide of angry suspicion and condemnation which was still running against them. But in spite of inevitable discouragement, they refused to regard their cause as a lost one." Church, *Life and Letters*, 68–9.

patience which all true service of mankind demands, where tasks are complex and results are almost sure to be deferred and mixed and fragmentary: he never trifled with the indefeasible right, the inevitable duty of each man ultimately in matters of conduct to make up his own mind."[156]

Dean Church took advantage of this "indefeasible right" himself by contriving to infuse all of his animadversions on Newman's last days in the Anglican fold with an elegiac wistfulness that is perhaps more touching than true. "How earnestly, how sincerely he clung to the English Church, even after he describes himself on his 'death-bed,' no one can doubt," Church writes.[157]

> The charm of the *Apologia* is the perfect candour with which he records fluctuations which to many are inconceivable and unintelligible, the different and sometimes opposite and irreconcilable states of mind through which he passed, with no attempt to make one fit into another. It is clear, from what he tells us, that his words in 1839 were not his *last* words as an Anglican to Anglicans. With whatever troubles of mind, he strove to be a loyal and faithful Anglican long after that. He spoke as an Anglican. He fought for Anglicanism. The theory, as he says, may have gone by the board, in the intellectual storms raised by the histories of the Monophysites and Donatists. "By these great words of the ancient father—*Securus judicat orbis terrarum*"—the theory of the Via Media was "absolutely pulverised." He was "sore," as he says in 1840, "about the great Anglican divines, as if they had taken me in, and made me say strong things against Rome, which facts did not justify." Yes, he felt, as other men do not feel, the weak points of even a strong argument, the exaggerations and unfairness of controversialists on his own side, the consciousness that you cannot have things in fact, or in theory, or in reasoning, smoothly and exactly as it would be convenient, and as you would like to have them. But his conclusion, on the whole, was unshaken. There was enough, and amply enough, in the English Church to bind him to its allegiance, to satisfy him of its truth and its life, enough in the Roman to warn him away. "We are all," he writes to an intimate friend on 22nd April 1842, a year after No. 90, "much quieter and more resigned than we were, and are remarkably desirous of building up a position, and proving that the English theory is tenable, or rather the English state of things. If the Bishops would leave us alone, the fever would subside."[158]

That Newman, in good faith, should have tried to find some apostolic tenability in the National Church does not mean that he was somehow convinced of that tenability before he undertook his trial—quite the opposite. The defining characteristic of Newman's tenure as an Anglican was his fairly continual discomfiture with a Church the apostolic *bona fides* of which were always questionable. In Tract 90, he could not have been more categorical about this: "it is a duty which we owe both to the Catholic Church and to our own, to take our reformed confessions in the most Catholic sense they will admit; we have no duties towards

---

[156] Francis Paget, "Preface," in Church, *Life and Letters*, xvi–xviii.
[157] For an example of this, see John Henry Newman, "Catholicity of the Anglican Church," in *Ess.*, ii, 55.
[158] Church, *Oxford Movement*, 281–2.

their framers."[159] If Newman can be seen as shaping the 19th-century Anglican Church, he did so by imposing questions upon it which were as importunate as they were unanswerable. Henry Chadwick certainly realized this in a centennial essay in which he wrote of how "Newman restates Hurrell Froude's question; Does the ambition of the Church of England to be national lead it ... to make their Church ... a wet and tolerant body ... not greatly interested in the notion of a visible Church that faithfully teaches a given revelation defined by Bible and sacred tradition? Anglicanism is periodically threatened by a do-it-yourself spirit of consumer choice." [160] Now that this same plebiscitary spirit threatens to vitiate the Church of Rome, Catholics can appreciate anew the salutary force with which Newman opposed the corruption when sworn to the Anglican ministry.

Yet Church is right to stress that Newman, for all of his reservations about the apostolicity of the Anglican Church, did remain loyal to it for at least the summer of 1839, even though that loyalty was increasingly beleaguered. What is fascinating about Church's reading of Newman's thinking leading up to his friend's "great revolution of mind"[161] is that it exhibits both faithful insight into the psychology of the incipient conversion, but also Church's own loyalty to the religion Newman was gradually abandoning. "In Mr. Newman's view of the debate between England and Rome, he had all along dwelt on two broad features, *Apostolicity* and *Catholicity*," Church writes;

> likeness to the Apostolic teaching, and likeness to the uninterrupted unity and extent of the undivided Church; and of those two features he found the first signally wanting in Rome, and the second signally wanting in England. When he began to distrust his own reasonings, still the disturbing and repelling element in Rome was the alleged defect of *Apostolicity*, the contrast between primitive and Roman religion; while the attractive one was the apparent widely extended Catholicity in all lands, East and West, continents and isles, of the world-wide spiritual empire of the Pope. It is these two great points which may be traced in their action on his mind at this crisis. The contrast between early and Roman doctrine and practice, in a variety of ways, some of them most grave and important, was long a great difficulty in the way of attempting to identify the Roman Church, absolutely and exclusively, with the Primitive Church. The study of antiquity indisposed him, indeed, more and more to the existing system of the English Church; its claims to model itself on the purity and simplicity of the Early Church seemed to him, in the light of its documents, and still more of the facts of history and life, more and more questionable. But modern Rome was just as distant from the Early Church though it preserved many ancient features, lost or unvalued by England. Still, Rome was not the same thing as the Early Church; and Mr. Newman ultimately sought a way out of his difficulty—and indeed there was no other—in the famous doctrine of Development.[162]

Readers can take exception to the claim that the Church of Rome was not the

---

[159] *VM*, ii, 344.
[160] Henry Chadwick, "Newman's Significance for the Anglican Church," in *Newman: A Man for Our Time*, ed. David Brown (London: SPCK, 1990), 67.
[161] *Apo.*, 191.
[162] Church, *Oxford Movement*, 228–9.

same thing as the Early Church without failing to credit Church for recognizing the force with which Newman's "great revolution of mind" hit him.

> But when the difficulty about *Apostolicity* was thus provided for, then the force of the great vision of the Catholic Church came upon him, unchecked and irresistible. That was a thing present, visible, undeniable as a fact of nature; that was a thing at once old and new; it belonged as truly, as manifestly, to the recent and modern world of democracy and science, as it did to the Middle Ages and the Fathers, to the world of Gregory and Innocent, to the world of Athanasius and Augustine. The majesty, the vastness of an imperial polity, outlasting all states and kingdoms, all social changes and political revolutions, answered at once to the promises of the prophecies, and to the antecedent idea of the universal kingdom of God. Before this great idea, embodied in concrete form, and not a paper doctrine, partial scandals and abuses seemed to sink into insignificance. Objections seemed petty and ignoble; the pretence of rival systems impertinent and absurd. He resented almost with impatience anything in the way of theory or explanation which seemed to him narrow, technical, dialectical. He would look at nothing but what had on it the mark of greatness and largeness which befitted the awful subject, and was worthy of arresting the eye and attention of an ecclesiastical statesman, alive to mighty interests, compared to which even the most serious human affairs were dwarfed and obscured. But all this was gradual in coming. His recognition of the claims of the English Church, faulty and imperfect as he thought it, did not give way suddenly and at once. It survived the rude shock of 1839. From first to almost the last she was owned as his "mother"—owned in passionate accents of disappointment and despair as a Church which knew not how to use its gifts; yet still, even though life seemed failing her, and her power of teaching and ruling seemed paralysed, his mother; and as long as there seemed to him a prospect of restoration to health, it was his duty to stay by her. This was his first attitude for three or four years after 1839. He could not speak of her with the enthusiasm and triumph of the first years of the movement. When he fought her battles, it was with the sense that her imperfections made his task the harder. Still he clung to the belief that she held a higher standard than she had yet acted up to, and discouraged and perplexed he yet maintained her cause.[163]

If one reads this sanguine interpretation against the last piece Newman wrote addressing the crisis of loyalty that he and so many others faced with regard to the Anglican Church, "The State of Religious Parties," which appeared in the *British Critic* in April of 1839—two months after the release of Tract 90—we can see that the "enthusiasm and triumph" of which Newman might have spoken in earlier days were, indeed, long gone. "The current of the age cannot be stopped, but it may be directed; and it is better that it should find its way into the Anglican port, than that it should be propelled into Popery, or drifted upon unbelief," he says at one point in the pitiably dispirited article. Yet he also says:

> At present not any one principle does it carry out logically; nor does it try to adjust and limit one by the other; but as the English language is partly Saxon,

---

[163] Ibid., 230–1.

partly Latin, with some German, some French, some Dutch, and some Italian, so this religious creed is made up of the fragments of religion which the course of events has brought together and has imbedded in it, something of Lutheranism, and something of Calvinism, something of Erastianism, and something of Zuinglianism, a little Judaism, and a little dogmatism, and not a little secularity, as if by hazard. It has no straightforward view on any one point on which it professes to teach; and to hide its poverty it has dressed itself out in a maze of words, which all inquirers feel and are perplexed with, yet few are able to penetrate. It cannot pronounce plainly what it holds about the sacraments, what it means by unity, what it thinks of Antiquity, what fundamentals are, what the Church; what again it means by faith. It has no intelligible rule for interpreting Scripture beyond that of submission to the arbitrary comments which have come down to it, though it knows it not, from Zuingle or Melancthon. "Unstable as water, it cannot excel." It is but the inchoate state or stage of a doctrine, and its final resolution is in Rationalism."[164]

In the *Apologia*, Newman wrote of the essay: "What will best describe my state of mind at the early part of 1839, is an Article in the *British Critic* for that April. I have looked over it now, for the first time since it was published; and have been struck by it for this reason:—it contains the last words which I ever spoke as an Anglican to Anglicans. It may now be read as my parting address and valediction, made to my friends. I little knew it at the time. It reviews the actual state of things, and it ends by looking towards the future."[165] In Newman's honest appraisal of this last halfhearted attempt to recommend the Via Media, one can see what a good and fair critic he was of his own work. "I concluded the Article by saying, that all who did not wish to be 'democratic, or pantheistic, or popish,' must 'look out for some Via Media which will preserve us from what threatens, though it cannot restore the dead. The spirit of Luther is dead; but Hildebrand and Loyola are alive. Is it sensible, sober, judicious, to be so very angry with those writers of the day, who point to the fact, that our divines of the seventeenth century have occupied a ground which is the true and intelligible mean between extremes? Is it wise to quarrel with this ground, because it is not exactly what we should choose, had we the power of choice? Is it true moderation, instead of trying to fortify a middle doctrine, to fling stones at those who do? … Would you rather have your sons and daughters members of the Church of England or of the Church of Rome?'"[166] In this last question, we can see a kind of polemical exhaustion, Newman, in effect, throwing up his hands. "And thus I left the matter. But, while I was thus speaking of the future of the Movement, I was in truth winding up my accounts with it, little dreaming that it was so to be;—while I was still, in some way or other, feeling about for an available Via Media, I was soon to receive a shock which was to cast out of my imagination all middle courses and compromises for ever."[167]

---

[164] *Ess.*, i, 296. Zwinglianism is the theology of H. Zwingli (1484–1531), the Swiss Protestant who broke with Luther in seeing the Eucharist as a merely symbolic matter.
[165] *Apo.*, 94.
[166] *Apo.*, 103–4.
[167] *Apo.*, 104.

The reluctance with which Newman was moving closer and closer to the Church of Rome may not have had as much to do with his love of his ecclesial "mother"—as Church suggests—as with his "savage and ungrateful" feelings towards those whom he styled "the controversialists of Rome." In the *British Critic* of January, 1840, Newman let rip against these hapless straw men.

> By their fruits ye shall know them ... We see it attempting to gain converts among us by unreal representations of its doctrines, plausible statements, bold assertions, appeals to the weaknesses of human nature, to our fancies, our eccentricities, our fears, our frivolities, our false philosophies. We see its agents, smiling and nodding and ducking to attract attention, as gipseys make up to truant boys, holding out tales for the nursery, and pretty pictures, and gilt gingerbread, and physic concealed in jam, and sugar-plums for good children. Who can but feel shame when the religion of Ximenes, Borromeo, and Pascal, is so overlaid? Who can but feel sorrow, when its devout and earnest defenders so mistake its genius and its capabilities? We Englishmen like manliness, openness, consistency, truth. Rome will never gain on us, till she learns these virtues.[168]

Newman deserves credit for calling his readers' attention to such effusions in the *Apologia*. Certainly, they are eloquent of the divided loyalties that exercised him during this time of crisis, especially since he was straightforward enough to admit that "No one ought to indulge in insinuations; it certainly diminishes my right to complain of slanders uttered against myself, when, as in this passage, I had already spoken in condemnation of that class of controversialists of that religious body, to which I myself now belong."[169] It was particularly ungracious of Newman to bring such charges in light of the brilliant and generous help that Fr. Charles W. Russell (1812–80) would give him in the following year. The sympathy, tact and good counsel that the ecclesiastical historian, student of Leibnitz, co-editor with Cardinal Wiseman of the *Dublin Review* and future president of Maynooth showed Newman could not have disproved such insinuations more thoroughly. Yet to make amends, Newman was later careful to attest that Russell "had, perhaps, more to do with my conversion than anyone."[170]

In composing his anatomy of that conversion for the *Apologia*, Newman also credited the confidential role that Church had played in it, which he makes plain in a letter he wrote to his old friend before sending the book off to print. Indeed, since Church had been such an intimate sounding board for the convert, Newman was naturally keen on having him confirm the accuracy of his anatomy.

The Oratory, Birmingham April 23. 1864

Private
My dear Church,
   Copeland encourages me to write to you. I am in one of the most painful trials in which I have ever been in my life, and I think you can help me.

---

[168] *Apo.*, 126–7. The quotation is from "The State of Religious Parties," which Newman reprinted as "The Catholicity of the Anglican Church" in *Ess.*, ii, with slight revision, 71–3.
[169] *Apo.*, 224.
[170] *Apo.*, 176.

It has always been on my mind that perhaps some day I should be called on to defend my honesty while in the Church of England. Of course there have been endless hits against me in Newspapers, Reviews, and Pamphlets but, even though the names of the writers have come out and have belonged to great men, they have been anonymous publications,—or else a sentence or two on some particular point has been the whole. But I have considered that, if any one with his name made an elaborate charge on me, I was bound to speak. When Maurice in the Times a year ago attacked me, I answered this at once.

But I have thought it very unlikely that anyone would do so—and then, I am so indolent, that, unless there is an actual necessity, I do nothing. In consequence, now, when the call comes on me, I am quite unprepared to meet it. I know well that Kingsley is a furious foolish fellow—but he has a name—nor is it any thing at all to me that men think I got the victory in the Correspondence several months ago—that was a contest of ability—but now he comes out with a Pamphlet bringing together a hodge podge of charges against me all about dishonesty. Now friends who know me say, "Let him alone, no one credits him—" but it is not so. This very town of Birmingham of course knows nothing of me, and his pamphlet on its appearance produced an effect. The evangelical party has always spoken ill of me, and the Pamphlet seems to justify them. The (R.) Catholic party does not know me,—the fathers of our schoolboys, the priests, etc etc, whom I cannot afford to let think badly of me. Therefore, thus publicly challenged, I must speak—and, unless I speak strongly, men won't believe me in earnest.

But now I have little more to trust to than my memory. There are matters in which no one can help me, viz. those which have gone on in my own mind—but there is also a great abundance of public facts, or again facts witnessed by persons close to me, which I may have forgotten. I fear of making mistakes in dates, though I have a good memory for them—and still more of making bold generalizations without suspicion that they are not to the letter tenable.

Now you were so much with me from 1840 to 1843 or even 1845, that it has struck me, that you could, if you saw in proof what I shall write about those years, correct any fault of fact which you found in my statement. Also, you might have letters of mine to throw light on my state of mind, and thus by means of contemporaneous authority. And these are the two matters I request of you as regards the years in question.

The worst is, I am so hampered for time. Longman thought I ought not to delay—so I began—and therefore of necessity in numbers. What I have to send you is not yet written. It won't be much in point of length.

I need hardly say I shall keep secret any thing you do for me, and the fact of my having applied to you
   Yours affectly John H Newman[171]

---

[171] Newman to R. W. Church (23 April 1864), *LD*, xx, 100–1. Here is an extract from Newman's reply to the Editor of the Times regarding Maurice's ill-founded charge: "I would rather be judged by my own words than by Mr. Maurice's interpretation of them. I distinctly repudiate his accusation that I maintained, either in Tract 90 or elsewhere, the right of a man's subscribing the Thirty-nine Articles in a non-natural sense. Nor ought he to speak from mere memory, as he seems to confess he did, when making a serious charge against another. I maintained in Tract 90 that the Thirty-nine Articles ought to be subscribed in their 'literal and grammatical sense'; but I maintained also

No one understood the risks Newman ran in revisiting his Anglican deathbed more than Church, as this letter of his to W. J. Copeland, one of the earliest historians of the Oxford movement attests. "I heard yesterday from Newman," Church wrote, "asking me to look over sheets, which of course I will gladly do. It must be very painful for him to have to go over all this ground again. I cannot help wishing that he had spared himself, or at any rate that he had left Kingsley alone, and said what was to be said without mixing it up with his quarrel with Kingsley. But he knows better than I do what best becomes him." Church also knew that his friend would be revisiting harrowing ground. "The truth is, he has a hard task before him. The whole question comes to be opened afresh, as to what people who don't agree with Newman are to think of the legitimacy of the position which he took up, while coming round to be what they so shrink from and dislike, it will be a hard matter to make explanations which will satisfy even candid ones among them. There is nothing so trying and so hard in the world as the position of a man who is changing his views, and doing so with due time, and deliberation, and caution." Here, one can see the discerning, moving note of the friendly critic in Church. "The more careful and conscientious and hesitating he is, the more people insist on flinging charges of dishonesty and inconsistency against him. If Newman's Apologia to the British public succeeds in bringing them round to judge him fairly, he will have accomplished a remarkable feat. He can do it if any man can; but he runs a risk. ... The public and the personal questions are so intermixed, that every one who is afraid of Rome, or dislikes it, will think himself bound to pronounce against Newman. But he must go on, and we must help him as well as we can."[172]

Something of what Newman expressed against "Catholic controversialists" at the time of his conversion might be thought to have stemmed from his fear that, if he did defect to Rome, he would leave Anglicans struggling to live the devout life in the lurch. "The unsettlement I am causing has been for a long time the one overpowering distress I have had," he wrote Pusey.[173] For Church, "As tutor at Oriel, Mr. Newman had made what efforts he could, sometimes disturbing to the authorities, to raise the standard of conduct and feeling among his pupils," and it was precisely because Newman's influence had had so profound an impact on Church himself that he could describe it so vividly.

> When [Newman] became a parish priest, his preaching took a singularly practical and plain-spoken character. The first sermon of the series, a typical sermon, "Holiness necessary for future Blessedness," a sermon which has made many readers grave when they laid it down, was written in 1826, before he came to St. Mary's; and as he began he continued. No sermons, except those which his great opposite,

that they were so drawn up as to admit, in that grammatical sense, of subscription on the part of persons who differed very much from each other in the judgment which they formed of Catholic doctrine." Newman to Editor of the Times (24 February 1863), *LD*, xx, 413.

[172] Church to Copeland (26 April 1864), *Life and Letters*, 2012.
[173] Newman to Pusey (14 March 1845), *LD*, x, 591. Cf. "God grant we may keep our faith, truth, innocence, conscience and the rest of our garments clean and close about us while better and brighter days may soon arise on our beloved Church," Charles Stephen Hassells wrote Newman after learning Newman had left Oxford for Littlemore. Hassells to Newman (9 February 1844), *LD*, x, 117.

Dr. Arnold, was preaching at Rugby, had appealed to conscience with such directness and force. A passionate and sustained earnestness after a high moral rule, seriously realised in conduct, is the dominant character of these sermons. They showed the strong reaction against slackness of fibre in the religious life; against the poverty, softness; restlessness, worldliness, the blunted and impaired sense of truth, which reigned with little check in the recognised fashions of professing Christianity; the want of depth both of thought and feeling; the strange blindness to the real sternness, nay the austerity, of the New Testament.[174]

Newman, however, was adamant that the tenability of a religion was not proved by the putative holiness of its adherents. He was unsparingly witty about this in his King William Street lectures. Addressing his old Anglo-Catholic friends, he confessed:

Really I am obliged in candour to allow, whatever part the evil spirit had in the work, whatever gross admixture of earth polluted it, whatever extravagance there was to excite ridicule or disgust, whether it was Christian virtue or the excellence of unaided man, whatever was the spiritual state of the subjects of it, whatever their end and their final account, yet there were higher and nobler vestiges or semblances of grace and truth in Methodism than there have been among you. I give you credit for what you are, grave, serious, earnest, modest, steady, self-denying, consistent; you have the praise of such virtues; and you have a clear perception of many of the truths, or of portions of the truths, of Revelation. In these points you surpass the Wesleyans; but if I wished to find what was striking, extraordinary, suggestive of Catholic heroism—of St. Martin, St. Francis, or St. Ignatius—I should betake myself far sooner to them than to you.[175]

Nevertheless, Church recognized the Via Media as the crucible of Newman's apostolic trial of the National Church, since it was on the ground of the Via Media—or "the English theory," as he strikingly put it—that Newman sought to reconcile the Anglican with the Roman Church.

It is in Newman's *Lectures on the Doctrine of Justification* (1838) that he makes this effort most pointedly by showing how the Via Media comports more with Rome than with the popular Protestantism of Evangelicalism or the Lutheranism of the Continental Reformation, a deliberately invidious comparison to which the Archdeacon of Lewes, Julius Charles Hare (1795–1855) took vehement exception in his *Vindication of Luther* (1855).

That Hare should have been so keen to criticize Newman for what he was convinced was his misreading of Luther followed from his unusual background. Born in Valdagno near Vincenza, Italy, where his distressed parents sought sanctuary for their ardent republicanism, Hare was educated at Charterhouse and Trinity College, Cambridge, though the influence of his well-read mother, who tutored him for five years before he entered school, was considerable. On the Continent, Hare's parents settled in Weimar and befriended Goethe, Schiller and the cosmopolitan diarist Henry Crabb Robinson. This continental upbringing left

---

[174] Church, *Oxford Movement*, 19.
[175] *Diff.*, i, 89.

Hare with an eccentricity that he would never shake. At Trinity, he befriended Connop Thirlwall, William Whewell, J. F. D. Maurice and John Sterling before entering the Anglican ministry and marrying Maurice's sister Esther. Although subsequently a good friend of Manning, Hare was always opposed to Newman's dogmatic Christianity, which his *Vindication of Luther* (1855) shows. Gladstone confided in Manning that he "found many horrors in Hare as I read on: [he was reading the Archdeacon's sermon, "The Unity of the Church" (1845)]: but many ... truths also."[176] Hare's other works include *Guesses at Truth* (1827) which he co-authored with his brother, translations of Niebuhr's *History of Rome* (1828–32), and *The Victory of Faith and Other Sermons* (1840).

Hare's response to Newman's *Lectures on Justification* was rather broad brush, though he was honest enough to admit that Newman's dissent from Luther's theology was "a part of the great contest by which our Church is so dismally torn." In other words, for Newman to assail Luther's theology was necessarily to assail the Protestant character of the National Church, which, of course, made Newman's point about the untenability of that Protestant character. "Whatever confidence in Luther's spiritual wisdom may have been inspired by the contemplation of his life, or the study of his writings," Hare wrote,

> it will often find occasion in these days to vindicate itself against the attacks which are continually made upon him and his cause. They have proceeded from more than one quarter, but chiefly, as might be expected, from that new School of Theology, which has set itself to depreciate and to counteract the work of the Reformation. By our modern Romanizers the mightiest enemy of the Romish corruptions is naturally regarded with dislike, with aversion, almost with hatred. His intense love of truth revolts those who dally with truth, and play tricks with it, until they cease to discern the distinction between truth and falsehood. His straight forwardness finds no sympathy among those who walk in crooked ways. His hunger and thirst after that which is spiritual, and his comparative indifference about out ward forms, are mortal offenses to those with whom forms, institutions, rites, ordinances are the main thing, and almost everything. Hence the contest about Luther's character now has a peculiar interest and importance. It is a part of the great contest by which our Church is so dismally torn. The enemy, the traducer has endeavoured to get possession of him, and to cover him with ignominy: there is urgent need of someone to defend him from his assailants; and as no one else has come forward, that I am aware of, I have felt bound to do what I can for him to whom I owe such a debt of gratitude and love as can never be paid.[177]

Apropos Newman's objections to Luther, Frederick Denison Maurice was not altogether mistaken when he wrote: "Dr. Newman's bitter dislike of Luther is due much more to his revolt from Aristotle and Aquinas than to his revolt from the Pope. When Luther, and still more Melanchthon, succumbed to propositions in

---

[176] Gladstone to Manning (20 February 1845), *The Correspondence of Henry Edward Manning and William Ewart Gladstone Volume II: 1844–1853*, ii, 62.
[177] Julius Charles Hare, *Vindication of Luther against his English Assailants* (London: John W. Parker and Son, 1855), 74.

their later days, when assent to the doctrine of justification was substituted for belief in the Justifier, Protestantism went into the lean, sickly, and yet contentious state of its existence, only to emerge from that into indifference—a mere denial of Romanism."[178]

In taking issue with the anti-Protestant musings of the *Lectures on Justification*, Hare is careful to concede that Newman is no bungling controversialist. He sees "a strong tendency toward the Church of Rome in Mr. Newman's *Lectures on Justification*, even as there was in our Arminian divinity of the seventeenth century," though he also sees little "practical wisdom and godliness" in them, attributes "which are ever indispensable to bridle in the runaway impetus of speculation." Nevertheless, notwithstanding Newman's "morbid subtilty," Hare recognizes that "In these *Lectures on Justification*, the Lutheran doctrine is assailed with great ingenuity and logical acuteness: and in the course of the argument Luther himself is often spoken of ... with respect, or at least with that exemplary decorum which has ever markt Mr Newman's controversial writings."[179] However, like so many of Newman's critics, Hare deplores Newman's unfamiliarity with the work of German theologians. "Verily, in reading the works of English censurers of Luther," he writes, "one is tempted at times to fancy that the History of Germany must have been omitted from the course of their studies."[180] At the same time, in several points of the pamphlet, Hare excuses himself from taking any specific issue with Newman's criticisms of Luther and his ideas of justification. For all of the superior knowledge he claimed of Luther and other German theologians, Hare was plainly unequipped to debate Newman on the matter. Indeed, there is something rather comical about a would-be controversialist entering the lists only to admit, as Hare admits, that "I cannot, as I have already said, enter here into the general argument concerning Mr Newman's view of Justification, and his objections to Luther's."[181] Reading what he and his brother did have to say of Luther in *Guesses at Truth by Two Brothers* (1827), one should be grateful to have been spared any detailed riposte, for there is nothing brilliant in comments like this: "[A]t the Reformation, Luther, having the true Apostolical spirit in him—the spirit of a Seminal, not of a Radical Reformer—was ever strenuous in resisting all attempts to carry out the Reformation by destructive, revolutionary, radical measures. Preach the word of God, he said,—preach the truth; and the truth will set us free."[182] Nevertheless, Hare's disinclination to debate the merits of Luther did not stay him from charging Newman with scepticism and sophistry, which

---

[178] Maurice to Bishop of Argyll (26 May 1870), *The Life of Frederick Denison Maurice Chiefly Told through his Letters*, ed. Frederick Maurice, 2 vols (London: Macmillan & Co., 1884), ii, 615.

[179] Hare, *Vindication*, 75. "Markt" is not a typo here: Hare, like Bernard Shaw, fancying himself a reformer of English spelling, gave all of his past tense verbs this idiosyncratic ending. Apropos Newman's mode of controversy, Hare repeats his praise of the convert in another passage where he says: "On the whole however, as has been acknowledged above, Mr Newman preserves that decorous tone, which so honorably distinguishes his polemical writings." Hare was obviously unacquainted with the rather indecorous swipes Newman took at Arnold of Rugby and R. D. Hampden, which are much more in keeping with the knockabout vitriol typical of Anglican controversy.

[180] *Ibid.*, 84.

[181] *Ibid.*, 93.

[182] Augustus and Julius Hare, *Guesses at Truth by Two Brothers* (London: Macmillan & Co., 1884), 202.

he does with a certain flourish at the end of his paper. "It is clear, Mr Newman, when he wrote these Lectures, had a very incorrect notion" he concludes:

> but probably it will have seemed to many, when they terminated their wanderings through the mazes of his *Lectures on Justification,* that the text prefixt to the first Lecture had been selected under a judicial blindness as the aptest motto for the whole work. Moreover, when we look back on the Author's subsequent career, when we reflect how he has gone on year after year sharpening the edge of his already overkeen understanding, casting one truth after another into his logical crucible, and persuading himself that he had dissolved it to atoms, and then exhibiting a like ingenuity in compounding the semblance of truths out of fictions,—when we call to mind how in this way he appeared to be gradually losing the faculty of distinguishing between truth and falsehood, and the very belief in the existence of any power for discerning truth, nay, as it seemed at times, in the existence of any positive truth to be discerned, and how, taking refuge from the encroachments of a universal scepticism, he has at length bowed his neck under a yoke, which a man, gifted with such fine qualities of mind and character, could hardly assume, until he had put out the eyes of his heart and of his conscience, as well as of his understanding,—it is not in scorn and triumph, but in deep sadness and awe, that we repeat, *Who is this that darkeneth counsel by words without knowledge?*[183]

Perhaps the most interesting gloss on the *Lectures on Justification* from an Anglican perspective is that of Henry Chadwick, who points out that "Newman's Protestant critics came to read his book as consciously preparing the ground for the conversion of 1845, reconciling the Thirty-Nine Articles with Trent (which on justification is not very difficult to do)" and "attempting a 'concordium' that might open the way for an ecumenical reconciliation between Canterbury and Rome. If there was any element of that in Newman's mind in 1838, it lay in his subconscious." Chadwick also notes the irony of Newman's dedicating the book to Richard Bagot, the Bishop of Oxford, who, when push came to shove after Tract 90, proved "cooly neutral, and was sadly felt by Newman to have done nothing to support him when critics were telling him to get out and go to Rome." That Chadwick believed the Lectures to be "among the major muniments of the modern ecumenical movement" does not say much for the common sense of the advocates of that movement.[184] Newman's ecumenical convictions whilst still an Anglican, such as they were, can be gleaned much more reliably from something he said in his *Lectures on the Prophetical Office of the Church* (1837), a year before the *Lectures on Justification,* in which he could not have been clearer about what he saw as the irreconcilability of the two religions.

> In Romanism there are some things absolutely good, some things only just tainted and sullied, some things corrupted, and some things in themselves sinful; but the system itself so called must be viewed as a whole, and all parts of it as belonging to

---

[183] Ibid., 99–100.
[184] Henry Chadwick, "The Lectures on Justification," in *Newman after a Hundred Years*, ed. Ian Ker and Alan G. Hill (Oxford: The Clarendon Press, 1990), 308.

the whole, and in connexion with their practical working and the end which they subserve. Viewed thus as a practical system, its main tenet, which gives a colour to all its parts, is the Church's infallibility, as on the other hand, the principle of that genuine theology out of which it has arisen, is the authority of Catholic Antiquity. In this and the following Lecture, I shall observe upon some of the characteristics of this main error, as we may consider it; viewing it first morally, and then what may be called politically. And the points to which I wish to direct attention, as involved in the doctrine of Infallibility, are such as the following: that Romanism considers unclouded certainty necessary for a Christian's faith and hope, and doubt incompatible with practical abidance in the truth; that it aims at forming a complete and consistent theology, and in forming it, neglects authority, and rests upon abstract arguments and antecedent grounds: and that it substitutes a technical and formal obedience for the spirit of love. I notice these peculiarities in order to draw intelligible lines of demarcation between members of the Roman Church and ourselves.[185]

The decorous controversialist in Newman only concluded his remarks by reassuring his Anglican readers that "If we are induced to believe the professions of Rome, and make advances towards her as if a sister or a mother Church, which in theory she is, we shall find too late that we are in the arms of a pitiless and unnatural relative, who will but triumph in the arts which have inveigled us within her reach. No; dismissing the dreams which the romance of early Church history and the high doctrines of Catholicism will raise in the inexperienced mind, let us be sure that she is our enemy, and will do us a mischief when she can. In speaking and acting on this conviction, we need not depart from Christian charity towards her. We must deal with her as we would towards a friend who is not himself; in great affliction, with all affectionate tender thoughts, with tearful regret and a broken heart, but still with a steady eye and a firm hand."[186] Reading this, one can easily imagine how it might have been the stylist in Newman—the witheringly agile rhetorician, not the co-religionist—whom Anglicans were most loth to lose when their erstwhile champion defected to Rome.

Here, one should stress that the fact that the *Lectures of Justification* show Newman moving steadily away from this unfavorable view of Rome is lively proof of the tenuity of his commitment to the Via Media before taking his final step to Rome. Even as he touts the Via Media, he is preparing to abandon it. One never quite gets this sense from reading Church: he is too intent on presenting Newman's dogged attachment to the Via Media, even after he had begun to doubt it. However, as we shall see, Church's special pleading on this score is never groundless, and, in any case, it is vital testimony to the criticism of friendship—a deeply sympathetic, forbearing, discerning criticism, bred, in the case of true pastors like Church and Newman, of shared discipleship. It is also an indispensable part of the record of the Oxford Movement, so much of which was propelled by friendship. Newman certainly saw himself as a beneficiary of its graces. "Rightly or wrongly," he wrote to Church, "I put down to you the review

---

[185] *VM*, i, 84–5.
[186] Ibid., 83–4.

of my Verses in the Guardian:—any how, they are the remarks of a friend rather than of a critic—and, as I cannot help liking kind friends better than impartial critics, I am extremely touched by a notice of me which breathes such delicate affection."[187]

IX

There are any number of passages that one might quote from Church's history to illustrate Church's criticism of friendship—especially at a time when men's religious loyalties were diverging and causing terrible strains within those friendships—but certainly his portrait of Charles Marriott (1811–58) before what he called the "catastrophe" of Newman's poping is admirably astute. "Marriott's great contribution to the movement was his solid, simple goodness," Church writes,

> his immovable hope, his confidence that things would come right. With much imaginativeness open to poetical grandeur and charm, and not without some power of giving expression to feeling, he was destitute of all that made so many others of his friends interesting as men. He was nothing, as a person to know and observe, to the genius of the two Mozleys, to the brilliant social charm of Frederic Faber, to the keen, refined intelligence of Mark Pattison, to the originality and clever eccentricity of William Palmer of Magdalen. And he was nothing as a man of practical power for organising and carrying out successful schemes: such power was not much found at Oxford in those days. But his faith in his cause, as the cause of goodness and truth, was proof against mockery or suspicion or disaster. When ominous signs disturbed other people he saw none. He had an almost perverse subtlety of mind which put a favourable interpretation on what seemed most formidable. As his master drew more and more out of sympathy with the English Church, Marriott, resolutely loyal to it and to him, refused to understand hints and indications which to others were but too plain. He vexed and even provoked Newman, in the last agonies of the struggle, by the optimism with which he clung to useless theories and impossible hopes. For that unquenchable hoping against hope, and hope unabated still when the catastrophe had come, the English Church at least owes him deep gratitude. Throughout those anxious years he never despaired of her.[188]

In his characterizations of Newman, the historian in Church is always at pains to chart the subtle twists and turns of the thinking that led to Tract 90, while putting it in some wider historical context, though it is the affectionate friend who manages to present these developments with such discerning accuracy. Indeed, in Church's criticism of friendship, for all its natural partiality, impartiality is never entirely sacrificed. Apropos Newman's treatments of his erstwhile Anglo-Catholic position in *Anglican Difficulties*, for example, he says: "Not from any studied impartiality, which is foreign to his character, but from his strong and keen sense of what is real and his determined efforts to bring it out, he avoids

---

[187] Newman to Richard William Church (27 February 1868), *LD*, xxiv, 22.
[188] Church, *Oxford Movement*, 88–9.

the temptation—as it seems to us, who still believe that he was more right once than he is now—to do injustice to his former self and his former position."[189] For Church, Newman "wanted, when all other parties were claiming room for their speculations, to claim room for his own preference for ancient doctrine," though, before he converted, he genuinely sought to claim this room for the benefit, not the embarrassment of the Anglican Church.

> He wished to make out that no branch of the Church had authoritatively committed itself to language which was hopelessly and fatally irreconcilable with Christian truth. But he claimed nothing but what he could maintain to be fairly within the authorised formularies of the English Church. He courted inquiry, he courted argument. If his claim seemed a new one, if his avowed leaning to ancient and Catholic views seemed to make him more tolerant than had been customary, not to Roman abuses, but to Roman authoritative language, it was part of the more accurate and the more temperate and charitable thought of our day compared with past times.

Yet Church also realized that "with this sincere loyalty to the English Church, as he believed it to be, there was, no doubt, in the background the haunting and disquieting misgiving that the attempt to connect more closely the modern Church with the ancient, and this widened theology in a direction which had been hitherto specially and jealously barred, was putting the English Church on its trial." This was, indeed, the crux of the matter. Would the Anglican Church bear the trial? "Would it respond to the call to rise to a higher and wider type of doctrine, to a higher standard of life? Would it justify what Mr. Newman had placed in the forefront among the notes of the true Church, the note of Sanctity? Would the *Via Media* make up for its incompleteness as a theory by developing into reality and fruitfulness of actual results? Would the Church bear to be told of its defaults? Would it allow to the maintainers of Catholic and Anglican principles the liberty which others claimed, and which by large and powerful bodies of opinion was denied to Anglicans? Or would it turn out on trial, that the Via Media was an idea without substance, a dialectical fiction, a mere theological expedient for getting out of difficulties, unrecognised, and when put forward, disowned? Would it turn out that the line of thought and teaching which connected the modern with the ancient Church was but the private and accidental opinion of Hooker and Andrewes and Bull and Wilson, unauthorised in the English Church, uncongenial to its spirit, if not contradictory to its formularies? It is only just to Mr. Newman to say, that even after some of his friends were frightened, he long continued to hope for the best; but undoubtedly, more and more, his belief in the reality of the English Church was undergoing a very severe, and as time went on, discouraging testing."[190]

The even-handedness of this assessment of Newman's circumstances before he composed Tract 90 is admirably characteristic of the friendly critic in Church, though he is equally balanced on the famous Tract's controversial impetus, arguing, as he did, that it "was occasioned by the common allegation, on the side of

---

[189] Church, "Newman's *Apologia*," in *Occasional Papers*, ii, 385.
[190] Church, *Oxford Movement*, 245–6.

some of the advanced section of the Tractarians, as well as on the side of their opponents, that the Thirty-nine Articles were hopelessly irreconcilable with that Catholic teaching which Mr. Newman had defended on the authority of our great divines, but which both the parties above mentioned were ready to identify with the teaching of the Roman Church." For Church, "The Tract was intended, by a rigorous examination of the language of the Articles, to traverse this allegation. It sought to show that all that was clearly and undoubtedly Catholic, this language left untouched." And Church quoted the Tract to substantiate his point: "That there are real difficulties to a Catholic Christian in the ecclesiastical position of our Church at this day, no one can deny; but the statements of the Articles are not in the number, and it may be right at the present moment to insist upon this."[191]

What is striking about Church's account of Tract 90 is his recognition that it was so logical—coldly, dispassionately, unmercifully logical. The Tract's approach to Anglicanism was precisely one that Newman always insisted could not be taken if one were to understand the appeal the Roman Church had for her converts.[192] The National Church, by contrast, could not enlist the sympathies of the whole man. "The Tract went through the Articles in detail, which were commonly looked upon as either anti-Catholic or anti-Roman," Church writes. "It went through them with a dry logical way of interpretation, such as a professed theologian might use, who was accustomed to all the niceties of language and the distinctions of the science. It was the way in which they would be likely to be examined and construed by a purely legal court. The effect of it, doubtless, was like that produced on ordinary minds by the refinements of a subtle advocate, or by the judicial interpretation of an Act of Parliament which the judges do not like; and some of the interpretations undoubtedly seemed far-fetched and artificial. Yet some of those which were pointed to at the time as flagrant instances of extravagant misinterpretation have now come to look different."[193] Here, the loyal Anglican in the Dean, whose churchmanship sprang so profoundly from his Tractarian sympathies, was clearly keen on putting the Tract in as favorable a light as possible, a light which the Catholic Newman would always find oddly unreal. In a letter of Newman's to Pusey one can see the comical divide that the Tract presented between the convert and his old Anglo-Catholic friends: "My dear Pusey," Newman wrote in 1863, "That Tract (Number 90) ... has been one among other means of keeping up a high Church party among the English clergy. For this I rejoice and am thankful—but that is no reason that you should be dragged through the mud by a composition of mine, which, viewed in the concrete, might have much in it, which had better not have been there."[194] Nevertheless, for Church, "the Tract had sufficient novelty about it to account for most of the excitement which it caused." Yes, "Its dryness and negative curtness were provoking," Church conceded. "It was not a positive argument, it was not an appeal to authorities; it was a paring down of language, alleged in certain

---

[191] Ibid., 282–6.
[192] Cf. "Newman's delight in exact logic made the argument [of Tract 90] sound clever, enjoyably if you wanted to agree, evasively sophisticated if you did not." Henry Chadwick, "Newman's Significance for the Anglican Church," in *Newman: A Man for Our Time*, ed. Brown, 42.
[193] Church, *Oxford Movement*, 286–7.
[194] Newman to Pusey (1 March 1863), *LD*, xx, 416.

portions of the Articles to be somewhat loose, to its barest meaning; and to those to whom that language had always seemed to speak with fulness and decision, it seemed like sapping and undermining a cherished bulwark." For its critics, "That it maintained without flinching and as strongly as ever the position and the claim of the English Church was nothing to the purpose; the admission, both that Rome, though wrong, might not be as wrong as we thought her, and that the language of the Articles, though unquestionably condemnatory of much, was not condemnatory of as much as people thought, and might possibly be even harmonised with Roman authoritative language, was looked upon as incompatible with loyalty to the English Church." Yet, Church was adamant that "The question which the Tract had opened, what the Articles meant and to what men were bound by accepting them, was a most legitimate one for discussion; and it was most natural also that any one should hesitate to answer it as the Tract answered it. But it was distinctly a question for discussion." Moreover, Church argued, "The course of events from that day to this has shown more than once in surprising and even startling examples, how much those who at the time least thought that they needed such strict construing of the language of the Articles, and were fierce in denouncing the 'kind of interpretation' said to be claimed in No. 90, have since found that they require a good deal more elasticity of reading than even it asked for. The 'whirligig of time' was thought to have brought 'its revenges,' when Mr. Newman, who had called for the exercise of authority against Dr. Hampden, found himself, five years afterwards, under the ban of the same authority."[195]

Another irony to which Church points is that W. G. Ward might have exerted an undue influence over Newman during his Anglican deathbed precisely because of his obsession with logic. Even if we do not find this interpretation of the fraught relationship between Ward and Newman persuasive, it does highlight what was always Newman's rather complicated relationship with logic, not to mention the Ultramontane who wished to have Pius IX issue a bull a day with his morning newspaper.

> Mr. Ward was continually forcing on Mr. Newman so-called irresistible inferences; "If you say so and so, surely you must also say something more?" Avowedly ignorant of facts and depending for them on others, he was only concerned with logical consistency. And accordingly Mr. Newman, with whom producible logical consistency was indeed a great thing, but with whom it was very far from being everything, had continually to accept conclusions which he would rather have kept in abeyance, to make admissions which were used without their qualifications, to push on and sanction extreme ideas which he himself shrank from because they were extreme. But it was all over with his command of time, his liberty to make up his mind slowly on the great decision. He had to go at Mr. Ward's pace, and not his own. He had to take Mr. Ward's questions, not when he wanted to have them and at his own time, but at Mr. Ward's. No one can tell how much this state of things affected the working of Mr. Newman's mind in that

---

[195] Church, *Oxford Movement*, 286–90. Cf. "Consider a moment. Is it fair, is it dutiful, to suffer our Bishops to stand the brunt of the battle without doing our part to support them?" *TT*, 1.

pause of hesitation before the final step; how far it accelerated the view which he ultimately took of his position. No one can tell, for many other influences were mixed up with this one. But there is no doubt that Mr. Newman felt the annoyance and the unfairness of this perpetual questioning for the benefit of Mr. Ward's theories, and there can be little doubt that, in effect, it drove him onwards and cut short his time of waiting.[196]

Certainly, the hammer-blows of Ward's "questions" sent his student and mentee Arthur Hugh Clough reeling, though if they inspired Newman to act, they had the direct opposite effect on his poor Balliol charge.

> 'Tis gone, the fierce inordinate desire,
> The burning thirst for action—utterly;
> Gone, like a ship that passes in the night
> On the high seas: gone, yet will come again:
> Gone, yet expresses something that exists.
> Is it a thing ordained, then? is it a clue
> For my life's conduct? is it a law for me
> That opportunity shall breed distrust,
> Not passing until that pass? Chance and resolve,
> Like two loose comets wandering wide in space,
> Crossing each other's orbits time on time,
> Meet never.[197]

As regards the behavior of the Heads of Houses who denounced Newman in the wake of the publication of Tract 90, Church put his finger on an aspect of Newman's more unscrupulous critics. "Unhappily Tract 90 was met at Oxford, not with argument, but with panic and wrath," he says in his history of the Movement. "There is always a sting in every charge, to which other parts of it seem subordinate. No. 90 was charged of course with false doctrine, with false history, and with false reasoning; but the emphatic part of the charge, the short and easy method which dispensed from the necessity of theological examination and argument, was that it was dishonest and immoral." Of course, this was Frank Turner's *modus operandi* in his attack on Newman's honesty and integrity in that ramshackle, venomous book of his with Yale, which Newman's latest detractors naturally extol as their *vade mecum*.[198] In the case of the Oxford of 1841, Newman was summarily traduced because the Heads of Houses knew that Tract 90 was a redoubtable challenge to their traditional interpretation of the Thirty-Nine Articles, on which the Protestant order not only of Oxford but of the country as a whole was based, and they brought the charge of dishonesty to

---

[196] Church, *Oxford Movement*, 364–5.
[197] From Arthur Hugh Clough, "Dipsychus," in *A Choice of Clough's Verse*, ed. Michael Thorpe (London: Faber & Faber, 1969), 134.
[198] The editors of *Receptions of Newman* (Oxford, 2015), for example, dedicate their volume to Turner "for opening up new historical … lines of inquiry," heedless of the fact that Turner's claim to be considered a proper intellectual historian is derisory. Yet since their own claims to any legitimate historical knowledge are bogus, it is perhaps unsurprising that they should tout one whose ignorance of history matches their own.

spare themselves the trouble of debating a challenge that they would have had a hard time refuting. Church paid his co-religionists the compliment of at least imagining that they might have joined the dispute. "The Professors of Divinity, and accomplished scholars, such as there were in Oxford, might very well have considered it an occasion to dispute both the general principle of the Tract, if it was so dangerous, and the illustrations, in the abundance of which the writer had so frankly thrown open his position to searching criticism. It was a crisis in which much might have been usefully said, if there had been any one to say it; much too, to make any one feel, if he was competent to feel, that he had a good deal to think about in his own position, and that it would be well to ascertain what was tenable and what untenable in it."[199] In the event, however, they excused themselves from any reasoned dispute. Church does not concede as much in his history but Newman would supply his own contribution to the dispute that did not happen in *Anglican Difficulties*, in which he took up the merits of the "general principle of the Tract" with not only "searching criticism" but what amounted to a dual perspective—the perspective, that is to say, of his former Anglo-Catholic friends when he was in league with those friends himself and that of the convert he would become once he left his erstwhile friends behind and took very seriously indeed "his own position" and "what was tenable and what untenable in it."

X

The best way to read Church's fascinating history is side-by-side with Newman's account of the same history, for even when their different accounts clash they illuminate the differences that finally made Newman's break with his Anglo-Catholic friends unavoidable. Here is Newman in *Anglican Difficulties* on the Via Media.

> And now you will ask me, what it is I saw in the history of primitive controversies and Councils which was so fatal to the pretensions of the Anglican Church? I saw that the general theory and position of Anglicanism was no novelty in ancient history, but had a distinct place in it, and a series of prototypes, and that these prototypes had ever been heretics or the patrons of heresy. The very badge of Anglicanism, as a system, is that it is a Via Media; this is its life; it is this, or it is nothing; deny this, and it forthwith dissolves into Catholicism or Protestantism. This constitutes its only claim to be recognized as a distinct form of Christianity; it is its recommendation to the world at large, and its simple measuring-line for the whole field of theology. The Via Media appeals to the good sense of mankind; it says that the human mind is naturally prone to excess, and that theological combatants in particular are certain to run into extremes. Truth, as virtue, lies in a mean; whatever, then, is true, whatever is not true, extremes certainly are false. And, whereas truth is in a mean, for that very reason it is very moderate and liberal; it can tolerate either extreme with great patience because it views neither with that keenness of contrariety with which one extreme regards the

---

[199] Church, *Oxford Movement*, 291.

other. For the same reason, it is comprehensive; because, being in a certain sense in the centre of all errors, though having no part in any of them, it may be said to rule and to temper them, to bring them together, and to make them, as it were, converge and conspire together in one under its own meek and gracious sway. Dispassionateness, forbearance, indulgence, toleration, and comprehension are thus all of them attributes of the Via Media. It is obvious, moreover, that a doctrine like this will find especial acceptance with the civil magistrate. Religion he needs as an instrument of government; yet in religious opinion he sees nothing else but the fertile cause of discord and confusion. Joyfully then does he welcome a form of theology, whose very mission it is to temper the violence of polemics, to soften and to accommodate differences, and to direct the energies of churchmen to the attainment of tangible good instead of the discussion of mysteries. This sentiment I expressed in the following passage, in the year 1837, which I quote with shame and sorrow; the more so, because it is certainly inconsistent with my own general teaching, from the very time I began to write, except for a short interval in 1825 and 1826 which need not be noticed here. However, it is an accurate exponent of the Anglican theory of religion. "Though it is not likely," I said, "that Romanism should ever again become formidable in England, yet it may be in a position to make its voice heard; and, in proportion as it is able to do so, the Via Media will do important service of the following kind. In the controversy which will ensue, Rome will not fail to preach, far and wide, the tenet which it never conceals, that there is no salvation external to its own communion. On the other hand, Protestantism, as it exists, will not be behind-hand in consigning to eternal ruin all who are adherents of Roman doctrine. What a prospect is this! two widely-spread and powerful parties dealing forth solemn anathemas upon each other, in the Name of the Lord! Indifference and scepticism must be, in such a case, the ordinary refuge of men of mild and peaceable minds, who revolt from such presumption, and are deficient in clear views of the truth. I cannot well exaggerate the misery of such a state of things. Here the English theology would come in with its characteristic calmness and caution, clear and decided in its view, giving no encouragement to luke-warmness and liberalism, but withholding all absolute anathemas on errors of opinion, except where the primitive Church sanctions the use of them." Such, then, is the Anglican Church and its Via Media, and such the practical application of it; it is an interposition or arbitration between the extreme doctrines of Protestantism on the one hand, and the faith of Rome which Protestantism contradicts on the other. At the same time, though it may be unwilling to allow it, it is, from the nature of the case, but a particular form of Protestantism. I do not say that in secondary principles it may not agree with the Catholic Church; but its essential idea being that she has gone into error, whereas the essential idea of Catholicism is the Church's infallibility, the Via Media is really nothing else than Protestant. Not to submit to the Church is to oppose her, and to side with the heretical party; for medium there is none.[200]

Reading this, one can see why the dispute was never joined by the Anglo-Catholics. Newman's definition of the true character of the Via Media was of an

---

[200] *Diff.*, i, 374–7.

irrefutability. Nevertheless, for the Anglo-Catholics, the consequences of such a debate never taking place, as Church so clearly realized, were epochal. "Things after No. 90 were never the same as to language and hopes and prospects," he wrote, "as they had been before; it was the date from which a new set of conditions in men's thoughts and attitude had to be reckoned. Each side felt that a certain liberty had been claimed and had been peremptorily denied. And this was more than confirmed by the public language of the greater part of the Bishops. The charges against the Tractarian party of Romanising, and of flagrant dishonesty, long urged by irresponsible opponents, were now formally adopted by the University authorities, and specially directed against the foremost man of the party. From that time the fate of the party at Oxford was determined. It must break up." While Church, in common with all of Newman's friends, discounted the charge of dishonesty—the charge to which Newman's detractors cling to this day—he was never unaware of the plausibility of the Romanizing charge. Indeed, on this vexed matter, Church shows himself to have been not only a good intellectual historian but an astute psychologist. "Mr. Newman had always been impressed with the greatness of the Roman Church," he writes.

> Of old it had seemed to him great with the greatness of Antichrist. Now it seemed great with the strange weird greatness of a wonderful mixed system, commanding from its extent of sway and its imperial authority, complicated and mysterious in its organisation and influence, in its devotion and its superstitions, and surpassing every other form of religion both in its good and its evil. What now presented itself to Mr. Newman's thoughts, instead of the old notion of a pure Church on one side, and a corrupt Church on the other, sharply opposed to one another, was the more reasonable supposition of two great portions of the divided Church, each with its realities of history and fact and character, each with its special claims and excellences, each with its special sins and corruptions, and neither realising in practice and fact all it professed to be on paper; each of which further, in the conflicts of past days, had deeply, almost unpardonably, wronged the other . The Church of England was in possession, with its own call and its immense work to do, and striving to do it. Whatever the Church of Rome was abroad, it was here an intruder and a disturber. That to his mind was the fact and the true position of things; and this ought to govern the character and course of controversy. The true line was not to denounce and abuse wholesale, not to attack with any argument, good or bad, not to deny or ignore what was solid in the Roman ground, and good and elevated in the Roman system, but admitting all that fairly ought to be admitted, to bring into prominence, not for mere polemical denunciation, but for grave and reasonable and judicial condemnation, all that was extravagant and arrogant in Roman assumptions, and all that was base, corrupt, and unchristian in the popular religion, which, with all its claims to infallibility and authority, Rome not only permitted but encouraged. For us to condemn Rome wholesale, as was ordinarily the fashion, even in respectable writers, was as wrong, as unfair, as unprofitable to the cause of truth and Christianity, as the Roman charges against us were felt by us to be ignorant and unjust. Rome professes like England to continue the constitution, doctrine, traditions, and spirit of the ancient and undivided Church: and so far

as she does so—and she does so in a great degree—we can have no quarrel with her. But in a great degree also, she does this only in profession and as a theory: she claims the witness and suffrage of antiquity, but she interprets it at her own convenience and by her own authority. We cannot claim exemption from mistakes, from deviations from our own standard and principles, any more than Rome; but while she remains as she is, and makes the monstrous claims of infallibility and supremacy, there is nothing for English Churchmen but to resist her. Union is impossible. Submission is impossible. What we have to beware of for our own sake, as well as for our cause, are false arguments, unreal objections, ignorant allegations. There is enough on the very surface, in her audacious assertions and high-handed changes, for popular arguments against her, without having recourse to exaggeration and falsehood; she may be a very faulty Church, without being Babylon and Antichrist.[201]

Yet, at the same time, Church was astute enough to realize that there was another factor—far short of any recrudescence of No Popery—that kept the majority of Anglo-Catholics from crediting Newman's shattering of the Via Media and following him to Rome, despite what might otherwise seem "the strong current in the direction of Rome" before and after Tract 90. Indeed, in the event, this was the factor that gave Newman's King William Street lectures their elaborate futility. Church's delineation of it is nicely appreciative of how the Englishry of Anglo-Catholic religion was always decisive.

> The constitutional frankness of Englishmen in finding fault with what is their own—disgust at pompous glorification—scepticism as to our insular claims against all the rest of Christendom to be exactly right, to be alone, "pure and apostolic"; real increase and enlargement of knowledge, theological and historical; criticism on portions of our Reformation history; admiration for characters in mediaeval times; eagerness, over-generous it might be, to admit and repair wrong to an opponent unjustly accused; all were set down together with other more unequivocal signs as "leanings to Rome." It was clear that there was a current setting towards Rome; but it was as clear that there was a much stronger current in the party as a whole, setting in the opposite direction. To those who chose to see and to distinguish, the love, the passionate loyalty of the bulk of the Tractarians to the English Church was as evident and unquestionable as any public fact could be.[202]

Their Englishness, then, not theological conviction was decisive for the Anglo-Catholics. Yet if Church realized that most of the Tractarians stayed put because of their Englishness—their English loyalty to their English Church—he also realized that Newman could not stay put despite his Englishness. In an essay entitled "Cardinal Newman's Course," Church paid Newman a handsome compliment on this score. "Never for a moment did his loyalty and obedience to his Church"—that is to say, the Church of Rome—"even when most tried, waver and falter," Church wrote of his beloved friend.

---

[201] Church, *Oxford Movement*, 179–81.
[202] Ibid., 301.

The thing is inconceivable to any one who ever knew him, and the mere suggestion would be enough to make him blaze forth in all his old fierceness and power. But perfectly satisfied of his position, and with his duties clearly defined, he could allow large and increasing play, in the leisure of advancing age, to his natural sympathies, and to the effect of the wonderful spectacle of the world around him. He was, after all, an Englishman; and with all his quickness to detect and denounce what was selfish and poor in English ideas and action, and with all the strength of his deep antipathies, his chief interests were for things English—English literature, English social life, English politics, English religion. He liked to identify himself, as far as it was possible, with things English, even with things that belonged to his own first days. He republished his Oxford sermons and treatises. He prized his honorary fellowship at Trinity; he enjoyed his visit to Oxford, and the welcome which he met there. He discerned how much the English Church counted for in the fight going on in England for the faith in Christ. There was in all that he said and did a gentleness, a forbearance, a kindly friendliness, a warm recognition of the honour paid him by his countrymen, ever since the *Apologia* had broken down the prejudices which had prevented Englishmen from doing him justice. As with his chief antagonist at Oxford, Dr. Hawkins, advancing years brought with them increasing gentleness, and generosity, and courtesy. But through all this there was perceptible to those who watched a pathetic yearning for something which was not to be had: a sense, resigned—for so it was ordered—but deep and piercing, how far, not some of us, but all of us, are from the life of the New Testament: how much there is for religion to do, and how little there seems to be to do it.[203]

Incisive sympathy suffuses such observations. After all, Church himself felt the same affection for things English. Yet, one has to say, he turned a strenuously blind eye to the King William Street lectures, which squarely disabused readers of any impression that *Lectures on the Prophetical Office of the Church: Romanism and Popular Protestantism* (1837) or Tract 90 might have given them that Newman somehow saw some compelling coherence in Anglican theology. Apropos the Gorham Case, for example, which sent Manning and Hope Scott across the Tiber once the real Erastian character of the National Church became undeniable, Church could write startling nonsense.

The English Church of George III, Charles II, Charles I, James, Elizabeth, and even of Henry VIII, however closely connected with the State,—or rather with the Crown,—however far it admitted its control, never for a moment lost sight of the principle, that if it held one set of powers from the Crown, it held another set of powers which no Crown or State on earth could, or pretended to, confer; powers which it held as a Church, powers which it inherited through a line distinct from that of a royal or a national succession. It never, we say, for a moment forgot that, however connected with the State, it was still a self-subsistent, even if not independent body, which would exist to-morrow if the State broke up into anarchy, or cast off the Church.[204]

[203] Church, "Cardinal Newman's Course," in *Occasional Papers*, ii, 477–8.
[204] Richard William Church, *"On the Relations between Church and State": An Article Reprinted from*

How a man of Church's intellectual honesty could have uttered something so demonstrably untrue is not difficult to understand if we consider another passage from the same essay, in which he speaks, again, of the loyalty enjoyed by the National Church: "This great nation of Englishmen is committed to her trust; if she cannot induce them, what other body has a more reasonable hope? If they will break away from her, or cast her off, let it be clearly their fault, not hers, or that of her clergy. She and her clergy have much to answer for; but the heaviest of their former sins will be in comparison light, if from impatience, from want of due consideration of the signs and changes of the time, from scruples, from theory, from fear of being taunted with inconsistency, or want of logic, or love of quiet, or insensibility to high views, or indifference to the maxims of saints—or any other of those faults of feeling or intellect, which are common at once to the noble and the feeble, the sensitive and the timid—she, or they, throw up that trust."[205] Some might be tempted to attribute such sentiments of loyalty to nationalism or even patriotism but they came of something much deeper: love of country. Speaking of what he construed as Newman's line of reasoning in the *Prophetical Office of the Church*, Church realized that Newman was directly challenging this love of country, ostensibly to strengthen the National Church, though, of course, the logic of such challenges would end by favoring Rome, not Canterbury.

> This line, though substantially involved in the theory of our most learned divines, from Andrewes to Wake, was new in its moderation and reasonable caution; in its abstention from insult and vague abuse, in its recognition of the *primâ facie* strength of much of the Roman case, in its fearless attempt, in defiance of the deepest prejudices, to face the facts and conditions of the question. Mr. Newman dared to know and to acknowledge much that our insular self-satisfaction did not know, and did not care to know, of real Christian life in the Church of Rome. He dared to admit that much that was popularly held to be Popish was ancient, Catholic, edifying; he dared to warn Churchmen that the loose unsifted imputations, so securely hazarded against Rome, were both discreditable and dangerous. All this, from one whose condemnation of Rome was decisive and severe, was novel. The attempt, both in its spirit and its ability, was not unworthy of being part of the general effort to raise the standard of thought and teaching in the English Church. It recalled men from slovenly prejudices to the study of the real facts of the living world.[206]

When it came to Newman's considered attitude towards Anglican theology on his Anglican death-bed, it is surprising that Church did not point to the following passage in "Catholicity of the Anglican Church" (1840), which Newman might have sought to repudiate in the King William Street lectures, but which nevertheless gives credence to Church's characterization of his friend as "clinging" to the same wreck of Anglicanism that he would exhort his Anglo-Catholic

---

the "*Christian Remembrancer*" April, 1850 (London: Walter Smith [Late Mozley & Smith], 1881), 4.
[205] Ibid., 54–5.
[206] Church, *Oxford Movement*, 209–10.

friends to abandon. Surely this was a friendly omission.[207] For Newman, before his "great revolution of mind,"[208] it was not altogether preposterous to argue that "our divines grow with centuries, expanding after their death in the minds of their readers into more and more exact Catholicism, as years rolled on. Nay, even our errors and heterodoxies turn to good: Wesleyanism in itself tends to heresy, if it was not heretical in the outset; but, so far as it has been in the Church, it has been overruled to rouse and stimulate us, when we were asleep. Moreover, look at the internal state of the Church at this moment; much that is melancholy is there, strife, division, error. But still on the whole, enlarge on the evils as you will, there is life there, perceptible, visible life; rude indeed, undisciplined, perhaps self-willed, but life; and not the life of death, not that heretical restlessness, which, as we have observed, only runs out the quicker for its activity, and hastens to be no more, but, as we may humbly trust, a heavenly principle after all, which is struggling towards development, and gives presage of truth and holiness to come."[209] Here is precisely the desperately sanguine view of Anglican theology that Newman would repudiate so roundly in his King William Street Lectures, though Church would have been within his rights to cite it as proof of Newman's loyalty to the National Church right up until the very end of his Anglican death-bed.

By revisiting *Anglican Difficulties*, we can see how Newman was careful to temper his account of what he called the "Movement of 1833" with passages from the Anglo-Catholic party—and in this case, something he had written himself from *Lectures on the Prophetical Office of the Church*. "We require a recognised theology," he confessed there, "and, if the present work, instead of being what it is meant to be, a first approximation to the required solution, in one department of a complicated problem, contains, after all, but a series of illustrations demonstrating our need, and supplying hints for its removal; such a result, it is evident, will be quite a sufficient return for whatever anxiety it has cost the writer to have employed his own judgment on so serious a subject."[210] Yet Newman's gloss on his own Anglo-Catholic musings shows that when it came to making fun of the unreality of Anglican theology, he could be as hard on himself as he was on others. "I must add, in justice to this writer," he says dryly of himself, "and it is not much to say for him, that he did not entertain the presumptuous thought of creating, at this time of day, a new theology himself; he considered that a theology true in itself, and necessary for the position of the Anglican Church, was to be found in the writings of Andrewes, Laud, Bramhall, Stillingfleet, Butler, and other of its divines, but had never been put together."[211] The elusiveness of Anglican theology notwithstanding, Newman returned to glossing the views of those who protested the Privy Council's ruling with a show of still more comical

---

[207] Here, one should quote Newman's letter to Pusey, in which he admitted: "I wrote the article on Catholicity of the English Church ... to satisfy my own mind. ... it was written by an unsettled person. I never simply acquiesced in it. When doubts of our Catholicity come powerfully on me, I did all I could to throw them from me—and I think I can never be ashamed of doing my utmost, as I have done for years, to build up the English Church against hope." Newman to Pusey (14 March 1845), LD, x, 591.
[208] *Apo.*, 191.
[209] *Ess.*, ii, 57.
[210] *Diff.*, i, 39.
[211] Ibid.

even-handedness. Eyewitness accounts of the lectures attest that their delivery was interrupted by a good deal of laughter. This passage shows why:

> Now, I grant that it has a narrow and technical appearance to decide the Catholicity of a religious body by particular words, or deeds, or measures, resulting from the temper of a particular age, accidentally elicited, and accomplished in minutes or in days. I allow it and feel it; that a particular vote of parliament, endured or tacitly accepted by bishops and clergy, or by the Metropolitans, or a particular appointment, or a particular omission, or a particular statement of doctrine, should at once change the spiritual character of the body, and *ipso facto* cut it off from the centre of unity and the source of grace, is almost incredible. In spite of such acts, surely the Anglican Church might be to-day what it was yesterday, with an internal power and a supernatural virtue, provided it had not already forfeited them, and would go about its work as of old time. It would be to-day pretty much what it was yesterday, though in the course of the night it had allowed an Anglo Prussian See to be set up in Jerusalem, and had disavowed the Athanasian Creed.[212]

The force of such satirical mockery simply proved too much for his Anglo-Catholic friends—even for Church, who was never shy of tackling fair criticism. Hence, their inability to grasp what Newman really found untenable about the National religion. One can see this almost pitiably in the Tractarian who accompanied Newman on his Anglican death-bed most closely. "There were especially two weak points in … Anglicanism," Church conceded in his history, and "Mr. Newman felt and admitted them, and of course they were forced on his attention by controversialists on both sides; by the Ultra Protestant school, whose modes of dealing with Scripture he had exposed with merciless logic, and by the now eager Roman disputants, of whom Dr. Wiseman was the able and not over-scrupulous chief." For Church, "The first of these points was that the authority of the undivided Church, which Anglicanism invoked, though it completely covered the great foundations of Christian doctrine, our faith as to the nature of God, did not cover with equal completeness other important points of controversy, such as those raised at the Reformation as to the Sacraments, and the justification of the sinner. The Anglican answer was that though the formal and conciliar authority was not the same in each case, the patristic literature of the time of the great councils, all that it took for granted and preserved as current belief and practice, all that resulted from the questions and debates of the time, formed a body of proof, which carried with it moral evidence only short of authoritative definition, and was so regarded in the Anglican formularies. These formularies implied the authority of the Church to speak; and what was defined on this authority was based on good evidence, though there were portions of its teaching which had even better."[213] Here one has an even-handedness of an almost pitiable sincerity. But even when Church dared to get to the heart of the matter and admit the real reason why Newman repudiated the Via Media, he could only go so far. "The other point was more serious," he writes.

---

[212] *Ibid.*, 49.
[213] Church, *Oxford Movement*, 186.

"Your theory," was the objection, "is nothing but a paper theory; it never was a reality; it never can be. There may be an ideal halting—place, there is neither a logical nor an actual one, between Romanism and the ordinary negations of Protestantism." The answer to the challenge then was, "Let us see if it cannot be realized. It has recognised foundations to build upon, and the impediments and interruptions which have hindered it are well known. Let us see if it will not turn out something more than a paper theory." That was the answer given at the time, abandoned ten years afterwards. But this at least may be said, that the longer experience of the last fifty years has shown that the Church of England has been working more and more on such a theory, and that the Church of England, whatever its faults may be, is certainly not a Church only on paper. But on the principles laid down in this volume, the Roman controversy, in its varying forms, was carried on—for the time by Mr. Newman, permanently by the other leaders of the movement. In its main outlines, the view has become the accepted Anglican view.[214]

About the denouement of this Roman controversy, begun by *Lectures on the Prophetical Office* and culminating in Tract 90, Church is the dispassionate historian *par excellence*. "The Tract was published on 27th February," he writes.

On the 8th of March four Senior Tutors, one of whom was Mr. H. B. Wilson, of St. John's, and another Mr. Tait, of Balliol, addressed the Editor of the Tract, charging No. 90 with suggesting and opening a way, by which men might, at least in the case of Roman views, violate their solemn engagements to their University. On the 15th of March, the Board of Heads of Houses, refusing to wait for Mr. Newman's defence, which was known to be coming, and which bears date 13th March, published their judgment. They declared that in No. 90 "modes of interpretation were suggested, and have since been advocated in other publications purporting to be written by members of the University, by which subscription to the Articles might be reconciled with the adoption of Roman Catholic error." And they announced their resolution, "That modes of interpretation, such as are suggested in the said Tract, evading rather than explaining the sense of the Thirty-nine Articles, and reconciling subscription to them with the adoption of errors which they are designed to counteract, defeat the object, and are inconsistent with the due observance of the above-mentioned statutes."[215]

Again, read against *Anglican Difficulties*, this foregoing account of the alacrity and unanimity with which the Heads circled the wagons might have been perfect satirical fodder for Newman's King William Street Lectures, exhibiting, as they do, the blatancy of the heads' bigotry.[216] In Church's description of the Heads we

---

[214] Ibid., 186.
[215] Ibid., 191.
[216] Cf. "Although 'system' is necessary to the human mind, the defining characteristic of bigotry, according to Newman, is an excessive love of system, combined with incomplete or insufficient knowledge: 'System, which is the very soul ... of Philosophy, when exercised upon adequate knowledge, does but make ... theorists, dogmatists, philosophists, and sectarians, when or so far as Knowledge is limited or incomplete.' [*US*, 200] This sentence describes the ignorant 'system' of bigotry that had led to the impulsive and furious response to Tract 90 by the Heads of Houses,

can see how thoroughly he agreed with Newman about the inherently corrupting influence of ecclesiastical establishments. "They were good and respectable men," Church says, "living comfortably, in a certain state and ease. Their lives were mostly simple compared with the standard of the outer world, though Fellows of Colleges thought them luxurious. But they were blind and dull as tea-table gossips, as to what was the meaning of the movement ... It perplexed and annoyed them; they had not imagination nor moral elevation to take in what it aimed at; they were content with the routine which they had inherited."[217] In censuring Newman, they sought somehow to invigorate that inherited routine. The unavailing desperation of such efforts was not lost on Liddon. For him, the censure of Newman in 1841 and of Pusey in 1845 "sealed the doom of the old *régime* ... Tories must have seen the hopelessness, Liberals the impossibility of things remaining as they were. It was a call for great University Reform. So far as the Church was concerned, it was disastrous ... It made men either despair of Anglicanism or realize what they had to expect if they remained true to their Church awaiting its deliverance."[218]

For the man who foiled the censuring, "It was an ungenerous and stupid blunder, such as men make, when they think or are told that 'something must be done,' and do not know what. It gave ... [Newman] an opportunity, of which he took full advantage, of showing his superiority in temper, in courtesy, and in reason, to those who had not so much condemned as insulted him. He was immediately ready with his personal expression of apology and regret, and also with his reassertion in more developed argument of the principle of the Tract; and this was followed up by further explanations in a letter to the Bishop. And in spite of the invidious position in which the Board had tried to place him, not merely as an unsound divine, but as a dishonest man teaching others to palter with their engagements, the crisis drew forth strong support and sympathy where they were not perhaps to be expected. It rallied to him, at least for the time, some of the friends who had begun to hold aloof. Mr. Palmer, of Worcester, Mr. Perceval, Dr. Hook, with reserves according to each man's point of view, yet came forward in his defence. The Board was made to feel that they had been driven

---

who were largely ignorant of church history and of all schools of theology except the evidential. Fifty years after Tract 90, R. W. Church scornfully criticized the intellectual laziness that prevailed among the Heads, who were High-and-Dry Churchmen with no excuse for such ignorance: "To one who, like Dr. [Martin Joseph] Routh of Magdalen, had gone below the surface, and was acquainted with the questions debated by those [sixteenth- and seventeenth-century Anglican] divines, there was nothing startling in what so alarmed his brethren, whether he agreed with it or not; and to him the indiscriminate charge of Popery meant nothing. But Dr. Routh stood alone among his brother Heads in his knowledge of what English theology was. To most of them it was an unexplored and misty region; some of the ablest, under the influence of Dr. Whately's vigorous and scornful discipline, had learned to slight it. But there it was ... Proof and quotation might lie before their eyes, but their minds still ran in one groove, and they could not realise what they saw. The words meant no harm in the venerable folio; they meant perilous heresy in the modern Tract." "Editor's Introduction," in John Henry Newman, *Fifteen Sermons Preached Before the University of Oxford*, ed. James David Earnest and Gerard Tracey (Oxford: Oxford University Press, 206), xcviii–xcix.

[217] Church, *Oxford Movement*, 246–7.
[218] Henry Parry Liddon, *The Life of Edward Bouverie Pusey*, 4 vols (London: Longmans, Green, & Co., 1893), ii, 363.

by violent and partisan instigations to commit themselves to a very foolish as well as a very passionate and impotent step; that they had by very questionable authority simply thrown an ill-sounding and ill-mannered word at an argument on a very difficult question, to which they themselves certainly were not prepared with a clear and satisfactory answer; that they had made the double mistake of declaring war against a formidable antagonist, and of beginning it by creating the impression that they had treated him shabbily, and were really afraid to come to close quarters with him. As the excitement of hasty counsels subsided, the sense of this began to awake in some of them; they tried to represent the off-hand and ambiguous words of the condemnation as not meaning all that they had been taken to mean. But the seed of bitterness had been sown."[219] Bitterness and clarity, though Church, looking back on the Movement's ecclesial crescendo, could only see a return to type.

> Sooner or later, there must be a secession more or less discrediting and disabling those who remained. And so the break up came, and yet, so well-grounded and so congenial to the English Church were the leading principles of the movement, that not even that disastrous and apparently hopeless wreck prevented them from again asserting their claim and becoming once more active and powerful. The Via Media, whether or not logically consistent, was a thing of genuine English growth, and was at least a working theory.

Church's qualification in that last sentence—"whether or not logically consistent"—was tell-tale, for there was little logic in the "English theory"—or authority. He might claim that Anglicanism was not "daring enough" for Newman. "With his ideas of the coming dangers and conflicts, he wanted something bold and thoroughgoing, wide reaching in its aims, resolute in its language, claiming and venturing much. Anglicanism was not that."[220] But what Newman really found unacceptable about Anglo-Catholicism is that it whetted an appetite for apostolic catholicity that Anglicanism could simply not satisfy. In September of 1839, Newman had written to Manning: "our Church has not the provisions and methods by which Catholic feelings are to be detained, secured, sobered, and trained heavenwards. Our blanket is too small for our bed ... we are raising longings and tastes which we are not allowed to supply—and till our Bishops and others give scope to the development of Catholicism externally and visibly, we *do* tend to make impatient minds seek it where it has ever been, *in* Rome."[221] This is the burden, over and over again, of nearly every one of the twelve King William Street lectures. Yet Church, like so many other Anglo-Catholics, could never bring himself to engage Newman's mockery of the "English theory" in *Anglican Difficulties*. There are many satirical set pieces in the King William Street lectures but this has to be one of the best.

> The idea, then, of the divines of the movement was simply and absolutely submission to an external authority; to such an authority they appealed, to it they

[219] Church, *Oxford Movement*, 293–4.
[220] Church, "Newman's 'Apologia,'" in *Occasional Papers*, ii, 389.
[221] Newman to Henry Edward Manning (1 September 1839), *LD*, vii, 133.

betook themselves; there they found a haven of rest; thence they looked out upon the troubled surge of human opinion and upon the crazy vessels which were labouring, without chart or compass, upon it. Judge then of their dismay, when, according to the Arabian tale, on their striking their anchors into the supposed soil, lighting their fires on it, and fixing in it the poles of their tents, suddenly their island began to move, to heave, to splash, to frisk to and fro, to dive and at last to swim away, spouting out inhospitable jets of water upon the credulous mariners who had made it their home. And such, I suppose, was the undeniable fact: I mean, the time at length came, when first of all turning their minds (some of them, at least) more carefully to the doctrinal controversies of the early Church, they saw distinctly that in the reasonings of the Fathers, elicited by means of them, and in the decisions of authority, in which they issued, were contained at least the rudiments, the anticipation, the justification of what they had been accustomed to consider the corruptions of Rome. And if only one, or a few of them, were visited with this conviction, still even one was sufficient, of course, to destroy that cardinal point of their whole system, the objective perspicuity and distinctness of the teaching of the Fathers. But time went on, and there was no mistaking or denying the misfortune which was impending over them. They had reared a goodly house, but their foundations were falling in. The soil and the masonry both were bad. The Fathers would protect "Romanists" as well as extinguish Dissenters. The Anglican divines would misquote the Fathers, and shrink from the very doctors to whom they appealed. The Bishops of the seventeenth century were shy of the Bishops of the fourth; and the Bishops of the nineteenth were shy of the Bishops of the seventeenth. The ecclesiastical courts upheld the sixteenth century against the seventeenth, and, regardless of the flagrant irregularities of Protestant clergymen, chastised the mild misdemeanours of Anglo-Catholic. Soon the living rulers of the Establishment began to move. There are those who, reversing the Roman's maxim, are wont to shrink from the contumacious, and to be valiant towards the submissive; and the authorities in question gladly availed themselves of the power conferred on them by the movement against the movement itself. They fearlessly handselled their Apostolic weapons upon the Apostolical party. One after another, in long succession, they took up their song and their parable against it. It was a solemn war-dance, which they executed round victims, who by their very principles were bound hand and foot, and could only eye with disgust and perplexity this most unaccountable movement, on the part of their "holy Fathers, the representatives of the Apostles, and the Angels of the Churches." It was the beginning of the end.[222]

XI

The lack of authority inherent in the Anglican Church notwithstanding, Church would always be inclined to believe that his friend embraced Catholicism not so much because he grew impatient with the Via Media as because he saw Rome's infallibility as the controversial means he needed to refute Liberalism. Yet we can

---

[222] *Diff.*, i, 150–2.

see in Church's own words how little he understood the doctrine of infallibility as the Church of Rome understands the thing. "Without infallibility, it is said, men will turn free thinkers and heretics," Church writes, "but don't they, with it? and what is the good of the engine if it will not do its work? And if it is said that this is the fault of human nature, which resists what provokes and checks it, still that very thing, which infallibility was intended to counteract, goes on equally, whether it comes into play or not." In other words, there can be no infallibility for a Church whose faithful are not infallible. But that is not what the Church claims. The Church's infallibility is Christ's infallibility, not those whom Christ came into the world to save. But Church himself is more eloquent of the incoherence and wrongheadedness of his understanding of infallibility than any paraphrase. "Meanwhile, truth does stay in the world," he declares,

> the truth that there has been among us a Divine Person, of whom the Church throughout Christendom is the representative, memorial, and the repeater of His message; doubtless, the means of knowledge are really guarded; yet we seem to receive that message as we receive the witness of moral truth; and it would not be contrary to the analogy of things here if we had often got to it at last through mistakes. But when it is reached, there it is, strong in its own power; and it is difficult to think that if it is not strong enough in itself to stand, it can be protected by a claim of infallibility. A future, of which infallibility is the only hope and safe guard, seems to us indeed a prospect of the deepest gloom.[223]

Here, one can see, clearly enough, whence Church derived his aversion to the claim of infallibility: from his very scepticism, and his concomitant notion that tolerance of error, not truth, should be the bond of charity. "People who talk glibly of the fearless pursuit of truth may here see a real example of a life given to it—an example all the more solemn and impressive if they think that the pursuit was in vain," he writes, appropriating Newman's failure to find truth in Anglicanism as a kind of emblem of what he imagined to be truth's more general elusiveness.

> It is easy to declaim about it, and to be eloquent about lies and sophistries; but it is shallow to forget that truth has its difficulties. To hear some people talk, it might be thought that truth was a thing to be made out and expressed at will, under any circumstances, at any time, amid any complexities of facts or principles, by half an hour's choosing to be attentive, candid, logical, and resolute; as if there was not a chance of losing what perhaps you have, as well as of gaining what you think you need. If they would look about them, if they would look into themselves, they would recognise that Truth is an awful and formidable goddess to all men and to all systems; that all have their weak points where virtually, more or less consciously, more or less dexterously, they shrink from meeting her eye; that even when we make sacrifice of everything for her sake, we find that she still encounters us with claims, seemingly inconsistent with all that she has forced us to embrace with appearances which not only convict us of mistake, but seem to oblige us to be tolerant of what we cannot really assent to.[224]

---

[223] Church, "Newman's 'Apologia,'" in *Occasional Papers*, ii, 393.
[224] Ibid., 394–5.

Newman's answer to such sentimental scepticism can be found in *The Idea of a University* where he says with memorable point: "[I]n a state of society such as ours, in which authority, prescription, tradition, habit, moral instinct and the divine influences go for nothing, in which patience of thought, and depth and consistency of view, are scorned as subtle and scholastic, in which free discussion and fallible judgement are prized as the birthright of each individual, I must be excused if I exercise towards this age as regards its belief in this doctrine"—as opposed to the dogmatic truth of Catholicism—"some portion of scepticism, which it exercises itself towards every received but unscrutinized assertion whatever."[225] Church may have thought that the Roman Church's claim to infallibility was, by definition, an untenable dogma, but, as Newman shows, he never stopped to question whether the dogma of fallibility—the dogma, that is to say, of Protestantism—could somehow take its place. When Thomas Arnold rejected the Church's infallibility to take his MA degree in 1865—which required him to repudiate his conversion of 1856 to the Church and recommence Anglican, Newman wrote: "Do not suppose I write these lines to trouble you with controversy, or to exact an answer—but I cannot bear to let you go from the one fountain of grace and spiritual strength, without saying a word, not of farewell, for well it cannot be so to direct your course, but to express my deep sorrowfulness at hearing the news. I will not believe that you have not found strength and comfort in Masses and Sacraments, and I do not think you will find the like elsewhere. Nor shall I easily be led to believe that the time will not come when you will acknowledge this yourself."[226] As it happened, Arnold, much to his poor wife's disgust, reconverted in 1876.

Church's animadversions on the "awful and formidable goddess" of Truth—not an epithet Newman would have found felicitous—show how little he understood the radical uneasiness with perplexity that drove Newman not only away from the dubiousness of Anglicanism but towards the certitude of Catholicism. One might be inclined to use the word "uneasiness" but, really, the apter word would be "fear." Newman feared remaining in a church that could not dispel perplexity. He feared perplexity separating him from the Truth. He feared the culpability he knew would be his if he acquiesced in a perplexity that failed to uphold the Truth. One can see this vividly in something he wrote in *An Essay in Aid of the Grammar of Assent* (1870): "I would maintain that the fear of error is simply necessary to the genuine love of truth," he writes in that probing, searching, radiant book.

> No inquiry comes to good which is not conducted under a deep sense of responsibility, and of the issues depending upon its determination. Even the ordinary matters of life are an exercise of conscientiousness; and where conscience is, fear must be. So much is this acknowledged just now, that there is almost an affectation, in popular literature, in the case of criticisms on the fine arts, on poetry, and music, of insisting upon conscientiousness in writing, painting, or singing; and that earnestness and simplicity of mind, which makes men fear to go wrong in these minor matters, has surely a place in the most serious of all undertakings.[227]

---

[225] *Idea*, 37.
[226] Newman to Thomas Arnold (4 June 1865), *LD*, xxi, 484.
[227] *GA*, 426.

Elsewhere, in answer to Gladstone, who had enquired after their mutual friend Blanco White, Newman responded that he "'loved and sought truth,' as liberals do, as Whately and Arnold that is, as mathematicians love and seek *mathematical truth … without fearing error*. Hence, he was not afraid of theological mistakes."[228]

Such "fear of error" does not rattle Church. He says himself that "Those who think that everything about religion and their own view of religion is such plain sailing, so palpable and manifest, that all who are not fools or knaves must be of their own opinion, will find plenty to wonder at in the confessions of awful perplexity which equally before and after his change Dr. Newman makes."[229] Before his change, yes; but not after. The serene certainty of Newman's Catholic faith once he converted is well-documented in his correspondence, not to mention his voluminous Catholic writings. "I have letters and notices come to me every week, and have had ever since I was a Catholic at least every month, to assure me that I have become an Anglican again or to ask me if I have not, or to entreat me to become one," Newman wrote to his good friend Thomas Henry Ellacombe in 1870. "My answers to them would make, if put together, really a respectable volume and, unless there was the trouble of rummaging them out, I have at times thought of making them into one." The very notion that he might be somehow perplexed in the faith to which he had converted brought out Newman's sense of the ridiculous in all its ebullience.

> Don't let me hurt you, my dear Ellacombe, by thus smiling over your letter, for I am not hurt at you—"make up my mind to return—" Why, I could as easily "make up my mind" to be a Garibaldian or a Siamese twin. Be sure there is as much chance of my turning an Anglican again as of my being the Irish Giant or the King of Clubs. Don't let impertinent Pamphleteers delude you. I am as certain that the Church in communion with Rome is the successor and representative of the Primitive Church, as certain that the Anglican Church is not, as certain that the Anglican Church is a mere collection of men, a mere national body, a human society, as I am that Victoria is Queen of Great Britain. Nor have I once had even a passing doubt on the subject, ever since I have been a Catholic. I have all along been in a state of inward certainty and steady assurance on this point, and I should be the most asinine, as well as the most ungrateful of men, if I left that Gracious Lord who manifests Himself in the Catholic Church, for those wearisome Protestant shadows, out of which of His mercy he has delivered me.[230]

---

[228] Newman to W. E. Gladstone (12 June 1845), *LD*, x, 702. Apropos White, Newman also said in the same letter: "I think one of the most influential and abiding feelings in B. W's mind was a hatred against the Church of Rome as a man might feel towards one who has injured him. It was a deep, awful, personal feeling. I am not here attempting to criticize it. It is a curious question whether one can feel sinful resentment towards an abstract body. The Church of Rome had, he considered, been the bane of his life—she was his enemy—he never forgave her. Every thing which reminded him of her was involved in the antipathy. People used to say when he became a Unitarian, 'O he will go round to his old Church at last'—I always said he never would.' *Ibid.*, 701.

[229] Church, "Newman's 'Apologia,'" in *Occasional Papers*, ii, 383–4.

[230] Newman to Thomas Henry Ellacombe (23 August 1870), *LD*, xxv, 194–5. Ellacombe (1790–1885) took his BA from Oriel in 1812 and went on to become rector of Clyst St George Devon, domestic chaplain to the Earl of Harrington, a learned antiquary and scholarly campanologist. Indeed, his delight in the ringing of bells was so passionate that one Devon clergyman feared that he might be actually possessed and in need of exorcism. According to Thomas Mozley, Ellacombe cared "for

Yet, paradoxically, it was Church's abiding uneasiness with Newman's certainty that enabled him to appreciate its nobility. Or, put another way, it was his reluctant acknowledgement of the divide between his old friend and himself that impelled him to recognize their indissoluble bond. We can see this most movingly in his essay on Newman's *Apologia*, in which he says of the book's appeal:

> The truth, in fact, is, that the interest is personal much more than controversial. Those who read it as a whole, and try to grasp the effect of all its portions compared together and gathered into one, will, it seems to us, find it hard to bend into a decisive triumph for any of the great antagonist systems which appear in collision. There can be no doubt of the perfect conviction with which Dr. Newman has taken his side for good. But while he states the effect of arguments on his own mind, he leaves the arguments in themselves as they were, and touches on them, not for the sake of what they are worth, but to explain the movements and events of his own course. … At any rate, the arguments to be drawn from this narrative, for or against England, or for or against Rome, seem to us very evenly balanced. Of course, such a history has its moral. But the moral is not the ordinary vulgar one of the histories of a religious change. It is not the supplement or disguise of a polemical argument. It is the deep want and necessity in our age of the Church, even to the most intensely religious and devoted minds, of a sound and secure intellectual basis for the faith which they value more than life and all things. We hope that we are strong enough to afford to judge fairly of such a spectacle, and to lay to heart its warnings, even though the particular results seem to go against what we think most right. It is a mortification and a trial to the English Church to have seen her finest mind carried away and lost to her, but it is a mortification which more confident and peremptory systems than hers have had to undergo; the parting was not without its compensations if only that it brought home so keenly to many the awfulness and the seriousness of truth; and surely never did any man break so utterly with a Church, who left so many sympathies behind him and took so many with him, who continued to feel so kindly and with such large hearted justice to those from whom his changed position separated him in this world for ever.[231]

XII

Church is an exemplary critic of Newman because, although not disinclined to find fault with his reasoning on certain matters, he had nothing of the impatient attitude towards religious faith *per se* that animated Newman's rationalist critics, of whom Thomas Henry Huxley was perhaps the most derisive. Chesterton wrote a nice sketch of the man. "If we take Macaulay at the beginning of the epoch and Huxley at the end of it," he wrote in his brilliant *Victorian Age in Literature* (1913),

---

everybody and everything" and one could not be in his company five minutes "without learning something worth knowing, and in a distinct and positive form." Before entering the Anglican ministry, he studied engineering in Chatham Dockyard under the direction of the greatest of all Victorian engineers, Isambard Kingdom Brunel, which could have only added to his native zest. Ellacombe corresponded with Newman until his death. See entry on Ellacombe in *ODNB*.

[231] Church, "Newman's 'Apologia,'" in *Occasional Papers*, ii, 385–6.

"we shall find that they had much in common. They were both square-jawed, simple men, greedy of controversy but scornful of sophistry, dead to mysticism but very much alive to morality; and they were both very much more under the influence of their own admirable rhetoric than they knew. Huxley, especially, was much more a literary than a scientific man. It is amusing to note that when Huxley was charged with being rhetorical, he expressed his horror of 'plastering the fair face of truth with that pestilent cosmetic, rhetoric,' which is itself about as well-plastered a piece of rhetoric as Ruskin himself could have managed. The difference that the period had developed can best be seen if we consider this: that while neither was of a spiritual sort, Macaulay took it for granted that common sense required some kind of theology, while Huxley took it for granted that common sense meant having none. Macaulay, it is said, never talked about his religion: but Huxley was always talking about the religion he hadn't got."[232]

One could quote any number of Huxley's jibes but this will suffice: "Dr. Newman's observation that the miraculous multiplication of the pieces of the true cross (with which 'the whole world is filled,' according to Cyril of Jerusalem; and of which some say there are enough extant to build a man-of-war) is no more wonderful than that of the loaves and fishes, is one that I do not see my way to contradict."[233] Huxley also famously held that a "Primer of Infidelity" could be extracted from Newman's books. Another of his characteristic sallies shows the extent to which his pretensions to learning kept pace with his impious flippancy:

> So far as Nazarenism differentiated itself from contemporary orthodox Judaism, it seems to have tended toward a revival of the ethical and religious spirit of the prophetic age, accompanied by the belief in Jesus as the Messiah, and by various accretions which had grown round Judaism subsequently to the exile. To these belong the doctrines of the resurrection, of the last judgment of heaven and hell; of the hierarchy of good angels; of Satan and the hierarchy of evil spirits. And there is very strong ground for believing that all these doctrines, at least in the shapes in which they were held by the post-exilic Jews, were derived from Persian and Babylonian sources, and are essentially of heathen origin.[234]

Newman's own reading of these matters inspired yet another gibe from Huxley: "Newman faces this question with his customary ability. 'Now, I own, I am not at all solicitous to deny that this doctrine of an apostate angel and his hosts was gained from Babylon: it might still be divine nevertheless. God who made the prophet's ass speak, and thereby instructed the prophet, might instruct his church by means of heathen Babylon.' (Tract 85, p. 83). There seems to be no end to the apologetic burden that Balaam's ass can carry."[235] Sarcasm of this sort abounds in Newman's rationalist critics. Church's response to such critics was an interesting amalgam of bewilderment, pity and revulsion. In one letter, he writes of John

---

[232] G. K. Chesterton, *The Victorian Age in Literature* (Oxford: Oxford University Press, 1961), 26.
[233] Thomas Henry Huxley, "Christianity and Agnosticism", *Christianity and Agnosticism, A Controversy Consisting of Papers by Henry Wace, D. D., Prof. Thomas H. Huxley, the Bishop of Peterborough, W. H. Mallook, Mrs. Humphry Ward.* (New York: Appleton & Co., 1889), 221.
[234] Ibid., 224.
[235] Ibid., 224-5.

Tyndall, the scientist, mountaineer and public intellectual, whose great claim to fame was discovering why the sky is blue: "It was said not to be one of his best; but his experiments were curious, and neat, and uniformly successful. But all the time I could not help a kind of sense of the insolence of the man, such as he appeared to be, claiming to bring all truth within what he called science. There was hardheadedness, originality, and sometimes a touch of imagination. But there seemed to be also a hard and hopeless onesidedness, as if nothing in the world would open his eyes to the whole domain of soul and spirit close about him, and without which, he would not be talking or devising wonderful experiments."[236] In his sermon, "Human Life and Its Conditions" (1877), Church delved more deeply into the ancient debate between religion and rationalism to show how it accentuated what Newman had famously called the "ventures of faith":

> A great conflict is going on between Christianity and ideas and beliefs which would destroy or supplant it. We look on, we cannot help it, for the world is full of it; we follow with interest the turns of the battle; we pass judgment on the skill of the combatants. It is conducted with ability, often with courtesy, with feeling, with conviction and purpose. We remark on the improved character of the discussion; the times at least of Voltaire, we observe, with satisfaction, are past. The old spectacle of unmannerly impertinence to such a thing as Christianity, though it has not wholly disappeared, is generally condemned, as unbecoming and out of place. But with all the literary power, and all the real and often pathetic earnestness shown in it, there is wanting often, as it seems to me, an adequate sense of the full issues raised by it, and of what in fact depends on it. I do not think, at any rate, that the majority of those who follow this tremendous debate reflect, or in any degree realise, what is involved in victory or defeat. It is not victory or defeat for a mere philosophical theory or criticism. It is not a question of something future and at a distance, something to be developed in time, something which raises the possibility of a future policy, which retards or brings near a future change in institutions. It is a present, instant result. If the opponents of Christianity are right, if the victory lies with them, it is much more than that Christians are mistaken, as men have been mistaken, and have corrected in time their mistakes, about science, about principles of government, about the policy or the economy of a state. It means that now as regards religion, as widely as men are living and acting, all that is now, is false, rotten, wrong. Our present hopes are utterly extinguished. Our present motives are as unsubstantial as bubbles on water. We are living in a dream. We are wasting on an idol the best love, the

---

[236] Church to J. B. Mozley (21 January 1868), Church, *Life and Letters*, 178. For a scholarly life of Tyndall, see Roland Jackson, *The Ascent of John Tyndall* (Oxford: Oxford University Press, 2018). See also Diarmid A. Finnegan, "Anglicans, Science and the Bible", *The Oxford History of Anglicanism*, ed. Rowan Strong (Oxford: Oxford University Press, 2017).416–39. Apropos the controversy that arose in England over the anonymous *Vestiges of the History of Creation* (1844), which contended that life, like the universe itself, had emerged from a process of evolution, Finnegan observes: "Church called for a return to a scholastic metaphysics of creation that did not place restrictions on inductive science but provided a philosophy of nature compatible with a Christian doctrine of creation. If this was done, Church saw little threat from an evolutionary account of life to orthodox Christian belief." P. 425.

highest affections, the purest tenderness which can dwell in human hearts.[237]

In light of this appraisal of how England's otherwise brilliant nineteenth-century scientists had cut themselves off from the life-affirming ventures of faith, it was apt that Newman should have dedicated the 1872 edition of his *Oxford University Sermons* to Church, the first of which, "The Philosophical Temper, First Enjoined by the Gospel" (1826) shows how perceptive an understanding the young Oriel don had of what accounted for the gap between scientists and the faithful. "It cannot be denied ... that the true philosophical spirit did not begin to prevail till many ages after the preaching of Christianity, nay, till times comparatively of recent date," Newman concedes. "Still, admitting this, it is also true that Scripture was, in matter of fact, the first to describe and inculcate that single-minded, modest, cautious, and generous spirit, which was, after a long time, found so necessary for success in the prosecution of philosophical researches."[238] To compare Newman's balanced treatment of the relationship between science and religion to Huxley's scattershot mockery shows what an infinitely more adept controversialist he was.[239] Moreover, whenever Newman warms to his subject, he tends to elevate it, to remove it from the usual fractiousness of polemical debate. Indeed, in this sermon, he makes his distinctions with a gravity utterly foreign to that fractiousness. He controverts not to win debating points, not to gore and toss opponents, but to impart wisdom. And here wisdom is needed, for despite the evil that ideologically warped science continues to visit upon the world, scientists still command an inordinate public trust. While granting them their merits, Newman is nevertheless unsparing about their inadequacies.

> It may be asked how it comes to pass, if a true philosophical temper is so allied to that which the Scriptures inculcate as the temper of a Christian, that any men should be found distinguished for discoveries in science, who yet are ill disposed towards those doctrines which Revelation enjoins upon our belief. The reason may be this: the humility and teachableness which the Scripture precepts inculcate

---

[237] Richard William Church, *Human Life and its Conditions* (London: Macmillan & Co., 1894), 76–7.
[238] *US*, 21.
[239] To be fair, Huxley was seen by some, especially those enrolled in the Metaphysical Society as not entirely unfair on the issue of science and religion. "Even the Catholic St. George Mivart, at the time engaged in a bitter biological dispute with Huxley, recalled, of 'one notable paper written by him, entitled "The Evidence of the Miracle of the Resurrection"', that the 'tact and delicacy with which he handled a subject about which so many members entertained strong convictions were as admirable as were the decision and firmness with which he stated what his own convictions were.' Hutton similarly considered that Huxley's contribution was 'conceived in a very reverent and even tender spirit, stating his views very frankly, though with great delicacy, on the miracle of the resurrection, and he concluded that the 'object of Huxley's paper was ... to seize an opportunity for a very eloquent apology for the incredulity of men of science.'" Gowan Dawson, "T. H. Huxley and the Resurrection," in *The Papers of the Metaphysical Society 1869–1880*, ed. Catherine Marshall, Bernard Lightman and Richard England (Oxford: Oxford University Press, 2015), 110–11. Newman, however, could not involve himself in such enterprises. To Church he wrote: "I hear that you and the Archbishop of York (to say nothing of Cardinal Manning etc) are going to let Professor Huxley read in your presence an argument in refutation of our Lord's Resurrection. How can this possibly come under the scope of a Metaphysical Society. I thank my stars that, when asked to accept the honour of belonging to it, I declined. Aren't you in a false position? Perhaps it is a ruse of the Cardinal to bring the Professor into the clutches of the Inquisition." Newman to R. W. Church (11 January 1876), *LD*, xxviii, 11.

are connected with principles more solemn and doctrines more awful than those which are necessary for the temper of mind in which scientific investigation must be conducted; and though the Christian spirit is admirably fitted to produce the tone of thought and inquiry which leads to the discovery of truth, yet a slighter and less profound humility will do the same. The philosopher has only to confess that he is liable to be deceived by false appearances and reasonings, to be biassed by prejudice, and led astray by a warm fancy; he is humble because sensible he is ignorant, cautious because he knows himself to be fallible, docile because he really desires to learn. But Christianity, in addition to this confession, requires him to acknowledge himself to be a rebel in the sight of God, and a breaker of that fair and goodly order of things which the Creator once established. The philosopher confesses himself to be imperfect; the Christian feels himself to be sinful and corrupt. The infirmity of which the philosopher must be conscious is but a relative infirmity—imperfection as opposed to perfection, of which there are infinite degrees. Thus he believes himself placed in a certain point of the scale of beings, and that there are beings nearer to perfection than he is, others farther removed from it. But the Christian acknowledges that he has fallen away from that rank in creation which he originally held; that he has passed a line, and is in consequence not merely imperfect, but weighed down with positive, actual evil. Now there is little to lower a man in his own opinion, in his believing that he holds a certain definite station in an immense series of creatures, and is in consequence removed, by many steps, from perfection; but there is much very revolting to the minds of many, much that is contrary to their ideas of harmony and order, and the completeness of the system of nature, and much at variance with those feelings of esteem with which they are desirous of regarding themselves, in the doctrine that man is disgraced and degraded from his natural and original rank; that he has, by sinning, introduced a blemish into the work of God; that he is guilty in the court of heaven, and is continually doing things odious in the sight of the Divine holiness. And as the whole system of the Christian faith depends upon this doctrine, since it was to redeem man from deserved punishment that Christ suffered on the cross, and in order to strengthen him in his endeavours to cleanse himself from sin, and prepare for heaven, that the Holy Spirit has come to rule the Church, it is not wonderful that men are found, admirable for their philosophical temper and their success in investigating nature, and yet unworthy disciples in the school of the Gospel.[240]

If judiciousness and equanimity characterize Newman's work, so too does an ability to enter into the psychology of his opponents. We can search the work of rationalists high and low and never find evidence of any readiness on their part to understand the arguments of their opponents. Gibbon is the most celebrated example. Content to caricature the faithful as creatures of credulity, he shows no interest in why men crave, struggle with, test and assent to faith. When Newman, by contrast, puts himself in his opponents' shoes, he reproduces the character of their thinking with a dazzling clairvoyance. Speaking of the attitudes that most men of science have towards men of faith, he writes: "Such men often regard

---

[240] US, 21–3.

Christianity as a slavish system, which is prejudicial to the freedom of thought, the aspirations of genius, and the speculations of enterprise; an unnatural system, which sets out with supposing that the human mind is out of order, and consequently bends all its efforts to overthrow the constitution of feeling and belief with which man is born, and to make him a being for which nature never intended him; and a pernicious system, which unfits men for this life by fixing their thoughts on another, and which, wherever consistently acted upon, infallibly leads (as it often has led) to the encouragement of the monastic spirit, and the extravagances of fanaticism."[241]

That Church was an apt student of Newman when it came to these matters is evident from a sermon he delivered in the Church of St. John the Baptist, Frome in 1876 entitled "The Life of Intellectual Self-Sufficiency." "I mean, by the life of Rationalism, the life of intellectual self-sufficiency," he wrote; "a life which fails in the essentials of self-discipline over the intellect and its temptations, which fails in humility, self-distrust, reverence, modesty, in the use of our faculties, in the pursuit of knowledge. And it must be remembered that such habits of mind, though naturally tending to produce error and unbelief, and the formidable phenomena characteristic of our time, are yet compatible with a right belief, which they are capable of so deeply injuring."[242] Like Newman, Church was opposed not to science *per se*—that would be tantamount to being opposed to reason *per se*—but to the misapplication of science. And in this misapplication, he saw the same insidious treachery that Newman saw. Indeed, Church is eloquent when it comes to this treachery.

> The plain, gross, open sins of the world and the flesh bear on them their own mark: they are "open beforehand, going before to judgment." We know also that there are the veiled and disguised sins of the self-deceiver and the double-minded; but besides, deeper and more impenetrable still, passing, it may be, through the world under the semblance and with the confidence of virtues, there are the subtle, refined sins of the intellect—sins of the hard, unbending, ungodly will, under the mask of passionless reason. And no one can cast ever so superficial a glance on the wild turmoil of opinions all round without seeing the fatal marks which point to sins of the intellect as surely as others point to sins of the passions.[243]

In his very Newmanian critique of the dangers of intellect undisciplined by faith, Church saw a number of moral consequences with which twenty-first-century readers are all too familiar. "First and foremost ... there is the sin of not caring: the sin of indifference and negligence amid the most awful issues that can be raised to man. It is the sin which raised the indignation of Bishop Butler; it is the sin which taxed the powers of Pascal ... And of all the amazing things in the world it is indeed the most wonderful, not that men should reject the Gospel, not that they should hate religion, not that they should disbelieve in God, but that they should write and speak continually, in the character of serious men and public teachers, as if they were insensible to the infinite and

---

[241] US, 23.
[242] Church, *Pascal and Other Sermons*, 238–9.
[243] Ibid., 244.

inexpressible import and gravity of these things; as if it really did not matter whether or not a man made up his mind and took his side about God, about immortality, about the Cross and Resurrection of Jesus Christ." With the rise of natural science throughout the nineteenth century, which both Huxley and Tyndall were so instrumental in advancing, Church saw the superficiality that came to characterize men's response to the appeal of faith. "They hold religion in their hands and look at it, as if it were a curious product of nature," he wrote, "to be examined, and turned round, and coldly taken to pieces ... They play with doubts. They amuse themselves with views. They who know so well what agitation and anxiety and alarm mean in their households, in their business, look on, as they call it, dispassionately, at questions on the decision of which must depend all that interests man—whether life is a shadow and delusion or the most inconceivable of treasures: whether a key can be found to its enigmas, so fatal if they cannot be answered, or whether all explanation of them is hopeless." And in this Church saw not only a betrayal of faith but an even more baffling betrayal of reason. "Men sin against their reason itself, who trifle with interests which reason itself shows them must be so tremendous."[244] Moreover, if this "off-hand, lazy-going fashion of disposing of the most solemn of claims by smart and shallow audacities is the sin of the negligent and the unthinking," Church saw an even graver sin in in those who did think: "the sin of self-confidence and pride, of trusting to ourselves to find our way."[245] For Church, one of the upshots of this intellectual self-sufficiency was that it bred determinism, the idea "that man's freedom of choice and action, his goodness, his sin, is the freedom of an automaton; that our consciousness, as we think, of a responsible self and immaterial soul, is, in theory at least, a delusion."[246] But there were other consequences to our neglecting the demands of faith that were, if anything, even more destructive, "when intellect and reasoning persuade us that this world after all is our best and satisfying portion; that we are wisest when we most follow our pleasure; that the lusts of the flesh and the pomps of the world have a good deal to say for themselves; that we were made for this world—made for things seen; and that of another, as we can know nothing, we were best believe nothing. Intellect will do this for us if we will let it; it will do it in hard-headed and powerful systems of abstract thought; it will do it in rich and passionate poetry, pathetic or tender or rapturous; it will do it in the beauty and magnificence of art. And descending to a yet lower deep, the questioning spirit which has called evil good finds it no hard task to prove that good is evil. Then intellect has indeed sinned its deadliest sin, when it has not only beguiled the will to break down the eternal barriers between goodness and sin, but has argued the soul out of its instinctive recognition and admiration of goodness; when by specious reasonings, the most easy of all things, it has taught the soul to revolt from its natural estimate of purity and unselfishness, and undermined its veneration of holiness—taught it to be disloyal to its own ideas of the highest and the best."[247] Those revolted by the apostate antinomianism that undermined

[244] Ibid., 244–5.
[245] Ibid., 245.
[246] Ibid., 248.
[247] Ibid., 248–9.

the doctrinal, sacramental and liturgical integrity of the Church of Rome under the papacy of Jorge Bergoglio will know exactly what the Dean of St. Paul's was getting at here.

For the purposes of any book on Newman's critics, Church's description of the final and most grievous result of rationalism is indispensable, precisely because it is "yet another sin, not so hateful as the sin of despising and explaining away goodness, yet very subtle and very fatal, which hangs about the excitement of religious inquiry. It is the sin of requiring undue and impossible conditions of proof. I call it a sin, because it is a rebellion against the natural conditions of the world and of our own constitution—a rebellion against those limitations and imperfections of our knowledge amid which we find ourselves—a demand that God should give us what it has not pleased Him to give us."[248] As I will show in subsequent chapters, this is precisely the sin to which most of Newman's hostile contemporary critics fell prey, especially Edward Abbott Abbott and James Fitzjames Stephen. Church's recognition of its gravity is a good example of how Newman's personal influence—the criticism of friendship—bound together two men who were so wide apart in other ways, though Newman's understanding of the challenges the man of science brings against the faith is rather different from Church's, which is to say, Newman sees them as a kind of effrontery. "The man of science ought to know that he has not proved that miracles are impossible; yet, he uses the assumption as confidently against the Catholic, as if it was the most necessary of truths. Before I can fairly be called upon to enter upon difficult questions which involve great study and research for the answering I have a right to make two conditions before I have that responsibility; first, does the inquirer allow the possibility of a miraculous revelation, and next, what are the *facts*, and what the *proof* of the alleged facts, which are supposed to interfere with the belief that such a revelation is to be found in Scripture." For Newman, "He brings no facts."[249]

When Church visited with Newman in 1886, fifty years after he had first met and befriended him, he rejoiced anew in his friend's incomparable company. "I dare say you have heard that we had three days of the Cardinal," Church wrote to the Warden of Keble. "He was so bright, so kind, so affectionate; very old and soon tired but also soon refreshed with a pause of rest, and making fun of his old age. 'You know I could not do an addition sum.' ... But the old smile and twinkle of the eye, and bright meaning εἰρωνεία are all still there."[250] When Newman died four years later, Church could not attend the funeral—he had come down with a bad case of bronchitis—but, as his daughter so movingly observed in her edition of his letters, the news must have come to him with "a peculiar sorrow," especially since:

> Such a loss sent back his thoughts to Oxford, and to the early days of companionship and work together, whilst it summed up, as it were, and completed in itself, the series of partings which had preceded it. The intercourse between the two friends—whether by correspondence, or by meetings at Whatley, or in London,

---

[248] Ibid., 250.
[249] Newman to St George Jackson Mivart (8 May 1884), LD, xxx, 359.
[250] Church, *Life and Letters*, 386–7.

where the Cardinal came as a guest to the Deanery, or in the Dean's visits to Birmingham—had gone on unbroken since its renewal in 1866. And in spite of the necessary changes which their changed positions had brought about, the friendship preserved to the end its distinct and peculiar character. On Cardinal Newman's side there was still the frank confidence and the reliance on sympathy and counsel which had belonged to the old Oxford days; while by those near the Dean, it was always recognised that Newman was a name apart, the symbol, as it were, of a debt too great and a friendship too intimate and complex to bear being lightly spoken of, or subjected to the ordinary measures of praise or blame. Where agreement was not possible, the Dean seldom allowed himself any criticism save that which was implied by silence. "I have not attempted a complete criticism of Newman," he wrote to Lord Acton, to whom he had shown the sheets of his book on the Oxford Movement, "partly because I feel it beyond me, partly because it is so against the grain."[251]

The friendly criticism that Church showed Newman—bred as it is of affectionate sympathy—might not be complete but it is faithful, just, and indispensable. It also reminds us of what these two extraordinary men had most in common, and that was their unswerving dedication to the cure of souls, which, of course, they exercised preeminently in their charges as pastors. Ian Ker, the greatest of Newman's critics, touches on this matter in his biography. "During 1858," Ker writes, Newman "had become seriously anxious and worried about the Oratory." Manifold reasons contributed to this anxiety.

> In January he had been to see a specialist in London about apparent heart palpitations; to his relief, the complaint was diagnosed as the effect of the indigestion he had long suffered from. On his return to Birmingham, he found Flanagan seriously ill in bed with bronchitis. He was the hardest worker in the community, ready to turn his hand to anything. Then, towards the end of February, Henry Bittleston (who had joined the community in 1850, after being received into the Church by Newman in 1849) fell seriously ill with pleurisy. Both went abroad to recuperate. Newman took on their confessional duties in the church ... He also replaced Flanagan as novice-master, having the previous year given his opinion that novices should be given as much freedom and personal responsibility as possible. A dozen novices could not make up for the loss of Flanagan; and while an Oratory should not normally "want novices except like so many drops now and then falling upon it," there was still an urgent need for new members. At one point in the summer holidays, Newman found himself virtually alone in the house, and felt ashamed when visitors came who witnessed the depleted state of the community. He was embarrassed by his new, unfamiliar, pastoral duties, afraid that he might confuse penitents, and worried that a baptism he had to perform was not valid ("The water was exhausted out of the abominable shell before I made the three crosses—and I made a hash of it"). There seemed no end to the troubles that befell the Oratory, but he wrote encouragingly to Flanagan:
>> from the first it has been my fortune to be ever failing, yet after all not to fail. From the first I have had bad strokes of fortune—yet on the whole

---

[251] Ibid., 416.

I have made way. Hardly had I begun life, when misfortunes happened to my family—then I failed in the Schools; then I was put out of office at College; then came Number 90—and later the Achilli matter. You talk of "brilliant success" as not our portion—it is not, because you are all joined to me. When I was a boy, I was taken beyond any thing in Homer, with Ulysses seeming "like a fool or an idiot," when he began to speak—and yet somehow doing more than others, as St Paul with his weakness and foolishness.

Newman was also trying to encourage himself. He felt he had the right, if not to despond, at least to complain of St Philip Neri that he could not be "detached" so long as he had Philip's Oratory on his hands: "*He* has implicated me in the world, in a way in which I never was before, or at least never since my sisters married and my mother died. For his sake I have given up my liberty, and have ... done, almost as much as if I had married." Anyway, it was a relief, and not "an unlawful one," to vent his feelings, like Job, to a few friends. He felt that "never in my life till this last year have I felt it any thing of a difficulty even for a moment to feel resignation."[252]

It is fitting that Ker should have set this scene so memorably since, as we all know, he was a pastor himself, with a pastor's solicitude for the faithful discharge of his duties. No one could have appreciated its fidelity to Newman's character better than Church, who knew something himself of the blessings of failure.

Indeed, this was his greatest affinity with Newman: he understood the place of failure in the life of faith.[253] He understood what Newman had said in the sermon that had so impressed him when he was an undergraduate at Oriel: "our duty as Christians lies in ... making ventures for eternal life without the absolute certainty of success."[254] In a sermon entitled "Failures in Life" preached in 1882 before St Mary the Virgin—Newman's old Tractarian pulpit—Church took up this most Newmanian of themes. "We see the failures of life in the ordinary incidents of our experience," Church wrote, "we see it when the good die young; when the bright promise is cut short or not fulfilled; when men miss their true calling, ignobly shrink from it or proudly scorn it; when a life of noble labour is wrecked within sight of the goal, as a ship sinks in sight of port; when men, who have served their brethren well grow too old for the new demands which each fresh generation brings with it, and for tasks that once were light; when, as age goes on, old friends not only are taken away from us year after year, but we who

---

[252] Ian Ker, *John Henry Newman: A Biography* (Oxford: The Clarendon Press, 1988), 469–70.

[253] Richard Holt Hutton saw something similar in the life of Frederick Denison Maurice: "[A] great deal of his work was undoubtedly tentative, awkward, 'inappropriate.' But the persevering and redundant laboriousness with which, when needful, it was all done over again, produced an effect which could hardly have been produced by the highest genius for adapting means to ends. There was the lavishness of the eternal world in all his efforts, though there was all the humiliation of human inadequacy too. 'We have this treasure in earthen vessels, that the excellency of the power may be of God and not of ourselves,' might be the motto of Maurice's career, so little did he feel the brightness of success, and so much nevertheless did he really attain." Richard Holt Hutton, *Essays on Some Modern Guides to English Thought in Matters of Faith* (London: Macmillan & Co., 1891), 351.

[254] Newman, "The Ventures of Faith" (1836), *PS*, iv, 195–6.

remain find ourselves drifting asunder, in judgment, in objects, in sympathies." Yet, for Church, "the failures which specially touch us are, when a man has aimed high, and has shot wide of his mark, or short of it. It is when care, and love, and toil, and hope, have been lavished on an idea or a cause; and the idea will not stand the test of conflict and time, or the cause dwindles into personal rivalries or strifes of words. It is when the purpose at starting was so honest, the thought so pure and high, but as time went on some secret mischief got entangled with them, and without any one feeling it, the enterprise was turned out of its course, and from that little angle of divergence the interval grew impassable which separated the original direction and the later one. It is when life and perhaps opportunity remain, and yet the strength is spent, just when the turning point arrives, and obstacles accumulate, and the path is confused and uncertain. ... It is when the sincere reformer sees his work taken out of his hands by a second generation of disciples of meaner and narrower thoughts; still worse when he becomes himself their prey and dupe, and leaves the evils of the world. greater than when he assailed them. The mark of our mortality and our weakness is set on the lives of men, the flower of our race, and on the history of institutions, founded for the highest ends."[255] Reading this, one might be tempted to see it as the cry of a man who made a choice at the crossroads and came to regret his choice. Yet the man who preached this sermon, for all his recognition of the deficiencies of the National Church, had no sectarian regrets.[256] Nor was he a defeatist, however aware of the ubiquity of defeat. He knew that the life of Christian discipleship must, perforce, embrace the life of Christ, and that: "'Toilsome and incomplete' must be the labour of him who, in daily contact with all that is horrible and desperate, spends a life to bring the mercies and peace of Christ into the coarse miseries and festering vices which girdle round all our brilliant capitals, all our great seats of industry and wealth. Only in after years does their work draw itself up to its true grandeur; only then do we lose sight of partial failures, of all that made it, while it was going on, so dreary, so unspeakably depressing,—and see it, at last, as it is."[257]

Here, in extolling the dignity of the devout life, a dignity no principled defeat could ever mar, Church showed that he was not only a good critic but a true confrere of Newman. "Don't let us be afraid, in a good cause, of the chances of failure," he urged his auditors.[258]

---

[255] Richard William Church, *Cathedral and University Sermons* (London: Macmillan & Co., 1892), 244–5.

[256] The beautiful eulogy that Church wrote for Pusey shows how magnificently he could transcend the unseemly sectarian fray. "All who care for the Church of God, all who care for Christ's Religion, even those—I make bold to say—who do not in many things think as he thought, will class him among those who in difficult and anxious times have witnessed, by great zeal, and great effort, and great sacrifice, for God and Truth and Holiness; they will see in him one who sought to make Religion a living and mighty force over the consciences and in the affairs of men, not by knowledge only and learning and wisdom and great gifts of persuasion, but still more by boundless devotedness, by the power of a consecrated and unfaltering will." Church quoted in Liddon, *Life of Edward Bouverie Pusey*, iv, 390.

[257] Church, *Cathedral and University Sermons*, 253–4.

[258] Leslie Stephen was also preoccupied with failure, convinced that he would only be a footnote in the history of English literature in the nineteenth century, an estimate with which his American friend James Russell Lowell disagreed. "I love you none the worse for your modesty, but you are

"Heaven is for those who have failed on earth," says the mocking proverb and since the day of Calvary no Christian need be ashamed to accept it. But even here, men have that within them which recognises the heroic aspect of a noble failure: they own the nobleness. in spite of the failure, in spite of the world's irony and amusement, which accompanies it as the jester of old accompanied what was greatest. Even here, it is better to have tried and failed, than not to have failed because we have not tried. It is better to have made the mistakes of high aspiration, of originality, of self-forgetfulness—better to have made the mistakes of the good, which it is said to be the business of the wise to correct, than never to have struck a blow for Christ and goodness, because so many before us have struck to little purpose. No one who makes the great ventures of duty and conscience can be so sure of himself as not to risk defeat, perhaps deserved defeat—but no one who does so in sincerity and humbleness knows what purpose he may be fulfilling beyond his own. If the great or the saintly life has been incomplete, at least there has been the great or the saintly life. If the great effort against error and sin and sloth has waxed feeble, at least there has been a new beacon of warning set up in the world's dangerous way. The world would have missed some of its highest examples, if men had always waited till they could make a covenant with success. Here, we can only give what we have to give, our faithfulness, our honesty, our singleness of purpose, our best powers of thought and endeavour, our life, in this short stage of the endless line of our being, which we call to-day. There, in the light beyond the veil, and not here, we shall really know which are the "lost causes," and which are the victorious.[259]

---

a swan taking yourself for a goose." Lowell quoted in Hermione Lee, *Virginia Woolf* (London: Chatto & Windus, 1996), 72–3.
[259] Church, *Cathedral and University Sermons*, 254.

RICHARD HOLT HUTTON

◆ 2 ◆

Richard Holt Hutton and Newman's Witness to the Unseen

> It grieves me ... to see the unfairness with which you are treated by those whose profession is 'liberalism.' ... I wanted simply to express that, underlying the wide and delicately sympathetic imagination which your writings show, there seems to me always to be a deep attachment to a dogmatic and systematic theological view of the universe, resting less on what I should call personal inspiration than on the *connected* view of a coherent body of theological truth.
>
> Richard Holt Hutton to John Henry Newman (28 February 1863),
> LD, xxi, 68

I

When the Pre-Raphaelite painter Edward Burne-Jones looked back on the influence that John Henry Newman had exerted on him, he recalled how "In an age of materialism, [Newman] taught me to venture all on the unseen, and this so early that it was well in me when life began, and I was equipped before I went to Oxford with a real good panoply and it has never failed me. If this world cannot tempt me with money or luxury—and it can't—or anything it has in its trumpery treasure-house, it is most of all because he said it in a way that touched me ... So he stands as a great image or symbol of a man ... who put all this world's life in one splendid venture."[1] Indeed, as a schoolboy, Burne-Jones would walk miles to hear Newman preach at the Birmingham Oratory. "Wherever he had told me to go then there I would have gone. Lord! What a whey-faced maniac I was."[2] For Burne-Jones, by contrast, Dean Stanley, the Broad-Church Anglican Divine "was a clever man and came at a very lucky time for himself." Why? "People were beginning to weary of the vehement ardour of Newman. [Stanley] brought a gentle kind of liberalism into religious questions that was very welcome to

---

[1] Edward Burne-Jones quoted in *Memorials of Edward Burne-Jones*, ed. Lady Georgiana Jones (London: Macmillan & Co., 1906), 59.

[2] Edward Burne Jones quoted in Fiona MacCarthy, *The Last Pre-Raphaelite: Edward Burne-Jones and the Victorian Imagination* (Cambridge: Harvard University Press, 2012), 22.

them. … They wanted to keep up the Church. Its downfall would be the signal of much mischief and they saw no good in handing it over to those who they thought would bring it to ruin by intolerance." Still, the uncompromising man of dogmatic faith in Newman would always command Burne-Jones's respect. "Dean Stanley was a clever man of course," he conceded, "but not anything like such a fine creature as Newman."[3] For the Brummagem Burne-Jones, the son of an impecunious frame-maker, who would leave the spectacular hideousness of Birmingham to paint the knights and dames of his unearthly imagination, "Newman was an unusually splendid character" precisely because no one could be "more unworldly." The painter who had had to make his own way in the world could not help but notice that Newman never sought out any of the world's or the Church's distinctions. "Wherever [the Church] chose to put him there he would be." Truly "humble minded," Newman "had to put up with a great deal of snubbing after his conversion," which "he took, in the prettiest way" possible.[4]

None of Newman's contemporary critics testified to his witness to the unseen as incisively as Richard Holt Hutton, the editor of the *Spectator*, with whom Newman entered into a long and fruitful friendship, starting with a favorable review that Hutton wrote of the *Apologia*.[5] In a review of Newman's *Parochial and Plain Sermons*, which he contributed to the *Spectator* in December 1868, Hutton speaks of this defining aspect of Newman with the acuity of a man who had personally benefited from the wisdom he recommends.

> Just as the scientific man trusts not to the signs by which he reasons but to the forces of which those signs are the mere calculus, Dr. Newman constantly teaches that faith is the act of trusting yourself to great and permanent spiritual forces, the tidal power of which, and not the power of your acts of faith, is commissioned by God to carry you into the clearer light. He uniformly speaks of faith as a "venture," an act of the soul by which it throws itself on what is beyond its own power, by which it gives itself up without either the power or the right to know the full consequences, gives itself up to some power higher than itself and beyond itself, as a man trusts to the sea, or to the railway, or to any natural power beyond his control. … To use his own words, it consists in risking "what we have for what we have not; and doing so in a noble, generous way, not indeed rashly or lightly, still knowing accurately what we are doing, not knowing either what we give up, nor, again, what we shall gain; uncertain about our reward, uncertain about the extent of sacrifice, in all respects leaning, waiting upon Him, trusting in Him to fulfill his promise, trusting in Him to enable us to fulfill our own vows, and so in all respects proceeding without carefulness or anxiety about the future."[6]

---

[3] Edward Burne-Jones quoted in *Burne-Jones Talking: His Conversations 1895–1898 Preserved by his Studio Assistant Thomas Rooke*, ed. Mary Lago (London: John Murray, 1982), 145.
[4] Ibid., 176.
[5] See Edward Short, "On the Track of Truth: Newman and Richard Holt Hutton," in *Newman and his Contemporaries* (London: T&T Clark, 2011), 303–34.
[6] Richard Holt Hutton, "Dr. Newman's Oxford Sermons," *Spectator* (5 December 1868), in *A Victorian Spectator: Uncollected Writings of R. H. Hutton*, ed. Robert Tener and Malcolm Woodfield (Bristol: The Bristol Press, 1989), 152–3. The sermon from which Hutton quotes is "The Ventures of Faith" (1836), *PS*, iv, 299.

A good example of how Newman practiced what he professed can be found in his *Oxford University Sermons* (1843), in which he delved into the nature of belief not altogether certain where his investigations might take him. "It is not too much to say," he wrote, "that the stepping by which great geniuses scale the mountains of truth is as unsafe and precarious to men in general, as the ascent of a skillful mountaineer up a literal crag. It is a way that they alone can take, and its justification lies in their success."[7] Here, Newman was speaking of a rather more rarefied mountaineer than LeNanin de Tillemont, Gibbon's "patient and sure-footed mule of the Alps" who could "be trusted in the most slippery paths."[8] Earlier, in 1836, in his sermon, "The Ventures of Faith," Newman had made his point even more explicitly. Taking as his theme, the words from Scripture, "They say unto Him, We are able" (Matt. 20.22), he exhorted an entire generation to "put all this world's life into one splendid venture."

> These words of the holy Apostles James and John were in reply to a very solemn question addressed to them by their Divine Master. They coveted, with a noble ambition, though as yet unpractised in the highest wisdom, untaught in the holiest truth,—they coveted to sit beside Him on His Throne of Glory. They would be content with nothing short of that special gift which He had come to grant to His elect, which He shortly after died to purchase for them, and which He offers to us. They ask the gift of eternal life; and He in answer told them, not that they should have it (though for them it was really reserved), but He reminded them what *they must venture for it*; "Are ye able to drink of the cup that I shall drink of and to be baptized with the baptism that I am baptized with? They say unto Him, We are able." Here then a great lesson is impressed upon us, that our duty as Christians lies in this, in making ventures for eternal life without the absolute certainty of success.[9]

In this chapter I shall revisit Hutton's work on Newman to demonstrate his appreciation for this essential aspect of Newman, on which so many of his contemporary critics cast unwarrantable doubt. I will also show how Hutton, although critical of Newman's embrace of Roman Catholicism in some respects, rose above his objections to enter into and prize not only the magnetism but the steadfastness of Newman's faith, which were such striking attributes of a life "fed ... from beginning to end on the substance of Divine Revelation."[10]

In his brief biography of Newman, written shortly after the Cardinal's death in 1890 and based on years of study of his work, Hutton charted the genesis of Newman's commitment to the unseen to the very beginning of his Anglican ministry.

> Take the very first sermon of which there is any record amongst Dr. Newman's printed writings, one preached in Oxford in January, 1825, and entitled "Temporal

---

[7] Newman, "Explicit and Implicit Reasoning" (1840), *US*, 177.
[8] Edward Gibbon, *The Decline and Fall of the Roman Empire*, 7 vols, ed. J. B. Bury (London: Methuen, 1909), iii, ch. xxv, 50–1, n. 126.
[9] *PS*, iv, 295–6.
[10] Richard Holt Hutton, *Cardinal Newman* (London: Methuen, 1891), 249.

Advantages", when he can only have been twenty-four years of age, from the text, "We brought nothing into this world, and it is certain we can carry nothing out; and having food and raiment, let us be therewith content," and consider if it be possible that that sermon could have been written by a man who did not feel to the full depth of his heart and soul the reality and power of the Christian faith: "What can increase their peace who believe and trust in the Son of God ? Shall we add a drop to the ocean, or grains to the sand of the sea? ... It is in this sense that the Gospel of Christ is a leveller of ranks; we pay indeed our superiors full reverence, and with cheerfulness, as unto the Lord; and we honour eminent talents as deserving admiration and reward; and the more readily act we thus because these are little things to pay." Here the utterly unworldly nature of the man, the vivid spiritual feeling that the inward life in God is everything of the smallest consequence to the soul, spoke out plainly, and at a time when Dr. Newman had not reached anything like the full maturity of his power. From that date onwards the vividness of his spiritual insight grew steadily, till it reached its highest point, and was recognized generally by the world when he wrote his religious autobiography in 1864. Writing of his own boyhood, when he was only just a man, he said of himself, "I used to wish that the Arabian tales were true; my imagination ran on unknown influences, on magical powers and talismans; I thought life might be a dream and I an angel, and all this world a deception, my fellow-angels hiding themselves from me, and deceiving me with the semblance of a material world." And in the sermon on "The mind of little children," he speaks professedly from his own experience when he says, "This we know full well—we know it from our own recollections of ourselves and our experience of children—that there is in the infant soul, in the fresh years of its regenerate state, a discernment of the unseen world in the things that are seen, a realization of what is sovereign and adorable, and an incredulity and ignorance about what is transient and changeable, which mark it as the first outline of the matured Christian, when weaned from things temporal, and living in the intimate conviction of the Divine presence." I quote these passages only to show how completely the spiritual reality of the Oxford preacher had its roots in his own past, how certain it is that Newman was speaking from the depths of his own experience when he said, that from a very early age he had rested "in the thought of two, and two only, supreme and luminously self-evident beings, myself and my Creator."[11]

Writing after Fitzjames Stephen and Andrew Fairbairn had brought their respective charges of scepticism against Newman, Hutton defended the Cardinal in terms that all who rejoice in his work will approve, even if Hutton's choice of the word "idealism" to describe his subject's Christian faith is obviously infelicitous.[12] "It is simply ridiculous for any one who knows intimately the whole series

---

[11] Ibid., 7–8.
[12] Hutton spent two years as a young man studying philosophy in Berlin under one of Hegel's severest critics, Friedrich Adolf Trendelenburg (1802–72). In speaking of the French Neo-Scholastic Jesuit Léonce de Grandmaison (1868–1927) and his response to Newman's essay on development, Andrew Meszaros says that, for Grandmaison: "Newman did more than anyone, except perhaps Möhler, to protect Christianity from the 'virus' of Hegelianism." Andrew Meszaros, "Some Neo-Scholastic Receptions of Newman on Doctrinal Development," *Gregorianum*, 97, i (2016), 123–50, at 141. Meszaros also nicely refutes Michael Shea's assertion that "The Neo-Scholastic Revival was ... a

of his writings to suppose for a moment that Newman's nature is sceptical, and his mind kept only by force of will from toppling over into unbelief," Hutton wrote.

> On the contrary, his nature is profoundly and entirely penetrated by the Christian idealism. And had it been otherwise, I believe that he would have been much more likely to ignore the sceptical aspects of the religious problems of the day altogether, instead of giving them so profound a study. It was his absolute confidence that nothing could shake his faith in the truth of revelation that induced him to master so completely as he did the various aspects of the objections which led so many men to withhold their faith from Christianity.[13]

Of course, this is altogether true. Newman took up the cudgels to defend the Church against her liberal critics precisely to show an increasingly irreligious age that these critics were not on anything like the impregnable ground they imagined: the Church could and would withstand the assaults of captious unbelief. Hutton was also right in recognizing that Newman's readiness to admit the appeal of scepticism was inseparable from his dedication to the cure of souls. "This then I regard as one certain test of Cardinal Newman's greatness," Hutton wrote, "that throughout a long life he has followed with singular tenacity and concentration of purpose one grand aim—that of winning his fellow-countrymen from their tepid and formal Christianity to a Christianity worthy of the name, in spite of obstacles in the way which he has recognized with a candour and a vivacity that have strangely misled some of his critics into imagining that he appreciated even more the obstacles to belief than he did the spiritual power by which those obstacles were to be surmounted."[14] Here, Hutton was clearly making reference to James Fitzjames Stephen, who, as we have seen, mischievously chose to argue that Newman's respect for scepticism somehow led him to become sceptical himself.[15]

---

strong factor in the turn away from the popularity of Newman's theory." Michael Shea, *Newman's Early Roman Catholic Legacy 1845-1854* (Oxford: Oxford University Press, 2017), 192. As Meszaros shows (p. 149), "Despite ... differences, the Neo-Scholastics were capable of appropriating what they deemed valuable in Newman's thought, and at times did so creatively. ... In short, any history of twentieth-century Newman reception that reduces the Neo-Scholastics' role to one of opposition or indifference will be an incomplete one."

[13] Hutton, *Cardinal Newman*, 8–9.
[14] *Ibid.*, 9.
[15] Hutton's response to Fitzjames Stephen's *Liberty, Equality, Fraternity* shows what a shrewd intellectual critic he could be. "The whole system of Mr. Stephen's book is artificial. His utilitarianism is artificial. His notion of liberty is wholly artificial. His idea of morality as a mere derivative from creed is most artificial of all. I maintain that morality lies at the root of religion and is its base rather than its superstructure; that men are much more agreed about the former than they are about the latter; that in choosing the latter the exercise of the most delicate and the highest kind of liberty is needed, and that to interfere with that exercise by pains and penalties, on an abstract theory that this or that is 'imposture,' is to mar what we shall never mend. Mr. Stephen's theory tramps over the most delicate blossoms of human life and character with a heavy elephantine tread. There is one view, and but one, which would justify him;—if religious truth were, as he seems to think, absolutely unattainable by any exercise of intellectual liberty, he might perhaps justify the manufacture of a sort of coarse substitute for it, to act as stays to the human conscience, which has an indestructible longing for truth. Indeed, Mr. Stephen glances once longingly at this notion; but is obliged to dismiss it with some reluctance as intrinsically hopeless,—in which I hold him to be right." Richard Holt Hutton, "Mr Stephen on Liberty, Equality, Fraternity" (1873), *Criticisms*

Apropos Fitzjames Stephen, Hutton was perceptive, rightly seeing the following boast as emblematic of the man. "I have always found myself one of the most unteachable of human beings," the judge claimed. "I cannot, to this day, take in anything at second hand. I have, in all cases, to learn whatever I want to learn in a way of my own. It has been so with law, with languages, with Indian administration, with the machinery I have had to study in patent cases, with English composition; in short, with everything whatever." As an example, he claimed in 1865 that F. D. Maurice's books "did their utmost to make me squint intellectually about this time, but I never learned the trick."[16] Perhaps one reason why Fitzjames Stephen was so dismissive of Newman was precisely the convert's tendency throughout his long life to consult others before committing to his various positions. Indeed, the first chapter of his *Apologia* is given over almost entirely to his praising the many individuals, living and dead, from whom he had learned to grow in faith. By contrast, when it came to Fitzjames Stephen's avowed "unteachableness," Hutton was withering:

> It seems to us that one of the chief lessons to be learned from the life of this great unteachable teacher,—one of the most powerful and sincerest of narrow-minded men,—is that many avenues to truth are closed to a mind that cannot learn from any experience but its own. So far as we can see, the life of Christ, the greatest source of true religious belief in this world, was to him almost a mere hieroglyphic, to be deciphered (if at all) by the study of the external accessories of that life, and of the light thrown upon these accessories by the study of science, the study of the long records of human credulity, and of the laws of legal evidence. These are important aids to the study of Christ's life, but they are only aids, and Sir Fitzjames Stephen seems to us to have treated them as if they were the main approaches to the explanation of it. We venture to think that both Mr. Maurice and Cardinal Newman might have taught him, had he been teachable, a good deal which would have prevented his "squinting" at the great subject of the gospel, through these subordinate and often misleading lights thrown upon the interpretation of its meaning.[17]

What makes Hutton's insights into Fitzjames Stephen so interesting is that they nicely illumine the very aspects of his own criticism that set him apart from so many other nineteenth-century critics. After all, it was the criticism of sympathy at which Hutton most distinguished himself, and here he makes good use of the malign example of Fitzjames Stephen to define that rare, deeply humanizing art.

---

on *Contemporary Thought and Thinkers: Selected from the Spectator*, 2 vols. (London: Macmillan & Co., 1900), i, 137–8.

[16] James Fitzjames Stephen quoted in Richard Holt Hutton, "An 'Unteachable' Teacher," *Spectator* (15 June 1885), 816. Cf. "I loved Frederick Maurice, as everyone who came near him; and have no doubt he did all that was in him to do of good in his day," Ruskin recalled. "Maurice was by nature puzzle-headed, and, though in a beautiful manner, *wrong*-headed; while his clear conscience and keen affection made him egotistic, and in his Bible-reading, as insolent as any infidel of them all. I only went once to a Bible-lesson of his; and the meeting was significant, and conclusive." John Ruskin, *Praeterita: Outlines of Scenes and Thoughts Perhaps Worthy of Memory in my Past Life*, ed. Kenneth Clark (London: Rupert Hart-Davis, 1949), 451–2.

[17] Hutton, "An 'Unteachable' Teacher," 816.

It would be the greatest mistake to suppose that because Sir Fitzjames Stephen was not teachable through his sympathy with others, he was not a man of strong and even passionately deep feeling. No one can read his brother's account of him without learning that what lent him his power was the great massiveness of that feeling. He wrote his thoughts on Lord Palmerston's death with tears streaming down his face. When he thundered against the "maudlin" view of life, or the pitiable weakness of philanthropic sentiment, he did it with a force of passion that had in it something of the sublime. There was nothing in him of the cold-blooded utilitarian, though he was a utilitarian in excelsis. He was a utilitarian of passionate fervour. But he was liable to no contagion from the feeling of others. He did not learn to understand a new kind of life, not primarily his own, by any capacity for appreciating the genius and life of others. Almost his only great literary hero, Carlyle, was a hero of his own mould. He learnt from the exaggeration of that mould in Carlyle to interpret his own mind and heart. Again, he felt most deeply for those whom, as a Judge, he had to condemn to death. He was profoundly sensitive to the rude and ignorant criticism with which some of his summings-up and sentences were received by the Press. Far from being thick-skinned, he was almost too thin-skinned, considering how strong and confident were his own convictions. But he never learned to enlarge his own feelings by entering into the feelings of others,— even those of the greatest of his contemporaries. We should describe him as a man of a great mind, of high magnanimity, of very deep feelings and a very sensitive nature, but who never enlarged the bounds of his own sympathies, even in the presence and by the help of natures higher and wider than his own, not even when these were of a quality which touched the region of the spiritual and the divine.[18]

By contrast, for all his impatience with the Roman Church and her claim to be the "*unam, sanctam, cathólicam et apostólicam Ecclésiam*," Hutton never lost sight of the value of Newman's unwavering fidelity in an age that increasingly came to convince itself that scepticism was somehow unavoidable. "Newman's life has been a continuous struggle against scepticism," Hutton declared.

> No one can read his long series of sermons, and his remarkable though much shorter series of poems, and still less re-read them by the light of his lectures "On Anglican Difficulties," his *Apologia* and his *Grammar of Assent*, without being profoundly convinced that the Roman Catholic in Newman is as deep as his thought, the High Church man as deep as his temperament, and the Christian as deep as his character, being intertwined with it inextricably ... I can understand what Dr. Newman was as an Anglican, because the first part of the most characteristic work of his life was done as an Anglican, and I believe that it was Reason, and Reason almost alone, working on the assumptions which were so deeply rooted in him in 1843, which made him a Roman Catholic. I cannot understand what he was as an Evangelical Protestant, because even so far as he ever was an Evangelical Protestant, it was only during his earliest youth, and the

---

[18] *Ibid.*

whole drift of his nature seems to have carried him away from the moorings of his early creed. But what would be left of Dr. Newman if you could wipe the Christian heart out of his life and creed I could as little guess as I could what would have been left of Sir Walter Scott if you could have emptied out of him the light of old romance and legend; or of Carlyle, if you could have managed somehow to graft upon him a conventional "gigmanic" creed.[19]

Again, if Newman's faith was unwavering, he never took the position that scepticism was somehow beyond the pale of debate. Daniel MacMillan (1813–57), the Scottish autodidact who founded the Macmillan publishing house, certainly saw the intellectual sympathy with which Newman entered into the allure of scepticism. In a letter of 29 April 1843, he wrote: "It is a very curious specimen of the sceptical turn of his mind. He very much reminds me of our great Scotch sceptic, David Hume. The same analytical power, the same carelessness about consequences. He is quite a logician, and a most powerful one. He holds fast by Christianity as developed 'in the Church,' *because the balance of probabilities seems in its favour*. If [Newman] had not been a Christian and a churchman, he would have been one of the powerfulest sceptical logic-mills we have had set going in this country for many years. For mere power, our friend, Archbishop Whately, is nothing to him. Newman is a true product of the nineteenth century— a genuine steam engine; and yet no one is more conscious of the weakness and self-sufficiency of 'our enlightened age.'"[20] That Newman's respect for scepticism, together with his readiness to refute it, won MacMillan's own respect is clear from another letter he wrote on 12 April 1843 recommending the book to a friend: "You will see that ... his notions about God are as sublime as anything you have ever read. I don't expect you to have much sympathy with the book. It was most painful for me. Still I could not help admiring the wonderful power of the man, and feeling that he was advancing much that was well worth thinking about, but was too much neglected. Above all it seemed most absurd to pretend to despise such men."[21] Here, one might say, was lively proof of the efficacy of Newman's approach to evangelizing his sceptical contemporaries. Yet MacMillan also shows how difficult a task Newman had set himself in an England where conceding the appeal of scepticism did not invariably lead men to entertain the antidote to scepticism. When Newman attacked what MacMillan referred to as the "weakness and self-sufficiency of 'our enlightened age,'" the publisher recognized that "some might think him an atheist." Indeed, for MacMillan,

> he seems to make the solid earth shake beneath you. And yet I think he is a good man; and he has great faith in goodness. One may learn many things from him, but I should be sorry to make him, or any of the class of which he is the most powerful member, my guide in spiritual matters. After leaving Newman, who

[19] Hutton, *Modern Guides*, 71–2.
[20] Thomas Hughes, *Memoir of Daniel Macmillan* (London: Macmillan & Co., 1883), 109–10. Another contemporary who found Newman's turn of mind upsetting was J. C. Hare, who wrote: "Logic is ever his favorite weapon, his Harlequin's sword, with which he works whatever transformations he pleases." Julius Charles Hare, *The Contest with Rome: A Charge to the Clergy* (London: John W. Parker & Son, 1852), 106.
[21] MacMillan quoted in James David Earnest and Gerard Tracey, "Introductory Essay," in *US*, cxiii.

somewhat bewilders one, it is such a relief to turn to Leighton, or Coleridge, or Maurice, or Trench, or Hare, men who have the most unwavering faith not merely "a balance of probabilities" on their side.[22]

Here, one can see that Newman's attempts to meet his sceptical audience half-way by invoking Butler's "balance of probabilities" was not always persuasive. Hutton would find this argument dubious as well.[23] Nevertheless, it is striking that Newman should have elicited the response he received from MacMillan, a man whose initial success as a publisher was attributable to the publication of Charles Kingsley's best-selling *Westward Ho!* (1853), an historical romance set in the time of Queen Elizabeth in which the author touted his "muscular Christianity." W. R. Greg got at the heart of the book's pell-mell ardor when he wrote:

> What unspeakable relief and joy for a Christian like Mr Kingsley, whom God has made boiling over with animal eagerness and fierce aggressive instincts, to feel that he is not called upon to control these instincts, but only to direct them; and that once having, or fancying that he has, in view a man or an institution that is God's enemy as well as his, he may hate it with a perfect hatred, and go at it *en sabreur*! Accordingly he reminds us of nothing so much as of a war-horse panting for the battle ... the dust of the combat is to him the breath of life; and when once, in the plenitude of grace and faith, fairly let loose upon his prey—human, moral, or material—all the Red Indian within him comes to the surface, and he wields his tomahawk with an unbaptized heartiness, slightly heathenish, no doubt, but withal unspeakably refreshing.[24]

After Daniel's death, Alexander took control of the family publishing firm and founded *Macmillan's Magazine*, in which Kingsley's attack on Newman's veracity appeared. If Daniel himself could not bring himself to be persuaded by Newman's *Oxford University Sermons*, the family's publishing business would willy-nilly advance Newman's exculpatory purposes by furnishing the spark for the *Apologia*.[25]

A good example of Hutton's preoccupation with the unseen, as well as his readiness to find fault with Newman's work where he felt fault was reasonably evident, can be seen in his preparation for a popular lecture on Newman's writings for the Working Men's College in Great Ormond Street, in which he wrote in

---

[22] MacMillan quoted in Thomas Hughes, *Memoir of Daniel MacMillan* (London: Macmillan & Co., 1882), 110.

[23] "The more I think of it the less can I understand how any accumulation of probabilities is to amount to certainty at all, or how moral certainty, short of mathematical, can be *in the strictest sense* certainty at all," Hutton wrote Newman in 1872. "If you put the letters of a line of Virgil into a box and after shaking them well up draw them out one by one, there is of course a mathematical possibility that you would draw them out in the old order; indeed there is *just* as much chance of that particular arrangement as of any other *specified* arrangement, and therefore there is of course a possibility. But no accumulation of practical probabilities such as you describe in the Grammar of Assent could come as near to certainty as the opinion of the man who expects that the letters will *not* be drawn out in that order." Richard Holt Hutton to Newman (20 February 1872), LD, xxvi, 39.

[24] W. R. Greg, *Literary and Social Judgments* (London: N. Trubner & Co., 1869), 114.

[25] Macmillan & Co. would also publish all of Hutton's books, with the exception of his biography of Newman, which was published in Methuen's "England's Leaders of Religion" series.

1883 to Newman: "in looking over your more popular writings again I am much struck by ... the apparent absence of any difficulty as to the moral degeneracy of the Papacy in the time preceding the reformation. To the ordinary Protestant mind it seems the most paradoxical of all assumptions that the centre of unity, doctrine, and even moral faith should be assumed to be in an office liable to be filled by absolutely wicked men, so that the Holy Spirit should have to overrule as it were, for the benefit of the Church, the words and acts of a Judas Iscariot almost—indeed of a Judas Iscariot without his remorse."[26] Newman's response can only have reassured Hutton of his correspondent's intellectual openhandedness, as well as his own respect for Newman's insights into the excursions of Providence. "As to your question, I have written very little certainly of the shocking spectacle the Popes presented to the world in the times introductory to the Reformation,[27] and I don't know the history well," Newman wrote to Hutton.

> But I am far from wishing to shirk the argument against us—just the reverse, I think 1. that nothing would do more good than a candid confession,—and that nothing is more stupid than to attempt to disguise facts. 2. I think that it would bring out much high religious excellence in the worst times, and how many powerful protests and denunciations there were on the part of holy men. And 3. it sets off the wonderful recovery which followed the bad time. Think of the life of St Philip, what he found in Rome and what he did there, so that his great title is "*Apostolo* di Roma." The recent life of him by Archbishop Capecelatro brings out this vividly.[28] Indeed the outburst of Saints in 1500–1600 after the monstrous corruption seems to me one of the great arguments for Christianity. It is the third marvellous phenomenon in its history; the conversion of the Roman Empire, the reaction under Hildebrand, the resurrection under Ignatius, Teresa, Vincent and a host of others. Think of the contrast between Alexander VI and Pius V, think of the Cardinals of the beginning, and then those of the end of the sixteenth century. One must not wish evil that good may come, but I am reminded of the Church's words on Holy Saturday, "O certe necessarium Adæ peccatum, quod Christi morte deletum est! O felix culpa, quae talem et tantum meruit habere Redemptorem!"[29]

Hutton recognized yet another proof of Newman's witness to the unseen world in his readiness to subordinate his considerable literary talent to the defence of

---

[26] Hutton to Newman (14 January 1884), *LD*, xxx, 263.

[27] Newman did, however, call Hutton's attention to something he said in his *Letter to the Duke of Norfolk* (1875) on the matter, namely that "For a while the Papal Chair was filled by men who gave themselves up to luxury, security, and a pagan kind of Christianity; and we all know what a moral earthquake was the consequence, and how the Church lost thereby and has lost to this day, one half of Europe." *Diff.*, ii, 254.

[28] Alfonso Capecelatro, *La Vita di S. Filippo Neri*, 2 vols (Naples 1879), English trans. by T. A. Pope (London, 1882).

[29] Newman to Hutton (12 October 1883), *LD*, xxx, 264. The Latin is from the *Exultet* and can be translated: "O surely necessary sin of Adam which was wiped out by the death of Christ, O happy fault, which merited such and so great a Redeemer." This is what the Church sings at every Easter in the first proclamation of the glory of the Resurrection at the Vigil. Her understanding of original sin in God's plan for our salvation was authoritatively expounded by St. Augustine of Hippo and the later councils of Orange in France, as well as the Council of Trent.

the Christian faith, for which he had sacrificed so much. For Hutton, "His literary power has been so great ... that the highest literary eminence was easily within his reach, had he cared to win it, long before his name was actually known to the world at large; and he would have been a great power in literature had he cared to devote himself to literature in the wider sense, before the Oxford movement had begun to cause anxiety in the Established Church." Although many acknowledged Newman's mastery of English prose in his own lifetime, few recognized how averse Newman was to exploiting this mastery for any meretricious success—"power of this kind," as Hutton rightly notes, being "precisely what he never coveted." Indeed, he could be amusingly disparaging of literary talent. Towards the end of his life, he wrote to his well-read sister Jemima:

> Apparently all my ailments have left me quite. And I have had no cold or cough for some years. I have nothing the matter with me but age—and I sensibly grow older. Now I fancy that, if I were careless and took too much work, paralysis would be my lot—as it was the lot of Keble, (Keble's brother), Whately, Milman, Walter Scott, Southey, and so many other literary men. There is a story in the middle ages of some sharp schoolman, who made a speech in proof of Christianity—and, when applauded by his hearers, said "O good Jesus, I could confute you as easily as I have proved you," on which he was immediately struck dumb and motionless, and never spoke again. I suppose it was paralysis; but I often think that that complaint, as attacking literary men, is the providential means of keeping them from over-estimation of their talent.[30]

Even the Dean of St. Paul's, William Inge (1860-1954), with whom Hilaire Belloc exchanged such choice, excoriating words, and who was never uncritical of Newman, recognized how indifferent the convert was to any literary distinction. "There are no cheap effects in any of Newman's writings," Inge wrote.

> He is the most undemocratic of teachers. Such men do what can be done to save a nation from itself, its natural enemy. They are not indifferent to fame, because they desire influence; but they will do nothing to advertise themselves. The public must come to them; they will not go to the public. There have been other great men who have been as indifferent as Newman to the applause of the vulgar. But they have been generally either pure intellectualists or pure artists, in whom
>
> > The intellectual power through words and things
> > Went sounding on a dim and perilous way.
>
> Newman's confidence towards God was of a still nobler kind. It rested on an unclouded faith in the Divine guidance, and on a very just estimate of the worthlessness of contemporary praise and blame. There have been very few men who have been able to combine so strong a faith with a thorough distrust of both logic-chopping and emotional excitement, and who, while denying themselves these aids to conviction, have been able to say, calmly and without petulance, that with them it is a very small thing to be judged of man's judgment.

---

[30] Newman to Mrs. John Mozley (25 January 1870), *LD*, xxv, 12–13.

"What [he asks] can increase their peace who believe and trust in the Son of God? Shall we add a drop to the ocean, or grains to the sand of the sea? Shall we ask for an earthly inheritance, who have the fulness of an heavenly one; power, when in prayer we can use the power of Christ; or wisdom, guided as we may be by the true Wisdom and Light of men? It is in this sense that the Gospel of Christ is a leveler of ranks: we pay, indeed, our superiors full reverence, and with cheerfulness as unto the Lord; and we honour eminent talents as deserving admiration and reward; and the more readily act we thus, because these are little things to pay."

Such unworldliness as this, in the well-chosen words of R. H. Hutton, "stands out in strange and almost majestic contrast to the eager turmoil of confused passions, hesitating ideals, tentative virtues, and groping philanthropies, amidst which it was lived." Another mark of greatness is unbroken consistency and unity of aim in a long life. There are few parallels to the neglect of his own literary reputation by Newman. Higher interests, he thought, were at stake; and so he had no dream of building for himself "a monument more durable than brass," and of claiming a pedestal among the great writers of English prose and verse. He accepted long years of literary barrenness; he wrote historical essays for which he had no special aptitude, and dogmatic disquisitions which even his genius could not save from dulness; he even descended into mere journalism. The "Apologia" would probably not have been written but for the accident of Kingsley's attack. It has, no doubt, been said with truth that Newman showed great dexterity in choosing opponents with whom to cross swords—Kingsley, Pusey, Gladstone, and his old Anglican self. But this does not alter the fact that a man who must have been conscious of rare literary gifts made no attempt to immortalise himself by them. It was for the Church, and not for himself, that he wrote as well as lived.[31]

Although Hutton might have been right about the admirable self-effacement with which Newman conducted his literary talents, he is oddly mistaken when he writes slightingly of Newman's Anglican writings, even if we concede that Newman's first book on the Arians did not exhibit his literary capabilities at their best. "The history of the Arian heresy is a very clear and accurate but a very homely, not to say dry, theological discussion," Hutton complained. "And for the next thirteen years at least, that is, from the thirty-second to the forty-fifth year of his life, it was only in a few short poems, and a few of the later University sermons, that he betrayed his strange mastery of literary effect."[32] Of course, this fails to take into account some of Newman's greatest writing, from a strictly literary standpoint, including his *Parochial and Plain Sermons*, his *Tamworth Reading Room*, his *Sermons on Subjects of the Day*, and, of course, his *Essay on the Development of Christian Doctrine*, though Hutton was right to acknowledge the peculiar excellence of his *Oxford University Sermons*, about which Newman might have said what Samuel Johnson said of his *Rambler* (1750–2) essays: "My

---

[31] William Ralph Inge. *Outspoken Essays* (London: Longmans Green, 1919), 202–3. The quotation within the passage is from Newman's sermon, "Temporal Advantages" (1825), *PS*, vii, 72–3.
[32] Hutton, *Cardinal Newman*, 10.

other works are wine and water; but my *Rambler* is pure wine."³³ For Newman, the *Oxford University Sermons*, pointing as they did not only to his *Essay on Development* and his *Grammar of Assent* but his *Apologia*, were "the best, not the most perfect book I have done. I mean there is more to develop in it though it is imperfect."³⁴ At the same time, as he told a correspondent in 1853, "I *stand by* my (Oxford) University Discourses ... and am almost a zealot for their substantial truth— ... if I have brought out one truth in any thing I have written, I consider it to be the *importance of antecedent probability* in conviction.³⁵ It is how you convert factory girls as well as philosophers."³⁶

II

To acknowledge Hutton's literary shortcomings is important because the value of his writings on Newman does not depend so much on their critical rigor as their critical sympathy. Coming as he did from a Socinian background, Hutton could hardly be blamed for not knowing the Church's profound tradition of

---

[33] Johnson quoted in *Samuel Roger's Table Talk* (1760). See *The Yale Edition of the Works of Samuel Johnson: Volume III: The Rambler* (New Haven: Yale University Press, 1958), xxiv.

[34] Newman quoted in Ward, *Life of Newman*, i, 58. See also Earnest and Tracey, "Editor's Introduction," *US*, cxiv. "After Newman arrived in Rome on 26 October 1846, he arranged for copies of some of his works, including the *University Sermons*, to be sent to him. At about the same time, at the suggestion of John Dobrée Dalgairns in France, the project of translating some of his *University Sermons* began. Dealing with a theologically sensitive topic, they were to be the first test of whether his Anglican writings would prove reasonably harmonious with Catholic doctrine, and the French translation was to make them more accessible to Catholic theologians, particularly in Rome, where he had been met warily. On 13 December, he wrote, 'I am curious to know what will be the fate of my University Sermons in my own judgment, when I have got up the subject catholicly.' On 10 January 1847, however, Newman was writing to Dalgairns, '... I am both surprised and pleased to hear what you say about my University Sermons—for though I feel confident they are in the main Catholic, yet I doubted whether they did not require considerable alteration in phraseology, as indeed I have hinted in the Preface.' Yet Newman's nervousness continued, and in the important letter to Dalgairns of 8 February he says he is 'terribly frightened lest the book ... should be brought before the Index.' Yet later in the same letter he remarks, 'after reading the Sermons I must say I think they are, as a whole, the best things I have written, and I cannot believe they are not Catholic, and will be useful.'"

[35] Cf. "*Revue Catholique*, 9 (June 1851), pp. 169–75, a review of the French translation of *US*. It accepted Newman's doctrine of the importance of antecedent probability, e.g., as to how an infinitely good God would act. "Nos inclinations, les désirs de notre cœur, des opinions préconçues, voilà donc les principaux motifs de crédibilité; et joints à l'évidence du témoignage quelque faible qu'elle soit d'ailleurs, ils font que l'esprit du croyant adhère à la vérité sans faiblesse comme sans témérité." This is one of several passages marked, almost certainly by Newman, in the copy at the Birmingham Oratory. *LD*, xv, 381, note 2.

[36] Newman to Edward Healey Thompson (12 June 1853), *LD*, xv, 381. What makes Newman's reference to factory girls so interesting is that he would quote Elizabeth Gaskell's novel *North and South* (1855) in the *Grammar of Assent* to show how factory girls could actually help convert readers of works of Christian epistemology. "I think," says the poor dying factory-girl in the tale, "if this should be the end of all, and if all I have been born for is just to work my heart and life away, and to sicken in this dree place, with those mill-stones in my ears for ever, until I could scream out for them to stop and let me have a little piece of quiet, and with the fluff filling my lungs, until I thirst to death for one long deep breath of the clear air, and my mother gone, and I never able to tell her again how I loved her, and of all my troubles,—I think, if this life is the end, and that there is no God to wipe away all tears from all eyes, I could go mad!" To which Newman tersely adds: "Here is an argument for the immortality of the soul." (*GA*, 312)

faith and reason—a tradition Newman sought to reintroduce into a pitiably de-Christianized England. And yet he made up for this ignorance, to some lively degree, by encountering truths in Newman's personal influence that he might never have encountered elsewhere. In reading his writings on Newman, we should always keep in mind that while Hutton might have begun life a Unitarian he grew into a High Church Anglican, and this largely as the result of Newman's influence, even though F. D. Maurice was also key to his abandoning Unitarianism. ("There was the lavishness of the eternal world in all his efforts," Hutton wrote of Maurice, "though there was all the humiliation of human inadequacy too.")[37] In this regard, Hutton was proof of Newman's contention that most people can find their religious convictions somewhere between the poles of atheism on the one hand and Roman Catholicism on the other. Another factor to bear in mind with regard to Hutton is how he appealed to Newman personally, even though the two men met only once in Hutton's London offices after the publication of the *Apologia*. Considering the dismay that Newman suffered on seeing his brother Francis fall prey to Unitarianism, after being brought up, as he had been brought up, in the Anglican Church, he would naturally have rejoiced to see Hutton taking the opposite path from Unitarianism to Anglicanism.[38] In Hutton's own relation of his religious development, one can see the grateful humility in the man that so endeared itself to Newman. "To me the most touching and satisfying words that have ever been uttered by human lips are those which no mere man could ever have uttered without jarring every chord in the human conscience," Hutton wrote, before quoting from Scripture.

> At that time Jesus answered and said, "I thank thee, O Father, Lord of heaven and earth, because thou hast hid these things from the wise and prudent, and hast revealed them to babes: even so, Father, for so it seemed good in thy sight. All things are delivered unto me by my Father; and no man knoweth the Son but the Father; neither knoweth any man the Father, save the Son, and he to whomsoever the Son will reveal him. Come unto me, all ye that labour and are heavy laden and I will give you rest. Take my yoke upon you, and learn of me, for I am meek and lowly in heart, and ye shall find rest unto your souls: for my yoke is easy and my burden is light."[39]

Here was the triumph of what Victorian Unitarians often called "Trinitarianism," and it infused Hutton's appreciation of Newman's work—indeed, Newman's work was largely responsible for instilling it in Hutton himself in the first place. In other words, it is sympathy that enables Hutton to speak of Newman's work so reliably and so luminously, the same sympathy to which a contemporary critic of Hutton's work attested when he wrote that "great imaginative sympathy ... is revealed ... in a great many of Mr Hutton's best essays."[40]

At the same time, it is important to stress that Hutton's sympathy with Newman

---

[37] Hutton, *Modern Guides*, 315.
[38] See Edward Short, "Frank Newman and the Search for Truth," in *Newman and his Family* (London: Bloomsbury, 2013), 141–208.
[39] Matthew 11:25–30.
[40] Richard Hogben, *Richard Hutton of the Spectator* (Edinburgh: Oliver and Bond, 1899), 29.

and his religious convictions had its distinct limits, though even when he took issue with the convert he did so with a certain *tenderness*, to use a word he uses himself when describing Newman's rhetorical suavity. A good example of this can be seen in the good word Hutton has for the Ultramontanes in the wake of Pius IX's *Syllabus* and the First Vatican Council.

> To our minds Rome does the Protestant world a great service, and even her own converts the very opposite of a disservice, by making them understand vividly, before they join her, the yoke she claims to impose upon their intellects. Nothing has had that effect more conspicuously than the teaching of the Ultramontane school, and we believe that without that teaching there might have been far more misunderstanding than there is. Converts, as a rule, import the habits of mind in which they have been trained into their new faith, and find it most difficult and painful, if not sometimes utterly destructive to their belief, to unlearn them. It is well, then, not to underrate the character of the change required of them, and were all Roman Catholic teachers as tender and subtle as Dr. Newman, that mistake would be oftener made. Englishmen may be apt to exaggerate what they think the idolatrous side of the Roman faith, but they hardly ever appreciate even adequately its steady intellectual pressure. There is far more danger of that being underrated than overrated. And to our minds, the sharp, imperious character attributed by the Ultramontane teaching to the Roman faith is far more likely to convey to Englishmen the practical truth about Rome than the delicate lights and shades, the subtleties, the distinctions, the anxious moderation of Dr. Newman's descriptions. Protestants need distinct warning against Rome. Romanizing Anglicans need a very difficult lesson as to the three requirements of the Church they are approaching. Without the Ultramontanes neither lesson would have been adequately taught. Dr. Newman certainly would never have taught it.[41]

Hutton's discomfiture with what he regarded as the inescapably Ultramontane character of Catholic dogma also colored his view of Newman's opposition to liberalism, which he expressed at the very end of his biography of the convert. While it is clear that many of Hutton's pieces on Newman commend the convert's readiness to take the rationalism of his age to task, it is not so clear that he was convinced that rationalism was an inveterate accompaniment of liberalism. "It is of course perfectly true that from the very beginning of his career Newman has been a steady advocate of what is called dogmatic Christianity," Hutton wrote,

> that is, Christianity which is not a formless and gelatinous mass of vague sentiment, but which springs from a deeply-planted seed of revealed doctrine, and has been, in his opinion, developed organically and providentially from that original germ. But is "Liberalism in Religion" a happy description of the anti-dogmatic attitude of mind? I should have thought not. Liberalism is probably

---

[41] Richard Holt Hutton, "Dr. Newman and Rome," *Spectator* (16 Rome 1875). Newman's own response to the *Syllabus* was bemused. "As to the Encyclical and Syllabus, I don't understand its meaning or its worth. Condemned propositions, as I have hitherto understood them, are propositions taken from the writings of *Catholics*. But what jurisdiction has the Church over statements which are made by the external world?" Newman to William Monsell (12 January 1865), *LD*, xxi, 385.

oftener used to signify the disposition to make concessions to popular demands than in any other sense, and it is by no means clear that the popular mind does demand the relaxation of dogmatic restraints on the Babel-like confusion of religious opinions. In one sense Newman has been a steady foe of dogmatic tyranny; virtually he received his Cardinal's hat because he had contended so boldly against any attempt to invade freedom of conscience in the Church. His doctrine has always been that private conscientiousness is the first step towards orthodoxy, and that any attempt to interfere with true liberty of conscience, or even to spur and hurry on its natural pace by external pressure, is in the highest degree dangerous to the cause of true belief.[42]

Here, we can see not only the pitfalls to which even incisive commentators fall prey when they take it into their heads to paraphrase Newman, especially on such involved matters as liberalism and the dogmatic principle, but the risks all commentators run when they make assumptions about what Newman may or may not have thought on such matters without paying close attention to his own stated views. No one who has studied Newman's anatomy of liberalism with any attentiveness would ever say that it is somehow wide of the mark because "Liberalism is probably oftener used to signify the disposition to make concessions to popular demands than in any other sense, and it is by no means clear that the popular mind does demand the relaxation of dogmatic restraints on the Babel-like confusion of religious opinions." Simply because Hutton imagined that liberalism inhered in making "concessions to popular demands" does not invalidate Newman's contention that it inhered precisely in the usurpation and infidelity to which rationalism gives rise, a contention for which there is too much demonstrable evidence for persuasive rebuttal.[43] Nor would anyone familiar with Newman's opposition to the extremer expressions of Ultramontanism cite it as somehow antagonistic to his advocacy of the dogmatic principle. Newman took issue with such Ultramontanism not because it was dogmatic *per se* but because it was heedless of the limitations of dogma. Still, if such statements shed little light on Newman's actual views on these matters, they do illumine Hutton's views. For example, in a commemorative piece on Dean Stanley, written in 1881, he was careful to stress that "Seldom has such a gallant knight-errant in ecclesiastical matters been so utterly without a dogmatic inspiration as Dean Stanley. There

---

[42] Hutton, *Cardinal Newman*, 242–3.
[43] See "Newman and the Liberals," Edward Short, *Newman and History* (Leominster: Gracewing, 2017), 135–202. The French theologian Yves Congar regarded Newman as "a great genius" precisely because of his sense of history. "Every time I return to Newman," he wrote in 1982, "I admire the extraordinary balance of this man—a rock from the point of view of the faith—I mean the dogmatic faith—and at the same time the openness, the sense of history; I believe he was so because of his sense of history. Though a historian of Arianism, he made many other great sketches of historical figures and epochs. I think it is to this that he owes his concrete realism … I admire this kind of wisdom that history gives him." For Congar, Newman's sense of history gave the prophetic convert not only "a knowledge of the past," but "a wisdom for the present and … the future." Congar quoted in Andrew Meszaros, *The Prophetic Church and Doctrinal Development in John Henry Newman and Yves Congar* (Oxford: Oxford University Press, 2016), 53. This nicely refutes the editor of Acton's letters to Richard Simpson, who claimed that Newman's "commitment to religion was too profound to allow him to submit to the rival discipline of history." See Josef L. Altholz, "Newman and History," *Victorian Studies*, 7, no. 3 (March 1964), pp. 285–94.

have been hundreds who, like Archdeacon Denison, would fight to the death for a dogma, to one who, like the late Dean of Westminster, would fight to the death in order to relax in all directions the binding force of dogmatic decisions. In truth, he discerned clearly enough how often dogmatic belief chokes religious life; but he was nearly incapable of understanding the equally important truth, how often dogmatic belief strengthens and ennobles the life which is honestly lived by its guidance."[44] Reading this, one might wonder with whom Hutton sympathized more: Newman or those of whom Burne-Jones spoke, who "beginning to weary of the vehement ardour of Newman," welcomed the "gentle kind of liberalism" that Stanley brought into religious questions to shore up, as he thought, an increasingly enfeebled National Church.

In a piece written the *Spectator* in 1879 after Newman received his red hat entitled "Cardinal Newman on Liberalism in Religion," Hutton spoke of Newman's lifelong campaign against liberalism with arresting ambivalence.

> For some time back a discussion has been going on in the English Press as to the proper word to describe Cardinal Newman's type of Roman Catholicism. Should he be called a Liberal, or a Conservative? Should he rank as one who wishes to modify the system of the Roman Church in the Liberal sense, or who wishes to fortify it in the Conservative sense? Cardinal Newman answers the question by an address, in which he rehearses and repeats what he has been saying for forty years as to the principle which he, at least, has always termed "Liberalism in Religion." To that principle he is as steadfastly opposed as ever. But what is it precisely that he means by it? He means by it the teaching that religion is a matter of feeling, rather than of truth; that it is a sentiment, not a revelation; that it need not rest on any positive basis of clear conviction; that it is a vague sensibility, which may be trusted to grope its way into a kind of sympathy with very many different forms of creed, without really accepting any; and that, consequently, all religious opinions should be treated as purely subjective, and so far as possible eliminated from public life and political organisation.

This is a fair paraphrase of the definition that Newman gave to his opposition to liberalism in his Biglietto speech, but Hutton goes on to suggest that Newman's adherence to this opposition had undergone a marked change as he aged.

> It is now a great many years since Cardinal Newman, then, we believe, Vicar of St. Mary's, Oxford, preached a sermon, on the "Religion of the Day," in which he avowed his firm conviction that "it would be a gain to this country were it vastly more superstitious, more bigoted, more gloomy, more fierce in its religion, than at present it shows itself to be. Not, of course, that I think the tempers of mind herein implied desirable, which would be an evident absurdity; but I think them eminently more desirable and more promising than a heathen obduracy, and a cold, self-sufficient, self-wise tranquillity." Referring to the then uppermost phase of religion of the educated world, "full as it is of security, and cheerfulness, and decorum, and benevolence," "I observe," said Dr. Newman, in the same sermon,

---

[44] Richard Holt Hutton, *Criticisms of Contemporary Thought and Thinkers: Selected from the Spectator* (London: Macmillan & Co., 1891), ii, 135.

"that these appearances may arise either from a great deal of religion, or from the absence of it; they may be the fruits of shallowness of mind and a blinded conscience, or of that faith which has peace with God through our Lord Jesus Christ. And if this alternative be proposed, I leave it to the common-sense of men to decide (if they could get themselves to think seriously) to which of the two the temper of the age is to be referred." That was an attack on the spirit of "Liberalism in Religion," by the Vicar of St. Mary's, Oxford, certainly sharper in tone than the new one delivered by Cardinal Newman to his Roman Catholic audience in Rome; and on the whole, we should say that the spirit of the new Cardinal's latest and maturest utterance, though identical in substance with convictions held by him long before he became a Roman Catholic, is milder and more hopeful than the spirit of his words on the same subject in his earlier days.[45]

For Newman, hope was never a vague, wishful, sentimental thing. "Hope," he said in his "Sermon on the Liturgy" (1830), "is the patient subdued tranquil cheerful thoughtful waiting for Christ."[46] For Hutton, Newman might still believe that "Liberalism in religion, as he calls it, is fatal to all religion, and ... imports (as who can doubt that it really does?) the speedy and rapid decay of all deep religious conviction. But he holds this belief now—if we may judge from the tone of his speech on Monday—with more sense of the misfortune of the case, and less of the sin, with more hope for the revival of serious belief under the very reign of secularism itself, and less indignation against the empty self-complacency of Liberalism in religion, than he did."[47] This may be true but it certainly does not take into account the context that Newman described as providing the spur for his campaign against liberalism. "Hitherto the civil Power has been Christian," Newman reminded his English, American and Italian auditors.

> Even in countries separated from the Church, as in my own, the *dictum* was in force, when I was young, that: "Christianity was the law of the land". Now, everywhere that goodly framework of society, which is the creation of Christianity, is throwing off Christianity. The *dictum* to which I have referred, with a hundred

---

[45] Richard Holt Hutton, "Cardinal Newman on Liberalism in Religion," *Spectator* (1879).
[46] Cf. "theological hope is necessary to perceive a path leading closer to the First Truth in all the debates ... surrounding the future of the Church's teaching. St. Thomas writes that in order for the object of hope to be what it is (namely, an object of *hope*), it be must be possible, but "arduous and difficult to obtain." But it nevertheless pertains to the virtue of hope that the Pilgrim and Prophetic Church, in her ongoing struggle can expect not only to obtain the Kingdom, but also to be provided with the means, such as endurance in her teaching, to attain it as promised. As Newman reminds us, 'the worse our condition is, the nearer to us is the Advent of our Deliverer." Meszaros, *The Prophetic Church*, 243. The quotation from Newman is from his sermon, "The Secrecy and Suddenness of Divine Visitations (1831), *PS*, ii, 115: "Let us carry this thought into our daily conduct," Newman exhorted his auditors at St. Mary's, "considering that, for what we know, our hope of salvation may in the event materially depend on our avoiding this or that momentary sin. And further, from the occurrences of this day let us take comfort, when we despond about the state of the Church. Perhaps we see not God's tokens; we see neither prophet nor teacher remaining to His people; darkness falls over the earth, and no protesting voice is heard. Yet, granting things to be at the very worst, still, when Christ was presented in the Temple, the age knew as little of it as it knows of His providence now. Rather, the worse our condition is, the nearer to us is the Advent of our Deliverer."
[47] Hutton, "Cardinal Newman on Liberalism in Religion."

others which followed upon it, is gone, or is going everywhere; and, by the end of the century, unless the Almighty interferes, it will be *forgotten*. Hitherto, it has been considered that religion alone, with its supernatural sanctions, was strong enough to secure submission of the masses of our population to law and order; now the Philosophers and Politicians are bent on satisfying this problem without the aid of Christianity. ... As to Religion, it is a private luxury, which a man may have if he will; but which of course he must pay for, and which he must not obtrude upon others, or indulge in to their annoyance.[48]

From this parlous state of affairs, Newman drew a conclusion that was as stark as it was prophetic: "The general character of this great *apostasia* is one and the same everywhere."[49] In response to Newman's assessment of matters, Hutton ventured his own theory of what he regarded as the real import of liberalism, which called into question Newman's lifelong campaign against it.

> For the defect of Dr. Newman's view of Liberalism in religion ... is this, that it does not account for the fact that on all sides of religious belief, the opinions which were once most rigid and definite seem to be those which have most rapidly become formal, hollow, and unreal. The old Evangelical system was rigid and definite, if ever a system was rigid and definite. Where is it now? To what school of thought does the sentimental decay of modem religion which Dr. Newman regrets, owe more of its adherents than to the school once called Evangelical? Again, where shall we look for less reality of intellectual life at least, than to the modern Ritualists, who found themselves, if ever any religious section of thinkers founded themselves, on most definite and rigid standards of orthodoxy, both theological and devotional? Again, probably Dr. Newman would himself be inclined to admit that it is the most rigid party in his own Church which has recently most endangered the hold of that Church on the world at large. It is the narrow kind of rigidity in relation to religious opinion which all over the world, among the Roman Catholics, among the Anglicans, among the Wesleyans, among the Independents, among the Scotch Presbyterians, and among the Unitarians, has most seriously endangered the belief of the world, and does most to prejudice Christianity in the eyes of those belonging to the same fold as the theological martinets themselves. Take which church you will, and you will find that in proportion to the definiteness and rigour of the systematic theology enforced by it, has been the reaction against faith,—that only those teachers who have given a large and genial and modest interpretation to the outlines of their creed have kept their hold on the adhesion of their disciples. Cardinal Newman can himself testify to this from a long personal experience, in relation at least to his own Church; and the chiefs of the more liberal movements in probably every other Church have had a good deal of the same experience. How, then, shall we account for this apparent paradox, that while "Liberalism in religion," when pushed to the point indicated by Cardinal Newman, is destructive of all faith, the stricter Conservatism seems even more destructive of it?

---

[48] John Henry Newman, "Biglietto Speech" (1879), *Addresses to Cardinal Newman with His Replies 1879–1881*, ed. W. P. Neville (London: Longmans, Green, & Co., 1905), 61–71.
[49] Ibid., 65–7.

Hutton's own view of the matter is one that has always won favor with those who confuse the doctrinal coherence of Rome with a kind of dogmatism for its own sake.

> Our own explanation would be this,—that the denial of all absoluteness in religious truth, and the attempt to make absolute truths of mere refinements of the human intellect, really play into each other's hands; that Revelation consisted in the presentation of certain great facts and divine objects to the conscience of mankind, real enough and imposing enough to kindle new life and new affections in men, but also far too great and too much beyond us, to admit of those strict, definite, and sharply-marked intellectual outlines which the active intellect of almost all Churches is always endeavouring to draw. Assuredly, no Church has suffered more from the attempt to over-define what is beyond us, than the Church which claims for herself infallibility,—an infallibility which the new Cardinal, while cordially accepting it, is, in conjunction with many others of his Church, most solicitous carefully to limit. Assuredly, if "Liberalism in religion" has been the immediate antecedent of the decay in faith, the immediate antecedent of that Liberalism has been a kind of dogmatism for which, in its relation to theology at least, the human mind is quite unfitted, and against which, in our belief at least, Revelation itself is full of warning.[50]

This, one might say, is an intriguing theory. Yet it is a theory that can only hold water if we assume, as Hutton assumed, that the Roman Church's claim to infallibility is unfounded. If we hold that the Church's claim to infallibility, derived as it is from God Himself, is not unfounded, Hutton's claim that this same infallibility is at once "unfitted" to the human mind and "destructive of all faith" is unsustainable. After all, the "dogmatism" that Hutton deplored, and, indeed, which Newman deplored, was not an expression of the dogma of infallibility; it was a travesty of that dogma. Moreover, the liberalism that Newman opposed from the 1820s onwards cannot be said to have been caused by Ultramontanism, which only emerges, in the sense in which Hutton refers to it, in the 1860s, in response to Pius IX's *Syllabus of Errors* (1864) and the fraught prelude to the First Vatican Council (1870). The liberalism that Newman opposed can be traced back to the Jacobinism of the French Revolution—or even further back to the Arian crisis of the fourth century.[51] Lastly, by Hutton's own admission elsewhere, the "stricter Conservativism" to which he adverts here was not destructive of belief: Pope Pius IX's hugely popular papacy is proof of that. Then, again, another aspect of liberalism, to which Hutton could hardly have referred, has been the degree of its destructiveness.[52] "The devastation wrought by Liberalism within the Church of England in the nineteenth century," Michael Davies wrote in 1978 in a preface to his selection of Newman's sermons, "has been magnified a thousandfold within the Catholic Church since the Second Vatican Council. It seems hard to believe that much of what is included in [Newman's *Parochial and Plain Sermons*]

---

[50] Hutton, "Cardinal Newman on Liberalism in Religion."
[51] Newman's shrewd sense of history made him peculiarly alive to the long-evolving evils of the rationalism inseparable from liberalism.
[52] See Ward's point regarding Newman's appreciation of this destructiveness, Ward, *Life of Newman*, i, 460–71.

was not addressed specifically to the contemporary situation within Western Catholicism."[53] In the same preface, he quotes W. J. Copeland, one of the first historians of the Oxford Movement, who said in his 1882 edition of the sermons: "To many of this generation [the *Parochial and Plain Sermons*] will appear in much of their original freshness; and to all with the greater power and reality, from the saddening aspect of the times, and the appalling prospects before us, replete as they are with those 'many secrets of religion, which are not perceived till they be felt, and not felt, but in the day of calamity.'"[54] Both Copeland and Davies, of course, were writing before the work of Pope John Paul II and Pope Benedict XVI sought to establish what the latter called "the hermeneutic of continuity,"[55] in the wake of the discontinuity brought about by those faithful to what they regarded as the spirit of the Council, though neither pope managed to stave off the calamitous liberalism of the twenty-first century, which has borne out all of Davies' worst suspicions as to what the real issue of the Council would be. Reinhard Hütter puts that issue in a nutshell: "One of the subtle strategies for advancing theological liberalism has been to co-opt Newman in such a way as to make him appear to support—indeed to legitimize—the very counterfeits produced by the spirit of liberalism in religion that he unmasks and refutes."[56]

In reading Hutton's assessment of Newman's campaign against liberalism, it is important to keep in mind that he formulated his theory five days after Newman delivered his speech on 12 May 1879. It was not his considered view of the matter. In light of the history of liberalism after Newman's death, one is tempted to speculate what Hutton would have made of the assessment Pio Nono's biographer made of the opposition against liberalism, in which both Newman and the controversial pope joined. "It was Pio Nono's fate, after traveling with sympathy, in his earlier years, more than half way to meet the Revolution, to be compelled, though not naturally a fighter, to turn and withstand its pretensions," Edward Hales wrote. "He died a hero to his followers, to the world, apparently, a failure. Few thoughtful men, in 1900, thought he had been right ... But we today [Hales was writing in 1954], who have met the children and the grandchildren of European Liberalism and the Revolution, who have seen Mazzini turn into Mussolini, Herder into Hitler, and the idealistic early socialists into the intransigent communists are able from a new vantage ground to consider once more whether Pio Nono, or the optimistic believers in an infallible progress, like his cultured friend Pasolini, will have in the eyes of eternity, the better of the argument."[57]

Nevertheless, Hutton was certainly right that Newman, as he aged, looked upon the accelerating menace of apostasy with a certain faithful aplomb. "Such is the state of things in England, and it is well that it should be realised by all of us," Newman told his auditors at the Palazzo delle Pigna where he gave his *Biglietto* speech;

---

[53] Michael Davies, "Preface," in *Newman against the Liberals: 25 Classic Sermons by John Henry Newman*, ed. Michael Davies (New York: Arlington Publishers, 1978), 10.
[54] Ibid., 10–11.
[55] Pope Benedict XVI, "Address of his Holiness Benedict XVI to the Roman Curia Offering Them his Christmas Greetings" (22 December 2005).
[56] Hütter, *Newman on Truth and its Counterfeits*, 4.
[57] Edward Elton Young Hales, *Pio Nono: A Study in European Politics and Religion in the Nineteenth Century* (New York: P. J. Kennedy & Sons, 1954), 331.

but it must not be supposed for a moment that I am afraid of it. I lament it deeply, because I foresee that it may be the ruin of many souls; but I have no fear at all that it really can do aught of serious harm to the Word of God, to Holy Church, to our Almighty King, the Lion of the tribe of Judah, Faithful and True, or to His Vicar on earth. Christianity has been too often in what seemed deadly peril, that we should fear for it any new trial now. So far is certain; on the other hand, what is uncertain, and in these great contests commonly is uncertain, and what is commonly a great surprise, when it is witnessed, is the particular mode by which, in the event, Providence rescues and saves His elect inheritance. Sometimes our enemy is turned into a friend; sometimes he is despoiled of that special virulence of evil which was so threatening; sometimes he falls to pieces of himself; sometimes he does just so much as is beneficial, and then is removed. Commonly the Church has nothing more to do than to go on in her own proper duties, in confidence and peace; to stand still and to see the salvation of God.[58]

One welcome proof of this salvation was the changed attitudes towards Catholics since the time of Newman's conversion, about which Newman himself wrote in his address to the citizens of Birmingham, "On the Relations between Catholics and Protestants in England" (1880). In his response to this address in the *Spectator*, Hutton again showed that he regarded the "stricter Conservatism" of Pio Nono as increasing, not undermining adherence to the Faith.

Cardinal Newman's striking address on the causes of the gentler and more friendly feeling towards Roman Catholics which is now to be found in English society, is, as he himself declared, by no means exhaustive. The reasons he assigns for that kindlier attitude are, first, that after every rush of exaggerated feeling, especially if it be unfair to a class, there is certain to be reaction so soon as it is discovered that the feeling was greatly and very unfairly exaggerated; next, that the terrible consequences which the Protestants had imagined as likely to result from the accession of a Catholic hierarchy in England have not shown themselves, so that the panic about Catholicism has died away; thirdly, that the regard felt in Protestant homes for many of the converts to Catholicism has itself done much to mollify the feeling towards Catholics, to remove prejudices, and to dissipate the idea that all Catholics must resemble Guy Faux or the Duke of Alva; and lastly, that the feeling inspired by the late Pope, Pio Nono,—who was the most perfect representative of high Papal claims, and who yet inspired so much respect and esteem, even among Protestants, by his kindness, eloquence, and humour,—went a great way to remove the notion that Catholics as Catholics, or even Popes as Popes, must be dangerous and malignant beings. Still, says Cardinal Newman, there is no change in the general dislike and distaste felt by Protestants for the religion of Catholics, though they have come to think so much better of those who profess that religion; but this state of things is hardly one, he imagines, which can be permanent. Either the friendly feeling entertained towards individual Catholics must inspire a higher estimate of the religion itself, or the distrust felt of the religion must in time restore the old aversion towards those who profess it.[59]

---

[58] Newman, "Biglietto Speech," 69–70.
[59] Richard Holt Hutton, "Cardinal Newman on England and the Roman Catholics," *Spectator* (31

In the more favorable estimate of Catholics that Newman discerned in his countrymen from the mid to the late nineteenth century, Hutton saw the salutary effect of the *Essay on the Development of Christian Doctrine* (1841). "Has not Dr. Newman's own 'doctrine of development' done much to foster this state of belief, by providing Protestants, no less than Catholics, with a distinct explanation of the mode in which Catholic doctrine might well have grown up, whether that growth were the overflow of a divine care, or simply the mere shooting and sprouting of human germs, sown in close proximity with the divine seed?" Hutton also perceptively recognized that the advocates of unbelief had brought English Catholics and Protestants together in a way that they had never been before. For Hutton, doctrinaire unbelief, "tended, and greatly tended, to mollify men's minds towards the older religion which our fathers used to think the only real seed-ground of Atheism. Say what men might a generation or two ago of the tendency of Sacerdotalism, as such, to turn men into unbelievers, no one now doubts that there are other causes at work in the very heart of the most liberal Churches which not only produce unbelief, but do so without the least pretence that it was the bad effect of a sacerdotal system which had helped to shake faith in God. Modern physics, modern physiology, modern philosophy have certainly much more disbelief to answer for, at the present day, than sacerdotal theories or sacramental principles." The jibes of No Popery no longer told. "The world knows very well where the greater number of its denials now originate, and knows that it is not in the overstraining either of ascetic or sacramental institutions, but rather in the probing of all principles of knowledge and of all principles of evidence. For every such modern victim of the ecclesiastical system, as Blanco White ... we have in our own day a hundred victims of the uncompromising inductive philosophy, or of the legal demand for sifted cross-examination. And clearly this has had the effect not only of making many Protestants think better of Roman Catholics, but also of making many Roman Catholics think better of Protestants,—in fact, of drawing Roman Catholics and Protestants together on the common ground of positive belief in God and in the Christian revelation."[60]

Here, we can see something of the charge that Wilfrid Ward would set himself in his work to show Roman Catholics and Protestants the shared interest they had in appreciating the untenability of positivist unbelief.

III

Since Hutton was a literary critic, with perceptive things to say of the work of Wordsworth, Sir Walter Scott, Jane Austen, Carlyle, Dickens, George Eliot, and Arthur Hugh Clough, among others, he attended closely to Newman's style, appreciating that if he occasionally addressed his readers with irony to disabuse

---

January 1880), 10–11.

[60] *Ibid.*, 11. Cf. entry for the word *Agnosticism* in *OED* corrected reissue (1961): "Suggested by Prof. Huxley at a party held previous to the formation of the Metaphysical Society, at Mr. James Knowles' house in Clapham Common, one evening in 1869 in my hearing. He took it from St Paul's mention of the altar to 'the Unknown God.' R. H. Hutton in letter of 13 March 1881." The first illustrative quotation for the word in is: "1870 *Spectator*, 29 January 135 In theory he [Prof. Huxley] is a great and even severe Agnostic, who goes about exhorting all men to know how little they know."

them of their misapprehensions, he also used style to lay bare his deepest convictions. Newman's famous passage in the *Apologia* on what he referred to as our "aboriginal calamity" certainly bears this out. If, as Leslie Stephen confirmed, James Fitzjames Stephen never bothered to treat the authors he criticized as authors, content, instead, to treat them as mere repositories of information, Hutton recognized that how a writer chose to say a thing often revealed what he was saying. For example, he quotes a passage from *Anglican Difficulties* in which Newman anticipates his Anglo-Catholic reader's objection to his conversion on the grounds of his having been an Anglo-Catholic himself by showing how his understanding of their shared experience, especially with respect to the Anglican episcopate, proved not only the false position in which Anglo-Catholics found themselves in the National Church but the very untenability of Anglo-Catholicism itself. Here, Newman's irony might be that of a Dutch uncle but it is no less effective for being unmerciful. "There are those who, reversing the Roman maxim, are wont to shrink from the contumacious and to be valiant towards the submissive; and the authorities in question gladly availed themselves of the power conferred on them by the movement against the movement itself," he wrote.

> They fearlessly handselled their Apostolical weapons upon the Apostolical party. One after another in long succession they took up their song and their parable against it. It was a solemn war-dance which they executed round victims who, by their very principle, were bound hand and foot, and could only eye with disgust and perplexity this most unaccountable movement on the part of those "Holy Fathers, the representatives of the Apostles, and the Angels of the Churches." … When bishops spoke against them, and bishops' courts sentenced them, and the universities degraded them, and the people were against them, from that day their "occupation was gone," … henceforward they had nothing left for them but to shut up the school and retire into the country. Nothing else was left for them unless, indeed, they took up some other theory, unless they changed their ground, unless they ceased to be what they were, and became what they were not; unless they belied their own principles, and strangely forgot their own luminous and most keen convictions; unless they vindicated the right of private judgment, took up some fancy religion, retailed the Fathers, and jobbed Theology.[61]

Another example of Newman's irony that Hutton shares with his readers is even more telling, though here he turns his genius for satire on himself. This is a passage worth keeping in mind whenever one encounters those commentators who insist that Newman only revisited the history of Tractarianism to indulge in self-vindication. It may be true, as Hutton writes, that "when Newman gives the rein to his irony, it is always with a certain earnestness, or even indignation against the self-deceptions he is ridiculing."[62] But this does not take into account that in *Anglican Difficulties* his own self-deception with regard to the *Via Media* serves as a kind of *leitmotif* for the book. "For me, my dear brethren, did I know myself well, I should doubtless find I was open to the temptation as well as others to take a line of my own, or what is called, to set up for myself; but whatever

[61] Hutton, *Modern Guides*, 59–60; *Diff.*, i, 152–3.
[62] Ibid., 56.

might be my real infirmity in this matter, I should, from mere common sense and common delicacy, hide it from myself, and give it some good name in order to make it palatable," he writes.

> I never could get myself to say, "Listen to me, for I have something great to tell you, which no one else knows, but of which there is no manner of doubt." I should be kept from such extravagance from an intense sense of the intellectual absurdity, which, in my feelings, such a claim would involve; which would shame me as keenly, and humble me in my own sight as utterly, as some moral impropriety or degradation. I should feel I was simply making a fool of myself, and taking on myself, in figure, that penance, of which we read in the lives of saints, of playing antics and making faces in the market-place. Not religious principle but even worldly pride would keep me from so unworthy an exhibition.

This was admonitory mockery that struck at the very essence of the Tractarian make-believe. Yet Newman upbraided his Anglo-Catholic friends more directly still in a subsequent passage. "Do not come to me at this time of day with views perfectly new, isolated, original, *sui generis*, warranted old neither by Christian nor unbeliever, and challenge me to answer what I really have not the patience to read. Life is not long enough for such trifles. Go elsewhere, not to me, if you wish to make a proselyte. Your inconsistency, my dear brethren, is on your very front. … I began myself with doubting and inquiring, you seem to say; I departed from the teaching I received; I was educated in some older type of Anglicanism—in the school of Newton, Cecil, or Scott, or … in the Liberal Whig school; I was a Dissenter or a Wesleyan, and by study and thought I became an Anglo-Catholic. And then I read the Fathers, and I have determined what books are genuine and what are not; which of them apply to all times, which are occasional, which historical, and which doctrinal; what opinions are private, what authoritative; what they only seem to hold, what they ought to hold; what are fundamental, what ornamental. Having thus measured and cut and put together my creed by my own proper intellect, by my own lucubrations, and differing from the whole world in my results, I distinctly bid you, I solemnly warn you, not to do as I have done, but to take what I have found, to revere it, to use it, to believe it, for it is the teaching of the old Fathers, and of your mother, the Church of England. Take my word for it that this is the very truth of Christ; deny your own reason, for I know better than you; and it is as clear as day that some moral fault in you is the cause of your differing from me. It is pride, or vanity, or self-reliance, or fulness of bread. You require some medicine for your soul. You must fast; you must make a general confession; and look very sharp to yourself, for you are already next door to a rationalist or an infidel."[63]

Again, Hutton's interpretation of this is accurate enough. "Newman's irony," he writes, "is directed against what he regarded as the real self-deception which went on in the minds of some of his own most intimate associates and friends of former days. He is all on fire to make them feel that if they had really given up private judgment in theology, they could not consistently hold a position which

---

[63] *Diff.*, i, 126–34, quoted in Hutton, *Modern Guides*, 59–60.

is tenable only on the score that a vast number of most uncertain and arbitrary private judgments, approved by no Church as a whole, nor even by any influential section of any, have concurred to define and fortify it." This is all true. As is this: "Keen as his irony is, there is a certain passion in it too. He cannot endure to see what he thinks such unreality, such self-deception, in those whom he has trusted and loved. He seeks to cut them almost by main force out of a position which he thinks humiliating to them, and which for himself he would certainly regard as wanting in candour and sincerity."[64] Yet what Hutton does not point out here is that throughout the passage Newman is taking to task his own unreality in leading his Tractarian friends to believe that they could somehow rid themselves of the private judgment of the National Church by taking refuge in the private judgment of the Via Media, a concoction, after all, almost entirely made up of his own highly idiosyncratic fashioning. What makes this irony so successful, in other words, is its humility. Newman sought to dissuade his Anglo-Catholic friends from continuing to subscribe to the self-deceptive unreality of the Via Media by showing them how implicated he was in subscribing to the unreality himself.[65]

Moreover, some of the most powerful passages of *Anglican Difficulties* are those in which Newman's insists on the reality of the Roman Catholic faith, especially as it is contrasted with Protestantism—the faith, that is to say, that he was so intent on sharing with his former Tractarian friends, and this is never more evident than when he writes of the practical, everyday relationship between Catholics and the unseen. "Protestants ... consider that faith and love are inseparable; where there is faith, there, they think, are love and obedience; and in proportion to the strength and degree of the former, are the strength and degree of the latter," he writes.

> They do not think the inconsistency possible of really believing without obeying; and, where they see disobedience, they cannot imagine there the existence of real faith. Catholics, on the other hand, hold that faith and love, faith and obedience, faith and works, are simply separable, and ordinarily separated, in fact; that faith does not imply love, obedience, or works; that the firmest faith, so as to move mountains, may exist without love,—that is, real faith, as really faith in the strict sense of the word as the faith of a martyr or a doctor. In other words, when Catholics speak of faith they are contemplating the existence of a gift which Protestantism does not even imagine. Faith is a spiritual sight of the unseen; and since in matter of fact Protestantism does not impart this sight, does not see the unseen, has no experience of this habit, this act of the mind—therefore, since it retains the word "faith," it is obliged to find some other meaning for it; and its common, perhaps its commonest, idea is, that faith is substantially the same as

---

[64] Ibid., 60–1.
[65] An amusing example of Newman's humility can be seen in his trying to dissuade the artist Walter Wiliam Ouless (1848–1933) from painting him. "As to your flattering proposal in regard to Mr Ouless, I have delayed my answer to it from a difficulty. I do not know how to consent that he should make so generous a sacrifice as that of a series of visits to this place, in the full London season, when his time must be most valuable to him; and, though I know that artists have their fancies which are beyond criticism, I too have mine, viz that, if he looks about him, he will find in London better subjects than me in Birmingham, to exercise his genius upon." Newman to James Bryce (24 January 1878), *LD*, xxviii, 319.

obedience; at least, that it is the impulse, the motive of obedience, or the fervour and heartiness which attend good works. In a word, faith is hope or it is love, or it is a mixture of the two. Protestants define or determine faith, not by its nature or essence, but by its effects. When it succeeds in producing good works, they call it real faith; when it does not, they call it counterfeit.[66]

This is the unreal faith that we see not only in liberal Protestantism but in liberal Catholicism as well, in both of which the same canting preoccupation with "social justice," the same moral vanity predominates. It was doubtless with this in mind that the poet Walter de la Mare spoke of the Church resembling a "cataleptic's countenance" with "no inward activity of its own."[67] By contrasting this spurious faith with the real Catholic faith, Newman may make himself as unwelcome to our contemporaries as he made himself to his own, but he nevertheless reaffirms an essential truth of Christianity, a truth liberals are never overzealous to concede: and that is that the Church does her own, not the world's work. To drive this point home, Newman expatiates on the Church's often unfashionable priorities.

> The Church, though she embraces all conceivable virtues in her teaching, and every kind of good, temporal as well as spiritual, in her exertions, does not survey them from the same point of view, or classify them in the same order as the world. She makes secondary what the world considers indispensable; she places first what the world does not even recognise, or undervalues, or dislikes, or thinks impossible; and not being able, taking mankind as it is found, to do everything, she is often obliged to give up altogether what she thinks of great indeed, but of only secondary moment, in a particular age or a particular country, instead of effecting at all risks that extirpation of social evils, which, in the world's eyes, is so necessary, that it thinks nothing really is done till it is secured. Her base of operations, from the difficulties of the season or the period, is sometimes not broad enough to enable her to advance against crime as well as against sin, and to destroy barbarism as well as irreligion. The world, in consequence, thinks, that because she has not done the world's work, she has not fulfilled her Master's purpose; and imputes to her the enormity of having put eternity before time.[68]

Here is Newman at his most judicious. And yet when he speaks of the genuine nature of Catholic faith—of its engagement with the unseen and what the issue of that engagement is—he transcends what might have been the lectures' merely polemical occasion and speaks for the ages.

> Now faith, in a Catholic's creed, is a certainty of things not seen but revealed; a certainty preceded indeed in many cases by particular exercises of the intellect, as conditions, by reflection, prayer, study, argument, or the like, and ordinarily, by the instrumental sacrament of Baptism, but caused directly by a supernatural influence on the mind from above. Thus it is a spiritual sight; and the nearest

[66] *Diff.*, i, 268–70.
[67] Walter de la Mare, "The Trumpet" (1938), *Walter de la Mare, Short Stores: 1927–1956*, ed. Giles de la Mare (London: Giles de la Mare Publishers, 2001), 334.
[68] *Diff.*, i, 263.

parallel by which it can be illustrated is the moral sense. As nature has impressed upon our mind a faculty of recognising certain moral truths, when they are presented to us from without, so that we are quite sure that veracity, for instance, benevolence, and purity, are right and good, and that their contraries involve guilt, in a somewhat similar way, grace impresses upon us inwardly that revelation which comes to us sensibly by the ear or eye; similarly, yet more vividly and distinctly, because the moral perception consists in sentiments, but the grace of faith carries the mind on to objects. This certainty, or spiritual sight, which is included in the idea of faith, is, according to Catholic teaching, perfectly distinct in its own nature from the desire, intention, and power of acting agreeably to it. As men may know perfectly well that they ought not to steal, and yet may deliberately take and appropriate what is not theirs; so may they be gifted with a simple, undoubting, cloudless belief, that, for instance, Christ is in the Blessed Sacrament, and yet commit the sacrilege of breaking open the tabernacle, and carrying off the consecrated particles for the sake of the precious vessel containing them. It is said in Scripture, that the evil spirits "believe and tremble"; and reckless men, in like manner, may, in the very sight of hell, deliberately sin for the sake of some temporary gratification.[69]

Here is the true, the terrible reality of fallen man's desperate need for faith, into which Newman's Protestant contemporaries, beguiled as they were by their equation of faith with what they imagined moral efficacy, could scarcely enter. Faith must not be confused with moralism, as the Calvinists, or their agnostic castaways, wished to imagine, and the reason for this has everything to do with the real nature of the human condition—and the vitality of the sacraments. "The case with most men is this ... that they grow up more or less in practical neglect of their Maker and their duties to Him," Newman pointed out to his auditors.

Nature tends to irreligion and vice, and in matter of fact that tendency is developed and fulfilled in any multitude of men, according to the saying of the old Greek, that "the many are bad," or according to the Scripture testimony, that the world is at enmity with its Creator. The state of the case is not altered, when a nation has been baptized; still, in matter of fact, nature gets the better of grace, and the population falls into a state of guilt and disadvantage, in one point of view worse than that from which it has been rescued. This is the matter of fact, as Scripture prophesied it should be: "Many are called, few are chosen"; "the kingdom of heaven is like unto a net gathering together of every kind." But still, this being granted, a Catholic people is far from being in the same state in all respects as one which is not Catholic, as theologians teach us. A soul which has received the grace of baptism receives with it the germ or faculty of all supernatural virtues whatever,—faith, hope, charity, meekness, patience, sobriety, and every other that can be named; and if it commits mortal sin, it falls out of grace, and forfeits these supernatural powers. It is no longer what it was, and is, so far, in the feeble and frightful condition of those who were never baptized. But there are certain remarkable limitations and alleviations in its punishment,

---

[69] *Diff.*, i, 270–1. James 2:19.

and one is this: that the faculty or power of faith remains to it. Of course the soul may go on to resist and destroy this supernatural faculty also; it may, by an act of the will, rid itself of its faith, as it has stripped itself of grace and love; or it may gradually decay in its faith till it becomes simply infidel; but this is not the common state of a Catholic people. What commonly happens is this, that they fall under the temptations to vice or covetousness, which naturally and urgently beset them, but that faith is left to them. Thus the many are in a condition which is absolutely novel and strange in the ideas of a Protestant; they have a vivid perception, like sense, of things unseen, yet have no desire at all, or affection, towards them; they have knowledge without love. Such is the state of the many; the Church at the same time is ever labouring with all her might to bring them back again to their Maker; and in fact is ever bringing back vast multitudes one by one, though one by one they are ever relapsing from her. The necessity of yearly confession, the Easter communion, the stated seasons of indulgence, the high festivals, Lent, days of obligation, with their Masses and preaching,—these ordinary and routine observances and the extraordinary methods of retreats, missions, jubilees, and the like, are the means by which the powers of the world unseen are ever acting upon the corrupt mass, of which a nation is composed, and breaking up and reversing the dreadful phenomenon which fact and Scripture conspire to place before us.[70]

Here was the best response Newman could have possibly given to Hutton's abiding complaint that the convert somehow did not make sufficient allowance, in his defense of his newfound faith, for the misdeeds of Catholics. Evelyn Waugh certainly understood the force of Newman's response when, in a piece retailing his conversion, he remarked: "The Protestant attitude seems often to be, 'I am good; therefore, I go to church,' while the Catholic's is, 'I am far from good, therefore I go to church.'"[71]

There were not many contemporary critical responses to Newman's *Anglican Difficulties*. When it was published in 1850, Newman's Anglo-Catholic friends largely ignored it, finding its satirical barbs too painful to parry. Owen Chadwick rightly speculated that "It was the only book by Newman which many Anglicans found it impossible to forgive." Chadwick wished to believe that the hard-hitting lectures were somehow uncharacteristic of Newman. According to the church historian, Newman "was suffering from the disease of being a new convert, of burning what once he had adored; but the occasion, while the high church party tottered upon the precipice of disruption, persuaded him to shout louder than his inward judgement truly approved. He confessed to Faber that he was writing them against the grain of his intellect." Taking these factors into account, Chadwick concluded that "the lectures were too extreme to persuade minds not already more than half persuaded," though he admitted that they did influence T. W. Allies, Edward Bellasis, and James Hope Scott.[72] He also omitted to share with his readers that the most damning criticism that Newman leveled against

---

[70] *Diff.*, i, 272–4.
[71] Evelyn Waugh, "Converted to Rome: Why it has happened to me," *Daily Express* (20 October 1930), 10.
[72] Owen Chadwick, *The Victorian Church*, 2 vols (London: Oxford University Press, 1966), i, 289.

Anglo-Catholicism—that it was a "paper" faith attached to an ineradicably Erastian National Church—was one that the disillusioned architect of the Via Media had mounted against the "Movement of 1833," as he called it, *before* his conversion. The lectures of *Anglican Difficulties* simply gave him the opportunity to refine and sharpen this criticism. It had nothing to do with a convert's zeal, especially since the lectures were composed five years after his conversion. Chadwick's response, like so much of his work on Newman, evades the actual matter in question.[73]

One Anglican contemporary of Newman's who delighted in the lectures of *Anglican Difficulties* precisely because they trounced the Anglo-Catholics whom he had deplored himself throughout the period when the Tractarians were publishing their Tracts was the Archdeacon of Lewes, Julius Charles Hare. "The main object of his *Lectures on the Difficulties of Anglicanism* (sic) is to shew the feebleness and untenableness of the opinions of which seventeen years ago he was the main promulgater and champion," Hare wrote in his charge of 1851.

> Nothing can exceed the contempt, the scorn, with which he speaks of those opinions. To all other modes of opinion, he can be indulgent. "I can understand (he says, p. 128), I can sympathize with those old-world thinkers, whose commentators are Mant and D'Oyly, whose theologian is Tomlin, whose ritualist is Wheatly, and whose canonist is Burns. Those also I can understand, who take their stand upon the Prayerbook; or who honestly profess to follow the consensus of Anglican divines, as the voice of authority and the standard of faith. Moreover I can quite enter into the sentiment, with which members of the liberal and infidel school investigate the history and the documents of the early Church. But (he adds, turning to his own *quondam* associates and followers), what a Catholic would feel so prodigious is this, that such as you, my brethren, should consider Christianity given from Heaven once for all, should protest against private judgement, should profess to transmit what you have received, and yet, from diligent study of the Fathers, from living, as you say, in the atmosphere of antiquity, should come forth into open day with your new edition of the Catholic Faith, different from that held in any existing body of Christians, which not half-a-dozen men all over the world would honour with their imprimatur; and then, withal, should be as positive in practice about its truth in every part, as if the voice of mankind were with you, instead of against you. You are a body of yesterday; you are a drop in the ocean of professing Christians; yet you would give the law to priest and prophet; and you fancy it a humble office forsooth, suited to humble men, to testify the very truth of revelation to a fallen generation, which has been in unintermittent traditionary error. You have a mission to teach the National Church, which is to teach the British Empire, which is to teach the world. You are more learned than Greece; you are purer than Rome; you know better than St Bernard; you judge how far St Thomas was right, and where he is to be read with caution, or held up to blame." By these, and similar stinging words he lashes his credulous admirers, if so he may again prevail upon them to follow him whom they have found so unerring a leader. The objections, which

---

[73] For a witty, indeed masterly, demolition of Chadwick's typically denigratory commentary on Newman, see Ian Ker, "Catholic Christianity," in *Newman and the Fullness of Christianity*, 103–22.

others have frequently urged against the Tractarian doctrines, but which were repelled with indignation, he himself brings forward in the most cutting form.[74]

Then, too, Hare revels in what he sees as Newman's tergiversating inconsistency. "Dr Newman indeed has a strange course to pursue in dealing with his former associates and disciples, a course which needs all the subtilty of his tortuous understanding. While on the one hand, as we have just seen, he speaks of them in language of unmeasured scorn, on the other hand he represents them as having been sent by God to revive the truth in our Church. When he was with them, they were the latter when he left them, they became objects of scorn."[75] The charge of inconsistency would become a staple of the abuse Newman received from English Protestants of various stripes throughout his career, though none of them, least of all Hare, ever thought to consider how conversion, without inconsistency of some sort, would not be possible.[76] In seeking to refute such inconsistency, Hare does not so much judge of Newman's evolving opinions on the merits of Rome, as opposed to those of Canterbury, as advocate for staying put, which he does with a kind of touching fatuity. After deploring what he sees as Newman's sophistical recourse to logic, he exhorts his Anglican readers to stand their ground:

> Therefore I would earnestly entreat his *quondam* followers to give no heed to his logical war-cry. If there be any extravagance of private judgement, it would be this. This is Rationalism in its baldest, wildest form. God has placed them where they are. He has given them the duties of their calling. He has girt them round with affections, that they may take root where they are, and not be blown about by every wind of Logic. Some outward necessity may indeed come, as it came to our ancestors at the Reformation, some revolutionary force, which may compel them, without their own act and deed, to quit their immediate position, or to make some material change in its relations. In such a case, of which however I cannot see a likelihood, it would behoove them to yield to the necessity, which they cannot change. We must not violate our conscience; we must not do what our conscience declares to be wrong. But so long as this lord of our being continues inviolate, we may bid Logic mind its own business, and content ourselves with doing our duty in that state of life to which it has pleased God to call us.[77]

The lively polemicist in Newman doubtless enjoyed the polemical exuberance of Hare's charge, in which the Archdeacon of Lewes might almost have been parodying the No Popery satire of Newman's *Present Position of Catholics in England* (1851). "On some other fallacies, by which men's minds have been beguiled of

---

[74] Julius Charles Hare, *The Contest with Rome: A Charge to the Clergy* (London: John W. Parker & Son, 1852), 98–9.
[75] Ibid., 104–5.
[76] Speaking of her father's assessment of Newman after his death, Mary Church touched upon this inconsistency but only in terms that Hare would have found dubious: "In an article in the *Guardian*," she wrote, her father's "intimate knowledge" of Newman "suggests a clue to an inner unity of thought and aim that might be traced beneath the outward and contradictory change of position of which the *Apologia* is the record." Church, *Life and Letters*, 417.
[77] Hare, *Contest with Rome*, 109.

late years into thinking too favorably of Rome, I have spoken in former Charges," Hare writes in an unwitting burlesque of Broad Church orthodoxy, the only core belief of which is that Roman Catholicism is inherently evil.

> But before I turn away from this subject, it behooves me to give some sort of brief general answer to the question which I propounded above: Why are we to resist and repel those who desire to draw us into the Church of Rome? why are we not to hail them as our benefactors, and to bow our necks thankfully beneath the yoke which they would impose on us? Because it is a yoke, and not an easy one, like that Divine yoke, which we are bid to take upon us, but a heavy and oppressive human yoke; whereas we are commanded to call no man master upon earth, seeing that we have One Master in heaven, who has called us all to be brethren and servants one to another. Because the dominion of Rome is a usurpation, founded upon no divine right, upon no human right, repugnant to both rights, destructive of both, destructive of the national individualities which God has markt out for the various nations of the earth, and which can only be brought to their perfection when the nations become members of His Kingdom. Because history shews, what from reflexion we might have anticipated, that the sway of Rome is degrading and corruptive to the spiritual and moral, and even to the political character of every nation that submits to it. Because the pretensions of Rome are built upon a primary imposture; and such as the foundation is, such is the whole edifice that has been piled upon it in the course of centuries, imposture upon imposture, falsehood upon falsehood. Because the evangelical truths, of which, from its portion in Christ's Church, it has retained possession, have been tainted and corrupted by its impostures, and thus have been prevented from exercising their rightful influence upon the moral growth of its members. Because it has gone on debasing the religion of Christ more and more from the religion of the Spirit into a religion of forms and ceremonies, substituting dead works for a living faith, the nominal assent to certain words for the real apprehension of the truths exprest by them, interposing all manner of mediators between man and the One Only Mediator, changing God's truth into an aggregation of lies, and, at least in its practical operation, worshiping the creature more than the Creator. Because so many of its principal institutions are designed, not so much to promote the glory of God, and the wellbeing of mankind, as the establishment and enlargement of its own empire, no matter at what cost of truth and holiness; because its celibacy is anti-scriptural and demoralizing, baneful to the sanctity of family life, and a teeming source of profligate licentiousness; because its compulsory confession taints the conscience, deadens the feeling of sin, and breeds delusive security; because its Inquisition enslaves and crushes the mind, stifling the love of truth; because its Jesuitism is a school of falsehood; because it eclipses the word of God, and withdraws the light of that word from His people. Therefore, because of these and divers other evils, inherent in, and almost inseparable from the system of the Papacy, evils, each of which has bred an untold mass of sin and misery, accumulated through centuries, and which have grievously hindered the saving and sanctifying power of the Gospel, therefore did our ancestors at the Reformation, under God's guidance, cast off the yoke and bondage of Rome, and deliver the State and people of England from it.

That a man who befriended Manning should have subscribed openly to such staples of No Popery is remarkable. Yet Hare's bigotry was shared by many Englishmen, who would have rallied to his words, especially when reminded that "the protest" against "the yoke and bondage" of Popery had been "maintained by the heart and mind of England for three centuries" despite "the softening influences of Time." Here was the Englishman's core Protestant identity, "handed down from father to son for nine generations." For Hare, "each generation has renewed it with determined, unflagging zeal. Therefore ... it is still the fixt purpose of the English heart and mind to reject the advances and to repell the assaults of the Papacy. Therefore, too, do we trust that, under God's blessing, we shall still have the heart and mind to repell them, yea, that, with His help, we shall repell them successfully, and shall preserve that pure treasure of Evangelical Truth, which He has so graciously committed to our keeping."[78] Catholic belief, as Edward Norman pointed out, especially its sacerdotal nature, which Whately called "religion by proxy," but also including "the primacy of St Peter and the See of Rome, the invocation of saints, veneration of the Virgin, transubstantiation, [and] popular miracles ... seemed to some Protestants mildly derisory, to others downright wicked, and to some, even perverted."[79] When it came to popery, Hare was in all three Protestant camps. If such prejudices seem outré to a later age, they were axiomatic to the Victorians. As G. M. Young reminded his readers, "To be misgoverned in this world and damned in the next seemed to many thousands of sober English families the necessary consequence of submission to Rome."[80] Yes, as Hutton appreciated, Newman's work would change these anti-Catholic views amongst certain Protestants but they were still widely held.

Hutton's response to the King William Street lectures shows his critical skills at their best. For Hutton, the lectures "were simpler and less ornate than the *Sermons Addressed to Mixed Congregations*, and more exquisite in form as well as more complete in substance than the *Essay on Development*, which was written under the heavy pressure of the dreaded ... rupture between himself and the Church of his baptism."[81] For Hutton, "the Lectures on *Anglican Difficulties* was the first book of Newman's generally read amongst Protestants, in which the measure of his literary power could be adequately taken. In the Oxford sermons there had been of course more room for the expression of religious feeling of a higher type, and frequently there had been more evidence of depth and grasp of mind; but here was a great subject with which Newman was perfectly intimate, giving the fullest scope to his powers of orderly and beautiful exposition, and opening a far greater range to his singular genius for gentle and delicate irony than anything which he had previously written." Since Hutton attended the lectures, he could recall their dazzling impact. "I shall never forget the impression which his voice and manner ... made on me. Never did a voice seem better adapted to persuade without irritating. Singularly sweet, perfectly free from any dictatorial note, and yet rich in all the cadences proper to the expression of pathos, of

---

[78] Ibid., 35–8.
[79] E. R. Norman, *Anti-Catholicism in Victorian England* (London: George Allen & Unwin, 1968), 14.
[80] G. M. Young, "Portrait of an Age," in *Early Victorian England 1830–1865*, 2 vols (Oxford: Oxford University Press, 1934), ii, 470.
[81] Hutton, *Cardinal Newman*, 207.

wonder, and of ridicule, there was still nothing in it that any one could properly describe as insinuating, for its simplicity, and frankness, and freedom from the half-smothered notes which express indirect purpose, was as remarkable as its sweetness, its freshness, and its gentle distinctness." The literary critic in Hutton was particularly struck by the exuberance of Newman's metaphors. "As he described the growth of his disillusionment with the Church of England, and compared it to the transformation which takes place in fairy tales when the magic castle vanishes, the spell is broken, 'and nothing is seen but the wild heath, the barren rock, and the forlorn sheep-walk,' no one could have doubted that he was describing with perfect truth the change that had taken place in his own mind. 'So it is with us,' he said, 'as regards the Church of England, when we look in amazement on that we thought so unearthly, and find so commonplace or worthless. Then we perceive that aforetime we have not been guided by reason, but biased by education, and swayed by affection. We see in the English Church, I will not merely say, no descent from the first ages, and no relationship to the Church in other lands, but we see no body politic of any kind; we see nothing more or less than an establishment, a department of government, or a function or operation of the State—without a substance,—a mere collection of officials, depending on and living in the supreme civil power. Its unity and personality are gone, and with them its power of exciting feelings of any kind. It is easier to love or hate am abstraction than so tangible a framework or machinery.' [*Diff.*, i, 6] This is, of course, an exaggerated view. It is not true that the State can do what it pleases with the English Church, can modify its theology or change its liturgy at will; but it is still less true that the Church can do as she will without the consent of the State."[82]

Considering that Hutton subscribed to High Church Anglicanism when he wrote this response to Newman's unsparing criticism of the National Church, it is remarkable that he should have shown the lectures such disinterested praise. For Hutton, the lectures delivered "one of the most powerful attacks ever opened on the Anglican theory of the Church as independent of the State. Not less powerful was Newman's delineation, in the fifth lecture, of the collapse of the Anglican theory of the Church when applied to practice. The Anglicans, he said, 'had reared a goodly house, but their foundations were falling in.'"[83]

At the same time, Hutton was not uncritical of the lectures. The intellectually honest High Church Anglican in him might have recognized that Newman's strikes against the Erastianism of the National Church were fairly unanswerable, but he still baulked at what he thought Newman's inadequate defense of the Roman Church herself, which, after all, was ostensibly one signal purpose of his delivering the lectures in the first place. "The lectures of which it was the intention to remove the objections felt towards the Roman Catholic communion were partly defective, partly inadequate," he wrote. "They did not deal at all with what seems to me the greatest of all objections to the Roman Catholic Church, the indifference she shows to reasonable criticisms, even in her most solemn acts, such as the sanction given to utterly unhistorical facts in the feast of the

[82] *Ibid.*, 207–9.
[83] *Ibid.*, 211.

Assumption of the Virgin Mary, and the sanction given to the doctrine of the plenary inspiration of the Scriptures in the decrees of the Council of Trent and (subsequently) of the Council of the Vatican. On the other hand, the eighth and ninth lectures on the 'Political state of Catholic countries no prejudice to the sanctity of the Church,' and the 'Religious character of Catholic countries no prejudice to the sanctity of the Church,' raise, I think, at least as many difficulties as they remove. And in effect they almost concede that comparative want of self-reliance and self-control in matters both political and religious which certainly characterizes Catholic countries, as distinguished from those Catholic communities which exist in the heart of Protestant countries, and which are surrounded on all sides by religious opponents."[84]

Hutton's animadversions on what he saw as Newman's refusal to own up to the real state of Ireland's relationship to the Church of Rome can only be seen as prophetic. "Newman's apology for the political and religious state of Ireland as given in 1850 seems even less effective," he wrote, "indeed much less effective, when read in 1890 than it seemed then. Almost all that Ireland has gained since 1850, she has gained by the resolute ignoring of Catholic principles; and all that she has lost, she has lost by the resolute ignoring of Catholic principles. And though the gain may be considerable politically, I fear the moral loss far outweighs the political gain."[85] No truer words have ever been written about Irish history.

IV

We can see Hutton at his best in his brilliant extended essay comparing Newman to the poet Matthew Arnold, in which he wrote:

> It may be thought that there is something incongruous between the two great Oxford thinkers whom I am associating together—Cardinal Newman and Matthew Arnold—the one a prince of the Church which holds as articles of faith the immaculate conception of the Virgin, the invocation of saints, and the efficacy of indulgences; the other a rationaliser who dissolves away the very substance, nay, the very possibility, of Revelation, recognises no God but "a stream of tendency not our selves which makes for righteousness," no saviour except "sweet reasonableness "in a human life, and no resurrection except the resurrection from a selfish to an unselfish heart.[86]

Here, Hutton compares and contrasts the two not merely to show how different they were, but to show how each reflected a culture reeling from the ever-accelerating erosion of Christian faith, "that melancholy, long, withdrawing roar" that left an entire civilization alone with the "night wind," as Arnold put it so memorably in his poem "Dover Beach" (1851). "Both give us the amplest sympathy in our desire to believe," Hutton points out,

> and both are merciless when they find us practically dispensing with the logic which they have come to regard as final. Both are witnesses to the great power

[84] Ibid., 212–13.
[85] Ibid., 213.
[86] Hutton, *Modern Guides*, 49.

of religion—the one by the imaginative power he shows in getting over religious objections to his faith; the other by the imaginative power he shows in clothing a vacuum with impressive and majestic shadows till it looks something like a faith. Again, both, with all their richness of insight, have had that strong desire to rest on something beyond that insight, something which they can regard as in dependent of themselves, which led Newman first to preach against the principle of private judgment, and to yearn after an infallible Church, while it led Matthew Arnold to preach what he calls his doctrine of verification—namely, that no religious or moral instinct is to be trusted unless it can obtain the endorsement on a large scale of the common consent of the best human experience. Surely there is no greater marvel in our age than that it has felt profoundly the influence of both, and appreciated the greater qualities of both—the leader who with bowed head and passionate self-distrust, nay, with "many a pause of prayer and fear," has led hundreds back to surrender their judgment to a Pope whose rashness Dr. Newman's own ripe culture ultimately condemned, and the poet who in some of the most pathetic verses of modern times has bewailed the loss of the very belief which, in some of the most flippant and frigid of the diatribes of modern times, he has done all that was in his power to destroy. Cardinal Newman has taught men to take refuge in the greatness of the past from the pettiness of the present. Mr. Arnold has endeavoured to restore the idolatry of the Zeitgeist, the "time-spirit," which measures truth by the dwindled faith of the existing generation, and which never so much as dreams that one day the dwindled faith of the existing generation may in its turn be judged, and condemned, by that truth which it has denied.[87]

What is arresting about this last insight regarding Arnold's sympathy with what Hutton nicely styles "the idolatry of the Zeitgeist" is that it is a sympathy that many within the Roman Church herself now share. It "measures truth by the dwindled faith of the existing generation," and it will most certainly be "judged, and condemned, by the truth which it has denied."[88] It is of the essence of Modernism—what the *Oxford English Dictionary* defines as "A tendency or movement towards modifying traditional beliefs and doctrines in accordance with modern ideas and scholarship; *spec.* a movement of this kind in the Roman Catholic Church around the beginning of the twentieth century."[89] Indeed, it is a movement that recrudesced in the twenty-first century under the Bergoglio papacy with a kind of pell-mell incoherence. Apropos Newman's opposition to this "idolatry of the Zeitgeist," Hutton writes: "His faith in the sacramental principle taught him to look for a created universe from which the Creator should be reflected back at every point; but he actually found one from which disorder, confusion, enmity to God, was reflected back at every point." And then he quotes from one of Newman's most famous passages:

[87] Ibid., 50–1.
[88] Ibid., 51.
[89] The *OED* cites the Modernist George Tyrell to illustrate this sense of the word: "1900 G. Tyrrell *Let.*, 3 September in T. M. Loome, *Liberal Catholicism* (1979), 30. The tension between the old & the young, between those who yield nothing to Modernism & can see no good in it, and those who would yield everything & can see no evil in it, is very acute."

> Starting then with the being of a God (which, as I have said, is as certain to me as the certainty of my own existence, though when I try to put the grounds of that certainty into logical shape I find a difficulty in doing so in mood and figure to my satisfaction), I look out of myself into the world of men, and there I see a sight which fills me with unspeakable distress. The world seems simply to give the lie to that great truth of which my whole being is so full, and the effect upon me is in con sequence, as a matter of necessity, as confusing as if it denied that I am in existence myself. If I looked into a mirror and did not see my face I should have that sort of feeling which actually comes upon me when I look into this living busy world and see no reflection of the Creator. This is to me one of the great difficulties of this absolute primary truth to which I referred just now. Were it not for this voice speaking so clearly in my conscience and my heart I should be an atheist, or a pantheist, or a polytheist when I looked into the world. I am speaking for myself only, and I am far from denying the real force of the arguments in proof of a God drawn from the general facts of human society; but these do not warm me or enlighten me; they do not take away the winter of my desolation or make the buds unfold and the leaves grow within me and my moral being rejoice. The sight of the world is nothing else than the prophet's vision, full of "lamentations and mourning and woe." To consider the world in its length and breadth, its various history, the many races of men, their starts, their fortune, their mutual alienation, their conflicts, and then their ways, habits, governments, forms of worship, their enterprises, their aimless courses, their random achievements and acquirements, and then the impotent conclusion of long-standing facts, the tokens so faint and broken of a superintending design, the blind evolution of what turn out to be great powers or truths, the progress of things as if from unreasoning elements, not towards final causes, the greatness and littleness of man, his far-reaching aims, his short duration, the curtain hung over his future, the disappointments of life, the defeat of good, the success of evil, physical pain, mental anguish, the prevalence and intensity of sin, the prevailing idolatries, the corruptions, the dreary hopeless irreligion, that condition of the whole race, so fearfully yet exactly described in the Apostle's words, "Having no hope, and without God in the world," all this is a vision to dizzy and appal, and inflicts on the mind the sense of a profound mystery which is absolutely beyond human solution.[90]

As Hutton points out, "This is a passage taken from the *Apologia*, but long before Dr. Newman became a Roman Catholic, even at a time when he held confidently that the Roman Catholic Church was anti-Christian, he had pressed home the same deep conviction that the spectacle of the moral universe and of human history is so utterly abhorrent to the heart taught from within, that it can only be explained at all on the principle that the human race has been implicated in some 'great aboriginal calamity' which can only be obviated by some equally great supernatural interference in human affairs, specially adapted to remedy that calamity. Even before he threw himself into the Tractarian movement, even before he went abroad with Mr. Hurrell Froude in 1832 on that memorable

---

[90] *Apo.*, 242.

journey in which, whether quarantined in lazarettos, or conversing with Roman ecclesiastics, or lying sick almost to death in Sicily, or tossing in an orange boat on the Mediterranean, he was so haunted by the belief that he had a 'work to do in England,' that he shrank from every kind of contact with influences which seemed to him incongruous with that work,—he had urged on Oxford students and Oxford audiences of every kind, with passionate earnestness, his warnings against trusting what Matthew Arnold delights to call the *Zeitgeist*, the 'modern spirit,' the spirit of the age."[91]

V

The fact that two men as different as Newman and Arnold should have at once mirrored and fascinated nineteenth-century England appealed to Hutton's deep sense of the mystery of history, which rationalist historians, taking their cue from Gibbon, always seek to rationalize away. "Surely, that the great University of Oxford should have produced first the one and then the other—first the great Romaniser, and then the great rationaliser—is such a sign of the times as one ought not lightly to pass by," Hutton wrote.

> When I consider carefully how the great theologian has vanished from his pulpit at St. Mary's, and how, finally transformed into a Cardinal, he has pleaded from his Birmingham Oratory with the same touching simplicity as in his old tutorial days for the truth that to the single heart "there are but two things in the whole universe—our own soul and God who made it"—and then how the man who succeeded him in exercising more of the peculiar influence of Oxford over the world than any other of the following generation—and where is there a promise of any younger Oxford leader who is likely to stand even in the place of Mr. Arnold?—tells us with that mild intellectual arrogance which is the leading characteristic of his didactic prose, "I do not think it can be said that there is even a low degree of probability for the assertion that God is a person who thinks and loves,"—when I consider this contrast, I realise more distinctly than in looking at any of the physical changes of the universe what Shakespeare meant when he wrote, "We are such stuff as dreams are made of."[92]

If Hutton could never follow Newman into the Church of Rome, finding her claim to infallibility not only incredible but dissolvent of credibility, he was fascinated by the Mass, to which he had been first drawn by Willis' description of it in *Loss and Gain*. Indeed, in his very first letter to Newman he spoke of his Oxford novel of conversion as "in some sense an era in my life."[93] In another letter not long after, he spoke of his inability to accept the Church's authority.

---

[91] Hutton, *Modern Guides*, 76.
[92] Ibid., 50–2.
[93] Richard Holt Hutton to Newman (25 February 1864), *LD*, xxi, 60. Fenton John Anthony Hort was also struck by the book, telling a correspondent "I have read … [Newman's] *Loss and Gain*; it is very painful in the early part from the sneers at the Prayer-book, etc., but it rises out of that, and is John Henry Newman all over. With all its faults and 'dangerousness,' it is a fine book, and much may be learnt from it." Hort to John Ellerton (22 May 1849), *Life and Letters of Fenton John Anthony Hort* (London: Macmillan & Co., 1896), i, 105–6.

> Your Apology has interested me very profoundly on its own account. I wish more than I can say that I could be nearer to you in faith for I feel the same fascination in all you write that I have always felt. I have struggled my way out of Unitarianism to a deep belief in the Incarnation, but not by the road of "authority" which you teach as the only road to theological truth. Surely God can and does teach us His own truth without confiding it to any visible Church. I have never got so far as any really authoritative visible Church, I don't think the apostles had. However, it is not for me to take up your time with my crude pinions. Such gleams of truth as God puts into our hearts—not systematically I think—I glean eagerly from all sides,—but I never could grasp the argument for supposing that the Church could teach us more than God can directly. I have always thought the Roman theology fuller of self-revealing truth than almost any other of the coherent *systems* and was delighted with Möhler's Symbolik, but my stumbling block has always been that a true theology ought to be (and I think is) self-revealing and does not need the organism of a visible institution to drive it home to the conscience and the heart. Of course I am not denying that a Church grows naturally out of a Theology: what I cannot see is that a Theology should grow out of a Church. The Church seems to me the expression of a faith once attained, not the means of giving it.[94]

The last objection reveals the extent to which Hutton could not enter into, not merely infallibility, but the sacramental vitality of the Church, which does give the faithful their faith, whether the ordinary faithful in the pews or the most exalted theologian. Nevertheless, Hutton's objections to Newman's understanding of the Church's infallibility exhibits his consummate fairmindedness, even if the objections themselves are wrongheaded.[95] "Where did he go wrong?" Hutton asks of Newman in one essay.

> Of course one does not like to say of a man of the highest genius, and of a kind of genius specially adapted to the subject on which he writes, that he is wrong, and that a man of no genius, who criticises him, is right; but still, as I believe that he did go seriously wrong, and should be a Roman Catholic myself if I did

---

[94] Richard Holt Hutton to Newman (15 June 1864) *LD*, xxi, 120.
[95] We can see something of the same readiness to show sympathy in Andrew Martin Fairbairn (1838–1912), even though his differences with Newman, at first, impelled him to attack the convert. Fairbairn's biographer is good on this matter. "Scotchman and Puritan though he was," Fairbairn was always fascinated "by the Anglo-Catholic revival ... The fact that the very constitution of his mind and faith made it the more difficult for him to understand it attracted him. Quite early in his career Newman's *Apologia* had appealed to him, as it did to so many others, and he would not rest until he had grasped, as far as might be, the secret of the man and of his teaching. He was deeply perplexed by the contrast between the real piety of the men who represented the Oxford movement, and their apparent insensibility to the finer and higher moralities of the mind. He recognised that they were as convinced in their way as he was in his, and he brought to the task of understanding them the sympathy born of that conviction. His criticism of them was never merely negative; he used it as a means of restating his own views on the Church and on religion, in terms which the revival of Catholicism seemed to demand. His whole treatment of the movement was a splendid and timely vindication of the Protestant position as he understood it. But it must be remembered that Fairbairn meant always by Catholicism not the Roman Church, but rather that movement which began with the revival of Anglicanism in Oxford, which had its Roman affinities and has so profoundly affected the recent course of religious history in this country." W. B. Selbie, *The Life of Andrew Martin Fairbairn* (London: Stodder and Houghton, 1914), 203.

not, I must give my explanation of the error I think I see. It seems to me, then, that he went wrong in his primary assumption that what he calls "the dogmatic principle" involves the existence of an infallible human authority, which can say, without possibility of error, "this is what God has revealed, and this again is radically inconsistent with what He has revealed." I will quote his own account of his convictions on this subject from the *Apologia*. It is a very striking passage, and very instructive as to the course of this great thinker's personal history:

> "Supposing, then, it to be the will of the Creator to interfere in human affairs, and to make provisions for retaining in the world a knowledge of Himself, so definite and distinct as to be proof against the energy of human scepticism, in such a case, I am far from saying that there was no other way, but there is nothing to surprise the mind, if He should think fit to introduce a power into the world invested with the prerogative of infallibility on religious matters. Such a provision would be a direct, immediate, certain, and prompt means of withstanding the difficulty; it would be an instrument suited to the need; and when I find that this is the very claim of the Catholic Church, not only do I feel no difficulty in admitting the idea, but there is a fitness in it which re commends it to my mind. And thus I am brought to speak of the Church's infallibility as a provision, adapted by the mercy of the Creator, to preserve religion in the world, and to restrain that freedom of thought, which of course in itself is one of the greatest of natural gifts, and to rescue it from its own suicidal excesses." *Apologia*, p. 382.

That seems to me a definite contention that the reason of man is naturally so restless, so disposed to devour its own offspring, as to need the bit and bridle of an infallible human authority in addition to the guidance of God's spirit. But is not that in a sense really putting man above God, or at best putting God's providence as revealed in human institutions above God's spirit as revealed in conscience and reason? I should have supposed that to a thinker with so passionate a belief in God as the deepest of all realities, the true security for the ultimate stability of our reason, for the ultimate subjection of our reason to the power and fascination of revelation, would have been simply this, that God after all sways our spirits, and draws them to Himself. But Newman has so keen an insight into the morbid side of the cravings of Rationalism for devouring its own offspring that he can hardly believe that we shall ever rest on what God has revealed, unless that revelation receives a genuinely human embodiment in an infallible institution set upon a rock for all men to recognise as stamped by Providence with one of God's greatest attributes, inability to err.[96]

Here Hutton is not simply disagreeing with Newman's idea of infallibility: he is trying to understand it. He may not understand the divine nature of the Church's infallibility—a nature fallible men cannot mar—but he does treat Newman's embrace of the doctrine with sympathetic respect, even if he disagrees with it.

If Hutton could not entirely enter into the grounds of the Church's authority, he could always enter into Newman's sense of wonder and awe, a good example of

---

[96] Hutton, *Modern Guides*, 80–2.

which the *Spectator*'s editor supplied in his essay on Newman and Arnold. "Can anything be more marvellous or startling," Newman asked in his sermon, "The Invisible World" (1837), "unless we were used to it, than that we should have a race of beings about us whom we do see, and as little know their state, or can describe their interests or their destiny, as we can tell of the inhabitants of the sun and moon. It is, indeed, a very overpowering thought, when we get to fix our minds on it, that we periodically use—I may say hold intercourse with—creatures who are as much strangers to us, as mysterious, as if they were the fabulous unearthly beings, more powerful than man, and yet his slaves, which Eastern superstitions have invented. We have more real knowledge about the angels than about the brutes; they have, apparently, passions, habits, and a certain accountableness; but all is mystery about them. We do not know whether they can sin or not, whether they are under punishment, whether they are to live after this life; we inflict very great sufferings on a portion of them, and they, in turn, every now and then, retaliate upon us, as if by a wonderful law ... Cast your thoughts abroad on the whole number of them, large and small, in vast forests, or in the water, or in the air, and then say whether the presence of such countless multitudes, so various in their natures, so strange and wild in their shapes, living on the earth without ascertainable object, is not as mysterious as anything Scripture says about the angels."[97] Hutton's commentary on this marvelous passage shows what a good close critic he could be: "Once more, how tender is the style in the only sense in which we can properly attribute tenderness to style, its avoidance of every harsh or violent word, its shrinking aside from anything like overstatement. The lower animals have, he says, 'apparently passions, habits, and a certain accountableness.' Evidently Dr. Newman could not have suggested, as Des Cartes did, that they are machines, apeing feelings without having them; he never doubts their sufferings; he could not, even by a shade, exaggerate the mystery he is delineating. Every touch shows that he wishes to delineate it as it is, and not to overcolour it by a single tint. Then how piercing to our dulness is that phrase, 'It is indeed a very overpowering thought when we get to fix our minds on it.' We are not overpowered, he would say, only because we cannot or do not fix our minds on this wonderful intercourse of ours with intimates, after a kind, of whose inner being we are yet entirely ignorant. And how reticent is the inference, how strictly it limits itself to its real object, to impress upon us how little we know even of the objects of sense, and how little reason there is in using our ignorance as the standard by which to measure the supersensual."[98]

Hutton's ability to share his subject's sense of wonder and awe shows why he was such an outstanding critic of Newman. In marveling at the fact that the mind of the nineteenth century should have been dominated by two such different thinkers as Newman and Arnold, he demonstrates how Newmanian his insights into contemporary history could be.

> What are messages flashed under the ocean, what is our more rapid flight through space, what is the virtual contraction of the distances on this little molehill of a

---

[97] Newman, "The Invisible World," in *PS*, iv, 205-6 quoted in Hutton, *Modern Guides*, 63-4.
[98] Ibid., 64-6.

planet till the most distant points upon it are accessible to almost all, compared with the startling mental revolution effected within thirty or forty years at most! When the highest intellect of a great place of learning in one generation says in effect, "Because I believe so utterly in God and His revelation, I have no choice but to believe also in the Pope," while the highest intellect of the same great school in the next generation says, "As there is not even a low degree of probability that God in the old sense exists, let us do all that we can with streams of tendency, and morality touched with emotion, to supply his place," we must at least admit that the moral instability of the most serious convictions of earth is alarming enough to make the whole head sick and the whole heart faint.[99]

Newman would spend most of his own adult life anatomizing and addressing the same "instability"—another proof of the extent to which Hutton entered into Newman's deepest preoccupations. But it is when Hutton engages in good old-fashioned physiognomical criticism that the reader begins to recognize the true character of his critical sympathy.

Most of us know, by bust, photograph, or picture, the wonderful face of the great Cardinal;—that wide forehead, ploughed deep with parallel horizontal furrows which seem to express his careworn grasp of the double aspect of human nature, its aspect in the intellectual and its aspect in the spiritual world,—the pale cheek down which "long lines of shadow slope/Which years, and curious thought, and suffering give,"—the pathetic eye, which speaks compassion from afar, and yet gazes wonderingly into the impassable gulf which separates man from man, and the strange mixture of asceticism and tenderness in all the lines of that mobile and reticent mouth, where humour, playfulness, and sympathy are intricately blended with those severer moods that "refuse and restrain." On the whole, it is a face full in the first place of spiritual passion of the highest order, and in the next, of that subtle and intimate knowledge of the details of human limitation and weakness which makes all spiritual passion look utterly ambitious and hopeless, unless indeed it be guided amongst the stakes and dykes and pitfalls of the human battlefield by the direct providence of God.[100]

If there was never any show of impersonality in Newman's work, it is only fitting that his faithful critics should acknowledge how not only the work but the man exuded personality.[101] Newman is sometimes rated for being self-absorbed, but once we take into account the richness of his personality we can see that its expression led not to self-absorption but self-giving. To share with others his true personality, in all of its splendor, was an exercise of *caritas*, especially since, as he said, "even those who think highly of me have the vaguest, most shadowy, fantastic notions attached to their ideas of me; and feel a respect, not for me, but

---

[99] Ibid., 52–3.
[100] Ibid., 53–4.
[101] At the same time, one must always bear in mind something that Muriel Spark expressed with her usual succinctness: "Newman approached practically everything from a personal point of view, not quite a 'subjective' one." Muriel Spark, *Letters of John Henry Newman*, ed. Derek Stanford and Muriel Spark (Westminster: The Newman Press, 1957), 158.

for some imagination of their own which bears my name."[102] The more deeply he delved into himself, the more capable he became of sharing with others the wit, brilliance, humility, generosity and fellow-feeling that were the hallmarks of his personality. Self-absorption, after all, cuts us off from our fellows, immuring us in the prison house of narcissism. No one was less narcissistic than John Henry Newman. Indeed, in his gregariousness we can find the key to his dedication to the cure of souls. In entering into the hopes and fears and spiritual yearnings of so many different people from so many different walks of life, from dukes to dustmen, from peeresses to governesses, Newman came to realize what they all had in common, their ineradicable need for God's love, and he could pinpoint this commonality with heart-piercing precision. In concluding his comments on Newman's style in his comparison of the convert with Arnold, Hutton gives some good examples of this when he writes: "And now to bring to a close what I have to say of Dr. Newman's style—though the subject grows upon one—let me quote one or two of the passages in which his style vibrates to the finest notes, and yet exhibits most powerfully the drift and undercurrent by which his mind is swayed. Perhaps he never expresses anything so powerfully as he expresses the deep pining for the rest of spiritual simplicity, for the peace which passes understanding, that underlies his nature. Take this from one of his Roman Catholic sermons: "Oh, long sought after, tardily found, the desire of the eyes, the joy of the heart, the truth after many shadows, the fulness after many foretastes, the home after many storms; come to her, poor children, for she it is, and she alone, who can unfold to you the secret of your being, and the meaning of your destiny."[103] Again, in the exquisite tale of martyrdom [*Callista* (1856)] … the destined martyr, whose thirst for God has been awakened by her intercourse with Christians, thus repels the Greek rhetorician, who is trying to feed her on the husks of philosophic abstractions, as she expresses the yearnings of a heart weary of its desolation: "O that I could find Him!" she exclaimed, passionately. "On the right hand and on the left I grope, but touch Him not. Why dost Thou fight against me?—why dost Thou scare and perplex me, O First and Only Fair? I have Thee not, and I need Thee."[104]

Hutton could readily enter into the longing for faith, the longing for certainty in faith to which Newman directed so much of his writing because he suffered it himself, as he wrote to Newman in one of his most moving letters to his admired friend.

> The tendency of the religion of the day to dissipate itself in the vaguest sentiment and smoke oppresses me more and more, and often makes me turn to your Church with a vague passionate yearning that I feel to be dangerous and even distrustful of God, for surely the knowledge of the truth should not come from a mere repulsion against error, and if God could bring Christianity out of the society of the heathen world, He can much more teach us, after a very much longer period of incredulity and scepticism than we have yet gone through, what the divine truth is at which we find it so hard to get. I feel as if the tendencies of

---

[102] Newman to Henry Wilberforce (13 December 1846), *LD*, xii, 294.
[103] "Mysteries of Nature and Grace" (1849), *Mix.*, 281.
[104] Hutton, *Modern Guides*, 67–8. *Call.*, 245.

the day were all witnessing against the only truth I can firmly grasp, and telling me that *that* at least is not what the common sense of mankind will accept. But when I look more narrowly at your Church I see nothing but what daunts me still more on the other side,—an apparent utter disregard of *evidence* in fixing the Creed in the days when the Creed acquired its first hold on the mind. Can you doubt that the early Fathers and even the Evangelists themselves, like the Saints of all days, supplemented the deficiencies of their intellectual case for many of their facts from the depth of their devotional feeling, and did not even question the right of the religious spirit, to keep to its facts in this, as we know now, utterly misleading fashion?[105]

Newman's response might have been too pat for someone as doubtful of the Church's authority as Hutton was. "Allowing the early Fathers were uncritical and rhetorical," Newman wrote, "this will show itself, not in the substance but in the method and mode of teaching. And among the articles they teach is the fact of an authoritative Catholic Church. In spite of its being in the Creed (which should hinder its surprising me) I *am* continually surprised how often the notion of the 'Catholic Church,' as the Christian power, polity, authority, is introduced into their writings, taken as a whole. Indeed what is meant by it as an article of the Creed, unless it has some great importance attached to it? And 'the Church' smoothes everything to us." Yet if such a response proved unavailing in encouraging Hutton to reconsider his opposition to the Church's authority, it doubtless left the editor reconfirmed in his view of the unity of Newman's thought.

It was precisely Newman's unity of thought that led Hutton to consider *Callista* "the most completely characteristic of Newman's books." It may be true that many of his other books "express with greater power his intellectual delicacy of insight, and his moral intensity," but for Hutton "none, unless it be *The Dream of Gerontius*, expresses as this does the depth of his spiritual passion, the singular wholeness, unity, and steady concentration of purpose connecting all his thoughts, words, and deeds. And yet it is not, and I think will never be, the most popular of his books."[106] The reviewer in Hutton knew that this unpopularity was the result of two inalienable attributes of the book: "the framework of the story involves a certain amount of antiquarian disquisition, which fatigues ordinary readers ... and the sentiment of the book is of too exalted a kind to make its way to the heart of a hasty reader in search of exciting incident."[107] Still, knowing Hutton's imaginative engagement with the best works of literature of his age, it is easy to see how he would have entered into the drama of this tale of conversion, especially since its heroine, like Hutton himself, had to defy the intellectual consensus of her time to embrace the Christian faith. Here, Newman describes the response of Callista's brother to her newly adopted faith with precisely the spiritual passion to which Hutton refers, a passion which must have seemed very baffling indeed to the rationalist intellectuals who found Newman's own faith so sceptical and dishonest. "It was as though she had never shown any tendency before to the proscribed religion," he writes.

---

[105] Richard Holt Hutton to Newman (20 February 1872), LD, xxvi, 38–9.
[106] Hutton, *Cardinal Newman*, 225.
[107] Ibid., 220–1.

> The words came to him with the intensity of something new and unimagined hitherto. He clasped his hands in emotion, turned white, and could but say, "Callista!" If she had made confession of the most heinous of crimes,—if she had spoken of murder, of some black treachery against himself,—of some enormity too great for words, it might have been; but his sister!—his pride and delight, after all and certainly a Christian! Better far had she said she was leaving him for ever, to abandon herself to the degrading service of the temples; better had she said she had taken hemlock, or had an asp in her bosom, than that she should choose to go out of the world with the tortures, the ignominy, the malediction of the religion of slaves.[108]

Newman gave another powerful expression of this same "spiritual passion" that Hutton so rightly admired in *Callista* in "Ignorance of Evil" (1836), which concludes the eighth and final volume of his *Parochial and Plain Sermons*:

> Men give good names to what is evil, they sanctify bad principles and feelings; and, knowing that there is vice and error, selfishness, pride, and ambition, in the world, they attempt, not to root out these evils, not to withstand these errors ... but to cherish and form alliance with them, to use them, to make a science of selfishness, to flatter and indulge error, and to bribe vice with the promise of bearing with it, so that it does but keep in the shade. But let us, finding ourselves in the state in which we are, take those means which alone are really left us, which alone become us. Adam, when he had sinned, and felt himself fallen, instead of honestly abandoning what he had become, would fain have hid himself. He went a step further. He did not give up what he now was, partly from dread of God, partly from dislike of what he had been. He had learnt to love sin and to fear God's justice. But Christ has purchased for us what we lost in Adam, our garment of innocence. He has bid us and enabled us to become as little children; He has purchased for us the grace of *simplicity*, which, though one of the highest, is very little thought about, is very little sought after. We have, indeed, a general idea what love is, and hope, and faith, and truth, and purity, though a poor idea; but we are almost blind to what is one of the first elements of Christian perfection, that simple-mindedness which springs from the heart's being *whole* with God, entire, undivided. And those who think they have an idea of it, commonly rise no higher than to mistake for it a mere weakness and softness of mind, which is but its counterfeit. To be simple is to be like the Apostles and first Christians. Our Saviour says, "Be ye harmless," or simple, "as doves." And St. Paul, "I would have you wise unto that which is good, and *simple concerning evil*." [Rom. 16.19.] Again, "That ye may be *blameless and harmless*, the sons of God, without rebuke, in the midst of a crooked and perverse nation." [Phil. 2.15.] And he speaks of the "testimony of" his own "conscience, that in *simplicity* and godly sincerity, not with fleshly wisdom, but by the grace of God," he had his conversation in the world and towards his disciples. Let us pray God to give us this great and precious gift; that we may blot out from our memory all that offends Him; unlearn all that knowledge which sin has taught us; rid ourselves of selfish

---

[108] *Call.*, 296–7.

motives, self-conceit, and vanity, littlenesses, envyings, grudgings, meannesses; turn from all cowardly, low, miserable ways; and escape from servile fears, the fear of man, vague anxieties of conscience, and superstitions. So that we may have the boldness and frankness of those who are as if they had no sin, from having been cleansed from it; the uncontaminated hearts, open countenances, and untroubled eyes of those who neither suspect, nor conceal, nor shun, nor are jealous; in a word, so that we may have confidence in Him, that we may stay on Him, and rest in the thoughts of Him, instead of plunging amid the thickets of this world; that we may bear His eye and His voice, and know no knowledge but the knowledge of Him and Jesus Christ crucified, and desire no objects but what He has blessed and bid us pursue.[109]

The greatest dividend that Hutton received from the critical sympathy he invested in his reading of Newman's work was precisely his understanding of Newman's deep respect for holy simplicity. This is not to say that he finally came round to agreeing with all of Newman's religious positions—he clearly did not. But early and late, the sympathetic critic in Hutton recognized that Newman was misinterpreted largely because unsympathetic critics failed to see or would not see the inestimable value he placed on the "grace of simplicity." One can see this rather movingly in his biography of the great convert, where, again, he applauds Newman not only for refusing to go along with the "idolatry of the Zeitgeist" but for never forgetting one of the two greatest of God's commandments: "You shall love the Lord your God with all your heart and with all your soul and with all your mind." Newman "has always been disposed to regard the material world as a mere hieroglyphic expression of deeper spiritual meanings," Hutton wrote.

> Even in dealing with Scripture, he has from a very early period inclined to mingle the mystical with the more obvious interpretation of the text. And even in accepting the guidance of a Church, he has ever been on his guard against any hasty and inadequate collation of its authoritative definitions. Hence he has vexed all impatient and eager minds, who cut their way to what they deem truth by rough and ready processes, and has laid himself open to the imputation of indirectness. There is a striking instance of this in the celebrated passage in the *Apologia* in which he contrasts the intimate, irresistible, indissoluble connection between belief in self and belief in God, with the mystery of the world as it actually presents itself to us in all its godlessness. "The tokens," he writes, "so faint and broken, of a superintending design, the blind evolution of what turn out to be great powers or truths, the progress of things as if from unreasoning elements, not towards final causes, the greatness and littleness of man, his far-reaching aims, his short duration, the curtain hung over his futurity, the disappointments of life, the defeat of good, the success of evil, physical pain, mental anguish, the prevalence and intensity of sin, the pervading idolatries, the corruptions, the dreary, hopeless irreligion, that condition of the whole race so fearfully yet exactly described in the Apostle's words, "having no hope, and without God in the world,"—all this is a vision to dizzy and appal; and inflicts upon the mind the sense of a profound

---

[109] *PS*, viii, 266–8.

mystery, which is absolutely beyond human solution." It was obvious that a mind which could grasp with such power the paradox of human life in its relation to Divine revelation, could not by any means have presented itself to a vivid and passionate imagination like Mr. Kingsley's as one which he would have called natural and straightforward; and yet its naturalness is naturalness of a very high order, and its straightforwardness as straightforward as any nature so wide and sensitive to all sorts of delicate attractions and repulsions could possibly be. The simplicity of minds such as Newman's, profound as it is, will seem anything but simplicity, will seem complexity, to other men, while the anxious forecast of it will seem artificial.

> "So dark a forethought rolled about his brain,
> As on a dull day in an Ocean cave,
> The blind wave feeling round his long sea-hall
> In silence."[110]

And yet this "dark forethought" is in Newman's case completely overruled and subdued by faith and love.[111]

Faith and love: if one were to single out two qualities that most characterize Newman, one could do worse than single out those. That Hutton singled them out was proof that he could vouch for that captivating personal influence on which Newman set such high store. "Men persuade themselves, with little difficulty, to scoff at principles, to ridicule books, to make sport of the names of good men," Newman wrote in his *Oxford University Sermons*, "but they cannot bear their presence: it is holiness embodied in personal form, which they cannot steadily confront and bear down: so that the silent conduct of a conscientious man secures for him from beholders a feeling different in kind from any which is created by the mere versatile and garrulous Reason."[112]

Newman saw an unlikely example of the influence of "holiness embodied" in Pius IX. Unlikely, because, as he points out, Pius might very well have had only a malign influence on the Protestants of England. "If there is any representative of the Roman Church, from whom Protestants ought to shrink, it is her Head," Newman wrote. "In their theory, in their controversial publications, in their traditions, the Pope is all that is bad. You know the atrocious name they give him; he is the embodiment of evil, and the worst foe of the Gospel. Then, as to Pope Pius IX, no one could, both by his words and deeds, offend them more. He claimed, he exercised, larger powers than any other Pope ever did; he committed himself to ecclesiastical acts bolder than those of any other Pope; his secular policy was especially distasteful to Englishmen; he had some near him who put into print just that kind of gossip concerning him which would put an Englishman's teeth on edge; lastly, he it was who, in the beginning of his reign, was the author of the very measure which raised such a commotion among us." Nevertheless, as Newman shows, none of these factors could weigh against "his personal presence,"

---

[110] Alfred Lord Tennyson, "Merlin and Vivien," in *Idylls of the King* (1869), 227–30.
[111] Hutton, *Cardinal Newman*, 233.
[112] Newman, "Personal Influence, The Means of Propagating the Truth" (1832), *US*, 72–3.

which "was of a kind which no one could withstand." Always attentive to what was of permanent value in the passing scene, Newman realized that

> one special cause of the abatement of the animosity felt towards us by our countrymen was the series of *tableaux*, as I may call them, brought before them in the newspapers; of his receptions of visitors in the Vatican. His misfortunes indeed had something to do with his popularity. The whole world felt that he was shamefully used as regards his temporal possessions; no foreign power had any right to seize upon his palaces, churches, and other possessions; and the injustice shown him created a wide interest in him; but the main cause of his popularity was the magic of his presence, which was such as to dissipate and utterly destroy the fog out of which the image of a Pope looms to the ordinary Englishman; His uncompromising faith, his courage, the graceful intermingling in him of the human and the divine, the humour, the wit, the playfulness with which he tempered his severity, his naturalness, and then his true eloquence, and the resources he had at command for meeting with appropriate words the circumstances of the moment, overcame those who were least likely to be overcome. A friend of mine, a Protestant, a man of practised intellect and mature mind, told me to my surprise, that, at one of the Pope's receptions at the Vatican he was so touched by the discourse made by his Holiness to his visitors, that he burst into tears. And this was the experience of hundreds; how could they think ill of him or of his children when his very look and voice were so ethical, so eloquent, so persuasive?[113]

In May of 1884, Newman wrote Hutton in the wake of the false account that his brother-in-law Thomas Mozley had written about him and his father.[114] "I can't expect that affectionate friends such as you (for the words 'affectionately yours' were in my own heart and at the end of my pen before I found them in your letter) that such can wait till my full years on earth have run out, before they speak of me; nor that the purveyors of gossip of the past should refrain from tearing off my morbidly sensitive skin, while they can with public interest," Newman wrote. But Hutton, of all his contemporary critics had been different. "Here I am but writing a letter of thanks," he wrote "It is about 20 years since I wrote to thank you for your Notice in the Spectator of my Apologia on its first publication. I dare say it was against the etiquette of the literary world, for no one was kind enough to answer me but you. In consequence I called on you at your Office. I have never seen you since, have I? but whenever in London, from the gratitude I ... [felt] for the continuance of the kindness you first showed in 1864, I have wished to do so. Now I suppose there is no chance of my ever going to London, at least for many hours. You will accept instead, I am sure, the blessing of a Cardinal of Holy Church, even though you cannot accept that title of 'Holy' as given her in the Creed."[115]

---

[113] *Addresses to Cardinal Newman with his replies 1879–81*, ed. W. P. Neville (London: Longmans Green, 1905), 242–3.

[114] See Thomas Mozley, *Reminiscences Chiefly of Oriel College and the Oxford Movement*, 2 vols (London: Longmans, Green, & Co., 1882), i, 11–18.

[115] Newman to Richard Holt Hutton (6 May 1884), *LD*, xxx, 357.

Richard Holt Hutton

Nothing better verifies the truth of the influence reserved for "holiness embodied" than the grateful fidelity with which Richard Holt Hutton entered into Newman's lifelong witness to the unseen, though the "venture of faith" necessary to join the "One True Fold of the Redeemer" was something he never managed. What he told Newman of his case in one of his earliest letters appears to have remained his case until the day he died. "When I was eighteen the passage in which Willis describes the mass in 'Loss and Gain' very nearly made a Willis of me," he confessed, "—a man I mean who *dives* experimentally into the Church in the hope of faith rather than one who goes into it because he sees it to be true. But since then I have got a growing conviction that faith however mysterious ought to prove itself to the mind and has the power to do so. Still that passage about the mass has a strange fascination for me which I cannot quite analyze. In this world I see no chance of ever following you. And yet there are passages in your teaching that cling to me still."[116]

---

[116] Richard Holt Hutton to Newman (15 June 1864), *LD*, xxi, 120–1.

MARK PATTISON

~ 3 ~

Mark Pattison and the Life of the Mind

March 12.—Have just finished Pattison's Memoir; curious as an unconscious confession of sordid egotism, mingling with a genuine ardour for an academic ideal of life. Very odd that a man of so much intellectual calibre appears never to have turned on his own character the cold and bitter criticism that he applies to others. In spite of my sympathy with his views, I cannot but admit that his life is a moral fiasco, which the orthodox have a right to point to as a warning against infidelity. The fiasco is far worse than Carlyle's, though the fall is from a lower pedestal.[1]

Henry Sidgwick

What a work it is to implant faith! what human power can do it?

John Henry Newman

All my energy was directed upon one end ... to free myself from the bondage of unreason, and the traditional prejudices which, when I first began to think, constituted the whole of my intellectual fabric.

Mark Pattison

I

In his *Memoirs* (1885), Mark Pattison recalled Dr. Arnold's biographer A. P. Stanley telling him, "'How different the fortunes of the Church of England might have been if Newman had been able to read German,'" a remark with which the Rector of Lincoln entirely agreed.[2] "That puts the matter in a nut-shell," Pat-

---

[1] Diary entry of Henry Sidgwick (12 March 1885) quoted in *Henry Sidgwick: A Memoir*, ed. Arthur Sidgwick and Eleanor Mildred Sidgwick (London: Macmillan, 1906), 404.
[2] Ruskin's mother was another figure from the Regency whose unfamiliarity with the German language left her open to the aspersions of Germanophiles. "Taking herself no interest in German studies," her son wrote, "and being little curious as to the events, and little respectful to the opinions, of Mayfair, she was apt to look with some severity ... on what she thought pretentious in the accomplishments, or affected in the manners, of the young people: while they, on the other hand, though quite sensible of my mother's worth, grateful for her good will, and in time really attached to her, were not disposed to pay much attention to the opinions of a woman who knew

tison wrote. "Newman assumed and adorned the narrow basis on which Laud had stood 200 years before. All the grand development of human reason from Aristotle down to Hegel was a sealed book to him."[3] Charging Newman with being remiss for somehow never seeing beyond the Archbishop of Canterbury's advocacy of the Elizabethan settlement (1558) was an eccentric aspersion; but it was not of the essence of Pattison's complaint. For Pattison, what was wrong with Newman was that he suffered from lack of knowledge; and not merely knowledge *per se* but the sort of historicist knowledge favored by Germany's rationalists and their liberal followers in England.[4] On this score, Edward Sillem (1916–64), the English editor of Newman's Philosophical Notebook is worth quoting:

> The growing desire for a scientific and fully rationalized system of philosophy amongst thinking people of education was clear from the increasing unwillingness shown by learned men to surrender their minds to mere faith in a creed. Educated people were looking for a philosophy, for something that is free (or not subject to authority), rational and personal. … Newman found [in this search on the part of the English and the Germans for a scientific faith] the problem of the *University Sermons*, i.e., that created by "the usurpation of reason." Obviously, he was no more impressed by the German than he had been by the English idea of "Reason," as Pattison considered he would have been if he had known something of German philosophy.[5]

Pattison's was not an original criticism: it was shared by nearly all of Newman's nineteenth-century rationalist critics. Johann Joseph Ignaz von Döllinger (1799–1890), who broke with the Roman Church over papal infallibility, had made the same criticism of the author of *A Letter to the Duke of Norfolk*: "whole stretches of Church history and the history of European culture are unknown to him, as the darkest Africa. There is no way of explaining his naïve and daring assertions." Newman, in other words, for all of his insights into the development of doctrine, was not sufficiently appreciative of how doctrine, like ideas, was

---

only her own language." John Ruskin, *Praeterita: Outlines of Scenes and Thoughts Perhaps Worthy of Memory in My Past Life*, ed. Kenneth Clark (London: Rupert Hart-Davis, 1949), 163.

[3] Mark Pattison, *Memoirs* (London: Macmillan, 1885), 111–12. Pattison's comment was ironic in light of the fact that it is the character Edward Casaubon in George Eliot's *Middlemarch* (1871–2) whose "Key to all Mythologies" remains unfinished because he did not read German. Pattison was long thought to have been the model for the proud, embittered, futile character of Casaubon, though the scholar Rosemary Ashton shows otherwise. After quoting the character in the book who uncovers Casaubon's ignorance of German—"I merely mean that the Germans have taken the lead in historical inquiries, and they laugh at results which are got by groping about in the woods with a pocket-compass while they have made good roads"—Ashton concludes her case with pithy irrefutability: "Ignorance of German scholarship is one criticism which could not be levelled at the Rector of Lincoln." Rosemary Ashton, "Lunch with the Rector: George Eliot and Mark Pattison Revisited," *Times Literary Supplement* (31 January 2014).

[4] The English don A. D. Nuttall nicely encapsulated this view by saying that "Pattison tends to assume that you explain a thing by eliciting its history rather than by exposing its metaphysical presuppositions." A. D. Nuttall, *Dead from the Waist Down: Scholars and Scholarship in Literature and the Popular Imagination* (New Haven: Yale University Press, 2003), 104.

[5] Edward J. Sillem, "General Introduction to the Study of Newman's Philosophy," John Henry Newman, *The Philosophical Notebook*, ed. Edward J. Sillem 2 vols. (Louvain: Nauwelaerts Publishing House, 1999), i, 230.

the product of historical time and space, which only a mastery of "the history of European culture" could bestow. Pattison's echoing of this criticism is worth singling out because it gave him the grounds to formulate an understanding of the place of scholarship in the life of the mind that would at once draw upon and renounce Newman's views on these matters. Revisiting Pattison's life and work can help us to gain a better understanding of Newman's rejection of this cardinal article of the rationalist faith. Of course, Newman's writings teem with rebuttals of the historicist fallacy, but his gloss on the proverb, "Wisdom is justified of her children" (Matt. 11.19) is a useful encapsulation of them. In his sermon, "The Usurpations of Reason" (1831), which he included in his *Oxford University Sermons* (1843), he paraphrased the parable thus: it was "as if [Our Lord] said, 'There is no act on God's part, no truth of religion, to which a captious Reason may not find objections; and in truth the evidence and matter of Revelation are not addressed to the mere unstable Reason of man, nor can hope for any certain or adequate reception with it. Divine Wisdom speaks, not to the world, but to her own children, or those who have been already under her teaching, and who, knowing her voice, understand her words, and are suitable judges of them. These justify her.'"

Pattison, for his part, once he repudiated his Christianity, agreed with the German historian of philosophy, Heinrich Moritz Chalybäus (1796–1862), whose classic *Historische Entwicklung der spekulativen Philosophie von Kant bis Hegel* (1837) Newman read in translation: "We feel no hesitation in stating that mere faith—we mean thereby a blind, traditionary belief—has lost its hold on the mind of men of education, and that all attempts to discover a formula wherewith to conjure it back, will prove abortive. The vain endeavours in that direction may be in fact characterised as the torment of our days. Nothing will satisfy any longer, on subjects so solemn and important, but a free, rational and personal conviction."[6] No one was more tortured on this account than Mark Pattison

On the first page of Pattison's autobiography, one of the more fascinating of the English nineteenth-century, he offered a possible genesis for what would become his rationalist preoccupations with the intellect. "If I cannot remember of myself the hidebound and contracted intellect, with which I entered upon life, and something of the steps by which I emerged from that frozen condition, I have nothing else worth recording to write."[7] For Pattison to claim that the only thing worth recording of his childhood was how he managed to survive his "hidebound and contracted intellect" shows how much his professed rationalism grew out of an impatience with the real self—his own or anyone else's. In 1833, when he was twenty, he wrote in his *Memoirs*, he "had no mind, properly so-called, merely a boy's intelligence,"[8] as though the latter were somehow of no account. Pattison's biographer H. S. Jones sidesteps this crucial issue of identity by arguing that Pattison actually understood himself well enough. "What was that 'real self,'" Jones asks. "It was a self fundamentally committed to the life of the mind. Even the gauche and naïve boy from Hauxwell had glimpsed that ideal." Reading Pattison's

---

[6] H. M. Chalybäus, *Historical Development of Speculative Philosophy from Kant to Hegel*, ed. Sir William Hamilton and trans. Alfred Edersheim (Edinburgh: T&T Clark, 1854), 20–1.
[7] Pattison, *Memoirs*, 78.
[8] Ibid., 120.

Memoirs, one cannot be at all certain that the boy who delighted in the beauty of the Yorkshire moors was preoccupied with "the life of the mind," despite his septuagenarian chronicler claiming otherwise. Nevertheless, when the life of the mind finally got round to presenting itself to Pattison, he felt utterly changed. "I now awoke to the new idea of finding the reason of things; I began to suspect that I might have much to unlearn, as well as to learn, and that I must clear my mind of much current opinion which had lodged there. Not that I saw this with the clearness, or thought of carrying it out with the thoroughness, of a Descartes; but the principle of rationalism was born in me, and once born it was sure to grow, and to become the master idea of the whole process of self-education on which I was from this time forward embarked."[9] Here was the "principle of rationalism" to which Pattison would dedicate his life. Apropos the "master idea" of Pattison's "process of self-education," John Morley, Gladstone's biographer remarked that although "Pattison conceived his ideal at the age of twenty, he was five-and-forty before he finally and deliberately embraced it and shaped his life in conformity to it. The principle of rationalism, instead of growing, seemed for twelve whole years to go under, and to be completely mastered by the antagonistic principles of authority, tradition, and transcendental faith."[10] This is one way of accounting for Pattison's development: under Newman's influence, he was stymied; once he rejected that influence, he came into his own. But in revisiting Pattison's development under and in rebellion against Newman's influence, we can see that those "twelve whole years" might not have been as antagonistic to the true life of the mind, let alone the whole person, as Morley suggests. Pattison's relation to "authority, tradition and transcendental faith" and, indeed, to Newman, was far more consequential than either Morley or Pattison himself supposed. Yet before revisiting Pattison's evolving understanding of this lively matter, it might be helpful to revisit the broad outlines of his life.

II

Mark Pattison (1813–84) was the son of Mark James Pattison, rector of Haukswell, Yorkshire and Jane, daughter of Francis Winn, banker, of Richmond, Yorkshire. He was the eldest of twelve children, ten of them girls. Growing up in a remote village, he was shy and sensitive, at once a voracious reader and an avid horseman, fisherman and naturalist. After going up to Oxford in 1832, he befriended Newman and his Tractarian friends and read deeply in classics and English literature, without, however, attaining the first on which he had set his heart. Graduating BA in 1836 and MA in 1840, he then took up residence with other young Tractarians in Newman's house in St. Aldate's, where he aided in the translation of St Thomas Aquinas' "Catena Aurea on the Gospels." After failing to obtain a fellowship from, first, Oriel and, then, Balliol, Pattison secured the Yorkshire fellowship from Lincoln in 1839, about which he later wrote: "Oh, the joy of relief! No joy in all my life has ever been so sweet as that Friday morning." At Lincoln, he continued to work with Newman and the Tractarians, writing lives

---

[9] *Ibid.*, 121.
[10] John Morley, *Critical Miscellanies*, 3 vols (London: Macmillan, 1898), iii, 139–40.

of two 13th-century saints, Stephen Langton and Edmund Rich, as well as the fifth-century St. Ninian, Bishop of Whithorn and Galloway, known in Scotland as the Apostle of the Southern Picts, for Newman's *Lives of the British Saints*. In what he referred to in his *Memoirs* as "the whirlpool of Tractarianism," he was even impelled to go to confession to Pusey, which he afterwards regretted when he learned that the Canon of Christ Church divulged details of the confession. In 1841, Pattison was ordained a deacon and in 1843 a minister of the National Church. In 1841 and 1842, respectively, he won theological prizes for papers on "The Sufficiency of Holy Scripture for the Salvation of Man" and "Original or Birth Sin and the Necessity of New Birth and Life." In 1843, he was appointed to a college tutorship, which constrained him to suspend his interests in theology and concentrate instead on Aristotle, logic, the classics and English literature. Despite these secular studies, Pattison briefly contemplated joining Newman when he seceded to the Church of Rome in 1845, confessing that "in some moment of mental and physical depression, or under the pressure of some arguing convert" he might have "dropped off to Rome."[11] At the same time, when he revisited his diary for that period, he saw that he was sufficiently removed from the Tractarian ethos—at least in his reading—to see Newman's secession more resignedly than some of the other Tractarians. "In the Diary which begins 1845 there is a much larger infusion of secular matter," he wrote in his *Memoirs*. "I find myself deep in the literary history of the eighteenth century, reading Gray's Correspondence, Prior's Life of Goldsmith, Hume's Life and Correspondence; and as all this was when Newman was preparing his going over, I must have been looking on with equanimity."[12]

In 1851, Pattison suffered the greatest disappointment of his life when he was passed over for the rectorship of Lincoln by a group of anti-reform electors, who appointed James Thompson, whom V. H. H. Green nicely describes as "a good-natured fellow but a clerical lowbrow of uncouth ways."[13] The setback was one about which Pattison admitted to feeling extravagant self-pity. "I dragged on a weary routine of tuition for the rest of the Michaelmas term and the Lent term of 1852," he recalled in his *Memoirs*; "went through the forms of lecturing, but the life and spirit were gone. I now loathed teaching as much as I had delighted in it. My tutor's back was broken; I knew that, whatever might happen about the appeal, I could never take up again college work with any spirit or hope of

---

[11] An amusing instance of such "arguing" can be found in the memoirs of the English author George Valentine Cox (1786–1875), which the editor Francis McGrath quotes in *LD*, ix, 567: "One of the earliest 'perverts' was Mr. Seager, of Worcester College. It was said that he went to Oscott 'for a literary enquiry'; that, after dinner, controversy was started by Dr. Wiseman, and was kept up till four o'clock next morning, when Mr. Seager 'cried for quarter!' Can we wonder that he, who thus rushed into the snare, should not have escaped? The account further added, that 'at 8 a.m. of the same morning he was baptised!' That act of baptizing converts from our Church is justly considered the most arrogant of all Romish proceedings; as ignoring our Church, our ministers, their orders and ministrations altogether. Only conceive such men as Newman, Manning, Oakley, Faber, &c., thus renouncing, or rather denouncing, the Church of their fathers, and condemning, as not Christian, their own previous ministrations!" G. V. Cox, *Recollections of Oxford* (London: Macmillan, 1868), 314.

[12] Pattison, *Memoirs*, 187–8.

[13] Vivian Hubert Howard Green, *Oxford Common Room: A Study of Lincoln College and Mark Pattison* (London: Edward Arnold, 1957), 157.

success."[14] Morley, who knew Pattison at Lincoln, could enter into the grounds for his disappointment, even betrayal, though he still marveled at its inordinate expression.

> His whole heart and pride had … been invested in the success of the college; it was the thing on which he had set all his affections; in a fortnight the foundation of his work was broken up; and the wretched and deteriorated condition of the undergraduates became as poison in his daily cup. That may all be true enough. Still, whatever elements of a generous public spirit sharply baffled may have entered into this extraordinary moral breakdown, it must be pronounced a painfully unmanly and unedifying exhibition … The world forgives almost anything to a man in the crisis of a sore spiritual wrestle for faith and vision and an Everlasting Yea, and almost anything to one prostrated by the shock of an irreparable personal bereavement. But that anybody with character of common healthiness should founder and make shipwreck of his life because two or three unclean creatures had played him a trick after their kind, is as incredible as that a three-decker should go down in a street puddle.[15]

Certainly, in retrospect, when it came to the theological preoccupations that had animated his work with Newman and the Tractarians, Pattison could only feel a kind of astonished revulsion. "Indeed I have great difficulty with the Diary in my hand in making intelligible the exact state of my mind and opinions in the whole of the four years from 1843 to 1847," he confessed. "I do not see a single page in the Diary which savours of rationalism, I mean the application of the common reason to religion. I see a great deal of degrading superstition, of fasting and attending endless religious services. I adopted the plan which many others did, of reciting the Hours of the Roman Breviary, and seemed to please myself for some time in this time-wasting and mind-drowning occupation."[16] The extent to which this was not only a retrospective but an unfair appraisal can be seen from the diary itself, one of the entries of which shows that the Tractarian Pattison was more rational—in the benign sense of that word—than the Post-Tractarian Pattison was prepared to allow. On Saturday, 30 September 1843, he went to see Newman at Littlemore for a fortnight, and one entry of his diary for that period reads: "Newman kinder, but not perfectly so. Vespers at eight. Compline at nine. How low, mean, selfish, my mind has been to-day; all my good seeds vanished; grovelling, sensual, animalish; I am not indeed worthy to come under this roof."[17] Another entry is equally revealing.

> 5th October.—Awoke poorly this morning, but got gradually better, yet did not make a thoroughly good use of my time. Coffin came to-day to stay; says the college at Chichester in great want of discipline. The principal does not live with them, and Lowe has not much authority. Men to be found in the billiard-rooms, and set up a tandem; many come only to cram for the Bishop's Examination …

---

[14] Pattison, *Memoirs*, 191–2.
[15] Morley, *Critical Miscellanies*, iii, 153–4.
[16] Pattison, *Memoirs*, 188–9.
[17] Ibid., 190.

How uncomfortable have I made myself all this evening by a childish fancy that once got into my head—I could not get out of it—a weak jealousy of N's good opinion. Oh, my God! take from me this petty pride; set me free from this idle slavery to opinion; fix my affections on things eternal.[18]

In yet another entry, he writes: "Thirty years old to-day; ripe and mature in age, but only beginning, if, indeed, I am beginning, Christian life. A child in knowledge and judgment. When I ought to be able to teach, guide, and influence others I am still only a learner. Spent nearly two hours this morning in devotion and self-examination; with some fervency and, by God's grace, I trust, profit, at least I have felt more peace and calm through the day than I have known for some time past."[19] Far from exhibiting any "degrading superstition," these entries show the winning humility that Pattison could show while still a Tractarian, a quality he would subsume in bitter irony once he repudiated Christianity for the donnish rationalism to which he would devote his life after Newman's secession to Rome.

This undue attention to intellect might have been planted in Pattison by his father, a high and dry Evangelical clergyman, who had read deeply but unsupervisedly at Brasenose. As Pattison says, "he had a veneration for intellectual eminence," insisting that his son read not only Pitt and Fox but Hume and Blackstone.[20] After Pattison left Hauxwell for Oxford, his father also had a nervous breakdown, which would only intensify his son's propensity for self-conscious brooding. By the time Pattison got round to writing his *Memoirs* (1885) choosing to see his youthful development almost exclusively in terms of intellect might almost have been inevitable, even though by his own account it was not intellect, but the human heart, with all its tenderness, joys and fears that animated his youthful fancy. After all, his heart's delight in the remote countryside of the North Riding suffused his first memories. "The idea of natural science was far above me," he recalled. "I only thought of collecting, first birds, then insects."[21] Collecting went hand-in-hand with observing. "Wandering over the moor whole days, haunting the skirts of the woods at night, on the look-out for birds and moths, the sense of the country, a delight in rural objects, grew within me, and passed insensibly into the more abstract poetic emotion."[22] There is little here that one would call intellectual. Or even here, which he wrote when he was much older: "I don't think that it was before two or three years after 1830 [when he was 30] that this transition from natural history to poetry proper began to take place in my mind. My removal to college diverted me from the pursuit of natural knowledge; my instinctive tastes were never developed into a science. The love of birds, moths, butterflies, led on to the love of landscape; and altogether, in the course of the next six or seven years, grew and merged into a conscious and declared poetical sentiment, and a devoted reading of the poets."[23] Although he acknowledges that the appeal of the aesthetic was one to which he was never

---

[18] Ibid., 195.
[19] Ibid., 205.
[20] Ibid., 8.
[21] Ibid., 32.
[22] Ibid., 33–4.
[23] Ibid., 34.

indifferent, he is rather dismissive about it in his *Memoirs*. "I don't suppose the temperament was more inclined to aesthetic emotion in me than in other youths," he recalled, "but I was highly nervous and delicate, and having never been at school had not had sentiment and delicacy crushed out of me."[24] Far from being "crushed out of him," responsiveness to beauty was central to Pattison. "When I came in after years to read The Prelude I recognised, as if it were my own history which was being told, the steps by which the love of the country boy for his hills and moors grew into poetical susceptibility for all imaginative presentations of beauty in every direction."[25] Still, the older man's obsession with the intellect could only perversely discount this "poetical susceptibility." "I see I am in danger of conveying an idea of myself as more advanced in intelligence, or power of perceiving beauty, than I was. I hasten to say that in these first years of the '30's there was nothing in me that could be called intelligence."[26]

Here, we can see, that if Pattison failed to do justice to Newman's influence in his memoir, for all of his incidental praise of his former mentor, he also failed to do justice to himself. Indeed, he recalled his entry into Oxford with the same barbed pitilessness that he recalled nearly everything else about his unhappy life. "I must have cut a laughably boorish figure that Thursday evening," he wrote, "marching up the High Street in an old brown greatcoat of my father's ... which had been reduced by a Richmond slop-tailor to fit me."[27] The Yorkshire clergyman's son had nothing of the polish or ease of his more conventional contemporaries. "I should never have done, were I to write down all I can recall about the young men among whom I now found myself, transported from a desert moor where were no inhabitants but Highland 'stots.'" If Pattison had looked forward to Oxford as the place where he would finally find not only teachers who could guide him in his reading but companions with whom he could share that reading, he was disappointed to find "that the differences between myself on the one side, and all the rest on the other, were greater than the resemblances; the points of antipathy more numerous than the points of sympathy."[28]

In specifying these differences, we see the Yorkshire solitary in Pattison avid for companions, yes, but never boon companions. We also see something of the captious fastidiousness that would always keep Pattison apart from his fellows.

> Large as was the part which the bodily appetites filled in my nature, in these youths they were still more rampant and imperious. If I was lazy, selfish, greedy, and rapacious, these youths were so to a degree which disgusted me. I wanted associates congenial with the better part of me, not with whom I could indulge the baser propensities. I had no taste for drinking. My father had great difficulty in getting me to drink a single glass on the occasions when he opened a bottle of his choice port. I was over forty before I even began to like wine, and it was later still in life before it became a daily beverage. In 1832 I had not begun to smoke, and did not desire to. I was not all at once made aware of this want of

---

[24] Ibid.
[25] Ibid., 35.
[26] Ibid.
[27] Ibid., 42–3.
[28] Ibid., 45–6.

conformity between myself and others of my age; I arrived at the apprehension of it slowly, after many vain experiments and successive failures to establish a good understanding with one after another.[29]

The moral, however, that he drew from these differences was striking. "As it was, my weakness of character was such that I came to the conclusion in the end that the fault or defect, whatever it might be, was in me. They could not be all wrong, and they seemed to have no difficulty in getting on with each other. My boyish inexperience was such, that I could not understand how it could be that the others, many of whom were below me in attainments, were before me in manliness of character; that they dared to assert themselves as they were, while I was deficient in character, and hid, instead of standing by, the small amount I possessed."[30] He itemizes what he regarded as the "small amount" of his attainments at the age of 18 in his *Memoirs*. Of Latin authors, he had read all of Sallust; about a dozen speeches of Cicero, twenty books of Livy, all of Vergil, all of Horace, all of Juvenal: all of Caesar, and all of Terence; and for Greek: the Gospels and Acts, Xenophon's Anabasis, Herodotus, Thucydides, Homer's Iliad, some of Demosthenes's speeches, Pindar, Sophocles, Aeschylus, Aristophanes, and Euripides. By any chalk, these were formidable attainments, though Pattison could only see their meagreness.

> None of the niceties of scholarship had ever been whispered to me. I was not well grounded even in the Greek grammar; as to accentuation and metrical law I had everything to learn. But the worst of all was that I had not been shown how to read, and that the general mystery of exact language was hidden from me. The book which had taken most hold of my mind was Thucydides; I had written out translations of all the speeches. The political pregnancy of certain words in these had excited my interest, and served afterwards as a kind of introduction to the study of philosophical terms. But I had no apprehension of the refined beauties of poetical expression, the exquisitely clean-cut wording of Sophocles, and no doubt preferred Horace to Vergil. All that my extensive reading had given me was a mere empirical familiarity with the languages, an enlarged vocabulary, and an idea of various and contrasted styles.[31]

Here, we can see a good example of the morbid scrupulosity that would keep Pattison from putting together any sizable or even coherent body of work. Since one could never know enough about any given subject, Pattison was always insisting, it was best to hold off on completing or even beginning any project. In his own case, this perfectionist defeatism would disable him from writing his most ambitious projects, his history of theology and his biography of J. J. Scaliger (1540–1609), the prodigious French scholar, who left behind an enormous body of scholarly work, despite his controversies with the Jesuits, who charged him with atheism and profligacy. The Oratorian Henry Tristram quotes Pattison as admitting that he was never tempted to subscribe to "the vulgar fallacy that a

---

[29] Ibid., 46–7.
[30] Ibid., 47–8.
[31] Ibid., 62–3.

literary life meant a life devoted to the making of books."[32] Like Lord Acton, another scholar more famous for the books he did not write than for those he did, Pattison exhibited a kind of phantom scholarship, which was all the more unassailable for being unpublished. Like George Eliot's Mr. Casaubon in *Middlemarch* (1871–2), Pattison would devote his entire adult life to planning an impossible scholarly work that would never be written. For Eliot, the delusive investment that Pattison made in his own "Key to all Mythologies" bespoke "a trait ... not quite alien to us, and, like the other mendicant hopes of mortals, claims ... our pity."[33] His biographer, H. S. Jones is good on this defining aspect of the man.

> He had the reputation of being the most learned man in England, but though he wrote extensively for a variety of periodicals, his published works did not do full justice to the depth and extent of his learning. "Mark Pattison is undoubtedly a researcher, so are we all," wrote Mandell Creighton in 1872, "but one Essay and Review and one edition of Pope's *Essay on Man* scarcely justify to the Philistine a large endowment" (L. Creighton, *Life and Letters of Mandell Creighton*, 1904, 1.135). Thus, while Pattison achieved a mastery of eighteenth-century literature and philosophy, it was a younger man, Leslie Stephen, who produced an authoritative and comprehensive work on the subject. ... "It takes me six weeks to write a sermon," he once complained, "and then I don't finish" (A. H. Sayce, *Reminiscences*, 1923, 36). Fortunately, he preached little. Arguably his research ethic was inherently sterile. His typical advice to an aspiring scholar—to choose a subject and then devote half a lifetime to reading all relevant sources—was daunting and often off-putting.[34]

When it comes to Pattison's inability to produce—a common enough bane of the would-be scholar critic toiling away in academic salt mines—John Morley was incisive, if unmerciful: "The ... key to Pattison's whole existence ... was [that he was] affected from first to last by a profound weakness of will and character. Few men of eminence have ever lived so destitute of nerve as Pattison was—of nerve for the ordinary demands of life, and of nerve for those large enterprises in literature for which by talent and attainment he was so admirably qualified. The stamp of moral *défaillance* was set upon his brow from the beginning."[35] Yet Morley could also see, as Newman saw, the good points in the man.

> Though nobody was ever much less of a man of the world in one sense, yet Pattison's mind was always in the world. In company he often looked as if he were thinking of the futility of dinner-party dialectics, where all goes too fast for truth, where people miss one another's points and their own, where nobody convinces or is convinced, and where there is much surface excitement with little real stimulation. That so shrewd a man should have seen so obvious a fact as all this was certain. But he knew that the world is the real thing, that the proper

---

[32] Pattison quoted in Henry Tristram, *Newman and his Friends: On Cardinal Newman's Dedications* (London: The Bodley Head, 1933), 25.
[33] George Eliot, *Middlemarch: A Study of Provincial Life*, ed. R. M. Hewitt (Oxford: Oxford University Press, 1947), 85.
[34] H. S. Jones, entry on Mark Pattison in *ODNB*, 43, 120.
[35] John Morley, "On Pattison's Memoirs," in *Critical Miscellanies*, iii, 140.

study of mankind is man, and that if books must be counted more instructive and nourishing than affairs, as he thought them to be, it is still only because they are the most complete record of what is permanent, elevated, and eternal in the mind and act of man.[36]

III

One can see something of the crippling perfectionism in Pattison in his fundamental objection to Leslie Stephen's two-volume history of the English eighteenth century. In his review of the book, apropos the Enlightenment, Pattison writes of the "yearning of the spirit for the years to come, this sense of waking at the dawn of day, when the night is past," which might have been "less perceptible in the English eighteenth century than in the French and German eighteenth century." Yet for Pattison, "it may not be out of place to make the observation, that it is not possible to place the history of English thought in a clear light without putting forward its relation to the contemporary thought of the progressive nations. Mr. Stephen has not attempted this."[37] In other words, Stephen should have written the history of English eighteenth-century thought in the context of continental thought. In his biography of Stephen, Lord Annan captured the essence of this objection when he said "Pattison complained that Stephen did not use the comparative method (always a safe card to play in a review.),"[38] even though Pattison does allow that Stephen might have objected that "one book cannot contain everything, nor one man write everything; and that to have tried to be all-comprehensive would have sacrificed the compactness and unity of his scheme." Indeed, this was the very criticism that Pattison leveled against Henry Thomas Buckle's sweeping *History of Civilization* (1857–61): it sought to be much too comprehensive. Pattison's criticism of Stephen is also the criticism leveled against Ian Ker's ruthlessly focused biography of Newman, which, for altogether justifiable aesthetic reasons, sacrificed context for critical depth and the coherence that only a single volume could accommodate. Yet for Pattison, to write proper intellectual history, such mundane considerations would have to be waved aside. "English thought is not a whole number, but a fraction … [and] the interest of its story lies in exhibiting this unity underneath the different aspects it presents in different countries."[39] Constricting his undertaking work to such severe prerequisites, it is no wonder Pattison never wrote any *magnum opus*.

Nevertheless, here, we should keep in mind that if Pattison took against teaching later in life, it was not because he lacked any talent for teaching—or solicitude for those he taught—until that is, he began regarding them as 'African savages.'"[40] Again, his biographer, Jones is emphatic about this: "Pattison developed few close friendships with his peers; perhaps his closest friend in that category was the

---

[36] Ibid., 166–7.
[37] Mark Pattison, "The Age of Reason," *The Fortnightly Review*, 27 (1877), 351.
[38] Noel Annan, *Leslie Stephen: The Godless Victorian* (London: George Weidenfeld & Nicholson, 1984), 231.
[39] Pattison, "The Age of Reason," 351.
[40] ODNB.

philosopher J. M. Wilson, president of Corpus Christi College.[41] On the other hand he evidently had, at his best, something of a genius for close friendship with the young, which clearly contributed to his success as a tutor. He was, effectively, the patron of a group of young university liberals of scholarly interests, some of whom he successfully steered towards distinguished research careers: these men included Ingram Bywater, A. H. Sayce, and Henry Nettleship. To exercise a personal authority of this kind he must have had an affectionate and generous side to his character. One former pupil, Richard Copley Christie, wrote of his 'magnetic influence' (*DNB*)."[42] One can also see from Pattison's essays the true devotion he had to teaching and to education, especially in his essay, "Oxford Studies" (1855), where he says: "education is only the natural result of the instinct to communicate our culture; an instinct active in proportion as the culture is vigorous and enlarged. An accomplishment, or a skill, its possessor desires to monopolize; talent excites admiration, not sympathy. Enlargement of mind, as of character, seeks to propagate itself; the more that share it, the greater our gain. Intellect attracts intellect in proportion to its capacity: there is a freemasonry of intelligence, as such; even while we are young, we are conscious of this before we can comprehend it. The young are worshippers of talent and contemn learning, yet they feel the power of genius and intellect; and, as Alcibiades held Socrates's robe, for the virtue that went out from him, the most intelligent pupil seeks the most intellectual instructor."[43] Yet after Pattison had secured his Lincoln Rectorship and Oxford had instituted so many of his pet reforms, he became disgusted with the place, as John Sparrow nicely relates. "Pattison was happier now in the smoking-room of the Athenaeum than in the senior common room of Lincoln. … Oxford was a 'desert of arid shop-dons; a day spent on College business was a day utterly wasted.'" When he gazed out of his windows at the undergraduates assembling for beginning of term, he could only say to himself, "Year after year, the same check suits! The same horse-shoe pins!"[44]

Another feature of Pattison's growing disillusionment with his chosen profession was his impatience with Oxford itself, particularly with the philistinism of the place, which might have called forth the genial satirist in Matthew Arnold in such effusions as *Culture and Anarchy* and *Friendship's Garland* but only elicited Pattison's saturnine contempt. "I had come up all eagerness to learn," he recalled in his *Memoirs*.

---

[41] Although a fluent talker, John Matthias Wilson (1813–81) was singularly slow in written composition. He did not produce any independent book, but was engaged for many years, in conjunction with Thomas Fowler, Wykeham professor of logic at Oxford, on a work entitled *The Principles of Morals*, the first part of which appeared posthumously in 1886, under their joint names, and the second part in 1887 under Fowler's name alone. In the book, Wilson took a strong position against Kant, deeming his system "without any regard to the facts of history, of human nature, and of human life" (*The Principles of Morals*, 1.83). He protested in particular against the notion of an Unknowable; for Wilson everything came within the compass of scientific understanding. The book was a clear statement of the empiricist school which continued to be represented at Oxford throughout the ascendancy of philosophical idealism by such figures as Wilson, Fowler, and Thomas Case. *ODNB*.

[42] *ODNB*.

[43] Pattison, *Essays*, i, 442.

[44] John Sparrow, *Mark Pattison and the Idea of a University* (Cambridge: Cambridge University Press, 1967), 119.

Having had next to no teaching at home, I exaggerated in imagination what a teacher could do for me. I thought that now at last I should be in the company of an ardent band of fellow-students, only desirous of rivalling each other in the initiation which the tutors were to lead into the mysteries of scholarship, of composition, of rhetoric, logic, and all the arts of literature. Philosophy did not come within my purview. I did not know there was such a thing. I was soon disillusioned. I found lectures regarded as a joke or a bore, contemned by the more advanced, shirked by the backward; Latin and Greek regarded as useless, except for the purpose of getting a degree; and as for modern literature, the very idea of its existence had never dawned upon these youths, none of whom knew any language but English. Such was my simplicity that I had believed that no one went to college but those who were qualified, and anxious, to study. Nor was the difference between the passman and the honour man a sufficient clearing up of the paradox ... that men should flock to a university not to study. It fairly puzzled me to find that even William Froude, whom his elder brother was compelling to read for classical honours, "hated Sophocles"—so he once told me—and regarded the whole job as a disgusting grind.[45]

After failing to secure the rectorship at Lincoln, Pattison would come to know something of the "disgusting grind" of academic work himself. "I now loathed teaching as much as I had delighted in it," he recalled. "I could never take up again college work with any spirit or hope of success."[46] His diary entries plumb the depths of his despond. "Dull, insensible wretchedness," reads one entry. "The miserable depression of these days is not to be forgotten" reads another.[47] Advent and Christmas only exacerbated his dejection.

> 18th December.—Began to read Carlyle's Life of Schiller. Very weary and wretched both yesterday and to-day; all the savour of life is departed.
> 26th December.—Very wretched all yesterday and to-day; dull, gloomy, blank. Sleep itself is turned to sorrow.[48]

If thwarted ambition made his days insufferable, it also gave him that sardonic aloofness that informs so much of his unsparing view of Oxford. Certainly, he was right to see that "Oxford was, at the time I write of ... a close clerical corporation, and ... talent was much scarcer here than it now is, since the secularisation of the University. A very little literature, and a modicum of classical reading, went a long way."[49] At every turn, readers of Pattison's *Memoirs* encounter a kind of anti-Tuckwell—morose, supercilious, aggrieved, implacable. That his wife Emilia Francis Strong (1840–1904), later Lady Dilke—a cultured, elegant, lively woman—should leave him for long periods to write art history in Paris—she wrote a monograph on Claude Lorrain—can only have made him unhappier still.

---

[45] Pattison, *Memoirs*, 53–4.
[46] Ibid., 292.
[47] Ibid., 296.
[48] Ibid., 298.
[49] Ibid., 69.

Unlike Newman, who would go to great magnanimous lengths to say glowing things about Oriel, especially in his *Apologia*, despite his distaste for its liberalism, Pattison delighted in cutting it down to size. "For about the first thirty years of this century Oriel fulfilled all the three conditions of renown. It contained all there was of original intellect at the time in the University; it was usually tutored by energetic and well-qualified (according to the narrow standard of qualification then known) tutors; and an entrance examination sifted the commoners. An examination did not directly bring in youths from good families; but as soon as it is understood that a college chooses to be 'select,' good families are anxious to get their sons into it. And as Oriel could only lodge some sixty men, it very soon became matter of favour and showing cause of preference to get a son in. There was a goodly array of silk gowns—gentlemen commoners they were invidiously called—at the high table. These being better born, or wealthier than the commoners, kept up a style of living such as is usual in large country houses."[50] As for the widely held belief that Oriel declined as the result of the Provost Edward Hawkins turning out Newman, Hurrell Froude and Robert Wilberforce from their tutorships, in response to their insisting that they be allowed to discharge them in a pastoral spirit, Pattison was unpersuaded. "What they were interested in themselves they were ready to give out to their pupils," he wrote, "and enthusiasm is contagious. At least they had nothing else to give, for their knowledge of the classics was extremely limited."[51] Ruskin was also struck by the effect the silk gowns had on Oxford—in his case, Christ Church. "In those days [1836–9] the happy servitor's tenure of his college-room depended on his industry, while it was the privilege of the noble to support with lavish gifts the college, from which he expected no return, and to buy with sums equivalent to his dignity the privileges of rejecting alike its instruction and its control. It seems to me singular, and little suggestive of sagacity in the common English character, that it had never occurred to either old dean, or a young duke, that possibly the Church of England and the House of Peers might hold a different position in the country in years to come if the entrance examination had been made severer for the rich than the poor; and the nobility and good breeding of a student expected to be blazoned consistently by the shield on his seal, the tassel on his cap, the grace of his conduct, and the accuracy of his learning."[52]

Pattison, trying to make sense of his early career at Oxford, perceptively saw that his personal detachment from others instilled in him not only self-abasement but a chameleon-like subservience to others. "This inability to apprehend the reason of my social ill success had a discouraging consequence upon the growth of my character," he wrote.

> I was so convinced that the fault was in me, and not in the others, that I lost anything like firm footing, and succumbed to or imitated any type, or set, with which I was brought in contact, esteeming it better than my own, of which I was too ashamed to stand by it and assert it. Any rough, rude, self-confident fellow, who spoke out what he thought and felt, cowed me, and I yielded to him, and even

---

[50] Pattison, *Memoirs*, 68.
[51] Ibid., 92.
[52] John Ruskin, *Praeterita* (London: Everyman, 2005), 184–5.

assented to him, not with that yielding which gives way for peace sake, secretly thinking itself right, but with a surrender of the conscience and convictions to his mode of thinking, as being better than my own, more like men, more like the world. My unlikeness to others alarmed me; I wanted to be rid of it, and tried to be so by conformity to whatever came close to me from time to time. All force impressed and moved me, and having no criterion of good and bad in style and manner, I was ready to adopt any that had success and fashion in its favour. Surely no boy ever reached eighteen so unformed and characterless as I was![53]

Pattison's diffidence also bred in him an intense self-consciousness, which, judging from his *Memoirs*, went beyond the usual fretfulness that adolescents feel when they imagine their discomfiture evident to others. "This constant ... considering how I looked in others' eyes, clung about me till very late in life. Had I been thrown more into an active profession I should have rubbed it off sooner, but living a student's life, and only emerging into the sunlight at intervals, this nervous self-consciousness adhered to me long. When I at last got rid of, it gave way, not to the ordinary social friction, but to the substantial development of the real self, which had been all the while dormant within me."[54] In another passage he returns to how this diffidence undermined his sense of self. "I was trying to suppress that which was, all the time, my real self, and to put on the new man—the type by which I was surrounded. The assimilating process, which was not wholly bad, was carried to a certain point, and there arrested ... and that is the history of my life, and its only interest, so far as it may have any." For someone who prided himself on being an exacting historian, this was a striking admission, and yet few of his commentators have paid it any mind. For Pattison himself, this tendency to take on the convictions and mannerisms of those around him had a "baneful influence" on his character, since "an endeavour to seem something I was not ... [slid] into an endeavour to seem something better than what I was," which, in turn, "gave my whole behaviour an insincerity and affectation which, when discovered, extremely displeased myself, but which I found it impossible to shake off, as it was bound up with the attempt to do and think as others do—an attempt which at that time was indispensable to my existence as a member of society . I could not continue the wild boy of Hanover such as I had been sent up to Oxford."[55] And yet this "wild boy of Hanover" might have had more to do with Pattison's "real self" than he ever realized.

Reading these autobiographical musings, one can see how Pattison's Tractarian phase might have been part and parcel of his search for his true identity—something which, sooner or later, must preoccupy all of us. The passage also suggests that his immersion in eighteenth-century studies after he disengaged from Tractarianism and threw in his lot with the rationalists of Jowett's Oxford might have been another part of that search. The question is which of the two was more reflective of his true nature, his yearning for faith or his delight in the belittling of faith. The literary critic, A. D. Nuttall was convinced that Pattison's fondness for Gibbon bespoke a defining sympathy. Pattison, he says, "had an

---

[53] Pattison, *Memoirs*, 49.
[54] Ibid., 56.
[55] Ibid., 55-6.

eighteenth-century mind."[56] This was probably so. In most of his writing, if any Christian affiliation is discernible, it is usually of an anticlerical Deism. Then, again, one suspects that another reason why Pattison swore off his Tractarianism and embraced what he saw as the rationalism of the eighteenth century—a rationalism that one will not find in Swift, Johnson or Burke—was because he saw what religious fervor had done to his mad Evangelical father, who would refuse to dine with his daughters after his son's fleeting Tractarianism turned them into Anglo-Catholics.[57] Indeed, the scholarly interest that Pattison took in Newman's *Lives of the Saints* stemmed from his interest in learning more of the early Church figures whom Gibbon traduced and mocked in his *Decline and Fall*. Certainly, Pattison would distance himself from what he saw as Newman's interest in Gibbon by reminding his readers that "When [Newman] studied, it was church history—the Fathers of the fourth century; Athanasius was his hero; he was inspired by the triumph of the church organisation over the wisdom and philosophy of the Hellenic world; that triumph which, to the Humanist, is the saddest moment in history—the ruin of the painfully constructed fabric of civilisation to the profit of the church. Religion was evidently to Newman, in 1830, not only the first but the sole object of all teachings."[58] Then, too, even before he began working with Newman on *The Lives of the Saints*, Pattison recalled how he could rub the charismatic critic of Socinianism the wrong way. Although Newman had praised an essay Pattison had written before succumbing to what he characterized as "the whirlpool of Tractarianism," he looked askance at the young Yorkshireman's view of the Socinian theology emerging from Oriel's Noetics in the 1830s, especially that of Renn Dickson Hampden, which Newman deplored so fiercely.[59] "I openly and ostentatiously took the side of Hampden in the matter of the Regius Professor of Divinity," Pattison recalled.

> The fact was, I was delighted with the Bampton lectures. Their tone of omniscience imposed upon me, and as I had not yet abandoned my nominalist foundations, the dissolving power of nominalist logic applied to the Christian dogmas was wholly to my mind. On a later occasion, I well remember a personal incident

---

[56] Nuttall, *Dead from the Waist Down*, 97.
[57] Dorothy, one of Pattison's sisters, became a Sister of the Christ Church Sisterhood, taking the name Sister Dora. A statue of her in Walsall commemorates the saintly nursing care she extended sufferers from industrial accidents. See *ODNB*.
[58] Pattison, *Memoirs*, 96.
[59] "As to Dr Hampden, your imagination, I am sure, cannot picture any thing a quarter so bad as he really is—I do think him worse than a Socinian—In the British Magazine of this month, you will see a Pamphlet called 'Elucidations etc' stitched in, which gives you some but a very faint notion of his opinions. There is no doctrine, however sacred, which he does not scoff at—and in his Moral Philosophy he adopts the lowest and most grovelling utilitarianism as the basis of Morals—he considers it is a sacred duty to live to this world—and that religion by itself injuriously absorbs the mind. Whately, whatever his errors, is openhearted, generous, and careless of money—Blanco White is the same, though he has turned Socinian—Arnold is amiable and winning—but this man, *judging by his writings*, is the most lucre loving, earthly minded, unlovely person one ever set eyes on." Newman to Simeon Lloyd Pope (3 March 1836), *LD*, v, 251. Apropos Dr. Arnold, Tuckwell remarked: "while Whately did not fail to challenge Arnold precipitancy in argument and action—'You have three faults, rashness, rashness, rashness'—none more truly appreciated the moral nobleness of his character." William Tuckwell, *Pre-Tractarian Oxford: A Reminiscence of the Oriel "Noetics"* (London: Smith, Elder & Co., 1909), 119.

on one of those evenings which must have wounded my vanity deeply. The conversation turned on some point of philosophy ... and I, who must always be pushing myself forward when something I did not understand was going on, offered some flippant remark, such as young B.A.'s are apt even now to deal in. Newman turned round and deposited upon me one of those ponderous and icy "very likelies"; after which you were expected to sit down in a corner, and think over amending your conduct. I am sure that up to April, 1838, the only sentiment Newman can have entertained towards me was one of antipathy.[60]

Reading this, one is tempted to wonder whether the interest in the heterodoxy of Gibbon and Hampden had been little more than a provocative pose. Who was the real Mark Pattison? Judging from the continual care he showed his old pupil, one is inclined to suspect that, for Newman, the real Pattison might have been the one who not only embraced the Christian faith in youth but bitterly missed it in his apostate adulthood. In all events, Pattison himself was shrewd enough to know that this question was at his life's core. "I was trying to suppress that which was, all the time, my real self, and to put on the new man—the type by which I was surrounded. The assimilating process, which was not wholly bad, was carried to a certain point, and there arrested ... [T]hat is the history of my life."[61]

IV

When Leslie Stephen published his *English Thought in the Eighteenth Century* (1876), Pattison, who had wished but failed to write something on the same subject, was generous in his notice of the book in the *Fortnightly Review*, which showed how he could rise above the rivalrousness to which dons are naturally prone, but he also gave his readers a good measure of how he believed intellectual history should be written, especially when dealing with the history of religion. "The tone is throughout one of perfect taste," he wrote of Stephen's history.

> It is possible that a shadow of the fashionable cynicism here and there flits across Mr. Stephen's page, but if it be there at all, it is but a passing shadow. He does not habitually quiz the subject he is expounding, or talk with condescending pity of Lord Bacon or Sir Isaac Newton. He is always serious, never enlisted as a partisan, though often refuting controversialists. He may not be earnestly zealous in behalf of truth, but he is a watchful guardian of the rights of reason. Writing of the eighteenth century—the rationalist century—Mr. Stephen is eminently rational; he applies the standard of common sense to every opinion that offers. We have no *a priori* system thrust upon us at every turn, no doctrine preached at us, no political nostrum for the regeneration of society advertised under the guise of a history. In Mr. Leslie Stephen's pages we seem to breathe the free air of common reason uninfected by the sickly miasmata generated by local or temporary party.[62]

[60] Pattison, *Memoirs*, 170–1.
[61] Pattison, *Memoirs*, 55–6.
[62] Pattison, "The Age of Reason," 343.

This sounds fair enough until one sees how Pattison's negotiates the challenges inherent in writing any history of thought. After acknowledging the daunting scale of such enterprises, even when limited to a given century in a given country,[63] he goes further and says that such history is only possible if the historian can identify a principle comprehensive enough to organize and measure his researches; and it is here that he lands on the principle of "progress," about which he writes with all of the tendentious bias that he had claimed the historian of ideas should eschew. For Pattison, the "theory of the decay of nations as the inevitable law of history held its ground till long after the Renaissance," but then

> the antagonist theory of Progress began to dawn upon thought. The history of this notion, that of progressive civilisation, would form by itself a long, and not the least interesting, chapter in the history of the eighteenth century thought. Long before it was brought out in explicit terms by Lessing and popularised by Herder, the theory of progress had been in the air. The mere fact that, though the Roman empire had perished, new political organisms had emerged from the ruins, supplied the ready induction that though the law of history for single states was death, society lived on. Bodin had even anticipated Lessing, and the Baconian aphorism, *Antiquitas seculi juventus mundi*, is pregnant with the new doctrine. Notwithstanding these symptoms of a new philosophy of history, it may still be said that the doctrine of the seventeenth century was, and remained, that the whole course of the race was a downward course of degradation. The superiority of classical civilisation over that of modern states was, on the whole, as much the faith of the statesmen and legists, as the superior purity of the Christianity of the apostolic age was the faith of the divines. The doctrine of "the ascent of man" was the antithesis of the doctrine of "the fall of man," and could not, therefore, make itself heard till the hold of theology over the mind of the West was loosened. ... In Germany the theory was sublimated into an obscure metaphysic, useless but harmless. In France the same theory attempted to be imposed on facts became—the Revolution. The Englishman, when at last he apprehended an idea so abstract as progress, set about laboriously proving it by collecting facts, and it became—Darwinism.[64]

We can see how poorly notions of this doctrine of progress put about by Herder and Kant applies to England's eighteenth-century thought by simply quoting at random from Boswell's *Life of Johnson*, in which the table talk of the great critic, poet, lexicographer and sage shows what very laughable things the schemes of intellectual history are. One would be hard pressed to extrapolate any theory of the "ascent of man" from Johnson's toughminded musings—or, more improbably still, any paean to intellectual progress.

[63] Samuel Johnson showed his own understanding of the far-ranging scope and complexity of the history of thought in conversation with James Boswell. "BOSWELL: Is there not less religion in the nation now, sir, than there was formerly? JOHNSON: I don't know, sir, that there is. BOSWELL: For instance, there used to be a chaplain in every great family, which we do not find now. JOHNSON: Neither do you find any of the state servants which great families used formerly to have. There is a change of modes in the whole department of life." *Boswell's Life of Johnson*, ed. George Birbeck Hill; revised and enlarged by L. F. Powell, 6 vols. (Oxford: Oxford University Press: 1934), ii, 96.

[64] Pattison, "Age of Reason", 349.

He much commended Law's *Serious Call*, which, he said, was the finest piece of hortatory theology in any language.

He observed that the established clergy in general did not preach plain enough; and that polished periods and glittering sentences flew over the heads of the common people, without any impression upon their hearts. Something might be necessary, he observed, to excite the affections of the common people, who were sunk in languor and lethargy, and therefore he supposed that the new concomitants of Methodism might probably produce so desirable an effect. The mind, like the body, he observed, delighted in change and novelty, and even in religion itself courted new appearances and modifications. Whatever might be thought of some Methodist teachers, he said, he could scarcely doubt the sincerity of that man [John Wesley], who travelled nine hundred miles in the month, and preached twelve times a week; for no adequate reward, merely temporal, could be given for such indefatigable labour.

Of Dr. Priestley's theological works, he remarked that they tended to unsettle everything, and yet settled nothing.

He was much affected by the death of his mother, and wrote to me to come and assist him to compose his mind, which indeed I found extremely agitated. He lamented that all serious and religious conversation was banished from the society of men, and yet great advantages might be derived from it. All acknowledged, he said, what hardly anybody practised, the obligations we were under of making the concerns of eternity the governing principles of our lives. Every man, he observed, at last wishes for retreat: he sees his expectations frustrated in the world, and begins to wean himself from it, and to prepare for everlasting separation.

He observed that the influence of London now extended everywhere, and that from all manner of communication being opened, there shortly would be no remains of the ancient simplicity, or places of cheap retreat to be found.

... He reproved me once for saying grace without mention of the name of our Lord Jesus Christ, and hoped in future I would be more mindful of the apostolical injunction.

He refused to go out of a room before me at Mr. Langton's house, saying he hoped he knew his rank better than to presume to take place of a Doctor in Divinity. I mention such little anecdotes merely to show the peculiar turn and habit of his mind.

He used frequently to observe that there was more to be endured than enjoyed in the general condition of human life; and frequently quoted those lines of Dryden:

> "Strange cozenage! none would live past years again,
> Yet all hope pleasure from what still remain."

For his part, he said, he never passed that week in his life which he would wish to repeat, were an angel to make the proposal to him.[65]

How the rationalist notions of progress of Pattison's Germans would have struck the man of these sentiments is not hard to imagine. Yet even in a con-

---

[65] *Boswell's Life of Johnson*, ed. Hill, ii, 122–4.

temporary of Pattison's, James Fitzjames Stephen, who was in many respects sympathetic to the rationalist enterprise, we can see a distinct uneasiness with the intellectual complacency bred of such notions. "What may be called the gospel of vagueness and sentiment has obtained a miserable currency in these times," Fitzjames Stephen wrote in *The Saturday Review* in 1859.

> It is, we think, one of the very greatest evils of the age in which we live. We think that the sea will never come, the waves never beat, the floods never rage again, and we accordingly build our houses most industriously on the sand. This is, we think, a fearful evil; for even if it be true that society is so firmly organized that we have got to the end of those trials which search the very heart and reins—if we have secured for ourselves and our heirs for ever that fair chance of being comfortable, provided we are industrious, which may be roughly taken as the meaning of the phrase's "civilization" and "social progress"—it is still not the less important that our mental foundations should be firmly settled. We have still got to live, to marry, to educate children, to discharge some duty in life, and, after all, to die, and go we know not where; and there is something infinitely contemptible in doing all this in a blind, helpless, drifting way, with nothing to guide us but a strange hash of inclinations and traditions. Perhaps no spectacle can be sadder than this; but, if there is any, it is the spectacle of clever, ingenious people who pass their lives in gossiping about the great principles in which their forefathers really did believe, and by believing in which they purchased for their children the inestimable privilege of being able, without conscious inconvenience, to do without any principles at all, and to pass their time in prattling over incongruities between their practice and the small remnant of their theories. *The Great Eastern*, or some of her successors, will perhaps defy the roll of the Atlantic, and cross the seas without allowing her passengers to feel that they have left the firm land. The voyage from the cradle to the grave may come to be performed with similar facility. Progress and science may, perhaps, enable untold millions to live and die without a care, without a pang, without an anxiety. They will have a pleasant passage, and, no doubt, plenty of brilliant conversation. They will wonder that people ever believed at all in clanging fights, and blazing towns, and sinking ships, and praying bands; and, when they come to the end of their course, they will go their way, and the place thereof will know them no more. But it seems very unlikely that they will have such a knowledge of the great ocean on which they sail, with its storms and wrecks, its currents and icebergs, its huge waves and mighty winds, as those who battled with it for years together in the little craft, which, if they had few other merits, brought those who navigated them full into the presence of time and eternity, their Maker and themselves, and forced them to have some definite views of their relations to them and to each other.[66]

As we shall see, Fitzjames Stephen's concern for his contemporaries' relation between "their Maker and themselves," never altogether strong, dissipated as

---

[66] *On the Novel and Journalism*, 196–7. Brunel's iron steamship, *The Great Eastern*, was the largest ship ever built at the time, about which Ricks remarks: "JFS's evocation of her and of 'sinking ships' was pointed since he would have known that on the maiden voyage of the ship, a month before his piece appeared, several men were killed in an explosion as she made her way into the English Channel."

he grew older, though here he recognized that it put the claims of progress in some clarifying light. Leslie Stephen, for his part, wrote his intellectual history to show that if the Deists of the Georges had failed to establish the credibility of Christianity, his own contemporaries had fared no better. For Noel Annan, "Stephen conceded that the conditions in the eighteenth century hardly favored the discovery of arguments which would convince men that revealed religion was false. That was why the work had to be done all over again in his own generation."[67]

If Stephen saw the "history of thought" as "in great part a history of the gradual emancipation of the mind from the errors spontaneously generated by its first childlike attempts at speculation," Pattison's innate pessimism impelled him to question not only the nature but the efficacy of such progress, though in deploring the susceptibility of the rationalists to a delusive trust in progress, Pattison succumbed to his own.[68]

> It is, perhaps, premature even in 1877 to speak of the epoch of the romantic and catholic reaction as over. It is not ended; it is in many departments of life in full career; but it is doomed. It was a reaction, and nothing more. It was the just and necessary penalty which the human mind had to pay for the excesses and exaggeration of the eighteenth century. It was not only in the domain of fact, in the streets of Paris, and the excesses of the Terror that this exaggeration took place; the "polite age" egregiously over-estimated its own worth and caricatured its own principles. Not content with knowing itself to be in advance of the past, it pronounced the whole past worthless, rotten, fit only to be swept away. It had invented the new faith—faith in progress—and this faith rapidly developed into a blind fanaticism of intolerance. Rationalism, in its passionate self-assertion, ceased to be reasonable, and became an imperious and arrogant despot. The revolt against this arrogant self-satisfaction with its own perfections was inevitable, and the romantic reaction repaid with scorn and contumely the self-complacency of the Age of Reason. The generation which is now passing to the grave has lived through this period of revolt. In many departments of mind, in the discipline of character, in the loftiest manifestations of feeling, such as religion, philosophy, art, architecture, it has been fifty years lost. But the rights of the legitimate monarch—the sovereign reason—have only been in abeyance the while; they are inalienable. The vices of the eighteenth century were indeed many, but it was withal on the true line of human progress. It had the excess of its own qualities. We are suffering for its over-confidence in our present mood of depression and despondency. How mournfully does our cynical indifference, which yawns over its own utterances, contrast with the sure and steadfast gaze with which Kant ... looks forward towards an unknown future of unlimited conquest![69]

With the exception here of the plug for Kant—hardly a figure to cite as an exemplar of reasoned progress, intellectual or otherwise—we might agree with

---

[67] Noël Annan, "Editor's Introduction," Leslie Stephen, *Selected Writings in British Intellectual History*, ed Noël Annan (Chicago: University of Chicago, 1979), xix.
[68] *Ibid.*, 5.
[69] Pattison, "Age of Reason," 350–1.

Pattison that the Regency and Victorian reaction against the eighteenth century was excessive. Yet when Pattison proceeds to articulate his own view of these matters, we goggle at its crudity.

> Although Positivism represents the present stage of human history as a transition period, or anarchy, the popular creed is that it is only one stage in the onward march, never interrupted, and that this Progress is represented by the perennial cause, Science v. Theology, in the pleading of which, point after point is contested by the defendant, and invariably adjudged in favour of the plaintiff. Our history is presented to us in this "cadre" in special books, such as Draper's Conflict of Science and Religion, or White's Warfare of Science. Even our general histories fall into the same lines, and we may, perhaps, say that this conception is the habitual attitude of the mind of all educated men in our day. This representation of Progress as the gradual wearing away of the rock of the Church by the ocean of Science is something more than a hypothesis; it cannot be denied that it approximately represents the facts. As such a conditional representation it may be allowably employed as the framework of modern history. Especially does it seem to fit the eighteenth century like a glove.

Such a view of the tensions between theology and science in the eighteenth century would have been scorned by Swift, Johnson, and Burke, to name but three of the age's more critical thinkers. None of them would have agreed that the century had been characterized by intellectual progress or that science, broadly defined, had somehow driven theology from the field. As Christopher Dawson noted in an incisive monograph, since "it is upon moral and spiritual unity of a culture that its external life ultimately depends," Europe is "not a group of peoples held together by a common type of material culture." On the contrary, "it is a spiritual society which owes its very existence to the religious tradition which for a thousand years moulded the beliefs, the ideals and the institutions of the European peoples." For Dawson, "Even the Reformation and the centuries of religious and international strife that followed it did not entirely destroy the common tradition. Europe remained Christendom, though it was a secularized Christendom and divided. The vision of its lost unity haunted the mind of Europe, and inspired the men of the eighteenth century with their enthusiasm for the abstract ideals of humanity and new social order."[70] It was the men of Pattison's nineteenth century that would come to realize, in Dawson's arresting words, that "the only ultimate progress conceivable in a mechanistic universe is a progress to eternal death."[71]

Nevertheless, Pattison was right to look askance at the *hubris* of the rationalists, whether in the eighteenth or the nineteenth century. We can see this in his review of Buckle's *History of Civilization*, the influential intellectual history which sought to tell the story of science's dynamic triumph over the reactionary conservatism of theological dogma. "Now it is not questioned that intellectual progress is a fact," Pattison writes;

---

[70] Christopher Dawson, *Progress and Religion: An Historical Enquiry* (London: Sheed & Ward, 1929), 169.
[71] Ibid., 173.

that its course can be traced; that it is an element of national history—perhaps the most attractive element. But what is of vital consequence to us to know is, whether intellectual advance is an inevitable necessity. Will society be regenerated by its intellect in spite of its passions? The condition of every society yet known to us has been, a small minority of educated persons in a combination, either of conflict or harmony, with an overwhelming unenlightened mass. The enlightened minority who are in possession of the knowledge, have, more or less, leavened the whole. Where this practice of leavening has proceeded, unchecked, for any considerable time, an appearance is presented which may easily be mistaken for an intrinsic power in knowledge to conquer every other motive of action. But is it more than an appearance? What security have we that the sleeping volcano of passion will not flame forth with irresistible violence? That the ocean of imagination, and false opinion, will not break in, submerge a continent, and sweep away every trace of the Palace of Truth?[72]

Newman, of course, entirely shared Pattison's distrust of any notion of the inevitability of knowledge's advance, as his criticism of the "march of mind" shows. Yet, despite his distrust of such claims, what sets him apart from Pattison is the quality of his hope—and his profoundly historical understanding of how the early Christians had managed not only to survive but prevail. Wilfrid Ward captures this aspect of Newman in his account of the wake of Newman's going over to Rome:

> The conversion of England—for which the English Catholics sighed during the long reign of Elizabeth, long retaining the phrase in Stuart times after hope for the reality was practically extinguished—was now once more seriously talked of and prayed for. Newman at no time ignored adverse omens; but Father Robert Whitty used to describe the scale of hope and feeling among Catholics at this moment as quite exceptional. There was a general sense that supernatural agencies were in operation, and there was in the atmosphere that faith which works wonders. For years the old English Catholics had laughed at the bare idea of the Oxford School submitting to the Holy See. Their Catholicism had been treated as unpractical antiquarianism. So unlooked-for a marvel as the conversion of Newman and his friends brought a reaction, and men were now prepared for any marvels that might follow. Newman's own imagination dwelt on the early triumph of the despised and superstitious sect of Christians in an empire yet greater in its day than the British Empire of the nineteenth century. Sanguine confidence of great visible achievement was utterly alien to his nature. But he never lost the sense that God can do all things even through insignificant instruments; and he saw day by day the accession of recruits conspicuous for piety or ability. Where would it end, and what might it not lead to? We cannot read his letters written at the time without seeing that the thought was present to him of great possibilities in the future.[73]

---

[72] Mark Pattison, "History of Civilization in England," *Westminster Review*, 1857; *Essays by Mark Pattison*, ed. Henry Nettleship, 2 vols. (Oxford: Oxford University Press, 1889), ii, 430.
[73] Ward, *Life of Newman*, ii, 99–100.

Pattison, for his part, in light of the failure of the converts who followed Newman to Rome effecting any reconversion of England might very well have seen the hope to which Whitty referred as wishful thinking but it was nevertheless a hope fulfilled as far as the condition of Catholics in England was concerned, if only in the sense that the amelioration of Catholic life that had begun after Catholic Emancipation (1829) proceeded apace throughout the nineteenth century. These might not have been advances to allay Pattison's impermeable pessimism but they certainly animated some of Newman's most endearing writing, especially his sermon, "The Second Spring" (1852), in which his cry of hope is that of all Catholics everywhere at all times. "One thing alone I know," Newman wrote in that beautiful sermon, "that according to our need, so will be our strength. One thing I am sure of, that the more the enemy rages against us, so much the more will the Saints in Heaven plead for us; the more fearful are our trials from the world, the more present to us will be our Mother Mary, and our good Patrons and Angel Guardians; the more malicious are the devices of men against us, the louder cry of supplication will ascend from the bosom of the whole Church to God for us. We shall not be left orphans; we shall have within us the strength of the Paraclete, promised to the Church and to every member of it."[74] Newman would echo these wonderfully defiant words in the Biglietto speech he gave after being given his red hat. Then, after deploring the Enemy's latest duplicity, the Cardinal declared: "I lament it deeply, because I foresee that it may be the ruin of many souls; but I have no fear at all that it really can do aught of serious harm to the Word of God, to Holy Church, to our Almighty King, the Lion of the tribe of Judah, Faithful and True, or to His Vicar on earth. Christianity has been too often in what seemed deadly peril, that we should fear for it any new trial now ... Commonly the Church has nothing more to do than to go on in her own proper duties, in confidence and peace; to stand still and to see the salvation of God."[75]

V

The storm over the latitudinarian *Essays and Reviews*, published in the autumn of 1860 coincided with Pattison's election to the Rectorship of Lincoln College, the prize which had so beguiled his academic ambitions. Pattison's contribution to *Essays and Reviews* (1860), "Tendencies of religious thought in England, 1688–1750" confirmed his break with the National Church, let alone whatever suppositious hankerings he might have had to follow Newman to Rome. As H. S. Jones points out, "The reception of his contribution to *Essays and Reviews* convinced [Pattison] that in England the hold of partisan churchmanship was so all-pervasive that the claims of theology and science were, for practical purposes, incompatible. That conviction hastened his gradual separation from the church. It seems beyond reasonable doubt that he died an agnostic. If not holding fast to God, however, he did hold fast to the clerical status that secured his office as rector. His growing unbelief did not prevent him from fulfilling his duties in

---

[74] OS, 180.
[75] *Addresses of Cardinal Newman with his Replies*, ed. W. P. Neville (London: Longman, Green & Co., 1905), 69–70.

attending college chapel, where he punctiliously took his turn in presiding at the eucharist. Likewise, on his visits to Yorkshire he assisted his brother-in-law, the rector of Richmond. 'Priests', he observed, 'are generally professional quacks trading in beliefs they don't share' (Sparrow, 58)."[76]

The publication of the piece was noted in correspondence that Newman had with Charles Crawley (1788–1871), the staunchly High Church country gentleman whom he had first befriended when living in Littlemore. "Thank you for your expressions of friendship and good will," Newman wrote in 1861. "Alas—what a history has past [sic] before us, and is over, since I saw you! As to Oxford, I feel bitterly its present state. But it must be so in the nature of things—Those infidel principles have an enormous force, and a dreadful battle is coming. If I had thought that the weapons which Anglicanism gave me were equal to meeting it, I never should have left persons and scenes so dear to me."[77] In response, Crawley wrote back: 'I trust your sad forebodings may not come true—tho' I must confess there is too much *apparent* cause for them—And yet on the other hand there is much to encourage a better hope—for look at the state of things in our Church 20 or 30 years ago, and compare it with what it is now—! If you could have foreseen the great advance that has been made amongst us in that time in true Catholic principles and practice, I cannot but think we should still have had you with us to help us fight that 'dreadful battle' which you fear is come—" Crawley only added: "I am sorry to say Mark Pattison one of those mischievous Essayists, has just been elected Rector of Lincoln College."[78] Newman's response was incredulous. "It astonished me to find that you think that the Church of England has made advance since I belonged to it. I don't know what can possibly weigh against the Gorham judgment, and the words of the Protest and Declaration of the 12 men—Keble, Mill, R. Wilberforce, Manning etc. etc. in prospect or consequence of it."[79] As for Pattison's essay, he stood up for it. "I can't help thinking Pattison must not be mixed up with the rest—at least not with such as poor Baden Powell or Mr R. Williams. I am truly sorry that he, or that Temple, should have connected themselves with men so different from themselves. Pattison professes no more than a survey or history—and so far is less to blame than Temple, who puts forth a theory."[80]

In March of 1861, Newman wrote Pattison to congratulate him on his ascension to the Rectorship of Lincoln.

---

[76] *ODNB*.
[77] Newman to Charles Crawley (15 January 1861), *LD*, xix, 453.
[78] Crawley to Newman (26 January 1861), *LD*, xix, 458.
[79] Newman to Crawley (11 February 1861), *LD*, xix, 458.
[80] Newman to Crawley (6 March 1861), *LD*, xix, 475. Dessain's notes are helpful here: "The letters that passed between Frederick Temple, then headmaster of Rugby School, and Bishop Phillpotts of Exeter were published in *The Times* (4 March 1861), p. 10. Temple mistakenly thought a passage from his contribution to *Essays and Reviews*, 'The Education of the World,' had been censured by Phillpotts as 'at variance with the fundamental doctrines' of the Church of England. Phillpotts explained that although this was not the case, *Essays and Reviews* as a whole was an attack on the Church's beliefs, and a contributor who did not dissociate himself from it, could not avoid responsibility." *LD*, xix, note 1, 475. "Baden Powell contributed to *Essays and Reviews* 'The Study of the Evidences of Christianity,' and Rowland Williams 'Bunsen's Biblical Researches.'" *LD*, xix, note 2, 475.

Rednall. March 7. 1861

My dear Pattison,

I was taking up my pen to write you a line of congratulation, as soon as I saw your election in the Papers, but something hindered it. Now Ornsby writes me word that he has done so, and stimulates me to do the same. Indeed I can sincerely say, it is a pleasure to me to think that justice is at length done to your merits; for, though I doubt whether I was in the country, yet I have certainly heard that you ought to have been head at the time of the vacancy made by Radford. What wonderful changes are on all sides of us! I cannot bring myself to lament that the reign of such men, as I suppose Thompson to have been, is gone out,—certainly for a very long time. Poor man, it is a shame perhaps that I should speak at all of one, of whom I knew so very little.

No friend of yours, nay, no one who has read what you have written, always so grave and sincere, can mix up your name with that of others with whom you have yourself felt it a duty to connect it. Indeed, I think the world at large feels this—tho' it pleased the Bishop of London the other day, if I read him rightly, to prefer the claims of friendship to those of truth, and to leave you in the mire, that he might attempt to extricate those who had given utterance to views and doctrines, while you had employed yourself upon historical facts, which, as such, cannot be found fault with in a writer.

It is my earnest trust and prayer, that in your new station you will serve and glorify God and save your own soul.

Ever Yours affectly John H Newman

Pattison was pleased by Newman's response to his contribution, and agreed with Newman's estimate of his contribution to *Essays and Reviews*, which he described as "a scientific history of the self-development of opinion." Pattison noted exceptions to the outcry which greeted his essay in England. "The Protestant historian—Dorner—going over the same ground a few years afterwards, accepted the essay for what it was intended to be—a history and not a party manifesto. Dorner's chapter, 'Der streitende und siegende Deismus,' makes much use and ample acknowledgment of my essay. Another exception to the chorus of blatant and ignorant howling, with which my poor venture was received … Soon after the publication of *Essays and Reviews*, happening to come down from town in the train with Father, since Cardinal, Newman, whom I had not seen for a long time, I was in terror as to how he would regard me in consequence of what I had written. My fears were quickly relieved. He blamed severely the throwing of such speculations broadcast upon the general public. It was, he said, unsettling their faith without offering them anything else to rest upon. But he had no word of censure for the latitude of theological speculation assumed by the essay, provided it had been addressed *ad clerum*, or put out, not as a public appeal, but as a scholastic dissertation addressed to learned theologians. He assured me that this could be done in the Roman communion, and that much greater latitude of speculation on theological topics was allowed in this form in the Catholic Church than in Protestant communities."[81]

---

[81] *Memoirs*, 314–16. The Protestant historian Isaak August Dorner (1809–84) studied under F. C.

After writing his letter to Pattison, Newman confided in his friend Robert Ornsby, the future biographer of his good friend, fellow convert and legal counselor James Hope-Scott: "I have written to Pattison, after your letter—but much as I feel for his state of doubt and discomfort, I cannot stomach his joining such men as Baden Powell and others—What has he in common with such men? they have said a great number of bold things, which I suppose he would not say, and for which he has made himself virtually answerable." Indeed, the Oratorian convert who lived so much outside of the world saw the publication of *Essays and Reviews* as an omen of an accelerating apostasy. "They say the growth of scepticism among educated women is something appalling. In short, Christianity is tending to go out in whole classes, as it has gone out in Germany. When then the evil shows itself in Heads of Houses, of public Schools, in Professors and other men of station, it is something very serious." Bishop Wilberforce and the Broad Church might have condemned the publication in vague terms, but Newman's appreciation of its import was much more dire. "It was serious enough, in spite of what I have said, a century ago. Bishop Butler stopped the evil, only by lowering by many pegs the pretensions of Christianity—for, without wishing to speak disrespectfully of a writer to whom I owe so much, as many others do, still it does seem as if the practical effect of his work was to make faith a mere *practical certainty*—i.e. a taking certain statements of doctrine, not as true, but as safest to act upon. The Anglican defenders of Christianity have all along been fighting and retreating. Paley half gave up the Old Testament—And there is every reason to anticipate that the antagonists of these seven Essayists, if such there shall be, will give up still more." It was characteristic of Newman, however, to see this radical erosion of faith not in abstract but personal terms. "All this being considered, it is very painful that Pattison, not only should not be a Catholic, but should have thrown himself into the first rank of the assailers of revelation."[82] Later, he would speak of Pattison to Ornsby almost as a representative of the general apostasy to come: "As to English religion, I cannot think there was a time in which such intense doubt, and such real misery in doubting, went through so many minds. What you say of Pattison is true in its degree of numbers. A notion is spreading that, as the Reformation unseated the Church, the present movement is to upset Christianity altogether. And the prospect of it is viewed, on the part of a great many, with simple dismay. May God bring good out of all this disorder!"[83]

When one revisits Newman's correspondence at this time, one can see how difficult it was for him to sympathize with Anglicans like Charles Crawley over the malignity of *Essays and Reviews* without ruffling feathers, a difficulty which would always color his relations with the lapsed Anglican in Pattison as well. "My dear Crawley," he wrote to his friend, "I did not in my last allude to your remark upon my probable sentiments about the Church of England, because I felt it would only lead to unprofitable controversy. If I thought I had a chance of convincing you, most gladly would I discuss—but I had no reason to hope

---

Baur at Tübingen and became known to English readers with his *History of the Development of the Doctrine of the Person of Christ*, 5 vols. (1861–3), his response to David Strauss's *Das Leben Jesu* (1835–6).

[82] Newman to Robert Ornsby (8 March 1861), *LD*, xix, 480–1.
[83] Newman to Robert Ornsby (14 June 1861), *LD*, xix, 515.

this, and knew too well my own sentiments, and therefore I felt that to keep silence was the only way in which I could avoid hurting your feelings." Crawley had responded rather sharply to Newman's last letter by saying that from his standpoint the Anglican Church had improved, despite the Gorham Judgment. Newman, however, was intent on driving home why he thought *Essays and Reviews* so pernicious. "As to the Volume in question, I deplore it extremely, but especially for a reason which bears on the difference of the two Creeds. The religion of England is 'the Bible, the whole Bible, and nothing but the Bible'—the consequence is that to strike a blow at its inspiration, veracity or canonicity, is directly to aim at whatever there is of Christianity in the country. It is frightful to think where England would be, as regards Revelation, if it once got to disbelieve or to doubt the authority of Scripture. This is what makes the Volume so grave a matter—and the responsibility of those who have had to do with it so great. This is the reason of the consternation of serious members of the Church of England at its appearance."[84] To Malcolm Maccoll (1831–1907), the Anglican who wrote in such zealous defense of Gladstone's political and religious policies, Newman was still more hortatory: "I assure you I look with the most anxious interest at the state of Oxford—the more so because I anticipated its present perplexities. And it was one of my severest trials in leaving it, that I was undoing my own work, and leaving the field open, or rather infallibly surrendering it to those who would break down and crumble to powder all religion whatever. As to the authors of 'Essays and Reviews,' some of them at least, I am sure, know not what they do. One of them I may still call my friend [Pattison], and for two others, though I do not know them, I feel great respect. These I trust are urged by a sincere feeling that it is not right to keep up shams—yet did they really see the termination, or rather the abyss, to which these speculations lead, surely they would see that, before attempting to sift facts, they ought to make sure that they have a firm hold of true and eternal principles. To unsettle the minds of a generation, when you give them no landmarks and no causeway across the morass is to undertake a great responsibility." In a later chapter—on James Anthony Froude—my readers will see that this very charge was levelled against Newman himself. Yet in his letter to Maccoll he saw *Essays and Reviews* as an undeniable milestone in the de-Christianization of England.

> The religion of England depends, humanly speaking, on belief in "the Bible and the whole Bible," etc., and on the observance of the Calvinistic Sabbath. Let the population begin to doubt in its inspiration and infallibility, where are they? Alas, whole classes do already; but I would not be the man knowingly to introduce scepticism into those portions of the community which are as yet sound. Consider the miseries of wives and mothers losing their faith in Scripture, yet I am told this sad process is commencing.

Of course, the attack on Scripture affected Protestants more than Catholics since, as Newman sensibly explained: "We indeed devoutly receive the whole Bible as the Word of God, but we receive it on the authority of the Church, and

---

[84] Newman to Charles Crawley (17 March 1861), *LD*, xix, 482–3.

the Church has defined very little as to the aspects under which it comes from God, and the limits of its inspiration." For Newman and his co-religionists, "though the whole Scripture were miraculously removed from the world as if it had never been, evil and miserable as would be the absence of such a privilege, [the Catholic] would still have enough motives and objects for his faith. Whereas, to the Protestant, the question of Scripture is one of life and death."[85] Here, incidentally, one might also remark that it is with the vanishing of Bible reading amongst the English, broadly defined, that one can date the deterioration of what had once been something of their shared cultural identity, so much of which was grounded in the Bible.

Maccoll had instigated this letter by writing to Newman what many devout Anglicans must have thought once the controversy of *Essays and Reviews* arose. "I do not know how you regard the *Essays and Reviews* in relation to the Church of England," he wrote, "but I know that it is the wish of many troubled minds that the book should receive its refutation from you. I was lately staying at Oxford, and heard many a sad regret expressed that you were no longer there to do battle for the truth. A distinguished Oxford man told me that the 'intellect of Oxford was at the feet of Jowett'; and I suppose there can be no doubt that the 'Essays and Reviews' have already precipitated a great many into infidelity, and will continue to do so."[86] Newman's response was shot through with his prophetical realization of the apostasy to come. "I feel no call on me to interfere in the controversy. And that the more, because we shall have a controversy of our own, viz with Atheism. My own belief is, that, if there be a God, Catholicism is true; but this is the elementary, august, and sovereign truth, the denial of which is in progress. May He Himself give grace to those who shall be alive in that terrible day. Then, again, although a redoubtable controversialist, Newman was never keen on controversy for the sake of controversy. "For myself, I don't think I have written anything controversial for the last 14 years," he told Pusey in September of 1865, oddly passing over the searing controversy in which he had engaged with Charles Kingsley. "

> Nor have I ever, as I think, replied to any controversial notice of what I have written. Certainly, I let pass without a word the various volumes which were written in answer to my Essay on Doctrinal Development, and that on the principle that truth defends itself, and falsehood refutes itself—and that, having said my say, time would decide for me, without any trouble, how far it was true, and how far not true. And I have quoted Crabbe's line as to my purpose, (though I can't quote correctly):—
>
> > Leaving the case to Time, who solves all doubt,
> > By bringing Truth, his glorious daughter, out.[87]

---

[85] Newman to Malcolm Maccoll (24 March 1861), *LD*, xix, 487–8.
[86] Maccoll to Newman, *LD*, xix, note 3, 487.
[87] Newman to Pusey (5 September 1865), *LD*, xx, 44. The lines from Crabbe, which Newman only slightly misquotes, are from *Tales of the Hall* (1819), ix.

VI

One of the striking ironies of Pattison's career is that the disaffected Tractarian in him should have set up shop as an intellectual historian intent on creating a kind of scholasticism without theology. Pattison's low view of theology came not simply of his revulsion from Tractarianism but his experience of the clergy in England, presumably that clergy charged with teaching and defending Anglican theology.

> It is true that complaints abound in English books of an earlier date than [Butler's] *Analogy* of the contempt into which the clergy had fallen before the end of the seventeenth century. Notwithstanding Mr. Babington's well-meant attempt to disprove Macaulay's statement, the picture drawn in the *History of England* is, I believe, little, if at all, exaggerated. Indeed, it will be difficult to select even from the language of Macaulay, always a little heated, stronger terms than are used by South (1698): "If we consider the treatment of the clergy in these nations since Popery was driven out, both as to the language and usage which they find from most about them, I do, from all that I have read, heard, or seen, confidently aver that there is no nation or people under heaven, Christian or not Christian, which despise, hate, and trample upon their clergy comparably to the English. So that as matters have been carried, it is really no small argument of the predominance of conscience over interest, that there are yet parents who can be willing to breed up any of their sons, if hopefully endowed, to so discouraged and discouraging a profession." [88]

The portrait of Newman that Pattison paints in his *Memoir* has something of this same grudging respect for "conscience over interest," though he is tempted, in Newman's case, to see conscience as somehow subject to interest. The memoirist is never entirely unfair about his old tutor, but he flatly refuses to enter into the conscientious appeal that the Christian religion held for him. Indeed, he treats it as though it were a kind of stultifying hobbyhorse. "In charge of a parish—first S. Clement's, then S. Mary's," Pattison recalls, Newman "spent much time upon the preparation of those weighty sermons by which he first became famous, and which were the foundation of his influence with young men." We have many eyewitness accounts of the influence the *Parochial and Plain Sermons* wielded in Tractarian Oxford but none as laconic as this. Expansiveness was never Pattison's mode. Yet the comments he makes on his old tutor, for all their exiguity, are fascinating.

> Religion was evidently to Newman, in 1830, not only the first but the sole object of all teachings. There was no thought then of ἐν κύκλῳ παιδεία, a genealogical chart of all the sciences; there was not even the lesser conception of education by the classics, as containing the essential elements of humanism. These teachers of the classics had sided with the enemies of humanism. Greek was useful as

---

[88] Pattison, "Age of Reason," 354–5. Samuel Johnson thought highly of Dr. Robert South (1634–1716), adjuring Boswell to read his sermons on prayer and ranking him one of the best of England's sermon writers, "if you except his peculiarities, and his violence, and sometimes coarseness of language." Boswell, *Life of Johnson*, ii, 204; iii, 248. Pattison's quotation from the combative divine can be found in Robert South, "Christ's Promise The Support of his Despised Ministers" (1668), *Sermons Preached upon Several Occasions*, 4 vols (London: Thomas Tegg, 1843), ii, 463–4.

enabling you to read the Greek Testament and the Fathers. All knowledge was to be subservient to the interests of religion, for which vague idea was afterwards substituted the definite and concrete idea of the Visible Church. Of the world of wisdom and sentiment—of poetry and philosophy, of social and political experience, contained in the Latin and Greek classics, and of the true relation of the degenerate and semi-barbarous Christian writers of the fourth century to that world Oxford, in 1830, had never dreamt. It is too much to require that the three Oriel tutors should have understood what no one about them understood. But their greater seriousness of purpose—their disinterested devotion to the cause of religion as they understood it—made them more dangerous than the pococurante plausibilities who displaced them. In the hands of the three tutors, all of them priests, narrow and desperate devotees of the clerical interest, the college must have become a seminary in which the pupils should be trained for church ends, and broken in, like the students of a Jesuit college, to regard the dictates of the confessor and the interests of the clergy as the supreme law of life. Religion is a good servant but a bad master. In the same volume in which Newman, in 1852, expounds the idea of an all-embracing university organisation, with a breadth and boldness which is not to be found elsewhere, I find the following notion on History, which he speaks of as a science:—" Revealed religion furnishes facts to other sciences, which those sciences, left to themselves, would never reach ... Thus, in the science of history, the preservation of our race in Noah's ark is an historical fact, which history never would arrive at without revelation" (p. 105).[89]

One can imagine such dry mockery going down well in Jowett's Oxford. Pattison, after all, was one of Jowett's most prestigious confreres. In a letter to Dean Stanley, Jowett set out the plan for *Essays and Reviews* after assuring the Dean that Pattison was on board. "It is ... an essential part of the plan," he wrote, "that names shall be given, partly for the additional weight which the articles will have if the authors are known, and also from the feeling that on such subjects as theology it is better not to write anonymously. We do not wish to do anything rash or irritating to the public or the University, but we are determined not to submit to this abominable system of terrorism, which prevents the statement of the plainest facts, and makes true theology or theological education impossible. Pusey and his friends are perfectly aware of your opinions ... but they are determined to prevent your expressing them. I do not deny that in the present state of the world the expression of them is a matter of great nicety and care, but is it possible to do any good by a system of reticence?"[90] If Pattison had any qualms about throwing his hat into the arena with such ramshackle companions, he never wrote them down.

Other comments that Pattison made about Newman would also have been met in liberal circles with amused chortles, though, for our purposes, they have to be seen as more than senior common room twaddle. Understanding Pattison's attitude to Newman's educational ideas, for all its glib dismissiveness, is necessary to understanding his own educational ideas.

---

[89] Pattison, *Memoirs*, 96–8.
[90] Evelyn Abbot and Lewis Campbell, *The Life and Letters of Benjamin Jowett, M. A., Master of Balliol College, Oxford*, 2 vols (London: John Murray, 1897), i, 275.

By 1830 Newman had enlarged his views upon the college beyond the circle of his pupils. He now aimed at a moulding of the college of fellows—there were at this date eighteen fellowships—on a mediæval system; at reviving the college of Adam de Brome and Laud, and mounting it as a reactionary machine to resist the formidable progress of "Liberalism" and the modern spirit. The elections were to be so manipulated that a body of like-minded fellows should be obtained, who should all reside and study the Fathers, not necessarily occupying themselves with tuition. They would form a nucleus of learned controversialists, destined to fight against the vicious tendencies of an unbelieving age.

The elections to fellowships for the ten years, from about 1830, were struggles between Newman endeavouring to fill the college with men likely to carry out his ideas, and the Provost endeavouring, upon no principle, merely to resist Newman's lead. Newman did not lose sight of the old Oriel principle of electing for promise rather than for performance; only, instead of looking for promise of originality, he now looked for promise of congeniality. Anyhow, in these contests, the old character of the Oriel fellowship was obliterated, and many inferior elections were made. It may be that the blame of the worst elections lay with the Provost's party, which was not so homogeneous as the opposing party, and possessed no one with the keen instinct, which Newman alone had, for recognising, through an examination paper, the kind of merit and character, which he wanted. The capital blunder which was patent to the whole university, when Burgon was taken over the head of Goldwin Smith, must have been made, I think, after Newman had done with the college.

It has often occurred to me to compare what took place at this period, in the fortunes of a small college, with the course of things in the great movement of the sixteenth century. About 1500 it seemed as if Europe was about to cast off at one effort the slough of feudal barbarism, and to step at once into the fair inheritance of the wisdom and culture of the ancient world. The Church led the van, and smiled on free inquiry and the new learning. About the third decennium of the century the resistance of the obscurantists was organised, the Catholic reaction set in, and in, and nascent humanism was submerged beneath the rising tide of theological passion and the fatal and fruitless controversies of Lutheran, Calvinist, and Catholic, to the rival cries of the Bible and the Church. The "sacrificio d'intelletto" of Loyola took the place of the free and rationalising spirit with which Erasmus had looked out upon the world of men. It was soon after 1830 that the "Tracts" desolated Oxford life, and suspended, for an indefinite period, all science, humane letters, and the first strivings of intellectual freedom which had moved in the bosom of Oriel.[91]

Rather than seeing the crisis of university education in the nineteenth century as one stemming from the university's abandonment of its scholastic foundations, where theology, understood properly as the means by which all of the other sciences could find their rightful place within the hierarchy of universal knowledge, Pattison saw it merely as a clash between classicists and utilitarians, a clash whose historical roots in the desuetude of scholasticism he never acknowl-

---

[91] Pattison, *Memoirs*, 101.

edges. It might be true, as he says, that that abandonment was accelerated by "the agitation of the matter of the King's divorce'; it might be true that "Ever since Henry VIII's first interference with opinion here, the Universities have been kept in dependence by the State"; but it is not true that proper liberal education "died out" because of "its severance from the living current of thought and opinion"; it died out because it became severed from the ancient faith, which, alone, could have properly elucidated that often turbid "living current of thought and opinion." Once we see this, the clash between classicists and utilitarians becomes otiose, though it is striking that this same clash would preoccupy John Sparrow in his classic study, *Mark Pattison and the Idea of a University* (1967), nearly a hundred years after Pattison took up his cry against what he regarded as the incoherence of Oxford's own understanding of its educational charge. In any case, what is striking about Pattison's animadversions on education is that they have nothing of Newman's large-mindedness—or precision. Pattison may insist on the prerogatives of the intellect, but he never gives that restive article any proper end. Cultivating the intellect for the sake of cultivating the intellect is not an ignoble object but it mistakes a means for an end. The mentee in Pattison learned many things from the mentor in Newman without ever apprehending the ultimate point of his mentorship, as their respective writings on education show. Here is Pattison:

> If I seem to coincide with a class of objectors who are dissatisfied with that idea of a University which would make it a great open school of all the useful arts and popular sciences, it is a coincidence from a diametrically opposite point of view. Those who remember the sneers with which the old Universities greeted the establishment of the London University, as a "new-fangled radical scheme of pantology," may measure the progress of opinion, by noting how differently they were then received, from what was felt by all educated men, when in the present year, Lord Derby attempted to jeer at science in the presence of the British Association. The classicist scorners, from their miserable rag of Latin writing and logic, looked then with the contempt of ignorance on all the wonders of the new learning. According to our view of a University, the whole body of sciences, inductive and exact, forms the indispensable groundwork, but only the groundwork, of that liberal education which it is the business of a University to provide. In the positions which each of the two parties in that controversy occupied, there was a point of right on either side. The classicists rightly maintained the principle of a liberal education versus useful knowledge; though the classical languages in their hands had ceased to be adequate instruments of such liberal culture. The friends of useful knowledge, on the other hand, saw clearly enough the grand error of the public schools and Universities, in shutting out the great bulk of generally accessible knowledge, and bringing up their *élèves* like Plato's men in the cave. They compared the learned languages with the physical sciences or mathematics, as acquisitions, and saw that the utility of the one was unlimited, of the other very narrow indeed. They did not know that the classical system in its origin was not a mere communication of the grammar of a couple of dead languages, but had comprehended a complete cultivation of mind, an expansion of the faculties adequate to the whole field of knowledge. It had dwindled in time

into a cramping pedantry, under which the herd of students learnt nothing, a few
only of the better sort acquired taste and skill in composition, but were utterly left
out of the whole region of thought in which their contemporaries were occupied.
University men in those days published essays or sermons, neatly worded, with
a classical allusion or two happily introduced; but they ceased to have anything
to say to the world without. Like those who, when Galileo's telescope was first
produced, refused to look through it, they declined to know anything of the
new movement, content with asserting in their rational moments, that it was
all superficies, glitter and show, and humbug; or, when irritated, that it was
materialist, godless, atheistical.[92]

Of course, this was the objection against the "march of mind," to which Newman lent his satirical voice, though Pattison did not recognize the true import of its godlessness. In any case, for the lapsed Tractarian, "As the movement advanced, triumphant contempt was succeeded by sorrowful lamentation over the decay of sound learning. All England was represented as rushing madly to folly and ruin, and Oxford as the one spot where the true old principles of English education were still understood. We are about, it was said, in 1840, 'to take precisely the same step in advance to ruin which was made at Athens by the first appearance of the foreign sophists.' [W. Sewell, *Introduction to Plato*, 1841, Oxford Essays, 1855] And in one respect these cries of despair did not exaggerate. They did not exaggerate the greatness of the crisis. It was, and is, a crisis in the history of the higher education in this country. Now, first, after two centuries of unbroken practice, not a reform, but a revolution in the system of our secondary education is in progress. The controversy between the impugners of an exclusively classical education, and the favourers of the modern sciences, is not an episode of that revolution; it contains the very pith of it." And once again Pattison saw these matters in terms of progress. "It is not a little curious," he says, "in reviewing the controversy … which has been going on for the last fifty years, to note that though the inevitable progress of things is gradually but silently giving the preponderance to the modern sciences, the advantage in the controversy has, till quite lately, been with the defenders of classical studies." Why?

> The classicists have not only written well, and brought out in a clear light many of the secondary benefits of the dead language training, but they have held to the fundamental idea of intellectual culture as the great end of education. Their error lies in their not understanding that the study of antiquity, of the past, even when much more profound than it usually is, cannot now convey that culture. Their opponents, on the other hand, in the free possession and enjoyment of the wonderful field of real knowledge, have lost sight of the truth, that for the purposes of education, knowledge is only a means,—a means to intellectual development. They will stake the issue on the comparative utility of the Classics and of Science, whereas they ought to place it on the comparative fitness of the two subjects to expand the powers, to qualify for philosophical and comprehensive view. In short, they confound life with education, and forget, or know not, that though a

---

[92] Mark Pattison, "Oxford Studies: Classics and Modern Science" (1855), *Essays*, i, 431–2.

useful and practical life may be the end of education, yet that the perfection of education consists in the perfection and enlargement of the intellect *per se*.⁹³

Yes, we might say, one object of education might be the "complete cultivation of mind" necessary to achieve "an expansion of the faculties adequate to the whole field of knowledge"; but if the "whole field of knowledge" was to be understood, as Pattison understood it, as one that should treat theology as so inalienably sectarian as to be "restricted," as it was in Pattison's Oxford, "to a blind getting up of the divinity of the seventeenth century which Dr. Pusey still wishes to enforce as the standard of the English Church," the field would necessarily be rather limited.⁹⁴ Here, Pattison could almost be touting the non-denominational Tamworth Reading Room of Lord Brougham and Sir Robert Peel. As the Rector himself admitted, "It is not enough that we systematize, methodize, theorize. Nothing less than the system, which explains all systems, the theory which places all the facts, the universal method, must be thought of."⁹⁵ Yes, but how could this "system of systems" ever be contemplated in a scheme of universal knowledge that consigned theology—for Newman, "the highest indeed, and widest" of the branches of knowledge—to scarcely tolerated margins?⁹⁶ Even Ruskin realized the bind in which the Victorians found themselves in refusing to own up to the incoherence of their notions of what ought to be the object of education. Apropos parents confronted with this matter, Ruskin observed: "They never seek, as far as I can make out, an education good in itself; even the conception of abstract rightness in training ... But, an education 'which shall keep a good coat on my son's back;—which shall enable him to ring with confidence the visitors' bell at double-belled doors; which shall result ultimately in establishment of a double-belled door to his own house;—in a word, which shall lead to advancement in life;—*this* we pray for on bent knees—and this is *all* we pray for.' It never seems to occur to the parents that there may be an education which, in itself, *is* advancement in Life;—that any other than that may perhaps be advancement in Death."⁹⁷

To show the superficiality of Pattison's notions of what ought to constitute the charge of university education, we can look at what R. W. Southern had to say on the subject. When the Anglican idea of the university as a finishing school for Anglican divines collapsed in Oxford in the mid-nineteenth century, many like Pattison and Newman naturally became avid to find some proper replacement. Newman, of course, drew on the perennial scholastic idea of education, and although his Oxford on the Liffey came to grief after Disraeli refused to give him a charter, the blueprint for his revival of scholastic education has been instrumental to the success of every proper Catholic educational shop ever since, mostly in America. Southern warrants quoting here because he understood the

---

⁹³ Ibid., 431–3.
⁹⁴ Ibid., i, 487.
⁹⁵ Ibid., i, 435.
⁹⁶ *Idea*, 63, 92.
⁹⁷ John Ruskin, "Of King's Treasuries," in *Sesame and Lillies: Two Lectures* (London, 1865). For an easily accessible copy of this lecture, see Ruskin, *The Lamp of Memory* (London: Penguin: Great Ideas, 2008), 38.

practical brilliance of the scholastic model, something Newman also prized.[98] In other words, he understood, as Newman understood, and Pattison did not, that this was the model of the future, especially in an English and American and European setting where apostasy was becoming general. Here is Southern.

> The first fundamental characteristic of the products of the schools is a strong sense of the dignity of human nature. Without this there can be no humanism of any description, and it is a conspicuous force in the schools of the twelfth and thirteen centuries. That Man is a fallen creature, who has lost that immediate knowledge of God which was the central feature of human nature before the Fall; that human instincts are now deeply disturbed and are often in conflict with reason; that human beings are now radically disorganized and disorientated—all this is common ground to all Christian thinkers at all times. We must not expect a denial of this condition in the Middle Ages, or in the Renaissance for that matter, or any time not blinded by excessive optimism about human capabilities. But what we may reasonably claim for the twelfth-century schools is that they were the first institutions in Europe to make it their main purpose to set about systematically restoring to the fullest possible extent the knowledge that had been forfeited at the Fall. The method employed for effecting this restoration was to study the works of the ancient scholars who had begun the slow process of repairing the ravages of sin in destroying man's knowledge of both the natural and supernatural worlds, and to elucidate and complete this process—so far as is possible in this world—by systemizing and elaborating the truth regained by ancient scholars or revealed in Old Testament prophets, and more fully available to later Christian Fathers and students. The expectation was that, when all had been gathered in, a very great part of the knowledge lost at the Fall would once more be available for the guidance and instruction of human beings.

For Southern, this was the first aim of scholasticism: but it had another, equally important one, which shows why scholastic humanism can be relied upon to extend our knowledge of the natural world in ways secular humanism cannot.

> Just as human nature has an inherent dignity which, though ruined by the Fall, has not been altogether lost, so too the whole natural order is in a similar situation. The continuing human power to recognise the grandeur and splendour of the universe, to understand the principles of the organization of nature, and to order human life in accordance with nature is symptomatic of the survival of human dignity, in however depleted a form, after the Fall. But it is also symptomatic of the continuing dignity of the natural world itself that it is intelligible. Consequently, when human beings understand the laws of nature, they not only achieve their true dignity as nature's keystone, holding the whole created order together in an intelligible union, but they also recognise the rationality of nature itself. Further, this position gives human minds access to the divine purpose in the Creation, and therefore, in some degree, access through reason, as well as Revelation, to the divine nature itself.[99]

---

[98] Cf. "the good is always useful," *Idea*, 143–4.
[99] Richard William Southern, *Scholastic Humanism and the Unification of Europe*, 3 vols (Oxford:

To quote from Newman's *The Idea of a University* (1873), where he has occasion to touch on these same issues, is to see the extent to which Southern drew on the convert's work, though it also shows the extent to which Pattison—and, indeed, nearly his entire Oxford generation—failed to learn the lesson of the master.

> [A]s health ought to precede labour of the body, and as a man in health can do what an unhealthy man cannot do, and as of this health the properties are strength, energy, agility, graceful carriage and action, manual dexterity, and endurance of fatigue, so in like manner general culture of mind is the best aid to professional and scientific study, and educated men can do what illiterate cannot; and the man who has learned to think and to reason and to compare and to discriminate and to analyze, who has refined his taste, and formed his judgment, and sharpened his mental vision, will not indeed at once be a lawyer, or a pleader, or an orator, or a statesman, or a physician, or a good landlord, or a man of business, or a soldier, or an engineer, or a chemist, or a geologist, or an antiquarian, but he will be placed in that state of intellect in which he can take up any one of the sciences or callings I have referred to, or any other for which he has a taste or special talent, with an ease, a grace, a versatility, and a success, to which another is a stranger. In this sense then ... mental culture is emphatically *useful*.[100]

Reading this, one might say that Newman and Pattison were in agreement, at least, in recognizing that the cultivation of intellect is not, as the utilitarians liked to claim, useless. But then Newman delves more deeply into the nature and scope of intellect, or reason, as he calls it, and draws a distinction which goes to the very heart of the liberalism to which Pattison and so many others succumbed in the Oxford that succeeded Tractarian Oxford.

> Right Reason, [Newman says], that is, Reason rightly exercised, leads the mind to the Catholic Faith, and plants it there, and teaches it in all its religious speculations to act under its guidance. But Reason, considered as a real agent in the world, and as an operative principle in man's nature, with an historical course and with definite results, is far from taking so straight and satisfactory a direction. It considers itself from first to last independent and supreme; it requires no external authority; it makes a religion for itself. Even though it accepts Catholicism, it does not go to sleep; it has an action and development of its own, as the passions have, or the moral sentiments, or the principle of self-interest. Divine grace, to use the language of Theology, does not by its presence supersede nature; nor is nature at once brought into simple concurrence and coalition with grace. Nature pursues its course, now coincident with that of grace, now parallel to it, now across, now divergent, now counter, in proportion to its own imperfection and to the attraction and influence which grace exerts over it. And what takes place as regards other principles of our nature and their developments is found also as regards the Reason. There is, we know, a Religion of enthusiasm, of superstitious ignorance, of statecraft; and each has that in it which resembles Catholicism,

Blackwell,1995), i, 22–3.
[100] *Idea*, 145.

and that again which contradicts Catholicism. There is the Religion of a warlike people, and of a pastoral people; there is a Religion of rude times, and in like manner there is a Religion of civilized times, of the cultivated intellect, of the philosopher, scholar, and gentleman. This is that Religion of Reason.[101]

For Newman, this "Religion of Reason" is knowable by its graduates. Some are upright and respectable enough but "The less aimable specimens of this spurious religion" are "proud, bashful, fastidious and reserved. Why is this? it is because conscience to them is not the word of a lawgiver, as it ought to be, but the dictate of their own minds and nothing more; it is because they do not look out of themselves, because they do not look through and beyond their own minds to their Maker, but are engrossed in notions of what is due to themselves, to their own dignity and their own consistency. Their conscience has become a mere self-respect. Instead of doing one thing and then another, as each is called for, in faith and obedience, careless of what may be called the keeping of deed with deed, and leaving Him who gives the command to blend the portions of their conduct into a whole, their one object, however unconscious to themselves, is to paint a smooth and perfect surface, and to be able to say to themselves that they have done their duty."[102] For Newman, this is the religion of civilization, which contrasts so sharply with the religion of primitivism..

> In rude and semi-barbarous periods, at least in a climate such as our own, it is the daily, nay, the principal business of the senses, to convey feelings of discomfort to the mind, as far as they convey feelings at all. Exposure to the elements, social disorder and lawlessness, the tyranny of the powerful, and the inroads of enemies, are a stern discipline, allowing brief intervals, or awarding a sharp penance, to sloth and sensuality. The rude food, the scanty clothing, the violent exercise, the vagrant life, the military constraint, the imperfect pharmacy, which now are the trials of only particular classes of the community, were once the lot more or less of all. In the deep woods or the wild solitudes of the medieval era, feelings of religion or superstition were naturally present to the population, which in various ways co-operated with the missionary or pastor, in retaining it in a noble simplicity of manners.[103]

Paradoxically, for Newman, the religion of civilization might have many advantages to that of primitivism but it is still beset with the same evils of human nature, the only difference being that civilized men do not tend to acknowledge those evils with anything like the same alacrity as primitive men, which only exacerbates the evils. Hence, the rise of the "march of mind," or "the practical benevolence of the day," as Newman calls it, which "has especially busied itself in plans for supplying the masses of our town population with intellectual and honourable recreations. Cheap literature, libraries of useful and entertaining knowledge, scientific lectureships, museums, zoological collections, buildings and gardens to please the eye and to give repose to the feel-

---

[101] *Idea*, 181–2.
[102] *Idea*, 191–2.
[103] *Idea*, 188.

ings, external objects of whatever kind, which may take the mind off itself, and expand and elevate it in liberal contemplations, these are the human means, wisely suggested, and good as far as they go, for at least parrying the assaults of moral evil, and keeping at bay the enemies, not only of the individual soul, but of society at large."[104]

Newman does not say as much but the intellectual cultivation, such as it was, offered to the town population, was, in some respects, not entirely dissimilar to the intellectual cultivation Jowett's university offered. It was designed preeminently "to take the mind off itself, and expand and elevate it in liberal contemplations." Pattison certainly was observant enough to recognize the inadequacy of such intellectual cultivation when he wrote: "It is not certainly the business of a University to provide a national literature. But in some sort it is responsible for its defects. A grave defect of taste or principle in the current literature of an age, is argument of a fault in the higher education which is administered. In the characteristics of our popular literature, in its aimlessness, its mixture of strength and sophistry, its vague baseless theorizing, in the utter absence of the true philosophical spirit, we must recognize the want of the harmonizing hand of liberal culture. Rude, native strength there is in plenty. This we owe to our freedom. Direction and purpose there is none; for the sacred central fire has been extinguished, and we go about sticking up lights in corners."[105]

Recognizing the consequentiality of this want, Pattison would have had no trouble recognizing the satirical force of Newman's famous definition of the gentleman produced by intellectual cultivation alone as one who "never inflicts pain":

> He is mainly occupied in merely removing the obstacles which hinder the free and unembarrassed action of those about him; and he concurs with their movements rather than takes the initiative himself. His benefits may be considered as parallel to what are called comforts or conveniences in arrangements of a personal nature: like an easy chair or a good fire, which do their part in dispelling cold and fatigue, though nature provides both means of rest and animal heat without them. The true gentleman in like manner carefully avoids whatever may cause a jar or a jolt in the minds of those with whom he is cast;—all clashing of opinion, or collision of feeling, all restraint, or suspicion, or gloom, or resentment; his great concern being to make every one at their ease and at home. He has his eyes on all his company; he is tender towards the bashful, gentle towards the distant, and merciful towards the absurd; he can recollect to whom he is speaking; he guards against unseasonable allusions, or topics which may irritate; he is seldom prominent in conversation, and never wearisome. He makes light of favours while he does them, and seems to be receiving when he is conferring. He never speaks of himself except when compelled, never defends himself by a mere retort, he has no ears for slander or gossip, is scrupulous in imputing motives to those who interfere with him, and interprets every thing for the best. He is never mean or little in his disputes, never takes unfair advantage, never mistakes personalities or sharp sayings for arguments, or insinuates evil which he dare not say out.

---

[104] *Idea*, 188–9.
[105] Pattison, "Oxford Studies: Classics and Modern Science," 449–50.

From a long-sighted prudence, he observes the maxim of the ancient sage, that we should ever conduct ourselves towards our enemy as if he were one day to be our friend. He has too much good sense to be affronted at insults, he is too well employed to remember injuries, and too indolent to bear malice. He is patient, forbearing, and resigned, on philosophical principles; he submits to pain, because it is inevitable, to bereavement, because it is irreparable, and to death, because it is his destiny. If he engages in controversy of any kind, his disciplined intellect preserves him from the blundering discourtesy of better, perhaps, but less educated minds; who, like blunt weapons, tear and hack instead of cutting clean, who mistake the point in argument, waste their strength on trifles, misconceive their adversary, and leave the question more involved than they find it. He may be right or wrong in his opinion, but he is too clear-headed to be unjust; he is as simple as he is forcible, and as brief as he is decisive. Nowhere shall we find greater candour, consideration, indulgence: he throws himself into the minds of his opponents, he accounts for their mistakes. He knows the weakness of human reason as well as its strength, its province and its limits. If he be an unbeliever, he will be too profound and large-minded to ridicule religion or to act against it; he is too wise to be a dogmatist or fanatic in his infidelity. He respects piety and devotion; he even supports institutions as venerable, beautiful, or useful, to which he does not assent; he honours the ministers of religion, and it contents him to decline its mysteries without assailing or denouncing them. He is a friend of religious toleration, and that, not only because his philosophy has taught him to look on all forms of faith with an impartial eye, but also from the gentleness and effeminacy of feeling, which is the attendant on civilization.[106]

That Newman himself could never be adjudged a gentleman by the lights of this definition only adds to its ironical point: the scourge of the establishment being the last person in the world to "look on all forms of faith with an impartial eye … from the gentleness and effeminacy of feeling."

No one can read Newman's *Apologia* without being struck by the generosity with which he treats his former colleagues there, some of whom were not altogether fair or decent to him. But in this marvelous set piece from the *Idea of a University*, we can see Newman putting in the knife, ever so gently, that he had withheld in the earlier book, especially with regard to the sort of gentleman whose "logical powers" might make him seem "a disciple of Christianity."

Not that he may not hold a religion too, in his own way, even when he is not a Christian. In that case his religion is one of imagination and sentiment; it is the embodiment of those ideas of the sublime, majestic, and beautiful, without which there can be no large philosophy. Sometimes he acknowledges the being of God, sometimes he invests an unknown principle or quality with the attributes of perfection. And this deduction of his reason, or creation of his fancy, he makes the occasion of such excellent thoughts, and the starting-point of so varied and systematic a teaching, that he even seems like a disciple of Christianity itself. From the very accuracy and steadiness of his logical powers, he is able to see what sentiments are consistent in those who hold any religious doctrine at all, and he

---

[106] *Idea*, 208–11.

appears to others to feel and to hold a whole circle of theological truths, which exist in his mind no otherwise than as a number of deductions.[107]

Here, the logical religion of the Noetics is fairly skewered, though Newman hastens to insist that the "lineaments of the ethical character" of such cultivation of intellect—"apart from religious principle'—is always varied. "They are seen within the pale of the Church and without it, in holy men, and in profligate; they form the beau-ideal of the world; they partly assist and partly distort the development of the Catholic. They may subserve the education of a St. Francis de Sales or a Cardinal Pole; they may be the limits of the contemplation of a Shaftesbury or a Gibbon. Basil and Julian were fellow-students at the schools of Athens; and one became the Saint and Doctor of the Church, the other her scoffing and relentless foe."[108] That they made Pattison the odd, conflicted, unhappy creature he was is certainly proof of that variousness, though the cultivation of intellect to which he dedicated his life scarcely gave the uprooted Yorkshireman the solace he craved.

As we can see, Pattison dedicated himself to advocating an ideal of scholarship that would at once plunder and seek to discredit Newman's own understanding of the idea of the university. He helped himself to Newman's insistence on the importance of the university providing its charges with cultivation of intellect, but rejected the faith that alone could give that cultivation its governing discipline, its life and its end. In his Catholic sermon, "Illuminating Grace" (1849), after all, Newman might have been addressing his old pupil directly.

> Faith and prayer alone will endure in that last dark hour, when Satan urges all his powers and resources against the sinking soul. What will it avail us then, to have devised some subtle argument, or to have led some brilliant attack, or to have mapped out the field of history, or to have numbered and sorted the weapons of controversy, and to have the homage of friends and the respect of the world for our successes,—what will it avail to have had a position, to have followed out a work, to have re-animated an idea, to have made a cause to triumph, if after all we have not the light of faith to guide us on from this world to the next? Oh, how fain shall we be in that day to exchange our place with the humblest, and dullest, and most ignorant of the sons of men, rather than to stand before the judgment-seat in the lot of him who has received great gifts from God, and used them for self and for man, who has shut his eyes, who has trifled with truth, who has repressed his misgivings, who has been led on by God's grace, but stopped short of its scope, who has neared the land of promise, yet not gone forward to take possession of it![109]

For Pattison, Newman's educational idea was too reactionary, too religiose, though he also acknowledged its superiority to anything Oriel was contemplating in the middle of the century. "If there were any one in the whole of Oxford who could be supposed capable of attaining to a complete conception of what instruction ought to be," Pattison wrote in his *Memoirs*, "it was the author of *Discourses*

---

[107] *Idea*, 210–11.
[108] *Idea*, 180–1.
[109] *Mix.*, 190–1.

on the Scope, etc., of University Education. Newman knew that 'ideas are the life of institutions social, political, literary'; and the idea which he would place as the basis of a university is the master idea"[110]—and here he quoted from Newman's Discourses: "Imagine a science of sciences, and you have attained the true notion of the scope of a university … A science is not mere knowledge; it is knowledge which has under gone a process of intellectual digestion … We consider that all things mount up to a whole; that there is an order and precedence and harmony in the branches of knowledge one with another, and that to destroy that structure is unphilosophical in a course of education."[111] For Pattison, "Nothing can be grander than the development of the idea which follows in the same volume." And, here, again, he quoted Newman: "All knowledge whatever is taken into account in a university, as being the special seat of that large philosophy which embraces and locates truth of every kind, and every method of attaining it."[112] However, while Pattison might have appreciated the far-sighted comprehensiveness of Newman's idea of the university, which was essentially a revival of the scholastic idea, he could not see the necessity of its theological basis.

> Thus thought Newman in 1852. Are we to suppose that this magnificent ideal of a national institute, embracing and representing all knowledge, and making this knowledge its own end, was the wisdom of riper years—a vision which grew up in Newman's mind in the course of the twenty or more years which elapsed between the Oriel tutorship and the Dublin presidency? Perhaps so; it required much time and mental enlargement for any of us, who were brought up under the old eight-book system of an Oxford college of 1830, to rise to the idea of a university in which every science should have its proper and appointed place. Newman may have been no exception.[113]

This poses an interesting question. When did Newman's idea of a university first begin to take root? I would say that there are stirrings of those roots taking hold as early as the Oriel Fellowship, culminating in *Loss and Gain* (1847), in which Newman depicts the unfulfilled yearnings of Tractarian Oxford with such sympathetic charm. In Pattison's comments about the novel, we can see a tell-tale dismissiveness. In discussing "Oxford novels," as he calls them, Pattison wrote:

> They present us only with one aspect of university life, and that its most superficial aspect. It is what I may call the street view of life. The novelist sets up his camera lucida in the middle of the High Street and lets the passing figures mirror themselves as they flit to and fro. He gives us what he sees. And he sees all from the student's side. And as the worst regulated student's life affords the most telling materials for fiction, it is the life of the idle and disorderly which is usually presented for our edification by the novelist. In all these drawings there is a level uniformity such as pervaded the new comedy at Athens. In that stage of dramatic development, the repertory of character was limited to the young scapegrace in

---

[110] Pattison, *Memoirs*, 94.
[111] Newman, *The Scope and Nature of University Education*, 142–4.
[112] Ibid., 153.
[113] Pattison, *Memoirs*, 94–5.

the capital, and his severe governor from the country, the designing hetaera, and the saucy slave who abetted his young master's dissipations; and on this slender cast of parts the changes were rung to infinite variety without novelty. So in the university novel we have the stereotyped parts of the fast undergraduate, beset by duns, contrasted with the slow reading man in woollen socks and spectacles, who is his foil and his butt—the deluded father, the inefficient proctor, a pompous and incapable tutor, a gyp thievish and patronizing, the breakfast and the wine-party, the ruffian of the playground, who is the admired hero of the bevy of charming girls who come up to Commemoration in pink ribands. The fast young man is the first part, the reading student is only brought on the scene to be quizzed, and the senior part of the university become stage dons, who are only there to provoke our derision by various forms of the witty definition of "donnism," "a mysterious carriage of the body intended to conceal the defects of the mind." If some of our fictionists have left this traditional groove, as, e.g., Dr. Farrar in Julian Home, it has been by sacrificing altogether the local colouring. *Loss and Gain* has some characteristic scenes—a tutor's breakfast is, or was, a peculiar institution of the place—was, I say, for we are too busy for breakfast now; and Dr. Newman has happily rendered it. But, on the whole, in *Loss and Gain*, only one transient phase of Oxford life was depicted—that, viz., which really passed over us in my own recollection, when our promising young men spent the time which ought to have been devoted to study in endeavouring to find the true Church.[114]

Yes, one wishes to respond to Pattison, the slow reading man in the woolen socks and spectacles may very well be a figure of fun, but if we do not answer his question as to what constitutes the true Church, we shall have no proper university for either the fast or the slow young man.

VII

If Pattison saw Newman as a beloved mentor, whose mentorship he could not bring himself to follow, Newman would come to see Pattison as a lost sheep, a casualty of liberal Oxford, who needed returning to the Christian fold. As Newman wrote one correspondent: "I have received and read the Article on dear Mr. Pattison, which you have been so good as to send me; and though I had seen him in brief interviews only twice or thrice in the course of forty years, and only knew him as a junior in age and standing to myself, and never had such intimacy with him as yours has been, still your interesting and vivid notices of him fitted on to my own recollections of him with remarkable exactness, and not only revived, but in good measure interpreted them. Much, alas, as, I fear, he differed from Catholics in religion, I must ever consider him a grave, cautious, conscientious thinker."[115] Throughout the years, although they went their separate ways, Newman and Pattison would always retain their high regard and affection for one another.

---

[114] Mark Pattison, "A Chapter in University History," *Macmillan's Magazine*, 1875, in his *Essays*, i, 309–10.
[115] Newman to Theodore Friedrich Althaus (13 January 1885), *LD*, xxxi, 10.

Newman even visited Pattison on his deathbed, convinced that the man who had helped edit the *Library of the Fathers* and the *Lives of the English Saints* could be converted. After all, he could not have known, what the reviewer of the *Memoirs* said in the *Spectator*, that "the interest of the whole volume is like the story of a wreck told without the reader being aware that in a wreck it is to end."[116] Before resolving to see him, Newman wrote him on Christmas Day, 1883: "I grieve to hear that you are anxiously unwell. How is it that I, who am so old, am carried on beyond my juniors? This turns me back in thought forty years, when you, with … so many others now gone, were entering into life. For the sake of those dear old times, I can't help writing to you. Is there any way in which I can serve you. At least I can give you my prayers, poor as they are."[117] Pattison wrote back:

> Lincoln College, Oxford 28 Decemb./83
>
> When your letter, my dear Master was brought to my bedside this morning, and I saw your well-known handwriting, my eyes filled so with tears that I could not at first see to read what you had said.
>
> When I found in what affectionate terms you addressed me, I felt guilty, for I thought, would he do so, if he knew how far I have travelled on the path, which leads quite away from those ideas which I once—about 1845-6—shared with him.
>
> Or is your toleration so large, that though you knew me to be in grievous error, you could still embrace me as a son?
>
> If I have not dared to approach you in any way of recent years, it has been only from the fear that you might be regarding me as coming to you under false colours. The veneration and affection which I felt for you at the time you left us, are in no way diminished and however remote my intellectual standpoint may now be from that which I may presume to be your own, I can still truly say that I have learnt more from you than from any one else with whom I have ever been in contact.
>
> Let me subscribe myself for the last time.
>
> Your affectionate son & pupil Mark Pattison.[118]

In response, Newman answered Pattison's question as to whether he could somehow show more toleration to him.

> My dear Pattison
>
> This requires no answer.
>
> On consideration I find it a duty to answer your question to me about toleration.
>
> I am then obliged to say that what Catholics hold upon it, I hold with them.
>
> That God, who knows the heart, may bless you now and ever is the fervent prayer of your most affectionate friend,
>
> John H Card. Newman[119]

---

[116] *Spectator* (14 March 1885).
[117] Newman to Pattison (25 December 1883), *LD*, xxx, 282.
[118] Pattison to Newman (28 December 1883), *LD*, xxx, 284.
[119] Newman to Pattison (2 January 1883), *LD*, xxx, 287–8.

Apropos the reference to "toleration," Dessain and Gornall note in Volume xxx of the *Letters and Diaries*: "This refers to Pattison's letter of 28 Dec. placed after that of 27 Dec. to him. Among the Pattison Papers at the Bodleian Library is a letter of 8 January 1884 to Meta Bradley, in which Pattison wrote: 'He [Newman] took my letter in an excellent spirit repeated his offer to come to me should I get stronger, but guarded himself from the sort of suggestion my words had conveyed that his toleration as a Catholic was exceptional and individual to himself.'"[120]

Weeks after his first letter, Newman wrote again: "I am now well enough, after a cold which has kept me to my room or my bed for a month, to ask you whether you are strong enough to see me, did I call on you. If you tell me yes, or at least do not say no, I am strongly moved to come to you next Monday, between 11.58 and 2.48. I hope this abrupt letter will not try you. Yours affectionately J. H. Newman."[121] Pattison's dictated response was pitiably agitated.

Lincoln College, Oxford 4. Jan/84.

My dear Master,

Is it possible that you at eighty three can be proposing to make the journey to Oxford and back only for the sake of visiting me?

Were you coming to this place on any other errand of your own, I could not but humbly petition you to let me look on you once more. But to come so far on purpose, that must not be. I could only see you for 3/4 hour and I should be so upset—more by the anticipation than by the visit, that I should not be able to collect my thoughts, to say one of the many things, or to ask one of the questions, which I would fain say, and ask.

I am a little stronger than I was 3 weeks ago, but only a little, and still in a very precarious and feeble state.

I do not think I could bear, what I should feel all the while was a final farewell.

You cannot tell what it costs me to be declining such an offer from you, an offer which thousands would esteem the highest honour that could be done them. Believe me, my dear Master, that I do not esteem it less, but it is too overwhelming and I shrink from it in terror. If I was looking forward to your coming on Monday, I should be in a state of nervous agitation from now till then.

I know if I live that I shall regret what I am now foregoing, but as I am at present, I dare not face it.

I am sure you will not misinterpret my motives and feelings in this letter, and will continue to believe that I am

Yours ever affectionately Mark Pattison[122]

Newman wrote back: My dear Pattison, I thank you for your touching letter. Of course I will be guided by your wish. As time goes on, if you find that can be, which is too trying for you at present, say the word, and I will come (if I can speak of the future). Yours affectionately John H. Card. Newman"[123] Yet, Newman's determination to see his old friend, despite his demurrals, is clear from Fr William

---

[120] LD, xxx, no. 1, 288.
[121] Newman to Pattison (4 January 1883), LD, xxx, 288–9.
[122] LD, xxx, 290.
[123] Newman to Pattison (5 January 1884), LD, xxx, 290.

Neville's account of the matter and the letter Newman wrote to Anne Mozley, the editor of his Anglican correspondence. Here is Fr Neville: "The Cardinal was rather seriously ill in bed with bronchitis when this sad news [about Pattison] came, but, at once he determined to do what he felt would be best—to go himself to the sick man. The doctors gave their forebodings of what would be the result to himself if he went, but he would not be deterred. 'Is the little life left me,' he said, 'to be weighed against the chance of good in a case such as this? Let the doctors say what they will, I shall go!'"[124] And here is the letter to Mozley:

> My dear Anne Mozley
> Thank you for your thoughtful present. I have been for the last five weeks confined to my room or even to my bed, with a cold
> I proposed to Pattison to call on him this very day, but he has refused to see me on the plea of his extreme weakness, and its being too much for him. I am intending to go tomorrow without leave; but what a work it is to implant faith! what human power can do it? I may only make him medically worse
> Don't tell this—I am burning your slip.
> I am better than I was.[125]

In the event, Pattison was not as ill as he had claimed, as Newman's letter to the Duke of Norfolk confirms. "My dear Duke, Your munificent present of wine has come, and I thank you for it. Also your gift of pheasants. I went to Oxford today and saw Mr Pattison who is much better and did not contemplate as I was told, being worse. I had been in correspondence with him some days."[126] Meanwhile, Pattison wrote to his friend Meta Bradley: "Nothing that has happened to me during my illness has moved me so much as this renewal of correspondence with my old Master after a very long interval ... And I had just been giving an account in my Memoirs of the steps by which I had passed beyond him leaving him as it were, wallowing in his fanaticism. I feel it hard-hearted now to let that page stand and yet it is the simple truth."[127]

Wilfrid Ward included Fr. William Neville's account of the meeting, which Dessain omits from the *Letters and Diaries*. "To Oxford ... the Cardinal went ... He had not had any extraordinary expectations when on his way, for he knew that the distance unbelief had travelled was immense, and that its cancerous wound was too deep, and had been too long lasting, and too long trifled with, to be cured quickly; but when leave-taking outside the house door in the college quadrangle, the appearance of both was singularly striking and pleasing to see. Perhaps the like had never occurred before—a parting such as that—two so far from ordinary men, each at the brink of his grave. They had passed some hours together alone; each knew that neither the other nor himself could live long; neither could say which was the likely one to be first called away. The result of the visit will no doubt be asked for, but it will be in vain; for the Cardinal was not the sort of person to say much on what was so grave, so anxious, so private

---

[124] *LD*, xxx, 288, note 3.
[125] Newman to Anne Mozley (7 January 1884), *LD*, xxx, 291.
[126] Newman to Duke of Norfolk (9 January 1884), *LD*, xxx, 293.
[127] Pattison quoted in *LD*, xxx, 394, note 4.

as this, the result of which must be in the hands of God. Never the less, what he did say was expressive of satisfaction and of hope. The journey, far from exhausting him, apparently quite set him up. Mr. Pattison died in the spring."[128] Neville also said that Pattison "allowed Cardinal Newman before leaving to send for and to introduce to him a priest of the place, expressly for the purpose of thus forwarding a priest's services to him at call," though, at the moment of truth, it is not clear that a priest was called.[129] Pattison's account had all of his characteristically vivid acerbity.

> Surely I told you all the particulars of Newman's visit, if I did not it was a strange omission, as it was the most remarkable event of this winter's illness, and has been the object of general wonder and curiosity here. After he had accepted, or acquiesced in my put off for the reasons I gave, on the Wednesday morning I got a note saying he would be here at 12. o'clock. I need not say how flurried I was by this, for other reasons, but also now my invalid routine of hours was upset. He came at 12 and left at 2.15 to return to Birmingham and out of that short time had to be taken lunch. The interview was most affecting. I was dreadfully agitated, distressed even. On the one hand I felt what a proof of affection he was giving, to one who had travelled so far, from what he regarded as important—On the other, I felt that it was not all personal regard which had brought him, but the hope, however slight, that I might still be got over in my last moments. And I could not tell in what proportion these two motives might have influenced N. to undertake a fatiguing journey. The conversation at first turned on old times and recollections. It gradually slid into religious discourse, when I found as I expected, that he had not realized the enormous distance at which I had left behind the stand-point of 1845. More than this he did not seem to apprehend more than any ordinary Catholic would have done, that there is such a space to travel, or that one can look back upon the ideas of those days as the ideas of childish ignorance. Of course I could not set about trying to put things in this light to a man of 84, let alone a Cardinal. On the other hand I did not feel it right to leave him under the illusion in which he evidently was that I was still hesitating about my road and doubting as we were in 1845 as to where the true church was to be found. In this dilemma having to be true and on the other hand having to avoid the futile attempt to explain to him, what it was evident could not be explained, I was in great embarrassment as to how to express myself. N. did not of course attempt the vulgar arts of conversion, nor was there anything like clerical cant, or affectation of unction like a parson's talk by a deathbed. He dwelt upon his own personal experiences since he had been reconciled to the Church, the secret comfort and support which had been given him in the way of supernatural grace under many great trials; that he had never been deserted by such help for a moment; that his soul had found sweet peace and rest in the bosom of the Church. Then we got for a moment, but only for a moment, on more controversial matter. Here he had nothing to say, but the old argument of the *Apologia* which I need not repeat to you. I said in answer three hypotheses each less probable than the one before it.

---

[128] Ward, *Life of Newman*, ii, 438.
[129] LD, xxx, 292, note 3.

After I had said this I regretted it, but was relieved to find that he had not taken the scope of the remark, so it passed harmless. We very soon changed the conversation; he allowing me to ask him several questions about Oriel before I became a member of it. This last conversation I should have liked to have prolonged as it interested me much more than the other, but I felt that that was not what he had come for and was therefore shy of pursuing it

There I have given you an outline of what took place; considering the busy life you are now leading it is probably more than you will care for. But it is the fullest account I have yet written and as you are so careful to keep my letters I consider that I have placed it upon record in as permanent a way as I could.[130]

Pattison died on 30 July, and on 20 September 1884 his widow wrote from Lincoln College: "Mrs Mark Pattison sends to Cardinal Newman by the same post as this letter a copy of the *Vie de Monseigneur Sibour* which she has found among the Rector's books and begs that H. E. [His Eminence] will permit her to offer it to his acceptance in memory of him to whom it so recently belonged. She also encloses several letters of Cardinal Newman's which were preserved with the Rector's other correspondence and which she thinks the Cardinal may like to have returned to him. The Rector spoke to Mrs Pattison in terms of strong feeling of Cardinal Newman's visit to him last January: he recapitulated every little incident of the meeting and turn of the conversation with a keen sense of the real meaning of the effort and deep gratitude for the affection which had prompted it."[131] Mrs. Arthur Johnson, a family friend, summed up Pattison's life in terms Newman might have approved. "The chief Oxford event to tell," she wrote, "is the death of the poor old Rector, whereby indeed the place loses a character ... It is very sad when a man's intellectual work is the best thing about him—you know how little I ever liked the poor old gentleman, how angry I felt with him ... and he has now gone to his God and we will keep silence."[132]

Nothing shows why Newman extended such charity and love to his old pupil better than Pattison's own account of his life.

While my contemporaries, who started so far ahead of me, fixed their mental horizon before they were thirty-five, mine has been ever enlarging and expanding. ... I seemed to my friends to have changed, to have gone over from High Anglicanism to Latitudinarianism, or Rationalism, or Unbelief, or whatever the term may be. This is not so; what took place with me was simple expansion of knowledge and ideas. To my home Puritan religion, almost narrowed to two points—fear of God's wrath and faith in the doctrine of the atonement—the idea of the Church was a widening of the horizon which stirred up the spirit and filled it with enthusiasm. The notion of the Church soon expanded itself beyond the limits of the Anglican communion and became the wider idea of the Catholic Church. Then Anglicanism fell off from me, like an old garment, as Puritanism

---

[130] *LD*, xxx, 292–3.
[131] *LD*, xxx, 293.
[132] Vivian Green, *Love in a Cool Climate: The Letters of Mark Pattison and Meta Bradley 1879–1884* (Oxford: The Clarendon Press, 1985), 229. Arthur Johnson joined Pattison and Henry Sidgwick in advocating for women's education at Oxford.

had done before. Now the idea of the Catholic Church is only a mode of conceiving the dealings of divine Providence with the whole race of mankind. Reflection on the history and condition of humanity, taken as a whole, gradually convinced me that this theory of the relation of all living beings to the Supreme Being was too narrow and inadequate. It makes an equal Providence, the Father of all, care only for a mere handful of the species, leaving the rest (such is the theory) to the chances of eternal misery. If God interferes at all to procure the happiness of mankind it must be on a far more comprehensive scale than by providing for them a church of which far the majority of them will never hear. It was on this line of thought, the details of which I need not pursue, that I passed out of the Catholic phase, but slowly, and in many years, to that highest development when all religions appear in their historical light, as efforts of the human spirit to come to an understanding with that Unseen Power whose pressure it feels, but whose motives are a riddle. Thus, Catholicism dropped off me as another husk which I had outgrown.[133]

After Pattison was gone, Dean Church wrote a piece on him in the *Guardian*, which shows what a good critic he was—sympathetic but just.

People have often not given Pattison credit for the love that was in him for what was good and true; it is not to be wondered at, but the observation has to be made. On the other hand, a panegyric, like that which we reprint from the Times, sets too high an estimate on his intellectual qualities, and on the position which they gave him. He was full of the passion for knowledge; he was very learned, very acute in his judgment on what his learning brought before him, very versatile, very shrewd, very subtle; too full of the truth of his subject to care about seeming to be original; but, especially in his poetical criticisms, often full of that best kind of originality which consists in seeing and pointing out novelty in what is most familiar and trite. But, not merely as a practical but as a speculative writer, he was apt to be too much under the empire and pressure of the one idea which at the moment occupied and interested his mind. He could not resist it; it came to him with exclusive and overmastering force; he did not care to attend to what limited it or conflicted with it. And thus, with all the force and sagacity of his University theories, they were not always self-consistent, and they were often one-sided and exaggerated.

Indeed, for the critic in Church, "Intellectually, in reach, and fulness, and solidity of mental power, it may be doubted whether [Pattison] was so great as it has recently been the fashion to rate him."[134]

In the same month, George Edwards, Secretary of the London Evangelization Society wrote Newman to say: "I fear the death of Mr Mark Pattison, the late Rector of Lincoln, has removed almost the last of your early Oxford friends. I heard with much interest of your visit to him shortly before the end, and I trust that 'at Evening time it was light'. Since the publication of the notorious *Essays and Reviews*, he seems to have taken little part in matters theological, though I hear he has left ready for publication some account of the Oxford Movement. I have no doubt he

---

[133] Pattison, *Memoirs*, 326–8.
[134] Church, *Occasional Papers*, ii, 354–6.

will be more accurate in his statement of facts than Mr Mozley, whose book I fear gave your Eminence pain, as it did indeed to many others," to which Newman replied: "Thank you for referring to my friend Mr. Pattison. Forty years ago he was on the point of becoming a Catholic. I fear nothing from his Reminiscences; he was an accurately-minded man—and never would pretend to know things about me before ever he saw or heard of me—or rather, before he himself was born. My fear is that his book will subserve the cause of infidelity, which is a dreadful thought."[135] A year later, another correspondent wrote Newman about his old friend, saying, in particular, that Pattison had kept a framed photograph of the Cardinal on his mantlepiece, to which Newman responded: "I have received and read the Article on dear Mr Pattison, which you have been so good as to send me; and though I had seen him in brief interviews only twice or thrice in the course of forty years, and only knew him as a junior in age and standing to myself, and never had such intimacy with him as yours has been, still your interesting and vivid notices of him fitted on to my own recollections of him with remarkable exactness, and not only revived, but in good measure interpreted them. Much, alas, as, I fear, he differed from Catholics in religion, I must ever consider him a grave, cautious, conscientious thinker." The fastidious stylist in Newman only added: "Since you have, as his gift, a copy of a volume of mine ["On the Office of Universities"], which went from me to him, on its first publication, with many imperfections in it, I venture, in return for your article about him, to send you my second Edition, in which I removed some of them."[136] When Pattison had first received his copy of the book, he wrote to Robert Ornsby: "It may have been sent me for review. But I have a lurking hope that it is just possible it was sent to me by JHN himself. Perhaps it is presumptuous even to hope this—but I should be greatly obliged if you would find out for me."[137] When Pattison learned that Newman had, indeed, sent the book himself, he responded with a lovely letter:

> My dear Dr Newman
>
> A letter from Ornsby to day confirms the truth of what I had ventured to hope, that a copy of your book On Universities had been sent me by your direction.
>
> Had I been sure that this was the case at first, I should not have allowed so long a time to pass without expressing to you the great gratification it is to me to find that I am not forgotten by you.
>
> If I have not ventured either to write to you, or to approach you in any way, it has been from no other feeling than the old one which used to keep me back in former days, that I had no claim to intrude on one who had so much else to think of.
>
> But I may be allowed to take this opportunity of saying that I can never forget the great obligations I am under to you. I do not exaggerate in saying that to the moral and mental influence derived from you I owe the formation of my mind, and a deep religious impression which has carried me through perplexities of no ordinary kind."[138]

---

[135] Newman to George Edwards (29 August 1884), *LD*, xxx, 393–4.
[136] *LD*, xxxi, 10. The volume to which Newman refers is his *The Office and Work of Universities* (London: Longman Brown, 1856).
[137] Pattison to Robert Ornsby (21 December 1856), *LD*, xvii, note 1, 481.
[138] Pattison to Newman (8 December 1856), *LD*, xvii, 481.

Since Newman, throughout his long life, was his own archivist, and an extraordinarily attentive one, he might very well have revisited this letter before resolving to visit Pattison on his death bed. Then, again, he had seen Pattison in 1877, when, passing through Birmingham, the Rector had stopped at the Oratory, and both men had had what Pattison described as an "affecting (to me) interview," in which they had "talked of old times." Pattison even asked him if he could not write down some anecdotes of famous men whom he had met."[139] Newman gave his old pupil his blessing before they parted.

Pattison's end was grim. His wife, Francis, who had become estranged from her unhappy husband, spending most of her time in France, returned home in the summer of 1884 to find a husband who had given way to the most appalling *timor mortis*. The dread of dying, and being dead, flashed afresh to hold and horrify. The scene in the sick room was frightful. "The nurses say they never saw anything like it," Francis remarked. "[T]he always uncontrollable temper, the rage, the pathos, the abject fits of terror, the immense vitality," of her dying husband was accompanied by "terrible fits of terror with shrieks which went through the house." Whether Francis called for a priest is not clear. She might have been too terrified. "Let not my last days be like his!" she thought to herself. "The moral misery is awful."[140]

Whether "moral misery" is a fair phrase with which to characterize Pattison's pitiable end—the poor man was suffering the agonies of stomach cancer—the end does remind one of something Newman says in *Anglican Difficulties*, which his old pupil obviously never credited.

> Every one is obliged, by the law of his nature, to act by reason; yet no one likes to make a great sacrifice unnecessarily; such difficulties, then, just avail to turn the scale, and to detain men in Protestantism, who are open to the influence of tenderness towards friends, reliance on superiors, regard for their position, dread of present inconvenience, indolence, love of independence, fear of the future, regard to reputation, desire of consistency, attachment to cherished notions, pride of reason, or reluctance to go to school again. No one likes to take an awful step, all by himself, without feeling sure he is right; no one likes to remain long in doubt whether he should take it or not; he wishes to be settled, and he readily catches at objections, or listens to dissuasives, which allow of his giving over the inquiry, or postponing it *sine die*. Yet those very same persons who would willingly hide the truth from their eyes by objections and difficulties, nevertheless, if actually forced to look it in the face, and brought under the direct power of the Catholic arguments, would often have strength and courage enough to take the dreaded step, and would find themselves, almost before they knew what they had done, in the haven of peace.[141]

---

[139] Pattison quoted in V. H. H. Green, *Oxford Common Room: A Study of Lincoln College and Mark Pattison* (London: Edward Arnold, 1957), 321.
[140] Ibid., 323.
[141] *Diff.*, i, xi–xii.

EDWIN ABBOTT ABBOTT

4

Edwin Abbott Abbott's Gibbering Phantom

Dr. Abbott has told us of the Cardinal's works that 'a young man loving Christ will find in them, as far as I can judge, little strength, stimulus, little sustenance.' The judgement lies with a generation which will know Dr. Abbott as little as he knows them.

Walter K. Firminger, "Dr. Abbott's Philomythus" (1891)

The handiwork which Newman fashioned so delicately and with such infinite pains, adding each year to the very end a finishing touch—new thoughts and new words as fresh truths broke on him, or old truths were seen better—all the beautiful and delicate ware utterly and hopelessly smashed by the invader [Edwin Abbott Abbott], as he advances with bovine stride, wholly unconscious of the value of the Dresden figures, of the antiquity of the Crown Derby, of the history of the Worcester vases, of the irredeemable and Philistine destruction he is perpetrating in his wild-goose chase after superstitions and deceptions. "Sad work, my masters, sad work!"

Wilfrid Ward, *Witness to the Unseen and Other Essays* (1893)

I

After resolving on writing his *Apologia pro Vita Sua* (1864), Newman shared with his readers what impelled him to answer the aspersions of Charles Kingsley in the way he did, with an intellectual rather than a conventionally autobiographical account of his life: "I recognized what I had to do," he wrote, in the prefatory piece to the *Apologia* entitled "True Mode of Meeting Mr. Kingsley," which was included in the 1864 edition of the book, "though I shrank from both the task and the exposure which it would entail. I must, I said, give the true key to my whole life; I must show what I am, that it may be seen what I am not, and that the phantom may be extinguished which gibbers instead of me. I wish to be known as a living man, and not as a scarecrow which is dressed up in my clothes. False ideas may be refuted indeed by argument, but by true ideas alone are they expelled. I will vanquish, not my Accuser, but my judges. I will indeed answer his charges and criticisms on me one by one, lest any one should say that they are unanswerable, but such a work shall not be the scope nor the substance of my reply. I will draw out, as far as may be, the history of my mind." For contemporary readers, this must have made for riveting reading. No one in nineteenth-century England, after all, was more celebrated than Newman for the quality of his mind, and to hear him pledging to share with readers the history of that mind promised a rare performance. Indeed, in these prefatory remarks, one can hear how Newman himself palpably thrilled to the prospect.

> Yes, I said to myself, his very question is about my *meaning*; "What does Dr. Newman mean?" It pointed in the very same direction as that into which my musings had turned me already. He asks what I *mean*; not about my words, not about my arguments, not about my actions, as his ultimate point, but about that living intelligence, by which I write, and argue, and act. He asks about my Mind and its Beliefs and its Sentiments; and he shall be answered;—not for his own sake, but for mine, for the sake of the Religion which I profess, and of the Priesthood in which I am unworthily included, and of my friends and of my foes, and of that general public which consists of neither one nor the other, but of well-wishers, lovers of fair play, sceptical cross-questioners, interested inquirers, curious lookers-on, and simple strangers, unconcerned yet not careless about the issue—for the sake of all these he shall be answered.[1]

However promising he might have initially found the project, he was scarcely unappreciative of the difficulties that stood in the way of his bringing it to a successful issue. "I must show,—what is the very truth,—that the doctrines which I held, and have held for so many years, have been taught me (speaking humanly) partly by the suggestions of Protestant friends, partly by the teaching of books, and partly by the action of my own mind," he wrote, "and thus I shall account for that phenomenon which to so many seems so wonderful, that I should have left 'my kindred and my father's house' for a Church from which once I turned away with dread;—so wonderful to them! as if forsooth a Religion which has flourished through so many ages, among so many nations, amid such varieties of social life, in such contrary classes and conditions of men, and after so many revolutions, political and civil, could not subdue the reason and overcome the heart, without the aid of fraud in the process and the sophistries of the schools." But there was an even keener and more personal difficulty, which went to the heart of the man whom so many of his contemporaries unfairly charged with self-absorption. He might aver, as he said, that "I am not expounding Catholic doctrine, I am doing no more than explaining myself, and my opinions and actions." But this would not forestall readers finding fault with his personal, historical account.

> Of course there will be room enough for contrariety of judgment among my readers, as to the necessity, or appositeness, or value, or good taste, or religious prudence, of the details which I shall introduce. I may be accused of laying stress on little things, of being beside the mark, of going into impertinent or ridiculous details, of sounding my own praise, of giving scandal; but this is a case above all others, in which I am bound to follow my own lights and to speak out my

---

[1] *Apo.*, 404–5.

own heart. It is not at all pleasant for me to be egotistical; nor to be criticized for being so. It is not pleasant to reveal to high and low, young and old, what has gone on within me from my early years. It is not pleasant to be giving to every shallow or flippant disputant the advantage over me of knowing my most private thoughts, I might even say the intercourse between myself and my Maker. But I do not like to be called to my face a liar and a knave: nor should I be doing my duty to my faith or to my name, if I were to suffer it. I know I have done nothing to deserve such an insult; and if I prove this, as I hope to do, I must not care for such incidental annoyances as are involved in the process.[2]

As it happened, the writing of the *Apologia*, composed as it was in six intense, harrowing weeks, was much more demanding than he could ever have anticipated, especially for a man past sixty. It also required him to revisit the painful parting of friends, which could only remind him of unallayable wounds. "I have no idea whatever of giving any *point* to what I am writing," he wrote to his dear friend Richard William Church, the historian of the Oxford Movement, "but that I did not act dishonestly. And I want to state the stages in my change, and the impediments which kept me from going faster. Argument, I think, as such, will not come in—though I must state the general grounds of my change."[3] Ludicrously, in the very midst of his ordeal, his sister Jemima sent him a parcel of marmalade; although averse from writing or speaking to him about anything related to the Christian faith that had meant so much to them when they were younger she could always send him parcels of marmalade; in his letter back to her, Newman replied, with strenuous gratitude: "Thank you for the Marmalade which has just come. I had not eaten Marmalade for years and years, till you sent me some. Yours is better than any other I ever ate. And it has made me eat it again. But it is only a luxury, so you should not go on sending it."[4] At the same time, John Keble sent a letter from Penzance, telling his old friend, from whom he had been estranged for over twenty years, "I feel as if I ought to write you a long letter, but it must be only a few lines just now, to implore you not to be seriously worried by such trash as Mr Kingsley's ... We (if I may say) want you, dear J. H. N.—all Christendom wants you—to take your stand against the infidelity which seems to be so fast enveloping us all ... Copeland has told me how you are now employed. I regret it so far as it will give you, I fear, much pain which I should have thought might be spared: but if I can be of the smallest use I shall be rejoiced."[5] Newman replied: "Thank you for your affectionate letter. When you see part of my publication, you will wonder how I ever could get myself to write it. Well, I could not, except under some very great stimulus. I do not think I could write it, if I delayed it a month. And yet I have for years wished to write it as a duty. I don't know what people will think of me, or what will be the effect of it—but I wish to tell the truth, and to leave the matter in God's hands."[6] Finally, when the manuscript had been dispatched to his publisher, he wrote

---

[2] *Apo.*, 407.
[3] Newman to R. W. Church (26 April 1864), *LD*, xxi, 102.
[4] Newman to Mrs. John Mozley (23 April 1864), *LD*, xxxi, 101.
[5] John Keble to Newman (25 April 1864), *LD*, xxi, 103.
[6] Newman to John Keble (27 April 1884), *LD*, xxi, 103.

W. J. Copeland, his old Tractarian friend: "I never have had such a time. It is the greatest effort I ever made … One time I went on for 22 hours running. But it is over—and, I trust, has done my work—so I must be content and thankful."[7]

Newman's *Apologia* did do his work: it gave readers "the history of his mind" and exculpated him from Kingsley's dual charge of dishonesty and mendacity. As Martin Svaglic shows in his critical edition of the *Apologia*, the best vindication in the book's reception came from Samuel Wilberforce, the Bishop of Oxford, the darling of the Broad Church, who had seen not only his two brothers but many of his friends defect from the Anglican Church as a result of Newman's influence. If ever there were a man who might have been interested in taking exception to Newman's defense of his religious convictions, it was the staunchly Anglican Wilberforce. And yet he exhibited precisely the "fair play" on which Newman relied from "sceptical cross-questioners, interested inquirers, curious lookers-on, and simple strangers, unconcerned yet not careless about the issue." Writing in the *Quarterly Review*, Wilberforce confirmed that the pages of Newman's book were written to lay open before his readers

> the whole secret of his moral and spiritual anatomy; they were intended to prove that he was altogether free from that foul and disgraceful taint of innate dishonesty, the unspoken suspicion of which in so many quarters had so long troubled him; the open utterance of which, from the lips of a popular and respectable writer, was so absolutely intolerable to him. From that imputation it is but bare justice to say he does thoroughly clear himself. The post-mortem examination of his life is complete; the hand which guided the dissecting-knife has trembled nowhere, nor shrunk from any incision. All lies perfectly open, and the foul taint is nowhere.[8]

Even F. D. Maurice took issue with Kingsley's bungling polemic. "I would have given much that Kingsley had not got into this dispute with Newman," he wrote. "In spite of all evidence I do believe Newman loves the truth in his heart of hearts, and more now than when he was an Anglican."[9] Svaglic notes Mrs. Kingsley's claim that if reviewers tended to see in the book an exoneration of Newman's integrity, it did not follow that they necessarily saw in it any exoneration of the integrity of the Catholic priesthood. Nevertheless, in the eyes of public opinion the *Apologia* had achieved both. "It was a triumph not only for Newman but for the Roman Church in general," Svaglic writes.[10] And he quotes Richard Holt Hutton to substantiate his point: the *Apologia*, for the editor of the *Spectator*, was "a book which, I venture to say, has done more to break down the English distrust of Roman Catholicism, and to bring about a hearty good fellowship between them

---

[7] Newman to W. J. Copeland (17 June 1864), *LD*, xxi, 118. After meeting Newman by accident in London on 3 June 1862, Copeland succeeded in reuniting the long estranged convert with his old friends Keble, Rogers and Church; and thus it was fitting that Newman should have contacted him first to tell him the good news that the *Apologia* was completed.
[8] Wilberforce quoted in Martin J. Svaglic, "Editor's Introduction," in *Apo.*, xvii.
[9] Maurice to Dean Stanley (19 April 1864), *The Life of Frederick Denison Maurice*, ii, 476.
[10] "Editor's Introduction," in *Apo.*, li. Readers should be forewarned that there is no acknowledgment of this widely favorable reception in the contemptibly biased *Receptions of Newman*, ed. Frederick Aquino and Benjamim King (Oxford: Oxford University Press, 2015).

and the members of other Churches, than all the rest of the religious literature of our time put together."[11]

II

But what is extraordinary about the *Apologia*, for all of its self-evident truthfulness and candor, let alone its literary distinction, is that it did not put to rest the aspersions against Newman's integrity that had dogged him since his Anglican days. If anything, in some respects, it exacerbated them. The very adroitness with which Newman defended himself was held against him as proof of what his liberal Protestant and rationalist critics insisted were his inalienable cunning and sophistry. After Newman's death, these aspersions returned with redoubled bitterness. We can hear something of this virulence in a letter that the otherwise mild-mannered Cambridge don and translator of the New Testament Fenton John Anthony Hort (1828–92) wrote to his wife a week or so after Newman's death.[12] Hort had been a keen admirer of Newman in his youth but later took the view that the convert had wasted most of his life in unjustifiable controversy. "It is rather trying to read the unqualified praises of Newman's 'saintliness,'" the friend of F. D. Maurice and Daniel MacMillan wrote.[13]

> As regards his old age they may be true, but certainly not as regards his early and middle life. Doubtless he lived always as in the sight of God. He was entirely free from self-seeking or ambition. To friends and pupils he was affectionate and tender to a rare degree. But he seemed to revel in religious warfare, and as a combatant he was bitter and scornful beyond measure. Doubtless he was often led by others; and in this respect he probably suffered great moral injury from association with men like Hurrell Froude. But the temptation to use his remarkable controversial powers unscrupulously must have been too strong for him;

---

[11] Hutton, *Cardinal Newman*, 230.
[12] Apropos the liberal churchman, the *ODNB* writes: "In 1887 Hort was elected to the Lady Margaret professorship of divinity, a post he held until his death. His reputation as a scholar now stood at its height. His achievements in textual and translation work were widely recognized, and he received honorary degrees from the universities of Dublin (1888) and Durham (1890); bad health obliged him to decline a similar offer from the University of Oxford. His stature was acknowledged by American and German scholars and in 1889 William Sanday, biblical scholar at Oxford, claimed that Hort was the greatest scholar in England or Germany. Contemporaries recall his striking appearance at this time: the keen, spare face, the piercing eyes, the prematurely white beard, moustache, and whiskers, and the broad forehead. His lectures were not popular with undergraduates, for his method was too austere. He would take almost a whole term to introduce a subject, for instance. He was always careful not to over-influence his students. One recalled that 'he seemed to regard the formation of opinion as a very sacred thing' (Robinson and Ramsay, 69). To another, who asked him to recommend books to help him study the synoptic problem, his answer was: 'I should advise you to take your Greek New Testament, and get your own view of the facts first of all' (*ibid.*, 69)." This last bit of advice should be heeded by the young who think they might wish to study Newman. Study Newman, not his dull and usually misguided academic commentators.
[13] Cf. "If Maurice had really been a futile, muddle-headed person without a clear idea in his head, he could never have exerted the influence on Hort which we know he did. If Maurice had done nothing more than help to form the mind of Hort, he would be entitled to our respect as a thinker and teacher." H. G. Wood, *Frederick Denison Maurice* (Cambridge: Cambridge University Press, 1950), 8.

and so towards opponents, or those whom he chose to consider such, it is sadly uncommon to find him showing gentleness, or forbearance, or even common fairness. It was so both at Oxford and in his early Roman Catholic days. Then came the collision with Kingsley, a tragic and shameful business. Kingsley was much to blame for his recklessly exaggerated epigram, though it had but too sad a foundation of truth. Newman's reply, however, was sickening to read, from the cruelty and insolence with which he trampled on his assailant. Kingsley's rejoinder was bad enough, but not so horribly unchristian. However, there was one good result. Newman learned, to his astonishment, from the public comments that there was not the least unwillingness in reasonable English people to do him justice, although he was a Roman Catholic and a pervert; and so he was emboldened to unbosom himself, and try to get his mental history understood, by writing his Apologia. From that day a change seemed to come over him. The antagonism against things English which had pervaded the Tracts and the early lectures delivered after his perversion died away, partly perhaps owing to recent experience as to the ugly realities of Italian Romanism. Another great experience of those days evidently told much upon him for good. He, the most conspicuous and brilliant of Roman converts, found but scanty recognition from the Pope and the Roman authorities. Except by a few friends, he was little more than tolerated as a troublesomely independent and eccentric person, not far removed from being a heretic. This terribly mortifiying lesson seems to have had a most salutary chastening effect, dispersing various delusions, and bringing back sympathy with Protestant England. After this the appreciation shown by Leo XIII. (when the Jesuits would let him) was only so much genial sunshine, and entirely salutary. If I am not much mistaken, these later years brought a far more peaceful frame of mind, and also at least an approach to a truer and wider view of human affairs than his old theories allowed. The end has been all one could desire, short of the (in his case impossible) return to the true Church of England. But it is misleading to keep out of sight the strife and violence of nearly all his active life.[14]

Scorn for the "ugly realities of Italian Romanism" also colored the work of Edwin Abbott Abbott (1838–1926), the Anglican schoolmaster and fantasist, whose intricately abusive two-volume *Anglican Career of Cardinal Newman* (1891) took no pains to conceal the author's opinion "that Newman's imagination dominated his reason, even more than his spiritual fears perverted his imagination; that he was led to wrong conclusions by hasty judgment and insufficient study; that the *Apologia* is by no means so accurate in its representation of facts as it is delight-

---

[14] Fenton John Anthony Hort to his Wife (24 August 1890), *Life and Letters of Fenton John Anthony Hort*, ed. by his Son (London: Macmillan & Co., 1896), 424–5. In referring to what he regarded in old age as the unsaintliness of Newman's "early and middle life," Hort omitted to recall his own earlier admiration of Newman at those times. In 1852, for example, he wrote his friend Brooke Foss Westcott (1825–1901), the Regius Professor of Divinity at Cambridge and later Bishop of Durham: "You must have misunderstood me about Newman. Many of his sayings and doings I cannot but condemn most strongly. But they are not Newman; and him I all but worship. Few men have been privileged to be the authors of such incalculable blessings to the world (though perhaps not a hundred acknowledge the fact), and therefore few have had his temptations. Unhappily the hard-hearted, scornful, and lying persecution which he had so long to bear did its work upon him but too effectually. Still even now it were most wrong to 'confound the cry of agony with a mocking laugh,' or rather to forget how both may be mingled in the same sound." *Ibid.*, i, 231.

ful in its literary style; and that the Sermons, full though they are of varied and subtle beauties, and of a marvellous insight into the imperfections of human nature, and though they may well have exercised a magnetic power over those who have had actual experience of the living magnet, are nevertheless deficient in the Pauline spirit of hope and love, and inconsistent, as well as inadequate, in their exposition of the meanings and claims of faith and reason."[15]

Abbott's two-volume hatchet-job was not his first book on Newman: he had published *Philomythus* (1890) an attack on the convert's *Two Essays on Biblical and Ecclesiastical Miracles* (1890), a year earlier. Mrs. Humphry Ward (1851–1920), the author of the bestselling *Robert Elsmere* (1888), whose hero abandons his Anglican ministry to devote himself to social work in the East End, wrote a glowing review of *Philomythus* in the *Nineteenth Century*. "In this acute, readable, and generally effective discussion of Cardinal Newman's famous essay," she told her readers, "Dr. Abbott has produced an important though fragmentary contribution to a book which has still to be written—to that scientific History of Miracle for which the materials are now accumulating on every side, waiting for some coordinating mind richly endowed enough to take up the great task."[16] As for Abbott's actual book, she might have considered it justifiable in principle, but she was curiously mum on whether he had altogether done the principle justice.

> Whether it be true or not that "the face of the Oxford movement would have been changed if Newman had known German," or, as Dr. Abbott says, that "Newman neither had nor pretended to have any critical knowledge whatever of the text of the New Testament," it is certainly true that the tendency to miraculous belief which almost everyone has, but which in most men and women of the present day is more or less corrected by the influences flowing from the world of physical science, is nowhere writ so large as in Newman, combined as it happens to be in him with a sensitive spiritual life and a wonderful rhetorical gift. If, as probably nobody will deny, this tendency and its fruits are still of great importance to thought and life, then to make a study of it in its foremost English representative, to watch how it works, how it affects a man's dealings with history and with the laws of rational statement, must be valuable.[17]

Oddly, she agreed with Abbott that Newman's literary gift somehow stood in the way of his assessing evidence, a contention that she would have had difficulty getting her friend Henry James to share, so much of whose own literary talent was dedicated to assessing the evidence for human destiny, which, in its way, can sometimes seem as inscrutable as divine destiny. Nevertheless, the eldest of Thomas Arnold's eight children had something of her mother's animus against the uncompromising convert and she was never afraid of showing it. "The real truth of course is, as Dr. Abbott points out repeatedly—that Newman does not care for facts, and in his heart despises argument," Ward wrote, with a virulence worthy of her mother.[18]

---

[15] Abbott, *Anglican Career*, i, viii–ix.
[16] Mrs. Humphry Ward, "Philomythus," *The Nineteenth Century* (May 1891), 768–9.
[17] Ibid., 769–70.
[18] Ward's mother Julia (*née*) Sorrell (1826–88) was no fan of Newman, blaming him for causing her

He is convinced already, and is in fact only playing round his readers with that wonderful literary gift of his. The crowning proof of this lies in the amazing passage defending the truth of the Assumption of the Virgin, where that mixture of poetry and what is surely, in essence, a non-sane conception of the world, which is characteristic of him, reaches its highest point. But it may be verified all through. Take the miracle of the Thundering Legion,—the story that, owing to the prayers of certain Christians serving in the army of Marcus Aurelius, a thunderstorm occurred and rain fell, which saved the army from perishing of drought. Newman accepts it with an absolute confidence. After recounting the facts, he does "not see what remains to be proved." Everything is as plain as daylight. But how does he recount the facts? Dr. Abbott's acute analysis must be read at length to appreciate the full force of it.[19]

In his conclusion, Ward praised the book as an admirable contribution to a more scientifically palatable, Socinian Christianity, to which her growing interest in social questions inclined her. J. W. Burrow, the intellectual historian, makes an interesting point regarding the emergence of such questions when he observes how: "In England a contrast has been drawn between *Lux Mundi* (1887), the collection of essays which constituted a kind of manifesto of liberal Anglicanism, and *Essays and Reviews* nearly thirty years earlier. *Lux Mundi* shocked some, but there was no attempt at persecution. More significantly, where *Essays and Reviews* was largely defensive, concerned to save essential Christianity from the damaging attacks of the secular intellect by jettisoning Biblical literalism, the latter essays were more affirmative, both of personal faith and of an outward-looking social concern."[20] It was to this latter group that Ward was drawn, comprised as it was of F. D. Maurice's Christian socialism and T. H. Green's Idealist philosophy and civic-mindedness.[21] In the *fin de siècle*, when the hapless converts Ernest Dowson and Lionel Johnson were drinking themselves to death in Piccadilly, Mary Ward took part in the establishment of a settlement house for the poor in Bloomsbury.[22]

> husband to convert not once but twice and causing her family a certain pecuniary sacrifice, to which she could never reconcile herself. Arnold's first conversion resulted in his losing his position as Inspector of Schools in Tasmania and the second forced him to settle for a position teaching English Literature at Newman's Catholic University in Dublin, which his wife considered *infra dignitatem*. Apropos the Arnold household, Newman was forbearing but clear-sighted. "He is a very good amiable fellow, but weak and henpecked. His wife is a Xantippe." Newman to Miss M. R. Giberne (11 February 1868), *LD*, xxiv, 34. One of Julia's finer maledictions bears quoting: "Sir, You have now for the second time been the cause of my husband's becoming a member of the Church of Rome and from the bottom of my heart I curse you for it. You know well how very weak and unstable he is, and you also know that he has a wife and eight children. You know well that he did nothing for the Roman Catholic Church in the ten years he belonged to it before, and you know well that he will do nothing for it now, but the temptation of having one of *his father's sons* under your direction was too much for you, and for the second time you counselled him to ignore every social duty and become a pervert. He has brought utter ruin upon us all, but what is that to you?." Mrs. Thomas Arnold to Newman (5 November 1876), *LD*, xxviii, 157–8.

[19] Ibid., 771.
[20] J. W. Burrow, *The Crisis of Reason: European Thought 1848–1914* (New Haven: Yale University Press, 2000), 203–4.
[21] Ibid., 204.
[22] The author of *The Tamworth Reading Room* (1843) would not have been surprised to hear that Lord Peel was present at the opening of the Passmore Edwards Settlement House, to which the *Daily News* referred as "Robert Elsmere's Scheme at Work." Rosemary Ashton, "Introduction,"

In her wrapping up of the review, one can hear the note of the social crusader.

> When the revolt against miracle has passed more fully than at present from the intellectual to the religious stage; when it is felt to rest upon a new conception of God, the world and life, a new faith, held not less tenaciously, and with a no less passionate humility than the old; when a visibly large number of persons, living the practical life of faith, and claiming the Christian name, have come to feel for themselves and to teach their children to feel that belief in miraculous births or possessed swine or bodily resurrection is, in its essence, a religious offense; then the decay of miraculous belief will have entered upon a new and much more rapid stage than that we see it in at present. Of that time, indeed, there are signs all about us.[23]

The Oratorian Father Ignatius Ryder chose to treat Ward's review of Abbott's book with studied cordiality, writing, in his own review of the book: "I am bound by etiquette ... to take some notice of the accomplished lady who eulogized [Abbott] last May. ... I am comforted, however, by the consideration that Mrs. Humphry Ward has raised no fresh point against the Cardinal which calls for an answer ... her presence may be regarded rather as that of a friendly goddess, who from some exalted sphere blesses her hero, than as his comrade in arms. So far, then, as I succeed in showing that Dr. Abbott's assault is at once barbarous and futile, I shall have sufficiently done my duty." His refusal to return Ward's thrusts against Newman notwithstanding, Ryder nicely summed up the Cardinal's view of the miraculous, a view which both Ward and Abbott misunderstood. When it came to elucidating Newman's true thinking, Ryder showed that his Oratorian formation gave him a distinct advantage.

> To put aside Church miracles altogether, without any reference to their evidence, or to demand as a *sine qua non* an absolute cogency of proof, in accordance with the ordinary Protestant spirit, appeared to Newman inconsistent with an ungrudging acceptance of Scripture miracles, and as threatening men so minded with an ultimate rejection of the Revelation of which miracles are an integral part, inasmuch as it implies an adhesion, conscious or unconscious, to the general principle that it is a mistake to believe in the miraculous. Thus we see how completely reasonable it was from his point of view for Newman to insist that the main matter to be considered was the question of antecedent probability. Once admit that miracles are antecedently probable, or at least not antecedently improbable under the circumstances, and then we shall admit the particular instances recorded, on such evidence as we should demand for any rare but admittedly possible occurrence such as had happened before and might happen again. It was to recommend this attitude of mind as the only one befitting a Christian, and not to prove this or that ecclesiastical miracle, that Newman wrote his essay. How completely his fears have been justified in respect to Scripture miracles let Dr. Abbott and his school declare.[24]

Mrs. Humphry Ward, *Robert Elsmere* (Oxford: Oxford University Press, 1987), xvii.
[23] Ward, "Philomythus," 773.
[24] Henry Ignatius Dudley Ryder, *Essays*, ed. Francis Bacchus (London: Longmans, Green, & Co.,

Newman makes reference to his application of the principle of antecedent probability in his understanding of miracles in the *Apologia* where he speaks of how the Anglican churchman, Joseph Milner (1744–97) had helped to sustain his youthful faith by calling attention to the lives of the devout in his *History of the Church of Christ* (1794–1809), a work which would inform his own later interest in the interior life of sanctity. "[A]s miracles accompanied the first effusion of grace, so they might accompany the later," Newman wrote. "It is surely a natural and on the whole, a true anticipation ... that gifts and graces go together," especially since "according to the ancient Catholic doctrine, the gift of miracles was viewed as the attendant and shadow of transcendent sanctity: and moreover, since such sanctity was not of every day's occurrence, nay further, since one period of Church history differed widely from another, and, as Joseph Milner would say, there have been generations or centuries of degeneracy or disorder, and times of revival, and since one region might be in the mid-day of religious fervour, and another in twilight or gloom, there was no force in the popular argument, that, because we did not see miracles with our own eyes, miracles had not happened in former times, or were not now at this very time taking place in distant places."[25] Nothing could better confute Abbott's own variation of this "popular argument."

Newman had written his first essay on miracles in 1825–6 and his second in 1842–3, though both could be said to be answering attacks on the miraculous that go back at least as far as David Hume's "Of Miracles" in his "An Enquiry concerning Human Understanding" (1748).[26] Then, again Newman shared his understanding of Christ's miraculous prerogatives with accustomed eloquence in "Christ Upon The Waters" (1850), the sermon he preached to celebrate what might be regarded as the miraculous restoration of the hierarchy in England. "The earth is full of the marvels of divine power," he reminded his auditors.

> "Day to day uttereth speech, and night to night showeth knowledge." [Psalm 19:2] The tokens of Omnipotence are all around us, in the world of matter, and the world of man; in the dispensation of nature, and in the dispensation of grace. To do impossibilities, I may say, is the prerogative of Him, who made all things out of nothing, who foresees all events before they occur, and controls all wills without compelling them. In emblem of this His glorious attribute, He came to His disciples in the passage I have read to you, walking upon the sea,—the emblem or hieroglyphic among the ancients of the impossible; to show them that what is impossible with man, is possible with God. He who could walk the waters, could also ride triumphantly upon what is still more fickle, unstable, tumultuous, treacherous—the billows of human wills, human purposes, human hearts. The bark of Peter was struggling with the waves, and made no progress; Christ came to him walking upon them; He entered the boat, and by entering it He sustained it. He did not abandon Himself to it, but He brought it near to Himself; He did not merely take refuge in it, but He made Himself the strength

---

1911), 207–8.
[25] *Apo.*, 33.
[26] See John Henry Newman, *Two Essays on Biblical and Ecclesiastical Miracles*, ed. Geoffrey Rowell (Leominster: Gracewing, 2010).

of it, and the pledge and cause of a successful passage. "Presently," another gospel says, "the ship was at the land, whither they were going." [John 6:21]²⁷

Forty years before Abbott wrote his attack on Newman's essays, Arthur Hugh Clough (1819–61), in a letter following his resignation of his Oriel fellowship, expressed doubts about miracles similar to those Abbott would express, though the poet was never in the least dismissive of Newman. "I think there is a general feeling that Miracles are poor proofs," Clough had written Edward Hawkins, the provost of Oriel. "Can we be sure that anything is really a miracle? … books like Strauss's life of Jesus have disturbed the historical foundations of Christianity." At the same time, Clough assured the provost that "young men" were not "inclined to part with Christianity, absolutely." The problem was that "they have no Christian ideal, which they are sure is really Christian, except the Roman Catholic"—an assessment of the matter that must have galled the man who had sent Newman and Robert Wilberforce packing—Oriel's star tutors—precisely because of their agreement with Clough.²⁸

Since so much of Abbott's criticism of Newman was given over to attacks on the convert's dogmatic beliefs, of which his belief in miracles was necessarily a vital part, it is good to hear Ryder point out how Abbott's aversion to dogma disabled him from having anything fair or insightful to say of Newman's ineradicably dogmatic witness to the One True Fold of the Redeemer. "Dr. Abbott's creed, on his own confession, contains but few dogmas," Ryder wrote. "So far as I can make out, it contains none of a distinctively Christian character. I have no interest in discussing his theology in detail, except so far as I have considered that it threw light upon the value of his criticism upon Cardinal Newman's. A critic, who only believes what he cannot help believing, is no judge of a theory of faith; and one who has committed himself to the position that miracles are not, is as little fitted to judge of the evidence of a particular miracle as a Quaker of the justice of a particular war."²⁹ Unfortunately, this disability afflicted many of Newman's contemporary critics. One can certainly see it in Leslie Stephen. "The most important biographical fact [regarding him] is naturally his confident agnosticism," Nöel Annan recognized. "Confident because Stephen said quite simply: 'You cannot believe in any meaningful sense of the word belief or these so-called dogmas of the church.' This was the citadel from which he went to war as an intellectual historian."³⁰ It was also the citadel that knew nothing of the Roman Church's tradition of faith and reason.

---

[27] *OS*, 121–2.
[28] Arthur Hugh Clough to Edward Hawkins (3 March 1849), *Correspondence of Arthur Hugh Clough*, 2 vols. (Oxford: Oxford University Press, 1957), i, 249. Cf. "Pattison entered the pre-eminent college of the time, but when he matriculated Oriel had imperceptibly passed its zenith. Provost Hawkins, recently elected to the headship in preference to Keble, had ousted a remarkable group of tutors, J. H. Newman, J. A. Froude, and R. I. Wilberforce, and had replaced them with lesser men whom Pattison, in a brilliantly acerbic account in his memoirs, denounced for their pedagogical and scholarly incompetence." *ODNB* entry for Mark Pattison.
[29] Ryder, *Essays*, 225–6.
[30] Annan, "Editor's Introduction," Stephen, *Selected Writings in British Intellectual History*, xvii.

III

Before revisiting Abbott's *Anglican Career of Cardinal Newman*, it might be helpful to say a few brief words about his life. Of all Newman's contemporary critics, Abbott was undoubtedly the most unbalanced. And yet he was not an untalented man. Born in London in the year that Newman began to look askance at his Via Media, Edwin Abbott Abbott (1838–1926) was educated at St. John's College, Cambridge, after which he took Anglican orders. From 1865 until 1889, he was a beloved headmaster at the City of London School, which he had attended himself. Hundreds of students learned their Latin and Greek from him. Indeed, under his charge, some even studied Sanskrit– including Cecil Bendall, who would become one of Victoria's greatest Sanskrit scholars. Abbott was also an innovative educator, being one of the first schoolmasters in England to require his charges to know chemistry and English literature, when neither subject was widely studied. He directed his sixth form boys to read Shakespeare along with the Greek playwrights, and even wrote a *Shakespearean Grammar* (1870), which, in an age fascinated by philology, went through many editions. One can see Abbott's understanding of the teacher's charge in his account of Richard Whately's influence on Newman. "Whately was like a June day with a north-east wind," Abbott writes, "and Newman rejoiced in the brightness and the bracing air. His trainer was also kind to him in other ways; spoke well of him to the Fellows of Oriel; declared that he was 'the clearest-headed man he knew'; and got him work for the *Encyclopædia Metropolitana*. The pupil responded to this appreciation and general kindness by what he himself calls an 'affectionate abandonment' of himself. So awkward, reticent, and uncouth among strangers, so unconventionally effusive among intimate friends, the Junior Fellow was in after days likened by the Provost [Hawkins] to the lion's cub in Aeschylus, bred up like a kitten in a household, at first plaything, presently the terror, of those who had fondled it."[31] The *Oxford Dictionary of National Biography* attests to the rigor and appeal of Abbott's own tutelage. "Of all the capacities that he strove to evoke in his pupils, Abbott valued most highly that of the clear expression of serious thought, which he conceived to be the chief result of the Oxford Greats training; and of all his pupils he was perhaps proudest of Herbert Henry Asquith, whom he regarded as its best representative."[32] Considering Asquith's delight in backgammon and brandy after he became Prime Minister, especially when the war in Flanders was not going well, this seems an odd boast; but then Abbott is credited with allowing the future prime minister to devote most of his time at school to writing speeches, a skill which would serve the ambitious young man well in both the law and politics. The other claims made by the *ODNB* for Abbott are less creditable. "A great moral and religious teacher, Abbott had the mark of the spiritual leader in that he could impart to others something of his own inspiration. Without driving or overtaxing his pupils, he made intellectual effort a kind of religion for them;

---

[31] Abbott, *Anglican Career*, i, 33–4.
[32] According to one of Asquith's more recent biographers, Abbott "was to have a huge influence on Asquith … [he] made him school captain … [and praised] him for 'keeping up the tone, as well as the intellectual standard of the higher classes.'" Colin Clifford, *The Asquiths* (London: John Murray, 2002), 3.

his deep reprobation of intellectual slackness and unveracity was such a spur to them that his sixth form became a most stimulating training ground for eager and receptive spirits." Again, if Asquith was the model beneficiary of Abbott's ministrations, it is difficult to see what effect, if any, spiritual leadership played in his development. Like Clough, Dr. Arnold's golden boy at Rugby, Asquith spent most of his adult life enjoying the fact that the days of his having to treat "intellectual effort" as "a kind of religion" were blessedly over. Then, of course, there is Churchill's remark that Asquith was always at his best in the House of Commons until dinner time—"but thereafter!"[33] The fact that the Prime Minister was often drunk in the Commons did not go unnoticed. "Sometimes he spoke while drunk. Sometimes he sat on the Government Front Benches helpless with drink: unable to speak."[34] As Churchill told his wife Clementine: "only the persistent free-masonry of the House of Commons prevents a scandal."[35] Asquith's infatuation with the enrapturing Venetia Stanley also bespoke his understandably keen desire to make up for lost time. But, again, what any of this had to do with spirituality is hard to see, even if we concede that the Edwardians had a fairly malleable sense of the meaning of that word. What induced the schoolmaster in Abbott to go on the attack against Newman is hard to pinpoint. Could it have been intellectual vainglory? A desire to ingratiate himself with the rationalist dons of Cambridge? An irrepressible strain of No Popery in the family genes? Having married his first cousin, could Abbott have been mad when he was writing his books on Newman? Possibly. Yet many sane mathematicians swear by the wit and even fun of his mathematical fantasy, *Flatland* (1884), which the back jacket of a current edition describes as "the fanciful tale of A. Square, a two-dimensional being who is whisked away by a mysterious visitor to The Land of Three Dimensions, an experience that forever alters his worldview—just as the book altered the worldview of its Victorian readers with the then-radical idea of a fourth dimension."[36] The book may not be the sort of thing that would engage every reader but it certainly does not give one the impression that its author would go in for Newman bashing, even though Abbott took the idea for the book from the popular mathematician Charles Howard Hinton (1853–1907), a convicted bigamist, whose pioneering work, "What is the Fourth Dimension?" appeared in the *Dublin University Magazine* in 1880. A *devoté* of table-tapping and the occult, Hinton associated the fourth dimension with ghosts and the afterlife and was deeply influenced by his father, James Hinton (1822–75), who was "something of a libertine, advocating free love and polygamy and eventually heading a cult," which obliged him to seduce an untold number of unsuspecting young women. Indeed, "He once said 'Christ was the Saviour of Man, but I am the saviour of women, and I don't envy Him a bit."[37] Hinton senior also had a major influence on the Victorian pornographer, Havelock Ellis (1859–1939), who thought the

---

[33] Winston Churchill quoted in *H. H. Asquith Letters to Venetia Stanley*, ed. Michael and Eleanor Brock (Oxford: Oxford University Press, 1982), 10.
[34] Marvin Rintala, "H. H. Asquith and Drink," *Biography*, 16, no. 2 (Spring 1993), 114.
[35] Churchill quoted in Andrew Roberts, *Churchill: Walking with Destiny* (New York: Random House, 2018), 150. One of Asquith's nicknames was "Squiffy."
[36] *The Annotated Flatland*, ed. Ian Stewart (New York: Basic Books, 2002).
[37] Ibid., xx.

polygamist's views on marriage brilliant.[38] Charles Hinton, for his part, took his father's polygamous teachings so much to heart that he was arrested for taking a second wife under an assumed name in Uppingham and imprisoned for three days before going abroad, first, to Japan, and, then, to America, where he became an instructor in mathematics at Princeton. (He is still remembered fondly there for designing a gunpowder-driven pitching machine for the university's baseball team.) Taking these associations into account, one could posit that what inspired Abbott to defame Newman so viciously was moral degeneracy, though this would necessarily be speculative. It would also be doing what Newman's detractors do routinely, which is to impute bad motives to their *bête noir* simply because they disagree with his uncompromisingly orthodox Catholic faith.

Of course, Newman had very distinct views when it came to speculating in controversy. Writing to Richard Frederick Littledale (1830–90), an Anglo-Irish clergyman, who had entered into controversy with Father Ryder after publishing an article in the *Contemporary Review* in November of 1878 charging that "conversion to Rome involves, in a large majority of instances, sudden, serious, and permanent intellectual and moral deterioration, especially as to the quality of truthfulness," Newman displayed the affable forbearance that would often distinguish his controversial conduct as a Catholic. "As to your controversy with Father Ryder, your language about the converts from Rome, you must let me say, gave very great, wide, and indeed just offence," Newman told Littledale. "It was impossible for me to stand in the way of his answering it when an answer was so earnestly urged and so natural. And I always feel that a writer under such circumstances must have elbow room, and that to tether him is unfair. In saying this, I do not mean to say that there are no rules in controversy, as well as in boxing. To introduce epithets of mere abuse, to deal in insinuations or to impute motives are as unworthy materials of combat as to hit in the stomach."[39]

This echoes an earlier letter that Newman had written over thirty years before to another correspondent, expressing his objection to personalities in controversy. "When we come to the second article, you impute motives to him, and call his conduct 'nasty,'" Newman wrote. "Motives have constantly been imputed to myself by various controversialists, down to Mr Brownson, Mr Hare and Dr Whately, and, I know, how very unfair I feel it to be. I am not aware that I have imputed motives to persons I have written against. It seems to me an unfair mode of fighting, like punching a man in the stomach. Perhaps feeling it so much myself, makes me quite angry when I see it used to another. The question is not whether the imputation is true or not, but whether it is fair—i.e. whether, whatever your private confidence may be you are right, you have a right to intrude it on the world. And whether it is your business to *judge* a man, which you do, where you impute motives—instead of confining yourself to judging his writings or his

---

[38] See *ODNB*.
[39] Newman to Richard Frederick Littledale (9 March 1879), *LD*, xxix, 69. Ryder responded to Littledale with "Ritualism, Roman Catholicism and Converts", the *Contemporary Review* (February 1879), pp. 482–9, remarking that "even if I were inclined to accept all Dr. Littledale's facts in the very colour he gives them, they are ludicrously insufficient to sustain his charge." His *Plain Reasons against joining the Church of Rome* (1880) proved a popular Anglo-Catholic attack on Roman Catholicism.

actions, whatever they are."⁴⁰

In writing of Newman's work, Abbott claimed in the second edition of *Philomythus*, which he re-titled *Newmanianism* (1891) that his criticisms were not *ad hominem*. "My book is intended as an attack, not against Newman himself, but against the whole of that theological 'system of safety' which would pollute the intellect with the suggestion that it is 'safe' to say this, and 'unsafe' to say that, about alleged historical facts. ... Is it not a fact—though a portentous fact—that men are expected to argue with scrupulous honesty about Thucydides or Aristotle, but not about the facts of the Bible or the history of the Christian Church? My war, then, is not with Newman, but with the system which Newman ... condemns.⁴¹ Such letters as I have received already (within little more than a fortnight from the date of publication), from eminent men well fitted to weigh evidence and to discuss the special questions here treated, lead me to hope that my book is not only substantially accurate but also helpful to the cause of religious truth. But it was of course impossible to attempt to dispel that kind of legendary exaggeration which had gradually attached itself to the popular estimate of Newman's work, without giving pain to some of his admirers."⁴²

IV

Abbot may have claimed that he did not bear Newman any personal ill will, but no one can read his attacks on Newman and his work without seeing in them animosity of the most flagrant personal malice. As for the "legendary exaggeration" that Abbott claimed attaches itself "to the popular estimate of Newman's work," it is unclear to what he was referring. It is true that Newman has always been held in high esteem by admirers and critics alike, but nowhere in his work on Newman does Abbott substantiate the contention that that esteem was based on "exaggeration," legendary or otherwise. Certainly, one could search the work of the critics favorable to Newman covered in the present study—whether Church or Hutton, Ward or Ker—and see nothing approaching exaggeration. It is the critics unfavorable to Newman, like Abbott himself, who indulge in exaggeration.

In *The Anglican Career of Cardinal Newman*, Abbott took especial offense to Newman's *Essay on the Development of Christian Doctrine*, which of course shared with his readers the reasoning he had followed in coming to the recognition that the Roman Catholic Church was the "One True Fold of the Redeemer"—not a departure from the Early Church but a verifiably authentic development from it. To appreciate the peculiar flavor of Abbott's criticism, it is necessary to quote him at length, especially since he still features in the bibliographies of Newman's more ardent detractors.⁴³ Readers unfamiliar with his criticism will benefit from

---

[40] Newman to Frederick Lucas (20 January 1848), *LD*, xii, 158–9.
[41] Eamon Duffy sees in Frank Turner's work the same disingenuous ploy of praising the man one means to tear to shreds in order to convince readers that one is interested in criticizing only the work, not the man. "Whatever lip-service Turner may have paid to Newman's greatness," Duffy writes, "his book is manifestly informed by loathing." Eamon Duffy, "Reception of Turner's Newman: A Reply to Simon Skinner," *Journal for Ecclesiastical History* (July 2012), 548.
[42] Edwin A. Abbott, *Newmanianism* (London: Macmillan & Co., 1891), v–vi.
[43] The Newman detractors J. M. I. Klaver and Benjamin King both list Abbott's attacks on Newman in

reading the man directly, if only because it will show them the sort of criticism that Newman's detractors regard as cogent.[44] If one of Abbott's central claims is that Newman was self-deceivingly irrational, relying too heavily on imagination in arriving at his religious convictions, it was necessary for the critic to establish that Newman's understanding of the authority of conscience was irrational as well, indeed, a figment of his excitable imagination; and so the censorious schoolmaster proceeded.

> In the first edition of the *Apologia* [Newman] puts it thus, "I determined to write an Essay on Doctrinal Development; and then, if at the end of it my convictions were not weaker, to make up my mind to seek admission into her fold." "Determined to make up my mind" is a curious expression; but it is in accordance with all that we know about Newman. "Making up his mind," in matters of religion, was, with him, equivalent to "leaping." It was not a deliberate act. What he says, then, expresses what he meant: "I determined to take the leap." In the second edition it runs thus, "I came to the resolution … of taking the necessary steps for admission into her fold." Both editions, however, make it clear that the Essay was not intended to convince himself of the claims of the Church of Rome; it was merely to ensure deliberation upon his present convictions. He was convinced already. It was to satisfy his conscience, not his reason, that he went through this (logically speaking) superfluous task of accumulating probabilities. What he felt was, that such an occupation as this, being a kind of duty, placed him in the best position for hearing the voice of conscience and ascertaining her will. He was ready to accept her terms at once if she would but let him know them. Thus regarded, the book would be a kind of flag of truce, a proposal to negotiate with conscience so far as this, that she would at least signify her will. That done, he would surrender at discretion.[45]

To grasp how misleading this characterization of Newman's understanding of conscience is, we can revisit the definition of conscience that Newman himself

---

the bibliographies attached to their contributions to *The Oxford Handbook of John Henry Newman*, a dreary exhibition of uncritical Newman-bashing. Eamon Duffy styles Abbott's two-volume *The Anglican Career of Cardinal Newman* "a formidable hatchet-job" in his "Reception of Turner's Newman," 548.

[44] The best specimen of the sort of criticism approved by Newman's latest batch of detractors is the criticism of Prof. Frank Turner, about which the *Spectator* observed: "Poor Professor Turner gets in an awful stew about discipline, monasticism and especially celibacy. Why do these fellows do these things? He is forever on the hunt for deep causes. Of Newman's decision for celibacy, he says that we don't know the reason and can only speculate. Why speculate? Why not just admit he does not know and get on with something he does know about? Instead, he speculates away about the young Newman avoiding nude swimming and suggests that he may have 'encountered confusion over his own sexual orientation'. Sexual orientation, abuse, deprecating of people of colour: it's all so hilariously predictable. It reaches a delicious height when Professor Turner speculates, again after admitting lack of evidence and consensus 'within the medical community' that Pusey, Newman and the others' fasting may be linked to anorexia nervosa and anorexia to confusion about homosexuality or doubt about sexual orientation. And, did you know, Newman's friends show 'evidence of depression and perfectionism, also linked to eating disorders'? There you are then. Now we know what's really behind this fasting lark." See Digby Anderson, "An Intolerant Sort of Liberal," *Spectator* (26 October 2002).

[45] Abbott, *Anglican Career*, ii, 374.

set out in his *Grammar of Assent* (1870), where he speaks of it as the "creative principle of religion," one which necessarily involves both the reason and the imagination.

> Conscience ... considered as a moral sense, an intellectual sentiment, is a sense of admiration and disgust, of approbation and blame: but it is something more than a moral sense; it is always, what the sense of the beautiful is only in certain cases; it is always emotional. No wonder then that it always implies what that sense only sometimes implies; that it always involves the recognition of a living object, towards which it is directed. Inanimate things cannot stir our affections; these are correlative with persons. If, as is the case, we feel responsibility, are ashamed, are frightened, at transgressing the voice of conscience, this implies that there is One to whom we are responsible, before whom we are ashamed, whose claims upon us we fear. If, on doing wrong, we feel the same tearful, broken-hearted sorrow which overwhelms us on hurting a mother; if, on doing right, we enjoy the same sunny serenity of mind, the same soothing, satisfactory delight which follows on our receiving praise from a father, we certainly have within us the image of some person, to whom our love and veneration look, in whose smile we find our happiness, for whom we yearn, towards whom we direct our pleadings, in whose anger we are troubled and waste away. These feelings in us are such as require for their exciting cause an intelligent being: we are not affectionate towards a stone, nor do we feel shame before a horse or a dog; we have no remorse or compunction on breaking mere human law: yet, so it is, conscience excites all these painful emotions, confusion, foreboding, self-condemnation; and on the other hand it sheds upon us a deep peace, a sense of security, a resignation, and a hope, which there is no sensible, no earthly object to elicit. "The wicked flees, when no one pursueth"; then why does he flee? whence his terror? Who is it that he sees in solitude, in darkness, in the hidden chambers of his heart? If the cause of these emotions does not belong to this visible world, the Object to which his perception is directed must be Supernatural and Divine; and thus the phenomena of Conscience, as a dictate, avail to impress the imagination with the picture of a Supreme Governor, a Judge, holy, just, powerful, all-seeing, retributive, and is the creative principle of religion, as the Moral Sense is the principle of ethics.[46]

Here, Newman might have been writing expressly to address Abbott's rationalist dismissal of his understanding of conscience, though he also implicitly recognizes that not all "inquiring minds" will be able to follow him in his explanation of this understanding.

> Of course I cannot hope to carry all inquiring minds with me in what I have been laying down in the foregoing Section. I have appealed to the testimony given implicitly by our conscience to the Divine Being and His Attributes, and there are those, I know, whose experience will not respond to the appeal:—doubtless; but are there any truths which have reality, whether of experience or of reason, which are not disputed by some schools of philosophy or some bodies of men? If we assume nothing but what has universal reception, the field of our possible

---

[46] GA, 75–6.

discussions will suffer much contraction; so that it must be considered sufficient in any inquiry, if the principles or facts assumed have a large following. This condition is abundantly fulfilled as regards the authority and religious meaning of conscience;—that conscience is the voice of God has almost grown into a proverb. This solemn dogma is recognized as such by the great mass both of the young and of the uneducated, by the religious few and the irreligious many. It is proclaimed in the history and literature of nations; it has had supporters in all ages, places, creeds, forms of social life, professions, and classes. It has held its ground under great intellectual and moral disadvantages; it has recovered its supremacy, and ultimately triumphed in the minds of those who had rebelled against it. Even philosophers, who have been antagonists on other points, agree in recognizing the inward voice of that solemn Monitor, personal, peremptory, unargumentative, irresponsible, minatory, definitive.[47]

It is also characteristic of Newman that he should use the example of the relationship of children to conscience to verify its authority, a relationship that would only have weakened the claim for that authority in the eyes of his rationalist critics, most of whom, like Dr. Simon Skinner, were adamant that only university dons could sort such things out.[48] "It is my wish to take an ordinary child, but still one who is safe from influences destructive of his religious instincts," Newman wrote in his *Grammar of Assent*.

Supposing he has offended his parents, he will all alone and without effort, as if it were the most natural of acts, place himself in the presence of God, and beg of Him to set him right with them. Let us consider how much is contained in this simple act. First, it involves the impression on his mind of an unseen Being with whom he is in immediate relation, and that relation so familiar that he can address Him whenever he himself chooses; next, of One whose goodwill towards him he is assured of, and can take for granted—nay, who loves him better, and is nearer to him, than his parents; further, of One who can hear him, wherever he happens to be, and who can read his thoughts, for his prayer need not be vocal; lastly, of One who can effect a critical change in the state of feeling of others towards him. That is, we shall not be wrong in holding that this child has in his mind the image of an Invisible Being, who exercises a particular providence among us, who is present every where, who is heart-reading, heart-changing, ever-accessible, open to impetration. What a strong and intimate vision of God must he have already attained, if, as I have supposed, an ordinary trouble of mind has the spontaneous effect of leading him for consolation and aid to an Invisible Personal Power!

[47] GA, 83–4.
[48] Dr. Skinner gave striking expression to this rather astringent view when he applied it to Turner's study of Newman. "Turner's *Newman*," he declared, "is a work of history. It was therefore written for a purpose which in most cases his reviewers literally could not comprehend because they were not engaged in the tasks of historical writing and teaching." Skinner, "History versus Hagiography," 776. The common reader owes a debt to Eamon Duffy for pointing out to the Keen Fellow and Tutor in History that "history is not an arcane discipline … The ordinary rules of historical evidence are intelligible to anybody and a *de haut en bas* restriction of the right to an opinion on Turner's book to the guild of professional historians runs the risk of seeming both arbitrary and condescending." Duffy, "Reception of Turner's Newman," 534.

Here was lively proof that the days Newman spent teaching the children of Littlemore before his conversion were not ill-spent. They clearly showed him that the "image brought before" the child's "mental vision is the image of One who by implicit threat and promise commands certain things which he, the same child ..., by the same act of his mind, approves; which receive the adhesion of his moral sense and judgment, as right and good. It is the image of One who is good, inasmuch as enjoining and enforcing what is right and good, and who, in consequence, not only excites in the child hope and fear,—nay (it may be added), gratitude towards Him, as giving a law and maintaining it by reward and punishment,—but kindles in him love towards Him, as giving him a good law, and therefore as being good Himself, for it is the property of goodness to kindle love, or rather the very object of love is goodness; and all those distinct elements of the moral law, which the typical child, whom I am supposing, more or less consciously loves and approves,—truth, purity, justice, kindness, and the like,—are but shapes and aspects of goodness. ... Such is the apprehension which even a child may have of his Sovereign Lawgiver and Judge."[49]

Of course, Abbott and his rationalist friends would never make such analogies favorable to childhood. For Leslie Stephen, "Old conceptions are preserved to us in the very structure of language: the mass of mankind still preserves its childish imaginations ... We start as infants with fetish worship ... and learn but slowly and with difficulty to conform our imaginative constructions to scientific truth"[50] For the discriminating epistemologist in Newman, by contrast, it was natural to see children, as Wordsworth had seen them, "appareled in celestial light." J. B. Mozley recognized the attention Newman brought to children when describing how he catechized them in Littlemore. "Newman's catechising has been a great attraction this Lent," Mozley told his sister, "and men have gone out of Oxford every Sunday to hear it. I heard him last Sunday, and thought it very striking: done with such spirit, and the children so up to it; answering with the greatest alacrity. It would have provoked some people's bile immoderately to have heard them all unanimous on the point of the nine orders of angels; the definiteness of the number being in itself a great charm to the minds of the children. He has also been teaching them to sing, during the week-time, and the fiddle has been brought into requisition, considerably to their astonishment; he found it the best way possible of keeping them in tune. St Mary's, as you may suppose, has been considerably thinned."[51] Needless to say, the uncatechized Abbott had neither the catechesis nor, indeed, the humility to catechize children himself.

Another important thing for readers to bear in mind in taking Abbott's measure as a critic is that there is no evidence in his two-volume thrashing of Newman that he ever read the convert's *Grammar of Assent*. In both volumes there are only three passing references to the book. One might say that Abbott was focused on the Anglican Newman and the *Grammar* lay outside his chosen remit; but this could never be the case for a book whose object was to invalidate Newman's epistemological engagement with the Christian faith, an engagement

---

[49] GA, 78–9.
[50] Stephen, *Selected Writings in British Intellectual History*, 5.
[51] *Letters of the Rev. J. B. Mozley*, edited by his sister (London 1885), 103. Gerard Tracey quotes this in *LD*, vii, note 1, 282.

which could only be assessed, even for the Anglican career alone, by consulting the *Grammar*, a book, after all, which had its genesis in Newman's days at Oriel when he was struggling to bring his brother Charles back to the Christian fold. For Abbott to ignore the *Grammar* exhibits surprising slackness in someone who preened himself on his scholarly thoroughness.

Additional samples of the schoolmaster's criticism of what he regarded as the dubious logic of the *Essay on Development* show what slackness typifies his response to Newman. It is doubtless tedious to plow through Abbott's dreary glosses on Newman's writings but it is necessary to read him directly to appreciate just how jaundiced they are.

> The Essay deals with the Notes of the Church and shows that Rome has these Notes. One of these is the Note of Logical Sequence; and here, if you concede to Newman his mechanical principle of the nature of the Forgiveness of Sins, you are led on to the acknowledgment of "Monastic Rule" as the perfection of Christian life, with a subtlety of gradation and logical cogency, which shows the author to great advantage. Newman regards forgiveness as an estate, so to speak, conveyable by God to man upon arbitrary conditions, one of which is the Sacrament of Baptism which washes away sins. What, then, as to sins after Baptism? Are they unpardonable? That would be too shocking. Hence, the Church must have the power to pardon. But there must be conditions, as before. Hence sprang four degrees of penance, through which offenders had to pass in order to obtain reconciliation. Then rose the question, Are these penances mere outward signs of inward contrition? If so, they might be dispensed with, as soon as true repentance was discovered. Newman does not clearly show why this should not be done; but if it could be dispensed with, penance would seem to fall from its sacramental footing. He points out that the Fathers considered penance more than an outward sign; it was an expiation, an act done directly towards God and a means of averting His anger. Penance, therefore, is of the nature of a "satisfaction" to God, paying to Him so much pain as a means of propitiating Him.

The tone of condescending contempt here is characteristic. Yet Abbott often treats his dead opponent thus—an opponent who obviously could not return fire. "But what if a man dies before he has paid this debt of pain; is he lost for ever?" he asks. "That again, would be too shocking. Therefore there must be a means of paying God that 'satisfaction' hereafter. Hence arises the logical need of a Purgatory. But the man who is once convinced that sin must have its punishment, here or hereafter … who believes that suffer he must, and that delayed punishment is the greater … has within his breast a source of greatness, self-denial, heroism. The inference appears to be that (in view of heavenly compensations) he will be absolutely indifferent to earthly pains and worldly motives, and that the actions accomplished in this spirit will be, according to the heading of this section, 'meritorious works.' But if we wish for a course of 'meritorious works,' where can we find it better than in 'the Monastic Rule'? Thus, by an easy, smooth descent of Logical Sequence, we are led on from the Dogma of Forgiveness to the Dogma of Pardons, and from Pardons to Penances, and thence to Satisfactions, and so to Purgatory, and then to Meritorious Works, and finally to the Monastic Rule:—which itself culminates in the greatest and highest 'penance,' or 'satisfaction,' that man can pay to God, the surrender of the mind, the intellect, the understanding, and the will, to some ecclesiastical superior: for 'it may fairly be questioned whether, in an intellectual age, when freedom both of thought and of action is so dearly prized, a greater penance can be devised for the soldiers of Christ than the absolute surrender of judgment and will to the command of another.' For Abbott, the conclusion to any rational critique of Newman's logic was ineluctable:

> All this symmetrical and subtly-connected fabric collapses like a house of cards if we reflect for a single moment that forgiveness of sins, whether between man and man or between man and God, is nothing but a spiritual process, and that no bodily pains, nor material penalties, inflicted or remitted, have any essential connection with it. But grant Newman's theory of forgiveness, and then—as the ancient false astronomy led on its supporters to their "eccentrics" and "epicycles": in order to "save the phenomena"—so the reader is led to adopt first this, and then that, development, in order to make things square and clear; and the result is a mechanical conclusion worthy of the mechanical premiss.[52]

No one could possibly blame readers familiar with Newman's *Essay on the Development of Christian Doctrine* for finding this précis of its reasoning unrecognizable. For all of his pretensions to scientific learning, Abbott clearly lacked what Newman had occasion to style in his response to Gladstone's fulminations against the doctrine of papal infallibility as "lawyer-like exactness and logical consecutiveness."[53] Yet even those unfamiliar with the book will marvel at Abbott's assertion that "forgiveness of sins, whether between man and man or between man and God, is nothing but a spiritual process, and that no bodily pains, nor material penalties, inflicted or remitted, have any essential connection with it,"—an assertion which not only denies Christ's Passion but refuses to acknowledge the Church's martyrs, let alone her legion patrons, the penitential largesse of which enriched at once the Church and the many states and cities in which the Church flourished. What is it that Walter Bagehot once said about indulgences, without which our guilt-ridden civilization should never have been put on the map in the first place?

> Whatever we may think of the doctrines of the Roman Church, she has a claim to at least this praise: it is her hand that has branded ineffaceably on the mind of Europe the belief in a certain retribution for sin: she found undoubtedly the outlines of the doctrine believed by those she came to teach; but it is her teaching that has given the idea fullness, depth, and permanence. The reality of the belief appears as much in some of her worst doctrines as in some of her best. What is the practice of indulgences, but the paying real money, possessing exchangeable value on earth, to avoid the punishment of sin in an unseen world? What do the

---

[52] Abbott, *Anglican Career*, ii, 375–7.
[53] *Diff.*, ii, 217. "[W]hatever we are bound to allow Mr. Gladstone ... [in his criticism of the First Vatican Council and what he saw as its implications for the loyalty of English Catholic subjects of the English crown] that does not warrant the passionate invective against the Holy See and us individually, which he has carried on through sixty-four pages. What we have a manifest right to expect from him is lawyer-like exactness and logical consecutiveness in his impeachment of us."

numerous bequests to the church remind us of, but that there was a belief that certain punishments were impending over the sinner, and that giving certain gifts to a body of men on earth was a means of avoiding them. No doubt these are gross superstitions; but surely it should come home to the hearts of a money-getting generation, that three centuries ago men were willing to give hard cash to save themselves from the pains of sin. We suspect that a priesthood in Greece would have got but little by putting up to auction the fee simple of the Elysian fields.[54]

To substantiate his objections to Newman's book, Abbott calls upon two liberal Anglican authorities, Connop Thirlwall (1797–1875) and Julius Hare (1795–1855), both of whom were critical of the *Essay on Development* when it first appeared. "Of course, the right of innovation, implied in this Essay, is irreconcilable with the claims of antiquity," Abbott contends. "Hence, as Bishop Thirlwall says, we have to enquire who, beside the Author of Revelation, has authority thus to innovate." In quoting Thirlwall, the Bishop of Saint David's and historian of Greece, whom the amiably broad-minded F. L. Cross assured us "took part in all of the ecclesiastical questions of the day in a liberal and unbiased spirit,"[55] Abbott was quoting an authority on whose sprightly calumnies all of Newman's nineteenth-century detractors repeatedly drew. Abbott himself, throughout his own criticisms of Newman, simply parrots Thirlwall.[56] In reading the Essay on Development, Thirlwall described himself as "drawn into a vicious circle."

> For the existence of this authority [to which Abbott refers] is no more explicitly attested, either by Scripture or Tradition, than any of the doctrines which rest upon its sanction. It must therefore witness to itself, and hang self-supported, like the prophet's tomb in the lying legend. For those who have been trained to look up to it with unquestioning veneration, this absence of all external warrant may create no difficulty. To them it may be sufficient to say, that belief is in itself better than unbelief; that it is safer to believe; that we must begin with believing, and that conviction will follow; that, as for the reasons of believing, they are for the most part implicit, and but slightly recognized by the mind that is under their influence; that they consist moreover rather of presumptions and guesses, ventures after the truth, than of accurate proofs, and that probable arguments are sufficient for conclusions which we even embrace as most certain and turn to the most important uses.'

In Thirlwall's conclusion we can see the defamatory thesis of Abbott's two volumes in a nutshell. "[F]or any one who has not been subject to the influence of such associations, who is required to make a deliberate choice, and to stake his all upon

---

[54] Walter Bagehot, "Festus," *Prospective Review*, 3 (November 1847), 516–17. I am indebted to James Grant for calling my attention to this wonderful quotation in his wonderful biography of Bagehot. See James Grant, *The Greatest Victorian: The Life and Times of Walter Bagehot* (New York: Norton & Co., 2019), 57.
[55] See entry on Thirlwall in *The Oxford Dictionary of the Christian Church*, ed. F. L. Cross (Oxford: Oxford University Press, 1957).
[56] Abbott's debt to Thirlwall is not sufficiently acknowledged in the otherwise astute article by Jonathan Smith, Lawrence I. Berkove and Gerald A. Baker, "A Grammar of Dissent: *Flatland*, Newman and the Theology of Probability," *Victorian Studies*, 39, no. 2 (Winter 1996), 129–50.

the adoption of a new belief, to content himself with such 'presumptions and guesses, and ventures after the truth' as those which form the best substitute this author has to offer for 'accurate proofs,' would argue a want either of judgment or of seriousness, which it may be hoped will not often be found in that class of readers for which his work is designed. Nor will that singular combination of the extremes of scepticism and credulity which it exhibits in a degree almost without precedent, recommend it to those who value either freedom of thought or earnestness of faith. To minds constituted and predisposed like his own, it may undoubtedly minister a welcome plea for yielding to that sentimental and imaginative bias, which, as I expressed my belief in my last Charge with regard to other cases, appears to have been the real cause of his own secession, and which alone enables us to reconcile the respect due to his abilities and attainments, with the esteem which we should wish to feel for his character."[57]

Here Thirlwall's objection to what he regarded as Newman's "sentimental and imaginative bias" could not have been plainer. Indeed, Thirlwall expressed this objection to Newman repeatedly throughout his writings: it is the cornerstone of his criticism of the convert.[58] For example, when a correspondent wrote to him to lament the fact that an Anglican of their acquaintance had poped, the historian could not have been clearer about what he regarded as the futility of trying to argue the man out of his "perversion."

> I had not heard the report which you have communicated. If it should prove true, I shall lament it the more, because I am afraid that every such perversion is contagious among persons of the same rank, but in itself hardly any could be more deplorable than the one you mention. I am much obliged to you for the expression of your good opinion of me. But as I am utterly a stranger to him, and without either a personal or official plea for interfering with his religious convictions, whatever way I might take of approaching him would be subject to great disadvantage, and much risk of doing harm rather than good, and for

---

[57] Thirlwall quoted in Abbott, *Anglican Career*, ii, 378–9.
[58] To be fair, the great diplomatic historian and historiographer, George Peabody Gooch had a good word for Thirlwall as an historian. One can recognize that Thirlwall was a dull, plodding, biased critic of Newman without losing sight of his achievements as an historian, though it is interesting to note that Gooch's central criticism of the historian in Thirlwall is that he lacks imagination. "Reserved in the expression of opinion and lacking colour and enthusiasm," he writes, "Thirlwall possessed none of the arts of popularity; but his faultless scholarship and his balanced judgment made him the companion of the student who was determined to understand Greek history and was willing to take some trouble to reach his goal. ... His survey of the golden period of Athens is clear and business-like, but lacks charm. There is no thrill of enthusiasm in the narrative of Marathon, and the art and literature of the age of Pericles occupy but little space. The struggle at Syracuse loses something of its tragedy and Alcibiades much of his brilliance. Thirlwall has no heroes except Socrates. His chapter on the internal condition of Athens during and after the Peloponnesian war is a rigidly judicial summary. ... The merits of Thirlwall's work are conspicuous. His classical scholarship was faultless, and he allows for the bias of his authorities. He was fully abreast of German scholarship. ... His judgment was equal to his scholarship. His pupil, Lord Houghton, when asked to name the most remarkable man he had ever known, replied without hesitation, 'Thirlwall.' The faults of the book are negative, not positive. It is almost too impersonal. The actors are a little shadowy, and the drama has the air of having been acted long ago. It was for Grote to bring the Athenian democracy back to life and to rivet the gaze of the world on its aspirations and achievements." George Peabody Gooch, *History and Historians in the Nineteenth Century* (London: Longmans, Green, & Co., 1913), 311.

such a cause as you suggest his own Diocesan is both eminently qualified and the person whose station might most naturally and fitly suggest such an attempt. But I must own that I should not think any one qualified for it who was not acquainted with the convert's character and turn of mind, and with the methods which have been employed to make a proselyte of him. I should be very much surprised to hear that they have been such as would be in the least affected by any discussion of the peculiar doctrines of the Church of Rome. I doubt very much whether a proselyte was ever gained to the Church by such discussion. An expert Romish controversialist would never willingly permit the question to be brought to that issue; he would anticipate such a result as that which you mention as related by Macaulay. It was not through any change of opinion as to particular dogmas that any of the Oxford Tractarians, Newman, or Manning, or Oakeley, or Ward, were won. Newman never believed in Transubstantiation before he became a Romanist. It was by wholly independent considerations of a general kind that they were led to adopt implicitly all Roman doctrine: such as the unity of the Church, our Lord's promise, the necessity of a visible infallible authority (the argument by which Le Maistre maintained the monarchy of the Pope). Such abstract considerations may have had a like effect in this case. Nothing appears to me less probable than that he has given way to any arguments which might be refuted by appeals to the evidence either of dogmatic theology or of ecclesiastical history. It is far more likely that he has been partly overawed by the dogmatic tone of his teachers, commanding him to submit to an infallible Church, and to seek safety and repose of conscience within her pale, and partly attracted, as most young persons and women, through the imagination and the sentiments, which are not merely incapable of being moved by the logical arguments, but absolutely deaf to them. If this is the case I see no remedy for the mischief."[59]

In the following passage from Abbott himself one can see how closely he followed Thirlwall in his attack on Newman, especially in associating assent to the certitude of faith with the young and gullible. Yet it is also a good example of how impatient the schoolmaster was with Newman's epistemological investigations into how we actually arrive at religious certainty.[60]

> To some it may perhaps occur that the man who can honestly say simply "I know," is "certain." He may be wrong, of course; but in that case he will be wrongly "certain." Still, he is "certain." If he is not, when is he? Newman replies, "when he knows that he knows." Perhaps he means that true certainty must be preceded

---

[59] Connop Thirlwall to W. Dundas, Esq. (23 April 1867), *Letters Literary and Theological of Connop Thirlwall*, ed. J. J. Stewart Perowne and Louis Stokes (London: R. Bentley, 1881), 258–60.

[60] Hutton called Abbott to account for this impatience in his review of the schoolmaster's first book on Newman, his *Philomythus* (1891). "Dr. Abbott is an eminent scholar, a genuinely Christian-minded writer, and a critic of considerable power. But he is a little too much of the schoolmaster, and when a great writer offends him as Cardinal Newman has offended him by some of his views,—views which are more or less open to sharp criticism, but not open to the kind of criticism which Dr. Abbott indulges in,—he is so indignant that he sets himself to a sort of theological caning which ill becomes him, and which to a certain extent, we must say, makes him, what it is hard to make a man of Dr. Abbott's power, even ridiculous." Richard Holt Hutton, "Dr. Abbott's Attack on Cardinal Newman," *Spectator* (18 April 1891), 10–11.

by reflection on what a man, before reflection, is sometimes hastily disposed to call his "knowledge"; and that a man often says, "I am certain," when he ought to say "I think." This, of course, sometimes happens. But the remedy is, to admit that it happens, and to caution people against rashly saying "I am certain" when the right words are "I think." Instead of doing this, Newman gives men a test of "certainty" which is wholly useless and largely mischievous—the power of saying "I know that I know." It is useless, because children, and positive people, will just as soon say "I know that I know," as "I know." It is mischievous, because over-meditative and self-introspective minds will go further, and say "I think I know that I know," but how am I to know "I know that I know?" And some still more subtle intellects, going further still, may crave to know that they know that they "know they know"—and so on *ad infinitum*, with the result of landing themselves in the port of Know-nothing, which is only another name (in some minds) for Believe-anything.[61]

If Abbott's readers did not find the testimony of the schoolmaster himself or the fair-minded historian in Thirlwall compelling, they could always consult his other authority, Julius Charles Hare, the Broad Church author of *Guesses of Truth* (1827), whose response to the Essay on Development had at least the virtue of brevity: "Take a sentence or two here and there from this Father, and a couple of expressions from another, add half a canon of this Council, a couple of incidents out of some ecclesiastical historian, an anecdote from a chronicler, two conjectures of some critic, and half-a-dozen drachms of a schoolman, mix them up in rhetoric *quant. suff.*, and shake them well together,—and thus we get at a theological development."[62]

Choosing to epitomize Abbott's criticism of Newman with extracts from his views of the Essay on Development might seem arbitrary, but such extracts epitomize his criticism of the Roman Catholic convert, as this summing up shows:

> It is an extraordinary instance of the thoroughness and depth of Newman's self-deception to find him—notwithstanding, and in the midst of, these splendid displays of misleading rhetoric—imitating the language of Socrates, who, having no religious issues at stake and nothing but the truth to seek, really did follow with single-hearted devotion wherever pitiless Logic led him. And Newman actually thinks he is doing the same thing: "We cannot manage our argument and have as much of it as we please and no more." Never was pantomimic sword of lath more "manageable" and capable of producing more sudden transformations than argument in Newman's hands. ... But what sort of argument was this? An argument appealing, not only to the weaknesses and moral infirmities of mankind, but also—which was far worse—to private judgment, and to experience. Such a view of the Roman Church could do no more than represent to his mind, somewhat more vividly than before, the connected subtlety, yet breadth, the symmetry of organic growth, the unity of vital principle, in the development of medieval from Christian Antiquity. But this, upon reflection, he must have perceived to be an appeal to the Imagination, not to the faculty that produces intellectual

---

[61] Abbott, *Anglican Career*, ii, 361–2.
[62] Hare quoted *ibid.*, 380.

convictions. Hence our study of the Essay itself drives us to the conclusion to which external evidence has pointed, viz., that Newman, in writing it, was simply spending his time in what seemed a pious manner, likely to be acceptable to God, and thereby to hasten the coming of that "sign" for which his soul panted, as for water in a dry desert.[63]

Again, in condemning Newman for making "an appeal to the imagination, not to the faculty that produces intellectual convictions," Abbott was simply repeating Thirlwall's criticism.[64] In the *Grammar of Assent*, Newman states categorically: "It seems a truism to say, yet it is all that I have been saying, that in religion the imagination and affections should always be under the control of reason."[65] At the same time, Newman recognized that imagination was vital to "that supra-logical argument, which … is not mere common-sense, but the true healthy action of our ratiocinative powers, an action more subtle and more comprehensive than the mere appreciation of a syllogistic argument."[66]

He also nicely confutes Thirlwall's and Abbott's objection by showing how it is sceptics, not believers, who suffer their imaginations to deceive their reason. "Philosophers of the school of Hume discard the very supposition of miracles," he writes, "and scornfully refuse to hear evidence in their behalf in given instances, from their intimate experience of physical order and of the ever-recurring connexion of antecedent and consequent. Their imagination usurps the functions of reason; and they cannot bring themselves even to entertain as a hypothesis (and this is all that they are asked to do) a thought contrary to that vivid impression of which they are the victims, that the uniformity of nature, which they witness hour by hour, is equivalent to a necessary, inviolable law."[67] At the same time, far from agreeing with the view that imagination somehow made the reception of faith untrustworthy, Newman was adamant that "assent, in its perfect, nay I might almost say, its normal state must be made to an imagination."[68]

V

It is in his treatment of the crucible of conversion that Newman underwent before leaving the Anglican Church for what he came to recognize as the One True Fold of the Redeemer that Abbott shows his own peculiar lack of imagination. In speaking of the heart-wrenching correspondence between Newman and Keble before Newman converted, Abbott makes reference to a postscript to one of Keble's letters, which reads: "Of course you make allowance for the longing

---

[63] Ibid., 383–5.
[64] In the cult of St Thomas of Canterbury, Abbott found an even more exasperating appeal to imagination. "Had St. Thomas been a St. Simeon Stylites, a cold blooded ascetic, or a mere ecclesiastical machine, it is doubtful whether he would have appealed, as he did, to the imagination of the people of England, and, through them, to Europe." Edwin Abbott, *St Thomas of Canterbury*, 2 vols. (London, 1898), ii, 303.
[65] GA, 83.
[66] GA, 317.
[67] GA, 58.
[68] Newman quoted in Ian Ker, "Editor's Introduction," in *An Essay in Aid of a Grammar of Assent*, ed. Ian Ker (Oxford: Clarendon Press, 1985), xxxviii–xxxix.

to be at rest, as a secondary influence possible in your case." And this duly gives the polemical schoolmaster the opening he needs to posit what he sees as the real reason why Newman converted.

> That P. S. was well meant; but, in its effects, it was a cruel cut and must have pierced deep. Up to this time, Newman had been able to think of his future conversion as a sacrifice, and to reckon the prospects, associations, plans, comforts, friendships, that he was giving up; and every such pleasant tie to be painfully snapped would be an additional proof of his sincerity, and of the depth and permanence of the convictions on which he proposed to act. But now, Keble had pointed out a new "temptation," and one perhaps that was the greatest of all,—the longing to be at rest from wearing doubts, to bathe his soul in spiritual peace at any cost. This must have made Newman distrust himself and "his own feelings" more than ever. Might it not be that the Enemy—that "skilful rhetorician"—was tempting him to Rome with the bait of what he prized most of all, peace for his troubled conscience?[69]

As this shows, Abbott had not a clue as to what motivated Newman or any Catholic to convert. In an age preening itself on its advances in knowledge, Newman wrote in *The Present Position of Catholics in England* (1851), "when the Alps are crested, and seas fathomed, and mines ransacked, and sands sifted, and rocks cracked into specimens, and beasts caught and catalogued, as little is known by Englishmen of the religious sentiments, the religious usages, the religious motives, the religious ideas of two hundred millions of Christians poured to and fro, among them and around them, as if, I will not say, they were Tartars or Patagonians, but as if they inhabited the moon." For Ian Ker, the irony was arresting. "[T]he English Protestant who despises the enclosed monk or nun is shown to be just as 'enclosed', while, in spite of his vaunted knowledge of the world, he is wholly ignorant of the Catholics about whom he has so much to say and so confidently."[70] Abbott is a perfect case in point.

In the closing pages of *The Anglican Career of Cardinal Newman*, Abbott returned to the charge with which he had begun his two-volume dossier, that Newman converted to salve his "troubled conscience," suppressing his reason in order to embrace a faith that was at once fanciful and irrational. In such pages, one can see where Lytton Strachey took the superciliously derisive style that would animate his *Eminent Victorians* (1918). "All was soon over," Abbott writes of Newman before he was received into the Church by the Passionist, Father Dominic Barberi.[71] "Newman had laid it down as a rule that men must not act

---

[69] Abbott, *Anglican Career*, ii, 366-7.
[70] Ian Ker, "John Henry Newman," in *The Oxford Handbook of English Literature and Theology*, ed. Andrew Hass, David Jasper, and Elisabeth Jay (2009; online edn, Oxford Academic, 2 September 2009). The quotation is from *Prepos*. 44.
[71] Blessed Dominic Barberi (1792-1849) was instrumental in reviving Catholicism in nineteenth-century England. In 1963, he was beatified by Pope Paul VI. Newman wrote the Passionist priest in March of 1847 from the Collegio di Propaganda: "My dear Father Domenico, I have thought of writing to you many times since I have been here, but am not sorry to have waited till I can tell you something about ourselves. We are to be Oratorians. The Pope has been very kind to us—suggested that others of us had better come here and pass their novitiate with us all together under an Oratorian Father. How long we shall remain here I do not know—when we return, we shall set up, I suppose, in some large town, and try to convert that numerous class of youths who

under 'exciting, tumultuous conviction.' But what was a man to do who could not act, in religious matters, under any but 'exciting and tumultuous' convictions? What could he do, what could he have done, more, in the way of attempting to act with deliberation and reasonableness? The thing was impossible. He could no more commit himself than Hamlet could, to the awful act before him, in cool deliberation."[72] Newman, in other words, converted to Roman Catholicism, after six years of the most excruciating deliberation, under precisely the "exciting, tumultuous conviction" that he would always counsel others to eschew, though for Abbott this was of a piece for a man who acted in as bad faith in his conversion as he acted in everything else. "Hence we can well believe the description of the final scene as Newman's biographers give it," Abbott writes, "telling us how the Passionist Father arrived late in the evening and amid torrents of rain; how he was shown into a room where he stood for a while alone, drying his drenched garments at the fire; and how, suddenly turning round, he saw the Leader of the Tractarian Party on his knees before him passionately declaring that he would not rise till he had received the Father's blessing and assurance of being received into the one true Church of Christ." Yet, for Abbott, the confession was perfunctory and half-hearted. To justify this reading of the confession, he quotes the letter Newman wrote to a friend the following day, which he characterizes as "written as if in a dream, with the spiritual faculties all benumbed, yet yearning for the touch that shall release them from their torpor."[73]

> May I have only one tenth part as much faith as I have intellectual conviction where the truth lies! I do not suppose any one can have had such combined reasons pressing in upon him that he is doing right. So far I am most blessed; but, alas! my heart is so hard, and I am taking things so much as a matter of course, that I have been quite frightened that I should not have faith and contrition enough to gain the benefit of the Sacrament. Perhaps faith and reason are incompatible in one person or nearly so.[74]

For Abbott, such deeply penitential, indeed humble words could have but one meaning: "Once more the soul had fallen beneath the cold spell of mere intellectual conviction; no fresh 'sign' had arrived; faith was felt to be chilled."[75] The refusal exhibited here to enter into the true nature of these proceedings was typical of Abbott, who, like Fitzjames Stephen, could never look at religious conviction of any Catholic without seeing weakmindedness and self-deceit. In his account of Newman's reception into the Church—indeed in his account of everything related to the convert—we can see Abbott's methods in all of their false, presumptuous vulgarity.

Yet there is perhaps nothing so distasteful in Abbott's book as his attempt to belittle Newman's holy fear, to charge, as he does in the preface, that "spiritual

---

at present have a little education and no religion." Newman to Dominic Barberi (14 March 1847), *LD*, xii, 62.

[72] Abbott, *Anglican Career*, ii, 405.
[73] Ibid., 406.
[74] Newman to T. W. Allies (9 October 1845), *LD*, xi, 12.
[75] Abbott, *Anglican Career*, ii, 406.

fear perverted his imagination." Richard Holt Hutton, who engaged in a brief controversy with Abbott after taking the schoolmaster to task for his first book on Newman, rose to the defense of his old friend on this score with eloquent indignation. "As to the question whether Newman's religion was or was not a religion of fear, it takes a greater familiarity than Dr. Abbott seems to possess with his writings as a whole to judge," Hutton wrote.

> That fear ... entered deeply into Newman's faith, nobody who knows anything about him doubts. If it had not been so, the depth of his love for God would not have been half as deep and passionate as it was. We hold heartily with him in adopting the teaching, "the fear of the Lord is the beginning of wisdom," and in believing that there is no true fear of God as God, fear of that which is holiest in God, that does not involve an active germ of love, and no true love of God which does not also inspire a very deep fear. As Wordsworth so finely says in the noble poem on Burns, "The best of what we do and are, just God forgive"; and he who asks for forgiveness for what is best in him, necessarily trembles lest there be more to forgive than his poor self-knowledge betrays. The expressions which Dr. Abbott quotes from Newman to show that he thought ill of himself, that he hated his own hollowness, that he saw in himself depths of evil which no one else saw in him, could be paralleled in the history of every exceptionally good man who ever lived, and their quotation appears to us to throw a very vivid light on the shallowness of Dr. Abbott's moral criticism.

No better insight into Newman's sanctity has ever been penned, and yet Hutton also recognized, what few contemporary critics recognized, the real profundity of the convert's relation to his beloved God, seeing as he did that "the fear in Newman's love of God is not half as remarkable as the love in Newman's fear of him." Indeed, for Hutton, "The picture of Callista, the martyr of his story, when the heathen philosopher attempts to find her good grounds for submitting to the Imperial decree, is, we are confident, a true picture of the sort of moral fear which had blossomed in himself into so deep a love. 'O that I could find Him!' she exclaimed, passionately. 'On the right hand and on the left I grope, but touch Him not. Why dost Thou fight against me, why dost Thou scare and perplex me, O First and Only Fair? I have Thee not, and I need Thee.' [*Call.*, 315] That is the language of a heathen seeking an object of love in whom the attributes that excite love and fear are closely blended; and it was Newman's own natural attitude, which an ever-growing faith and gratitude deepened more and more into one of over-flowing thankfulness. Dr. Abbott cannot enter into Newman's complexity of religious feeling, and so he grossly exaggerates the proportion of what he calls his religious fear. The true complexity, and also the true simplicity, of Newman's religious attitude are so finely expressed in the sermon on 'The State of Grace,' that we will close our unwelcome controversy with Dr. Abbott by a sentence taken from it. 'All the necessary exactness of our obedience,' he says, 'the anxiety about failing, the pain of self-denial, the watchfulness, the zeal, the self-chastisements which are required of us, as little interfere with this vision of faith, as if they were practised by another, not by ourselves. We are two or three selves at once in the wonderful structure of our minds, and can weep while we smile, and labour while we meditate.' Perhaps Dr. Abbott is not in the same sense two or three selves at once; at all events, he grossly misreads one who was, and this has drawn him into a violent attempt at iconoclasm of which we do not doubt that he will one day repent."[76]

As persuasive as this is, we should also quote Newman himself to show how central fear of the Lord was to his understanding of the Christian faith, an understanding which partakes of none of the impetuosity or arrogance that infuses Abbott's criticism. "Consider the Bible tells us to be meek, humble, single-hearted, and teachable," Newman reminded his auditors in one of his earliest Anglican sermons, "Inward Witness to the Truth of the Gospel" (1825).

> Now, it is plain that humility and teachableness are qualities of mind necessary for arriving at the truth in any subject, and in religious matters as well as others. By obeying Scripture, then, in practising humility and teachableness, it is evident we are at least *in the way* to arrive at the knowledge of God. On the other hand, impatient, proud, self-confident, obstinate men, are generally wrong in the opinions they form of persons and things. Prejudice and self-conceit blind the eyes and mislead the judgment, whatever be the subject inquired into. For instance, how often do men mistake the characters and misconstrue the actions of others! how often are they deceived in them! how often do the young form acquaintances injurious to their comfort and good! how often do men embark in foolish and ruinous schemes! how often do they squander their money, and destroy their worldly prospects! And what, I ask, is so frequent a cause of these many errors as wilfulness and presumption? The same thing happens also in religious inquiries. When I see a person hasty and violent, harsh and high-minded, careless of what others feel, and disdainful of what they think;—when I see such a one proceeding to inquire into religious subjects, I am sure beforehand he cannot go right—he will not be led into all the truth—it is contrary to the nature of things and the experience of the world, that he should find what he is seeking. I should say the same were he seeking to find out what to believe or do in any other matter not religious,—but especially in any such important and solemn inquiry; for the *fear* of the Lord (humbleness, teachableness, reverence towards Him) is the very *beginning* of wisdom, as Solomon tells us; it leads us to think over things modestly and honestly, to examine patiently, to bear doubt and uncertainty, to wait perseveringly for an increase of light, to be slow to speak, and to be deliberate in deciding.[77]

VI

The best contemporary rebuttal of Abbott's wrongheaded attacks on Newman came from Wilfrid Ward (1856–1916), the son of the Ultramontane editor of the *Dublin Review*, William George Ward (1812–82), about whom Richard Holt Hutton nicely observed: "Never did a mind of great power luxuriate so heartily in the bars of what an outsider thought his intellectual prison." Wilfrid Ward would

---

[76] Ricard Holt Hutton, "Dr. Abbott and Cardinal Newman: Dr. Abbott's Long Letter Published," *Spectator* (25 April 1891), 11.
[77] *PS*, viii, 113–14.

write excellent biographies not only of his lively father and Cardinal Newman but of Cardinal Wiseman and Cardinal Vaughan, as well as several collections of essays, which, as I shall endeavor to show in a separate chapter on Ward, abound with insightful assessments of Newman and his work. Here, I will simply detail Ward's criticism of Abbott's attack on Newman's idea of miracles.

Like Hutton, Ward realized that one of Newman's governing concerns in his various writings was to address the rationalist objections to Christianity, especially those of professed agnostics, and in order to do this justice he put himself in the shoes of the agnostics themselves, oftentimes in ways that baffled them. Ward wittily shows that the purblind schoolmaster in Abbott, in his zeal to discredit Newman, entirely missed this object. "The writer never sees that he is cutting the ground from under his own feet by his assault," Ward wrote.

> that Newman is really inquiring with great delicacy into the nature of that very Faith and Love which his critic professes to be the basis of his own Christianity, but fails to justify against the Agnostic. Newman as the reflective thinker, as the man to whom himself and his Creator were ever the two most luminous of realities (*Apologia*, p. 5), as the man who is bringing all his gifts of profound analysis and religious imagination to justify belief in God and Immortality, never enters into the limited range of this writer's vision; and while the great Oxford thinker's own mind and soul are concentrated on securing from assault those primary truths on which the religious life of every Christian depends, the critic can only see an artificial theory, planned with the express purpose of tricking unwary souls into believing in miraculous Madonnas with moving eyes, or giving their confidence to priests intent on fraud and extortion.[78]

Here, Ward captured the cross purposes that would repeatedly vex Newman and his critics. He also exhibited the faithful sympathy that distinguishes his own criticism of a man whose work cannot be understood without such sympathy. Ward might still be remembered principally for his lopsided biography of Newman—in which he breezed over Newman's first forty-six years in a single chapter of fifty odd pages—but this should not obscure the genuine distinction of his criticism of Newman's work, which is often essential for understanding how Newman's unsympathetic critics go astray in trying to judge the same work. Ward's rebuttal of Abbott is a good case in point, especially since the schoolmaster "only once catches a glimpse of the very necessity of justifying, for the satisfaction of those in whom questions inevitably arise, that loving trust which is popularly called Faith; and then simply remarks that to 'entertain questions of this kind leads to insanity.'" For Ward, Abbott

> does not see, with the full tide of Agnosticism at his door, what Newman foresaw fifty years ago, that the question will force itself upon many a religious mind: is my loving trust a groundless delusion? Is it a sentiment corresponding to no reality, as the Agnostics say? And where Newman with patient anxiety devotes volumes to this question, the critic, hardly looking at his solution in its fundamental

---

[78] Wilfrid Ward, "Philalethes," in *Witness to the Unseen and Other Essays* (London: Macmillan & Co., 1893), 138–9.

application, but scared beyond words at the superstitious horrors it will be made to sanction, endeavours with blind violence to dislocate and disable words and sentences whereby Newman meant to convey principles with which no Christian can dispense, however little many may consider them applicable, as Newman ultimately did, to belief in the Catholic Church. All the deep, candid, careful analysis of the springs of Faith, all the subtle introspection into the ultimate unconscious basis of every degree of belief; all the fine comparisons and contrasts between the definiteness and shallowness of the unbelieving view of the world, and the imperfect form and yet conscious depth of the religious view; between the conclusions of mere logic and the conviction of the whole man; between vivid living belief and deep restful certitude; between the credulity of superstition and the confident faith which is protected by love; between the formal dogmatism of bigotry and the teachableness of faith, and the wide, calm, all-seeing vision of the spirit of wisdom—all this remains unnoticed, as this writer blunders on, eagerly moving his single eye, looking for St. Walburga's oil in one corner, Papal infallibility in another, Newman's own hollow heart in a third. Oh, the pity of it![79]

In his response to Abbott's rationalist objections to Newman's understanding of the miraculous, which he set out in a crudely polemical book, Ward described the contempt for miracles that still exercises our own rationalists. "It is not to be expected at the present hour that the question of miracles should receive very patient or serious consideration from those to whom the judgment of what has been called the Zeitgeist is a final test of truth," Ward writes.

> The present age, instead of learning effectually the one true lesson which Agnosticism suggests—how much there is in the supernatural region which we can neither prove nor disprove has passed rapidly to a new Gnosticism, and considers direct Providence or Miracle not only unproved, but utterly at variance with the conclusions of physical and critical science. Consequently the title-page of a work published not long after Cardinal Newman's death, "Philomythus, an Antidote against Credulity. A discussion of Cardinal Newman's 'Essay on Ecclesiastical Miracles,' by Edwin Abbott, D. D., late Head-Master of the City of London School," is not calculated to astonish any. Nor would the present writer have been surprised to find in it a stringent and even contemptuous criticism of Cardinal Newman's conclusions. But the wholesale condemnation of the man, which it contains, the systematic, though no doubt unintentional, misrepresentations by which this condemnation is supported, the charges which involve nothing less than accusations of habitual dishonesty in dealing with evidence, are graver matters.[80]

Ward also remarked the vituperative language to which Abbott resorted to express his impatience with his subject, citing, in particular, Abbott's use of such phrases as "foulness and falsehood", "immoral shiftiness", and "insolent aggressiveness,"—which, as Ward said, "would have been simply impossible to one who knew either the man or his works intimately, however much he

---

[79] Ibid., 139.
[80] Ibid., 119–20.

dissented from the views which those works contain."[81] Moreover, it is vital to keep in mind just how thoroughgoing Abbott's "misrepresentations" of Newman's treatment of miracles are, especially since Newman expressly assures his reader that "It does not strictly fall within the scope of this Essay to pronounce upon the truth or falsehood of this or that miraculous narrative" and he has only taken up his pen on the subject "to throw off the abstract and unreal character which attends a course of reasoning."[82] Agnosticism and scepticism vis-à-vis miracles, in other words, were of the very essence of Newman's preoccupations in the essay, if Abbott had only had the patience—or, perhaps, one should say, the fairmindedness—to see it.

The question to which we are returned, therefore, is why Abbott was so intent on seeking to discredit Newman and his work. Ward's answer certainly has logical force. "The union of Christianity with belief in the miraculous is in this writer's eyes the most disastrous obstacle to the cause of religion; Catholicism is committed to that union; Newman is the most influential name among Catholics in this land." Therefore, Abbott perforce had to discredit the man and his work. Yet the sad mystery remains of why the mathematician and so many other contemporary detractors could not enter into the real richness of the man they were so avid to diminish. Ward, whose distinction as a critic of Newman inheres most in his sympathy with his subject, captures this mystery nicely.

> Little dreaming—apparently not able to comprehend—the extent and depth of reflection, the wide vision from different points of view, which were characteristic of the man he assails, he seizes on the work whose title promises to be most directly to his purpose—the "Essay on Ecclesiastical Miracles"—and goes through it, without to the end understanding what Newman's attitude towards miracles is. He treats his phrases and sentences as a man unacquainted with the art of watch-making would behave, if by way of ascertaining how a watch was constructed, he should hastily pull it wheel from wheel, and should suppose that scrutiny of some of the fragments taken at random, would explain to him the mechanism of the whole.

Moreover, Ward saw that Abbott's quoting of Newman's work—not only from his essay on miracles but his Essay on Development—was of a tell-tale undigested randomness. "By a similar process of hastily setting down passages from Newman's writings," Ward recognized, "without taking the pains to enter into his mind or to understand their organic connection, the writer has accomplished the feat of covering most of his 259 pages with an assault not on Newman, but on a lay figure, first constructed and then demolished by himself. True, he has clothed it in some of Newman's language, but as in the case of most persons who are burnt in effigy, the clothes are the only, and not very essential, point of resemblance."[83]

Ward was also astute enough to see that Abbott's partisan attack on Newman's work was representative of most of the partisan attacks mounted against the convert in his own lifetime by would-be critics who only read his work to

---

[81] Ibid., 120.
[82] Mir., 238.
[83] Ward, "Philalethes," 120–1.

confirm their prejudicial misreading of it. "In conclusion," Ward wrote, "after this imperfect estimate of a most misleading book, let me say that if the author had written with a little more of Cardinal Newman's candour and accuracy, his work might have been a contribution to problems of real difficulty, which even those who rejected its conclusions could read with profit. ... But such a work as this, inaccurate in statement, partisan in character, and based throughout on the travesty of a misconception of the man whom its author assails, can satisfy no one, except other blind partisans, who welcome any attack on views they dislike, caring more for statements in harmony with their prejudices than for statements accurate in fact. As a serious contribution to the important matters it reviews it can have no value, whether for those who agree with the author's conclusions or for those who do not."[84]

That Newman himself welcomed Ward's sympathetic appreciation of his solicitude for agnostics and their rejection of Christian faith is clear from an exchange of letters between the two men in Newman's old age. On 19 June 1886, Ward had written Newman: "I saw Lord Tennyson yesterday who told me that his son Lionel, who lately died on his way back from India, asked a few hours before his death that "Lead kindly light" should be read to him. It seemed to help him to pray, his wife said, more than anything else. Lord Tennyson seemed to wish that you should know this. I was especially glad as Lionel, whom I knew well, was *apparently* something of a sceptic during his life. But this seems to show that religious influences had still a hold on him.' Newman's response of 21 June richly confirmed Ward's sense of how moving this must have been for the cardinal. "My dear Wilfrid Ward," Newman wrote:

> I wish my fingers and my general feebleness allowed me to say how touched I was by what you told me, in relation to myself, about Mr Lionel Tennyson, and how very kind I think it in his Father to wish me to be told of it. It is remarkable and cheering, as leading to the thought that the agnosticism of Englishmen is in many or most Englishmen only skin deep, and that, as careless Catholics in so many instances at the last send for a Priest so, when the awful future is immediately before many a sceptic, he sees what that future really implies and *to whom* he must look.[85]

On 22 June, Ward added with a poignancy that recalls Newman's own understanding of the yearning for home in the most exiled of hearts: "Lionel Tennyson repeated three times the words 'far from home' when his wife reached them, on the day of his death, in reading your hymn."[86]

VII

To conclude, I shall quote another good contemporary critic of Newman, Walter K. Firminger (1870–1940), who was educated at Merton before becoming Archdeacon of Calcutta. In 1892, Firminger responded to Abbott's attack on Newman

---

[84] Ibid., 154.
[85] LD, xxxi, 150–1.
[86] LD, xxxi, 151. See Short, *Newman and his Family*, 24–5, 248, 254, 399–400.

with genuinely devout dismay, which is something rather different from merely critical disapprobation. "Dr. Abbott has written a book which merits the severest criticism," he wrote;

> but O the pity of it! Dr. Abbott is, first and foremost, a scholar, and yet we find that he has attacked the writings of a man whose principal work he has only too plainly left unstudied—perhaps unread. To bring home his charges, he has interpolated quotations with his own miserable glosses, and attempted to twist his author's words into meanings they were never intended to convey. He has inadequately quoted and grossly misconstrued. All this deserves the most detailed and most ruthless exposure; but we frankly confess that we have no heart for such a task. "Philomythus" has convicted its author of a worse failing than slovenly scholarship, it has proved that he has little or no capacity for gauging the elements of true religion. It has, in fact, not so much weakened our veneration for a "lost leader," as saddened us by a description to be read between the lines of the author himself. "What," we cannot refrain from asking ourselves, "what can a man who speaks so slightingly of reverential fear know of God?"[87]

Hutton and Firminger might have been in the minority when it came to writing criticism of Newman that was at once full of reservations and yet ultimately laudatory, but they were indispensable in calling to account detractors of Newman like Abbott, whose gibbering phantom bears no resemblance whatever to the living man he had chosen to traduce.

---

[87] Walter K. Firminger, *Some Thoughts on the Recent Criticism of the Life and Works of John Henry Cardinal Newman* (London: James Parker & Co., 1892), 52.

JAMES FITZJAMES STEPHEN

◈ 5 ◈

Uncle Fitzy, Newman and God Almighty

Half the controversies in the world are verbal ones; and could they be brought to a plain issue, they would be brought to a prompt termination. Parties engaged in them would then perceive, either that in substance they agreed together, or that their difference was one of first principles ... When men understand what each other mean, they see, for the most part, that controversy is either superfluous or hopeless.

John Henry Newman,
"Faith and Reason, Contrasted as Habits of Mind" (1839)

>   The matron smiled, but she observed a frown
>   On her son's brow, and calmly sat her down;
>   Leaving the truth to Time, who solves our doubt,
>   By bringing his all-glorious daughter out—
>   Truth: for whose beauty all their love profess,
>   And yet how many think it ugliness!
>
>   George Crabbe, *Tales of the Hall* (1819)

Christ comes not in pride of intellect, or reputation for philosophy. These are the glittering robes in which Satan is now arraying. Many spirits are abroad, more are issuing from the pit; the credentials which they display are the precious gifts of mind, beauty, richness, depth, originality. Christians, look hard at them with Martin in silence, and ask them for the print of the nails.

John Henry Newman, "Martin and Maximus" (1840)

I

On 5 May 1870, the jurist and littérateur James Fitzjames Stephen wrote his brother Leslie Stephen a letter from Simla that nicely epitomized his view of John Henry Newman, in which he observed:

> You tell me the story of your controversy with the Spectator and Maurice. I read the letters, for I take in the Spectator, with profound astonishment at the

idiocy of Stanley and Maurice. It appears to me that a curse has descended upon the religious world of all denominations. I really think that Newman, and his God Almighty, liable to be misled by the Jesuits on the one hand, subject to some chance of being kept right by Athanasius and Co. on the other, are such an incomprehensible couple of idiots, that it is difficult to say whether the man himself, or the creature of his imagination, is the greater fool. Imagine too the monstrosity of the notion that the question in which God is being lugged this way and that by the notable authorities in question, is as to the exact moment at which it would be most expedient for him to prompt a parcel of quarrelsome old bigots to tell a pack of infernal lies. [An apparent reference to the First Vatican Council, which was taking place at the time.] I have no patience at all with the turn of mind which affects to print all this contemptible drivel with respect, as a sort of thing which may be held by, what the Spectator describes as a really great man, in good faith. I have asked Froude to let me review the old idiot's Grammar of Assent, and if he says yes, I will try by September to give him a kick from a once familiar toe, which I hope will reach across the Ocean. The only fault I have to find with your manifestations on these subjects is, that you are too civil to these idiots. I long for an opportunity of saying in the very broadest and plainest English words, what I think of [the] Broad way that leadeth to the destruction of all honesty, manliness, and common sense. It is only less disgusting than Newman, which again is simple drivel—systematic lying carried to the point of justifying falsehood on principle.[1]

Never one to put too fine a point on the contempt he felt for those whose reasoning did not tally with what he regarded as the requirements of rationalist proof, Fitzjames Stephen revealed here not only how vituperative but also how intellectually crude he could be. As his brother Leslie Stephen observed, "I venture to think that he had few equals in good downright sledgehammer controversy."[2] Indeed, one of the reasons why Fitzjames Stephen might have chosen to try to engage Newman in controversy was precisely to cross swords with someone whose polemical skills were renowned for their subtlety and force. For anyone as proud of his controversial swordplay as Fitzjames Stephen, engaging an opponent as redoubtable as Newman would naturally be tempting, though Charles Kingsley certainly thought twice about the wisdom of his succumbing to the temptation. Fitzjames Stephen, for his part, clearly found the temptation irresistible. That Newman did not deign to respond to his provocations may account for the especial bitterness to which the judge gave expression in his letter to his brother, though later, as I shall show, Newman did respond (indirectly)

---

[1] Fitzjames Stephen to Leslie Stephen (5 May 1870) in *Selected Writings of James Fitzjames Stephen: The Life of Sir James Fitzjames Stephen by his Brother Leslie Stephen*, ed. Christopher Tolley (Oxford: Oxford University Press, 2017), 332. With Newman's "illative sense," which the convert set forth in his *Grammar of Assent*, Fitzjames was unimpressed, regarding it as "a new faculty, the function of which appears to be to draw positive conclusions from insufficient premisses." James Fitzjames Stephen, "On the Certitude in Religious Assent," *Fraser's Magazine* (January 1872), 36.

[2] Ibid., xxiv. Cf. "The very strength of the Stephens was rooted in weakness; the prodigious capacity for hard work, the ability to take risks, the athletic feats"—and I would argue the readiness to scoff at professed Christianity—"were but the sorties of a garrison that has no walls." Quentin Bell, *Virginia Woolf: A Biography* (New York: Harcourt Brace Jovanovich, 1972), 19.

to a piece that the judge wrote for the *Pall Mall Gazette* called "Old and New Creeds" in November of 1880.

Nonetheless, Fitzjames Stephen's letter exhibits more than his pugnacity. While the controversy to which he refers in the *Spectator* need not detain us, it is striking that both he and his brother should have found fault with the theology of the quixotic Anglican minister F. D. Maurice, whom Newman charitably regarded as "a man of great powers as well as of great earnestness" but "hazy."[3] If the Stephen brothers were united in regarding Newman's defense of Catholicism as unpersuasive, they found Maurice's defense of Anglicanism even more so. As Noel Annan points out in his biography of Leslie Stephen: "To Stephen [Maurice] was anathema, and of all theologians whom Stephen handled none got rougher treatment. He portrayed him as intricate, futile, bewildering, a 'melancholy instance of the way in which a fine intellect may run to waste in the fruitless endeavour to force new truth into the old moulds.'"[4] In this assessment, as Annan showed, Stephen was following his father, a committed Evangelical, who nevertheless baulked at Maurice's peculiarly elusive Christianity. "Sir James Stephen had regarded Maurice's teaching as an attempt to wed 'the gospel to some form of philosophy … to conceal its baldness. But Paul of Tarsus many years ago forbade the banns,' and his son added that to see Maurice graft Coleridgean metaphysics on to Christianity was like watching the struggles of a drowning creed"—a characterization of Maurice's travails and those of countless other Anglicans with which Newman would not have disagreed.[5] Indeed, one irony of the Stephen brothers' criticism of Newman is that they took issue with his response to a problem with which they took issue themselves—the indefensibility of Anglicanism's "drowning creed"—the only difference between them in this regard being that while Newman responded to the shipwreck of Anglicanism by taking refuge in what he regarded as "the one true Fold of the Redeemer," his rationalist critics took their refuge in agnosticism.[6] At the end of a review

---

[3] Newman to Lord Lyttelton (26 July 1864) in *LD*, xxii, 504.
[4] Leslie Stephen quoted in Annan, *Leslie Stephen: The Godless Victorian*, 245.
[5] Ibid., 245–6.
[6] G. K. Chesterton is a good guide to what agnosticism meant in the Age of Huxley. "The general background of all my boyhood was agnostic. My own parents were rather exceptional, among people so intelligent, in believing at all in a personal God or in personal immortality. I remember when my friend Lucian Oldershaw, who introduced me to this Bohemian colony, said to me suddenly, looking back on the tired lessons in the Greek Testament at St. Paul's School, 'Of course, you and I were taught our religion by agnostics'; and I, suddenly seeing the faces of all my schoolmasters, except one or two eccentric clergymen, knew that he was right. It was not specially our generation, it was much more the previous generation, that was agnostic after the fashion of Huxley. It was the period of which Mr. H. G. Wells, a sportive but spiritual child of Huxley, wrote truly enough that it was 'full of the ironical silences that follow great controversies'; and in that controversy, Huxley had been superficially successful. So successful, that Mr. Wells, in the same passage, went so far as to say that the Bishops, 'socially so much in evidence, are intellectually in hiding.' … How dear and distant it all seems! I have lived to see biological controversies, in which it is much truer to say that the official Darwinians are in hiding. The 'silence' following on the first evolutionary controversy was a good deal more 'ironical' than Mr. Wells was then aware. But then certainly the silence seemed to be one of religion defeated; a desert of materialism. Men no more expected the myriad mystical reactions now moving all nations than the flat-chested mansions of Pimlico and Bloomsbury had expected to see spreading through the land the crested roofs and cranky chimneys of Bedford Park. But it was not in *this* that Bedford Park was eccentric. There

he wrote in the *Pall Mall Gazette* in 1868 discussing the limits of philosophical enquiry, Fitzjames Stephen appended a parable that vividly captured the character of this agnosticism. Leslie Stephen, in his biography of his brother paraphrased it thus:

> I dreamt, he says, after Bunyan's fashion, that I was in the cabin of a ship, handsomely furnished and lighted. A number of people were expounding the objects of the voyage and the principles of navigation. They were contradicting each other eagerly, but each maintained that the success of the voyage depended absolutely upon the adoption of his own plan. The charts to which they appealed were in many places confused and contradictory. They said that they were proclaiming the best of news, but the substance of it was that when we reached port most of us would be thrown into a dungeon and put to death by lingering torments. Some, indeed, would receive different treatment; but they could not say why, though all agreed in extolling the wisdom and mercy of the Sovereign of the country. Saddened and confused I escaped to the deck, and found myself somehow enrolled in the crew. The prospect was unlike the accounts given in the cabin. There was no sun; we had but a faint starlight, and there were occasionally glimpses of land and of what might be lights on shore, which yet were pronounced by some of the crew to be mere illusions. They held that the best thing to be done was to let the ship drive as she would, without trying to keep her on what was understood to be her course. For 'the strangest thing on that strange ship was the fact that there was such a course.' Many theories were offered about this, none quite satisfactory; but it was understood that the ship was to be steered due north. The best and bravest and wisest of the crew would dare the most terrible dangers, even from their comrades, to keep her on her course. Putting these things together, and noting that the ship was obviously framed and equipped for the voyage, I could not help feeling that there was a port somewhere, though I doubted the wisdom of those who professed to know all about it. I resolved to do my duty, in the hope that it would turn out to have been my duty, and I then felt that there was something bracing in the mystery by which we were surrounded, and that, at all events, ignorance honestly admitted and courageously faced, and rough duty vigorously done, was far better than the sham knowledge and the bitter quarrels of the sickly cabin and glaring lamplight from which I had escaped.[7]

In his admirable critical edition of Stephen's biography of his brother, Christopher Tolley calls attention to Richard Holt Hutton's response to the parable, a response which Newman himself might have echoed, if we recall his correspondence with the equally skeptical William Froude, the naval engineer and brother of Hurrell

---

was nothing new or odd about not having a religion. Socialism, mostly upon the rather wallpaper pattern of Morris, was a relatively new thing. Socialism, in the style of Bernard Shaw and the Fabians, was a rising thing. But agnosticism was an established thing. We might almost say that agnosticism was an established church. There was a uniformity of unbelief, like the Elizabethan demand for uniformity of belief; not among eccentric people, but simply among educated people. And, above all, among the educated people older than myself." G. K. Chesterton, *Autobiography* (San Francisco: Ignatius Press, 2006), 144–5.

[7] *Life of Sir Fitzjames Stephen*, 132.

and James Anthony. In a letter dated 27 November 1868, the shrewd editor of the *Spectator* told Fitzjames Stephen that this "parable seems to me to point itself to a real knowledge of a life below phenomena, though you insist upon it that all we have in our power is to make guesses at what is behind the phenomena, from the phenomena. I don't believe that is what you do yourself, though you think you do, and there pervades that parable a feeling of greater reality in God than in any of the feelings it describes, though it appears to be written to inculcate the opposite view."[8] For Hutton, in other words, Fitzjames Stephen's agnosticism might not have been as thoroughgoing as the jurist imagined. Was his preoccupation with what he regarded as the inadmissibility of Christian faith a criticism against the "dogmatic principle" of which Newman was so fond, or an unwitting criticism of his own lack of such a principle? In 1881, Mark Pattison captured the predicament of his and the Stephens' generation far more radically when he confessed, apropos the Yorkshire Dales of his childhood: "Protestantism took away the saints who were once invisibly all about us, and now agnosticism has taken away Providence as death takes away the mother from the child, and leaves us forlorn of protection and love."[9]

With such matters in mind, in this chapter I shall take up the criticism that Fitzjames Stephen leveled against Newman to show how both its agnosticism and its rationalism[10] defined a good deal of Newman's opposition to liberalism, an aspect of his work which it will be one purpose of the present study to probe and illuminate.

Newman defined liberalism throughout his career many times but this is the definition to which Fitzjames Stephen objected most: "Now by Liberalism I mean false liberty of thought, or the exercise of thought upon matters, in which, from the constitution of the human mind, thought cannot be brought to any successful issue, and therefore is out of place. Among such matters are first principles of whatever kind; and of these the most sacred and momentous are especially to be reckoned the truths of Revelation. Liberalism then is the mistake of subjecting to human judgment those revealed doctrines which are in their nature beyond and independent of it, and of claiming to determine on intrinsic grounds the truth and value of propositions which rest for their reception simply on the external authority of the Divine Word."[11] While some have sought to deny the accuracy of Newman's opposition to liberalism, the attacks mounted against him by Fitzjames Stephen not only corroborate that accuracy but reveal the contradictions that have always animated Newman's rationalist critics, of whom Fitzjames Stephen or "Uncle Fitzy," as he was known by his niece Virginia Stephen is perhaps the most fascinating.[12]

---

[8] Ibid.

[9] Pattison quoted in Jo Manton, *Sister Dora: The Life of Dorothy Pattison* (London: Methuen, 1971), 112.

[10] There is a certain aptness in the fact that the man who defines *rationalism* most precisely should have been the same man who gave Newman his red hat. "The fundamental doctrine of rationalism is the supremacy of the human reason, which, refusing due submission to the divine and eternal reason, proclaims its own independence, and constitutes itself the supreme principle and source and judge of truth." Pope Leo XIII, *Libertas Praestantissimum* (20 June 1888).

[11] *Apo.*, 255–6.

[12] See Hermione Lee's "Introductory Essay," in *Life of Sir James Fitzjames Stephen*, xxvi.

Reading Newman's wonderfully satirical *Anglican Difficulties*, in which he showed his Anglo-Catholic friends what an incoherent Erastian make-believe Anglo-Catholicism was, one can see how the convert would often substantiate his case by quoting the Erastian absurdities of the Anglo-Catholics themselves, from Bishop Warburton in the eighteenth century to William Palmer of Worcester in the nineteenth.[13] One can quote from Fitzjames Stephen as well to the same purpose. In an article entitled "Dr Newman and Liberalism" (1865), for example, the jurist explains in a memorable passage why he finds Newman's first principle not only unacceptable but outrageously unacceptable. "This is an ingenious and indeed courageous *petitio principii*," Fitzjames Stephen wrote.

> No sane man ever claimed to subject to human judgment doctrines which he admitted to be revealed by God as true. What Liberals say is—We must subject to our human, judgments the question, whether what you tell us is really a "revealed doctrine" or not, and, in considering that question, we must take into account, the moral character of the doctrine itself. If we did not do this, we should be at the mercy of the first impostor who chose to claim our belief. It is possible to imagine a kind and degree of evidence which would induce the most sturdy Liberal to make his children pass through the fire to Moloch, but surely it is at least a respectable prejudice to think that the evidence ought to be carefully examined, and that nothing short of something approaching to demonstration ought to be sufficient for such a purpose. The vilest of all practices—murder, human sacrifices, sexual iniquities of every sort—have been presented to mankind as divine revelations. Nearly every form of idolatry is more or less cruel and licentious. Would Dr. Newman stigmatize as a Liberal everyone who objected on moral grounds to the practices connected with the worship of Juggernaught and Bowanee, and who was so much shocked by them as to proceed to investigate somewhat strictly the question whether they were really revealed doctrines, or only the product of human passions and prejudices? If he allows this "exercise of thought," where does he draw the line? May a man brought up as a Mahometan lawfully compare Christian and Mahometan morality as one part of the evidence bearing on the question whether either, and which, of the two sets of doctrines is revealed? May a Protestant properly exercise his thoughts on the question, whether the social or the ascetic theory of morals is the true one, as part of the evidence relevant to the inquiry whether the Protestant or Roman Catholic doctrines are revealed? Might a Pagan, when Christianity was first preached, consider the question whether it was true or false, and might he exercise his thoughts on its morality as part of the evidence for its truth? To answer all these questions in the negative involves, amongst other things, the consequence that there are no legitimate natural means by which Christianity itself can ever have been propagated. To answer them in the affirmative is to concede everything for which Liberals contend. The great majority of Liberals in the present day would admit that they are perfectly willing to believe any doctrines which can be proved to their satisfaction to have been revealed to men by God. All that they contend for is, that the question whether,

---

[13] See John Henry Newman, *Difficulties of Anglicans*, vol. i, ed Edward Short (Leominster: Gracewing, 2021), 223–31.

in fact, alleged revelations are real is a question of evidence, to be decided by the common rules of evidence, and that the moral character of an alleged revelation is one item of the evidence to be considered. Where is the error in this? Dr. Newman is so far from pointing it out that he never will state his opponents' case fairly, but always ascribes to them a view which is notoriously not held by the greater and most influential part of them.[14]

Here, far from disproving Newman's first principle, Fitzjames Stephen substantiates it by showing why human judgment alone cannot verify "the external authority of the Divine Word." If that authority were verifiable by human judgment alone, faith would be superfluous. At the same time, Newman never discounts the evidence of natural theology *per se*. If that were the case, he would never have credited Bishop Butler's *Analogy of Religion* (1836), on which he based his understanding of antecedent probability. In attempting to wrongfoot Newman, the judge distorts the convert's work. As for the "moral character" of Revelation," Newman commended Wilfrid Ward for articulating the Catholic understanding of the matter in his essay, "The Wish to Believe" (1884): "Firstly, to take the Christian evidences alone. A man who looks at them for the purposes of religious inquiry must necessarily feel their strength to be supplemented by those very considerations in his own mind which prompted the inquiry. The need he has for a religion, the completeness of satisfaction which Christianity affords to that need, the powerful appeal of Christ's character to his moral nature, here are specimens of the supplementary personal evidences which an individual inquirer has over and above the historical evidences viewed on their own merits."[15] As to whether Newman never stated his opponents' cases fairly, the present study, replete as it is with the saint's responses to his various critics, disproves that idle assertion. Lastly, there was Newman's riposte to Fairbairn after he had claimed that the convert was somehow a "secret sceptic" for holding that the reason of the World is not the reason of the infallible Church. "The World, then, has its first principles of religion, and so have we. If this were understood, I should not have my present cause of protest against its Reason as corrosive of our faith. I do not grudge the World its gods, its principles, and its worship; but I protest against its sending them into Christian lecture-rooms, libraries, societies, and companies, as if they were Christian—criticizing, modelling, measuring, altering, improving, as it thinks, our doctrines, principles, and methods of thought, which we refer to divine informants."[16]

Yet putting these matters to one side, we should know what Newman meant by first principles when it came to our apprehending the truth of Christianity, and he gives a good two-fold explanation in the *Grammar of Assent*. First, broadly, he contends: "I assume the presence of God in our conscience, and the universal

---

[14] James Fitzjames Stephen, "Dr. Newman and Liberalism" (1865), *Selected Writings of James Fitzjames Stephen: On Society, Religion and Government*, ed. Thomas E. Schneider (Oxford: Oxford University Press, 2015), 183–4. For a thoroughgoing refutation of the assertion that Newman never stated his opponents' claims fairly or accurately, see Edward Short, "Newman and the Liberals," in *Newman and History* (Leominster: Gracewing, 2017), 134–202.

[15] Newman to Wilfrid Ward (20 December 1884), *LD*, xxx, 446.

[16] Newman, "The Development of Religious Error," *The Contemporary Review* (October 1885), 463.

experience, as keen as our experience of bodily pain, of what we call a sense of sin or guilt. This sense of sin, as of something not only evil in itself, but an affront to the good God, is chiefly felt as regards one or other of three violations of His law. He Himself is Sanctity, Truth, and Love; and the three offences against His Majesty are impurity, inveracity, and cruelty. All men are not distressed at these offences alike; but the piercing pain and sharp remorse which one or other inflicts upon the mind, till habituated to them, brings home to it the notion of what sin is, and is the vivid type and representative of its intrinsic hatefulness." Then, Newman argues that it is from these first principles that we can begin to enter into the other evidences of Christianity. "Starting from these elements, we may determine without difficulty the class of sentiments, intellectual and moral, which constitute the formal preparation for entering upon what are called the Evidences of Christianity. These evidences, then, presuppose a belief and perception of the Divine Presence, a recognition of His attributes and an admiration of His Person viewed under them; a conviction of the worth of the soul and of the reality and momentousness of the unseen world, an understanding that, in proportion as we partake in our own persons of the attributes which we admire in Him, we are dear to Him; a consciousness on the contrary that we are far from exemplifying them, a consequent insight into our guilt and misery, an eager hope of reconciliation to Him, a desire to know and to love Him, and a sensitive looking-out in all that happens, whether in the course of nature or of human life, for tokens, if such there be, of His bestowing on us what we so greatly need. These are specimens of the state of mind for which I stipulate in those who would inquire into the truth of Christianity."[17]

Yet, more fundamentally still, Newman articulates what, forty years later, would become one of the guiding truths of the *Grammar of Assent* in "Love the Safeguard of Faith Against Superstition" (1830): "If children, if the poor, if the busy, can have true Faith, yet cannot weigh evidence, evidence is not the simple foundation on which Faith is built. If the great bulk of serious men believe, not because they have examined evidence, but because they are disposed in a certain way,—because they are 'ordained to eternal life,' this must be God's order of things. Let us attempt to understand it.[18]

II

Before delving further into Fitzjames Stephen's criticism of Newman and his work, it will be helpful to say a few words about his life. The grandson of the evangelical and abolitionist, James Stephen (1758–1832) and the second of four children of Sir James Stephen (1789–59), the colonial administrator and his wife, Jane Catherine Venn (1793–1875), James Fitzjames Stephen (1829–94) was born into that "aristocracy of intellect," as Lord Annan called it, made up of the Darwin, Maine, Huxley, Macaulay, Strachey and Thackeray families, all of whom epitomized the intellectual elite within England's nineteenth-century professional

---

[17] GA, 417–18.
[18] OS, 231–2.

middle classes.[19] He began his education at Eton, where, bullied for being a day boy, he acquired the disputatiousness that would never leave him. Indeed, to prove his extraordinary skill in disputation, he even went so far as to defend the ritualists. His favorite book growing up was Macaulay's *Essays*, the self-assured Whiggery[20] of which he would seek to emulate in his own books, though he took lively issue with the great historian on the impeachment of Warren Hastings.[21] Upon leaving Eton, Fitzjames Stephen went on to King's College, London and Trinity College, Cambridge, where, after failing to secure a fellowship, he decided to pursue a legal career. Although a poor scholar, he was an intrepid disputant. At the Union, where he often crossed swords with William Harcourt, Gladstone's future Chancellor of the Exchequer, he was affectionately known as the "British Lion"—a "roaring, crushing, rampageous debater," who was also a member of the "arch-intellectual society," the Apostles, chosen for the "brightness of his intellect and his manifest intellectual integrity."[22] After leaving Cambridge, he entered the Inns of Court and, thereafter, his legal posts included membership of the Indian Vicegeral Council (1869–72), a law professorship at the Inns of Court (1875–9), and a judgeship on the High Court (1879–93). He was called to the Bar in 1854 and worked on the Midland Circuit. In 1879, he took silk. In 1855, he married Mary Richards, daughter of John William Cunningham, vicar of Harrow and editor of the Evangelical *Christian Observer*, with whom he had seven children, one of whom, Jem, his papa's pride and joy, who had had great success at Eton and Cambridge, went mad after suffering a head injury. Fitzjames Stephen's friends included Lord Lytton, James Anthony Froude, Carlyle, Jowett and Dean Stanley, many of whom he met once he commenced littérateur.

---

[19] Quentin Bell, in his amusing biography of Virginia Woolf, says of Fitzjames Stephen's brother Leslie that he and his wife "belonged to what one might call the lower division of the upper middle class. ... They kept seven maid servants and no man-servant. They might sometimes travel in a cab but kept no carriage; when they went by rail they traveled third class. The ladies had their clothes made by a reasonably good dressmaker." Quentin Bell, *Virginia Woolf: A Biography* (New York: Harcourt Brace Javonovich, 1972), 20–1. Fitzjames Stephen was more or less of the same social standing.

[20] Proof of Fitzjames Stephen's own impeccable Whiggery can be found in a letter he wrote to his eight-year-old daughter, Katherine (1856–1924), who would go on to become principal of Newnham College, Cambridge: "Many Roman Catholics are good people but they are taught a great many very false doctrines, and especially they are taught to believe a great deal too much in the wisdom of their clergy. They are taught to think that God appointed the clergy to teach them all about religion infallibly, that is without the possibility of being wrong which is a great mistake and altogether untrue. ... Now the Roman Catholic clergy persuaded James II to try to make the English people Roman Catholics and to alter all the laws which had been made for the purpose of keeping up the Protestant church which was set up at the Reformation—the greatest event in the history of England. As you get older you will get to understand that the English people for a great many excellent reasons are thoroughly determined ... not to be Roman Catholics and not to let their laws be altered as James II wanted to alter them." Fitzjames Stephen to Katherine Stephen (15 March 1864), *Life of Sir James Fitzjames Stephen*, 329–30.

[21] Manning, too, was very taken by Macaulay when a young man. "Macaulay's life of public activity and utility," the Cardinal recalled when he reread the historian in old age, "his contact with men, his share in events: all this was what I once thirsted for; not, I believe with any low ambition or any empty vanity. So I willed, but God willed otherwise." Manning quoted in Purcell, *Life of Carinal Manning*, ii, 675.

[22] Bell, *Virginia Woolf: A Biography*, 7.

Fitzjames Stephen's brother Leslie looked with distaste on the reviewer's charge, regarding it, as he told a correspondent, as *infra dig*. "Reviewing is an employment which I have never held in great esteem," he wrote. "It is generally a self-sufficient, insolent, superficial, and unedifying style of writing, and I had fully persuaded myself that I should never be enlisted in the Craft. But I am not the first example of self-ignorance and of the frailty of human resolution."[23] Amusingly enough, the writer whose work actually betrayed him into reviewing was Newman. Fitzjames Stephen, for his part, had no qualms about reviewing and wrote extensively for various journals, including the *Pall Mall Gazette*, *Fraser's Magazine*, the *Saturday Review*, *Cornhill Magazine*, the *Contemporary Review*, the *Edinburgh Review*, *Nineteenth Century*, and the *Fortnightly Review*. Although the publication of essay collections struck him as tantamount to an author offering his readers "stale buns," he published several himself, including *Essays of a Barrister* (1862) and *Horae Sabbaticae* (3 vols, 1892).[24] If criticism is a kind of betting, his wagers were not always winners. "It does not appear to us certain," he wrote of Dickens in 1858, "that his books will live, nor do we think his place in literary history will be by the side of such men as Defoe and Fielding."[25] The judge's books include *A General View of the Criminal Law of England* (1863), which set out his views on what he saw as the primacy of coercion in the criminal law; *The Story of Nuncomar and the Impeachment of Sir Elijah Impey* (1885), which opposed Macaulay's reading of Nuncomar and Impey; and what many consider his masterpiece, *Liberty, Equality and Fraternity* (1873), his response to John Stuart Mill's *On Liberty* (1859), which took issue with what his biographer K. J. M. Smith refers to as Mill's "radical democratic liberalism."[26] For Fitzjames Stephen, the "great defect of Mill's later writing seems to me to be that he had formed too favourable an estimate of human nature."[27] As a judge, defending and prosecuting criminals, Fitzjames Stephen had no illusions about the perfectibility of man; to address man's imperfection, he believed in coercion, not liberty. "Estimate the proportion of men and women who are selfish, sensual, frivolous, idle, absolutely commonplace and wrapped up in the smallest of petty routines," he enjoined his readers, "and consider how far the freest of free discussion is likely to improve them. The only way by which it is practically possible to act upon them at all is by compulsion or restraint."[28] Mill might speak of one's having the moral right to do as one pleases just so long as it did not harm one's neighbor. "The liberty of the individual must be thus far limited," he declared, with his accustomed insouciance: "he must not make himself a nuisance to other people." The hard-headed jurist in Fitzjames Stephen thought otherwise.

> The punishment of common crimes, the gross forms of force and fraud, is no doubt ambiguous. It may be justified on the principle of self-protection, and

---

[23] Leslie Stephen to the Rev. John Venn (25 August 1838), *The Life and Letters of Leslie Stephen*, 14.
[24] Fitzjames Stephen quoted in *On the Novel and Journalism*, xvi.
[25] *Ibid.*, 159.
[26] K. J. M. Smith, *James Fitzjames Stephen: Portrait of a Victorian Rationalist* (Cambridge: Cambridge University Press, 1988), 103, 108–13.
[27] *The Selected Writings of James Fitzjames Stephen: Liberty, Equality, Fraternity*, ed. Julia Stapleton (Oxford: Oxford University Press, 2017), 45.
[28] *Ibid.*, 39.

apart from any question as to their moral character. It is not, however, difficult to show that these acts have in fact been forbidden and subjected to punishment not only because they are dangerous to society, and so ought to be prevented, but also for the sake of gratifying the feeling of hatred—call it revenge, resentment, or what you will—which the contemplation of such conduct excites in healthily constituted minds. If this can be shown, it will follow that criminal law is in the nature of a persecution of the grosser forms of vice, and an emphatic assertion of the principle that the feeling of hatred and the desire of vengeance above-mentioned are important elements of human nature which ought in such cases to be satisfied in a regular public and legal manner.[29]

Henry Sidgwick's review of the judge's riposte to Mill is one with which many readers will concur: "Throughout the book, there is a great want of clearness of method," Sidgwick lamented: "applications of utilitarian principles and appeals to popular prejudice, the logic of Bentham and the rhetoric of Carlyle, succeed each other with bewildering incoherence."[30] Newman never wrote any formal response to Mill's "On Liberty"—apparently agreeing with Lord Acton that the Catholic journalist Richard Simpson should respond to him in the *Rambler*—but his opposition to liberalism *per se* was suffused with an opposition to precisely the false liberty that Mill's essay commended.[31] For Newman, the definition of "false liberty" was straightforward: "the exercise of thought upon matters, in which, from the constitution of the human mind, thought cannot be brought to any successful issue."[32] At the same time, as he wrote to his good friend Mrs. William Froude: "We can believe what we choose," though "We are answerable for what we believe."[33] Hutton nicely paraphrased Newman's general view of liberty thus: "Liberty, he insisted, is only valuable to those who can find the highest guidance for its exercise, and is even injurious to those who are satisfied with the mere possession of it, and regard the mode in which it is to be exercised as something more or less irrelevant to the joy of being at liberty to be wrong. He could not endure the jauntiness with which men riot in the possession of one of the most responsible of gifts."[34]

Fitzjames Stephen, despite his disagreement with Mill on how the country should define liberty in response to the challenges posed by the Reform Bill of 1867, which gave the vote to the urban working classes for the first time in England and Wales and doubled the electorate from one to two million, would never entirely forswear liberalism. After all, his response to Mill, as Julia Stapleton points out in her introduction to her critical edition of *Liberty, Equality, Fraternity*

---

[29] Ibid., 102.
[30] Henry Sidgwick quoted in Appendix 6, *ibid.*, 265.
[31] *LD*, xix, note 1, 166. Newman was always fond of the versatile Simpson, despite his liberalism. "It is a happy thing to have a number of resources," he once wrote the editor. "When you are not making displays of ecclesiastical fireworks, you can, like Cincinnatus or Cato, turn (as I am told) to gardening, to Shakespearian criticism, and to musical creations." Newman to Richard Simpson (3 January 1869), *LD*, xxiv, 200.
[32] *Apo.*, 493.
[33] Newman to Mrs. Froude (27 June 1848), *LD*, xii, 228.
[34] R. H. Hutton, "Newman and Tennyson," in *Brief Literary Criticisms* (London: Macmillan & Co., 1906). 197.

"sought to protect liberalism from ... the dangerous encroachment of radicalism, especially of a continental kind."[35] He never attacked liberalism *per se*. Indeed, it was his liberal rationalist convictions that impelled him to become an ardent member of the Metaphysical Society, at one of whose dinners at the Grosvenor Hotel in London he gave a paper entitled "On a Theory of Dr. Newman's as to Believing in Miracles" (1875), a characteristically cocksure disquisition, in which he sought to demolish Newman's belief in miracles by adducing what he considered its unreality.

> I cannot understand how a mystery, as Dr. Newman defines it, can possibly be the object of assent or belief in any case. If reached in the manner described by him, it is a mere absurdity, a contradictory proposition testifying to the weakness of human language, and its inadequacy to describe certain facts. Under such circumstances, language surely becomes useless, and all that a rational person can do, is to confess his own ignorance and incompetence to deal with the subject at, or rather away from, which his language impotently points. The mystery, the proposition combining incompatible notions, suggests not that the premise which leads to it represents the truth, but that it does not represent the truth. This is no mystery at all, but a confession of ignorance, an admission that we have got into a region of which we know nothing, and therefore ought to say nothing. To speak of a combination of contradictory words as in any sense the object of belief is, I think, a mere abuse of language; such words mark the point at which belief, knowledge, distinct or profitable thought of any kind, becomes impossible.[36]

Here is precisely the glib, injudicious language that mars so much of Fitzjames Stephen's criticism of Newman, though, in this case, he was impugning not only Newman's delight in mystery but that of all of the great doctors of the Church.[37] In her introductory essay to the new critical edition of Leslie Stephen's life of his brother, the biographer of Virginia Woolf, Hermione Lee acknowledges Leslie's distaste for his brother's abrasiveness.[38]

---

[35] Stephen, *Liberty, Equality, Fraternity*, xix.

[36] James Fitzjames Stephen, "On a Theory of Dr. Newman's as to Believing Miracles" (1875), *The Papers of the Metaphysical Society 1869–1880*, ed. Marshall, Lightman and England (Oxford: Oxford University Press, 2015), 2:245.

[37] Newman gives voice to this delight in his sermon, "Mysteries in Religion" (1834), *PP*, 2, 18: "What has been now said about the Ascension of our Lord comes to this; that we are in a world of mystery, with one bright Light before us, sufficient for our proceeding forward through all difficulties. Take away this Light, and we are utterly wretched – we know not where we are, how we are sustained, what will become of us, and of all that is dear to us, what we are to believe, and why we are in being. But with it we have all and abound. Not to mention the duty and wisdom of implicit faith in the love of Him who made and redeemed us, what is nobler, what is more elevating and transporting, than the generosity of heart which risks everything on God's word, dares the powers of evil to their worst efforts, and repels the illusions of sense and the artifices of reason, by confidence in the Truth of Him who has ascended to the right hand of the Majesty on high?"

[38] To be fair, Fitzjames Stephen's manner was not entirely without its redeeming points, as the historian Simon Heffer shows: "Stephen had a wit and a bluntness in deploying it that minced his opponents: such as when he ruminated, in response to Mill's saying that he would rather go to hell rather than worship a God who punished people by sending them there, on what Mill would say after being there half an hour." Simon Heffer, *High Minds: The Victorians and the Birth of Modern Britain* (London: Random House, 2013), 587.

He had "a tendency to leave raw edges", in his legal work as well as in his journalism. Words flowed out of him so fast into his articles that "he has not taken time to make them short". Leslie is openly critical of his rough, bludgeoning tone, his "want of quick and versatile sympathy", and a grim, uncompromising voice which made "the ordinary reader [find] himself in company with a stern, proud man who obviously thinks him foolish but scarcely worth denouncing for his folly". He thought Fitzjames's literary judgements almost comically obtuse, making "little allowance for the historical position of the writer" and lacking in any sensitivity to language: "He was generally more interested in the information to be got from books than in the mode of conveying it."[39]

This insensitivity to language—not to mention his heedlessness of "the historical position of the writer"—scarcely made Fitzjames Stephen an ideal critic of Newman, so much of whose rhetorically subtle work is steeped in history.[40] The judge was always at his best mocking far easier targets. "Mr. Arnold's sympathies," he says in an essay on the cultural critic in Arnold, "would evidently gravitate towards what George Eliot somewhere calls 'a great, roomy, universal Church,' but he has a nervous horror of all kinds of 'religious organizations' for active purposes, and, we suspect, would look on any systematic efforts, say for the conversion of the heathen, or the promotion of Ragged Schools ... or the reclaiming of prostitutes, as scarcely less ... vulgar than the 'hideous and grotesque illusions of middle-class Protestantism.'"[41]

Hutton recalled Cardinal Manning coming to the defense of miracles after Fitzjames Stephen spoke at a dinner of the Metaphysical Society when the uniformity of Nature was being debated. "Mr. Stephen's investigations into the evidence of the interference of unseen agents in human affairs are hardly on a par with some of those undertaken by the Church to which I belong," Manning informed his auditors, who included not only Fitzjames Stephen but such eminent Victorians as George Ward, Walter Bagehot and John Ruskin.

> In canonizing, or even beatifying those who are lost to us, the Holy See has long been accustomed to go into the evidence of such events as those to which Mr. Stephen has just referred, and that with a disposition to pick holes in the evidence, which, if he will allow me to say so, could hardly be surpassed even by so able a sifter of evidence as Mr. Stephen himself. Nor is it indeed necessary to go into the archives of these laborious and most sceptically conducted investigations. If there were but that predisposition amongst Protestants to believe in the evidence of the unseen which Dr. Ward desired to see, there would, I am convinced, be many believers in miracles of the most astounding kind ... I do not, however, apprehend that Mr. Stephen will sift the evidence, or even regard it as worth his serious attention. He has hardly assigned sufficient force to that strong predisposition to incredulity which is so widely spread at this moment in the Protestant

---

[39] Lee, "Introductory Essay," in *Life of Sir James Fitzjames Stephen*, xxxiv–xxxv.
[40] See Edward Short, "Newman, Superstition and the Whig Historians," *Newman and History*, 81–115.
[41] James Fitzjames Stephen, "Mr. Matthew Arnold on Culture," in *On the Novel and Journalism*, 253. The quotation from Eliot is brilliant: "Altogether this world, with its partitioned empire and its roomy, universal Church, seemed to be a handsome establishment for the few who were lucky or wise enough to reap the advantages of human folly." *Romola* (1862–3), ch. xxi.

world, a predisposition which I cannot entirely reconcile with Mr. Bagehot's very striking remarks on the universal credulousness of the natural man. Perhaps, however, there may be such credulousness where there is no prejudice, and yet incredulity still more marked where there is. I have been a careful observer of the attitude of Protestants in relation to the controversy between the natural and supernatural. I have seen its growth. I have watched its development. I am persuaded that Mr. Stephen is quite wrong in supposing that the matter can be settled as one of evidence alone. You must first overcome that violent prejudice in your minds which prevents you from vouchsafing even a glance at the evidence we should have to offer you.[42]

As Smith shows, Fitzjames Stephen's reluctance to credit the evidence for Christianity with any critical evenhandedness may not have had a rational explanation. It is true that he felt an animus against the Christian faith, but that is not to say that he was never unambivalent about it.

Stephen's beliefs were obscure beyond inclining towards holding to the existence of a god and some sort of Providence: seeming to hang suspended between a form of basic lay Christianity and agnosticism. Applying the Butlerian formula[43] and performing the delicate psychological feat of rationing belief in proportion to the state of evidence at any given time became steadily more demanding. But, however vaguely, Stephen still believed that the "soul must survive the body," which, for him, implied the existence of *some* god. Without biblical foundations, however, belief was largely thrown on to a naturalistic or final cause basis. In someone of Stephen's mentality the durability of such beliefs was surprising, though their ultimate demise was reasonably predictable. Yet in the same way that the mental source of revelatory truth along with the reasons for its decline and eventual total evaporation defy serious investigation, so also does Stephen's ultimate abandonment of final cause reasoning. In William Hale White's *Autobiography of Mark Rutherford* (1881) loss of faith is dramatic: "silently the foundation is sapped while the building stands fronting the sun … but at last it falls suddenly with a crash." With Stephen both the process and the final outcome were without spectacle; no sudden catharsis expelled Stephen's faith; instead there grew a contained yet sustained resentment. Hutton detected this mood in Stephen's Metaphysical Society performances, where he sometimes appeared to be "avenging himself on what he could not believe, for the disappointment he

---

[42] Manning quoted in R. H. Hutton, "The Metaphysical Society: A Reminiscence," *Nineteenth Century* (1885), *On Society, Religion, and Government*, 306. For a compelling study of the evidence for Christianity from the standpoint of natural theology, readers may wish to look at Richard Swinburne, *Was Jesus God?* (Oxford: Oxford University Press, 2008).

[43] Like Newman, Fitzjames Stephen was a proponent of the views of the Anglican divine, Joseph Butler (1692–1752), one of whose most famous convictions from his highly influential work of natural theology, *The Analogy of Religion* (1736), was that "probability is the very guide of life." Although both cited the work of Butler in many of their writings, Newman and Fitzjames Stephen drew different inferences from it, Newman seeing it as a confirmation of the reasonability of Christian faith and Fitzjames Stephen seeing it as a confirmation of the inescapability of agnosticism. "Butler does not prove Christianity to be true by his famous argument," Newman says, "he removes a great obstacle of a prima facie character to listening to the proofs of Christianity." *GA*, note ii, 497.

had felt in not being able to retain the beliefs of his youth."⁴⁴

One factor that might have caused Fitzjames Stephen's "revolt from awe," to borrow George Meredith's memorable phrase, was his relationship with his Evangelical father, Sir James Stephen.⁴⁵ Unfortunately, Lee settles for a caricature of the colonial administrator, which hardly does justice to the man or his influence.

> The Right Honourable James Stephen was one of the most influential colonial administrators of the nineteenth century, known, only half-admiringly, as "Mr Over-Secretary Stephen" or "Mr Mother-Country Stephen". His main life's task (like his father's) was to work for emancipation in the Colonies, as Counsel to the Colonial Office and Board of Trade, and as Under-Secretary (and in reality the dominant administrator) to the Colonies. He drafted the Emancipation Bill in 1833. (He was also, after his retirement from the Civil Service, a privy councillor, KCB, and professor of modern history at Cambridge.) He was an unpopular as well as a powerful figure. Public hostility to his campaign for emancipation encouraged what he himself described as "a sort of morbid self-esteem". Leslie described his father as "a thin skinned man". Austere, learned, brilliant, and self-destructively hard-working, he was intensely shy, his shyness taking the form of an extremely formal public manner and an unstoppable flow of rapid talk, usually with his eyes fixed on the ceiling.⁴⁶ He was impatient, unable to delegate and sharply critical of his colleagues. His domestic life was regulated by an ascetic piety ("a theatre was as remote from us as an elephant", Leslie noted) and forbiddingly high standards of behaviour. His daughter said that it was like being brought up in a cathedral.⁴⁷

Fitzjames Stephen's autobiographical fragment on his father is worth quoting at length, not only because it serves as a corrective to Lee's caricature but shows how, in some respects, the judge took issue with his father's faith for much the same reason that he took issue with Newman's: in both cases, it was their treating their faith as a first principle and their wariness of the intellect in religious matters that the judge found objectionable.⁴⁸ "He was essentially an intensely

---

⁴⁴ K. J. M. Smith, *James Fitzjames Stephen: Portrait of a Victorian Rationalist* (Cambridge: Cambridge University Press, 1988), 236–7.
⁴⁵ This is from George Meredith's sonnet, "Lucifer in Starlight," which can be found in Sir Arthur Quiller-Couch's *Oxford Book of English Verse* (1900).
⁴⁶ Newman's friend, Frederic Rogers, later Lord Blachford (1811–89), who was in the Colonial Office himself, said of Sir James's conversation: "I like Stephen. He is the most consecutive, or rather continuous, talker I ever heard ... with a great deal in what he says, and singular precision of thought and expression and a spice of humour running through the whole." *Letters of Frederic Lord Blachford: Under-Secretary of State for the Colonies 1850–1871*, ed. George Eden Marindin (London: John Murray, 1896), 131.
⁴⁷ Lee, "Introductory Essay", *Life of Sir James Fitzjames Stephen*, xxiv.
⁴⁸ A good example of Newman's understanding of first principles can be seen in a letter he wrote to his good friend, Mrs. William Froude: "I agree with what you say about Faith and Reason, the doctrine of the Divine Being, Attributes, Providence etc etc—nor do I think it possible to prove what is the truth on these great subjects, except to minds under the influence of certain principles—but this in fact is the very thing I should aim at logically bringing out.' Wisdom is justified by her children—' not by those who are not children of wisdom. I certainly do think that the world is tending to Atheism, because its principles are working freely. This thesis may be widely illustrated, and, when

pious man with a natural turn for asceticism," Fitzjames Stephen wrote. If Lee took her mocking view of Sir James from Virginia Woolf, Fitzjames Stephen took his from filial respect and love,[49] not qualities that would be likely to appeal to the author of *To the Lighthouse* (1927).[50] "He ate and drank hardly anything and brought on (so his doctor said) the illness which made the first great break in his constitution, by abstaining almost entirely for many years from any dinner beyond a little pudding," Fitzjames Stephen wrote of his father.

> His only pleasures were reading and talking ... His piety was of a most singular kind. He was brought up in the evangelical party. His wife my mother was the daughter of John Venn the rector of Clapham and the spiritual head of what was called the Clapham Sect. He used to go to church twice on a Sunday with unfailing regularity. He not only read prayers daily and for years twice a day but he used to pray extempore and to expound the Bible to us every morning. Nearly the last words I ever heard him speak were about Jesus Christ, for whom he had a semi-mystical adoration and love which I could never sympathize with in the smallest degree. He deferred in all kinds of ways to his wife's brothers who were leading evangelical clergymen, but all this was in the strictest privacy. He took in public hardly any part in religious or ecclesiastical matters being wholly occupied by his official duties, and though a sort of saint at heart I should doubt if he was much known in that capacity out of his own household. Moreover he united a singularly clear piercing sceptical intellect to his pious feelings. An acquaintance of mine, lately told me, that Charles Austin, the famous parliamentary lawyer, had told him, that he had talked with my father about the evidence of Christianity, and that my father had said that he thought the historical evidence for it very weak. This I can very well believe. He used to be always talking about theology, and his favourite text was "Whoso doeth the will of my father, he shall know of the doctrine." He used to be impressing on me the doctrine that one must begin by taking Christianity for granted, throwing oneself into the system praying and so forth, and then as a reward you would get to see how true it was. I took his advice. I did give the system as well as I understood it a thoroughly fair trial. I prayed and lived a good life according to my lights and threw my mind into it all

---

it is so done, it assumes in philosophy the dignity of being a Principle. Men may agree with it or not, but they are obliged to recognise and respect it. Thus, within the last day or two, the Times in a leading article against Dr Ellicott, Bishop of Bristol, says, that his charge against the Reason of the day, is a *railing*, *because* he has no remedy;—it ends in itself—whereas Dr Newman, with whom he Dr E. agrees, has a word *more* to say, viz that the *remedy* of this abuse of reason is the infallibility of the Church. It is not that the Times agrees with me—but it seems to recognise in Catholic doctrine intelligibility and practical tangibleness and availableness which are not found in Anglicanism." Newman to Mrs. William Froude (6 October 1864), *LD*, xxi, 255.

[49] "Fitzjames revered our father even more than I did." Sir Leslie Stephen quoted in *The Life and Letters of Leslie Stephen*, 12.

[50] One exception appeared in an affecting piece about her father that Woolf wrote when she was fifty. "To read what one liked because one liked it, never to pretend to admire what one did not—that was his only lesson in the art of reading. To write in the fewest possible words, as clearly as possible, exactly what one meant—that was his only lesson in the art of writing ... [James Russell] Lowell, when he called him 'L. S., the most lovable of men' has best described the quality that makes him, after all these years, unforgettable." Virginia Woolf, "Leslie Stephen: The Philosopher at Home," *The Times* (28 November 1932), 15–16.

as well as I could but I did not find it answer at all. One bit broke away and then another bit, and by degrees when I had reached middle age I gave it up and now that I am on the verge of old age I feel altogether estranged from it and convinced in a quiet way without any conscious indirect motive that it is not true at all. However that is my history and not my father's.[51]

Again, what is fascinating about Fitzjames Stephen's autobiographical fragment is how it shows the degree to which Sir James shared the one trait that his son found most blameworthy in Newman: his distrust of what the convert called "the all-corroding, all dissolving scepticism of the intellect in religious inquiries."[52] Of course, the son spins this distrust in his father to make it seem evasive and irresolute; but he is also faithful enough to the old man's memory to testify to the fact that his father had a "semi-mystical adoration" for Our Lord and Saviour and went to his grave a believer, even if his belief exasperated his son.[53] Yet it is best not to paraphrase, especially when it comes to such deeply personal matters. "He never allowed himself to think freely on religious subjects," the judge writes of his father.

> though he thought about them incessantly, devising with singular ingenuity all sorts of reasons for not following the obvious roads which led to disbelief. I recollect one day talking with him about my reluctance to be a clergyman, because it involved the wearing of mental chains. "My dear boy" said he "we all have to wear chains." I remember at another time some years later (it was at Haileybury in 1857 or 1858) asking him if he really believed the whole of the Bible to be true? He said that there were no doubt mistakes arising from corrupt readings and so forth. I persisted and asked Whether allowing for this he thought it all substantially true and what was to be said to people who honestly believed parts of it to be untrue, and how if serious errors or the possibility of serious errors were admitted any sort of supernatural character could in practice be preserved for it? I do not precisely recollect his answer, but I know that he appeared much pained and embarrassed, and said "Well well my dear boy perhaps it is as you say but don't tell your mother and sister." Nothing could make a deeper impression on me than these reluctant admissions torn from him as they were by arguments of which he was too honest to deny the force though not bold or truth loving enough to measure the full force. He had a genuine distrust of the powers of his own mind in reference to such subjects or rather a genuine reluctance to be guided solely by his own reason. I watched the outward signs of his mental struggles for many years without fully understanding them. I understand now well enough, and much as I reverence his memory I wish he had been bolder and more decisive. He must however have sacrificed much that was most attractive in his character and most characteristic of him in every way if he had been so.[54]

---

[51] "Extracts from James Fitzjames Stephen's Autobiography," in *Life of Sir James Fitzjames Stephen*, 324.
[52] *Apo.*, 218.
[53] Here, it might be useful to quote Newman's dear Irish friend, the poet and convert Aubrey de Vere, who said that Sir James "had taken no offence at being called 'a transcendental Quaker with a tendency to popery.'" Aubrey de Vere quoted in *The Life and Letters of Leslie Stephen*, 17.
[54] "Extracts From James Fitzjames Stephen's Autobiography," 324–5.

Another striking thing about this fragment is that it calls to mind Newman's recognition of the tendency of the unshriven intellect to deny the truths of religion, a recognition which demonstrates his readiness to enter in the reasoning of his opponents, something one rarely finds in any of Fitzjames Stephen's criticism.[55]

> I know that even the unaided reason, when correctly exercised, leads to a belief in God, in the immortality of the soul, and in a future retribution; but I am considering the faculty of reason actually and historically; and in this point of view, I do not think I am wrong in saying that its tendency is towards a simple unbelief in matters of religion. No truth, however sacred, can stand against it, in the long run; and hence it is that in the pagan world, when our Lord came, the last traces of the religious knowledge of former times were all but disappearing from those portions of the world in which the intellect had been active and had had a career. And in these latter days, in like manner, outside the Catholic Church things are tending,—with far greater rapidity than in that old time from the circumstance of the age,—to atheism in one shape or other. What a scene, what a prospect, does the whole of Europe present at this day! and not only Europe, but every government and every civilization through the world, which is under the influence of the European mind![56]

While Sir James' son was baffled by his father's refusal to follow "the obvious roads which led to unbelief," Newman clearly understood why the old Evangelical demurred—why, indeed, any proper Christian would demure, cognizant, as Sir James was cognizant, that "Whoso doeth the will of my father, he shall know of the doctrine."[57] Nevertheless, that Fitzjames Stephen sought to emulate his father in the practice, not merely the profession of Christianity and *failed* is a piteous reminder of what a gift faith is—and a discipline.

If Fitzjames Stephen inherited his father's penchant for overworking—a compulsion that killed him at the age of sixty-five after he lost the use of his reason—he also shared something else with his father: they both corresponded with Newman. Sir James had written Newman in 1835 to apologize for "having imputed to you a contempt for that Body in the Church who are usually called 'Evangelical,'" before assuring him of his "no ordinary feelings of Esteem,"[58] to which Newman responded by saying that he did not despise Evangelicals;[59] "I

---

[55] Lady Gwendolen Cecil called attention to this trait in Newman in her biography of her father, Robert, Lord Salisbury (1830–1903) the conservative prime minister. "Lord Robert," she wrote, "never examines—he rarely discusses—the reasons which influence his adversary. A House of Commons debater, alone among controversialists, argues in the actual presence of his opponents; he is not called upon to state their case, but is intent only on destroying it. The habit thus induced becomes an undoubted defect when transferred to literature: to what degree will be appreciated by those who have recognised the effectiveness of the contrary method in the hands of a master. The fulness with which Newman, for instance, states the case of his opponent adds immeasurably to the force of his subsequent reply to it." Lady Gwendolen Cecil, *Life of Robert, Marquis of Salisbury* (London: Hodder and Stoughton, 1922), i, 76. Elsewhere, Lady Gwendolen notes that her father "always entertained a supreme admiration" for Newman's writings. Ibid., 24.
[56] *Apo.*, 218–19.
[57] John 7.17: "If any man will do his will, he shall know of the doctrine."
[58] James Stephen to Newman (26 February 1835), *LD*, v, 31.
[59] *Pace* Frank Turner and his friends, Newman was never obsessed with Evangelicals when he was an Anglican, as he showed repeatedly in the *Apologia*. "I thought little of the Evangelicals as a class,"

James Fitzjames Stephen

have every reason the other way," though he admitted that he did oppose them insofar as "the spirit of their school ... tends to liberalism and Socinianism." He also took exception to their preaching, which he thought was composed to "melt" rather than to convert their hearers.[60] When Stephen responded by saying that he acknowledged the limitations of the preaching of Evangelicals, even though he had chosen to rear his children in the Evangelical tradition,[61] the greatest writer of sermons in the nineteenth century replied: "I cannot consider Sermons to be the principal Ministration under the Gospel." Why? "Exposition of Scripture or Catechising, both have a definite object—but neither are compatible ... with the formal and measured style of a sermon. For myself, I should be contented to hear that Sermons were merely unmeaning and harmless, as they will almost be except ... in the instance of the (so-called) orthodox School."[62] Later, in 1836, Newman dined with Stephen at his home in Kensington, an encounter about which he wrote to Hurrell Froude:[63]

> He did not like my Arians which (if I understood him) jumped about from one subject to another and was hastily written, though thought out carefully. My two

---

he recalled. "I thought they played into the hands of the Liberals. With the Establishment thus divided and threatened, thus ignorant of its true strength, I compared that fresh vigorous Power of which I was reading in the first centuries. In her triumphant zeal on behalf of that Primeval Mystery, to which I had had so great a devotion from my youth, I recognized the movement of my Spiritual Mother. 'Incessu patuit Dea.' The self-conquest of her Ascetics, the patience of her Martyrs, the irresistible determination of her Bishops, the joyous swing of her advance, both exalted and abashed me. I said to myself, 'Look on this picture and on that'; I felt affection for my own Church, but not tenderness; I felt dismay at her prospects, anger and scorn at her do-nothing perplexity. I thought that if Liberalism once got a footing within her, it was sure of the victory in the event. I saw that Reformation principles were powerless to rescue her. As to leaving her, the thought never crossed my imagination; still I ever kept before me that there was something greater than the Established Church, and that that was the Church Catholic and Apostolic, set up from the beginning, of which she was but the local presence and the organ. She was nothing, unless she was this. She must be dealt with strongly, or she would be lost. There was need of a second reformation." *Apo.*, 40. See also Ker, *Newman and the Fullness of Christianity*, 19–30.

[60] Newman to James Stephen (27 February 1835), *LD*, v, 31–2.
[61] James Stephen to Newman (16 March 1835), *LD*, v, 41–2.
[62] Newman to James Stephen (16 March 1835), *LD*, v, 44.
[63] After Froude's death, when Newman and Keble published *The Remains of the Late Reverend Richard Hurrell Froude* (1838), which included their friend's letters and journals, Sir James wrote a witty review of the two-volume book, in which he famously wrote: "Whatever may be thought of the propriety of disclosing such passages ... they will provoke a contemptuous smile from no one who knows much of his own heart. But they may relieve the anxiety of the alarmists. Luther and Zwingli, Cranmer and Latimer, may still rest in their graves. 'Take courage, brother Ridley, we shall light up such a flame in England as shall not soon be put out,' is a prophecy which will not be defeated by the successors of the Oxonian divines who listened to it, so long as they ... publish, contrite reminiscences of a desire for roasted goose, and of an undue indulgence in buttered toast." It was a mark of the colonial administrator's forbearance that although he might have goggled at Froude's views of the natives of the West Indies in the wake of their manumission; Froude admitted, as he said, that "I have felt it a kind of duty to maintain in my mind an habitual hostility to ... [the former slaves], and to chuckle over the failures of the new system, as if these poor wretches concentrated in themselves all of the Whiggery, dissent, cant, and abomination that have been ranged on their side." Nevertheless, Sir James concluded that the Tractarian firebrand was "a good and able man, a ripe scholar, and a devout Christian," though at the same time he doubted whether Froude and his colleagues were any proof that Oxford had "given birth to a new race of giants, by whom the Evangelical founders of the Church of England are about to be expelled." Sir James Stephen, "The Lives of Whitfield and Froude: Oxford Catholicism," *Edinburgh Review* (July 1838), 67, 500–35.

> volumes of Sermons he looked on as … important as showing we had something in us which would be of essential service in the present state of philosophy and religion. He seemed to treat with utter scorn the notion that we favoured Popery. This age of Mammon, and this shrewd minded nation, was in no danger of it. … Further, the most subtle enemy Christianity ever had had was Benthamism. He had had a dream of attacking it in his latter years himself. He saw *every one* infected with it. Now he thought our views had it in … [[them]] that which could grapple with it—and he wanted me to throw myself out of active business, and think and write; that was my mission. That was my function—the more I wrote the better—He wanted from me a new philosophy—he wanted Christianity developed to meet the age. He thought that the gospel had a kingly sway, and of right might appropriate all Truths everywhere, new and old.[64]

Newman came away from the dinner encouraged: "Indeed go where I will here, 'the fields are ready to harvest' and none to reap them. If I might choose my place in the Church, I would (as far as I can see) be Master of the Temple. I am sure from what very little I have seen of the young Lawyers I could do something with them. You and Keble are the philosophers and I the rhetorician."[65] That it should have been the father of one of his fiercest critics who helped to instill this confidence in Newman was an amusing irony. Yet, at the same time, it is important to see that Sir James Stephen corroborated Newman's view of the development of liberalism, which he articulated in 1864 in his *Apologia*.

> I am not going to criticize here that vast body of men, in the mass, who at this time would profess to be liberals in religion; and who look towards the discoveries of the age, certain or in progress, as their informants, direct or indirect, as to what they shall think about the unseen and the future. The Liberalism which gives a colour to society now, is very different from that character of thought which bore the name thirty or forty years ago. Now it is scarcely a party; it is the educated lay world. When I was young, I knew the word first as giving name to a periodical, set up by Lord Byron and others. … Afterwards, Liberalism was the badge of a theological school, of a dry and repulsive character, not very dangerous in itself, though dangerous as opening the door to evils which it did not itself either anticipate or comprehend. At present it is nothing else than that deep, plausible scepticism, of which I spoke above, as being the development of human reason, as practically exercised by the natural man.[66]

Of course, Benthamism was an early manifestation of this "deep, plausible scepticism," and Sir James was not unaware of the celerity with which it was gaining recruits thirty years before Newman wrote his *Apologia*. Earlier still, Newman had warned his contemporaries of the futility of statesmen looking to Benthamite utilitarianism to govern an increasingly democratic age. "People say to me, that it is but a dream to suppose that Christianity should regain the organic power in human society which once it possessed," he wrote.

---

[64] Newman to Richard Hurrell Froude (17 January – 1 February 1836), *LD*, v, 224.
[65] Newman to Richard Hurrell Froude (17 January – 1 February 1836), *LD*, v, 225. The quotation is from John 4:35.
[66] *Apo.*, 233–4.

I cannot help that; I never said it could. I am not a politician; I am proposing no measures, but exposing a fallacy, and resisting a pretence. Let Benthamism reign, if men have no aspirations; but ... do not attempt by philosophy what once was done by religion. The ascendancy of Faith may be impracticable, but the reign of Knowledge is incomprehensible. The problem for statesmen of this age is how to educate the masses, and literature and science cannot give the solution.[67]

Another striking irony is that Sir James should have elicited from Newman one of his most incisive observations on the ephemerality of falsehood, an ephemerality that should buck those up who deplore the grossly false interpretations of Newman's idea of development that continue to be put about by Modernists. Such false claims, for all their assiduity, never stick. After Sir James had written Newman complaining that he had made oblique unfavorable reference to him in his novel *Loss and Gain* (1847), the convert wrote him back: "Now I have never been dissatisfied with my Tale on the grounds which have caused you to introduce it into your Essay: and I shall not feel the adverse judgement even of good and sagacious men, till I have reason to accuse myself." All of the characters in the novel, although representative of various religious schools in Oxford at the time, were strictly fictitious. For Newman, the "clearness of conscience" that absolved him of impugning Stephen, even if obliquely, gave him "a sort of prophetic confidence, which the experience of the past justifies, that not a few of those excellent persons, who criticize me now, will see cause at length to soften their unfavorable sentiments." And from this, he reaffirmed his trust in truth's perdurability.

> It used to be a proverb often in the mouth of Dr Whately, "Fling dirt enough and some will stick." I have not found it true in my own case. Misconceptions from many quarters have been attached to my words, acts, and motives, for 20 years and more. But they have been inconsistent with each other, and unreal in themselves: and having no life, have faded away. It has been so in time past, it will be so in time to come. Do not think me arrogant when I say, that, with ten thousand failings, I have a witness within me to singleness of mind and purpose, and to a heart bared before my Maker and Judge. Time is the test of facts. What I am conscious of myself now, I think will one day be granted by others.[68]

Now that Newman has been canonized, despite the distortions of many within and outside of the Roman Church, his confidence in Truth prevailing over defamatory caricature has been duly vindicated, even if the pope responsible for the canonization is at radical odds with the true import of Newman's "singleness of mind and purpose." In the case of Fitzjames Stephen, whatever misjudgments might have been made of him and his work during his lifetime, he is now enjoying something of a revival, especially in the wake of the full-dress critical edition of his works that Oxford University Press has brought out under the general editorship of the literary critic, Christopher Ricks. As Smith writes in the *Oxford Dictionary of National Biography*, "No distillation of him can be bettered than that of Lytton

---

[67] "Tamworth Reading Room," in *DA*, 292.
[68] Newman to Sir James Stephen (17 July 1853), *LD*, xv, 398.

Strachey, whose first-hand observation suggested that Stephen 'preponderated with a character of formidable grandeur, with massive and rugged intellectual sanity and colossal commonsense.'"[69] One of the editors of the critical edition, Thomas Schneider puts this "sanity" (always an arresting word when used to describe any rationalist) in a larger context.

> As Leslie Stephen tells it, [Fitzjames] Stephen "sympathised as heartily as any man could do in the general spirit of rationalism ... Every attempt to erect a supernatural authority roused his uncompromising antagonism." But it was for him a question of evidence, whether or not an appeal to a supernatural authority should be seen as a human attempt to "erect" one. Nevertheless, Stephen's antagonism was directed against one authority in particular, the Roman Catholic Church, in a way that suggests the effect of some deep-seated personal trait as much as it does his concern with the canons of evidence.[70]

What the source of this "deep-seated personal trait" was remains a mystery. In the *Apologia*, Newman speculated, apropos rationalists, that "in many men of science or literature there may be an animosity arising from almost a personal feeling; it being a matter of party, a point of honour, the excitement of a game, or a satisfaction to the soreness or annoyance occasioned by the acrimony or narrowness of apologists for religion, to prove that Christianity or that Scripture is untrustworthy."[71] Elsewhere, he asked: "Are there pleasures of Doubt?" In the *Grammar of Assent*, he answered his own question with characteristic insight into the prepossessions of his opponents; and, at the same time, refuted their long-standing contention that certainty in matters of religion was somehow not on offer. For Newman, there definitely were pleasures inherent in doubt.

> Not indeed, if doubt simply means ignorance, uncertainty, or hopeless suspense; but there is a certain grave acquiescence in ignorance, a recognition of our impotence to solve momentous and urgent questions, which has a satisfaction of its own. After high aspirations, after renewed endeavours, after bootless toil, after long wanderings, after hope, effort, weariness, failure, painfully alternating and recurring, it is an immense relief to the exhausted mind to be able to say, "At length I know that I can know nothing about anything"—that is, while it can maintain itself in a posture of thought which has no promise of permanence, because it is unnatural. But here the satisfaction does not lie in not knowing, but in knowing there is nothing to know. It is a positive act of assent or conviction, given to what in the particular case is an untruth. It is the assent and the false certitude which are the cause of the tranquility of mind. Ignorance remains the evil which it ever was, but something of the peace of Certitude is gained in knowing the worst, and in having reconciled the mind to the endurance of it.[72]

---

[69] Giles Lytton Strachey, "The Earl of Lytton," *The Independent Review*, 12 (January–March 1907) (London: John Lane, 1907), 333.
[70] *On Society, Religion and Government*, xxvi.
[71] *Apo.*, 234.
[72] *GA*, 130.

Whatever the specific motive might have been of Fitzjames Stephen's antagonism to Christianity, he wrote his wife in 1863 to confirm that his belief in God was firm.[73] By 1879, however, his religious views had undergone a sea change, which is evident in a letter he wrote to his close friend, Lord Lytton.[74]

> The clever young men at Cambridge have no theological beliefs at all. My sons have none. They know my views, and seem to me to take them as a matter of course, and my own opinion is that, though the existence of some sort of intelligent maker of the world is probable, and a future state of existence suggested by certain considerations, both are incapable of proof, and that the Christian history is obviously not true. All this notwithstanding, better, more moral, more respectful, more affectionate more careful and domestic sons I could not wish to have. They are all fine sturdy fellows too, full of life and spirit. If I had pretended to believe what I don't believe, and had left them to find out that I regarded as a forgery that which I had alleged to be the bond and final sanction of human society, I fancy things would have been very different.[75]

Sadly, in his own life Fitzjames Stephen could scarcely boast of any "singleness of mind and purpose." As this candid letter to his friend shows, double-mindedness and doubt would always accompany his uneasy apostasy. Yet it was from these troubled wellsprings that he wrote his increasingly bitter attacks on Newman and his unflagging faith.

III

In his admirably fraternal, sympathetic biography of his difficult brother, Leslie Stephen chronicles the start of what became Fitzjames Stephen's obsession with Newman.

---

[73] See letter to his wife (22 October 1863), W. L. Burn, *The Age of Equipoise: A Study of the Mid-Victorian Generation* (New York: W. W. Norton & Co., 1964), 274.

[74] Edward Robert Bulwer Lytton (1831–91), poet and diplomatist, served as Viceroy of India from 1876 to 1880. His stint as viceroy was not an unalloyedly happy one. "Lytton's viceroyalty served the ends of the new imperialism and the growing assertiveness of British power in the world. But they were ways which provoked high levels of controversy and revealed deepening contradictions in Britain's imperial project. Lytton's term of office was one of the most turbulent in viceregal history, ending in widespread public outcry, the defeat of Lord Beaconsfield's government, and the near bankruptcy of the government of India." *ODNB*. According to Lady Balfour, the editor of Lytton's correspondence, Fitzjames Stephen wrote a pamphlet for Lord Lytton on the Indian administrative system which Lytton compared to "a police man's bull's-eye," and said that it had given him "the master-key to the magnificent mystery of Indian administration." *Personal and Literary Letters of Robert, first earl of Lytton*, ed. Lady Betty Balfour (London: Longmans Green, 1906), 347. The alacrity with which Fitzjames Stephen and Lytton became close friends might have been attributable to the earl's religious views. "I am reading Pascal," he wrote his father in 1868 at the age of 37. "His life interests me more than his thoughts, only a very few of which I can agree with. His life, however, is to me, though a very painful, a deeply interesting and suggestive story—that of the deliberate intellectual suicide of a magnificent mind. Such men as Pascal and John [Henry] Newman are solemn and terrible warnings against taking Theology *au serieux*. They fill me with profound melancholy, and make me almost execrate the name of Religion." *Personal and Literary Letters of Robert, First Earl of Lytton*, i, 242.

[75] Fitzjames Stephen to Lord Lytton (1 October 1879), *Life of Sir James Fitzjames Stephen*, 339.

Fitzjames had some personal acquaintance with Newman. He had been taken to the Oratory, I believe by his friend Grant Duff; and had of course been impressed by Newman's personal charm. Fitzjames, however, was not the man to be awed by any reputation into reticence. He had a right to ask for a serious answer to serious questions. Newman represented claims which he absolutely rejected, but which he desired fully to understand. He had on one occasion a conversation which he frequently mentioned in later years. The substance, as I gather from one of his letters, was to this effect: "You say," said Fitzjames, "that it is my duty to treat you and your Church as the agents and mouthpiece of Almighty God?" "Yes." "Then give me anything like a reasonable ground for believing that you are what you claim to be." Newman appears to have replied in substance that he could not argue with a man who differed so completely upon first principles. Fitzjames took this as practically amounting to the admission that Newman had "nothing to say to anyone who did not go three-fourths of the way to meet him." "I said at last," he proceeds, "If Jesus Christ were here, could He say no more than you do?" "I suppose you to mean that if He could, I ought to be able to give you what you ask?" "Certainly, for you profess to be His authorized agent, and call upon me to believe you on that ground. Prove it!" All he could say was, "I cannot work miracles," to which I replied, "I did not ask for miracles but for proofs." He had absolutely nothing to say."[76]

Leslie Stephen's own response to this account was at once honest and fair-minded, if one-sided. "I need hardly say that Newman's report of the conversation would probably have differed from this," he admitted, "which gives a rough summary from Fitzjames's later recollections. I do not hesitate, however, to express my own belief that it gives a substantially accurate account; and that the reason why Newman had nothing to say is simply that there was nothing to be said."[77] For Newman's account of the encounter, we can go to a letter he wrote to the convert Jonathan Henry Woodward (1805–79), who became Perpetual Curate at St. James, Bristol:

[76] *Ibid.*, 127–8. Cf. Hutton, "An 'Unteachable' Teacher." "We venture to say, not from our own inner consciousness, but from a study of Newman's writings, that this report, though no doubt perfectly truthful on Sir Fitzjames Stephen's part, could not have been correct. Newman could never have said that it was the duty of Sir Fitzjames Stephen, with his education and in his then state of mind, to have swallowed the Roman Catholic Church whole … at one gulp. Newman always insisted that anything like conversion must usually be a long and complex process. He maintained for years that it would have shown unfaithfulness for himself to have become a Roman Catholic. He was very careful to point out that it was by obedience to the highest attainable authority really set over a man, that any step was gained towards the guidance of a better authority; that, for instance, the most dutiful dissenter who guided himself in early life by his father's lights, had a far better chance of gaining a higher guidance in the end, than one who broke loose passionately and early from parental authority. He knew by his own experience that it was impossible to leap into a new theological belief at one bound, and though he no doubt thought that if Sir Fitzjames Stephen was true to his own convictions, he would, or might in time, reach the Roman Catholic Church, it was quite inconsistent with convictions constantly reiterated in his writings that he should have given the "Yes" here recorded, to Stephen's bald question, "You say that it is my duty to treat you and your Church as the agents and mouth-piece of Almighty God."
[77] In 1881, Newman wrote to W. S. Lilly that Fitzjames Stephen "went away and told his friends that I had acknowledged that I had been unable to answer what he had said. This great misinterpretation of my words he has since thrown into a formula, his only defence of Catholicity is that atheism is its alternative." Newman to W. S. Lilly (17 February 1881), *LD*, xxix, 338.

James Fitzjames Stephen

The Oratory (Rednall) April 20. 1870

My dear Mr Woodward

Your letter with its inclosure of this morning astonished me, as showing how completely Mr Stephen and I were at cross purposes when he (twice) was so good as to call on me. I thought he came to make it up with me, or to apologise, for some severe things that he had said of me in Frazer, and he thought he came to hear me refute, or try to refute him. I had turned over the pages of his review of me and had said to myself "This is shallow," "this is unfair," "this is shameful"; and I thought he felt that, in accusing me of want of honesty, as he did in some places, he had been a little too strong, and, as he happened to be passing through Birmingham, he, as a good hearted man, had thought he would see how I bore it, and make it up. So, when he came, the first thing I did, was to draw his attention to the fact of his severity, which he took very well, and made a sort of apology. Then we talked of many things at random; but, as I perfectly well knew that any real controversy would be like a fight between a dog and a fish, it never occurred to me to *argue*, nor, to tell the truth, had I any dream that he was arguing either. I recollect his asking (or suggesting the question) how we are to treat a man who does not believe in a God, and I recollect answering that I had no means of persuading him—and "was I God, to make alive"? And this I should ever maintain, that there *must* be first principles which cannot be proved and must be assumed, and that, unless the phenomenon of conscience brought home to a man the existence of God, I could say nothing to convince him. Between such a man and me there was a difference so fundamental, that neither could argue with the other.

As to the article in Frazer, I thought it far more like a lawyer's argument from his brief, than the writing of a philosopher—and I said to myself, The time may come some day, when I may have my own say, and put down in extenso, what I think—but to answer an argument which makes a thousand assumptions, none of which I grant, is to write a book. I had not heard of your loss, and grieve to hear it.

Most truly Yours John H Newman[78]

Fitzjames Stephen's piece on the *Apologia* in *Fraser's Magazine* does not exhibit his controversial skills at their best. For all of its laborious mockery and would-be logical rigor, it is, as Newman noted, "shallow." Charles Kingsley's doting biographer, J. M. I. Klaver predictably commends the article for being "densely argued," and proceeds to cite as a specimen of this admirable argumentation Fitzjames Stephen's claim that "as [Newman] believes in God, he sees no difficulty in believing in anything. Such a method smacks of reckless scepticism."[79] Under the circumstances, considering the offensiveness of the piece, it was surprising that Newman chose to receive the judge; but then, when it came to those hostile to him, he could often be forbearing to a fault: it was part and parcel of his good faith. One can see this in another account of his meeting with his rationalist antagonist. "I have been trying to think what else passed between us, which he might think a confession of weakness in me," Newman confessed.

---

[78] Newman to Jonathan Henry Woodward (20 April 1870) in LD, xxv, 103–4.
[79] J. M. I. Klaver, "The *Apologia*," in *The Oxford Handbook of John Henry Newman*, 463.

I know perfectly we did not argue—he stated what he thought, I what I thought. I recollect I used the words "Abstract ideas," and he got animated and protested against them in toto—and I laughed. Also, when, in answer to something he said about those who followed, as well as they could, what they thought right, I gave the Church's doctrine about invincible ignorance, he replied "That is a very different doctrine to the Duke of Alva's, when he slaughtered Protestants," and I did not make any answer. The amusing thing is that I thought, and still think, that what I said did on the whole *soften* him, and I thought I had gained a victory.[80]

Far from gaining any "victory," Newman only exacerbated the long-simmering animus in his guest against a faith he could neither believe nor altogether disbelieve. For our purposes, what is most striking about the judge's piece is how scattershot its fire is. When Newman said that he could not answer the piece's argument, such as it was, because it "made a thousand assumptions" and answering them would be "to write a book," he was only speaking the truth. A few excerpts will suffice to show Newman's point. At the opening of the piece, Fitzjames Stephen brings the charge of dishonesty against Newman, which he may attempt to qualify but ends by compounding.

> The main questions at issue ... are deeply interesting to the community at large. And upon those questions, all transitory and personal matters being waived, we feel deeply that Mr. Kingsley was right, though he expressed himself incautiously and clumsily; and that Dr. Newman was wrong, though he managed his cause with great skill. Mr. Kingsley's original accusation was as follows:—"Truth, for its own sake, had never been a virtue with the Roman clergy. Father Newman informs us that it need not, and on the whole ought not to be; that cunning is the weapon which heaven has given to the saints wherewith to withstand the brute male force of the wicked world." It would be more bold than wise to undertake the defence of these loose and general statements as they stand. Truth, in the sense of veracity, has always been recognized as a virtue by all moralists; and though there has been a considerable difference of opinion as to the cases in which deviations from truth are justifiable, there is nothing to show that either in theory or in practice Dr. Newman has maintained any doctrine on this subject which honest men may not, and indeed have not, held. If, and in so far as, Mr. Kingsley meant to "call him a liar," as Dr. Newman says he did, we think he was wrong. Neither Dr. Newman's life nor his writings sustain such a charge. There is, however, another question between the parties. Besides vindicating his individual moral character, Dr. Newman attempts to meet another and a wider charge. In his general answer to Mr. Kingsley, he says that many Protestants start with the suspicion "that our creed is actually set up in inevitable superstition and hypocrisy." He, on the contrary, affirms that this is not so; that the system of Romanism "is in no sense dishonest"; and that its "upholders and teachers, as such, have a claim to be acquitted in their own persons of that odious imputation." Of course no one makes these imputations in the terms in which Dr. Newman states it. No doubt many Roman Catholics, especially those who have been born and brought

---

[80] Newman to Jonathan Henry Woodward (26 April 1870), *LD*, xxv, 110.

up in it. hold their creed without superstition or hypocrisy; but Dr. Newman's account of the principles by which he has been guided, and his statement of the conclusions at which he has arrived, appear to us to prove to demonstration, that he at least—and he is surely a favourable specimen of Protestants who have become Romanists—has been brought to accept superstition by sophistry. He may be an honest man, but his system is dishonest.[81]

Here Fitzjames Stephen's claiming that Protestants did not impute "superstition or hypocrisy" to Catholics was patently false. His own defamatory misrepresentations proved otherwise, as did nineteenth-century England's rampant No Popery, about which Newman was so witty in his *Lectures on the Present Position of Catholics in England* (1851). Yet Fitzjames Stephen was intent not so much on finding fault with the book itself—with its chronicling of an involved, uncompromising, highly deliberative conversion—as with the mere fact of Newman's belief in dogmatic Christianity, a belief which the judge insisted on finding "sophistical."[82]

> The difference between mind and mind is so great that it is hardly possible to say what may or may not be honestly believed by particular people. It is no doubt possible that evidence which most men would reject with contempt, and that arguments which to most men would seem childish, may honestly appear conclusive to others. When, therefore, it is asserted that a system is dishonest, or that a man is intellectually dishonest, all that is meant is, that the system is sophistical; that the man's mind has in fact taken a tortuous course; that the arguments to which it gives way are such as might have been accepted by a mind in search, not of the truth, but of proofs for a foregone conclusion; and that the evidence with which he has been satisfied is not such as would generally be required by reasonable men to support the propositions at which it is pointed. This of course may be morally wrong; but no one can say that it is so in a particular case. No one can pretend to dive into the mind of another person, and pass sentence upon the way in which he has managed his own intellect. Human critics can look only to results. It must also be observed that it is difficult to connect the notion of dishonesty in any form with Dr. Newman. His *Apologia* is a winning, and in some ways, a touching book. It is full of courage and straightforwardness; every word that the author says of himself and his opinions bears upon it the stamp of truth. The vigour and spirit with which, in his old age, he stands up for his good name; the price which he sets upon the good opinion of the world at large; his anxiety to be freed from the most odious of all imputations on the character of a straight-forward Englishman; the simple dignity with which he tells the story of his life—all these things go straight to the hearts of his readers. Almost all of us, he seems to think, are to be damned to all eternity; but with amiable inconsistency he wishes for our good opinion. He would like us to think kindly of him in hell

---

[81] James Fitzjames Stephen, "Dr. Newman's Apologia," *Fraser's Magazine*, 70 (September 1864), 265–303.

[82] T. H. Huxley would later echo this charge: "That man is the slipperiest sophist I have ever met with. Kingsley was entirely right about him." Huxley to Sir James Hooker (30 May 1880), *Life and Letters of Thomas Henry Huxley* (London: Macmillan, 1900), ii, 226.

> fire. ...We have no intention to say a word inconsistent with the respect due to an old and distinguished man, who appeals so manfully to the good feeling of his countrymen; but high as Dr. Newman's personal character is, we cannot read his book without feeling that his theology is dangerous sophistry, calculated to serve no other purpose than that of drugging the minds of men who care more for peace of mind than for truth, and whose *ultima ratio* is found not in their reason, but in their fears of their fancies.[83]

To assert that Newman, of all people, preferred "peace of mind" over truth betrays a fundamental misunderstanding of the man and his work. What was it that G. K. Chesterton said? "Whatever else is right, the theory that Newman went over to Rome to find peace of mind and end of argument is unquestionably wrong. He had far more quarrels after he had gone over to Rome. But, though he had far more quarrels, he had far fewer compromises: and he was of that temper which is tortured more by compromise than by quarrel."[84] After all, Thomas Scott's dictum, "Holiness rather than peace"[85] was of the very essence of Newman's conversion, as it was of his life. Similarly, to assert that Newman's *Apologia* teaches its readers to fear their fancies—assuming that by *fancies* the judge meant *thoughts*—is equally false. The *Apologia* is suffused with thought: it is, after all, an intellectual, not a spiritual autobiography. No one familiar with Newman's life or character would ever credit such groundless assertions.

In another passage, Fitzjames Stephen reiterates the charge of sophistry, though here he introduces a note of would-be jocularity into his otherwise churlish dismissal of Christian belief, a note which was obviously meant to offend his celibate opponent.

> It is fair to Dr. Newman to admit, and indeed to insist upon, the fact that his mental obliquity is neither fraudulent nor sordid. It is of that kind which goes with the fondness of a lover. He appears to us in the light of a man who, having been infatuated by a woman neither young, lovely, nor virtuous, marries her at the expense of destroying all his prospects in life, and of throwing up all his connexions, and who then exhausts every resource of his mind in proving that she combines, in ideal perfection, eternal youth, perfect beauty, and every moral and mental grace which could adorn such a person. Such conduct produces mixed feelings. It can neither be approved nor despised. But surely it is neither unjust nor uncharitable to say of such a man that he does not care for truth as truth; that he builds castles in the air and not on the ground; and that the general tendency of his writings and speculations is unfavourable to honesty in its widest sense. This fault is a very common one. The same accusation might be brought on very similar grounds, against such men as Pascal and Joseph le Maistre; and, indeed, perfect honesty in the conduct of the mind is a rare virtue. To exemplify this in detail, let us begin with Dr. Newman's cardinal article—his belief in God.

---

[83] Stephen, "Dr. Newman's Apologia," 265–303.
[84] Chesterton, *The Victorian Age in Literature*, 46.
[85] *Apo.*, 19 Cf. Newman's Private Journal for 16 September 1824: "*Holiness* is the great end. There must be a struggle and a trial here. Comfort is a cordial, but no one drinks cordials from morning to night." (*A. W.*, 172.).

If his views upon this great subject appear to be fundamentally sophistical, it will be no wonder if every other part of his creed is tainted with the same fault.[86]

Here, we can see something of the same frivolity that characterizes so much of the criticism of Newman's detractors, whether Abbott, Froude, Kingsley, Meyrick or the ineffable Hare.

Nonetheless, to his credit, if Fitzjames Stephen thought Newman's belief in Roman Catholicism dishonest, he did not follow many of his contemporaries in finding the convert's former allegiance to Anglicanism so. "We do not think that there was anything dishonest in Dr. Newman's relations to the Church of England," he states. "The imputation under which he says he long laboured in popular estimation of having sailed under false colours, is certainly not true. It is clear enough that he was all along under a perfectly *bona fide* mistake as to the nature and capabilities of the Church of England, and that it was only by a long and troublesome series of investigations that he discovered that his own principles were those of the Church of Rome." Yet it is when Fitzjames Stephen delves into the principles underlying Newman's conversion—especially his adherence to the "dogmatic principle"—that he betrays the sheer incomprehension with which he regarded the very idea of dogma. "Read [Newman's] autobiography from end to end, and what is its leading principle," the reviewer asks.

> Hatred to liberals and liberalism. And on what is this based? On an instinctive antipathy, imbibed apparently at fifteen years of age; waived for a short time; and under the influence of illness resumed and persisted in without inquiry, without hesitation, with no better warrant than the impulse of a fierce mental passion, for nearly fifty years. What Dr. Newman means by the "principle of dogma," which was the foundation of the movement of 1833, and which he had held from 1816, it is not very easy to say with precision; but the nearest approach to an explanation of it contained in this volume, is in these words (p. 120):—"From the age of fifteen dogma has been the fundamental principle of my religion. I know no other religion; I cannot enter into the idea of any other sort of religion; religion as a mere sentiment is to me a dream and a mockery. As well can there be filial love without the fact of a father, as devotion without the fact of a Supreme Being." This seems to mean that religion is a set of thoughts, feelings, sentiments, and habits of mind excited by external objects, the description of which external objects constitutes dogma. Thus God himself is the external fact.[87]

What Newman's "dogmatic principle" entailed might not have been "very easy to say with precision" for James Fitzjames Stephen, but in venturing a definition the judge certainly tells his readers a good deal about his own notions of dogma. "The proposition that there is a spirit, without body, parts, or passions, whom we call God, is the dogma. Our mental relations towards God, and the sentiments with which we regard him, as excited by the contemplation of this dogma, are our religion. Thus dogma is essential to religion. If this is Dr. Newman's theory it is simple enough, though it neglects the possibility that the feelings in question

---

[86] Stephen, "Dr. Newman's Apologia," 265–303.
[87] Ibid.

might exist, and that their operation might be beneficial to mankind, even if there were no object by which they were excited. A man's love for his family might remain, and might restrain him from bad courses, even though his family were all dead and gone in his absence. Religion need not be a mockery, nor a dream, even if it had no object. It might be an ultimate fact in human nature of which no account could be given, but from which benefits might arise."[88] This echoes Matthew Arnold's Christianity, something we should preserve, not for its truth, but for its sentimental and aesthetic benefits. For the poet, when "sacerdotalism and superstition are gone, Catholicism is not, as some may suppose, gone too. Neither is it left with nothing further but what it possesses in common with all the forms of Christianity, the curative power of the word, character, and influence of Jesus. It is, indeed, left with this, which is the root of the matter … It is left with the beauty, the richness, the poetry, the infinite charm for the imagination, of its own age-long growth."[89]

While such musings may not constitute any fair or, indeed, coherent criticism of Newman's "dogmatic principle," they do richly corroborate Newman's recognition of the deep-seated antipathy of the English to the Church of Rome, an antipathy to which he gave memorable expression in a letter to a correspondent at the height of the period known as "papal aggression," when Cardinal Wiseman set about restoring the English Catholic hierarchy: "I don't agree with you at being troubled at the present row," Newman wrote in 1850. "It is always well to know things as they *are*. … It has but brought out what all sober people knew,—though one is apt to forget it,—that the English people is not Catholicly-minded. Many foreigners, many old Catholics, have thought they were. I dislike our smoothing over the nation's aversion to our doctrines, just as I dislike smoothing over those doctrines themselves."[90] No one better exhibits the form this aversion took among England's professional classes than James Fitzjames Stephen. His defense of the exception Kingsley took to Newman's commendation of the faithful Irish beggar-woman over the State's pattern man makes this plain.

> In the volumes of sermons to which we have referred, he delights to contrast the good Protestant with the good Catholic; the eminently respectable Englishman, utterly material and fundamentally selfish, and the eminently unrespectable Irishman, whose rags cover a heart warmed by divine faith and love. As a typical illustration, we may take a few lines from his Apology. "Mr. Kingsley has said that I was demented if I believed, and unprincipled if I did not believe, in my statement, that a lazy, ragged, filthy, story-telling beggar-woman, if chaste, sober, cheerful, and religious, had a prospect of heaven which was absolutely closed to an accomplished statesman, or lawyer, or noble, be he ever so just, upright, generous, honourable, and conscientious, unless he had also some portion of the divine Christian grace; yet I should have thought myself defended from criticism by the words which our Lord said to the chief priests—'the publicans and harlots go into the kingdom of God before you.'" This certainly favours the notion that

---

[88] Ibid.
[89] Matthew Arnold, "Irish Catholicism and British Liberalism," in *Mixed Essays* (London: Macmillan, 1879), 88–9.
[90] Newman to Mrs. Wood (7 December 1850), *LD*, xiv, 160.

truth, honour, justice, conscience, and the like, are mere worldly virtues, the whitewash of the sepulchre; and that chastity and religious faith are spiritual virtues of altogether a different sort of importance. It is the fundamental tenet of Protestantism, though it is not to be found in creeds or text-books, that the earth is the Lord's and the fulness thereof; that all virtues stand on the same footing; that courage, justice, honour, uprightness, and generosity are as good evidence of Christian grace as chastity or a taste for the practices of religion; and that Dr. Newman's contrast involves an impossible case, as the statesman could no more be just and upright without the grace of God than the beggar-woman could be chaste. Protestants, moreover, would say that as a fact, honourable, upright, and conscientious statesmen, nobles, and lawyers, were usually more chaste and more religious than lazy, ragged, lying beggars. ... The constant glorification of the ascetic life as the highest form of human goodness, the preference of virginity over marriage, the admiration of voluntary mortifications, and the like, do unquestionably tend to depreciate the domestic and civic virtues, to place them on a lower level, and to attach a less degree of criminality to offences against them than the Protestant theories on those subjects.[91]

As this passage shows, to make his points, Fitzjames Stephen was never above appealing to the stock prejudices of No Popery. He certainly had no qualms insinuating that the Roman Catholic in Newman was somehow foreign and contemptuous of his Protestant countrymen. Yet these incidental aspersions are not what is most noteworthy about the passage. Some of its comments sound almost as though they had been written to satirize the judge's worldly view of religion; indeed, they put one in mind of one of Jonathan Swift's most amusing satires.[92] For Fitzjames Stephen, Newman's "notion of English society appears to be that it is selfish, worldly, and godless," and the judge's response to this is wonderfully characteristic.

> It never seems to occur to [Newman] that men can honestly believe that God sent them into the world expressly for the purpose of doing the business of the world; that the objects of the statesman, the lawyer, the doctor, the merchant, the shopkeeper, the day labourer, are as sacred as those of the priest; that when the

---

[91] Stephen, "Dr. Newman's Apologia," 265–303.

[92] Cf. "I am very sensible what a weakness and presumption it is to reason against the general humour and disposition of the world. I remember it was with great justice, and a due regard to the freedom, both of the public and the press, forbidden upon several penalties to write, or discourse, or lay wagers against the—even before it was confirmed by Parliament; because that was looked upon as a design to oppose the current of the people, which, besides the folly of it, is a manifest breach of the fundamental law, that makes this majority of opinions the voice of God. In like manner, and for the very same reasons, it may perhaps be neither safe nor prudent to argue against the abolishing of Christianity, at a juncture when all parties seem so unanimously determined upon the point, as we cannot but allow from their actions, their discourses, and their writings. However, I know not how, whether from the affectation of singularity, or the perverseness of human nature, but so it unhappily falls out, that I cannot be entirely of this opinion. Nay, though I were sure an order were issued for my immediate prosecution by the Attorney-General, I should still confess, that in the present posture of our affairs at home or abroad, I do not yet see the absolute necessity of extirpating the Christian religion from among us." Jonathan Swift, "An Argument Against Abolishing Christianity" (1711), *Satires and Personal Writings*, ed. William Alfred Eddy (Oxford: Oxford University Press, 1932), 3.

scavenger cleans the street, or the stockbroker sells shares, or the publican serves his customers, he is discharging a divinely imposed duty, and playing his part—an essential part, too—in a divine scheme, as much as a priest administering the sacrament to a dying man.[93]

After attacking Newman's faith on the grounds that it exhibited insufficient respect for Protestant England's "honourable, upright, and conscientious statesmen, nobles, and lawyers," Fitzjames Stephen returned to Newman's "dogmatic principle," which he found credulous and puerile.

> Let us consider a little what this dogmatic principle, fully carried out, implies. The "principle of dogma," as Dr. Newman understands, and has since the age of fifteen years understood and maintained it, appears to be the foundation of his creed, and not the superstructure. A belief that somewhere or other there is and must be a collection of absolutely true dogmas precedes, as we understand him, the belief in specific dogmas. He believes in the Trinity, the Incarnation, &c., because it appears clear to him that some such doctrines there must be, not on account of the evidence appropriate to each of them; for if he believed them on the evidence appropriate to each, he would, of course, have to examine that evidence, and might from time to time modify his conclusions. This conviction he attained at the age of fifteen. Might not any other boy in any other part of the world attain the same conviction, and would not this lead either to the conclusion that all religious dogmas, Mahometan, Buddhist, heathenish, &c., are true, or else that none of them are true? The dogmatic principle as he seems to understand it must either prove the truth of all the dogmas of all creeds, or be insufficient to prove the truth of any dogmas whatever. The plain fact is, that the "principle of dogma" is nothing else than an obscure way of describing the process of begging the question.[94]

The logic-chopping on display throughout the review justified Newman in seeing it as a "lawyer's speech," even though the reviewer's appeal to logic is seldom persuasive; indeed, in many instances it puts the judge's reasoning in a very unflattering light.[95] One example of his lack of cogency will suffice. "If it be doubtful whether there is any God at all," Fitzjames Stephen asserts, "(and though Dr. Newman will not admit that it is, we shall see immediately that the result of his argument is that it is doubtful in the highest degree), it must be still more doubtful whether Christ was his messenger; and if this again is as doubtful as the existence of a God, the natural doubtfulness of the claims of the Roman Catholic Church to be the Church which Christ established must be weakened still further." Reading this, one can hardly be surprised that Newman refrained from responding. There is a kind of soliloquist's remorselessness in the piece, which finds an eerie echo in something Fitzjames Stephen's father wrote in a letter to his wife: "Alone I am sometimes oppressed by myself. I seem to come

---

[93] Stephen, "Dr. Newman's Apologia," 265–303.
[94] Ibid.
[95] "I do feel very strongly that his Article was a lawyer's speech." Newman to Jonathan Henry Woodward (26 April 1870), xxv, 110.

too closely into contact with myself," Sir James confessed. "It is like the presence of some unwelcome, familiar, and yet unknown visitor. This is a feeling for which I have no description in words. Yet I suppose everyone has now and then felt as if he were two persons in one, and were compelled to hold a discourse in which soliloquy and colloquy mingle oddly and even awfully."[96] Fitzjames Stephen's review of the *Apologia* is a perfect example of the sort of "discourse" his father had in mind. Indeed, its insistence that the Christian faith be subject to the rules of evidence is reminiscent of one of the propositions condemned by Pope Pius IX in his *Syllabus of Errors* (1864): "All the dogmas of the Christian religion are indiscriminately the object of natural science or philosophy, and human reason, enlightened solely in an historical way, is able, by its own natural strength and principles, to attain to the true science of even the most abstruse dogmas; provided only that such dogmas be proposed to reason itself as its object."[97] After reading Fitzjames Stephen, one can see that in condemning rationalism for trying to usurp the prerogatives of faith, the pope was trying to spare the world not only heterodoxy but tediously bad logic.

In light of the pope's censure of rationalism, it is interesting to see what the legal profession had to say of Fitzjames Stephen and his rationalist principles. Smith quotes the *Law Times* apropos his subject's last days on the bench to the effect that he was "brief, terse and to the point, and as lucid as in the old days."[98] The *Law Journal*, however, took a more searching view of the judge:

> To deal ... with the least agreeable of the topics which the late judge's career suggests, it cannot, we think, be denied that his elevation to the Bench diminished, and unduly diminished, his fame. It was expected of him that he should be a great judge. Taking the whole of his judicial service together, the later years when his mental powers were affected by overwork and illness as well as those of unclouded strength, he was not even a good judge, at least in civil causes. In these he was but little interested. He had never had, as his biographer suspects, that constant practice in everyday business by which alone he could have "acquired the practical instinct which qualifies a man for the ordinary work of the Law Courts," although he appears to have had between his call in 1854 and the time when he took silk in 1868 a good deal of business on circuit and at sessions, and both then and after his return from India to have been occasionally employed in a big case. "The steady gale never blew." Blackstone declares that not less than twenty years' constant work at the Bar will qualify an advocate for judicial service, and in Stephen's case the twenty-five years of intermittent employment, interrupted by many other absorbing occupations, were not sufficient to give him the easy and confident touch which enables an experienced barrister of no extraordinary ability to discharge judicial functions with regular and competent success. His confident habit of mind, too, and even his strongly-held opinion that the State ought to act as guardian and teacher of morality, to be "the organ of the moral indignation of mankind," as he said, were probably hindrances rather than aids to

---

[96] James Stephen quoted in Lee, "Introductory Essay," in *Life of Sir James Fitzjames Stephen*, xxiv.
[97] Letters to the Archbishop of Munich, *Gravissimas inter*, 11 December 1862, and *Tuas libenter*, 21 December 1863.
[98] Entry for Sir James Fitzjames Stephen in *ODNB*.

him when he came to sit as a judge. He had grown accustomed, in his abundant journalistic labours, to express his opinions dogmatically and as forcefully as possible, to choose rather than avoid the manner of expression least agreeable to his opponents, and often to speak with contempt of opponents with whose arguments he did not agree; and when he found himself in a position of authority he could not always restrain the inclinations fostered by his old habits, and not infrequently he met what he deemed to be undue persistency by a manner which was certainly overbearing. He was too much like a schoolmaster on the Bench, and the fault was more unfortunate because, from the causes suggested above, his knowledge, if upon some subjects, and especially criminal law, extensive and perhaps unparalleled, was deficient upon some other matters falling within the competency of even an undistinguished junior. He could not always control the indignation which his theory of criminal jurisprudence directed him to express in sentencing a criminal until the verdict had been given, and the complaint of his conduct in the unfortunate *Maybrick Case*, made, not by reckless and ignorant scribblers in the Press, but by persons who were aware of the facts and entitled to form an opinion upon them, was that he dwelt so much on the offence of adultery, which was not in question, as possibly to over-influence the jury in regard to the crime of murder, which was. A judge must add to clearness of thought and power of mind quickness of apprehension and a moderate fluency of expression, if he is to deliver lucid and satisfactory judgments impromptu. He cannot wait, as a writer may, for the most appropriate or the most forcible word, and these qualifications Mr. Justice Stephen possessed in small degree. As a writer a very different verdict must be passed upon his memory. And writing was the substantial occupation of his life. Even after he was made a judge he continued the enormous activity of production of his earlier years, and his most elaborate work, the "History of the Criminal Law," was written in vacations and in the leisure his judicial duties afforded him. De Tocqueville has described the American system as a democracy qualified and made workable by the influence of lawyers. That influence is not now what it once was, either in England or in America, but one can see in the accounts given in this biography of the mass of articles and essays poured out by Stephen, and all infected by a view which is essentially that of the common law, all preaching the doctrine that order is the first social good, and law and legal method the chief available agents for the remedy of social evils, for the punishment of offenders and the guiding of conduct, how very great an influence one lawyer, at any rate, must have exerted on the general average of newspaper doctrines which we call public opinion. The tests applied may have been too coarse at times; they may have been unsafe in cases lying outside the ordinary actions of ordinary people. But there are no others available, and upon them the common law acts in dealing with life and liberty, as well as with questions affecting reputation or property. In the search for truth among disputed facts, which constitutes after all the principal business of law Courts and lawyers, it refers all questions to the standard of an average man's conduct, either explicitly by summoning a jury, or implicitly. And if this is justifiable in the administration of the law, it is justifiable also in resolving all the problems of practical affairs. Stephen applied the process to morals, to religion, and, so far as he went, to philosophy. When he was introduced to Cardinal Newman, he made,

James Fitzjames Stephen

with characteristic promptitude, against that eminent divine a "peremptory order for particulars," to be delivered forthwith, of the claims of his Church to authority in matters of faith and conduct. And he regarded the Cardinal's refusal to argue with one who differed so fundamentally from him as almost tantamount to an admission of imposture. Perhaps the method of the common law is not quite adequate for the investigation of the claims of an ancient Church.[99]

There are any number of passages from Newman's work that one might cite to refute Fitzjames Stephen's contention that the truths of Christianity must somehow pass the tests of rationalists, or be presumed false, but here is one that certainly fits the bill from the *Grammar of Assent* (1870), which could have been composed expressly with the circuit judge in mind.

> A learned writer says, "In criminal prosecutions, the circumstantial evidence should be such, as to produce nearly the same degree of certainty as that which arises from direct testimony, and to exclude a rational probability of innocence." By degrees of certainty he seems to mean, together with many other writers, degrees of proof, or approximations towards proof, and not certitude, as a state of mind; and he says that no one should be pronounced guilty on evidence which is not equivalent in weight to direct testimony. So far is clear; but what is meant by the expression "*rational* probability"? for there can be no probability but what is rational. I consider that the "exclusion of a rational probability" means the "exclusion of any argument in the man's favour which has a rational claim to be called probable," or rather, "the rational exclusion of any supposition that he is innocent"; and "rational" is used in contra-distinction to argumentative, and means "resting on implicit reasons," such as we feel, indeed, but which for some cause or other, because they are too subtle or too circuitous, we cannot put into words so as to satisfy logic. If this is a correct account of his meaning, he says that the evidence against a criminal, in order to be decisive of his guilt, to the satisfaction of our conscience, must bear with it, along with the palpable arguments for that guilt, such a reasonableness, or body of implicit reasons for it in addition, as may exclude any probability, really such, that he is not guilty,—that is, it must be an evidence free from anything obscure, suspicious, unnatural, or defective, such as (in the judgment of a prudent man) would hinder that summation and coalescence of the evidence into a proof.[100]

Having established what courts of law accept as "rational probability" in ascertaining proof of guilt, Newman then proceeds to remind his readers what the limits of such proof are. "Now here I observe," he says, "that whereas the conclusion which is contemplated by the Judge, is what may be pronounced (on the whole, and considering all things, and judging reasonably) a proved or certain conclusion, that is, a conclusion of the truth of the allegation against the prisoner, or of the fact of his guilt, on the other hand, the *motiva* constituting this reasonable, rational proof, and this satisfactory certitude, needed not, according to him, to be stronger than those on which we prudently act on matters of important

---

[99] From *Law Journal* (22 June 1885) in *Life of Sir James Fitzjames Stephen*, 314–15.
[100] GA, 324–5.

interest to ourselves, that is, probable reasons viewed in their convergence and combination. And whereas the certitude is viewed by the Judge as following on converging probabilities, which constitute a real, though only a reasonable, not an argumentative, proof ... which, of course, might have been ten times stronger than it was, but was still a proof."[101] In other words, courts of law, like individuals, necessarily accept proof that falls short of absolute certainty, and thus the force of the convergence of probabilities obtains for both.

IV

Newman's treatment of faith and reason in the sermons he collected in his *Fifteen Sermons Preached before the University of Oxford* (1843) nicely anticipated the attacks that he would later receive from Fitzjames Stephen and other rationalists. James David Earnest and Gerard Tracey, the editors of the superb critical edition of the Oxford University Sermons make this point in their introductory essay to the edition. "The truly polemical passages in the *University Sermons* are aimed at critics of Christianity—the Benthamite utilitarians and rationalists," the editors point out.

> But on the whole the sermons are more prophecy than polemic. Newman was predicting the direction from which future attacks on Christianity would come and trying to prepare a generation of young clerics for the battles they would one day have to fight. Wilfrid Ward remarks in his *Life* of Newman that the *University Sermons* were "caviare to the general", because their audience was largely unaware of religious scepticism. "But", Ward adds, "by the more speculative minds in Oxford, such as W. G. Ward and the students of Coleridge, they were regarded, as by Newman himself, as containing his best and most valuable thoughts." Whether or not his hearers understood all that was at stake, his stature in Oxford guaranteed a captivated audience.[102]

Twenty-first century readers are not so unaware of the stakes involved in the evils of rationalism: they see them wherever they turn in a Western society contemptuous not only of God but of God's Divine Law, and, consequently, Newman's anatomy of rationalism finds an audience more receptive than ever. Examples for the grounds of this abound. First, in his sermon, "The Usurpation of Reason" (1831), addressing an age that had begun to follow the rationalists in exalting the intellect at the expense of faith, Newman reminded his readers that this exaltation could find no sanction in Scripture.

> When we consider how common it is in the world a large to consider the intellect as the characteristic part of our nature, the silence of Scripture in regard to it (not to mention its positive disparagement of it) is very striking. In the Old Testament scarcely any mention is made of the existence of the Reason as a distinct and chief attribute of mind; the sacred language affording no definite and proper terms expressive either of the general gift or of separate faculties in which it

---

[101] *GA*, 212.
[102] James David Earnest and Gerard Tracey, "Editor's Introduction," in *US*, xxvi–xxvii.

exhibits itself. And as to the New Testament, need we but betake ourselves to the description given us of Him who is the Only-begotten Son and Express Image of God, to learn how inferior a station in the idea of the perfection of man's nature is held by the mere Reason? While there is no profaneness in attaching to Christ those moral attributes of goodness, truth, and holiness, which we apply to man, there would be an obvious irreverence in measuring the powers of His mind by any standard of intellectual endowments, the very names of which sound mean and impertinent when ascribed to Him. St. Luke's declaration of His growth "in *wisdom* and stature," with no other specified advancement, is abundantly illustrated in St. John's Gospel, in which we find the Almighty Teacher rejecting with apparent disdain all intellectual display, and confining Himself to the enunciation of deep truths, intelligible to the children of wisdom, but conveyed in language altogether destitute both of argumentative skill, and what is commonly considered eloquence.[103]

Next, in "Faith and Reason, Contrasted as Habits of Mind" (1839), he set out the "especial dignity and influence of Faith, under the Gospel Dispensation," which nicely rebuts Fitzjames Stephen's continual disparagement of faith in all of his criticisms of the convert.

Whatever be the particular faculty or frame of mind denoted by the word, certainly Faith is regarded in Scripture as the chosen instrument connecting heaven and earth, as a novel principle of action most powerful in the influence which it exerts both on the heart and on the Divine view of us, and yet in itself of a nature to excite the contempt or ridicule of the world. These characteristics, its apparent weakness, its novelty, its special adoption, and its efficacy, are noted in such passages as the following:—"Have faith in God; for verily I say unto you, that whosoever shall say unto this mountain, Be thou removed, and be thou cast into the sea, and shall not doubt in his heart, but shall believe that those things which he saith shall come to pass, he shall have whatsoever he saith. Therefore I say unto you, what things soever ye desire, when ye pray, believe that ye receive them, and ye shall have them." And again: "If thou canst believe, all things are possible to him that believeth." Again: "The preaching of the Cross is to them that perish foolishness, but unto us which are saved it is the power of God. Where is the wise? where is the scribe? where is the disputer of this world? For after that in the wisdom of God the world by wisdom knew not God, it pleased God by the foolishness of preaching to save them that believe." Again: "The word is nigh thee, even in thy mouth and in thy heart, that is, the word of faith which we preach … Faith cometh by hearing, and hearing by the word of God." And again: "Yet a little while, and He that shall come will come, and will not tarry; now the just shall live by faith." … And then, soon after, the words of the text: "Now faith is the substance of things hoped for, the evidence of things not seen."[104]

In thus sharing with his readers the incomparable wonder of faith, as it was not only perceived but experienced during the rise of Christianity—a wonder,

---

[103] *US*, 49.
[104] *US*, 177–8.

indeed, which accelerated and sustained that rise—Newman showed how much at variance he was with Gibbon and the school of rationalist history, with which Fitzjames Stephen was enamoured.[105] The judge was particularly fond of W. E. H. Lecky's *Rise and Influence of the Spirit of Rationalism in Europe* (1865),[106] which set forth the approved rationalist view of the Middle Ages as "that gloomy period" when "the only scholars in Europe were priests and monks, who conscientiously believed that no amount of falsehood was reprehensible which conduced to the edification of the people." For Lecky, "Not only did they pursue with the grossest calumny every enemy to their faith, not only did they encircle every saint with a halo of palpable fiction, not only did they invent tens of thousands of miracles for the purpose of stimulating devotion—they also very naturally carried into all other subjects the indifference of truth they had acquired in theology."[107] If Gibbon and his rationalist friends wished to argue that the rise of Christianity was tantamount to the rise of episcopal imposture and lay credulity, Newman insisted that its rise could only be attributed to its faith, especially the faith of the martyrs.[108] In his 1839 sermon on faith and reason, he makes no mention of Gibbon, but when he speaks of faith "as an instrument of knowledge and action, unknown to the world before, a principle *sui generis*, distinct from those which nature supplies, and in particular ... independent of what is commonly understood by Reason," he undermines the whole rationalist foundation on which Gibbon builds his Socinian history.

> Certainly if, after all that is said about Faith in the New Testament, as if it were what may be called a discovery of the Gospel, and a special divine method of

---

[105] Even Ruskin was sensible enough to know that Gibbon and his rationalist heirs falsified their history of the rise of Christianity by treating only of its externals. "It seems almost wholly lost sight of by ordinary historians, that in the wars of the last Romans with the Goths the great Gothic captains were all Christians; and that the vigorous and naïve form which the dawning faith took in their minds is a more important subject of investigation, by far, than the inevitable wars which followed the retirement of Diocletian, or the confused schisms and crimes of the lascivious court of Constantine." John Ruskin, *Our Fathers have told us: Sketches of the History of Christendom for Boys and Girls who have been held at its Fonts* (Orpington, Kent: George Allen, 1882), 103.

[106] *Life of Sir James Fitzjames Stephen*, 133.

[107] William Edward Hartpole Lecky, *History of the Rise and Influence of Rationalism in Europe* (London: Longmans Green, 1910), 397-8. If Lecky shared Fitzjames Stephen's contempt for Newman's dogmatic Catholicism, he also shared his fascination with the man himself, as this passage from his letters shows: "At Vevey, where I was staying until driven away by a band, was no less a person than Dr. Newman ... Had I been more brazen I would have ventured to introduce myself, as I happen to know that he knows me in my disembodied state, but I had not courage. However, he did not look engaging, speaking to no one, rarely smiling, and on the whole looking very melancholy—a striking face, though, with a very large nose (bending about a good deal in different directions to economise space), very gentlemanly, ... and a general look, till you observed closely, of an English clergyman. He was travelling with—, whom, if I remember rightly, he puffs immensely in the "Apologia," who had a general look of being his keeper, beckoning him with his eyes when to leave the room, and who at tea kept his hat on and read a book, leaving poor Dr. N. very sadly gazing at the bottom of his teacup. They were only there, I am happy to say, two or three days, for I own it tantalised me exceedingly, there being no one (scarcely anyone, indeed) I should so much have liked to know." *A Memoir of the Right Hon. William Edward Hartpole Lecky*, ed. Elisabeth van Dedem Lecky (London: Longmans Green & Co., 1910), 47. Newman's traveling companion when he was in Switzerland in the summer of 1866 was his fellow Oratorian, Ambrose St. John (1815–75).

[108] See Edward Short, "Newman, Gibbon and God's Particular Providence," in *Newman and History*, 3–80.

salvation; if, after all, it turns out merely to be a believing upon evidence, or a sort of conclusion upon a process of reasoning, a resolve formed upon a calculation, the inspired text is not level to the understanding, or adapted to the instruction, of the unlearned reader. If Faith be such a principle, how is it novel and strange?[109]

This last point shows the respect that Newman, unlike Fitzjames Stephen, was always prepared to show the "unlearned," who would necessarily marvel at what had become of God's "miracles and wonders and signs"[110] if told that they could somehow be explicated by "a sort of conclusion upon a process of reasoning." To reinforce Newman's point, the editors of the critical edition of the *Oxford University Sermons* call the reader's attention to Newman's sermon, "Subjection of the Reason and Feelings to the Revealed Word" (1840), in which he asks, "what is faith itself but an acceptance of things unseen, from the love of them, *beyond* the determinations of calculation and experience? Faith outstrips argument."[111] Yet, again, at the same time, Newman, unlike Gibbon, always insisted that it was the collective testimony of the martyrs that provided the key to the rise of Christianity. Speaking of "the age of Martyrs," in his *Lectures on the Present Position of Catholics in England* (1850), Newman was careful to insist on the compelling breadth of that testimony.

> The most horrible tortures which imagination can fancy, the most appalling kinds of death, were the lot, the accepted portion, the boast and joy, of those abject multitudes. Not a few merely, but by thousands, and of every condition of life, men, women, boys, girls, children, slaves, domestics, they willingly offered their life's blood, their limbs, their senses, their nerves, to the persecutor, rather than soil their faith and their profession with the slightest act which implied the denial of their Lord.[112]

Another passage from the same sermon could have been written in response to Fitzjames Stephen's criticisms of what the judge wrongly perceived to be Newman's denigration of reason, especially since it makes explicit references to the part judges play in the weighing of evidence.

> Now, in attempting to investigate what are the distinct offices of Faith and Reason in religious matters, and the relation of the one to the other, I observe, first, that undeniable though it be, that Reason has a power of analysis and criticism in all opinion and conduct, and that nothing is true or right but what may be justified, and, in a sense, proved by it, and undeniable, in consequence, that, unless the doctrines received by Faith are approvable by Reason, they have no claim to be regarded as true, it does not therefore follow that Faith is actually grounded on Reason in the believing mind itself; unless, indeed, to take a parallel case, a judge can be called the origin, as well as the justifier, of the innocence or truth of those

---

[109] *US*, 128–9.
[110] δυνάμεσι καὶ τέρασι καὶ σημείοις, Acts 2.22 "Men of Israel, listen to this. Jesus of Nazareth was a man duly accredited to you from God; such were the miracles and wonders and signs which God did through him in your midst, as you yourselves well know."
[111] *PS*, vi, xviii, 258–9.
[112] *Prepos.*, 396–7.

who are brought before him. A judge does not make men honest, but acquits and vindicates them: in like manner, Reason need not be the origin of Faith, as Faith exists in the very persons believing, though it does test and verify it. This, then, is one confusion, which must be cleared up in the question,—the assumption that Reason must be the inward principle of action in religious inquiries or conduct in the case of this or that individual, because, like a spectator, it acknowledges and concurs in what goes on;—the mistake of a critical for a creative power.[113]

We can conclude this section with Newman's characteristically practical contention in his sermon, "Implicit and Explicit Reason" (1840) that "No analysis is subtle and delicate enough to represent adequately the state of mind under which we believe, or the subjects of our belief, as they are presented to our thoughts." Rationalists like Fitzjames Stephen might insist on these matters being somehow established in the measurable, verifiable way that evidence is brought before courts of law, but Newman calls attention not only to the presumptuousness but the stunning unreality of such a demand.

> The end proposed is that of delineating, or, as it were, painting what the mind sees and feels: now let us consider what it is to portray duly in form and colour things material, and we shall surely understand the difficulty, or rather the impossibility, of representing the outline and character, the hues and shades, in which any intellectual view really exists in the mind, or of giving it that substance and that exactness in detail in which consists its likeness to the original, or of sufficiently marking those minute differences which attach to the same general state of mind or tone of thought as found in this or that individual respectively. It is probable that a given opinion, as held by several individuals, even when of the most congenial views, is as distinct from itself as are their faces. Now how minute is the defect in imitation which hinders the likeness of a portrait from being successful! how easy is it to recognize who is intended by it, without allowing that really he is represented! Is it not hopeless, then, to expect that the most diligent and anxious investigation can end in more than in giving some very rude description of the living mind, and its feelings, thoughts, and reasonings? And if it be difficult to analyze fully any state, or frame, or opinion of our own minds, is it a less difficulty to delineate, as Theology professes to do, the works, dealings, providences, attributes, or nature of Almighty God?[114]

V

If Newman never deigned to respond to Fitzjames Stephen's reviews of his books, he did respond, as we have noted, to a piece the judge wrote in the *Pall Mall Gazette* on Frederic Harrison's positivism in which the judge referred to "Cardinal Newman's way of writing about atheism. He has always treated thoroughgoing unbelief with the greatest respect. He has never attempted to argue against it, and he has confined his defence of his own creed to the proposition that it forms the

---

[113] US, 131.
[114] US, 183.

only possible alternative to it. By this means he has done as much for the diffusion of general disbelief as any living writer."[115] Although Newman's response to this misrepresentation of his work was withering, it is worth noting that neither Fitzjames Stephen's biographer, K. J. M. Smith nor his brother make any mention of it. "Now, what do I hold, and what do I not hold," Newman wrote in a note to the revised edition of the *Grammar of Assent* (1870).

> The present volume supplies an answer to this question. From beginning to end it is full of arguments, of which the scope is the truth of the Catholic religion, yet no one of them introduces or depends upon the alternative of Catholicity or Atheism; how, then, can it be said that that alternative is the only defence that I have proposed for my creed? The Essay begins with refuting the fallacies of those who say that we cannot believe what we cannot understand. No appeal to the argument from *Atheism* here. Incidentally and *obiter* reasons are given for saying that causation and law, as we find them in the universe, bespeak an infinite Creator; still no *argumentum ab atheismo*. This portion of the work finished, I proceed to justify certitude as exercised upon a cumulation of proofs, short of demonstration separately; nothing about atheism. Then I go to a direct proof of theism ... as a conclusion drawn from three departments of phenomena; still the threat of atheism is away. I pass on to the proof of Christianity; and where does the threat of atheism come in here? I begin it with prophecy; then I proceed to the coincident testimony of the two covenants, and thence to the overpowering argument from the testimony borne to the divinity of Catholicism by the bravery and endurance of the primitive martyrs. And there I end.
>
> Nor is this my only argumentative work in defence of my "creed" which I have given to the public. I have published an "Essay on Development of Doctrine", "Theological Tracts", "A Letter to Dr. Pusey", "A Letter to the Duke of Norfolk", works all more or less controversial, all defences of the Catholic creed; does the very word "atheism" occur in any one of them?
>
> So much, then, on what I do not hold and have not said:—now as to what I have avowed and do adhere to. This brings me at once to the saying to which I have committed myself in *Apologia*, page 198, viz., "that there is no medium, in true philosophy, between Atheism and Catholicity, and that a perfectly consistent mind, under those circumstances in which it finds itself here below must embrace either the one or the other";—a saying which doubtless my critic has in mind, and which, I am aware, has been before now a difficulty with readers whom I should be sorry to perplex.[116]

In defending this saying—one with which, incidentally, the agnostic Thomas Huxley agreed[117]—Newman was careful to stress that in actually believing or disbelieving in Christianity most men did not engage in the logic chopping of

---

[115] "Old Creeds and New", *St. James's Gazette* (18 November 1880), 11–12.
[116] GA, note ii, 318–19.
[117] For Huxley, Newman "believed that his arguments led either Romeward, or to what ecclesiastics call 'Infidelity,' and I call Agnosticism. I believe that he was quite right in this conviction, but while he chooses the one alternative, I choose the other." Thomas Henry Huxley, *Science and Christian Tradition* (New York: D. Appleton & Co., 1898), 345.

which Fitzjames Stephen and his rational friends were so fond.

> The multitude of men indeed are not consistent, logical, or thorough; they obey no law in the course of their religious views; and while they cannot reason without premises, and premises demand first principles, and first principles must ultimately be (in one shape or other) assumptions, they do not recognize what this involves, and are set down at this or that point in the ascending or descending scale of thought, according as their knowledge of facts, prejudices, education, domesticities, social position, and opportunities for inquiry determine; but nevertheless there is a certain ethical character, one and the same, a system of first principles, sentiments and tastes, a mode of viewing the question and of arguing, which is formally and normally, naturally and divinely, the *organum investigandi* given us for gaining religious truth, and which would lead the mind by an infallible succession from the rejection of atheism to theism, and from theism to Christianity, and from Christianity to Evangelical Religion, and from these to Catholicity. And again when a Catholic is seriously wanting in this system of thought, we cannot be surprised if he leaves the Catholic Church, and then in due time gives up religion altogether. I will add, that a main reason for my writing this Essay on Assent, to which I am adding these last words, was, as far as I could, to describe the *organum investigandi* which I thought the true one, and thereby to illustrate and explain the saying in the *Apologia* which has been the subject of this Note.[118]

When William Samuel Lilly (1840–1919), the convert editor of *Characteristics from the Writings of John Henry Newman* (1875), urged Newman to write a response to Fitzjames Stephen's attack for the *Fortnightly Review*, Newman declined, telling his good friend: "I thank you for your zealous consideration for me, but it is unlike my ways, and repugnant to my feelings, to do what you recommend. My brain works too slowly, and my hand too feebly to allow of my interfering in the work of an abler controversialist—you."[119] Here, Newman was paying his friend a handsome compliment by making reference to the letter that Lilly himself had sent to the *Pall Mall Gazette* protesting the inaccuracy of Fitzjames Stephen's accusation. There, the critical sympathy that Lilly brought to his treatment of Newman and his work is patent—a sympathy rarely shown by the judge in his pieces on Newman. "Cardinal Newman's main defence—not his sole defence—of his creed amounts, then, to this," Lilly had written to the editor, "that religion is an integral part of our nature, and that Catholicism alone adequately fulfils the expectation of a revelation which natural religion raises. This may be a good or a bad defence; but, whether good or bad, it is very different from the crude proposition 'that Catholicism is the only possible alternative to atheism.'"[120]

Putting aside the falsity of Fitzjames Stephen's claim that Newman's only defense of Catholicism was that it saved one from atheism, one can readily see that what is arresting about the claim is that he should have made it at all, since

---

[118] *GA*, note ii, 321.
[119] Newman to W. S. Lilly (17 February 1881), *LD*, xxix, 337.
[120] Lilly to Editor (17 February 1880), *Pall Mall Gazette* (23 November 1880), 5. Newman published extracts from the letter in note ii of the revised edition of his *Grammar of Assent*.

his own descent into unbelief as a result of his skeptical convictions proved the accuracy of Newman's actual reading of the matter. The author of *Victorian Bloomsbury* (2013), Rosemary Ashton makes this point in a review of Smith's biography: "If one wished to test Newman's claim that in the mid-nineteenth century the only choice was between Catholicism and unbelief, one might do worse than consider the life of James Fitzjames Stephen, barrister brother of Leslie Stephen. Newman's warning to his own brother Francis that the 'low arrogant ultra-Protestant principle' by which 'every one may gain the true doctrines of the gospel for himself from the Bible' would lead to infidelity—'You will unravel the web of self-sufficient inquiry'—proved true not only for Francis but also for Fitzjames Stephen."[121]

VI

If Fitzjames Stephen was unprepared to treat Newman's understanding of the relationship between Catholicism and atheism with any critical fairness, he was even less prepared to do so with Newman's opposition to liberalism. "The truth appears to be that the liberal cast of thought is so unfamiliar to Dr. Newman that he cannot do it justice," the judge claimed in a piece entitled "Dr. Newman and Liberalism," which he wrote for the *Saturday Review* in 1865. Newman's response was one of weary resignation: "I was amused at having at length to take in the Saturday," he confessed. "Of course it must have come sooner or later. I wonder whether the wounds I have received will do me any good with the people in London who go about telling people I am a liberal. As they have said this up to now, in spite of my Apologia, I suppose the testimony of the Saturday in my favor may go for nothing—still, it ought to tell."[122] Since one of the people whom he wished to disabuse of his being a liberal was Manning, it is striking that a day after writing this letter he was in London for Manning's consecration, about which an eyewitness recorded: "'Dr. Newman was there, and I just saw him to shake hands with him. As his manner is, he kept retired but had come up for the ceremony, and immediately afterwards was seen in the sacristy on his knees before the archbishop, who hastened to raise him up and embrace him.'"[123] Two of the most uncritical acolytes of the former Yale Professor, Frank Turner (who pinched his own claim that Newman did not understand liberalism from the same piece by Fitzjames Stephen) follow Turner by quoting the judge's assertion that Newman had misapprehended "so completely" the tenets of liberalism "as to fall into the double error of ascribing to Liberals principles which hardly any of them hold, and of drawing from those principles inferences which have nothing to do with them."[124] Readers may decide for themselves whether this charge is sustainable. In the case of Fitzjames Stephen, who, by any chalk, was liberal in his religious views, even if he took issue with Mill's views on liberty, one can see that he held

---

[121] Rosemary Ashton, "Leaving It," *London Review of Books* (16 February 1989).
[122] Newman to J. Walker of Scarborough (2 July 1865), *LD*, xxii, 4–5.
[123] Richard Waldo Sibthorp quoted in J. Fowler, *Richard Waldo Sibthorp* (London, 1880), 173. See also *LD*, xxii, note 2.
[124] Colin Barr and Simon Skinner, "Political and Social Thought," in *The Oxford Handbook of John Henry Newman*, 413.

several of the propositions cited by Newman as representative of liberals.[125] As was the case with his objection to Newman's understanding of Catholicism and atheism, his objection to Newman's understanding of liberalism only called attention to the fact that his own life proved the accuracy of Newman's view of liberals: in matters of faith, he trusted to what Newman called "the immense energy of the aggressive, capricious, untrustworthy intellect" and ended his days an apostate.[126] His numerous pieces attacking Newman make this indisputably plain. Fitzjames Stephen held that "no religious tenet is important unless reason shows it to be so"; he held that "it is immoral in a man to believe more than he can spontaneously receive as being congenial to his moral and mental nature"; he held that "No revealed doctrines or precepts may reasonably stand in the way of scientific conclusions"; he held that "There is a right of private judgment; that is, there is no existing authority on earth competent to interfere with the liberty of individuals in reasoning and judging for themselves about the Bible and its contents as they severally please"; and he held that "There are rights of conscience, such that everyone may lawfully advance a claim to profess and teach what is false and wrong in matters religious, social, and moral, provided that to his private conscience it seems absolutely true and right." These are all propositions that Newman set out in his *Apologia* to define liberalism, and his fiercest liberal critic held every one of them. Fitzjames Stephen may have been tolerably well read in the classics—his brother notes that he reread Aeschylus, Aristotle, Plato, Demosthenes and Cicero when he returned from India before writing *Liberty, Equality, Fraternity*—but he clearly never took to heart Socrates's great dictum, γνῶθι σεαυτόν—"Know thyself."

Since a good deal of Fitzjames Stephen's criticism of Newman turns on his contention that Newman not only misrepresented but misunderstood liberals and liberalism, it might be helpful to see how Fitzjames Stephen defined such terms himself. Lee rightly points out that Leslie Stephen is most concerned in his biography of Fitzjames with two subjects: his brother's critique of John Stuart Mill and his "insistence on the need for coercion and compulsion in social relations." For Lee, the two subjects were "linked aspects of the brothers' disagreements over liberalism."

> Leslie, an admirer of John Stuart Mill's adherence to "rationalism and liberty", profoundly disagreed with his brother's argument against Mill, to which he gives a long chapter at the centre of the biography. Leslie described in detail Fitzjames's view that Mill was espousing the wrong kind of liberalism, the kind which "restricted the legitimate sphere of government", leaned towards socialism, wanted to withdraw from imperial commitments, and entertained "a smug,

---

[125] According to Leslie Stephen in the *DNB*, Fitzjames Stephen "was a disciple of Mill and the utilitarians, but in the application to political questions rather followed Hobbes, and was in sympathy with Carlyle's approval of strong government. He agreed, too, with Carlyle in retaining much of the old puritan sentiment, while abandoning the dogmas as indefensible. In spite of this, he still considered himself to be on the liberal side." See also Thomas Schneider's introduction to *James Fitzjames Stephen: On Society, Religion, and Government*, xxvi. "Stephen was happy to be counted a liberal. He understood himself to be a liberal in the same sense in which Newman understood himself not to be one."

[126] For the propositions that Newman cited to substantiate his definition of liberalism, see *Apo.*, 220.

placid, contemptible optimism" about the perfectibility of the human race. Mill's idea of the law as a neutral machinery "for enabling each man to go his own way, virtuous or vicious", and not as an instrument of moral force, was anathema to Fitzjames. In his view Mill's recommendations for equality between the sexes flew in the face of "the necessary subordination of the weaker to the stronger". "Life is a battle", Leslie concluded his summary of his brother's opinions, and "the strongest, in one way or other, will always rule."[127]

There was a certain audacity in Fitzjames Stephen accusing Newman of not understanding liberals sufficiently to define or criticize them when he ran so completely afoul of liberals himself, especially those like his brother Leslie, who regarded Mill as liberalism's most admirable and, indeed, compelling advocate. As if to prove just how wide of the mark Fitzjames Stephen's own understanding of liberalism was, he finished last in the polls in 1873 when he stood as one of three Liberal candidates contesting the parliamentary seat of Dundee. One might say that political liberalism was an altogether different thing from religious liberalism, but in Fitzjames Stephen's handling of them the two were never separate. In his work, as Julia Stapleton confirms, "law, morality, and religion form a seamless whole to which all history bears testimony."[128] Accordingly, in 1862, he submitted a piece to the *Cornhill Magazine* entitled "Liberalism," in which he offered a definition of liberalism that could not have been more revealing. "Those only are entitled to the description as well as to the name of liberals, who recognize the claims of thought and learning," he wrote, in his best pontifical manner, "and of those enlarged views of men and institutions which are derived from them, to a permanent preponderating influence in all the great affairs of life. The highest function which the great mass of mankind could ever be fitted to perform, if the highest dreams of the most enlightened philanthropists were fully realized, would be that of recognizing the moral and intellectual superiority of the few who, in virtue of a happy combination of personal gifts with accidental advantages, ought to be regarded as their natural leaders, and of following their guidance, not slavishly but willingly, and with an intelligent cooperation. It is in the hands of such persons only that national affairs will be handled in a magnanimous and truly liberal temper, and that the vast wealth and power which ages of peace and plenty have stored up can be directed to adequate purposes." In other words, the real liberals were those who obeyed their betters—not a definition with which most of Queen Victoria's liberals would have been comfortable, especially since, in the judge's estimation, one's betters were the "prudent, steady, hardy, enduring race of people, who are neither fools nor cowards, who have no particular love for those who are, who distinctly know what they want, and are determined to use all lawful means to get it. Some such religion as this is the unspoken deeply rooted conviction of the solid, established part of the English nation."[129] Here was how Fitzjames Stephen defined liberals—*they knew what they wanted and how to get it*. Moreover, what they wanted could not have been clearer. "India," he declared, with an imperial zest that only Disraeli could have rivalled, "is the

---

[127] *Life of Sir James Fitzjames Stephen*, xxxvi.
[128] Stephen, *Liberty, Equality, Fraternity*, xix.
[129] Ibid., 179–80.

problem which true liberals must solve successfully if their success is to be a blessing and not a curse."[130] In other words, it was the colonial administrator in Fitzjames Stephen's father that gave his son his understanding of the true liberals. "Hitherto they have been critics," the judge wrote.

> They are now to be authors; and if they fail, their success will prove nothing but imbecility. There is hardly an institution in the country from which good fruit is not to be got, if they will only catch the spirit which presided over its formation. In many cases, this has been done with great skill. Very many of the reforms which have succeeded each other so rapidly for the last thirty years have been liberal, in the positive as well as the technical sense; but as the class which governs the country grows more numerous, and, as the slight and hasty opinions of persons who are doomed by their circumstances to a contented, and, for the most part, unconscious ignorance, gradually come to be invested with increasing importance, it becomes a matter of the first necessity to impress upon them the responsibilities under which they lie, and to give them, if possible, a glimpse of the sort of temper in which they must approach the great problems of government, if they are worthily to sustain the burden which eight centuries of greatness and glory have laid on their shoulders.[131]

In light of this passage, the reader must ask himself who had the better understanding of the nineteenth-century liberal: Newman, who defined him as someone who contends that "No religious tenet is important, unless reason shows it

---

[130] *Selected Writings of James Fitzjames Stephen: On Society, Religion and Government*, ed. Thomas Schneider (Oxford: Oxford University Press, 2015), 96. It was a speech that Fitzjames Stephen gave at Eton regaling his auditors with descriptions of a British eastern empire "more populous, more amazing and more beneficent than that of Rome" that inspired young George Curzon to devote himself to becoming one of India's most resplendent Viceroys. After listening to Fitzjames Stephen, Curzon "prepared himself for a historic role in the Raj. He excelled at Oxford. He married an American heiress. He travelled widely in the East, having first hired from a theatrical costumier a galaxy of foreign decorations, huge gold epaulettes, enormous Wellington boots with spurs, and a gigantic curved sword." Piers Brendon, *The Decline and Fall of the British Empire 1781-1997* (London: Jonathan Cape, 2007), 239.

[131] *Ibid.*, 96. Fitzjames Stephen might have put matters more succinctly if he had simply quoted Lord Mayo (1822-72), who told Sir Henry Durand, after making him lieutenant-governor of the Punjab: "Teach your subordinates that we are all British gentlemen engaged in the magnificent work of governing an inferior race." Lord Mayo quoted in David Gilmour, *The British in India: Three Centuries of Ambition and Experience* (London: Allen Lane, 2018), 11. Sir James was Law Member of Mayo's Council and Gilmour argues that when it came to Indian policy Mayo entirely agreed with Sir James, whose view it was that "the Indian government was an absolute government which could never represent native principles of life unless it wanted to represent 'heathenism and barbarism.'" David Gilmour, *The Ruling Class: Imperial Lives in the Victorian Raj* (London: John Murray, 2005), 24. Although fond of the empire, the fortunes of which he followed closely, Newman naturally was jealous of the talent it took away from England, talent which, as he saw it, might be accomplishing good at home, rather than far afield, especially for the Church, as he made plain to his friend, the convert Marquis of Ripon, who was Viceroy of India between 1880 and 1884: "That you are doing a great work in India, none of us doubts, and it is selfish to complain you are not doing work at home, but be sure that Catholics here all feel how much you would be doing for us if your duty did not call you away. Especially do I often think how many young men there are, of position and with a future, who are sadly [deprived] of what only you can do for them." Newman to the Marquis of Ripon (1883), *LD*, xxx, 168.

to be so,"¹³² or Fitzjames Stephen who defined him as someone who should be prepared "to sustain the burden which eight centuries of greatness and glory have laid on [his] shoulders" by keeping the civil servants of the Raj scribbling at their desks.

VII

There is one sense, however, in which Fitzjames Stephen and Newman were both of the same mind and that is in their insistence that religion, in order to be compelling, must be true, though, of course, they each of them differed fundamentally on how that truth should be ascertained. After all, Fitzjames Stephen chose to represent the liberal Welsh biblical scholar Rowland Williams (1817–70) after he faced legal action for heresy as a result of his contribution to the radically liberal *Essays and Reviews* (1860) precisely because he believed strongly that the enquiries made by religious liberals like Williams as to whether the truth of Christianity could survive the new developments in scholarship and science had consequences for people of all political persuasions.¹³³ His defense of the challenges made by Williams and his liberal friends is worth quoting.

> There is only one course which the clergy can take with credit and consistency, and that is the course of saying that Christianity is true, and that they or some of them can prove it to be true, and can answer the objections brought against it. No doubt this involves the admission that it is conceivable that Christianity may not be true, in which case it must be given up; but that admission can be avoided only by withdrawing the whole subject from discussion, and by thus depriving religion at once of all influence over men of educated and powerful minds, and gradually over the human race. It is of the highest importance that the world in general, and the clergy in particular, should understand that a proposition of whatever kind becomes utterly worthless as soon as it is placed beyond the reach of argument or possible contradiction. The only propositions which cannot be contradicted are those which relate to matters about which we can have no knowledge. If I say, "Perhaps a child will be born to-morrow with eyes in the back of his head," no one can contradict me, but the proposition is totally worthless. If I say, "Such a child was born last week at such a place," the proposition is curious and may be highly important, but it derives its curiosity and importance from the fact that its truth can be tested. So, if I say, "I do not affirm the truth of the Christian religion, but I will teach a number of poor people to go through certain Christian ceremonies," my position is unassailable, but it

---

¹³² *Apo.*, 260–1.
¹³³ See the entry on Williams in the *ODNB* "W. K. Hamilton, bishop of Salisbury, took proceedings against Williams for heterodoxy before the court of arches of the province of Canterbury. He was defended by J. P. Deane and J. F. Stephen in a hearing which lasted ten days in December 1861 and January 1862. The subsequent judgment sustained three charges relating to inspiration, propitiation, and justification, but dismissed the others. In retrospect, however, the liberty that the judgment allowed seems more significant than these three particular condemnations. Williams himself wrote: 'Whatever freedom I have claimed is judicially conceded as permissible by the Church of England. If we gain nothing more, I feel this day that I have not lived in vain; my Master has done a work by me which will abide.'" In February, 1864, the unfavorable charges were reversed.

is also unmeaning. If, on the other hand, I say, "I teach this religion because it is true," I take a great responsibility, no doubt, and am open to contradiction, but if I can establish my point I can move the world and change the face of society. With a definite creed, founded on a rational conviction, everything is possible. Without it, men may say what they like about being humble and practical, but in fact they will never get beyond beating the air.[134]

One of the reasons why Fitzjames Stephen was so preoccupied with this question of the truth of Christianity—especially with regard to the after-life—is that he recognized that it had a great bearing on what ought to be the limits of liberty, about which he had parted ways so sharply from John Stuart Mill. In the second edition of *Liberty, Equality, Fraternity* he elaborates on the implications of this preoccupation in response to a review of the book by Frederic Harrison, the Comtean positivist, who had complained that Mill's critic treated the after-life as a given and, even worse, as a given bound up with eternal reward and punishment.[135] "The great instrument by which priests rule is an appeal not merely to heaven and hell, personal hope and fear, but to a variety of hopes and fears, sympathies and antipathies, which depend upon and refer to an unseen and future world," Fitzjames Stephen wrote.

> These hopes and fears, sympathies and antipathies, affect people's conduct in reference to this present life as directly as law affects them, and in this sense religion is as temporal as law. ... To point the matter still more, let us assume, for the sake of argument, that the doctrine which [Harrison] twits me with so lavishly, and I must add, so coarsely—the doctrine of eternal damnation—were indisputably proved to be true, and were heartily accepted as such by all mankind. Surely it would have a most direct and powerful influence both upon law and upon religion. To take one instance out of a million, it would have a direct and important bearing on the question of capital punishment in the province of law, and it would obviously determine the whole character of religious teaching.
>
> Suppose, on the other hand, it were to be established beyond all doubt whatever, that there is no life at all beyond the grave, and that this doctrine was accepted by the whole human race with absolute confidence. This would have an equally powerful and direct influence both on law and morals. The value which is set upon human life, especially upon the lives of the sick, the wretched, and superfluous children would at once appear to be exaggerated. Lawyers would have occasion to reconsider the law of murder, and especially the law of infanticide; priests would have to pass over in a body to some such creed as Mr. Harrison's, or to give up their profession altogether.[136]

In effect, what Fitzjames Stephen is saying here is that either religion is the bond of society or it is not, and if we agree that it is not, certain rather appalling things follow. Indeed, in our own apostate social order, they *have* followed—anarchy duly abounds in every sphere of life. Newman defined liberalism in the way he

---

[134] James Fitzjames Stephen, "Sceptical Humility," *The Saturday Review* (9 April 1864), 435.
[135] See Harrison's review in Stephen, *Liberty, Equality, Fraternity*, 226–8.
[136] *Ibid.*, 20–1.

defined it precisely because he agreed with Fitzjames Stephen: the question of whether or not Christianity was true was an inescapably consequential question for Britain's radically changing social order. That Newman chose to answer the question in a way that entirely opposed the way most liberals answered it does not invalidate his definition of liberalism—it gives it its abiding appeal, an appeal which we dismiss at our peril at a time when so much of the evil of liberalism so clearly prophesied by Newman is now on our doorsteps. In rereading the definition, we can only marvel at how perfectly it describes the convictions that animate that ramifying evil.

> Liberalism in religion is the doctrine that there is no positive truth in religion, but that one creed is as good as another, and this is the teaching which is gaining substance and force daily. It is inconsistent with any recognition of any religion, as true. It teaches that all are to be tolerated, for all are matters of opinion. Revealed religion is not a truth, but a sentiment and a taste; not an objective fact, not miraculous; and it is the right of each individual to make it say just what strikes his fancy. Devotion is not necessarily founded on faith. Men may go to Protestant Churches and to Catholic, may get good from both and belong to neither. They may fraternize together in spiritual thoughts and feelings, without having any views at all of doctrine in common, or seeing the need of them. Since, then, religion is so personal a peculiarity and so private a possession, we must of necessity ignore it in the intercourse of man with man. If a man puts on a new religion every morning, what is that to you? It is as impertinent to think about a man's religion as about his sources of income or his management of his family. Religion is in no sense the bond of society.[137]

VIII

Liberal commentators on Newman have tried again and again to use Fitzjames Stephen's criticisms of Newman to justify their own detractions of the man and his work, detractions which they contrive to present as somehow corroborated by "history" or "objective criticism," as opposed to what they style, in the vulgar sense of the word, "hagiography."[138] Intent on nullifying Newman's criticism

---

[137] Newman, "Biglietto Speech," 62.

[138] Simon Skinner, Professor of History at Balliol, argued some years ago that if scholars convinced of Newman's integrity did not concede the tenability of Turner's smears against that integrity they were somehow guilty of not being proper historians. "What is at stake," the professor declared, "is the legitimacy and remit of historical inquiry itself." For Skinner, "The difference between [Turner] ... and his critics" was nothing less than the difference "between history and hagiography"— hagiography, that is to say, in the vulgar sense of "whitewashing." And the professor sought to seal his argument by invoking the historian most responsible for laying bare the misrepresentations of Whig history—the very type of history of which Turner and Skinner are themselves unabashed practitioners. "Herbert Butterfield warned as long ago as 1931," Skinner wrote, "that 'The study of the past with one eye on the present is the source of all sins and sophistries in history.'" What is comical about this argument from authority is that the quotation from Butterfield validates not Turner and his acolytes but those whom Skinner accuses of hagiography. Newman's "hagiographical" critics, after all, have never been interested in conforming Newman and his work to any present ideological agenda—certainly not a present liberal agenda. They do not write of Newman to extoll the work of Professor Frank Turner or Cardinal Walter Kasper. They are not neo-Modernists. They

of the liberal creed to which they subscribe themselves, they have cynically appropriated the judge's criticisms to advance their own polemical enterprises. Yet if one looks at the historical record critically, one can see that Fitzjames Stephen's criticisms of Newman were neither accurate nor fair, though they say a good deal about the resentment he felt towards the faith of his youth and, what amounted to the same thing, his inability to share the faith of his father. Like Gibbon, Fitzjames Stephen had embraced the truths of Christianity when young with a certain perfervidity, but once this zealous faith foundered, he took against it with an obsessional vengeance. If reading Gibbon hastened his apostasy, his contempt for Roman Catholicism was inseparable from the prejudices against Rome typical of England's professional middle classes.[139] Nevertheless, what impelled him to abandon Christianity with such passionate animosity cannot be altogether ascribed to the influence of his reading or his class. At the same time, his rejection of Christianity was never thoroughgoing. As his differences with Mill show, he would always have trouble entertaining the possibility of a sustainable social order in which the deterrent terrors of Hell were absent.[140] Moreover, like his father, Fitzjames Stephen believed in providential destiny, at least for the imperial English. Sir James, when engaged in settling northern Australia, for example, had no doubt that colonizing the country was, as he said, "one of those vast schemes of national policy into which Great Britain has been drawn and ... which must be regarded as one of the most impressive movements of Divine Providence in the government of the world."[141] His son would regard England's duty to rule India in a similar light, even though his idea of Providence was a good deal fuzzier. Then, again, like Henry Sidgwick, he might have preened himself on being disabused of what he considered the more fantastic aspects of Christianity, but he still feared that, when it came to embracing agnosticism, his contemporaries might not be so stoical.[142] "I feel much alarmed at the spread of my own opinions," he confessed. "I do not doubt their truth but I greatly doubt the capacity of people to bear them."[143] In all events, as he wrote to Lord Lytton,

---

write of Newman to extoll the work of Newman. For the references to Skinner's article above, see Simon Skinner, "History versus Hagiography: The Reception of Turner's Newman," *Journal of Ecclesiastical History*, 16, no. 4 (October 2010), 781.

[139] Cf. "He admires Gibbon enthusiastically; he has read the 'Decline and Fall' four or five times, and is always wishing to read it again." *Life of Sir James Fitzjames Stephen*, 228.

[140] Frederic Harrison might claim that Fitzjames Stephen "clung to Hell for its utility as a moralising agent in deterring the weak and the vicious from sin and crime," but surely his inability to let go of this central Christian dogma was more complicated than that. Frederic Harrison, *Autobiographic Memoirs* (London: Macmillan, 1911), ii, 88. See also "Introductory Note," in *LD*, xxxi, xiii for Newman's reading of eternal punishment, which he accepted, as he said in "The Development of Religious Error" (1885), later collected in *Stray Essays* (1890), "on the simple word of the Divine Informant."

[141] *ODNB*.

[142] "The reason why I keep strict silence now for many years with regard to theology," Sidgwick wrote [Thomas] Mozley in 1881, "is that while I cannot myself discover adequate rational basis for the Christian hope of happy immortality, it seems to me that the general loss of such a hope from the minds of average human beings as now constituted, would be an evil of which I cannot pretend to measure the extent. I am not prepared to say that the dissolution of the existing social order would follow but I think the danger of such a dissolution would be seriously increased, and the evil would certainly be very great." Sidgwick quoted in Short, *Newman and his Family*, 347–8.

[143] *Life of Sir James Fitzjames Stephen*, 339.

by the time he was fifty his faith was in tatters: "The whole theory about the relations (if any) between God (whatever that may be) and man is so hopelessly obscure that one is reduced to silence."[144] Of course, as his prolific publications show, his silence could often bear an odd resemblance to the most voluble chattering. He certainly spent much of his life obsessing over "the relations (if any) between God (whatever that may be) and man," and, seen in this light, his criticisms of Newman are always more about himself and his lack of faith than they are about Newman, which is another way of saying that they substantiate something Newman said in an essay on rationalism that he wrote long before he became a Catholic: "The rationalist makes himself his own center, not his Maker; he does not go to God, but he implies that God should go to him."[145]

The last epistolary exchange between the two men may serve as a suitable conclusion to their vexed relationship. On 12 February 1876, Fitzjames Stephen wrote Newman: "I daresay you have forgotten my existence, but I had the pleasure of calling upon you in 1854 in company with our common friend Mr. Grant Duff, and again in 1864 in consequence of a review which I wrote on your Apologia when we had a conversation which interested me very much. After twelve years I have an engagement which will lead to my spending a day (Saturday the 26th) in Birmingham. I shall be engaged for the evening, but shall hope to be free during the greater part of the day. It would give me great pleasure to call upon you at any hour you like to appoint and to talk over some of the subjects on which we formerly conversed and on which the varied events of 12 years full of the deepest interest and very varied experience have not changed, but have I think considerably matured and extended my views." Newman's response was cordial but decided.

Feb 14/76

Dear Mr Stephen

I am far indeed from forgetting, as you seem to fancy I may, your kindness in seeking me out in past years, and I feel the honour you do me now in going out of your way to ask of me a controversial meeting. But I hope, my dear Mr Stephen, you will think it neither an uncourtesy to yourself nor a distrust in my own religious professions, if I beg your leave to decline it.

I am no extempore disputant; I never had that presence of mind, happy memory, readiness in argument, and coolness in the "keen encounter of wits,"[146] which are learned in parliamentary debates and courts of law, and are necessary not only for defending but even for stating one's opinion.

And now at my age I have turned from controversy to personal duties suggested by my great change in prospect, and moreover have had all spirit for fight knocked out of me by special bereavements in the course of the last year.

But my main reason for thus writing to you is one which would hold, though my mind were ever so vigorous. The conversations which have already passed between us have served to show me that in matters of religion we unhappily differ

---

[144] Burn, *The Age of Equipoise: A Study of the Mid-Victorian Generation*, 274–5.
[145] Newman, "On the Introduction of Rationalist Principles into Revealed Religion" (1836), *Ess.*, i, 33–4.
[146] *Richard III*, I.ii.115.

in first principles; that each of us assumes, at least implicitly, what the other will not grant, and that in consequence discussion must, from the nature of the case, be nothing else but a melancholy waste of time.

Bear with me in thus writing, and believe me &c &c
J H N[147]

At the end of the copy of his letter, Newman appended this explanatory note: "'NB Mr Stephen has, as he says, called on me three or four times in past years—and, with great modesty of manner, and not saying what he was about, picked my brains, and then gone away reporting to others to my disadvantage, what I had said to him in utter unconsciousness that I was undergoing a cross-examination. This must be considered as a preliminary to a judgment upon the following answer which I propose sending him J H N'" On 15 February, Stephen replied: "I assure you that I fully appreciate the kindness of your letter, and understand the reasons which lead you to the conclusion which it expresses. I will only ask you to acquit me of the great impropriety, for I am sure I should feel it as such, of having wished to challenge you to 'a controversial meeting.' I had wished to talk over matters of the deepest interest with you for the sake of learning if possible where I am wrong. I see however that the conversation would be useless and I hope that you will forgive me for having suggested it."[148] According to Grant Duff, the man who had first introduced Fitzjames Stephen to the convert, Newman replied on 21 February: "I shall be seventy-five; if you chance to remember me then, give me a kind thought."[149]

Was Newman right to refuse to see Fitzjames Stephen? Was the judge asking to meet him merely to engage the cardinal in a "controversial meeting"? Would their meeting result, as Newman thought, in "a melancholy waste of time"? Or was the judge being sincere when he said that he wished to meet in order to see where he had been wrong? We shall never know. Yet considering how frequently Fitzjames Stephen strove to follow in his father's footsteps, one is inclined to believe that he might have wished to meet Newman to apologize. As Quentin Bell shrewdly notes, Fitzjames Stephen might have presented "a façade of stern commonsensicality," but behind it lay "a quivering bundle of vulnerable feelings."[150] His pose of jaunty agnosticism was never as cocksure as he might have wished it to appear. Moreover, men who find themselves in the wrong do occasionally come round. After all, this is what Sir James did, and did rather graciously, after he realized that he had misconstrued Newman's intent in *Loss and Gain*. After receiving Newman's letter of explanation, the old proconsul appended a footnote to his *Essays in Ecclesiastical Biography* (1853), the humility of which might very well have inspired the son to try to reconcile with the man whom he had spent nearly half his life egregiously misrepresenting.

It was on the 18th of July 1853, [Sir James wrote] that I for the first time learnt (and

---

[147] Newman to James Fitzjames Stephen (14 February 1876), *LD*, xxviii, 25–6.
[148] *Ibid.*, 26.
[149] Newman quoted in Sir Mountstuart Elphinstone Grant Duff, *Notes from a Diary, 1873–1881* (London: John Murray, 1898), i, 185.
[150] Bell, *Virginia Woolf: A Biography*, 19.

the evidence which then reached me was altogether conclusive and irresistible …), that I had been mistaken in representing Mr. Newman as having aimed the ridicule and the sarcasms of his novel against those who had formerly been his own disciples, and whose imputed errors were the result of his own teaching; and that those caustic passages had really been designed to chastise the follies of a different class of persons. This discovery imposes on me the obligation of thus publicly and unequivocally apologising to Mr. Newman for having done him that injustice, and for the asperity of the terms in which, under my misconception of his meaning, I referred to him. … While utterly dissenting from the doctrines which [Newman] has recently adopted, I render a willing homage to his genius and his learning, to his mastery of all the resources of our English tongue, to the integrity with which, for conscience sake, he has abandoned so many brilliant prospects and long-cherished attachments, and to the spirit with which he stands erect and fearless in the presence of antipathies and of calumnies before which many a brave man might have quailed. My solicitude not to be numbered among his enemies and calumniators is dictated by my regard, not for him, but for myself; for I am well aware that neither his estimation in the world nor his tranquility of mind is at all dependent on any thing which I have ever written or could ever write respecting him.[151]

---

[151] Sir James Stephen, *Essays in Ecclesiastical Biography* (London: Longman, Brown, Green, and Longmans, 1853), 194–5.

JAMES ANTHONY FROUDE

∽ 6 ∾

The Ambivalent Newmania of James Anthony Froude

> Of all the constituents of human society, an established religion is that which religious men themselves should most desire to be let alone, and which people in general when they are healthy-minded are most sensitive about allowing to be touched.
>
> J. A. Froude, *Short Studies on Great Subjects*

> Far different from Keble, from my brother, from Dr. Pusey, from all the rest, was the true chief of the Catholic revival—John Henry Newman. Compared with him, they were all but as ciphers, and he the indicating number.
>
> J. A. Froude, *Short Studies on Great Subjects*

> Were the Church to treat but one man or woman in these days of ours as three centuries ago she treated tens of thousands, she would be rent in pieces by the common indignation of the entire human race. As it is, she remains doing the work which is still appointed for her. But if an institution with such a history behind it is an exceptional instrument to bear witness to God's existence; if it be the voice through which alone He speaks to man, and makes known His nature and His will; then the attempt to understand this world, and what goes on in it, had better be abandoned in despair.
>
> J. A. Froude, *Short Studies on Great Subjects*

In a memorable passage from his Oxford sermons, John Henry Newman pointed out a truth vital to understanding not only his life's work but how that work was received by his contemporary critics. "Men persuade themselves, with little difficulty, to scoff at principles, to ridicule books, to make sport of the names of good men" he wrote; "but they cannot bear their presence: it is holiness embodied in personal form, which they cannot steadily confront and bear down: so that the silent conduct of a conscientious man secures for him from beholders a feeling different in kind from any which is created by the mere versatile and garrulous Reason."[1] What distinguished James Anthony Froude from Newman's rationalist critics—whether James Fitzjames Stephen, Charles Kingsley or

---

[1] *OS*, 92.

Edwin Abbot—is that as a young man at Oxford he had had a chance to know something of Newman's personal influence, and although he spilled a fair amount of ink afterwards scoffing at the convert's Catholic faith, he could never forget the integrity, grace and magnetism inseparable from that influence. In 1881, in a piece devoted to his memories of Newman at Oriel, he captured this allure with his characteristic élan.

> When I entered at Oxford, John Henry Newman was beginning to be famous. The responsible authorities were watching him with anxiety; clever men were looking with interest and curiosity on the apparition among them of one of those persons of indisputable genius who was likely to make a mark upon his time. His appearance was striking. He was above the middle height, slight. His head was large, his face remarkably like that of Julius Cæsar.[2] The forehead, the shape of the ears and nose, were almost the same. The lines of the mouth were very peculiar, and I should say exactly the same. I have often thought of the resemblance, and believed that it extended to the temperament. In both there was an original force of character which refused to be moulded by circumstances, which was to make its own way, and become a power in the world; a clearness of intellectual perception, a disdain for conventionalities, a temper imperious and wilful, but along with it a most attaching gentleness, sweetness, singleness of heart and purpose. Both were formed by nature to command others; both had the faculty of attracting to themselves the passionate devotion of their friends and followers; and in both cases, too, perhaps the devotion was rather due to the personal ascendency of the leader than to the cause which he represented. It was Cæsar, not the principle of the empire, which overthrew Pompey and the constitution. *Credo in Newmannum* was a common phrase at Oxford, and is still unconsciously the faith of nine tenths of the English converts to Rome.[3]

---

[2] That Froude should have likened Newman to Caesar was typical of his imperial imagination. In his history of the British empire, Piers Brendon (who wrote an excellent biography of Froude's brother Hurrell) notes that the imperial English were fond of seeing themselves in terms of their imperial antecedents. "J. A. Froude opened his biography of Julius Caesar with the statement that 'the English and the Romans resemble one another.' Lord Bryce said that the men who won the Roman Empire and the British Raj 'triumphed through force of character.' In his comparative study of Greater Rome and Greater Britain Sir George Lucas asserted that both peoples possessed 'an innate capacity for ruling'. Such avowals were usually made to boost the confidence of British imperialists." Piers Brendon, *The Decline and Fall of the British Empire 1781–1997* (London: Jonathan Cape, 2007), xvii. Froude took a passionate interest in imperial matters, as his book *Oceana* (1886) attests, though his own views were rather more visionary than those of even the most ardent proconsuls. Speaking of New Zealand, he wrote: "This desert promontory, with its sad green lake and Maori huts and distant smoke-columns, will hereafter be an enormous cockney watering-place, and here it will be that in some sanatarian salon Macaulay's New Zealander, returning from his travels, will exhibit his sketch of the ruins of St. Paul's to groups of admiring young ladies. I have come to believe in that New Zealander since I have seen the country. (Froude, *Oceana*, 236–7). For Froude, New Zealand, not London, would be the new hub of the British Empire and would last even longer than Macaulay's perdurable Catholic Church. See Macaulay's review of Ranke's *History of the Popes* (written in 1840) where, writing of the Catholic Church, he says: "She may still exist in undiminished vigour, when some traveller from New Zealand shall, in the midst of a vast solitude, take his stand on a broken arch of London Bridge to sketch the ruins of St. Pauls."

[3] James Anthony Froude, "The Oxford Counter-Reformation," in his *Short Studies on Great Subjects*, 4 vols. (London: Longmans, Green & Co., 1905), iv, 273–4.

Even here Froude could not resist disparaging the faith that animated much of what he otherwise admired about Newman's "singleness of heart and purpose." Why this should have been the case is a lively question. In this chapter, I shall revisit Froude's work to show how much of it was driven by the historian's deeply personal ambivalence towards a figure whom he could neither follow nor forget. In the course of the chapter, I shall look at what Froude had to say not only about Newman and the Roman Catholicism to which he converted but history, the English Reformation, Protestantism, Anglicanism, the Oxford Movement, the Catholic Revival, dogma, theology, established as opposed to doctrinal religion, and the relation between faith and the affections. Lastly, I shall share with my readers Froude's reviews of two of Newman's most brilliant books, *Essay on the Development of Christian Doctrine* (1845) and the *Essay in Aid of a Grammar of Assent* (1870), from which we can take the historian's critical measure.

I

Before delving into Froude's ambivalence about Newman, I should say something of his life, for his childhood and youth had a great bearing on how he responded to Newman. James Anthony Froude (1818–94) was born at Dartington Rectory in Devon, the son of Robert Hurrell Froude (1770–1859) rector of Denbury and of Dartington from 1799 and archdeacon of Totnes from 1820 until his death. The family consisted of eight children, five sons and three daughters. James Anthony was the younger brother of Hurrell (the eldest), Newman's Tractarian comrade-in-arms and William, the naval engineer, with whom Newman would have a long correspondence. English life teems with stories about how boys were tortured at school—George Orwell had fun with this tradition in his satirical reminiscence "Such, Such Were the Joys" (1952) about his own miserable schooldays—but Froude's case was exceptionally lurid. For three years, he was bullied at Buckfastleigh Vicarage School, his schoolmates stealing his books, mutilating his clothes, beating him unmercifully and depriving him of food. James Anthony's mother, Phyllis Hurrell died when he was two, and even when he was finally taken out of Buckfastleigh the sickly boy was bullied and beaten at home by a father who would not believe that his son had not brought his troubles on himself. Once enrolled in Westminster School, his ordeals only worsened. At home, his brother Hurrell (1803–36) joined gaily in his father's torture of the unhappy boy by taking particular delight in "holding him by the heels over a stream and stirring the mud at the bottom with his head."[4] Froude's first biographer, Herbert Paul adds that "At the mature age of three," James Anthony "was ducked every morning at a trough, to harden him, in the ice-cold water from a spring, and whenever he was in the least degree naughty he was whipped."[5] Throughout most of his childhood, James Anthony had as his "chief consolation" the thought, as he confessed later, that "the consumption which had proved so deadly in our family and was already working in my elder brother's constitution … would soon take me away. I was indifferent about the future, because I did

[4] ODNB.
[5] Herbert Paul, *The Life of Froude* (New York: Charles Scribner's Sons, 1906), 5.

not believe that any future lay before me."[6]

Considering the mistreatment that Froude suffered at the hands of his father, one might be inclined to expect that he would have rebelled against his influence wholesale. Instead, he made his father into something of a paragon. It is speculative to say but one of the reasons he might have done this was to rehabilitate his otherwise fractured relationship with his father. After all, when it came time for him to have a family of his own, he enjoyed fatherhood.[7] Then, again, his kind words about his father and his father's religion might have been written to lay claim to the old man's legacy. Judging from William Froude, the archdeacon went to his grave fond of Newman, which might account for James Anthony's trying to appropriate the old man's memory for his own purposes.[8] His criticism of Newman can often seem an oblique rebuke to his father for cozying up to a man who was, in effect, sabotaging not only his father's but the national religion. In any case, in the same essay in which he spoke at length about his memories of Newman, Froude included this passage about his father and his father's religion—probably the single most useful key to understanding why Froude spent so much of his life not only obsessing about but abusing Newman. "My father was rector of the parish," the historian recalled.

> He was archdeacon, he was justice of the peace. He had a moderate fortune of his own, consisting chiefly in land, and he belonged, therefore, to the "landed interest." Most of the magistrates' work of the neighborhood passed through his hands. If anything was amiss, it was his advice which was most sought after, and I remember his being called upon to lay a troublesome ghost. In his younger days he had been a hard rider across country. His children knew him as a continually busy, useful man of the world, a learned and cultivated antiquary, and an accomplished artist. My brothers and I were excellently educated, and were sent to school and college. Our spiritual lessons did not go beyond the Catechism. We were told that our business in life was to work and to make an honorable position for ourselves. About doctrine, Evangelical or Catholic, I do not think that in my early boyhood I ever heard a single word, in church or out of it. The institution had drifted into the condition of what I should call moral health. It did not instruct us in mysteries, it did not teach us to make religion a special object of our thoughts; it taught us to use religion as a light by which to see our way along

---

[6] Froude quoted in Waldo Hilary Dunn, *James Anthony Froude: A Biography*, 2 vols (Oxford: Oxford University Press, 1961), i, 39. Paul confirms this source of his subject's puerile gloom: "Before Anthony Froude, the youngest of eight, was three years old, his mother died of a decline [consumption], and within a few years the same illness proved fatal to five of her children. The whole aspect of life at Dartington was changed. The Archdeacon retired into himself and nursed his grief in silence—melancholy, isolated, austere." Paul, *Life of Froude*, 5.

[7] Ciaran Brady, *James Anthony Froude: An Intellectual Biography of a Victorian Prophet* (Oxford: Oxford University Press, 2013), 175. Dunn says that Froude's fatherhood influenced the historian's view of the Dissolution of the Monasteries. "In his opinion the Reformation was mainly a protest against the vile habits of the clergy. As a decent family man, Froude naturally objected to a celibate clergy." Dunn, *Froude: A Biography*, 8.

[8] When writing on 23 February 1859 to Newman of the Archdeacon's death, William Froude described "with what unfailing interest he always spoke of your Mediterranean expedition … and how in going over these scenes, he has always dwelt with particular pleasure on the share you had in them." *LD*, xix, 49.

the road of duty. Without the sun our eyes would be of no use to us; but if we look at the sun we are simply dazzled, and can see neither it nor anything else. It is precisely the same with theological speculations. If the beacon lamp is shining, a man of healthy mind will not discuss the composition of the flame. Enough if it shows him how to steer and keep clear of shoals and breakers. To this conception of the thing we had practically arrived. Doctrinal controversies were sleeping. People went to church because they liked it, because they knew that they ought to go, and because it was the custom. They had received the Creeds from their fathers, and doubts about them had never crossed their minds. Christianity had wrought itself into the constitution of their natures. It was a necessary part of the existing order of the universe, as little to be debated about as the movements of the planets or the changes of the seasons.[9]

This was the serene, unreflecting idyll that Froude would never forgive Newman for unsettling—an idyl in which bothering oneself about "the metaphysics of doctrine,"[10] to use the historian's phrase, was considered not only bad form but vicious. What makes the idyll particularly arresting, however, is that although variations of it appear throughout Froude's work it was largely imaginary. We have already seen what a miserable childhood Froude had with a father who was cold, unjust, abusive and the reverse of philoprogenitive. Young Froude, solitary and desolate, spent most of his time reading; like Gibbon, he read for company; one can see the extent of his reading in his essays.[11] But one can also see that such morose reading led Froude, as it had led Gibbon, to indulge in a certain amount of unhappy make-believe. And nowhere was this make-believe more manifest

---

[9] Froude, "The Oxford Counter-Reformation," 241–2. Surtees has an amusing passage on the nostalgia for better days. "He had lived in good times, when gentlemen were gentlemen, and trusted their land agents implicitly, never troubling themselves with farming or interfering with their tenants' occupations in any shape or way, taking everything for granted, including both facts and figures. Still Lonnergan was a noted old screw in his own affairs, never missing a chance anywhere, and always on the watch for discount. He was too good a judge to receive tenant-farmer testimonials himself, but Mrs. Lonnergan was open to the reception of any number—vases, inkstands, butter-coolers, fruit-stands, etc. A guest leaving his house one dark night mistook his lordship for the servant in the passage, and gave him a shilling, saying, 'There, there's a shilling for you, and mind your master doesn't get hold of it.'" R. S. Surtees, *Mr. Facey Romford's Hounds* (London: Bradbury & Evans, 1865), 126.

[10] Ibid., 239.

[11] In one of Froude's essays, comparing English writers of the 18th-century with those of his own day, he writes: "Our English-speaking forefathers in the last century it seems were poor creatures, yet they had contrived to achieve considerable success in most departments of human affairs. They founded empires; they invented steam engines; they produced a Chatham, a Clive, a Warren Hastings, a Washington, a Franklin, a Nelson—a longer list of illustrious names than there is need to mention. Their literature might not equal the Elizabethan, but it was noteworthy in its way. A period which had produced Pope and Swift, Sterne and Fielding, Johnson and Goldsmith, Hume and Gibbon, Butler and Berkeley, was not so entirely shallow. Men had fixed beliefs in those days. Over the pool of uncertainties in which our own generation is floundering there was then a crust of undisturbed conviction on which they could plant their feet and step out like men. Their thoughts, if not deep, were clear and precise; their actions were bold and strong. A good many years, perhaps a good many hundreds of years, will have to pass before as sound books will be written again, or deeds done with as much pith and mettle in them." Froude, "The Oxford Counter-Reformation," 244–5. It is interesting that Froude should exclude Burke from his pantheon here, perhaps because he thought him too associated with Roman Catholicism. See Emily Jones, *Edmund Burke and the Invention of Modern Conservatism, 1830–1914* (Oxford: Oxford University Press, 2017), 48, 80.

than in the utopia he concocted to accommodate his father's established religion, a utopia which, as G. M. Young notes, "Froude declared to be the golden age of the Church, when her princes were still princes, and her pastors enforced the simple morality and administered the simple consolations of village life, with the authority due rather to personal character, birth and learning, than to any pretensions as priests."[12] It was also an idyll, the sardonic wit in Froude noted, in which the National Church had "drifted into ... what I should call moral health," by which the historian meant that it actually practiced what it professed. In other words, the Church was "not to be an object of thought, but a guide to action. Life was a journey in which there were many temptations and many pitfalls. Religion was the lanthorn by which we could see our way on the dark road." For the retrospective Froude, "The Christianity of my childhood was the light to our feet and the lamp of our ways, perhaps the ideal conception of what religion ought to be."[13] His abiding adult complaint was that this eminently moral religion should have devolved into the broad church idea of national religion—a thing which was neither instructive nor edifying. Indeed, it was best personified by the character of Grimes in Evelyn Waugh's Decline and Fall (1928), the same Grimes who assures the novel's hapless hero, Paul Pennyfeather: "When you've been in the soup as often as I have, it gives you the sort of feeling that everything's for the best, really. You know, God's in His heaven; all's right with the world. I can't quite explain it, but I don't believe one can ever be unhappy for long provided one does exactly as one wants to and when one wants to."[14]

Once enrolled in Oriel College in 1835, where his father had also gone, Froude's brother Hurrell duly died of consumption. After leaving Oxford, Froude decided against the church, medicine and schoolmastering to set up shop as an historian. Working with Newman on his *Lives of the Saints* had opened his eyes to the appeal of history, though he claimed that Newman was hardly an exemplary mentor. "Rationalise when the evidence is weak," Froude claimed Newman had told him, "and that will give credibility when you can show the evidence is strong." In concluding his life of St. Neot, Froude quipped: "This is all, and perhaps rather more than all that is known of his life." No hagiographer ever had so memorable a debut, though it is hard to imagine Newman uttering such flippant nonsense.

Froude might have been ordained in 1845, but after Oxford banned and, indeed, burned his autobiographical novel, *The Nemesis of Faith* (1849) and stripped him of his Exeter Fellowship, he was ripe for repudiating an Anglican faith in which he could no longer believe and converting to another faith more suitable to the contrarian in him, though Froude's contrarianism was always laced with an odd amalgam of conformity.[15] The biographer Julia Markus is

[12] G. M. Young, *Portrait of an Age: Victorian England*, 2nd edn (Oxford: Oxford University Press, 1953), 55.
[13] From Froude's autobiographical fragment, quoted in Algernon Cecil, *Six Oxford Thinkers* (London: John Murray 1909), 109.
[14] Evelyn Waugh, *Decline and Fall* (London: Chapman & Hall, 1928), 42–3.
[15] Cf. "I have done your bidding and read Froude's book [*The Nemesis of Faith*] with what depth of interest I need not tell you. It is ... a very profitable book. ... For myself I have felt more than ever since I read it how impossible it is to find any substitute for the old faith. If after all that experience a man cannot ask the God of Truth to give him His Spirit of Truth to guide him into all truth, what is left? but just what he describes—doubt—not merely of existence, but of doubt

good on how the publication of the scandalous novel affected Froude's already strained relationship with his father.

> The archdeacon was disgraced by the book. His close associate, the Archbishop of Exeter, wrote to the rector with compassion for the "truly venerable" octogenarian. For he had suffered one of the heaviest afflictions of this world, "the consciousness of having given birth to one who perverts no ordinary endowments to the corruption of his fellow men—and to the more presumptuous defiance of his God!" His father was at the end of his rope and disinherited Anthony. "Perplexed as I believe he was, he came to the wisest resolution possible," Anthony wrote years later. "As I had persisted in declining the established roads and choosing a way of my own, he determined that I should be made to feel the meaning of what I was doing. As I would not do what he had wished, I must be left in the water to find bottom for myself where I could." The archdeacon would not support him, would not talk to him, write to him, or allow him to return home. So sharp and clean was this separation that Anthony, in the first throes of liberation, felt no pain, only release."[16]

And, fittingly, it was at this point, when father and son had completely fallen out, that Froude fell under the sway of Thomas Carlyle, to whom he was introduced in London in 1849.

The influence Carlyle had on Froude was immense. Everything in the younger man's life before he met the Scottish author could almost have been combined to make its reception inevitable. The breakdown of his relationship with his father, his estrangement from his father's faith, his loss of his Exeter fellowship, his experience of death, his experience of the tyranny of power, his delight in the written word, his fascination with history, his longing for belief—all conduced to make Carlyle's influence not only pervasive but creative. His unflinchingly critical biography of Carlyle bears this out. And yet, for all its creativity, Carlyle's influence was deleterious. It reinforced Froude's *penchant* for flippancy; it exacerbated his many unresolved contradictions, especially as regards his vexed relationship to Christian belief; and, perhaps most lamentably, it caused him to assume the pose of Carlylean prophecy, which might have given his writings their literary *frisson* but denied them any intellectual, moral or spiritual coherence. If the

---

itself, doubt whether every superstition may not be real, every lie a fact. It is undoubted that such a state of mind is possible, yes, is near to all of us; Froude is no false witness. But if it is possible there must be some one to bring us out of it, clearly the deliverance is not in ourselves. And what is the Bible after all but the history of a deliverer—of God proclaiming Himself as man's deliverer from the state into which he is ever ready to sink, a state of slavery to systems, superstitions, the world, himself,—Atheism? The book is good for this, it brings us to the root of things, and there is nothing, or there is God. It is good for this, it shows that God must come forth and do the work for us, and that all the religions we make for ourselves, whatever names we give them, are miserable mutilated attempts to fashion Him after our image, with yet such fragments of truth as show that we are formed in His. What is His admirable sketch of Newmanism and its effects but a declaration of this truth? In fact, the whole book read backwards, aye or forwards ... is a book of evidences which to my mind at least is worth all Paley and Lardner." Frederick Denison Maurice to Charles Kinglsey (9 March 1849), *The Life of Frederick Maurice Denison*, i, 516–17.

[16] Julia Markus: *James Anthony Froude: The Last Undiscovered Great Victorian* (New York: Scribner, 2007), 43–4.

pose of Carlylean prophecy degenerates in Carlyle into unreadable self-parody, it descends to travesty in Froude. This was especially the case in his attempts to make Henry VIII and Oliver Cromwell Carlylean heroes. Carlyle's conception of the hero and hero-worship might have been inherently wrongheaded but it was always more nuanced than Froude's.[17] As Chesterton nicely observed: "The supreme glory of Carlyle was that he heard the veritable voices of the Cosmos. He left it to others to attune them into an orchestra. Sometimes the truth he heard was this truth, that some men are to be commanded and some obeyed; sometimes that deeper and more democratic truth that all men are above all things to be pitied."[18] The problem with Froude is that he adopted the first truth without ever making allowance for the second.

In his biography of Carlyle, Froude wrote of how the Scottish writer struggled to earn a living from writing without ruining his talent. According to Froude, after publishing *Sartor Resartus* (1833), Carlyle prepared "to find … if possible, some humble employment to which his past work might have recommended him; to launch himself, at any rate, into the great world, and light on something among its floating possibilities to save him from drowning, which of late had seemed likely to be his fate."[19] Making his wife's family farm at Craigenputtock his home in the remote moorlands of Scotland had proven unsustainable. Moreover, Carlyle found, as many before and after him have found, that submitting articles to reviews did not pay the bills, while the drudgery and time required for potboiling distracted him from proper work. Even the higher journalism, Froude recognized, "if it was to be profitable, must become an intellectual prostitution"; and it was to escape this all-too-common fate that Carlyle decided to leave Scotland and settle in London. As it was, although for a time he tried his hand at lecturing, at which he was only modestly successful, he did manage to dedicate most of his time to the writing of books, the royalties from which kept

---

[17] G. K. Chesterton is good on Carlyle's preoccupation with the heroic. "Carlyle set himself the impossible task of making heroes out of the successful men of history and politics", he wrote in one of his pieces for the *London Illustrated News*. "It was not much more hopeful than that of making heroes out of the successful men in soap or petrol. In one sense that sort of hero-worship is heroic, in the sense of being impossible. The task is heroic because the subject is unheroic. In Carlyle's characteristic work it soon ran into absurdity. It reached the point of praising Frederick the Great—a form of hero-worship which is clearly a *reductio ad absurdum*, and even almost a contradiction in terms. The character of Cromwell had more human elements; but what was best in it was human and emphatically not heroic. The best case for Cromwell is that he was a moderately sane man in a very insane age. His best work was done as a moderator and maker of compromises; not as an originator or inspirer of enthusiasms. He saved works of art which the wilder Puritans would have destroyed; but we cannot picture him as a great patron of art in the sense of a friend of artists. He insisted that there must be good pay for good soldiers; but he was not the sort of man to be a romance to his own soldiers, like Napoleon. He was a seventeenth-century English squire, whose family had grown rich in the great pillage; and morally he was no worse than most of his kind, and perhaps better than many of them. He was certainly much better than Frederick the Great, whom Carlyle made even more of a hero, and even a god." G. K. Chesterton, "On Heroes and History" (18 October 1924), *The Collected Works of G. K. Chesterton: Volume 33: The Illustrated London News 1923–1925*, ed. Lawrence Clipper, George Marlin and Edwin Swan (San Francisco, 1990), 425–6.

[18] G. K. Chesterton, *Collected Works: Volume XVIII: Carlyle, Tolstoy, Stevenson, Chaucer*, with introduction and notes by Russell Kirk (San Francisco: Ignatius Press, 1991), 27.

[19] J. A. Froude, *Life of Thomas Carlyle*, 2 vols (New York: Scribner's & Son, 1882), i, 129–30.

the bailiffs at bay. By the 1850s, however, even after his *Collected Works* (1856) had received glowing reviews, he could still not shake the feeling that his work had left him immured within "enormous rubbish-mountains."[20] Froude's own far-ranging essays—ultimately gathered together into the five-volume *Short Studies on Great Subjects* (1890)—left him overshadowed by similar mountains.

Yet, what was ultimately most destructive about Carlyle's influence on Froude was that it accelerated the younger man's loss of faith. Frederick Denison Maurice saw this clearly enough. "I am quite certain that we do not become reconciled to any confused or manichæan views of God," he wrote to his good friend Charles Kingsley,

> but that the Bible helps us out of them, and that, not by suggesting cunning explanations and apologies for the acts which it speaks of, but by leading us to look at them more simply, more according to the letter. I speak confidently. I wish to put all upon this issue. Froude's hero did not. He gave himself no fair chance. He adopted the Newmanic theory. He gave God credit for being a tyrant. Then he plunged into Carlyleism and believed that he could look all things in the face and make no theories. Then he took orders, undertook to preach of God, whom he believed that the Bible misrepresented, [and] undertook to face Nature while he was shirking it. Out of such a confusion the result must have been what he says it was. But if he had clung to his belief in God which his childhood gave him instead of falling into a religion about God which the Puseyites gave him, or into a religion of Man which he drew from Carlyle, would it not have been just otherwise? Would not that belief in God have made him capable of meeting the new problem of boyhood and manhood instead of being merely linked as he supposes it was to the associations and memories of infancy? Yes! Religion against God. This is the heresy of our age, as Irving said long ago,—how often have I blessed him for the words,—and this is leading to the last most terrific form of infidelity.[21]

After his father cut him off, Froude had no alternative but to earn his living by his pen. He wrote reviews and long essays for the *Westminster Review*, *Quarterly Review*, *Nineteenth Century*, *Longman's Review* and *Fraser's Magazine* to free himself to write his wonderfully *outré* Tudor and Irish histories.[22] For fourteen years, he was editor for *Fraser's*, a tenure which enabled him to give voice to most of his abiding preoccupations, including "his anticlericalism, his high esteem for the Reformation and all its works, his hatred of current Ritualist and Ultramontane movements and of all dogmatic views, his distrust of democracy, his reluctant but inescapable 'rationalism.'"[23] It is true that the precariousness of professional scribbling was made not entirely intolerable by the £300 a year that his wife, Charlotte Grenfell brought to their marriage, but it is also true that he was indefatigably

---

[20] Froude quoted in *ODNB*.
[21] Maurice to Charles Kingsley (9 March 1849), Maurice, *The Life of Frederick Denison Maurice*, i, 518.
[22] For a complete list of Froude's reviews and essays, see Brady, 74–81.
[23] Oscar Maurer, Jr, "Froude and *Fraser's Magazine*, 1860–1874," *The University of Texas Studies in English*, 28 (1949), pp. 213–43.

prolific. The essays and books that resulted are not of an invariably high quality. Improvisational zest, rather than scholarly exactitude characterizes much of his work. Still, a good English style gives his writings a consistent readability.

Certainly, the bookman Augustine Birrell recognized that the bookman in Froude appealed to an audience fond of having its history served up with a certain *panache*, without worrying unduly whether it was accurate. "Never let us speak disrespectfully of accuracy, of research, of stern veracity, of unbiassed judgments, or lightly confer the grave title of historian upon hasty rhetoricians who have refused to take pains," Birrell wrote in an essay on Froude; "but the fact remains that for the ordinary thinking man who has taken his degree, an ounce of mother-wit is often worth a pound of clergy, and that even the so-called history of an inaccurate genius may be not only more amusing but more profitable reading than the blameless work of a duller nature."[24]

It was the "ordinary thinking man" to whom Froude appealed, not dons; all of his books, including his 12-volume history of England and his history of the English in Ireland in the eighteenth century sold well; and although the accuracy of his scholarship was attacked in his own day by the now unreadable historian of the Anglo-Saxons, Edward A. Freeman, it has since been defended by G. R. Elton, whose anti-Catholic Tudor histories opened the door to the popular scurrilities of Hilary Mantel. For Elton, Froude "reversed the common judgment of the day on the two foremost members of the House of Tudor, elevating Henry VIII and depressing Elizabeth." As a result, "Henry VIII remained a hero to his next biographer, A. F. Pollard, who prudently discarded some of Froude's extravagant praise but concurred in the general view that here was a great king personally building a nation's greatness and behaving as morally as a statesman, constrained by circumstances, might."[25] Pollard would also write an excellent entry on Froude in the *Dictionary of National Biography*, remarking dryly in one passage: "His 'History of England' is an historical drama, representing the triumph of the Reformation over the powers of darkness typified by Philip of Spain and the pope of Rome; and Froude himself admits that the dramatic poet 'is not bound when it is inconvenient to what may be called the accidents of fact.'"[26]

---

[24] Augustine Birrell, "Essays and Addresses" (New York: Charles Scribner's Son, 1907), 165.

[25] J. R. Elton, "J. A. Froude and his History of England," in *Studies in Tudor and Stuart Politics and Government*, iii: *Papers and Reviews 1973-1981* (Cambridge: Cambridge University Press, 1983), 410.

[26] A. F. Pollard, *DNB*, xxii, Supplement. Curiously enough, Froude's "dramatic" sense of historical interpretation influenced Hilaire Belloc, who attended his Oxford lectures after Salisbury made the historian Oxford's Regent Professor of History. While most readers assume that Belloc's unabashedly biased history came of his devotion to the Faith; this is only partially true. It also came of his delight in Froude, about whom he wrote: "Froude had this merit—a merit he shared with Huxley alone of his contemporaries—that he imposed his convictions. He fought against resistance. He excited (and still excites) violent animosity. He exasperated the surface of his time and was yet too strong for that surface to reject him. This aggressive and combative quality in him ... should arrest any one who may make a general survey of the last generation in letters." Hilaire Belloc, "Introduction," in Froude, *Short Studies on Great Subjects*, 2 vols. (Londong, J. M. Dent & Sons, 1906), i, ix. Belloc also convinced himself that Froude was a "borderland" Catholic: "He was, I think, like a man who has felt the hands of a woman and heard her voice, who knows them so thoroughly well that he can love, criticize, or despise according to his mood; but who has never seen her face." *Ibid.*, xxi.

Readers should always keep this in mind when reading Froude on Newman.

The historian John Pemble, in a review of Brady's intellectual biography, nicely captured the provocative *éclat* of Froude's history:

> A mammoth work on the Tudors was the last thing anyone wanted; and when Froude's appeared it was the last thing anyone expected. It exasperated and thrilled as it pushed back the frontier of modernity by 150 years and overturned traditional evaluations. Henry VIII wasn't a coarse and cruel tyrant, but the deliverer of his people and the founder of the modern state. Anne Boleyn wasn't the innocent victim of a monster's caprice, but a nymphomaniac and serial adulteress who was properly tried and legally executed. Thomas More, the genial philosopher, was not a saint but a sadistic bigot. The real Mary Tudor wasn't the hate figure of myth. Pious, well-meaning and emotionally fragile, she'd been manipulated by Cardinal Pole, a ruthless éminence rouge with his sights on the papacy. Mary Queen of Scots wasn't a tragic romantic heroine but a lethal combination of beauty, intelligence and homicidal infatuation—"a dangerous animal which had run into a trap ... a bad woman, disguised in the livery of a martyr." Elizabeth I wasn't an Amazonian mastermind rallying the free world against the forces of darkness. Although her portraits "are usually without shadow, as if her features radiated light," she was muddled, volatile, indecisive and impulsive, and would have floundered without Burghley, the power behind the throne and saviour of her and her realm. The navigators and privateers weren't despicable buccaneers, but knights of the sea upholding chivalry and national honour. Most startling of all was Froude's reassessment of the age as a whole. "For the rack, the thumbscrew, the Tower dungeons," he wrote, "no detestation can be too strong, no gratitude too vehement that we have left them, with stake and wheel and red-hot pincers ... long and forever behind us." Yet here were all those "ferocious refinements of another age" graphically recalled, with the message attached that this was an epoch to make England proud.[27]

In addition to coming to the defense of Henry VIII,[28] when his reputation was at an all-time low,[29] Froude was one of the first English historians to follow Ranke's lead and mine archives, though he never shared the German historian's

---

[27] John Pemble, "Resurrecting the Tudors," *London Review of Books*, 35, no. 10 (23 May 2013).

[28] Cf. "In his history, Froude portrayed the English Reformation as a moral victory in the struggle for human freedom and intellectual honesty. The Reformation was not political and unprincipled; the reformers were not frightened sycophants; the opponents of the reform such as More and Mary of Scotland were not heroes or heroines; there was no mediaeval Catholic Utopia destroyed by iconoclastic Protestants. Instead, there were strong, good men fighting a strong, good fight. So Froude saw the Reformation as something not politically but morally necessary. The monasteries were dissolved not because Henry needed money but because they were offensive; the spoils went to serve educational and national defence purposes and not to line the pockets of Henry and his courtiers. England's independence of Rome was declared because she would govern herself and not be ruled by loathsome priests. Henry rid himself of Anne Boleyn because she was guilty. Lord Burghley was not simply a canny statesman but also a defender of the faith." Rosemary O'Day, *The Debate on the English Reformation* (London: Methuen, 1986), 91.

[29] Dickens followed most of his contemporaries in regarding the Eighth Henry as "a most intolerable ruffian, a disgrace to human nature, and a blot of blood and grease upon the History of England." Charles Dickens, *Master Humphrey's Clock and A Child's History of England*, ed. Derek Hudson (Oxford: Oxford University Press, 1958), 390.

simple-minded belief that archives *per se* could enable the historian to present the past *wie es eigentlich gewesen ist*. Although often associated with German historians because of his association with Carlyle, Froude was sceptical of their grandiose philosophizing of history.

> There is the philosophy of the German idealists, of which I was once a more ardent student than I have been in later years. Hegel was a supremely eminent man, to be spoken of with all possible respect. Hegel said when he was dying, "that after all his efforts there was but one man in Germany who understood what he meant," and then added, as a painful after-thought, "and he does not understand me." It is a notice-board warning strangers against trespassing on such uninviting premises: we live in an age when much that is real is to be learnt, and when the time to learn it is no longer than it used to be.[30]

While Froude liked to imagine that he was wary of the unreal—a wariness that never left Newman—he did not always bother to be accurate about facts. Indeed, when it came to accuracy, he was skeptical. Facts, after all, come to us "through the minds of those who recorded them, neither machines nor angels, but fallible creatures, with human passions and prejudices." Indeed, "The address of history is less to the understanding than to the higher emotions," he wrote in "The Science of History" (1864). "We learn in it to sympathize with what is great and good; we learn to hate what is base. In the anomalies of fortune we feel the mystery of our mortal existence, and in the companionship of the illustrious natures who have shaped the fortunes of the world, we escape from the littlenesses which cling to the round of common life, and our minds are turned to a higher and nobler key."[31] Since Froude was keen on making invidious comparisons between English writers of the eighteenth and nineteenth centuries in order to show up the deficiencies of the latter, it is worth noting what a pallid echo the passage just quoted from his work is of Samuel Johnson's in *A Journey to the Western Islands* (1775), where the great moralist famously observed:

> Whatever withdraws us from the power of our senses; whatever makes the past, the distant, or the future predominate over the present, advances us in the dignity of thinking beings. Far from me: and from my friends, be such frigid philosophy as may conduct us indifferent and unmoved over any. ground which has been dignified by wisdom, bravery, or virtue. That man is little to be envied, whose patriotism would not gain force upon the plain of Marathon, or whose piety would not grow warmer among the ruins of Iona![32]

If relying on history to understand the past was problematic, relying on it to predict the future was even more so. "We live in times of disintegration," Froude reminded his readers, "and none can tell what will be after us."[33] History itself was eloquent of how wrong historical prognostications had been over the cen-

---

[30] "Scientific Method Applied to History," in *Short Studies*, ii, 594.
[31] "The Science of History," in *Short Studies*, i, 37.
[32] *The Yale Edition of the Works of Samuel Johnson Volume IX: A Journey to the Western Islands of Scotland* (New Haven: Yale University Press, 1971), 148.
[33] "The Science of History," in *Short Studies*, i, 37.

turies. Froude himself was grossly wrong when he gave out that the Tractarians' opposition to liberalism was misguided, indeed alarmist. For Froude, there was a certain "inflation" about the way in which "the Catholic revivalists went to their work." Why? "Our age perhaps has a mistaken idea of its consequence. All its geese are swans, and every new enemy is a monster never before heard of. The *Edinburgh Review* and Brougham, and Mackintosh and the Reform Ministry, and Low Church philosophy and the London University were not so very terrible. But as the windmills were giants to the knight of La Mancha, so the Whigs of those days were to young Oxford apostles the forerunners of Antichrist. Infidelity was rushing in upon us. Achilles must rise from his tent, and put on his celestial armor. The Church must reassert herself in majesty to smite and drive back the proud aggressive intellect. The excitement was unnecessary."[34] Now, when the unshriven intellect continues to dehumanize men at the behest of an ever more progressive liberalism, the historian's dismissal of Newman's warnings against "the all-corroding, all-dissolving scepticism of the intellect" can be seen to have been deeply mistaken.[35] Indeed, the unreliability of Froude's own prognostications illustrates the unreliability of most of the historical predictions made in his own time, about which he was clear-sighted. "The temper of each new generation is a continual surprise," Froude wrote.

> The Fates delight to contradict our most confident expectations. Gibbon believed that the era of conquerors was at an end. Had he lived out the full life of man, he would have seen Europe at the feet of Napoleon. But a few years ago we believed the world had grown too civilized for war, and the Crystal Palace in Hyde Park was to be the inauguration of a new era. Battles bloody as Napoleon's are now the familiar tale of every day; and the arts which have made greatest progress are the arts of destruction. What next? We may strain our eyes into the future which lies beyond this waning century; but never was conjecture more at fault. It is blank darkness, which even the imagination fails to people.[36]

Another aspect of history that the literary historian in Froude recognized was its necessary selectiveness, which also complicated the contention that history could somehow be regarded as scientific. In a lecture delivered at the Royal Institution in February of 1864, he confirmed that there was "something incongruous in the very connection of such words as Science and History. It is as if we were to talk of the colour of sound, or the longitude of the rule-of-three. Where it is so difficult to make out the truth on the commonest disputed fact in matters passing under our very eyes, how can we talk of a science in things long past, which come to us only through books? It often seems to me as if History was like a child's box of letters, with which we can spell any word we please. We have only to pick out such letters as we want, arrange them as we like, and say nothing about those which do not suit our purpose."[37] After Ruskin attended the lecture, he wrote his friend with his usual candor: "I am very glad to have

---

[34] "The Oxford Counter-Reformation," in *Short Studies*, iv, 245.
[35] *Apo.*, 243.
[36] "The Science of History," in *Short Studies*, i, 27.
[37] *Ibid.*, 1.

the lecture. It is very nice, but it seems to me a great talk, and wise one, about what nevertheless could have been settled in two sentences. There is no law of history any more than of a kaleidoscope. With certain bits of glass—shaken so, and so—you will get pretty figures, but what figures, heaven only knows. Add definite attractions and repulsions to the angles of the tube—your figures will have such and such modifications. But the history of the world will be for ever new."[38]

Froude justly poured scorn on the extravagant claims made for history in the age of Ranke and Acton, though Newman's understanding of the matter was infinitely more incisive. In one of his Oxford sermons, Newman wrote of how the very patterns of history could conceal the Truth:

> the warfare between Error and Truth is necessarily advantageous to the former, from its very nature, as being conducted by set speech or treatise; and this, not only for a reason already assigned, the deficiency of Truth in the power of eloquence, and even of words, but moreover from the very neatness and definiteness of method required in a written or spoken argument. Truth is vast and far-stretching, viewed as a system; and, viewed in its separate doctrines, it depends on the combination of a number of various, delicate, and scattered evidences; hence it can scarcely be exhibited in a given number of sentences. If this be attempted, its advocate, unable to exhibit more than a fragment of the whole, must round off its rugged extremities, and unite its straggling lines, by much the same process by which an historical narrative is converted into a tale. This, indeed, is the very *art* of composition, which, accordingly, is only with extreme trouble preserved clear of exaggeration and artifice; and who does not see that all this is favourable to the cause of error,—to that party which has not faith enough to be patient of doubt, and has just talent enough to consider perspicuity the chief excellence of a writer?[39]

Interestingly enough, Ruskin nicely confirmed the truth of Newman's point here, when, in a lecture delivered at Oxford in 1884, entitled "Protestantism: The Pleasures of Truth" he quoted a passage from Carlyle's life of Frederick the Great to show how "the very *art* of composition" could falsify. Here is the passage from Carlyle to which Ruskin referred:

> Protestant or not Protestant? The question meant everywhere: "Is there anything of nobleness in you, O Nation, or is there nothing? Are there, in this Nation, enough of heroic men to venture forward, and to battle for God's Truth versus the Devil's Falsehood, at the peril of life and more? Men who prefer death, and all else, to living under Falsehood, who, once for all, will not live under Falsehood; but having drawn the sword against it (the time being come for that rare and important step), throw away the scabbard, and can say, in pious clearness, with their whole soul: "Come on, then! Life under Falsehood is not good for me; and we will try it out now. Let it be to the death between us, then!"[40]

---

[38] Ruskin to Froude (February, 1864), *The Works of John Ruskin: The Letters of John Ruskin, 1827–1889*, ed. E. T. Cook And Alexander Wedderburn (London: George Allen, 1909), 465.
[39] OS, 89–90.
[40] Carlyle quoted in John Ruskin, *Selected Writings*, ed. Richard Lansdown (Oxford: Oxford University Press, 2019), 366.

The art critic's response to Carlyle's paean to Protestantism, which the historian saw, with his typical rhetorical exuberance, as wholly beneficial to the nations it transformed, was a nice critique of the zeal Froude would never question

> Protestantism is ... the appeal of Truth against wanton or impious imagination, essential truth of character against the Desire and Love of Lies; and truth of observation against insanity or conjecture; in Religion it is the strength of simplicity, which knows the law of duty and, by experience, the Help of God in answer to prayer, and asserts this personal knowledge of God against theology which is only tradition, or history which is intentionally fictitious. But, since denial is always easy, understanding always difficult, and experience only the reward of perseverance (patience worketh experience, and experience hope), the strength of Protestantism is only found among laborious and unambitious peasantry; in all its half-educated and aggressive forms it merely means the scorn of persons incapable of thought for the things they have never thought of, and of persons who will not look for the things they have not. It is the natural enmity of the material to the spiritual, and of the base to the pure; the law which it arrogantly fulfils becomes its worst corruption; and the truth to which it narrowly consents, a totality of lie.[41]

In the same lecture, Ruskin quoted Froude haranguing his readers on what he claimed was the Catholic faith's culpability not only for the Massacre of St Bartholomew but nearly every other murderous outrage committed in Europe. For Froude, the "horrors of the French Revolution were a mere bagatelle, a mere summer shower" compared to "the atrocities committed in the name of religion, and with the sanction of the Catholic Church." Ruskin's response to this sectarian hyperbole was that: "the Catholic religion [was] no more answerable for the death of Coligny than that of Joan of Arc, and ... no more to be judged in the person of her corrupt kings and priests than the Law of Moses in Herod and Caiaphas." As far as Ruskin could see, "in the disputes between men of the world professing contrary views of religion ... either side will commit crimes of which their adversaries will rejoice to tell the story ... but the wonderful thing is that, professing the strictest love of truth, Protestant history is always the falsest."[42] And the case in point to which he referred was the historian whom he called "one of the ... faithfullest of Protestant historians—wholly candid in heart—Froude."[43] However, being a loyal friend of Froude, Ruskin admirably defended the historian against the criticisms of Charles Eliot Norton: "I don't like what you say of Froude. I like the man, and have learned much from his work. If it is romance, it is unintentionally so, and at present, to me, unique among history-work since Thucydides, for being of no side."[44]

---

[41] *Ibid.*, 372.
[42] Ruskin quoted in *Ruskin: Selected Writings*, 369.
[43] Froude quoted *ibid.*, 369.
[44] Ruskin to Charles Eliot Norton (5 October 1875), *The Letters of John Ruskin*, 181.

II

Like Carlyle, Froude was drawn to history because he had things to say that only the writing of history could enable him to say. In his novel, *The Nemesis of Faith* (1849), Froude has his hero exclaim:

> Oh, how I wish I could write! I try sometimes; for I seem to feel myself overflowing with thoughts, and I cry out to be relieved of them. But it is so stiff and miserable when I get anything done. What seemed so clear and liquid comes out so thick, stupid, and frost-bitten, that I myself, who put the idea there, can hardly find it for shame if I go look for it a few days after. Still, if there was chance for me! To be an author—to make my thought the law of other minds!—to form a link, however humble, a real living link, in the electric chain which conducts the light of the ages! O how my heart burns at the very hope.[45]

This echoes something Carlyle wrote in his journal in 1848 after he had written some of his best work—including *The French Revolution* (1837), *Heroes and Hero Worship* (1841), and *Past and Present* (1843)—but was uncertain whether the draft of his *Latter Day Pamphlets* (1850) was up to snuff:

> All these paper bundles were written last summer, and are wrongish, every word of them. … The worst is, however, I am not yet true to myself; I cannot yet call in my wandering truant being, and bid it wholly set to the work fit for it in this hour. Oh, let me persist, persist—may the heavens grant me power to persist in that till I do succeed in it![46]

The merit of Froude's biography of Carlyle is that he often articulates what preoccupied the historian's "wandering truant being" better than the historian himself. Carlyle, Froude wrote,

> had stripped himself of "Formulas" as a Nessus shirt, and flung them fiercely away from him, finding "Formulas" in these days to be mostly "lies agreed to be believed." In the record of God's law, as he had been able to read it, he had found no commendation of "symbols of faith, of church organisation, or methods of government." He wrote, as he said to Sterling, "in the character of a man' only; and of a man without earthly objects, without earthly prospects, who had been sternly handled by fate and circumstances, and was left alone with the elements, as Prometheus on the rock of Caucasus. Struggling thus in pain and sorrow, he desired to tell the modern world that, destitute as it and its affairs appeared to be of Divine guidance, God or justice was still in the middle of it, sternly inexorable as ever; that modern nations were as entirely governed by God's law as the Israelites had been in Palestine—laws self-acting and inflicting their own penalties, if man neglected or defied them. And these laws were substantially the same as those on the Tables delivered in thunder on Mount Sinai. You shall reverence your Almighty Maker. You shall speak truth. You shall do justice to your fellow-man.

---

[45] James Anthony Froude, *The Nemesis of Faith* (London: J. Chapman, 1849), 43–4.
[46] Carlyle quoted in James Anthony Froude, *Thomas Carlyle: A History of His Life in London 1834–1881* (London: Longmans, Green & Co., 1883), i, 22.

If you set truth aside for conventional and convenient lies; if you prefer your own pleasure, your own will, your own ambition, to purity and manliness and justice, and submission to your Maker's commands, then are whirlwinds still provided in the constitution of things which will blow you to atoms."[47]

The tune to which Froude adopted Carlyle's undogmatical faith as his own can be seen in how his own writings echo those of the implacable sage.[48] For both men, the truth of God's law was to be found not in Catholic or Protestant "formulas," but in history, though, as we have seen, Froude was always sceptical of any claims made for history being a science. By contrast, Newman's view of the limitations of history was that of the Schoolmen, who might have conceded that history could have a bearing on the emergence of truth but could not be, in and of itself, the source of truth. Unlike the misguided Protestant historians of Tübingen in the nineteenth century and their Modernist friends in the twentieth and twenty-first centuries, Newman never subscribed to historicism.[49] "History," as he wrote in *The Idea of a University* (1875), "is invaluable in its place; but, if it assumes to be the sole means of gaining Religious Truth, it goes beyond its place. We are putting it to a larger office than it can undertake." For Newman, as for the Schoolmen, to "countenance" such a "usurpation" would be "turning a true guide and blessing into a source of inexplicable difficulty and interminable doubt."[50] For Froude, the literary historian *par excellence*, "The most perfect English history which exists is to be found ... in the historical plays of Shakespeare. In these plays, rich as they are in fancy and imagination, the main bearings of the national story are scrupulously adhered to, and, wherever attainable, verbal correctness. Shakespeare's object was to exhibit, as faithfully as he possibly could, the exact character of the great actors in the national drama—the circumstances which surrounded them and the motives, internal and external, by which they were influenced. To know this is to know all. The reader can form his own

[47] Carlyle quoted *ibid.* (London: Longmans, Green & Co., 1883), ii, 87.
[48] For all of his own prophesizing, Carlyle was skeptical of prophecy. "It is no very good symptom either of nations or individuals, that they deal much in vaticination," he wrote as a young man. "Happy men are full of the present, for its bounty suffices them, and men wise also, for its duties engage them." Carlyle quoted in Simon Heffer, *Moral Desperado: A Life of Thomas Carlyle* (London: Weidenfeld and Nicholson, 1995), 3. At the same time, it was what he fancied the prophetical quality in Oliver Cromwell that he found so attractive. "Poor Cromwell—great Cromwell! The inarticulate Prophet: Prophet who could not *speak*. Rude, confused, struggling to utter himself, with his savage depth, with his wild sincerity ... Sorrow-stricken, half-distracted; the wide element of mournful *black* enveloping him,—wide as the world. It is the character of a prophetic man: a man with his whole soul *seeing* and struggling to see." Thomas Carlyle, *On Heroes, Hero-Worship, and the Heroic in History*, ed. Sorensen and Kinser (New Haven: Yale University Press, 2013), 177.
[49] Of course, the historicism against which Newman argued was a staple of Tübingen. It also animated the work of such popular apostates as Renan. For R. W. Southern, the biographer of Anselm, Renan "had had his first shock of a changing world in the same summer of 1838 when Newman had seen his vision of the two Churches, the one static, the other changing; he walked out of the seminary of St Sulpice as a convert to historicism, three days before Newman at Littlemore entered the Catholic Church. Faced with a choice between the grand but impossible stability of his youth (the only Catholicism he could accept) and the petty shifting Catholicism of Paris, Renan chose to construct his own Catholicism of the human spirit in history." R. W. Southern, "The Historical Experience" (1977), in *History and Historians: Selected Papers of R. W. Southern*, ed. R. J. Bartlett (Oxford: Blackwell, 2004), 116.
[50] *Idea*, 96. See also R. W. Southern, "The Truth about the Past," in *History and Historians*, 120–34.

theories."[51] In his reading of the historian in Shakespeare, Froude's respect for what he regarded as the moral force of history was reconfirmed. "It is in this characteristic that we are accustomed to say Shakespeare's supreme *truth* lies," Froude wrote in "The Science of History":

> He represents real life. His drama teaches as life teaches—neither less nor more. He builds his fabrics, as Nature does, on right and wrong; but he does not struggle to make Nature more systematic than she is. In the subtle interflow of good and evil; in the unmerited sufferings of innocence; in the disproportion of penalties to desert; in the seeming blindness with which justice, in attempting to assert itself, overwhelms innocent and guilty in a common ruin, Shakespeare is true to real experience. The mystery of life he leaves as he finds it; and, in his most tremendous positions, he is addressing rather the intellectual emotions than the understanding—knowing well that the understanding in such things is at fault, and the sage as ignorant as the child.[52]

Its brio notwithstanding, the view of religion to which such convictions gave rise was always rather jejune. Speaking of his own highly fanciful notion of Calvinism—the faith that "overthrew spiritual wickedness" and "hurled kings from their thrones"[53]—Froude refers to it as "the spirit which rises in revolt against untruth; the spirit which ... has appeared, and reappeared, and in due time will appear again, unless God be a delusion and man be as the beasts that perish. For it is but the inflashing upon the conscience with overwhelming force of the nature and origin and of the laws by which mankind are governed—laws which exist, whether we acknowledge them or whether we deny them, and will have their way, to our weal or woe, according to the attitude in which we place ourselves towards them—inherent, like electricity, in the nature of things, not to be altered by us, but to be discerned and obeyed by us at our everlasting peril."[54]

This notion of religion as little more than the handmaiden of duty, the safeguard of morality, the scourge of retribution is a theme that Froude returns to again and again. He gave it particularly droll expression in a piece called "Party Politics" (1874):

> The world of outward experience has been conquered slowly and with difficulty. The invisible world lies beyond experience; where experience ceases to be tangible, emotion and conjecture hold their own with exceptional tenacity, and intellect and observation have been comparatively powerless to check them. Something, however, has been done, and something continues to be done, without which our religious insanities would rapidly make us intolerable to each other. From the earliest recorded times the lawgivers have endeavoured to connect the service of the gods with moral duty, as duty has been from time to time understood. Moral duty standing at length on a ground of its own, they content themselves with preventing men from killing one another in the name of religion. They

---

[51] "Scientific Method Applied to History," in *Short Studies*, ii, 596–7.
[52] "The Science of History," in *Short Studies*, i, 29.
[53] "Calvinism," in *Short Studies*, ii, 57.
[54] Ibid., 57–8.

have established, so far as the law can be a guide, that differences of opinion upon subjects on which all men are equally ignorant shall not be punished as crimes. If the advocates of different creeds continue to hate each other, the law has compelled the more tolerant to confess that the hatred shall not be carried into act. This is called religious liberty, and by some religious indifference. It may be said rather that by keeping steadily before it the principles of justice, the law has become the witness and the sanction of the highest religion yet attained, or perhaps attainable, by man, that the service of God is obedience to the moral commandments.[55]

Dr. Jane Garnett is good at showing how Froude applied his preoccupations with what he thought the central moral force of religion to both his sixteenth-century studies and his criticisms of Victorian Protestantism: "In the context of the Reformation Froude had a respect for the extremists—for an intense Calvinist like John Knox who could bring about change more decisively than the intellectuals whom he also admired, Erasmus or the sixteenth-century Scottish poet and statesman Maitland of Lethington," she writes.

> He recognized that the fanatics went too far, but in contextualizing their intolerance, he wheeled round to attack the lack of intensity and inconsistency of religious behaviour of mid-Victorian Protestants. He compared the Calvinist burning of witches in the seventeenth century with the modern-day inviting of spirit mediums to dinner to conjure up dead relations: "The first method is but excess of indignation with evil; the second is complacent toying with it."[56] The uncomfortable comparison, and the focus on Calvinism itself, which to most of Froude's readers was a by-word for religious narrowness, helped to sharpen Froude's critique of the religious flabbiness of the present. But he was not calling for a Calvinist revival; nor did he romanticize, as Carlyle did, the Calvinist activists whom he admired—Knox or Cromwell. Calvinism stood as the type of Protestantism, in its negative and positive senses. It stood for Froude's conviction that Protestantism had an inherent tendency to support the ideal of the nation as the sphere of moral action.[57]

III

This view of religion was also of the essence of Froude's contempt for theology. "We have no hope from theologians, to whichever school they may belong," he says in "The Condition and Prospects of Protestantism" (1868). "They and all belonging to them are given over to their own dreams, and they cling to them with a passion proportionate to the weakness of their arguments."[58] If the national

---

[55] "Party Politics," in *Short Studies*, iii, 462–3.
[56] "Calvinism," in *Short Studies*, i. 53.
[57] Jane Garnett, "Protestant Histories: James Anthony Froude, Partisanship and National Identity," in *Politics and Culture in Victorian Britain: Essays in Memory of Colin Matthew*, ed. Peter Ghosh and Lawrence Goldman (Oxford: Oxford University Press, 2006), 183–4.
[58] "The Condition and Prospects of Protestantism," in *Short Studies*, ii, 178–9. Froude here echoes what Gibbon had to say on the matter: "Those persons who, from their age, or sex, or occupations,

religion were "to support the ideal of the nation as the sphere of moral action," it would have to do without theology, which was as futile as it was fractious. This rather comports with Mark Pattison's impatience with dogmatic religion. "[D]ogma, consecrated by the blood of the martyrs, becomes in lapse of time a tyrant over reason," he wrote in a piece on Calvin, "and from having been the bulwark of faith, settles into its chief impediment. Systems, and institutions founded on them, thus doom themselves to destruction. A new revolution becomes necessary to displace the charter which the old had inaugurated."[59]

In a review of Newman's *Essay on the Development of Christian Doctrine* (1845), Froude gave another reason why he was dismissive of theology. "The present theological crisis furnishes abundant matter for speculation as well as for sorrow," he wrote about an England still embroiled in theological controversy thanks to the distaste of Anglo-Catholics for their theologically incoherent National Church. "Connexions are broken, friendship severed, families divided," Froude wrote, doubtless with his own differences with his Romanizing elder brother Hurrell in mind, one of the chief architects of Tractarianism, but also with Newman as well. "People enquire after each other in much the same kind of tone that they do after a long separation, half expecting to hear that one or other of them is dead. Men are afraid of writing to their friends, lest they should be told, by return of post, that they are heretics."[60]

In light of such crass objections to dogma, Newman's brilliant discussion of the matter in his *Grammar of Assent* accentuates something of the chasm that always lay between him and his contemporary critics. Indeed, in many respects, it is a chasm that continues to this day. Apropos "the common mistake of supposing that there is a contrariety and antagonism between a dogmatic creed and vital religion," Newman wrote:

> People urge that salvation consists, not in believing the propositions that there is a God, that there is a Saviour, that our Lord is God, that there is a Trinity, but in believing in God, in a Saviour, in a Sanctifier; and they object that such propositions are but a formal and human medium destroying all true reception of the Gospel, and making religion a matter of words or of logic, instead of its having its seat in the heart. They are right so far as this, that men can and sometimes do rest in the propositions themselves as expressing intellectual notions; they are wrong, when they maintain that men need do so or always do so. The proposi-

were the least qualified to judge, who were the least exercised in the habits of abstract reasoning, aspired to contemplate the economy of the Divine Nature: and it is the boast of Tertullian, that a Christian mechanic could readily answer such questions as had perplexed the wisest of the Grecian sages. Where the subject lies so far beyond our reach, the difference between the highest and the lowest of human understandings may indeed be calculated as infinitely small; yet the degree of weakness may perhaps be measured by the degree of obstinacy and dogmatic confidence." Gibbon, *Decline and Fall*, ii, ch. xxi, 361.

59   Mark Pattison, "Calvin at Geneva," *Westminster Review* (1858); *Essays*, ii, 3–4.
60   *Oxford and Cambridge Review*, 2 (January–June 1846), 186. Froude also makes oblique reference here to the conversion of William Froude's wife and children, in which Newman was instrumental. See Edward Short, "The Certainty of Vocation: Newman and the Froudes," in *Newman and his Contemporaries*, 135–63. Mrs. William (Catherine) Froude had become a Catholic in 1857. In 1859 the two eldest of her five children were received into the Church, and two more later. See *LD*, xix, 49.

tions may and must be used, and can easily be used, as the expression of facts, not notions, and they are necessary to the mind in the same way that language is ever necessary for denoting facts, both for ourselves as individuals, and for our intercourse with others. Again, they are useful in their dogmatic aspect as ascertaining and making clear for us the truths on which the religious imagination has to rest. Knowledge must ever precede the exercise of the affections. We feel gratitude and love, we feel indignation and dislike, when we have the informations actually put before us which are to kindle those several emotions. We love our parents, as our parents, when we know them to be our parents; we must know concerning God, before we can feel love, fear, hope, or trust towards Him. Devotion must have its objects; those objects, as being supernatural, when not represented to our senses by material symbols, must be set before the mind in propositions. The formula, which embodies a dogma for the theologian, readily suggests an object for the worshipper. It seems a truism to say, yet it is all that I have been saying, that in religion the imagination and affections should always be under the control of reason. Theology may stand as a substantive science, though it be without the life of religion; but religion cannot maintain its ground at all without theology. Sentiment, whether imaginative or emotional, falls back upon the intellect for its stay, when sense cannot be called into exercise; and it is in this way that devotion falls back upon dogma.[61]

Considering Froude's impatience with dogmatic theology, it is surprising that he should have reviewed Newman's theological works at such length. And yet his criticisms, however mistaken, are worth reading precisely because they shed such useful light on his anti-dogmatic prejudices, which he would never shake. Thus, he puts Newman's defection from the National Church in a polemical historical context by comparing him to Origen, of whose case, Froude argues, Newman's is reminiscent.[62] Origen, Froude says, was "a man in whom were very many gifts so rare, so singular, so strange, that in the beginning any one would have thought that his opinions might have been believed of all men. For if life procureth authority, he was a man of great industry, of great chastity, patience and labour." For Froude, Newman puts one particularly in mind of Origen because

[61] *GA*, 120–1. Ian Ker's gloss on this passage is typically apt. "The dogmatic formulations that Newman had once seen as necessary but undesirable are now seen as indispensable ... Of course, he knew when he wrote the *Arians* that the believer cannot worship Christ without *some* knowledge of who Christ is, but he seemed to think that it was a pity that the faith could not rest on the simplest kind of *kerugma*. Forty years later he is very clear that far from there being any kind of opposition between a personalistic and a propositional faith, the two are in fact indivisible." Ian Ker, *Newman on Vatican II* (Oxford: Oxford University Press, 1914), 112–13.

[62] Origen (*c*. 184/5–*c*. 253/4): theologian and biblical critic in the Alexandrian school. The founder of Neoplatonism, Origen sought to introduce Neoplatonic elements into Christianity. His *Principles*, which were rejected by the Church as heretical, were translated by St Jerome and quoted by St Bernard, and he influenced the allegorical method of literary criticism developed by St Augustine, *Oxford Companion to English Literature*, 4th edition, ed. Margaret Drabble. In the *Apologia*, Newman wrote of Origen: "I love ... the name of Origen; I will not listen to the notion that so great a soul was lost; but I am quite sure that, in the contest between his doctrine and followers and the ecclesiastical powers, his opponents were right and he was wrong." *Apo.*, 232. However, he also observed how "The free thought of Origen is visible in the writings of the Western Doctors, Hilary and Ambrose; and the independent mind of Jerome has enriched his own vigorous commentaries on Scripture, from the stores of the scarcely orthodox Eusebius." *Apo.*, 237.

"if, in our own church, we heard mention of some highly gifted soul, whose character seemed painted to the very life in the above glowing description, whom else could we bring to our minds but him who has just forsaken us?—one, who by his unblemished life, vast learning, and surpassing intellect, was well fitted to have been a second Athanasius, had he not chosen to be a second Origen."[63]

Of course, many did regard Newman as the English Athanasius, before and after his conversion, which was proof that there was more continuity than discontinuity between the so-called Anglican and the convert Newman. Indeed, Froude himself quotes from *Lectures on the Prophetical Office of the Church* (1837) to show how very Romish the Anglican Newman could be. In the passage he shares with his readers one can see not only a foreshadowing of Newman's *Essay on Development* but his trouncing of Anglo-Catholicism in *Anglican Difficulties*, the lectures he gave in King William Street in London in 1850 to try to coax his old Tractarian friends to join him in abandoning Canterbury for Rome.

> A religious principle, or idea, however true, before it is realized in a substantive form, is but a theory; and since many theories are not more than theories, and do not admit of being carried into effect, it is exposed to the suspicion of being one of these, and of having no existence out of books. The proof of reality in a doctrine is its holding together when actually attempted. Practical men are naturally prejudiced against what is new, on this ground, if on no other, that it has not had the opportunity of satisfying this test. Protestantism and Popery are real religions; no one can doubt about them; they have furnished the mould in which nations have been cast; but the via media has never existed except on paper, it has never been reduced to practice; it is known not positively but negatively, in its differences from the rival creeds, not in its own properties; and can only be described as a third system, neither the one nor the other, partly both, cutting between them, and as if with a critical fastidiousness, trifling with them both, and boasting to be nearer antiquity than either. What is this but to fancy a road over mountains and rivers, which has never been cut?[64]

Froude also marvels at the *sangfroid* with which Newman accounts for his secession from the National Church—a rhetorical self-assurance that Froude would try to emulate himself, especially when sharing with his readers his often outrageous views on English and Irish history.[65] "We did not, indeed, consider

---

[63] J. A. Froude, "Mr. Newman's Theory of Development," *The Oxford and Cambridge Review* (February 1846), 137.

[64] *VM*, i, 16–17.

[65] Froude's defense in his three-volume *The English in Ireland* (1872–4) of Oliver Cromwell's atrocities in Ireland was of a piece with his defense of those of Henry VIII in his history of England. In effect, he treated both as the necessary frightfulness of admirably ruthless Carlylean strongmen. The anti-British Irish in America objected so passionately to what they regarded as Froude's anti-Irish bigotry that they forced him to cancel his planned American lecture tour in 1873. Even Lecky regarded the polemical historian as beyond the pale. "A writer who seriously regrets the penal code," Lecky wrote in a review of Froude's Irish history, "and implies that the whole Catholic population of Ireland ought as far as possible to be deprived of every description of political representation, is not deserving ... of a serious answer. However much it may please literary gentlemen in search of sensational paradox to coquet with such views, any responsible statesmen who acted on them would be more fit for a place in Bedlam than a place in Downing Street." *Macmillan's Magazine*

absolute silence on Mr. Newman's part necessary," he says. "We were prepared for such an apology, or defence of his secession, as should be in fact an attack on the position of the English church; but we expected certainly that a tone of deep humility and self-distrust would have been apparent through all that he put forth at such a time." But there was little humility and no self-doubt. "The treatise itself, instead of being in the form of an apology, is dogmatic, and the tone is not only, as Mr. Newman fears it may at times appear 'positive and peremptory,' but throughout is one of the most unqualified dogmatism. There is nothing in it like doubt or hesitation, nothing like a feeling of self-distrust—scarcely an admission of the possibility of present error. Nay, there even seems to us to be some attempt to gloss over the extent of those changes of opinion which are admitted in the preface." One can detect in Froude's response to what he sees as the effrontery of the essay an unspoken admiration. "Notwithstanding the misdirection hitherto of all his efforts and energies, he comes forward ... within little more than a month of his conversion, to instruct and direct us, with as much calmness and assurance as if he had lost nothing in intellectual position by recent events, as if he were not stultified by the sudden and complete change which his opinions have undergone—as if he were now to be as thoroughly trusted, as much looked up to, as though all his life he had taken one consistent course, and taught one uniform system of divinity." For a man full of inconsistencies himself, this was an attractive rhetorical gambit. Of course, what Froude mistook for effrontery was consistency, though it is still fascinating to see the historian claiming that he wishes the book had shown "a sad and chastened, a doubting and an humble tone." For the joyous convert in Newman, such strictures must have seemed peculiarly unreal. Why would he have gone through with the ordeal of conversion if he suffered from doubt?

In the readiness of English Protestants to allow for doubt in their religious opinions, Newman always saw a tell-tale faithlessness. In "Faith in Private Judgment" (1849), for example, he described a kind of doubt that he regarded as characteristically Protestant. To describe this doubt, he asked: "What is faith?" And he defined it as an "assenting to a doctrine as true, which we do not see, which we cannot prove, because God says it is true, who cannot lie. And further than this, since God says it is true, not with His own voice, but by the voice of His messengers, it is assenting to what man says, not simply viewed as a man, but to what he is commissioned to declare, as a messenger, prophet, or ambassador from God." Now, for Newman, "Such is the only rational, consistent account of faith; but ... Protestants ... laugh at the very notion of it. They laugh at the notion itself of men pinning their faith ... upon Pope or Council; they think it simply superstitious and narrow-minded, to profess to believe just what the Church believes, and to assent to whatever she will say in time to come on matters of doctrine. That is, they laugh at the bare notion of doing what Christians undeniably did in the time of the Apostles. Observe, they do not merely ask whether the Catholic Church has a claim to teach, has authority, has the gifts;—this is a

(June 1874). Froude's reluctance to grant the Irish any say in the political conduct of Ireland stemmed in large measure from his low view of the Irish, whom he thought "more like tribes of squalid apes than human beings." Froude quoted in F. S. L. Lyons, *Culture and Anarchy in Ireland 1890–1939* (Oxford: Oxford University Press, 1979), 12.

reasonable question;—no, they think that the very state of mind which such a claim involves in those who admit it, namely, the disposition to accept without reserve or question, that this is slavish. They call it priestcraft to insist on this surrender of the reason, and superstition to make it. That is, they quarrel with the very state of mind which all Christians had in the age of the Apostles." Here Newman rejected the quintessentially Protestant claim that it was Protestants who upheld the faith of the primitive Church by showing that they had no faith in the sense in which the Apostles understood the term. On the contrary, they reserved the right to judge for themselves; they recognized no authority; they prided themselves on their private judgment. And if the Protestants of nineteenth-century England were cast back into the primitive Church, their prejudices would not have credited what the Apostles had to say. For Newman, "those who thus boast of not being led blindfold, of judging for themselves, of believing just as much and just as little as they please, of hating dictation, and so forth, would have found it an extreme difficulty to hang on the lips of the Apostles." They "would have simply resisted the sacrifice of their own liberty of thought, would have thought life eternal too dearly purchased at such a price, and would have died in their unbelief. And they would have defended themselves on the plea that it was absurd and childish to ask them to believe without proof, to bid them give up their education, and their intelligence, and their science." And this, as Newman argued, in spite of "those difficulties which reason and sense find in the Christian doctrine, in spite of its mysteriousness, its obscurity, its strangeness, its unacceptableness, its severity." Protestants, with their skeptical principles, would never "surrender themselves to the teaching of a few unlettered Galilæans, or a learned indeed but fanatical Pharisee." They would have insisted on their Protestant prerogatives and shown St. Paul and the Apostles the door. And, for Newman, if "This is what they would have said then; … is it wonderful they do not become Catholics now? The simple account of their remaining as they are, is, that they lack one thing,—they have not faith; it is a state of mind, it is a virtue, which they do not recognise to be praiseworthy, which they do not aim at possessing."[66] Of course, we cannot say with any definiteness whether Newman had James Anthony Froude in mind when he wrote this withering sermon, but he might very well have.

What is striking about Froude's review of Newman's *Essay on Development* is its close and, on the whole, fair reading, despite its fundamental wrongheadedness. Other critics—Edwin Abbott Abbott and James Fitzjames Stephen come to mind—refused even to acknowledge the terms of Newman's argument before taking him to task for what they chose to see as his sophistry and bad faith. Froude is careful to advert to Newman's own words.

> For the theory itself, we shall give it, as far as possible, in his own words; it is this. Firstly :—'That the increase and expansion of the Christian Creed and Ritual, and the variations which have attended the process in the case of individual writers and churches, are the necessary attendants on any philosophy or polity which takes possession of the intellect and heart, and has had any wide or

---

[66] "Faith and Private Judgment" (1849), *Mix.*, 192–213.

extended dominion; that from the nature of the human mind, time is necessary for the full comprehension and perfection of great ideas; and that the highest and most wonderful truths, though communicated to the world once for all by the inspired teachers, could not be comprehended all at once by the recipients, but, as received and transmitted by minds not inspired, and through media which, mere human, have required only the longer time and deeper thought for their full elucidation."—p. 27. Secondly, that the existing religion of the Roman Catholic Church, both as laid down in the decrees of the Council of Trent, and also as carried out in act through the churches in communion with Rome, is the legitimate and due development of primitive Christianity, the very right and true sequel of that faith once delivered to the saints, which was unalterable indeed in its outlines, but admitted of indefinite expansion. And here we would call attention to the fact, that it is not simply Tridentine Romanism of which Mr. Newman undertakes the defence, but that whole existing practical system of which, four years ago, he said, that it went far to substitute another gospel for the true one; instead of setting before the soul the Holy Trinity, and heaven and hell, seeming to him, as a popular system, to preach the blessed virgin and the saints, and purgatory,—recalling to our minds, with very unpleasant sensations, the awful words, 'Though we, or an angel from heaven, preach any other gospel unto you, let him be accursed.' The papal supremacy in the most ultramontane sense, the worship of the Virgin as practised, the adoration of images and relics, persecution, all are admitted to be parts of the system, and, as such, have each of them a portion of the work devoted to their justification.[67]

Again, Froude calls attention not only to what he regards as the inconsistency of Newman's thinking but its extravagance, papal supremacy and devotion to the Virgin, not to mention respect for relics being precisely the aspects of the Roman Church that English Protestants had been reared since the sixteenth century to scorn and revile. However incredible Froude himself might find Newman's defense of such things, he gives his readers an accurate account of Newman's defense of them.

> This, then, is Mr. Newman's present view;—he believes that the whole of the existing Roman system has been evolved ... from the original doctrines of Christ, in the same way that the oak is developed from the acorn, the bird from the egg, the butterfly from the caterpillar. He grants that there is a very wide difference between the religion of ancient Christendom, and the system of modern Rome, and he would admit, we suppose, the far greater resemblance of our own system, than the Roman, to that of the primitive church, but he considers this close resemblance to make against us rather than for us, and the diversity in the other case to be not only no disadvantage to the claims of Rome, but to be actually an argument in their favour. Change he considers an evidence of life and growth; stationariness he looks upon as implying the absence of a living principle (p. 32). He holds that Christianity could not be communicated to men all at once, and that a power of gradually working out the truth was therefore committed to the

---

[67] Froude, review *of Essay on Development*, 145–6.

church, whereby, in process of time, the system of Rome has been formed. This, we believe, is a fair statement of Mr. Newman's view; a view which is no novelty, but has, as he observes, been implicitly adopted by Romanist theologians at all times ... It is the same view which he himself thus described six years ago in the British Critic:

> When we object to the Romanists that their church has changed in the course of years, they not unfrequently acknowledge it, and are philosophical on the subject. They say that all systems have their development; that nothing begins as it ends; that nothing can come into the world *totis numeris*; that the seed becomes a tree, and the child a man. And they urge, moreover, that the full blown development, to superficial observers, necessarily seems different to what it was in its rudiments; just as a friend not seen for many years, is strange to us at first sight, till, by degrees, we catch the old looks, or the well-remembered tones, or the smile, or the remark, which assure us that, with whatever changes of age or circumstances, he is the same. ["Catholicity of the Anglican Church," *Ess.*, ii, 43–4]

> Mr. Newman has adopted this philosophy, and the treatise which we are considering is an exposition and defence of it.[68]

If Froude accurately sets out the terms of Newman's case for doctrinal development, he shows the superficiality, indeed crudity of his own thinking when he attempts to refute the case.

> And first, with regard to the theory itself, let us consider what it implies—whether, despite a certain magnificence which is well calculated to dazzle the imagination, it has not at least as many difficulties as that Anglican hypothesis which Mr. Newman has discarded from it. Is it not then sufficiently startling, that on Mr. Newman's view the primitive Christians were mere children in the faith, the most ignorant of all Christians? The best instructed amongst them, Clement, Ignatius, Polycarp, less knowing, less built up in Christian doctrine, than the worst instructed Roman Catholic of the present day? Yet assuredly this must be believed, if it be considered that the doctrine of the Trinity was really worked out gradually by the Arian controversy, that of the Incarnation by the Nestorian and Eutychian, that of Baptism by the Novatian, that of original sin by the Pelagian, the early Christians having mere dim and indistinct notions on these matters; while on the subject of St. Mary's dignity, the duty of praying to the Saints, the existence of purgatory, the necessity of submission to the Bishop of Rome, they were wholly ignorant.[69]

Newman does not argue that the Fathers were ignorant of the Faith: he argues that they were in possession of a Faith that the Church would require time to apprehend fully. Nor does he argue that the doctrines of the Church—whether the Trinity, the Incarnation, Baptism, or Original Sin—were unknown to the Fathers:

---

[68] *Ibid.*, 145–7.
[69] *Ibid.*, 155–6.

he argues that the doctrines were clarified and reaffirmed whenever disputed. In his essay "Trials of Theodoret," which Newman included in his *Historical Sketches*, he encapsulated this hallmark of the Church's doctrinal infallibility: "truth is wrought out by the indirect operation of error and sin."[70] Earlier still, in his King William Street lectures, Newman was more categorical still.

> It is imprudent in opponents of the Catholic Religion to choose for their attack the very point in which it is strong. As truth is tried by error, virtue by temptation, courage by opposition, so is individuality and life tried by disturbance and disorder; and its trial is its evidence. The long history of Catholicism is but a coordinate proof of its essential unity. I suppose, then, that Protestants must be considered as turning to bay upon their pursuers, when they would retort upon us the argument available against themselves from their religious variations.[71]

Froude is equally mistaken with regard to the principle of development itself, a principle which he could simply not see in the life of faith, nor, indeed, in any historical phenomenon. With passages like the following, it is not surprising that he never chose to include the review in his *Short Studies on Great Subjects*, which he published between 1867 and 1883, especially after the appearance of Charles Darwin's *Origin of Species* (1859).

> Even in human religions and philosophies, when a master-mind has struck out a complete system, there is no after growth. So Platonism was corrupted, but did not develop, and there has been no development of Mahometanism. Much more is original completeness, a property of a divine creation—if there are analogies such as Butler notices in God's ordinary Providence of a gradual and as it were painful progress from weakness and imperfection to full strength and maturity, yet at least in his extraordinary manifestations of his power it is otherwise not the "herbs and plants" only, but all that moved in the waters or upon the earth, or in the open firmament of heaven, fish and fowl, and cattle, and beast, and creeping thing—all were created in maturity. Adam, too, was made not a child, not a youth, but a man. Eve, not a girl, but a woman. May it not be also, that the

---

[70] *HS*, ii, 213.
[71] *Diff.*, i, 313. Wilfrid Ward is vivid on the lectures that have never ceased to annoy those who would make excuses for or defend the Anglican imposture: "The brilliant irony of the King William Street lectures," Ward writes in his biography of the Cardinal, "delighted such intellectual critics as Mr. Hutton. The lectures also attracted the Broad-Church members of the Establishment, who attended in considerable numbers. They rejoiced the heart of that born controversialist, Dr. Wiseman, who sat listening to them, vested in a cope, swaying to and fro, his ruddy face beaming with delight as the war-dance of the Anglican episcopate was described by the lecturer. Conversions to the Church immediately followed—notable among them being those of Sir George Bowyer and Mr. T. W. Allies." Ward, *Life of Newman*, i, 251. For the war-dance, see *Diff.*, i, 152. Sir George Bowyer (1811–83), 7th baronet, received much of his early education in Italy before studying law at Lincoln's Inn. Having been a fervent follower of the Oxford Movement, he converted in August of 1850 and, in addition to being a constitutional adviser to Manning and Wiseman, defended the Church of Rome throughout his long life in the pages of the *Dublin Review*. Later he became MP for Dundalk and County Wexford but was expelled from the Reform Club once his fellow liberals could no longer bear the unreliable eccentricity of his political views. Certainly, Newman, amongst all his wide circle of friends and admirers, never attracted one who was so ardent an admirer of Lord Henry Brougham, chief advocate of the "march of mind."

material world itself was created a perfect and mature world, and that this is the solution of that enigma which geologists find it so hard to unriddle? Even in that part of what is called God's ordinary providence which is most like to his extraordinary, the sending forth into the world from time to time of high art, or philosophy of a diviner kind, a similar law prevails. They start up suddenly in full vigour and full majesty, and what follows is a gradual deterioration, with at best here and there a dim reflection and faint shadow of the ancient glory.[72]

To argue that Newman's idea of development is unpersuasive because it does not allow for the lack of development in Mahometanism is typical of the flippancy that could often play havoc with Froude's reasoning—an abiding tendency, as he must have known, of scribblers working against deadlines or littérateurs beguiled by their own vagrant rhetoric. Indeed, the historian shows himself an even more dubious disputant when he takes issue with the scriptural implications of Newman's argument. The Victorian English might have been more familiar with their Bibles than most of their successors, but here it is clear that their understanding of the theological character of the book was not always as sound as it might have been. Froude showed his own defective understanding of Scripture when he claimed that Newman's understanding of doctrinal development "is disparaging to Scripture"—a wild aspersion. Despite his adoption of Carlyle's prophetic poses, Froude shared the *sola scriptura* fallacies of many of his Protestant contemporaries.

> It is not indeed admitted, that Scripture is silent concerning those additions to the Primitive faith, which Rome imposes as fundamental truths under the sanction of an anathema, rather every nerve is strained, every effort made, and the most violent interpretations advocated for the purpose of shewing that Scripture does contain intimations of them but it cannot with any face be argued that they are in such sort contained in Scripture, as that Scripture can really prove them. Mr. Newman indeed observes that he is not aware that Post-Tridentine writers deny that the whole Catholic faith may be proved from Scripture (*Dev.*, 323) and this may be the fact; probably they do not deny it; but do they venture to assert it? or could they do so with any decency?[73]

When Froude leaves off quoting Newman directly and paraphrases him, he can be rather amusing. Here, he takes up what he considers the implicit *argumentum ad hominem* in Newman's case, demanding that Anglicans account for the development on which they themselves rely in their own church.

> What is your own ceremonial, we are asked, your set forms, your cathedrals, your altars and altar-pieces, your vestments, your chanting, your church consecrations, your coronation service;—what is this but the very thing you condemn, a development? What, again, is your church polity—your archdeacons, and deans, and canons, and prebends, and chapters, and *congés d'élire*,[74] and royal

---

[72] Froude, review of *Essay on Development*, 161.
[73] Ibid., 156–7.
[74] *congé d'élire*: Permission to elect a bishop, granted in the Church of England by the Crown to the dean and chapter of the cathedral of the diocese.

supremacy, and Queen's arms in churches, and ecclesiastical courts with their lay judges, and archbishops and primates of England and of all England? Is this apostolic? Is this primitive? Can you defend it on any other ground but that despised one of development? What, finally, are your articles? your decisions on the subject of the lawfulness of taking oaths, and bearing arms, your whole system of doctrine therein contained; what is all this again, right or wrong, but a development of the ancient faith? and how then can you oppose the theory?"[75]

Froude clearly recognized that there would be consequences for Anglicans denying to Rome what they reserved for themselves. For Froude, "the *argumentum ad hominem*, which [Newman] urges against Anglicans—namely, that they, too, hold a development exactly the same in kind as that which they oppose in the case of Romanism, and that such opposition on their part, is suicidal, since their arguments 'strike at Rome through England'; and if valid against the creed of Pope Pius, are equally so against the Athanasian. (*Dev.*, 9)"[76] Froude may not have always entered into the niceties of theological argument with any reliability but he could recognize logical inconsistency.[77]

Acting himself as though the person addressed in Newman's argument, he provides not only a summary of his response to Newman's book as a whole but a good example of what rhetoricians call *ignoratio elenchi*, which the *Oxford English Dictionary* defines as "an argument that appears to refute opponent while actually disproving something not advanced by him." "We reply, by granting the theory, to a certain extent," Froude writes.

> We have argued hitherto against such a development as Mr. Newman advocates, not against all development. We proceed to make our meaning clearer. We hold, then, that the saving faith, that faith which was once for all delivered to the saints, as a deposit to be kept and guarded—that this, which is the sum and substance of Christianity, was possessed from the first in its fulness, if not by all Christians, yet by some. We cannot doubt but that by the apostles it was more vividly apprehended and more thoroughly understood than it has ever been by

---

[75] Froude, review of *Essay on Development*, 159–60.
[76] Ibid., 158.
[77] Cf. Father John Hunwicke on the "Anglican Patrimony": "People still sometimes ask what *is* this Anglican Patrimony of which Professor Ratzinger wrote in *Anglicanorum coetibus*. Does it just mean occasional Choral Evensong? I believe dear old Archdeacon ... oops, *Cardinal* ... Manning summed it up thus: 'I see much danger of an English Catholicism of which Newman is the highest type. It is the old Anglican, patristic, literary, Oxford tone transplanted into the Church.' Bang on, except for that strange word 'danger'. I have often wondered whether our own Professor Henry 'Patrimony' Chadwick had Manning's words consciously in mind when he wrote: 'The fact that [Newman] had been converted to Catholicism by Oxford and the study of the Church Fathers, not by any personal friendship with Roman Catholics, meant that everything he wrote and said sounded almost Anglican.' That's the Patrimony: Anglican tone. Including, of course, Saint John Henry Newman's old Anglican gifts of Irony, Satire, and especially, above all, and pretty well daily, the *Argumentum ad hominem*. And an adherence to Saint John Henry's belief in the iniquities of Liberalism. And his resolute opposition to Ultrahyperuberpapalism. And his emphasis on getting one's guidance from the Fathers. And writing decent English. Those are things I would have concentrated upon if anybody had ever asked me to contribute to the endless Conferences that keep happening in order to pin down and identify the meaning of 'the Anglican Patrimony.'" See Hunwicke's blog, *Mutual Enrichment*.

any since—nor can we do otherwise than think, that by those, who, having learnt their religion from the apostles themselves, were selected by them as the fittest of all their converts to succeed them in the governance of the infant church, it was appreciated only less fully than by the inspired apostles themselves. We can see no force in the assertions that on the first uninspired recipients of the gospel, the revealed truths must have fallen vaguely and generally' (*Dev.*, 95), and that 'the inspired teachers could not be comprehended by those to whom they first addressed themselves' (*Dev.*, 27); to us it seems that Polycarp was as fit to receive gospel truth as Augustine, and more likely to learn it accurately from St. John, than Augustine from St. Ambrose; we cannot but think, that the apostolical fathers were the best informed of all Christians, next to the apostles themselves, and that the greatest saints, the most finished Christians of later ages have but approximated to, without reaching, the perfection of their knowledge.

In fine, Froude sensibly acknowledged his limitations in passing judgment on so learned, rich and intricate a work. For all of his delight in paradox, he was not incapable of intellectual honesty. "Thus have we endeavoured to put before our readers the broad features of the case as it stands between us and Rome, between the Anglican and Mr. Newman's theories," he wrote.

> With regard to the details of his book, a review article is not the place in which to attempt an examination of them. We trust that our church retains within her pale divines learned enough to answer Mr. Newman's treatise, in the way in which alone it can be satisfactorily answered—by a treatise as elaborate. We hope that they who are plainly incompetent to the task, from want of learning or of controversial skill, will abstain from the attempt, by which our cause can only be prejudiced. We trust that no one will be precipitate, or think that it is a light thing to engage in set controversy with such an antagonist. He has brought forward, it is true, no new theory; but he has advocated the theory of Le Maistre and Möhler, as it never before was advocated in this country, with a power, an eloquence, a depth of learning, a grasp of mind, which are seldom found united, much less conjoined with such a weight of personal character. Mr. Newman's desertion of us is a severe blow in itself; it will be rendered severer, if sciolists in patristic learning, or tyros in polemic encounter, put themselves forward to answer a book which is the most finished production of a most accomplished theologian.[78]

Here, we can put Froude's response to Newman's work in some larger context by quoting a letter that Newman wrote to the historian's sister-in-law, Mrs. William Froude from Littlemore on Christmas Eve, 1845, after the publication of the *Essay*, which shows the extent to which stationariness played no part in the development of his own Christian apostolate. Faithful dynamism was of its essence.

> You may think what a pain it is to quit this neighbourhood. I am now beginning my thirtieth year since my matriculation. Thus I have spent nearly two thirds of

---

[78] Froude, review of *Essay on Development*, 160, 167.

my life here. And that for the most part summer as well as winter, unlike most Oxford residents And then a new generation is springing up in Littlemore whom I might influence towards the Catholic Church. Yet I have no position in this place and no calling. I have no better reason for staying than at any place along the road, beyond the fact that I am here. It comes upon us all that life is short, and that one must not stay all the day idle, when there is one that hires us, and work to be done.[79]

IV

What sets Froude apart from other critics of Newman's work is his appreciation of the limits of the rationalism on which he draws to find fault with that work. One can see this strikingly in a piece of his entitled "Conditions and Prospects of Protestantism" (1868), in which he shows that he was not entirely dissimilar from Newman in finding the intellect estranged from religion in an unhappy fix.

> In the present alienation of the higher intellect from religion, it is impossible to foresee how soon or from what quarter any better order of things is to be looked for. We spoke of an eddy in the stream, but there are "tides in the affairs of men" which run long and far. The phenomena of spirit-rapping show us that the half-educated multitudes in England and America are ready for any superstition. Scientific culture seems inclined to run after the will-o'-the-wisp of positivism; and as it is certain that ordinary persons will not live without a belief of some kind, superstition has a fair field before it; and England, if not Europe generally, may perhaps witness in the coming century some great Catholic revival.

Not only Newman but all of the figures of the Catholic Revival in England would have found this prescient observation amusing.[80] It baffled so many of Froude's convictions about the untenability of the Church in a ruthlessly rationalist world. However, Froude stuck to his guns. He was not merely content to equate superstition with Catholicism, he touted the preferability of rationalism, even though it might degenerate into table rapping. Indeed, he admitted that there would be radical inadequacies in any rationalist alternative to Catholicism. "We are indulging, perhaps, in visionary fears," he writes;

> but if experience shows that in the long run reason will prevail, it shows also that reason has a hard fight for it; and in the minds even of the most thoughtful rarely holds an undisputed empire. We expect no good from the theory of human things with which men of intellect at present content themselves. We look for little satisfaction to our souls from sciences which are satisfied with phenomena, or much good to our bodies from social theories of utility—utility meaning the gratification of the five senses in largest measure by the greatest number. We believe that human beings can only live and prosper together on the. condition

---

[79] JHN to Mrs. William Froude (24 December 1845), *LD*, xi, 78.
[80] For an excellent critical overview of the writers of the Catholic Revival, see Ian Ker, *The Catholic Revival in English Literature 1845–1960* (South Bend: University of Notre Dame Press, 2003).

of the recognition of duty, and duty has no meaning and no sanction except as implying responsibility to a power above and beyond humanity. As long as the moral force bequeathed to us by Christianity remains, the idea of obligation survives in the conscience. The most emancipated philosopher is still dominated by its influence, and men continue substantially Christians while they believe themselves to be only Benthamites. But the feebleness of Protestantism will do its work of disintegration at last, and a social system which has no religion left in it will break down like an uncemented arch.[81]

Here, Froude might be alive to the indispensability of faith, but he sees it in terms of moralism. Faith is useful because it is the sanction of duty. Like his friend James Fitzjames Stephen, he saw faith as the only bulwark against moral and civil disorder, though as Leslie Stephen nicely remarked "it would be hard to say which of them had the most unequivocal hatred of popery."[82]

Froude explained one reason why he had such contempt for popery in his review of Newman's *Grammar of Assent*, the opening paragraph of which elaborates on how he saw, on the one hand, a rationalism not entirely free of the allure of superstition, and, on the other, a Roman Catholicism demanding full, undoubting assent.

> Thirty years ago, when the tendencies Romewards of the English High Churchmen were first becoming visible, Dr. Arnold expresses his own opinion of the reasonableness of the movement in the brief sentence, "Believe in the Pope! I would as soon believe in Jupiter." Whether belief in Jupiter may hereafter become possible time will show. Necromancy has been revived in spirit-rapping. We have converts to Islam among us, and England is the chosen recruiting ground of the Mormon Apostles; while this book before us is an attempt on the part of one of the ablest of living men to prove that there is no reasonable standing ground between Atheism and submission to the Holy See—submission not outwardly only, or partially, or conditionally, as to an authority which has historical claims upon us, and may possibly or probably deserve our allegiance; but submission complete and entire, the unreserved resignation of our moral and spiritual intelligence. The Church of Rome, and indeed all religious dogmatic systems, are not content with insisting that there is a high probability in their favor. They call themselves infallible. They demand, on our part an absolute certainty that they are right, and although they disagree among themselves and cannot all be right, and although points on which those competent to form an opinion differ, in all other things we agree to hold doubtful, they tell us that doubt is a sin, that we can be and ought to be entirely certain, that a complete and utter acquiescence which excludes the possibility of mistake is a frame of mind at once possible and philosophically just.[83]

For Froude, this was "the seeming paradox which Dr. Newman undertakes to prove." And the reviewer then proceeds to encapsulate the argument of this

---

[81] "Condition and Prospects of Protestantism," in *Short Studies*, ii, 177–8.
[82] *Life of Sir James Fitzjames Stephen*, 133.
[83] "Father Newman on 'The Grammar of Assent,'" in *Short Studies*, ii, 101–2.

most demanding of all Newman's books. "He commences with an analysis of the elementary mental processes," Froude writes.

> He divides "assent" into "notional" and "real." He calls notional "assent" that which we give to general propositions, scientific, literary, or philosophical; real assent, the conclusions which we form in matters of fact, either in our sensible perceptions, or in the application of principles to details. He professes to show how, from our intellectual constitution, we are unable to rest in probabilities, and rightly or wrongly pass on to a sensation of certainty; how, notwithstanding exceptions which cannot wholly be got over, the conviction that we have hold of the truth is an evidence to us that we have hold of it in reality. Our beliefs are borne in upon our minds, we know not how, directly, indirectly, by reason, by experience, by emotion, imagination, and all the countless parts of our complicated Nature. We may not be able to analyze the grounds of our faith, but the faith is none the less justifiable. And thus, after being led by the hand through an intricate series of mental phenomena, we are landed in the Catholic religion as the body of truth which completely commends itself to the undistorted intellectual perception.[84]

However broad brush, this is not an unfair precis of Newman's argument. Froude is also faithful to Newman in acknowledging how central conscience is in the convert's explanation of how we arrive at certainty in our religious convictions.

> "Can we," Father Newman asks, "give a real assent to the proposition that there is one God—not an *anima mundi* merely or an initial force, but God as the word is understood by the Theist and the Christian, a personal God, the Author and Sustainer of all things—the Moral Governor of the world?" He says that we can, and that we can be certain of it; that it is a truth which every reasonable person is able and ought to acknowledge. He does not look for what has been called scornfully "a clock-making Divinity." The evidences of a contriving intellect in nature, of the adaptation of means to ends, weigh but little with him. There is no morality in the physical constitution of things. The elements know nothing of good and evil; and we can arrive only at a power adequate to the effects which we witness. The water will not rise higher than its source. The created world is finite, and can tell us nothing of an Infinite Creator. The root of religious belief lies in the conscience and in the sense of moral obligation.[85]

Unlike so many other critics of Newman, Froude at least does his readers the courtesy of quoting, not paraphrasing his subject and, what is more, quoting him in context. Thus, since he provides his readers with passages from the *Grammar of Assent* illustrative of Newman's understanding of conscience, readers can decide for themselves whether the reviewer's response to them are just or not. Here is a good case in point, in which Froude quotes Newman on the vitality of conscience.

> I assume (says Father Newman) that Conscience has a legitimate place among our mental acts; as really so as the action of memory, of reasoning, of imagination,

[84] Ibid., 102–3.
[85] Ibid., 110–11.

or as the sense of the beautiful; that, as there are objects which, when presented to the mind, cause it to feel grief, regret, joy, or desire, so there are things which excite in us approbation or blame, and which we in consequence call right or wrong; and which, experienced in ourselves, kindle in us the specific sense of pleasure or pain, which goes by the name of a good or bad conscience. This being taken for granted, I shall attempt to show that in this special feeling, which follows on the commission of what we call right and wrong, lie the materials for the real apprehension of a Divine Sovereign and Judge. The feeling of conscience being, I repeat, a certain keen sensibility, pleasant or painful,—self-approval and hope, or compunction and fear,—attendant on certain of our actions, which in consequence we call right or wrong, is twofold: it is a moral sense, and a sense of duty; a judgment of the reason, and a magisterial dictate.[86]

To assure his readers that he has followed Newman's understanding of conscience, Froude adds: "Conscience, it is evident, does not furnish a rule of right conduct. It has sometimes been the sanction of crime. Sometimes it is at a loss to decide. Sometimes it gives contradictory answers. Conscience made St. Paul into a persecutor. Conscience has made kings into tyrants, and subjects into rebels. It is not a rule of right conduct, but it is a sanction of right conduct. It assures us that there is such a thing as right, and that when we know what it is we are bound to do it."[87] But it is after Froude quotes the following passage from the *Grammar of Assent*, one of the most brilliant in the book, that he takes issue with Newman. Here is the quote:

If, as is the case, we feel responsibility, are ashamed, are frightened, at transgressing the voice of conscience, this implies that there is One to whom we are responsible, before whom we are ashamed, whose claims upon us we fear. If, on doing wrong, we feel that same tearful, broken-hearted sorrow which overwhelms us on hurting a mother; if, on doing right, we enjoy the same sunny serenity of mind, the same soothing, satisfactory delight which follows on our receiving praise from a father, we certainly have within us the image of some person, to whom our love and veneration look, in whose smile we find our happiness, for whom we yearn, towards whom we direct our pleadings, in whose anger we are troubled and waste away. These feelings in us are such as require for their exciting cause an intelligent being: we are not affectionate towards a stone, nor do we feel shame before a horse or a dog; we have no remorse or compunction on breaking mere human law: yet, so it is, conscience excites all these painful emotions, confusion, foreboding, self-condemnation; and, on the other hand, it sheds upon us a deep peace, a sense of security. a resignation, and a hope, which there is no sensible, no earthly object to elicit. "The wicked flees, when no one pursueth"; then why does he flee? whence his terror? Who is it that he sees in solitude, in darkness, in the hidden chambers of his heart? If the cause of these emotions does not belong to this visible world, the Object to which his perception is directed must be Supernatural and Divine; and thus the phenomena of Conscience, as a dictate, avail to impress the imagination with the picture of a

---

[86] GA, 105–6.
[87] *Short Studies* ii, 111–12.

Supreme Governor, a Judge, holy, just, powerful, all seeing, retributive, and is the creative principle of religion, as the moral sense is the principle of ethics.[88]

The reason why it is here, as Froude says, "that our acquiescence in Father Newman's reasoning comes to an end, and we henceforth part company with him," is rather striking. Like Carlyle, Froude affected to despise the feelings—his blithe defense of the manifold enormities of Henry VIII and Oliver Cromwell show this amply enough—and, as a result, he imagined Newman's respect for the feelings a sign of weakness: for the rationalist historian it was proof that Newman resorted to feelings when reasonings failed him. Froude was also distrustful of his own feelings when it came to matters of faith, especially Newman's faith, as we shall see. Indeed, Froude's distrust of the dogmatic extended to what he himself nicely called "the imaginative intellect." "His book is a counterpart to Butler's 'Analogy,'" Froude wrote

> and as the first part of the "Analogy" has been in these bad times a support to many of us, when the formulas of the established creeds have crumbled away, so we give cordial welcome to this addition to our stock of religious philosophy, which addresses itself to the intellect of the nineteenth century as Butler addressed that of its predecessor. But just as with Butler, when we pass from his treatment of the facts of nature to the defense of the dogmatic system of Christianity, we exchange the philosopher for the special pleader, so Father Newman at the same transition point equally ceases to convince. Assumption takes the place of reasoning. Facts are no longer looked in the face, and objections are either ignored altogether or are caricatured in order to be answered. Hitherto he has been pleading the cause of religion as it has existed in all ages and under countless varieties of form. We are now led across the morasses of technical theology. We spring from tuft to tuft and hummock to hummock. The ground shakes about us, and we are allowed no breathing time to pause, lest it give way under our feet altogether. The promised land lies before us, the land of absolute repose in the decisions of the Infallible Church. Once there we may rest for ever; and we are swung along towards it, guided, if we may use the word for an absolute surrender of reason, by the obscure emotions and half realized perceptions of what is called the imaginative intellect. We leave behind us as misleading the apparatus of faculties which conduct us successfully through ordinary life. We are told to believe, and accept it on Father Newman's authority, that we are not after all chasing a will-o'-the-wisp, and that the other side to which he points the way is really solid ground, and not a mere fog-bank.[89]

The objections that Froude raises here to Newman's locating the springs of religious assent in the affections, as well as the intellect, would influence two other ardent rationalists. First, we can quote what the Anglo-Irish historian William Edward Hartpole Lecky (1838–1903) had to say of Newman after his death in an essay attacking the convert, the very wording of which suggests that Lecky had Froude in mind when he wrote it, even though he wrote his work

[88] Ibid., ii, 113–14, GA, 109–10.
[89] Short Studies, ii, 116–17.

on eighteenth-century Ireland to refute what he regarded as the "anti-Catholic calumnies" of Froude:[90]

> In an age remarkable for brilliancy of style he was one of the greatest masters of English prose. His power of drawing subtle distinctions and pursuing long trains of subtle reasoning made him one of the most skilful of controversialists, and he had a great insight into spiritual cravings and an admirable gift of interpreting and appealing to many forms of religious emotion. But though he was a man of rare, delicate, and most seductive genius, we have sometimes doubted whether any of his books are destined to take a permanent and considerable place in English literature. He was not a great scholar, or an original and independent thinker. Dealing with questions inseparably connected with historical evidence, he had neither the judicial spirit nor the firm grasp of a real historian, and he had very little skill in measuring probabilities and degrees of evidence. He had a manifest incapacity, which was quite as much moral as intellectual, for looking facts in the face and pursuing trains of thought to unwelcome conclusions. He often took refuge from them in clouds of casuistry. The scepticism which was a marked feature of his intellect allied itself closely with credulity, for it was directed against reason itself; and though he has expressed in admirable language many true and beautiful thoughts, the glamour of his style too often concealed much weakness and uncertainty of judgment and much sophistry in argument.[91]

Secondly, there is this passage from Fitzjames Stephen's *Liberty, Equality and Fraternity* (1873), which shows how ready the literary jurist was to reinforce Froude's line of attack against a Roman faith that both dismissed as credulous and absurd. When it came to what they regarded as the casuistry of papists, the two Englishmen were as one. "It is easy to understand why men passionately eager about the propagation of their creed should persistently deny the force of … [evidence], and should try by every means in their power to prove that in regard to religious subjects insufficient evidence may and ought to produce an unnatural effect," Fitzjames Stephen wrote in his best knockabout polemical manner.

> This does not justify the attempt to give evidence a weight which does not belong to it. Our feelings ought to be regulated by the facts which excite them. It is a great mistake, and the source of half the errors which exist in the world, to yield to the temptation to allow our feelings to govern our estimate of facts. Rational religious feeling is that feeling, whatever it may be, which is excited in the mind by a true estimate of the facts known to us which bear upon religion. If we do not know enough to feel warmly, let us by all means feel calmly; but it is dishonest to try to convert excited feeling into evidence of facts which would justify it. To say, "There must be a God because I love him," is just like saying, "That man must be a rogue because I hate him," which many people do say, but not wisely. There are in these days many speculations by very able men, or men reputed to

---

[90] See William Edward Hartpole Lecky, *The History of Ireland in the Eighteenth Century*, 5 vols. (1892–6).
[91] William Edward Hartpole Lecky, *Historical and Political Essays* (London: Longman, Green & Co., 1908), 249–50.

be of great ability, which can all be resolved into attempts to increase the bulk and the weight of evidence by heating it with love, Dr. Newman's "Grammar of Assent," with all its hair-splitting about the degrees of assent, and the changes which it rings upon certainty and certitude, is a good illustration of this, but it is like the wriggling of a worm on a hook, or like the efforts which children sometimes make to draw two straight lines so as to enclose a space, or to make a cross on a piece of paper with a single stroke of a pencil, not passing twice over any part of the cross. Turn and twist as you will, you can never really get out of the proposition that the Christian history is just as probable as the evidence makes it, and no more; and that to give a greater degree of assent to it, or, if the expression is preferred, to give an unreserved assent to the proposition that it has a greater degree of probability than the evidence warrants, is to give up its character as an historical event altogether.[92]

One could quote a good many responses from Newman to this appraisal of how the feelings inform religious assent—his sermons take up the theme again and again—but here is a characteristic one from his *Parochial and Plain Sermons* (1842). There he defines the dogma of the Trinity thus: the "Eternal Three are worshipped by the Catholic Church as distinct, yet One;—the Most High God being wholly the Father, and wholly the Son, and wholly the Holy Ghost; yet the Three Persons being distinct from each other, not merely in name, or by human abstraction, but in very truth, as truly as a fountain is distinct from the stream which flows from it, or the root of a tree from its branches." Then, doubtless with the rationalist impatience with dogma in mind, he says:

> Now should any one be tempted to say that this is dark language, and difficult speculation to set before a Christian people, I answer that it is not more dark and difficult than the sacred mystery which is our great subject today; that it is in fact but the *exposition* of the sacred mystery as the Church has received it; that I am not engaged in defending the Creed of St. Athanasius, but am stating its meaning; and, My Brethren, that you may well bear once in the year to be reminded that Christianity gives exercise to the whole mind of man, to our highest and most subtle reason, as well as to our feelings, affections, imagination, and conscience. If we find it tries us, and is too severe, whether for our reason, or our imagination, or our feelings, let us bow down in silent adoration, and submit to it each of our faculties by turn, not complain of its sublimity or its range.[93]

Froude's contempt for dogma recalls that of Edward Gibbon. Gibbon hated dogma because he could never forgive himself for falling prey to it when he poped as a Magdalen undergraduate—to his own eventual chagrin, not to mention that of his father, who saw to it that his bookish son was sent off to Lausanne to be reindoctrinated into the family's Protestantism. The connoisseur of classical culture in Gibbon saw dogma as a threat to that culture's polytheistic broadmindedness. Froude hated dogma because it had caused division not only between his family and himself but between families throughout Oxford and the nation

---

[92] Stephen, *Liberty, Equality, Fraternity*, 189–90.
[93] Newman, "The Mystery of the Holy Trinity" (1838), *PS*, vi, 352–3.

beyond. "Wives have quarrelled with their husbands, and husbands with wives; the son has been set against the father, and the father against the son; thousands of households have been made miserable by young people dissatisfied with their spiritual condition, and throwing themselves upon Catholic priests because they require, as they fancy, 'something deeper and truer' than was enough for the last century."[94] This was an obvious exaggeration but it still exhibits the deep, personal hatred that impelled Froude to take issue with Newman's argument in the *Grammar of Assent*.[95] "There are two roads on which it is possible to travel," he wrote, "after starting from conscience and the acknowledgement of God to whom obedience is due. There is the theological road, and there is the road of experience and fact."[96] This could almost be said to be an epitome of Gibbon's ruthlessly superficial account of the rise of Christianity, an account which would only concern itself with externals. Martyrdom and the dogmatic Faith articulated by the Fathers meant nothing to the glib, sardonic historian. Yet Froude borrows again and again from Gibbon's Socinianism to try to discredit the place Newman gives to dogma in the appeal of Christianity. Indeed, in attacking Newman, Froude writes a kind of parody of Gibbon. If the enlightenment historian contrasted a malign, barbarous, dogmatic Christianity with a benign, civilized, non-dogmatic polytheism, the rationalist historian contrasts an oppressive Catholicism with a decadent Protestantism to argue that both are as unbelievable as they are obsessed with "imaginary speculative theories" precisely because they are in thrall to the phantasmagoria of dogma—a captivity first brought about by the Vicar of St. Mary's. "Religion has had two parts," Froude says:

> the inward moral and spiritual, the outward ritualistic, or speculative; and the division between them, and the history of their effects upon mankind, when one or the other has preponderated, is the most signal testimony to their real character, and to the relations in which they stand to each other and to the world. Where the moral element has been foremost, where men have been chiefly bent upon contending with practical evil, and making so much as they can understand of the law of God the rule of their dealings among themselves, there the religion has spread over the earth like water for the purifying the nations. Where the superstitious or theological element has been in the ascendant, where charity has been second to orthodoxy, and religion has been an affair of temples and sacrifices and devotional refinements, there as uniformly it has lost its beneficent powers, it has fraternized with the blackest and darkest of human passions, and has carried with it as its shadow, division and hatred and cruelty. The power in the universe, whatever it be, which envies human happiness, has laid hold of conscience and distracted it from its proper function. Instead of looking any more for our duties to our neighbors, we go astray, and quarrel with each other over imaginary speculative theories. We wonder at the failure of Christianity, at the small progress which it has made in comparison with the brilliancy of its rise: but if men had shown as much fanaticism in carrying into practice the Sermon on the

---

[94] "The Oxford Counter-Reformation," in *Short Studies*, iv, 242.
[95] See Edward Short, "Newman, Gibbon and God's Particular Providence," in *Newman and History*, 3–80.
[96] *Short Studies*, ii, 117.

Mount as in disputing the least of the thousand dogmatic definitions which have superseded the Gospel, we should not be now lamenting with Father Newman that "God's control over the world is so indirect, and His action so obscure."[97]

In musings such as these, one can see what an indelible mark the divisions of Tractarian Oxford left on Froude. He will not enter into Newman's case for dogmatic certainty because it is too redolent of those divisions, and he justifies leaving the case unexamined by claiming that it is grounded on inadmissible evidence.

> Prejudices, prepossessions, "trifles light as air," irregular emotions, implicit reasons, "such as we feel, but which for some cause or other, because they are too subtle or too circuitous, we cannot put into words so as to satisfy logic," these, and such as these, in matters of religion, are genuine evidences to which, we are told, a reasonable man is expected to defer. Having once passed the line where evidence can be produced and tested, we are at the mercy of imagination, and the reader who has thus committed himself can now be led forward blindfold through the analytical labyrinth. The intellectual faculties, "looking before and after," are touched as it were by a torpedo. Our criteria of truth leave us.[98]

Indeed, Froude may begin his review by claiming that Newman's "object, from the beginning to the end, is to combat and overthrow the position of Locke, that reasonable assent is proportioned to evidence, and in its nature, therefore, admits of degrees."[99] But Froude omits to quote Newman's refutation of Locke in this regard, where the deft disputant in Newman demonstrates that his evidence is every bit as admissible as Locke's. Apropos the empiricist philosopher, Newman writes: "This celebrated writer, after the manner of his school, speaks freely of degrees of assent, and considers that the strength of assent given to each proposition varies with the strength of the inference on which the assent follows; yet he is obliged to make exceptions to his general principle,—exceptions, unintelligible on his abstract doctrine, but demanded by the logic of facts. The practice of mankind is too strong for the antecedent theorem, to which he is desirous to subject it."[100] Here, as in so much of the *Grammar*, Newman insists on consulting not so much the contentions of philosophy as the experience of ordinary life in order to establish the tenability of his claims for certainty. Andrew Meszaros certainly recognizes as much: "According to Newman, in religious matters, it is the antecedent considerations more than the evidences that actually bear the brunt of the proof. If the reverence or the 'spontaneous or traditional feeling of Christians' towards the Virgin Mary is strong enough, then actually little evidence is needed to convince them that she was immaculately conceived or assumed into heaven."[101] Indeed, Newman shows that even Locke was constrained to concede

---

[97] Ibid., 118–19.
[98] Ibid., 131–2.
[99] Ibid., 102.
[100] GA, 106.
[101] Andrew Meszaros, "John Henry Newman and the Thomistic Tradition: Convergences in Contribution to Development Theory," *Nova et Vetera*, English edition, 19, no. 2 (2021), 454. The quotation within the quotation is from *Dev.*, 145.

the vitality of the same experience.

> First he says, in his chapter "On Probability", "Most of the propositions we think, reason, discourse, nay, act upon, are such as we cannot have undoubted knowledge of their truth; yet some of them *border so near* upon certainty, that we *make no doubt at all* about them, but *assent* to them *as firmly*, and act according to that assent as resolutely, *as if they were infallibly demonstrated*, and that our knowledge of them was perfect and certain." Here he allows that inferences, which are only "near upon certainty", are so near, that we legitimately accept them with "no doubt at all", and "assent to them as firmly as if they were infallibly demonstrated". That is, he affirms and sanctions the very paradox to which I am committed myself.[102]

Despite the fact that Newman did adduce proper evidence to make his case, Froude shows that it is not Newman's evidence that he finds discreditable but Newman's Church. As Ian Ker points out in his excellent critical edition of the *Grammar of Assent*, Froude's review is suffused with "anti-Catholic invective."[103] Here is but one specimen of this impassioned animus.

> Whether the Church has really gained in philosophical cogency by the Reformation and its consequences is a matter on which Father Newman has a right to his opinion; but others have also a right to theirs, which will probably be different. To ourselves it appears that what vitality she possesses is proportioned to the degree in which she has adopted the principles of her enemies; that so far as she retains her own she becomes every hour more powerless to act upon them. If it be vitality to have lost her hold on nine tenths of the educated laymen in her own communion; if it be vitality to have compelled every Catholic Government to take from her the last fibre of regular and civil authority, to deprive her even of her control over education, and relegate her to the domain of mere opinion; if it be a sign of vigor that her once world-wide temporal authority is now limited to a single state, and supported there by the bayonets of a stranger, then indeed the evidence of her divinity may be said to have gained strength. In the sixteenth and seventeenth centuries the Church destroyed by sword and fire many hundreds of thousands of men and women in the effort to recover her dominion. She still professes intolerance, and Father Newman himself claims it as her right. Let her lay her hand upon one single heretic and dispose of him, as she used to do, at the stake; let but one man, now on the occasion of this brilliant Council, be publicly burnt in Rome for want of orthodoxy, and who does not know that the whole ecclesiastical fabric would be torn to pieces by the indignation of mankind?[104]

This can serve as a good example of how anti-Catholic prejudice disabled a good number of Newman's contemporary critics from understanding his work. The strenuous champion of Henry VIII was too intent on defending the English Reformation to give Newman's book the critical attention it deserves. The lengths

---
[102] *GA*, 106–7.
[103] *GA*, liii.
[104] *Short Studies*, ii, 133–4.

to which he would go to defend the Reformation, however, had a kind of quixotic doggedness about them. Even when one disagrees with Froude, he is still worth reading. On this score, Birrell is right: there was an "inaccurate genius" in Froude, or perhaps one should say a genius for inaccuracy, as this proves:

> The conclusion contains a beautiful sketch of the rise of Christianity, with an analysis of the causes assigned by Gibbon in explanation of its spread, and an exhibition of their insufficiency. We are not concerned to defend Gibbon, whose reasoning on this subject has always appeared to us singularly unconvincing. Still less do we wish to question the nature of the power which enabled Christianity to diffuse itself; though we may mean by Christianity something else than Father Newman means, and by the power which enabled it to grow, a spiritual influence working from mind to mind, rather than an external supernatural force. Father Newman identifies Christianity with the complex doctrinal system embodied in the formulas and represented in the constitution of the Catholic Church. We mean by it the code of moral duties which were taught by our Lord upon the Mount, and which, as the type of human perfection, He illustrated in his own character. In so far as the Catholic Church has adhered to the original pattern, in so far as it has addressed itself to the moral sense, and has aimed rather at making men good than at furnishing their intellects with orthodox formulas, so far it has fulfilled its function of regenerating mankind. Under this aspect the spread of it ceases to be a mystery. The Roman world was sunk in lies, insincere idolatry, and the coarsest and most revolting profligacy. There is something in human nature, in all times and in all countries, which instinctively recoils against such things, something which says that lies are to be abhorred, and that purity is nobler than bestiality; and when the bad side of things is at its worst the nobler sort of men refuse to put up with it longer. The Roman government offered to the devotion of the empire a Divus Nero or a Divus Domitianus. The image of a peasant of Palestine, a being of stainless integrity, appeared simultaneously, pointing to a Father in heaven, and requiring men in his name to lead pure and self-sacrificing lives; and if it be true that man is more than a beast, and that conscious and moral sense are a part of his natural constitution, we require no miracles to explain why millions of men and women with such alternatives before them were found to choose the better part. Father Newman thinks it unexampled: if he will study the history of the Reformation he will find its exact counterpart among "the miserable deeds" of the sixteenth century.[105]

To see Froude trying to justify this outrageous claim is to see the paradoxical polemicist in him in all his glory. "Protestantism, like Christianity itself, began from below," he writes.

> The Marian martyrs were nine tenths of them petty tradesmen and mechanics. The Christian brothers who first imported Tyndal's New Testament were weavers, carpenters, and cobblers; and the Catholic missionaries who came over in Elizabeth's time to reconquer England declared that their only opponents were to be found among the vilest of the people. The Catholic religion in the sixteenth

---

[105] Ibid., 141–2.

century had become like the heathen religions in the first. It had forgotten moral duty in the development of its theology. The service of God had become a juggler's game; the only visible fruits of it were tyranny and simony and lasciviousness: and the uncorrupted part of Europe rose in indignation and declared that they would remain in it no longer: that God was a Spirit, and those who worshipped Him should worship in spirit and in truth. The Church treated them as the Roman Empire had treated the Church in its infancy. They suffered martyrdom like the early Christians in defense of the same principles, and like them they conquered.[106]

Even though such polemical fireworks are amusing, they overshadow the occasional good points in Froude's criticism. Throughout the review, he makes a number of just and insightful observations. "The argument is extremely subtle, and often difficult to follow, but the difficulty is in the subject rather than in the treatment," he writes. "Dr. Newman has watched and analyzed the processes of the mind with as much care and minuteness as Ehrenberg[107] the organization of animalculae. The knotted and tangled skein is disengaged and combed out till every fibre of it can be taken up separately and examined at leisure; while all along, hints are let fall from time to time, expressions, seemingly casual, illustrations, or notices of emotional peculiarities, every one of which has its purpose, and, to the careful reader, is a sign-post of the road on which he is travelling."[108] Elsewhere, he notes, with succinct relish: "Every line, every word tells, from the opening sentence to the last."[109] Then, again, he has nothing but praise for the mastery with which Newman makes his case, even though he feels obliged to withhold assent from its conclusions. "Nowhere in the English language will be found the reasons for believing in a moral power as the supreme ruling force in the universe, drawn out more clearly or more persuasively. There are no gratuitous assumptions—no appeals to the imagination. He lays the facts of personal experience before us: he indicates the conclusion at which they point: and when the conclusion is conceded, the obligations of obedience follow."[110] Good criticism is impossible without good sympathetic reading. His biases notwithstanding, Froude extends this sympathy to Newman, even when it tends to undermine his own captious digressions. For example, at one point Froude admits, with winning humility:

> When the mind is ... devotionally pervaded, the Catholic theology will be developed by the theological intellect as naturally as geometrical theorems from the elementary axioms and propositions. The difficulty is with the preparation of the soil; and if we find Father Newman unpersuasive, the fault may be simply in ourselves. Persuasiveness implies agreement in first principles between the teacher and the taught. It is possible that we may be color blind, or be without ear

---

[106] *Short Studies*, ii, 143–4.
[107] Christian Gottfried Ehrenberg (1795–1876), German naturalist, zoologist, biologist, and microscopist.
[108] *Short Studies*, ii, 103.
[109] *Ibid.*, 102.
[110] *Ibid.*, 110.

to follow the harmony of the theological variations. The Catholic doctrines may carry conviction only to the elect. Those who are chosen to inherit the blessing, may alone have grace to apprehend its conditions. If it be so, we are beyond help; but we claim for the present to belong to those who believe in God and in the moral laws, and to those, therefore, to whom Father Newman says that his book is addressed. In this character we have a right to speak, and when he fails to convince us, to give reasons for withholding our assent.[111]

That this concern for his own Protestant limitations was not a passing concern is borne out in the review's conclusion, where he writes, apropos these limitations, that a good number of his contemporaries, despite Newman's certainty, or perhaps because of it, are "perplexed and disheartened," "looking back into Egypt" or "staggering into Atheism."[112] Indeed, it is the very certitude on which Newman insists that Froude could not abide. To claim that faith without doubt was not only possible but an inalienable hallmark of the Roman Catholic struck him as an epistemological conjurer's trick. "You feel that you are in the hands of a thinker of the very highest powers," Froude writes,

> yet they are the powers rather of an intellectual conjuror than of a teacher who commands your confidence. You are astonished at the skill which is displayed, and unable to explain away the results; but you are conscious all the time that you are played with; you are perplexed, but you are not attracted; and unless you bring a Catholic conclusion ready made with you to the study, you certainly will not arrive at it. For it is not a simple acknowledgment that Catholicism may perhaps be true that is required of us, or even that it is probably true, and that a reasonable person might see cause for joining the Roman communion. This is not conviction at all, nor is it related in any way to a religious frame of mind. We are expected rather to feel Catholicism to be absolutely necessary and completely true—true, not as an inference from argument, but as imposed by a spiritual command—true, in a sense which allows no possibility of error, and cannot and ought not to endure contradiction.[113]

Obviously, this is a misreading of Newman's understanding not only of religious certitude but of the Church's infallibility. Froude's misconstrual of these things is clear from the moral he attempts to draw from them. Quoting Newman, he writes: "'The highest opinion of Protestants in religion … is, generally speaking, assent to a probability, as even Butler has been understood or misunderstood to teach, and therefore consistent with the toleration of its contradictory.' The creed, therefore, which we are to accept is the Romanism with which we are familiar in history; persecuting from the necessity of the case, for it cannot, where it has the power, permit opposition. No heterodox opinion can be borne with, or be even heard in its own defense."[114] Newman's clarification of the matter could only have exasperated the rationalist in Froude still more.

---

[111] Ibid., 120–1.
[112] Ibid., 121.
[113] Ibid., 104.
[114] Ibid., 105.

> It is very common, doubtless, especially in religious controversy, to confuse infallibility with certitude, and to argue that, since we have not the one, we have not the other, for no one can claim to be certain on any point, who is not infallible about all; but the two words stand for things quite distinct from each other. For example, I remember for certain what I did yesterday, but still my memory is not infallible; I am quite clear that two and two make four, but I often make mistakes in long addition sums. I have no doubt whatever that John or Richard is my true friend, but I have before now trusted those who failed me, and I may do so again before I die. A certitude is directed to this or that particular proposition; it is not a faculty or gift, but a disposition of mind relatively to a definite case which is before me. Infallibility, on the contrary, is just that which certitude is not; it *is* a faculty or gift, and relates, not to some one truth in particular, but to all possible propositions in a given subject-matter. I am quite certain that Victoria is our Sovereign, and not her father, the late Duke of Kent, without laying any claim to the gift of infallibility; as I may do a virtuous action, without being impeccable. I may be certain that the Church is infallible, while I am myself a fallible mortal; otherwise, I cannot be certain that the Supreme Being is infallible, until I am infallible myself. ... Therefore, we may be certain of the infallibility of the Church, while we admit that in many things we are not, and cannot be, certain at all.[115]

Newman's discriminations notwithstanding, Froude refused to concede the convert's argument for certitude or infallibility, content to regard Rome and her adherents as involved in a kind of organized fantasy. "The Church evidently is the true *Deus ex machinâ*," he writes. "The Church, in virtue of its infallibility, will resolve this and all ... difficulties; and the infallibility, it seems, is somehow or other its own witness, and proves itself."[116] To this objection, Newman could have pointed his implacable critic to a memorable passage of his book, where he says, apropos the infallibility of the Church and our assent to it:

> He who believes that Christ is the Truth, and that the Evangelists are truthful, believes all that He has said through them, though he has only read St. Matthew and has not read St. John. He who believes in the *depositum* of Revelation, believes in all the doctrines of the *depositum*; and since he cannot know them all at once, he knows some doctrines, and does not know others; he may know only the Creed, nay, perhaps only the chief portions of the Creed; but, whether he knows little or much, he has the intention of believing all that there is to believe whenever and as soon as it is brought home to him, if he believes in Revelation at all. All that he knows now as revealed, and all that he shall know, and all that there is to know, he embraces it all in his intention by one act of faith; otherwise, it is but an accident that he believes this or that, not because it is a revelation. This virtual, interpretative, or prospective belief is called a believing *implicitè*; and it follows from this, that, granting that the Canons of Councils and the other ecclesiastical documents and confessions, to which I have referred, are really involved in the *depositum* or revealed word, every Catholic, in accepting the *depositum*, does

---

[115] *GA*, 224–48.
[116] *Short Studies*, ii, 126.

implicitè accept those dogmatic decisions.[117]

Imagining what Froude and his rationalist friends might have thought and felt while reading such passages is rather comical. Newman reaffirmed everything about the Faith that they abominated. Yet the fact that he devoted so much of his time to reaffirming truths that his contemporaries found insufferable was one measure of the necessity of his apostolate. That our own contemporaries should also find such truths equally repellent gives Newman's witness its perennial appeal. No one speaks of how the individual Christian enters into the infallible Truth of the Church and makes it his own as clearly or as usefully as Saint John Henry Cardinal Newman.

> The word of the Church is the word of the revelation. That the Church is the infallible oracle of truth is the fundamental dogma of the Catholic religion; and "I believe what the Church proposes to be believed" is an act of real assent, including all particular assents, notional and real; and, while it is possible for unlearned as well as learned, it is imperative on learned as well as unlearned. And thus it is, that by believing the word of the Church *implicitè*, that is, by believing all that that word does or shall declare itself to contain, every Catholic, according to his intellectual capacity, supplements the shortcomings of his knowledge without blunting his real assent to what is elementary, and takes upon himself from the first the whole truth of revelation, progressing from one apprehension of it to another according to his opportunities of doing so.[118]

V

Another comical aspect of Froude's obsession with Newman's Catholicism is that if he could not embrace it, neither could he have done with it. In "Revival of Romanism" (1874), he marvels at the resilience of a faith that should by rights be rejected wholesale by the modern rational world and yet continues to meet with conversions. "The proverb which says that nothing is certain but the unforeseen was never better verified than in the resurrection, as it were out of the grave, during the last forty years, of the Roman Catholic religion," he writes.

> In my own boyhood it hung about some few ancient English families like a ghost of the past. They preserved their creed as an heirloom which tradition rather than conviction made sacred to them. A convert from Protestantism to Popery would have been as great a monster as a convert to Buddhism or Odin worship. … The singular change which we have witnessed and are still witnessing is not due to freshly-discovered evidence of the truth of what had been abandoned as superstition. The intellect which saw the falsehood of the papal pretensions in the sixteenth century, sees it only more clearly in the nineteenth. More than ever the assumptions of the Holy See are perceived to rest on error or on fraud. The doctrines of the Catholic Church have gained only increased improbability

---

[117] *GA*, 152.
[118] *GA*, 153.

from the advance of knowledge. Her history in the light of critical science is a tissue of legend woven by the devout imagination.[119]

Yet despite "the tide of knowledge" moving against Romanism, the Catholic Church, "as a kite rises against the wind," has "once more shot up into visible and practical consequence." She may be losing Spain and Italy, her old bastions, but "she is gaining in the modern energetic races, which had been the stronghold of Protestantism"—Germany, England and America. The papacy's relinquishment of the Papal States, far from eroding, increases her power.

> Her numbers increase, her organisation gathers vigour. Her clergy are energetic, bold, and aggressive. Sees, long prostrate; are re-established; cathedrals rise, and churches, with schools, and colleges, and convents, and monasteries. She has taken into her service her old enemy the press, and has established a popular literature. Her hierarchy in England and America have already compelled the State to consult their opinions and respect their pleasure; while each step that is gained is used as a vantage-ground from which to present fresh demands. Hildebrand, in the plenitude of his power, was not more arrogant in his claim of universal sovereignty than the present wearer of the tiara.[120]

For Froude, the evidence of this exasperating revival was peculiarly striking in France. "The France of the Revolution and the Goddess of Reason, the France of Science and the Academy, the France, which, however dark her outward fortunes, held with easy pre-eminence the intellectual sovereignty of Europe" was now re-evangelized, especially in light of the testament to the Faith of Bernadette Soubirous (1844–75), the miller's daughter, whose visions of Our Lady of Lourdes in 1858 so outraged Protestants.[121] Now instead of deploring the imposture of the Church and her dogmas, France had become a place where her "most accomplished sons and daughters" were "flocking as pilgrims to the scenes of a pretended miracle; and a woman who deserved rather a year's hard labour in jail is erected into a saint."[122]

---

[119] *Short Studies*, iii, 130–1.
[120] Ibid., 132.
[121] In 1858, at the age of fourteen, Bernadette experienced fourteen visions of the Blessed Virgin Mary over a period of six months at the rock of Massabielle, Lourdes. According to the Protestant hagiographer, David Hugh Farmer: Bernadette was "an undersized ailing child who suffered from asthma; her intellectual equipment was simple, and some witnesses thought her stupid. But her veracity, courage and complete disinterestedness are beyond dispute. She was subjected to a series of searching investigations both by the clergy and minor state officials; and from all of these she emerged with her story unshaken." In 1866, Bernadette joined the Sisters of Notre Dame of Nevers, with whom she spent the rest of her life, dying at the age of thirty-five after prolonged illness "heroically borne." *Oxford Dictionary of the Saints*. In 1862, after exhaustive canonical review, Soubirous's encounters with Our Lady of Lourdes were declared "worthy of belief." Since her death, Soubirous's body has remained internally incorrupt. The Marian shrine at Lourdes has become a major pilgrimage site, drawing over five million pilgrims of all denominations each year. On 8 December 1933, Pope Pius XI declared Soubirous a saint of the Catholic Church. Her feast day, initially specified as 18 February—the day Mary promised to make her happy, not in this life, but in the other—is now observed in most places on the date of her death, 16 April.
[122] *Short Studies*, iii, 136.

Despite such crude anti-Catholicism, Froude was fair enough to attribute such renewed faith, however improbable, to the auspices of the Church herself. Like Newman, he saw clearly that the vitality and appeal of the Church had a good deal to do with her readiness to eschew the Erastianism that defined the Protestant churches. Rome's stalwart anti-Erastianism ensured not only a certain integrity but a thoroughgoing discipline, both of which the Church would periodically muster in her long, checquered, resilient history.[123] "Never was the Church better disciplined, never more completely denationalised and unpatriotic than at the present moment," Froude wrote.

> When her creed was really and universally received and believed, her bishops and archbishops were engaged in the local government of their several countries. They were English, they were French, they were Spanish. They shared in national aspirations; they were swayed by national prejudices. The Popes themselves were often rather Italian princes than vicegerents over the mystic organism which was co-extensive with mankind. As temporal governments have become secularised, the influences have ceased which so long interfered with the centralising tendencies of the system. As division of opinion grows among the masses, those who remain or who become members of the Catholic Church find a closer bond of union in their creed than in their temporal allegiance. The Church of Rome is now herself and nothing else. From the Pontiff to the humblest parish priest, her ecclesiastics acknowledge no object save the assertion of the Catholic cause. Her bishops and clergy all over the world are as completely obedient to orders from Rome, they work together as harmoniously and enthusiastically as the officers of a perfectly organised army. Whether in their own minds they approve or disapprove the orders which they receive—it is no matter—they obey them. The Immaculate Conception is proclaimed; there is a murmur of surprise, but it dies away: the miracle in the womb of St. Anne becomes thenceforth a matter of faith. Papal infallibility claims to be acknowledged; clamour follows, and even active resistance, but when the decree is past, submission is absolute. The hierarchy regard themselves as soldiers of a cause to which all minor interests, all personal opinions must yield. Unanimity and cooperation are essential to success; and with a heartiness, an enthusiasm, a singleness of purpose which is never forgotten, and to which every enjoyment and occupation of life is deliberately postponed, the entire ecclesiastical order devotes itself, body and soul, to the propagation of the principles of the Roman Church.[124]

In seeking culprits to blame for the revival of Romanism, Froude turned, first, to Protestants themselves for abandoning their Protestantism, which, again, he sees in exclusively moral terms. "The Reformation of the sixteenth century was the waking up, after a long slumber, of a living conviction," he contended, "and the Reformers were not more distinguished from the Catholics by the simplicity of their doctrines than by the austerity and purity of their lives." Yet

---

[123] For a detailed look at Newman's witty, prescient reading of Erastianism, see "Newman's Anglican Difficulties: A Conversation with the Editor," Edward Short, *What The Bells Sang: Essays and Reviews* (Leominster: Gracewing, 2023), 459–68.
[124] *Short Studies*, iii, 146–7.

> The veil of imposture which had so long shut out the light of the sky had suddenly been rent away. The ritualistic paraphernalia which had usurped the functions of piety appeared as the tawdry furniture of a theatre when surprised by daylight. Masses, penances, absolutions, pilgrimages to the shrines of saints—mechanical substitutes, all of them, for a life of righteousness—were recognized in their infinite contemptibility as but the idle mummery of a spiritual puppet-play. The true nature of human existence, the tremendous responsibilities of it; the majesty and purity of God, and the assurance of his judgment, came home as they had never come before to the hearts of those whose eyes were opened. Thus, while in their consciousness of sin and infirmity, the Reformers repudiated with passionate earnestness every notion of human merit; while they denied that by the fullest obedience men could either deserve God's favour, or escape his wrath, they endeavoured, nevertheless, with all their souls, to learn and to do his will. They loved what they knew to be good; they hated what they knew to be evil. They lived soberly, purely, modestly, honestly, and industriously. They modelled themselves after the highest conceptions of duty which they were able to form. Wealth would have been showered on Luther had he cared to receive it: his scale of expenditure was that of a modern artisan. Calvin might have commanded any income that he liked to name from the revenues at Geneva: he was contented with the average wages of a clerk.[125]

Yet, after the Roman imposture had been shown the door, Froude contended, the Reformers fell from their former commanding heights and began to throw away the moral gains they had so heroically won. Froude's refusal to enter into any consideration of dogma in this licentious assessment might discredit his understanding of Protestantism, but his very insistence on the moral at the expense of the dogmatic was an implicit concession that there could be no doctrinal defense of the Protestant religion. Indeed, Froude's moral defense of Protestantism betrayed him into equating the taboos of Calvinism with the Sacraments of Catholicism, which could only call attention to the dogmatic hollowness of the former.

> A religion which holds possession of our lives, which directs us at each step which we take, becomes part of our own souls. Unless, in some shape or other, it prescribes a rule of conduct, it inevitably loses its hold. The Catholic system scarce leaves an hour without its stated duties; such and such forms to be gone through, such and such prayers to be repeated. Night and day, morning and evening, at meals and in the intervals between meals, the Catholic is reminded of his creed by a set form. Calvinism superseded these formal observances by yet more noble practical observances. It was ever present with its behests in fixing the scale of permitted expenditure, in regulating the dress, the food, the enjoyments, the hours of sleep and labour; sternly cutting short all idle pleasure and luxury; sternly insisting on the right performance of all practical work, the trade, the handicraft, or whatever it might be, as something for every thread and fibre of which a man would one day be called to account.[126]

---

[125] Ibid., 152–3.
[126] Ibid., 154–5.

That Protestants might have abandoned such Calvinist "observances" precisely because they had no dogmatic warrant is not a possibility Froude entertains. Instead, he simply chronicles their abandonment. "After the middle of the seventeenth century Protestantism ceased to be aggressive," he writes. "It no longer produced men conspicuously nobler and better than Romanism, and, therefore, it no longer made converts. As it became established, it adapted itself to the world, laid aside its harshness, confined itself more and more to the enforcement of particular doctrines, and abandoned, at first tacitly and afterward deliberately, the pretence to interfere with private life or practical business."[127]

If Froude's reading of the character of Protestantism as opposed to Catholicism is not altogether reliable, he nicely captures the desuetude into which the Protestant virtues fell once the creed of Protestantism, such as it was, could no longer command respect. Or perhaps one should say that it was when Protestants could not present themselves as morally better than their neighbors as a result of their creed that they deserted the creed. For Froude, when Protestant countries were "no longer able to boast of any special or remarkable moral standard ... the effect of the creed on the imagination ... [was] analogously impaired."

In his sensibly realistic way, Newman never imagined Christianity would turn most fallen men into choir boys. In one memorable passage, he writes: "It is indeed by no means clear that Christianity has at any time been of any great spiritual advantage to the world at large. The general temper of mankind, taking man individually, is what it ever was, restless and discontented, or sensual, or unbelieving. In barbarous times, indeed, the influence of the Church was successful in effecting far greater social order and external decency of conduct than are known in heathen countries; and at all times it will abash and check excesses which conscience itself condemns. But it has ever been a restraint on the world rather than a guide to personal virtue and perfection of a large scale; its fruits are negative."[128] Then, again, nearly twenty years later, in his King William Street lectures, he would make the same point: the Church's "best fruit is necessarily secret: she fights with the heart of man, her perpetual conflict is against the pride, the impurity, the covetousness, the envy, the cruelty, which never gets so far as to come to the light; which she succeeds in strangling in its birth. From the nature of the case, she will ever do more in repressing evil than in creating good."[129]

Newman was similarly struck by the attenuated Christianity of Protestants when considering the faith of America's moneyed Episcopalians: "A religion which neither irritates their reason nor interferes with their comfort, will be all in all in such a society," he wrote in his essay, "The Anglo-American Church" (1839).

> Severity whether of creed or precept, high mysteries, corrective practices, subjection of whatever kind, whether to a doctrine or to a priest, will be offensive to them. They need nothing to fill the heart, to feed upon, or to live in; they despise enthusiasm, they abhor fanaticism, they persecute bigotry. They want only so much religion as will satisfy their natural perception of the propriety of being

---

[127] Ibid., 155.
[128] "Sermon 3. Evangelical Sanctity the Completion of Natural Virtue" (1831), OS, 40. See also Short, *Newman and his Contemporaries*, 221.
[129] *Diff.*, i, 264.

religious. Reason teaches them that utter disregard of their Maker is unbecoming, and they determine to be religious, not from love and fear, but from good sense.[130]

Although Froude's reading of the same phenomenon may put one in mind of Newman's, the historian claims that the nominalism characteristic of this peculiar strand of Christianity comes not from too little but too much doctrine.

> Protestant individuals, who profess the soundest of creeds, seem, in their conduct, to have no creed at all, beyond a conviction that pleasure is pleasant, and that money will purchase it. Political corruption grows up; sharp practice in trade grows up, dishonest speculations, short weights and measures, and adulteration of food. The commercial and political Protestant world, on both sides of the Atlantic, has accepted a code of action from which morality has been banished; and the clergy have for the most part sate silent, and occupy themselves in carving and polishing into completeness their schemes of doctrinal salvation. They shrink from offending the wealthy members of their congregations. They withdraw into the affairs of the other world, and leave the present world to the men of business and the devil.[131]

Froude also blamed Protestants for aiding their Roman enemy by investing in the *sola scriptura* misreading of the Bible, a Bibliolatry by which, in effect, they were hoist by their own petard. "The Bible was to be the religion of Protestants," Froude writes; though the flipside of this conviction was that "From an Infallible Church they appealed to the Infallible Book."

> We have erected dogmas, and made idols of them. The idol falls down broken. The man of the world concludes that God Himself has been ejected from his throne, that religion is folly, and that atheism is the only reality. The conscientious and devout, perplexed by doubts and thirsting for certainty, take refuge in the communion which claims to speak with an authority from which there is no appeal. Weary of the hesitating utterances of Evangelical theologians, they fail to see that the Church of Rome is unchanging, not because it is in possession of the truth, but because it is impervious to it.[132]

The other culprits Froude blamed for the revival of Romanism were the Tractarians, whose assault on the Reformation owed so much to the vituperative genius of Froude's brother Hurrell.

> Forty years ago a knot of Oxford students, looking into the Constitution of the Church of England, discovered principles which, as they imagined, had only to be acted on to restore religion to the throne of the empire. With no historical insight into the causes which had left these peculiar forms in the stratification of the Church like fossils of an earlier age, they conceived that the secret of the Church's strength lay in the priesthood and the sacraments; and that the neglect of them was the explanation of its weakness. The Church of England so renovated

---

[130] *Ess.*, i, 349.
[131] *Short Studies*, iii, 156.
[132] *Ibid.*, 165–6.

would rise, they thought, like Achilles from his tent: clad in celestial armor, it would put to flight the armies of infidelity, and bring back in a modern shape, adapted to modern needs, the era of Hildebrand and Becket. They and only they stood on ground from which they could successfully encounter atheism. They and they only, as tracing their lineage through imposition of hands to the apostles, could meet and vanquish the pretensions of Rome.

Singular imagination![133]

Of course, this presents a grossly false picture of the Oxford Movement. Tractarianism was not formed "to vanquish the pretensions of Rome," nor did it seek "to restore religion to the throne of the empire." While it might have wished to "put to flight the armies of infidelity," it had no yearning "to bring back in a modern shape, adapted to modern needs, the era of Hildebrand and Becket." It might have been deluded on some matters—certainly it underestimated the extent to which the Anglican Church is ineradicably Erastian—but it was never an exercise in nostalgic antiquarianism. G. K. Chesterton was much nearer the mark when he wrote how

> the more it is studied, the more it would appear that it was a movement of mere religion as such. It was not so much a taste for Catholic dogma, but simply a hunger for dogma. For dogma means the serious satisfaction of the mind. Dogma does not mean the absence of thought, but the end of thought. It was a revolt against the Victorian spirit in one particular aspect of it; which may roughly be called (in cosy and domestic Victorian metaphor) having your cake and eating it too. It saw that the solid and serious Victorians were fundamentally frivolous—because they were fundamentally inconsistent. A man making the confession of any creed worth ten minutes' intelligent talk, is always a man who gains something and gives up something. So long as he does both he can create; for he is making an outline and a shape. Mohamet created, when he forbade wine but allowed five wives: he created a very big thing, which we have still to deal with. The first French Republic created, when it affirmed property and abolished peerages; France still stands like a square, four-sided building which Europe has besieged in vain. The men of the Oxford Movement would have been horrified at being compared either with Moslems or Jacobins. But their sub-conscious thirst was for something that Moslems and Jacobins had and ordinary Anglicans had not: the exalted excitement of consistency.[134]

The good English Protestant in Froude, however, was right about one aspect of the Oxford Movement and that was its treachery. From the standpoint of English Protestantism, after all, Tractarianism, with all of its rooted criticism of the Erastian Protestant order, was, by definition, treacherous. And here is where we see the centrality for Froude of what he regarded as Newman's perfidy. Indeed, this is why there is always a double-edged quality to Froude's admiration of Newman:

---

[133] *Ibid.*, 171.
[134] G. K. Chesterton, "The Victorian Compromise and its Enemies," in *The Collected Works of G. K. Chesterton. Volume XV: Chesterton on Dickens.*, ed. Alzina Stone Dale (San Francisco: Ignatius Press, 1989), 439–40.

he admired the man's gifts but deplored what he saw as the anti-Anglican uses to which he put the gifts. "The ablest of ... [the Tractarians] after all their passionate denials, were the first to see that if their principles were sound, the Reformation had been a crime, and that they must sue for admission into the bosom of their true mother," Froude wrote, clearly referring to Newman and those most deeply influenced by Newman, though he could never bring himself to imagine that his brother would have poped if he had lived longer. In all events, as far as Froude was concerned, the Tractarians most loyal to their true Anglo-Catholic colors did secede from the Established Church.

> They submitted; they were received; they and the many who have followed them have been the most energetic knights of the holy war; they have been the most accomplished libellers of the institution in which they were born. The Anglican regiment, which pretended to be the most effective against the enemy in the whole Protestant army, is precisely the one which has furnished and still furnishes to that enemy the most venomous foes of the English Church and the largest supply of deserters.[135]

Again, if we look at these fraught matters through the eyes of a loyal English Protestant, even one whose loyalty was not without criticism of a feckless and incoherent Establishment, the cogency of Froude's reading of Tractarianism vis-à-vis the National Church is difficult to deny. Moreover, even though his view of the matter could not have been more different from his Tractarian brother, he made his case with the same rhetorical decidedness that Hurrell made his, which shows that relish for the controversial resources of rhetoric constituted something of a shared family tradition between the two otherwise dissentient brothers.[136] "What these gentlemen have really accomplished is the destruction of the Evangelical party in the Established Church," Froude wrote.

> While the most vigorous of the Anglo-Catholics have gone over to the Papacy, the rest have infected almost the entire body of the Episcopal clergy with principles which seem to add to their personal consequence. The youngest curate affects the airs of a priest. He revives a counterfeit of the sacramental system in which he pretends to have a passionate belief. He decorates his altar after the Roman pattern; he invites the ladies of his congregation to confess to him and whispers his absolutions; and having led them away from their old moorings, and filled them with aspirations which he is unable to gratify, he passes them on in ever-gathering numbers to the hands of the genuine Roman, who waits to receive them.[137]

Froude's conclusion to his long essay could not have been more categorical: "The Episcopal Church of England, with its collateral branches in this and other countries, no longer lends strength to the cause of Protestantism. It is the enemy's

---

[135] *Short Studies*, iii, 172.
[136] William Froude (1810–79) was too immersed in his naval work to write of theological matters, though his letters to Newman show that it was the claim of infallibility that kept him from following his wife and children into the Church. See Short, *Newman and his Contemporaries*, 135–63.
[137] *Short Studies*, iii, 172–3.

chief depot and recruiting ground."[138] And for that, without saying it expressly, he blamed Newman.

VI

If Froude had never written anything related to Newman after his essay of 1874 on Rome's revival, we might be inclined to regard his view of the convert as simply that of many of his rationalist critics, who saw the Oratorian as little more than a casuist—brilliant, charming, gifted, redoubtable—but still a casuist. Instead, Froude wrote a rather double-edged paean to his old mentor, which puts much of what he had previously written of the man in a more coherent, if not entirely favorable light.

In "The Oxford Counter-Reformation" (1881), the littérateur in Froude acknowledged that one of the first impressions that Newman made on his contemporaries was that of a uniquely gifted stylist, in poetry as well as prose. At the time that he first met Newman, Froude recalls, the Oriel don had written a few short poems which would later be published in "Lyra Apostolica." For Froude, despite their brevity: "They were unlike any other religious poetry which was then extant. It was hard to say why they were so fascinating. They had none of the musical grace of the "Christian Year." They were not harmonious; the metre halted, the rhymes were irregular, yet there was something in them which seized the attention, and would not let it go. Keble's verses flowed in soft cadence over the mind, delightful, as sweet sounds are delightful, but are forgotten as the vibrations die away. Newman's had pierced into the heart and mind, and there remained." In summing up the effect Newman's poetry made on readers, Froude summed up the effect that he had on his critics. "The literary critics of the day were puzzled. They saw that he was not an ordinary man; what sort of an extraordinary man he was they could not tell."[139] If one of the unfortunate findings of my book is that Newman had few contemporary critics—critics, that is to say, who truly entered into what he was doing and could write intelligently of his work—it is a mark of Froude's being an exception to this rule that he did recognize the severe limitations of these would-be critics.

First and foremost, it was Newman's personal influence that made so deep and abiding an impression on Froude. "Here was a man who really believed his creed, and let it follow him into all his observations upon outward things," he recalled. His literary work certainly demonstrated this, as Froude attested.

> We had been hearing much in those days about the benevolence of the Supreme Being, and our corresponding obligation to charity and philanthropy. If the received creed was true, benevolence was by no means the only characteristic of that Being. What God loved we might love; but there were things which God did not love; accordingly, we found Newman saying to us,
>
>> Christian, would'st thou learn to love?
>> First learn thee how to hate.

---

[138] *Ibid.*, 173.
[139] "The Oxford Counter-Reformation," in *Short Studies*, iv, 274.

> Hatred of sin and zeal and fear
> Lead up the Holy Hill;
> Track them, till charity appear
> A self-denial still.

For Froude, "It was not austerity that made him speak so. No one was more essentially tender-hearted. But he took the usually accepted Christian account of man and his destiny to be literally true, and the terrible character of it weighed upon him. *Sunt lacrymæ rerum et mentem mortalia tangunt.*"[140] Yet Froude stresses that Newman was not simply the sum of his literary attainments.

> It has been said that men of letters are either much less or much greater than their writings. Cleverness and the skilful use of other people's thoughts produce works which take us in till we see the authors, and then we are disenchanted. A man of genius, on the other hand, is a spring in which there is always more behind than flows from it. The painting or the poem is but a part of him inadequately realized, and his nature expresses itself, with equal or fuller completeness, in his life, his conversation, and personal presence. This was eminently true of Newman. Greatly as his poetry had struck me, he was himself all that the poetry was, and something far beyond. I had then never seen so impressive a person. I met him now and then in private; I attended his church and heard him preach Sunday after Sunday; he is supposed to have been insidious, to have led his disciples on to conclusions to which he designed to bring them, while his purpose was carefully veiled. He was, on the contrary, the most transparent of men. He told us what he believed to be true. He did not know where it would carry him.[141]

Froude also shows that it was not merely charm that gave Newman's influence its appeal. For Froude, "He was never condescending ... never didactic or authoritative ... Perhaps his supreme merit as a talker was he never tried to be witty or to say striking things. Ironical he could be, but not ill-natured. Not a malicious anecdote was ever heard from him. Prosy he could not be. He was lightness itself—the lightness of elastic strength –and he was interesting because he never talked for talking's sake, but because he had something to say."[142] These winning attributes notwithstanding, it was Newman's uncompromisingly real Christianity and his recognition of the consequences of setting such reality at naught that lent his influence its power. "Newman's mind was world-wide," Froude wrote.

> He was interested in everything which was going on in science, in politics, in literature. Nothing was too large for him, nothing too trivial, if it threw light upon the central question, what man really was, and what was his destiny. He was careless about his personal prospects. He had no ambition to make a career, or to rise to rank and power. Still less had pleasure any seductions for him. His

---

[140] *Ibid.*, 276. The Latin verse is from book I, line 462 of the *Aeneid* (c. 29–19 BC) which the crack translator of both Homer and Virgil, Dr. Robert Fagles, translates: "The world is a world of tears, and the burdens of mortality touch the heart."
[141] *Short Studies*, iv, 278.
[142] *Ibid.*, 282–3.

natural temperament was bright and light; his senses, even the commonest, were exceptionally delicate. I was told that, though he rarely drank wine, he was trusted to choose the vintages for the college cellar. He could admire enthusiastically any greatness of action and character, however remote the sphere of it from his own. Gurwood's "Dispatches of the Duke of Wellington" came out just then. Newman had been reading the book, and a friend asked him what he thought of it. "Think?" he said, "it makes one burn to have been a soldier." But his own subject was the absorbing interest with him. Where Christianity is a real belief, where there are distinct convictions that a man's own self and the millions of human beings who are playing on the earth's surface are the objects of a supernatural dispensation, and are on the road to heaven or hell, the most powerful mind may well be startled at the aspect of things. If Christianity was true, since Christianity was true, (for Newman at no time doubted the reality of the revelation), then modern England, modern Europe, with its march of intellect and its useful knowledge and its material progress, was advancing with a light heart into ominous conditions.[143]

The sceptic in Froude also appreciated that Newman never underestimated the force of scepticism, even though, as I shall show, his appreciation of this aspect of Newman was not unalloyed. If Newman personally had the certitude necessary to know that the "One True Fold" of the Roman Catholic Church, as he called it, was the true Church, he recognized that many others did not have this certitude, and it was thus reasonable of them to question whence Newman's came. Moreover, Froude respected Newman for not simply acquiescing in the Bible religion to which most English Protestants subscribed, though, again, he was ambiguous about the wisdom of Newman's sharing these reservations with English Protestant undergraduates. For Froude, Newman "could not, being what he was, acquiesce in the established religion as he would acquiesce in the law of the land, because it was there, and because the country had accepted it, and because good general reasons could be given for assuming it to be right. The soundest arguments, even the arguments of Bishop Butler himself, went no farther than to establish a probability. But religion with Newman was a personal thing between himself and his Maker, and it was not possible to feel love and devotion to a Being whose existence was merely probable." This was certainly true. For Newman, faith was real or it was unreal. For Froude, "The Anglican Church had a special theology of its own, professing to be based on the Bible. Yet to suppose that each individual left to himself would gather out of the Bible, if able and conscientious, exactly these opinions and no others, was absurd and contrary to experience. There were the creeds; but on what authority did the creeds rest? On the four councils? or on other councils, and, if other, on which? Was it on the Church? and, if so, on what Church? The Church of the fathers? or the Church still present and alive and speaking? If for living men, among whom new questions were perpetually rising, a Church which was also living could not be dispensed with, then what was that Church, and to what conclusions would such an admission lead us?"[144] These were all questions that exercised Newman.

[143] Ibid., 279–80.
[144] Ibid., 280–2.

Such a sympathetic reading of Newman's struggles with the legitimacy of Anglicanism recalls the sympathetic reading that the historian made of Newman's sermons. "They appear to me to be the outcome of continued meditation upon his fellow-creatures and their position in this world," Froude wrote; "their awful responsibilities; the mystery of their nature, strangely mixed of good and evil, of strength and weakness. A tone, not of fear, but of infinite pity, runs through them all, and along with it a resolution to look facts in the face; not to fly to evasive generalities about infinite mercy and benevolence, but to examine what revelation really has added to our knowledge, either of what we are or of what lies before us."[145] This, in turn, recalls a well-known passage from *The Nemesis of Faith*, where Froude spoke of his Newman-like character Mornington as one who had spellbound him when an undergraduate at Oxford: "How often in old college years he had hung upon those lips; that voice so keen, so preternaturally sweet, whose very whisper used to thrill through crowded churches, when every breath was held to hear; that calm grey eye; those features, so stern, and yet so gentle!"[146] Froude's later description of Newman the homilist was clearly lifted from this earlier recollection. Newman, according to Froude, had been giving a sermon on Christ's passion and then, as the historian recalled, he paused.

> Then, in a low, clear voice, of which the faintest vibration was audible in the farthest corner of St. Mary's, he said, "Now, I bid you recollect that He to whom these things were done was Almighty God." It was as if an electric stroke had gone through the church, as if every person present understood for the first time the meaning of what he had all his life been saying. I suppose it was an epoch in the mental history of more than one of my Oxford contemporaries.[147]

Was this a recollection of an actual sermon, or simply a rhetorical set piece inserted to provide prelude to the essay's denigratory upshot? Since at this point in the essay Froude's sympathy for his subject comes to an abrupt end, the question poses itself. For the polemical historian, if Newman was a riveting homilist, he was also one who sowed doubts in the minds of his suggestible young auditors. Indeed, for Froude, there was something of a Socrates in Newman: he was encouraging the young to reject the State's religion. Froude could vouch for the unsettling impact of Newman's sermons because, as he claimed, he was not susceptible to such doubts until he heard the sermon. "I had supposed up to that time that the chief events related in the Gospels were as well authenticated as any other facts of history," he recalled.

> I had read Paley and Grotius at school, and their arguments had been completely satisfactory to me. The Gospels had been written by apostles or companions of apostles. There was sufficient evidence, in Paley's words, "that many professing to be original witnesses of the Christian miracles had passed their lives in labors, dangers, and sufferings in attestation of the accounts which they delivered." St. Paul was a further and independent authority. It was not conceivable that such

---

[145] *Ibid.*, 284.
[146] J. A. Froude, *Life of Thomas Carlyle*, 2 vols. (New York: Scriber & Son, 1882), i, 129–30.
[147] *Short Studies*, iv, 286.

men as St. Paul and the other apostles evidently were should have conspired to impose a falsehood upon the world, and should have succeeded in doing it undetected in an age exception ally cultivated and sceptical. Gibbon I had studied also, and had thought about the five causes by which he explained how Christianity came to be believed; but they had seemed to me totally inadequate.[148]

Froude follows this testimonial to his own settled Christian faith as an undergraduate with a reminiscence of what he claims was a jarring admission from Newman. "I was something more than surprised, therefore, when I heard Newman say that Hume's argument against the credibility of miracles was logically sound," Froude relates.

> The laws of nature, so far as could be observed, were uniform, and in any given instance it was more likely, as a mere matter of evidence, that men should deceive or be deceived, than that those laws should have been deviated from. Of course he did not leave the matter in this position. Hume goes on to say that he is speaking of evidence as addressed to the reason; the Christian religion addresses itself to faith, and the credibility of it is therefore unaffected by his objection. What Hume said in irony Newman accepted in earnest. Historically, the proofs were insufficient, or sufficient only to create a sense of probability. Christianity was apprehended by a faculty essentially different. It was called faith. But what was faith, and on what did it rest? Was it as if mankind had been born with but four senses, by which to form their notions of things external to them, and that a fifth sense of sight was suddenly conferred on favored individuals, which converted conjecture into certainty? I could not tell. For myself, this way of putting the matter gave me no new sense at all, and only taught me to distrust my old ones.

Having expressed praise of certain aspects of Newman's personal influence, Froude went on to question its ultimate salubrity. Would it not have been better to leave the undergraduates in his charge alone with their unexamined Bible religion? Froude's answer to his own question was nicely barbed: "I say at once that I think it was injudicious of Newman to throw out before us thus abruptly an opinion so extremely agitating."[149] Newman himself must have been particularly struck by this turn in the essay. Basil Willey certainly recognized its import. "Froude had done his work," the intellectual historian realized; "he had vindicated the Reformation, and he could afford to be magnanimous to its arch-enemy, whom after all, he had loved and admired. But he has taken his stand, and in the last section of the essay he dissociates himself finally from Newmananism."[150]

For the Oratorian who had advised his fellow Oratorians that he did "not want a panegyric written of me, which would be sickening, but a real fair downright account … according to the best ability and judgment of the writer," Froude's indictment of his influence must have come as a jolt. The essay was "downright"

---

[148] Ibid., 286–7. For a discussion of Newman's criticism of Gibbon's account of the rise of Christianity, see Short, *Newman and History*, 3–80.
[149] *Short Studies*, iv, 288.
[150] Basil Willey, *More Nineteenth Century Studies: A Group of Honest Doubters* (London: Chatto & Windus, 1956), 135.

enough but it was based on a number of patent falsehoods.[151] And yet it confirmed Newman's longstanding suspicions about the character of his Protestant contemporaries' Christianity. In objecting to Newman's allegedly entertaining rationalist arguments against the teachings of Christianity, Froude was conceding that those teachings were not capable of withstanding such arguments. Their doubtfulness being what they were, it would have been better to leave them unexamined. Froude was also criticizing Newman for exactly the same sort of truth-telling that he had been criticized for himself in writing frankly of Carlyle's deficiencies in his biography of the Scottish historian. Nevertheless, for Froude, and for an entire Anglican culture,

> To remove the foundation of a belief, and to substitute another, is like putting new foundations to a house, the house itself may easily be overthrown in the process. I have said before that in a healthy state of things religion is considered too sacred to be argued about. It is believed as a matter of duty, and the why or the wherefore is not so much as thought about. Revolutions are not far off when men begin to ask whence the sovereign derives his authority. Scepticism is not far off when they ask why they believe their creed. We had all been satisfied about the Gospel history; not a shadow of doubt had crossed the minds of one of us; and though we might not have been able to give a logical reason for our certitude, the certitude was in us, and might well have been let alone.[152]

In other words, Newman was a marvelous man—an inspiring, an unforgettable man—but he was still responsible for tearing down what Cromwell, Cranmer and Jewell had built and unsettling the undergraduates of Oxford—a claim to which Wilfrid Ward gave understandably short shrift. "What is the bearing of the history of the Oxford Movement upon those great problems concerning religious knowledge and religious truth which agitate the world of English thought at the present day," Ward asked in the waning of Victoria's century.

> Mr. J. A. Froude, in his fascinating recollections of the Oxford Movement, speaks of the scepticism which is fast leavening all classes of English society, and maintains that its leading principles were first brought before the English popular mind by Newman himself. He says, "But for the Oxford Movement scepticism might have continued a harmless speculation of a few philosophers." I make a claim for the Movement, equally important but opposite. It did not, I maintain, sow the seeds of scepticism; it saw that they were already sown. Its philosophy did not create, it only recognised frankly the new difficulties. Its object—so far as it disseminated sceptical views—was not that of the poison which seeks to destroy life, but of the inoculation which gives disease under such favourable conditions that death is averted.[153]

Ciara Brady seeks to defend Froude's reductionist claim by simply reiterating it without offering any case for its validity. "Froude's objection to Newman," he

---

[151] John Henry Newman, "Memorandum as to a Biography" (24 July 1876), LD, xxviii, 92.
[152] *Short Studies*, iv, 292.
[153] Ward, *William George Ward and the Oxford Movement*, 380.

writes, "was that in protesting against the cruel caprice of Calvinist predestination, and in subtly exploiting the devastating critiques of the *philosophes*, without having fixed upon a clear idea of the direction in which his own thoughts were leading him, Newman was behaving in an extremely irresponsible manner. He was undermining the confidence of his hearers in the intellectual authority of the teachings of the Established Church, which for them was based largely on the arguments of Paley and Butler, without providing them with anything on which they could rely except blind dependence on Newman's good faith."[154]

"Intellectual authority"? There was no "intellectual authority" for the Established Church. Of course, Jewell and Hooker had written to commend it, not to mention the sensational Foxe, and after them, William Palmer of Worcester, the great champion of the preposterous "branch theory," but they hardly provided any "intellectual authority." Nor had Paley or Butler. After all, if there had been any intellectual authority for Anglicanism, Newman and Froude's brother Hurrell would never have had to launch the Oxford Movement in the first place. Moreover, to claim that Newman did not give the undergraduates of Oxford any "clear idea of the direction in which his own thoughts were leading him" with respect to the challenges that had been mounted against orthodox Christian belief is wildly false. Newman's *Fifteen Sermons Preached Before the University of Oxford* (1843) abounds with arguments against the rationalism that Newman regarded as the chief contemporary challenge to Christianity. The sermons are the very essence of his lifelong campaign against rationalist liberalism. Here, at random, is one:

> No one will say that Conscience is against Reason, or that its dictates cannot be thrown into an argumentative form; yet who will, therefore, maintain that it is not an original principle, but must depend, before it acts, upon some previous processes of Reason? Reason analyzes the grounds and motives of action: a reason is an analysis, but is not the motive itself. As, then, Conscience is a simple element in our nature, yet its operations admit of being surveyed and scrutinized by Reason; so may Faith be cognizable, and its acts be justified, by Reason, without therefore being, in matter of fact, dependent upon it; and as we reprobate, under the name of Utilitarianism, the substitution of Reason for Conscience, so perchance it is a parallel error to teach that a process of Reason is the *sine quâ non* for true religious Faith. When the Gospel is said to require a rational Faith, this need not mean more than that Faith is accordant to right Reason in the abstract, not that it results from it in the particular case.[155]

And here is another:

> Now, in attempting to investigate what are the distinct offices of Faith and Reason in religious matters, and the relation of the one to the other, I observe, first, that undeniable though it be, that Reason has a power of analysis and criticism in all opinion and conduct, and that nothing is true or right but what may be justified,

---

[154] Ciaran Brady, *James Anthony Froude: An Intellectual Biography of a Victorian Prophet* (Oxford: Oxford University Pres, 2013), 90.
[155] *OS*, 182–3.

and, in a certain sense, proved by it, and undeniable, in consequence, that, unless the doctrines received by Faith are approvable by Reason, they have no claim to be regarded as true, it does not therefore follow that Faith is actually grounded on Reason in the believing mind itself; unless, indeed, to take a parallel case, a judge can be called the origin, as well as the justifier, of the innocence or truth of those who are brought before him. A judge does not make men honest, but acquits and vindicates them: in like manner, Reason need not be the origin of Faith, as Faith exists in the very persons believing, though it does test and verify it. This, then, is one confusion, which must be cleared up in the question,—the assumption that Reason must be the inward principle of action in religious inquiries or conduct in the case of this or that individual, because, like a spectator, it acknowledges and concurs in what goes on;—the mistake of a critical for a creative power.[156]

No undergraduate paying even cursory attention to Newman in Oxford in the 1830s or 1840s would have thought the Oriel Fellow was crediting the plausibility of rationalist attacks on Christianity without acknowledging their fallaciousness. Here, Froude set up a straw man. Ciaran Brady might imagine the straw man a real man; but none of those who were listening to Newman's sermons would have mistaken the one for the other. James David Earnest and Gerard Tracey, the superb editors of the critical edition of *Fifteen Sermons Preached Before the University of Oxford* were certainly not taken in by Froude's man of straw. In their introduction, they point out:

> In his essay Froude scores Newman for having criticized evidential theology as a dangerously lopsided apologetical method. Yet Froude does not deny the validity of Newman's thesis, that on purely logical grounds the Evidences do not constitute an incontrovertible or irresistible proof of Christianity. Because of the old High Church sympathies of his clerical family, Froude had grown up assuming the infallibility of the Evidences. And his response to Sermon X ["Faith and Reason Contrasted as Habits of Mind"] illustrates, in confirmation of Newman's analysis, the pernicious effects of this naively rationalistic, insular theology, which had become the norm in eighteenth-century England. The Evidences were taken to be sufficient for all practical purposes; and, thanks also to English anti-Catholicism, traditional theology was all but forgotten, together with the pre-Reformation history of the Church. The religious milieu thus created in the Church of England was dangerously intellectualized and removed from the life of the faithful. Moreover, evidential theology by its very nature implied that the available evidence for the truth of Christianity approached the standards of legal evidence. The evidential method also subtly suggested that proof was necessary to faith—an attitude that affected, or afflicted, Froude and

---

[156] *OS*, 182. James David Earnest and Gerard Tracey reaffirm Newman's critical engagement with rationalism in their excellent introduction to the *Oxford University Sermons*: "The truly polemical passages in the *University Sermons* are aimed at critics of Christianity—the Benthamite utilitarians and rationalists. But on the whole the sermons are more prophecy than polemic. Newman was predicting the direction from which future attacks on Christianity would come and trying to prepare a generation of young clerics for the battles they would one day have to fight." John Henry Newman, *Fifteen Sermons Preached before the University of Oxford*, ed. Earnest and Tracey (Oxford: Oxford University Press, 2006), xxvi–xxvii.

many of his contemporaries. Throughout his writings, in *The Nemesis of Faith* and "The Oxford Counter-Reformation" and elsewhere, Froude chronicled his religious anguish. He longed for a kind of proof, at once historical and logical, that Newman realized was simply not available. Froude in his essay complains, peevishly, that his youthful religious "certitude", based on a customary reliance on the Evidences, "might well have been let alone" by Newman. He surely missed the point. Newman had not created the historical and cultural processes, the challenges to Christianity, that he and the Tractarians were anticipating and attempting to counter.[157]

The point for Froude of summing up Newman's Oxford work thus was not to treat fairly with a man who had influenced his youth but to confirm his rejection of theological inquiry, about which he wrote tellingly in an essay entitled "Origen and Celsus" (1878):

> The early Christians did not inquire, and therefore have left no record of inquiry. St. Paul was converted by a vision. The vision was sufficient for him, and he pointedly abstained from examining witnesses or strengthening his conviction by outward testimony. To us the ultimate fact is the existence of belief—belief created by such evidence as was convincing to the minds of the first converts. The evidence was sufficient for them, but they did not argue as we argue; their methods of inference were not our methods of inference; we can see only Christianity coming into existence as a living force; and, as of the oak tree, we do not ask, Is it true or is it false? we ask, Is it alive?[158] so with Christianity, we see a spiritual germ, quickened suddenly into active being, which grew and took possession of the human race, overthrowing every other force with which it came into collision, and eventually revolutionizing the entire character of human thought and energy. Life is not truth merely, but it is, as Plato says, τὸ ἐπέκεινα τῆς ἀληθείας, something above truth and more than truth; a force in visible operation which remains a mystery to the intellect; and it is immortal, not as the properties of the circle are immortal, but as it propagates itself in eternal descent, body after body which it has animated successively perishing, but forever reorganizing itself anew in fresh and developed forms.[159]

This was a strange argument coming from someone who sought to justify the

---

[157] John Henry Newman, *Fifteen Sermons Preached before the University of Oxford*, ed. James David Earnest and Gerard Tracey (Oxford: Oxford University Press, 2006), lxxxi.

[158] In his *Anglican Difficulties* (1850), Newman argued that the Anglican Church was dead precisely because it was false. He would not have thought it possible to inquire after a church's life irrespective of its truth. When he wrote of the deadness of the Anglican Church, for example, he did so by fully allowing that it had every outward semblance of life. "For this is the truth: the Establishment, whatever it be in the eyes of men, whatever its temporal greatness and its secular prospects, in the eyes of faith is a mere wreck. We must not indulge our imagination, we must not dream: we must look at things as they are; we must not confound the past with the present, or what is substantive with what is the accident of a period. Ridding our minds of these illusions, we shall see that the Established Church has no claims whatever on us, whether in memory or in hope; that they only have claims upon our commiseration and our charity whom she holds in bondage, separated from that faith and that Church in which alone is salvation." *Diff.*, i, 4-5.

[159] "Origen and Celsus," in *Short Studies*, iv, 365-6.

English Reformation on the grounds that it bought the English liberty—liberty to think as they pleased, liberty to believe as they pleased—though not so much liberty, if we are to credit what Froude has to say here, to inquire into the tenability of their Protestant religion. Newman, however, did bear out the justness of Froude's praise of him by sending the historian a gracious letter of thanks, even though when he wrote the letter he had not seen the piece itself (he had only seen extracts of it in the *Birmingham Post*) and consequently he had not seen the bit accusing him of unsettling the faith of Oxford undergraduates. Later, Newman would write his friend, the Old Etonian, convert and Jesuit priest, Henry James Coleridge (1822–93), "Till your letter came, I had not a dream of his having accused me of unsettling him."[160] In any case, here is the letter from Newman to Froude.

> The Oratory Birmingham March 2, 1881
>
> My dear Anthony Froude
>
> I have seen some portions of what you have been writing about me, and I cannot help sending you a line to thank you.
>
> I hope this will reach you before you set off.
>
> I thank you, not as being able to accept all you have said in praise of me. Of course I can't.
>
> Nor again as if there may not be other aspects of me which you cannot praise, and which you may in a coming chapter of your publication find it a duty, whether I allowed them or not, to remark upon.
>
> But I write to thank you for such an evidence of your affectionate feelings towards me, for which I was not prepared, and which has touched me very much.
>
> May God's fullest blessing be upon you, and give you all good.
>
> Yours affectionately, John H. Cardinal Newman[161]

Despite its praise, Froude's essay was payback for what the litterateur regarded as Newman's treachery. It also showed why Froude refused to consult affections in matters of faith. In replying to Newman's letter, the historian may have written: "For you personally I have always felt and must feel an affectionate veneration."[162] Yet the champion of the Reformation in Froude could never let his affection for Newman get in the way of his contempt for the foreign Church to which his old mentor converted. After Newman read the offending passages, and questioned the accuracy of Froude's account,[163] he explained to Coleridge

---

[160] John Henry Newman to Henry James Coleridge (29 March 1881), *LD*, xxix, 351.
[161] John Henry Newman to James Anthony Froude (2 March 1881), *LD*, xxix, 343–4.
[162] James Anthony Froude to John Henry Newman (4 March 1881), *LD*, xxix, 344.
[163] "As to the Sermon to which J. A. Froude refers, it was preached on 6 January, when he would be, I consider, almost the only Undergraduate in Oxford. How he got leave to stay up I cannot imagine; for Oriel, where he was then, did not allow of residence in the Vacation. Perhaps he was already at Exeter. Any how, I was not preaching to *undergraduates*—rather to empty benches." John Henry Newman to Henry James Coleridge (29 March 1881), *LD*, xxix, 352. As Charles Dessain pointed out: E. S. Estcourt wrote a defense of Newman, "Mr. Froude on Cardinal Newman" in the *Month* (April, 1881), in which he identified Newman's sermon as "Faith and Reason contrasted as habits of the Mind," in *US*, pp. 176–201, and showed that it did not contain the sentences Froude quoted. On the contrary, Newman had spoken about the fallacy of Hume's argument against miracles (p. 195), and maintained that they could provide evidence enough for conviction in the judgment of

what had motivated him to write the historian: "I did this because I heard last year that he was in distress of mind about religion."[164] Indeed, a fellow passenger who had met Froude on shipboard on his way back from South Africa recalled how "Sometimes there was something almost fearful in the gloom and utter disbelief and defiance of his mind."[165] One can see this in the sad, lost, brooding eyes of the portrait painted of him by Sir George Reid. In any case when all was said and done, Froude had the satisfaction of settling a long-simmering score with an eighty-year-old priest. In return, the priest, who was destined to become a saint, gave the historian "God's fullest blessing."

In conclusion, to understand what lay at the heart of Froude's ambivalence towards a man for whom he otherwise had so much genuine admiration—an ambivalence suffused with hostility—we might end with a passage from his History of England where he speaks of the ordeal of another eighty-year-old priest.

> Ridley withdrew, and Latimer was then introduced—eighty years old now—dressed in a threadbare gown of Bristol frieze, a handkerchief on his head with a night-cap over it, and over that again another cap, with two broad flaps buttoned under the chin. A leather belt was round his waist, to which a Testament was attached; his spectacles, without a case, hung from his neck. So stood the greatest man perhaps then living in the world, a prisoner on his trial, waiting to be condemned to death by men professing to be the ministers of God. As it was in the days of the prophets, so it was in the Son of man's days; as it was in the days of the Son of man, so was it in the Reformers' days; as it was in the days of the Reformers, so will it be to the end, so long and so far as a class of men are permitted to hold power, who call themselves the commissioned and authoritative teachers of truth. Latimer's trial was the counterpart of Ridley's: the charge was the same, and the result was the same, except that the stronger intellect vexed itself less with nice distinctions. Bread was bread, said Latimer, and wine was wine; there was a change in the sacrament, it was true, but the change was not in the nature, but the dignity. He too was reprieved for the day. The following morning the court sat in St Mary's Church, with the authorities of town and university, heads of houses, mayor, aldermen, and sheriff. The prisoners were brought to the bar. The same questions were asked, the same answers were returned, and sentence was pronounced upon them, as heretics obstinate and incurable.[166]

Here, again, we are in the country of Carlyle's "rubbish mountains." Indeed, in the odd bagatelle with which Froude ends the last volume of his *Short Studies on Great Subjects*, "A Siding at a Railway Station" (1879), he portrays himself as rendering an account before four grave-faced examiners, and his description of the scene shows that he had no illusions himself about the quality of his work. "A fluid was poured on the pages, the effect of which was to obliterate entirely every untrue proposition, and to make every partially true proposition grow faint in

---

reason. *LD*, xxix, 352.
[164] John Henry Newman to Henry James Coleridge (29 March 1881), *LD*, xxix, 351.
[165] Dunn, *Froude: A Biography*, ii, 442.
[166] James Anthony Froude, *History of England from the Fall of Wolsey to the Defeat of the Spanish Armada* (London: Longman, Green & Co., 1860), v, 553.

proportion to the false element which entered into it. Alas! chapter after chapter vanished away, leaving the paper clean, as if no compositor had ever labored in setting type for it. Pale and illegible became the fine-sounding paragraphs on which I had secretly prided myself."[167] Yet this was only the literary judgment made upon him: there was also another judgment, and it was made by "those which in the course of my life I had devoured, either in part or whole, to sustain my unconscionable carcass." And here is how he describes these inquisitors.

> There they stood in lines with solemn and reproachful faces oxen and calves, sheep and lambs, deer, hares, rabbits, turkeys, ducks, chickens, pheasants, grouse, and partridges, down to the larks and sparrows and blackbirds, which I had shot when a boy and made into puddings. Every one of them had come up to bear witness against their murderer; out of sea and river had come the trout and salmon, the soles and turbots, the ling and cod, the whiting and mackerel, the smelts and white bait, the oysters, the crabs, the lobsters, the shrimps. They seemed literally to be in millions, and I had eaten them all.[168]

Obviously, his account of his judges was meant as a joke, a rather elephantine joke, but it is a joke nevertheless that reveals the startling frivolity, one might almost say nihilism with which Froude regarded the Judgment that awaits us all—believers and nonbelievers, Catholics and Protestants, dogmatists and rationalists—whether we acknowledge the fact or not. To quote from the sermon Newman gave in 1848 on the Last Judgment is to be reminded of how different Newman and Froude were—different and yet ineluctably bound by the same reckoning.

> And oh! what a sight it will be, what an unexpected sight, at the last day and public judgement to be present at that revelation of all hearts! How different persons will then seem, from what they seem now! How will the last be first, and the first last! Then those whom the world looked up to, will be brought low, and those who were little esteemed, will be exalted. Then will it be found who are the real movers in the world's affairs, those who sustained the cause of the Church or who influenced the fortunes of empires, were not the great and powerful, not those whose names are known in the world, but the humble despised followers of the Lamb, the meek saint, the man full of prayer and good works whom the world passed by; the hidden band of saintly witnesses, whose voice day by day ascended to Christ; the sufferers who seemed to be living for nothing; the poor whom the proud world thought but an offence and a nuisance. When that Day comes, may it reveal good for each of you, my brethren.[169]

---

[167] "A Siding in the Railway Station," in *Short Studies*, iv, 568.
[168] *Ibid.*, 569–70.
[169] John Henry Newman, "Preparation for the Judgment" (1848), *Faith and Prejudice and Other Unpublished Sermons of Cardinal Newman* (New York: Sheed & Ward, 1956), 40.

FREDERICK MEYRICK

◦ 7 ◦

Frederick Meyrick and the Church Triumphant

There are many reasons one could cite to explain why the High Churchman Frederick Meyrick (1827–1906) took against Newman. He had no use for Newman's Tractarianism. He had even less use for the Roman Catholicism to which Newman converted. He cannot have relished the mockery to which Newman subjected the Anglican Establishment in his *Lectures on Certain Difficulties felt by Anglicans in submitting to the Catholic Church* (1850). He blamed Newman for abandoning Oxford to liberalism. Yet although all of these reasons weighed heavily on the resentment of the man there was another, more personal, more visceral reason why Meyrick took against Newman, and it is clear from his memoirs, in which he recalled:

> My cousin Thomas Meyrick was scholar of Corpus Christi College, Oxford, and took a first class in Classics ... After taking his degree he resided in Oxford, and became a popular private tutor. He was an enthusiastic admirer and follower of Newman. In 1844, during my first year of residence as an undergraduate, I received a note from the Rev. R. G. Macmullen of Corpus Christi College, saying that my cousin was very ill. Going to see him, I found him in a state of great mental excitement, and hardly master of himself. He said that he wished to join the Church of Rome but was bound by a promise to Newman not to do so. I went to Littlemore, where Newman was then living, to consult him, and he gave me a letter for my cousin, in which he said that he could not authorize his secession, but he relieved him from the obligation of any promise made to him. Recovering to a certain degree, my cousin went to his home to ask his father's permission to become a Romanist. His father, an old Tory Protestant parson, said that to save him from losing his mind (which appeared likely from his excitement) he would give the leave, though if it had been to save his life, he would not. Soon afterwards he was received into the Roman Church, and went to live for a time at the Roman Catholic College at Prior Park, near Bath where I paid him a visit. Later on he joined the Jesuits, and became extravagantly attached to the worship of St. Mary. But ever since the excitement that he underwent at the time of his secession he had been liable to temporary fits of deep depression, followed sometimes by unusually high spirits. The Jesuits, wearied with his distressed and variable bearing, sent him to an asylum. The asylum was very ill-managed in respect to the moral control exercised over the patients, and it was governed by

great violence. On one occasion my cousin tried to escape, and, being caught, was brought back and placed in a padded room with a strong man, who knocked him down and then provoked him to fight, knocking him down every time that he stood up, till "the devil of insubordination" was supposed to be subdued in him. On a later occasion he succeeded in escaping; and having hidden himself under the willows that fringe the Thames at Putney during the day, he set off as soon as it was dark and walked all the way to Wiltshire, and begged his brother to take him in and protect him. Indignant and angry with the Jesuits, he broke off from them, and wrote a pamphlet (printed 1827–42 but not published) called *My Imprisonings; or, Why I left the Jesuits*. Time passed, and an imagination suggested itself to him that he had committed a sin in leaving the Jesuits after having once been enrolled among them and taken oaths of obedience. He again joined them, but once more the depression and excitement seized him, and he was sent by the Jesuits to an asylum in Ireland, from which he was delivered by the Inspector of Asylums. After this he made a solemn vow never to rejoin the Jesuits, and he went to live in a lodging-house at Bournemouth, refusing either to leave the Roman Church or to see a Roman priest, or to go near the Roman or the English Church. Thus many years passed. At length he had a partial recovery, and again officiated as a Roman priest; but the recovery was not complete, and, indignant at not receiving all his "faculties," he went to Rome in 1899 for redress, at the age of eighty-two, and was there consigned to the care of some charitable nuns, who looked after him until his death in 1903. Few know the wrench that it was to those who left the Church of England for Rome before Newman's secession in 1845 had made it easier to do so. Thomas Meyrick never recovered from it.[1]

Many English Protestants in Victoria's reign associated the Church of Rome with superstition, backwardness, treason and credulity, but that it was also associated, in Meyrick's case, with lunacy and straitjackets might very well explain why he was so extraordinarily hostile to the Church of Rome and her most brilliant English convert.

Despite Meyrick's prejudices, it is important to stress that he was not an uncharitable or spiteful man. The Trinity diarist and later housemaster at Eton, Wharton Booth Marriott (1823–71) confided to his journal: "I never yet met with the man before whom I could pour out my *whole self*, or rather my two selves, but my *better self* seems to yearn for such a friend as Frederick—and he seems not disinclined to meet one half way."[2] Tuckwell, too, had a good word for Meyrick. "Residents at Oxford in the later Forties were frequently aware of a very good-looking junior Don taking his walks abroad with young Lord Robert Cecil, Lord Lothian ... and others of the *jeunesse dorée*, who apparently looked up to him as guide, philosopher, and friend," the chronicler of Tractarian Oxford recalled. "It was Frederick Meyrick, a lately elected Fellow of Trinity."[3] Nevertheless, Meyrick's loyalty to the Church of England was too fierce for him

---

[1] Frederick Meyrick, *Memories of Life at Oxford, and Experiences in Italy, Greece, Turkey, Germany, Spain and Elsewhere* (London: John Murray, 1905), 5–7.
[2] Marriott quoted in Clare Hopkins, *Trinity: 450 Years of an Oxford College Community* (Oxford: Oxford University Press, 2005), 235.
[3] William Tuckwell, *Reminiscences of Oxford* (London: Smith, Elder & Co., 1907), 227.

to have anything but loathing for the man whom he thought sabotaged it.

Meyrick's attachment to the National Church was intertwined with the Meyrick family history. From 1530, the Meyricks were farmers in Carmarthenshire until Edward (1750–1830) was ordained and became a schoolmaster, first in Cardigan and then at Hungerford. In 1785 he became vicar of Ramsbury, Wiltshire, and transferred the Hungerford school there. He married first Anne Graves and second, Caroline Habersham. His son by the first marriage, A. Edward Graves (1780–1839) was also vicar of Ramsbury and married Myra Howard from Aldbourne, a nearby village. They had nine children of whom the seventh, Frederick (1827–1906) was tutor and Dean of Trinity College, Oxford, then HM Inspector of Schools and from 1868 Rector of Blickling in Norfolk. In 1859, Frederick married Marion Danvers whose ancestor Sir Roland de Alvers or Auvers came, possibly with the Conqueror, from Auvers, Normandy. The Danvers claim descent from the English kings back from Edward I, the French kings back from Louis VIII, and from Duncan first king of Scots. Frederick and Marion had nine children of whom the seventh Frederick James (1871–1945) was vicar of St Peter Mancroft, Norwich (1902–29).

Meyrick was convinced that his cousin had not been the only man whose mind had been deranged by the Romanizing Newman. Long before he published his memoirs, he compiled a volume of letters written by his brother James, Vicar of Westbury in Wiltshire and his sister when James was recovering from pleurisy for two winters at Malaga in Spain entitled *The Practical Working of the Church of Spain* (1851), which "served," as he said, "as a counterpoise to some extravagant imaginations as to the perfection of the Roman Catholic Church entertained at the time in England by men whose minds had been disturbed by Newman's secession."[4]

Reading the book, one has to say that it is striking to see how Meyrick's wish to be fair-minded is continually foiled by his and his siblings' irrepressible prejudices. "There is something pleasant in the gay careless character of the people here," he quotes his sister as writing in one of her letters. "They do not seem to suffer want as our poor do. The country people who come in to market wear silver tags on their jackets, and silver clasps and buttons. They are very friendly, and say, '*Vaya. con Dios*,' which means, 'May you go with God,' when they pass us. Sometimes my English dress makes them laugh; but they will go out of the way to shew us the road, and it is a friendly laugh." However, the scolding Protestant in her could not resist adding: "I have not said a word of what I most dislike: the worship of the Virgin. To me it ruins every thing. The Churches are full of her images, ugly dolls, absurdly dressed, with wax and artificial flowers, and far more prominent than the Crucifix. A Clergyman at Gibraltar told me, that it had sadly grown of late years there."[5]

Richard Ford in his classic *The Handbook for Travellers in Spain* (1845) took a less censorious view of how the Spanish expressed their faith. Speaking of the pilgrimage and festival of San Isidro, patron saint of Madrid, he managed to put

---

[4] Meyrick, *Memories*, 4–5.
[5] Frederick Meyrick, *The Practical Working of the Church in Spain* (London: John Henry Parker, 1851), 10.

away his English prejudices.

> The chief act in this fair is to kiss the saint's image and receive the blessing of the priest who holds it. 10,000 kiss this image in one day, and each drops at its feet a farthing. This fair is to the Madrilenian what Greenwich was, on Easter Monday, to the Cockney; the holy ceremony has degenerated into a St. Bartholomew fair, but most classes refer to it with pleasure in recollection of their sweet days of youth, fun, and frolic. ... The early popes, by countenancing this and similar pilgrimages of piety and fun, rendered acts of devotion sources of enjoyment to its believers; and their flocks, wedded to festivals which suited themselves and their climate, will long prefer them to the dreary Sundays of our purer Protestantism.[6]

Spain's flocks did exult in such festivals—they still do—but Meyrick actually preferred the "dreary Sundays" of the "purer Protestantism," unlike Charles Dickens, who "used to entertain friends in his garden on Sunday mornings [in Tavistock Square in the 1850s] with trays of bottled stout and church-warden pipes—his way of protesting against the dullness of the British Sabbath," though he would have been startled if anyone had suggested that there was anything papist in such conviviality.[7] In *Sunday Observance: An Argument and Plea for the old English Sunday* (1902), Meyrick advocated for the preservation of the British Sabbath. "Every day as it passes shows the great and greater need that there is to make a protest in behalf of the old English Sunday before it is too late. Its overthrow is part of a system which is attempting to bring back the mediaeval doctrines and practices of the Church of Charlemagne, which originated in the ninth century, in place of the primitive doctrines and practices of the Church of Constantine and the ages before Constantine." What was it about the Sunday as the Edwardians observed it that jarred with the Rector of Blickling?

> There is the hurried rush from bed to a morning Eucharist or Mass ... a consequently late breakfast, preventing servants from attending morning church; private morning prayers and family prayers often cut short or neglected; a contemptuous disregard of the Morning service, to which the Evening service is preferred, because it contains the Magnificat, and can be called vespers; a dawdling in the garden or the drawing-room over the novels that were being read during the week; a waking up after luncheon for a reception of young men and women to chatter over the last ball, the last ping-pong, the last hunt, the last races, the last Society gossip; or, it may be, a golf match, attended by boys, as caddies, who used to be at Sunday School taught by young ladies who are now golfing; the large evening dinner party of from-Saturday-to-Monday friends or acquaintances, which disables the servants of the household, if not their masters and mistresses, from attending the Evening Church service, and sets them the example of profanation of the Lord's Day ... What dressing of the soul is there in such a day as that?[8]

---

[6] Richard Ford, *The Handbook for Travellers in Spain*, 8th, edn (London: John Murray, 1890), 88.
[7] Norman Gash, *Robert Surtees and Early Victorian Society* (Oxford: Oxford University Press, 1993), 319.
[8] Frederick Meyrick, *Sunday Observance: An Argument and Plea for the Old English Sunday* (London:

Here we can see something of the prig in Meyrick, who, when dean of Trinity, banned supper parties in the college, deeming them "noisy and ill-conducted" affairs, full of "gross language" and "filthy songs."[9] By contrast, the legendary Trinity Fellow Thomas Short, who encouraged Newman to sit for the exam that made him an Oriel Fellow, was partial to the more exuberant undergraduates. The "hunting and sporting men were rarely refused leave of absence from lecture," the memoirist James Pycroft recalled: "I think [Short] had a secret satisfaction in the remark, then often heard, that Trinity turned out more red coats than most of the colleges twice its size."[10]

When Meyrick visited Spain as a young man, his prejudices in favor of the "purer Protestantism" were already pronounced. Meeting his brother and sister in Seville, he asked them how they had found the ceremonies of Holy Week, and he was happy to record that his sister found them "a most instructive lesson on the evil of making religion a spectacle." She also noted how: "Worse behaviour in church we never saw." As for the processions, they were "very splendidly arranged" but "mere shows"; indeed, "the cloak of the Blessed Virgin and the dress of the Nazarenes" were "discussed just as a gentleman's or lady's dress at a ball."[11] What also recommended such responses to Meyrick is that they were offered with an eye to Newman's conversion, as is clear from another of the letters.

> At one time I used in my own mind to compare the English Church to a sickly tree, that was throwing off all its healthy leaves. Those words of Newman's seemed so true to me: "How is it that all that is warm and tender in feeling, or true and noble in performance, thy flower and thy promise, falls from thy bosom, and finds no home in thy arms." Now the Church has proved her vitality. Though some whom we loved and trusted are gone from us, others have sprung up to take their places. Still we have guides, still friends, only we have learnt the lesson that we must not idolize: and now the English Church compared with the Roman reminds me of two oaks in Marlborough forest, called the Queen and the King. The King was a giant, covering a huge space of ground when I remember him, but held together with bands of iron, and now falling to pieces: while the Queen in vigorous youth and health, which in my childhood no one would compare with him, is now almost as large, and will soon be the largest of the two.[12]

Such an invidious comparison was one with which Meyrick entirely agreed, though his sister's paraphrase of the passage from Newman's last Anglican sermon, "The Parting of Friends" (1843) entirely misses Newman's point. For Newman, as one can see from the passage itself, the lesson of the defections from the Anglican Church was not that "we must not idolize" but that the Anglican Church betrayed the faithful.

Skeffington & Son, 1902), 210–11.

[9] Meyrick quoted in Peter Hinchliff, "Religious Issues, 1870–1914," in *The History of the University of Oxford, Volume VII: Nineteenth-Century Oxford, Part 2*, ed. M. G. Brock and M. C. Curthoys (Oxford: Oxford University Press, 2000), 138.

[10] Pycroft quoted in Clare Hopkins, *Trinity: 450 Years of an Oxford College Community* (Oxford: Oxford University Press, 2005), 232–3.

[11] Meyrick, *Memories*, 154.

[12] Meyrick, *Church in Spain*, 9–10.

O my mother, whence is this unto thee, that thou hast good things poured upon thee and canst not keep them, and bearest children, yet darest not own them? why hast thou not the skill to use their services, nor the heart to rejoice in their love? how is it that whatever is generous in purpose, and tender or deep in devotion, thy flower and thy promise, falls from thy bosom and finds no home within thine arms? Who hath put this note upon thee, to have "a miscarrying womb, and dry breasts," to be strange to thine own flesh, and thine eye cruel towards thy little ones? Thine own offspring, the fruit of thy womb, who love thee and would toil for thee, thou dost gaze upon with fear, as though a portent, or thou dost loathe as an offence;—at best thou dost but endure, as if they had no claim but, on thy patience, self-possession, and vigilance, to be rid of them as easily as thou mayest.[13]

Meyrick's very compiling of the correspondence of his brother and sister was an answer to Newman's barbed departure from the National Church, which he makes clear in his dedication.

TO
ALL WHO HAVE DREAMED
THAT THE PERFECTIONS OF THE
CHURCH TRIUMPHANT
BELONG TO THE
CHURCH MILITANT
AND THAT THEY ARE TO BE FOUND IN ANY OTHER
PART
OF THE CHURCH CATHOLIC
IN A GREATER DEGREE THAN IN THE
CHURCH OF ENGLAND
THESE PAGES ARE ADDRESSED
EARNESTLY, AFFECTIONATELY, SADLY[14]

What Meyrick styled the "Church Triumphant" was something that he never tired of defending. It altogether colored his reading of the Oxford Movement.

When the Tractarian movement first began, its leaders had no idea of going beyond the standing-ground of the English seventeenth-century divines; but Dr. Newman, who resolutely seized and held the direction of the movement, had not a mind that was evenly balanced. Full of enthusiasm, he embraced with all his heart certain principles of thought and action, and he carried them out to their extreme limit, regardless of other principles, equally true, which should have qualified them and restrained their application. Pusey followed Newman up to a certain point from personal love of the man, and so for a time did Keble, till he found and acknowledged that he was misled, and drew back. Newman s influence pushed the older Tractarian movement beyond its original aim.[15]

[13] SD, 407–8.
[14] Meyrick, *Church in Spain*, iii.
[15] Frederick Meyrick, *Old Anglicanism and Modern Ritualism* (London: Skeffington & Son, 1901), 1–2.

In other words, the Oxford Movement would only have been a benign movement if it had joined Meyrick in defending the Church Triumphant. When it questioned the *bona fides* of that Erastian Church, it became intolerable.

So certain was Meyrick of the appeal of this Church that he even convinced himself that it should come to the rescue of Spain. The "indifference, unbelief, and superstition prevalent throughout Spain," he believed, could only be resolved by the sort of reforms championed by Bishop Juan Cabrera (1837–1916), the founder of the Reformed Episcopal Church of Spain.[16] It is a mark of Meyrick's humorlessness that he actually thought that one could evangelize Spaniards with Anglicanism. Here one is reminded of Rose Macaulay's amusing novel, *The Towers of Trebizond* (1956), in which Aunt Dot proposes to liberate the women of Turkey by converting them to Anglicanism and showing them the benefits of the bathing hat.

Curiously enough, Meyrick contrived to see the same unsuspected yearning for Anglicanism among the people of Ireland that he saw among the Spanish. "The general charge against the Irish missions in Connemara was that they did not teach a positive Christianity, but only a negation of Romanism," he tells his readers in *Memories of Life at Oxford, and Experiences in Italy, Greece, Turkey, Germany, Spain and Elsewhere* (1905). But going to Protestant churches in and around the town of Clifden, he found the charge unjustifiable.

> Several orphan institutions had been established for the children of those who had died in the late famine. I examined the girls in the orphan house at Clifden, to see what the character of their positive teaching was.
> "What religion were they of?"
> "The Christian religion."
> "Why are we called Christians?"
> "Because we trust in Christ."
> "Are we Catholics?"
> "Yes."
> "Do we hold the Catholic faith?"
> "Yes."
> "Where is that to be found?"
> "In the Bible."
> "And where its chief articles?"
> "In the Creed."
> "How many creeds are there?"
> "Three."
> "What are they?"
> "The Apostles' Creed, the Nicene Creed, and the Athanasian Creed"
> "Is it right to speak of Roman Catholics as the Catholics?"
> "No."
> "Why not?"
> "Because they are Roman Catholics."[17]

---

[16] Meyrick, *Memories*, 150.
[17] Ibid., 195–6.

If Meyrick warmed to those, like Bishop Wordsworth, who joined him in extolling Anglicanism, he could be rather unforgiving towards those, like William Palmer of Magdalen (1811–79), who wanted out of the National Church. His description of the interview that Palmer had with the Fanar, the headquarters of the Eastern Church in Constantinople, when he was attempting to see if the Easter Church would have him as her convert is amusing.[18]

> Had he been baptized with three immersions? No; it was not the Anglican custom. Had he, at least, had water three times poured upon him? Probably not; he could not be certain of it. Then he must be baptized again. But that would mean that he had not been a Christian down to the present moment, and he could not believe that; and he knew that his father, by whom he had been baptized, was a very careful ministrant. That might be so; but it was a rule of the Church that a child should be thrice immersed, and he must now submit to regard his previous baptism as null, and be baptized aright. Thus, it appeared that Constantinople was stiffer in its unbending adherence to rules than St. Petersburg. Palmer bowed and withdrew. He could not acknowledge that he had now to begin the Christian life.[19]

After this unpromising exchange, Palmer went to Rome and consulted Carlo Passaglia (1812–87), the Italian Jesuit, whose initial catechizing left the restive Anglican unmoved. His heart might have been willing but his reason baulked. As Meyrick described him: "He was dissatisfied with the English Church, the Greek Church would not accept him except on a condition to which he could not assent, and he could not believe the Roman doctrines. Newman had built a bridge for himself, and had crossed by it; but as [Palmer confessed] 'as soon as I try to do the same, I find myself in the position of an elephant under whose feet the planks give way at the first step.'" Eventually, however, Palmer did convert, despite his intellectual reservations, which led Meyrick to conclude: "There was … only one thing that William Palmer lacked, and that was the common sense which looks at a thing all round and makes allowance for conflicting principles. Not having this, he became an ecclesiastical Don Quixote; he was a man of noble soul, unselfish, honest, true, lovable, but lost to his friends, to his Church, to the name and fame that might have been his, by his inability to reconcile himself to the conditions of imperfect humanity and human institutions, untaught by the wisdom of Butler."[20] Another defender of the National Church, Owen Chadwick

---

[18] Whatever his shortcomings as a critic, Meyrick could be an entertaining storyteller. Of Martin Joseph Routh, the celebrated President of Magdalen, he wrote: "He was born in 1755, and died in December, 1854. He was elected to the headship of his college in 1791. His appearance in his later life was that of a man of a previous generation. He always wore his academical gown, even when in his study, and there he sat surrounded by his books as his intimate friends. It was reported that he died at last by his having mounted a ladder to reach a large folio which fell upon him. This was not altogether true, but it was true that some years previously he had severely injured his leg in this manner. In giving an account of the accident to his medical man, the President pathetically complained that the injury had been done by 'a worthless book, sir—a worthless book,' as though," says Burgon, 'he would not have minded if it had been done by a volume of Chrysostom or Augustine.'" Meyrick, *Memories*, 111.

[19] Meyrick, *Memories*, 78–9.

[20] Ibid., 79. Butler: in *The Analogy of Religion* (1736) Joseph Butler (1692–1752), Bishop of Durham, drew on natural theology to argue the probability, rather than the evidentiary proof, of Christianity,

would bring the same charge against Newman, claiming that he had left the Anglican Church not in search of the true but "an ideal Church."[21]

While Meyrick might have been dismayed by Palmer's defection from the Anglican ranks, he was even more so by that of Manning and Newman. Speaking of what he claims to have been the "petty personal squabble between the two leading English Roman Catholic ecclesiastics lasting for forty years," Meyrick remarks:

> Who could have believed that the Newman and the Manning that we knew in the Anglican Church could have been kept in permanent hostility to each other by jealousy, spitefulness, and unforgiving tempers, which continued to operate until death closed the career of one of them? Had they both remained in the Anglican Church, and had Manning become Archbishop of Canterbury, can we imagine his whispering, intriguing, plotting to keep Newman shut up at Littlemore, lest he should rival him in influence? And had he done so, can we imagine Newman irritated beyond endurance by such treatment, and refusing all advances towards friendship or social intercourse with him? There is something more wholesome in the wider, larger, fresher atmosphere of the Church of England than in the confined air of the Roman Catholic body in England.[22]

In other words, one should forget about the schismatical, indeed heretical reality of the Act of Supremacy; the preferability of the Established to the Roman Church could be seen plainly in the decorum it inspired in its adherents.

The putative constrictions of the Church of Rome exercised another critic of Newman, whom Meyrick would go out of his way to befriend. When the Archbishop of Munich demanded that Ignaz von Döllinger (1799–1890) accept the definition of papal infallibility promulgated at the First Vatican Council, the German theologian famously refused, which resulted in his excommunication by Pius IX in 1871. Like Lord Acton, Döllinger tended to condescend to Newman as someone whose learning was not quite up to snuff and whose theological insights were jejune.[23] "Whole stretches of Church history and the history of European culture are unknown to him, as the darkest Africa. There is no way of explaining his naïve and daring assertions," he wrote.[24] While Döllinger was prepared to concede that Newman "is an uncommonly gifted and also deeply

---

convinced, as he said, that "probability is the very guide of life." For Butler's considerable influence on Newman, see *Apo.*, 22–3. Despite this, Newman saw the dangers of a theory of probability that could seem to undercut the "absolute certainty" of Christian faith. See *Apo.*, 30. See also the 1877 revision of Lectures on the Prophetical Office of the Church, Viewed Relatively to Romanism and Popular Protestantism (1837), in which Newman says: "Faith may *follow* after doubt ... but the two cannot co-exist" *VM*, i, 108.

[21] See Ian Ker's witty refutation of Chadwick's characteristically false claim in his *Newman and the Fullness of Christianity*, 103–22. Chadwick made the claim in the introduction to Susan Foister, *Cardinal Newman 1801–90: A Centenary Exhibition* (London: National Portrait Gallery Publications, 1990), 7.

[22] Meyrick, *Memories*, 212–13.

[23] For Owen Chadwick, the convert's detractors could never resist suspecting that "the original genius of Newman's mind consisted in an infinite capacity for not reading important books." Owen Chadwick, *From Bossuet to Newman*, 2nd edn (Cambridge: Cambridge University Press, 1987), 111.

[24] Döllinger to Gladstone, 17 February 1875, BL Add. 44140/348–9 (German), quoted in Hill, *Lord Acton*, 271.

religious man" and "writes excellently," he was nonetheless convinced that "his insights into Church history are too scanty." Indeed, for the German theologian, "with [Newman's] theory of development he transplants Darwinism into religion except that where Darwin lets the ape develop into Caucasian man, in Newman's case in contrast man gradually degenerates into ape."[25] Here was a Catholic whom Meyrick could admire. "At this time, I paid a visit to Munich, and spent the greater part of two days with Dr. Döllinger," he related in his memoirs.

> It was a most interesting visit to make at such a moment. Döllinger was firm and decided without the shadow of a disposition to yield to the Archbishop's pressure. "When they tell me to believe that the Bishop of Rome has been regarded by the Church as infallible, they might as well tell me to believe that two and two make five." He was still in hopes that Bishop Hefele and Bishop Strossmayer might refuse to accept the Vatican dogmas. Dupanloup had not yet submitted, and Hungary had not given the *Regium Placitum* to the publication of the Bull, nor had Bavaria, although it had been published there. He gave me a copy of the Declaration to the Archbishop of Munich, which he had published, and I left with him some tracts relating to the Anglican Church. As we parted, he said, with a bright smile: "We are walking in parallel paths with scarcely a barrier between us." By the action of Döllinger and his thirteen associates at Nuremberg, the Old Catholic community was formed as a body separate from Rome, and by Conferences held at Munich in the autumn of 1871 and at Cologne in 1872 a beginning was made of its organization.[26]

Newman saw Döllinger rather differently. Before the excommunication, he was prepared to see an understandable, even commendable conscientiousness in the dissentious German. "I think, certainly, Dr Döllinger has been treated very cruelly," Newman wrote in November of 1871.

> And I fear your account of the Italian Catholics is true; for other persons make the same contrast between them and the Germans. Every consideration, the fullest time should be given to those who have to make up their minds to hold an article of faith which is new to them. To take up at once such an article may be the act of a vigorous faith; but it may also be the act of a man who will believe anything because he believes nothing, and is ready to profess whatever his ecclesiastical, that is, his political party requires of him. There are too many high ecclesiastics in Italy and England, who think that to believe is as easy as to obey—that is, they talk as if they did not know what an act of faith is. A German who hesitates may have more of the real spirit of faith than an Italian who swallows. I have never myself had a difficulty about the Pope's Infallibility—but that is no reason I should forget Luke xvii.[27]

---

[25] Döllinger to Lady Blennerhassett, 20 February 1875, Ignaz von Döllinger *Briefwechsel mit Lady Blennerhassett, 1865–1886*, ed. Victor Conzemius (Munich: Beck, 1963–81), 597–8 (German), quoted in Hill, *Lord Acton*, 270.

[26] Meyrick, *Memories*, 257.

[27] JHN to Malcolm MacColl (11 November 1871), *LD*, xxv, 430. There is a good deal in Luke's chapter 17 but here Newman appears to be referring to that portion of it which enjoins sinful men to be forbearing of the sins of other sinful men. "If your brother sins, rebuke him, and if he repents,

After the ex-communication, however, when Döllinger made common cause with Anglicans like Meyrick, Newman distanced himself from the learned apostate. "As to Dr Döllinger I shall always think and hear of him with interest, and I may say, with affectionate solicitude," the Oratorian wrote,

> but also I must say frankly that what the Papers have lately told me of him has filled me with dismay, and I am prepared to hear any thing, however dismal, of him. He is not an Anglican getting nearer to the truth, but a Catholic receding from it. It is not a yearning after unity which made him turn from Rome, such as has made Liddon and others journey to Bonn. I do not see what is to save him ... from giving up all Councils and Creeds, and falling back upon a private-judgment induction from the works of St Irenæus or St Cyprian, of Origen or Tertullian, as the ultimate standard of Christian Truth. And then, since such a standard is sure to be no standing point, he must, if he lives long enough, give up dogma altogether, or at least his party must ... and then how long will they be separate from Renan?[28]

Here we can see how appreciative Newman was of how Renan's historicist blind alley awaited all who rejected "Councils and Creeds" for the primitive church of private judgment. For the historian in R. W. Southern, Renan's misguided preoccupation with history had landed him in "complete historical relativity, with the curious result that he wished everything to remain unchanged in a kind of gigantic museum of historical experience." In an echo of Newman's point about the necessary subordination of disciplines in the *Idea of the University*, Southern observed how "We have in Renan an example of what happens when any single experience takes control, and makes claims which cannot be sustained. From the unwarranted conviction that history is everything, it is but a small step to the further conviction that it will soon be nothing."[29] Döllinger and Meyrick certainly fell prey to this fallacy, a fallacy, one might say, tailormade to bamboozle those who mistake historical development for Revelation.

Of course, historical development can witness to Revelation, but it cannot replace it. After all, one of the reasons why history was only recognized as an academic discipline in 1850 was rather simple; as Southern observes: "it was thought impossible for historical investigation to discover a body of systematic, reliable, and important general truth, which would qualify for placing it alongside those subjects which had long been recognized as having all of those qualities." The subjects which included all of these qualities were, first, theology, and then law, medicine, arithmetic, geometry and the arts of the Trivium, grammar, rhetoric and logic. Again, to quote Southern: "All of these subjects had been offered for study by Oxford University since the early thirteenth century, and any reasonable person might think that they offered enough for all important

---

forgive him."

[28] JHN to Alfred Plummer (6 October 1874), *LD*, xxvii, 129. Joseph Ernest Renan (1823–92) studied for holy orders in Paris but left the seminary of Saint-Sulpice in 1845 as a result of religious doubts to become a writer. His *La Vie de Jèsus* (1863) was a more popular variation on the Socinian Christ of historicist Tübingen first touted by David Strauss's *Das Leben Jesu* (1835–6).

[29] R. W. Southern, "The Historical Experience," in *History and Historians: Selected Papers of R. W. Southern*, ed. R. J. Bartlett (Oxford: Blackwell Publishing, 2004), 117–18.

purposes of learning and for the conduct of life in this world, and in preparation for the next."[30] Amusingly, if one reason the University took it into its head to deviate from this view of history was because it had wearied of the *odium theologicum* that the Tractarians had introduced into the university in the 1840s, Newman's *Essay on Development* was a witty reminder to his erstwhile Oxford colleagues that no proper investigation into history could lead anywhere but to a renewed appreciation of the inescapable primacy of theology. Döllinger might have imagined that he was turning the new view of history to some theologically useful account, while, in fact, he was only proving its severe limits.

The accuracy of Newman's assessment of Döllinger and his Old Catholic friends can also be seen in a fairly deluded letter that Döllinger wrote to Meyrick before the first Bonn Conference of 1874, in which Old Catholics, the Eastern Churches and the Anglican Church participated:[31]

> I firmly believe that we, who claim to be true Catholics and professors of genuine, unadulterated Christianity, are obliged in conscience to make great concessions, and to introduce gradually considerable modifications wherever the departure of the embryo Vatican Church, as you call it, from the Ancient Church and its principles is evident. You have pointed out with perfect justice some of the indispensable corrections, and I trust that by personal discussion we may come to an agreement, or at least mutual toleration, respecting several other difficult questions. "Believe me, my dear Meyrick, Always to be yours affectionately and respectfully," I. Döllinger[32]

In reply, Meyrick stipulated "That the attention of the Conference be concentrated on the teaching of the first five (or six) centuries, and that no documents of later date be taken into consideration."[33] Like all good Protestants, he was sworn

---

[30] Ibid., 120.
[31] Cf. "[After] the Vatican Council definitions closed the door to dialogue with Rome, Anglican ecumenical attention turned to the Eastern Churches and those of the continent which had broken away from Rome, in particular the Old Catholic Church. These episcopal Churches, national in character and deeply anti-papalist, were seen by many Anglicans as more promising partners in dialogue than Rome. The Bonn Reunion Conferences of 1874 and 1875, organized by Professor Ignaz von Döllinger, who had left the Church of Rome after the Vatican Council's definition of infallibility, were a moment of hope. The Bonn Conferences brought together some Anglicans, Orthodox, Old Catholics, and representatives of other Churches. The conferences also marked a convergence of ritualism with traditional High Churchmanship, facilitated by the former's growing anti-Romanism as the result of recent events; for example, this convergence later made it possible for the High Church Christopher Wordsworth, bishop of Lincoln, to join R. F. Littledale and other ritualists in their liturgical conferences at All Saints, Margaret Street. Traditional High Churchmen, like bishops Christopher Wordsworth and Edward Harold Browne, took now a central role in the conferences, as also did Henry Parry Liddon, Pusey's disciple and biographer. The original optimism was short-lived. Pusey, who was not taking part in the conferences, reacted strongly against Orthodox intransigence in respect to the *Filioque*, writing a long pamphlet against its removal from the Creed. The various parties to the conferences drifted inevitably away from each other. Ecumenical paths seemingly closed, the Church of England, for the time being, turned its attention towards building up the Anglican Communion around the globe." James Pereiro, "The Oxford Movement and Anglo-Catholicism," *The Oxford History of Anglicanism, Volume III: Partisan Anglicanism and its Global Expansion 1829–c. 1914*, ed. Rowan Strong (Oxford: Oxford University Press, 2017), 207.
[32] Meyrick, *Memories*, 259.
[33] Ibid. See Henry Wace and Frederick Meyrick, *An Appeal from the New to the True Catholics, or*

to the very theological stasis that Newman wrote his *Essay on Development* to explode. Like the historicist in Renan, he wished to confine Christianity to a kind of "gigantic museum of historical experience" where everything would "remain unchanged."[34] That Döllinger accepted such a stipulation shows how little he understood the real relationship between history and theology. Of course, it also shows that it was more than papal infallibility that the German apostate found dubious about Roman Catholicism. Moreover, his very founding of the Old Catholic movement put him at odds with the Church to which he claimed to be faithful, though for some time after the Council he imagined that he could have matters both ways: he could break from the Church and yet somehow remain faithful to her. The Döllinger scholar Thomas Albert Howard nicely shows this in his treatment of Döllinger's interactions with the liberal Catholic historian, Lord Acton (1834–1902), who also looked askance at the definition of papal infallibility.

> While not relinquishing his misgivings about the Vatican Council, Acton nonetheless viewed the Old Catholic movement as fundamentally schismatic and he questioned Döllinger about his involvement in it. In his response, Döllinger recognized the validity of Acton's concerns, but told him that although he would rather withdraw from the public eye to scholarly solitude, his status as a professor, member of the Academy, and, not least, public official (Reichsrath) did not permit him the luxury of disengagement. But he also made clear to Acton his desire that the movement stay within the Church: "In order that the false teaching [Infallibility] not master the church and so that it can later be ejected, there must be some people who, repeatedly and loudly, reject and dispute [the teaching], but who do not separate themselves from the Church." Such sentiments partially allayed Acton's concerns, even as he continued to view the Old Catholic movement and Döllinger's proximity to it with misgivings.[35]

The euphoria that the movement inspired in some quarters can be seen in the response of the American Protestant theologian John Nevin (1803–86) who saw "immense meaning" and "true world-historical importance" in the Old Catholic movement. Germany, he believed, is "now destined, even more than in the sixteenth century, to lead the way in any great spiritual revolution having to do with the religion and civilization of the Christian world."[36] Indeed, Nevin saw the Old Catholic Movement as a possible response to the need for what Newman referred to as "ecclesiastical liberty"[37] in the wake of the Gorham

---

the Faith and Practice of the First Six Centuries (London, 1904).

[34] Southern, "Historical Experience," 117.
[35] Thomas Albert Howard, *The Pope and the Professor: Pius IX, Ignaz von Döllinger and the Quandary of the Modern Age* (Oxford: Oxford University Press, 2017), 186.
[36] Nevin, "The Old Catholic Movement," quoted in Howard, *The Pope and the Professor*, 187.
[37] Cf. "I say, [Anglo-Catholicism] has been definite in its principles, though vague in their application and their scope. It has been formed on one idea … That idea, or first principle, was ecclesiastical liberty; the doctrine which it especially opposed was in ecclesiastical language, the heresy of Erastus, and in political, the Royal Supremacy. The object of its attack was the Establishment, considered simply as such." *Diff.*, i, 124. Although, as a High Churchman, Meyrick was never in sympathy with the Anglo-Catholics, either before or after Newman's secession, he did wish to prevail upon the Establishment to follow his lead in aligning itself with the anti-papal Old Catholic Movement.

Case.³⁸ The Old Catholic Movement, in other words, could offer an alternative to the Erastian national churches—proof, at this time of turmoil, that Meyrick was not the only churchman suffering from bizarre delusions. Dean Church poured cold water on the scheme.

> If Germany were the world, or if the world were like Germany, these expectations might appear better grounded. But large elements have been left out of the calculation. If the Eastern Church were attracted, what about the Latin populations? What about Italy, Spain, and Ultramontane France? What about the strong anti-Catholic element in the English Church? What about the 126 sects of English Nonconformists, fiercely insular, fiercely suspicious of Popery, or of anything which their ignorance or their instinct confounds with Popery? What about the land of triumph ant sectarianism, the United States? Do they give much promise of coming into a scheme of reunion like this?³⁹

The moral of such questions for Church was undeniable: "nations may make peace, Churches are irreconcilable. In the whole course of Church history, it is hard to find a single clear instance of genuine voluntary reunion between separated bodies."⁴⁰

Nevertheless, Döllinger's scheme was never without support. Although American and German Protestants welcomed the theologian's break with Rome, Anglicans "were arguably the most smitten by the movement, precisely because they saw 'a tradition-minded, ecumenical ethos of the sort that they sought to cultivate.'" For Howard, 'John Newenham Hoare, rector of an Anglican parish in Killiskey, Ireland ... observed that 'it may be that Old Catholicism is attracting towards itself much that is great and noble in the Church of Christ' and it is therefore poised to help all Christians 'reach that highest end of Christian development, the union of the now divided Christians.' Similarly, Bishop Wordsworth of Lincoln hailed the movement as 'a great and holy cause.'"⁴¹

What, if anything, came of the Bonn conferences is not clear,⁴² though Meyrick gratefully acknowledges that they introduced him to the fabulously wealthy patron of the National Church, Alexander Beresford Hope (1820–87), the Conservative Member of Parliament for Cambridge, who foot the bill for

---

³⁸ In 1847, Henry Phillpotts (1778–1869), Bishop of Exeter, refused to institute G. C. Gorham, who had been presented to the living of Brampford Speke, after Gorham refused to subscribe Baptismal Regeneration, which gave rise to the Gorham Case, in which the Privy Council overruled the Bishop in favour of Gorham, thus undermining the longstanding Anglican doctrine of Baptismal Regeneration and reaccentuating the Erastian character of the National Church, in which "ecclesiastical liberty" could always be undermined by the English state. The ruling resulted in several Anglicans defecting to the Church of Rome, including Henry Edward Manning and Robert Wilberforce.

³⁹ Richard William Church, "Döllinger on the Reunion of Christendom," in *Occasional Papers*, i, 374.

⁴⁰ *Ibid.*, 368.

⁴¹ Howard, *The Pope and the Professor*, 187.

⁴² Cf. "The story of these Conferences deserves to be better known, since it provides a good example of the external factions that both promise and restrict the possibilities of ecumenical dialogue. Ultimately ... the claims of nationalism triumphed over the reunion of Christendom." Mark D. Chapman, *The Fantasy of Reunion: Anglicans, Catholics and Ecumenicism 1833–1882* (Oxford: Oxford University Press, 2014), 223.

much of the work of the Anglo-Continental Society and was married to Lord Salisbury's sister. With this redoubtable lady, Meyrick was clearly besotted. "I once saw Lady Mildred in a Court dress resplendent with the famous Hope diamonds," he gushes in his memoir. "The Queen had given her a diamond ring, which she therefore wore in going to Court; but it was by no means equal to many of the other diamonds that she was wearing." Still, for obvious pecuniary reasons, it was her husband whom Meyrick primarily sought to cultivate. "No one set a nobler example of liberality in connection with the Church than Mr. Beresford Hope."[43]

For Meyrick, "Such men are not prodigies of asceticism to make the world go wondering after them, and they are marked by a simplicity and common-sense which makes those who seek after a sign think lightly of them. Why is this, but that their minds are evenly balanced, each quality being duly developed in proper proportion with the rest, the result of which is to produce a *man* in the highest perfection of man's nature? Out of the best men are formed the best Christians— the truest saints of God. Such were, in the generation that has passed away, Sir John Patterson, Sir John Coleridge, Sir William Martin, Mr. J. H. Markland, Mr. W. Gibbs, Mr. J. G. Hubbard, and Roundel, Lord Selborne. May such laymen be never wanting to the Church of England!"[44]

Newman's understanding of sanctity as it relates to the Anglican Church was strikingly different. As he wrote to Catherine Ward (c. 1813–97) in 1848, when she was on the brink of converting to Rome after finding Pusey's High Church Anglicanism unsatisfactory:

> the Anglican Church cannot take support from the high religious excellence of *individuals* who are found in her. It is that the *direction* of their holy feelings, views, and works is, not *towards* that Church, but *away from* it, and bears testimony consequently, not to it, but against it; whereas the whole company of Catholic Saints, not only are indefinitely higher in sanctity than the best Anglicans, but are the natural fulfilment of the idea, the due ex-emplification of the teaching, of the Catholic Church. Who will say that fasting, devotion, and the like are in any sense the fruit of the historical, real, tangible Church of England? Is not *the idea* of an Anglican Bishop or clergyman, that of a gentleman, a scholar, a good father of a family, a well conducted, kindhearted, religiously minded man, and little more?[45]

---

[43] Meyrick, *Memories*, 280. According to the *ODNB*, Beresford Hope was "an architectural pundit of considerable influence. Having inherited a fortune in 1841, a great London mansion (Arklow House, Connaught Place) in 1843, and sizeable estates in Kent and Staffordshire (Bedgebury Park and Beresford Hall), he placed his resources at the service of the Gothic revival. ... Yet although he was a Gothicist to his heart's core, he eventually discovered Gothic principles—of skyline, composition, and planning—in Venice and Amsterdam alike, and in seventeenth-century Paris and fifteenth-century Bruges. ... In the politics of ecclesiology Beresford Hope played an ambivalent role. Although he will be forever linked with Benjamin Webb and John Mason Neale—the high-church trinity of Trinity College, Cambridge—his churchmanship was rather different to theirs. He was less of a sacramentalist than Neale, less of a ritualist than Webb. He was, after all, a layman. His Anglicanism was establishmentarian, moderate, paternal, tory. He was a high-churchman of the Hook and Hooker type—rather different from being a ritualist."

[44] Meyrick, *Memories*, 295. See the *ODNB* for biographies of all of these worthy individuals.

[45] JHN to Catherine Ward (25 September 1848), *LD*, xii, 273. See also Short, *Newman and his*

Meyrick's criticism of Newman reflects what he imagined his respect for "simplicity" and "common sense"—attributes that he considered Newman lacked.[46] In his judgment, Kingsley was right to impugn Newman's veracity in the controversy that led to the *Apologia* because it was always right to impugn the veracity of Catholics. In his pamphlet in defense of Kingsley, Meyrick addressed Newman directly:

> Sir, All England has been laughing with you, and those who knew you of old have rejoiced to see you once more come forth, like a lion from his lair, with undiminished strength of muscle, and they have smiled as they watched you carry off the remains of Mr. Charles Kingsley (no mean prey), lashing your sides with your tail, and growling and muttering as you retreated into your den. But, after all, is not Mr. Kingsley, substantially right? He was certainly not right in charging you personally with having made the statement which he has attributed to you. Nor was he right in not at once withdrawing words which he could not maintain. But is he wrong in saying that you not Dr. Newman the individual man, but Dr. Newman the representative of a school,—are unable to declare what we in England mean by untruthfulness to be immoral?[47]

Gladstone found Meyrick's line of reasoning persuasive: "Dr. Newman has had immeasurably the best of it in the rest of the controversy, but I think he will find it difficult to make a sufficient answer to you."[48] Others may find it indistinguishable from Kingsley's own circular reasoning. Newman was untruthful because Catholics were untruthful—or, to be more precise, Newman was untruthful because St. Alfonso Liguori was untruthful.[49] Years later, Lord Acton wrote to Meyrick to commend his criticism of Newman's defense of the Church's veracity *vis-à-vis* Liguori: "Some would deny that what Newman said to mitigate the shock of his own rejection of Liguori amounted to an actual defence of his teaching ... Newman's way of getting out of scrapes is worse than his occasional habit of getting into them."[50] However, Acton's biographer supplies a more cogent explanation of Liguori's understanding of what amounted to the pastoral advisability of probabilism. "The issue involved the moral theology of Alfonso Maria di Liguori (1696–1787), founder of the Redemptorist order, who was canonized in 1839," Roland Hill writes.

Contemporaries, 205–8.
[46] For Newman's recognition of the place of simplicity in the practice of faith, see the last of his *Parochial and Plain Sermons*, "Ignorance of Evil" (1836), *PS*, viii, 256–68.
[47] Frederick Meyrick, *But isn't Kingsley right, after all? A Letter to Dr. Newman* (London: Rivingtons, 1864), 3–4.
[48] Gladstone to Meyrick (31 October 1864) quoted in Meyrick, *Memories*, 24.
[49] Meyrick, *But isn't Kingsley right?*, 4. In 1854, over ten years before the Kingsley controversy, Meyrick wrote an article attacking Liguori, which Kingsley might very well have had in mind when he brought his charge against Newman. See *The Christian Remembrancer*, 27 (January 1854), Article II, pp. 38–87, "St Alfonso de Liguori's Theory of Truthfulness." Newman's response to the piece can be found in JHN to Capes (5 January 1854), *LD*, xvi, 9–10, the gist of which was this: "St. Alfonso's views are not binding on us, we may dissent from them."
[50] Unpublished letter from Acton to Meyrick (24 March 1874), Meyrick Papers, Pusey House Catalogue no. 9.

As an opponent of the dominant rationalism of the eighteenth century, he developed a pastoral approach or system of casuistry, that, on disputed questions of conscience, was more compassionate and relied more on divine grace than did harsh and pessimistic judgments. The system was intended to counter Jansenists, Liguori's particular opponents, who admitted only a model of perfection. On these disputed questions Liguori's "probabilism" allowed a more liberal course to be followed ... Newman's view of equivocation, which Liguori permitted under certain circumstances, was: "Much as I admire the high points of the Italian character, I like the English rule of conduct better" and "follow other guidance in preference to this."[51]

Newman, as Hill points out, stressed that Liguori's allowance for probabilism was meant to guide confessors, not preachers. Again, Liguori offered it as a pastoral option.[52] He was not an advocate of Laxism. "When I know that the rigid view is more probable, I say that it has to be followed," Liguori wrote; "but when the rigid opinion is only equally probable or very doubtfully more probable, then it is safe to follow the more benign opinion."[53] There is no acknowledgement of this lively qualification in either Meyrick's or Kingsley's charges against Liguori or Newman, though Meyrick did allow that Newman himself could not be accused of untruthfulness: it was only his Roman Catholic faith that bound him, as Meyrick imagined, to subscribe to what he regarded as Liguori's untruthfulness.

The *Oxford Dictionary of National Biography* may claim that Meyrick was "a clever disputant" but there is no clever disputation in Meyrick's pro-Kingsley pamphlet. Rather than a disputant, Meyrick was a raconteur. He is marvelous, for example, on Newman's return to Trinity to receive its honorary degree.

> I did not meet Dr. Newman again until he came to Oxford at the invitation of Dr. Percival (Bishop of Hereford), who was then President of Trinity College, in 1880, to dine at the High Table after having been elected an honorary Fellow of Trinity. He was then a bent old man, bedizened with pieces of red indicating that he was a Cardinal. I happened to have gone up to my old college on the same day, and I sat next but one to him at dinner, Henry Coleridge sitting between us. On hearing my name, he leant across, and said: "I think I used to know Mr. Meyrick formerly?" "Yes," I said, "thirty-five years ago." After dinner he went to the President's lodgings, and entered into unpolemical conversation with any of us that pleased to talk to him. At dinner his health was given by Professor Bryce, who congratulated him on having brought about a state of theological liberalism or indifferentism in Oxford, the one thing which from the beginning of his life to its end he abhorred. In the course of the day he paid a visit to his old and beloved friend, Dr. Pusey. "Newman," said Pusey, after the first greetings, "the Oxford Liberals are playing you like a card against us who are trying to

---

[51] Hill, *Lord Acton*, 150–1. See also the editor's introduction to Martin Svaglic's Oxford critical edition of the *Apologia*, xxv–xxx. Cf. "Falsehood and delusion are allowed in no case whatsoever. But there is an economy of truth ... a sort of temperance, by which a man speaks truth with reason that he may continue to speak it longer." Edmund Burke, *Regicide Peace* (1796).
[52] *Apo.*, 244, 248, 270–1.
[53] Liguori quoted in *Alphonsus de Liguori: Selected Writings*, ed. F. M. Jones (New York: Paulist Press, 1999), 329.

preserve the religious character of the University." He was made much of during this visit. College Gardens were lighted in his honour, and he held receptions of admirers. But it was his old enemies, whom he had fought *à outrance*, and whose principles he hated now from the bottom of his heart, who flocked round him as their champion, and thanked him for what he had done in demolishing the power of the Church of England in Oxford.[54]

The historian in Newman was the first to see the victory of liberalism as the upshot of the Oxford Movement.[55] Bryce's making reference to it in his after-dinner speech showed what an apt reader he was of Newman's King William Street lectures and his *Apologia pro Vita Sua* (1864). By the time William Burgon wrote his *Lives of Twelve Good Men* (1888), it had become an interpretive commonplace. In his chapter on Samuel Wilberforce, Burgon recalled:

> The desertion of Dr Newman to the opposite camp (1845) had brought matters to a crisis. That event took place in the year when Wilberforce was called to the episcopate; and only those who were resident in the University at the time can have any idea of the atmosphere of unhealthy excitement which prevailed before and after the date referred to,—the result chiefly of the publication of Ward's *Ideal* and of Newman's *Tract No. 90*. A terrible shock had been given to the moral sense of the place by the monstrous claim to read English formularies in Romish senses,—a shock which it has not to this day recovered. There followed a terrible recoil.[56]

With that shock still reverberating in Oxford nearly thirty years later, Newman wrote Bishop Ullathorne for his blessing before the Trinity dinner:

> The Oratory: Dec. 18, 1877.
> My dear Lord,—I have just received a great compliment, perhaps the greatest I have ever received, and I don't like not to tell you of it one of the first.
>
> My old College, Trinity College, where I was an undergraduate from the age of 16 to 21, till I gained a Fellowship at Oriel, has made me an Honorary Fellow of their Society. Of course it involves no duties, rights or conditions, not even that of belonging to the University, certainly not that of having a vote as Master of Arts, but it is a mark of extreme kindness to me from men I have never seen, and it is the only instance of their exercising their power since it was given them.
>
> Trinity College has been the one and only seat of my affections at Oxford, and to see once more, before I am taken away, what I never thought I should see again, the place where I began the battle of life, with my good angel by my side, is a prospect almost too much for me to bear.
>
> I have been considering for these two days, since the offer came to me, whether there would be any inconsistency in my accepting it, but it is so pure a compliment in its very title that I do not see that I need fear its being interpreted by the world as anything else.

---

[54] Meyrick, *Memories*, 25–6.
[55] *Diff.*, i, 1; *Apo.*, 184–5, 193.
[56] John William Burgon, *Lives of Twelve Good Men* (London: John Murray, 1888), 50.

Begging your Lordship's blessing, I am your obedient and affectionate servant in Christ,
John H. Newman.[57]

After the dinner, Newman wrote his old friend Maria Giberne: "I assure you I made no record of my feelings when I went to Oxford, and recollect nothing. I know it was a trial to me and a pleasure—but I could not say more, if you put me on the rack." Reticence in Newman always betokened deep feeling. However, he did add that "the Trinity Fellows seem to be a pleasing set of men and very kind to me," though he supposed them "very far from the Church."[58] Bryce's account of the Trinity Dinner (which he gave to Newman's biographer Wilfrid Ward) is also worth quoting:

> In response to the toast of his health [Newman] made a speech of perhaps ten minutes in length or a little more in a delightfully simple, natural and genial vein. My recollections of what he said are now unfortunately comparatively faint, but I remember the exquisite finish of his expressions and the beautiful clearness of his articulation and the sweetness of his voice. The subject was so far as I recollect mainly reminiscences of his college days at Trinity, and in particular he referred to one occasion when he went to call upon one of the former tutors who was still living, but who, if I remember right, had become so feeble in body that he was not able to come to the dinner. He was then Senior Fellow. That was Mr. Thomas Short, who was the Cardinal's senior by, I should think, 8 or 10 years. He mentioned to us that he found Mr. Short at lunch, and I remember how he entertained us by conveying indirectly and by a sort of reference that Mr. Short was lunching off lamb chops. ... He spoke with the greatest respect and reverence of Mr. Short, who by that time had outlived all his contemporaries.
>
> There was something tenderly pathetic to us younger people in seeing the old man come again, after so many eventful years, to the hall where he had been wont to sit as a youth, the voice so often heard in St. Mary's retaining, faint though it had grown, the sweet modulations Oxford knew so well, and the aged face worn deep with the lines of thought, struggle and sorrow. The story of a momentous period in the history of the University and of religion in England seemed to be written there.[59]

Meyrick's seeing the honorary Trinity degree as proof of what he regarded as Newman's failure in Oxford was of a piece with his discrediting Newman's work *per se*. When it came to Newman's Tractarian work, Meyrick was categorical: "It is an entire mistake to suppose that the religious movement in Oxford of the last century owes its origin to Newman, or required his help for its success. It would have taken place had Newman not existed, though the fire would not have blazed up so rapidly nor so fiercely if he had not been there to feed it."[60] For

---

[57] JHN to Bishop Ullathorne (18 December 1877), *LD*, xxviii, 283–4.
[58] JHN to Miss M. R. Giberne (Feast of St. Joseph, 1878), *LD*, xxviii, 331.
[59] James Bryce quoted in Ward, *The Life of Newman*, ii, 429–30.
[60] Meyrick, *Memories*, 26. Peter Nockles pinched the thesis of his ahistorical monograph, *The Oxford Movement in Context: Anglican High Churchmanship, 1760–1857* (Cambridge: Cambridge University Press, 1997) from this passage in Meyrick. To see the Oxford Movement in proper

the High Churchman, the Oxford Movement would only have been beneficial if it had been conducted by sensible High Church committee men like William Palmer of Worcester.[61] As it was, it was led by someone antagonistic to the High Church, and this, for Meyrick, accounted for its failure. Although "the Oxford revival would have been less picturesque without Newman, it would have been more beneficial," he held.

> It would then have been under the direction of Keble, Pusey, Palmer, Sewell, Rose, and others, who would have kept it in its proper course. As soon as he had joined it, Newman could not but be the controlling power. He was one of those men who must be first, and must stamp his own personality on others without making concession in turn to them. From the first he was the disquieting element in the body of associates; when Palmer tried to restrain his individuality by giving a revising power to a committee, he broke away from the shackles which would have been thus cast around him. The result was that he made himself master of the situation, and led his followers full upon the rocks, on which they were broken to pieces, like a wave when it dashes against a cliff. The Tractarian Movement, as a concerted movement, failed, and turned out a fiasco, because Newman led it. Keen as was his intellect, Newman was never guided by his reason, but always by his emotions; and a man so constituted cannot lead a host to victory, though he may stir up in them the enthusiasm which, if directed aright, insures success.[62]

The portrait drawn here of a man who was domineering, intransigent, irrational, unduly emotional and heedless of the wellbeing of those with whom he worked will only tally with those antagonistic to Newman or the Roman Church to which he converted, though Meyrick's defamatory catalogue helps us to see where Newman's later detractors derive their copycat libels. The ghost of Meyrick will always haunt the school of Frank Turner.[63]

If Meyrick found Newman too clever by half, he had to find a way to discredit the cleverness, even though, for the English readership to whom he addressed his writings, cleverness was suspect in and of itself. For Meyrick, "It is interesting to see the employment to which Newman put his intellect. It was not the directing force within him, but it was a faculty of extraordinary power which he used, like a powerful slave to which he gave his orders for reconciling to his own

---

critical and historical context, see Newman's *Anglican Difficulties* (1850, rev. edn 1876).

[61] Newman's treatment of Palmer in the *Apologia* is wonderfully acid: "Mr Palmer had a certain connexion, as it may be called, in the Establishment, consisting of high Church dignitaries … [who] were far more opposed than even he was to the impossible action of individuals. Of course, their beau ideal in ecclesiastical action was a board of safe, sound, sensible men. Mr. Palmer was their organ … and he wished for a Committee … with rules and meetings, to protect the interests of the Church in its existing peril." *Apo.*, 47. In the *ODNB*, Peter Nockles says that after Newman's conversion, Palmer "remained outspoken in defence of church principles and deplored the Gorham judgment," without acknowledging that the Erastianism on which the judgment of the Gorham case was decided is not any incidental but the core principle of the National Church founded on the Act of Supremacy (1534).

[62] Meyrick, *Memories*, 27.

[63] Frank Turner (1944–2010), former John Hay Whitney Professor of History at Yale University, many of whose scurrilous attacks on Newman were derived from Meyrick, still inspires various Newman detractors.

conscience any course that his will and affections had previously determined upon. It was so subtle that it beguiled him, and easily persuaded him that anything that he chose to do or to say was right." Thus, Newman's mind was not only servile, but sceptical. Indeed, for Meyrick, "His mind was naturally sceptical, like his brother's;[64] but his affections forced him to resolve by an act of will to be a believer, and his intellect was then called on to justify his resolution to himself and to the world. The more that this process went on—and it grew upon him with his years—belief lost the true character of belief, and became acceptance." What exactly the distinction between "belief" and "acceptance" is, Meyrick does not say. But he does hold that what Newman accepted was unacceptable. "Whether he gave an inward assent to a tenet or whether he did not, he would accept it if it came from a quarter to which he was inclined to pay deference. We know that in his heart he regarded the doctrine of the Pope's Infallibility the work of an "insolent and aggressive faction"; nevertheless, as soon as it was declared, he accepted it, not with what we understand by belief, but with assent. So with the dogma of the Immaculate Conception: he accepted it when declared, and condescended to justify it by arguing in its favour from a known misreading in Irenæus, the true character of which he ignored until he was compelled to acknowledge it."[65]

The charges here, such as they are, can be readily refuted. For Newman's understanding of the relationship between faith and reason fundamental to the Catholic understanding of Catholic dogma, readers can consult his *Oxford University Sermons* (1843), which hardly corroborate Meyrick's wild claim that Newman's reason was uncritical. Newman did not favor "acceptance" over "belief": he gave "inward assent" to tenets when they came "from a quarter to which he was inclined to pay deference," and since that quarter was the magisterial deposit of the Faith, it was hardly unreasonable for him to pay it deference.[66] Newman "in his heart" did not reject the doctrine of papal infallibility: he rejected those who wished to overstate the definition of the doctrine.[67] And Newman's acceptance of the dogma of the Immaculate Conception was not founded on a misreading of something in Irenaeus but on his reading of the development of doctrine.[68] Again, such feeble reasoning hardly shows Meyrick's power of disputation in any laudable light.

---

[64] For a critical study of Newman's fraught relationship with his brother, Francis Newman (1805-97), see "Frank Newman and the Search for Truth" in Short, *Newman and his Family*, 141-208.
[65] Meyrick, *Memories*, 27-8.
[66] Newman was always appreciative of the often indiscernibly fine line between belief and acceptance: "Though the meaning of the Creed be extended ever so far, it cannot go beyond our duty of obedience, if not of active faith; and if the line between the Creed and the general doctrine of the Church cannot be drawn, neither can it be drawn between the lively apprehension and the submission of her members in respect to both the one and the other. Whether it be apprehension or submission, it is faith in one or other shape, nor in fact can individuals themselves ever distinguish what they spiritually perceive from what they merely accept upon authority. It is the duty of every one either to believe and love what he hears, or to wish to do so, or at least, not to oppose, but to be silent." *VM*, i, 254-5.
[67] For an account of Newman's response to the definition of papal infallibility. see *LD*, xxv, xv-xvi.
[68] In accepting the doctrine of the Immaculate Conception, declared by Pope Pius IX in *Ineffabilis Deus* in 1854, Newman followed the Fathers. See JHN to Bishop Ullathorne (19 October 1854), *LD*, xvi, 281. See also Ker, *John Henry Newman: A Biography*, 610-11.

Yet, for someone so intent on taking another to task for being emotional and irrational, Meyrick was remarkably emotional and irrational himself. One can see something of his obsessive anti-Romanism in the following passage—an anti-Romanism, which he shared with so many English Protestants brought up to abominate priestly celibacy:

> His method of putting on an innocent face and passing off some fallacy as an undoubted axiom—e.g., that it is the world, the flesh, and the devil, not celibacy, which has caused and causes immoral life in a celibate clergy (as though no one had ever heard of the distinction between a cause and an occasion)—becomes provoking and monotonous when it has been noticed more than a certain number of times, and observed to be habitual.[69]

Hypocrisy was another charge that Meyrick brought against the convert, hypocrisy and treachery, two staples of the vituperation of No Popery.

> Few men have been so conspicuous for bringing about that which they specially aimed at resisting as Dr. Newman. He organized the forces of Belief against Unbelief, and then, deserting his soldiers in the conflict, he fell back and hurled weapons on them from behind till they lost half their confidence. He was a dogmatist to his marrow, and yet his teaching and example drove man after man of his followers (to whom he gave only the choice of all or nothing) into scepticism. He loved the ecclesiastical character of Oxford, and he destroyed it. He loved the Church of England, and he assailed it with all his force and with envenomed weapons of offence. He loved the party which he led at the University, and he scattered it to the winds. His one object of abhorrence throughout his life was Liberalism, and he became the darling and the cat's-paw of Liberals, while he spread dismay and disorganization through the ranks of their opponents, whom he had betrayed.[70]

What made these perceived failings so personally odious to Meyrick is that he saw them as proof of what he regarded as Newman's cardinal sin: his betrayal of the National Church, or, as he called it in his polemical book on Spain, the "Church Triumphant." If unconvincing, these aspersions have at least the logic of malevolence. Newman had many critics but what sets Meyrick apart is the straightforwardness with which he identified the source of his contempt. For the unswerving High Churchman, Newman was treachery personified: he attacked the Church that he had been sworn to uphold and defend. Yet paraphrase is poor stuff compared to Meyrick's own elaborate abuse.

> Newman lived long enough to see the very men who would have stoned him as a bigot in his earlier career build his sepulchre, to the sound of drums and fifes in honour of one who had done so much to undermine and weaken the institution on which the continuance of religion as a powerful influence in England depends. The record of Newman's life is a sad one. It is the record of one who, endowed

---

[69] Meyrick, *Memories*, 28.
[70] Ibid., 28–9.

with great powers, warm affections, strong will, high purpose, and a desire to do right, damaged profoundly the cause which he had most at heart, and promoted that which he most abhorred. On Dr. Newman's death he became the object of a hero-worship which was most creditable to the generosity of Englishmen, but in many respects, as I thought, undeserved.[71]

Something of the "hero-worship" of which Meyrick complains can be seen in many of the obituaries of Newman that appeared in the public prints throughout the English-speaking world, though it is amusing that the ardently liberal *Daily Chronicle* should have put this almost universal esteem in perspective when it noted that: "To the mass of Englishmen ... [Newman] was a conspicuous example of that welding together of genius, talent, and self-effacement which are the prime elements of a popular hero."[72] Another unlikely quarter, the *Daily Free Press* seconded these sentiments, which were precisely those of the common sense Meyrick claimed to prize.

> There is something strange, and yet not difficult to explain, in the unbroken chorus of admiration that has followed the death of Cardinal Newman. A man that never once in his long life sought popularity, whose work lay so distant from that of our present democracy, and whose later years have been passed in ascetic seclusion, is now the object of loving recollection. Above all, one who renounced the religion of the great majority in this country, and who took what must be regarded by that majority as a great retrograde step has passed away without a note of bitterness from those whom his memorable action disappointed most.

For the obituarist at the *Daily Free Press*, it was not the "learned theologian who had the courage to act up to his convictions" that his countrymen admired, even though "the act of his becoming a Roman Catholic made his name more widely known than it would otherwise have been." No, "of all his great qualities," it was his "beautiful personal character" that the nation singled out for praise." Personal influence, in other words, accounted for the esteem in which he was held. "He was singularly free from the narrowness and sharp temper that are the usual concomitants of the faculty for polemical controversy. There are many great divines who, by their austerity, repel sympathy; Newman, the greatest of them all, never did."[73]

Meyrick attacked more than the popular hero in Newman: he also attacked the theologian in him. In a book aptly entitled, *Is Dogma A Necessity?* (1883), he charged Newman not only with falsification but fabrication. "In order to erect some sort of intellectual scaffolding for dogmas of the modern Roman Church," the High Churchman wrote, "which are without the support of Scripture, tradition, or history (numbering, as we have seen, fourteen or fifteen, while those of the Oriental Church are only two), Petavius[74] invented, and Dr. Newman has

---

[71] Ibid., 29–31.
[72] Obituary of Newman in *Daily Chronicle*, LD, xxxii, 589–90.
[73] *Daily Free Press* obituary of JHN, LD, xxxii, 590.
[74] Petavius, Dionysius (1583–1652), Jesuit historian and theologian who recognized the validity of doctrinal development.

embellished, a theory, called the theory of development, by which are justified any innovations in doctrine or discipline which actually arise within that communion, however originating; the very fact of their existence being regarded as a proof that it was the Divine intention that they should emerge, even though it may be demonstrated that they actually took their origin from misapprehension, ignorance, or superstition."[75] Some critics have taken issue with Newman's understanding of doctrinal development, but few with anything like Meyrick's blithe crudity. In thus attacking Newman along dogmatic lines, Meyrick followed an approved Whig tradition. The intellectual historian J. W. Burrow is good on this score: "Of course, in so far as the Whig tradition was constitutionalist, tolerant and Erastian, it had no concern with theological questions as such." Macaulay might have supported Catholic Emancipation (1829) but that was only because it advanced the purposes of political Whiggery; after all, "it was persecution that turned sects into factions."[76] And as for Froude, Whiggery's most paradoxical advocate, he "hated theologians more than Macaulay disliked theoretical republicans or Stubbs and Freeman lawyers."[77] Meyrick's impatience with Newman's theological preoccupations may not have been cut out of exactly the same latitudinarian cloth as theirs—he concedes that dogma is key to Christianity—but he does insist that the dogma of the reformed Anglican Church is the only true dogma because it rejects what he regarded as Rome's unscriptural accretions.[78] In the wake of the definition of the dogmas of the Immaculate Conception (1854) and Papal Infallibility (1870), Meyrick was convinced that: "We are not to suppose that even the exploitation of Mariolatry and Papal authority have come to an end with the dogmas of the Vatican Council and Pius IX. We see new extravagances on both heads forming before our eyes and awaiting the hour when a future Pope shall declare them revelations of God." For Meyrick, as it was, Leo XIII had already shown his disposition to such "exploitation" by

---

[75] Meyrick, *Is Dogma a Necessity?* (London: Hodder and Stoughton, 1883), 94–5.
[76] J. W. Burrow, *A Liberal Descent: Victorian Historians and the English Past* (Cambridge: Cambridge University Press, 1981), 244.
[77] Ibid., 271.
[78] Cf. "An expression was used by the late Canon Shirley, in preaching a remarkable sermon before the University of Oxford, that Christianity was 'dogmatic to its core; 'and again, in a paper written so soon before the close of his career that it was published after his death, he declared that 'the teaching of positive doctrine, entailing dogma in the inevitable progress of things, is of the very essence of Christian preaching.' In spite of the strong prejudices felt against dogma, and the protests raised from many quarters against definite teaching and the intervention of authority in matters of opinion or belief, no thoughtful man, brought face to face with the question, can deny the truth of the Canon's statement. For it is, and must be, the belief of Christians that Christ, during His sojourn on earth, made a revelation of truth which it is necessary for all men who would be saved by Christianity to hold and cherish." *Is Dogma A Necessity*, 165–6. According to the *ODNB*, the ecclesiastical historian Walter Shirley (1828–66) began a life of Wyclif while a fellow at Wadham that he never finished. Moreover, his "theological views underwent considerable change and began to lean more towards the opinions of the Tractarians. Having been in his early days a disciple of Arnold, he ultimately came to regard 'undogmatic Christianity' as a contradiction in terms. Finally, in May 1863, he preached in the university church a sermon—which created a great impression at the time of its delivery and was subsequently published—in which he sought to demonstrate the unreasonableness of Arnold's teaching." However, "The theological position which Shirley occupied at the time of his death was still regarded by him as a provisional one, as he believed that any moral or intellectual position should always be open to revision." Meyrick, to say the least, was not always happy in the choice of his authorities.

going out of his way to encourage devotion to the Blessed Virgin, "taking under his protection all the wilder legends which do her honour."[79]

Meyrick's dismissal of Newman's theory of the development of Christian doctrine is of a piece with his impatience with papal authority.

> It is plain that every corruption, whether of the Jewish Church, or of any section of the Christian Church, or of any religious body, might be thus justified; and that if the theory be true, there is virtually no such thing as a "faith delivered to the saints" (Jude 3), to be "kept" as a deposit "committed to" the Church's trust (1 Tim. 1.3, 6.20) for the salvation of mankind; and that St Paul's heat in twice repeating, "If any man preach any other gospel unto you than that ye have received, let him be accursed" (Gal. 1.8, 9) was quite out of place; and that he should have said, instead of "other than that ye have received," "other than that which, perhaps, after centuries of hesitancy and doubt and denial, may receive the sanction of the Bishop of Rome."[80]

The amusing thing about this criticism of Newman's idea of development is that Newman would have surely agreed with Meyrick about any false development, though, of course, it was a different matter altogether when it came to genuine dogmatic developments.

In addition to his contempt for the development of dogma, there might have been something else that contributed to Meyrick's opposition to Newman: disappointed ambition. Tuckwell is intriguing on this possibility:

> We thought that a man starting with qualifications so marked, academic, social, personal, must become a shining University light: but he married, became a School Inspector, for a time disappeared, then suddenly came into notice during the *horrida bella* between Newman and Charles Kingsley, as author of a pamphlet bearing the cumbrous title—"But isn't Kingsley right after all?" It was a rather vigorous production, touching with an Ithuriel spear of commonsense Newman's dexterous subterfuge and Kingsley's bungling incompetence; and it won Gladstone's admiring approbation. It had no effect upon the public mind; men could not all appreciate reasoning; they could all enjoy the "Apologia" to which the controversy gave rise. Kingsley was entirely discredited, and for several years the sale of his books fell off. Exchanging his School Inspectorship for a living, Meyrick devoted himself to theological controversy. More than fifty pamphlets stand against his name in the British Museum Catalogue ... He was a friend and supporter of Döllinger, a vehement opponent of Manning, of Huxley, of Pattison, of Jowett. How could such a man escape promotion? His youthful friend, afterwards Lord Salisbury, quarrelled with him when in 1865 he voted for Gladstone at Oxford, and his displeasure was possibly permanent. But what was Gladstone about, in his numerous Episcopal creations, to pass over a man so like-minded, so active, and above all so safe? Perhaps it was as well for

---

[79] Frederick Meyrick, *Scriptural and Catholic Truth and Worship or The Faith and Worship of the Primitive, the Mediæval and the Reformed Anglican Churches* (London: Skeffington & Son, 1901), 251–2.

[80] Ibid., 251.

Meyrick: endowment with mitral consequence might not have compensated for deterioration of moral fibre: anyhow, he remained Vicar of Blickling till his death. Dignified, learned, pious, with high College honours and good social position, he preserved the old type of humanistic University training in the past. Intransigent in youth, and sturdy to the end, he remained through life a faithful champion of lost and losing causes.[81]

Meyrick's crusade against Newman and the Church to which he converted was the most seductive of these lost causes. It was also the one that he probably never recognized as lost, his championship of the "Church Triumphant" being so imperturbably zealous.

The epigraph that he chose for his book on Spain is a case in point. He took it from an address delivered by the father of the architect A. W. N. Pugin in 1850 during the time known as "papal aggression," when Pius IX was reconstituting the English Catholic hierarchy: "Pleasant meadows, happy peasants, all holy monks, all holy priests, holy everybody. Such charity and such unity when every man was a Catholic—I once believed in this Utopia myself, but when tested by stern facts it all melts away like a dream."[82] Read out of context, the quotation could almost have been the recantation of a disenchanted papist; in context, it was quite otherwise. It is clear that the young Meyrick decided to use it despite its context, no doubt imagining that most of his readers would never know or inquire after its provenance. In all events, his choice of epigraph does not reflect well on his diligence, let alone his intellectual probity. "It is, indeed, remarkable, that in no official act is the Church of England committed to the term Protestant," the French émigré wrote;

> it does not occur in the Liturgy or any authoritative office, nor in the Articles or Canons, and in the bidding prayer, she prays for the whole state of Christ's Catholic Church, and especially for that part of it established in this dominion— language which can only admit of one interpretation. Now in opposition to this, the vulgar Protestant idea is that before the Reformation there was an entire reign of idolatry and superstition, that the clergy were all ministers of anti-Christ, worshippers of false gods, and in fine, that the first dawning of Christian light and truth commenced with the spiritual headship of the eighth Henry; that all the old clergy were turned out, and that Cranmer, Ridley and Latimer were the fathers of the new system, to whom it owed its very existence, and to such an extent has this false idea prevailed, that a few years ago men filling high positions in the leading university, got up a cross to commemorate those arch heretics as founders of the English church. Such is the low and popular Protestant view. Now, let us examine the ordinary Catholic idea that prevails among our own body, and which is very little nearer to the truth than the one I have described. All, anterior to the Reformation, is regarded and described as a sort of Utopia:—pleasant

---

[81] W. Tuckwell, *Reminiscences of Oxford*, 2nd edition (London: Smith Elder & Co., 1907), 228–9. For a lively study in contrast between the humanist tradition to which Meyrick subscribed and that of the scholastic humanists, see R. W. Southern, *Scholastic Humanism and the Unification of Europe, Volume I: Foundations* (Oxford: Blackwell, 1995).

[82] Meyrick, *Church in Spain*, 5.

meadows, happy peasants, merry England—according to Cobbett bread cheap, and beef for nothing, all holy monks, all holy priests,—holy everybody. Such charity, and such hospitality, and such unity, when every man was a Catholic. I once believed in Utopia myself, but when tested by stern facts and history, it all melts away like a dream. The Catholic religion was founded in England as in any other country, on a political system that was barbarous; the people were barbarous, the customs were barbarous, the traditions were barbarous, hence from the very beginning the pure Catholic faith was, in temporal matters, mixed up with barbarism, and most assuredly the conquest of the Norman kings was accompanied with every possible barbarity and injustice. Let any reasonable man then reflect on the enormous difficulties that the Catholic religion had to contend with in preserving its position, and maintaining the truth in such a state of society, and which will be evident to all who attentively study the chronicles of English church history in all their bearings and details.[83]

Instead of writing to impugn the Catholic Church, Pugin senior wrote to commend her. His son's characterization of the address was memorably searing.[84]

> This pamphlet was written at a time of great hope for the Church in England. The edifice which had been so ruthlessly levelled at the time of the Reformation as not to leave a stone standing upon a stone, had to be erected anew from its foundation. There was not even rubbish to clear away, the ground was unencumbered and level. Good workmen, too, were at hand, for the scattered remnant which, true to the old faith, had survived ages of persecution and of social outlawry, had at their head in Dr. Wiseman a leader worthy of their sacred cause. Untrammelled by party ties or personal associations, large-minded, modest, full of trust in those who had to work with him, or under him, inspiring confidence in all who came in contact with him, our great English Cardinal was peculiarly fitted for the work of building up again the Church in England. To one less open than my father to great ideas, less keenly alive to great occasions, the beginning of such a work could not be a common occurrence, but in him it awoke the highest hopes and aspirations, not unmingled however, with grave apprehensions. He had pondered more fully perhaps than any man of his time over the remoter causes which led to the shameful apostacy of the English clergy and bishops in the sixteenth century. Had not wide spread corruption and venality prevailed, had churchmen of the highest grade not been worldlings addicted to the pomps and vanities of the court, hirelings who abjectly served the State instead of safeguarding religion, the Church in England would never at the bidding of a tyrant have basely surrendered the faith and bartered the cross of Christ for the sceptre of a king. The guilty cause of this shameless betrayal of a divine trust, my father rightly traced, not indeed to the legitimate union of the two Powers entrusted by God with the government of the world, but to that adulterous intercourse

---

[83] A. Welby Pugin, *Christian Liberty in Church and State. An Earnest Address on the Subject of the Re-establishment of the Hierarchy*, with an introduction and notes by his son (London: Longmans & Co., 1875), 35–6.

[84] For Newman's response to Auguste Pugin's address, see JHN to E. W. Pugin (10 February 1875), *LD*, xxviii, 217.

between things divine and human, which in due course has begotten, as we see, the godless State.[85]

Here was betrayal of another sort, which did not altogether comport with Meyrick's exalted view of his Church Triumphant. It is also a clear-eyed indictment of precisely the Erastianism that Newman skewered so unsparingly in his *Anglican Difficulties*, an Erastianism that Meyrick spent nearly his entire life defending and promoting. Wilfrid Ward was certainly clear-eyed about this defining aspect of Meyrick's Church Triumphant.

> The history of Anglican doctrine, from the Gorham case to the Public Worship Regulation Act, has been one long assertion of the [undogmatic] principle for which Arnold contended, and a denial of the principle which Newman maintained. It is Parliament and the Privy Council which ultimately determine what doctrines and practices are admissible within the Established Church, whether they do so directly or by delegating their work to specialists. Bishops who, as Bishop Philpotts did, have attempted to assert their prerogative as exponents of Anglicanism have been overruled. The Erastianism which it was the object of the Movement to overthrow has, beyond question, come forth triumphant.[86]

Manning, too, saw the same Erastianism as one of Newman's chief foes, though he could not foresee that the forces Newman opposed in the National Church would prevail as thoroughly as they did. "It is too soon to measure the work that has been silently wrought by the life of Cardinal Newman," Manning told the faithful at Newman's Solemn Requiem Mass at the Oratory, South Kensington, 20 August 1890.

> No living man has so changed the religious thought of England. His withdrawal closes a chapter which stands alone in the religious life of this century. It has, for the most part, been wrought in silence; for the retiring habits of the man, and the growing weight of age, made his later utterances few. Nevertheless, his words of old were as "the hammer that breaks the rocks in pieces," and as the light that works without a sound. It has been boldly and truly avowed that he is "the founder, as we may almost say, of the Church of England as we see it. What the Church of England would have become without the Tractarian movement, we can faintly guess; and of the Tractarian movement Newman was the living soul and the inspiring genius." This sentence will be implacably resented and fiercely attacked; but it is true as the light of day. This intellectual movement

---

[85] Pugin, *Christian Liberty in Church and State*, 8–9. Of course, Newman entirely agreed with Pugin when it came to the magnificent part Wiseman played in the period known as "papal aggression": "He is made for the world," Newman told Sir George Bowyer,"and he rises with the occasion. Highly as I put his gifts, I was not prepared for such a display of vigour, power, judgment, sustained energy as the last two months have brought. I heard a dear friend of his say before he got to England that the news of the opposition would kill him. How he has been out. It is the event of the time. In my own remembrance there been nothing like it. It is an anxious thing, that he is the only one among us equal to the work Providence has laid upon him; yet, again, not anxious, because he is in the hands of that Providence, and because Providence ever works with few instruments." Newman to Bowyer (1 December 1850), *LD*, xiv, 185.
[86] Ward, *William George Ward and the Oxford Movement*, 376.

was begun and sustained by one man. But for this movement, Erastianism and Rationalism would by this time have reigned supreme in the National religion. The penetrating influence of this one mind has pervaded also the bodies separated from the Established Church, and most opposed to it. They have been powerfully attracted, not to the Tudor Settlement, but to primitive Christianity. And the same sweet voice and luminous words have been working among them, all the more persuasively because he had rejected all things of this world, even more than themselves. He spoke to them as a simple voice of truth, which could neither be warped by prejudice nor bribed to silence.[87]

How to conclude? *Pace* Meyrick, Newman did not set about destroying the National Church: it destroyed itself.[88] The seeds of its self-destruction were sown in its very Erastian founding, a piece of worldly triumphalism that could only have ended badly. Of course, one might say that Pugin was beguiled by a triumphalism of his own in seeking to revive a kind of Catholic mediaevalism in the hope that it would somehow come to the rescue of an England bereft of her former Catholic faith and coherence—something which never tempted the more level-headed Newman.[89] "During the Middle Ages Rome is spoken of, not only as the world, but even as Babylon," he reminded his friend T.W Allies. "How strong is St. Thomas of Canterbury upon it! How the saints are used to look upon the Pontifical Court as in fact almost a road to perdition! Consider

---

[87] Manning quoted in Purcell, *Life of Cardinal Manning*, ii, 750–1.
[88] For Newman's last-ditch effort to salvage the National Church, see his article "Catholicity of the Anglican Church" which appeared in the January issue of the *British Critic* in 1840 and collected in his essays. "Now if there ever were a Church on whom the experiment has been tried whether it had life in it or not, the English is that one. For three centuries it has endured all vicissitudes of fortune. It has endured in trouble and prosperity, under seduction and under oppression. It has been practised upon by theorists, browbeaten by sophists, intimidated by princes, betrayed by false sons, laid waste by tyranny, corrupted by wealth, torn by schism, and persecuted by fanaticism. Revolutions have come upon it sharply and suddenly, to and fro, hot and cold, as if to try what it was made of. It has been a sort of battle-field on which opposite principles have been tried. No opinion, however extreme any way, but may be found, as the Romanists are not slow to reproach us, among its bishops and divines. Yet what has been its career upon the whole? Which way has it been moving through three hundred years? Where does it find itself at the end? Lutherans have tended to Rationalism; Calvinists have become Socinians; but what has it become? As far as its formularies are concerned, it may be said all along to have grown towards a more perfect Catholicism." *Ess.*, ii, 55.
[89] Cf. "Christianity in the middle ages impressed its image on society, it did not succeed equally with literature and science. Society at the time bore witness to this serious incompleteness in the regeneration of human nature ... And no one will deny that, as in primitive and in these times, the intellect of the world in the medieval period was untamed. If then Christianity has not compelled the intellect of the world, viewed in the cultivated classes, to confess Christ and follow His teaching, why insist, as some triumphant success that it has influenced the soldier and the magistrate? If there was to be a grand progress according to which first the individual, the family, then civil polity, was to be converted, why was the conquest of literature and science to have no place in the series of triumphs?" For Newman, "since the object of Christianity is to save souls, and St. Paul says that he endures all things for the sake of the elect, I ask what reason have we to suppose that more souls were saved, relative to the number of Christians, under the Catholic theocracy, than under the Roman Emperors or under the English Georges. There are no means of course of proving the point, but we ought to have some good reason for answering in the affirmative, before we lay any stress upon the glories of the medieval system." JHN to T. W. Allies (22 November 1860), *LD*, xix, 422.

St. Philip's title of the Apostle of Rome, and that the correlation to Apostle is a state of heathenism. St. Bernard, I think, speaks as if a man could scarcely be saved who did not enter the cloister. Surely Christian society was the world still, and nothing short of it."[90]

Yet at least Pugin knew which was the false and which the true English Church. He certainly would have recognized the accuracy of what the convert in Newman had to say of both in the first lecture of his *Anglican Difficulties*.

> It is this keen feeling that my life is wearing away, which overcomes the lassitude which possesses me, and scatters the excuses which I might plausibly urge to myself for not meddling with what I have left for ever, which subdues the recollection of past times, and which makes me do my best, with whatever success, to bring you to land from off your wreck, who have thrown yourselves from it upon the waves, or are clinging to its rigging, or are sitting in heaviness and despair upon its side. For this is the truth: the Establishment, whatever it be in the eyes of men, whatever its temporal greatness and its secular prospects, in the eyes of faith is a mere wreck. We must not indulge our imagination, we must not dream: we must look at things as they are; we must not confound the past with the present, or what is substantive with what is the accident of a period. Ridding our minds of these illusions, we shall see that the Established Church has no claims whatever on us, whether in memory or in hope; that they only have claims upon our commiseration and our charity whom she holds in bondage, separated from that faith and that Church in which alone is salvation. If I can do aught towards breaking their chains, and bringing them into the Truth, it will be an act of love towards their souls, and of piety towards God.[91]

---

[90] Newman to T. W. Allies (22 November 1860), *LD*, xix, 421.
[91] *Diff.*, i, 4–5. See also Edward Short, "Editor's Introduction," in *Difficulties of Anglicans*, ed. Edward Short (Leominster: Gracewing, 2021), i, xv–clxxxii.

CHARLES KINGSLEY

8

Kingsley, Newman and God's Kind Providence

Of your belief in a special providence, of a perpetual education of men by evil as well as good, by small things as well as great, I cannot speak too highly. If I did not believe that, I could believe nothing.
          Charles Kingsley to Horace Field (3 November 1867)

It was by a wonderful Providence that I got through my trial last year; but I felt at the time it was like dancing on a tight rope à la Blondin.
          Newman to Henry James Coleridge (28 April 1865)

I

In July of 1848, Charles Kingsley wrote to his wife, "I know the miserable, peevish, lazy, conceited, faithless, prayerless wretch I am, but I know this, too, that One is guiding me, and driving me when I will not be guided, who has made me, and will make me go His way and do His work, by fair means or foul."[1] Much speculation has been spent trying to ascertain what could have induced Kingsley to impugn John Henry Newman's veracity in his notorious review of James Anthony Froude's *History of England*, in which the clergyman, poet, novelist and historian went out his way to impugn both Newman and his co-religionists. "Truth, for its own sake, had never been a virtue with the Roman clergy," Kingsley wrote in *Macmillan's Magazine* in January of 1864. "Father Newman informs us that it need not, and on the whole ought not to be; that cunning is the weapon which Heaven has given to the saints wherewithal to withstand the brute male force of the wicked world, which marries and is given in marriage. Whether his doctrine be doctrinally correct or not, it is at least historically so." The claim was made in reference to one of Newman's sermons, "Wisdom and Innocence" (1843), in which, apropos Matthew x, 16, "Behold, I send you forth as sheep in the midst of wolves; be ye therefore wise as serpents, and harmless as doves," Newman had remarked:

---

[1] *Charles Kingsley: His Letters and Memories of his Life*, ed. by his wife 2 vols. (London: Henry S. King & Co., 1877), i, 170.

Christians were called crafty, because "they were, in fact, so strong, though professing to be weak." And next, in mere consistency, they were called hypocritical, because "they were, forsooth, so crafty, professing to be innocent." And thus whereas they have ever, in accordance with our Lord's words, been wise and harmless, they have ever been called instead crafty and hypocritical. The words "craft" and "hypocrisy" are but the version of "wisdom" and "harmlessness," in the language of the world. It is remarkable, however, that not only is harmlessness the corrective of wisdom, securing it against the corruption of craft and deceit, as stated in the text; but innocence, simplicity, implicit obedience to God, tranquillity of mind, contentment, these and the like virtues are themselves a sort of wisdom;—I mean, they produce the same results as wisdom, because God works for those who do not work for themselves; and thus Christians especially incur the charge of craft at the hands of the world, because they pretend to so little, yet effect so much.[2]

That Kingsley should have construed Newman's point to mean that he agreed with the world's misunderstanding of Christ's exhortation to his disciples to be "wise" and "harmless" not only proved the necessity of Christ's words but Kingsley's inability to understand Newman's gloss on them. Reading incomprehension, in other words, played a livelier part in the controversy than most realize. It must also be remembered, apropos Kingsley's defamatory outburst, that it came from a man who had never met Newman, who was not particularly well-read in Newman's voluminous work, and who had no understanding whatever of the Roman Church's mission in the world. Why Kingsley, a dutiful clergyman and esteemed, popular author, should have gone out of his way to cross swords with one of the deftest controversialists of his own or any age is a question that it will be the object of this chapter to answer.

Some hold that Kingsley attacked Newman because he genuinely believed that Newman and the Church to which he converted were indifferent to the truth—and, moreover, had good grounds for such a belief. James Fitzjames Stephen, as we have seen, was a sedulous advocate of this still widespread view.

Some argue that Kingsley attacked Newman because he saw him as living proof of the effeminacy and indeed deviance that many Englishmen associated not only with Catholicism but Anglo-Catholicism. In 1851, when the English, led by their prime minister Lord John Russell were fulminating against what came to be known as "Papal Aggression" (set off by Pope Pius IX's restoration of the Roman Catholic hierarchy in the country), Kingsley had written of Catholics and Anglo-Catholic Tractarians:

> In ... all that school, there is an element of foppery—even in dress and manner; a fastidious, maundering, die-away effeminacy, which is mistaken for purity and refinement; and I confess myself unable to cope with it, so alluring is it to the minds of an effeminate and luxurious aristocracy; neither educated in all that should teach them to distinguish between bad and good taste, healthy and unhealthy philosophy or devotion.[3]

[2] SD, 298–9.
[3] *Charles Kingsley: His Letters and Memories of his Life*, ii, 260.

This view of the inherent unmanliness of Romanism, whether Catholic or Anglo-Catholic, can be traced back to the reports Thomas Cromwell's visitors produced claiming that the practice of sodomy vitiated the monasteries before King Henry VIII had them dissolved, though the No Popery view of the incidence of that practice was exaggerated: the monasteries had many more whoremasters than sodomites.[4]

Some, like Martin Svaglic, the brilliant editor of the Oxford critical edition of the *Apologia*, argues that the main source of Kingsley's bitterness and hostility to Newman was psychological.

> The ultimate basis of Kingsley's hostility to Newman, the Tractarians, and Rome itself—more important than his distrust of casuistry or "economy" or sacerdotalism—appears to have been psychological. As a young man Kingsley had been torn between the exclusive demands of an austere Evangelical religion and such worldly concerns as scientific pursuits and the attractions of physical love. The scepticism, indulgence, and vigorous physical activity of his early years at Cambridge were an attempt at a resolution which proved impossible for a man of Kingsley's temperament and inheritance. Some religious faith was necessary to him. At one point he confessed that he was wavering between "deism or the highest and most monarchical system of Catholicism." And Catholicism, as Kingsley understood it, led even more than his childhood faith to a Manichean asceticism, not without a beauty of its own, which turned its back on the natural world. The same inability to make distinctions which made the work of Roman casuists like Alfonso Liguori so abhorrent to him made it possible for him to write: "Were I a Romanist, I should look on a continuance in the state of wedlock as a bitter degradation to myself and my wife."[5]

Some have argued that it was the *fracas* that Kingsley had with Dr. Edward Pusey in 1863 over an Oxford D. C. L. that fired his animus against Newman. When Pusey effectively barred Kingsley from receiving the honorary degree, Kingsley's contempt for Anglo-Catholicism in general and Newman in particular, according to this supposition, was reignited. "Puseyism is dead, & knows it," Kingsley wrote to his good friend Frederick Denison Maurice, "& is therefore, like an evil sprite, venomous & querulous."[6]

Some hold that Kingsley attacked Newman because he detested Newman's celibacy and sought to discredit the convert and the Church of Rome in order somehow to discredit celibacy *per se*. There were many grounds for Kingsley's complicated distaste for celibacy. As a young man, reared as he had been in a strict Evangelical country rectory, he had actually contemplated following a life

---

[4] "The *Compendium Compertorum* carefully read … offers very little in support of the substantial association of monks and homosexuality." G. W. Bernard, *The King's Reformation: Henry VIII and the English Church* (New Haven: Yale University Press, 2005), 259.
[5] Martin J. Svaglic, "Editor's Introduction," in *Apologia pro Vita Sua: Being a History of His Religious Opinions by John Henry Newman* (Oxford: Oxford University Press, 1967), xxxi. The quotation from Kingsley is from Guy Kendall, *Charles Kingsley and his Ideas: A Biography* (London: Hutchinson, 1947), p. 147.
[6] Kingsley quoted in R. B. Martin, *The Dust of Combat: A Life of Charles Kingsley* (New York: W. W. Norton & Company, Inc., 1960), 231–2.

of celibacy himself. "I once formed a strange project," he confessed, "I would have travelled to a monastery in France, gone barefoot into the chapel at matins (midnight) and confessed every sin of my whole life before the monks and offered my naked body to be scourged by them."[7] Then, too, his wife Fanny had come under Newman's Tractarian influence before marrying and even contemplated becoming an Anglican nun. Before their marriage, Kingsley had been obliged to persuade her of the evils of celibacy and what he saw as the transcendental blessings of erotic love. Lastly, his brother Henry had sworn himself to a uniquely misogynistic celibacy when an undergraduate at Oxford, which must have intensified Kingsley's revulsion from what he regarded as an inhuman abstention. At Oxford, Henry had founded the "Fez" Club with Edwin Arnold.

> It was a society of fifty members, all haters of women, all pledged to pass their lives in celibacy and to diffuse the principles of misogyny in every section of English life ... At their luxurious breakfasts everyone wore a fez and insignia on the masonic pattern and smoked oriental tobacco from oriental pipes. Each man was allowed to rise and address the company provided he could tell some story against "the sex which would serve to confirm members in their conviction that women must be held in subjection as weak-minded and incorrigibly frivolous creatures."[8]

If Charles was opposed to celibacy, he was also opposed to marital sexual relations unless treated as a preparation for the sexual relations that he believed would obtain in Heaven. "Rather than being merely idiosyncratic," the scholar Charles Barker argues, "Kingsley's ideas about sex prefigured important aspects of the modern construction of sexuality. Kingsley has, for instance, been credited with the first use of the word 'sexuality' to refer to intercourse rather than to the differences between male and female (the word's earlier meaning).[9] Kingsley, in fact, went a step further. In effect, he distinguished sexuality from sex—from the mere act of intercourse—by conceiving of a heavenly mode of passion ... Kingsley's claim that erotic touch is a conduit to God often had the unintended effect of equating sexuality with experiencing the deity. Kingsley's eroticized Christianity was a precursor for a modern discourse in which sex implicitly replaces God as a transcendent locus of meaning."[10]

Still others have pointed to Kingsley's preoccupation with alleviating the difficulties of the poor as a source of his hostility to Newman. For the scholar Norman Vance, "Kingsley, the embattled activist, sensed that Catholic spirituality exemplified by Newman could sanction serene, even disdainful, withdrawal from the everyday problems and responsibilities of secular life and from ordinary moral accountability."[11] Newman's correspondence—which is full of instances of the alms he gave to the poor and the necessitous—disproves such a theory,

---

[7] Kingsley quoted in Susan Chitty, *The Beast and the Monk: A Life of Charles Kingsley* (New York: Mason Charter, 1974), 59.
[8] Una Pope Hennessy, *Canon Charles Kingsley* (London: Chatto & Windus, 1948), 131.
[9] Kingsley's usage is confirmed by the citation from his *Yeast* in *OED*, s.v. "sexuality 3".
[10] Charles Barker, "Erotic Martyrdom: Kingsley's Sexuality beyond Sex," *Victorian Studies*, 44.3 (2002), 466.
[11] ODNB.

though it is true enough that Newman never shared Kingsley's view that Christian socialism could somehow come to the rescue of the inherent theological incoherence of the Anglican Church. On Christmas Day in 1841, he wrote his good friend R. W. Church:

> Has not all our misery, as a Church arisen, from people being afraid to look difficulties in the face? They have palliated acts, when they should have denounced them. There is that good fellow Worcester Palmer can whitewash the Ecclesiastical Commission and the Jerusalem Bishoprick. And what is the consequence? that our Church has through centuries ever been sinking lower and lower? till good part of its pretensions and professions is a mere sham;—though it be a duty to make the best of what we have received. Yet though bound to make the best of other men's shams, let us not incur any of our own. The truest friends of our Church are they who boldly say when her rulers are going wrong and the consequences—and (to speak catachrestically) they are most likely to die in the Church who are (under these black circumstances) most prepared to leave it.

For Newman, "considering the traces of God's grace which surround us," he was, as he said, "very sanguine, or rather confident (if it is right so to speak) that our prayers and our alms will come up as a memorial before God, and that all this miserable confusion tends to good."[12] Less than ten years later, in *Anglican Difficulties*, Newman would temper this view. In the book's third lecture, he returns to the question of whether "inward evidences of grace" legitimate a party within the Establishment otherwise illegitimate on external grounds. "I have no intention at all of evading their position," he says of the Anglo-Catholics' position, "I mean to attack it."[13] And so he does by quoting long passages from his sermon "Grounds for Steadfastness in Our Religious Profession" (1841) in which he had strenuously sought to commend such evidences of grace, only to conclude: "No one can read the series of arguments from which I have quoted, without being struck by the author's clear avowal of doubt, in spite of his own reasonings ... He longed to have faith in the National Church, and he could not."[14] Here, incidentally, is a good example of Newman's readiness to criticize himself when he recognized that he had been in the wrong. Nevertheless, unsurprisingly, his conclusion to these discriminations has never found much warm receptivity from Anglicans or Catholics favorable to the claims of Anglicanism: "The highest gifts and graces are compatible with ultimate reprobation."[15] According to the *OED*, *reprobation* means "rejection by God; the state of being so rejected or cast off and thus ordained to eternal misery." If one had the means of knowing that the Anglican Church was a "sham" and the Roman Catholic Church was the "One True Fold of the Redeemer," one had an inescapable obligation to convert. Alms, in other words, whether tendered by Anglo-Catholics or Christian socialists, would not inoculate one from the consequences of reprobation if one persisted

---

[12] Newman to R. W. Church (Christmas Day, 1841), *LD*, viii, 387.
[13] *Diff.*, i, 74.
[14] *Diff.*, i, 79.
[15] *Diff.*, i, 84.

in affiliating oneself with a church that one knew to be a sham.[16]

In this chapter, I shall argue that while it is true that Kingsley regarded Catholics and Anglo-Catholics as unmanly deviants, opposed Catholic celibacy and felt Newman and his Catholic co-religionists did too little to help the poor, it is also true that he was a man who placed great store by Providence and, as such, was driven to malign Newman for reasons he might not have entirely understood. Taking, as I take, a hagiographical view of the matter, I wish to argue that the explanations for Kingsley's conduct that posit deliberate motivation on the part of the defamatory clergyman are wide of the mark. What impelled Kingsley to act as he did were impulses of Providential destiny.

II

Charles Kingsley was born on 12 June 1819 at Holne in Devon, a child of the Reverend Charles Kingsley (died 1860) and his wife Mary (Lucas). He was educated at Bristol Grammar School and Helston Grammar School before studying at King's College London and Cambridge. He entered Magdalene College in 1838, and graduated in 1842, having decided to enter the Anglican ministry. He left Cambridge with a low view of dons, regarding them as implicated in "a system of humbug," even though "the dons get their living by it; and their livings too, and their bishoprics now and again."[17] In 1844 he married Frances Eliza Grenfell, daughter of Pascoe Grenfell (1761–1838), MP, a rich industrialist who had married as his second wife Georgiana St Leger, daughter of the first Viscount Doneraile. Kingsley and his wife had four children. Like James Joyce, who would commemorate the date he met his wife Nora Barnacle—16 June—in *Ulysses* (1922), Kingsley would always regard the day he met Fanny—6 July 1839—as the most fortuitous of his life.[18] In 1844 he became Rector of Eversley in Hampshire. He wrote a string of novels in the 1850s that made his name: *Alton Locke* (1850), *Yeast* (1851) *Hypatia* (1853), and *Westward Ho!* (1855). In 1859 he was appointed chaplain to Queen Victoria. In 1860, he was appointed Regius Professor of Modern History at Cambridge, where, despite the disesteem of colleagues, he drew large crowds of undergraduates to his impassioned lectures. In 1861 he became a private tutor to the Prince of Wales.[19] In 1863, he wrote what remains his most popular book,

---

[16] See Edward Short, "Introduction," in *Difficulties of Anglicans*, i, lxii–lix.

[17] *Alton Locke*, chapter XIII.

[18] If Kingsley shared something of Joyce's gratitude for having married a good wife, he did not share the Irish novelist's fascination with his Irish countrymen. Traveling through Sligo in 1860, Kingsley wrote a letter to his wife from Mackree Castle, in which he confessed: "I am haunted by the human chimpanzees I saw along that hundred miles of horrible country ... [for] to see white chimpanzees is dreadful; if they were black, one would not see it so much, but their skins, except where tanned by exposure, are as white as ours." Kingsley quoted in Pope Hennessy, *Kingsley*, 197.

[19] "In January, 1861, Bertie enrolled at Trinity College. ... Here Charles Kingsley, the regius professor, came to lecture him on history. Kingsley was nervous as to whether the interpretation that he gave on the Glorious Revolution of 1689 accorded with the royal parents' historical views. 'The responsibility terrified me,' he wrote. He needn't have worried. Bertie thought Kingsley one of the best lecturers he had ever heard—'though of course my experience is not very great'—and he had nothing to say about the contents." The prince's father insisted that Bertie not take notes, believing that committing the contents of lectures to memory was the more effective course of study—a wise bit of advice, considering what would become Bertie's masterly grasp of diplomacy, which

Water Babies, about which Owen Chadwick wrote:

> Never has there been a successful nursery book like this. This nursery book defended the establishment of the Church of England, denounced David Hume's philosophy about miracles, advocated the Darwinian theory of evolution, introduced for the first time into an English novel the new found gorilla, and its discoverer Du Chaillu, denounced the tendency towards State education, recommended "the good old Cambridge hours of breakfast at eight and dinner at five" in order to get more work done in the day, mocked professors of science who make over-dogmatic speeches at meetings of the British Association, ridiculed confidence tricksters in the medical profession, denounced tight stays for women and corporal punishment for schoolboys and ladies who wear shoes when swimming.[20]

In 1870–3, Kingsley served as a canon of Chester Cathedral. While there, he founded the Chester Society for Natural Science, Literature and Art. In 1873 he was made a canon of Westminster Abbey. Influenced by Frederick Denison Maurice, whose rejection of the doctrine of Hell appealed to his sentimental notions of eschatology, Kingsley took a lifelong interest in the Christian socialist movement (1848–54), though he never approved of the seditious schemes of the more violent Chartists. Under the pseudonym "Parson Lot," he contributed to *Politics for the People* (1848) and *The Christian Socialist* (1850–1). In 1854, he was an enthusiastic supporter of Maurice's institution of a Working Men's College. His novel *Two Years Ago* (1857) concerned itself with sanitation problems, as well as the Crimean War. Yet Kingsley bristled at being known as a "muscular Christian." Given to self-doubt and nervous breakdowns, he regarded the epithet as impertinent and a mockery, as he said, of the "weakness of character, sickness of body, and misery of mind, by which I have brought what little I know of the human heart."[21] Nevertheless, there is an aptness in the epithet if we take into account that Kingsley came to his Christianity the long way round, after rebelling against it as a young man at Cambridge, where he gave himself up to much impious dissipation. Once he managed to return to the faith of his fathers, Kingsley wrote to his son that, as a gentleman, he must bring up his own family on the two principles that animated all Christian gentlemen: modesty and honesty. After all, these were the principles that had guided his great grandfather, the father of Kingsley's father, the Rector of Chelsea, who was a Christian gentleman himself, "and never did in his life, or even thought, a mean or false thing." When Kingsley and his wife set up house in Eversley on Kingsley's salary of £670 per annum, they did so modestly with a maid, a cook, and a man who served as groom, gardener and butler. Although offered entombment at the Abbey, Kingsley decided to be buried in Eversley churchyard.

---

cannot be understood without some understanding of diplomatic history. Jane Ridley, *Edward the Seventh: The Playboy Prince* (London, 2013), 60–1.
[20] Owen Chadwick, *The Spirit of the Oxford Movement: Tractarian Essays* (Cambridge: Cambridge University Press, 1990), 119–20. Owen Chadwick may have spent decades misrepresenting Newman in his various books but his essay on Kingsley in this collection is not only amusing but insightful.
[21] *Charles Kingsley: His Letters and Memories of his Life*, ed. by his wife 2 vols. (London: Henry S. King & Co., 1877), ii, 186.

Like Newman, Kingsley was profoundly influenced by his mother. We can see this influence in a letter that Mrs. Kingsley wrote her son in 1842 when she was staying in Eversley visiting him.

> Eversley, 1842.
>
> Here I am, in a humble cottage in the corner of a sunny green, a little garden, whose flower-beds are surrounded with a tall and aged box, is fenced in from the path with a low white paling. The green is gay with dogs, and pigs, and geese, some running frolic races, and others swimming in triumph in a glassy pond, where they are safe from all intruders. Every object around is either picturesque or happy, fulfilling in their different natures the end of their creation ... Surely it must have been the especial providence of God that directed us to this place! and the thought of this brightens every trial. There is independence in every good sense of the word, and yet no loneliness. The family at the Brewery are devoted to Charles, and think they cannot do enough for him. The dear old man says he has been praying for years for such a time to come, and that Eversley has not been so blessed for sixty years. Need I say rejoice with me. Here I sit surrounded by your books and little things which speak of you."[22]

In this one can see the mother's delight in the natural world, her attentiveness to her immediate physical surroundings, her strong Christian faith, and her alertness to the "especial providence" of one's living in accordance with God's plan—all of which helped to shape her son.

Similarly, one can see the influence of Mrs. John Newman (1772–1836) on her son in letters they exchanged when Newman was gradually becoming disillusioned with the Oriel Senior Common Room in the early 1830s, a disillusionment in which her simple but deeply held Christian faith offset the liberalism of such Oriel colleagues as Edward Copleston, Edward Hawkins and Richard Whately. In one of these letters, *apropos* her wayward son, Charles, Mrs. Newman wrote to her son:

> June 12. 1834
>
> The style of C's letter pains me greatly, and I fear, if he is left quite desolate, his nervous symptoms may increase, so as to render him incapable of helping himself. I do not ask you to approve what I have determined to do, I only ask you not to condemn me, and to allow for my decision, as I feel, if any melancholy results should ensue, I should condemn myself for having omitted my duty as a Mother and a Christian. I think you will anticipate that I intend to ask him down here for a short time, that is, I mean to devote a fortnight to him, instead of going to Burford. As you purposed reading at Oxford during my absence, I hope the plan will not [be] inconvenient to you. I feel every day I shall lose from enjoying your company alone, a sacrifice, as I had anticipated much delight and profit in enjoying your individual attention, but the hope of giving consolation to such a poor desolate being, makes me yield it.[23]

---

[22] *Ibid.*, i, 67.
[23] *LD*, iv, 267.

Charles Kingsley

In another letter, she expressed her keen appreciation of her son's providential destiny. More than many of his contemporaries, she recognized what a blessing his influence would be for ages to come. "I have ever felt it a source of deep thankfulness," she wrote her son on 26 September 1834, two years before her death, "that we were enabled to put you in the way of those advantages, that your gifts and merit claimed ... and I often reflect with heartfelt delight and gratitude on the prospect of your labours being valuable to future generations. But you must not spend yourself too much ... In these times, with your talents and energy, you cannot say what you may be called to, and no one can be very efficient without spirits and health."[24] If the Huguenot in Mrs. Newman knew that it was to conversion to Rome that her son would be called, she might very well have blanched; as it was she died nine years before that final step. Still, it is fitting that it was with his mother that Newman should have first given voice to the dilemma that would eventually carry him off to Rome. While he assured her that he was made uncomfortable by Rome's "unedifying dumbshow" and the spectacle of "the Pope's foot being kissed," he nevertheless had to admit that he could not be sure that the Catholic religion he beheld in the churches of Rome was entirely bogus. "As I looked on," he told his mother, "and saw all Christian acts performing the Holy Sacrament offered up, and the blessing given, and recollected I was in church, I could only say in very perplexity my own words, 'How shall I name thee, Light of the wide west, or heinous error-seat?'"[25]

Something of Kingsley's abiding character was captured by Richard Cowley Powles, a friend of his from boyhood, who wrote: "Looking back on those schoolboy days, one can trace without difficulty the elements of character that made his maturer life remarkable. Of him more than of most men who have become famous it may be said "the boy was father of the man." The vehement spirit, the adventurous courage, the love of truth, the impatience of injustice, the quick and tender sympathy, that distinguished the man's entrance on public life, were all in the boy, as any of those who knew him then and are still living will remember; and there was, besides, the same eagerness in the pursuit of physical knowledge, the same keen observation of the world around him, and the same thoughtful temper of tracing facts to principles."[26]

Despite the fact that Kingsley was inept at games—he was particularly hopeless at cricket—he was remarkably tough. Powley recalled an episode from their childhood that vividly bears this out.

> I remember his climbing a tall tree to take an egg from a hawk's nest. For three or four days he had done this with impunity. There came an afternoon, however, when the hawk was on her nest, and on the intruder's putting in his hand as usual the results were disastrous. To most boys the surprise of the hawk's attack, apart from the pain inflicted by her claws, would have been fatal. They would have loosed their hold of the tree, and tumbled down. But Charles did not flinch. He came down as steadily as if nothing had happened, though his wounded hand was streaming with blood. It was wonderful how well he bore pain. On one occasion,

---

[24] LD, iv, 332.
[25] Newman to Mrs. Newman (25 March 1833), LD, iii, 268.
[26] Richard Cowley Powles quoted in *Charles Kingsley: His Letters and Memories of his Life*, i, 15.

having a sore finger, he determined to cure it by cautery. He heated the poker red-hot in the school room fire, and calmly applied it two or three times till he was satisfied that his object was attained. His own endurance of pain did not, however, make him careless of suffering in others. He was very tender-hearted—often more so than his school-fellows could understand; and what they did not understand they were apt to ridicule. The moral quality that pre-eminently distinguished him as a boy, was the generosity with which he forgave offence. He was keenly sensitive to ridicule; nothing irritated him more.[27]

Surely no one could have tried this last trait more excruciatingly than John Henry Newman, once he resolved to hold up Kingsley's reckless accusations to the general derision.

Another contemporary, the publisher Charles Kegan Paul (1828–1902) recognized a fatal flippancy in the popular writer. "Kingsley was altogether a stimulating neighbour, co-worker, and friend," Kegan Paul recalled. Yet "His eagerness led him into many situations in which it could only be asked, 'Quel diable allait il faire dans cette galère?' There was scarce a question on which he would not give an answer to persons who wrote to him as if he had been in possession of the whole counsel of God, and his great fluency enabled him to put words now and then in the place of thought."[28] Such glibness was certainly at play in his wild misrepresentation of Newman and his work.

Kingsley's place in English literature is justly assessed by G. K. Chesterton. "Charles Kingsley was a great publicist: a popular preacher; a popular novelist; and (in two cases at least) a very good novelist," the sympathetic critic in Chesterton wrote.

> His *Water Babies* is really a breezy and roaring freak; like a holiday at the seaside—a holiday where one talks natural history without taking it seriously. Some of the songs in this and other of his works are very real songs: notably, "When all the World is Young, Lad," which comes very near to being the only true defence of marriage in the controversies of the nineteenth century. But when all this is allowed, no one will seriously rank Kingsley, in the really literary sense on the level of Carlyle or Ruskin, Tennyson or Browning, Dickens or Thackeray: and if such a place cannot be given to him, it can be given even less to his lusty and pleasant friend, Tom Hughes, whose personality floats towards the frankness of the *Boy's Own Paper*; or to his deep, suggestive metaphysical friend Maurice, who floats rather towards *The Hibbert Journal*. The moral and social influence of these things is not to be forgotten: but they leave the domain of letters.[29]

One thing that Chesterton overlooks here is the extent to which Providence was a great pillar of Kingsley's Broad-Church Christianity. One can see this clearly in many of his sermons. Here, he expresses his understanding of the thing with all of his accustomed gusto

---

[27] Ibid., i, 16.
[28] Charles Kegan Paul, *Biographical Sketches* (London: Kegan, Paul, Trench & Co., 1883), 136.
[29] Chesterton, *The Victorian Age in Literature*.

Charles Kingsley

For, believe me, my friends, whatever nation or whatever man Christ chooses to be His own, and to be holy and noble and glorious with Him, He makes them perfect through suffering. First, He stirs up in them strange longings after what is great and good. He makes them hunger and thirst after righteousness, and then He lets them see how nothing on this earth, nothing beautiful or nothing pleasant which they can get or invent for themselves will satisfy; and so He teaches them to look to Him, to look for peace and salvation from heaven and not from earth. Then He leads them, as He led the Jews of old, through the wilderness and through the sea, through strange afflictions, through poverty, and war, and labour, that they may learn to know that He is leading them and not themselves; that they may learn to trust not in themselves, but in Him; not in their own strength: but in the bread which cometh down from heaven; not in their own courage, but in Him; and just when all seems most hopeless, He makes one of them chase a thousand, and by strange and unexpected providences, and the courage which a just cause inspires, brings His people triumphant through temptation and danger, and puts to flight the armies of the heathen, and the inventions of the evil fiend, and glorifies His name in His chosen people.[30]

Like Dean Stanley, Kingsley was impatient of dogma, associating it with what he regarded as the malign power and superstitious chicane of the papacy. In choosing to make Kingsley a canon of Westminster Abbey, Stanley knew that Kingsley agreed with him that "The Sacraments—the Clergy—the Pope—the Creeds—will take a long time dying": but die they must.[31] For both men, following the founder of muscular Christianity, Dr. Arnold of Rugby, the modern world required a modern religion and it was only providential that Protestantism should supplant a Roman Church no longer responsive to modern needs. This is one reason why Newman was such a thorn in their side: he was thwarting this providential trajectory, as they saw it, by insisting that Christians return to an exploded dogmatism. After all, for Arnold and the Broad Church, if Christianity was the salt of the earth, then an ever more emollient Protestantism should have to be that modern Christianity's salt: no other ecclesiastical preservative would do.

Stanley, the epitome of the Broad Church, is nicely summed up by J. Mordaunt Crook who writes in a piece he contributed to a recent paean to Westminster Abbey, of which Stanley was Dean:

> Stanley was a Protestant Whig, He believed in progress; in civil and religious liberty; in the evolution of Christian thinking within a context of cohesive liberalism. Above all he supported the union of Church and crown. He believed in religious diversity, sheltered by the framework of an established Church, guaranteed by the crown in parliament. "A free development of religious thought," he came to see, was the only pathway appropriate to an "age of flux and transition" like the mid-nineteenth century. "No one creed or confession," he explained, "has exhausted the whole of Christian truth"; "each form of theology is but an approximation to

---

[30] Charles Kingsley, "The Englishman Trained by Toil," in *True Words for Brave Men: A Book for Soldiers and Sailors* (London: Kegan Paul Trench & Co., 1886), 42.
[31] Stanley quoted in J. Mordaunt Crook, "Towards a Broad Church Valhalla 1837–1901," in *Westminster Abbey: A Church in History*, ed. David Cannadine (New Haven: Yale University Press, 2020), 300.

the truth." The Church of England, as he put it in 1850, "was meant to include, and always [has] included, opposite and contradictory opinions." After all, the prayer book has been a statement of faith, composed by Protestants; but the Thirty-Nine Articles was a statement of law, formulated by parliament. Ambivalence, not doubt, was thus built into the very fabric of Anglicanism.[32]

This catalogue of the defining principles of the Broad Church, political and ecclesiastical, is worth keeping in mind when trying to understand Kingsley because, although he deviated from its orthodoxy when backing the Confederacy in the American Civil War and taking sharp issue with the exceedingly liberal *Essays and Reviews*, he adhered to most of its Latitudinarian pieties. When Samuel Wilberforce, "Soapy Sam," as he was called, another pillar of the Broad Church, was enthroned in his Cathedral Church of Winchester, Kingsley exclaimed: "A born ἄναξ ἀνδρῶν he is, and I will do my best to support him on his throne."[33]

If it was with the Broad Church that Kingsley allied himself throughout his life, he had rather surprising reservations about a Protestantism that left the religious life of so many of his compatriots arid and lifeless. Nevertheless, in *Alton Locke* (1850), his Chartist novel, he has his hero call for a manifesto for the new undogmatical Christianity. After sharing with his readers how he read the whole of the Bible and Shakespeare to find guidance for his new faith, he writes:

> Then I waded, making copious notes and extracts, through the whole of Hume, and Hallam's "Middle Ages," and "Constitutional History," and found them barren to my soul. When ... will some man, of the spirit of Carlyle—one who is not ashamed to acknowledge the intervention of a God, a Providence, even of a devil, in the affairs of men—arise, and write a "People's History of England"?[34]

Kingsley even had his hero see the building of new churches, despite the assiduity of the "Puseyite sectarians" in that line, fulfilling Providence, noting in particular "morning and evening prayers—for there were daily services there, and saint's day services, and Lent services, and three services on a Sunday, and six or seven on Good Friday and Easter day." New churches also came with new schools, from which "troops of children poured in and out, and women came daily for alms; and when the frost came on, every morning I saw a crowd, and soup carried away in pitchers, and clothes and blankets given away; the giving seemed endless, boundless; and I thought of the times of the Roman Empire and the "sportula" when the poor had got to live upon the alms of the rich, more and more, year by year till they devoured their own devourers, and the end came; and I shuddered." Even when history revealed little more than the persistence of injustice, it reinforced Kingsley's affinity for the providential. "[I]t was a pleasant sight, as every new church is to the healthy-minded man," he wrote, "let his religious opinions be what they may. A fresh centre of civilization, mercy,

---

[32] *Ibid.*, 297.
[33] Charles Kingsley quoted in Reginald G. Wilberforce, *Bishop Wilberforce* (Oxford: A. R. Mowbray & Co., 1905), 225.
[34] Charles Kingsley, *Alton Locke, Tailor and Poet: An Autobiography*, 2 vols. (London: Chapman and Hall, 1850) ii, 137.

comfort for weary hearts, relief from frost and hunger; a fresh centre of instruction, humanizing, disciplining, however meagre in my eyes, to hundreds of little savage spirits; altogether a pleasant sight."[35] Newman would have recognized the justness of Kingsley's point. In his heartfelt sermon, "The Church a Home for the Lonely" (1837), he, too, speaks of Christianity as a refuge from the cold, cruel, unbelieving world. "The mind finds nothing to satisfy it in the employments and amusements of life, in its excitements, struggles, anxieties, efforts, aims, and victories," he told his auditors at Saint Mary's in Oxford.

> Supposing a man to make money, to get on in life, to rise in society, to gain power, whether in a higher or lower sphere, this does not suffice; he wants a home, he wants a centre on which to place his thoughts and affections, a secret dwelling-place which may soothe him after the troubles of the world, and which may be his hidden stay and support wherever he goes, and dwell in his heart, though it be not named upon his tongue. The world may seduce, may terrify, may mislead, may enslave, but it cannot really inspire confidence and love. There is no rest for us, except in quietness, confidence, and affection; and hence all men, without taking religion into account, seek to make themselves a home, as the only need of their nature, or are unhappy if they be without one. Thus they witness against the world, even though they be children of the world; witness against it equally with the holiest and most self-denying, who have by faith overcome it. Here then Christ finds us, weary of that world in which we are obliged to live and act, whether as willing or unwilling slaves to it. He finds us needing and seeking a home, and making one, as we best may, by means of the creature, since it is all we can do. The world, in which our duties lie, is as waste as the wilderness, as restless and turbulent as the ocean, as inconstant as the wind and weather. It has no substance in it, but is like a shade or phantom; when you pursue it, when you try to grasp it, it escapes from you, or it is malicious, and does you a mischief. We need something which the world cannot give: this is what we need, and this it is which the Gospel has supplied.[36]

Kingsley also saw the history that followed the fall of Rome in peculiarly providential terms. At the beginning of *Hypatia* (1853), for instance, his historical novel, set in 5th-century Alexandria, in which Hypatia, the beautiful proponent of Neoplatonism comes to grief after trying to introduce some reasonable tolerance into a world riddled with fanatical intolerance, he gives expression to his notions as to why monasticism triumphed over what he calls the "stern yet wholesome discipline" of the Gothic races. For Kingsley, "some great Providence forbade to our race, triumphant in every other quarter, a footing beyond the Mediterranean, or even in Constantinople, which to this day preserves in Europe the faith and manners of Asia." Why this should have been the case was clear to the fatalistic historian in Kingsley.

> The Eastern World seemed barred, by some stern doom, from the only influence which could have regenerated it. Every attempt of the Gothic races to establish

---

[35] Ibid., 143–4.
[36] John Henry Newman, "The Church a Home for the Lonely" (1837), *PS*, iv, 188–90.

themselves beyond the sea, whether in the form of an organised kingdom, as the Vandals attempted in Africa; or of a mere band of brigands, as did the Goths in Asia Minor, under Gainas; or of a praetorian guard, as did the Varangens of the middle age; or as religious invaders, as did the Crusaders, ended only in the corruption and disappearance of the colonists. That extraordinary reform in morals, which, according to Salvian and his contemporaries, the Vandal conquerors worked in North Africa, availed them nothing; they lost more than they gave. Climate, bad example, and the luxury of power degraded them in one century into a race of helpless and debauched slave-holders, doomed to utter extermination before the semi-Gothic armies of Belisarius; and with them vanished the last chance that the Gothic races would exercise on the Eastern World the same stern yet wholesome discipline under which the Western had been restored to life.[37]

In order to appreciate the interest of *Hypatia* for the study of Newman it is necessary to put the book in its immediate Victorian context. Written only two years after the period known as Papal Aggression, *Hypatia* could be seen as something of a salve to the battered sensibilities of Newman's Protestant contemporaries. It also gave rise to two Catholic fictional accounts of the Early Church: Nicholas Wiseman's *Fabiola* (1854) and John Henry Newman's *Callista* (1856). Moreover, it was *Hypatia* that led to Kingsley being passed over for an Oxford D. C. L. in 1863 when Edward Pusey and his High-Church friends thwarted his being nominated by the Prince of Wales. The retrospective significance of the book for later scholars is nicely captured by a good commentator on Kingsley's work, Prof. Larry K. Uffelman. "Kingsley's *Hypatia* has always been a problem for students of nineteenth-century fiction, as well as for students of Broad Church religion," Prof. Uffelman explains, "because it so flagrantly flouts both the sociodocumentary realism that attracts readers to his earlier novels and the broad-mindedness that modern religious liberals usually attribute to their spiritual forebears. Even though it has a historical basis, it is, as most critics agree, visionary, perfervid, overwrought."[38] "Polemical" might be more accurate here than "visionary," especially since Kingsley follows Gibbon fairly closely in finding celibate monasticism the sworn enemy of the sort of rationalist order to which the Romans—and the Protestant English—aspired. Yet Uffelman is right: liberal Christians with any pretentions to learning must always recoil from the crudity of Kingsley's church history. Of course, Gibbon's history is crude, too, but at least he expresses it in a style as ornamental as it is entertaining.

> Prosperity and peace introduced the distinction of the *vulgar* and the *Ascetic Christians*. The loose and imperfect practice of religion satisfied the conscience of the multitude. The prince or magistrate, the soldier or merchant, reconciled their fervent zeal, and implicit faith, with the exercise of their profession, the pursuit of their interest, and the indulgence of their passions: but the Ascetics,

---

[37] Charles Kingsley, *Hypatia* (London: J. M. Dent Co., 1906), 9–10.
[38] Larry K. Uffelman, "Kingsley's *Hypatia* in Context," *Nineteenth-Century Literature*, 41, no. 1 (June 1986), pp. 87–96. See also Prof. Uffelman's book on Kingsley in Twayne's English Authors series (1979). Free of the tiresome psychobabble that mars so much more recent work on Kingsley, it gives readers a more reliable understanding of the author in his historical context.

who obeyed and abused the rigid precepts of the gospel, were inspired by the savage enthusiasm which represents man as a criminal, and God as a tyrant. They seriously renounced the business, and the pleasures, of the age; abjured the use of wine, of flesh, and of marriage; chastised their body, mortified their affections, and embraced a life of misery, as the price of eternal happiness. In the reign of Constantine, the Ascetics fled from a profane and degenerate world, to perpetual solitude, or religious society. Like the first Christians of Jerusalem, they resigned the use, or the property of their temporal possessions; established regular communities of the same sex, and a similar disposition; and assumed the names of Hermits, Monks, and Anachorets, expressive of their lonely retreat in a natural or artificial desert. They soon acquired the respect of the world, which they despised; and the loudest applause was bestowed on this Divine Philosophy, which surpassed, without the aid of science or reason, the laborious virtues of the Grecian schools.[39]

Here is as succinct a précis of the polemical preoccupations of Kingsley's historical novel as one might wish to find; it is also proof of the profound impact that Gibbon's anti-Catholic church history had on the Victorian imagination, an impact which impelled Newman to put education at the very forefront of his apostolate once he converted, convinced as he was that three-hundred years of Protestant Christianity had all but de-Christianized his English compatriots. As I shall show, Kingsley was not unaware of this de-Christianization. Indeed, one of the reasons why he wrote *Hypatia* was to beguile this naturally galling awareness, about which Chesterton is so insightful. "There are ... genuinely eloquent things in *Hypatia*," Chesterton wrote in his *bravura* critical overview of Victorian literature, "and a certain electric atmosphere of sectarian excitement that Kingsley kept himself in, and did know how to convey. He said he wrote the book in his heart's blood. This is an exaggeration, but there is a truth in it; and one does feel that he may have relieved his feelings by writing it in red ink."[40] He certainly relieved the feelings that made him resent how Newman's Catholicism showed up the ahistorical unreality of the English National Church. Moreover, for someone of Kingsley's fiery imagination, Gibbon's red ink must have been irresistible. The eighteenth-century historian's description of the death of Hypatia is a good case in point. "Hypatia, the daughter of Theon the mathematician,[41] was initiated in her father's studies," Gibbon writes;

her learned comments have elucidated the geometry of Apollonius and Diophantus, and she publicly taught, both at Athens and Alexandria, the philosophy of

---

[39] Gibbon, *Decline and Fall*, ch. xxxvii, vol. iv, 62–3.
[40] *The Collected Works of G. K. Chesterton*, xv, 479.
[41] "We have no evidence of research Mathematics on the part of either father or daughter. What we can reconstruct of their Mathematics suggests to us that they edited, preserved, taught from and supplied minor addenda to the works of others. A great deal of Theon's work survives and at most a small part of Hypatia's. In other words, Theon was seen as the better text-writer ... Where Hypatia does quite clearly outshine Theon is in her reputation as a teacher. She was revered as such and no similar endorsement of Theon has come down to us. ... We are left with a well-attested account of a popular, charismatic and versatile teacher. And that, I suggest, is the best picture we can form of her." Michael A. B. Deakin, "Hypatia and her Mathematics," *The American Mathematical Monthly*, 101, no. 3 (March 1994), 242.

Plato and Aristotle. In the bloom of beauty, and in the maturity of wisdom, the modest maid refused her lovers and instructed her disciples; the persons most illustrious for their rank or merit were impatient to visit the female philosopher; and Cyril beheld, with a jealous eye, the gorgeous train of horses and slaves who crowded the door of her academy. A rumor was spread among the Christians, that the daughter of Theon was the only obstacle to the reconciliation of the praefect and the archbishop; and that obstacle was speedily removed. On a fatal day, in the holy season of Lent, Hypatia was torn from her chariot, stripped naked, dragged to the church, and inhumanly butchered by the hands of Peter the reader, and a troop of savage and merciless fanatics: her flesh was scraped from her bones with sharp oyster shells, and her quivering limbs were delivered to the flames. The just progress of inquiry and punishment was stopped by seasonable gifts; but the murder of Hypatia has imprinted an indelible stain on the character and religion of Cyril of Alexandria.[42]

Yet, one has to say, even from a Catholic standpoint, despite his delight in Gibbon's lurid periods, it would not be fair to dismiss Kingsley simply as an anti-Catholic polemicist. By his own lights, even though they were fairly flickering lights, he yearned to know, love and serve his Creator. The very sincerity of this yearning on his part is reflected in how the man was perceived by his contemporaries. Una Hennessy quotes a portrait Justin McCarthy (1830–1912), the Irish nationalist politician, historian and journalist drew of the man.

Rather tall, very angular, surprisingly awkward, with thin staggering legs, a hatchet face adorned with scraggy whiskers, a faculty for falling into the most ungainly attitudes and making the most hideous contortions of visage and frame; with a rough provincial accent and an uncouth way of speaking which would be set down for caricature on the boards of a theatre. Since Brougham's day nothing so ungainly and eccentric had been displayed upon an English platform. Needless to say Charles Kingsley had not the eloquence of Brougham, but he had a robust way of plain speaking which soon struck home to the heart of a meeting. Even those, who began by laughing or heartily disliking what he stood for, were won over by his sincerity.[43]

In the last sermon Kinglsey preached before returning to Eversley, "The Beatific Vision," one can see that the Christian faith meant a good deal to him. As Una Pope Hennessy says in her excellent biography of Kingsley: "After a kind of petition that both he and his hearers might have their souls gladdened by the vision of God and live in a spirit of adoration for the glory of His justice and the glory of His love,"[44] Kingsley concluded:

And now friends—almost all friends unknown—and alas never to be known by me—you who are to me as people floating down a river; while I the preacher stand upon the bank, and call in hope that some of you may catch some word

---

[42] Gibbon, *Decline and Fall*, v, ch. xlviii, 117.
[43] Justin McCarthy quoted in Pope Hennessy, *Kingsley*, 121.
[44] Ibid., 275.

of mine, ere the great stream shall bear you out of sight—oh! catch at least this one word—the last which I shall speak here for many months, and which sums up all that I have been trying to say to you of late. Fix in your minds—or rather ask God to fix in your minds—this one idea of an absolutely good God; good with all forms of goodness which you respect and love in man; good as you and I and every honest man understand the plain word good. Slowly you will acquire that grand and all-illuminating idea; slowly and most imperfectly at best: for who is mortal man that he should conceive and comprehend the goodness of the infinitely good God? But see, then, in the light of that one idea whether all the old-fashioned Christian ideas about the relation of God to man; whether a Providence, Prayer, Inspiration, Revelation, the Incarnation, the Passion, and the final triumph of the Son of God—whether all these, I say, do not seem to you, not merely beautiful, not merely probable, but rational, and logical, and necessary, moral consequences from the one idea of an Absolute and Eternal Goodness, the Living Parent of the Universe. And so I leave you to the grace of God.[45]

Una Pope Hennessy, the mother of James Pope Hennessy, the author of that wonderfully good biography of Queen Mary, remarks in her book on Kingsley that Dean Stanley confirmed "that the vergers and everyone connected with the Abbey were very proud of Kingsley's fame as author and preacher: it delighted them to know how much he enjoyed Westminster "just as if he had never had anything else to enjoy". His power of attraction, said the Abbey staff, was unusual in a Church dignitary: there was something about him that fascinated."[46] After reading his various sermons and his letters, one has the sense that what might have fascinated his contemporaries most about Kingsley was the ardor of his Christian faith, which was animated, to a lively degree, by his sense of the Providential.

III

Newman, too, was fascinated by Providence. As a saint, he could not but be caught up in its ineluctably mysterious proceedings. In a letter he wrote to Richard Bagot, Bishop of Oxford in the wake of the publication of Tract 90, the author of that unintentionally incendiary effusion showed the extent to which he felt himself driven by Providence.

> I assure your Lordship I was altogether unsuspicious that my Tract would make any disturbance. No one can enter into my situation but myself. I see a great many minds working in various directions and a variety of principles with multiplied bearings, I act for the best. I sincerely think that matters would not have gone better for the Church had I never written. And if I write I have a choice of difficulties. It is easy for those who do not enter into these difficulties to say, "He ought to say this and not say that"; but things are so wonderfully linked together, and I cannot, or rather I would not, be dishonest. When persons too interrogate

---

[45] Kingsley quoted *ibid.*, 275–6.
[46] *Ibid.*, 276.

me, I am obliged in many cases to give an opinion, or I seem to be underhand. Keeping silence looks like artifice. And I do not like persons to consult or to respect me, from thinking differently of my opinions from what I know them to be. And again, to use the proverb, what is one man's food is another man's poison. All these things make my situation very difficult. Hitherto I have been successful in keeping people together—but that a collision must at some time ensue between members of the Church of opposite opinions <sentiments> I have long been aware. The time and mode have been in the hand of Providence: I do not mean to exclude my own great imperfections in bringing it about, yet I still feel obliged to think the Tract necessary.[47]

Since Newman always chose his words precisely, his use of the word "necessary" here is striking, capturing as it does a twofold meaning: (i) the tracts were both "necessary" in the sense that they were needed in order to meet the uncertainty that obtained throughout the country at the time about the real nature of what Anglicans tended to see as Newman's unacceptable "Romanism" and (ii) they were necessary in the sense that they were providential: they had to be published in order to carry out God's Providence. Reading the correspondence pertaining to the fallout of Tract 90, we might almost be at a Providential play, with everyone involved speaking their parts exactly as a directorial God should wish them spoken. Newman signs off his letter to the Bishop of London with a becoming submissiveness: "Dr Pusey has shown me your Lordship's letters to him. I am most desirous of saying in print anything which I can honestly say to remove false impressions created by the Tract." Yet, as Archbishop Howley's letter to Bagot shows, the Anglican episcopate also played their part in the Providential comedy. After Bagot had apprised the Archbishop of Newman's response to the discomfiture that the Tract had caused, Howley wrote on the 22nd of March:

> Dr Pusey and Mr Newman have received your communication as from my knowledge of their disposition and principles I expected they would. This is so far satisfactory, and holds out a prospect of a peaceful termination which, if continued, would very possibly be productive of incalculable injury to the Church. The passages to which your Lordship refers are very objectionable, and I doubt whether they would admit of an explanation satisfactory in all respects. I am therefore of opinion that it would be advisable to let things rest, at least for the present, rather than to come forward with explanations inconsistent with the apparent sense of the propositions which have given offence, or expressing the same sense, with little variation, in different words. ... I have this instant seen Mr Newman's Postscript to his second edition, and as he can go no further in explanation he should, in my opinion, explain no more; but it seems most desirable that the publication of the Tracts should be discontinued for ever.[48]

Of course, things would not rest; there would be no "peaceful termination" of the matter; "incalculable injury" would be visited upon the National Church; and Newman's conversion became, what Providence had always intended it

---

[47] Newman to Richard Bagot, Bishop of London (20 March 1841), *LD*, viii, 100–1.
[48] Howley quoted in Liddon, *Life of Pusey*, 4 vols (London: Longmans, Green, & Co., 1893), ii, 190.

should become, ineluctable. Such ineluctability may seem to fly in the face of the contingency of history; it may even conjure up the fallacy of determinism, the very thing of which Marxist historians have always been fond; yet Providence does not nullify the contingency of history nor free will; it completes them: and in doing so it reveals God's glory, for God does operate in the world—and one proof of this operation is the lives of His saints.[49]

In the sermon preached at the University Church, Dublin in 1857, "Omnipotence in Bonds," Newman gave memorable expression to the restiveness that most of us experience when called upon to cooperate in God's providential plans for us—a restiveness that shows that God's Providence never bundles away human contingency. The saint is simply the Christian who conquers such restiveness in order to cooperate with God's good will.

> O my Brethren, let us blush at our own pride and self-will. Let us call to mind our impatience at God's providences towards us, our wayward longings after what cannot be, our headstrong efforts to reverse His just decrees, our bootless conflicts with the stern necessities which hem us in, our irritation at ignorance or suspense about His will, our fierce, passionate wilfulness when we see that will too clearly, our haughty contempt of His ordinances, our determination to do things for ourselves without Him, our preference of our own reason to His word,—the many, many shapes in which the Old Adam shows itself, and one or other of which our conscience tells us is our own; and let us pray Him who is independent of us all, yet who at this season became as though our fellow and our servant, to teach us our place in His wide universe, and to make us ambitious only of that grace here and glory hereafter, which He has purchased for us by His own humiliation.[50]

Nothing demonstrated Newman's own willingness to cooperate in "grace here and glory hereafter" more than his abandonment of his Anglican ministry, his Oxford fellowship, his Oxford friends and relations, the snapdragon growing on the wall in Trinity. Yet in following God's Providence, Newman was actually following an old English tradition, one which the English Reformation might have mutilated but which still survived in Newman's nineteenth century. Indeed, Charles Kingsley would be one of its last hurrahs.

In the *Grammar of Assent*, Newman had occasion to argue that the religion of England consisted "not in rites or creeds, but mainly in having the Bible read in Church, in the family, and in private." Many good things came of this. "At

---

[49] Cf. "I still lie on a sofa—till Sunday last I have been all day in bed. For thirty years I have not had so anxious an illness. And the worst is, it came on so suddenly and without notice, that it makes me dread to leave home ever again, lest I should be seized in a railway carriage, or at a friend's house. The doctor puts it down to the fidget caused by the Letter I have written to Pusey—but, though any application of mind tries me, I cannot credit him. It has been most providential that it did not come on two years ago, when I was in controversy with Kingsley—most merciful again, that I had finished my Letter before the really bad attack came on, and that I have been up and downstairs on Christmas Day, Epiphany, and every Sunday, and now, wishing you and Lady Rogers and all who are dear to you a very happy New Year." Newman to Sir Frederic Rogers (16 January 1866), LD, xxii, 127–8.

[50] OS, 89–90.

least in England, it has to a certain point made up for great and grievous losses in its Christianity. The reiteration again and again, in fixed course in the public service, of the words of inspired teachers under both Covenants, and that in grave majestic English, has in matter of fact been to our people a vast benefit. It has attuned their minds to religious thoughts; it has given them a high moral standard; and it has served them in associating religion with compositions which, even humanly considered, are among the most sublime and beautiful ever written." However, the shortcomings of this *sola scriptura* Christianity were no less numerous. "It has been comparatively careless of creed and catechism; and has in consequence shown little sense of the need of consistency in the matter of its teaching. Its doctrines are not so much facts, as stereotyped aspects of facts; and it is afraid, so to say, of walking round them. It induces its followers to be content with this meagre view of revealed truth; or, rather, it is suspicious and protests, or is frightened, as if it saw a figure in a picture move out of its frame, when our Lord, the Blessed Virgin, or the Holy Apostles, are spoken of as real beings, and really such as Scripture implies them to be." Still, for Newman, "what Scripture especially illustrates from its first page to its last, is God's Providence; and that is nearly the only doctrine held with a real assent by the mass of religious Englishmen."[51]

Kingsley certainly confirms this, as does another bluff Englishman, the novelist Arnold Bennett (1867–1931), who had occasion to remark in his wonderful novel, *The Old Wives' Tale* (1908): "It is to be remembered that in those days [the novel is set in the 1870s] Providence was still busying himself with everybody's affairs, and foreseeing the future in the most extraordinary manner."[52] In another passage, Bennett writes:

> The era of good old-fashioned Christmases, so agreeably picturesque for the poor, was not yet at an end. Yes, Samuel Povey had won the battle concerning the locus of the family Christmas. But he had received the help of a formidable ally, death. Mrs. Harriet Maddack had passed away, after an operation, leaving her house and her money to her sister. The solemn rite of her interment had deeply affected all the respectability of the town of Axe, where the late Mr. Maddack had been a figure of consequence; it had even shut up the shop in St. Luke's Square for a whole day. It was such a funeral as Aunt Harriet herself would have approved, a tremendous ceremonial which left on the crushed mind an ineffaceable, intricate impression of shiny cloth, crape, horses with arching necks and long manes, the drawl of parsons, cake, port, sighs, and Christian submission to the inscrutable decrees of Providence.[53]

Apropos Bennett's novel, it is worth noting that Max Beerbohm once said of it: "I regard *The Old Wives' Tale* as the finest novel published in my time. Henry James, having read it, said that one asked oneself what it was all about. Well, it was, it is, all about a very important thing: the passage of youth into old

---

[51] GA, 56–7.
[52] Arnold Bennett, *The Old Wives' Tale* (London: Chapman and Hall, 1908), 43.
[53] Ibid., 146.

age."⁵⁴ Coincidentally enough, when the charming stylist recalled Newman in a speech he gave at his seventieth birthday party in London, he spoke, too, of the inscrutability of Providence. "There had been no recurrent snapdragon on the walls of the Oxford College in which I was an undergraduate," Beerbohm said, "but even as John Henry Newman had thought he was destined to be always an Anglican, so I had I believed that I should be a caricaturist to the end of my days. Fate saw otherwise."⁵⁵

IV

If Newman's idea of the bishop was one that confirmed the dogmatical reality of the Catholic faith, Kingsley's idea was rather different. In *Hypatia*, he has a scene in which Raphael, clearly a stand-in for Kingsley himself, approaches Bishop Synesius of Cyrene, who figures in the novel as a foursquare, married, ostrich-hunting bishop, and says, "I had a dream one night, on my way, which made me question whether I were wise in troubling a Christian bishop with any thoughts or questions which relate merely to poor human beings like myself, who marry and are given in marriage," at which Synesius urges the young man to relate his dream, and Raphael tells him he dreamed of a "philosopher, an academic and a believer in nothing" who tried to share with Christian priests how moved he was by reading the Song of Songs, which confirmed what he considered the holiness of erotic love, and how the priests had responded:

> O blasphemous and carnal man, who pervertest Holy Scripture into a cloak for thine own licentiousness, as if it spoke of man's base and sensual affections, know that this book is to be spiritually interpreted of the marriage between the soul and its Creator, and that it is from this very book that the Catholic Church derives her strongest arguments in favour of holy virginity, and the glories of a celibate life.

When Synesius hears this, he falls silent. But Raphael continues, relating that when he received this response "he cursed the day he was born," convinced that the "most sacred books" of Christians "'mean anything or nothing' as the case may suit your fancies; and there is neither truth nor reason under the sun." At which:

> Synesius remained a while in deep thought, and said at last—"And yet you came to me?"

---

⁵⁴ Max Beerbohm to Geoffrey Bemrose (February 1954), *Letters of Max Beerbohm 1899–1956*, ed. Rupert Hart-Davis (Oxford: Oxford University Press, 1989), 224.
⁵⁵ *Ibid.*, 235. The famous passage in the *Apologia* to which Beerbohm refers is this: "I left Oxford for good on Monday, February 23, 1846. On the Saturday and Sunday before, I was in my house at Littlemore simply by myself, as I had been for the first day or two when I had originally taken possession of it. I slept on Sunday night at my dear friend's, Mr. Johnson's, at the Observatory. Various friends came to see the last of me; Mr. Copeland, Mr. Church, Mr. Buckle, Mr. Pattison, and Mr. Lewis. Dr. Pusey too came up to take leave of me; and I called on Dr. Ogle, one of my very oldest friends, for he was my private Tutor, when I was an Undergraduate. In him I took leave of my first College, Trinity, which was so dear to me, and which held on its foundation so many who had been kind to me both when I was a boy, and all through my Oxford life. Trinity had never been unkind to me. There used to be much snap-dragon growing on the walls opposite my freshman's rooms there, and I had for years taken it as the emblem of my own perpetual residence even unto death in my University." *Apo.*, 213.

"I did, because you have loved and married; because you have stood out manfully against this strange modern insanity, and refused to give up, when you were made a bishop, the wife whom God had given you. You, I thought, could solve the riddle for me, if any man could."[56]

Synesius, however, will not solve the riddle. "Alas, friend! I have begun to distrust, of late, my power of solving riddles," says the sporting bishop. "After all, why should they be solved? What matters one more mystery in a world of mysteries? 'If thou marry, thou hast not sinned,' are St. Paul's own words; and let them be enough for us. Do not ask me to argue with you, but to help you. Instead of puzzling me with deep questions, and tempting me to set up my private judgment, as I have done too often already, against the opinion of the Church, tell me your story, and test my sympathy rather than my intellect. I shall feel with you and work for you, doubt not, even though I am unable to explain to myself why I do it." Synesius, in other words, exercises no episcopal authority; he regards the Church as animated by "opinion"; and he imagines Christians only bound by feelings, not by the faith and reason of God's Truth revealed in His Church. This is the undogmatical faith of the Broad Church and it could not be more different from the faith of St John Henry Cardinal Newman.

As one can see clearly in the foregoing passages, *Hypatia*, among other things, is Kingsley's fictional plug for his religion of erotic love, which consisted mostly in an abomination of celibacy. Norman Vance, in his entry for Kingsley in the *Oxford Dictionary of National Biography*, is good on the source, character and culmination of this muddled faith.

> [Kingsley] had spent the difficult years just before his marriage in a bizarre religiously erotic correspondence with Fanny, and in reading Coleridge, F. D. Maurice, and Carlyle under her guidance to develop some kind of intellectual framework to reconcile his poetic, almost pantheistic love of the physical world, his developing social concern, and his powerful awakened sexuality with traditional religious belief. He also began to write and illustrate a prose life of St Elizabeth of Hungary, a conspicuously married saint, as a wedding present for Fanny; it was an early instalment in his lifelong crusade against the celibate ideal of the religious life which had threatened to keep Fanny from him. The material was eventually reworked as a rather uneven quasi-Shakespearian verse tragedy, *The Saint's Tragedy*, and published in 1848 with an aggressively protestant preface. It seemed to attract little attention at the time except among critics of the Oxford Movement in Oxford itself, but Baron von Bunsen, the Prussian ambassador, and Prince Albert greatly admired it, as did Daniel Macmillan, later Kingsley's publisher.

In reading Kingsley's depiction of his ideal bishop in *Hypatia*, one has the strange sensation of reading a parody of Surtees. "Before sunrise the next morning, Raphael was faring forth gallantly, well armed and mounted, by Synesius's side," he writes, "followed by four or five brace of tall brush-tailed greyhounds, and by the faithful Bran, whose lop-ears and heavy jaws, unique in that land of

---

[56] *Hypatia*, 290.

prick-ears and fox-noses, formed the absorbing subject of conversation among some twenty smart retainers, who, armed to the teeth for chase and war, rode behind the bishop on half-starved, raw-boned horses, inured by desert training and bad times to do the maximum of work upon the minimum of food." Apropos the sportsman in Kingsley, Norman Gash says that his "sporting instincts were never far below the clerical surface," though "he could not afford to go out with Sir John Cope's (now the Garth) Hunt" and "thought that shooting would cause trouble in his notoriously poaching parish." Reluctantly, he had to restrict himself to "Izaak Walton's quieter recreation of angling." Nevertheless, he was known to be a great follower of the hunt and was admired by grooms and huntsmen alike.[57]

Although Kingsley found time for sport when he could, it is also important to remember that he was a dutiful minister, seeing to the needs of his parish diligently and even staying up all night to look after cholera patients when necessary. Indeed, he wrote an unforgettable letter to his wife during one outbreak of cholera, which nicely demonstrates how his preoccupations with the egregious living conditions of the Victorian lower orders animated his love of neighbor.[58]

> Chelsea: October 24, 1849.
> I was yesterday with George Walsh and Mansfield over the cholera districts of Bermondsey; and, oh, God! what I saw! people having no water to drink—hundreds of them—but the water of the common sewer which stagnated full of ... dead fish, cats and dogs, under their windows. At the time the cholera was raging, Walsh saw them throwing untold horrors into the ditch, and then dipping out the water and drinking it!! Oh, entreat Mr. Warre (a Member of Parliament) to read the account of the place in the Morning Chronicle of last week, and try every nerve to get a model lodging-house there; why should people spend money and time in making a plaything model parish of St. Barnabas,[59] where there are three rich to one poor, while whole square miles of other parts of London are in the same state as two or three streets only of Upper Chelsea! And mind, these are not dirty, debauched Irish, but honest hard-working artisans. It is most pathetic, as Walsh says, it makes him literally cry—to see the poor souls struggle for cleanliness, to see how they scrub and polish their little scrap of pavement, and then go through the house and see society leaving at the back poisons and

---

[57] Norman Gash, *Robert Surtees and Early Victorian Society* (Oxford: Oxford University Press, 1993), 118.

[58] In entering into Kingsley's care for the poor, one must always be careful to dissociate it from the Marxist-Leninism of latter-day socialists. The shrewd critic John Derbyshire is good on this point. "Kingsley is tagged in all brief biographies as a 'Christian Socialist,'" he argues in the *New Criterion*, "but this gives a misleading impression to the modern mind. Certainly, he was a reformer, and in sympathy with the radical Chartist movement of 1837–48; *Alton Locke* was a Chartist novel, the only one of any distinction. Kingsley's ideal, however—shared, as A. N. Wilson points out, by many of the Chartists—was the old Tory ideal of ordered liberty. What he objected to in the society around him was the dirt, ignorance, impiety, and indignity in which the lower classes dwelt. He evinces no desire, in anything of his that I have read, to cast down the mighty from their thrones and lift up the lowly. He was happy that the lowly should remain lowly; but he wanted them cleaner, better housed, better instructed, and better treated." John Derbyshire, "Divine Order, Divine Love," *New Criterion* (September 2006). See also A. N. Wilson, *The Victorians* (London: Hutchinson, 2002), 36, 135, 276, 487.

[59] The first purpose-built Anglo-Catholic church in England, erected in 1847–50 in Pimlico.

filth—such as would drive a lady mad, I think, with disgust in twenty-four hours. Oh, that I had the tongue of St. James, to plead for those poor fellows! to tell what I saw myself, to stir up some rich men to go and rescue them from the tyranny of the small shopkeeping landlords, who get their rents out of the flesh and blood of these men. Talk of the horrors of the middle passage. Oh, that one-tenth part of the money which has been spent in increasing, by mistaken benevolence, the cruelties of the slave-trade, had been spent in buying up these nests of typhus, consumption, and cholera, and rebuilding them into habitations fit—I do not say for civilized Englishmen—that would be too much, but for hogs even! I will say no more. Remember it is not a question of alms. It is only to get some man to take the trouble of making a profitable investment, and getting six per cent, for his money. I will put him in communication with those who know all the facts if he will help us. Twenty pounds sent to us, just to start a water-cart, and send it round at once—at once—for the people are still in these horrors, would pay itself. I can find men who will work the thing. Ludlow, Mansfield, the Campbells, will go and serve out the water with their own hands, rather than let it go on. Pray, pray, stir people up, and God will reward you. Kiss my darlings for me.

P. S.—Do not let them wait for committee meetings and investigations; while they will be maundering about "vested interests" and such like, the people are dying. I start to-morrow for Oxford to see the bishop about these Bermondsey horrors. Direct to me there. The proper account of Bermondsey is in the Morning Chronicle of September 24, published a month ago, and yet nothing done, or likely to be!![60]

As Una Pope Hennessy shows, Kingsley also endured the daily exasperations of parish life with forbearance and grace. Since Newman had to endure the same exasperations, this is a part of Kingsley's life and character that we need to take into account if we are to understand the man, let alone fairly assess his engagement with Newman. "There was nothing very cheering about daily life in the parish," Pope Hennessy writes.

Much of it is recorded in private letters, sometimes querulous, sometimes tart in tone. There are references to rebuilt pews, to preferential seats for the households of the gentry, to enclosures of common land, to enlarging the church yard and so on. No one seemed to be anxious to oblige the rector or to consider his interest. When, for example, the question arose of finding extra land for graves everyone seemed to take it for granted that the rector should surrender part of his glebe. It was even broken to him that the parish had set its mind on his rick-yard. From time-to-time Kingsley's relations with his flock tended to irritate him, and had it not been for his innate unselfishness and amiability, open quarrelling might have ensued.[61]

Such matters might seem trifling. Yet they recall that exchange in the *Life of Johnson* where Boswell confesses to being afraid that he has filled his journal with too many little incidents, to which the old philosopher in the brown coat

---

[60] *Charles Kingsley: His Letters and Memories of his Life*, i, 191–2.
[61] Pope Hennessy, *Kingsley*, 187.

replies: "There is nothing, Sir, too little for so little a creature as man. It is by studying little things that we attain the great art of having as little misery and as much happiness as possible."[62] Kingsley proved the wisdom of Johnson's point by never neglecting the littlenesses inherent in ministering to a parish, and thus obviated much sublunar misery, though he would never leave off lamenting the lifelessness of his parishioners' nominal Christianity. Newman, too, recognized how important it was not to neglect what might seem the little act of charity. "One little deed," he was convinced, "done against natural inclination for God's sake, though in itself of a conceding or passive character, to brook an insult, to face a danger, or to resign an advantage, has in it a power outbalancing all the dust and chaff of mere profession."[63]

A wonderfully vivid portrait of Kingsley the exuberant clergyman in his country rectory is given by Kegan Paul. "The picturesque bow-windowed rectory rises to memory as it stood with all its doors and windows open on certain hot summer days," he recalled,

> the sloping bank with its great fir-trees, the garden—a gravel sweep before the drawing-room and dining-room, a grass plot before the study hedged off from the walk—and the tall active figure of the rector tramping up and down one or the other. His energy made him seem everywhere, and to pervade every part of house and garden. The MS of the book he was writing lay open on a rough standing desk, which was merely a shelf projecting from the wall; his pupils, two in number, and treated as his own sons, were working in the dining-room, his guests perhaps lounging on the lawn or working in the study. And he had time for all, going from his writing to lecturing on optics, or to a passage in Virgil, from this to a vehement conversation with a guest, or tender care for his wife, who was far from strong, or a romp with his children. He would work himself into a sort of white heat over his book till, too excited to write more, he would calm himself down by a pipe, pacing his grass plot in thought, with long strides. He was a great smoker, and tobacco was for him a needful sedative. He always used a long clean *churchwarden*, and these pipes used to be bought a barrel-full at a time. They lurked in all sorts of unexpected places. A pipe would suddenly be extracted from a bush in the garden, filled and lighted as by magic, or one has been even drawn from a whin bush on the heath, some half mile from the house. But none was ever smoked which was in any degree foul, and when there was a vast accumulation of old pipes, enough to fill the barrel, they were sent back again to the kiln to be rebaked, and returned fresh and new. This gave him a striking simile, which in Alton Locke he puts into the mouth of James Crosthwaite, "Katie here believes in purgatory, where souls are burnt clean again like 'bacca pipes."[64]

---

[62] James Boswell, *The Life of Samuel Johnson* with an introduction by Claude Rawson (London: Everyman's Library, 1992), 272. Hilaire Belloc, a great admirer of Johnson, wrote a poem entitled "On a Great Name," which was inspired by Boswell's subject. "I heard today Godolphin say/ He never gave himself away./ Come, come, Godolphin, scion of kings,/ Be generous in little things."

[63] OS, 93.

[64] Kegan Paul, *Biographical Sketches*, 119–20. A *churchwarden* is "a small clay pipe with a stem from sixteen to twenty inches long." OED.

Kingsley's impatience with what he would later call "Popular Protestantism" sheds light on his long-standing quarrel with Newman. If Kingsley found Newman's celibacy objectionable because he had once thought of pursuing celibacy himself, he found Newman's Catholicism objectionable because he saw the shortcomings of Protestantism as clearly as Newman but could never bring himself to entertain the necessary papist remedy. Like Newman before his "great revolution of mind," he was captive to a bogus National Church: the only difference in this respect between the two men being that Newman contrived to extricate himself from his captivity and Kingsley did not.[65] And why this should have been the case is not difficult to see. Newman had the courage to change his mind and change his heart when he saw what a wreck Anglicanism was.[66] He had the courage to convert. Kingsley might have been courageous in his way, but we can never imagine him choosing to accept the paradoxical truths that Newman describes in *Anglican Difficulties* as the natural dictates of conversion:

> It is not an easy thing to prove to men that their duty lies just in the reverse direction to that in which they have hitherto placed it; that all they have hitherto learned and taught, that all their past labours, hopes, and successes, that their boyhood, youth, and manhood, that their position, their connections, and their influence, are, in a certain sense, to go for nothing; and that life is to begin with them anew. It is not an easy thing to attain to the conviction, that, with the Apostle, their greatest gain must be counted loss; and that their glory and their peace must be found in what will make them for a while the wonder and the scorn of the world.[67]

Still, it is important to recognize that Kingsley might have actually suffered more than Newman for not changing his heart and mind when he, too, saw the wreck of Anglicanism for what it was. In a letter to Derwent Coleridge of 1851, Kingsley even admitted that:

> If I were inclined to make my own "tastes and thoughts" the test of what should be restored I should have long ago adopted daily services, the Litany read from the nave, ceremonials as gorgeous and intricate as I could afford and lights and censors –the whole machinery of St. Barnabas. ... The sense of deadness, desolation, unreality ... weighs me down Sunday after Sunday ... All things are lawful to me—crucifixes, images, processions, chantings, incense, flowers, festivals, fasts—but all things are not expedient.

---

[65] *Apo.*, 191.
[66] In addressing his former Anglo-Catholic friends in his King William Street lectures, which would be published as *Anglican Difficulties*, Newman wrote: "It is this keen feeling that my life is wearing away, which overcomes the lassitude which possesses me, and scatters the excuses which I might plausibly urge to myself for not meddling with what I have left for ever, which subdues the recollection of past times, and which makes me do my best, with whatever success, to bring you to land from off your wreck, who have thrown yourselves from it upon the waves, or are clinging to its rigging, or are sitting in heaviness and despair upon its side. For this is the truth: the Establishment, whatever it be in the eyes of men, whatever its temporal greatness and its secular prospects, in the eyes of faith is a mere wreck." *Diff.*, i. 4–5.
[67] *Diff.*, i, 126.

Why should such things be thought inexpedient? Kingsley's answer was intriguing: "Many have unfortunately learnt to connect them with Romanism, the creed which they abhor and despise, sooner than have which, they would remain heathen."[68] In other words, he tended to abjure his own anti-Protestant leanings to assuage his parishioners' No Popery. At the same time, in the same year, in the preface of the fourth edition of *Yeast* (1851) he praised the Anglo-Catholics for attempting to redress the deadness that characterized so much English Protestantism, arguing that one "cause for the improved tone of the landlord class, and of the young men of what is commonly called the aristocracy" was "a growing moral earnestness," which he attributed "to the Anglican movement," as he called it.

> How much soever Neo-Anglicanism may have failed as an ecclesiastical or theological system; how much soever it may have proved itself, both by the national dislike of it, and by the defection of all its master-minds, to be radically un-English, it has at least awakened hundreds, perhaps thousands, of cultivated men and women to ask themselves whether God sent them into the world merely to eat, drink, and be merry, and to have "their souls saved" upon the Spurgeon method, after they die; and has taught them an answer to that question not unworthy of English Christians.
>
> The Anglican movement, when it dies out, will leave behind at least a legacy of grand old authors disinterred, of art, of music; of churches too, schools, cottages, and charitable institutions, which will form so many centers of future civilization, and will entitle it to the respect, if not to the allegiance, of the future generation. And more than this; it has sown in the hearts of young gentlemen and young ladies seed which will not perish; which, though it may develop into forms little expected by those who sowed it, will develop at least into a virtue more stately and reverent, more chivalrous and self-sacrificing, more genial and human, than can be learnt from that religion of the Stock Exchange, which reigned triumphant for a year and a day in the popular pulpits.[69]

Here, we can see a certain magnanimity in Kingsley, something we do not always associate with the man, which proves that it was not simple hot-headed inconsistency that drove his contradictory attitude to Newman and his Roman religion: there was also a certain generosity in his conflicted response to a man and a religion that he was otherwise inclined to admire *malgré lui*. "I have said that Neo-Anglicanism has proved a failure, as seventeenth-century Anglicanism did," he wrote.

> But now peace to its ashes. Is it so great a sin, to have been dazzled by the splendor of an impossible ideal? Is it so great a sin, to have had courage and conduct enough to attempt the enforcing of that ideal, in the face of the prejudices of a whole nation? And if that ideal was too narrow for the English nation, and for

---

[68] Charles Kingsley to Derwent Coleridge (12 February 1851) quoted in Margaret Farrand Thorp, *Charles Kingsley: 1819–1875* (Princeton: Princeton University Press, 1937), 31.
[69] Charles Kingsley, *Yeast: A Problem*, 4th edition (London: Macmillan & Co., 1891), x. Kinglsey composed the preface in 1859.

the modern needs of mankind, is that either so great a sin? Are other extant ideals, then, so very comprehensive? Does Mr. Spurgeon,[70] then, take so much broader or nobler views of the capacities and destinies of his race, than that great genius, John Henry Newman? If the world cannot answer that question now, it will answer it promptly enough in another five-and-twenty years.[71]

After the publication of the heterodox *Essays and Reviews* (1864)—heterodox, even by the Broad Church's rather elastic notions of heterodoxy[72]—Kingsley returned to his reservations about the Protestantism of his countrymen, a Protestantism which the editor of the controversial volume, the Rev. Henry Wilson had only made more blatant.

> I have marked with deep concern a growing desire under Lord Palmerston's government to throw more power into the hands of the Bishops and their representatives. If that scheme has a chance of taking effect then I at least will meet it with whatsoever powers God has given me whether of logic or oratory, ridicule or denunciation, and all the more because it proceeds from that section of the clergy who have the lowest views of a Bishop's office and who magnify that office in the hope that the existing majority of Bishops if their power be increased will enable them to establish a doctrine which is contrary to Episcopacy, to the Liturgy, and (as I believe) to the Articles viz . the modified Puritanism which is now called Popular Protestantism.[73]

Newman, too, had experience of the same "deadness," "desolation," and "unreality" of the "Popular Protestantism" to which Kingsley refers, though, once having turned papist, he naturally saw it through the lens of conversion—and God's Providence. "A person who has taken the step which I have naturally wishes all others to take the same," he wrote to an Anglican who had not followed him into the Church of Rome. "But it pleases Divine wisdom to leave many good and sincere Christians in (apparently) simple deadness to the claims of the one Church—nay even in strong prejudices against her, or in violent opposition. Such persons we are obliged to leave as God leaves them—fearing to make matters worse instead of better, if we attempt anything—to unsettle them for nothing, to take away what they have, without prevailing on them to accept what they have not, or to increase their misconceptions and consequent hatred of the Mother of Saints."[74] If he was wary of trying to convert those in the Protestant swim whom he regarded as inconvertible, he made an exception for the Anglo-Catholics with whom he constructed the castle of cards that became the Oxford Movement, even though his efforts in this line, set forth in the lectures he gave

---

[70] Charles Haddon Spurgeon (1835–92), popular Baptist preacher based in London famous for his contempt for Romanizing Anglicanism.
[71] Kingsley, *Yeast*, x–xi.
[72] Edward Pusey's view of one of the most famous contributors to *Essays and Reviews* is worth quoting: "I do not know what the common Christianity of myself and Professor Jowett is. I do not know what single truth we hold in common, except that somehow Jesus came from God, which the Mohammedans believe too." Pusey to A. P. Stanley (28 February 1864), Liddon, *Life of Pusey*, iv, 65.
[73] Charles Kingsley quoted in Pope Hennessy, *Kingsley*, 191.
[74] Newman to Julius Plumer (19 June 1846), *LD*, xi, 178.

in his *Anglican Difficulties*, were hardly well-received by his intended audience. Pusey, Keble and most of their Anglo-Catholic friends ignored the lectures, perhaps unavoidably, Newman never being one to extenuate the culpability of willful error.[75] "The want of congeniality which now exists between the sentiments and ways, the moral life of the Anglican communion, and the principles, doctrines, traditions of Catholicism," he told his Anglo-Catholic friends in the lectures, "show that that movement of 1833 was from its very beginning engaged in propagating an unreality."[76]

However, it is important to recognize that in order for Newman to come to this realization, he had to repudiate the nonsense he had written himself when still within the Anglican pale. We can see something of this nonsense in *Lectures on the Prophetical Office of the Church: Viewed Relatively to Romanism and Popular Protestantism* (1837), in which he explained to his readers how:

> To prevent misconception as to the meaning of the Title-page, he [that is to say, Newman himself; he refers to himself in the third person] would observe, that by Popular Protestantism he only wishes to designate that generalized idea of religion, now in repute, which merges all differences of faith and principle between Protestants as minor matters, as if the larger denominations among us agreed with us in essentials, and differed only in the accidents of form, ritual, government, or usage. Viewed politically, Protestantism is at this day the rallying point of all that is loyal and high-minded in the nation; but political considerations do not enter into the scope of his work. He has endeavoured in all important points of doctrine to guide himself by our standard divines, and, had space admitted, would have selected past sages from their writings in evidence of it. This is almost a duty on the part of every author, who professes, not to strike out new theories, but to build up and fortify what has been committed to us. In the absence of such a collection of testimonies, he hopes it will not look like presumption to desire to make his own the following noble professions of the great Bramhall.[77]

To identify the fallacies of popular Protestantism, in other words, Newman in that embarrassing book sought to rely on Anglican bishops like John Bramhall, a tack on which the author of *Anglican Difficulties* would pour immitigable scorn.[78]

In fine, when it came to the deficiencies of English Protestantism, as to the tenability of Tractarianism, Kingsley and Newman had more in common than is usually realized. The biographer of Tennyson and Hopkins, Robert Bernard Martin held that "Layer after layer of belief and personality show how fundamentally opposite the two men were: Catholic and Protestant; Roman and English

---

[75] Regarding Pusey's silence in face of the criticism that Thomas Harper, SJ mounted against the *Eirenicon*, the Jesuit was amusingly sardonic: "I hope I may say, without offence, that the whole procedure [that is to say Pusey's inability to follow through with any riposte] recalls to one's mind the words of the memorable Pym, 'I dare not fight; but I can wink, and hold out my iron. It is a simple one; but what though? It will toast cheese; and it will endure cold as another man's sword will; and there's the humour of it.'" Thomas Harper, *Peace through Truth, Or Essays connected with Dr. Pusey's Eirenicon* (London: Burns, Oates & Co., 1874), xi.

[76] *Diff.*, i, 48.

[77] *VM*, i, xi–xii.

[78] John Henry Newman, *Difficulties of Anglicans*, i, ed. Short, xlix–li.

(one is tempted to write 'Teuton'); traditionalist and modern; even Oxford and Cambridge, which all of those terms conveyed in the 1860s; subtlety and bluntness; misogamy and uxoriousness: it is difficult to find any point of reference on which they were not opposed, and on which their terms of battle might not have been declared."[79] Some of these differences might have been real enough, but they need to be seen in the context of the two controversialists' similarities.

Kingsley's Christian socialism provided him with a cause with which he could stave off his exasperation with the "deadness" of English Protestantism. "Another day is dawning for England," the rather eccentric Chartist in him would prophesy, in a broadside addressed to the country's labourers, "a day of freedom, science, industry. ... But there will be no freedom, without virtue, no true science without religion, no true industry without the fear of God, and love to your fellow citizen. Workers of England, be wise, and then you must be free, for you will be fit to be free."[80] Whether harangues of this sort edified or merely bemused England's working classes is a nice question.[81] For the biographer Guy Kendall, the upshot of Kingsley's Christian Socialism points to an ideological dead end that the would-be social reformer never outgrew—amounting as it did "to the old cliché ... that socialism will not come till all are good, and then it will not be necessary."[82] Yet this is not altogether fair. Plucked out of context, the manifesto that the crusading socialist in Kingsley wrote might be given this interpretation. But if one reads what he actually wrote in full one can see that Kingsley's crusade was actually rather ambivalent.

> Workmen of England!! You say you are wronged. Many of you are wronged and many beside yourselves know it—above all the working clergy know it. They go into your houses, they see the shameful filth and darkness in which you are forced to live crowded together; they see your children growing up in ignorance and temptation for want of fit education; they see intelligent and well-read men among you, shut out from a Freeman's just right of voting; they see, too, the noble patience and self-control with which you have as yet borne these evils, and God sees it. You think the Charter will make you free—would to God it would. The Charter is not bad; if the men who use it are not bad. But will the Charter make you free? Will it free you from slavery to ten-pound bribes? Slavery to beer and gin? Slavery to every spouter who flatters your self-conceit and stirs up bitterness and headlong rage in you? There will be no true freedom without virtue, no true science without religion, no true industry without the fear of God, and love of

---

[79] Robert Bernard Martin: *The Dust of Combat: A Life of Charles Kingsley* (New York: W. W. Norton & Company, 1960), 241.
[80] Kingsley quoted in Kendall, *Kingsley and his Ideas*, 47–8.
[81] After the Chartist mass meeting of April 1848 fizzled out in what *Punch* called a "rain of terror," Chartism faded from popular consciousness, hastened to its oblivion by a reference to its failure in *Alton Locke* in which Kingsley described how "the monster petition crawled ludicrously away in a hack cab, to be dragged to the floor of the House of Commons amid roars of laughter." See Robert Tombs, *The English and their History* (London: Allen Lane, 2014), 455–7. "The Jacobin or Chartist who ... held back from actual revolutionary preparation," the Marxist historian E. P. Thompson noted, "was always exposed, at some critical moment, both to the loss of the confidence of his own supporters and the ridicule of his opponents." E. P. Thompson, *The Making of the English Working Class* (London: Victor Gollancz, 1963), 176.
[82] Kendall, *Kingsley and his Ideas*, 48.

your fellow citizens. Workers of England be wise, and then you must be free, for you will be fit to be free.[83]

Here, Kingsley was speaking of a dilemma at the very heart of human fallenness—not a merely ideological dilemma, as some might infer from reading Kendall. Moreover, he was an odd socialist to speak to his would-be socialist converts in such unWhiggish terms.

Newman also had some rather striking things to say of fallen man's condition. In his sermon, "St. Paul's Gift of Sympathy" (1857), delivered in the University Church in Dublin, he says:

> There is no one who has loved the world so well, as He who made it. None has so understood the human heart, and human nature, and human society in its diversified forms, none has so tenderly entered into and measured the greatness and littleness of man, his doings and sufferings, his circumstances and his fortunes, none has felt such profound compassion for his ignorance and guilt, his present rebellion and his prospects hereafter, as the Omniscient. What He has actually done for us is the proof of this. "God so loved the world, as to give His Only-begotten Son." He loved mankind in their pollution, in spite of the abhorrence with which that pollution filled Him. He loved them with a father's love, who does not cast off a worthless son once for all, but is affectionate towards his person, while he is indignant at his misconduct. He loved them for what still remained in them of their original excellence, which was in its measure a reflexion of His own. He loved them before He redeemed them, and He redeemed them because He loved them. This is that "philanthropy" or "humanity" of God our Saviour, of which the inspired writers speak.
>
> I say the word "disappointing" is the only word to express our feelings on the death of God's saints. Unless our faith be very active, so as to pierce beyond the grave, and realize the future, we feel depressed at what seems like a failure of great things. And from this very feeling surely, by a sort of contradiction, we may fairly take hope; for if this life be so disappointing, so unfinished, surely it is not the whole. This feeling of disappointment will often come upon us in an especial way on happening to hear of or to witness the deathbeds of holy men. The hour of death seems to be a season, of which, in the hands of Providence, much might be *made*, if I may use the term; much might be done for the glory of God, the good of man, and the manifestation of the person dying.[84]

Newman might very well have had his father in mind when he wrote his sermon on the littleness and greatness of man—after all, misfortune struck the private banker down before he could ever turn his considerable talents to account—though his son might also have had Kingsley in mind as well when he spoke of the "philanthropy" of God the Saviour.[85] In a sermon entitled, "Endurance,"

---

[83] Kingsley quoted in Pope Hennessy, *Kingsley*, 76–7.
[84] OS, 106–7.
[85] If asked how I know that Newman had his father in mind when writing this sermon, I should be obliged to say that I do not know: I am only guessing, though I have good grounds for guessing, which I shared with my readers in *Newman and his Family*. "Newman pointed to the suppositious case of a man who might almost be the double of his father. 'I mean,' he explained, 'when one sees

Kingsley gave vent to his best oratorical vein to speak about how ordinary people partake in this "philanthropy."

> The statesman debating in Parliament; the conqueror changing the fate of nations on bloody battlefields; these all do their work; and are needful, doubtless, in a sinful, piecemeal world like this. But there are those of whom the noisy world never hears, who have chosen the better part which shall not be taken from them; who enter into a higher glory than that of statesmen, or conquerors, or the successful and famous of the earth. Many a man—clergyman or lay man—struggling in poverty and obscurity, with daily toil of body and mind, to make his fellow-creatures better and happier; poor woman, bearing children in pain and sorrow, and bringing them up with pain and sorrow, but in industry, too, and piety; or submitting without complaint to brutal husband; or sacrificing all her own hopes in life to feed and educate her brothers and sisters; or enduring for years the peevishness and troublesomeness of some relation;—all these (and the world which God sees is full of such, though the world which sees takes no note of them)—gentle souls, humble souls, uncomplaining souls, suffering souls, pious souls—these are God's elect; these are Christ's sheep; these are the salt of the earth, who, by doing each their little duty as unto God, not unto men, keep society from decaying more than do all the constitutions and acts of parliament which states men ever invented . These are they—though they little dream of any such honour—who copy the likeness of the old martyrs, who did well and suffered for it; and the likeness of Christ, of whom it was said, "He shall not strive nor cry, neither shall his voice be heard in the streets."[86]

What is interesting about such sentiments is that they show that Kingsley, like Newman, never placed an undue emphasis on the intellect in his understanding of God's creatures—or his destiny. Intellect, of course, had its place but that place was not paramount. Action was also important; duty was important; faith was important. Simply by committing himself to the Broad Church, Kingsley might have been tainted by the rationalism that taints all forms of Protestantism; but, as we have seen, he was not at peace with the "deadness" to which that rationalism gave rise. As much as Newman, he craved the life of reality—a life he saw in inalienably Christian terms. One can see this in one of his poems, aptly entitled "The Dead Church":

> Wild wild wind, wilt thou never cease thy sighing?
> Dark dark night, wilt thou never wear away?
> Cold cold church, in thy death sleep lying,

> some excellent person, whose graces we know, whose kindliness, affectionateness, tenderness, and generosity,—when we see him dying (let him have lived ever so long; I am not supposing a premature death; let him live out his days), the thought is forced upon us with a sort of surprise; Surely, he is not to die yet; he has not yet had any opportunity of exercising duly those excellent gift s with which God has endowed him. Let him have lived seventy or eighty years, yet it seems as if he had done nothing at all, and his life were scarcely begun.' Of course, these are words that can apply to multitudes, but they especially evoke the talented, good-hearted, unfortunate man, whose enterprise and acuity were no match for the vagaries of the post-Napoleonic financial markets or the unpredictability of breweries." Short, *Newman and his Family*, 395.

[86] Charles Kingsley, *Discipline and Other Sermons* (London: Macmillan, 1868), 266-7.

> The Lent is past, thy Passion here, but not thine Easter-day.
> Peace, faint heart, though the night be dark and sighing;
> Rest, fair corpse, where thy Lord himself hath lain.
> Weep, dear Lord, above thy bride low lying;
> Thy tears shall wake her frozen limbs to life and health again.

Yet if Kingsley could not reconcile himself to what Protestantism had wrought in his beloved land, he could resent what Newman had done to the dead church of which he speaks in his poem by going over to Rome, and this leads us to the hapless conduct of his controversy with Newman.

V

In revisiting the controversy between Kingsley and Newman, it might be best to remind readers of its terms. In the preface to the second edition of his *Apologia*, Newman set out these terms fairly and squarely.

> It was in the number for January 1864, of a magazine of wide circulation, and in an Article upon Queen Elizabeth, that a popular writer took occasion formally to accuse me by name of thinking so lightly of the virtue of Veracity, as in set terms to have countenanced and defended that neglect of it which he at the same time imputed to the Catholic Priesthood. His words were these:—
>
>> "Truth, for its own sake, had never been a virtue with the Roman clergy. Father Newman informs us that it need not, and on the whole ought not to be; that cunning is the weapon which heaven has given to the Saints wherewith to withstand the brute male force of the wicked world which marries and is given in marriage. Whether his notion be doctrinally correct or not, it is at least historically so."
>
> These assertions, going far beyond the popular prejudice entertained against me, had no foundation whatever in fact. I never had said, I never had dreamed of saying, that truth for its own sake, need not, and on the whole ought not to be, a virtue with the Roman Clergy; or that cunning is the weapon which heaven has given to the Saints wherewith to withstand the wicked world.[87]

Newman's initial response was to the Macmillan brothers, the proprietors of *Macmillan's Magazine*.

> Gentlemen,
> I do not write to you with any controversial purpose, which would be preposterous; but I address you simply because of your special interest in a Magazine which bears your name.
> That highly respected name you have associated with a Magazine, of which the January number has been sent to me by this morning's post, with a pencil mark calling my attention to page 217.

---

[87] *Apo.*, 2–3.

There, apropos of Queen Elizabeth, I read as follows:—

> "Truth, for its own sake, had never been a virtue with the Roman clergy. Father Newman informs us that it need not, and on the whole ought not to be; that cunning is the weapon which Heaven has given to the saints wherewith to withstand the brute male force of the wicked world which marries and is given in marriage. Whether his notion be doctrinally correct or not, it is at least historically so."

There is no reference at the foot of the page to any words of mine, much less any quotation from my writings, in justification of this statement.

I should not dream of expostulating with the writer of such a passage, nor with the editor who could insert it without appending evidence in proof of its allegations. Nor do I want any reparation from either of them. I neither complain of them for their act, nor should I thank them if they reversed it. Nor do I even write to you with any desire of troubling you to send me an answer. I do but wish to draw the attention of yourselves, as gentlemen, to a grave and gratuitous slander, with which I feel confident you will be sorry to find associated a name so eminent as yours.

I am, Gentlemen, Your obedient Servant, John H. Newman.[88]

Kingsley's response altogether evaded the real question at hand, which was whether Newman had actually said what Kinglsey had charged him with saying: that he and the priests of the Roman Church repudiated the virtue of truth. His apology, in fine, apologized for nothing.

> Dr. Newman has, by letter, expressed in the strongest terms his denial of the meaning which I have put upon his words. No man knows the use of words better than Dr. Newman; no man therefore, has a better right to define what he does or does not mean by them. It only remains, therefore, for me to express my hearty regret at having so seriously mistaken him, and my hearty pleasure at finding him on the side of truth, in this, or in any other matter.[89]

Edward Badeley, one of Newman's ablest legal counselors, echoed Newman's response to the pseudo-apology: "[S]o far from making any proper apology, he concludes with a most offensive and insolent sneer—Such an apology, I think, would not be deemed sufficient in any Court of Justice, or in any society of Gentlemen, and I have no hesitation in declaring that I consider it a disgrace to the writer."[90]

In a letter to Alexander Macmillan, Newman justified his "severe" response to Kinglsey's unrepentant response. "Had Mr Kingsley shown a particle of frankness which your own letter displayed, my trouble would have been spared. All of us are liable to error; it is a pity when any of us forget it. For myself, I can truly say that, had he, in his justification, been able, contrary to my expectation, to produce any passage from any work of mine, of an ambiguous character, I should

---

[88] Newman to Macmillan (30 December 1863), *LD*, xx, 571–2.
[89] Kingsley quoted in Pope Hennessy, *Kingsley*.
[90] *LD*, xxi, 35, n.1.

have felt obliged to him for giving me the opportunity of explaining it; and the candour, which I feel I could have shown myself, when assailed, I had a right to expect in him, the assailant. The absence of it in him has obliged me to be severe; but, after all, my severity in my necessary defence is far less than the severity of his unprovoked attack."[91] If there was anything amiss in this self-defense, Macmillan never shared it with his understandably aggrieved correspondent.

Since Newman's detractors have always been fond of claiming that nothing Newman says in defense of himself can be regarded as anything other than self-vindicating eyewash, one is grateful to be able to point to what James Fitzjames Stephen had to say of the matter in *The Saturday Review*, which shows that even someone unsympathetic to Newman and his Catholic religion could see the groundlessness of Kingsley's charge.

> In fact, Father Newman never wrote the sermon on Wisdom and Innocence at all. It was not Father Newman, but Mr. Newman, an Anglican vicar, who preached and published it. Next, the word Truth only occurs once in the sermon at all, and quite in another connexion, when the preacher observes that "the truth has in itself the gift of spreading without instruments." Neither does the sermon contain one single word about the moral obligations of the clergy, whether Roman, Greek, or Anglican. Neither of the words "Roman" or "Clergy" occur in the whole sermon. Nor is there any discussion whatever about truth or its claims, general or partial, seeing that truth is not named in the sermon. Nor again does Dr. Newman inform us that "cunning is the weapon given to the saints," seeing that he says "Christians were allowed the arms—that is, the arts—of the defenceless. ... And then he goes on to argue from this illustration, as his text suggested:—"The servants of Christ are forbidden to defend themselves by violence, but they are not forbidden other means. For instance, *foresight ... avoidance ... prudence and skill*, as in the text, 'Be ye wise as serpents.'" And, lastly, as to the somewhat offensive language attributed to Dr. Newman—"cunning is given to the saints wherewith to withstand the brute male force of the wicked world which marries and is given in marriage"—there is not one single word in the sermon, from end to end, about males or marriage or giving in marriage. The explanation of the whole matter is this:—Mr. Kingsley had some vague and indistinct recollections of a sermon of Mr. Newman's which, when he read it, made a great impression upon him—an impression so deep that it "shook off the strong influence which Dr. Newman's writings had excited in him," and which sermon seemed to Mr. Kingsley's mind to convey a sort of apology for unmanliness and unstraightforwardness, and to suggest a theory and Christian philosophy of slyness and artifice and insincerity. If Mr. Kingsley had said this, he would have been perfectly justified in saying it; but what he was not justified morally in doing was deliberately to assign to Dr. Newman express language and plain words which Dr. Newman never used, without any reference or quotation. And what he was not justified merely as a literary man in doing was to imagine for a moment that Dr. Newman—of all men in the world, so consummate a master of language, so subtle, so indirect and suggestive, so pregnant with qualifications, so refined, and so judicious, not to

---

[91] Newman to Alexander Macmillan (10 February 1864), LD, xxi, 47.

say so crafty, in statement—should ever deliver himself of such a coarse, vulgar, stupid saying as, "Truth need not, and on the whole ought not, to be a virtue," and "cunning is the virtue which Heaven has given to the saints to withstand the brute male force of the wicked world."[92]

If James Fitzjames Stephen cannot be regarded as an adequate witness to the falsity of Kingsley's claim, we can turn to Kingsley's beloved friend Maurice, who told the Dean of Westminster: "I would have given much that Kingsley had not got into this dispute with Newman. In spite of all apparent evidence, I do believe that Newman loves truth in his heart of hearts, and more now than when he was an Anglican."[93] George Eliot's having sided with Newman must also be included in the defense. "I have been made so indignant by Kingsley's mixture of arrogance, coarse impertinence and unscrupulousness with real intellectual incompetence," the author of *Middlemarch* wrote, "that my first interest in Newman's answer arose from a wish to see what I consider thoroughly vicious writing thoroughly castigated. But the Apology now mainly affects me as the revelation of a life."[94] *The Irish Ecclesiastical Gazette* was equally balanced in its notice of the pamphlets exchanged between Kinglsey and Newman, saying of the latter that although he "is now separated by a wide gulph from us in the matter of doctrine ... we will not follow Mr. Kingsley's example in repudiating a man who once exercised over English Churchmen ... a very definite intellectual influence ... He has left deeply upon our Church the impress of a sovereign mind, and has, among other benefits conferred upon us, been indirectly the means of preventing Christianity in the Anglican Church from degenerating into the phantom of mere outward arrogant profession."[95]

On 7 January 1864, Thomas Harper, SJ, who would take issue with Newman's *Grammar of Assent*, wrote the Oratorian to express his "disgust at the shameless and wanton insult offered you by the Revd C. Kingsley" and to thank him for his Pamphlet. A day later he added, in reference to the Newman's letter to Macmillan, "I would not dare to obtrude my own opinion against your own judgment that you are unpopular and down; but I think I may safely say that there are multitudes still in the city of confusion who look out wistfully now, as in past years, for the writings of Dr Newman," which prompted a grateful response from the maligned convert.

---

[92] James Fitzjames Stephen, "Dr. Newman and Mr. Kingsley," *Saturday Review* (27 February 1864).
[93] Maurice to A. P. Stanley (19 April 1864), *The Life of Frederick Denison Maurice*, ii, 478–9.
[94] George Eliot quoted in *The George Eliot Letters 1862–1868*, ed. Gordon Sherman Haight, 4 vols. (New Have: Yale University Press, 1958), iv, 158. Eliot's good sense here should be contrasted with something she had occasion to say of Kingsley in a review of his *Westward Ho!* (1855), where, disagreeing with his perfectly sound preference for the Bible's account of the Fall, rather than that of the science to which Alexander von Humboldt (1769–1859) subscribed, she deplored "Kingsley's cool arrogance in asserting that a man like Humboldt, the patriarch of scientific investigators, is 'misled by the dogmas of so-called science, which has *not a fact* whereon to base its wild notions.' Indeed, it is rather saddening to dwell on the occasional absurdities into which anomalous opinions can betray a man of real genius." George Eliot, *Selected Essays, Poems and Other Writings*, ed. A. S. Byatt (London: Penguin Books, 1990), 319. Of course, in these once hotly contested matters, Kingsley has been proven right and Eliot wrong.
[95] *The Irish Ecclesiastical Gazette* (20 April 1864), 89–90.

Charles Kingsley

My dear Fr Harper

I thank you with all my heart for your kind letter, and I shall keep it as a pledge of what you say, that there are many, though I am removed from them, who do not forget me, nor the special needs which a person of my age has on their religious thoughts and good prayers.

When I say that I am "unpopular" and "down," I state what is a simple fact, but not at all in the way of complaint or regret.

It is impossible that the thought of me should remain so steadily in the minds of the religious parties who do not agree with me, if I were not still doing work. I accept it as a token that I am still feared, because I am still abused, and, to take the case of Oxford itself, I have within this week been shown the following most astonishing extract from the letter of an Ultraliberal resident there of high name—In quoting it, I must beg you not to show it about, as it was written in the confidence of private friendship: "We are all becoming High Church again as fast as we can, a fact which it is difficult for the country to understand. It is so nevertheless. England will awake one morning, astonished to find itself Tractarian."

But further than this, let me say to you, (what I trust I may say without taking a liberty in speaking so personally about myself,) that I take this long penance of slander and unpopularity, which has been on me for thirty years, nay rather I have taken it almost from the time when that thirty years began,—and have said so indeed more or less clearly in print,—as the price I pay for the victory, or at least the great extension, of those principles which are so near my heart;—and, I think, while I live, I shall go on paying it, because I trust that, even after my life, those principles will extend

Very sincerely Yrs John H Newman[96]

Perhaps the most interesting response to the Kingsley-Newman controversy came from Basil Willey (1897-1978), the intellectual historian and literary critic, who fought in the Great War with the West Yorkshires and became King Edward VII Professor of English Literature at Cambridge and President of Pembroke College.[97] Sympathetic to those in the nineteenth century whom he regarded as honest doubters, Willey was also appreciative enough of good writing to recognize the power of Newman both as a rhetorician and a thinker, and his reading of why Kingsley was provoked into tussling with Newman is at once intellectually and theologically persuasive. "To the average Englishman and Churchman of the time—to a man like Kingsley, for example," Willey wrote, "it was so shocking to hear proclaimed as truths, doctrines long regarded as exploded superstitions, so disturbing to find the charges of ignorance and inconsistency

---

[96] Newman to Thomas Harper, SJ (18 February 1864), *LD*, xxi, 53-4.
[97] "Willey went to University College School in Hampstead in 1912. He excelled in his studies, and in December 1915 he won a scholarship in history to Peterhouse, Cambridge. But war service intervened; commissioned into the West Yorkshire regiment, he saw active service on the western front, chiefly as his battalion's signals officer. He was wounded and captured in the German offensive of March 1918, spending the rest of the war as a prisoner. His account of his war service in his memoir, *Spots of Time*, dwells more on the moments of Wordsworthian oneness with nature than with military matters, though it offers a rueful, occasionally touching, account of how the shy, bookish, Methodist teetotaller struggled to adjust to the earthier natures of his comrades." ODNB.

retorted upon themselves that one explanation alone seemed possible: these Catholics were crafty priests who did not, could not, mean or believe what they said." This could apply not only to Kingsley but to all of the Victorian rationalists from Thomas Huxley to Fitzjames Stephen who took issue with Newman, and, indeed, to most of his later detractors. Newman had to be regarded as a liar because no one as bright as he could ever have truthfully claimed to believe the dogmatical truths that he claimed to believe. For Kingsley and so many others, Newman was a skeptic only masquerading as a dogmatist. Yet in pondering this odd assumption on the part of so many Victorian thinkers, Willey was led to see the conflict as one between genuine faith and anxious unbelief. "Few … would be inclined to dismiss Newman as a reactionary dreamer, out of touch with his time," Willey writes.

> If he lacked interest in what was specifically of the nineteenth century, it was because he was a spectator of all time and all existence. What concerns him is not the local and the transient, but the perennial plight of fallen man. The solution which he proposed seemed to many, as it did to Arnold, "frankly impossible"; indeed, to the average Englishman, for whom Catholicism had long been an object of scorn and fear (associated with Guy Fawkes and hocus-pocus), it seemed preposterous. Yet in so far as Catholicism meant really believing what others only professed, and really using means of grace which others had abandoned or used as mechanical routine: in so far as it meant a return and a recall to spiritual first principles, it could, again, as of old, form the advance column in the holy war against the principalities and powers. The current of the Reformation had run its course, and its spent energies were losing themselves in the flats and shallows of worldliness and unbelief; could it be that Rome had been right all along?[98]

Willey hits the bullseye here. The challenge of Newman's deeply held dogmatical faith is what led to the obsessive detestation of Newman's Catholicism on the part of so many Victorian rationalists; and it certainly had a great deal to do with Kingsley's maniacal determination to discredit Newman and the faith to which he had converted—a faith which could only highlight the unreal velleities of Protestantism and, worse, the negations of unbelief.

Once in receipt of the defamatory reference to his own and the Roman Catholic priesthood's veracity, Newman set out a strategy of parrying its falsehood, which shows how nicely appreciative he was of the advantages of his position. In his introduction to the 1864 and the 1865 editions of the *Apologia*, Ward summarizes this plausible strategy.

> He had first to rivet general attention on the contest, and to write without being tedious to the average reader;—to make such a reader ready to follow the dispute further. This he succeeded in doing in the witty pamphlet, published in this volume, in which he summarized his correspondence with Kingsley,—a brief and amusing jeu d'esprit which all could enjoy. That this pamphlet made Kingsley so angry as to forget himself and strike random blows in his retort entitled "What,

[98] Basil Willey, *Nineteenth-Century Studies: Coleridge to Matthew Arnold* (London: Chatto & Windus, 1949), 86–9.

then, does Dr. Newman mean?" was, probably, a result foreseen by its author: and it was all in Newman's favour. Then Newman had to keep the ball rolling, to avoid any such delay or dullness as might lose for him the general attention he had won. For this purpose, it was desirable that the *Apologia* should be published in weekly parts, and the first parts had to sustain the note of humorous banter which his pamphlet had struck. This meant work at the very highest pressure. Easy reading means hard writing in such a case. Again, he had to find successfully the tone which could make the advocate of an unpopular cause win general sympathy. It was necessary to bring vividly home to every one the fact that he was deeply wronged, that a serious charge had been brought, that when challenged its bringer had wholly failed to justify it, and had also failed to make any adequate apology for his slander. When once Newman had completely won public sympathy, he could say things that could only be told to sympathetic ears. He could then relate the whole story of his life, and could make plain its utter sincerity. The first two parts of the *Apologia* were brief, brilliant, and full of indignant passion. Then came the bulk of the narrative, so touching to those who had become really interested in the man. Lastly, as an Appendix, came the thirty-nine "blots," as he called them,—with a humorous suggestion in their number of the Anglican articles—in which the worst of Kingsley's random charges were swept away in such a tone of contempt as could only be securely adopted after the reader's sympathy was entirely won. The occasion was great; the work was exacting; but Newman rose to it and emerged triumphant. The *Apologia* carried the country by storm. It became a classic of the language.[99]

The "amusing *jeu d'esprit*" to which Ward refers was indeed a brilliant sally. The withering satirist of "The Tamworth Reading Room" (1841), *Anglican Difficulties*, and *Lectures on the Present Position of Catholics in England* (1851), came to the fore in this preliminary salvo, and it set in motion what would become his ebullient demolition of his accuser's ill-considered case. "I shall attempt a brief analysis of the foregoing correspondence," Newman wrote in his publication of the correspondence that went back and forth between Kingsley and himself, "and I trust that the wording which I shall adopt will not offend against the gravity due both to myself and to the occasion. It is impossible to do justice to the course of thought evolved in it without some familiarity of expression." Newman's irony was never more playful or more minatory.

> Mr. Kingsley begins then by exclaiming,—"O the chicanery, the wholesale fraud, the vile hypocrisy, the conscience-killing tyranny of Rome! We have not far to seek for evidence of it. There's Father Newman to wit: one living specimen is worth a hundred dead ones. He, a Priest writing of Priests, tells us that lying is never any harm."
> I interpose: "You are taking a most extraordinary liberty with my name. If I have said this, tell me when and where."
> Mr. Kingsley replies: "You said it, Reverend Sir, in a Sermon which you preached, when a Protestant, as Vicar of St. Mary's, and published in 1844; and

---

[99] Wilfrid Ward, "Introduction," in *Newman's Apologia pro Vita Sua: The Two Versions of 1864 and 1865*, ed. Wilfred Ward (Oxford: Oxford University Press, 1913), vi–vii.

I could read you a very salutary lecture on the effects which that Sermon had at the time on my own opinion of you."

I make answer: "Oh ... Not, it seems, as a Priest speaking of Priests;—but let us have the passage."

Mr. Kingsley relaxes: "Do you know, I like your tone. From your tone I rejoice, greatly rejoice, to be able to believe that you did not mean what you said."

I rejoin: "Mean it! I maintain I never said it, whether as a Protestant or as a Catholic."

Mr. Kingsley replies: "I waive that point."

I object: "Is it possible! What? waive the main question? I either said it or I didn't. You have made a monstrous charge against me; direct, distinct, public. You are bound to prove it as directly, as distinctly, as publicly;—or to own you can't."

" Well," says Mr. Kingsley, "if you are quite sure you did not say it, I'll take your word for it ; I really will."

My word! I am dumb. Somehow, I thought that it was my word that happened to be on trial. The word of a Professor of lying, that he does not lie!

But Mr. Kingsley re-assures me: "We are both gentlemen," he says: "I have done as much as one English gentleman can expect from another."

I begin to see: he thought me a gentleman at the very time that he said I taught lying on system. After all, it is not I, but it is Mr. Kingsley who did not mean what he said. "Habemus confitentem reum."

So we have confessedly come round to this, preaching without practicing; the common theme of satirists from Juvenal to Walter Scott! "I left Baby Charles and Steenie laying his, duty before him" says King James of the reprobate Dalgarno: "O Geordie, jingling Geordie, it was grand to hear Baby Charles laying down the guilt of dissimulation, and Steenie lecturing on the turpitude of incontinence."

While I feel then that Mr. Kingsley's February explanation is miserably insufficient in itself for his January enormity, still I feel also that the Correspondence, which he has between these two acts of his, constitutes a real satisfaction to those principles of historical and literary justice to which he has given so rude a shock.

Accordingly, I have put it into print, and make no further criticism on Mr. Kingsley.

J. H. N.[100]

While admirers of Newman's style might revel in these sprightly salvos, not everyone found them amusing.[101] Lady Jane Franklin found them unseemly. For her more rarefied taste, Newman's send-up of his assailant's epistolary impertinence gave her "a more unfavourable impression of Dr. Newman than before." Why? "[T]he more apology Mr. Kingsley makes for his original rash utterance, the more does the other taunt & press upon him & ends with a low comic paraphrase of the correspondence in a colloquial style, utterly unworthy of a priest

---

[100] Ibid., 20–1.
[101] Readers desirous of seeing the stylist in Newman at his best should read his eulogy for his good friend James Hope-Scott (1812–73), Josephine Ward's papa, generally deemed the handsomest man in Victorian England, which shows what an elegant English the convert could write, though, as his various writings show, he was master of many different registers from the elegiac to the satirical. See OS, 263–80.

& a gentleman."[102] *The Edinburgh Review* saw the book as a kind of ventilator for all the grievances Newman felt against the crowing of Anglicans at what appeared to be the convert's displeasure with his adopted Church, even though "The aristocratic hauteur of the *civis Romanus* living among barbarians lives on in the sentiment of the Roman Catholic towards Protestants. When Newman was publicly charged with intending to return to Anglicanism, this spirit broke out in a disagreeable and insulting manner." Consequently, Kinsley's slur "roused him to put on his armour and fight for his reputation. There had always been an element of combativeness in Newman's disposition. '*Nescio quo pacto*, 'my spirits most happily rise at the prospect of danger,' he wrote early in life. And when he could persuade himself that not only his honour but that of the Church was at stake, he could feel and show the true Catholic ferocity, the cruellest spirit on earth."[103] Another quarter unimpressed by Newman's initial conduct of his controversial response was the editor of the *Athenaeum*, who wrote:

> Except that it makes yet another controversy of the season, a subject for club-gossip, and a dinner-table tattle ... this discussion can have no particular result. It is famous sport; the world is amused, the athletes get admired, and there is an end. Of all the diversions of our dining and dancing season, that of a personal conflict is ever the most eagerly enjoyed ... And how briskly we gather round a brace of reverend gentlemen, when the prize for which they contend is which of the two shall be considered as the father of lies![104]

However funny, this ignores the true character—indeed, the stakes—of the controversy. It also ignores the way Newman's defense of himself and the Catholic priesthood was received by his contemporaries, most of whom agreed that Kingsley's calumny had to be answered and that Newman had answered it splendidly.

In preparing the second edition of the *Apologia* for publication, Newman would remove the controversial materials of the first edition, knowing that they would give his book an unnecessarily polemical cast. He was careful, however, never to repent of writing them in the first place. "Even if I could have found it consistent with my duty to my own reputation to leave such an elaborate impeachment of my moral nature unanswered," he wrote in the preface to the 1865 edition, "my duty to my Brethren in the Catholic Priesthood would have forbidden such a course. *They* were involved in the charges which this writer, all along, from the original passage in the Magazine, to the very paragraph of the Pamphlet, had so confidently, so pertinaciously made. In exculpating myself ...

---

[102] Lady Jane Franklin quoted in Robert Bernard Martin: *The Dust of Combat: A Life of Charles Kingsley* (New York: W. W. Norton & Company, 1960), 247.
[103] *The Edinburgh Review* (April, 1912), 268. The passage quoted appears in a review of Wilfrid Ward's biography of Newman, in which the reviewer, for all his antipathy to Catholicism, appreciates the false position into which the convert's assailant put himself: "The coarseness of [Kingsley's] attack upon an elderly man of saintly character and acknowledged intellectual eminence, who had to all appearance blighted a great career by honestly obeying his conscience, offended the British public, which was now fully disposed to give a respectful and favourable hearing to whatever Newman might care to say in reply. In a Catholic country it would have been useless for a Protestant, however falsely attacked, to appeal to Catholic public opinion for justice; but Newman understood the English character, and saw his splendid chance." *Ibid.*, 269.
[104] *The Athenaeum* (26 March 1854), 432.

I was making my protest in behalf of a large body of men of high character, of honest and religious minds, and of sensitive honour."[105]

Nevertheless, Newman did retain some of the passages from the first edition, one of the most pointed of which explains that another reason why he was impelled to respond to his accuser was to refute the attack that Kingsley subsequently mounted on the very marrow of his character, an attack designed to invalidate anything Newman might say in his defense by charging that nothing could be credited from so discreditable a source. In the course of their correspondence, Kingsley's charge had gone from claiming that Newman and the Catholic priesthood were untruthful to calling into question the integrity of the convert's entire life. If he could not substantiate the truthfulness of the initial charge of mendacity with respect to the sermon, "Wisdom and Innocence" (1843), he had no compunction going in search of a much wider, deeper dossier, to which Newman responded in the preface of the *Apologia*'s first edition:

> [H]ere I will but say that I scorn and detest lying, and quibbling, and double-tongued practice, and slyness, and cunning, and smoothness, and cant, and pretence, quite as much as any Protestants hate them; and I pray to be kept from the snare of them. But all this is just now by the by; my present subject is my Accuser; what I insist upon here is this unmanly attempt of his, in his concluding pages, to cut the ground from under my feet;—to poison by anticipation the public mind against me, John Henry Newman, and to infuse into the imaginations of my readers, suspicion and mistrust of everything that I may say in reply to him. This I call *poisoning the wells*.[106]

Once Newman realized the extent of Kingsley's calumny, comprising as it did not only his initial defamatory reference in *Macmillan's Magazine* but his subsequent pamphlet, he recognized how he should refute it.

> My perplexity had not lasted half an hour. I recognized what I had to do, though I shrank from both the task and the exposure which it would entail. I must, I said, give the true key to my whole life; I must show what I am, that it may be seen what I am not, and that the phantom may be extinguished which gibbers instead of me. I wish to be known as a living man, and not as a scarecrow which is dressed up in my clothes. False ideas may be refuted indeed by argument, but by true ideas alone are they expelled. I will vanquish, not my Accuser, but my judges. I will indeed answer his charges and criticisms on me one by one, lest any one should say that they are unanswerable, but such a work shall not be the scope nor the substance of my reply. I will draw out, as far as may be, the history of my mind; I will state the point at which I began, in what external suggestion or accident each opinion had its rise, how far and how they developed from within, how they grew, were modified, were combined, were in collision with each other, and were changed; again how I conducted myself towards them, and how, and how far, and for how long a time, I thought I could hold them consistently with the ecclesiastical engagements which I had made and with the position which I

---

[105] *Apo.*, 4.
[106] *Apo.*, 5–6.

held. I must show—what is the very truth—that the doctrines which I held, and have held for so many years, have been taught me (speaking humanly) partly by the suggestions of Protestant friends, partly by the teaching of books, and partly by the action of my own mind: and thus I shall account for that phenomenon which to so many seems so wonderful, that I should have left "my kindred and my father's house" for a Church from which once I turned away with dread;—so wonderful to them! as if forsooth a Religion which has flourished through so many ages, among so many nations, amid such varieties of social life, in such contrary classes and conditions of men, and after so many revolutions, political and civil, could not subdue the reason and overcome the heart, without the aid of fraud in the process and the sophistries of the schools.[107]

The last extract that Newman published from the first edition of the *Apologia* bespeaks not only the author's veracity but his integrity, which detractors can impugn but never confute. "I purpose to set nothing down in [the *Apologia*] as certain," he wrote, "of which I have not a clear memory, or some written memorial, or the corroboration of some friend. There are witnesses enough up and down the country to verify, or correct, or complete it; and letters moreover of my own in abundance." The correspondence which Newman conducted with so many of his erstwhile Anglo-Catholic friends to verify the accuracy of his recollections—correspondence with William John Copeland, Dean Church, Edward Pusey, John Keble and Sir Frederic Rogers, among others—richly bears this out. Newman and his work have always been a magnet for unbalanced detractors, from Edwin Abbott Abbott in the nineteenth to Frank Turner in the twenty-first century; detractors who cannot abide his sanctity and will go to any lengths to discredit his work. But the foil to such denigrators has always been Newman himself and the work that so embodies his integrity. While Newman anticipated these naysayers, he was naturally too modest to anticipate how the *Apologia* would continually baffle them. "I mean to be simply personal and historical," he wrote in the book's first edition; "I am not expounding Catholic doctrine, I am doing no more than explaining myself, and my opinions and actions. I wish, as far as I am able, simply to state facts, whether they are ultimately determined to be for me or against me." Indeed, the degree of self-criticism in the book is rarely acknowledged. It was part and parcel of Newman's intellectual honesty to call a spade a spade, especially when such truth-telling required him to critise himself. And this extended to his readiness to welcome the criticisms of those who saw the history of his religious opinions differently. "Of course there will be room enough for contrariety of judgment among my readers, as to the necessity, or appositeness, or value, or good taste, or religious prudence, of the details which I shall introduce," he wrote. "I may be accused of laying stress on little things, of being beside the mark, of going into impertinent or ridiculous details, of sounding my own praise, of giving scandal; but this is a case above all others, in which I am bound to follow my own lights and to speak out my own heart. It is not at all pleasant for me to be egotistical; nor to be criticized for being so. It is not pleasant to reveal to high and low, young and old, what has

---

[107] *Apo.*, 12–13.

gone on within me from my early years." Nevertheless, the very act of writing the *Apologia* was an act of humility—this is why it proved so lacerating. No one who lived so controversial, so self-sacrificing, so harrowing a life as Newman's could have relished defending its integrity against so many groundless charges of untruthfulness and duplicity; and yet he undertook the task out of duty and an unwavering trust in his own probity. The assumption that anyone writing of his own life and convictions, held by so many of Newman's detractors, is necessarily unreliable and, indeed, self-vindicatingly deceitful is to take an oddly cynical view of the autobiographical impulse in all writers. Do we all wish to throw sand in the eyes of our readers when speaking of our lives and convictions? Do none of us wish to tell the truth about ourselves and our relations with others and with God? If it were axiomatic that one's own reading of one's life and character were necessarily false, what assurance could we have that anyone else's reading of one's life would not be tainted by comparable falsehoods? The contention that such low polemical anti-Catholic fellows as Abbott and Turner would somehow know more about Newman than Newman himself, or be more inclined to be more truthful about his life than the man who actually lived it is patently absurd, and yet contentions of this sort have always been the governing contentions of Newman's detractors, especially those masquerading as his critics. If we return to Newman's own reading of matters, we immediately see not only the honorableness but the embattled dignity of the man. "It is not pleasant to be giving to every shallow or flippant disputant the advantage over me of knowing my most private thoughts," he wrote; "I might even say the intercourse between myself and my Maker. But I do not like to be called to my face a liar and a knave; nor should I be doing my duty to my faith or to my name, if I were to suffer it. I know I have done nothing to deserve such an insult, and if I prove this, as I hope to do, I must not care for such incidental annoyances as are involved in the process."[108]

Here was the nub of the controversy: did Newman, in fact, do or say anything to deserve Kingsley's insult? R. H. Hutton surely spoke for most of Newman's contemporaries and most of ours when he responded to the correspondence between the two men that Newman published by saying that "Mr. Kingsley made a random charge against Father Newman in *Macmillan's Magazine*. The sermon in question certainly contains no proposition of the kind to which Mr. Kingsley alludes. Mr. Kingsley ought to have said, what is obviously true, that on examining the sermon no passage will bear any colourable meaning at all like that he had put upon it."[109] When Hutton wrote Newman about the controversy, the Oratorian responded: "Your letter gave me extreme pleasure. Though I contrive to endure my chronic unpopularity, and though I believe it to be salutary, yet it is not in itself welcome; and therefore it is a great relief to me to have from time to time such letters as yours which serve to show that, under the surface of things, there is a kinder feeling towards me than the surface presents."[110] Of course, once the *Apologia* was published, this kinder feeling would become altogether general.

Instead of retreating from the fray, after Hutton's review, Kingsley dug in and

---

[108] *Apo.*, 13.
[109] Hutton quoted in Ward, *The Life of Newman*, ii, 6.
[110] Newman to Hutton (26 February 1864), *LD*, xxi, 60–1.

set off a fresh barrage of calumnies against his opponent in a pamphlet about which Susan Chitty is sensibly fair-minded.

> Kingsley all too hastily snatched up his pen and dashed off the pamphlet *What then Does Dr. Newman Mean?* "I am answering Newman now," Kingsley told a friend, "and though I give up the charge of conscious dishonesty, I trust to make him and his admirers sorry that they did not leave me alone. I have a score of more than twenty years to pay, and that is an instalment of it." The person who was made to feel sorry, however, was not Newman, for the pamphlet was a disastrous failure. Having already accepted Newman's explanation of the meaning of "Wisdom and Innocence," Kingsley could now only appeal to the lowest prejudices of his readers by showing that no man could be honest who believed in such things as the virginity of Christ's mother and, of course, celibacy.[111]

Yet such stooping to the jeers of No Popery only confirmed Kingsley's unfitness for the proper cut and thrust of controversy. No one has captured the deludedness of Kingsley's assault on Newman with more succinct mordancy than Una Pope Hennessy. "Kingsley had thought of himself as the manly Englishman showing up the shifty papist, but there was little left of manliness when the shifty papist had done with him."[112] Even after the publication of the *Apologia*, Kingsley could not bring himself to admit defeat. "Here is my ultimatum on the Newman question which please shew privately to anyone and everyone you like, including Mr. Hutton," he wrote to Alexander Macmillan. "I have determined to take no notice whatever of Dr. Newman's apology." He had "nothing to retract, apologise for, explain." The injudicious hot head in Kingsley was not only unbowed but unrepentant.

> Deliberately, after twenty years of thought I struck as hard as I could. Deliberately I shall strike again, if it so pleases me, though not one literary man in England approved. I know too well of what I am talking. ... I cannot trust, I can only smile at the autobiography of a man who (beginning with Newman's light, learning and genius) ends in believing that he believes in the Infallibility of one Church, and in the Immaculate Conception. If I am to bandy words it must be with sane persons.[113]

Kingsley's defiant reference to Hutton was tell-tale. As Wilfrid Ward points out, Hutton's defense of Newman in the controversy was pivotal.

> In spite of the extreme brilliancy of [of Newman's riposte to Kingsley's "What, then, eoes Dr. Newman mean?"] it is likely enough that the British public, with its anti-Catholic prejudices, would have charged Newman with hyper-sensitiveness and ill-temper, and considered that the popular writer against whom the sally

---

[111] Susan Chitty, *The Beast and the Monk: A Life of Charles Kingsley* (New York: Mason/Charter, 1974), 231.
[112] Pope Hennessy, *Kingsley*, 221.
[113] Letter of Kingsley to Alexander Macmillan (8 June 1864) quoted in Martin Svaglic, "Editor's Introduction," John Henry Newman, *Apologia pro Vita Sua* (Oxford: Clarendon Press, 1967), xlvii–xlviii.

was directed had really made ample amends by his apology. But at this juncture there intervened a man who was already becoming a power, by force of intellect and character, in the world of letters. Richard Holt Hutton, editor of the *Spectator*, was a Liberal in politics, until lately a Unitarian in religion, a known admirer of Kingsley, a sympathiser with the Liberal theology of Frederick Denison Maurice. It was to his intervention that an able critic—the late Mr. G. L. Craik, who well remembered the controversy and whose theological sympathies were with Kingsley—used confidently to ascribe the direction which public opinion, in many instances trembling in the balance, took at this moment, and ultimately took with overwhelming force. All Hutton's antecedents seemed to be against any unfair partiality on Newman's behalf. But he had been for years keenly alive to spiritual genius wherever it showed itself—in Martineau, in Maurice, as well as in Newman. He had followed Newman's writings and career with deep interest and had been present (as we have seen) at the King William Street lectures in 1849. Endowed with a justice of mind which only a few men in each generation can boast, and which makes them judges in Israel, he had an ingrained suspiciousness of the unfairness of the English public where "popery" was concerned, and felt the need to guide it aright. He saw fully the injustice of Kingsley's method. On February 20 he published in the *Spectator* an estimate of the controversy, raised on that judicial platform of thought from which the most unfailingly effective argument proceeds. He allowed for the popular feeling that Newman's retort was too severe, and even admitted it. But in his fine psychological study of the two men, he pointed out a looseness of thought, a prejudice, a want of candour in Kingsley, which were at the root both of his original offence and of his insufficient apology, and summed up very strongly in Newman's favour.[114]

In certain anti-Catholic quarters of the nineteenth century, the tendency was to admit that Newman might have gored and tossed his opponent but he was still in the wrong because his religion was in the wrong. "I have read the *Apologia* with great interest," Bishop Cotton of Calcutta[115] wrote, "and though it gives me the impression that Newman has a subtle and tortuous mind, I do not think him dishonest.—His victory over Kingsley is complete; his book is in beautiful English, his autobiography is a curious chapter of Church history, his defence of Rome places its pretensions in a clearer sight [*sic*] than I ever saw them before, and perhaps on a more logical basis, but he entirely fails to convince me that I should find any refuge from modern difficulties under the auspices of the Pope. The questions of fact, critical and other, which disturb people now-a-days, are surely no more solved by the assurances of Pius IX that they are not difficulties, than by the assurances of the 'Record.' And this assurance of Pius IX that all is right is, in fact, the sole security which Newman gives us. Strange that it should

---

[114] Ward, *Life of Newman*, ii, 4–5.
[115] George Edward Lynch Cotton (1813–66), bishop of Calcutta, responsible for founding schools in India modelled on the English public school. The original of the Master in *Tom Brown's School Days*, Cotton came under the influence of Dr. Arnold at Rugby and remained a persevering liberal churchman throughout his life until he met an unexpected end by slipping while boarding a steamer in the dusk after consecrating a cemetery at Kushtia, on the River Gorai, a branch of the Ganges, after which he fell into the river and was never seen again. See *ODNB*.

be a security to so able a man as he is."¹¹⁶ Newman's response to his critic could apply to many of the critics covered in the present volume.

> It is amusing to me to see how blind men often are, who consider themselves especially qualified to be critics and judges of their brethren.... Dr Cotton coolly takes upon himself to pronounce on the question whether another is honest or dishonest in his subscriptions, who did but follow Laud, Bull, and the school of the greatest Anglican divines. And then what can be so *il*logical as to compare the Pope ... to the Record—as if the Record had existed 1800 or 1200 years, and had been acknowledged as the back bone of Christianity for more years than can be counted—and then moreover can say, *I* believe in the Pope, when there are hardly two words about the Pope in my whole Apologia.¹¹⁷

One of Newman's best critics, Wilfrid Ward is good on the malice aforethought that animated Kingsley's side of the controversy when, after writing the unacceptable apology to Newman, the rash canon returned to the fray. "Kingsley, who was doubtless persuaded that his apology to Newman was a very handsome one, and unconscious how his own judgment was warped by his antipathy to everything that Newman represented in his eyes," Ward writes,

> now changed his tone, and, in a pamphlet called "What then does Dr. Newman mean?" fully justified the estimate Newman had formed of his true attitude of mind—an attitude which had prevented Newman, at the outset, from accepting an apology which he felt to be grudging and not in the fullest sense sincere. How deep and habitual Kingsley's feeling of animosity was, we see from some words written while his pamphlet was in preparation, to a correspondent who had called his attention to a passage in W. G. Ward's "Ideal of a Christian Church" which appeared to justify Kingsley's charge against Newman and his friends. "Candour," Mr. Ward had written, "is an intellectual rather than a moral virtue, and by no means either universally or distinctively characteristic of the saintly mind." If "candour" meant "truthfulness," such an admission was surely significant.¹¹⁸

Yet, Kingsley's trying to mine "Ideal" Ward's book to implicate Newman in dishonesty only accentuated the weakness of his original charge vis-à-vis Newman's sermons. As Wilfrid Ward points out, Hutton was certainly alive to Kingsley's casting about for what he imagined more telling evidence when the initial accusations were shown to be unfounded, and excoriated him for it unsparingly in the *Spectator*:

> Mr. Kingsley replies in an angry pamphlet, which we do not hesitate to say aggravates the original injustice a hundredfold. Instead of quoting language of Dr. Newman's fairly justifying his statement, he quotes everything of almost any sort, whether having reference to casuistry, or to the monastic system, or the theory of Christian evidences, that will irritate,—often rightly irritate,—English

---

[116] Cotton quoted in R. D. Middleton, *Newman and Bloxam* (Oxford: Oxford University Press, 1947), 233.
[117] Newman to J. R. Bloxam (30 April 1871), *LD*, xxv, 325–6.
[118] Ward, *The Life of Newman*, ii, 7.

taste against the Romish system of faith, and every apology or plea of any kind put in by Dr. Newman in favour of that faith. He raises, in fact, as large a cloud of dust as he can round his opponent, appeals to every Protestant prepossession against him, reiterates that "truth is not honoured among these men for its own sake," giving a very shrewd hint that he includes Dr. Newman as chief amongst the number, and retires without vindicating his assertion in the least, except so far as to prove that there was quite enough that he disliked or even abhorred in Dr. Newman's teaching to suggest such an assertion to his mind,—his latent assumption evidently being that whatever Mr. Kingsley could say in good faith it could not have been unjustifiable for him to say. Mr. Kingsley evidently holds it quite innocent and even praiseworthy to blurt out raw general impressions, however inadequately supported, which are injurious and painful to other men, on condition only that they are his own sincere impressions. He has no mercy for the man who will define his thought and choose his language so subtly that the mass of his hearers may fail to perceive his distinctions, and be misled into a dangerous error,—because he cannot endure making a fine art of speech. Yet he permits himself a perfect licence of insinuation so long as these insinuations are suggested by the vague sort of animal scent by which he chooses to judge of other men's drift and meaning. Mr. Kingsley has done himself pure harm by this rejoinder.[119]

For Wilfrid Ward, "The phrase 'animal scent' was an expressive one, and told with great effect. It characterised mercilessly the sheer prejudice which led to Mr. Kingsley's insinuations."[120]

Other critics treated Newman's controversial victory as though the convert had taken unfair advantage of Kingsley, who, after all, despite his polemical ineptitude, had only spoken the truth when he said that Newman was untruthful. This was James Fitzjames Stephen's tack. The judge in him might have nicely itemized the many ways in which Kingsley had fallen short in his attempt to condemn Newman and the Roman priesthood for mendacity, but this in no way exculpated Newman or the priesthood. "We think that, substantially, what [Kingsley] really meant to say about the Roman Church was right," Stephen wrote, "and that even what he meant to say about a certain aspect of Dr. Newman's teaching in a particular sermon had some justification; but then what he meant to say was what he did not say."[121] So Kingsley's poor showing was attributable not to any failure of truth but a failure of rhetoric.

How a man of James Fitzjames Stephen's smarts could have subscribed to such feeble reasoning might seem puzzling, but, then, if we consult what he had to say of the reason why Englishmen could not stomach the Roman Church the puzzle disappears. Here is a defense of the truth to which both Stephen and Kingsley subscribed, set out in all of its theological vacuity. "For, although there are many minds which desire theological certainty, the great majority of minds are indifferent about it," Stephen wrote in 1859 in the *Saturday Review* in response to Newman's lectures on university education.

[119] Hutton quoted *ibid.*, ii, 11–12.
[120] *Ibid.*, ii, 12.
[121] James Fitzjames Stephen, "Dr. Newman and Mr. Kingsley," *Saturday Review* (27 February 1864).

Charles Kingsley

The objections of Englishmen to the Church of Rome are not principally theological—they are far more political, social, and moral. The dilemmas, the comparisons of methods, the forms of *reductio ad absurdum* which Romish theologians shoot forth to confound their enemies, fall dead on the obtuse British public. That public wants a religion that shall be consistent with political freedom, sanctify material prosperity, and protect the purity of families. The religion of the Church of Rome does not seem to Englishmen such a religion, and therefore they will not have anything to do with it. But, as Dr. Newman is so fond of crowing on logical grounds over the Church of England, we may go on to remark that the religion of the Church of England is exactly such a religion. The moral atmosphere which a creed tends to produce is the real test of its probable suitableness to a nation; and the moral atmosphere of the Church of England is so exactly suited to the majority of Englishmen, that the more religion advances in England the stronger the Church becomes. The success of the Church of Rome in making converts among the upper classes of late years has been loudly trumpeted, and is great enough to make its causes worth considering. But a success of infinitely more importance is that thorough adhesion of the great bulk of the educated classes which has been gained by the Church of England. We do not see why we should be prevented by modesty from speaking of this success, but still it is not as a matter of triumph that we are now concerned with it. It is of its causes that we are speaking; and very little reflection will convince any one that the recent success of the Church of England has been mainly due to the establishment of a habit of thought which makes the moral and social tendency of a belief one of the principal criteria of its truth. A person, once impressed with this way of thinking is not attracted by the ecclesiastical system represented by Cardinal Wiseman, nor by the dogmatic certainty offered by Dr. Newman.[122]

Nevertheless, in reading the passages from the preface of the *Apologia*'s first edition quoted above, one can clearly see that Newman's motivation for responding to Kingsley was a straightforward wish to defend a life that had been under assault since his Anglican days from precisely the sort of tribal rationalist that James Fitzjames Stephen had in mind. There was nothing meanspirited in Newman's response. Even his mockery was playful. He was simply defending himself, as any man would defend himself, against a "grave and gratuitous slander," though the way he set about this defense was striking. In his magisterial biography of Newman, Ian Ker sheds bright critical light on the means Newman chose to present the history of his religious opinions to his contemporaries. "To call the book an autobiography, even a religious autobiography, could be misleading, as it is hardly more concerned with the author's spiritual life than with his personal life," Ker writes.

> In this sense it is quite unlike St Augustine's *Confessions*, and much more like *The Force of Truth*, the story of Newman's old mentor Thomas Scott's progress from Unitarianism to Calvinism. For this is an intellectual—or rather, theological—autobiography. It is unique among Newman's published works, not only in

---

[122] James Fitzjames Stephen, "Dr. Newman's University Lectures," *Saturday Review* (28 May 1859).

its form and content, but also in its style and tone. This is not surprising when one considers that far from attempting to persuade by argument, the main autobiographical part of the book convinces by deliberately abandoning all argument in favour of facts, by adopting an almost dry documentation in the place of polemical rhetoric in order to prove the integrity of the author's own life. It is thus a curious anomaly that the very book on which Newman's literary reputation is usually presumed principally to rest, itself so strikingly differs from his other works of controversy, which give him so distinctive a place in the history of English literature. Its power lies indeed in the (almost) disconcertingly calm, limpid tone of the author's conversational, indeed confidential, voice. Eloquence is as rigorously excluded as self-defence: "I am not setting myself up as a pattern of good sense or of any thing else: I am but giving a history of my opinions, and that, with the view of showing that I have come by them through intelligible processes of thought and honest external means." Nor is there any overt appeal to the reader's sympathy—"I have no romantic story to tell."[123]

Stepping back from the controversy as a whole, however, and from the way Newman chose to respond to it, one has to say that there is an arresting irony in the fact that Kingsley, of all people, never particularly keen himself on establishing the force of objective truth, religious or otherwise, should have set upon the one man in England who was, *par excellence*, the Servant of Truth. Newman anatomized the misrepresentations to which Truth had been subjected in the nineteenth century with a prophetic force that must always make reading his work a tonic for those in the twenty-first century still contending with the rationalist rejection of Truth that he identified so brilliantly.

> I am speaking of evils, which in their intensity and breadth are peculiar to these times. But I have not yet spoken of the root of all these falsehoods—the root as it ever has been, but hidden; but in this age exposed to view and unblushingly avowed—I mean, that spirit of infidelity itself which I began by referring to as the great evil of our times, though of course when I spoke of the practical force of the objections which we constantly hear and shall hear made to Christianity, I showed it is from this spirit that they gain their plausibility. The elementary proposition of this new philosophy which is now so threatening is this—that in all things we must go by reason, in nothing by faith, that things are known and are to be received so far as they can be proved. Its advocates say, all other knowledge has proof—why should religion be an exception? And the mode of proof is to advance from what we know to what we do not know, from sensible and tangible facts to sound conclusions. The world pursued the way of faith as regards physical nature, and what came of it? Why, that till three hundred years ago they believed, because it was the tradition, that the heavenly bodies were fixed in solid crystalline spheres and moved round the earth in the course of twenty-four hours. Why should not that method which has done so much in physics, avail also as regards that higher knowledge which the world has believed it had gained through revelation? There is no revelation from above. There is no

---

[123] Ian Ker, *John Henry Newman: A Biography*, 548–9.

exercise of faith. Seeing and proving is the only ground for believing. They go on to say, that since proof admits of degrees, a demonstration can hardly be had except in mathematics; we never can have simple knowledge; truths are only probably such. So that faith is a mistake in two ways. First, because it usurps the place of reason, and secondly because it implies an absolute assent to doctrines, and is dogmatic, which absolute assent is irrational. Accordingly you will find, certainly in the future, nay more, even now, that the writers and thinkers of the day do not even believe there is a God. They do not believe either the object—a God personal, a Providence and a moral Governor; and secondly, what they do believe, viz., that there is some first cause or other, they do not believe with faith, absolutely, but as a probability.[124]

Here, it is striking that Newman should have singled out Providence to the men of St Bernard's Seminary as something in which the English were losing faith, for, as we have seen, belief in Providence had been the great hallmark of English religion, the one hallmark to survive the deliberate destruction of so much else of the country's traditional faith in the wake of the Reformation. If belief in Providence were to go, Newman recognized, not only the English but the whole Western world would be in very dark waters indeed.

The controversy that arose between Kingsley and Newman as the result of Kingsley's aspersions might have involved two men of deeply different affiliations—for all of their surprising similarities when it came to Protestantism and Providence—but at heart it was a controversy about faith and reason. Hovering always over the whole controversy was what Newman called "the great *Apostasia*." That the man who worked more unflaggingly than anyone else in the modern era to restore the reasonableness of faith should have been accused of mendacity was typical of the moral, spiritual and intellectual confusion of Newman's age, a confusion bred, in large part, of the sundering of faith and reason.[125]

Ironically, in 1861 Newman told a correspondent: "As to my writing on Faith and Reason, I feel most keenly the vast controversy which is in progress; but I am too old for such an undertaking."[126] Four years later, as the result of the controversy with Kingsley, in writing the fifth section of the *Apologia*, he would

---

[124] John Henry Newman, "The Infidelity of the Future" (2 October 1873), *Faith and Prejudice and Other Unpublished Sermons of Cardinal Newman*, ed. The Birmingham Oratory (London: Sheed and Ward, 1956), 123-4.

[125] Cf. "With the rise of the first universities, theology came more directly into contact with other forms of learning and scientific research. Although they insisted upon the organic link between theology and philosophy, Saint Albert the Great and Saint Thomas were the first to recognize the autonomy which philosophy and the sciences needed if they were to perform well in their respective fields of research. From the late Medieval period onwards, however, the legitimate distinction between the two forms of learning became more and more a fateful separation. As a result of the exaggerated rationalism of certain thinkers, positions grew more radical and there emerged eventually a philosophy which was separate from and absolutely independent of the contents of faith. ... In short, what for Patristic and Medieval thought was in both theory and practice a profound unity, producing knowledge capable of reaching the highest forms of speculation, was destroyed by systems which espoused the cause of rational knowledge sundered from faith and meant to take the place of faith. "*Fides et Ratio*: Encyclical Letter of the Supreme Pontiff John Paul II (September 1998).

[126] Newman to Malcolm Maccoll (20 May 1861), *LD*, xix, 499. See also Ker, *John Henry Newman: A Biography*, 550-1.

return to the subject that he had dealt with so extensively in his *Oxford University Sermons* (1843) with masterly brilliance.

What is striking about the reception of the *Apologia* is that it should have received such a favorable response from John Keble, one of Newman's closest confidants throughout the Oxford Movement, though after his conversion they had had a falling out of nearly twenty years. On 25 April 1864, Newman contacted his old friend to tell him that he needed his help in verifying portions of what would become the *Apologia*, and Keble replied: "I feel as if I ought to write you a long letter, but it must be only a few lines just now, to implore you not to be seriously worried by such trash as Mr Kingsley's ... We (if I may say) want you, dear J. H. N.—all Christendom wants you—to take your stand against the infidelity which seems to be so fast enveloping us all ... I wish, if it please God, we may meet before very long."[127] On 27 April, Newman responded: "Thank you for your affectionate letter. When you see part of my publication, you will wonder how I ever could get myself to write it. Well, I could not, except under some very great stimulus. I do not think I could write it, if I delayed it a month. And yet I have for years wished to write it as a duty. I don't know what people will think of me, or what will be the effect of it—but I wish to tell the truth, and to leave the matter in God's hands."[128] This was to be Newman's own account of his conversion and he was writing it at breakneck speed. Proofs of Newman's genius abound in his life and work but none is quite as astonishing as the fact that he managed to compose the *Apologia* in less than three months. "I am writing from morning to night, hardly having time for my meals," he wrote to Keble. "I write this during dinner time—This will go on for at least 3 weeks more." What is remarkable is that he knew that Keble would not take issue with his account of their pivotal relationship, which shows how confident he was of his own veracity. "I dare say, when it comes to the point, you will find nothing you have to say as to what I send you—but I am unwilling not to have eyes upon it of those who recollect the history. You will be startled at my mode of writing."[129] Keble could scarcely contain his delight with what Newman sent. On 28 June, he wrote: "My very dear Newman I will not wait any longer before thanking you with all my heart for your loving words to me and far too loving of me—If I wait till I write as I could wish, I should never write at all—for indeed dear friend the more and the more intently I look at this self drawn photograph (what a cruel strain it must have been to you) the more I love and admire the Artist—Whatever comes of controversial points, I see no end to the good which the whole Church, we may reasonably hope, may derive from such an example of love and candour under most trying circumstances. You have said things which by the blessing of God will ... materially help us in our sad weary struggle against Unbelief."[130] Newman naturally rejoiced when he received this letter. To have his old Tractarian friend understand the "love and candour" that impelled him to write the *Apologia* was a blessing indeed, a providential blessing after their long estrangement.

[127] John Keble to Newman (25 April 1864), *LD*, xxi, 103.
[128] Newman to John Keble (27 April 1864), *LD*, xxi, 103.
[129] Newman to John Keble (27 April 1864), *LD*, xxi, 103–4.
[130] John Keble to Newman (28 June 1864), *LD*, xxi, 143.

One of the very best accounts of the reception of the *Apologia*, however, is probably the one written by Father Ignatius Ryder:

> Ever since the publication of the "Apologia," Cardinal Newman has been accepted by the general public of his countrymen not merely as a religious writer of consummate genius but as emphatically an honest thinker and writer, one who might be trusted never consciously to overstate his case or undervalue the position of an adversary; who was an Englishman with his heart in the right place—no "Inglese Italianato" as the old phrase went, but one in whose affections his country and his countrymen had never ceased to hold their own. Thus it often happened that persons who could not find a civil word to say of the Pope or of aught to him appertaining, always made an exception in favour of Father Newman, adding, more frequently than not, that of course he did not count, seeing that he was in his present position a sort of *lusus naturæ*, an exception proving the rule. Still, he did count notwithstanding, and for a good deal; and Englishmen have got to think better of Catholics for the sake of Cardinal Newman. His popularity found a safe guard and support in a condition of things which on other grounds we might be inclined to deprecate, his seclusion from public life. He has not been forced by his position to take a decided line on each question as it has arisen; to assume the character of a partizan or the scarcely less odious *rôle* of an officious neutral. It has been open to him almost always to keep silence except when he has elected to break it. He has been allowed to choose the subject and the moment and the manner of his intervention, to calculate nicely his point of incidence, until people learned to recognise that the mere fact of his opening his mouth implied that he had something to say which, whether they agreed with it or not, was well worth listening to.[131]

VI

Far from holding any grudges against Kingsley for casting such wild aspersions, Newman would always be grateful to his blundering antagonist for being "the instrument in the good Providence of God by whom I had the opportunity given me ... of vindicating my character and conduct in my Apologia." Moreover, one can see the forbearance that Newman showed Kingsley throughout their controversy in the response that he made to the Irish novelist and convert Geraldine Penrose Fitzgerald who had encountered the convert's old antagonist before his death in 1875: "As you mention Kingsley, it is pleasant to think that he had no feeling of resentment against me, (as you showed me in your letter after meeting him at Chester) as I am sure I had none against him."[132]

Fitzgerald herself, who had come of an Irish Protestant family in Cork, was actually converted by the *Apologia*—more proof of the providential hand God took in what would become the far-ranging controversy between Newman and Kingsley. In a letter of 9 March 1938 to Francis Brown S. J., Fitzgerald related how she had begun reading the *Apologia* before a disapproving cousin hid it

---

[131] Ignatius Ryder quoted in Ward, *Life of Newman*, ii, 358.
[132] Newman to Geraldine Penrose Fitzgerald (27 January 1875) *LD*, xxvii, 206–7.

away. "[B]ut it had set me off on the road to Popery," she recalled. "I longed to read more, but it was a dear book. I had but little pocket money, ... I pawned a valuable gold and ruby brooch one of my aunts had given me, and bought it ... Finally, I was praying in the chapel he [Newman] built in Stephens Green, when the truth of the Catholic Church came over me like a thunderclap: but I would not join, I was afraid of being turned out of the house." In May of 1869, a friend took her to see T. F. Knox at the Brompton Oratory, who received her into the Church, and became her confessor.[133]

Kingsley, for his part, might have been a rash, hot-tempered, imprudent man but he was not altogether imperceptive. In 1868, he wrote of Newman's "Dream of Gerontius," which Edward Elgar set to such an incomparable music:

> I read the Dream with awe and admiration. However utterly I may differ from the entourage in which Dr. Newman's present creed surrounds the central idea, I must feel that that central idea is as true as it is noble, and it, as I suppose, is this : The longing of the soul to behold the Deity, converted by the mere act of sight, into a self-abasement and self-annihilation so utter, that the soul is ready, even glad, to be hurled back to any depth, to endure any pain, from the moment that it becomes aware of God's actual perfection and its own utter impurity and meanness. How poor my words are in expressing in prose what Dr. N, has expressed in poetry, I am well aware. But I am thankful to any man, who under any parabolic, or even questionably true forms, will teach that to a generation which is losing more and more the sense of reverence, and beginning confessedly to hate excellence for its own sake, as the Greek ostracised Aristides, because he was tired of hearing him called the Just.[134]

If it was providential that Kingsley should defame Newman in order to induce him to write the *Apologia pro Vita Sua*, it was also providential that he should express how much he shared Newman's longing to behold the Just and Holy Judge.

It was only fitting that Dean Stanley should offer the eulogy at Westminster Abbey in 1875 for Kingsley, about whom he spoke with sincere affection, though, in the course of his remarks, he could not resist adverting to the National Church's inability to attract more ordinands to what he styled the "noblest ... and most sacred of all professions." For Stanley, Kingsley

> was sent by Providence as it were, "far off to the Gentiles,"—far off, not to other lands, or other races of mankind, but far off from the usual sphere of minister or priest, to "fresh woods and pastures new," to find fresh worlds of thought, and wild tracts of character, in which he found a response for himself, because he gave a response to them. Witness the unknown friends that from far or near sought the wise guidance of the unknown counsellor, who declared to them the unknown God after whom they were seeking if haply they might find Him. Witness the tears of the rough peasants of Hampshire, as they crowded round the open grave, to look for the last time on the friend of thirty years, with whom

---

[133] *LD*, xxiv, 415.
[134] *Charles Kingsley: His Letters and Memories of his Life*, edited by his wife (London, Henry S. King & Co., 1877), ii, 239.

were mingled the hunter in his red coat and the wild gipsy wanderers, mourning for the face that they should no more see in forest or on heath. Witness the grief which fills the old cathedral town of my own native county and of the native county of his ancestors, beside the sands of his own Dee, for the recollection of the energy with which he gathered the youth of Chester round him for teachings of science and religion. Witness the grief which has overcast this venerable church, which in two short years he had made his own, and in which all felt that he had found a place worthy of himself, and that in him the place had found an occupant worthy to fill it. In these days of rebuke and faintheartedness, when so many gifted spirits shrink from embarking on one of the noblest, because the most sacred of all professions, it ought to be an encouragement to be reminded that this fierce poet and masculine reformer deemed his energies not misspent in the high yet humble vocation of an English clergyman—that, however much at times suspected, avoided, rebuffed, he yet, like others who have gone before him, at last won from his brethren the willing tribute of honour and love, which once had been sturdily refused or grudgingly granted.[135]

Although delivered nearly ten years after Kingsley's controversy with Newman, Stanley's eulogy, for all its praise of the energetic, solicitous clergyman, could not entirely dispel the damage the controversy had done to his reputation. Wilfrid Ward, in a lecture he gave on Newman at Harvard in 1914, had occasion to quote Max Müller on the impact the controversy with Newman had had on his friend's literary fortunes:

Kingsley felt his defeat most deeply; he was like a man that stammered, and could not utter at the right time the right word that was in his mind. What is still more surprising was the sudden collapse of the sale of Kingsley's most popular books. I saw him after he had been with his publishers to make arrangements for the sale of his copyrights. He wanted the money to start his sons, and he had the right to expect a substantial sum. The sum offered him seemed almost an insult, and yet he assured me that he had seen the books of his publishers, and that the sale of his books during the last years did not justify a larger offer. He was miserable about it, as well he might be. He felt it not only the pecuniary loss, but, as he imagined, the loss of that influence which he had gained by years of hard labour.[136]

How to conclude? Kingsley had many of the same convictions as Newman—he loved God, he loved his neighbor, he strove to act in accordance with God's Providence. Indeed, in attacking Newman as provocatively as he did, he served God's Providence. Yet, as an Englishman, a proud, tribal, uncatechized Englishman, he could not bring himself to embrace the Church where such convictions would have found a proper home. He chose to remain within a Broad Church where the one true Fold of the Redeemer was excluded. Nevertheless, by embracing

---

[135] Ibid., 467.
[136] Müller quoted in *Last Lectures by Wilfrid Ward, Being the Lowell Lectures 1914 and Three Lectures Delivered at the Royal Institution, 1915*, edited and introduced by Josephine Ward (London: Longmans, Green & Co., 1918), 119. Ward's explanation for quoting the passage is worth quoting itself: "I quote it as testimony to Newman's power of carrying public opinion with him even in so unpromising a task as the defence of popery in 1864 against a popular writer."

the Athanasian Creed, when so many in the Broad Church were abandoning it, he showed how the Providence he had served did not deserve him. As for Newman, his last words regarding Kingsley confirm the *caritas* with which he dealt with this "furious foolish fellow," as he called him, who might have been mistaken but was not contemptible.[137] After all, he had paid a high price for his folly.[138] "The death of Mr Kingsley, so premature, shocked me," Newman wrote to one of his correspondents. "I never from the first have felt any anger towards him. As I said in the first pages of my Apologia, it is very difficult to be angry with a man one has never seen. A casual reader would think my language denoted anger—but it did not. ... I heard too a few years back from a friend that she chanced to go into Chester Cathedral, and found Mr K. preaching about me kindly though of course with criticisms on me. And it has rejoiced me to observe lately that he was defending the Athanasian Creed, and, as it seemed to me, in his views generally nearing the Catholic view of things." Whether this was true is anyone's guess, though it was good of Newman to give his former assailant the benefit of the doubt. What is indubitably true is that Newman not only forgave but prayed for Charles Kingsley. "I have always hoped that by good luck I might meet him," Newman confessed, "feeling sure there would be no embarrassment on my part, and I said Mass for his soul, as soon as I heard of his death."[139]

---

[137] Newman to R. W. Church (29 April 1864), *LD*, xxi, 100.

[138] Cf. "Newman's reply [to Kingsley's pamphlet] turned Kingsley into a laughing stock for a good part of educated England. From that moment all the lean and hungry men started to put in their swords. In the novel *Hereward the Wake* comes a sentence, written during the autumn of 1864, which moves the reader if he knows the inner torments of the author. 'If a man once fall, or seem to fall, a hundred curs spring up to bark at him, who dared not open their mouths while he was on his feet.'" Owen Chadwick, *The Spirit of the Oxford Movement: Tractarian Essays* (Cambridge: Cambridge University Press, 1990), 124.

[139] Newman to William Henry Cope (13 February 1875), *LD*, xxvii, 219–20.

WILFRID WARD

⁓ 9 ⁓

Wilfrid Ward and the "Wide Kingdom of Spiritual Genius"

> The main outcome of [Newman's] writings is that they convey his own vision of Christianity to the intellect and imagination of his readers, and his own resulting passionate conviction; his principal aim being to form in them the Christian mind and the Christian character—to bind fast to Christianity with numerous and fine tendrils the imagination, the conscience, and the intellect of his disciples; to draw them within the ark of the Christian Church while the deluge of unbelief is being poured throughout the world at large (to use his own chosen metaphor), while the old Christendom is being transformed into a new and non-Christian civilisation.
>
> Wilfrid Ward, "The True Nature of Newman's Genius" (1914)

I

Sheridan Gilley gives an incisive summary of Wilfrid Ward's appraisal of Newman in his entry on the writer in the *Oxford Dictionary of National Biography*: "The biography which Ward eventually completed was almost wholly devoted to Newman's life as a Catholic, his forty-four years as an Anglican being dispatched in one chapter of fifty-two pages. In this respect Ward was writing a Roman Catholic 'Tract for the Times' on the need for orthodoxy to be self-critical, though this preoccupation hardly appears on the smooth surface of the narrative." For Gilley, the Oratorians, who commissioned the long-gestating work, "disliked Ward's stress on the suffering side of Newman's personality," portraying the convert as though he "were 'hyper-sensitive, a *souffre-douleur*' in Abbot Butler's phrase." Nor were they altogether comfortable with the intellectual cast of the work, "which argued, that Newman's Catholicism had dissented strongly from both the liberal Catholicism of Richard Simpson and Sir John Acton and the new ultramontanism of William George Ward and Manning." Instead, Ward sought to "hold the balance between the two schools by combining the critical sense of the one with the orthodoxy of the other." Gilley recognized clearly enough that "This was, at least in part, a backward projection of Ward's own difficult mediating position between modernists and integralists and, in part, his own final resolution of his father's great battle with Newman, in Newman's favour." After many revisions, *The Life of John Henry Cardinal Newman* (2 vols.) appeared in 1912 to critical acclaim.

This is all true. Ward can be seen as the biographer who presented Newman as unduly sensitive and as a kind of referee between ultramontane and liberal Catholics. Yet in engaging so discriminatingly and so faithfully with Newman's wide-ranging work, he showed unusual insight into its depth and judiciousness—indeed, its genius. Moreover, by presenting it in the context of the work of Ultramontane and Liberal Catholics, as well as Protestants, unbelievers and would-be believers, he proved himself to be Newman's best contemporary critic. In this chapter, I shall endeavor to identify Ward's strengths and weaknesses as a critic and biographer without losing sight of the admirable scale of his achievement.

If Ward shared his father's love of opera, he went his own way in intellectual matters. Yet what is perhaps not generally appreciated is that it was his father's influence—not Newman's—that made him initially see that Catholics could gain from paying attention to thinkers outside the Catholic tradition when it came to strengthening and renewing their tradition. Indeed, as he shows in an autobiographical fragment, it was the interest his father took in the work of the positivist Auguste Comte that first impressed upon him the need for Catholics to put their apologetical house in more impregnable order, a revelation which clearly had a profound impact on his son. Too often William George Ward is seen simply as Ultramontanism's most rabid advocate—the fellow who wished to be served a papal bull every morning with his breakfast and morning paper—but as his work and conduct in the Metaphysical Society shows he was highly respected by his non-Catholic contemporaries. "As a quick-witted dialectician," Huxley was convinced, "thoroughly acquainted with all the weak points of his antagonist's case, I have not met Dr. Ward's match."[1]

This readiness on the part of Ward to engage his opponents in the scrimmage between religion and science made an indelible impression on his son. "Our intercourse at the opera led us to talk about other things and even when I was a boy religious philosophy came in," Wilfrid Ward recalled.

> When I began serious philosophical reading at the Catholic University College ... my father's philosophical talks grew more frequent. The question of the foundations of all belief, especially a belief in religion, had a great interest for me quite early in life and this was my father's special subject. In discussing it his curious theological narrowness entirely disappeared. He was most helpful and most real in his thought, and it was wholly candid and without theological preoccupation or bias. He had from his early Oxford days been keenly alive to the sceptical attitude in religion, therefore this fundamental philosophy was a very practical matter to him. But he had also a deep interest in thought for its own sake. He especially loved wide and suggestive speculations and complete theories and was a good deal taken with Auguste Comte's scheme of positive philosophy and positive religion.

---

[1] Thomas Henry Huxley quoted in *The Metaphysical Society (1869–1880): Intellectual Life in Mid-Victorian Society*, ed. Catherine Marshall, Bernard Lightman and Richard England (Oxford: Oxford University Press, 2019), 263.

It seemed to him really a proof of the Catholic Church. Some such complete scheme in my father's eyes responded to a universal need for a religious system as a basis for social and personal life, yet Comte's attempt to establish it while he denied all validity to the transcendental element in religious belief—to establish a theocracy without God as it were—was so unreal as to leave its Catholic rival in possession. But my father did feel a certain justification for Comte's dissatisfaction with the Church in the inadequate fundamental philosophy set forth in many scholastic textbooks. One of his strongest feelings in this connection was that the current proofs of theism and Christianity needed supplementing by the general view of the foundations of belief set forth by Cardinal Newman in the *University Sermons*, and *The Grammar of Assent*.[2]

Here, we can see what would become Wilfrid Ward's *raison d'être*, his vocation. He would show his Catholic and non-Catholic contemporaries how vital it was to establish a *modus vivendi* between Catholic tradition and modern thought not only for the good of the Church but for modern civilization, and he would justify this charge by pointing to how St. Thomas Aquinas had reconciled faith and reason in the thirteenth century by reconciling Catholic doctrine with the work of Aristotle.

Those who were disposed to believe in the Christian theology, and yet were troubled by the antagonism between what they regarded as the genius and learning of the day, and the old theological writings which took no account of them, found rest in this reconciliation of the truths of philosophy and faith by one who united the reverent temper of a Saint with a mind of consummate ability. And when the generation incurably habituated to rationalistic discussion had passed away, the orderly structure of theological science provided by Aquinas prevailed so completely, that within fifty years of his death *il buon fra Tommaso* towers with almost the authority of an inspired writer over the epoch of Dante, as we plainly see in the *Divina Commedia* itself.

For Ward, the analogy between what Saint Thomas faced in the thirteenth century and what Newman and his contemporaries faced in the nineteenth century—and, indeed, what Ward faced in the twentieth century—was compelling. "This is the lesson which appears to me to be at the present hour the more universally valuable, just because it speaks to those who are most alive to the perverse elements of the characteristic thought of our own time and to its excesses," Ward wrote.

Let it be granted that some of the extremely speculative conclusions put forth by exponents of the higher criticism are as extravagant as the medieval belief that the syllogism could discover the secrets of nature, that they are sometimes as unreliable from their extreme fancifulness as the replies to the most insoluble problems made by those medieval schoolmen whose excessive subtlety Leo XIII gently reproved. Yet to proscribe the really scientific use of that critical method which has hold of all minds which think on such subjects, would be as ineffectual

---

[2] Ward quoted in Maisie Ward, *The Wilfrid Wards and the Transition*, 2 vols (London: Sheed & Ward, 1934, 1937), i, 42–3.

now as the bonfires fed by living rationalists were in the Paris of 1209. On the other hand, a strenuous effort to deal with modern criticism, to keep it within its reasonable limits, to restrain by its own principles a method which professes to be cautious and experimental, but which is constantly proving itself in the highest degree theoretical, speculative and adventurous, is just the medicine which will remedy the ills of the hour after the manner of Albertus and Thomas.[3]

Ward would also justify his charge by arguing that it was one that Newman not only understood but undertook himself throughout the nineteenth century, whether he was confronting the errors of the "march of mind," the Anglo-Catholic imposture, rationalism of various sorts, or what he called the "great *apostasia*" in the later years of the century. In tackling all of these matters, Newman willy-nilly found himself, as Sheridan Gilley realized, "crushed between W. G. Ward's friends and John Acton's Liberal Catholics, the former intolerant of a proper freedom of thought, the latter of a proper authority."[4] Moreover, for Ward, Newman "was sure that posterity would see the necessity of conscientious fidelity to historical and scientific fact with a view to preserving the influence of Christianity among the educated classes in the age to come."[5] For corroboration of his point, Ward could have quoted from the *Apologia*, in which Newman reminds his readers: "There never was a time when the intellect of the educated class was more active, or rather more restless, than in the middle ages."[6] Engaging intellectual challenges to Catholic tradition was itself a Catholic tradition. In an essay entitled "St. Thomas Aquinas and Mediaeval Thought," Ward wrote:

> Cardinal Newman, in speaking of the scholastic theology which emerged from the new apologetic of St. Thomas, and from his attempt to reconcile the thought of his day with the essence of Christian tradition, points out that it "involved a creative act of the intellect." In the earlier period, popularly known as the Dark Ages, theology had been, he reminds us, mainly in the hands of devout Benedictine monks, whose "intellect attempted no comprehension of this multiform world." It had consisted in "a loving study and exposition of Holy Scripture according to the teaching of the Fathers, who had studied and expounded it before them. It was a loyal adherence to the teaching of the past, a faithful inculcation of it, an anxious transmission of it to the next generation." Theology was receptive, not creative. The period in question was not marked by that intellectual activity which makes on the one hand brilliant heresiarchs, on the other great constructive theologians. But if we go back earlier again to the patristic period, we have once more a creative movement of thought. "Origen, Tertullian, Athanasius, Chrysostom, Augustine, Jerome, Leo," writes Cardinal Newman in his *Historical Sketches*, "are authors of powerful original minds, and engaged in the production of original works." Yet earlier we have another period of simple receptivity. The earlier sub-apostolic days had been in this respect like the later epoch of the

---

[3] Wilfrid Ward, *Men and Matters* (London: Longmans, Green & Co., 1914), 345–6.
[4] Sheridan Gilley, "An Intellectual Discipleship: Newman and the Making of Wilfrid Ward," *Louvain Studies*, 15 (1990), 340.
[5] Ward, *Life of Newman*, ii, 439. Cf. *The Saturday Review* (10 February 1912), 178.
[6] *Apo.*, 266–7.

monks. Theology had meant the anxious and reverent transmission of what had been received—of the teaching of the Apostles. In the modern sense, indeed, theology did not exist. It did not profess to be a science. The Christian brotherhood belonged mainly to the uncultured classes and was one in mind. The first Pontiff had been a fisherman, and vivid faith rather than learning or intellectual subtlety characterized the community. Each man received in unquestioning simplicity what he was taught. Creative and constructive Christian thought was first demanded when this simple, unquestioning, unanalytical attitude of mind became impossible, because the character of the community changed. When thinkers and philosophers became Christians, and attempted, each in his own way, the intellectual explication of the faith, sects and heresies arose of necessity, and called in response for the work of the creative theologians. These men dealt with the philosophical theories broached by various thinkers, and rejected or assimilated them as the essential character of the Christian revelation demanded.[7]

What particularly confirmed the necessity of such a discriminating charge in Ward's own day was the emergence of the Modernist crisis, which is usually dated between Pope Leo XIII's encyclical *Providentissimus Deus* (1893) and Pope Pius X's encyclical *Pascendi Dominici Gregis* (1907), a crisis which culminated in what Pius called "a synthesis of all the heresies." Readers of Ward's biography of Newman can see the care he took to ensure that there should be no mention of the crisis, the biographer's Oratorian commissioners being averse to having their founder even rumored to have been tarred with any Modernist brush. However, in both the biography and the lectures he gave at Harvard on Newman after the publication of the biography, Ward reaffirms how brilliantly cognizant Newman was of the Church's need to confront modern challenges to the Faith. If Newman's greatness can only be adequately measured by showing him in his immediate historical setting in order to show how he transcends that setting, nothing accomplishes this better than showing how Newman met these challenges throughout his work. What makes Wilfrid Ward so apt a witness to these festivities is that he had been preoccupied with what one might call proto-Modernism from the very start of his writing career. This is doubtless why he was precipitate enough to imagine that *Pascendi* might have been indirectly critical of Newman. As he wrote to the Duke of Norfolk shortly after the publication of the encyclical: "I don't believe the Pope *meant* to condemn Newman. But he has done so beyond all doubt so far as the words of the Encyclical go—not only on development but on so much else."[8] Of course, here, the proprietorial interest that Ward took in his subject warped his judgment, though, as we shall see, once the Modernist crisis arose, he was not alone in worrying that the crisis might taint Newman's reputation.

At the same time, we have to appreciate that, early on in their correspondence, Newman praised Ward for his astute understanding of the scepticism that animated so much late-Victorian rationalism among the educated classes, a scepticism which found something of its apotheosis in Modernism. "Thank you for your letter which was very acceptable to me," Newman wrote to the young author.

---

[7] Ward, *Men and Matters*, 347–8.
[8] Wilfred Ward Papers VI/24 (36), University of St Andrews Libraries and Museums.

I have read your article ["The Clothes of Religion," which appeared in the *National Review* (June, 1884)] with great interest and like it much—but my brain works so slowly and my fingers are so stiff, that writing is a difficulty and a trial to me.

I should say that the theories of Mr Spencer and Mr Harrison have that hearing and acceptance from the public, as to need an answer, and, that your answer to them is unanswerable, but in saying this, I am not paying you so great a compliment as it appears to be at first sight; for I say so from the impatience I feel at able men daring to put out for our acceptance theories so hollow and absurd. I do not know how to believe that they are in earnest, or that they preach the Unknowable and Humanity except as stop gaps, while they are in suspence and on the look out for the new objects of worship which Sir James Stephen thinks unnecessary as well as impossible.

I then am too impatient to refute carefully such theorists; if it was to be done, it required to be done with both good humour and humour, as you have done it. You have been especially happy in your use of Mr Pickwick; but this is only one specimen of what is so excellent in your article.[9]

It is striking that Newman should have had so high an opinion of Ward's early essays because the essays, early and late, are indispensable supplements to his biographies, especially those on Newman. "In the [Harvard] lectures on Cardinal Newman he allowed himself as a lecturer the space and the abandon which he had sternly denied himself as a biographer," his wife Josephine wrote.

> In them he claims for his master a greater position in the world of thinkers than had been habitually conceded by the Cardinal's contemporaries. In this final apology and justification Wilfrid Ward is still painting the picture of a great personality. The subject gives him a last opportunity of using to the full his powers of psychological insight. He is no longer occupied with portraiture in narrative form, he is not presenting the long story of nearly ninety years of a human life, human suffering, heroism, and frailty. He is in a more purely intellectual sphere, the wide kingdom of a spiritual genius. Without the intimate knowledge of Newman gained in seven years' toil as a biographer, he could not have acquired the freedom of touch he shows in these lectures.[10]

One of the reasons why Ward would become so perceptive a critic of Newman is that, as his wife noted, he was always most comfortable with men and women of his father's generation. Accordingly, early on in his life, he formed friendly relations with Gilbert Keith Chesterton and Alfred Lord Tennyson. "I believe it was a deep satisfaction to the author of 'In Memoriam,'" she says, "that a 'papist' boy, son of an Ultramontane of the deepest dye, studied and learnt and made his own the poet's thoughts on the philosophy of religion. It was one of the earliest and most unconscious signs of a vocation—he was already beginning to be, as Dr. Sadler wrote of him after his death, a 'liaison officer' between the historic Church and religious thinkers outside of it. He loved to see similarities,

---

[9] Newman to Wilfrid Ward (3 April 1884), *LD*, xxx, 389.
[10] Ward, *Last Lectures*, vii–viii.

to draw cognate elements together, to synthesise."[11] Perhaps the most definitive expression of the Ultramontane position, Pius IX's *Syllabus of Errors* (1868) had made such an officer necessary, especially when the pope, disenchanted with liberalism after the assassination of the prime minister of the Papal States, Count Pellegrino Rossi, declared that it was erroneous to imagine that "The Roman Pontiff should and can reconcile and harmonise himself with progress, with liberalism, and with recent civilization." Ward would make it his business to qualify Pio Nono's categorical rejection of such things by seeking to reconcile the Church and her modern critics in circumstances in which the reception of the *Syllabus* among liberal intellectuals could not have been more hostile, though Ward, like Newman, would always recognize that sensible, as opposed to the extreme Ultramontanism of which his father was fond, was a useful antidote to anti-Catholic liberalism, one of the most virulent manifestations of which was Modernism. Yet before delving into the work, we need to revisit Ward's life and his pointedly sympathetic approach to criticism.

II

Born on 2 June 1856, Wilfrid Philip Ward was the sixth surviving child and second son of the Catholic convert and apologist William George Ward (1812–82) and his wife Frances, née Wingfield (1816–98), the daughter of an Anglican clergyman, John Wingfield (1760–1825). Ward grew up in Old Hall House, one of Pugin's neo-Gothic buildings, set in the grounds of St. Edmund's, Ware, "where English Catholics had been educated from the reign of Elizabeth onwards," as Ward himself noted in an autobiographical fragment[12] and where his father was a lecturer. His upbringing was exuberantly Catholic. Three of his sisters became nuns and his younger brother, Bernard Nicholas Ward (1857–1920) became bishop of Brentwood and wrote a splendid history of Catholicism 1781–1850. Ward was named after St. Wilfrid (633–709), the indefatigable bishop, whose church building, patronage of the arts and founding of monasteries made him one of the most dynamic figures of the early English Church. St. Wilfrid was also the patron of the Wilfridians, Frederick Faber's order of priests. Augusta Marie Minna Catherine (1821–86), younger daughter of Admiral Sir Edmund Lyons, the ambassador at Athens, and, later, duchess of Norfolk, the wife of the fourteenth duke,[13] was his godmother. In addition to the society of the Catholic aristocracy, Ward moved as a young man in the company of his father's highly placed prelatical friends, including the Archbishops of Westminster Nicholas

---

[11] Ward, *Last Lectures*, x.
[12] Ward quoted in Ward, *The Wilfrid Wards and the Transition*, i, 17.
[13] See *ODNB* for entry on Henry Granville Fitzalan-Howard, fourteenth duke of Norfolk (1815–60): "Norfolk's faith had two wellsprings. One was the early intimacy with Montalembert, from whom he derived an acute sense of Europe's Catholic past. The vanished simplicity of master and servant holding a common faith greatly appealed to him. In later years greater influence was exerted by John Henry Newman and Frederick Faber. Faber—who acted as his confessor—considered him a near saint. With his wife he devoted much of his time and wealth to charity on a vast scale. 'There is not a form of want', Cardinal Wiseman noted, 'or a peculiar application of alms which has not received his relief or co-operation' (*The Times*, 4 Dec 1860). Diffident, ascetic, indifferent to fashionable opinion, he achieved much as a philanthropist, less as a politician."

Wiseman, Henry Edward Manning and Herbert Vaughan. He also imbibed the work of Newman. After attending Downside Abbey, he took his BA from the University of London, his father refusing to allow him to study at Oxford on religious grounds, an embargo which his son would always lament. After university, he attended the English College in Rome and Ushaw College in County Durham, only to find that he had no vocation for the priesthood, though he prized the time he spent at the seminaries, especially Ushaw, where, as Maisie Ward noted, "he saw what specially appealed to him—the putting into practice of the Church's ideals in typically English fashion. For Ushaw is *par excellence* the heir of the old English Catholic tradition, the lineal descendant of Douai, the college of Challoner, the college of Lingard and of Wiseman. All his life my father loved Ushaw."[14] Subsequently, Ward enrolled in the Inner Temple, London in preparation of becoming a barrister, a career at which he might well have excelled, but left after finding the law uncongenial as well. Thenceforward, after the sale of the family living, he set up as an independent scholar, edited the *Dublin Review*, as his father had before him, and wrote a number of exceptional books, including his two-part biography of his father, *William George Ward and the Oxford Movement* (1889) and *William George Ward and the Catholic Revival* (1893), a number of collections of essays, the first biography of Newman with any scholarly pretensions, and biographies of Wiseman, Vaughan and Aubrey de Vere. Apropos *The Life of Cardinal Wiseman* (2 vols., 1897), Sheridan Gilley wrote justly that "This careful documentary history combined a lively critical narrative of high religious politics with a warm portrait of the most exuberant of the great English ecclesiastics of his generation. It also led to Ward's most ambitious undertaking, a life of his intellectual patron, Cardinal Newman."[15] Worn out by the labor and anxiety exacted by the Newman biography, Ward died in London in 1916, after two highly successful lecture tours of America.

To appreciate the degree to which Ward became saturated in the life and work of Newman from his earliest youth one has to appreciate the great regard that Ward Senior had for the convert, which his son chronicles so movingly. "Dinner can scarcely pass," Wilfrid recalled, "without some reference to Oxford and Newman—a subject which arouses deep feeling. 'Was there ever anything in the world like Newman's influence on us?'" he recalls his father asking, "for the hundredth time."[16] Testimonials to this regard abound but Dean Church's is probably one of the best. "Mr. W. G. Ward had learned the interest of earnest religion from Dr. Arnold, in part through his close friend Arthur Stanley," Church wrote in his history of the Oxford Movement.

> But if there was ever any tendency in him to combine with the peculiar elements of the Rugby School, it was interrupted in its *nascent* state, as chemists speak, by the intervention of a still more potent affinity, the personality of Mr. Newman. Mr. Ward had developed in the Oxford Union, and in a wide social circle of the most rising men of the time—including Tait, Cardwell, Lowe, Roundell Palmer—a

---

[14] Ward, *The Wilfrid Wards and the Transition*, ii, 46.
[15] ODNB.
[16] Wilfred Ward, *William George Ward and the Catholic Revival* (London: Macmillan & Co., 1893), 386.

very unusual dialectical skill and power of argumentative statement: qualities which seemed to point to the House of Commons. But Mr. Newman's ideas gave him material, not only for argument but for thought. The lectures and sermons at St. Mary's subdued and led him captive. The impression produced on him was expressed in the formula that primitive Christianity might have been corrupted into Popery, but that Protestantism never could. For a moment he hung in the wind. He might have been one of the earliest of Broad Churchmen. He might have been a Utilitarian and Necessitarian follower of Mr. J. S. Mill. But moral influences of a higher kind prevailed. And he became, in the most thoroughgoing yet independent fashion, a disciple of Mr. Newman. He brought to his new side a fresh power of controversial writing; but his chief influence was a social one, from his bright and attractive conversation, his bold and startling candour, his frank, not to say reckless, fearlessness of consequences, his unrivalled skill in logical fence, his unfailing good-humour and love of fun, in which his personal clumsiness set off the vivacity and nimbleness of his joyous moods. "He was," says Mr. Mozley, "a great musical critic, knew all the operas, and was an admirable buffo singer."—No one could doubt that, having started, Mr. Ward would go far and probably go fast.[17]

A gregarious, energetic, guileless man, Wilfrid Ward made many friends throughout his life, including Friedrich von Hügel, Alfred Lord Tennyson, Thomas Henry Huxley, Henry Sidgwick, and Frederic Myers—all former members of his father's Metaphysical Society. In tandem with A. J. Balfour, Charles Gore, and Edward Talbot, Ward founded his own metaphysical club, the Synthetic Society in 1896, with a few former surviving members of the older club, including James Martineau, Richard Holt Hutton, Sidgwick, Myers as well as some new members such as Lord Hugh Cecil, George Wyndham, and A. V. Dicey. Ranging from nonconformists and Anglicans to agnostics and Catholics, the club took up scientific and religious issues similar to those taken up by the Metaphysical Society, though the fact that it included George Tyrrell and von Hügel embroiled Ward in what became the Modernist controversy.

In 1887, Ward married Josephine Mary (1864–1932), the second daughter of James Robert Hope-Scott of Abbotsford (1812–73), one of Newman's most trusted counselors, and his second wife, Victoria Howard (1840–70), daughter of the fourteenth duke of Norfolk. As a consequence of his marriage, Ward befriended the fifteenth duke of Norfolk, whom he advised on ecclesiastical matters, the admission of Catholics to Oxford, the validity of Anglican orders, and the Modernist controversy.[18] The Wards had five children, one of whom, Wilfrid Hope Ward (1890–1902), died young; the eldest, Mary Josephine Ward (1889–1975), known as "Maisie," founded the publishing house of Sheed & Ward with her husband, Frank Sheed, the brilliant apologist, whom she met through the Catholic Evidence Guild after serving as a nurse's aide in medical hospitals during the Great War. After marrying, Maisie became a leading figure of Catholic life between the wars in both England and America, writing an entertaining

---

[17] Church, *Oxford Movement*, 339–40.
[18] ODNB.

biography of Chesterton, as well as lively books about Newman and her parents. Of the latter, she observes in *The Wilfrid Wards and the Transition* (1934–7): "If Wilfrid and Josephine Ward were united in their absorption in certain ideas they were no less so in their intense interest in character. To both of them it seemed of the first importance to observe how ideas work in the individual mind, and again how character shapes life and destiny. The chosen medium of one was biography, of the other fiction; and both of these demand—in very different ways—a study of character, its interpretation, even its creation."[19] Proof of this can be seen in Ward's appreciation of Newman's musings on the English character in his epistolary review of the country's misadventures in the Crimea. "Besides the types produced by various callings, Newman's psychology notes the types produced by various nationalities," Ward wrote.

> He was impressed by the conspicuous practical success of Englishmen, and yet their inability to theorise or systematise. The Crimean War was the occasion of his observations. It found Englishmen wholly unprepared—so little was this unimaginative race impelled to forecast the future or prepare for its eventualities systematically. Yet when Englishmen were actually in the field of war, and face to face with its practical necessities, their efficiency was amazing. It was the individual Englishman in action who did great deeds. The Government which represented the department of systematic planning and arrangement was again and again at fault. This was conspicuous in the story of the Empire. Our Colonies began for the most part in private enterprises. The United States are the outcome of the endeavours of individual Englishmen. Even our great Indian Empire was the outcome of the labours of the men who united and formed the East India Company. The turning-point was the unofficial military exertion of Clive. Newman's psychological analysis of our national character in this respect, at this moment offers an interesting contrast to the German who does all by the medium of planned organisation under official authority. He leads off with Clive's work:[20]
>
>> Suddenly a youth, the castaway of his family, half-clerk, half-soldier, puts himself at the head of a few troops, defends posts, gains battles, and ends in founding a mighty empire over the graves of Mahmood and Aurungzebe. It is the deed of one man; and so, wherever we go all over the earth, it is the solitary Briton, the London agent, or the *Milordos*, who is walking restlessly about, abusing the natives, and raising a colossus, or setting the Thames on fire, in the East or the West. He is on the top of the Andes, or in a diving-bell in the Pacific, or taking notes at Timbuctoo, or grubbing at the Pyramids, or scouring over the Pampas, or acting as prime minister to the King of Dahomey, or smoking the pipe of friendship with the Red

---

[19] Ward, *The Wilfrid Wards and the Transition*, i, 232. See also Dana Greene's entry on Maisie Ward in *ODNB*.

[20] Robert Clive (1725–74), English solider and colonial administrator, raised to the Irish peerage as Clive of Plassey in 1762. As governor and commander-in-chief of Bengal, he rooted out corruption, restored military order, and was instrumental in establishing British rule over India. Nevertheless, Parliament charged him with mishandling the affairs of the East India Company and although vindicated, he despaired over the public abuse he suffered and took his own life.

> Indians, or hutting at the Pole. No one can say beforehand what will come of these various specimens of the independent, self-governing, self-reliant Englishman. Sometimes failure, sometimes openings for trade, scientific discoveries, or political aggrandisements. His country and his government have the gain; but it is he who is the instrument of it, and not political organisation, centralisation, systematic plans, authoritative acts. The polity of England is what it was before,—the Government weak, the Nation strong,—strong in the strength of its multitudinous enterprise, which gives to its Government a position in the world, which that Government could not claim for itself by any prowess or device of its own.[21]

Then, again, Ward calls his readers' attention to the character of Bateman in *Loss and Gain* (1848) as an example of Newman's delight in character.

> They saw before them a tall, upright man, whom Sheffield had no difficulty in recognising as a bachelor of Nun's Hall, and a bore at least of the second magnitude. He was in cap and gown, but went on his way, as if intending, in that extraordinary guise, to take a country walk. He took the path which they were going themselves, and they tried to keep behind him; but they walked too briskly, and he too leisurely, to allow of that. It is very difficult duly to delineate a bore in a narrative, for the very reason that he is a bore. A tale must aim at condensation, but a bore acts in solution. It is only on the long-run that he is ascertained. Then, indeed, he is felt; he is oppressive; like the sirocco which the native detects at once, while a foreigner is often at fault. *Tenet, occiditque*. Did you hear him make but one speech, perhaps you would say he was a pleasant, well-informed man; but when he never comes to an end, or has one and the same prose every time you meet him, or keeps you standing till you are fit to sink, or holds you fast when you wish to keep an engagement, or hinders you listening to important conversation,—then there is no mistake, the truth bursts on you, *apparent dirae facies*, you are in the clutches of a bore.[22]

Yet more proof of how the Ward marriage delighted in character can be seen in Josephine's reading of the artist in Charles Dickens, about whom she wrote: "The child who had been over-stimulated in the nursery, escaped the drill of the boys' school, had nothing to crush his originality, nothing to conquer the awful nervous terrors of his age, nothing to make him learn the ordinary worldliness of the ordinary boys' school. The streets of London by night or day were his preparatory school, and after he had learnt his huge lesson by heart, after his imagination had been moulded in an indelible form, he went to learn enough of books and grammar, and what little more teachers far more ignorant of life than himself could teach him, so that he might be able to express the fiery vision in language that we all may read. But it was that first period, that first terrible

---

[21] Ward, *Last Lectures*, 133–4. The quotation from Newman is from "Who's to Blame?" in *DA*, 337–8.
[22] *LG*, 11–12. In his critical edition of *Loss and Gain*, Sheridan Gilley translates and identifies these Latin tags thus: *Tenet, occiditque*: "he holds on and kills," like a leech. Horace, *Ars Poetica*, 475. *apparent dirae facies*: "dreadful apparitions make themselves known." Virgil, *Aeneid*, book II, line 622. Ward quotes the passage in *Last Lectures*, 111–12.

development, that produced the great Dickens characters, the great Dickens horrors, the great Dickens knowledge of how the selfishness and cruelty and mercy and love of men do actually fulfil themselves in life."[23] Kathleen Tillotson, the great Dickens scholar, would have agreed.

Josephine, who would become not only her husband's trusted confidante but an acclaimed novelist, is one of our best sources of knowledge for Ward's life and character.[24] She certainly understood how important the relationship between father and son was in Ward's makeup. "His devotion to his father was one of the strongest influences in his life," Josephine wrote; "he delighted in his society and in his keen sense of humour and of the drama of life. In their tastes, in love of literature, the theatre, and above all the opera, they were drawn very close together. But as a guide in practical matters for a young man he could never believe in his father's judgment."[25] The son of William Ward (1787–1849), a Director of the Bank of England and the proprietor of Lord's cricket ground, William George Ward inherited a fortune on the Isle of Wight from a childless uncle and only agreed to teach moral theology at St Edmund's Hall, Ware at the insistence of Nicholas Wiseman, after being given a doctorate of philosophy by Pope IX. (The men of the nineteenth century were not in thrall to the credentialism that stultifies learning in the twenty-first century.) Being independently wealthy, Ward's father could not understand why his son should be anxious to have a career.[26] For Josephine, "Once it was clear that Wilfrid had no vocation to the priesthood, it was very difficult to make his father enter into the question of what he was to do. He expected a life of the highest ideals, but he did not see the danger of too much freedom and leisure. He was, on the other hand, in 1882 intensely interested in Wilfrid's first attempt as author, and exclaimed after reading 'The Wish to Believe,' with his usual vehemence: 'I prophesy an immense success for it.'"[27] In the end, Wilfrid followed his father in becoming a gentleman scholar, though it will always be interesting to imagine what he might have done if he had taken Bishop Vaughan's advice, who told the unsettled young man: "Go to America. There are plenty of nice Catholic girls over there. Find one with plenty of wool on her back. They like to marry Englishmen. Sing

[23] Josephine Ward quoted in Ward, *The Wilfrid Wards and the Transition*, i (London: Sheed & Ward, 1934), 233–4.
[24] See Julia Meszaros's critical edition of Josephine Ward, *One Poor Scruple* (Washington: Catholic University Press, 2023).
[25] Ward, *Last Lectures*, xii.
[26] Upon learning that "Ideal" Ward had come into a fortune, Newman wrote to him with characteristic suavity: "If there is one who can bear wealth, it is you." Newman quoted in Ward, *William George Ward and the Catholic Revival*, 10. See JHN to Ward (30 September 1849), LD, xii, 265.
[27] Ward, *Last Lectures*, xii. Stripped of his Oxford degrees after the publication of his Romanizing book *The Ideal of a Christian Church Considered in Comparison with Existing Practice* (1844), "Ideal Ward," as Wilfrid's father was known, was astounded when contemporaries ridiculed him for what they regarded as the ludicrous hypocrisy of his marrying. "How anyone can imagine that I have ever professed any vocation to a high and ascetical life, I am utterly at a loss to conceive," he told the *Times* on 3 March 1845. Yet his candor on this score was of a piece with his candor in everything else. For Tennyson, Ward was "the most truthful man I ever knew ... He was grotesquely truthful." After Ward's death, the Laureate composed a lovely little poem in Ward's honor, the last lines of which are "How subtle at tierce and quart of mind with mind/How loyal in the following of the Lord." See Sheridan Gilley's entry on W. G. Ward in the *ODNB*.

to her and she will marry you soon enough. Then you can come back here and go into Parliament or do anything else that you like. The first thing is to have enough money to make you independent."[28]

Josephine also astutely appreciated the influence that the Ward family had on her husband. "The early education of the family was very like that of other families who were under the influence of Father Faber and the Oxford converts of 1845," she remarked in her introduction to her husband's *Last Lectures* (1918).

> My own mother and her brothers and sisters were educated in the same idealistic atmosphere. The world was most carefully excluded from the domestic life, and there was an intense interest in religious practices. All this other-worldliness was no doubt intensified by the special characteristics of "Ideal Ward" [William George Ward], who always carried logic into action. But in these homes, narrowly bounded as they were, with no doubt too many devotional practices, there was a peculiar sunshine, a radiant life and happiness. In those days the upbringing of children was very unlike what it is now, but with the Howards or the Wards there was nothing of the Puritan severity towards children pictured in such a book as "Father and Son."[29]

Then, as now, the outside world did not know what to make of the joy the Catholic religion instilled in families faithful to her doctrines, teachings and sacraments, and the wit in Mrs. Ward could not but delight in this, at times, comical chasm.[30] "In *Villette*," she noted, "Charlotte Bronte, after her first visit to a Catholic country, describes the methods of the Roman Church towards children as an artful system whereby they are kept healthy and happy" so as "not to think for themselves!"[31] Yet Mrs. Ward also shows that it was precisely the faithful Catholic upbringing that she and her husband and many of their English Catholic contemporaries were given by their faithful parents that enabled them to enter into the unity of the Catholic faith that meant so much to Newman. "All of these early habits and enthusiasms stamped indelibly on us the main ideals of a Catholic," she quotes from a reminiscence of childhood that her husband left behind.

> And this was undoubtedly a personal possession of great value. Even apart from its importance from a Catholic standpoint it helped immensely towards unity of view and—strange as some may think it—it eventually told in my own case for large-mindedness. Anxiety about the fundamentals of faith leads some persons to be nervous of relinquishing any beliefs hitherto entertained—lest it

---

[28] Ward, *The Wilfrid Wards and the Transition*, i, 51.
[29] Ward, *Last Lectures*, ix.
[30] Elsewhere, Josephine notes of her husband: "He had great enjoyment of fun with children, but he also delighted in the society of young men. With his own sons as with his daughters he was in the closest sympathy conceivable, but on his relations with his children I will not dwell, as I do not feel equal to speaking here of the happiness of our family life. There is an old prayer in the Breviary—I do not know if it is in the Anglican Prayer Book—which speaks of the 'trials and aspirations of young men.' The aspirations of an undergraduate full of life and promise always attracted Wilfrid, and he was especially pleased when he knew that they enjoyed his society. This love of his sons' contemporaries added to the sorrows of the great war. In his last hours he used to sigh over the losses in this 'beautiful generation.'" Ward, *Last Lectures*, xlvii.
[31] Ibid., ix.

may prove the first step towards a more general denial. When one has no doubt that in fundamentals one is right and secure, one shrinks the less from complete candour. One does not tremble lest to face a new fact may mean to dissolve one's faith. This feeling of perfect security was engendered by the nature of our life as children. Thus in a sense the very narrowness of my early training told for breadth in the long run—because the narrowness meant the exclusiveness which gives depth and stability to belief.[32]

The gloss Mrs. Ward gives of these observations confirm one's sense of the reliability of her insights into her husband, whose whole life can be seen to have been dedicated to a defense of the "depth and stability of belief," especially as these were exhibited in the work of Newman. "This brief account of his freedom of intellectual action and sympathy written by himself very near the end explains him in a singularly true way," she writes.

> His faith was the simplest and clearest thing possible. The light that shone so visibly in his last weeks had been with him ever since that experience of his youth. It was for this reason that he could be at once so loyal and so bold. He could be sympathetic with every honest form of thought, and he made men more honest with themselves by his belief in their intellectual integrity. "To be with your husband is to live in the palace of truth," Father Waggett once said to me.[33]

That Josephine reveled in her husband's deep faith could hardly have been otherwise for the daughter of James Robert Hope-Scott, about whom Newman spoke with such unearthly eloquence. "Judging as we do from the event," Newman said of the conversion of Josephine's brilliant, munificent, saintly papa, "we thankfully recognize in him an elect soul, for whom, in the decrees of Omnipotent Love, a seat in heaven has been prepared from all eternity,—whose name is engraven on the palms of those Hands which were graciously pierced for his salvation."[34] Since Wilfrid, too, had been the child of a convert, a most passionate convert, he could not have been better matched than with the child of the convert in Hope-Scott.

No one captured the admirable essence of Josephine Ward better than her friend Hilaire Belloc, who wrote in a letter to Reginald Balfour in 1932: "On the grave news of the moment, graver to you and me: I have not written to you because I myself heard it very late; only just in time to attend the Requiem. It is the death of Joe Ward. You will have felt it keenly, for I know how fond you were of her and she of you, and I felt it profoundly. I have known her for 50 mortal years, ever since I was a schoolboy ... Lately, I had come to see a great deal more of her. She received me kindly, which is more than all the old Catholics do. She had an excellently active and intelligent mind, based on a fundamental humility.

---

[32] Ibid., xiv.
[33] Ibid. Philip Napier Waggett SSJE (1862–1939) was an Anglican priest with the Cowley Fathers, scholar, and military chaplain. By all accounts, Waggett was a wonderful conversationalist, as well as a "bridgebuilder between traditions." See *ODNB*. In his biography of Chesterton, Ian Ker says that Waggett may have been GKC's confessor. Ian Ker, *G. K. Chesterton: A Biography* (Oxford: Oxford University Press, 2011), 279.
[34] OS, 276.

That was really her great virtue. ... I have come to that stage in life in which the death of such few friends as remain must be expected, but it is in a way more grievous than in earlier life, both because the diminishing number becomes so small and because the imagination is less vivid. On the other hand, with age philosophy grows firmer, and one is more fixedly certain that all the trouble is for us, *nos qui vivemus*, and all the benefits for the dead. I have much more than I used to have the feeling that they have become alive, and we are only half alive. This is particularly true with the death of the exceptionally good; and she was exceptionally good."[35] That Josephine entirely reciprocated Belloc's fondness is clear from something she said of a visit she and her son made to Paris after Belloc had published his little book about the city, *Paris* (1900), which Speaight regarded as a "little masterpiece of historical topography." Josephine and her son Leo looked upon the visit "as one of the great experiences of their lives to have dined with Belloc in a small Paris restaurant (Aux Vendages de Bourgoyne) and then to have walked with him the streets of that glorious city while he discoursed of its past."[36] Josephine always saw the point of how the French do civilization. After all, she had spent summers as a child with her family in Hyères, as her father's biographer vividly describes. "From 1859," Robert Ornsby writes, "it was thought necessary that the surviving child of his first marriage should spend every winter in a warm climate. Hyères, in the south of France, was selected for this purpose, which led to Mr. Hope-Scott's purchasing a property there, the Villa Madoña, on a beautiful spot near the Boulevard d'Orient. Here he spent several winters with his family, in the years 1863–70. He added to the property very gradually, bit by bit; first a vineyard, and then an oliveyard, as opportunities offered, and indulged over it the same passion for improvement which he had displayed at Abbotsford ... He took the most practical interest in all the culture that makes up a Provençal farm, the wine, the oil, the almonds, the figs, not forgetting the fowls and the rabbits. He laid out the ground and made a road, set a plantation of pines, and adorned the bank of his boulevard with aloes and yuccas and eucalyptus—in short, astonished his French neighbours by his perfection of taste and regardlessness of expense."[37] That Josephine had been thus cradled in French country living would naturally have endeared her to the Francophile in Belloc.

III

Confirming the sympathy that would become a hallmark of Wilfrid Ward's work, Maisie Ward remarked about her father's treatment of Newman in his 2-volume biography: "In a way the amazing fairness commented on by so many reviewers with which Wilfrid Ward held the scales between Newman and his foes, was easier for him than it might have been for another biographer. For if he loved Newman, he loved no less deeply his own father, and if in philosophy and in

---

[35] *Letters from Hilaire Belloc*, ed. Robert Speight (New York: The Macmillan Company, 1958), 233–4.
[36] Josephine Ward quoted in Robert Speight, *The Life of Hilaire Belloc* (London: Carter & Hollis, 1957), 155.
[37] Robert Ornsby, *Memoirs of Robert James Hope-Scott*, 2 vols (London: John Murray, 1884), ii, 170–1.

his views of Church politics he was a Newmanite, he could, brought up in the opposite camp, yet see the reason for the opposition Newman encountered."[38]

Another proof of the sympathy Ward showed his hero can be seen in the very charge of hypersensitivity that he brought against him.[39] While some readers might regard the charge as unbalanced—Ward was not sufficiently appreciative of just how tough the man of action in Newman could be—he was nevertheless right to see that, for all of his toughness, Newman *was* sensitive.[40] Chesterton is very good on this point. "It was ... after his passage to Rome, that Newman claimed his complete right to be in any book on modern English literature," he writes.

> This is no place for estimating his theology: but one point about it does clearly emerge. Whatever else is right, the theory that Newman went over to Rome to find peace and an end of argument, is quite unquestionably wrong. He had far more quarrels after he had gone over to Rome. But, though he had far more quarrels, he had far fewer compromises: and he was of that temper which is tortured more by compromise than by quarrel. He was a man at once of abnormal energy and abnormal sensibility: nobody without that combination could have written the *Apologia*. If he sometimes seemed to skin his enemies alive, it was because he himself lacked a skin. In this sense his *Apologia* is a triumph far beyond the ephemeral charge on which it was founded; in this sense he does indeed (to use his own expression) vanquish not his accuser but his judges. Many men would shrink from recording all their cold fits and hesitations and prolonged inconsistencies: I am sure it was the breath of life to Newman to confess them, now that he had done with them for ever. His *Lectures on the Present Position of English Catholics*, practically preached against a raging mob, rise not only higher but happier, as his instant unpopularity increases. There is something grander than humour, there is fun, in the very first lecture about the British Constitution as explained to a meeting of Russians. But always his triumphs are the triumphs of a highly sensitive man: a man must feel insults before he can so insultingly and splendidly avenge them. He is a naked man, who carries a naked sword. The quality of his literary style is so successful that it succeeds in escaping definition. The quality of his logic is that of a long but passionate patience, which waits until he has fixed all corners of an iron trap. But the quality of his moral comment on the age remains what I have said: a protest of the rationality of religion as against the increasing irrationality of mere Victorian comfort and compromise.[41]

---

[38] Ward quoted in Ward, *The Wilfrid Wards and the Transition*, ii, 350.

[39] In addition to the Newman biography itself, see "Cardinal Newman's Sensitiveness" in Ward, *Men and Matters*, 273–89.

[40] Putting the man of action aside, one should say here that even as a scholar Newman was tough. Fielding criticism of the *Grammar of Assent*, he wrote to one correspondent: "I am heartily obliged both to yourself and to any others, for your kind and welcome sollicitude about me—but I smile to think of M. Veuillot's being able to plague an old soldier, whose skin has been hardened by 40 years of warfare. If the words were not far too solemn for the occasion, I should say to him, 'Contemsi Catalinae [sic] gladios, non pertimescam tuos.'" Newman to John Thomas Walford, SJ (21 May 1870), *LD*, xv, 132. The line from Cicero translates: "I scorned the swords of Catiline, I will not quail before yours." Louis Veuillot, the extreme Ultramontane editor of *L'Univers* had accused Newman, wrongly as it happens, of ingratitude. See *LD*, xv, 124, note 1.

[41] Chesterton, *The Victorian Age in Literature*, 30–1.

In the biography, Ward defends his characterization of his subject's sensitivity in ways that show that, fundamentally, it was sympathy for his subject that animated the characterization, not censoriousness. "In his letters," Ward writes, we can see "the intensely affectionate and sensitive nature which won him such devoted friendships and brought at the same time so much suffering." Surely, no one would deny this.

> We find him telling Mr. Hutton that nothing could be said about him in praise or in blame which did not tear off his morbidly sensitive skin. And there was something in the depth of his affections distinct from the temperament of the artist of which I have already spoken. My picture would not be true or living if I omitted from the correspondence as published the indications of this feature and its consequences. I am aware that the unsympathetic reader may find matter for criticism in some manifestations of Newman's sensitiveness, and in a certain self-centeredness which so often goes with genius, and which had in Newman's case been fostered by his almost unique leadership at Oxford. But I do not think that anyone who appreciates the overmastering love of holiness, the absolute devotion to duty, as well as the intellectual force and wisdom evident in the letters as a whole, will feel any disposition so to belittle the great Cardinal when he reaches the end of this book. In reading Newman's correspondence, as when we watch a man in great pain, we hear, perhaps, at moments cries which are not musical, we witness movements not wholly dignified. But the feeling when all is read can hardly fail to be (the present writer speaks at least for himself) one of deep love and reverence. If the biographer has not conveyed his sense of proportion in this respect the fault is wholly his own. But, on the other hand, he did not feel that he would be justified in suppressing the signs of those defects which make the individuality stand out, and publishing a merely conventional biography, painting a "court portrait." There are men of genius in respect of whom the world has a right to know the facts as they are, and whose great gifts and qualities enable them to bear an entirely truthful representation. Such was Johnson. Such was Carlyle. One cannot bear the thought of these great men being shorn of their real individuality. John Henry Newman is such another. And his very holiness and devotion to duty are brought into relief by the trials which his own nature enhanced. His brightness of temperament made him keenly alive to the joys of life. It made him at times the most charming of companions. There probably would be few symptoms of undue sensitiveness or of angry and resentful feeling to record had he led a life according to human inclination. But at the call of duty, he attempted tasks which were intensely trying. He had strength to put his hand into the fire and keep it there. He had not strength never to cry out with pain, or always to preserve an attitude of studied grace.[42]

These are all fair points, with the exception of Ward's claim that Newman regarded any praise or blame as tearing off his "morbidly sensitive skin," which is false. In his letter to Hutton, Newman was only alluding to the objectionably erroneous references Tom Mozley had made about his father, not making any general

---

[42] Ward, *Life of Newman*, i, 20–1.

statement, as Ward suggests.[43]

Josephine also saw her husband's sympathy at play in his handling of the Anglican sources for his life of Newman. "From Dean Church's time to that of Dr Figgis, he welcomed whatever in the Anglican Church helped the cause of truth," she observed.

> And this drew to him the single-hearted and earnest Anglicans with whom he was thrown. There was much to charm him in the descendants of the Oxford Movement, and no one was ever more attracted than was Wilfrid by intellectual gifts, by culture, and that traditional standard of life and manners that makes so glaring a contrast with the rough and ready ways of a plutocratic world. That he grasped their intellectual point of view, and that to a degree at times bewildering alike to his own co-religionists and to the ordinary Protestant, can be seen by his little book on the Oxford Movement for the "People's Books" series. When I congratulated him on the way he had stated the case for the High Church party, "I've done it better than they could do it themselves," was his laughing retort.[44]

Wilfrid Ward, it has to be remembered, took Figgis' call for an Anglicanism purged of its broad-church inanities seriously; he agreed with the Anglican theologian that the ersatz Pelagian faith of Protestant reformers like Mrs. Humphry Ward's character Richard Meynell would only embolden the errors that true Christianity was charged to correct. "If Mr. Figgis is right in holding that the Church of England can still remain the home at once of learning and of traditional Christianity," Ward wrote, "it cannot be justifiable to open its doors, as Richard Meynell demands, to men who preach so meagre a gospel as that of 'reduced Christianity,' driven thereto not by hard facts but by ingenious theories. Pantheism and optimism are congenial enough to human society in the heyday of life: the Christian Church has been forcibly depicted by Newman as the providential antidote against them—as set up to remind us of 'the hateful cypresses'—of death, sin, judgment, and of the beliefs which are needed to face these ugly facts. If the Church of England can share in this work and still be a bulwark or breakwater against infidelity, can it be wise to cripple her power in this respect by admitting to her ministry those who go so very near to holding the very attitude towards life which Christianity is set up to oppose ...?"[45] If Catholics are now more likely to pose such questions to themselves than Anglicans, Ward's point is doubly well made.

Another winning trait about Ward's criticism is its lucidity. Like Jonathan Swift, who would assemble his servants to attend and approve any piece of writing he was composing before he gave it over to the printer's boy, Ward was intent that

---

[43] Cf. "I can't expect that affectionate friends such as you ... can wait till my full years on earth have run out, before they speak of me; nor that the purveyors of gossip of the past should refrain from tearing off my morbidly sensitive skin, while they can with public interest." Newman to Hutton (6 May 1884), *LD*, xxx, 356.

[44] Ward, *Last Lectures*, xxiv. See Mark Chapman's superb entry on John Neville Figgis (1866–1919), political theorist and theologian, "who regarded 'the boneless Christ of the German liberals' as 'incapable of producing the mighty fact of the Christian Church'" in the *ODNB*.

[45] Wilfrid Ward, "Reduced Christianity," in *Men and Matters* (London: Longmans, Green & Co., 1914), 416. See Mrs. Humphry Ward, *The Case of Richard Meynell* (London, 1920).

everyone in his household, including his wife and children, should read what he had written to verify its intelligibility, even if they disagreed with its reasoning. "As to myself," Mrs. Ward wrote in her reminiscence, "I can recall the head-splitting experience of his refusing to send an article on Mr. Balfour's 'Foundations of Belief' to the *Quarterly Review* before he was quite sure I had mastered the argument. I was at the time absorbed in nursery cares. I had not had a philosophical training, and it was a tough bit of work. But there was immense enjoyment in such moments of intellectual energy—which can only be understood by those who have worked in close companionship with a mind of absolute candour and absorbing earnestness. In an article written last summer Mr. G. K. Chesterton said of Wilfrid Ward that 'thinking was to him like breathing.'"[46]

Ward returned the compliment by praising Chesterton's *Orthodoxy* (1908) to the skies, regarding the chapter on "The Paradoxes of Christianity" as especially good, even going so far as to say that Chesterton's "pages are marked by freshness and often by the insight of genius." Ward singled out Chesterton's account of his discovery of the appeal of Christianity, in which "he gives us a rough and unphilosophical expression of the line of reasoning in a book which he has, perhaps, never read—Cardinal Newman's *Essay in Aid of a Grammar of Assent*. He tells us, in popular language, that it is by the cumulative argument, by the 'illative sense', which cannot express all the latent reasons which influence its decision, that he, like others, really reached his conclusions." For Ward, *Orthodoxy* was "a book to upset the pedant, to irritate Mr Chesterton's *bêtes noires*, the "dreary and well-informed." It was also one in complete accord with what he thought should be the object of all good defenders of Christianity in the modern world. "Our faculties are in danger of losing what they have already grasped and possessed," he wrote, "—truth which is substantial and divine—while they pursue shadows—or substances ever retreating among the shadows. To concentrate our main attention on this fact is a one-sided insistence for the age on old aspects of truth which are being forgotten, not a denial of new aspects to be recognized in due time and in due proportion. Such an attitude is undoubtedly reinforced by some of Mr Chesterton's best pages. And it is likely to be as unpopular in many quarters as the Church is ever unpopular with the world."[47]

Of course, Josephine Ward entirely shared her husband's delight in Chesterton. It was one of the bonds of taste and judgment that made their marriage such a joy. At the same time, while it might have been the accustomed thing for many eminent Victorians to have their wives compile their epistolary biographies, few wives knew the intellectual preoccupations of their subjects as well as Mrs. Ward knew hers. "Between my wife and myself," Ward himself averred, "there was complete unity of interests so far as all serious things were concerned."[48] That Mrs. Ward should have quoted the passage she quoted from Chesterton on her husband shows how finely she understood his rare critical distinction, for no one captured that distinction better than GKC. "One admirable quality he had which is exceedingly difficult to describe," Chesterton wrote

---

[46] Ward, *Last Lectures*, xv.
[47] Wilfrid Ward, "Mr. Chesterton among the Prophets," *Dublin Review* (January 1909), 1–32.
[48] Ward quoted in Ward, *The Wilfrid Wards and the Transition*, i, 158.

but which in a book like *William George Ward and the Catholic Revival* makes the son and father singularly at one. I know not whether to call it a curiosity without restlessness, or a gigantic intellectual appetite rather amplified than moderated by patience. It is common to say of a man so acute that he had a restless activity of mind; for in the effort to evade the platitudes of praise a phrase like "restless" has almost become a compliment. But the mind of Wilfrid Ward had very notably a restful activity.[49]

Indeed, Ward's ability to enter into and recreate the intellectual and spiritual qualities of Newman and his other biographical subjects was directly tied to his own "gigantic intellectual appetite," as well as his sympathy. Moreover, Chesterton was right to see these critical gifts as essential to Ward the biographer, about whom he could be eloquent.

Wilfrid Ward was a biographer in a sense as exact and more exalted than we apply to a biologist; he really dealt with life and the springs of life. Some are so senseless as to associate the function with merely indirect services to literature like those of the commentator and the bibliographer. They level the great portrait-painter of the soul with the people who put the ticket on the frame or the number in the catalogue. But in truth there is nothing so authentically creative as the divine act of making another man out of the very substance of oneself. Few of us have vitality enough to live the life of another. Few of us therefore can feel satisfied with our own competence in or for biography, however fertile we may be in autobiography. But he was so full of this disinterested imagination of the biographer that even his short journalistic sketches were model biographies. He made a death-mask in wax with the firmness of a sculptor's monument in marble.[50]

This quality of sympathy, of being able to enter into and understand the thoughts of others with a kind of empathetic clairvoyance—Chesterton called his friend "that great clearing-house of philosophies and theologies"—made Ward a consistently fair-minded critic of Newman.[51] "Certainly he could not ... have undertaken to write the life of any man with whom he was out of sympathy," Mrs. Ward confirmed, though there were limits to his sympathy, as there were to Newman's. As her daughter, Masie Ward pointed out: "If nature had given Wilfrid Ward a "sympathetic voice" his education and temperament both supplied him with the other necessary side to his equipment for the difficult task of liaison officer. For it is not enough merely to enter with sympathy into the minds of others. A man who does this to excess may end by losing his own standpoint." His daughter, then, proceeded to give a few striking examples of the decided limits of her father's sympathy.

Wilfrid used to quote a saying of Tennyson with which on the whole he disagreed but of which he saw the full force "In religion you must choose between bigotry and flabbiness." Much as he hated bigotry he hated flabbiness still more, and every

---

[49] Chesterton quoted in Ward, *Last Lectures*, xv.
[50] Ibid., xvi.
[51] *The Collected Works of G. K. Chesterton: volume XVI, The Autobiography of G. K. Chesterton*, ed. Fr. Scott Randall Paine (San Francisco: Ignatius Press, 1988), 248.

kind of sentimentality or emotionalism in religion. In a letter to my mother soon after *Lux Mundi* appeared [1889] he wrote:

> "Scott Holland's article on Faith has very striking bits, but the tone is far too rationalistic and there is a touch of disgusting Robert Elsmere *gush* which I *hate*, and which is evidently in the air at Oxford now. It is the one thing when I groan over the opening Oxford could have been for one with my tastes, which I console myself with—that I have kept free from that horrid sentimental emotionalism in religion."[52]

Maisie Ward also recalled another instance in which her father's sympathy gave way. "Where fighting must be done, he fought," she wrote. "On one occasion, when he was dining at the British Embassy in Rome, the Ambassador (Sir Philip Currie) and others made a direct attack on the Church. Wilfrid Ward retorted with astonishing vigour—and Sir Philip later expressed the view that Mr. Ward was certainly the most intelligent of the Roman Catholics. His fighting made no enemies because it was direct. Because he saw the 'why' of the other side, he never sneered. The nearest he ever got to a sneer was against Mivart. For once he could not get inside another's mind—and did not realise that that other was no longer in full possession of his mind!"[53] St. George Jackson Mivart (1827–1900), English Catholic biologist and controversialist, was excommunicated after contending that the whole Roman Church, including the pope, was guilty of antisemitism in the Dreyfus affair. According to Mivart's biographer, "Friends and family excused his latest and strongest arguments [regarding, in addition to antisemitism, faith and science] on the grounds that in his last months his mind was diseased or he suffered from a hubris-induced madness. It was the final insult to his life as a constant protestant."[54] Newman, too, had his otherwise forbearing sympathies give way when, as a Tractarian, he encountered the incoherent theological musings of Renn Dickson Hampden (1793–1868), one of Oriel's Noetics, whom he could not resist attacking in a memorably virtuosic broadside, in which he wrote:

> [Dr. Hampden] considers that the only belief necessary for a Christian, as such, is belief that the Scripture is the word of God; that no statement whatever, even though correctly deduced from the text of Scripture, is part of the revelation; that no right conclusions about theological truth can be drawn from Scripture; that Scripture itself is a mere record of historical facts; that it contains no dogmatic statements, such as those about the Trinity, Incarnation, Atonement, Justification, &c. that theological statements, though natural and unavoidable, are in all cases but human opinions; that even the juxtaposition of the actual sentences of Scripture, is a human deduction; that an individual is not abstractedly the worse for being a Unitarian; that it does not follow that another is worse because I should be worse for being so; that, though a deduction be correct, logical, and true, yet a denial of it must not be pronounced to be more than an error of judgment that infinite theories may be formed about the text of Scripture, but

---

[52] Ward, *The Wilfrid Wards and the Transition*, i, 102.
[53] Ibid., 103.
[54] Entry on Mivart by Jacob W. Gruber in *ODNB*.

that they ought not to be made of public importance to Christian communities, badges of fellowship, reasons for separation, and the like; that the Articles of the Nicene and Athanasian Creeds are merely human opinions, scholastic, allowing of change, unwarrantable when imposed, and, in fact, the produce of a mistaken philosophy; and that the Apostles' Creed is defensible only when considered as a record of historical facts.[55]

If Newman and Ward could be impatient with those, like Hampden and Mivart, whose errors were not only blatant but scandalous, they could also turn their sympathy to critical account. In this regard, Chesterton was right when he wrote that Ward did more than efface himself from his biographies and critical essays in order to showcase the thought of his subjects; he could also "be strongly co-operative with another's mind";[56] and, of course, this was another trait that he shared with Newman, in whose work we can see a like cooperation with such varied subjects as Thomas Scott and Bishop Butler, Father Charles Russell, SJ and Father Dominic Barberi, St Philip and St Ignatius—to name but a few. Yet it was a mark of the saint in Newman that he shrank from certain displays of sympathy, as he told Mary Holmes, the orphan governess whom he befriended for many years. "Thank you for your anxiety about me," he told his solicitous friend. "As to the Achilli matter, it was a trouble while it lasted—none now that it is over. Publicity tries me, but not to be let alone. The extreme overpowering kindness and sympathy of Catholics has, from its very fulness, tried me almost as much as the attacks of my opponents; as involving publicity."[57]

Another of Newman's biographers, Meriol Trevor, whose account of Newman's life was so deeply influenced by the Fathers of the Birmingham Oratory, interpreted Ward's ascribing oversensitivity to Newman as proof of his own lack of sensitivity. Indeed, she related the dream Ward's father had, in which he found himself at a dinner party sitting next to a veiled lady whose conversation was so fascinating that he exclaimed, "I have not heard such conversation since I knew John Henry Newman at Oxford," whereupon the lady lifted her veil and declared, "I am John Henry Newman!" For Trevor, the dream said less about

---

[55] John Henry Newman, *Elucidations of Dr. Hampden's Theological Statements* (Oxford: W. Baxter, 1936), 5–6. Newman's delight in taunting opponents is evident in his third-person response to Hampden's public protest against what he regarded as Newman's persecution of him. "As to the charge of 'dark malignity,' which Dr Hampden asserts to be founded in Mr Newman's case on a 'fanatical spirit,' and Dr Hampden's remark that he has 'done no wrong or unkindness to' Dr Newman, 'but on the contrary always treated' him 'with civility and respect,' he observes that he should rejoice at nothing more than a return to that state of good understanding with Dr Hampden which he has before now enjoyed, and that he shall be ever watchful and eager to discern any approach to a removal of the differences which separate him from Dr Hampden. At the same time, he certainly does recognize as conceivable the existence of motives for approving or disapproving the conduct of another, distinct from those of a personal nature." Newman to Hampden (24 June 1835) *LD*, v, 84–5. In the *Apologia*, the wit in Newman confessed: "My behaviour had a mixture in it both of fierceness and of sport; and on this account, I dare say, it gave offence to many; nor am I here defending it." *Apo.*, 44 It has certainly caused great offense to his more dull-witted detractors, though they might at least give their *bête noir* credit for restraining his more polemical impulses. After all, as he admitted himself, "not even when I was fiercest, could I have ... cut off a Puritan's ears, and I think the sight of a Spanish *auto-da-fé* would have been the death of me." *Ibid.*, 47.

[56] Chesterton quoted in Ward, *Last Lectures*, xvii.

[57] Newman to Mary Holmes (22 April 1853), *LD*, xv, 360.

Newman than the dreamer. "That Ward identified Newman in his dream with a fascinating lady does not prove that Newman ought to have been one; it tells us nothing about Newman, but quite a bit about Ward." W. G. Ward, in her view, "was very much the intellectual, his mind concentrated on logical reasoning, and noticeably deficient in those qualities of imagination, intuition and sympathy which are associated with the feminine side of human nature ... Newman was certainly one in whom the intuitive region of the personality was as profoundly developed as the reasoning faculty, and in his antagonism to Newman, Ward was opposing the sense of mystery and the sympathy with others that he himself so signally lacked."[58] While it is true that W. G. Ward could take an unwarrantably intellectual approach to men and their affairs, it would be demonstrably false to suggest that his son followed suit. The friend of such a wide-ranging, variegated lot as Lord Tennyson, Lord Halifax, Lord Emly, Fr. Ignatius Ryder, T. H. Huxley, R. H. Hutton, A. J. Balfour, Charles Gore, Henry Sidgwick and Baron von Hügel could hardly be charged with lacking "sympathy with others." Moreover, Wilfrid Ward was insistent that Newman's "sensitive temperament, which was so apparent in voice, manner of speech, and personal bearing, went with a piercing appreciation of what was beautiful and happy in the world around him and in life."[59] The reason why Sheridan Gilley is right to single out Ward as a conciliating force between men espousing belief and those espousing unbelief, as well as between ultramontanes and liberals, is precisely because Ward's sympathies were so catholic, without ever undermining his orthodox Roman faith.[60]

Yet W. G. Ward's dream also says a good deal about the dreamer because it captures the old provocateur's delight in theatricality, the fun of theatricality, a trait he shared with his fun-loving son. Wilfrid Ward confirms this himself in his autobiographical fragment apropos the plays he put on in his home when a young man, "plays," in which, as he said, he would

> dress up as a Highlander or a gipsy or a bravo, and amuse, bore or terrify my neighbours by appearing suddenly in strange-coloured garments, and if I really succeeded in thoroughly frightening anyone my mother especially enjoyed the fun. I used to experiment in this way both on our servants and on the Professors and students at St. Edmund's College. On one occasion, however, when I blacked my face and posed as an oriental in peculiarly fantastic garb and armed with knives and daggers, the disguise was so complete that my mother, seeing this strange being suddenly quite close to her in the garden with a drawn dagger, was herself really terrified before I had time to give her the information that it was only I, and that I was about to embark on a fresh campaign—presumably welcome to her—of alarming the neighbourhood.[61]

---

[58] Meriol Trevor, *Newman: Light in Winter* (London: Macmillan, 1962), 517–18. Trevor's biography, for all its limitations, is still very much worth reading, though few even favorably-disposed readers will disagree with Edward Kelly that "There is perhaps no more painfully tedious passage in all of biographical literature—almost one hundred pages—than her account of the battle between the Birmingham and London Oratories." Kelly, "Newman's Reputation and the Biographical Tradition," *Faith and Reason* (Winter 1989), 4. Score settling has its place but the Oratorians overdo it.

[59] Wilfrid Ward, *Ten Personal Studies* (London: Longmans, Green & Co., 1908), 225.

[60] ODNB.

[61] Ward quoted in Ward, *The Wilfrid Wards and the Transition*, i, 37.

If W. G. Ward was given to dreams simply as a result of his teeming imagination, his son was also prone to dreaming—and fending off nightmares—as a result of the stress and strain of work, particularly when at work on his life of Newman. At one point in the composition of the biography, he wrote to the Duke of Norfolk: "On Sunday night I dreamed I was condemned to death by the Inquisition. The trial had been most unfair and Newman's Life had been represented as an attack on the Holy See; I was vividly aware I was to die next day. I said to [Josephine], 'I shall ask Norfolk to telegraph to the Pope to say proceedings must be stayed.' She replied, "You really must not bother Uncle Henry to do things for you."'[62]

Josephine was all too well aware of the enormous anxiety the writing of the book caused her husband. In one letter to one of her uncles, quoted in Maisie Ward's biography of her parents, Ward's wife disclosed the tune to which she sympathized with her husband's literary grief: "I think you know something of what the strain of these last years has been to Wilfrid," Josephine wrote. "The Cardinal's Life was a big enough job to break a stronger man's health than Wilfrid's," she wrote.

> The mental strain, and I may say it, his absolute conscientiousness has made that worse, is really too much for him. He was promised a free hand but he has constantly sent the work as it went on to Fr. John.[63] The other day I saw Fr. John and he had read to the end of the first volume and he told me that he was quite satisfied, except that he wished certain allusions to be left out. He spoke with the utmost sympathy of the work. Now as you know proofs that have laid neglected for months are made the subject of attack. Wilfrid has been allowed to overwork himself at a tension of which they have no notion. They have no consideration for his health and they will break his nerve effectually without knowing what they are doing, or perhaps caring! I don't know whether to try to get him away for a complete rest or what to do. Do you think the Fathers even suspect that they are spoiling or stopping a great work for souls? I wonder if they would tease a portrait painter while he was at work as they tease a biographer? And yet if it is to do a great work it must be a work of art. I am getting many prayers for help in this trying time. Is it not curious that Cardinal Newman's own sons should treat Wilfrid just as the Irish Bishops treated him? It will make a strange chapter in the life of Wilfrid when that comes to be written. The unkindness of good men is to me one of the greatest trials there are.[64]

IV

Whether "Cardinal Newman's own sons" were altogether wrong to be anxious about how Ward presented their founder in his biography is a complicated question. It is true that both the biographer and the Oratorians might have had grounds for grievance—Ward for the pettifogging oversight to which he was occasionally subjected and the Oratorians for what they feared, rightly as it

---

[62] Ward quoted *ibid.*, 347.
[63] Father John Norris (1843–1912), the third provost of the Birmingham Oratory.
[64] Josephine Ward quoted in Ward, *The Wilfrid Wards and the Transition*, ii, 347.

turned out, might be the biographer's distortion of certain aspects of Newman's character and work, especially with regard to his temperament. Nevertheless, whatever tensions obtained between the two should not obscure the fact that their collaboration resulted in what is, on balance, a fairly good biography.[65] After all, even Boswell's *Life of Johnson*, the greatest of all biographies, neglects Johnson's early years and does not do justice to the nuances of his political and moral thought.[66] The reviewer of the *Pall Mall Gazette* captured what many must have felt who had looked forward to the book's publication over the years: "Long expectation as a rule means deep disappointment. Here for once is a sovereign exception. Mr. Ward has brought his well-known powers to a happy consummation. He has treated a great theme with magnificent ability, and if Newman had never written the *Apologia* he would have found his vindication here."[67] Owen Chadwick certainly saw the merits of the book accurately enough.

> Wilfrid Ward's life of Newman appeared at last in 1912, when its author had four years to live. It was excellently done—very surprisingly, after all the pressure which Ward suffered. It was excellent for three reasons: first the author hid himself, and wove the letters together, standing back and not obtruding his own judgment; secondly, his selection of the material was coherent and even more … fair-minded … thirdly, he was a moderate man who saw the strength in liberalism and yet was a strong servant of the papacy, and therefore had a rapport with Newman's own mind; and fourthly, he happened to be using material which is exceedingly interesting.[68]

Everything Chadwick says here is true, with the exception of the bit about Ward seeing "the strength in liberalism," which, of course, is misleading.[69] Yes, Ward

---

[65] For an opposing view of this estimate, see *The Edinburgh Review*, which argued that "it is misleading to give the title 'The Life of Cardinal Newman' to a work which is only, as it were, the second volume of a biography. There are very few men, however long-lived, who have not done much of their best work before the age of forty-five, and Newman was certainly not one of the exceptions. From every point of view, except that of the Roman Catholic ecclesiastical historian, Newman's Anglican career was far more interesting and important than his residence at Birmingham. He will live in history, not as the recluse of Edgbaston, nor as the wearer of the Cardinal's hat which fell to his lot, almost too late to save the credit of the Vatican, when he had passed the normal limit of human life, but as the real founder and leader of nineteenth century Anglo-Catholicism, the movement which he created and then tried in vain to destroy." *The Edinburgh Review* (April 1912), 263–4.

[66] Ward admired Boswell, about whom he wrote: "biography reaches perfection only if the biographer's art … [gives] a living picture of the man who is revealed by the evidence before him," and "in this respect Boswell stands and is likely to remain supreme. He is supremely accurate and supremely vivid." Yet Ward also understood that accuracy must always discipline the biographer's vividness, precisely because "in biography there is an obvious risk in giving free rein to the imaginative method. Boswell was no doubt greatly assisted by this keen perception. It helped him immensely in making his record of Johnson's conversation quite exact, for he could test its accuracy by his close knowledge of the Johnsonian *ethos*. But the precision of Boswell's perception was due to a really exhaustive study of his material, and his mind was constantly held in check by that material." Ward, *Last Lectures*, 172 and 161.

[67] *Pall Mall Gazette* (22 January 1912).

[68] Owen Chadwick, "Newman and the historians," in *The Spirit of the Oxford Movement* (Cambridge: Cambridge University Press, 1990), 164–5.

[69] Apropos Wilfrid Ward's conservatism, Fr. Cuthbert once wrote: "He could hardly have been a liberal if he had tried, any more than he could have been a democrat in politics. By temperament,

saw good aspects to liberal notions of liberty and free intellectual inquiry—they were notions, after all, rooted in the Catholic tradition, even though liberals would be the last to acknowledge as much. Yet, as Maisie Ward pointed out, "My father doubted the possibilities of Liberalism as a basis for any ordered society: still more did he question: could there be a Liberalism that was not at bottom illiberal to Catholicism."[70] In this regard, Ward, like Newman, saw the actual liberalism progressing throughout the nineteenth century in England and Europe following the French Revolution as nothing less than ruinous. Asking what Newman's mission in life was, Ward answered:

> It was one of relentless war against the "Liberalism" in thought that was breaking up ancient institutions in Church and State, and would not cease from its work until it had destroyed religion. In England its aims were comparatively moderate and its tendencies disguised, but we are now witnessing its inevitable results in Continental Europe [Maisie was writing in the late 1930s]. Newman foresaw them in 1828. He saw fresh symptoms of an un-Christian movement in the revolution of 1830 in France, and on one occasion refused even to look at the tricolor that was hoisted on the mast of a French ship. It was not his way to spread a panic or to indulge in alarmist talk of the incoming flood of infidelity. But this was in reality, as we know from a letter written in old age, the anticipation which early haunted him. We learn from this letter that for fifty years he had looked forward to the gradual rising of such a flood until only the tops of the mountains will be seen like islands in the waste of waters. To rescue his own countrymen from this danger, or to show them an ark of safety, appeared to be a mission especially suited to one keenly alive to the plausibility of scepticism, yet profoundly convinced that modern science and research were compatible with Christianity, and that in Christianity alone could be found the meaning of life and the happiness of mankind.[71]

One Victorian critic who recognized the consistency of Newman's lifelong campaign against liberalism, without ever conceding its justification, was Leslie Stephen, who, in a passage from his essay "An Agnostic's Apology" (1893) wrote:

> Newman is, like Mill, a lover of the broad daylight; of clear, definite, tangible statements. There is no danger with him of losing ourselves in that mystical haze which the ordinary common-sense of mankind irritates and bewilders. From

---

he was essentially conservative; it required the full weight of his intellectual ability to make him an open-minded conservative, that is to say, a conservative who believes the world has a future as well as a past." Fr. Cuthbert quoted in Ward, *The Wilfrid Wards and the Transition*, ii, 364.

70 Ward, *The Wilfrid Wards and the Transition*, ii, 362.
71 Ward, *Life of Newman*, 4–5. Cf. "I have all that time thought that a time of widespread infidelity was coming, and through all those years the waters have in fact been rising as a deluge. I look for the time, after my life, when only the tops of the mountains will be seen, like islands in the waste of waters." Newman to Mrs. William Maskell (6 January 1877), *LD*, xxviii, 156. For a good example of how the academy ignores the ruinousness of liberalism by contriving to imagine liberalism indefinable, see the following: "If we share anything with the 1870s debates, it is a cumulative, conceptual anxiety about what liberalism actually means or entails." Andrew Vincent, "Liberalism and the Metaphysical Society," in *The Metaphysical Society (1869–1880)*, ed. Marshall *et al.*, 87. Needless to say, neither Newman nor Ward suffered from this anxiety—nor, indeed, Leslie Stephen.

the age of fifteen, he tells us, dogma has been the fundamental principle of his religion. Upon this point he has nothing to retract or to repent. Liberalism was his enemy, because by liberalism he meant the anti-dogmatic principle; the principle which would convert religion into a sentiment, and therefore, for him, into a dream and a mockery. No one, of course, could be more sensitive to the mysterious element of theology; but, in his view, that dogma is not the less definite for being mysterious. If, on one side, it leads us to the abysses where the highest reason faints, yet, on the other, it may serve as a basis for truths as clear-cut and peremptory as those of the physical sciences.[72]

Chadwick's inability to grasp the real nature of Ward's handling of liberalism in his biography notwithstanding, he did recognize that the biography succeeded because of its balance. If Ward sometimes bristled under the supervision of the Oratorians, it forced him to determine how he should structure his biography, as Maisie Ward recognized.

> One good perhaps arose out of these troubles [between Ward and the Oratorians]. Wilfrid had always intended in the Biography to use Newman's letters far more freely than his father's or Wiseman's because of their literary quality. Newman had always stood supreme in Wilfrid's thoughts even when he was writing his other biographies. When the Cardinal before he died sent Wilfrid his own side of the correspondence with W. G. Ward, the biographer's insight was curiously illustrated. The chapter dealing with the relations between the two men was already in proof. Not one line had to be altered. Wilfrid printed the letters as an illustrative appendix, and people thought the chapter was based on them. When then he came to write the Life, the necessity to show that his own view was never subjective determined him to make it all but a mosaic of letters.[73]

This was not dissimilar to how Newman believed biographies should be structured. In a letter to his sister Jemima, he confessed: "It has ever been a hobby of mine (unless it be a truism, not a hobby) that a man's life lies in his letters. This is why Hurrell Froude published St Thomas a Beckett's Letters, with nothing of his own except what was necessary for illustration or connection of parts."[74] Indeed, Newman was convinced that "for the interest of a biography ... for arriving at the inside of things, the publication of letters is the true method. Biographers varnish—they assign motives, they conjecture feelings—they interpret Lord Burleigh's nods, but contemporary letters are facts."[75] That Newman's definitive

---

[72] Leslie Stephen, *An Agnostic's Apology and Other Essays* (London: Smith Elder & Co., 1893), 179. Cf. "My Newman has appeared ... in the November number of the Fortnightly ... I should like you to look at it if it comes in your way, for he is a curious cuss, and has interested me a good deal." Stephen to Charles Eliot Norton (22 October 1877) *The Life and Letters of Leslie Stephen*, 303. It is strange that Leslie Stephen did not cotton more to Newman's wit, for he could be witty himself. Quentin Bell recalls that when Leslie's "old friend Frederick Weymouth Gibbs had, for a space of twenty minutes," held forth "on the Dominion of Canada, Leslie would produce an enormous groan and remark, in a deafening whisper: 'Oh, Gibbs, what a bore you are.'" Bell, *Virginia Woolf: A Biography*, 24.
[73] Ward, *The Wilfrid Wards and the Transition*, i, 348.
[74] Newman to Mrs. John Mozley (18 May 1863), *LD*, xx, 443.
[75] *LD*, xx, note 4, 443.

biographer Ian Ker would follow Ward's lead in this epistolary method confirmed its soundness, though Ker improved on the method exponentially by integrating Newman's letters directly into the narrative of his text.

Here, incidentally, we might also cite the revelatory importance that Dean Church accorded letters, especially in his essay on Gregory the Great (590–604), whose letters bring alive "the history of his age and country," though for Church "the collection [had] a further interest," as he relates.

> The history of forsaken and helpless Italy, abandoned by the Empire to which it had given birth, and, after having been for ages the flower and glory of the world, the chosen and privileged home of luxury and power, delivered over defenceless to the barbarians, to be dealt with at their insolent pleasure, is perhaps the most pathetic spectacle to be found in history of a fallen nation ; and the piercing and expressive sense of this degradation thrills through every line of Gregory's letters. We see in them the evidence of one of those times of apparent chaos, when the power and hope of remedy, of repair, of resource, seem exhausted among men. But those times of chaos are only apparent; there is always something forming, organizing itself, growing under them. And the special interest of Gregory's letters is that, amid the desolations of Italy and these wails of despair, in this record of lamentation and mourning and woe, they exhibit in the clearest and most instructive way the nascent Papacy of the Middle Ages: the early steps by which the Primacy of St. Leo, the head of the hierarchy of the early times, *Primus inter pares* among the great Patriarchs of the undivided Church, developed into the administrative all-controlling monarchy of Gregory VII, Innocent III, and Boniface VIII . And they show not only the steps by which it took shape and became established; they show it was a necessary and inevitable consequence of the conditions of the time.[76]

Ward's understanding of how essential letter writing was to his hero certainly enabled him to execute his epistolary method with fidelity and panache. He shows this clearly in his introductory remarks to the biography where he writes:

> With Newman the writing of letters was a very important part of his daily life. It was the chief means of communication with others for one whose affections were singularly keen and clinging. It was a vehicle for expressing the thoughts of his full mind, without the great anxiety attaching to words that were printed, and, therefore, in some sense irrevocable. And it was the means of exercising personal influence on the large numbers who sought his advice and judgment in difficulties or troubles. He devoted immense labour to his letters. When the subject of writing was at all difficult he would make a rough draft and keep it, sending to his correspondent a letter based on this first draft, but generally including some changes in order to bring out his meaning more clearly. He kept the letters he received and endorsed them with any specially important passage in his own reply. He devoted many hours in the day to writing, and this habit continued as long as he was physically able to write at all.[77]

---

[76] Richard William Church, *Miscellanous Essays* (London: Macmillan & Co., 1888), 208–9.
[77] Ward, *Life of Newman*, i, 20–1.

If both Ward and Ker were naturally leery of resorting to paraphrase in the case of letters that tended to be of such rich subtlety, neither followed Newman in imagining that letters alone, without the biographer's superintending admixture of context and point, could somehow constitute a proper biography. "Letters … are nearly always material of great value in the hands of a good biographer," Ward recognized, "but it is essential that before the biographer uses them in his work he should estimate their true place in the particular instance as revelations of character and give his readers the clue to their interpretation." In other words, there could be no "mosaic of letters" without the mosaicist. After all, the biographer "must locate … [the letters] and interpret them. He must also judge what selections are really representative of the man's individuality and what are not. Moreover, he has to consider in the case of letter-writers who lack the literary gift, whether to quote correspondence *in extenso* will not make his book very dull. If in your book you delineate a bore *in extenso*—it has been well said—the book is as much a bore as the man it describes. And there are men who are bores in their letters though not in private life. It is probably for this reason that Lord Morley has used Mr. Gladstone's letters with a very sparing hand."[78] Newman's biographer is faced with the opposite situation: a subject whose letters are so numerous, so well-written, and so incisive as to confront the biographer with not only an embarrassment of epistolary riches but, in effect, a rival biographer, one who writes of matters, as Newman wrote of them, with a kind of immersed detachment. Gilley sees one measure of Ward's biographical achievement in the creditability his self-effacement made possible. "The biography," he says, "is almost bland, its author properly buried beneath his subject, whose great correspondence controls the flow of the narration. Newman need not have feared his Catholic biographer; through his letters, Newman writes his life."[79] Of course, this is not entirely true: to give just one example, Ward misrepresents Newman's work in Dublin with the Catholic University by neglecting the contemporary letters and relying instead on Newman's retrospective Memorandum;[80] but Gilley is nevertheless right to argue that the role the letters play in Ward's biography is commanding

Some, of course, question the reliability of the letters, for all of their unquestionable brilliance; but no one conversant with the considerable primary materials on which any biographical work on Newman must be based can plausibly claim that the convert, as a rule, or even incidentally, sought to falsify facts to burnish or exculpate his own role in events. On the contrary, he rarely spares himself the sort of deft, satirical mockery that he visited upon others whenever he thought his own behaviour blameworthy—especially in his conduct of the

---

[78] Ward, *Last Lectures*, 181.
[79] Sheridan Gilley, "Wilfrid Ward and his Life of Newman," *Journal of Ecclesiastical History*, 19, no. 2 (April 1978), 193.
[80] Cf. "Ward's almost exclusive reliance on the Memorandum and disregard of any correspondence … gave him a very partial view of his subject." Paul Shrimpton, "Editor's Introduction," John Henry Newman, *My Campaign in Ireland, Part II, My Connection with the Catholic University*, ed. Shrimpton (Leominster: Gracewing, 2022), xc–xci. While Dr. Shrimpton might be warranted in taking Ward to task for neglecting the Dublin correspondence in his account of the Catholic University in Dublin, he has no grounds for blaming him for Constantine Curran's nationalist misrepresentation of Newman's efforts.

Oxford Movement. The lectures that he published in his *Anglican Difficulties* amply demonstrate this.[81] The reason why his former Tractarian friends Pusey and Keble never responded to his critical reassessment of the Anglo-Catholic Via Media is that they naturally resented being implicated in its unreality, an unreality in which Newman never flinched from implicating himself. For his erstwhile comrades-in-arms, it was best to ignore the lectures and pray that they might somehow be forgotten as pieces of superannuated controversy.

If Ward took Newman's epistolary cornucopia in stride, he set himself two criteria in the selection and deployment of the letters, which merit relating:

> (1) the whole of Newman's story and attitude of mind at every stage of his career had to be mastered by the biographer, so that when printing an individual letter which by itself would give a one-sided impression, he could remind the reader of the other side which the particular letter itself did not present; (2) letters had to be given so selected as to represent, in Newman's own words, his very various points of view and obviously to justify the biographer's explanations, to prevent the charge that they were based on his own personal views, and thus to preserve the objectivity of the picture. A mere summary of Newman's attitude on the points in question would not have sufficed and would have been impossible. His own words had to be given. I may be allowed to make use of what I said on this subject in an essay published a year ago—The man's nature was so complex and subtle that the biographer dared not trust to a summary. A subjective estimate must always be open to dispute. The documents must speak for themselves.[82]

Ward is particularly good at meeting these criteria when negotiating the difficulties inherent in Newman's own negotiation of the tensions between the liberal Catholicism of his friends Lord Acton and Richard Simpson and the imperatives of authority. When, for example, Ward quotes the following letter of Newman to Acton on how the *Rambler* should be conducted in light of these tensions, the reader has been given enough of the involved context by Ward to appreciate the wisdom of the convert's good counsel. "Let [the *Rambler*] ... go back to its own literary line," Newman advised Sir John.

> Let it be instructive, clever, and amusing. Let it cultivate a general temper of good humour and courtesy. Let it praise as many persons as it can, and gain friends in neutral quarters, and become the organ of others by the interest it has made them take in its proceedings. Then it will be able to plant a good blow at a fitting time with great effect—it may come down keen and sharp, and not only on Protestants—and without committing itself to definite statements of its own, it may support authority by attacking views which authority will be the first to be jealous of, if the *Rambler* is not the first to attack them—Power, to be powerful, and strength, to be strong, must be exerted only now and then—It then would be strong and effective, and affect public opinion without offending piety or good sense.[83]

---

[81] See *Difficulties of Anglicans*, i, ed. Short.
[82] Ward, *Last Lectures*, 189–90.
[83] Newman to Acton (31 December 1858), *LD*, xviii, 562.

At first, the advice was taken, but when it was flouted, Newman became understandably exasperated. "I despair of Simpson being other than he is," Newman wrote Acton of the paper's incorrigible editor. "He will always be clever, amusing, brilliant, and suggestive. He will always be flicking his whip at Bishops, cutting them in tender places, throwing stones at Sacred Congregations, and, as he rides along the high road, discharging peashooters at Cardinals who happen by bad luck to look out of the window. I fear I must say I despair of any periodical in which he has a part."[84] When Newman suggested that his friends either shut down the *Rambler* or reform it under a new name, they chose the latter course, naming the new paper, *The Home and Foreign Review*. In all of this, Ward nicely shows the lengths to which Newman went to appease not only his liberal Catholic friends but his Ultramontane friends as well, especially Ward's excitable father. No one has captured the impossible position in which these diplomatic embassies cast Newman better than Ward:

> W. G. Ward, who had been earnestly hoping for the termination of the *Rambler*, did not at all like the news that a new Quarterly was to rise from its ashes. And Simpson, who took a malicious pleasure, as he said, in making Ward's 'hair stand on end' by startling and unwelcome news, assured him that the new Review had the full sympathy of Newman. Ward, greatly distressed, wrote to Newman proposing a visit that he might talk over the situation. There is a touch of sad irony in Newman's reply:

> My dear Ward,
> I shall be glad to see you at any time and so far as I know shall be here or at Rednal for months.
> If things are to go as they have gone, I should anticipate that our conversation would have this result,—viz. you would begin by stating that I held something very different from, or the reverse of, what I really hold. I should undeceive you, and you would confess you were mistaken. Then we should branch off to some independent subject of theology, and you would be pleased to find that I agreed with you when others did not. You would leave; and then, in a few weeks, you would write me word that it pained you bitterly to think that we were diverging from each other in theological opinion more and more. If I then wrote to inquire what you could mean, you would answer that you really could not, at the moment, recollect the grounds on which you had been led to say so,—but you would not withdraw it.
> Thus, I have to endure, in spite of your real affection for me, a never-dying misgiving on your part that I am in some substantial matter at variance with you; while I for my part sincerely think that on no subject is there any substantial difference between us as far as theology is concerned,
> Ever yours affectly. J. H. N[85]

Here, Ward quotes a letter to delineate aspects of character that could not have meant more to him—not only his father's fractiousness and Newman's forbear-

---

[84] Newman to Lord Acton (5 July 1861), *LD*, xx, 4–5.
[85] Newman to W. G. Ward (22 April 1862), *LD*, xx, 191.

ance of that fractiousness but the unanimity both men shared when it came to bed-rock theological matters, always allowing for what Newman called "the allowable, inevitable differences ... which must ever exist between mind and mind."[86] Yet, Ward decided to go further and transcribe conversations he had had with Newman to give his readers a sense of the living presence of his subject, in much the same way Boswell had given life to his subject in his *Life of Johnson*. In one conversation, held on 30 January 1885, Ward has Newman ask:

> "And now I want to talk to you a little about your father. I wish you could let me know, for it would be news to me, the real secret of our estrangement latterly. He seemed determined to differ from me. I knew too well how much he had the advantage of me in theological reading—he had begun earlier and had given more time to it—to wish to differ from him. I followed him in all I could. But he seemed determined to make the most of our points of difference. I endorsed one of his letters: 'See how this man seeketh to find a quarrel against me.' Can you tell me more of it?" I did not like to go into many particulars, but I said: "Well, as you ask me does not the history of the *Home & Foreign Review* suggest something to your mind?" "But surely," he said, "your father never thought I agreed with Acton and Simpson?" "Not entirely," I said, "but he thought they were a great danger to the Church, and that they gained support from your countenance." "But I never really countenanced them," he said.[87] "Still, I could fancy that your father may have thought some of their views the outcome and result of my views; and that I ought explicitly to have disclaimed all solidarity with them. I own I was angry with him for not seeming to see the importance of avoiding the danger of alienating such able men from the Church. And perhaps I erred on the opposite side. I say it partly in praise, but perhaps partly in blame of myself, that I had a great tenderness for those learned men and excellent scholars, and wished to do all I could to prevent our losing the great advantage which might accrue to the Catholic cause from their services which we should lose if they were simply treated as rebels. But from first to last my opinions were with your father on the questions they raised, tho' I was angry with his tone. Then again, what did he mean by saying to Allies (who repeated it to me) directly the *Apologia* came out: "There I told you so"?—"so" meaning that I was unsound in my opinions. "I said that I thought things ran so high in those days that there was occasionally a want of perspective in my father's way of looking at things—tho' of course it was not for me to speak of the actual points at issue. He seemed at times to

---

[86] Newman to W. G. Ward (9 May 1867), *LD*, xxii, 216–17.
[87] According to Ward, what his father found objectionable about the *Home and Foreign Review* was the paper's "sweeping advocacy of all modern instruments of progress"; its "almost habitual treatment of Papal teaching as antiquated"; and its tendency to regard "modern liberties" and "modern scientific theories" as entitled to "supreme and unreserved allegiance." Ward, *William George Ward and the Catholic Revival*, 140. For an example of its Liberalism, Ward quoted this from the paper: "Is it not scandalous to allow congregations like those of the Index and Holy Office to come forth with all the pomp of authority, and to condemn as false and heretical theories which the Church, as teacher of the truth, has not so condemned? As if the only object were to impose on weak minds and to force them to obedience by pretending an infallible authority which really has nothing to do with the matter in hand." Ward, *William George Ward and the Catholic Revival*, 145. In Simpson's witty use of the word "congregations," one can see why the polemicist in Newman must have had a soft spot for the man.

exaggerate the importance of things important in the abstract, and not to see that practically people were not logical enough to make the things in question so important in them. For instance, where certain decisions of the Holy See were practically accepted, it was possible that his occasionally laying such stress as he did on their actual infallibility, which was at least a matter disputed, might practically give the Pope's words less rather than more weight, as raising a dispute and arousing party feeling.

I then said that his affection for the Cardinal had never diminished. "In one sense I knew that," he said, smiling. "In fact, I think his theory was that I was all the more dangerous because I was so attractive—that I was a sort of siren of whose fascination all should beware." But by degrees I convinced him that my father's reverence for him, as well as his affection, had never diminished. I told him that my father had wanted me to go to Edgbaston to be under his influence, as he thought I could judge for myself in points of theological difference between them, and that his personal influence would be invaluable. This touched and surprised the Cardinal extremely. He seemed at first almost incredulous. "It pleases and gratifies me much to hear that," he said. I told him also—which pleased him—that my father said to me on his death bed: "If ever I recover, one lesson I hope I have learnt in all the pain I have suffered, is that of being gentler and more tolerant. There is an inevitable and natural difference between one mind and another for which I have never made enough allowance." After a little further conversation, the Cardinal said: "It has been a real pleasure to me to have this talk with you about your father, and I hope you will not forget me and will pray for me." Then he gave me as a parting present the last edition of *The Grammar of Assent* ... I sent a letter afterwards thanking him for his kindness, and he wrote in reply: "It pleases me very much to find that you take so kindly the real affection I have for you which has come to me as if naturally from the love I had for your father. You can give me in return your prayers, which I need much."[88]

Here, the reader is given a picture not only of Newman's affection for Ward's father—despite all that impossible man's love of disputation—but his readiness to mediate between men of opposing opinions to prosper Church unity. From all we know of Newman through his letters and other writings, not to mention contemporary accounts of him, we can see that the transcription has the ring of truth, even if its Boswellian liberties flout scholarly protocol. The transcription certainly confirms the genius Newman had for befriending whole families. Josephine, as was only fitting for a daughter of James Hope-Scott, was devoted to Newman, as was her Aunt Philippa.[89] Indeed, as Sheridan Gilley points out, "The

---

[88] Ward, *Life of Newman*, ii, 495–7.
[89] Apropos, James Hope-Scott, his Christ Church friend, Sir Francis Doyle recalled: "Hope Scott was a sufficiently remarkable person ... there were not many of his contemporaries entitled, morally or intellectually, to rank with him ... I have said that James's sudden melancholy was not the outgrowth of any religious impulse, if anything, it worked in the opposite direction. I do not suppose that he was at any time a real sceptic, but if he ever dallied with scepticism, it would have been during those months of despondency when he sat alone in his long dismal room at Christ Church brooding over French and German metaphysics. In truth his mental state was such that I feared he might go mad. It was not long, however, before he found safety and peace by giving up his whole heart to the Church, and seeking, through her influence, to raise the moral and religious condition of the university

chief intellectual influence on Josephine ... was Newman, whom she had known since childhood when he visited Abbotsford and whom she remembered sitting in the family carriage becoming ever graver with her father's every pun. ... In her middle teens, she began to read his works in earnest ... and developed a strong devotion to him, taking passages from his books for her daily meditation."[90] In the case of the Ward family, Maisie's son, Wilfrid Sheed (1930–2011), the sprightly essayist, biographer and novelist remarked: "Cardinal Newman remained a spectral presence in the Ward household for ... three generations. 'He's just a fellow who lives at our place,' I once described him to a young friend."[91] Maisie Ward gave a less jocose account of why Newman fascinated the family. "My mother always thought that it was the failure to show the illuminating and vivifying relation of theology to life which prevented it from going home to the average mind," Maisie wrote.

> With what delight, then, did she discover Newman—through the strongest intellectual influence of those years, her aunt Philippa. They read him together, and for years the Newman habit was so strong that my mother kept a volume on her dressing-table and read a short passage daily. It was a curious unconscious preparation for her future vocation. My mother left a paper entitled "On reading Newman," which shows the line she followed and the way in which she was later able to supplement my father's Newman studies. Her approach is primarily personal: it is through the personality of "our great teacher" that she learns his doctrine. The Apologia, the Verses read as illustrating his life, The Parting of Friends, the unconscious self-revelation in Loss and Gain, but far more in Callista, are her chief themes. The style and the thought are one thing: *Cor ad cor loquitur*; and she concludes,
>
> > "It was the personal love of Our Lord that was to John Henry Newman the beginning and the end of his inner life. That love was the consecration and the consolation of a life marked out as a sacrifice to truth. If he had not been set apart in a desert place, should we of this generation go out to learn from his voice? Indeed he was one of the few great men who are alone while they live that they may leave immortal thoughts to be the companions of those that come after them." [92]

after a fashion of his own. It is a curious instance of the intense zeal with which he embraced his religious opinions, that no friendship, apparently, could keep its hold upon him unless in harmony with them. He withdrew from all personal intimacy with Mr. Gladstone on becoming a Catholic even more formally and decisively than he withdrew from mine on becoming a High Churchman. It was not, I am sure, that he ceased to regard either Mr. Gladstone or me with a certain affection, only he settled that it was better for him not to give way to it, but as it were 'to pass by on the other side.' No such necessity, that I am aware of, has ever suggested itself to Cardinal Newman. He retains his kindly feelings towards those whom he knew of old, and interests himself in his former friends and favourites with the old warmth of heart, Protestants though they be. It was Cardinal Newman, I think, whose example operated most strongly in leading Hope to the Catholic Church. That great man's extraordinary genius drew all those within his sphere, like a magnet." *Reminiscences and Opinions of Sir Francis Hastings Doyle 1813–1885* (London: Longmans, Green & Co., 1886), 144–5.

[90] Gilley, "An Intellectual Discipleship," 332. Abbotsford is Walter Scott's estate in the Scottish Borders where Hope-Scott brought up his family.
[91] Wilfrid Sheed, *Frank and Maisie: A Memoir with Parents* (New York: Simon & Schuster, 1985), 43.
[92] Ward, *The Wilfrid Wards*, i, 151.

Maisie Ward was never at a loss for giving vivid life to the figures she presented in her biography of her parents. Yet, if Wilfrid Ward managed the vividness necessary for good biography, he occasionally fell short of the requisite accuracy. For example, we can take the letter to which his transcription of Newman's conversation refers:

The Oratory. Birmingham. May 9th 1867

My dear Ward,

Fr Ryder has shown me your letter to him, in which you speak of me; and though I know that to remark on what you say will be as ineffectual now in making you understand me, as so many former times in the last 15 years, yet, at least as a protest in memoriam, I will, on occasion of this letter and of your letter to myself, make a fresh attempt to explain myself.

Let me observe then, that, in former years and now, I have considered the theological differences between us as unimportant in themselves, that is, such as to be simply compatible with a reception, both by you and by me, of the whole theological teaching of the Church in the widest sense of the word "teaching"; and again, now and in former years too, I have considered one phenomenon in you to be "momentous," nay portentous, viz. that you will persist in calling the said unimportant, allowable, inevitable differences (which must ever exist between mind and mind,) not unimportant, but of great moment.

In this utterly uncatholic, not so much opinion, as feeling and sentiment, you have grown in the course of years, whereas I consider that I remain myself in the same temper of forbearance and sobriety which I have ever wished to cultivate.

Years ago you wrote me a letter, in answer to one of mine, in which you made so much out of such natural difference of opinion between us, as exists, that I endorsed it with the words "See how this man seeketh a quarrel against me!"[93]

Now you are running on, as it appears to me, into worse excesses. [Here Charles Stephen Dessain, the founding editor of *The Letters and Diaries of John Henry Newman*, notes: "This sentence was omitted by Wilfrid Ward when he printed this letter in *William George Ward and the Catholic Revival*, and again in *Ward II*."]

Pardon me if I say that you are making a Church within a Church, as the Novatians of old did within the Catholic pale, and as, outside the Catholic pale, the Evangelicals of the Establishment. As they talk of "vital religion" and "vital doctrines," and will not allow that their brethren "know the Gospel" or are "Gospel preachers" unless they profess the small shibboleths of their own sect, so you are doing your best to make a party in the Catholic Church, and in St Paul's words are "dividing Christ" by exalting your opinions into dogmas, and shocking to say, by declaring to me, as you do, that those Catholics who do not accept them are of a different religion from yours. [Here Dessain notes: "All the words after 'dogmas' were again omitted by Wilfrid Ward on the two occasions when he published this letter."]

---

[93] Actually, this letter of 13 December 1861 is no longer to be found, though Newman did scrawl this across a letter dated 22 December 1861: "Observe how he *persists*, in spite of all I have written, all I have proved, all I have challenged him to prove, to say ... that we seriously differ from each other. Why, our last letter was an *agreement!*" *LD*, xx, 168, note 5.

I protest then again, not against your tenets, but against what I must call your schismatical spirit. I disown your intended praise of me viz that I hold your theological opinions "in the greatest aversion," and I pray God that I may never denounce, as you do, what the Church has not denounced.

Bear with me. Yrs affectly in Xt

John H. Newman[94]

Although Newman himself might have regarded these as pardonable omissions from a son protective of his father's reputation, the rest of us might simply see them as proof of the incidental shortcomings of Ward's work—shortcomings, after all, from which not even the best biographers are immune. They also dramatize how very personal Ward's engagement with these matters were. If we cannot expect to have Ward be an entirely dispassionate witness to the jousts between Newman and his father, we can be grateful for a witness for whom the jousts were never trifling or abstract. Nonetheless, the omissions certainly confirm the prudence of the Oratorians' blocking Ward from bringing out a volume of Newman's letters separate from his 2-volume biography, after he had completed the biography, even though this decision fueled speculation for some time that there might be something unspeakable in the Cardinal's correspondence. Whether the Oratorians knew of these omissions might be a moot point: they certainly knew that the biographer was not likely to bring out a creditable edition of even a sampling of the letters. In all events, in their providential wisdom, the Oratorian fathers left the door open to Father Stephen Dessain to lay the groundwork for what became *The Letters and Diaries of John Henry Newman*, which, for all its incidental flaws, is still a magnificent edition. In the introduction to the first volume of that edition, which appeared in 1962, Dessain laid out his vision for the projected work in terms of what he saw as Ward's comparative failure to do the letters or, indeed, the life justice. "Wilfrid Ward hoped to be allowed to bring out a third volume, supplementary to the *Life*, containing only letters," Dessain wrote.

> He began work on it, and "counted on this volume to complete the presentation of his hero to the world," but permission for it was not forthcoming from the Cardinal's literary executors. Masterly and admirable as Ward's *Life* was in so many respects, they felt that it had not been altogether successful, precisely in its presentation of the hero. They wanted as much of the correspondence as possible to be inserted in the *Life* itself, because that was what Newman had wished, and they "protested against a third volume of letters appearing after the *Life* on many grounds, but chiefly because it would make the letters subordinate to Mr Ward's presentation of Newman." Maisie Ward has stated her father's case, but she writes with such generous candour as to enable the reader to gather something of what prompted the literary executors' action. The Modernist crisis was at its height, and Wilfrid Ward, whose sister described him as "a prodigious blab," was maintaining that Newman too had been condemned. It is not surprising that in those anxious days the confidence of the executors in one who was appearing as

---

[94] Newman to W. G. Ward (9 May 1867), *LD*, xxii, 216–17.

Newman's official exponent should have been shaken, or that they should have been dissatisfied with his exposition. Wilfrid Ward claimed to know Newman's teaching through and through, but a real disciple ought to have been less easily perturbed. Subsequent history has vindicated the executors on this point. Also Wilfrid Ward seemed too inclined to set up as Newman's judge when writing the *Life*, which he treated as a tragic drama, "the tragedy of the Church in the Nineteenth Century." It was felt that a simpler approach, with the reader allowed to interpret more for himself, would have been preferable.

Dessain's objection to Ward, however, was more radical. "What had perhaps greater weight with the executors was their feeling that the picture of Newman which emerged from Wilfrid Ward's biography was not that of the natural, energetic, humorous and practical man they had known. 'It has become the fashion to speak of Newman as hyper-sensitive, a *souffre-douleur*,' said Abbot Butler, in 1926, by way of exordium to an excellent rebuttal of the charge, and surely it must be admitted that Wilfrid Ward bears some of the responsibility for this fashion. However, it is on the wane, and there has been enough material at hand for judgments independent of it to be formed. 'His integrity he never lost, however bleak and dreary some days and months and years might be; therefore he had resources, a power of stillness, a sense of order, which did not fail. Everyone who knew him felt his composure and stillness; as we who read him feel these qualities in his style.'"[95] For Dessain, Ward had failed to capture not only the toughness but the joy of his subject.

While Dessain's criticisms are not entirely unjust, and it is true that Ward unnerved the easily unnerved William Neville,[96] it is also true that Father Norris, Neville's successor, felt bound to write a letter to the *Times* exculpating Newman from any Modernist imputation, as did Cardinal Gasquet, who would later advise Ward "to hold nothing back in his *Life of Newman* in the interests of edification," though he also enjoined him to "Be careful … in your philosophical statements. There are heresy hunters after you."[97] Edward E. Kelly, chosen by Dessain to help him edit the twenty-first volume of the *Letters and Diaries*, subtitled "The Apologia," covering the years 1864–5, touted the merits of Ward's biography, especially since "Wilfrid Ward was given neither the originals nor the full collection of Newman's letters to work with; nor was he allowed, according to Newman's own wish, to add to the "record given in those letters [edited by Anne Mozley] and in the *Apologia*." In other words, the biography's unbalanced treatment of the early Newman was caused by the Oratorians refusing to grant him access to the earlier letters, not by any ineptitude on Ward's part. "As a result," Kelly continues, "only one chapter in the two volumes deals with Newman's life before 1845. This part of Newman's life was apparently considered complete and final in Newman's letters, and no interpretation was wanted from Ward."[98] Still, apropos Ward's treatment of the life as a whole, *The Spectator* made a striking

---

[95] Dessain quoted in *LD*, xi, xix–xx.
[96] Fr. Ignatius Ryder counselled Ward to treat Neville "as an old aunt from whom you have expectations." Ward, *The Wilfrid Wards and the Transition*, ii, 334.
[97] Gasquet quoted in Shane Leslie, *Cardinal Gasquet* (London: Burnes & Oates, 1953), 188.
[98] Kelly, "Newman's Reputation," 1–9.

observation when it said that: "We sometimes find ourselves wishing that the letters and papers had been left to tell their own tale, as were the Anglican letters in Miss Mozley's volumes, with just enough annotation as to clear up obscurities. However, Mr. Ward has decided otherwise; he clearly wished to point what he considered the moral of the life unmistakably; and we should think it now could escape nobody, not even the Congregation of the Propaganda, against whom it would appear to be especially directed." And for the reviewer the moral of the tale was unmistakable: "Mr. Ward's thesis is that the career in the Roman Church which Newman had planned for himself as the vindicator of Catholicism to his own nation was rendered nugatory, and his influence among Roman Catholics in every way restricted by the jealous fears of the narrow party which then, as now, was dominant at the Vatican."[99] What Dessain does not tell his readers is that this was precisely the thesis Neville feared might emerge from the Catholic correspondence, since, for the Oratorian, "Newman's Catholic period ... was a time of nothing else but disappointments, quarrels and failures."[100] Whether the thesis described by the *Spectator* reviewer is, in fact, Ward's thesis is another matter. Yes, Ward does not look away from the "disappointments, quarrels and failures," but nor does he stint the triumph of the life and work. In his introductory chapter to the biography, he is quite definite on this point: "The story more than once threatens to prove a tragedy," he writes, "but ends, as it begins, in peace and happiness."[101] Indeed, Ward understood, as Newman understood, how failure had been an inalienable part of his subject's spiritual development. "It is the rule of God's Providence," Newman wrote to the old Etonian Lord Braye in the fall of 1882, "that we should succeed by failure."[102] He would counsel Sir George Bowyer (1811–83) similarly once that exuberant convert became downhearted as the result of what he regarded as the failure of the church he founded in Great Ormond Street to serve as the chapel of the Hospital of St John and St Elizabeth. "My dear Bowyer," Newman wrote after he had brought the *Apologia* and all its troubles to a successful conclusion, "I am deeply grieved at what you tell me. It was only a few days ago, that in passing thro' London, I went to see your beautiful church, little dreaming what you tell me about it. But be sure, it will come all right—whatever be your trouble just now—such a work must command its legitimate place, as time goes on, and you must look steadily to the future. ... You must not be discouraged—who is there who has not had disappointment when he had a right to look forward hopefully?—a little time and the clouds will disperse."[103] Yet even earlier, in March of 1840—a pivotal time for the converting Newman—he wrote with fair prescience of what his future life as a Catholic would entail: "This world is a scene of conflict between good and evil. The evil not only avoids, but persecutes the good; the good cannot conquer, except by suffering. Good men seem to fail; their cause triumphs, but their own overthrow is the price paid for the success of their cause. When was it that this conflict, and this character and

---

[99] *Spectator* (2 March 1912), 350.
[100] Neville to Ward (6 April 1899), Wilfred Ward Papers, quoted in Gilley, "Wilfrid Ward and his Life of Newman," 184.
[101] Ward, *Life of Newman*, i, 4.
[102] Newman to Lord Braye (29 October 1882) quoted in Ward, *Life of Newman*, ii, 485.
[103] Newman to Bowyer (27 November 1864), *LD*, xxi, 315–16.

issue of it, have not been fulfilled?"[104] Weighing the conflicting claims of Ward and the Oratorians as to the import of Ward's biography, one has to conclude that it was not Ward but the Oratorians, despite all of their protestations to the contrary, who were inclined to see Newman's life as a "tragic drama."

Apropos the warrantability of Dessain's attack on Ward *vis-à-vis* the Modernist crisis, Kelly is, again, persuasive. "The Oratorians of 1912 and 1961 criticized Ward most for thinking Newman was implicated in the condemnation of Modernism in 1907," Kelly writes.

> Dessain was indignant with Ward for not succeeding in his portrait of Newman as "hero": "a real disciple ought to have been less easily perturbed." These are strangely unscholarly words. In point of fact, Ward wrote nothing about Newman and Modernism in his biography. He had hoped to defend Newman's thought against Modernist heresy but neither the Oratorians nor Cardinal Mercier wanted this. Ward did not think less of his hero because of his possible connections with Modernism; if there was fault anywhere, it was in the papal encyclical, "Pascendi Gregis." Despite all of the problems Ward had to face, he produced a very good biography of Newman. Martin Svaglic claims that it is the best one.[105]

Another factor that Dessain omitted to share with his readers was the publication of a separate pamphlet defending Newman against the charge of Modernism by Edward Thomas O'Dwyer, the Bishop of Limerick (1842–1917), whom Ward characterised as a "regular little fighting cock," a pamphlet, which, I shall show, is still very much worth reading, even though Ward found it wanting.[106] Thus, Ward was not the only one sworn to transmitting Newman's legacy faithfully who felt the need to defend him against the imputation of Modernism. "I observe that some of the persons who feel the severity of the Pope's condemnation try to shield themselves under the venerable name of Newman," O'Dwyer wrote.

> They would make believe that, in his writings, they can find, if not in express terms, at least in germ and embryo, the very doctrines for which they are now condemned, and they seem to hope that, in England, the name of Newman will be more authoritative on Catholic doctrine than the teaching of the Holy See.
>
> It is an uncatholic position, in principle, but it is as untrue to fact as it is unsound in faith. There is nothing in Newman to sustain, or extenuate, or suggest a particle of their wild and absurd theories.
>
> Newman was a Catholic to the tips of his fingers. Years before he thought of entering the Holy Catholic Church, he got a firm grip, by the grace of God, of some of the first principles of Catholic faith, and he never let them go, until by the

---

[104] John Henry Newman, "Endurance of the World's Censure" (29 March 1840), *PS*, viii, 141.
[105] Kelly, "Newman's Reputation." Martin Svaglic was the editor of the Clarendon critical edition of Newman's *Apologia* (1967).
[106] Ward, *The Wilfrid Wards and the Transition*, ii, 53. Although considered a "castle bishop" in his earlier career for refusing to support Parnell and Dillon and the Liberal Party over Home Rule, O'Dwyer shocked his contemporaries after the Easter Rebellion of 1916 when he threw his support behind Sinn Fein. Of course, there could be no defensible theological basis for support of "a movement which contemplated revolutionary violence." O'Dwyer's politics may have been askew, but he understood Newman clearly enough, as his pamphlet shows. See David M. Miller's entry on O'Dwyer in *ODNB*.

same grace, they led him into the true fold. And for us, who have been reared in that fold, and have had the blessing of living in a land where the spirit of faith, like an atmosphere, like the light of heaven, as with a robe, invests the very material world around us, it has always been a source of wonder and admiration to observe the extraordinary insight of Newman into Catholic theology, and the almost preterhuman power and grasp—at the same time, prevision and caution—with which he, a convert, dealt so fully with almost every phase of Catholic life.

Manning, in his striking funeral oration, said that by Newman's death we had lost a great witness to the faith. In a sense it was true. But yet that witness lives. It speaks in the great works which for several generations have been a help and a consolation to many; and what I propose to do now is to set his views, and opinions, on the questions involved in the errors of the Modernists, side by side with the teaching of our Holy Father, the Pope, and then I think it will appear that, as if by prophetic vision, he foresaw the evil with which we are now confronted, and bore his witness against it.[107]

In addition to giving *Pascendi* the robust defense it deserved, O'Dwyer demonstrated how little Modernists could lay claim to Newman's idea of development. "I cannot see how there can be room for doubt," he wrote.

Newman's whole doctrine was not only different from that of the Modernists, but so contrary to it in essence and fundamental principle, that I cannot conceive how, by any implication, it could be involved in their condemnation. ... Newman starts with the revelation of the Christian faith by Christ our Lord; "it is a *revelatio revelata*; it is a definite message from God to man, distinctly conveyed by chosen instruments, and to be received as such a message; and, therefore, to be positively acknowledged, embraced and maintained as true, on the ground of its being Divine, not as true on intrinsic grounds, not as probably true, or partially true, but as absolutely certain knowledge, certain in a sense in which nothing else can be certain, because it comes from Him who can neither deceive nor be deceived" (*Grammar of Assent*, p. 387).

Consequently, he holds that, whatever may be the processes of development with regard to that message, they are bound to it, and become a corruption if they change it. In other words, his theory is governed by the doctrine of the *depositum fidei*—the great body of truths which make up the complete system, if I may use the phrase, of the Christian faith, e.g., the doctrine of the Blessed Trinity, the Incarnation, the Redemption, the Sacraments, the Church; these and many other great truths would constitute, in Newman's view, the contents of the Divine message, that is, "the whole revealed dogma as taught by the Apostles, as committed by the Apostles to the Church, and as declared by the Church" (*Apologia*, p. 250).

Now the whole scope and purpose of the Essay on Development was to show that in the Church this original revelation has been preserved, that whatever

---

[107] Edward Thomas O'Dwyer, Bishop of Limerick, *Cardinal Newman and the Encyclical Pascendi Dominici Gregis: An Essay* (London: Longmans, Green & Co., 1908), 5–6.

definitions have been pronounced, in the course of ages, they but declare authoritatively, what it has contained from the beginning, and, consequently, that the faith of every Catholic of the present day is identical with that of the Church from the Apostolic times. As this is important let me quote his own words:—

"That the increase and expansion of the Christian creed and ritual, and the variations which have attended the process in the case of individual writers and Churches, are the necessary attendants of any philosophy or polity which takes possession of the intellect and heart, and has any wide or extended dominion; that from the nature of the human mind time is necessary for the full comprehension and perfection of great ideas; and that the highest and most wonderful truths, though communicated to the world once for all by inspired teachers, could not be comprehended all at once by the recipients, but, as being received and transmitted by minds not inspired, and through media which were human, have required only the longer time and deeper thought for their elucidation. This may be called the Theory of the Development of Doctrine." (*Development of Christian Doctrine*, Introduction, p. 30).

Now whether this theory be sound or not, and mind it is put forward only as a theory, and whether one is willing or not to admit implicit revelation to the extent which it postulates, it presents to the mind a well-defined view, which is based on the assumption that Christianity was revealed as a complete system, analogously to a philosophical system, with its own special doctrines, which required time for their comprehension and elucidation, but being revealed once for all in their fulness, could never admit any addition or change.[108]

One may ask, then, what on earth has a theory such as this to do with the views of these Modernists, which the Pope condemns? They begin with no deposit of faith; they do not admit any revelation in the Catholic sense; they deny the existence of any body of objective truth, authenticated for us by Divine revelation, as the source from which faith has to draw its doctrines and the criterion by which all human speculations as to faith are to be tested. With Newman the one question to be put to every proposition which claimed to be accepted on Divine faith was, is it in the primitive revelation?[109]

The fact that Ward turned O'Dwyer's piece down for the *Dublin* riled the Oratorian Fr Joseph Bacchus, who edited a good edition of Newman's correspondence with Keble. "The Catholics of these countries," he fulminated, "will not forget that, on flimsy grounds, *The Dublin Review* refused the hospitality of its columns to Dr. O'Dwyer's unanswerable vindication of Newman's integrity."[110] Yet, *pace* Bacchus, there were grounds for Ward's not running the piece: O'Dwyer had not sufficiently interpreted the anti-Modernist bull, which, without more detailed interpretation, could be construed as too sweeping. Ian Ker noted how Newman

---

[108] Newman puts this rather more precisely: "The absence, or partial absence, or incompleteness of dogmatic statements is no proof of the absence of impressions or implicit judgments, in the mind of the Church. Even centuries might pass without the formal expression of a truth, which had been all along the secret life of millions of faithful souls." *US*, 323.

[109] O'Dwyer, *Cardinal Newman and the Encyclical Pascendi Dominici Gregis*, 35–41. For a good, learned, far-ranging discussion of Newman's idea of development, see Hütter, *Newman on Truth and its Counterfeits*, 130–66.

[110] Bacchus to Longman (5 April 1911) quoted in Gilley, "Wilfrid Ward and his Life of Newman," 191.

had made a similar point regarding Pius IX's bull on papal infallibility: "At the outset [Newman] emphasizes a point that he had made in a private letter in 1870, namely that the definition of 1870, like all definitions and teachings of Councils and popes, did not speak for itself—it required interpretation by theologians, just as 'lawyers explain acts of Parliament.'"[111] In fact, Ward was open to running O'Dwyer's response to the bull if it included some practical guidance as to the bull's scope, but when the bishop refused to modify what he had written, Ward withdrew his offer of publication. In making his decision, Ward obviously had in mind the precedent of Bishop Joseph Fessler's *True and False Infallibility* (1875), which set out the exact scope of papal infallibility.[112] Indeed, it was Fessler's reading of the bull that guided Newman in his handling of the matter in his *Letter to the Duke of Norfolk* (1875), upon the publication of which Bishop David Moriarty of Kerry wrote the author: "Many thanks for the *coup de grace* you have given to the faction who would allow none to be Catholics but Dublin Reviewers and Tablet Editors ... You and Dr Fessler have shut them up."[113] The son of W. G. Ward naturally wished Bishop O'Dwyer to write something equally useful for *Pascendi*.

Here, parenthetically, it might be useful to make the point that if readers wish to see a practical application of Newman's idea of development, they should attend to his response to the doctrine of papal infallibility, a truly authentic doctrinal development, which, as any even cursory study of the response will show, has nothing whatever to do with the heretical fantasies of our more recent Modernists.

Another factor that we should take into consideration in weighing Dessain's criticism of Ward is Newman's fondness for his biographer. "Every one speaks well of young Mr. Ward," Newman wrote their mutual friend Baron von Hügel in 1884, "and I hope he will do much service to the philosophical side of religion in our English controversies."[114] Two years later, after meeting with the son of his most exasperating critic, Newman wrote the budding author: "Everything you write is like yourself and makes a reader love you."[115] That Newman should have described the successful author as one who induced love in his reader was characteristic. Writing, if successful, should prosper salutary personal influence. Heart should speak to heart. Newman could extoll such influence with some authority because he had written of it in his Oxford University Sermon, "Personal Influence: The Means of Propagating the Truth" (1832) with masterly discernment and made his own influence throughout his life a radical blessing to others.

After the publication of the *Apologia*, he wrote Lord Coleridge (1820–94), the friend of Mathew Arnold and Arthur Hugh Clough and biographer of John

---

[111] Ker, *Newman on Vatican II*, 35. Cf. Newman to E. S. Froude (30 March 1870), *LD*, xxv, 71–2.

[112] Cf. "The official countenance of Fessler's weighty theological judgment was a reminder that the co-operation of theologians of different views—the theological Schola—secured the constitution of the Church against absolutism and the excesses of individuals." Ward, *Life of Newman*, ii, 373. It was translating Fessler's German that killed Ambrose St John. See *LD*, xxvii, 412.

[113] Bishop Moriarty to Newman (24 February 1875), *LD*, xxviii, 237.

[114] Newman to Baron Von Hügel (21 July 1884) *LD*, xxx, 384.

[115] Newman to Wilfrid Ward (2 April 1886), *LD*, xxxii, 473. Newman was referring to Ward's "The Clothes of Religion: A Reply to Popular Positivism" (1884), which appeared in the *National Review*.

Keble, to thank him for kind words he had written about the book. "It has been the great mercy of God towards me," Newman wrote "that a season of especial trial has had its especial compensation in the extreme personal sympathy shown towards me, by so many men, of such various characters of mind and shades of opinion. I have, indeed, had most equitable and lenient judges." This was especially welcome to Newman because, as he said, "I am often led to call my life a history of failures. It is a great consolation to me to receive evidence, as I do from time to time, that all was not lost, when so much time and anxiety was expended."[116]

Coleridge had disabused his old friend on this score in words that must have touched Newman deeply: "of my own personal friends there are many who from that day to this have lived better lives and tried more earnestly to love and serve God because of your influence — and I am sure that what I can say in this respect many others can say also. No lapse of time, no difference of opinion can ever destroy or even weaken the feeling with which men must regard you who know that in a true sense under God they owe you their own souls."[117]

In judging Ward's work, we should be leery of imagining Dessain's the only tenable assessment. Sheridan Gilley, for one, is a good deal more balanced. Yes, for Gilley, "Ward was a 'prodigious blab,' 'vehement, rash and excitable'[118] and given to writing angry letters which his wife and daughter tried to stop him from posting. His temperament was not one conducive to mental peace." Yet, "in the anti-modernist climate in the Church Ward's theological view of a careful, critical, and discriminating, if not a 'liberal', Catholicism obscured to hyper-orthodox Catholics the great gulf which lay between him and a modernist like Tyrrell, who denied fundamental credal doctrines."[119]

V

Ward's relationship with George Tyrrell highlights the risks the biographer was prepared to run in order to understand the *soi-disant* "historical-critical" methods of the more unorthodox religious thinkers of his time, and certainly Tyrrell epitomized those thinkers. Born in Dublin in 1861 to Protestant parents, he converted in 1879 and joined the Society of Jesus in 1880. His staunchly Church of Ireland mother, whom Tyrrell adored, found his poping particularly grievous, bewailing, as she said, "that a son of mine should go to Mass with the cook."[120] After reading Newman's *Grammar of Assent* no less than four times, Tyrrell set himself the task of seeing whether it would be possible to have his study of Newman enable the Church "to pour Catholic truth from the scholastic into the modern mold without losing a drop in the transfer"—thus having the best, as he thought, of Newman and St. Thomas Aquinas combined.[121] Of course, this

---

[116] Newman to John Duke Coleridge (12 October 1864), *LD*, xxi, 259–61.
[117] *LD*, xxi, 261, n.1.
[118] Ward, *The Wilfrid Wards and the Transition*, i, 103.
[119] Gilley, *ODNB*.
[120] Tyrell quoted in Nicholas Sagovsky, *'On God's Side': A Life of George Tyrrell* (Oxford: Oxford University Press, 1990), 10.
[121] Ibid., 40.

was an otiose transference, Aquinas and Newman never being at odds, though, as I shall show, the compatibility of the two lay at the very heart of the Church's response to the Modernist crisis. Despite what detractors and even champions of Newman imagine, Neo-Scholastics during and after Newman's lifetime approved of his theological work; indeed, they saw it as complementary to their own.[122] Moreover, as we shall see, Newman was never suspected of unorthodoxy by Pius X or the prelates with whom he surrounded himself, all of whom were trained in scholasticism. Nevertheless, Tyrrell's biographer is right to see that the *Grammar* had a profound impact on his hero precisely because "Newman's stress on the moral and intuitive dimension of certainty in religious belief provided a necessary complement to the intellectualism of nineteenth-century scholastic teaching."[123] Like Newman, Tyrrell would always credit personal influence as crucial to his personal development. Apropos Robert Dolling, the Irishman whom Harrow and Cambridge had turned into a Christian Socialist, Tyrrell would write: "All my love of the *benignitas et humanitas Dei Salvatoris nostri*; all that people care for in *Nova et Vetera*; all my evangelical sympathies; all my revolt against the Pharisees and the canon-lawyer is the outgrowth of the seeds of his influence."[124] Indeed, it was at Dolling's library in Mountjoy Square that the young Tyrell was first introduced not only to Pusey's biographer Liddon but to Aquinas, in whose work he would become steeped once he joined the Jesuits. As a result, Tyrrell was always appreciative of the Church's majesty, even after he chose to reject it. One can see this clearly in one of his sermons, where he bid his parishioners to

> Look for a moment ... at the great Kingdom of God the Catholic Church whose root is at Rome ... and whose branches are in all lands, stretching from sea to sea and to the uttermost bounds of the earth; look at her highly developed organisation, her hierarchy, her discipline, her doctrine. What a gigantic power she is! How rationalists and misbelievers are at a loss to account for her origin, her spread, her persistence.[125]

---

[122] Meszaros, "Some Neo-Scholastic Receptions of Newman." If the Neo-Scholastics were appreciative of Newman's work, Newman was also appreciative of theirs. Cf. "Newman had a keen awareness of how the *schola theologarum* and their theological argumentation played key roles in the ultimate determination of doctrines. In this sense, Marín-Sola, Schultes, Garrigou-Lagrange, and others find renewed relevance, for they are exemplary in their theological reasoning and argumentation." Meszaros, "Newman and the Thomistic Tradition," 467. Cf. "No Catholic theologian working on the inherently complex and ongoingly contested question of the development of doctrine could afford to ignore Marin-Sola's *magnum opus*," The Homogenous Evolution of Catholic Doctrine (1924) ... [M]ost Catholic theologians still dealing with the development of Catholic doctrine embrace the notion of paradigm shift ... This purported shift makes possible the unexamined dismissal of Marin-Sola's theory as belonging to an outdated 'neo-Scholastic' past. Theologians who adopted this ... dismissal" are oblivious "of a nuanced, profound and coherent tradition of discourse on the development of doctrine stretching from the sixteenth century right up to the threshold of the Second Vatican Council. It is this very oblivion that makes post Vatican II theologies of doctrinal development vulnerable to the very pitfalls and dead-ends Marin-Sola astutely identifies and ably navigates around in *The Homogenous Evolution of Catholic Dogma*." Hütter, *Newman on Truth and its Counterfeits*, 158.
[123] Sagovsky, 'On God's Side', 40.
[124] Tyrrell quoted *ibid.*, 9.
[125] Tyrrell quoted *ibid.*, 41. Cf. Edward Short, "Fair Triumph or Foul," *City Journal* (7 April 2023).

Ironically enough, it was the epilogue of Ward's life of Wiseman, "The Exclusive Church and the Zeitgeist" that hastened Tyrrell down the road of Modernism. In the epilogue, the biographer insisted, as he wrote in his essay, "New Wine in Old Bottles," that the Church find "a *modus vivendi* with what is really valuable in intellectual movements, or really true in scientific achievement." Tyrrell, in his review of the book, inferring from it what he thought its upshot, did Wilfrid Ward no favors. "The first endeavour," Tyrrell wrote, "must be to create ... [the] 'wish to believe' by drawing attention to the human and attractive side of Catholicity, its social utility, its universal sympathy with every effort in the cause of truth, justice, and charity; or at least by removing all false impressions to the contrary." The failure of any mention of Jesus Christ in these musings was tell-tale enough, but when the agitated Jesuit proceeded to hold forth on the place of dogma in the Faith his dissent not only from Catholic orthodoxy but from Newman, the arch defender of the dogmatic principal, became patent. "The Church ... binds only so far as she is absolutely urged by necessity ... definitions are simply forced from her by the cavillings of the rationalistic or heretical mind," Tyrrell wrote,

> that though final, so far as they exclude some definite error, her dogmas are never final in the sense of stating exhaustively truths that, being supernatural, are inexhaustible; that if she arrests the inopportune discussion or proclamation of some new discovery in history or science, it is really in the essential interest of truth, lest the wheat should be uprooted with the tares, and the minds of millions perplexed in matters of supreme practical consequence for the sake of a detail of little or no practical consequence; or it is because the truth is urged in an heretical spirit, not as creating an interesting difficulty, but as founding a right to doubt. When once we recognize that there is in all men, so far as unregenerate, a spirit of unauthorized dogmatism essentially heretical, against whose tyranny the authorized dogma of the Church is the Divine safeguard of liberty, we shall not be surprised to find that many who belong to the Church are prone at times, all unconsciously, to gratify this dogmatizing instinct by urging orthodox beliefs upon others in an intolerant and narrow spirit, really because they are their own, ostensibly because they are divinely authorized; and even to try to bring their purely private opinions under the aegis of ecclesiastical infallibility, and to impose them upon others under pain of anathema.[126]

After gradually becoming more and more dismissive of Catholic dogma, and, indeed Catholic orthodoxy *per se,* Tyrrell left the Jesuits and was finally excommunicated after writing mocking rebuttals of Pius X's encyclical condemning Modernism. In one salvo, we can see a fair specimen of the heretical Irishman's talent for mockery. "In spite of the long and strenuous efforts of Leo XIII to enforce Scholasticism," he wrote, "it seems that the ailment of modernists, for the most part educated in seminaries, is a profound ignorance of Scholasticism. One wonders irresistibly whether a profound knowledge of Scholasticism may not have something to do with their defection." Maude Petre, the editor of Tyrrell's *Autobiography,* was good on her friend's sardonic view of the world and of the

---

[126] George Tyrrell, "Wiseman: His Aims and Methods," The Month, 91 (Jan.–June 1898), 149–50.

Church. "The sense of humour is a close ally" to the "fundamental sense of truth, and it was an insuppressible element of [Tyrrell's] temperament," she wrote.[127]

> It played over the most serious events of his life as irresistibly as over the lighter ones; it was with him in joy and in sorrow, in rest and in work; it flashed over his most strenuous efforts and flickered over his death-bed. He had, indeed, a fund of sheer merriment, but his was, in general, the humour of the tragic, and not of the cheerful temperament; the humour that is associated with a sense of sin and sorrow, and that is not bestowed on the innocent and happy. God and His perfectly holy ones are without it; faulty man is less faulty when he possesses it. It is associated with the pathos of wrong-doing and short-coming, with the sad clear vision of those who gauge the puny efforts of man in comparison with the vast universe in which he moves.[128]

What Petre does not allow for is Tyrrell's delight in mockery for its own sake, a good an example of which can be found from his introduction to Bremond's book:

> I would advise somebody to read Newman from one end to the other, for the sole purpose of extracting from his works a literary and religious manual of "economy." We should thus have a delightful book, a commentary on the text "Sufficient for the day is the evil thereof" applied to teaching, to the popularising of knowledge, and to controversy. Christian literature would gain much by a revival of those too much neglected methods which, in other fields, have made Jouberts and Sainte-Beuves; and, besides, we should learn gradually to familiarise the simple-minded with those necessary revelations which would often frighten them less if they were not presented to them with a sort of masterful brutality.[129]

Apropos Maud Petre and her Modernist friends Tyrrell and Bremond, Hilaire Belloc was predictably unsparing. Conversing with a friend, he once remarked, "They think we've got the text wrong, and that what Our Blessed Lord really said was 'Thou art Maud Petre, and upon this rock I will build my Church.'" Belloc's biographer, Robert Speaight, however, did not altogether share his hero's con-

---

[127] Maude Petre (1863–1942), "author and writer on religion, was born on 4 August 1863 at Coptfold Hall near the village of Margaretting in Essex, the seventh of eleven children of Arthur Petre (1828–82), younger son of the thirteenth Lord Petre, and Lady Catherine Howard (1831–82), fifth daughter of the earl of Wicklow. Her mother was a convert to Roman Catholicism and her father, a gentleman farmer and justice of the peace, belonged to one of the old Roman Catholic families. Her parents died within two months of each other when Maude was nineteen. She was educated at home. In her memoirs … she described her Victorian Catholic childhood and adolescence and reflected on her spiritual journey. She saw herself as 'passionately religious' and 'innately sceptical' (Petre, 187). When she was twenty-two, at the suggestion of her confessor as a remedy for her religious doubts, she studied scholastic philosophy under private instruction in Latin from professors of the college of the propaganda fide in Rome." *ODNB*. A zealous Modernist, Petre was denied the sacraments in her own diocese after she refused to take Msgr. Benigni's anti-modernist oath, though she regained access to the sacraments when she moved in old age to London. When Petre's friend Tyrrell was shown the door by the Jesuits, she provided a home for him in her own home at Storrington, Essex.
[128] *Autobiography and Life of George Tyrrell*, 2 vols, ed. Maude Petre (London: Arnold, 212), ii, 9–10.
[129] Tyrrell, "Introduction," in Henri Bremond, *The Mystery of Newman* (London: Williams and Norgate, 1907), 6.

tempt for Petre and her friends. For Speight, Belloc "may not have done justice to the niceties of Modernist hesitations and [he] certainly did not grasp the tragedy of what was going on around him. It needed a mind more sympathetic and theologically trained—a mind like Wilfrid Ward's—to see that while the Papal condemnations might have been necessary, the handling of the crisis on the human side was both clumsy and cruel." Moreover, Speaight added, "When Ward remarked to someone at the Athenaeum that the Pope was 'narrow,' Belloc assumed that he was ... fellow-travelling with the persecuted trio," which was demonstrably false. "Ward was as orthodox as Belloc," Speaight insisted, and "he knew much more about the working of other people's minds."[130]

Ward experienced some of this clumsy cruelty himself when he received a letter from Cardinal Rampolla criticizing the epilogue he had written for his Wiseman biography, a letter which caused him, as he said, "a quite extraordinary degree of misery." Rampolla's disapproval was all the more crushing because Cardinal Mercier had written Ward in 1902 to say that he regarded the epilogue as "beautiful and suggestive." Once he learned of Rampolla's views, Mercier even offered to act as Ward's "Mémoire justificative" with Rampolla, a show of sympathy which moved Ward. "Nothing could be kinder than the Cardinal," he wrote. "He will write me a letter to quote. Also he will write to Rampolla on my behalf. He thinks all will quiet down in Rome. His view is that it means 'take care not to write a biography of Newman which is a defence of Modernism.'" Yet Rampolla was adamant: the epilogue must be suppressed. After conferring with Rampolla in Rome, Archbishop Bourne tried to give Ward useful advice, which Maisie Ward paraphrased thus: "give no explanations; make no requests ... simply withdraw the chapter as an obedient son of the Church."[131] In response, Ward might have withdrawn the errant chapter but he could not refrain from giving explanations. In the event, his explanations extended not only to the epilogue but his friendship with Tyrrell, which he could reasonably fear as incurring guilt by association, and Pius X's Encyclical *Pascendi* condemning Modernism. In his defense of the epilogue, what Maisie thought "in substance Wilfrid Ward's Apologia," one can see Ward's pitiable inability to leave well enough alone, but also his recognition that the Church could not simply sidestep the modern thinking that she was bound to condemn.

The distress this episode caused Ward understandably distracted him from recalling something Newman had written to Pusey, which Ward might very well have adduced to parry Rampolla, for in remonstrating with his old Tractarian friend for not answering the criticism that Thomas Harper, S. J. had made against his *Eirenicon* Newman got at the essence of Ward's perennial plea for open debate: "[F]or myself I do not sympathise at all in the policy of suppression," Newman wrote. "I have no fear that it will harm the cause of what I think truth, that some things, nay strong things can be adduced against it. There are objections, and grave objections, to the simplest truths, and the cause of Truth gains by their being stated clearly and considered carefully."[132]

---

[130] Speight, *The Life of Hilaire Belloc*, 251.
[131] Ward, *The Wilfrid Wards and the Transition*, ii, 319–20.
[132] John Henry Newman to Edward Pusey (4 August 1867), *LD*, xxiii, 284.

The failure of the Church adequately to refute Modernism has had rather appalling consequences: the recrudescence of hydra-headed heresy in the twenty-first century is baleful proof of that. Yes, *Pascendi* showed the bad actors off the stage but their errors remained. In a witty journal essay, Stephen Bullivant shows that it was not Tyrrell's heretical views *per se* that caused him to be excommunicated, though these were heretical enough, but "his insubordination and contempt for the magisterium in the secular press." To substantiate his point, Prof. Bullivant quotes what Canon James Moyes wrote in the *Tablet* (in an article soon reprinted in full in *L'Osservatore*):

> That a priest could so far forget himself ... as to publish in the columns of the chief journal of the land a vehement attack upon the Encyclical, and the specific body of teaching which the Holy See has solemnly addressed to the whole Catholic world, holding up to contempt the august person of the Vicar of Christ as one who has not sufficient intellectual capacity even to comprehend the meaning of what he is condemning, is a scandal, which it is impossible to condone.
>
> The spectacle of a priest waging battle against the Holy See in the columns of *The Times* is one which even the few sympathisers whom he may have in this country will be very glad to forget.'[133]

Prof. Bullivant also shows that, for authority, Newman was never the source of suspicion or disapproval that Ward and so many others feared. Indeed, Newman was actually a favorite of Pius X's Secretary of State, the impeccably ultramontane, Merry del Val. "[C]ontrary to frequent reports ... there was no campaign against Newman within the Curia at the time of the publication of *Pascendi*," Prof. Bullivant writes. "While the wording of *Pascendi* may perhaps have been ambiguous in this regard, it was nobody's intention to condemn him, or to cast aspersions on his theology in any way." Indeed, Prof. Bullivant goes so far as to say that "had Merry del Val or St Pius been less zealous in their defence of Newman, then a doubt would surely have been cast over him that even his latter-day supporters John Paul II (who declared him Venerable) and Benedict XVI (who broke his own protocol to beatify him personally, and who has previously suggested Newman to be a Doctor of a Church) might have been wary of overturning. Blessed John Henry might then forgive us if, just this once and on his behalf, we toast first a pope—and afterwards, his Cardinal Secretary of State."[134]

Shortly before his death, Tyrrell wrote a friend, "My own work—which I regard as done—has been to raise a question, which I have failed to answer." For Tyrrell's biographer, Nicholas Sagovsky, "The question was that of the meaning of Christianity in the modern world." Tyrrell's insistence on believing that the

---

[133] Stephen Bullivant, "Newman and Modernism: The 'Pascendi' Crisis and its Wider Significance," *New Blackfriars* (March 2011), 92, no. 1038, 194–5.

[134] *Ibid.*, 207–8. If Merry del Val was fond of Newman, he looked askance at Wilfrid Ward, as Prof. Bullivant shows. "Writing to the vice-president of Ushaw in 1908, he noted: I am glad to see that among your speakers [for the centenary] you have not W. Ward who is so unsafe. He is an acrobat and performs the trick of teaching or insinuating unsound doctrines and of wriggling out of them within twenty-four hours, and then tells everybody that all that is Newman. Poor Newman. We don't want this humbug at Ushaw where we like the genuine article in everything." "Newman and Modernism," 200.

Church lacked an answer to the question finally caused him to part ways with Wilfrid Ward, whose complaint was not that the Church lacked an answer but that it would not articulate its answer in modern terms. Maisie Ward saw the chasm between the Modernists and orthodoxy in terms Newman set down in his *Essay on Development*:

> They are ever hunting for a fabulous primitive simplicity; we repose in Catholic fullness. They seek what never has been found; we accept and use what even they acknowledge to be a substance. They are driven to maintain, on their part, that the Church's doctrine was never pure; we say that it can never be corrupt. We consider that a divine promise keeps the Church Catholic from doctrinal corruption; but on what promise, or on what encouragement, they are seeking for their visionary purity does not appear.[135]

Father Alfred Loisy was another controversial figure at the time whose relationship with Catholic dogma became hardly orthodox. A pupil of Renan and an esteemed biblical scholar at the *Institut Catholique*, Loisy was at first regarded as a defender of orthodoxy. Indeed, in *L'Évangile et l'Église* (1902), he was applauded by Catholics for seeming to refute, as they imagined, the claim of the Protestant historian, Adolf Harnack that the divinity of Christ was nothing more than an accretion of the post-primitive Church. Looking back on his monograph, the Frenchman squarely disabused his erstwhile sympathizers of their misapprehensions and admitted that "Historically speaking, I did not admit that Christ founded the Church or the Sacraments; I professed that dogmas formed themselves gradually, and that they were not unchangeable; and it was the same for ecclesiastical authority which I conceived as a ministry of human education without allowing it an absolute and unlimited right on the intelligence and conscience of the believers."[136] More bluntly still, he confessed: "Christ has even less importance for my religion than he has in that of the liberal Protestants, for I attach little importance to the revelation of God the Father for which they honour Jesus. If I am anything in religion, it is more pantheist-positivist-humanitarian than Christian."[137] As Mark Vickers, the witty biographer of Cardinal Bourne observes: "There are those who judge Loisy 'the most impressive, because the most learned, subtle and eloquent, of the Modernist leaders' ... but his memoirs ... justified every fear Pius X entertained about Modernism."[138]

Yet when we read Ward's account of Loisy's first discovery of Newman's *Essay on Development*, we can begin to understand how he might have allowed himself

---

[135] *Dev*, 382.
[136] Loisy quoted in Mark Vickers, *By the Thames Divided: Cardinal Bourne in Southwark and Westminster* (Leominster: Gracewing, 2013), 215. Proof that the Church's theological young are not infected with the Modernist virus can be seen in the work of Prof. Andrew Meszaros, who confirms in his monograph on Congar and Newman: "certain key principles must be maintained: namely, the unity and finality of revelation based on, and culminating in, the coming of Jesus Christ; the homogeneity of revelation based on the truth that is God who neither deceives nor is deceived; and the communicability and knowability of revelation implied in the very notion of revelation" Meszaros, *The Prophetic Church*, 198.
[137] Loisy quoted in Vickers, *By the Thames Divided*, 215.
[138] *Ibid*.

to be diddled by this imposing man. "A note of genuine surprise is visible in [Loisy's] remarks on the scientific quality of this great work," Ward remarks, apropos Loisy; and then he quotes Loisy from a piece the French scholar wrote in *Revue du Clergé Français* (December, 1898).

> A large conception of the history of dogma and of Christian development [he writes], a conception truly scientific, in which all legitimate conclusions of historical criticism can find a shelter, had been formulated by a Catholic thinker long before certain Protestant publications which have made a stir in these latter days. Harnack's "History of Dogma" is more learned than "The Development of Christian Doctrine," but how inferior it is to that essay in the general understanding of Christianity, with its varied life and the intimate connection which exists between all forms and all phases of that life! As to readers of Augusta Sabatier's "Esquisse de la philosophie de la religion" who have been struck by some of its generalizations', who have regretted, it may be, that a similar book had not been written in defence of Catholicism, we may tell them that such a book exists already, better documented than that of the learned Dean of the Protestant theological faculty, showing a more complete religious experience, a mind more open and more impartial. Catholic theology has had in our days that great doctor whom it has needed. There has been wanting to him [Loisy concludes] no element of the scientific spirit.[139]

How so many fairly learned Catholics could have been taken in by Loisy is a nice question. For Maisie Ward, "It seemed so improbable at first view that priests who had dedicated their lives to the service of the Church, who celebrated daily the Holy Sacrifice of the Mass, who declared that their one object was to make the Church acceptable to the world of to-day, should really mean the things they were apparently saying. It was easier to think that they were being misunderstood than to accuse them at once of what was not merely an error but a complete abandonment of revelation, the miraculous and the whole supernatural order."[140]

In all events, Maisie Ward saw her father's friend, Baron von Hügel as Loisy's agent. All the favorable notices of *L'Évangile et l'Église* in the English press were orchestrated by the baron; and Maude Petre had no doubts about his central role in the advancement of Modernism. "He was undoubtedly our leader, she wrote in *My Way of Faith* (1937), "through all the first stages of the Modernist Movement and his influence extended over at least four countries. He was our centre, our link with others whom we did not personally know. He diffused our writings and extolled our efforts; while criticizing our shortcomings."[141] He was particularly impatient with what he regarded as Ward's shortcomings. Again, Maisie Ward is clear about this: "As early as 1899 von Hügel wrote irritably to Loisy about my father's mania for discussing the orthodoxy of points of view and methods" when what is needed is to bring our people to look at the reality

---

[139] Loisy quoted in Ward, *Last Lectures*, 19. After quoting Tyrrell and Loisy, Ward wrote: "I need hardly say that in quoting these writers I imply no sympathy with their theological views. I appeal to them only as acknowledged experts in their own line."
[140] Ward, *The Wilfrid Wards and the Transition*, ii, 171.
[141] Ibid., 492–3.

of things and the legitimacy of scientific methods. "Wilfrid Ward," he said, "manoeuvres to get air for us," but "meanwhile he is always tending to trace limits, to set up no thoroughfare signs, *ce qui n'est que nous enfermer dans la vieille cage*.'"[142] In summing up a man about whom she was deeply ambivalent, finding him at once "rebellious" and "deeply Catholic," a "contemplative by nature and intensely prayerful by practice," Maisie Ward nevertheless saw him as a kind of Tertullian—a deaf, unworldly, purblind Tertullian.[143] "It seems to me that if harm was done by the Baron's commerce with the Modernists, greater was done by [his] visits to Rome. For the obvious goodness, sincerity and deep piety of the Baron induced the Roman authorities to trust him in his representations about his friends. Then when Loisy's real meaning was unmasked, came disillusionment that led very far. Was it likely that rulers who were also the guardians of a divine deposit of truth would listen again to a plea for the rights of scholarship when that plea had once led them into such dangers? Better far an uncritical unscholarly Church holding fast the divine truth to a Church of scholars which had let go the one thing necessary."[144] Certainly Newman would have agreed with this assessment, since he had no time for the "Church of scholars" that his friend Döllinger was so keen to establish after rejecting the First Vatican Council's definition of papal infallibility. In all events, one reason why Ward might have allowed himself to become embroiled in the depredations of the Modernists is suggested by something Maisie Ward says about Loisy and his correspondent, von Hügel.

> A close study of Loisy's *Mémoires* gives the best clue I have found to the characters and career of both men. Depressing as is Loisy's own mental and spiritual history, I think there is one virtue discernible in these three volumes of 2,000 pages: the possession of a literary conscience. He usually gives the point of view of his correspondent with plentiful quotation. He never depends on memory but on his diaries and correspondence in speaking of the past, and wherever I have been able to check his account by contemporary reference I have found it accurate. So much so that in places he gives quite frankly the evidence that destroys his own conclusions.[145]

The biographer of Newman would doubtless have found such documentary meticulousness irresistible.

After it became undeniable that Tyrrell and Loisy were heretics, Wilfrid Ward wrote an account of his unfortunate association with both of them, in which he wrote of how: "I entreated the Tyrrells and the Loisys to show ... practicalness and moderation as would make authority regard them as friends."[146] The futility of such an approach would, in time, become all too clear. In this instance, Ward's otherwise admirable willingness to show the thought of others some modicum of sympathy badly betrayed him. Yet, since Ward's very involvement in the

---

[142] *Ibid.*, 491.
[143] *Ibid.*, 490, 496, 512.
[144] *Ibid.*, 495.
[145] *Ibid.*, 503.
[146] Ward quoted in *Last Lectures*, xxxii.

Modernist crisis eventually helped to vindicate the orthodoxy of Newman's work, it would be unfair to rate him for alarmism. In retrospect, we can see that he played a providential part in Newman's apostolate. The writer of Ward's obituary in the *Tablet* certainly recognized this: "That Mr. Ward's independence of judgment should have led him to be suspected of modernist tendencies by some narrow folk only rendered his loyal acceptance of Catholic teaching the more striking as an object lesson in submission to authority. Intellectually, Mr. Ward was a man who counted."[147]

One Modernist by whom Ward was not deceived was Henri Bremond (1865–1933), whose *The Mystery of Newman* (1907) ignored the writings to speculate on the character of the man who composed the writings—a wonderfully perverse enterprise, especially since Bremond concluded that the man responsible for the writings suffered from a kind of religiose solipsism. Gilley's contention that it was from this Gallican caricature that Ward willy-nilly drew his hypersensitive Newman was ingenious but unpersuasive.[148] Bremond, his thesis being what it was, could not have done better than to have Tyrrell write the forward. Ward's review in the *Dublin* was justly contemptuous. "M. Bremond has taken as a model for his work a smaller man cut out of the real Newman—and a good deal altered and damaged in the cutting. He has dressed him partly in French clothes and partly in a raiment of his own exuberant fancy. I am bound to add that he has constructed so lively a marionette that at moments one thinks he is a real human being."[149] The Frenchman betrayed his blithe disregard for his subject's writing when he admitted at the very start of the book that "The study of Newman's doctrine is relegated to a sort of appendix at the end of the volume, which I should like to have made still shorter."[150] Maisie Ward is amusing on the exasperated fury the book induced in her combustible father.

> Towards the end of these three years came the appearance of Bremond's book, *The Mystery of Newman*, which intensely exasperated my father. A lifelong study of Newman had given him alike familiarity with his lines of thought and a profound personal love for him. I shall never forget the violent irruptions into our own work that my mother and I suffered while Wilfrid was reading this book, or the number of indignantly scored passages to which we had to listen. To Mgr. Benson, who had asked his advice about a review he was writing, Wilfrid wrote:
>
> "I think Bremond's book should be treated very severely. It is a very impertinent book. Such an account of a great man, deducing far more than there are real premises to warrant, can only be justified by a very reverent attitude and a real mastery of the character. The book shows neither.
>
> "I should single out as flagrant blots the fact that the Chapter on Newman as a Historian has practically nothing about the Arians or the Development. It is these two works which show a complete mastery of early Church

---

[147] Obituary, *Tablet* (15 April 1916), 489.
[148] "yet while strongly dissenting from Bremond's argument, Ward carried over the themes of *ego solus* and Newman's sensitivity." Gilley, "Wilfrid Ward and his Life of Newman."
[149] *Dublin Review*, no. 141 (1907), 1ff.
[150] Bremond, *The Mystery of Newman*, vii.

history. Yet Bremond deals with neither, but instead dwells on the slight Historical Sketches. The true reason is that he cannot understand J. H. N.'s more serious work."[151]

Maisie Ward's summary of what her father found objectionable about Bremond is compelling.

> My father never thought that Bremond was a complete Modernist, but he did think that he did not understand Newman, and he thought part of the lack of understanding was due to the difference between Frenchman and Englishman. Moreover, he felt very keenly that *The Mystery of Newman* was an exceedingly unfair book. While asserting that he had the greatest possible admiration for Newman, Bremond constantly questioned the latter's sincerity, assumed that no satisfactory answer had been given to the attacks of Kingsley and of Abbott, asserted that Newman was a man of cold heart, who had the gift of winning friends, but did not return their love. What made the attack so very much more serious was that it was put forward under the guise of an explanation, so that the casual reader was almost sure to say: "The case against Newman's sincerity must be a very strong one if even such an admirer as the Abbé Bremond can find no answer to it." My father also felt that Bremond had written without sufficient knowledge of Newman's works. He based all his theories on the *Plain and Parochial Sermons*, the *Essay on Miracles*, of which he clearly had not understood the drift, and one or two other books, while as we have seen he left aside almost entirely the *University Sermons* which my father thought Newman's deepest book.[152]

Indeed, Ward regarded the *Oxford University Sermons* in the same light in which Samuel Johnson regarded his *Rambler* essays—they were the unmixed wine—and pivotal to the composition of the *Essay on Development* and the *Grammar of Assent*, the most intellectually incandescent of Newman's books, though Ward was careful to stress that the *Grammar* was but "a fine supplement" to the earlier sermons.[153] That Bremond had nothing to say of any of these works exposed the superficiality on which he based his licentious speculations. Ward, by contrast, had made the epistemological joy of these books so much his own that he spent his lifetime sharing it with others. Indeed, this is precisely why he could recognize it so clearly when he saw it in his friend Chesterton's *Orthodoxy*, which, as he said in his *Dublin* essay, was a plug for the illative sense almost as good as Newman's own. "A man is not really convinced of a philosophic theory when he finds that something proves it," Chesterton wrote. "He is only really convinced when he finds that everything proves it. And the more converging reasons he finds pointing to this conviction, the more bewildered he is if asked suddenly to sum them up. Thus, if one asked an ordinary intelligent man, on the spur of the moment, 'Why do you prefer civilization to savagery?' he would look wildly round at object after object, and would only be able to answer vaguely: 'Why, there is that bookcase ... and the coals in the coal scuttle ... and pianos ...

---

[151] Ward, *The Wilfrid Wards and the Transition*, ii, 172–3.
[152] Ibid., 173.
[153] Ward, *Ten Personal Studies*, 251.

and policemen.' The whole case for civilization is that the case for it is complex. It has done so many things. But that very multiplicity of proof which ought to make reply overwhelming makes reply impossible."[154]

Once the work of Tyrrell and Loisy was recognized as clearly heretical, Pius X issued his encyclical against Modernism, *Pascendi Dominici Gregis*, which was issued on the nativity of Our Lady in 1907. Of all the sources of Modernism, the pope saw hatred of Scholasticism as paramount.

> Whether it is ignorance or fear, or both, that inspires this conduct in them, certain it is that the passion for novelty is always united in them with hatred of scholasticism, and there is no surer sign that a man is on the way to Modernism than when he begins to show his dislike for this system. Modernists and their admirers should remember the proposition condemned by Pius IX: The method and principles which have served the doctors of scholasticism when treating of theology no longer correspond with the exigencies of our time or the progress of science (Syll. Prop. 13). They exercise all their ingenuity in diminishing the force and falsifying the character of tradition, so as to rob it of all its weight. But for Catholics the second Council of Nicea will always have the force of law, where it condemns those who dare, after the impious fashion of heretics, to deride the ecclesiastical traditions, to invent novelties of some kind … or endeavour by malice or craft to overthrow any one of the legitimate traditions of the Catholic Church.

Keen on pleasing the Oratorians, Ward was careful to include the following letter in his biography of Newman, which attests to how much the convert shared Leo XIII's respect for what he called "the Catholic tradition of philosophy." The encyclical to which Newman refers is *Aeterni Patris* (1879), in which Leo decreed that the Church revive the work of Saint Thomas Aquinas, about whom Newman once asked: "who so large and so minute and exact in thought as St. Thomas?"[155] Here, where he says that the work of theologians and controversialists must be "grafted on the Catholic tradition of philosophy"—not on novelty with no roots in tradition—he is describing his own work.

---

[154] Gilbert Keith Chesterton, *Orthodoxy* (London: The Bodley Head, 1908), 135–6.
[155] *Ess.*, ii, 415, In Leo XIII's Bull, St Thomas is praised to the rooftops: "Among the Scholastic Doctors, the chief and master of all towers Thomas Aquinas, who, as Cajetan observes, because "he most venerated the ancient doctors of the Church, in a certain way seems to have inherited the intellect of all." The doctrines of those illustrious men, like the scattered members of a body, Thomas collected together and cemented, distributed in wonderful order, and so increased with important additions that he is rightly and deservedly esteemed the special bulwark and glory of the Catholic faith. With his spirit at once humble and swift, his memory ready and tenacious, his life spotless throughout, a lover of truth for its own sake, richly endowed with human and divine science, like the sun he heated the world with the warmth of his virtues and filled it with the splendor of his teaching. Philosophy has no part which he did not touch finely at once and thoroughly; on the laws of reasoning, on God and incorporeal substances, on man and other sensible things, on human actions and their principles, he reasoned in such a manner that in him there is wanting neither a full array of questions, nor an apt disposal of the various parts, nor the best method of proceeding, nor soundness of principles or strength of argument, nor clearness and elegance of style, nor a facility for explaining what is abstruse."

To Pope Leo XIII
[14 December 1879]

Beatissimo Padre,
    I hope it will not seem to your Holiness an intrusion upon your time if I address to you a few lines to express to your Holiness those thanks which we all cannot but feel for the very seasonable and important Encyclical which you have bestowed upon us. All good Catholics must feel it a first necessity that the intellectual exercises, without which the Church cannot fulfil her supernatural mission duly, should be founded upon broad as well as true principles, that the mental creations of her theologians, of her controversialists and pastors, should be grafted on the Catholic tradition of philosophy, and should not start from a novel and simply original tradition, but should be substantially one with the teaching of St Athanasius, St Augustine, St Anselm, and St Thomas, as those great Doctors in turn are one with each other.
    At a time when then there is so much cultivation of mind, so much intellectual excitement, so many new views true and false, and so much temptation to overstep the old truth, we need just what your Holiness has supplied us with in your recent Pastoral, and I hope my own personal gratitude for your wise and seasonable act may be taken by your Holiness as my apology, if I seem to outstep the limits of modesty and propriety in addressing this letter to your Holiness.
    Asking the Apostolical Benediction[156]

Although naturally appreciative of St Thomas' work, to the extent that he knew it, Newman was drawn more to the early Fathers because of their letters. For Newman, letters "always [had] the charm of reality." To a correspondent who had sent him a batch of historical letters, he wrote:

> I have before now given this as the reason why I like the early Fathers more than the Medieval Saints viz: because we have the letters of the former. I seem to know St. Chrysostom or St. Jerome in a way in which I never can know St. Thomas Aquinas.—and St. Thomas of Canterbury (himself medieval) on account of his letters as I never can know St. Pius Vth. There is something always to be gained by the sight of a religious man, as he is—whether he be in partial error, or on the other hand a Doctor of the Church—[157]

When the Irishman Robert Whitty, SJ wrote Newman to express his own confidence that the brilliant convert's work in *The Grammar of Assent* could not be construed to be at any variance with the work of the Angelic Doctor, Newman replied: "Thank you for what you say about the *Grammar of Assent*. If any one

---

[156] Newman to Pope Leo XIII (14 December 1879), *LD*, xxix, 212–13. Ward included the following commentary before his quoting of the letter: Newman's "general feeling as to the necessity of basing Christian thought on that of the great masters in theology, is shown in the draft of a letter written to Leo XHI. himself in the early years of his pontificate—whether it was sent I cannot say—welcoming his Encyclical on the Philosophy of St. Thomas Aquinas on the ground that at a time of new theories it was all-important to remember the great thinkers of old." Ward, *Life of Newman*, ii, 501–2. According to Fr. Dessain, the letter was actually sent to the Provost of the Birmingham Oratory while in Rome, John Norris, who presented it to the pope.

[157] Newman to Mrs. Sconce (15 October 1865), *LD*, xii, 73–4. Cf. *HS* ii, 271–24.

is obliged to say 'I speak under correction' it is I; for I am no theologian and am too old, and ever have been, to become one. All I can say is I have no suspicion, and do not anticipate, that I shall be found in substance to disagree with St Thomas."[158] There was never anything perfunctory about Newman's expressions of gratitude whenever readers let him know that they enjoyed or approved of what he had written. In 1877, he wrote to Father Coleridge: "I write to thank you for the favorable critique, which you have admitted in the *Month*, of my Preface to the *Via Media*. And I am pleased that you *could* admit it. I mean, I have been so bullied all through my life for what I have written, that I never publish without forebodings of evil."[159] Ward's comment on Newman's comment was predictably barbed: "As late as 1877 ... we find at once the smart of past censure remaining, and gratitude for present kindness keen and fresh."[160]

VI

Ward's break with Tyrrell has to be seen in light of his grudging recognition of the wisdom of Leo XIII's pontificate (1878–1903), despite his misgivings about reviving Scholasticism in the modern era, a revival Pius X's pontificate (1903–14) would fully perpetuate. For Dom Paschal Scotti, the author of a study of Ward's editorship of the *Dublin*, Leo in many ways defined the challenges that beset the Church before and after the turn of the nineteenth century. "His conciliatory policy achieved an end to the *Kulturkampf* in Germany and his failure to rally French Catholics to the Third Republic (the *ralliement*) was due to the intransigence of others. He approved and encouraged the very successful International Scientific Congresses started by Mgr. d'Hulst, to which Ward so often referred in his articles. He opened the Vatican Archives to scholars, promoted the revival of scholastic theology and philosophy with *Aeterni Patris* ... and in his encyclicals he elaborated a complete, and in some ways, a new vision of society and the Catholic's place in it. He elevated to the Sacred College not only Thomists, but also Hergenröther and Ward's idol, Newman, who represented a very different theological method."[161]

Yet in Ward's characterization of Leo's relationship to liberalism we can see his own ambivalent attitude to the Church's opposition to liberalism. For Ward, Leo "never had the belief in liberty, as such, which led Pius IX, in 1846, so nearly to accept the partial alliance of Mazzini. He never had the belief in free criticism in history or Biblical research which characterised a Döllinger or a Bickell. His wish to come to terms with modern civilisation was quite of a different kind. It was rather of the kind indicated in his *Encyclical on Human Liberty*. There was no disposition to idealise the tendencies of modern civilisation. On the contrary, civilisation was ever regarded by him as having in most important matters deteriorated. Yet that was not, in his judgment, a reason for despairing of it. In its present imperfect state, then, we must fully accept its conditions in

---

[158] Newman to Robert Whitty, SJ (20 December 1878), *LD*, xxviii, 430–1.
[159] Newman to Henry James Coleridge (5 November 1877), *LD*, xxviii, 263.
[160] Ward, *Life of Newman*, ii, 347.
[161] Dom Paschal Scotti, "Wilfrid Ward: A Religious Fabius Maximus," *The Catholic Historical Review* (January 2002), 52.

order to improve it. We must use the modern liberties—our ultimate ideal being largely to get rid of them. Pius IX. began with a certain sanguine trust in the more generous features of modern Liberalism. Disappointment led to reaction, and made him the intransigent opponent of all that savoured of Liberalism. Leo never idealised Liberalism, and, consequently, he was kinder to it. There was never in his utterances any enthusiasm for the sacred rights of liberty, or even much appreciation of the value of liberty in the search for truth. His constant denunciations of free discussion have not been tempered by any recognition of its indispensable necessity in certain fields of inquiry. Truth was ever referred to by him as the possession of the Church, not only in the sense in which all Catholics so regard it, but almost without qualification—without direct contemplation of that important work of correcting its analysis and defining its limits in relation to advancing secular knowledge, which needs free discussion for its successful accomplishment. How little liberty, as such, has been valued by him in philosophy may seen from Leo's policy in reference to Thomism—his tendency to treat it as the last word in philosophy, rather than merely as a profound and admirable work of the human reason at a certain epoch. How little liberty, as such, was valued by him in Biblical criticism is seen in his letter on the study of the sacred Scriptures in the early nineties. But the wisdom of the statesman, who knows that to rule effectively the ruler must often tolerate what he does not approve, that you must be conciliatory and considerate if you hope to win conciliation and consideration, these are of the essence of Pope Leo's policy."[162]

Whether this is a fair or even accurate summation of Leo's pontificate is questionable. For example, Ward made no mention here of the pope's attacks on socialism, communism and nihilism in *Quod apostoli muneris* (28 December 1878). He made no mention of *Rerum novarum* (15 May 1891), which upheld the rights of property, as well as those of workers. As for the "sacred rights of liberty," the pope in *Libertas praestantissimum* (29 June 1881) followed Newman in recognizing that while the Church might not sanction false liberty, it had always been the custodian of proper liberty.[163] In Ward's conclusion to his portrait of Leo, we might not be able to see the pope but we can see Ward trying to see if he

---

[162] Ward, "Leo XIII," *Ten Personal Studies*, 192–3.
[163] Although he naturally saw the responsible exercise of liberty as necessary to the devout life, Newman also recognized that an insistence on undue liberty was often at odds with religion. "I wish it were possible, my brethren, to lead men to greater holiness and more faithful obedience by setting before them the high and abundant joys which they have who serve God," he wrote: "but this is, I know, just what most persons will not believe. They think that it is very right and proper to be religious; they think that it would be better for themselves in the world to come if they were religious now. They do not at all deny either the duty or the expedience of leading a new and holy life; but they cannot understand how it can be pleasant: they cannot believe or admit that it is more pleasant than a life of liberty, laxity, and enjoyment. They, as it were, say, "Keep within bounds, speak within probability, and we will believe you; but do not shock our reason. We will admit that we *ought* to be religious, and that, when we come to die, we shall be very glad to have led religious lives: but to tell us that it is a *pleasant* thing to be religious, this is too much: it is not true; we feel that it is not true; all the world knows and feels it is not true; religion is something unpleasant, gloomy, sad, and troublesome. It imposes a number of restraints on us; it keeps us from doing what we would; it will not let us have our own way; it abridges our liberty, it interferes with our enjoyments; it has fewer, far fewer, joys at present than a worldly life, though it gains for us more joys hereafter." This is what men say, or would say, if they understood what they feel, and spoke their minds freely." "Religion Pleasant to the Religious" (1840), *PS*, vii, 195–6.

could tolerate what he did not entirely approve. Leo's "ideal of a universal reign of Thomistic philosophy alarmed some able Catholic thinkers," Ward wrote, "but it was not, in the long run, pressed to practical excess. His sympathy with Christian democracy was in his public utterances carefully safe guarded. In the matter of Biblical criticism, if he did not fully appreciate the situation intellectually, his practical action was in course of time guided by the real needs of the hour." Such qualifications notwithstanding, Ward was prepared to concede that Leo would "unquestionably rank ... among our holy Pontiffs" for having "steered the bark of Peter with judgment and wisdom in a very troublous and difficult time." Yet this was tepid praise of a pope who had written profound encyclicals on the Blessed Virgin and the Rosary, greatly expanded Catholicism outside Europe, consecrated humanity to the Sacred Heart, and restored the papacy to international respect after the controversies of Pio Nono's reign.[164] Here, in Ward's small-minded reservations, we can see the captious intellectual in him, obsessing over suppositious restrictions to intellectual freedom while losing sight of the pontiff's far-ranging services to the cause of Truth. One wishes to be fair to Ward—he did so much that was admirable—but he was demonstrably unfair to Leo XIII.

Why is this important? Ward's disapproval of what he regarded as Leo XIII's unreceptiveness to Catholic thinkers *per se*, not just Modernists, colored his attitude to Pius X. Maisie Ward, who paid close attention to these matters, relates that Cardinal Mercier once wrote her father saying that "We need a campaign against the anti-Modernists,"[165] and for Masie this was telling, since the views of Mercier and her father on the advisability of such a campaign were "identical":[166] Maisie Ward elaborates in her biography of her parents.

> No Pope has fostered learning more eagerly than Leo XIII. But before his death the disintegration later called Modernism had so far begun that he had been forced into an attitude of suspicion. True, Sabatier declares that he would have ended by creating Modernist Cardinals, but the correspondence of the period tells a different tale. Pius X was more repressive and, as we have seen, his reign saw an outburst of almost persecution by a political party veiled by a pretext of religious zeal. But the reaction had already begun in Leo's reign, after a period of the greatest possible encouragement of scholarship. It was the Modernists who produced that reaction. It was the Modernists who gave Benigni his opportunity.[167]

Msgr. Umberto Benigni (1862–1934) was Pius X's close advisor and leader of the Society of St Pius V, the charge of which was to root out Modernists from seminaries and schools. Maisie Ward quotes a vivid description of the man from a Vatican commentator: "Behold now the darling of the day, the master of the hour, the man before whose shattering good fortune the whole Church beyond the Alps stands stupefied, Mgr. Benigni, the left arm of His Holiness, drawn no

---

[164] Ward, "Leo XIII," *Ten Personal Studies*, 197.
[165] Ward, *The Wilfrid Wards and the Transition*, ii, 299.
[166] Cf. "My father's position and Mercier's were practically identical; in that both maintained the possibility of genuine untrammelled thought within the Church." *Ibid.*, 316.
[167] *Ibid.*, 304–5.

one knows how or by whom from the obscurity of the little diocese where he lived his little life and borne suddenly upwards to the most brilliant honours. He is a large man, round as a ball, his eyes sparkling with cleverness, cunning and curiosity, gold-spectacled, grossly fat, stammering; wriggling and writhing in an arm-chair too deep for him like a devil in a holy-water stoup. His arms, legs, head and tongue are all on the go together ... And *au fond*, behind the spectacles and the greasiness and the vulgarity, he has intelligence in plenty."[168] It is doubtless this lurid view of the anti-Modernist Benigni that confirmed Eamon Duffy in his view that *Pascendi* unleashed a "reign of terror."[169] In all events, what both Wilfrid Ward and his daughter Maisie underplay is the degree to which both Leo XIII and Pius X admired Newman, though this in no way mars Ward's published work on Newman, whether in the biography or the essays.

VII

After the Modernist crisis and all of its ramifications, as well as the writing of his biography of Newman, Ward resolved to give his readers a summation of his work on Newman in the Lowell Lectures that he gave at Harvard in the winter of 2014–15, about which Maisie Ward observed:

> These lectures rounded off my father's life work. I cannot but think that if Mr. Belloc's words come true concerning Wilfrid's great, permanent and certainly increasing effect upon his countrymen in the only thing that matters, these lectures will be recognised as especially important and significant. "They are on the highest level," wrote Mr. Balfour. Yet at the time neither the reviews nor the sales of the book were on a scale at all proportioned to those of the Newman biography. No doubt this was in part owing to the war, but it was also in part, I think, owing to the idea that Wilfrid had already said his say about Cardinal Newman. Yet, in fact, he had much to say on Newman's psychological insight, on the sources of his style, on his philosophy and his personality, which could not have been developed in a biography. By far his best work on Newman is in this book and this was realised by some of the critics.[170]

America agreed with Ward. He loved its extravagant attentiveness—the "private sitting-rooms and bathrooms everywhere, a golf professional put at his disposal, a drawing-room on the train taken by his hosts for a long journey, another car following for fear of accidents as he drove to another engagement."[171] At the same time, he could not help but be embarrassed by how some of his countrymen behaved in America, convinced, as he was, that "the English swagger and the Americans are at their feet though they are far cleverer in reality."[172] At Harvard, he delighted in what he regarded as the intelligence of the Americans. A lunch at

---

[168] Ibid., 328.
[169] Eamon Duffy, *Saints and Sinners: A History of the Popes* (New Haven: Yale University Press, 1997), 250–1. Pace Duffy, the necessity of the Society of Pius V has been made crystal clear by the recrudescence of Modernism in the papacy of Jorge Bergoglio but that is another story.
[170] Ward, *The Wilfrid Wards and the Transition*, ii, 516.
[171] Ibid., 442–3.
[172] Ibid., 446.

the University Club in New York he recalled as "*most memorable*—forty people of different creeds all doing homage to J. H. N. and speaking in some cases with real knowledge and keen appreciation of my own work."[173] This was obviously preferable to what the popular English humorist Jerome K. Jerome encountered when he went on his lecture tour to America.

> I have been described, within the same period of seven months, as a bald-headed, elderly gentleman, with a wistful smile; a curly-haired athletic Englishman, remarkable for his youthful appearance; a rickety cigarette-smoking neurotic; and a typical John Bull. Some of them objected to my Oxford drawl; while others catalogued me as a cockney, and invariably quoted me as dropping my aitches.[174]

Ward's Lowell Lecture on Newman is full of choice insights. Here he is on how the teacher affected the stylist in Newman. "[O]ne quality was more marked in him than in many great writers, namely, his close touch on the minds of those whom he is directly addressing," he wrote.

> "My own motive for writing," [Newman] says in a letter to W. G. Ward, "has been the sight of a truth and the desire to show it to others." And what he wrote had so to be written that those others could see it. *Cor ad cor loquitur*—the motto he chose as a Cardinal—conveys this quality which communicates itself to his style. His style, therefore, differs considerably according to the particular audience he is addressing. It differs not only according to the particular stage in his history which it represents, but according to the readers or hearers he has in view. Refinement and self-restraint are apparent at Oxford. This restraint is sometimes due to a certain tentativeness in his thought. But it also arises from the milieu in which he speaks. His audience belonged mainly to the cultivated classes, and included persons of considerable intellectual refinement. The Birmingham Sermons are of a more popular character—more pictorial, less analytical. And he paints in broader colours and introduces more scenic effects for an audience drawn from a commercial town which is presumably less fastidious and less sensitive to delicate lights and shades.[175]

The versatility of Newman's style—even within individual works—should be given some proper study. The many different stylistic registers he deploys in the lectures of *Anglican Difficulties* are dazzling, ranging as they do from declamation to satire to historical exposition to irony to advocacy to prayer. For Chesterton, the "quality of [Newman's] literary style is so successful that it succeeds in escaping definition."[176] Ward's animadversions on the style are perceptive, recognizing as he does that

> The fact … that his writing is largely a reflection of his mental and moral history leaves its deep impress on the style, and gives it its depth, its gravity, its volume.

---

[173] *Ibid.*, 445.
[174] Jerome K. Jerome, *Life and Times*, 187, quoted in Philip Waller, *Writers, Readers and Reputations: Literary Life in Britain 1870–1918* (Oxford: Oxford University Press, 2006), 589.
[175] Ward, *Last Lectures*, 52.
[176] Chesterton, *The Victorian Age in Literature*, 31.

The brooding imagination so often apparent tells of deep and hard-won conviction as distinguished from mere ingenuity expended in defending this or that position. The style has qualities which a mere literary man does not possess—for whom artistic effect is the beginning and end of his aim. It conveys, in one place, his own suffering and labour; in another the sense of triumph at conviction laboriously won. The outcome of this experience possesses the whole man, gradually making his views deeper and wider; and his aim is to convey to others the solemn lesson of his own life. This imparts a deep note as of a great bell to their expression, where a mere master of phrases can, at the very best, only ring out, however skilfully, his thinner tones.[177]

These are welcome observations because they show how little Newman saw himself in literary terms, even though his literary talents were prodigious. When we place him alongside other masters of English style in the nineteenth century— say, Ruskin or Arnold—we always do so conscious that the power of Newman's English always comes of the power of what it is he is saying. It is his command of Catholic Truth that makes the great English style possible, not the resources of style *per se*, though his command of those resources is of a staggering virtuosity. Again, as Ward recognized so clearly, it is his determination to share this Truth with the reader that elicits from him all of his rhetorical genius. We delight in Ruskin and Arnold because we delight in their literary fireworks, their rhetorical sumptuousness, their phrase-making, their music—not because we care about what they have to say of the sins of Venetian architects or the barbarities of the Bullingdon.[178] Or take the exquisite twaddle of Landor. No one ever wrote a finer English and yet it is trained on such elaborate trifles.[179] With Newman, our experience as readers is the direct opposite. We delight in the style because we delight in what it tells us of the profundities of religion—for some of us vital, deeply consequential profundities. G. K. Chesterton once said of Tennyson that "he suffered by the very splendour and perfection of his poetical powers. He was quite the opposite of the man who cannot express himself; the inarticulate singer who dies with all his music in him. He had a great deal to say; but he had much more power of expression than was wanted for anything he had to express. He could not think up to the height of his own towering style."[180] With Newman, it is always precisely his towering theme that demands of him the "towering style" But, here, again, is Ward:

---

[177] Ward, *Last Lectures*, 50.
[178] This may not be altogether fair to Ruskin, who often had insightful things to say of the Protestant order in which he found himself. Apropos the Victorian insistence on doing as one pleases, which Arnold would examine in *Culture and Anarchy* (1869), Ruskin observed in *Sesame and Lilies* (1865): "Our National wish and purpose are only to be amused; our National religion is the performance of church ceremonies, and preaching of soporific truths (or untruths) to keep the mob quietly at work, while we amuse ourselves; and the necessity for this amusement is fastening on us, as a feverous disease of parched throat and wandering eyes—senseless, dissolute, merciless."
[179] See the conversation between La Fontaine and La Rochefoucauld. "We pray the more commodiously and of course the more frequently, for rolling up an ell of stocking round about our knees; and our high-heeled shoes must surely have been worn by some angel, to save those insects which the flat-footed would have crushed to death." Walter Savage Landor, *Imaginary Conversations* ed by Charles G. Crump 6 vols (London: J. M. Dent & Co., 1901), iv, 373.
[180] Chesterton, *The Victorian Age in Literature*, 101.

Newman himself more than once expressed his feeling that really great writing can be achieved only by something very different from the aim at diction for its own sake. Familiarity with good models—for we know that Gibbon and Cicero both affected him—is only a preparation. His artist's nature, his sense of form, was cultivated and perfected by such reading. It tuned the instrument, so to speak. But the really great style, the great performance on the instrument, is achieved (so he maintains in a paragraph I shall read directly) primarily by conviction and thought stimulating the writer to their expression. It can never be gained merely by a study of the tricks of graceful diction.

"A great author [he writes in one of the Dublin Lectures] is not one who merely has a *copia verborum*, whether in prose or verse, and can, as it were, turn on at his will any number of splendid phrases and swelling sentences; but he is one who has something to say and knows how to say it. ... He is master of the two-fold Logos, the thought and the word, distinct, but inseparable from each other. He may, if so be, elaborate his compositions, or he may pour out his improvisations, but in either case he has but one aim, which he keeps steadily before him ... That aim is to give forth what he has within him; and from his very earnestness it comes to pass that, whatever be the splendour of his diction or the harmony of his periods, he has with him the charm of an incommunicable simplicity."[181]

Nowhere is this "incommunicable simplicity" on more moving display than in Newman's *Parochial and Plain Sermons*, which he preached at St Mary the Virgin in Oxford before converting. They "are extremely simple in style—self-restrained, even austere," Wards notes. They make "frequent use of the Old Testament, which [Newman] knew almost by heart." And they apply "the lessons of [Scripture] with great felicity and reality"—a point to keep in mind whenever Newman is compared to St Thomas Aquinas, for Newman shared the Angelic Doctor's mastery of Scripture: it was an inalienable part of all he wrote. With the exception of "The Parting of Friends," Ward sees no formal eloquence in the Anglican sermons, equating eloquence as he does with rhetoric, though he is certainly right to maintain that "There is nothing in the earlier sermons in the least parallel to the splendid rhetoric with which he describes Mary Magdalen in the Birmingham discourse on 'Purity and Love,' nothing parallel to the triumphant march of the 'Second Spring.' The characteristic developments of the later manner are at their highest point in these two sermons."[182] Here, he might also have pointed to "The Glories of Mary for the Sake of her Son" (1849) and "Christ upon the Waters" (1850), in both of which Newman abandons the simplicity of the earlier sermons to achieve an almost Baroque orotundity.

Reading Ward on Newman's *Parochial and Plain Sermons*, one is surprised that he does not have more to say of their style. It is not that his observations about them are unjust: they are simply inadequate. Dean Church is much more descriptive of the power of their appeal. "The contrast of Mr. Newman's preaching was not obvious at first," Church wrote.

---

[181] Ward, *Last Lectures*, 50–1; *Idea*, 291–2.
[182] Ibid., 55–6.

The outside form and look was very much that of the regular best Oxford type—calm, clear, and lucid in expression, strong in its grasp, measured in statement, and far too serious to think of rhetorical ornament. But by degrees much more opened. The range of experience from which the preacher drew his materials, and to which he appealed, was something wider, subtler, and more delicate than had been commonly dealt with in sermons. With his strong, easy, exact, elastic language, the instrument of a powerful and argumentative mind, he plunged into the deep realities of the inmost spiritual life, of which cultivated preachers had been shy. He preached so that he made you feel without doubt that it was the most real of worlds to him; he made you feel in time, in spite of yourself, that it was a real world with which you too had concern. He made you feel that he knew what he was speaking about; that his reasonings and appeals, whether you agreed with them or not, were not the language of that heated enthusiasm with which the world is so familiar; that he was speaking words which were the result of intellectual scrutiny, balancings, and decisions, as well as of moral trials, of conflicts and suffering within; words of the utmost soberness belonging to deeply gauged and earnestly formed purposes. The effect of his sermons, as compared with the common run at the time, was something like what happens when in a company you have a number of people giving their views and answers about some question before them. You have opinions given of various worth and expressed with varying power, precision, and distinctness, some clever enough, some clumsy enough, but all more or less imperfect and unattractive in tone, and more or less falling short of their aim; and then, after it all, comes a voice, very grave, very sweet, very sure and clear, under whose words the discussion springs up at once to a higher level, and in which we recognise at once a mind, face to face with realities, and able to seize them and hold them fast.[183]

Flannery O'Connor once confessed, as she said, that "I've read almost all of Henry James—from a sense of High Duty and because when I read James I feel like something is happening to me, in slow motion but happening nevertheless."[184] Church might have said the same about his experience of attending to Newman's sermons, as could many others, including your humble historian.

Apropos the satirist in Newman, Ward reveled in his hero's ability to show his countrymen what buffoons their prejudices made them. "For exhibitions of his higher powers of humour and irony he needed a direct and urgent call of duty," Ward writes.

> These powers are fully visible in only two publications—the lectures on "The Present Position of Catholics"—delivered at the time of the agitation of 1850 against the "Papal Aggression," as it was called—and the controversy with Kingsley. In both cases he felt that only by exerting to the full his brilliant gift of irony could he make an effectual impression on public opinion. The lectures of 1851 aimed at discrediting a really gross libel on Catholics which had become current coin. Not only did he let out his full force of sarcasm and humour, but his style was

---

[183] Church, "Newman's Parochial Sermons," in *Occasional Papers*, ii, 444–6.
[184] O'Connor to "A" (28 August 1955), *The Habit of Being: Letters of Flannery O'Connor* (New York: Farrar, Straus, Giroux, 1979), 99.

transformed to suit the occasion. Little is visible of those cross currents of which I spoke in my last lecture, which in most of his works represent and anticipate the objections and exceptions to the views he set forth. The very close perception of facts which, in ordinary cases, made him alive to objections to general statements or strong statements, made him now alive to the absence of material objections or exceptions. The hue and cry against Catholics at that time was grossly unjust, and was not based on really plausible objections to the action of the Catholic religion to which he was as keenly alive as anyone. It was based on sheer ignorance and fanatical bigotry. Therefore he let himself go for all he was worth in ridiculing it. We have the very curious spectacle of a grave religious apologist giving rein for the first time at the age of fifty to a sense of rollicking fun and gifts of humorous writing, which if expended on other subjects would naturally have adorned the pages of Thackeray's *Punch*.[185]

Nevertheless, Ward is right to see praise of the famous style as the means by which generations of critics have contrived to ignore or disparage the style's content. Apropos the celebrated style of the *Apologia*, Ward remarks: "We have ... to face the fact that the 'regal English' which the critics have glorified, including indeed many of the passages they have singled out for admiration, was directly inspired by the theology—the controversy—so many of them have despised. The two can no more be separated than the beauty of the human expression of a Saint can be separated from the soul that speaks through it."[186] Yet this did not stop A. N. Wilson—a blithe offender in this regard—from separating them completely in an essay he wrote for Newman's centennial.

> Newman's religious temperament was highly developed—for some Laodicean readers, disconcertingly so—but in England a religious mind has seldom been gifted with such a capacity for self-description. In the English language, I know no author except Wordsworth who can match him in this particular field, and few to rival him as a prose stylist. But then I am drunk with the Newman music, and even when my mind moves in a direction directly opposite to his own, even when the particular matters which distressed or excited him seem to me as distressing or exciting as the controversies of Tweedle-dum and Tweedle-dee, even when his hysterical assaults on Liberalism make me glad to be, in his terms, a Liberal, I warm to him, and feel, as did those undergraduates in St Mary's during the 1830's, the strength and charm of the man.[187]

Tyrrell, in his introduction to Bremond's book, is also guilty of adverting to the style to disparage Newman's work, giving out that "In truth, almost always, and even in the works which followed his conversion, it is as well to consider whether Newman is not keeping something back, whether the play of adverbs or of adjectives does not cover some reserve or contain some innuendo, whether there is nothing to be read between the lines, whether the printed text, retouched, repolished twenty times, is anything else than a passage of discovery

---

[185] Ward, *Last Lectures*, 112–13.
[186] Ibid., 64.
[187] A. N. Wilson, "Newman the Writer," in *Newman: A Man for Our Time*, ed. Brown, 137–8.

or a temporary expedient. In this delicate art of saying a thing without appearing to say it he is a past-master."[188] Newman's own contemporaries were notorious for seeing manifold deceit in the subtle style. "Lord Morley in his essay on J. S. Mill treats the fascination of Newman's style as the sole cause of the influence of one whose powers of thought were, so far as he could see, inconsiderable," Ward writes, and then he quotes the liberal *littérateur*, who argues that "Mill had none of the incomparably winning graces by which Newman made mere siren style do duty for exact, penetrating, and coherent thought; by which, moreover, he actually raised his Church to what would not so long before have seemed a strange and inconceivable rank in the mind of Protestant England. Style has worked many a miracle before now, but none more wonderful than Newman's."[189] Amongst the Victorians, equating Newman's style with sophistry was a defamatory commonplace, which Ward nicely refutes by appealing to his readers' common sense, not to mention their aesthetic sense: "those who admire the style and ignore the thinker and the apostle are really separating what it is impossible to separate. They want the flower, but condemn planting and watering as empty ritual."[190]

Then, too, Ward sees the very variousness of Newman's output as a cause for his having been dismissed by critics convinced that such variousness was the mark of superficiality.

> When we turn to Newman's writings in order to analyse that genius ... we are met by a difficulty—a difficulty which at once seems to account in part for the hesitation of so many critics to commit themselves to an ungrudging recognition of his intellectual greatness, Newman's claims, when we look at his life-work and his books, seem to be so multifarious that notably in these days of specialism they savour at first sight of superficiality, almost of dilettantism. He is at once a religious leader, a preacher, a father confessor, a religious philosopher, an historian, a theologian, and a poet—even a novelist. He was the leader of the Oxford Movement, and, as such, to be ranked with Loyola, Luther, Wesley—with the great religious leaders of history. Principal Shairp, Dean Lake, and others have chronicled the marvellous effect of his Oxford sermons, and he would seem at first sight to claim rank among the great preachers. He was a religious guide to very many, having over them an influence rarely surpassed in the annals of spiritual direction. In this respect he ranks with Fenelon or St. Francis de Sales. He wrote as Pascal did on the philosophy of faith in his *Oxford University Sermons* and ... in *The Grammar of Assent*. His book on the Arians and his *Essay on the Development of Christian Doctrine* are historical. So are his *Sketches of the Church of the Fathers*. ... He published poetry and two books of fiction—*Loss and Gain* and *Callista*. This multifariousness, as I have said, cannot fail to suggest superficiality; a want of thoroughness in any one sphere of his activity; the qualities rather of a dilettante than of a great thinker.[191]

---

[188] Tyrrell, "Introduction," in Bremond, *The Mystery of Newman*, 5–6.
[189] Ward, *Last Lectures*, 2.
[190] Ibid., 45.
[191] Ibid., 6.

Yet Ward responded to this charge by calling attention to two qualities in Newman's work that show him to have been the reverse of the dilettante. "One is that his best work, even when slight, limited, or unfinished, was nearly always first-hand work—which a dilettante's never is. The philosophic thought was genuine and creative, the theological and historical research based on original sources. The other quality is that the variety of his work, instead of being due, like a dilettante's, to want of concentration, was due to the exact opposite—to the absolute unity of his purpose, and his concentration on one object. That object was the preservation of religion against the incoming tide of rationalism and infidelity. It was this passionate concentration which won him the devotion of so many disciples. Dilettantes do not inspire men with enthusiasm."[192]

Since the preservation of religion necessarily required men and women to understand the force of what Newman styled the "dogmatic principle," Ward nicely upheld the convert's defense of dogma as the guardian of the "living and inspiring part of religion."

> Many thinkers have been contemptuous and impatient of theological subtleties. But Newman points out that they have not faced the necessities of history and of human nature. These subtleties are, of course, not in themselves the living and inspiring part of religion. But they have been necessary to the preservation of what is living and inspiring. Both the simple prayers of the early Church and the complex theology of the later represent one and the same religion, the definitions protecting those simple truths which are the life of the prayers. They have been essential to actual operative religion as the dry details of the Statute Book and the proceedings of the Law Courts are necessary to the welfare of a nation, to its healthy life and best energies. Had Christians attempted to dispense with the subtleties of orthodox theology, the heterodox speculations of Gnostics and Arians would have defaced the gospel teaching, and the process, if continued long enough, might have reduced Christianity to a fable. Mr. Froude has left it on record that Carlyle in his old age was forcibly impressed by this fact in respect of the Arian controversy. Mr. Froude's own words on the subject are worth quoting:
>
> > In earlier years [Carlyle] had spoken contemptuously of the Athanasian controversy, of the Christian world torn in pieces over a diphthong, and he would ring the changes in broad Annandale on the Homoousian and the Homoïsion. He told me now that he perceived Christianity itself to have been at stake. If the Arians had won, it would have dwindled away into a legend.[193]

Yet another example of Ward's lively appreciation of Newman's "dogmatic principle" can be seen in one of his essays, in which he says: "The personal love of Christ, visible alike in an Augustine, a Loyola, a Fénelon, the simplicity and freedom with which they walk in the theological clothing which, to an outsider,

---

[192] Ibid., 6–7. See Edward Short, "Newman, Superstition and the Whig Historians," in *Newman and History*, 81–115, for a discussion of how the underrated historian in Newman availed himself of primary sources in his *Essay on Development*.

[193] Ward, *Last Lectures*, 42. The quotation from Carlyle is from Froude, *Thomas Carlyle's Life in London*, ii, 494.

seems so entangling and elaborate, are a practical witness that the dogmatic system is in fact what it pretends to be, an instrument whereby the unchangeable God, of infinite simplicity, has ever communicated, in the changing and complex conditions of human history, with finite man. It is like the infinitely complex machinery of a pipe organ, which may yet play to a child the simplest melody."[194]

Ward also recognized how vital the dogmatic principle was to Newman's understanding of the development of Christian doctrine, the very vitality of which exposed the paralytical stasis of Anglican theology.[195]

> Newman, like Renan, finds in history the law of development. But the principal sphere in which he finds this great key to the understanding of the world, is the very department in which Renan denies its existence namely, dogmatic theology. To Newman it was Protestantism and not Catholicism which contradicted the philosophy of the nineteenth century; which denied the necessity and the possibility of dogmatic evolution. However little Catholic theologians had analyzed "development" in dogma, the Church had in practice (he held) admitted it. It was Protestantism and not Catholicism which strove to test the accuracy of Christian dogma in these latter days by its not going beyond the primitive Apostolic and Biblical forms of expression, which denied to it that history and that development the records of which constitute its true science ; which claimed for the expression of the revealed Word absolute immobility as though an idea could live amid ever-changing civilisation without expressing itself anew in response to the innumerable other living ideas which press upon it and attempt to influence its course. Catholicism, no doubt, affirmed the *semper eadem* of revealed dogma, but this identity of dogma has never been treated by the Church as an unchangeableness of theological forms. The Scholastic form differed widely from the Patristic. New definitions were admitted to meet new emergencies. Plato aided the Fathers of Nicaea in their terminology; Aristotle was used at Trent. St. Vincent of Lerins, the early prophet of the unchangeableness of dogma, in his "*Quod semper, quod ubique, quod ab omnibus*," had also indicated the complementary truth which Protestantism denies. He had compared the progress of religion to that of a living man, from boyhood to maturity a progress in which identity is preserved not by a stationary fixity of form, but by its growth. The single abiding soul of a man expresses itself through bodily organs which grow and change. Newman embodied St. Vincent's two positions in a profound philosophy. Religion "changes," he said, "in order to remain the same." This is

---

[194] Wilfrid Ward, "Two Mottoes of Cardinal Newman," in *Problems and Persons* (London: Longmans, Green & Co., 1903), 282.

[195] Cf. "Antiquarianism and presentism, two unfortunate post Vatican II counterfeits of the authentic development of doctrine, are static, reductive, and eventually unsustainable; in short, *they lack chronic vigor*. They therefore lack ecclesial authenticity and tend to display the characteristics Newman would regard as typical for corruption of doctrine. Precisely for this reason, in order to identify and repel antiquarianism and presentism whenever they raise their heads, a robust understanding of the development of doctrine greatly matters." Hütter, *Newman on Truth and its Counterfeits*, 154. Since the liberal notion of development stems, in part, from the antiquarianism and presentism of Anglican theology—the notion, that is to say, that development has something to do with what the liberals call "paradigm shift"—it is useful to appreciate how Wilfrid Ward anatomized Newman's lifelong resistance to it. By "presentism" Dr Hütter means the truckling to the *Zeitgeist* typical of liberal theology.

the condition of all that lives on this earth. With the fossil it is not so. In another world, too, it may be otherwise. But on our earth "to live is to change, and to be perfect is to have changed often." The Catholic dogma is Divine truth in human language.[196]

Apropos the theological and historical content of Newman's writings, Ward makes another good point: "theological controversy is never allowed in his pages to become parochial or out-of-date, for it knows its place and its relation with those deeper, universal, and eternal problems to which it ministered in his own mental history. And his historical writing, far from being special pleading in the ordinary sense, has no more prominent characteristic than its frankness and its patient recognition of all that tells against his own conclusions."[197] This "patient recognition of all that tells against its own conclusions," so redolent of the barristerial quality of Newman's mind, is also what links him to the *quaestio* method of St. Thomas Aquinas. "If we consult Aquinas's masterpiece, the *Summa theologiae*," the popular apologist Bishop Robert Barron writes, "we find that he poses literally thousands of questions and that not even the most sacred issues are off the table, the best evidence of which is article three of question two of the first part of the *Summa*: "*utrum Deus sit?*" (whether there is a God). If a Dominican priest is permitted to ask even that question, everything is fair game; nothing is too dangerous to talk about." And one can see that in tackling vexed questions Saint Thomas and Newman shared a common method, as Bishop Barron shows.

> After stating the issue, Thomas then entertains a series of objections to the position that he will eventually take. In many cases, these represent a distillation of real counter-claims and queries that Aquinas would have heard during *quaestiones disputatae*. But for our purposes, the point to emphasize is that Thomas presents these objections in their most convincing form, often stating them better … than their advocates could. … Having articulated the objections, Thomas then offers his own magisterial resolution of the matter: "*Respondeo dicendum quod* … (I respond that it must be said …). … Finally, having offered his *Respondeo*, Aquinas returns to the objections and, in light of his resolution, answers them. It is notable that a typical Thomas technique is to find something right in the objector's position and to use that to correct what he deems to be errant in it.[198]

The fact that Protestant England knew so little of St. Thomas rendered Newman's use of the mediaeval saint's method suspect. Oxford might have had a long tradition of close study of the Bible, but it tended to look askance at the medieval Fathers, in much the same way that they looked askance at "papists, schismatics and enthusiasts."[199] Consequently, James Fitzjames Stephen and Andrew Martin Fairbairn, to name but two Victorian critics, could only have imagined Newman's

---

[196] Ward, "Renan and Newman," 285.
[197] Ward, *Last Lectures*, 50.
[198] Robert Barron, "Thomas Aquinas and the Art of Making a Public Argument," *Word on Fire* (21 June 2016).
[199] R. Greaves, "Religion in the University 1715–1800," in *The History of the University of Oxford: Volume V: The Eighteenth Century*, ed. L. S. Sutherland and L. G. Mitchell (Oxford: Clarendon Press, 1986), 408–9.

entertainment of scepticism, for purposes of disputation, an endorsement of scepticism as the result of not knowing Aquinas's *quaestio* method. Of course, granting the plausibility of an argument in order to demonstrate its untenability shows intellectual probity, not scepticism.[200]

For Ward, another reason why nineteenth-century critics found fault with Newman is that he did not write for the academy. "His positions ... [were] outlined in controversial pamphlets. He turned out nothing which was in its form designed to satisfy the learned world's ideal of a *magnum opus*. This was due largely to the apostle in him—to his intense practicalness, his wish to act on living, earnest, practical men, not on the learned world which cared far less for what he judged most important. He took up the existing controversies in the religious world—those which were actually occupying religious minds of very various capacities. But people are very slow to believe that one who takes his place among the sectarian controversialists of the day has done historical or theological work of the first order."[201] Newman expressly chose to join the lists of such "sectarian controversialists" to prosper the cause of truth, not only for its own sake but for that of his readers, whose practical need of the truth was, of course, always pressing. As Ward reminds his readers, Newman "cared for the reality of looking for truth, not about the etiquette of the learned world." He cared much to help men who were in earnest and in difficulty. He cared little or not at all to win a reputation in intellectual circles. He wished to go deep and to touch vital issues."[202] Another, perhaps even more fundamental reason why a number of Newman's contemporary critics scorned him is that Newman's idea of what constituted the deep and vital was not theirs. "Those who have been helped out of difficulty and doubt by Newman's lines of thought, have had the motive to penetrate beneath the surface," Ward saw, but "his higher gifts [were] easily overlooked even by the ablest outsider—by the Carlyles and the Morleys." Readers might question the critical acuity that Ward attributes to Carlyle and Morley but his analysis of why more highly regarded critics failed to appreciate Newman's genius is nonetheless just.

---

[200] For Fairbairn, Newman had "a deep distrust of the intellect ... he dares not trust his own, for he does not know where it might lead him, and he will not trust any other man's." Regarding *The Grammar of Assent*, Fairbairn had written: "The book is pervaded by the intensest philosophical scepticism." *Contemporary Review* (May 1885), 667. Ward's riposte was the obvious one any sensible reader of Newman would make: "Dr. Fairbairn fell into the usual error of supposing that, despairing of reason, Newman had thrown himself for refuge into the arms of an infallible Church." Ward, *Life of Newman*, ii, 505. To understand Fairbairn's objections to Newman's conversion to Catholicism, one must understand his ecclesial allegiances. "Perhaps no man did more than Fairbairn to rescue Nonconformity from the political reproach that had so long attached to it," his biographer remarks. "He turned it back on its spiritual and theological beginnings, and bade it find in the fulfilment of these its true bent, and the best policy for its present needs. Though he did not himself shrink from controversy where necessary, as ... his discussions on Catholicism, Roman and Anglican [show], he regarded it always as merely incidental, and was much more concerned with the positive and constructive expression of the Christian life and message, which, he believed, could only be found in its purest form in the Free Churches." W. B. Selbie, *The Life of Andrew Martin Fairbairn* (London: Hodder and Stoughton, 1914), 148–9.

[201] Ward, *Last Lectures*, 8.

[202] *Ibid.*, 8. One can contrast Newman in this respect with Leslie Stephen, who once confessed, "I find a good bit of metaphysical puzzling the best distraction." Stephen to Charles Eliot Norton (5 March 1876), *The Life and Letters of Leslie Stephen*, 287.

Such men dismiss without real examination the deeper side of Newman's work as mere *controversy* on outworn subjects, of no interest now to the serious thinking world. Its relation to the search for truth in a penetrating and earnest mind is simply overlooked, because mere theological controversy is not supposed in the nineteenth and twentieth centuries to go really deep, or to have any relation to such a deeper quest. The really profound thoughts in such writings are simply passed over and the discussions are politely set aside. The pleasanter task is undertaken of paying tributes to what is not controversial—the English style, the poetic beauty of the *Dream of Gerontius*, the engaging frankness of the *Apologia* as an autobiography, the picturesque account of the history of the Turks, the subtle and humorous delineation of the typical gentleman in the *Idea of a University*. Thus an imaginary Newman is formed out of his more superficial gifts. It may be a graceful figure, but it is not the Newman whose ... power transformed the lives of scores of young men at Oxford, and led hundreds who felt the magic of a genius at once spiritual and intellectual, which they could not explain, to subscribe to the formula: *Credo in Newmannum*.[203]

For all of the undeniable glamor that Newman had for undergraduates throughout his life, even after he left the snap-dragon growing on the wall opposite his freshman rooms in Trinity, he was always keenly appreciative of the apostasy that was overcoming the world beyond Oxford's dreaming spires.[204] As Ward shows, he saw this particularly in the rise of scepticism, precisely because he recognized the speciousness "of the negative position in religion," however much "his moral nature bound him closely to theism and Christianity." In other words, Newman's prescience when it came to the scepticism that would overtake England and so much of Europe beyond came of his own susceptibility to scepticism.[205] Both Liddon in his *Life of Pusey* and Ward in his *Last Lectures* quote the unforgettable letter Newman wrote to Pusey in 1845, in which the convert admitted to his dear friend: "Each one has his temptations. I thank God that He has shielded me morally from what intellectually might so easily come on me—general scepticism." As this shows, the solicitude Newman felt for the faith of his contemporaries—or, as the case might be, their loss of faith—could not have been more personal.

> Why should I believe the most sacred and fundamental doctrines of our faith, if you cut off from me the ground of development? But if that ground is given me,

---

[203] Ward, *Last Lectures*, 21–2.
[204] Cf. "My old College, Trinity College, where I was an undergraduate from the age of 16 to 21, till I gained a Fellowship at Oriel, has made me an Honorary Fellow of their Society. Of course, it involves no duties, rights or conditions, not even that of belonging to the University, certainly not that of having a vote as Master of Arts, but it is a mark of extreme kindness to me from men I have never seen, and it is the only instance of their exercising their power since it was given them. Trinity College has been the one and only seat of my affections at Oxford, and to see once more, before I am taken away, what I never thought I should see again, the place where I began the battle of life, with my good angel by my side, is a prospect almost too much for me to bear." Newman to Bishop Ullathorne (18 December 1877), *LD*, xxviii, 383–4.
[205] Cf. "When I was fourteen, I read Paine's Tracts against the Old Testament, and found pleasure in thinking of the objections which were contained in them. Also, I read some of Hume's Essays; and perhaps that on Miracles. So at least I gave my father to understand; but perhaps it was a brag. Also, I recollect copying out some French verses, perhaps Voltaire's, in denial of the immortality of the soul, and saying to myself something like 'How dreadful, but how plausible!'" *Apo.*, 3.

> I must go further. I cannot hold precisely what the English Church holds and nothing more. I must go forward or backward, else I sink into a dead scepticism, a heartless *acedia*, into which too many in Oxford, I fear, are sinking. You cannot take them a certain way in a line, and then, without assignable reason, stop them. If they find a bar put on them, a prohibition, from within or without, they come to think the whole matter a dream, a sham, and fall back to an ordinary life.[206]

For Ward, this is what made Newman "awake to the signs of the times in modern civilisation pointing to the impending break-up of Christendom with its corporate faith and to the imminence of general doubt or disbelief."[207] Moreover, seeing this movement against religion emerging so grievously, Newman resolved to expose and repel it. And, for Ward, it was this resolve that made Newman such a connoisseur of his contemporaries' peculiar scepticism. Indeed, it leant his musings on the character of this anti-Christian movement an unerring exactitude and prescience. "Further, Newman's prescience was notable in respect of the distinctive character of the movement against religion." Why?

> The term "agnostic" [Ward writes] belongs to the early seventies. It was invented by Huxley at an early meeting of the Metaphysical Society. The agnostic's strength as a dangerous force lies in his moderation. He does not say in his heart with the fool "There is no God." He says "Even if there is a God, He cannot be known by man." Mr. Huxley once compared speculation on the realities of another world to speculation on the politics of the inhabitants of the moon. This attitude is, in many quarters, a commonplace of our own day—though it takes various shapes in its detail. I think it a very remarkable fact that an attitude which was first fully recognised and expressed in the early seventies had been vividly delineated by Newman in the early fifties.[208]

To appreciate the force of Ward's point, we can turn to what Leslie Stephen had to say of the word in his essay, "An Agnostic's Apology" (1878). "It is sometimes used to indicate the philosophical theory which Mr. Herbert Spencer ... developed," Stephen wrote; but he used the word in:

> a vaguer sense, and am glad to believe that its use indicates an advance in the courtesies of controversy. The old theological phrase for an intellectual opponent was Atheist—a name which still retains a certain flavour as of the stake in this world and hell-fire in the next, and which, moreover, implies an inaccuracy of some importance. Dogmatic Atheism the doctrine that there is no God, whatever may be meant by God—is, to say the least, a rare phase of opinion. The word Agnosticism, on the other hand, seems to imply a fairly accurate appreciation of a form of creed already common and daily spreading. The Agnostic is one who

---

[206] Newman to Pusey (14 March 1845), *LD*, x, 593. This is one of those letters in which Newman shared his own doubts about the Anglican Church in order to impel his Tractarian friends to join him in considering conversion. He did this with Keble as well. Cf. "By making his friend [Keble] so privy to the doubts of conversion, Newman was preparing him for an understanding of how such doubts could be overcome." Short, *Newman and his Contemporaries*, 76.
[207] Ward, *Last Lectures*, 23.
[208] Ibid., 24.

asserts—what no one denies that there are limits to the sphere of human intelligence. He asserts, further, what many theologians have expressly maintained, that those limits are such as to exclude at least what Lewes called "metempirical" knowledge. But he goes further, and asserts, in opposition to theologians, that theology lies within this forbidden sphere.[209]

In other words, according to Stephen's biographer, Lord Annan: "When Stephen said that dogmatic Christianity was unreal, he meant that there was no possible way of knowing whether the propositions put forward by theologians were true or false. There was a simple answer to the theologians. You denied that their subject had any right to exist. The agnostic declared that there were limits to human knowledge and that beyond those limits no man had the right to be dogmatic."[210] It followed for Stephen that "we are all agnostics, though some people choose to call their ignorance God or mystery."[211]

Such are indeed the professions of agnosticism, and to provide his auditors with a good example of Newman's ability to enter into the thinking of those sworn to such doctrinaire doubt Ward read passages from one of the convert's Dublin lectures of 1854, "in which," as he said, "Newman puts into the mouth of an imaginary philosopher what we must at once recognise as being in essence the attitude of many a modern agnostic." In exhibiting the passages at such length, Ward shows how finely attuned Newman was to the peculiar idiosyncrasies of the agnostic *Zeitgeist*, which, he was convinced, the Church of Leo XIII and Pius X ignored at their peril. Here, then, is the first passage he quotes:

> Without denying that in the matter of religion some things are true and some things false [says Newman's imaginary philosopher], still we certainly are not in a position to determine the one or the other. And as it would be absurd to dogmatise about the weather, and say that 1860 will be a wet season or a dry season, a time of peace or war, so it is absurd for men in our present state to teach anything positively about the next world—that there is a heaven, or a hell, or a last judgment, or that the soul is immortal, or that there is a God. It is not that you have not a right to your own opinion, as you have a right to place implicit trust in your own banker, or in your own physician ; but undeniably such persuasions are not knowledge, they are not scientific, they cannot become public property, they are consistent with your allowing your friend to entertain the opposite opinion ; and, if you are tempted to be violent in the defence of your own view of the case in this matter of religion, then it is well to lay seriously to heart whether sensitiveness on the subject of your banker or your doctor, when he is handled sceptically by another, would not be taken to argue a secret misgiving in your mind about him, in spite of your confident profession, an absence of clear, unruffled certainty in his honesty or in his skill.

Here, Newman turns the agnosticism he wishes to refute into a most doctrinaire agnostic, though he is careful to have the imaginary sage refute

---

[209] Leslie Stephen, *An Agnostic's Apology and Other Essays* (London: Smith, Elder & Co., 1893), 1–2.
[210] Annan, *Leslie Stephen: The Godless Victorian*, 234.
[211] Stephen to Charles Eliot Norton (5 March 1876), *The Life and Letters of Leslie Stephen*, 287.

himself,[212] especially in the passage where we encounter him explaining the futility he experiences whenever he tries to escape the faith he has resolved to deny.

> And the misery is, [continues Newman's imaginary philosopher] that, if once we allow it to engage our attention, we are in a circle from which we never shall be able to extricate ourselves. Our mistake reproduces and corroborates itself. A small insect—a wasp or a fly—is unable to make his way through the pane of glass; and his very failure is the occasion of greater violence in his struggle than before. He is as heroically obstinate in his resolution to succeed as the assailant or defender of some critical battle-field; he is unflagging and fierce in an effort which cannot lead to anything beyond itself. When, then, in like manner, you have once resolved that certain religious doctrines shall be indisputably true, and that all men ought to perceive their truth, you have engaged in an undertaking which, though continued on to eternity, will never reach its aim; and, since you are convinced, it ought to do so, the more you have failed hitherto, the more violent and pertinacious will be your attempt in time to come. And further still, since you are not the only man in the world who is in this error, but one of ten thousand, all holding the general principle that Religion is scientific, and yet all differing as to the truths and facts and conclusions of this science, it follows that the misery of social disputation and disunion is added to the misery of a hopeless investigation, and life is not only wasted in fruitless speculation but embittered by bigoted sectarianism.

The conclusion Newman gives his imaginary friend nicely sums up the agnostic's refusal to concede the admissibility of faith as an object of knowledge. "'Such is the state in which the world has lain,' it will be said, 'ever since the introduction of Christianity. Christianity has been the bane of true knowledge, for it has turned the intellect away from what it can know, and occupied it in what it cannot.'"[213] Swift himself could not have improved on the deliciousness of this satirical sally.[214]

Ward's appreciation of the apologetical uses of Newman's satire is also incisive. "I lay great stress on these passages as showing how clearly Newman saw the signs of the times, and how persuasively, and even sympathetically, he could delineate this anti-Christian view of life which he held to be so dangerous, yet so plausible," he writes.

---

[212] Newman had done this to witty effect in *Anglican Difficulties* by having Bishop Warburton (1698-1779) refute Erastianism by touting what he imagines its virtues. "When Religion is in alliance with the State ... its purity must needs be reasonably well supported and preserved. For truth and public utility coinciding, the civil magistrate ... will see it for his interest to seek after and promote the truth in religion." *Difficulties of Anglicans*, i, ed. Short, 226. Apropos Warburton, Pattison wrote: "his peremptory despotic temper unfitted him for dealing with men. Regarding the Church, as he did, exclusively as an institution of government, his manner with his clergy was that of an officer to the common soldier. He knew not the arts of persuasion; and if he was resisted, he could only either sulk or cajole." Pattison, *Essays*, ii, 155.

[213] Ward, *Last Lectures*, 24-6. The passages from Newman can be found in *Idea*, 387-9.

[214] Cf. "Swift's strategy was to lash his victims with their own whip, to inoculate them with their own poison, to deride them with their own sophistries." William Alfred Eddy, "Introduction," in *Swift: Satires and Personal Writings*, ed. Eddy (Oxford: Oxford University Press, 1932), xxv.

It is a view which, as stated by him, will seem to many men of the world to be the merest common sense. It reflects human nature in a certain mood. This Newman saw clearly. He fully recognised the fact that just as Christian heroism and asceticism seem in certain moods to be unpractical and one-sided enthusiasm, so Christian faith appears in certain moods to be at variance with the common-sense view of life and of the limits of human knowledge. But he held that in both cases these were moods in which we do not realise life or the world in its deeper aspects.

For Ward, Newman's "direct antidote to agnosticism, therefore, was not mere argument against a position that did not itself rest on mere argument, but the persuasive delineation of what he held to be a deeper view than the agnostic's—a view which appeals to men in deeper moods—moods which he held to be more truly representative of normal human nature when it is completely aroused and awake and alive to life as a whole. Thus also the good man is alive to consequences of human actions which the sensualist or epicure in his picture of life according to nature necessarily banishes from his purview. Newman's apologetic is primarily of this nature—a delineation of motives actually influencing the believing mind, chiefly of his own mind when analysing the sources of its belief, rather than a merely objective statement of arguments. Arguments are, of course, included among these sources, but in the form and with the surrounding imagery amid which they stood in his own mind. His aim is not only to sound the logic of the matter, but to paint what actually affects and convinces the concrete man with all his existing sympathies and dispositions." Newman, in other words, seeks to plumb the epistemological depths of faith, rather than the shallows of logic, since "the whole man is won over to one side or the other by larger influences than logic—by influences which appeal to the heart and imagination as well as to the reason. This view of the case is apparent in his persuasive style even when he deals with the philosophy of faith, and with Christian history and theology. He is not content with opposing what he accounts a deeper intellectual view to a shallower one. Recognising how much the actual influence of the shallower view owes to the effect of a worldly and secularist atmosphere, he seeks to steep the imagination in a religious atmosphere which shall be a counterbalancing force. His writing reproduces the atmosphere in which he himself lives; and that, or something like it, is judged by him to be necessary to persuasion from the very fact that it is necessary to expel and replace the agnostic atmosphere which is continually finding entrance in modern society."[215]

Here, Ward, like Newman, recognizes that it is with sympathy, not polemics that we bring round agnostics—by appealing to their affections.[216] Thus, Ward writes not to convince his readers with arguments but to share with them his admiration for an apostle whose solicitude for the cure of souls continues to

---

[215] Ward, *Last Lectures*, 26–7.
[216] Since generalities must always be arguable, here is a lively objection from a Newman-friendly source. "Putting truths into logical form helps to crystallize the highest principles at stake in any particular assertion. With solid logical argumentation, one can better show how, if one denies a conclusion, one is also denying the principles from which it is vividly inferred." Meszaros, "Newman and the Thomistic Tradition," 468.

evangelize our own agnostics.[217] That Ward responded so deeply to Newman's appeal to the affections confirmed its efficacy. After all, it was an efficacy deeply appreciated by St. Thomas Aquinas, who knew that "Not merely learning about divine things but also experiencing them ... does not come from mere intellectual acquaintance with the terms of scientific theology, but from loving the things of God and cleaving to them by affection."[218] Ward's openness to Newman's appeal also vindicated his biographical and critical method, for it was sympathy that enabled him not only to understand but to love Newman, a love which entitles him to be regarded, *pace* Dessain, as one of Newman's finest contemporary critics. Of course, for some, love of one's subject will hardly count as an acceptable criterion for sound critical judgement. "The assumption of the rationalistic liberals was that mere sentiment ... stood on one side, cold reason on the other," Ward wrote in his Lowell Lectures.[219] Yet love enabled Ward not only to understand the struggles that made the beauty of Newman's style possible but that "triumph over difficulties," that "peace of conviction," which give all of his subject's life and work their defining nobility. In this case, as in so many others in the life of Newman, heart had spoken to heart. Without his love of Newman, Ward would never have understood the profound legacy his subject has left the world. He would certainly not have understood what he says in another passage: that in the work of Newman, "we can never escape from the truth of Buffon's often quoted aphorism, *Le style c'est l'homme meme*."[220] The greatest gift that Newman gave his contemporaries and, indeed, posterity, Ward recognized, was himself.

Here, Ward elaborates on how the aphorism's truth preeminently applies to a writer in whom style and the gift of self are inseparable.

> The 'Essay on the Development of Christian Doctrine' is the first of his works which at all shows the full extent of his literary power.... There is not in this essay the sustained beauty and uniformly high level which are visible in the *Apologia*, or even in the *Lectures on Anglican Difficulties*, in spite of their controversial character. But its finest pages show Newman at his very best. In imaginative sweep, in eloquence, in richness of language ... we find a combination which opens a new chapter in Newman's history as a writer. In no other of his writings is the white heat of eloquence more manifest. As that eloquence is all directed towards a particular conclusion, the charge of special pleading is an inevitable consequence, and no charge is more fatal to a reputation for historical thoroughness. Yet those who make the charge have missed the essential character of the work. The elo-

---

[217] Cf. "Logic makes but a sorry rhetoric with the multitude ... Logicians are more set upon concluding rightly, than on right conclusions. They cannot see the end for the process. Few men have that power of mind which may hold fast and firmly a variety of thoughts. We ridicule 'men of one idea;' but a great many of us are born to be such, and we should be happier if we knew it. To most men argument makes the point in hand only more doubtful, and considerably less impressive. After all, man is not a reasoning animal; he is a seeing, feeling, contemplating, acting animal. He is influenced by what is direct and precise." *GA*, 93. See Meszaros's amusing objection to this in the journal article above, p. 423.

[218] St. Thomas Aquinas, Opusc. XIV, Expositio, *De Divinis Nominibus*, ii, *lect.* 4, *St. Thomas Aquinas: Philosophical Texts*, ed. Thomas Gilby (Oxford: Oxford University Press, 1951), 92.

[219] Ward, *Last Lectures*, 106.

[220] Ibid., 70.

quence, the beauty of style, is largely a direct result of the writer's very candour. It speaks of triumph over difficulties directly faced and explicitly stated, which the uncandid special pleader would ignore, of a rough road traversed. But the journey had been accomplished when he wrote the book, and in the actual writing the triumphant note of arrival is apparent. The obstacles are recorded, but the pain and anxiety they once caused are lost in present happiness. We know from his letters and diaries that the time of waiting—during which it was written—was a period of heartache, of impending separation from dearest associations at Oxford and in the Church of England. The stress of his fateful inquiry left an ineffaceable mark. The vision of Rome beckoned him in the distance; the Church of his birth, lifelong friendships, the clinging hold of early and sacred memories, held him back. In the *Apologia* he compared the struggle to that of the death agony. ... Yet we know also that he emerged from [the agony] ... into a repose and peace of conviction which never left him. Both aspects of his story are visible in the style of this famous essay. A trail of glory is visible in many of its pages—thrown in retrospect on a rugged path which has led to a scene to him so inspiring. Hence the peculiar character of the style. Let the anti-Roman theological critic of the work say what he may against its argument, if he has any sense of the deep pathos of the drama of a soul, he cannot read without emotion those pages in which the intensity and rich colouring of the drama become apparent.[221]

To conclude, it might be best to hear what Josephine had to say of her brilliant, faithful, lovable husband once the end came round, for her encapsulation of his life would have profoundly moved the man who meant so much to both of them.

His last Communion was of extraordinary joy to him, and his reserve on spiritual matters was wearing thin. I don't think he knew what he was showing. His voice was failing, but he kept saying "Thank God! How wonderful!" and once he added, "No one knows what it is to be a Catholic." No one could doubt of his joy or fail to be comforted by it—the deep Christian penitence so constant and so complete for months past was turned into joy. It seemed then as if his life unfolded before us in a clear picture first of energy and, as this chequered world goes, of happiness, then of the trials, very deep and very great, of the last months, ending in almost visible triumph. The greatness of human nature, the immense scope of man's destiny, the fresh wind blowing from an infinite future filled the chamber of death. At first it was impossible not to be happy. As he had strengthened the faith of others during life, he opened to us at the end a vision of daylight clearness. His vocation was an intellectual vocation, and it was by absolutely honest use of his intellectual powers that he had to make his way. There are spiritually minded men and women who are not especially candid in affairs of the intellect, but who have other beautiful charities and virtues. Wilfrid was a man faithful

---

[221] *Ibid.*, 62–4. Cf. "From the end of 1841, I was on my death-bed, as regards my membership with the Anglican Church, though at the time I became aware of it only by degrees. ... A death-bed has scarcely a history; it is a tedious decline, with seasons of rallying and seasons of falling back; and since the end is foreseen, or what is called a matter of time, it has little interest for the reader, especially if he has a kind heart. Moreover, it is a season when doors are closed and curtains drawn, and when the sick man neither cares nor is able to record the stages of his malady. I was in these circumstances, except so far as I was not allowed to die in peace." *Apo.*, 147.

with his "whole mind." It is carved on his gravestone that "The desire of wisdom bringeth to the Everlasting Kingdom."[222]

---

[222] Ward, *Last Lectures*, lxxii.

IAN KER

≈ 10 ≈

Ian Ker and the Criticism of "Due Formation"

> The critical sense is so far from frequent that it is absolutely rare, and the possession of the cluster of qualities that minister to it is one of the highest distinctions. It is a gift inestimably precious and beautiful; therefore, so far from thinking that it passes overmuch from hand to hand, one knows that one has only to stand by the counter an hour to see that business is done with baser coin. We have too many schoolmasters; yet not only do I not question in literature the high utility of criticism, but I should be tempted to say that the part it plays may be the supremely beneficent one when it proceeds from deep sources, from the efficient combination of experience and perception. In this light one sees the critic as the real helper of the artist, a torch-bearing outrider, the interpreter, the brother.
>
> Henry James, "The Science of Criticism" (1891)

I

In the *Grammar of Assent*, Newman takes Edward Gibbon to task for failing to acquire what he called the "due formation" necessary to understand Christianity and for resolving, instead, to write of its rise as a matter of episcopal fraud, lay credulity, barbarity and the most tediously futile theological hairsplitting.[1] "It is very remarkable that it should not have occurred to a man of Gibbon's sagacity to inquire what account the Christians themselves gave of the matter," Newman wrote. For the convert, reading the *Decline and Fall* could only leave the fair-minded with a litany of questions. "Would it not have been worth while for him to have let conjecture alone, and to have looked for facts instead? Why did he not try the hypothesis of faith, hope and charity? Did he never hear of repentance towards God, and faith in Christ? Did he not recollect the many

---

[1] In his entertaining biography of Carlyle, James Anthony Froude writes: "In speaking of Gibbon's work to me [Carlyle] made one remark which is worth recording. In earlier years he had spoken contemptuously of the Athanasian controversy, of the Christian world torn in pieces over a diphthong, and he would ring the changes in broad Annandale on the Homo*o*usion and the Homo*i*ousion. He told me now that he perceived Christianity itself to have been at stake. If the Arians had won, it would have dwindled away into a legend." Froude, *Thomas Carlyle: A History of his Life in London*, ii, 462.

words of Apostles, Bishops, Apologists, Martyrs, all forming one testimony?" Newman's own answer to these questions was summary. "No; such thoughts are close upon him, and close upon the truth; but he cannot sympathize with them, he cannot believe in them, he cannot even enter into them because he needs the due formation for such an exercise of mind."[2] This same lack of "due formation," the humility and sympathy necessary to understand anything worth understanding, hobbled the majority of Newman's contemporary critics. In the present study, I have only touched upon a select number of these unsympathetic critics—Abbott and Fitzjames Stephen are two of the most egregious—but I have certainly adduced enough evidence to show to what poor, perverse, imperceptive criticism such lack of formation leads. The point of my defying the set scope of my study and including a chapter on the finest of all Newman scholar critics, Ian Ker, is to show my readers what criticism can look like once animated by this "due formation." But before I share examples of Ker's unmatched mastery of the unity, coherence and force of Newman's work, I shall say a few words about his life, since it is in his life that we can see why he was so ready to acquire the "due formation" that so many other critics, favorable and unfavorable lack.

II

Born in Naini Tal in India on 30 August 1942, Ian Turnbull Ker was the son of Charles Murray Ker of the India Civil Service and his wife Joan May Knox, the daughter of another official in the India Service who was first cousin of Ronald Knox. He had two sisters, one younger and one older, though the younger died tragically when still in her twenties. Naini Tal had been set up in the 1860s and 1870s under the Raj as the summer hill station for the North Western Provinces. In 1947, Ian Ker and his parents and two sisters left India after independence was declared and settled in Wimbledon. As Ker recalled, "I arrived in a bitterly cold England at the age of 5 where there was still no central heating (to the disgust of my Canadian-born paternal grandmother) and where wartime rationing was still in force. Apart from a nanny and maid, there were no servants as contrasted with India where there were servants for every possible task."[3] The English in India often had to employ more servants than they wished if only because religion and caste limited what any given servant could perform. Being, as he was, a child of the Raj, Ker had always a certain imperiousness, but also a delicious sense of humor, the absurdities of misrule, whether in the ecclesiastical, political or academic sphere, always appealing to his delight in the ridiculous.

As a boy, Ker recalled entering into the Sacred Heart Church in Edge Hill, Wimbledon and finding it at once impressive and welcoming. "I remember as a small boy wandering into the cathedral-like Jesuit church out of curiosity and being welcomed by an old Irishman at the back. There were an unusual number of Catholics in Wimbledon in South London, where I grew up, no doubt because there were a Jesuit school and an Ursuline convent school. The service—which

---

[2] GA, 297.
[3] All of the remarks quoted here from Ian Ker are taken from a series of interviews the author conducted with the scholar before his death.

of course, being the Tridentine Mass, I didn't understand—was utterly unlike the middle-of-the-road Church of England matins we attended as a family." However intriguing Ker found the Jesuit church, his view of Catholics at the time was conventional enough. "Thanks to history, not religion, lessons at school about Good Queen Bess as opposed to Bloody Mary and to the threatened Spanish Armada, I thought of Catholics as disloyal quasi-foreigners." If his first five years in India had given Ker a certain detachment from his English fellows, a detachment not unlike the one Newman had as a result of his having a father who was a private banker in the cosmopolitan City and a mother of Huguenot Norman stock, he nevertheless grew up in an Anglican ethos that was not altogether different from the one in which Newman had grown up.

It was his uncle, a Classics don at Trinity College, Cambridge, who recommended that Ker go to Shrewsbury School, whose brightest pupils in the 1960s went to Balliol or Trinity College, Cambridge. That the most famous of Shrewsbury's Old Boys should have been Charles Darwin gives Ker's time there an apt twist—the theme of development that would so preoccupy Newman being in the air even when Ker was a schoolboy. From Shrewsbury, Ker duly went to Balliol, about which he was somewhat ambivalent. "Balliol was the pre-eminent college at Oxbridge for Classics and I only got there through excellent teaching and hard work," he recalled.

> I read "Mods and Greats," which in those days oddly encompassed both ancient history and ancient and modern philosophy. I loathed ancient history for the very reason that my Classics school teacher had commended it, the paucity of sources/documents; it seemed to consist of reading endless articles in learned journals of an extremely hypothetical nature (if …, then …); exactly the sort of argumentation I was later to encounter in Biblical studies. After completing Mods and Greats, I was taught by the top scholars in their fields. Gordon Williams (who taught me to think) later occupied the Yale chair in Latin; Russel Meiggs (one of the pre-eminent ancient historians of his time and editor of J. B. Bury's *History of Greece*); and R. M. Hare, then the pre-eminent moral philosopher in the English-speaking world. The theory for which Hare was famous—prescriptivism, or "preference utilitarianism," as it was called, the contention that one should act in such a way as to maximize people's preferences—seemed to me to be obviously refuted as it made no provision for moral weakness, a fact which taught me how very silly very clever people could be.

Ker's conversion to Catholicism was gradual. After falling away from the conventional Church of England faith in which he had been brought up, he ceased going to church services altogether until he had a conversion experience in Florence, wither he had gone in his second year at Oxford to learn Italian. As he recalled, it was while looking at Italian Old Master paintings that he was reminded of Christ's words on the Cross: "Father, forgive them for they know not what they do." [Luke 23: 34–8] After this encounter with Christ in his Passion, which impressed upon him the heart-rending reality of Christianity, Ker returned to Oxford and set about finding a church that would nurture his newfound faith. He began attending services at the Anglo-Papalist Saint Mary Magdalene because it was conveniently near his college, though he soon found the preaching of the vicar, John Hooper "spell-binding."[4] Indeed, the vicar's mimic Catholicism fascinated Ker. "Being by nature rather rebellious and subversive of authority, I enjoyed the way extreme Anglo-Papalists like Father Hooper behaved like Roman Catholics within what was obviously a Protestant church." Eventually, however, he found "the whole thing unreal."[5] Thereafter, before leaving Oxford, he was received into the Church of Rome, though his personal experience of the unreality of the Via Media naturally prepared him to appreciate Newman's disenchantment with the same unreality.[6]

Regarding his conversion at Oxford, Ker remarked: "Although my father was a professed atheist, I think his dogmatic dismissal of Christianity provoked in me the opposite reaction and in my teens, I was greatly influenced by C. S. Lewis's *Mere Christianity* (1952)." The brilliant apologist Origen (185–254) also sent Ker down the road to conversion. As Ker recalled, "his argument that either Christ was who he claimed to be or a scoundrel influenced my conversion to Catholicism as exactly the same argument seemed to me to apply to the pope." Between writing his great biographies, Ker would write a brilliant response to Lewis with a work of apologetics of his own, *Mere Catholicism* (2007), which argued that mere Christianity, ineluctably, could not be other than mere Catholicism. Over the years, to Ker's delight, this gem of a book has brought many converts into the Church from around the world, though later he would admit to me that he ought to have paid more attention to miracles in the book. Like Newman and, for that matter, Waugh, Ker was very alive to the operation of grace in the fallen world. After all, he was directly instrumental in the two miracles that canonized Newman.

Once Ker decided to convert, the reaction of his parents was mixed. "My father was indifferent to my becoming a Catholic, my mother wasn't pleased—although she eventually became a Catholic herself. There were already several Catholics in the English Department at York. I always saw my teaching role, as Newman had seen his, as a pastoral as well as an educational role. One reason why I became a priest was because I thought I would like to teach people about Catholicism as opposed to English literature. My colleagues were amazed when they heard I was going to become a priest. Although I went to daily Mass I never advertised the fact, nor did I give the appearance of being pious."

If Ker's mother converted to the Church of Rome, his father, elder sister and several friends did not, which must have reminded him of something Newman told Sophia Ryder (1817–1901) regarding the Catholic understanding of "invincible ignorance." "We know perfectly well, and hold with all our hearts that the Catholic Church is the sole communion in which there is salvation," Newman wrote.

---

[4] Ker, "The Hall and the Side Rooms," 50.
[5] Ibid.
[6] Cf. "Protestantism and Popery are real religions; no one can doubt about them; they have furnished the mould in which nations have been cast: but the *Via Media*, viewed as an integral system, has never had existence except on paper; it is known, not positively but negatively, in its differences from the rival creeds, not in its own properties; and can only be described as a third system, neither the one nor the other, but with something of each, cutting between them, and, as if with a critical fastidiousness, trifling with them both, and boasting to be nearer Antiquity than either." *VM*, i, 16.

But we know too, that there is such a state of mind as invincible ignorance, and the present Pope in one of his Allocutions has expressly recognised it. [Pius IX, *Singulari quadam*, 9 December 1854.] He has said too, if my memory is correct, that no one can decide who is in invincible ignorance and who is not—indeed, it seems plain that it would require a particular revelation in order to be able to do so. For myself, I certainly do not consider, speaking under correction, that in order to be in invincible ignorance one must be out of sight and hearing of Catholicism; and that to be near Catholics is incompatible with such an ignorance. Habit, formation of mind, prejudice, reliance and faith in others, may be as real walls of separation as mountains. Members of one and the same household may be more distant from each other in the intercommunion and mutual apprehension of ideas, than they would be made by the interposition of an ocean.

Ker had long painful experience of this salt, estranging sea, though he also recognized, with Newman, that such estrangement partook of an unfathomable mystery. "Your dear Mother may have been in perfect good faith," Newman wrote to Sophia after her Protestant mother died. "And, if we once get so far as to feel the possibility of this, then we may take comfort to ourselves and believe, that all those tokens of sincerity and devotion which we see in our Protestant friends, are not mere appearances and pretences, but real evidence that their ignorance was not vincible, and their separation from the Church not voluntary." Since all Catholics have experience of this heartbreaking divide, we can take solace from the solace Newman derived from his experience, which he describes so movingly. "I cannot get myself to believe that the many dear friends and relatives I have lost are without the hope of salvation; I do not know what obliges me to think so; I do not see why I should adopt the contrary views of this Catholic or that who is narrowminded in his view of doctrine, and has not the experience of fact, of the lives of Protestants, as I have. Till then I am called by the voice of the Church to think otherwise, I shall think hopefully, where others who have no means of judging, rashly despair. Do pray for me."[7]

After Balliol, Ker won a scholarship to study English at Corpus Christi, Oxford where he was taught by another notable figure, the English don F. W. Bateson. In 1951, Bateson founded *Essays in Criticism*, which succeeded F. R. Leavis's *Scrutiny* as the pre-eminent scholarly journal in its field after the latter folded in 1953. Advocating for what he called the "scholar-critic," Bateson once wrote that "Dr Leavis at his best is a much better literary critic than I am but when it comes to scholarship, I am perhaps the better man of the two" In a witty piece on Bateson in *Essays in Criticism*, the literary critic Valentine Cunningham quoted the don's conclusion that "The scholar-critic must be a scholar, a researcher, *before* he can become a really competent critic. There are therefore almost no reputable scholar-critics," to which Cunningham added: "And so it

---

[7] Newman to Sophia Ryder (4 September 1862), *LD*, xx, 268–9. Sophia Ryder (1817–1901), youngest daughter of the Bishop of Lichfield and Coventry, and sister of George Ryder, one of Newman's godsons, with whom she converted to Rome in 1846, became a Good Shepherd Nun. George had been a pupil of Newman's at Oriel. "To think that I have a godson a Catholic," Newman wrote on hearing of George's conversion, "—he is the first of them. I do trust others will follow." Newman to George Ryder (22 May 1846), *LD*, xi, 165.

was with Freddy Bateson."[8] Yet Bateson may have been surprised to know that in having Ian Ker as his student he had someone who would go on to become one of the most talented scholar critics that Oxford has ever produced. His work on Newman, Chesterton, and the authors of the Catholic Revival amply attest to this. Indeed, his essay on Evelyn Waugh is the single best thing ever written about the great Catholic novelist.[9]

One extract, apropos Gervase Crouchback, the pivotal character in Waugh's masterpiece, *Sword of Honour* (1965) will show what a fine literary critic Ker is, one of the many distinctions which made him such an incomparably fine critic of Newman. "One obvious way of conveying holiness in fiction is to hint at a certain naiveté—one has to be a little naïve to be quite so good—but that, of course, undermines the holiness," Ker writes,

> and Waugh has no intention of taking that easy way out. Far from it, he insists on the self-awareness of Mr. Crouchback. "As a reasoning man Mr. Crouchback had known than he was honourable, charitable and faithful a man who by all the formulations of his faith, should be confident of his salvation." But that doesn't lead to pride because "as a man of prayer he saw himself as totally unworthy of divine notice." And when we are told that "to Guy his father was the best man, the only entirely good man he had ever known," we do not feel we are being manipulated because that is how we feel too. The mercenary proprietor of the boardinghouse where Mr. Crouchback lives as a permanent resident, who knows as little or less than Kirstie [the publicist for the Halberdiers] about holiness, can only conclude in his "invincible ignorance": "He's a deep one and no mistake. I never have understood him, not properly. Somehow his mind seems to work different than yours and mine." His wife knows from the many grateful letters she has seen in his rooms that Mr. Crouchback "gives it away, right and left," handouts which include "a weekly allowance to an unfrocked priest." When Mr. Crouchback dies, it seems entirely appropriate that his solicitor should observe that, although none of Mr. Crouchback's furniture is "of any value," nevertheless "it was all well made." A man who has done the job of being a Catholic, of doing Catholic things, so perfectly would naturally also have well-crafted furniture.[10]

Waugh could be comically dismissive of the generation that succeeded his own. "It is tedious for the young to be constantly reminded of what fine fellows their fathers were and what a much more enjoyable time we had," he wrote in one of his last book reviews. "But there you are: we were and we did."[11] However, he did have a good eye for the talent of young writers coming up when he was already long established, as his praise of William Trevor, Sybille Bedford and Muriel Spark shows. Could he have been around when Ker's chapter on his work was published, he certainly would have relished its appreciation of how

---

[8] Bateson quoted in Valentine Cunningham, "F. W. Bateson, Scholar Critic," in *Essays in Criticism* 29/2 (April 1979), 139.
[9] See Ian Ker, "Evelyn Waugh: The Priest as Craftsman," in *The Catholic Revival in English Literature 1845-1961* (Leominster: Gracewing, 2003), 149–202.
[10] Ibid., 202.
[11] *The Essays, Articles and Reviews of Evelyn Waugh*, ed. Donat Gallagher (London: Methuen, 1984), 611.

his Catholic faith transformed his understanding and, indeed, his practice of the art of writing.

From Oxford, Ker went to Trinity College, Cambridge where he undertook doctoral work on George Eliot, which the university rejected. Ian Jack, the editor of Emily Brontë and Robert Browning, was apparently not interested in hearing what Ker had to say of George Eliot's treatment of the Christian religion in her fiction. "If God is anywhere," the agnostic Jack told his obituarist, "he is in the mind of man"—not a sentiment which would have made Jack receptive to Ker's Catholic sensibility.[12] However, the honorary doctorates that Ker received subsequently from several universities in England and North America more than made up for his unrewarded labors at Cambridge, though Cambridge did eventually award him a doctorate for his published work. In his biography of Newman, Ker has occasion to touch on George Eliot in a way that shows something of what Jack and Cambridge lost when they rejected Ker's project. "Newman may have abandoned Evangelicalism," Ker writes, "but there can be little doubt that he had learned much from the kind of rigorous self-analysis to which the Evangelical habit of self-examination led and which was encouraged so strenuously by such standard spiritual books as William Wilberforce's *Practical View* and Hannah More's *Practical Piety*. In so far as this kind of introspection replaced a Christocentric spirituality, Newman rejected it, but it was certainly as important for the psychological penetration of his own sermons, as it was significant for the creative achievement of another former Evangelical, George Eliot, whose probing of intention and motive, and especially of self-delusion, was to raise the delineation of character in the novel to an altogether new level."[13]

From Trinity College, Ker went to teach at the University of York, about which he recalled: "I got the job at York because it was a department of English and Related Literature and I was able to teach Latin as well as English literature. I was very lucky to get a job in one of the best English departments in the country and in such a historic and beautiful city at a time when academic jobs in the humanities were growing increasingly scarce." Coincidentally enough, it was also at York that he encountered Leavis as a colleague, whom he found dour and unapproachable. At York, Fr. Ian liked to relate, the famously astringent critic was wary of other faculty, with whom he rarely spoke, though he could often be seen walking about the grounds picking up litter. When a visitor noticed Leavis engaged thus and remarked on the extraordinary neatness of the grounds, the vice chancellor replied that, yes, York did indeed have an unusually dedicated grounds staff.

That Ker came up with first-rate literary critics still on the scene (all progeny in one way or another of T. S. Eliot) accounts for something of his own critical rigor. Indeed, in later years, Ker often confided that he would have liked to have written a critical biography of Eliot—something the world still lacks. No conversation with the fastidious scholar critic about Eliot would exclude his fulminations against what he regarded as the uncritical vacuousness of Robert Crawford's two-volume biography.

---

[12] The obituary of Ian Jack (1923–2008) by Howard Erskine-Hill appears on the Cambridge website.
[13] Ker, *John Henry Newman: A Biography*, 95.

After his stint at York from 1969–74, Ker was ordained in 1979 and served as Assistant Priest at St. Edmund's, Southampton University from 1979 to 1982. He was Catholic chaplain at Southampton from 1987 to 1989 before becoming Senior Chaplain at Oxford from 1989 to 1990 and Chaplain at St. Mary's, Ascot from 1991 to 1993. From 1987 to 1989 he held the Endowed Chair in Theology and Philosophy at the University of St. Thomas in Minnesota. In 1993, he was Visiting Professor in the Humanities at Franciscan University, Steubenville. From 1995, he was Senior Research Fellow at St. Benet's Hall, Tutor at Campion Hall and Member of the Oxford University Theology Faculty.

As for his decision to work on Newman, it was serendipitous in the way that providential choices often are. "I knew a bit about Newman from reading Victorian literature and I had read the *Apologia* (1864) once when I was ill in bed—without I am afraid it making much of an impression on me. It was a chance encounter that got me writing about Newman: a colleague invited me to dinner in London where I met an Italian academic who was aiming to publish a selection of Newman's works in Italian and who invited me to edit *The Idea of a University* (1873), which he later suggested I turn into an Oxford critical edition." Ker's friendship with the brilliant Newman scholar, Fr. Charles Stephen Dessain, would also inform his work on Newman—proof of the vitality of that personal influence of which Newman was always so appreciative. Moreover, Newman's devotion to his sister, Mary, who died young, particularly appealed to Ker, who was devoted to his own sister, Susan, who also died young. He kept a photograph of Susan on his mantlepiece and dedicated his Newman biography to her. There is a corresponding poignancy to Ker's quoting Newman's letter to a domestic servant, in which the Oratorian wrote:

> I am sorry that you should still be so far from well—but God will bless and keep you in His own good way, We never can trust Him too much. All things turn to good—to them who trust Him. I too know what it is to lose a sister. I lost her 49 years ago, and, though so many years have past, I still feel the pain.[14]

After his conversion, Ker, as he recalled, was "offered an endowed chair not in English but in theology and philosophy at the University of St Thomas in St Paul, Minnesota on the basis of what I had published about Newman. even though I had no degree in theology, having studied privately for ordination (like Pope St Paul VI)." St Thomas suited Ker. "I had been given to understand that mid-western Americans were dull characterless people but I certainly didn't find that there: I lived in a residence for priests teaching at the university and I found myself in the company of some wonderful eccentrics. It was one of the happiest times in my life and I made many friends there, I returned to England because my parents were growing old and needed care (my only surviving sibling had long lived in Canada). I also regretted no longer doing pastoral work apart from supplies and hearing confessions at the local seminary."

Ker's fondness for the many students, scholars, priests and religious he met over the years in North America, Europe and elsewhere points to another similarity

---

[14] Newman to a Domestic Servant (9 January 1877), *LD*, xxviii, 159. See Ker, *John Henry Newman: A Biography*, 699.

he had with Newman, and that was his talent for friendship. Although not always adept at suffering fools gladly, especially fools given to distorting Newman or the Catholic Faith, Ker always inspired fondness in those who reveled in his wit, his bonhomie, his learning, and his very real, if inconspicuous *pietas*.

Upon returning to England to look after his aging parents, Ker joined the theology faculty of Oxford and became parish priest of the Church of SS Thomas More and John Fisher at Burford in the Cotswolds, thus ensuring that in his critical, biographical, theological and apologetical work he would always be grounded, as Newman had been grounded, in pastoral work. For both, in all they did, the cure of souls was paramount.

Towards the end of his life, Ker retired to Cheltenham Spa, where he was lovingly looked after by Mrs. Julia Kadziela, of whom he was immensely fond. From accounts of his Cotswold parishioners, one can see that if not particularly ingratiating in the way that smarmy, popular pastors tend to be, Ker was dutiful, devoted and decisive. Whenever parishioners were in need, at whatever time of day or night, he attended to them himself. Delegating such duties was unthinkable. He was particularly attentive to the bereaving, a trait he shared with Newman, whose letters to the bereft could be of the most eloquent fellow feeling. "What you say about Mother Prioress' troubles is a great lesson to me," Newman wrote his friend Sister Mary Imelda Poole, when she had confided in him about the loss of various nuns.

> but the Oratory is a body unlike any other (at least Congregation of men) in the Church. Since it is local and isolated it does not want novices except like so many drops now and then falling upon it. But since it has no vows, it cannot well part with those who at length by long trial and habit have become knit into it. Here emphatically "the old are better," a dozen novices could not (humanly speaking) make up for one Fr Flanagan. In the loss of dear Fr Gordon five years ago, we suffered what was irreparable. If it be God's blessed will to take Fr Flanagan that again would be an irreparable blow—but He who gave eyes to the blind and limbs to the maimed can supply for bereavements even as great as these—, but it must be almost as miraculously.[15]

After a week of suffering intermittent chest pains, in the early morning of 5 November, Ian Ker died in hospital in Gloucester, not far from his home in Cheltenham Spa. That he should have died on Guy Fawkes Day, his friend Bishop James Conley remarked, must have made for "many smiles in Heaven."

III

In the second half of the twentieth century, biography, especially literary biography, enjoyed something of a renaissance—one thinks of such gifted critical biographers as Peter Brown on Saint Augustine, Leon Edel on Henry James, Richard Holmes on Coleridge, Robert Baldrick on J. K. Huysmans, and Walter Jackson Bate on Samuel Johnson. As a critical biographer, Ker very much belongs

---

[15] Newman to Sister Mary Imelda Poole (29 April 1858), *LD*, xviii, 339.

in this distinguished company. In his biography of Newman, he encapsulated his subject's quest for reality by translating Newman's epitaph, *Ex umbria et imaginibus in veritatem*: "Out of unreality into Reality." In his biography of Chesterton, Ker persuasively argued that GKC was Newman's successor precisely because he shared the convert's passion for reality, a quality which Hilaire Belloc also discerned in his friend. "Truth had for him," Belloc recalled, "the immediate attraction of an appetite. He was hungry for reality. But what is much more, he could not conceive of himself except as satisfying that hunger […] it was not possible for him to hold anything worth holding that was not connected with the truth as a whole."[16] Here was the hunger that drove the Christian witness of both Newman and Chesterton, and Ker brilliantly recreates it in his magisterial biographies.

Another virtue of the Chesterton biography is its identifying and setting out the major themes that preoccupied GKC in his massive, though uneven *oeuvre*, including not only his well-known philosophy of wonder but the principle of limitation that governs his thinking about art, literature, history and religion and the role of the imagination in enabling us to see familiar matters anew.[17] Distillation is one of the hallmarks of Ker's work as a biographer and it is radiantly evident in his biography of Chesterton.

The reception of Ker's Newman biography was overwhelmingly favorable. "That there is never a dull page out of the seven hundred and forty-five of text is due not only to the vigour and elegance of Newman's prose and the excitement of his ideas," one reviewer wrote, "but the skill of a presentation which never obtrudes, nor seeks to vie with the subject himself. The book reads with the effortlessness which belies the magnitude of the task so well accomplished."[18] As for the negative reviews he occasionally received over the years to his various books, Ker so delighted in their abuse that he actually gave a talk once sharing a kind of compendium of it with a conference audience. He had nothing of the rancorous vanity of most academics.

Ker's biography of Newman, in all its amplitude and acuity, is a model life not only because of its critical rigor but its unusual precision. Newman lay great store by what he called "clearness," which he found preeminently in Cicero. "I may truly say that I have never been in the practice since I was a boy of attempting to write well, or to form an elegant style," Newman once confessed to a correspondent; "my one desire and aim has been to do what is so difficult—viz., to express clearly and exactly my meaning."[19] Ker follows Newman in this most demanding of

---

[16] Hilaire Belloc, *Saturday Review* (4 July 1936), 4.
[17] Ker, *G. K. Chesterton: A Biography*, xi.
[18] Gordon Wakefield, review of Ker's *John Henry Newman: A Biography*, *Scottish Journal of Theology*, 43:3 (August, 1990), 427–9.
[19] Newman to John Hayes (13 April 1869), *LD*, xxiv, 241. Ruskin shared Newman's respect for clarity. "I never for an instant compared Johnson to Scott, Pope, Byron, or any of the really great writers whom I loved. But I at once and for ever recognized in him a man entirely sincere and infallibly wise in the view and estimate he gave of the common questions, business and ways of the world. I valued his sentences not primarily because they were symmetrical but because they were just, and clear; it is a method of judgment rarely used by the average public, who ask from an author always, in the first place, arguments in favor of their own opinions in elegant terms." John Ruskin, *Praeterita* with an introduction by Tim Hilton (New York: Everyman's Library, 2005), 198–9.

all literary virtues. In his limpid prose, there is an unfailing fidelity to both the complexity and the simplicity of Newman's work. He eschewed paraphrase. In all that he wrote of Newman, he was careful to present his subject in his own words.

A good stylist, Ker was never oblivious to how style informs thought, a quality he shared with Dean Church, who once remarked of the sermons of Lancelot Andrewes: "If the stupendous facts of the Christian Creeds are true, no attention, no thought is too great for them; and their greatness, their connections, their harmony, their infinite relations to the system of God's government and discipline of mankind, and to the hopes and certain ties of human life, are here set forth with a breadth, a subtlety, a firmness of touch, a sense of their reality, a fervour and reverence of conviction, which have made the Sermons worthy and fruitful subjects of study to English theologians." Indeed, for Church, "the style is like the notes of the unceremonious discourses of a very animated and varied talker rather than the composition of a preacher," and consequently the thought of the discourses pivots on the style's "perpetual and unexpected allusions, its oddly-treated quotations, its abrupt and rapid transitions, its fashion of tossing about single words."[20] Ker, too, recognizes how thought finds shape in style. Throughout his books, one can see the scholar critic in him hammering this home, usually at the expense of duffers intent on distorting Newman's work, as here:

> Professor Owen Chadwick has written that as an Anglican Newman "slaughtered the Catholic Church with scorn and satire." The observation seems plausible enough ... But, in fact, neither the work he published nor the private letters he wrote as an Anglican support the point. For what is so interesting and noteworthy about all that he said as an Anglican about the Roman Catholic Church—and he said some very rude and scathing things—is the almost total absence of any satire in all his various critical comments and strictures. Indeed, there appears to be only one place where Newman allows himself anything approaching ridicule or satire, and that is a passage ... in his 1840 article on the "Catholicity of the Anglican Church," which was a desperate attempt to shore up the theory of the *via media* ... The passage I have in mind is actually only a single sentence which occurs at the end of an attack on Roman Catholicism.
>
>> When we go into foreign countries, we see superstitions in the Roman Church which shock us; when we read history, we find its spirit of intrigue so rife, so widely spread, that "jesuitism" has become a by-word; when we look round us at home, we see it associated everywhere with the low democracy, pandering to the spirit of rebellion ... We see it attempting to gain converts among us, by unreal representations of its doctrines ... We see its agents smiling and nodding and ducking to attract attention, as gipsies make up to truant boys, holding out tales for the nursery, and pretty pictures, and gold gingerbread, and physic concealed in jam, and sugar-plums for good children.[21]

---

[20] Church, *Pascal and Other Sermons*, 59–60.
[21] Ian Ker, "Newman the Satirist," in *Newman after a Hundred Years*, 11.

Such comments show the meticulous precision of Ker's criticism, which arose naturally from his confining himself to what Newman actually wrote, not what he might be thought to have written. "The satirical dig at the end [of the passage Newman quotes above] is quite exceptional," Ker writes, "but the word 'unreal' prepares us for the apologetic, explanatory sentence that follows: 'Who can but feel shame when the religion of Ximenes, Borromeo, and Pascal is so overlaid?' In other words, for once the Roman Catholic Church is satirized because she is seen as inconsistent, and therefore unreal, and therefore ridiculous. Normally, while Newman was a Tractarian, confident in the *via media*, there was never any doubt as to the Church of Rome's *consistency*, whatever else could be urged against her. Criticism and invective were in order, but not satire because there was nothing ridiculous about a Church so massively, even objectionably, not to say alarmingly, consistent."[22] By any chalk, this is brilliant criticism. Having been engaged in pastoral work of various sorts for over ten years before he wrote this, Ker knew what he was about when he extolled Newman's appreciation of the consistency of the Roman faith, without which the faithful exercise of the pastoral charge would be impossible. In turn, Ker is also insistent that "One of the most consistent themes of Newman's preaching is the difficulty of consistency in the Christian life." Sin, of course, predisposes us to inconsistency, but if we are to live the devout life, we must resort to the confessional to restore the consistency of grace. Ker quotes Newman reminding his readers that "in the heart and life of even the better sort of men ... continual repentance must ever go hand in hand with our endeavors to obey." [*PS*, i, 171] "And so [Newman] can conclude," Ker writes, quoting Newman again, 'The very test of a mature Christian, of a true saint, is consistency in all things.'" [*PS*, vi, 186][23]

If Newman was chary of satirizing the Church of Rome, he had no such reservations when it came to the Church of England. Ker is marvelously attentive to how Newman satirizes what he regarded as the unreality of the National Church. As *Anglican Difficulties* (1850) and *The Present Position of Catholics* (1851) so richly attest, Newman was a satirist of the first order—his only peer is Swift—and one of the best things about Ker's writings on Newman is how nicely they capture this satirical wit in all of its exquisite fun. In an essay on Newman that he contributed to *The Oxford Handbook of English Literature and Theology* (2009), for example, Ker remarks:

> Newman's first novel, *Loss and Gain*, which was also the first book he published as a Roman Catholic, opens his most creative period as a satirist. Running through the novel is a strong, often comic, sense of the real and the unreal. The issue for the hero Charles Reding becomes not so much which is the true religion, but which is the real religion. The doctrinal comprehensiveness of the Church of England is perceived not as a source of strength but as fatal to its reality, for two contradictory views cannot 'both be real'. In the face of broad or liberal Anglicanism, it is no longer a question of satirizing inconsistencies, but of satirizing

---

[22] *Ibid.*, 12.
[23] Ian Ker, "Introduction," in *John Henry Newman: Selected Sermons*, ed. Ian Ker (New York: Paulist Press, 1994), 51–2. Ker's fullest critical exposition of the sermons is set out in this incisive introduction.

inconsistency itself as an ideal.²⁴

And then Ker proceeds to quote this brilliant effusion from the junior don, Mr. Vincent, who was "ever […] converting pompous nothings into oracles and had a great idea of the *via media* being the truth."

> "Our Church," he said, "admitted of great liberty of thought within her pale. Even our greatest divines differed from each other in many respects; nay, Bishop Taylor differed from himself. It was a great principle in the English Church. Her true children agree to differ. In truth," he continued, "there is that robust, masculine, noble independence in the English mind, which refuses to be tied down to artificial shapes, but is like, I will say, some great and beautiful production of nature—a tree, which is rich in foliage and fantastic in limb, no sickly denizen of the hothouse, or helpless dependent of the garden wall, but in careless magnificence sheds its fruits upon the free earth, for the bird of the air and the beast of the field, and all sorts of cattle, to eat thereof and rejoice."²⁵

Reading this, one thinks of Johnson's "Life of Pope," in which the great moralist reminds his readers: "All truth is valuable, and satirical criticism may be considered as useful when it rectifies error and improves judgment; he that refines the publick taste is a publick benefactor."²⁶ Unfortunately, there are so few Anglo Catholics going the roads nowadays that Newman's benefaction will not have much effect in that attenuated quarter. However, there are hordes of Roman Catholics who imagine themselves sworn to a Church of "great liberty of thought," and they can certainly be edified by Newman's gentle mockery.

Since Ker brought out several works supplemental to his Newman biography, including essays on different aspects of the saint's life and work, critical editions of the *Idea of a University*, the *Apologia*, and the *Grammar of Assent*, as well as monographs on his spiritual development, engagement with the full spectrum of Christianity, and what the great convert might have made of Vatican II in a book full of shrewd theological insights, he has given his readers an incomparably well-rounded portrait of Newman. All who delight in Newman owe him an inestimable debt.

Once, when speaking with Ker over lunch in a charming little Italian restaurant in Cheltenham, I asked him which proof for the existence of God he found most persuasive, and, without hesitation, he replied, "the lives of the saints." Since Ker spent so much of his long, prolific, faithful life celebrating the gifts of sanctity, which only God bestows, there was an undeniable authority in this decided judgement. But even on that occasion, a touch of comedy, typical of any meeting with the great scholar critic, intervened. When we had finished our lunch and went outside to wait for a taxi, the restaurant's proprietor, an elegant Italian gentleman accompanied us and while Fr. Ian was getting into the taxi, he turned to me and

---

²⁴ *LG*, 74.
²⁵ Ian Ker, "John Henry Newman," in *The Oxford Handbook of English Literature and Theology*, ed. Andrew Hass, David Jasper, and Elisabeth Jay (Oxford: Oxford University Press, 2009), 624–38. The quotation from Loss and Gain is *LG*, 84–5.
²⁶ Samuel Johnson, *The Lives of the Most Eminent English Poets with Critical Observations on their Works*, ed. Roger Lonsdale, 4 vols (Oxford: Clarendon Press, 2006), iv, 75.

asked, "Who is this gentleman? He always comes to my restaurant with others from around the world who treat him with the greatest respect. Is he a famous man?" "Tolerably famous," I replied. "Fr. Ian Ker is the greatest biographer of England's greatest saint."

IV

One can see how thoroughly Ker possessed the "due formation" necessary to write of Newman with insight and authority in his treatment of the convert's various works, starting with his sermons. Church and Ward, I endeavored to show in previous chapters, had bright things to say of the preacher in Newman, but Ker's handling of the sermons is far better, exhibiting as it does the distillation that is one of the hallmarks of his critical method, as well as his close reading. Here, rather than simply summarizing, Ker weaves quotations from the sermons, the letters and his Oratorian papers into his narrative to show their incandescent unity. In one section of the critical biography, he calls attention to what he calls the "paradox" of Newman's "ideal of holiness" being "as elevated and lofty as the means to attaining it are humble and mundane," and thus highlights a major theme not only of Newman's sermons but of all his pastoral work.

> For Newman, real spirituality is characterized by its utter unpretentiousness. He preached that "the self-denial which is pleasing to Christ consists in little things … in the continual practice of small duties which are distasteful to us". He warned his congregation not to be "content with a warmth of faith carrying you over many obstacles", but to practise "daily self-denial" in "those little things in which obedience *is* a self-denial". [*PS*, i, 67, 69] There is the typically realistic reminder that nothing is more difficult than to be disciplined and regular in our religion. It is very easy to be religious by fits and starts, and to keep up our feelings by artificial stimulants; but regularity seems to trammel us, and we become impatient." [*PS*, viii, 242–3]. Real holiness is attained by concrete acts of no particular significance in themselves, for we should remember "how mysteriously little things are in this world connected with great; how single moments, improved or wasted, are the salvation or ruin of all-important interests" [*PS*, ii, 114] The hallmark of the truly spiritual person is that he or she "is *consistent*" in a "jealous carefulness about all things, little and great". [*PS*, ii, 159] One day as a Catholic he would say, "I have ever made consistency the mark of a Saint", the greatest mortification being "to do well the ordinary duties of the day". [*LD*, xi, 191; *LD*, xiv, 153] As an Anglican, he preached that real self-denial lies not in "literally bearing Christ's Cross, and living on locusts and wild honey, but in such light abstinences as come in our way". [*PS*, iii, 211] In his spirituality, as in other things, there was not discontinuity but development after 1845; as the Superior of the Birmingham Oratory, he would one day warn his community:
>
> > Unless you prune off the luxuriances of plants, they grow bare, thin, and shabby at the roots. The higher your building is the broader must be its base—So it is with sanctity—Acts, words, devotions, which are suitable in saints, are absurd in other men.

The imagery may have become richer and subtler, but the teaching has not changed:

> if we would aim at perfection, we must perform well the duties of the day. I do not know any thing more difficult, more sobering, so strengthening than the constant aim to go through the ordinary day's work well.

And arguing that, "if we wish to be perfect, we have nothing more to do than to perform the ordinary duties of the day well", Newman draws out the logic of his realism to its humorous conclusion, "Go to bed in good time, and you are already perfect." [*NO*, 235, 359–60][27]

Since the saints meant so much to Newman, Ker is particularly adept at delineating why his hero so insisted on sanctity.

> His favourite early Father, St Athanasius, is characterized by this kind of Christian humanism, as is St Paul. St Philip Neri, too, who "lived in an age ... when literature and art were receiving their fullest development", was anxious "not to destroy or supersede ... but ... to sanctify poetry, and history, and painting, and music". [*OS*, 118–19] Very different, he emphasizes, is "the religion of the natural man", even when "embellished ... with the refinements of a cultivated intellect"; for when "virtue is something external" and "has little to do with conscience and the Lord of conscience", the devotees of such a religion "pace round and round in the small circle of their own thoughts and of their own judgments", with "self" as "their supreme teacher". Instead of allowing conscience to lead them "into the fulness of religious knowledge", they "succeed in pleasing themselves" by fulfilling the "contracted, defective range of duties" which they allow conscience to put before them. [*OS*, 20–3, 25][28]

Reading this, one can see how Ker takes advantage of quotation to show not only the unity but the development of Newman's thought. He also weaves his quotations so seamlessly into his narrative as to efface himself from it.[29] He is never the obtruding biographer. Like James Joyce's artist, he is "within or behind or beyond or above his handiwork, invisible, refined out of existence ... paring his fingernails." Yet, however removed from the book's center stage, where he has Newman alone command our attention, his psychological acuity is always in charge of the biography's critical intelligence. This is clear from his portrait of the psychological acuity that Newman himself displays in his sermons.

Far from assuming that Christians want to be holy, the sermons start from the eminently realistic assumption that the reason why people sin is that they want

---

[27] Ker, *John Henry Newman: A Biography*, 94, quoting *Newman the Oratorian: His Unpublished Oratorian Papers*, ed. Placid Murray, OSB (Dublin, 1969), 235, 359–60.
[28] Ibid., 434.
[29] Cf. "A happy effect of the extensive use of quotation is to highlight what should never have been in doubt, Newman's sparkling wit and fertility in imagery, often satirically directed, sometimes simply exuberant. Dr Ker is occasionally reminded of Dickens, a comparison not inapt and independent of their generally opposed views." Kathleen Tillotson, review of Ian Ker's Newman biography, *The Modern Language Review* (July, 1991), 672.

to. It is not just that it is unrealistic to expect sudden transformations, and that if there is to be change there has to be the will to change, but this willingness is itself something that only gradually develops: "Is not holiness the result of many patient, repeated efforts after obedience, gradually working on us, and first modifying and then changing our hearts?" [PS, i, 11] Prayer itself has to be realistic: it is quite unreal to pray to be good when one does not in fact particularly want to be good, and when it is in fact this desire to be good for which one should be praying. A shrewdly practical psychology informs a highly idealistic spirituality. Thus, for example, voluntary acts of self-denial are recommended as a means to acquiring self-control in order to guard against unexpected temptations like anger, which "are irresistible perhaps when they come upon you, but it is only at times that you are provoked, and then you are off your guard; so that the occasion is over, and you have failed, before you were well aware of its coming". [PS, i, 69] False illusions about self are mercilessly exposed. A man"s real "trial", for instance, lies in his "weak point", and "not in those things which are easy to him, but in that one thing, in those several things, whatever they are, in which to do his duty is against his nature". [PS, i, 69] "Any *one* deliberate habit of sin", Newman warns severely, "incapacitates a man for receiving the gifts of the Gospel." [PS, i, 95[A total commitment to Christ, he remarks, is "rare", for most Christians retain "a reserve" in their obedience, a "corner" in their heart which they intend not to give up, if only because they feel they would not "*be*" themselves any longer, if they did "not keep some portion" of what they "have been hitherto", with the result that they take up only "a pretence of religion instead of the substance". People may "profess in general terms to wish to be changed", but "when it comes to the point, when particular instances of change are presented to us, we shrink from them, and are content to remain unchanged." [PS, viii, 238; PS, iv, 5; PS, v, 244–5][30]

As an exercise in distillation, this is masterly, especially since its understanding of Newman's preaching proceeds not simply from close reading but pastoral discernment, which can only come of genuine pastoral experience. Here, Ker brings "due formation" to his interpretations of Newman because he has sat in the confessional long enough to understand what it truly means for penitents to change—or, as the case may be, not change.

Yet another passage in the biography exhibits both Ker's critical and psychological astuteness. If self-deception is a recurring theme in Newman's sermons—"Let us put off all excuses, all unfairness and insincerity, all trifling with our consciences, all self-deception, all delay of repentance," Newman exhorts his auditors in his sermon, "Faith and the World" (1838)—Ker draws upon the sermons to anatomize its insidious sway.

> In one of the most penetrating sermons he ever preached, "Unreal Words", Newman pointed out that when we subscribe to religious beliefs, we have to use words, and "Words have a meaning, whether we mean that meaning or not", so that "To make professions is to play with edged tools, unless we attend to what we are saying." The expression of religious feelings, too, may be unreal, since someone

---

[30] Ker, *John Henry Newman: A Biography*, 94–5.

may "not really believe" the doctrines of Christianity "absolutely, because such absolute belief is the work of long time, and therefore his profession of feeling outruns the real inward existence of feeling, or he becomes unreal". Unreality also affects religious, like other, knowledge: people who "do not understand the difference between one point and another", who "have no means of judging, no standard to measure by", are in consequence "inconsistent" and "unreal". The conclusion is that "unreality ... is a sin; it is the sin of every one of us, in proportion as our hearts are cold, or our tongues excessive." [PS, v, 33, 39, 36, 43] For God "meant us to be simple, and we are unreal", with the result that "the whole structure of society is ... artificial". [PS, viii, 265][31]

Taking this rather general claim from Newman as his starting point, Ker looks at how this structure of artificiality is specifically set out in the sermons, and he sees it tied to another major theme in Newman's work—the primacy of action, especially for those who wish to live the devout life, the imperative, that is to say, to practice what one professes. "A real religion reveals itself above all in actions as opposed to feelings and words," Ker quotes Newman as insisting.

> In "Unreal Words" he remarked that "Literature is almost in its essence unreal; for it is the exhibition of thought disjoined from practice." [PS, v, 42] The point is developed in one of the most interesting of the sermons, "The Danger of Accomplishments", which argues that the danger of a literary education is that "it separates feeling and acting". Newman complains that the effect of reading novels, for example, is that "We have nothing to do; we read, are affected, softened or roused, and that is all; we cool again,—nothing comes of it." But
>
>> God has made us feel in order that we may go on to act in consequence of feeling; if then we allow our feelings to be excited without acting upon them, we do mischief to the moral system within us, just as we might spoil a watch, or other piece of mechanism, by playing with the wheels of it. We weaken its springs, and they cease to act truly. [PS, ii, 371][32]

Again, Ker can elucidate these points creditably because he was himself, to a lively degree, the product of a "literary education." Indeed, he chose to become a priest because he wished to instruct young people in the truths of the Faith, not merely the niceties of literature. Yet it is precisely because he has been trained as a scholar critic that he can identify the cogency with which Newman pursues his wide-ranging theme. At the same time, indirectly, Ker shares with his readers how, in becoming a priest, he is emulating Newman by going beyond what the convert characterized in his King William Street lectures as "smart articles in newspapers and magazines ... clever hits, spirited attacks, raillery, satire, skirmishing on posts of [one's] own selecting."[33] In other words, Ker, like Newman, practices what he professes; he does not simply write about it; and he can criticize Newman's sermons on the theme of artificiality with a certain authority because he

---

[31] Ibid., 97–8.
[32] Ibid., 98.
[33] Diff., i, 226.

has dedicated his own life to tackling the same deeply human temptation, even among religious people, or, perhaps, one should say, especially among religious people, of allowing oneself to be ruled by "unreal words."[34] But rather than paraphrase, we should let Ker make his point in his own words—or, rather, words he has selected with such illuminating care from Newman's sermons.

> "It is easy", [Newman] remarks in another sermon, for religious people "to make professions, easy to say fine things in speech or in writing, easy to astonish men with truths which they do not know, and sentiments which rise above human nature". But in order to prove that faith is real, "Let not your words run on; force every one of them into action as it goes …". [*PS*, i, 70] It is not "by giving utterance to religious sentiments" that we "become religious", but "rather the reverse", by "obeying God in practice". [*PS*, i, 233] To do "one deed of obedience for Christ's sake" is better than any amount of religious eloquence, feeling, and imagination. [*PS*, i, 270] People who talk of love in general terms come in for some of Newman's sharpest sarcasm:
>
>> Such men have certain benevolent feelings towards the world,—feelings and nothing more;—nothing more than unstable feelings, the mere off-spring of an indulged imagination, which exist only when their minds are wrought upon, and are sure to fail them in the hour of need. This is not to love men, it is but to talk about love.—The real love of man must depend on practice, and therefore, must begin by exercising itself on our friends around us, otherwise it will have no existence.[*PS*, ii, 55]
>
> He condemns "mere feeling" as "a sort of luxury of the imagination", which has no place in this world, which is intended to be "a world of practice and labour", a place for "obedience" not "excellent words". [*PS*, ii, 367] Speaking, indeed, is positively discouraged, in terms strongly reminiscent of Carlyle: "Let us avoid talking, of whatever kind"—for "That a thing is true, is no reason that it should be said, but that it should be done". We shall, for example, be more moved by the thought of the Cross by "bearing" it than by "glowing accounts of it". The call to silence may be terse, but it is not lacking in eloquence.
>
>> Think of the Cross when you rise and when you lie down, when you go out and when you come in, when you eat and when you walk and when you converse, when you buy and when you sell, when you labour and when you rest, consecrating and sealing all your doings with this one mental action, the thought of the Crucified. Do not talk of it to others; be silent, like the penitent woman, who showed her love in deep subdued acts. [*PS*, v, 45; *PS*, v, 338–9][35]

---

[34] Ker influenced many Newman scholars but never formed anything that could be called a school. Still, one can see the influence of his reading of the sermons in an excellent essay that the literary critic Eric Griffiths contributed to a collection of essays celebrating Newman's centennial. Newman, he says, "specially mistrusts the power of imagination to doll up religious life and deliver it over as a toy for the delectation of a consumer who then 'appreciates' it rather than being judged by it. The sermons persistently warn against religious allure." Eric Griffiths, "Newman: The Foolishness of Preaching," in *Newman after a Hundred Years*, 64.

[35] Ker, *John Henry Newman: A Biography*, 98–9.

Or, one could add, like St Joseph, whose silence speaks so eloquently of his awe before the majesty of God.

If Ker's reading of the major themes of the sermons is of a *bravura* incisiveness, his conclusion is bracing: "The realism of the sermons can be quite disconcerting, even shocking," he writes. "[H]e is remarkably unencouraging and unsanguine about the progress of Christianity in the world. The revival of religion in the nineteenth century did not impress him very much. He owned to being 'suspicious of any religion that is a people's religion, or an age's religion'. The 'token' of 'true religion' was rather 'The light shining in darkness', and, 'though doubtless there are seasons when a sudden enthusiasm arises in favour of the Truth ... yet such a popularity of the Truth is but sudden, comes at once and goes at once, has no regular growth, no abiding stay'. It is, unfortunately, 'error alone which grows and is received heartily on a large scale'. Even though truth 'has that power in it, that it forces men to profess it in words', still, 'when they go on to act, instead of obeying it, they substitute some idol in the place of it'. In the face of any manifestation of religion, 'a cautious mind will feel anxious lest some counterfeit be, in fact, honoured instead of it'. [*PS*, i, 61–2] The fact of the matter is that people's 'real quarrel with religion ... is not that it is strict, or engrossing, or imperative, not that it goes too far, but that it *is* religion." [*PS*, iv, 14][36]

Here, we might be inclined to see a certain provocative hyperbole in Ker's reading of the sermons. Yes, Newman always insisted that it is "a weariness to the natural man to serve God humbly and in obscurity" [*PS*, vii, 22]. And yes he did wonder whether three centuries of Protestant Christianity had not left his English neighbors not so much Latitudinarian as de-Christianized; but, by the same token, by commending "A Short Road to Perfection" to his Oratorians he surely recognized that the devout life was not as unattainable as some might imagine.[37] Later, in *Newman on Vatican II* (2014), in a discussion of how Callista is converted by the appeal the Faith makes to her affections, Ker quotes from Newman's great sermon, "The Thought of God: The Stay of the Soul" (1839) to remind his readers of the Augustinian *aperçu* that God "alone is sufficient for the heart who made it," an appeal that was not as ineffectual in the nineteenth century as Ker suggests, even allowing for Newman's ruthless realism.[38] Nevertheless, Ker is right that the Christianity Newman presents in the Anglican sermons is the Christianity of Scripture, not that of the ingratiating accommodations of the Broad Church—or liberal Catholicism.[39] "For the preacher's aim," Ker writes,

---

[36] *Ibid.*, 99.
[37] John Henry Newman, *Prayers, Verses and Devotions* (London: Longmans, Green & Co., 1903), 328.
[38] *PS*, v, 316. See also Ker, *Newman on Vatican II*, 140.
[39] The same liberal Catholicism that Newman opposed throughout his long life is nicely anatomized by Fr Gerald Murray, who shows how it "consists of the effort to do away with Catholicism as a dogmatic revealed religion centered upon the eternal salvation of souls and remake it into a religion of human benevolence promoting personal fulfillment, social harmony, and material well-being. Eternal salvation for everyone is now assumed. God is too good and loving to condemn anyone to Hell. Jesus should not be taken literally when he speaks about souls being punished eternally. This is obviously a bracing, if puzzling, type of hyperbole to get people's attention, not something we should take literally. Belief in unchangeable doctrines that must be believed in order to be saved is an artifact of a forgettable past in which believers were naively fixated upon the mistaken notion that Christ's teaching is the only divinely revealed, and hence normative, way to live in union

"was to present the person of Christ not in an 'unreal way—as a mere idea or vision', but as 'Scripture has set Him before us in His actual sojourn on earth, in His gestures, words, and deeds'. Instead of using 'vague statements about His love, His willingness to receive the sinner, His imparting repentance and spiritual aid, and the like', the sermons present 'Christ as manifested in the Gospels, the Christ who exists therein, external to our own imaginings ... really a living being.'" [*PS*, iii, 130–1][40] Again, this is the criticism of the pastor in Ker, who knows that, in ministering to his refractory flock, as Newman had ministered to his, he had his work cut out for him. Yet it is also Ker's criticism of the historian in Newman—the historian who knew how to look at primary sources and assess their import with dispassionate fidelity. What is ironic about the *Parochial and Plain Sermons* is that Newman's primary source was the Bible—the very thing that so many of his Anglican and, indeed, Dissenting contemporaries were presumed to know so well. Needless to say, Newman's reading of the book did not always tally with theirs. That the literary historian Oliver Elton, friend of John Butler Yeats, was not entirely exaggerating matters when he said that the "religion" to be found in the sermons was "often one of gloom, denunciation, fear, and distrust of human nature"[41] is borne out by the memorable sermon, "The Immortality of the Soul" (1833), in which Newman did not pull his punches:[42]

> Let us, then, seriously question ourselves, and beg of God grace to do so honestly, whether we are loosened from the world; or whether, living as dependent on it, and not on the Eternal Author of our being, we are in fact taking our portion with this perishing outward scene, and ignorant of our having souls. I know very well that such thoughts are distasteful to the minds of men in general. Doubtless many a one there is, who, on hearing doctrines such as I have been insisting on, says in his heart, that religion is thus made gloomy and repulsive; that he would attend to a teacher who spoke in a less severe way; and that in fact Christianity was not intended to be a dark burdensome law, but a religion of cheerfulness and joy. This is what young people think, though they do not express it in this argumentative form. They view a strict life as something offensive and hateful; they turn from the notion of it. And then, as they get older and see more of the world, they learn to defend their opinion ... They hate and oppose the truth, as

with God. God would never be so exclusive. He is the inclusive God who loves everyone just as they are. The purpose of religious rites and teachings is to help man find peace with himself and with his neighbor. Any Church doctrine or law that creates barriers and separates people from each other must be cast aside." Of course, as this shows, the satirical irony with which Fr Murray exposes the self-complacent hollowness of liberal Catholicism is deeply Newmanian. Fr Gerald Murray, "'Outing' the Liberal Catholic Project," *The Catholic Thing* (15 September 2023).

[40] Ker, *John Henry Newman: A Biography*, 100.
[41] Oliver Elton, *A Survey of English Literature 1830–1880* 2 vols. (London: Edward Arnold, 1927), i, 186. That Oliver Elton (1861–1945) had some fair critical smarts is evident in his estimate of William Butler Yeats, about whom he once said: "He believed in his occult rubbish and in his own rigmarole as much as he could believe in anything ... He had no formal education but a natural God-given style and genius, and could say the most imbecile things as perfectly as the things that were inspired." Elton quoted in *The Collected Letters of W. B. Yeats. Volume V: 1908–1910*, ed. John Kelly and Ronald Schuchard (Oxford: Oxford University Press, 2018), 948.
[42] Oliver Elton, *A Survey of English Literature: 1780–1880*, 6 vols (London: Macmillan & Co., 1920), iii, 186.

it were upon principle; and the more they are told that they have souls, the more resolved they are to live as if they had not souls. But let us take it as a clear point from the first, and not to be disputed, that religion must ever be difficult to those who neglect it. All things that we have to learn are difficult at first; and our duties to God, and to man for His sake, are peculiarly difficult, because they call upon us to take up a new life, and quit the love of this world for the next. It cannot be avoided; we must fear and be in sorrow, before we can rejoice."[43]

Here was precisely the "rigorism" that put Baron von Hügel off the sermons.[44] But, at the same time, it was the very uncompromising gravity with which Newman spoke of the stakes of religion that left so indelible an impression on his contemporaries. "After hearing these sermons," Professor Shairp famously recalled, "you would be harder than most men … if you did not feel the things of faith brought closer to the soul."[45] Not everyone present at St Mary's when Newman preached the sermons can have benefited equally from their attestation to the force of the Gospels. After all, as Newman reminded his auditors, "A man who loves sin does not wish the Gospels to be true, and therefore is not a fair judge of it; a mere man of the world, a selfish and covetous man, or a drunkard, or an extortioner, is from a sense of interest, against that Bible that condemns him."[46] But, at the same time, "those who try to obey God evidently gain a knowledge of themselves at least; and this may be shown to be the first and principal step towards knowing God. … Wishing … and striving to act up to the law of conscience, he will yet find that, with his utmost efforts, and after his most earnest prayers, he still falls short of what he knows to be right, and what he aims at. Conscience, however, being respected, will become a more powerful and enlightened guide than before; it will become more refined and hard to please; and he will understand and perceive more clearly the distance that exists between his own conduct and thoughts, and perfection. He will admire and take pleasure in the holy law of God, of which he reads in Scripture; but he will be humbled withal, as understanding himself to be a continual transgressor against it."[47] Certainly, no one who heard the sermons took their wisdom to heart more deeply than Dean Church, who confided in his son-in-law, Francis Paget shortly before his death:

> I often have a kind of waking dream; up one road, the image of a man decked and adorned as if for a triumph, carried up by rejoicing and exulting friends, who praise his goodness and achievements; and, on the other road, turned back to back to it, there is the very man himself, in sordid and squalid apparel, surrounded not by friends, but by ministers of justice, and going on, while his friends are exulting, to his certain and perhaps awful judgment. That vision rises when I hear, not just and conscientious endeavours to make out a man's character, but

[43] *PPS*, i, 23–4.
[44] See Edward Short, "Saint John Henry Newman and the Standard of Saintliness," in *Heart Speaks to Heart: Saint John Henry Newman and the Call to Holiness*, ed. Kevin J. O'Reilly (Leominster: Gracewing, 2021), 30–1.
[45] Professor C. Shairp quoted in Church, *Oxford Movement*, 143.
[46] Newman, "Inward Witness to the Truth of the Gospel" (1825), *PS*, viii, 114.
[47] *PS*, viii, 116.

when I hear the loose things that are said—often in kindness and love—of those beyond the grave.[48]

In concluding his remarks on the sermons, Ker echoes what Dean Church and so many others recognized, though he points to more substantive grounds for his praise than the preacher's "mesmeric influence." For Ker, "Newman's 4 o'clock Sunday sermons in St Mary's [were] the most potent spiritual force of the Oxford Movement" and they have a "permanent place among the classics of spirituality."[49]

V

One can also see Ker's "due formation" when he addresses the "dogmatic principle" that was so quintessential an element of Newman's work. Knowing how embattled the very notion of dogma had become after the Second Vatican Council, Ker draws on both his extensive theological knowledge and his forensic skills to defend Newman's principle. In 1837, "Newman began another series of lectures in the Adam de Brome chapel at St Mary's, returning again to the crucial question of the relation of the Bible to Christianity," Ker writes.

> Of the twelve "Lectures on the Scripture Proof of the Doctrines of the Church", the last of which was given on 7 August, eight were published as Tract 85. Newman begins by arguing that it is inconsistent for Bible Protestants to deny a Church doctrine like the Apostolic Succession "because it is not clearly taught in Scripture", while accepting "the divinity of the Holy Ghost, which is nowhere literally stated in Scripture". The "kill-or-cure remedy" for such "inconsistency" lies either in "adding to their creed, or ... giving it up altogether". It was a similar "fearful" alternative with which one day he would confront Anglo-Catholics themselves. [DA, 112–13] Now he insists that it is facile to suppose that doctrines are either in or not in Scripture: "Indeed ... the more arguments there are for a certain doctrine found in Scripture, the more objections will be found against it." [DA, 125] Moreover,
>
>> The arguments which are used to prove that the Church system is not in Scripture, may as cogently be used to prove that no system is in Scripture. If silence in Scripture, or apparent contrariety, is an argument against the Church system, it is an argument against system altogether. No system is on the surface of Scripture; none, but has at times to account for the silence or the apparent opposition of Scripture as to particular portions of it.
>
> The conclusion is relentlessly pressed home: "either Christianity contains no definite message, creed, revelation, system ... nothing which can be made the

---

[48] Church quoted in Francis Paget, "Preface," Church, Life and Letters, xxiv.
[49] Ker, John Henry Newman: A Biography, 100. It was Sir Francis Hastings Doyle (1810–88), the poet and Professor of Poetry at Oxford, who wrote, apropos the preacher in Newman: "That great man's extraordinary genius drew all those within his sphere, like a magnet ... Nay, before he became a Romanist, what we call his mesmeric influence acted not only on his Tractarian adherents, but even in some degree on outsiders like myself." Doyle quoted in Church, Oxford Movement, 143.

subject of belief at all; or, secondly, though there really is a true creed or system in Scripture, still it is not on the surface of Scripture, but is found latent and implicit within it." ... [DA, 126–7]

It is hard to take liberal Protestantism seriously: "Why should God speak, unless He meant to say something? Why should he say it, unless He meant us to hear?" If there has been a Revelation, then "there must be some essential doctrine proposed by it to our faith"; and therefore it is difficult "to be a consistent Latitudinarian", because even he will hold on to "his own favourite doctrine, whatever it is".[DA, 130–1] It is against "the common sense of mankind" to have "a religion without doctrines": "Religion cannot but be dogmatic; it ever has been."[DA, 134] Not only do the New Testament writers themselves acknowledge that they "did not in Scripture say out all they had to say", but they actually refer to a "system" of doctrine and worship which has existed from the earliest times and which would have survived even if Scripture had been lost. [DA, 136–7] To suppose that all beliefs are equally true in the eyes of God, provided they are sincerely held, is simply "unreal" and a "mere dream of religion". On the contrary, says Newman, invoking the pragmatic principle to which he was so often to appeal, "We must take things as we find them, as God has given them", however inconvenient or unsatisfactory we may find them. [DA, 140–1][50]

Ker also has occasion to observe how crucially the dogmatic principle figures in the notes of the Church that Newman set out in his *Essay on the Development of Christian Doctrine* (1845) to argue that the primitive and the Roman Catholic Church were one and the same. "One of the most important of the principles which arise out of the discussion of the second 'Note,'" he writes, "and which characterize Christianity and the development of its doctrines, that of dogmatism ('a religion's profession of its own reality as contrasted with other systems')" [Dev, 439] is described in a famous passage calculated to provoke many readers:

> That there is a truth then; that there is one truth; that religious error is in itself of an immoral nature; that its maintainers, unless involuntarily such, are guilty in maintaining it; that it is to be dreaded; that the search for truth is not the gratification of curiosity; that its attainment has nothing of the excitement of a discovery; that the mind is below truth, not above it, and is bound, not to descant upon it, but to venerate it; that truth and falsehood are set before us for the trial of our hearts ... this is the dogmatical principle.

And this he contrasts with what he calls "the principle of liberalism," which he quotes Newman defining thus:

> That truth and falsehood in religion are but matter of opinion; that one doctrine is as good as another; that the Governor of the world does not intend that we should gain the truth; that there is no truth; that we are not more acceptable to God by believing this than by believing that; that no one is answerable for his opinions; that they are a matter of necessity or accident; that it is enough if we sincerely hold what we profess; that our merit lies in seeking, not in possessing;

[50] Ker, *John Henry Newman: A Biography*, 160–1.

that it is a duty to follow what seems to us true, without a fear lest it should not be true; that it may be a gain to succeed, and can be no harm to fail; that we may take up and lay down opinions at pleasure; that belief belongs to the mere intellect, not to the heart also; that we may safely trust to ourselves in matters of Faith, and need no other guide ... [*Dev.*, 357–9][51]

Knowing how repellent dogma is to liberal Christians, Catholic and Protestant alike, Ker quotes both passages with a certain admonitory relish, knowing that what was controversial about Newman's work in the nineteenth century remains controversial in our own age. The natural man's distaste for dogmatic religion has not changed much over the centuries. This is why those who speak of "secularism" as some new dissolvent of religion's appeal betray an odd ignorance of history, not to mention human nature. Yet Ker knows that presenting Newman's lifelong advocacy of the dogmatic principle fully and fairly is essential if readers are to understand why it meant so much to the apologist. On one level, as Ker shows, Newman's respect for the dogmatic was of a piece with his respect for common sense. When the *fracas* over whether Catholics should send their sons to Oxford was at its height in the 1860s, Newman confided to a correspondent:

> I love Oxford too well to wish its dogmatism destroyed, tho' it be a Protestant dogmatism. I had rather it was dogmatic on an error, than not dogmatic at all. At present I had rather it excluded us, from dogmatism, than admitted us, from liberalism. Dogmatism is not so common in these days, that we can dispense with any one of its witnesses. Oxford has been a breakwater against latitudinarianism; I don't wish to have part in letting the ocean in. It is another thing altogether what one ought to do when the breakwater is gone.[52]

Ker's comment regarding this amusing admission is characteristically apt. "The paradox was typical. But so too was the opposite conclusion, acknowledging the practical rather than advocating the ideal: Catholics were bound to want to go to Oxford, and therefore it was better not to oppose a Catholic college or hall there. Nevertheless, he personally could not bring himself to support the idea; apart from anything else, it would be inconsistent with his position on mixed education, it would be tacitly admitting that the Catholic University had failed, and it would involve opposition to Rome. His predicament was that the Catholic University was not in fact meeting the needs of English Catholics and that some provision had to be made for them. Perhaps the time might be coming when a Catholic presence at Oxford would turn out to be a welcome ally for Anglicans in the fight to defend religion there. Privately, he was embarrassed by the consideration that he had himself once written to Propaganda opposing English Catholics going to Oxford and Cambridge in order to protect the interests of the Catholic University; he had also urged the granting of a charter for the University as an alternative to the English universities opening their doors to Catholics. The irony was that it

---

[51] *Ibid.*, 312.
[52] Newman to Edmund S. Foulkes (3 June 1863), *LD*, xx, 455–6, quoted in Ker, *John Henry Newman: A Biography*, 525.

was the only time Propaganda had ever supported him!"[53] When Rome turned against Newman's plan for the proposed Oxford Oratory, and left him in the lurch after he had enlisted the support of a number of subscribers and spent his own money on land for the proposed enterprise, Newman might have shown something of the overly sensitive pique to which he was thought to be so prone, but, instead, as Ker writes, "Newman had become accustomed to 'neglect and unkind usage': it was his 'cross and the easiest one I could have—how much easier than ill health or bereavement or poverty! I would not change if for any other—and somehow I don't think it will ever leave me.'" [LD, xxiii, 150–1] Of course, here the cardinal-to-be was wrong, but it is true that he was much tougher than some supposed. Ker also quotes the beleaguered advocate of the Oxford Oratory assuring a concerned correspondent: "As for 'the actual attack upon me, I shall outlive it, as I have outlived other attacks—but it is not at all easy to break that formidable conspiracy which is in action against the theological liberty of Catholics.'" [LD, xxiii, 187][54] Of course, the "theological liberty of Catholics" was what also exercised Wilfrid Ward.

Ker shows Newman's respect for dogma in other contexts. Apropos *The Tamworth Reading Room* (1847), for example, Ker writes of Newman's satirical response to Sir Robert Peel and Lord Brougham's rationalist library to show how preposterous the impulse to extirpate the dogmatic could become. Again, the literary critic in Ker never fails to bring alive Newman's literary brilliance, though that brilliance is always trained, as here, on defending the understanding of faith and reason at the core of the Catholic religion.

> In establishing a library where all discussions or lectures on denominational or political lines will be excluded, Sir Robert treats religious distinctions exactly as if they were mere local party differences—"such, I suppose, as about a municipal election, or a hole-and-corner meeting, or a parish job, or a bill in Parliament for a railway." However,
>
>> Christianity is faith, faith implies a doctrine; a doctrine propositions; propositions yes or no, yes or no differences. Differences, then, are the natural attendants on Christianity, and you cannot have Christianity, and not have differences.
>
> Sir Robert "advocates concessions", but "he must be plainly told to make presents of things that belong to him, nor seek to be generous with other people's substance. There are entails in more matters than parks and old places." It is not that Sir Robert "considers all differences of opinion as equal in importance; no, they are only equally in the way". It is a "remarkable example of self-sacrifice" to become "the disciple of his political foe, accepting from Lord Brougham his new principle of combination, rejecting Faith for the fulcrum of Society, and proceeding to rest it upon Knowledge". Whereas faith was "once the soul of social union", now it is "but the spirit of division". So far as Sir Robert is concerned,

---

[53] Ibid., 525.
[54] Ibid., 606.

> We must abandon Religion, if we aspire to be statesmen. Once, indeed, it was a living power, kindling hearts, leavening them with one idea, moulding them on one model, developing them into one polity. Ere now it has been the life of morality: it has given birth to heroes; it has wielded empire. But another age has come in, and Faith is effete; let us submit to what we cannot change; let us not hang over our dead, but bury it out of sight. Seek we out some young and vigorous principle, rich in sap, and fierce in life, to give form to elements which are fast resolving into their inorganic chaos; and where shall we find such a principle but in Knowledge? [DA, 283–6][55]

Here, Ker deploys something of his own talent for satire to capture Newman's satirical mockery of the "march-of-mind," but he does so fully cognizant that the issues raised by Newman are still with us. Indeed, the "inorganic chaos" bred of rationalism is more prevalent in the twenty-first century than it was in the nineteenth, and this is precisely why Ker also appreciates the vitality of Newman's understanding of the importance of the Church's dogmatic infallibility.

VI

No one can read Dean Church without recognizing how averse he was to Newman's insistence on Roman Catholicism's infallibility, which he thought as unpersuasive in theory as it was ineffectual in practice. In his review of Newman's *Apologia*, he could not have been clearer on these matters:

> Dr. Newman has stated, with his accustomed force and philosophical refinement, what he considers the true idea of that infallibility, which he looks upon as the only power in the world which can make head against and balance Liberalism—which "can with stand and baffle the fierce energy of passion, and the all-corroding, all-dissolving scepticism of the intellect in religious inquiries; which he considers "as a provision, adapted by the mercy of the Creator, to preserve religion in the world, and to restrain that freedom of thought which is one of the greatest of our natural gifts, from its own suicidal excesses." He says, as indeed is true, that it is "a tremendous power," though he argues that, in fact, its use is most wisely and beneficially limited. And doubtless, whatever the difficulty of its proof may be, and to us this proof seems simply beyond possibility, it is no mere power upon paper. It acts and leaves its mark; it binds fast and overthrows for good. But when, put at its highest, it is confronted with the "giant evil which it is supposed to be sent into the world to repel, we can only say that, to a looker-on, its failure seems as manifest as the existence of the claim to use it."[56]

If one were to cite one passage from Ker's work illustrative of its superiority over Newman's contemporary critics it would be this one, in which he answers Church's objection with a presentation of Newman's understanding of infallibility that is at once nuanced and exacting. "The argument proceeds," Ker writes, "by thesis, antithesis, and synthesis," though "the question now is not whether

---

[55] Ibid., 207.
[56] Church, *Occasional Papers*, ii, 392.

it is possible to believe honestly in particular Catholic doctrines, but whether, more fundamentally, the Catholic 'system' as such is dishonest." Here, we have to keep in mind that in the *Apologia*, from which the passage comes, Newman was parrying the charge of Charles Kinglsey that the Church and her clergy *were* "dishonest." In any case, the passage Ker takes up is the celebrated one with which anthologists are so justly fond.

> Newman begins by stating, "the being of a God ... is as certain to me as the certainty of my own existence." But the "world seems simply to give the lie to that great truth, of which my whole being is so full", for when "I look out of myself into the world of men ... I see a sight which fills me with unspeakable distress". It is as if "I looked into a mirror, and did not see my face", when "I look into this living busy world, and see no reflexion of its Creator". It is not that he wishes to underrate the usual arguments for God's existence, "but these do not warm me or enlighten me; they do not take away the winter of my desolation, or make the buds unfold and the leaves grow within me, and my moral being rejoice", as he looks out at a world without God, "a vision to dizzy and appal". There is only one resolution of the dilemma which does justice to both truths: "if there be a God, since there is a God, the human race is implicated in some terrible aboriginal calamity." [*Apo.*, 216–18]

For Ker, "This is the background to the explanation of infallibility which follows and which contains much the same movement of argument." He then proceeds to unpack Newman's intricate, affecting, faithful reasoning with masterly dispatch.

> Granted that "truth is the real object of our reason", then "right reason" when "correctly exercised "arrives at religious truth." But unfortunately, "reason as it acts in fact and concretely in fallen man" has a "tendency ... towards a simple unbelief", and there is no denying "the all-corroding, all-dissolving scepticism of the intellect", which has resulted in an "anarchical condition of things". Just as "in the pagan world, when our Lord came, the last traces of the religious knowledge of former times were all but disappearing from those portions of the world in which the intellect had been active and had had a career," so too, in the modern world, "What a scene, what a prospect, does the whole of Europe present at this day!" The necessity "to arrest fierce wilful human nature in its onward course" in order to preserve "some form of religion for the interests of humanity" led to the establishment of religion at the Reformation in Protestant countries, "but now the crevices of those establishments are admitting the enemy"; nor can the Bible as "a book ... make a stand against the wild living intellect of man". The conflict between the claims of reason and religion is resolved through "the Church's infallibility, as a provision, adapted by the mercy of the Creator, to preserve religion in the world, and to restrain that freedom of thought, which of course in itself is one of the greatest of our natural gifts, and to rescue it from its own suicidal excesses". This "power ... is happily adapted to be a working instrument ... for smiting hard and throwing back the immense energy of the aggressive, capricious, untrustworthy intellect". [*Apo.*, 218–20] There follows a severely uncompromising exposition of the Church's authority "viewed in its fulness" and

"viewed in the concrete, as clothed and surrounded by the appendages of its high sovereignty ... a supereminent prodigious power sent upon earth to encounter and master a giant evil". Although infallibility strictly only belongs to solemn dogmatic definitions, Newman professes to submit not only to the traditions of the Church, but also "to those other decisions of the Holy See, theological or not ... which, waiving the question of their infallibility, on the lowest ground come to me with a claim to be accepted and obeyed". Nor does he feel any "temptation at all to break in pieces the great legacy of thought" which the Church has inherited from her greatest thinkers.

This unequivocal statement of the "thesis" provokes the "antithesis", the obvious objection that "the restless intellect of our common humanity is utterly weighed down" by such an authority, "so that, if this is to be the mode of bringing it into order, it is brought into order only to be destroyed". This leads to the "synthesis", the claim that in fact the "energy of the human intellect ... thrives and is joyous, with a tough elastic strength, under the terrible blows of the divinely-fashioned weapon, and is never so much itself as when it has lately been overthrown". The resolution of the conflict lies in the remarkable argument that far from being mutually contradictory, authority and reason need each other precisely because, paradoxically, each is actually sustained by conflict with the other:

> it is the vast Catholic body itself, and it only, which affords an arena for both combatants in that awful, never-dying duel. It is necessary for the very life of religion ... that the warfare should be incessantly carried on. Every exercise of Infallibility is brought out into act by an intense and varied operation of the Reason, both as its ally and as its opponent, and provokes again, when it has done its work, a re-action of Reason against it; and, as in a civil polity the State exists and endures by means of the rivalry and collision, the encroachments and defeats of its constituent parts, so in like manner Catholic Christendom is no simple exhibition of religious absolutism, but presents a continuous picture of Authority and Private Judgment alternately advancing and retreating as the ebb and flow of the tide;—it is a vast assemblage of human beings with wilful intellects and wild passions, brought together into one by the beauty and the Majesty of a Superhuman Power,—into what may be called a large reformatory or training-school, not as if into a hospital or into a prison, not in order to be sent to bed, not to be buried alive, but (if I may change my metaphor) brought together as if into some moral factory, for the melting, refining, and moulding, by an incessant, noisy process, of the raw material of human nature, so excellent, so dangerous, so capable of divine purposes. [*Apo.*, 224–6]

Throughout this critical commentary, one can see the extent to which the literary critic in Ker helps him to understand and appreciate the theologian in Newman. Ker never deploys his critical skills merely to effuse over the beauty of Newman's English style, though, he recognizes clearly enough that, without that beauty, the precision and depth of Newman's thought could never have been shared with his readers. Precision and depth also characterize Ker's commentary, as here:

The startling chain of imagery that concludes this richly metaphorical passage hints at a new, divergent movement of argument, and reminds us that Newman has other than Protestant or unbelieving readers also in mind. The infallible authority, he insists with a typically secular metaphor, "is a supply for a need, and it does not go beyond that need", for its purpose is "not to enfeeble the freedom or vigour of human thought in religious speculation, but to resist and control its extravagance". Having begun by freely admitting the wide powers enjoyed by ecclesiastical authority, he now emphasizes both the narrow limits of infallibility in defining as explicit doctrine what is already implicit in revelation, and also its rare occurrence (normally by a "Pope in Ecumenical Council"). But, more important, he recognizes what "is the great trial to the Reason", namely, that the Church claims jurisdiction over a wide area of "secular matters which bear upon religion". These disciplinary rather than doctrinal judgements are not, however, infallible—but they do claim obedience (although not faith). Again, "because there is a gift of infallibility in the Catholic Church", it does not necessarily follow that "the parties who are in possession of it are in all their proceedings infallible". Indeed, "I think history supplies us with instances in the Church, where legitimate power has been harshly used." The unequivocal assertion of the Church's legitimate authority is thus sharply qualified by these reminders of its limits and limitations. But the apparent discrepancy is resolved by the consideration that it does not "follow that the substance of the acts of the ruling power is not right and expedient, because its manner may have been faulty". In fact, Newman remarks tartly, "high authorities act by means of instruments", and "we know how such instruments claim for themselves the name of their principals, who thus get the credit of faults which really are not theirs". [*Apo.*, 226–31][57]

Here, Ker shows that barristerial, indeed Thomistic readiness on Newman's part to entertain objections to his reasoning in order to reaffirm its conformity to the Truth. He also puts his reader in mind of the antithetical prose of Gibbon and Johnson, which gave Newman the rhetorical models he needed to capture the equipoise of the Church's conduct of her infallible authority. Yet by showing how Newman prefaced his argument with a relation of his own experience of the need for infallibility—a fairly lacerating experience—Ker shows how Newman lends his argument an affecting personal appeal. Indeed, one of the great virtues of Ker as a biographer is that he never loses sight of the deep sensitivity of the man whose thinking he expounds. Some mistake his biographical portrait by seeing it as merely intellectual. No, as this passage shows, he never omits to include the priest in his discussion of the priest's thinking. Of course, he does not exaggerate Newman's sensitivity, as Wilfrid Ward sometimes did. But he nevertheless pays it the attention it deserves, judiciously, faithfully, as here.

While he was out at Littlemore, he finally completed the extraordinary account of his illness in Sicily in 1833, which he had begun writing in 1834. The last part, which is dated 25 March 1840, concludes with a reflection on the ideal and the pain of celibacy:

---

[57] Ker, *John Henry Newman: A Biography*, 550–3.

> The thought keeps pressing on me, while I write this, what am I writing it for? For myself, I may look at it once or twice in my whole life, and what sympathy is there in my looking at it? Whom have I, whom can I have, who would take interest in it? I was going to say, I only have found one who ever took that sort of affectionate interest in me as to be pleased with such details—and that is H. Wilberforce and what shall I ever see of him? This is the sort of interest which a wife takes and none but she—it is a woman's interest—and that interest, so be it, shall never be taken in me. Never, so be it, will I be other than God has found me. All my habits for years, my tendencies, are towards celibacy. I could not take that interest in this world which marriage requires. I am too disgusted with this world—And, above all, call it what one will, I have a repugnance to a clergyman's marrying. I do not say it is not lawful-I cannot deny the right—but, whether a prejudice or not, it shocks me. And therefore I willingly give up the possession of that sympathy, which I feel is not, cannot be, granted to me. Yet, not the less do I feel the need of it. Who will care to be told such details as I have put down above? Shall I ever have in my old age spiritual children who will take an interest such as a wife does?[58]

Here, again, Ker brings his pastoral "due formation" to bear to capture the human complexity of his subject, though the artful biographer rounds out this complexity with a brilliant aside. Newman, he says, apropos the journal account he made of his Sicilian expedition "had not yet ended his account. There was still the story of his parting with Gennaro at Palermo. His faithful Neapolitan servant had hinted he would like as a parting-present

> an old blue cloke of mine which I had since 1823; a little thing for him to set his services at—at the same time a great thing for me to give for I have an affection for it. It had nursed me all through my illness; had even been put on my bed, put on me when I rose to have my bed made … I had nearly lost it at Corfu—it was stolen by a soldier but recovered. I have it still. I have brought it up here to Littlemore, and on some cold nights I have had it on my bed. I have so few things to sympathize with me, that I take to clokes. [AW, 137–8][59]

VII

In his last book, *Newman on Vatican II*, Ker summarized Newman's life with *bravura* concision.

> In 1878 Newman delivered in Rome his famous biglietto speech following his elevation to the College of Cardinals. He began by referring to the "many trials" he had suffered, a clear reference to his persecution by the Ultramontanes for his alleged liberal Catholicism. In fact, the "one great mischief" he had opposed "from the first" was "the spirit of liberalism in religion".

---

[58] Ibid., 196–7.
[59] Ibid., 197. Gennaro had nursed Newman back to health after he fell sick with fever: Indeed, he had saved his life.

> Liberalism in religion is the doctrine that there is no positive truth in religion, but that one creed is as good as another ... It is inconsistent with any recognition of any religion, as true. It teaches that all are to be tolerated, for all are matters of opinion. Revealed religion is not a truth, but a sentiment and a taste; not an objective fact.

But he does not hesitate in the heart of papal Rome to introduce the important modification, "that there is much in the liberalistic theory which is good and true; for example ... the precepts of justice, truthfulness". But then it is precisely because of the positive side of liberalism that "There never was a device of the Enemy, so cleverly framed, and with such promise of success." [Campaign 393, 395, 398–9]

Having abandoned the attempt as a Tractarian Anglican to construct a *via media* ... between Rome and Geneva, Newman found that he had to forge another *via media* as a Catholic between the Ultramontane and liberal wings of the Church. Neither simply conservative nor liberal, he is best described again as a conservative radical or conservative reformer.[60]

In fine, for Ker, Newman was "Open to development and reform, yet insistent on the tradition and authority of the Church"—a steadfast proponent, in other words, of that dynamic continuity for which Benedict XVI was such a redoubtable advocate.[61] Indeed, Ratzinger exulted in Newman. In a paper delivered to a Workshop for Bishops in 1991 in Dallas, Texas, entitled "Conscience and Truth," he praised Newman's life and work as "a single great commentary on the question of conscience"—a judgment he might have come to after reading Ker's brilliant exegesis of Newman's view of conscience, which I shall quote at length. It displays so many of his virtues as a critic: his powers of perception, his sympathy, his faith, his responsiveness to the exhilarating explorations of Newman's thought, his respect and solicitude for "the man at the cross-roads," to borrow a phrase from Chesterton.[62] No one can read Ker on Newman without coming away more enamoured of Newman—and more grateful to Ker. But here is the passage:

> At the heart of *A Letter to the Duke of Norfolk* is the celebrated treatment of the sovereignty of conscience. Newman, of course, had often written on conscience as the basis of religious belief. But here he discusses the individual believer's conscience in its relation to legitimate ecclesiastical authority. He first defines

---

[60] Ker, *Newman on Vatican II*, 38–9.
[61] Ibid., 39.
[62] "All Christianity concentrates on the man at the cross-roads. The vast and shallow philosophies, the huge syntheses of humbug, all talk about ages and evolution and ultimate developments. The true philosophy is concerned with the instant. Will a man take this road or that? that is the only thing to think about, if you enjoy thinking. The aeons are easy enough to think about, any one can think about them. The instant is really awful: and it is because our religion has intensely felt the instant, that it has in literature dealt much with battle and in theology dealt much with hell. It is full of danger, like a boy's book: it is at an immortal crisis. There is a great deal of real similarity between popular fiction and the religion of the western people. If you say that popular fiction is vulgar and tawdry, you only say what the dreary and well-informed say also about the images in the Catholic churches. Life (according to the faith) is very like a serial story in a magazine: life ends with the promise (or menace) "to be continued in our next." Also, with a noble vulgarity, life imitates the serial and leaves off at the exciting moment. For death is distinctly an exciting moment." Chesterton, *Orthodoxy*, 353–4.

conscience as the law of God "as apprehended in the minds of individual men"—which, "though it may suffer refraction in passing into the intellectual medium of each ... is not therefore so affected as to lose its character of being the Divine Law, but still has, as such, the prerogative of commanding obedience". On this view of conscience it is "the voice of God", whereas the world regards it as little more than "a creation of man". Far from being "a long-sighted selfishness" or "a desire to be consistent with oneself", Newman declares in ringing tones that "Conscience is the aboriginal Vicar of Christ, a prophet in its informations, a monarch in its peremptoriness, a priest in its blessings and anathemas, and, even though the eternal priesthood throughout the Church could cease to be, in it the sacerdotal principle would remain and would have a sway." In earlier times "its supremacy was assailed by the arm of physical force", but "now the intellect is put in operation to sap the foundations of a power which the sword could not destroy". The threat is grandiloquently conveyed, but for all its fragile vulnerability, conscience has a strange, indestructible life:

> All through my day there has been a resolute warfare, I had almost said conspiracy against the rights of conscience, as I have described it. Literature and science have been embodied in great institutions in order to put it down. Noble buildings have been reared as fortresses against that spiritual, invisible influence which is too subtle for science and too profound for literature. Chairs in Universities have been made the seats of an antagonist tradition.

The secularized idea of conscience merely concerns "the right of thinking, speaking, writing, and acting" as one sees fit, "without any thought of God at all". Paradoxically, it has become "the very right and freedom of conscience to dispense with conscience". In effect, conscience "has been superseded by a counterfeit", namely, "the right of self-will". [*Diff.*, ii, 247–50] Were the Pope himself to "speak against Conscience in the true sense of the word, he would commit a suicidal act. He would be cutting the ground from under his feet." Indeed, continues Newman, "we shall find that it is by the universal sense of right and wrong, the consciousness of transgression, the pangs of guilt, and the dread of retribution, as first principles deeply lodged in the hearts of men, it is thus and only thus, that he has gained his footing in the world and achieved his success". It is the "championship of the Moral Law and of conscience" which is "his raison d'être", and the "fact of his mission is the answer to the complaints of those who feel the insufficiency of the natural light; and the insufficiency of that light is the justification of his mission". Once again Newman emphasizes the precarious nature of the moral sense, which "is at once the highest of all teachers, yet the least luminous; and the Church, the Pope, the Hierarchy are ... the supply of an urgent demand". But if revelation is the fulfilment of natural religion, it is in no sense "independent of it": "The Pope, who comes of Revelation, has no jurisdiction over Nature." [*Diff.*, ii, 252–4]

Turning to the crucial question of the relation of the individual conscience to authority, Newman begins by laying down that since "conscience is not a judgment upon any speculative truth, any abstract doctrine, but bears immediately ... on something to be done or not done", it "cannot come into direct collision with the Church's or the Pope's infallibility; which is engaged on general propositions, and in the condemnation of particular and given errors". But because conscience is "a practical dictate", conflict is possible "only when the Pope legislates, or gives particular orders, and the like". However, "a Pope is not infallible in his laws, nor in his commands, nor in his acts of state, nor in his administration, nor in his public policy." After all, St Peter was not infallible at Antioch when St Paul disagreed with him, nor was Liberius when he excommunicated Athanasius. However, the "dictate" of conscience, "in order to prevail against the voice of the Pope, must follow upon serious thought, prayer, and all available means of arriving at a right judgment on the matter in question". The onus of proof, then, lies on the individual conscience: "Unless a man is able to say to himself, as in the Presence of God, that he must not, and dare not, act upon the Papal injunction, he is bound to obey it, and would commit a great sin in disobeying it." [*Diff.*, ii, 256–8] As usual, the bold admission about the fallibility of the first Pope in no way excludes a rigorous emphasis on loyalty and obedience to a legitimate superior. But on the other hand, to obey a papal order which one seriously thinks is wrong would be a sin—even if one is culpably mistaken (a person may be to blame for having a false conscience, but not for acting in accordance with it). In the last analysis, conscience, however misguided, is supreme; and Newman concludes the discussion calmly, even casually, with the famous declaration:

> I add one remark. Certainly, if I am obliged to bring religion into after-dinner toasts, (which indeed does not seem quite the thing) I shall drink—to the Pope, if you please—still, to Conscience first, and to the Pope afterwards. [*Diff.*, ii, 261][63]

This is criticism of a very high order. However finely intricate Newman's thought, Ker always does it faithful justice. For another example, here is Ker on Newman's handling of the Sacraments.

> The great Johnine and Pauline doctrine of the indwelling of the Holy Spirit lies at the heart of Newman's deeply personal spirituality. In his novel *Callista* (1858), the pagan heroine is attracted to Christianity precisely because it is represented to her as a religion of persons rather than abstractions, and made to consist in "the intimate Divine Presence in the heart. It was the friendship or mutual love of person with person." [Cal, 293] But how do we receive this Presence and enter into this loving relationship? From the Fathers Newman learned that the Sacraments were the concrete means of our union with God. "He inhabits us personally, and his inhabitation is effected by the channel of the Sacraments." [Ath, 193] For Christ, "shines through them, as through transparent bodies without impediment." [PS, iii, 277] In the Sacraments, Newman declares in a magnificently mysterious passage,

---

[63] Ker, *John Henry Newman: A Biography*, 688–90. Cf. "In responding to W. E. Gladstone's charge that papal infallibility would impede the exercise of conscience, indeed disable English Catholics from being loyal subjects, Newman wrote *his Letter to the Duke of Norfolk* (1875), which 'upholds,' as Newman's biographer Ian Ker remarks, 'the sovereignty, but not the autonomy, of the individual conscience.' The conscience, in other words, needs forming, and, for Catholics, it is formed by the Church's infallible teachings, not the counsels of self will." Short, *What the Bells Sang: Essays and Reviews*, 472.

In these is manifested in greater or less degree, according to the measure of each, that Incarnate Saviour, who is one day to be our Judge, and who is enabling us to bear His presence then, by imparting it to us in measure now. A thick black veil is spread between this world and the next. We mortal men range up and down it, to and fro, and see nothing. There is no access through it into the next world. In the Gospel this veil is not removed; it remains, but every now and then marvellous disclosures are made to us of what is behind it. At times we seem to catch a glimpse of a Form which we shall hereafter see face to face. We approach, and in spite of the darkness, our hands, or our head, or our brow, or our lips become, as it were, sensible of the contact of something more than earthly. We know not where we are, but we have been bathing in water, and a voice tells us that it is blood. Or we have a mark signed upon our foreheads, and it spake of Calvary. Or we recollect a hand laid upon our heads, and surely it had the print of nails in it, and resembled His who with a touch gave sight to the blind and raised the dead. Or we have been eating and drinking; and it was not a dream surely, that One fed us from His wounded side, and renewed our nature by the heavenly meat He gave. [*PS*, v, 10–11][64]

Whence came the luminous precision of this critical writing is a nice question. Yes, Ker was a gifted critic, scholar and biographer. He was even something of a theologian, as his monographs, *Newman and the Fullness of Christianity* (1993) and *Healing the Wound of Humanity: The Spirituality of John Henry Newman* (1993) show, though his commendations of the hermeneutic of continuity in *Newman and Vatican II* (2014) might now seem quixotic pleading. The discontinuity brought into the Church by the ripping out of altar rails has yet to be properly acknowledged, let alone remedied. But there is still something else in Ker that gives his work on Newman its rare distinction, and that is his love of Newman. I know I said the same of Wilfrid Ward but Ker's love is rather different, being at once subtler and more profound. We can see this in his understanding of Newman's conception of love. For Ker,

> There is a problem about taking love as the measure of holiness. As Newman put it strikingly in a sermon he never published.
>
>> To attempt to be guided by love alone, would be like attemptiong to walk in a straight line by steadily gazing on some star It is too high—we must take nearer objects to steady our course. … Love must be wrought out by fear and trembling. It is the offspring of self-abasement and self-discipline. [John Henry Newman: Sermons 1824–1843, vol i, ed Placid Murray, OSB (Oxford: Clarendon Press, 1991), 133]
>
> The ultimate source of happiness is of course for Newman the "indwelling of the Holy Spirit," for "Christ brings us into it by coming to us through his Spirit; and, as His Spirit is holy, we are holy, if we are in the state of grace." [*PS*, v, 179, 181] But if holiness is indistinguishable from His love that God pours into our hearts, it is attainable, humanly speaking, by "nearer objects" than love. And nothing

---

[64] *John Henry Newman: Selected Sermons*, ed. Ian Ker (New York: Paulist Press, 1994), 38.

can take "the place of careful obedience, of that *self-denial*, which is the very substance of true practical religion." [*PS*, i, 30] If one had to define the authentic Christian in terms of Newman's spirituality, one would have to say that he or she is characterized by *obedience*.[65] This is not because obedience is more important than faith and love, but because it is the concrete proof and realization of things more important than itself, things too easily corrupted or counterfeited.[66]

As this makes clear, Ker loved Newman because he loved God and God's Church, and now that I have revisited the books that had so abiding an influence on my own life, I see with renewed admiration that his work on Newman has perennial appeal not only because it is so well-researched and so well-written but because it is a prayer of thanksgiving.[67] Like Newman, Ker recognized that "Prayer, praise, thanksgiving, contemplation are the peculiar privilege and duty of the Christian," and his critical work on the saint is a living up to and dispatch of that privilege and duty.[68] In *Newman on Vatican II*, Ker shows not only why he was thankful for the Faith but why he believed Newman was thankful for it as well. In the first passage, Ker follows Newman in considering objections to his understanding of conscience as it is set out in the convert's work.

> Newman has been criticized for "concentrating his energies so exclusively on one aspect of our experience, our awareness of moral obligation", for "a unilateral concentration on moral experience", that is, "our experience of conscience". [Aidan Nichols, OP, *A Grammar of Consent: The Existence of God in Christian Tradition* (Edinburgh: T&T Clark, 1991), 1, 19, 35] But the criticism can only apply to his philosophical writings. Neither in his novel of conversion nor in his preaching does he stress the argument from conscience, but rather that self-fulfilment that human nature demands: the need to love and to be loved, the need for a mutual sympathy that cannot be broken and that is all-satisfying: "the soul of man is made for the contemplation of its Maker; and ... nothing short of that high contemplation is its happiness". And "if we are allowed to find that real and most sacred Object on which our heart may fix itself, a fullness of peace will follow, which nothing but it can give". [*PS*, v.315, 321][69]

---

[65] Since Ker was a keen admirer of the art critic Kenneth Clark, it might be useful to see what he had to say of obedience and the Roman Church from a distinctly English perspective. As a result of the Counter-Reformation, says Clark, "Rome and the Church of Rome regained many of the territories it had lost, and ... became once more a great spiritual force. But was it a civilizing force? In England, we tend to answer no. We have been conditioned by generations of liberal Protestant historians, who tell us that no society based on obedience, repression and superstition can be really civilized. But no one with an ounce of historical feeling or philosophic detachment can be blind to the great ideals, to the passionate belief in sanctity, to the expenditure of human genius in the service of God, which are made triumphantly visible to us with every step we take in Baroque Rome. Whatever it is, it is not barbarian or provincial. Add to this that the Catholic revival was a popular movement, that it gave ordinary people a means of satisfying, through ritual, images and symbols, their deepest impulses, so that their minds were at peace; and I think one must agree to put off defining the word civilization until we have looked at the Rome of the Popes." Kenneth Clark, *Civilization: A Personal View* (London: John Murray, 1969), 115–16.
[66] Ker, "Introduction," in *John Henry Newman: Selected Sermons*, 49.
[67] See Hutton's insight into Newman's "overflowing thankfulness," above, pp. 229–30.
[68] Newman, "Moral Effect of Communion with God" (1837), *PPS*, iv, 227. See Fr James Tolhurst's superb critical edition of *Anglican Difficulties* (Leominster: Gracewing, 2023), ii, xxxv.
[69] Ker, *Newman on Vatican II*, 141.

Here was the peace for which Ker and, indeed, Newman was so thankful. Indeed, Ker calls attention to this same longing in Newman's character. "Now a reader of the *Grammar of Assent* might well assume that Callista is suffering from a troubled conscience, a sense of sin, and looking for possible forgiveness from the God of the Christians. But in fact, conscience is not the issue, rather something quite different." And he quotes Callista herself:

> Here am I a living, breathing woman, with an over-flowing heart, with keen affections, with a yearning after some object which may possess me. I cannot exist without something to rest upon. I cannot fall back upon that drear, forlorn state, which philosophers call wisdom, and moralists call virtue ... I must have something to love; love is my life ... You have thrown me back upon my dreary, dismal self. [*Call.*, 126][70]

What is extraordinary about this commentary is that it reminds us of the young English professor at York who converted to share with others the "self-fulfillment that human nature demands," the peace that only God and His Church make possible in a world rife with the most despondent war "with the dreary, dismal self." In this light, all of Ker's work can be seen as a thanksgiving for that peace, since, as Newman realized so clearly, "All God's providences, all God's dealings with us, all his judgments, mercies, warnings, deliverances, tend to peace ... as their ultimate issue."[71] And *Callista* (1856), Newman's novel about the conversion of a girl in the third century, is key to understanding that peace, as Ker explains.

> Years after publishing the novel, Newman expressed his disappointment that Catholics had never "done justice to the book; they read it as a mere story book". In fact, he thought, "Protestants are more likely to gain something from it." [*LD*, xxvi, 130] He surely had in mind the whole generations of Victorian Protestants who, like Matthew Arnold, had abandoned the Christian faith, who were no longer in fact Protestants but secularized post-Christians, to whom he felt the book had something important to say. And the absence of any reference to the novel in contemporary discussions of Newman's philosophy of religion shows that the neglect of Callista as a serious work of apologetics continues to this day.
> As in *Callista*, so too in the *Grammar of Assent* Newman was to maintain that Christianity of all the religions in the world alone "tends to fulfil" human "aspirations, needs", for it is Jesus Christ who "fulfils the one great need of human nature, the Healer of its wounds, the Physician of the soul". [*GA*, 277, 299] And the way we encounter Christ is the way that Callista met him—through reading the Gospels. The reason, Newman thought ... why so many Catholics abandon their religion is because "They have not impressed upon their hearts the life of our Lord and Saviour as given us in the Evangelists", they do not believe "with the heart", and lack "a faith founded in a personal love for the Object of Faith". [*LD*, xxvi, 87] To the question, how do we learn to love God, he answered simply in one of his Catholic sermon notes, "By reading of our Lord in the Gospels". [*SN*, 125] But, of course, Newman also knew that we encounter Christ, albeit less

---

[70] *Ibid.*, 135.
[71] *PS*, vi, 369.

directly, through the Church, through Christians. For it was "that wonderful unity of sentiment and belief in persons so dissimilar from each other" as Chione, Agellius, and Caecilius, "so distinct in their circumstances, so independent in their testimony, which recommended to [Callista] the doctrine which they were so unanimous in teaching". [*Call.*, 293-3][72]

Thanks to Ker"s monograph, *Callista* no longer suffers any scholarly neglect. Nevertheless, it was brilliant of Ker to cite Newman's sermon "The Thought of God: The Stay of the Soul" (1839) in his discussion of the novel because it so marvelously encapsulates Newman's recognition—which was Ker's recognition as well—that it is not conscience alone that brings us to Christ but our yearning for happiness. Sin is many things, after all, many rather lurid things, but it does not conduce to the happiness for which our God-given hearts yearn. The sermon also demonstrates, as the extract that follows will show, that Newman practiced what he professed when he recommended that the best way to learn to love God was to read Scripture. Like Aquinas, Newman thought with the mind of the Church precisely because he thought with the mind of Scripture, and he does just that in his meditations on the Bible verse "Ye have not received the spirit of bondage again to fear, but ye have received the Spirit of adoption, whereby we cry Abba, Father." Rom. 8.15.[73]

> I say, by birth we are in a state of defect and want; we have not all that is necessary for the perfection of our nature. As the body is not complete in itself, but requires the soul to give it a meaning, so again the soul till God is present with it and manifested in it, has faculties and affections without a ruling principle, object, or purpose. Such it is by birth, and this Scripture signifies to us by many figures; sometimes calling human nature blind, sometimes hungry, sometimes unclothed, and calling the gift of the Spirit light, health, food, warmth, and raiment; all by way of teaching us what our first state is, and what our gratitude should be to Him who has brought us into a new state. For instance, "Because thou sayest, I am rich, and increased in goods, and have need of nothing; and knowest not that thou art wretched, and miserable, and poor, and blind, and naked: I counsel thee to buy of Me gold tried in the fire, that thou mayest be rich; and white raiment, that thou mayest be clothed, ... and anoint thine eyes with eye-salve, that thou mayest see." Again, "God, who commanded the light to shine out of darkness, hath shined in our hearts, to give the light of the knowledge of the glory of God, in the face of Jesus Christ." Again, "Awake, thou that sleepest, and arise from the

---

[72] Ker, *Newman on Vatican II*, 141-2.
[73] "Newman loves to quote from Scripture in his sermons—lavishly, almost extravagantly. As an Anglican, of course, he quoted from the Authorised Version, that great mounument to the golden prose of the English Renaissance. He used biblical quotations less profusely in his Catholic sermons, and the effect is correspondingly less compelling as the translation is inferior from the literary point of view. But it is surely also less effective from a spiritual point of view too, as the emotional impact of of the language of the Authorised Version is so overwhelming that the preacher frequently and for long periods simply freewheels, as it were, on the strength of what becomes in fact an extended reading of Scripture." Ian Ker, "Introduction," in *John Henry Newman: Selected Sermons*, 11. This is only partially true. There is nothing in the Anglican sermons as beautiful as the Baroque majesty of "The Glories of Mary for the Sake of Her Son" (1849).

dead, and Christ shall give thee light." Again, "Whosoever drinketh of the water that I shall give him, shall never thirst; but the water that I shall give him shall be in him a well of water springing up into everlasting life." And in the Book of Psalms, "They shall be satisfied with the plenteousness of Thy house; and Thou shalt give them drink of Thy pleasures as out of the river. For with Thee is the well of life, and in Thy Light shall we see light." And in another Psalm, "My soul shall be satisfied, even as it were with marrow and fatness, when my mouth praiseth Thee with joyful lips." And so again, in the Prophet Jeremiah, "I will satiate the souls of the priests with fatness; and My people shall be satisfied with My goodness … I have satiated the weary soul, and I have replenished every sorrowful soul." [Rev. 3.17, 18; 2 Cor. 4.6; Ephes. 5.14; John 4.14; Ps. 36.8, 9; Ps. 63.5. Jer. 31.14, 25]

Newman then echoes St Augustine by reminding his readers "that the soul of man is made for the contemplation of its Maker; and that nothing short of that high contemplation is its happiness; that, whatever it may possess besides, it is unsatisfied till it is vouchsafed God's presence, and lives in the light of it." And this leads Newman to speak of the real life of man's often misunderstood happiness. "I say, then, that the happiness of the soul consists in the exercise of the affections; not in sensual pleasures, not in activity, not in excitement, not in self esteem, not in the consciousness of power, not in knowledge; in none of these things lies our happiness, but in our affections being elicited, employed, supplied. As hunger and thirst, as taste, sound, and smell, are the channels through which this bodily frame receives pleasure, so the affections are the instruments by which the soul has pleasure. When they are exercised duly, it is happy; when they are undeveloped, restrained, or thwarted, it is not happy. This is our real and true bliss, not to know, or to affect, or to pursue; but to love, to hope, to joy, to admire, to revere, to adore. Our real and true bliss lies in the possession of those objects on which our hearts may rest and be satisfied." Evoking the commonest experience to make his point is typical of Newman. Yet having convinced his reader that they have real hungers that need sating, he proceeds to speak of "another reason why God alone is the happiness of our souls.. and that is "the contemplation of Him, and nothing but it." Only this can "fully … open and relieve the mind, to unlock, occupy, and fix our affections." And again, Newman resorts to real-life analogy to drive home the importunity of our need for happiness.

> We may indeed love things created with great intenseness, but such affection, when disjoined from the love of the Creator, is like a stream running in a narrow channel, impetuous, vehement, turbid. The heart runs out, as it were, only at one door; it is not an expanding of the whole man. Created natures cannot open us, or elicit the ten thousand mental senses which belong to us, and through which we really live. None but the presence of our Maker can enter us; for to none besides can the whole heart in all its thoughts and feelings be unlocked and subjected. "Behold," He says, "I stand at the door and knock; if any man hear My voice and open the door, I will come in to him, and will sup with him, and he with Me." "My Father will love him, and We will come unto him, and make Our abode with him." "God hath sent forth the Spirit of His Son into your hearts." "God is greater than our heart, and knoweth all things." [Rev. 3.20; John 14.23; Gal. 4.6; 1

John 3.20.] It is this feeling of simple and absolute confidence and communion, which soothes and satisfies those to whom it is vouchsafed. We know that even our nearest friends enter into us but partially, and hold intercourse with us only at times; whereas the consciousness of a perfect and enduring Presence, and it alone, keeps the heart open. Withdraw the Object on which it rests, and it will relapse again into its state of confinement and constraint; and in proportion as it is limited, either to certain seasons or to certain affections, the heart is straitened and distressed. If it be not over bold to say it, He who is infinite can alone be its measure; He alone can answer to the mysterious assemblage of feelings and thoughts which it has within it. "There is no creature that is not manifest in His sight, but all things are naked and opened unto the eyes of Him with whom we have to do." [Heb. 4.12.][74]

Here is the union Callista craves, the love that alone satisfies the hearts of those born into "a state of defect and want." It is also the union Ker and, indeed, all Newman's best critics crave.

Yet, in recommending the Faith's appeal to our affections, Ker shows, Newman does not lose sight of the role conscience plays in that appeal: he simply sees it as working in tandem with the appeal to the affections. "In *Callista* the apologetic approach of this great sermon is simply given dramatic actuality," he writes.

Faced with the unbelief of secular man, Newman unabashedly appeals to the universal human desire for happiness and self-fulfilment, emphasizing not the dictates of conscience but the demands of self-interest, the need to respond to the "affections and aspirations pent up within" the human heart.[*PS*, iii, 124] Nevertheless the human "need" that the gospel "supplies" also, of course, includes the need to respond to the promptings of conscience, and, just as conscience is not excluded (although not given first place) in *Callista*, so too elsewhere in another sermon Newman includes conscience in his account of the human "need" that the gospel "supplies":

There is a voice within us, which assures us that there is something higher than earth. We cannot analyze, define, contemplate what it is that thus whispers to us. It has no shape or material form. There is that in our hearts which prompts us to religion, and which condemns and chastises sin. And this yearning of our nature is met and sustained, it finds an object to rest upon, when it hears of the existence of an All-powerful, All-gracious Creator. [*PS*, iv, 339–40][75]

In Ker's masterly critical work, rooted as it is in the most trenchant "due formation," many around the world will continue to encounter the "All-powerful, All-gracious Creator" as He is set out in the works of St John Henry Cardinal Newman, and for that we can all be thankful. No critic has read that work with more dazzling perspicacity or more fidelity than Ian Ker, though he would have been the first to admit that he was only a witness to the work's prophetical truth,

---

[74] *PS*, v, 314–19.
[75] Ker, *Newman on Vatican II*, 140.

which no hostile criticism could long obscure. We can see the indefectibility of this truth in a lively exchange of letters towards the end of Newman's life. In 1877, John Morley sent Newman a letter out of the blue, in which he wrote:

> 4, Chesham Place, Brighton. Nov. 19. 77.
>
> Reverend Sir,
>
> I hope you will not think it very presumptuous in me to venture to address you, without a formal introduction. The matter in which I take the liberty of approaching you is this. Mr. Leslie Stephen is publishing in my Review two papers in which he examines what he calls Dr. Newman's Theory of Belief. Though personally I am not very full of admiration for the modern fashion of provoking tournaments among great knights, it has occurred to me that you might care to rejoin to Mr. Stephen's arguments. He is at least a painstaking and honourable disputant. If you should deign to reply in the same Review in which the criticism appears, I should hold it a singular honour and distinction. I hope you will accept my apologies for writing to you, and that you will believe that I am, with sincere respect,
>
> Yours very obediently, John Morley.[76]

Leslie Stephen's criticism was of the *Grammar of Assent* (1870), the "whole pith" of which, he argued, "was in the assertion that belief is a personal product in such a sense that no common measure between different minds is attainable. Therefore, agreement can only be produced by supernatural intervention; or, in other words, rational agreement is impossible." As misreadings of Newman's epistemological essay go, Stephen's was fairly unoriginal. Martin Fairbairn (1838–1912) had also charged the essay with scepticism, without ever taking into account Newman's rigorous criteria for the attainment of certitude.[77] Yet what is amusing about Stephen is that he contrived to criticize the book for not being sceptical enough. Nevertheless, Stephen's objections are worth quoting, if only because they constitute a kind of magazine of misconceptions

---

[76] John Morley to Newman (19 November 1877), *LD*, xxviii, 270. Ian Ker's defense of Newman's plea for our ability to attain certitude in our religious opinions needs quoting here, as well, since it can serve as a final exhibition of his critical acumen. "Now it is perfectly true that Newman says that certitude 'carries with it an inward assurance … that it shall never fail'. [*GA*, 145] But this subjective confidence only reflects a *general rule* to which exceptions are always possible; Newman's concern, in his own words, is merely 'to show, that, as a general rule, certitude does not fail'. [*GA*, 145] Far from confusing indefectibility with incorrigibility, the latter of which does not entail the former, Newman proceeds immediately to enlarge upon but also to qualify this 'inward assurance': 'Indefectibility almost enters into its very idea, enters into it at least so far as this, that its failure, if of frequent occurrence, would prove that certitude was after all and in fact an impossible act.' [*GA*, 145] In claiming that 'failures of what was taken for certitude are the exception', [*GA*, 145] … The possibility of error is freely allowed, but 'if we are never to be certain, after having been once certain wrongly, then we ought never to attempt a proof because we have once made a bad one'. [*GA*, 150] And indeed error itself presupposes certitude because if 'I have been mistaken in my certitude, may I not at least be certain that I have been mistaken?' [*GA*, 151] But the fact is that for Newman false certitudes are conceivable 'in many cases' even as 'false consciences abound'. *GA*, 153; Ian Turnbull Ker, "Introduction," in *GA*, lxviii.

[77] Tempted to write a second response to Fairbairn, Newman rightly thought better of it. Speaking of himself in the second person to Lord Blachford, he wrote: "You yourself know better than any man else that your submission to Rome was not made at all as a remedy against a personal, or against a controversial scepticism." Newman to Lord Blachford (4 February 1886), *LD*, xxxi 113.

about Newman's understanding of the Roman Church's long tradition of faith and reason, a tradition of which most of Newman's contemporary critics were sorely ignorant. "The *depositum* of faith which we must accept is not that which is guarded by any single Church, however august in its history and imposing in its pretensions," Leslie declared. "It is that body of scientific truth which is the slow growth of human experience through countless ages, and which develops by the labour of truth-loving men, and under the remorseless pressure of hard facts. We cannot accept as proved the rash solutions of the eternal riddle which have commended themselves to savages, or to philosophers, or to any arbitrary selection of men who happen to agree with us, or to any organisation which has enabled men to find a common mouthpiece for the utterance of their emotions. Dreams, however gorgeous, however richly they embody the thoughts of old poets and sages, and generations of the noblest men on earth, cannot pass muster. We can take nothing as proved but that which has stood the hard test of verification by multitudinous experience. The authority, we must admit, of any individual is infinitesimal; his chances of error innumerable. No man can say, This is true because I think it; no man can hold that he has grasped the full and ultimate truth upon any subject."[78]

Newman's response to Morley and, by extension, Stephen was eloquent of his attitude to the unfavorable criticism that had been levelled against him by all his contemporary critics.

[20 November 1877]

Dear Sir

I thank you for the very courteous and kind proposal which is the occasion of your writing to me. But with many thanks I decline it. I shall have nothing to complain of in Mr Leslie Stephen's second Paper upon me, if it is in tone and character like that of this month. The views to which I have at various times given expression in print are worth nothing if they cannot sustain the criticism of an acute and calm mind like his; such criticism is a necessary step in the process of the general recognition of their soundness, if such recognition is to be; and, though I do not acknowledge as mine all that he has ascribed to me, and do not expect of his December critique what I do not find in his November, I shall cheerfully leave it to Time to do for me what Time has so often done in the last 40 or 50 years. Time has been my best friend and champion: and to the future I lovingly commit myself with much resignation to its award.

J H N[79]

Part of that award for Newman was certainly the cardinalate bestowed upon him in 1879 by Pope Leo XIII, but part of it, too, was the good providential fortune of having Ian Ker become his definitive biographer and most discerning critic. As for his red hat, Newman wrote to his good friend, John O'Hagan: "Of course, I view the wonderful change of things as you view it. It was the reason which when the Holy Father so considerately allowed me to live here, made me put away every other thought and constrained me to accept the honour. I felt that

[78] Leslie Stephen, *An Agnostic's Apology* (London: Smith, Elder & Co., 1893), 239–40.
[79] Newman to John Morley (20 November 1877), *LD*, xxvii, 270.

he was generously and tenderly clearing me from the charges which were made against me. I used to say to myself, 'Time will set me right, I must be patient, for Time is on my side.' But the Pope has superseded Time. How should I not be most grateful to him!"[80] Ian Ker's gloss on this cry of thankfulness is apt: Newman "could not help thinking of all those now dead who would have rejoiced at the extraordinary event. He had always thought that in time he would be vindicated."[81] Indeed, he had prefigured this vindication in his sermon, "Many Called, Few Chosen" (1837). "We know that the man, in the parable, who came to the feast without a wedding garment, was 'cast into outer darkness,'" Newman wrote, alluding to Matt. 22.13.

> Let us then set at nought the judgment of the many, whether about truth and falsehood, or about ourselves, and let us go by the judgment of that line of Saints, from the Apostles' times downwards, who were ever spoken against in their generation, ever honoured afterwards ... And, in proportion as we attain to their judgment of things, let us pray God to make it live in us; so that at the Last Day, when all veils are removed, we may be found among those who are inwardly what they seem outwardly,—who with Enoch, and Noah, and Abraham, and Moses, and Joshua, and Caleb, and Phineas, and Samuel, and Elijah, and Jeremiah, and Ezekiel, and the Baptist, and St. Paul, have "borne and had patience, and for His Name-sake laboured and not fainted," watched in all things, done the work of an Evangelist, fought a good fight, finished their course, kept the faith.[82]

---

[80] Newman to John O'Hagan (15 April 1879), *LD*, xxix, 105–6. It was altogether fitting that Newman should express the full extent of his joy on receiving his cardinalate to such a good friend as O'Hagan, who, upon hearing of the appointment, wrote to the Cardinal-to-be, "I am sure no one desired it more or rejoiced at it more than I did. ... during such a time as awaits the Church ... nothing could be more fortunate for the Cause of truth than that your works should go forth as the writings of a Cardinal of the Church." O'Hagan to Newman (13 April 1879), *LD*, xxix, 105. John O'Hagan (1822–90), judge, was born at Newry, County Down. Entering Trinity College, Dublin, in 1837, he graduated BA in 1842 and MA in 1865. He was called to the Irish bar in 1842, and thereafter joined the Munster circuit. A member of the Young Ireland party, he represented Sir Charles Gavan Duffy when tried for his role in the 1848 rebellion. He also contributed verse and prose to *The Nation*. As a lawyer he was renowned for his integrity and hailed as "a nineteenth-century edition of Blessed Thomas More." In 1854 Newman appointed him Lecturer in Political Economy at the Catholic University, after which the two became good friends. After Newman's return to Birmingham, O'Hagan frequently visited him. He was made a Commissioner of the Board of National Education in 1861, and Gladstone appointed him Chief Judicial Commissioner for the Irish Land Commission in 1881. Duffy praised O'Hagan as "the safest in council, the most moderate in opinion, [and] the most considerate in temper" (Duffy, *Young Ireland*, 1896, 1.133). *ODNB* and *LD*, xxi.

[81] Ker, *John Henry Newman: A Biography*, 719. See also Carleton P. Jones, OP, "Three Latin Papers of John Henry Newman: A Translation with Introduction and Commentary," in *Dissertatio ad Lauream in Facultate S. Theologiae apud Pontificiam Universitatem S. Thomae in Urbe* (Rome, 1995), 256.

[82] *PS*, v, 18, 268–9.

EPILOGUE

It costs a very peculiar kind of suffering to conduct a controversy, after his personal intervention, with the one man in all England on whose lips the words of the dying Polycarp sit with equal truth and grace. Not that Cardinal Newman has been either a hesitating or a soft-speaking controversialist. He has been a man of war from his youth, who has conquered many adversaries—amongst them the most inveterate and invincible of English prejudices. He was one who not only changed sides when the battle was hottest, but led a goodly company with him: yet the change, so far from lessening, increased the honour and admiration in which he was held. He has, as scarcely any other teacher of our age, made us feel the meaning of life, the evil of sin, the dignity of obedience, the beauty of holiness and his power has been due to the degree in which men have been constrained to believe that his words, where sublimest, have been but the dim and imperfect mirrors of his own exalted spirit. He has taken us into the secret places of his soul and has held us by the potent spell of his passionate sincerity and matchless style, while he has unfolded his vision of the truth, or his quest after it. He has greatly and variously enriched the religious life of our people, and he lives in our imagination as the last at once of the Fathers and of the Saints. Whatever the degree of our theological and ecclesiastical difference, it does not lessen my reverence for the man, or my respect for his sincerity.

Andrew Martin Fairbairn, *Contemporary Review* (1885)

❦ FINIS ❧

INDEX

Abbott, Edwin Abbott
  and Aristotle 415
  and Asquith, Herbert Henry 212–13
  and Bagehot, Walter 221–2
  and Bible 215
  and Churchill, Winston 213
  and *Essay in Aid of a Grammar of Assent* (1870), no evidence of having read 219
  and frivolity 265
  and Hare, Julius Charles Hare 225
  and Hinton, Charles 214
  and Hinton, James 213–14
  and Hutton, Richard Holt 229
  and Ryder, Fr. Ignatius 207–9
  and Stephen, James Fitzjames 229
  and Strachey, Lytton 227
  and Thirlwall, Connop 222–5
  and Thucydides 215
  and "tone of condescending contempt," characteristic of his criticism of Newman 220–1
  and Ward, Mrs. Humphry 207–9
  and Ward, Wilfrid 231–4
  OPINIONS
  on Bible 216
  claim that fear, not hope or love, animated Newman's Chistian faith; that his judgement was precipitate; that the *Apologia*, however well written, was riddled with inaccuracies 206
  claim that literary gift stood in the way of his ability to assess evidence 207
  claim that Newman's imagination impaired his reason 206, 226
  on conscience 216–17
  on conversion 228; claim that Newman converted "to bathe his soul in spiritual peace at any cost" 227
  on *Essay on the Development of Christian Doctrine* (1845) 216, 220–1
  on fear, and claim that Newman's holy fear "perverted his imagination" 229
  on forgiveness of sins 221
  on miracles 206–9
  on Newman's reasoning, what he sees as its "mechanical" quality 221
  on Oxford Greats 213
  on popular estimate of Newman's work 215
  on Whately, Richard 212
Acton, John Emerich Edward Dalberg, 1st Baron Acton of Aldenham xiv, xvi, 114, 158, 247, 363, 364, 367, 371, 444, 470, 471, 472
  on Kinglsey's case against Newman 370
Aethelbert, king of Kent and first English king to adopt Christianity 42
Albert, Prince Consort of Queen Victoria, and admiration of Kingsley's *Hypatia* 406
Agnosticism 88, 121, 211, 232, 233, 234, 239–41, 250, 277, 288, 511, 512, 514
Alphonso Ligouri, St, and "probalism" 370–1
Ambrose, St 50, 311, 320
Andrewes, Lancelot 42, 43, 529
Anglo-Catholicism 413; and "paper religion" 522
Annan, Lord Noel
  and "aristocracy of intellect" 244
  on the campaign to prove revealed religion false 169
  on Leslie Stephen's judgment of the work of Frederick Denison Maurice 239
Apostasy 119, 175, 184, 259, 286, 510
Arianism 112
Aristotle 150
Arnold (*née* Sorrell), Julia 207–8
Arnold, Matthew 139–40, 141, 160, 249, 266, 422, 554
  and "idolatry of Zeitgeist" 133–5
  and "that mild intellectual arrogance which is the leading characteristic of his didactic prose" 136
  and style 501

Arnold, Thomas 85, 207, 208
Arnold, Thomas of Rugby 2, 64, 149, 150, 164, 322, 378, 395, 430, 448
  and undogmatic principle 382
Asquith, Herbert Henry 212–13
Athanasius, St 444
Atheism 112, 121, 157, 177, 254, 260, 276, 277, 278, 279, 280, 333, 340, 511
Augustine of Hippo, St 2, 24, 42, 57, 108, 300, 311, 320, 362, 433, 444, 493, 506, 527, 556
  and *Confessions* 2, 24

Bacchus, Fr. Joseph 481–2
Bacon, Francis 44, 165
Baden-Powell, Robert Stephenson Smyth, 1st Baron Baden-Powell 173
Barberi, Blessed Dominic 227–8
Becket, St Thomas 42
Beerbohm, Max 404–5
  Bell, Quentin
  on the Stephen brothers 238
  on Stephen, James Fitzjames 288
Belloc, Hilaire 409
  on Modernists 486–7
  on Mrs. Josephine Ward 454–5
Bennett, Arnold
  and *The Old Wives Tale* (1908)
  on Providence 404–5
Benthamism 31, 247, 256, 257, 272, 322, 350
Bible
  and Abbott, Edwin Abbott 215
  Bible reading central to English shared cultural identity 177
  and claim by James Anthony Froude that Newman's idea of doctrinal development was "disparaging to Scripture" 318
  "Day to day uttereth speech, and night to night showeth knowledge" [Psalm 19:2] 210
  and Froude, James Anthony and *sola scriptura* misreading of the Bible 340
  and Froude's contention that Newman's undergraduate charges might have been better left to their "unexamined Bible religion" 347
  and Froude's respect for Newman for not acquiescing in England's Bible religion 345
  and Kinglsey's misreading of "Behold, I send you forth sheep in the midst of wolves; be ye therefore wise as serpents and harmless as doves" [Matt. 10:16] 385
  main source for *Parochial and Plain Sermons* (1834–44), though unpopular with the natural man 539
  and Maurice, Frederick Denison 297
  and Newman, John Henry 230
  Newman's contention that Bible cannot make any effective stand against "the wild living intellect of man" 545
  and Newman's thoughts on the Bible verse "Ye have not received the spirit of bondage again to fear, but ye have received the Spirit of adoption, whereby we cry Abba, Father." [Rom. 8.15] 555
  Newman's quoting of Chillingworth's old saying: "The religion of England is the Bible, the whole Bible, and nothing but the Bible" 176, 403–4
  and Oxford 508
  and Pattison, Mark 180
  and private judgment 280
  and "the publicans and harlots go into the kingdom of God before you" [Matt. 21:31] 261, 266;
  and Roman Catholicism 322
  "Wisdom is justified of her children" [Matt. 11:19] 151
  and what Newman called the "low, arrogant ultra-Protestant principle' 279
Blackstone, Sir William 155, 269
Bonn Conference of 1874 366
Boswell, James xii, 2, 166, 167, 178, 408, 409, 472, 473
  and Ward, Wilfrid, admiration of 465
Bourne, Cardinal Francis Alphonsus, and advice to Wilfrid Ward regarding Modernists 487
Bowles, Emily 8–9
Bowyer, George 317
Bramhall, John 413
Bremond, Henri 492–3

Index

Brendan, Piers, on fondness of imperial English to see themselves in terms of their ancient imperial antecedents 292
Broad Church 395–6
Brougham, Henry Peter, 1st Baron Brougham and Vaux 317
Brown, Peter, on Gibbon and his distortion of the character of late antiquity 37
Bryce, James
  and Bunsen, Christian Karl Josias, Baron 406
  and dinner for Newman's honorary degree at Trinity 371
  on Manning, Cardinal 51–2
  on Newman's receiving Trinity honorary degree 373
Buckle, Henry Thomas 159, 170, 405
Buddhism 6
Bullivant, Stephen, on Newman and Modernism 488
Burgon, William, on *dénouement* of Oxford Movement 372
Burke, Edmund viii, 17, 35, 170, 295, 371
  On economy of truth 371
Burne-Jones, Edward 99, 100, 115
  on Stanley, Dean 99–100
  on Newman's teaching "to venture all on the unseen" 99–100
Burrow, J. W., on *Essays and Reviews* and *Lux Mundi*, difference of reception 208
Butler, Joseph 33, 36, 78, 92, 107, 243, 250, 295, 325, 333, 349, 362, 462

Carlyle, Thomas
  compared to Pattison, Mark 149
  compared to Stephen, James Fitzjames 105–6
  and Chesterton's view of 298, 394
  and Froude, James Anthony 297–9, 301, 306–7, 309, 312, 318, 325, 346, 348, 353, 506, 519
  and Hutton, James 121
  and Ian Ker's view that Newman shared Carlyle's respect for reticence about grave matters that required obedience and action, not "excellent words" 536
  and Kingsley, Charles 396, 406
  and Pattison, Mark 161, 245
  and Ruskin, John 304–5
  and Henry Sidgwick's appraisal of James Fitzjames Stephen's *Liberty, Equality and Fraternity* (1873) 246
  and James Fitzjames Stephen's preference for strong government 280
  and Wilfrid Ward's view of 457, 509
Catholic Emancipation 172
Cecil, Algernon on Dean Church 26
Chadwick, Henry
  on Anglicanism 56
  on ecumenical reconciliation between Canterbury and Rome 63–6
  on English Reformation 44
  on Newman's *Lectures on the Doctrine of Justification* (1838) 65
Chadwick, Owen
  and *Difficulties of Anglicans* (1850 rev. 1876), 127–8
  on Kingsley, Charles 440
  on Kingsley's *Water Babies* (1863) 391
  on Newman's search for an "ideal," not the true Church 362–3
  on Newman's writings about Rome while still an Anglican 529
  on Wilfrid Ward's biography of Newman 465–7
Chalybäus, Heinrich Moritz 151
Chesterton, Gilbert Keith
  on agnosticism 239–40
  on childhood and children 41, 118
  on Huxley, Thomas 87–8
  on *Hypatia* (1853) 399
  on Kingsley's *Water Babies* (1863) 391
  on Newman's sensitiveness 456
  on Oxford Movement 341
  on Ward, Wilfrid 456, 459, 460
Chrysostom, St John 444
Church, Richard William
  and childhood and early schooling in Italy 3–4
  and cosmopolitanism 4, 9
  and "criticism of friendship" 66, 67, 68, 95;
  and death 25
  death of Liddon 25
  death of Newman 25
  and delight in books 9

and elevation to deanship of St
  Paul's 23–4
and Englishmen, Jesuits and
  despotism 4
and English gentleman 8
and English insularity, freedom
  from 7–8
and Englishness 7
and error, patient of 5
and Evangelical formulae 9
and Evangelicalism 9
and exploits of soldiers and sailors,
  fascinated by 3
and faith and reason 30–1
and French Revolution 6–7
and German Protestantism, evolving
  view of 5–6
and Gladstonian Liberalism 4
and history, student of 36
and intellectual currents of the age 37
and Keble 9, 40
and literary criticism 43–4
and mother, close relationship to 16
and Newman's charm 2–3
and Newman's conversion 17, 41
and Newman's death 94–5
and Niebuhr, Stolberg, Neander,
  Schleiermacher, Jacobi, view of 5
and Oriel 9–10
and Oxford Union 10
and Pattison, Mark 10
and personal affinity with
  Newman 21–2
and post-Tractarian Oxford 22
and religious liberalism, 4–6
and Puseyism and "effete, plausible,
  hollow Toryism" 14
and ritualist crisis 22
and Roman Catholicism 9, 40–1
and schooling at Redlands in Bristol 9
and sense of humor 37–9
and travel 7
and Wadham College 9
and Whatley village church 19–20
  OPINIONS
on Andrewes, Lancelot 43, 529
on Athens 4
on Augustine's *Confessions* and Newman's *Apologia* 2
on *Catholicity* and *Apostolicity* 56–7
on charm of Newman 94
on charm of *Apologia* 55
on conversion 2, 48
on conversion as set out in
  Apologia 87
on conversion as "catastrophe" 39
on conversion as means of refuting
  Liberalism 83
on the Counter-Reformation
  Church 43
on dangers of reason undisciplined by
  faith 92–4
on Dante 29–30
on debate regarding faith and science,
  consequentiality of 32–3
on devout life 97–8
on English Reformation 42–3
on "English theory" 82–3
on Englishry as factor in keeping
  Anglo-Catholics within Anglican
  pale 75–6
on error as "bond of charity" on failure, blessings of 96–8
on *Essays and Reviews* as proof that
  "intellect of Oxford at the feet of
  Jowett" 177
on faith and natural science 30–1, 32–3
on faith and reason 30–1
on fear of God 26
on Germans and Germanism 4–6
on Gibbon, Edward 36–7
on Gospel 93
on Hampden, Renn Dickson, and the
  "whirligig of time" 70
on Heads of Houses and Tract 90
  (1841) 71–2, 80–2
on Hooker, Richard 43–4
on the "idea of the English Reformation," as seen from abroad 47
on infallibility, Catholic Church's claim
  to 52–3
on letters, historical importance of for
  ecclesiastical history 468
on liberalism's rise in the wake of the
  French Revolution 6–7
on Marriott, Charles 9–10
on Milman, Henry Hart 24
on mystery 11, 12
on National Church, "gingerly defence
  of" 42–7

on National Church, grounds for loyalty to 76–7
on Newman's affection for things English 76
on Newman's Anglican deathbed 55
on Newman's Anglican sermons, defining character of 11
on Newman's English style 34–5
on Newman's "great revolution of mind" 57
on Newman's readiness to forgo loyalty to National Church in light of the claims of Rome 40–1, 76–7
on Newman's Tract 90 (1841) 69–70, 71–2
on Newman's understanding of Catholicity and Apostolicity before conversion 56–7
on Newman's view of Anglican theology before converting 78
on Pattison, Mark 193
on practice in relation to the profession of faith 31, 32
on the presence of Christ 26
on Pusey, Edward 97
on rationalism 89–90, 92
on rationalism as "a rebellion against those limitations and imperfections of our knowledge amid which we find ourselves" 94
on rationalism as "a failure in humility, self-distrust, reverence, modesty, in the use of our faculties" 92
on Renan and influence of *Vie de Jésus* (1863) 12–13
on reunion between separated churches 368
on reverence due God 26
on Rome, first impressions of 7
on science 30–1
on scientists heedless of the consequentiality of the venture of faith 89–90
on scientists on socialism 37
on sin 92–3, 94
on Spenser and the *Faerie Queen* 8
on style, literary 31, 502–3
on Tyndall, John 88–9
on "vast masses of practical evil in the Roman Church" 40–1

on vergers at St Paul's Cathedral, officious insolence of 24
on *Via Media* 42–3
on Ward, W. G. 448–9
on Western Civilisation 8
CHURCH'S WORKS
Occasional Papers (1897) 3, 13, 24; *Oxford Movement 1833–1845* 3, 15, 31, 39; *Spenser* (1879) 8; "Dean Milman's Essays" in *Occasional Papers* 24; "Responsibility for Our Belief" (1877) 32; *Human Life and its Conditions: Sermons Preached before the University of Oxford in 1876–1878* 32, 89–90; *Christianity and Civilization* (1914), 37; *Pascal and Other Sermons* (1895) 36; *The Gifts of Civilization and other Sermons and Lectures* (1891), 37; "The French Revolution of 1848" (1848), *Essays and Reviews* (1854), 37; "The Call of God" (1876) 32; "Responsibility for Our Belief" (1877) 32; "Failures in Life" (1882) 96–8; "The Life of Intellectual Self-Sufficiency" (1876) 92; *Cathedral and University Sermons* (1892) 97–8
Refs. to Newman's works: *Apologia pro Vita Sua* (1864) 2, 87; "The Tamworth Reading Room" (1841) 14
Newman's Sermons: "The Ventures of Faith" (1836) 10–11; "Obedience the Remedy for Religious Perplexity" (1830) 13;
Churchill, Winston 213
Clive of Passey, Robert, Baron 450–1
Clough, Arthur Hugh 71, 121, 211, 213
Coleridge, Henry 371
Confucius 6
Conversion 41
Copeland, W. J.
  on Newman's Anglican sermons 12
  on *Parochial and Plain Sermons* (1834–43) 119
Conley, James, Bishop of Lincoln, Nebraska, on Guy Fawkes Day 527
Crabbe, George 177–8
  on Truth 237
Currie, Sir Philip 461
Curzon, George, and James Fitzjames Stephen 282

Dawson, Christopher, on progress, material 170
Derrida, Jacques 49
Dessain, Fr. Charles Stephen of the Oratory
and Ward's biography of Newman 476–9
and Ward's excision of content unfavorable to his father from a letter of Newman's 475
Dickens, Charles 121, 246, 341, 358, 394, 451, 452, 533
on Gorham Case, Puseyism and Newman 46
on King Henry VIII 301
Dolling, Robert, and George Tyrrell 484
Döllinger, Ignaz von
on history 365–7
on Newman's putative ignorance of history 363–4
on the "professors of genuine, unadulterated Christianity" 366
Dowson, Ernest 208
Doyle, Sir Francis, on James Hope-Scott 473–4
Dryden, John 167
Duffy, Eamon, on the rules of historical evidence 218

Earnest, James David
on English anti-Catholicism 336–7
on Froude, James Anthony 350–1
on *Oxford University Sermons*, charge of and intended audience for 272
on response to Tract 90 by Heads of Houses 80–1
Eliot, George
and Ker, Ian 525
and *Romola* (1862–3), good quote from deployed by James Fitzjames Stephen to mock Matthew Arnold 249
on Kinglsey, Charles 420
Eliot, T. S.
and Ker, Ian 525
on Andrewes, Lancelot 43–4
on literary criticism, best when sympathetic 43–4
Elizabethan Settlement (1558) 150
Erastianism 381–3
Essays and Reviews (1860) 172–7, 179, 197, 208, 283, 396, 412

Fairbairn, Andrew 137
Faith and Reason 30, 211, 228, 272, 275, 349, 352, 375, 406, 443, 543
Fathers of the Church 16, 44–5, 46, 83, 142, 184, 192, 316, 320, 328, 495, 507, 524, 551, 561
Fessler, Bishop Joseph, and *True and False Infallibility* (1875) 482
Figgis, John Neville 458
Firminger, Walter K. 201, 234–5
French Revolution 6–7
Froude, Hurrell 1, 162, 205, 240, 255–6, 293–3, 296, 310, 340, 349, 467
and delight in rhetorical decidedness shared by his brother James Anthony 342
opinions on West Indies, view that mismanagement of epitomised Whiggery 255
Froude, James Anthony
and ambivalence towards Newman 353
and anti-Catholic prejudice typical of Newman's unfavorable contemporary critics 330
and Arnold of Rugby, Thomas 322
and biographical details 293–7
and Brady, Ciara, and defense of Froude's criticism of Newman for unsettling Oxford's undergraduates 348
and Carlyle, Thomas, and "rubbish mountains" 353
and contempt for theology 309
and Cromwell, Oliver 325
and defense of Henry VIII and Oliver Cromwell consonant with his refusal to be swayed by feelings or emotions or affections 325
and doubt 313–14
and evidential theology, according to crack editors of Oxford critical edition of *Fifteen Sermons Peached Before the University of Oxford* 350–1
and faith and reason, offices of, according to Newman 349–50
and flippancy 318
and France, and re-evangelisation 336
and frivolity 265, 354

and Froude's charge that Newman unsettled Oxford's undergraduates 348
and Froude's rejection of theological enquiry 251
and Gibbon, Edward 295, 327
and imperial imagination 292
and "intellectual authority" of Anglican Church 349
and Henry VIII, King of England 325, 330
and history 300–9
and "imaginative intellect" 325
and influence of Thomas Carlyle 297–9
and Judgement 354
and Ker, Ian, and anti-Catholic prejudice 330
and Maistre, Joseph Marie, Comte de 320
and Möhler, Johann Adam 320
and Newman's warning Oxford's undergraduates of the evils of substituting Reason for Conscience 349
and Orwell, George, and "Such, Such were the Joys" (1952)
and rationalism 321–2
and Reformation, English 352
and Reid, Sir George, and portrait of Froude 353
and Socrates 346
and sympathy, example of 332–3
and "vindication of Reformation" 347
and Ward, Wilfrid, response to Froude's recollections of Oxford Movement 348
and Waugh, Evelyn, and Decline and Fall (1928) 296
and Willey, Basil, 347
and Young, George Malcolm, and Froude's fantasies about the world of his father's youth 296
OPINIONS
on ambivalence towards Newman 293
on Burke, Edmund, and exclusion from pantheon of great Georgian writers 295
on conscience, as the pivotal topic of Grammar of Assent 323–4
on Credo in Newmanuum 292
on divisiveness of dogma 328–9
on dogma, contempt for, reminiscent of Edward Gibbon's contempt for same 327–8
on eighteenth-century English literature 295
on Essay on the Development of Christian Doctrine (1845) 314–21
on evidence, which, once abandoned, leaves us at "the mercy of imagination" 326, 329
on father, Robert Hurrell Froude, Archdeacon 393–5
on feelings and emotions as opposed to reason 325–7
on Gospels, and claim that Newman unsettled belief of undergraduates in 329, 346–8
on Grammar of Assent (1870) 323–35
on history 300–8, 327–9, 346–7, 353
on Hume, David, and argument against miracles 347
on infallibility claimed by Church of Rome, contempt for 322, 325, 334–5
on "mystery of our life" 308
on "mystery of our mutual existence" 302
on Newman as the "indicating number" of the Catholic revival" 291
on Newman, likeness to Julius Caesar 292
on Newman, personal influence of 343–6
on Newman, as poet 343–4
on Newman, resemblance to Origen 311–12
on Newman, the rhetorical "calmness and assurance" of 313
on Newman, and "singleness of heart and purpose" 292
on New Zealand, as future hub of British Empire 292
on Oxford Movement and Anglo-Catholicism 340–3
on popery, contempt for 322
on Protestantism
on rationalism, tolerable limits of 321–2
on Reformation, English 331–2, 337–8
on religion, established 291

on religion, healthy, something one does not argue about 348
on religion, as moralism 338–9
on revival of Romanism 335–6
on Roman Catholic Church, contempt for 291, 330
on Roman Catholic Church as *Deus ex machina* 334
on Roman Catholic Church, and the "indignation of mankind" 330
on Roman Catholicism 322
on sermons preached by Newman in Oxford 346
on *sola scriptura* misreading of the Bible 340
on Soubirous, Bernadette, and Our Lady of Lourdes 326
on scripture, claim that Newman's idea of doctrinal development was "disparaging to" 318
on theology, Anglican 345
on Tractarianism, treachery of 341
on truth 263–4, 351
WORKS
Short Studies on Great Subjects (1867–83) 291
The Nemesis of Faith (1849) 296, 346
"Oxford Counter-Reformation" (1881) 343-
Oceana (1886) 292
"Origen and Celsus" 351
"Revival of Romanism" (1874) 335
"A Siding at a Railway Station" 353–4
Froude, William, and career of naval engineer, uncongenial to pursuit of theological enquiry 242

German, Germans and Germanism 4–6, 149; and Ruskin, Mrs. and Sillem, Edward 150
Gibbon, Edward 24, 30, 36, 37, 91, 101, 16, 163, 189, 274, 274, 295, 303, 309, 31, 327, 328, 331, 347, 502, 519, 547
and Kingsley, Charles 398–400
and Pattison, Mark and Early Church 164–5
and Roman Catholicism, contempt for inseparable from prejudices of England's professional middle classes 286

Gilley, Sheridan vii–viii
and *Loss and Gain* 451
on Wilfrid Ward 441–2, 444, 448, 468, 469, 473–4, 478, 481, 483, 492
Gladstone, Wiliam Ewart 27, 28
and fear of error 86
and Gladstonian Liberalism, 4
and sanctity 1
Gooch, George Peabody, on Connop Thirlwall 223
Gorham Case 46, 173, 368
Grandmaison, Léonce de 102
Grant Duff, Sir Mountstuart Elphinstone 27, 260, 287, 288
Grant, James viii, 222
Greg, W. R. on Kingsley, Charles 107

Hales, Edward Elton Young, and Pius IX and liberalism 119
Hampden, Renn Dickson 164–5, 461–2
Hanmer, A. J. 50–1
Hare, John Julius
and frivolity 265
on Newman's criticism of Luther in *Lectures on the Doctrine of Justification* (1838) 63–5
on Newman's *Difficulties of Anglicans* 128–30
on Roman Catholicism, why English must continue to abjure 130–1
Harper, Thomas, SJ
on Kingsley, Charles 420–1
on Pusey, Edward 413
Harrison, Frederic, on sin and James Fitzjames Stephen 286
Hawkins, Edward 211
Hegel, Georg Wilhelm Friedrich 150
History 114
Holland, Canon Henry Scott, on "Church of Oriel" 1
Homer 5, 12, 31, 42, 56, 89, 172
Hope, Alexander Beresford, and Frederick Meyrick 368–9
Hooker, Richard 43–4
Hope-Scott, James
and delight in south of France 455
and Doyle, Sir Francis, and reminiscence of 473–4
and Newman 454
and Ward, Josephine 45

Index

Horace 24
Hort, Fenton John Anthony
  on *Apologia* (1864) 205–6
  on *Loss and Gain* (1846) 136
  on Newman's "unsaintliness" 206
Howard, Thomas Albert, on Ignaz von Döllinger 367
Hügel, Baron von
  and distaste for perceived "rigorism" of Newman's sermons 539
  and friendship with Wilfrid Ward 449, 463
  and letter to Loisy complaining of Wilfrid Ward's obsession with orthodoxy 490–1
  and letter to Newman about young Wilfrid Ward 482
  and Modernism 491
Hume, David 22, 34, 106, 105, 155, 210, 295, 252, 391, 396, 510
  and Froude, James Anthony 347
  and miracles 226, 347
Hütter, Reinhard, Dr.
  and Newman's genius for identifying the counterfeits of Christianity 6
  on the advance of theological liberalism 119
Hutton, Richard Holt
  and ambivalence towards Newman's understanding of liberalism 115
  and "criticism of sympathy" 103–4
  and deep sense of history 136
  and grateful humility 112
  and inability to share Newman's view of Church's authority 136–7
  and longing for faith 141–2
  and Pius IX's popularity 118–20
  and pitfalls of paraphrasing Newman 114
  and physiognomical critique of Newman 140
  and religious development from Unitarianism to High Anglicanism 112
  OPINIONS
  on Abbott, Edwin Abbott, and holy fear 229
  on Abbott, Edwin Abbott, and "shallowness of moral criticism" 229
  on agnosticism 241
  on *Apologia* 202–3
  on Arnold, Matthew, and Newman compared and contrasted 133–6
  on Butler, Joseph, unpersuasiveness of Newman's citing accumulated probabilities as proof of certainty in religion 107
  on Callista, picture of 229
  on *Callista* (1856), which Hutton thought "the most completely characteristic of Newman's books" 142–3
  on Catholics and Protestants, differences with regard to the unseen 124–5
  on charge of scepticism against Newman 103–5
  on disagreement with Newman on the Church's infallibility 137–8
  on Englishmen's changed views of Roman Catholicism 120
  on faith and love in Newman 144–5
  and impact of Willis's description of the Mass in *Loss and Gain* 147
  on infallibility 118
  on James Fitzjames Stephen's *Liberty, Equality and Fraternity* (1873) 103
  on James Fitzjames Stephen's claim that he was "unteachable" 104–5
  on liberalism in religion, Newman's opposition to 115–16
  on Maurice and failure 96
  on Maurice, debt to 112
  on Maurice and reading of Bible 104
  on mystery of history 136
  on Newman's encouragement of an entire generation to make "ventures for eternal life without the absolute certainty of success" 101
  on Newman's enjoining readers to regard life as a venture of faith 100–1
  on Newman's mastery of objections to Christian faith 103
  on Newman's novel *Loss and Gain* (1847) 136–7
  on Newman and the Catholic tradition of faith and reason 110–11
  on Newman's opposition to Liberalism 113–19

on Newman's opposition to liberalism and the Church's infallibility 117–19
on Newman's own experience, depths of 102
on Newman's King William Street lectures, later published as *Anglican Difficulties* (150) 131–3
on Newman's putative refusal to own up to the "moral degeneracy of the Papacy" 108
on Newman's sanctity 229
on Newman's view of faith as a venture 99
on Newman's "wide and delicately sympathetic imagination" 99
on Newman in relation to Sir Walter Scott and Thomas Carlyle 105–6
on Newman and Matthew Arnold 138–9
on Newman's Anglican work, erroneous appraisal of 110–11
on Newman's style 121–2
on Newman's thankfulness 229
on Newman's use of Irony 122–4
on personal influence 145
on Pius IX 119–20, 145–6
on scepticism, Newman's struggle against 105–6
on Stanley, Arthur Penrhyn 114–15
on subordination of literary talent to evangelisation of English contemporaries 108–9
on true complexity and true simplicity of Newman's religious attitude "The State of Grace" (1836) 229
on Ultramontanism, dogmatism of 113, 117, 118;
on Ward, William George 230;
Huxley, Thomas Henry
and impious flippancy 87–8
and sarcasm 88
on Balaam's ass 88
on Newman "as slipperiest sophist I have ever met" 263

Infallibility and liberalism 118
Inge, William, on Newman's "very just estimate of the worthlessness of contemporary praise and blame" 109–10; on indifference to literary fame 110

Islam 6, 322

James, Henry 207, 519
Jerome, St 444
Jerome, Jerome K., on American lecture tours 500
Johnson, Lionel 208
Johnson, Manuel 17;
Johnson, Samuel vii, xii, xiii, xvi, 44, 164, 170, 179, 295, 302, 457, 465, 472, 493, 527, 531, 547
on general human condition: "more to be endured than enjoyed" 167
on "studying little things" 408–9
and "Preface to the English Dictionary" (1755) xii; and *Idler* No. 103 xii–xiii; "the secret horror of the last" xiii; *Rambler* essays compared to *Oxford University Sermons* 110–11
on Priestley, Joseph: his theological works unsettled everything and settled nothing 168
and progress 166–7
Jones, H. S. (biographer of Pattison) 151, 158, 159, 172–3

Kant, Immanuel 169
Keble, John 1, 9, 33, 34, 38, 44, 211, 226, 255, 256, 343, 374, 427, 470, 511
and loyalty to National Church 40–2
on *Apologia* 436, in draft 203; and praise of Newman for "your stand against infidelity" 203
Ker, Ian
and Abbott, Edwin Abbott 520
and Bateson, F. W. 523–4
and biographical details 520–7
and Callista, and our yearning for happiness 555–7
and Christ of Scripture 6
and Church, Dean 539–40, 544–5
and context, sacrifice of for critical depth 159
and conversion 520–2
and Crawford, Robert, and critical biographical ineptitude of 525
and criticism of due formation 519–60
and criticism as thanksgiving 553–4
and Cunningham, Vincent 523

Index

and Darwin, Charles 523
and dogmatic principle 541
and "due formation" 519–20, 540, 548, 557
and Eliot, George 525
and Eliot, T. S. 525
and Gibbon, Edward 519–20
and *Grammar of Assent* (1870) 519
and invincible ignorance 522–3
and James, Henry 519
and Joyce, James 533
and Leavis, F. R. 525
and love of Newman 552–3
and Morley, John 558
and pastoral discernment 534
and Ryder, Sophia 522–3
and saints, lesson of for Newman 560
and self-effacement 533
and Stephen, James Fitzjames 520
and Stephen, Leslie 558
and *Sword of Honour* (1965) 524
and thankfulness 393, 553, 560
and truth as it relates to both Newman and Chesterton 527–8, 560
and truth as it relates to his own conversion and priesthood 535
and *Via Media* 522
and virtues of critical approach 549–60
and Waugh, Evleyn 524–5
OPINIONS
on Newman's anatomy of self-deception 534–5
on Newman's appeal to affections 557
on Newman's Biglietto speech 548
on Newman's celibacy 547–8
on Newman's conversion 227
on Newman's "dogmatic principle" as opposed to "principle of liberalism" 540–2
on Newman's experiencer of failure 95–6
on Newman's handling of his pastoral charge 95–6
on Newman's insistence on the primacy of action in the exercise of faith 535
on Newman's opposition to "march of mind" 544
on Newman's preoccupation with unreality, artificiality and self-deception 533–6
on Newman's realism 537
on Newman's sensitivity 543, 547–8
on Newman's sermons 10, 537–40
on Newman's style an inseparable element of his matter 529
and Newman's thankfulness for red hat 559–60
on Newman's understanding of certitude in religious faith 558
on Newman's understanding of conscience 549–51, 553–4
on Newman's understanding of dogmatic principle 541
on Newman's understanding of faith and reason 543
on Newman's understanding of infallibility 544–7
on Newman's understanding of the "mixed education" 542–3
on Newman's understanding of the "principle of liberalism" 541–2
on Newman's understanding of sanctity 533
on Newman's understanding of sacraments 551–2
on Newman's understanding of truth and error, their respective appeals 537, 538–9
on Newman's understanding of the relationship between truth and saints 560
on Newman's understanding of the yearning for happiness 555–7
on Newman's work, summary of 548–9
on Roman Catholics as opposed to Anglo-Catholics 41
Kingsley, Charles 262
and ambivalence of Christian socialism 414–15
and American Civil War 396
and Arnold, Thomas, of Rugby 395
and attack on Newman, reasons why he might have been induced to proceed with 385–90
and "Behold, I sent you forth as sheep in the midst of wolves; be ye therefore wise as serpents, and harmless as doves" [Matt. 10:16] 385
and biographical details 390–1

and Broad Church 395–6
and Bunsen, Baron 406
and celibacy 387–8
and Chadwick, Owen 529–30
and Chartism 414–15
and Christian socialism 388–9, 391, 407, 414–16
and controversy with Newman 385, 412–37
and controversy with Newman, fallout and effect on legacy 437–40
and country rectory 409
and craving for life of reality 416
and dictates of conversion, as Newman saw them 410
and good word for church building of "Puseyite sectarians" 396
and hagiography 390
and Henry VIII, King of England 387
and *Hypatia* (1853) 397–400, 405–7
and Froude, James Anthony 385
and Gibbon, Edward 398–400
and Ignatius Loyola, St 462
and Johnson, Samuel 408–9
and Macmillan, Daniel 406
and mother, close relationship with 392
and muscular Christianity 35
and Palmerston, Lord 412
and parish life 408
and Paul, Kegan 409
and poor 388–9, 407–8
and Providence 394. 437–40
and psychology 387
and Pusey, Edward 387
and religion of erotic love 406
and repugnance for dead religion 416–17
and St Barnabas, parish of 407
and Stanley, A. P. 438–9
and Surtees, Robert 406–7
and truth 385
and Walton, Izaak 407
and Westminster Abbey, and pride of staff in Kingsley, his fame as author and preacher 401
OPINIONS
on Anglican Church, disenchantment with the "sense of deadness" it inspires 410
on Anglo-Catholics, praise for 411–12
on bishops and the bishop's office 412
on cholera districts 407–8
on Christ's sheep 416
on effeminacy of Catholics and Anglo-Catholics 386–7
on God's elect 416
on history 396–400
on "modesty and honesty" 391
on mystery 406
on new churches 396–7
on Newman, and truth 385
on Newman, "that great genius" 412
on Popular Protestantism 410–12
on Providence 385
on "salt of the earth" 416
on sin 388, 412, 416
on Truth, not being a virtue with the Roman clergy 385
on "Wisdom and Innocence" (1843), Newman's sermon 385–6
CHARACTERISTICS
dutiful 386, 407
faithful 438
flippant 394
frivolous 265
generous 394, 411
hot-headed 411
impatient of dogma 395
magnanimous 411
self-critical 385
"sensitive to ridicule" 394
sincere 400
"tender-hearted" 394
tough and physically brave 393–4

Landor, Walter Savage, and style 501
Laud, William 150
Law, William, and Samuel Johnson's high regard for his *Serious Call* (1728) 167
Lecky, William Edward Hartpole
on Froude, James Anthony 312
on Newman's "credulity," "scepticism" and "sophistry," despite the "glamour" of his style 325–6
Lee, Hermione, on Sir James Stephen 251–2
Leo the Great, St 444
Leo XIII, Pope
on liberalism 241, 496–7
on Thomas Aquinas, St 494

Index

Liberalism
  European character of, 4
  religious liberalism, R. W. Church's view of 4–5
  R. H. Hutton's view of Newman's opposition to 113–19
  and what Newman called "the great *apostasia*" 117
  and Newman's definition of in *Apologia* 241
  and James Fitzjames Stephen's response to Newman's definition of 242
Liddon, Heny Parry 16, 25, 39, 81, 97, 365, 366, 412, 510
  on Heads of Houses 81
Lilly, William Samuel 278
Loisy, Alfred 489–90
Louis XVI, king of France 6
Louis XVIII, king of France 6
Lytton, Edward George Lytton Bulwer, 1st Earl of
  and friendship with Stephen, James Fitzjames 259
  on Newman 259
  on Pascal 259

Macaulay, Rose, and *The Towers of Trebizond* (1956) 361
Macaulay, Thomas Babington 14, 34, 87–8, 178, 244, 245, 292, 378
Maccoll, Malcolm 176, 177, 364, 435
MacMillan, Daniel
  on Hume in comparison with Newman 106
  on logician in Newman 106–7
  on Newman's "sublime" notions of God 106
  on Newman's treatment of scepticism 106–7
  on Whately in comparison with Newman 106
Maistre, Joseph Marie, Comte de 264
Manning, Henry Edward 1, 14, 28, 29, 51, 63, 76, 82, 90 153, 173, 224, 245, 249, 250, 279, 317, 319, 363, 379, 382, 383, 446, 480
  on delight in Macaulay, Thomas Babington 245
  on evidence, Holy See's careful investigation of 249
  on Newman, eulogy for 29
  on Newman, stand against Erastianism and Rationalism in the National Church 383
  on Stephen, James Fitzjames, and "evidence of the interference of unseen agents in human affairs" 249–50
  on Stephen, James Fitzjames, and "strong predisposition to incredulity" 249
  OPINIONS
  on *Essay on the Development of Christian Doctrine* (1845) 28–9
  on passage from Essay on Development commending Virgin Mary 29
  on sanctity 1
Mare, Walter de la, on Anglican Church resembling a "cataleptic's countenance" with "no inward activity of its own" 125
Marie Antoinette, Queen of France 6
Martin, G. Murphy 4
Mary, Mother of God, and worship of the Virgin in Spain 357
Maurice, Frederick Denison 37, 60, 63, 64, 96, 107, 204, 205, 208, 237, 239, 391, 394, 420, 430
  and Bible, his "insolent" reading of 104
  and Bible, means of being delivered of atheism 297
  and Bible, means of being delivered from the sort of "confused or Manichean views of God" that led Carlyle and James Anthony Froude astray 299
Meredith, George 251
Metaphysical Society 248, 249
Meszaros, Andrew
  and citation of Congar, Ives to highlight Newman's sense of history 112
  and response of Neo-Scholastics to Newman 101–2
  and St Thomas Aquinas 116
  and "virus of Hegelianism" 102
  on hope and Newman's insistence that "the worse our condition is, the nearer to us is the Advent of our Deliverer" 116

on Neo-Scholastics and respect for
  Newman's work 484
on "unity and finality of
  Revelation" 489
Meyrick, Frederick
  and Acton, Lord 362
  and Anglican ecumenism 366–7
  and biographical details 356–7
  and Chapman, Mark 368
  and Dickens, Charles 358
  and Döllinger, Ignaz von 363–8
  and frivolousness of 265
  and grounds for taking against
    Newman 355
  and Kingsley, Charles 370
  and Ireland 361
  and Manning, Edward Henry
    Cardinal 382–3
  and Nockles, Peter
  and old English Sunday 358
  and Palmer, William of Magdalen 362
  and Pugin, August Welby
    Northmore 380–2
  and Spain 357–61
  and unhappy tenure with Jesuits 355–6
  and Ward, Wilfrid 382
  OPINIONS
  on Newman, and development of
    doctrine 379–80
  on Newman, and hero-worship 326–7
  on Newman, and honorary degree at
    Trinity 371–2
  on Newman's hypocrisy and treachery
    (alleged) 376
  on Newman's intellect 374–5
  on Newman's return to Trinity for
    honorary degree 371–2
  on Newman's theology 377–8
  on Newman's views on faith and rea-
    son, dogma, acceptance and belief,
    papal infallibility, and Immaculate
    Conception 374–5
  on Oxford Movement 374
  on Palmer, William of
    Magdalen 362–3
  on "Saints" of the Church of
    England 369
Meyrick, Thomas 355–6
Milbank, John 49
Milman, Henry Hart 24

Moberly, George 9
Modernism 483–96
Möhler, Johann Adam 102, 137
Monsell, William, and *Syllabus of Errors*
  (1864) 113
Moriarty, David, Bishop of Kerry 482
Morley, John 469, 505, 509, 558–9
  on Mark Pattison 152–8
Mozley, J. B., on Newman's teach-
  ing children their catechism at
  Littlemore 219
Mozley, Thomas, on W. G. Ward 440
Murray, Fr Gerald, Pastor of St Joseph
  Church, New York City, on liberal
  Catholicism 537

Neo-Scholastics 102–3
Nevin, John 367–8
Newman, St John Henry Cardinal
  and ability to enter into the psychology
    of his opponents 91–2
  and Abraham 560
  and accumulation of probabilities 107
  and Achilli affair 96, 462
  and Acton, Lord, and negotiating
    divide between ultramontane and
    liberal Catholicism 470
  and adage "Answer a fool according to
    his folly" 44
  and agnosticism 88, 121, 211, 232, 233,
    234, 239–41, 250, 277, 288, 511, 512,
    514
  and antecedent probability 36, 111, 243
  and anti-Catholicism 336–7
  and *Apologia pro Vita Sua*, contem-
    porary responses to 420, 424–5,
    428–33
  and atheism 112, 121, 157, 177, 254, 260,
    276–7, 280, 297, 322, 333, 341, 511
  and autobiography 102, 264, 265, 428,
    433–4
  and Bagot, Richard, Bishop of
    London 401–2
  and Barberi, Fr Dominic 462
  and belief 22, 24, 26, 32–3, 53, 57, 64–5,
    68, 5, 89, 90, 92, 94, 101, 103–4, 113–
    78, 121, 126, 130–1, 134, 137–8, 144,
    151, 162, 173, 176, 207–9, 211, 221–3,
    231–3, 240, 242, 244, 248, 250–1, 253,
    254, 259, 260, 263–5, 268, 276–9, 297,

299, 314, 319, 322–3, 336, 342, 348–9, 351, 375, 376, 378, 385, 406, 413, 435, 441–3, 453–4, 458, 461, 463, 485, 514, 534, 537, 541, 545, 553–4, 557, 558
and Biglietto Speech 115, 119, 120, 172, 285, 548
and Blessed Sacrament 126
and Birmingham Oratory vii, xiii, 99, 136, 464, 495
and bishops, Anglican 46
and Bremond, Henri 492–3
and Broad Church 130, 175, 204, 225, 395, 396, 406, 416, 439–40, 449, 537
and Bryce, James 373
and Buffon, George-Louis Leclerc, Comte de 515
and Burke, Edmund, and the "economy of truth" 371
and Butler, Joseph 36, 107, 175, 243, 462
and celibacy 130, 216, 376, 387–9, 406, 410, 421, 548
and Caleb 560
and casuistry 431
and Catholic faith, certitude 30, 85, 232, 258, 271–2, 277, 327, 333–5, 348, 351, 558–9
and champion of Anglo-Catholicism 44–5
and charm with which he treats Tractarian Oxford in *Loss and Gain* (1846) 190
and childhood 118
and Church, R. W. 1–98
and Christianity, evidence for 104, 121, 142, 173
and communion of saints 1
and conversion 17, 40–1, 48, 48–50, 52, 56, 59, 61, 85, 100, 108, 122, 128, 122, 128, 142, 171–2, 195, 208, 219, 249, 260, 263–5, 310, 312–13, 317, 359, 393, 410, 436, 454, 504, 511, 521, 522–3, 524–5
and correspondence to verify accuracy of *Apologia* 427
and Crawley, Charles 173, 175–6
and daughters of R. W. Church 17–18
and detractors 71, 74, 214, 215, 216, 222, 223, 235, 363, 373, 422, 427, 428, 462, 484
and development of doctrine 29, 277, 481, 484, 507

and dogmatic principle vii, 114, 138, 265, 266, 268, 421–2, 467, 506, 507, 541, 542
and Döllinger, Ignaz von
and early Church 45, 56, 57, 66, 83, 164, 215, 398, 492, 506, 541
and education viii, 150, 160, 178, 180, 181, 182, 183, 187, 196, 228, 260, 317, 385, 399, 460, 535, 538
and election to Oriel Fellowship 14–15
and Elgar, Edward 438
and Elijah 560
and English gentleman 8–9
and Englishness 76
and Enoch 560
and equivocation 371
and Erastianism 46, 49, 58, 76, 128, 132, 242, 337, 341, 361, 368, 374, 382–3, 513
and Evangelicals and Evangelicalism 9, 12, 27, 52, 62, 105, 117, 130, 131, 155, 164, 244, 245, 252, 254, 255, 278, 339, 342, 387, 475, 525
and Ezekiel 560
and falsehood 335, 347, 348, 371, 428, 434, 541, 560
and father, John Henry Newman Sr. 415–16
and Fathers of the Church 16, 50, 561
and Fitzgerald, Geraldine Penrose 437–8
and friendship, delight in 1–2
and Gospel 31, 33, 90, 91, 102, 14, 110, 230, 273, 274–5, 310, 349, 397, 475, 534, 538, 539, 554, 557
and gratitude to Hutton for his favorable notice of the *Apologia* 156
and Gibbon, Edward 274
and Giberne, Maria 373
and Gladstone, Willam Ewart xiv, 14, 22, 27, 28, 29, 40, 41, 63, 86, 110, 152, 221, 245, 370, 379, 474, 551, 460
and Gorham Ruling 46, 76, 173, 367, 368, 374, 383
and Guy Fawkes 423
and Hare, Julius Charles 62, 64, 106, 128, 129
and Heads of Houses 15, 16, 71, 80–2, 175, 353
and Heaven 98, 112, 266, 284, 306, 317, 331, 385, 395, 417, 418, 480, 527

and Hell 88, 263, 284, 286, 315, 345, 391, 511, 512, 537, 549
and history 6, 36,7, 44, 72, 76, 103, 108, 14, 118, 136 139–40, 150, 164, 169–70, 171, 196–7, 210, 215, 218, 221–5, 243, 249, 259, 274, 285–6, 292, 293, 296, 300–1, 302, 303–5, 306, 307, 308, 312, 346–7, 348, 363–4, 365–6, 387, 374, 381, 382, 385, 395, 402–3, 414, 533
and history, and primary sources 506
and historical perspective granted by Rome's "greater latitude of theological speculation" 174
and hope, and Newman's insistence that "the worse our condition is, the nearer to us is the Advent of our Deliverer" 116
and his "immediate historical context" xiii
and influence on the critic in Dean Church 44
and Harper, Thomas SJ, with regard to Kingsley's attacks leading to *Apologia* 420–1
and Hope-Scott, James 454–5
and Howley, William 402
and humor vii, 477, 504, 510, 533
and Huxley, Thomas 277
and "idolatry of Zeitgeist" 144
and imagination 99, 171, 206, 216, 231, 303, 339, 441, 455, 460, 501, 514
and infallibility 137–8
and intellectual authority for Established Church 348–9
and Jeremiah 560
and John the Baptist 560
and Joshua 560
and Keble, John 436
and Ker, Ian, and unusual autobiographical character of *Apologia* 433–4
and Kingsley, Charles 385–440
and Kingsley, Charles, and death of 439–40
and Kingsley, Charles, and wider dossier against Newman in *Apologia* controversy 426
and Laud, William 150, 180
and Lecky, William Edward Hartpole 274, 312, 325, 326
and letter-writing, a vital part of Newman's daily life throughout his long life 468
and liberalism 4, 5 6, 83, 99, 113–19, 180, 185, 241, 243, 246, 247–8, 254, 255, 256, 265, 266, 279, 392, 465–6, 466–7, 472, 496, 497, 504, 541, 542
and Loisy, Alfred 489–90
and love of Our Lord 474
and Manning, Henry Edward 1, 14, 28, 29, 51, 63, 76, 82, 90 153, 173, 224, 245, 249, 250, 279, 317, 319, 363, 379, 382, 383, 446, 480
and "march of mind" 14
and Maurice, Frederick Denison 297
and Metaphysical Society 90, 121, 248, 249, 250, 442, 449, 466, 511
and Modernism and Wilfrid Ward 483–96
and mother, close relationship with 16, 392–3
and Moses 560
and Mozley, Thomas 146
and Marriott, Charles 9–10
and Maurice, F. D., and Newman's love of truth 204
and Meyrick, Frederick 355 -384
and miracles 207–11
and mystery 11, 12, 139, 145, 233, 248, 255, 327, 346, 463, 523
and natural theology 12, 243, 250
and Noah 560
and notes of Church 68, 230, 541
and O'Hagan, John 560
and papal infallibility 150
and Pascal 34, 39–40, 59, 92, 259, 264, 505, 530
and pastor, role as 18
and Paul, St 560
and personal influence 2, 468, 473
and preaching 11, 21, 35, 51, 62, 127, 255, 270, 273, 252, 378, 424, 440, 502, 522, 530, 534, 536, 553
and Philip Neri, St 96, 533
and Phineas 560
and Polycarp 561
and Popular Protestantism 413
and Primitive Church 541
and private judgment 9, 30, 45, 47, 122, 123, 124, 134, 225, 280, 406, 546

Index

and proof for truth of religion 434
and Providence 401–3, 437–40
and publication of Tracts 402
and Pusey, Edward 61, 78, 403
and rationalism 89–90, 113–14, 129, 151, 152, 155, 164, 169, 196, 241, 258, 269, 272, 274, 280, 287, 299, 321, 349, 371, 383, 416–17, 435, 445, 544
and red hat 115, 173, 241, 559–60
and religion of civilisation 186
and reunion with Rogers and Church 3
and rhetoric 255
and Rogers, Frederic, later Lord Blachford 2, 3, 4, 5, 14, 21, 23, 38, 204, 403, 427
and Ryder, Ignatius 209–11, 437
and saints xiv, xvi, 1, 16, 21, 47, 77, 98, 108, 131, 133, 153, 164, 172, 192, 241, 243, 252, 262, 296, 301, 315, 319, 335, 336, 353, 354, 357, 358, 365, 366, 369, 379, 385, 401, 403, 406, 415, 417, 41, 425, 435, 447, 462, 495, 508, 530, 531, 532, 533, 539, 560, 561
and sanctity 1, 47, 68, 133, 210, 229, 244, 339, 369, 427, 531, 532, 553
and Samuel 560
and satire 423, 503–4, 513
and St Paul's Cathedral 24
and Scott, Thomas 433–4, 462
and Scripture 6, 8–9, 42, 58, 112, 133, 139, 144–5, 153, 209, 318, 444, 497, 502, 537
and self-criticism 469–70
and sermons 10, 346
and sin 26, 53, 74, 86, 108, 116, 126, 135, 143, 144, 222, 244, 285, 316, 364–5, 458, 530
and sophistry, commonly held to be inseparable from style by contemporary detractors 209, 505
and Stanley, Arthur Penrhyn, and eulogy for Charles Kingsley 438–9
and Stephen, James Fitzjames, meeting with 260
and Stephen, James Fitzjames, and evidence 326–7, 329, 330, 347
and Stephen, Lesley 467
and style 46–7, 66, 500–5, 513, 515
and *Syllabus of Errors* (1864) 269

and Swift, Jonathan 267–8
and Tennyson, Lord Alfred 501
and theology, Catholic 332, 480, 490
and Tracts 402
and Trinity College 371–3
and truth 36, 47, 49, 50, 52, 59, 61, 62, 65, 66, 68, 72, 73 78, 84, 85, 87, 89, 91, 94, 99, 103, 113 115, 118, 123, 125, 126, 128, 130, 134, 136, 137, 142, 144, 158, 171, 177, 182, 184, 190, 201, 202, 204, 215 237, 248, 263–4, 283, 284, 434, 435, 480, 481, 507, 508, 509, 510
and truth for the benefit of "living, earnest men," not merely the applause of the learned world 509
and Tyrrell, George 483–9
and Ullathorne, William Bishop 372–3
and unseen world 102, 127
and unshriven intellect 254
and Warburton, William 513
and Ward, Mrs. Humphry 207–9
and Ward, William George, 472–3, 474–6
and Willey, Basil 421–2
OPINIONS
on affections 554
on agnosticism 234
on ancient philosophers, tendency in most when engaging matters of religious gravity to be frivolous 30–1
on Anglican Church 78, 173
on Anglican divines 44, 83, 183
on Anglican theology 76, 77, 78, 178, 507
on Anglo-Catholicism 45–6, 78–9, 389
on Anglo Catholics, and "propagating an unreality" 412
on apostasy 119, 175, 177, 184, 259, 286, 510
on Apostles' Creed 462
on Athanasian Creed 462
on atheism 254, 277–9
on atheism, "no medium in true philosophy between Atheism and Catholicity" 277
on authority of Church 549
on belief and acceptance, fine line between 375
on Bible, and religion of England 176–7, 403–4

- on Bible, its dreariness for the natural man 539
- on Bible's relation to Christianity 540
- on Bible, inability to make any effective stand against the "wild living intellect of man" 545
- on Bible verse: "Ye have not received the spirit of bondage again to fear, but ye have received the Spirit of adoption, whereby we cry Abba, Father" Rom. 8.15 555
- on Bible, John 7.17: "If any man will do his will, he shall know of the doctrine."
- on biographical principle that "a man's life lies in his letters" 467
- on Bramhall, John 413
- on Butler, Joseph, "stopped the evil [of scepticism] only by lowering by many pegs the pretensions of Christianity" 175
- on Catholic faith 86
- on Catholicism whilst on Anglican deathbed 65–6
- on certitude in faith 30, 85, 232, 258, 271–2, 277, 327, 329, 333–5, 348, 351, 558–9
- on children, the little minds of 102
- on children as exemplars of the force of conscience 218–19
- on Church, notes of
- on Church and the World 243
- on church as home for the lonely 397
- on Clive of Passey, Robert, Baron 450–1
- on conscience 549–51
- on conscience as "the creative principle of religion" 217–18
- on conscience as "proof of the presence of God… and the experience… of what we all call sin or guilt" 243–4
- on conscience, as supplying the imagination "with the picture of a Supreme Governor, Judge, holy, just powerful, all-seeing, retributive" 325
- on controversy 177–8
- on controversialists of Rome 59
- on conversion 50–1
- on criticism xvi
- on "deadness to the claims of the true Church" 412
- on dead religion, despite every semblance of life 351
- on death 15
- on definition of gentleman 187–8
- on development of Chrisitan doctrine and dictates of conversion, difficulty of accepting 410
- on Divine Wisdom 151, 412
- on Divine Word 241
- on dogmatic principle 421–2, 461
- on dogmatic statements, such as those on the Trinity, Incarnation, Atonement and Justification 461
- on Dollinger, Ignaz von 365
- on doubt 258, 313–14
- on doubt and Protestantism 313–14
- on Early Church, whilst gasping on his Anglican deathbed 66
- on eclecticism of Anglican Church 45–6
- on educated women, growth of scepticism among "something appalling" 175
- on elevation of friends to high positions 23–4
- on Eliot, George 525
- on Episcopalians, moneyed, and Anglo-American Church 339–40
- on error, fear of 85–6
- on *Essays and Reviews* (1860) 173
- on Establishment 410
- on Evangelicalism
- on Evangelicals 254–5
- on evidence for Christianity 12, 151, 243–4, 250, 263–4, 362–3
- on evidence not being the "simple foundation on which Faith is built" 244
- on evidence, weighing of 275–6
- on Evangelicals as a class, the Established Church and Roman Catholicism 254–5
- on faith "as an instrument of knowledge and action, unknown to the world before, a principle *sui generis*" 274
- on faith and reason 251–2, 275–6, 435
- on falsehood, ephemerality of 257

on Fathers of the Church 44–5, 50–1
on faith and reason, offices of 349–50
on faith, Roman Catholic 125–6, 149
on faithful Irish beggarwoman and state's pattern man 266
on fallen man 415
on falsehood 434–5
on fear of the Lord 230
on "feelings, affections, imagination and conscience" 327
on first principles 237, 241, 243, 244, 251–2, 260, 261, 278, 288, 550
on Gibbon, Edward 37
on God's Love for the "greatness and littleness of man" 415
on grace 389–90
on "grace now and glory hereafter" 403
on *Grammar of Assent*, précis of argument 277
on hallmark of Church's infallibility 317
on Hampden, Renn Dickson 461–2
on "hatred of the Mother of Saints" 412
on Heaven 6, 9, 26, 29, 78, 82, 91, 126, 273, 434–5, 454, 552
on history 6, 24, 50–1, 122–3, 135, 173, 189, 201, 433–4, 426–7, 500–1, 547
on holiness 40, 61, 78, 91, 145, 147, 264, 273, 291, 457, 497, 524, 532, 533, 534, 539, 552–3
on hope 118
on humanity of Saviour 415
on Hume, David, school of and miracles 226
on humility and style 36
on "humility and teachableness which the Scripture precepts inculcate" 90–1, 230
on Huxley and Manning and the Metaphysical Society 90
on imagination 58, 102, 141, 188, 217, 226, 275, 311, 561
on imputing motives in controversy 214–15, 426
on infallibility 66, 334–5
on infallibility and certitude, confusion of 334
on "intrinsic hatefulness of sin" 244
on invincible ignorance 262, 523–4
on knowledge
on Last Day 560
on Laud, William 78, 431
on letters and letter writing 468
on letters of St Gregory 468
on liberalism 241, 242, 285, 349–50
on liberty 497
on limits of rational probability 271–2
on Locke, John 329
on logic 278
on London 24
on "long penance of slander and unpopularity" 421
on love 552–3
on martyrs 275
on Milman, Henry Hart 24
on miracles 210–11
on mystery 327
on music 3
on Moral Sense as the principle of ethics 217
on "Mother of Saints" 412
on natural man, and Church's continual attempts to rescue from his own folly 126–7
on natural virtue 8–9
on Nicene Creed 462
on notes of the Church 51, 68, 541
on *odium theologicum* 50
on old Adam 403
on Origen 311, 444
on Oxford Movement and Fathers of the Church 45, 123
on Palmer, William of Worcester, "that good fellow" 389
on papal infallibility 325
on paradoxical truths dictated by conversion 410
on Pattison, Mark, whose work he commends as "always grave and sincere" 174
on Pattison, Mark as "grave, cautious, conscientious thinker" 191
on personal influence, "holiness embodied in personal form" 291
on "philanthropy" of God 415
on pride 403
on private judgment 313–14
on Providence 385, 403–4, 415, 435

on *Rambler*, what ought to its editorial policy 469
on rationalism 57–8, 321–2, 349–50
on reason, unaided, tends towards "a simple unbelief in matters of religion" 254
on rebuff of proposed visit by Stephen, James Fitzjames to Oratory, and letter setting out reasons 287–8
on Reformation, English 175
on religion of civilisation and religion of primitivism 186
on religion of England 403
on reprobation 389
on Revelation
on rhetoric 256
on Right Reason 185–6
on Roman Catholic Church as "oracle of truth" 335
on "rules in controversy, as well as in boxing" 214
on Russell, SJ, Fr. Charles 59
on Sacraments 551–2
on saints 560
on saints, death of 415
on saints, outburst of after "monstrous corruption" 108
on salvation of God 120, 172
on Satan 237
on scepticism 256
on science 30–2, 90–1
on scientists, tendency to have low view of Christian faith 91–2, 94
on scientists, tendency to be "unworthy disciples in the School of the Gospel" 90–1
on Scripture 20–1, 80–101, 126–7, 176, 177, 230, 258, 272–3, 404, 461, 538, 539, 540–1, 555–6
on self-absorption, anticipation of charge from readers of *Apologia* 202–3
on self-will 403
on Simpson, Richard 471
on sin 91, 244, 364–5, 533–5, 539, 551, 557, 561
on sermons, low view of 255
on *sola scriptura* Christianity 403–4
on Stephen, Sir James, encounter with 255–6, 260–2

on teachableness 230
on Tennyson, Lionel 234
on tests of rationalists 271
on Thirty-Nine Articles as a test of humility 46
on time as "test of facts" 257, 560
on "time of widespread infidelity" 466
on Tract 90, and indifference to Sheldonian fallout of 16
on Tract 90 and Pusey 69
on tradition of Church 549
on truth viii, 13, 21 24, 29, 30, 31, 35, 101, 111, 116, 135 141 145, 151 219, 230, 241–4, 251, 296–7, 304, 307, 384, 434–5
on truth being mysterious 327
on truth, the Broad Church version of 395–6
on truth, leading his Tractarian friends to, being the object of his writing *Anglican Difficulties* 384
on truth being "wrought out by the indirect operation of error and sin" 317
on Truth's perdurability 257
on university education, utility of 185
on unsettling the "minds of a generation" 176
on Via Media 72–3
on "wayward longings" 403
on Ward, William George, criticism of extreme ultramontane carry on of 475–6
on Whately, Richard 257
on White, Blanco 27

CHARACTERISTICS
austerity 35
barristerial ability to state views of opponents better than opponents themselves 513
charm 1, 2–3, 21, 39, 44–5, 55, 94–5, 190, 260, 343, 344, 504
delight in children 219
delight in the "dogmatic principle" 43–4, 99, 114, 138, 241, 265, 266, 268, 466–7, 506, 507–8, 540, 541
directness 46–7
failure, acceptance of as means of spiritual growth 95–6
humility 36, 124, 428

Index

irony 44–5, 123–4
mastery of objections that "made so many men withhold their faith from Christianity" 103
openness to the good counsel of others 104
personality, proof not of self-absorption but self-giving 140–1
priesthood, dedication to 95–6
realism 458
reality, respect for 124
scepticism, readiness to treat seriously 103
scepticism, susceptibility to 510–11
readiness to enter into the reasoning of those with whom he disagreed 254
reticence about personal matters that touched him most deeply 373
satirical mockery, gift for 78–9, 513, 529
self-criticism 124, 389, 427
self-effacement 110
sense of history 114
sensitivity 457, 458
Servant of Truth 434
simplicity, respect for the grace of 143–4
snubbing, ability to put up with 100
solicitude for cure of souls, an example of which being his enjoining the lapsed Pattison to "glorify God and save your own soul" 174
sophistry, perceived susceptibility to 264
subtlety 221, 238, 414, 469
trust in the "principle that truth defends itself" 177
unworldliness 102
wariness with respect to the notion of progress, though always full of hope 171
WORKS
Apologia pro Vita Sua (1864) viii, xiii, 2, 14, 55, 59, 61, 68, 76, 82, 84, 87, 104, 107, 100, 110, 112, 129, 135-38, 144, 146, 162, 188, 195, 201, 203, 204, 205, 206, 210, 216, 231, 254, 256, 258, 261, 263, 264, 267, 269, 274, 277-8, 279-80 287, 311, 370, 371-2, 374, 379, 387, 405, 410, 417, 422–3, 425, 426, 427–33, 435–7, 440, 444, 456, 462, 465, 474, 477–80, 482, 504, 510, 515, 526, 531, 545; Biglietto Speech (1879) 115, 117, 119, 120, 172, 548; *Difficulties of Anglicans* (1850, rev. edn. 1876) 41, 44, 45, 50, 52, 62, 73, 78, 83, 108, 122, 123, 125, 126, 127, 132, 199, 317, 339, 367, 384, 389, 410, 413, 470, 535, 550, 551; "The Tamworth Reading Room" (1841) 14, 110, 183, 257, 423, 543; *Historical Essays*, ii, 24; *Idea of a University* (1873) 8, 19, 37, 85, 160, 181, 183, 184, 185, 186, 187, 188, 189, 190, 307, 365, 510, 513, 526, 531; *An Essay in Aid of a Grammar of Assent* (1870) 85, 105, 107, 111, 217, 218, 219, 226, 238, 243, 244, 271, 291, 310, 322, 324, 328, 403, 443, 459, 473, 483, 495, 505, 509, 520, 531, 554; *Essay on the Development of Christian Doctrine* (1845) 28–9, 110, 121, 215, 221, 257, 310, 318, 379, 480, 490, 505, 507, 515, 541; "The State of Religious Parties" (1839) 57–8; *Lectures on the Doctrine of Justification* (1838), 63–5; Tract 90 (1841) 71–2, 401; *Parochial and Plain Sermons* (1834–43) 119, 537, 539, 554, 557, 560; *Loss and Gain* (1847) 136, 147, 288, 451; *Callista* (1856) 142–3, 398, 554–5; *A Letter to the Duke of Norfolk* (1875) 108, 150, 277, 445, 447, 482, 549, 551; *Present Position of Catholics in England* (1851) 129, 227, 263, 275, 503; "The Development of Religious Error" (1885) 243; *Fifteen Sermons Preached before the University of Oxford* (1843) 2, 30, 90, 101, 107, 110, 111, 145, 151, 272, 349–50, 375, 436, 493, 505; *Historical Sketches* (1872–3) 317, 444, 493; *Sermons Preached on Various Occasions* (1857) 276, 409, 415; *Lectures on the Prophetical Office of the Church* (1837) 45, 65, 78, 312, 413; *Lectures on Justification* (1838) 63, 64, 65
Sermons: "The Ventures of Faith" (1836) 10, 96; "Obedience the Remedy for Religious Perplexity" (1830) 13; "The Parting of Friends" (1843) 20–1; "The Philosophical Temper First Enjoined by the Gospel" (1826) 30–1; "Knowledge of God's Will without

Obedience" (1832) 51; "Explicit and Implicit Reasoning" (1840) 101; "The Secrecy and Suddenness of Divine Visitations" (1831) 116; "The Invisible World" (1837) 139; "Inward Witness to the Truth of the Gospel" (1825) 230; "Ignorance of Evil" (1836) 143–4; "The Usurpations of Reason" (1831) 151, 272; "The Second Spring" (1852) 172; Bigiletto Speech (1879) 172; "Inward Witness to the Truth of the Gospel" (1825) 230; "The State of Grace" (1836) 229; "Love the Safeguard of Faith Against Superstition" (1830) 244; "Mysteries in Religion" (1834) 248; "Faith and Reason, Contrasted as Habits of Mind" (1839) 273; "Subjection of Reason and Feelings to the Revealed World" (1840) 275; "Implicit and Explicit Reason" (1840) 276; "The Mystery of the Holy Trinity" (1838) 327; "Preparation for the Judgment" (1848) 354; "Wisdom and Innocence" (1843) 385–6; "Grounds for Steadfastness in our Religion Profession" (1841) 389–90; "The Church A Home for the Lonely" 397; "Omnipotence in Bonds" (1857) 403; "Saint Paul's Gift of Sympathy" (1857) 415; "The Infidelity of the Future" (1873) 435; "Endurance of the World's Censure" (1840) 479; "The Glories of Mary for the Sake of her Son" (1849) 535

Newton, Sir Isaac 165

Noetics 189

Norton, Charles Eliot 22, 305, 467, 509, 512

Nuttal, A. D. 150

O'Dwyer, Edward Thomas, Bishop of Limerick 479–82

Old Catholic Movement 367

Oxford and Bible 508

Paget, Francis
  OPINIONS
  on Dean Church's "perfect simplicity and lightness of manner" 38
  on Church's sense of humor 37–9
  on Church's humility 54

Palmer, William of Magdalen 67, 362

Palmer, William of Worcester 43, 81, 242, 349, 374

Papal infallibility 150

Pascal, Blaise 34, 39–40, 59, 92, 259, 264, 505, 530

Pastoral charge and bond between Newman and Church, R. W. 95–6

Pattison, Mark
  and A. P. Stanley's view that the Church of England's fortunes might have been different if Newman knew German 149–50
  and Annan, Noel 159
  and autobiographical musings 163–4
  and Bacon's aphorism, *Antiquitas saeculi Juventus* ("Ancient times were the youth of the world") 166
  and being passed over for rectorship of Lincoln 153–4
  and biographical details 152–3, 155
  and Bodin, Jean 166
  and Boswell's *Life of Johnson* (1791–9) 166–7
  and Bradley, Meta 10, 193, 194, 196
  and comparative method 159
  and criticism of Ian Ker's biography of Newman for not being contextual enough 159
  and Dean Church's appraisal of Pattison 197
  and death of Pattison 196–9
  and Edward Sillem on whether Newman's knowing German would have changed his understanding of the "usurpation of reason" that so characterised the rationalists of his age 150
  and eighteenth century and Swift, Johnson and Burke 164
  and Elizabethan Settlement (1558) 150
  and *Essays and Reviews* (1860) 172–7
  and George Eliot's *Middlemarch* (1871–2) 150
  and Gibbon, Edward, and *Decline & Fall* 164
  and Herder, Johann Gottfried 166
  and historian of ideas 166
  and inability to produce books 158

and influence of high and dry father 155
and John Sparrow's characterisation of Pattison's disenchantment with Oxford and Oxford undergraduates 160
and Johnson, Samuel 166–7
and Lessing, Gotthold Ephraim 166
and likelihood Pattison died an agnostic, though clinging to clerical status that made his rectorial position at Oxford possible 172–3
and Morley, John 152, 154, 158–9
and Newman's correspondence with and visit to Pattison on his deathbed 192–9
and Newman's criticism of the "march of mind" 171
and Newman's favorable view of Pattison's contribution to *Essays and Reviews* (1860) 173
and Newman's secession 153
and Nuttall, A. D. 163–4
and Oxford 156–7
and Pattison's criticism of Oxford lacking in geniality of Arnold's criticism of the place in *Culture and Anarchy* and *Friendship's Garland* 160
and Pattison's interest in cobbling together a "scholasticism without theology: 178
and principle of rationalism 152
and progress and eighteenth century 166–7
and progress and Stephen, James Fitzjames 168
and quoting of Robert South's view of English clergy 178
and relationship to "authority, tradition and transcendental faith" 152
and repudiation of Tractarianism 154–5
and Ruskin, John 162
and Ruskin, Margaret, and not knowing German 149–50
and sisters 155
and *Spectator* review of Pattison's *Memoir* (1885) 193
and Stephen Leslie, 159
and teaching 153–4

and the life of the mind 151–2
and *timor mortis* 199
and view of how intellectual history should be written 159, 165
and view that human reason from Aristotle to Hegel was a closed book to Newman 150
and view that the only thing memorable about his childhood was his "hidebound and contracted intellect" 151
and wife Francis, later Lady Dilke 161, 199
and Wilfrid Ward's portrayal of Newman's sense of hope with respect to conversion of England 171
and Yorkshire Dales 241
and "defeatist perfectionism" 157
and "extravagant self-pity" 153
conviction that Wordsworth's *Prelude* his own history 156
delight in natural world as a child 155
his rationalism the result of his impatience with the real self 151
reputation for learning 158
OPINIONS
on Bible 180
on Church, R. W, 10
on "clash between classicist and utilitarians" 180–1, 182–3
on Darwinism 166
on decay of nations theory 166
on delusiveness of faith in progress not being itself cause for losing faith in "the rights of the legitimate monarch – the sovereign reason" 169
on the desolating influence of the Tracts 180
on disenchantment with teaching profession and Oxford 160–2
on growth of his own character 162–3
on Hampden, Renn Dickson 164–5
on intellectual progress and the "sleeping volcano of passion" 171
on Kant, Immanuel 169
on low view of Anglican priests, whom he regarded as "professional quacks trading in beliefs they don't share" 173
on need to free himself from "the

bondage of unreason ... and traditional prejudices" 149
on Newman and Oxford 178–9, 180
on Newman's idea of university education 189–90
on Newman, *Loss and Gain* (1847) 191
on Newman's visit to Pattison when the rector of Lincoln was gravely ill 195–6
on the objectionable sweep of Thomas Buckle's *History of Civilization* (1857–61) 159
on Oriel 162
on Oxford novels 190–1
on progress 166
on Providence 241
on university education 181–2
on Warburton, Bishop William 49
Pemble, John, on James Anthony Froude and his provocative history 301
Percival, John, Bishop of Hereford and President of Trinity College 371
Pius IX 118–19
and *Syllabus of Errors* (1864) 118
Plato 6
Pole, Reginald 42
Progress 169–70
Providence 382, 385
Public Worship Regulation Act of 1874 22
Pusey, Edward Bouverie 1, 9 16, 23 39, 40, 42, 44, 46, 52, 69, 78, 81, 97, 153, 177, 183, 216, 291, 366, 369, 371–2, 374, 387, 398, 402, 405, 412, 413, 427, 470, 487, 510
and Harper, Thomas, SJ 413
and Pattison's charge that Pusey called for Oxford religion to be restricted to "the blind getting up of the divinity of the seventeenth century" 183
OPINIONS
on Jowett's Christianity 412
on proposed censure of Newman over Tract 90 at Sheldonian 16

Rationalism
and evils of 272
and Pattison, Mark 151
and Sillem, Edward 150
Reform Bill of 1867 247–8

Reformation, Continental 43, 62, 63, 64, 79, 108, 170, 175, 545
Reformation, English 42, 47, 130, 255, 293, 294, 295, 299, 300-1, 309, 330-1, 337-8, 342, 350, 352, 380-1, 387, 422
Rogers, Frederick, later Lord Blachford 3, 7
Roman Catholicism
and Dean Church's objection to on the grounds of what he considered its unpersuasive claim of infallibility 544
and Ignaz von Döllinger's unreliable view of 367
and faith and reason, 30
and English distrust of 204
and J. A. Froude's view of 322
and Julius Charles Hare's detestation of 130
and Hutton's never being tempted to follow Newman into 101
and R. F. Littledale's urging Anglo-Catholics to steer clear of Church of Rome 214
and Frederick Meyrick's low view of 355
and Newman's contention that all Christianity definable between the two poles of Roman Catholicism and atheism 112
and Newman's opposition to liberalism in religion definitive of his type of Catholicism 115
and Newman's satirical treatment of in "Catholicity of the Anglican Church" (1840) 529
Routh, Dr. Joseph Martin 81–2
Ruskin, John
and Gibbon's insistence on treating the rise of Christianity merely in terms of externals 274
on advancement in life 183
on the Victorians' incoherent view of education 162
on silk gowns 162
on style 501
on what ought to be the object of university education 183
Russell, SJ, Fr Charles 462
Ryder, Fr Ignatius
on Abbott, Edwin Abbott 209–11
on *Apologia* 437

Index

Salisbury, Lady Gwendolen 254
Salisbury, Lady Mary 27–8
Salisbury, Lord Robert 254
Science scientific faith 150; and science vs. theology according to Pattison 170
Scholasticism 183–5
Shakespeare, William 44
Sheed, Wilfrid, on the Ward family's long affection for Newman 474
Short, Edward John Joseph Sebastian viii–ix
Short, Jane viii
Short, John Francis viii
Short, Karina viii
Short, Sophia Thérèse Mariana viii–ix
Short, Thomas
  and fondness for red coats
  and Newman's visiting whilst receiving honorary degree at Trinity 373
Skinner, Simon, and preposterous claim that only history dons are entitled to a view of history 218
Sibthorp, Richard Waldo 51–2
Sidgwick, Henry low regard for Mark Pattison 149
Simpson, Richard, on the Holy Office and Index 472
Smith, Albert 50–1
Smith, B. A. (Church's brilliant biographer) 2
Sophistry 263, 264
South, Robert, and low repute in which English clergy were held 178
Southern, R. W.
  on Renan 365–7
  on university education 183–5
Southey, Robert *Life of Nelson* (1813) 3
Spurgeon, Charles Haddon 412
Stanley, Dean 99–100, 395–6
  on Kingsley, Charles 438–9
Stanley, Venetia 212
Stephen, James Sir
  and admiration of Newman's first two volumes of sermons 256
  and Benthamism, regarded as "the most subtle enemy Christianity ever had" 256
  and Bible reading 252, 253
  and dislike of Newman's *Arians of the Fourth Century* (1832) 255
  and dismissive of view that Newman and Tractarians favored Popery 256
  and Gospel, trust in its "kingly sway" 246
  and letter of apology to Newman 288–9
  and reminiscences by James Fitzjames Stephen 252–3
  on Froude, Hurrell, the Tractarians and *The Remains of the late Reverend Richard Hurrell Froude* (1838) 255
  on Newman 255–6
Stephen, James Fitzjames
  and agnosticism 250
  and apostasy, uneasy 259
  and Ashton, Rosemary 279
  and *Autobiography of Mark Rutherford* (1881) by William Hale White 250
  and Butler, Joseph 250
  and charge of casuistry against Newman 326
  and charge of dishonesty against Newman 262
  and charge of sophistry against Newman 263–5, 314
  and Chesterton, Gilbert Ketih and whether Newman poped to be done with quarrels 264
  and Christianity, loss of faith in 251–4
  and critical edition of works from Oxford University Press edited by Christopher Ricks 257
  and Curzon, George 282
  and Darwin, Charles, and *Origin of Species* (1859) 317
  and Disraeli, Benjamin, 1st Earl of Beaconsfield 281
  and criticisms of Newman by Stephen, James Fitzjames appropriated by later detractors of Newman 285–6
  and dogma, Newman's insistence on "sophistical" 263
  and doublemindedness and doubt 259
  and evidence 258
  and favorable to rationalism, according to his brother, Stephen Leslie 258
  and filial respect and love 252
  and Harrison, Frederic 275–6

and Hutton, Richard Holt, and contention that James Fitzjames Stephen, throughout his adulthood, "was avenging himself on what he could not believe, for the disappointment he had felt in not being able to retain the beliefs of his youth" 250–1
and Hutton's response to Fitzjames Stephen's *Liberty, Equality, Fraternity* 103–4
and Hutton's response to parable regarding agnosticism 440–1
and Kingsley, Charles 238
and *Law Journal* appraisal of James Fitzjames Stephen's rationalist principles 269–71
and Lilly, William Samuel and clarification about what Newman meant when he said that one must choose between Catholicism and Atheism 278
and logic-chopping, lawyerly 268
and Lytton, Edward George Lytton Bulwer, 1st Earl of 259
and Macaulay, Thomas Babington 245
and Mayo, Richard Southwell Bourke, Earl of 282
and mystery 258
and overworking, inheritance of his father's penchant for 254
and proposed calling on Newman in Edgbaston rejected by the Oratorian 287–8
and rejection of Christianity, possible reasons for 286–7
and relationship with father 251–3
and reviewing 246
and Stephen, Leslie 238
and Strachey, Lytton 257–8
and tests of rationalists, which Christianity must pass or be presumed false 271
and Whiggery 245
and Williams, Rowland, contributor to *Essays and Reviews* (1860) charged with heresy in court of arches and defended by James Fitzjames Stephen 283–4
OPINIONS
on agnosticism, parable of 240
on *Apologia pro Vita Sua* (1864) 262–9
on Arnold, Matthew 249
on beggarwoman vs. State's pattern man 266–7
on Christian faith, ambivalence towards 250–1
on civilisation and social progress 168–9
on Dickens, Charles 246
on doctrine of eternal damnation, and bearing on law and religion 284–5
on doctrinal development, Newman's understanding of 312–30
on "dogmatic principle," Newman's understanding of 265, 268, 274
on evidence 224, 242–3, 250, 258, 267–8
on father, Sir James Stephen, son's reminiscence of 252–3
on *Grammar of Assent* 238
on Hastings, Warren 245
on India, British Raj in 281–3
on India and liberals 281–3
on Kingsley, Charles, and controversy with Newman leading to *Apologia* 419–20
on Lecky, William Edward Hartpole 274
on liberalism 242, 256, 279–83
on making any claims regarding what one might imagine the truths of Christianity "an abuse of language" 248
on Mill, John Stuart 246–8
on miracles, and Newman 248
on mystery 240, 248
on "mystery of Indian administration" 259, 331
on objections of Englishmen to the Church of Rome 433
on rearing of sons with the conviction that Christianity is a "forgery" 59
on religion of "solid, established part of the English nation" 281
on sin 338
on Stanley, Dean and Maurice, Frederick Denison 237–8
on suitability of National Church to the English 433
on time and eternity 168

on "the Christian history" 259
on "the inestimable privilege of being able, without conscious inconvenience, to do without any principles at all" 168
on truth of Christianity, and bearing on limits of liberty 284–5
  WORKS
  "Dr. Newman's Apology" 262–9
  "Dr Newman and Liberalism" 242
  "Dr. Newman and Mr. Kingsley," 419–20
  "Dr. Newman's University Lectures," 433
  "Mr. Newman's Theory of Development," 312–20
  "On the Certitude in Religious Assent" (1872)
  "Old and New Creeds" (1880) 239
  "On a Theory of Dr. Newman's as to Believing in Miracles" (1875) 348
Stephen, Leslie
  An Agnostic's Apology (1893) 465–6
  and faith and reason 211
  and Pattison Mark, 159, 165–6
  and revealed religion 169
  and reviewing 246
  and wit 407
  OPINIONS
  on abrasiveness of James Fitzjames Stephen 248–9
  on dogma, incredibility of 211
  on imagination, childishness of 219
  on mystery 512
  on Newman's campaign against Liberalism, consistency of 466–7
  on Stephen, James Fitzjames 238; and "insensitivity to language" 249; and "heedlessness of history" 249
Strachey, Lytton
  and "superciliously derisive style" 227
  and *Eminent Victorians* (1918) 227
Swift, Jonathan 34, 170, 295, 458, 513, 530
  "An Argument Against Abolishing Christianity" (1711) 267
Sympathy and Newman's critics xiii, 99

Tennyson, Alfred, Lord 145, 234, 247, 394, 413, 446, 449, 460, 463
  and style 501

Tennyson, Lionel 234
Tertullian 444
Temple, Frederick, contributor to *Essays and Reviews* 173
Thirlwall, Connop
  on Newman and evidence 223–4
  on Newman and his "sentimental and imaginative bias" 223
  and Abbott, Edwin Abbott's parroting of Thirlwall's criticism 224–6
Thomas Aquinas, St 63, 116, 152, 443, 444, 484, 494, 495, 503, 508, 509, 515, 551
Tillotson, Kathleen 452
  on Ker, Ian and his Newman biography 533
Tocqueville, Alexis de, and American democracy 270
Tracey, Gerard
  on English anti-Catholicism 336–7
  on Froude, James Anthony 350–1
  on *Oxford University Sermons*, charge of and intended audience for 272
  on response to Tract 90 by Heads of Houses 80–1
Trendelenburg, Friedrich Adolf 102
Tuckwell, William 27–8
  on Meyrick's disappointed ambition 379–80
Turner, Frank, and aspersions against Newman and his friends, no evidence for 216
Tyrrell, George 483–8
  on Newman's style 504–5

Ullathorne, William Bishop, and Newman's letter asking permission to attend Trinity College ceremony for awarding of honorary degree 372–3
Unbelief 27, 33, 57, 103, 121, 194, 196, 254, 279, 314, 361, 422, 436, 254, 441, 463, 545, 557

Via Media 43, 44, 52, 54, 55, 58, 62, 66, 68, 72, 73, 75, 79, 82, 83, 122, 124, 212, 312, 470, 496, 522, 529, 531, 549
Victoria, queen of United Kingdom of Great Britain and Ireland and empress of India 86, 212, 281, 334, 348, 390
Victorians and travel 7

Ward, Mrs. Humphry 6
   and Abbott's attack on Newman's understanding of miracles 207–9
   and *Robert Elsmere* (1888) 5, 461
Ward, Josephine Mary (*née* Hope-Scott)
   and Belloc, Hilaire 455
   and Bronte, Charlotte 453
   and delight in France 455
   and one of best sources of knowledge for Wilfrid Ward 452–5
   OPINIONS
   on Dickens, Charles 451–2
   on "enormous anxiety" incurred by her husband in writing Newman biography 464
   on Figgis, John Neville 458
   on "personal love of Our Lord" being "the beginning and end" of Newman's "inner life" 474
   on science 31
   on Ward family, influence of Catholic faith of on Wilfrid and Josephine Ward 453–4
   on Wilfrid Ward's criticism of Newman in his late lectures 446
   and *One Poor Scruple* (1899) 31
Ward, Maisie 449
   on Josephine Ward's discovery of Newman 474
   on Wilfrid Ward's biography of Newman 455–6
Ward, Wilfrid
   and Acton, Lord 470
   and America 499–500–1
   and anti-Semitism, and Mivart, St George Jackson 461
   and "shared interest" both Anglicans and Roman Catholics have in "appreciating the untenability of positivist unbelief" 121
   and Benigni, Monsignor Umberto 498–9
   and biographical details 447–8
   and Boswell, James, admiration of 465
   and character, interest in 451–1
   and Chesterton, Gilbert Ketih, and Newman's perceived sensitiveness 456
   and Church's need to confront modern challenges 445
   and Church, R. W. 448
   and Currie, Sir Philip 461
   and Dreyfus Affair 461
   and *Dublin Review* 448
   and Emly, Lord 463
   and epistolary structuring of Newman biography 457
   and excisions from a letter from Newman to his father 475–6
   and friends of varying religious and political opinions, including A. J. Balfour, Charles Gore, Richard Holt Hutton, Lord Hugh Cecil, George Wyndham, A. V. Dicey Friedrich von Hügel, James Martineau, Thomas Henry Huxley, Henry Sidgwick, and Frederic Myers 449
   and friendships with Tennyson and Chesterton 446–7
   and Halifax, Lord 463
   and limits of sympathy 460–1
   and Lingard, John 448
   and lucidity 458–9
   and Manning, Henry Edward 441, 448, 480
   and Mivart, St George Jackson 461
   and Modernist crisis 445
   and Newman, correspondence with 234
   and Newman, high regard for Ideal Ward's son 446
   and Newman, influence on Ward, father and son 448–9, 452
   and Newman, "regal style" of 500–5
   and Norfolk, Henry Fitzalan Howard, fifteenth duke of 449
   and O'Dwyer, Edward Thomas, Bishop of Limerick, and Modernism 479–82
   and Oratorian Fathers and Newman biography 476–9
   and *Pascendi Dominici Gregis* (1907) 445, 494
   and Pius X 445
   and *raison d'être* 443
   and rationalism 445
   and scepticism among educated classes 445–6
   and Simpson, Richard 470
   and Stanley, Arthur Penrhyn 448
   and Swift, Jonathan 458

Index

and theatricality 463
and Ushaw 448
and Vaughan, Herbert Alfred, and advice to Wilfrid Ward in youth 452–3
and Ward, Josephine, and encapsulation of her husband's achievement 516–17
and Ward, Maisie, and Wilfrid Ward's biography of Newman 455–6
and Ward, W. G. and Newman, fraught relationship between 471–3, 475–6
and Wiseman, Nicholas 448
OPINIONS
on Abbott, Edwin Abbott 231–4
on affections, and evangelisation 514–15
on agnosticism, Newman's ability to apostrophise 512–13
on Americans 500
on *Anglican Difficulties* 317
on Anglicanism 458
on apostasy, about which Newman was so prescient 510–11
on Bateman in Newman's *Loss and Gain* 451
on Boswell, James 465
on Bremond's book, *The Mystery of Newman* 492–3
on Catholic tradition as "involved in a creative act of the intellect" 44–5
on Chesterton's *Orthodoxy* (1908) 459
on Comte, Auguste 442–3
on conversion 49
on "disgusting Robert Elsmere gush" 461
on Holland, Canon Scott 47
on *Home and Foreign Review, The* 471, 472
on Leo XIII, Pope 497–8
on miracles 232
on Newman's affection for him 473
on Newman's antidote to agnosticism 514–15
on Newman, caricature of, formed by those uninterested in his "deeper side" 510
on Newman, and charge of dilettantism 505–6
on Newman's dogmatic principle 506–8
on Newman's entertainment of objections to whatever argument he mounts 508–9
on Newman's "gift of self" 514–15
on Newman's interest in character 450
on Newman's letters, how best to plunder for biography 470
on Newman's Oxford University Sermons 493
on Newman's personal influence 473
on Newman's satire, genius for 512–13
on Newman's sensitiveness 457–8
on Newman's style 500–5
on Newman's treatment of Faith and Love 232
on Newman's wariness of progress, tempered always by hope 170
on Newman's work, true outcome of 441
on Renan and Newman 507–8
on scepticism, about which Newman was so perceptive 510–12
on Tennyson, Lionel 234
on theology, evolving need for creativity in the writing of 444–5
on Thomas, St, lesson for nineteenth century 443–4
on Thomas, St, and *quaestio* method 508–9
on Ward, William George (Father) 442–3
on wife, and "unity of interests" with 459
WORKS
Problems and Persons (1903) 13
References to Newman's Works
on Newman's understanding of "the *semper eadem* of Catholicism" 13
on his charm, especially on conversion and logic 48–9
Ward, William, biographical details 452
Ward, William George
and Newman's exasperation with his extreme ultramontane positions 471, 475–6
and father and son 452
on mystery 463
Warham, Archbishop William 42
Waugh, Evelyn 127, 296, 522, 524
Whiggery 245, 255, 378

White, Blanco 27–8; and fear of error 86
White, William Hale, and *Autobiography of Mark Rutherford* (1881) 250
Wilberforce, Samuel, on *Apologia* 204
Willey, Basil, on why Kinglsey chose to assail Newman 421–2
Williams, Isaac
 and loyalty to National Church 40
 on Newman's conversion 39
Williams, Rowland, and contribution to *Essays and Reviews* (1860) 173; and reference to by Newman 173
Wilson, A. N., on Newman's style 504
Wiseman, Archbishop Nicholas 52, 381
Wolsey, Archbishop Thomas 42
Wordsworth, Bishop of Lincoln 368
Woolf, Virginia, on her father, Leslie Stephen, and the art of reading 252

Yeats, William Butler 538

Edward Short is the author of *Newman and his Contemporaries* and *Newman and his Family*, both now reissued by Gracewing in uniform revised editions to the present volume, as well as *Newman and History*. The first volume of his collected essays and reviews, *Adventures in the Book Pages*, was acclaimed by the *Catholic Herald* as "wise, witty and entertaining." His critical edition of the first volume of Newman's *Difficulties of Anglicans* introduces and annotates the lectures that Newman delivered in London in 1850, which, taken together, constitute a dress rehearsal for his *Apologia pro Vita Sua*. The doyen of Newman scholars, Ian Ker, hailed the book as "a lively, well-researched, well-written edition, which all faithful readers of Newman will enjoy." Edward Short also edited the *Saint Mary's Book of Christian Verse* (2022), which Prof. Emma Mason of Warwick University called "a mesmerizingly beautiful anthology." His latest collection, *What the Bells Sang: Essays and Reviews* (2023) includes far-ranging pieces on poets, novelists, moralists and historians. Lord Andrew Roberts, Churchill's biographer, called the book "beautifully written," "brave" and "wise." Mr. Short studied history and art history at Hunter College in the City University of New York. He lives in New York with his wife and two children.

www.ingramcontent.com/pod-product-compliance
Lightning Source LLC
Chambersburg PA
CBHW021228300426
44111CB00007B/465